CORPORATION LAW AND ECONOMICS

by

STEPHEN M. BAINBRIDGE
Professor, UCLA School of Law

NEW YORK, NEW YORK

FOUNDATION PRESS

2002

Mat #18145839

COPYRIGHT © 2002 By FOUNDATION PRESS

        395 Hudson Street
        New York, NY 10014
        Phone Toll Free 1–877–888–1330
        Fax (212) 367–6799
        fdpress.com

All rights reserved
Printed in the United States of America

ISBN 1–58778–139–5 (hard cover)
ISBN 1–58778–140–9 (soft cover)

TEXT IS PRINTED ON 10% POST
CONSUMER RECYCLED PAPER

For Helen

*

PREFACE

Law students taking the basic course in corporations or business associations are the target audience for this text, although I hope the analysis will also prove useful to lawyers and judges seeking a fresh perspective on corporate law problems. Virtually all law students take the basic course in corporation law. At the various law schools at which I have taught, 80–90 percent of each graduating class typically take the introductory Business Associations class. For many of these students, the prospect of studying corporate law is a daunting one. They may lack training in economics, business, and accounting—indeed, some went to law school precisely because they wanted to avoid those subjects. But now they discover that Corporations is a "must take" class, if only because it is on most state bar examinations.

Corporations classes present such students with two not wholly unrelated problems: First, they cannot understand the cases studied if they do not understand the transactions giving rise to those cases. Consider the classic case of *Smith v. Van Gorkom*,[1] found in all corporations casebooks. The transactional background essential to understanding that case includes such complexities as leveraged leasing, investment tax credits, a leveraged buyout structured as a merger, a stock lock-up, a best efforts clause in the merger agreement, and an attempted auction of corporate control. A student cannot understand why the court held against the defendant directors without understanding exactly what the defendant directors did wrong, which the student cannot understand unless he understands the underlying transactions.

Second, corporations classes at many law schools are taught from a law and economics perspective. This is as it should be, of course. Law and economics remains the most successful example of intellectual arbitrage in the history of corporate jurisprudence. It is virtually impossible to find serious corporate law scholarship that is not informed by economic analysis. Even those corporate law scholars who reject economic analysis spend much of their time responding to those who practice it. Perhaps the most telling evidence of the success of law and economics in this field, however, is that many leading judicial opinions rely on it, including a number stud-

1. 488 A.2d 858 (Del. 1985).

2. 692 F.2d 880 (2d Cir. 1982), cert. denied, 460 U.S. 1051 (1983).

3. 947 F.2d 551 (2d Cir. 1991), cert. denied, 503 U.S. 1004 (1992).

v

ied in the basic corporations course: e.g., *Joy v. North*,[2] *United States v. Chestman*,[3] *Basic Inc. v. Levinson*,[4] *Edgar v. MITE Corp.*,[5] *Amanda Acquisition Corp. v. Universal Foods Corp.*,[6] and others.

This text is addressed to both of those problems. I sought to produce a readable text, with a style that I hope is simple, direct, and reader-friendly. Even when dealing with complicated economic or financial issues, I tried to make them readily accessible to legal audiences. At the same time, however, I have not shied away from bringing theory to bear on doctrine. While the text has a strong emphasis on the doctrinal issues taught in today's corporations classes, it also places significant emphasis on providing an economic analysis of the major issues in that course. The text thus offers not only with an overview of the black letter law of corporations, but also a unifying method of thinking about the subject. Using a few basic tools of law and economics—such as price theory, game theory, and the theory of the firm literature—the reader, I hope, will come to see corporate law as the proverbial "seamless web."

I hasten to reassure the potentially worried reader that I do not regard corporate law pedagogy, whether in the classroom or this text, as an appropriate forum for the sort of recreational mathematics that has become fashionable in some avant-garde scholarly circles. This text is designed for lawyers and law students—not graduate finance or economics students. Economic analysis is done solely qualitatively—no mathematical models or formal game theory—and kept as intuitive as possible. Even more important, economic analysis is never done for its own sake. In his well-known critique of modern legal scholarship, Judge Harry Edwards remarked: "Theory wholly divorced from cases has been of no use to me in practice."[7] My practice experience confirms that criticism, at least as long as we put strong emphasis on the phrase "wholly divorced." Theory brought to bear on specific legal issues often can be quite illuminating, as I hope to illustrate in this text. Economic analysis nevertheless is brought into play gradually and only in instances where it adds significant value.

In the interests of full disclosure, a goal that ought to be near and dear to the hearts of all transactional lawyers, I should admit at the outset that this is neither an encyclopedia nor a traditional hornbook. You will find no stultifying discussions of minutiae (I hope) nor lengthy string citations of decades-old cases (or, at least, not very many). A student who wants to know Alaska's black letter law of ultra vires should look elsewhere. My goal is to help the student (or lawyer or judge) who needs to understand why the nexus of contracts model of the firm leads to a preference for default rather than mandatory rules.

---

4. 485 U.S. 224 (1988).

5. 457 U.S. 624 (1982).

6. 877 F.2d 496 (7th Cir.), cert. denied, 493 U.S. 955 (1989).

7. Harry T. Edwards, The Growing Disjunction Between Legal Education and the Legal Profession, 91 Mich. L. Rev. 34, 46 (1992) (quoting a former law clerk).

A note on citation forms

In general, citations herein follow standard Blue Book form. To the despair of my research assistants, almost all of whom were law review editors, however, I have kept footnotes to the bare minimum. In particular, I generally refrained from using "id.," short form citations, and jump cites. Hence, unlike most modern law review articles, not every statement in the book is footnoted. Instead, I typically provide a source citation and allow interested readers to seek out pinpoint citations on their own. I trust that this approach will help produce a more readable text. Finally, note that frequently referenced statutes and Restatements are cited in abbreviated form without dates, as follows:

Agency Restatement: American Law Institute, Restatement (Second) of Agency (1958).

ALI PRINCIPLES: American Law Institute, Principles of Corporate Governance: Analysis and Recommendations (1994).

CAL. CORP. CODE: California General Corporation Law, California Corporations Code § 100 *et seq.* (West 1998).

DGCL: Delaware General Corporation Law, Delaware Code Annotated tit. 8 (1999).

Exchange Act: Securities Exchange Act of 1934, as amended, 15 U.S.C. § 78a *et seq.* (1999).

MBCA: Model Business Corporation Act (1984 and supp.).

N.Y. Bus. Corp. L.: New York Business Corporation Law (McKinney 1999).

Rule: A rule adopted by the Securities and Exchange Commission under either the Securities Act or the Securities Exchange Act, 17 C.F.R. § 230.100 *et seq.* (1999) and 17 C.F.R. § 240.0-1 *et seq.* (1999), respectively.

RULPA: [Revised] Uniform Limited Partnership Act (1976, with 1985 amendments).

Securities Act: Securities Act of 1933, as amended, 15 U.S.C. § 77a *et seq.* (1999).

ULLCA: Uniform Limited Liability Company Act (1996)

ULPA: Uniform Limited Partnership Act (1916).

UPA (1914): Uniform Partnership Act of 1914.

UPA (1997): Uniform Partnership Act of 1997 (also known as the Revised Uniform Partnership Act).

Acknowledgments

I am grateful to the many colleagues who read portions of this text while it was in draft: David Binder, Mitu Gulati, Lynn LoPucki, Richard Painter, Mark Ramseyer, Lynn Stout, and Bob Thompson. Special thanks go to my friend and UCLA colleague William Klein, who read vast chunks of the text, and provided especially constructive criticism throughout. I also thank Professor Michael P. Dooley for permission to include adapted portions of a planned joint project in Chapters 6 and 12. Valuable research assistance was provided by Steven Chasin, Hsin Chau, Peggy Chen, Melissa Gilbert, Sarah McGonigle, and Stephanie Thomas-Hodge. I also owe a deep debt of gratitude to the reference librarians at the UCLA and Harvard schools of law.

SUMMARY OF CONTENTS

*

TABLE OF CONTENTS

TABLE OF CONTENTS

xxi

TABLE OF CONTENTS

TABLE OF CONTENTS

CORPORATION LAW AND ECONOMICS

*

Chapter 1

AN INTRODUCTION TO THE CORPORATION

Analysis

---

§ 1.1   What is a corporation?

By every measure except sheer number of firms, the corporation is the predominant form of business organization in the United States. According to recent census data, U.S. business organizations include approximately 17 million unincorporated proprietorships, 1.7 million partnerships, and 4.6 million corporations. Although corporations thus account for only about one-fifth of all business organizations, they bring

1

in almost 90% of all business receipts.[1]

What is this economic giant and why does it dominate our economy? A leading legal dictionary defines the corporation as "an artificial person or legal entity created by or under the authority of the laws of a state or nation...."[2] Although technically correct, this definition is not especially enlightening. You may find it more helpful to think of the corporation as a legal fiction characterized by six attributes: formal creation as prescribed by state law;[3] legal personality; separation of ownership and control; freely alienable ownership interests; indefinite duration; and limited liability.[4] Taken together, these six attributes give the corporate form considerable advantages for large businesses as compared to the other forms of business organizations available under U.S. law. Each of these attributes will be discussed in far greater detail during the course of this text, but an overview at the outset may prove helpful.

A. Some fundamental distinctions

Corporations come in a wide variety of flavors: business corporations, municipal corporations, and ecclesiastical corporations, to name a few. In this text, we are concerned solely with business corporations. Even with that limitation, however, here are a number of fundamental distinctions to bear in mind:

- *Not-for-profit versus for-profit corporations*. Many charitable organizations are organized as corporations, even though they do not carry on for-profit business activities. Special "non-profit" corporation statutes govern these organizations. Not-for-profit corporations can also qualify for special tax treatment under both state and federal law. As the name implies, the profit motive is what distinguishes business corporations from nonprofit corporations.

- *Public versus private corporations*. The term public corporation is sometimes used to refer to corporations created by the government (be it federal, state, or local) to carry out some public function. In this terminology, private corporations are created by and owned by private individuals to carry out private functions. Almost all business corporations fall into the latter category.

§ 1.1

1. U.S. Census Bureau, Statistical Abstract of the United States 545 (1999).

2. Black's Law Dictionary 307 (5th ed. 1979).

3. Virtually all U.S. corporations are formed ("incorporated") under the laws of a single state by filing articles of incorporation with the appropriate state official. (A very few exceptions are formed under federal law.) The state in which the articles of incorporation are filed is known as the "state of incorporation." The founders of a company are free to select any state as the state of incorporation; they need not select the state in which the company is currently doing business. Selecting a state of incorporation has important consequences, because corporate law matters usually are governed by the law of the state of incorporation, irrespective of the jurisdiction in which suit is brought or the residence of the other parties to the dispute.

4. Note that the latter four of these attributes are default rules. Some corporations opt out of one of more of them. In particular, close corporations often unify ownership and control to one degree or another and/or restrict transfer of ownership interests.

• *Close versus public corporations*. Business corporations generally are divided into two main categories: close corporations (a.k.a. closely held corporations) and public corporations (a.k.a. publicly held corporations). As a general rule of thumb, close corporations tend to be smaller than public corporations, but size is not what distinguishes the two categories. Instead, they are distinguished by the presence or absence of a secondary trading market for their shares of stock. Public corporations are those whose stock is listed for trading on a secondary market, such as the New York Stock Exchange or the NASDAQ system. Close corporations are those whose stock is not listed on such a market. In this text, the term public corporation will be used in this sense.

Of these three distinguishing characteristics, the last is most salient for our purposes. Corporate securities, like all commodities, is traded in markets. Corporate lawyers distinguish between two basic types of markets in which a corporation's securities (such as stocks or bonds) are traded: the primary market and the secondary market. The primary market is the one in which the corporation sells its shares to investors. An initial public offering (IPO), for example, takes place on the primary market.

The secondary market is a trading market: the one in which investors trade stocks among themselves without any significant participation by the original corporate issuer of the shares. The New York Stock Exchange and the American Stock Exchange are well-known, highly organized, and thoroughly regulated examples of secondary markets. Market professionals working on these exchanges facilitate the trading process by matching buy and sell orders from investors.

Having a corporation's securities listed for trading on a secondary market is significant because it makes the securities liquid. In other words, investors can freely sell their securities without involving the firm. Liquidity, in turn, makes it easier and cheaper for the company subsequently to raise capital in the primary market, because investors generally prefer (and are willing to pay more) for liquid securities. The difference in liquidity of publicly held corporate stock and that of close corporation stock has important theoretical and doctrinal consequences.

B. Some key terminology

Bonds: Long-term debt securities.

Classes of shares: A class of shares is a type or category of stock. Thus, common stock is considered to be a class of stock. Preferred stock would be a second class of shares. Multiple classes must be authorized by the articles, which must set forth the number of shares of the class the corporation is authorized to issue and the class' basic rights.

Debentures: Unsecured long-term debt securities.

Directors: Although shareholders nominally own the corporation, they do not control it. Instead, control of the firm is vested in the board of directors, a body of individuals elected by the shareholders to manage the business.

Dividend: A pro rata distribution of the corporation's assets to shareholders. A liquidation dividend occurs when the firm dissolves and has assets remaining after all other claims have been satisfied. The residual assets are distributed pro rata to the corporation's shareholders as a final dividend.

Issuer: Used in connection with sales of securities to refer to the corporation that originally sold the securities.

Junk bonds: High yield, high risk corporate bonds frequently used to finance takeovers.

Notes: Short-term debt securities, usually unsecured.

Series of shares: A series of shares is a subclass of stock. Thus, the corporation might have a class of preferred shares that is divided into series. All members of the class will have some preference over the common stock, but each series may have different rights and preferences from the others.

Shares: The units into which the ownership interest of a corporation is divided. Shares typically carry two basic rights: (1) voting rights, which allow their owners to elect the corporation's directors and to vote on certain other matters; and (2) economic rights, which entitle their owners to a pro rata share of dividends and, in the event of liquidation, any residual assets remaining after all other claims on the corporation have been paid.

Shareholder: Person or legal entity who owns shares.

Stock: Sometimes used interchangeably with the term "shares," but also used in a more technical sense to refer to the corporation's aggregate outstanding shares; hence the term, "a share of corporate stock."

§ 1.2 Essential attributes

No one type of business organization is always appropriate. Rather, one of the business lawyer's most important jobs is considering the unique facts and circumstances of the particular client and providing advice as to which organizational form best serves that client's needs. Alternatives to the corporation include the sole proprietorship, the general or limited partnership, and the limited liability company.

In general, the corporation's economic dominance stems from the advantages it offers large businesses when compared to these other forms of business organizations. This section first introduces the key alternatives to the corporation and then outlines the six essential attributes of the corporation relevant to the choice between it and these other forms of business organization.

A.   Alternatives to the corporation

General partnerships: A partnership is an association of two or more persons to carry on as co-owners a business for profit. Modern partnership law is a mixture of common law decisions and statutory rules. Most states adopted the Uniform Partnership Act of 1914, with only minor variations. An increasing number of states have adopted the more recent Uniform Partnership Act of 1996, albeit with modifications in may cases, which has reduced the uniformity of partnership law.

Limited partnerships: In a general partnership, there is one type of investor: a general partner having full rights of management, control and profit-sharing. Limited partnerships have two classes of partners: general partners, whose rights are largely the same as in a general partnership; and limited partners, who have much less expansive rights, but whose obligations are correspondingly limited. Limited partnerships would have long since faded out of existence except for certain quirks of the federal tax laws, which made them a tax advantageous vehicle in some situations. Tax reforms during the last decade have largely eliminated these advantages and the limited partnership may gradually fade away. Most states have adopted the Uniform Limited Partnership Act (ULPA) or the more recent Revised Uniform Limited Partnership Act (RULPA).

Limited liability company: The limited liability company (LLC) is an unincorporated business organization providing its members with pass through tax treatment, limited liability, and the ability to participate actively in firm management. Although LLCs date from a 1977 Wyoming statute, they were rare until the late 1980s. In 1988, the Internal Revenue Service concluded that LLCs could be classified as partnerships for federal tax purposes. With that development, the concept took off. Virtually all states have adopted LLC statutes and numerous LLCs have been formed. State statutes vary considerably, although the promulgation of the Uniform Limited Liability Company Act should gradually introduce a greater degree of uniformity.

B.   Formal creation

One creates a corporation by filing a document called the articles of incorporation (a.k.a. charter) with the appropriate government office of the chosen state of incorporation. The articles are the most important of the corporation's organic documents. They set out the corporation's essential rules of the road—the basic terms under which it will operate. Each state corporate statute sets forth the minimum provisions the articles must contain. MBCA § 2.02, for example, requires the articles to include the corporation's name, the number of shares the corporation is authorized to issue, the name and address of the corporation's registered agent, and the name and address of the incorporator.[1] In addition, § 2.02 lists numerous other provisions that must be included in the articles if the corporation wishes to avail itself of certain statutory options. Among the more important of these are provisions relating to division of shares into classes and series and liability of directors.

Once prepared, the articles are filed with the appropriate state agency, which in most states is the Secretary of State's office. In some states, the Secretary of State's office then issues a document called the certificate of incorporation. In other states, the Secretary of State will simply return a copy of the articles of incorporation, along with a receipt, to the incorporator. At this point, the corporation comes into existence.[2] The initial board of directors thereupon holds an organizational meeting at which corporate bylaws are adopted, officers are appointed,[3] and other loose ends are tied up.

The bylaws adopted at that meeting are the corporation's basic internal operating rules. Other than certain provisions that must be contained in the articles of incorporation, most of the corporation's internal affairs will be governed by the bylaws. Virtually anything may be contained in the bylaws. MBCA § 2.06, for example, allows the bylaws to "contain any provision for managing the business and regulating the affairs of the corporation that is not inconsistent with law or the articles of incorporation."

Although the formal steps necessary to create a corporation are quite straightforward, glitches sometimes occur. In some of these cases, the founders begin doing business in the belief that they properly formed a corporation, but the company in fact remains unincorporated due to some technical defect in the filing process. This "defective incorporation" problem embroils one in a complex body of doctrine all too likely leading to undesirable results.[4] The competent lawyer and well-counseled client take pains to ensure compliance with the requisite formalities.

Most of the alternatives to the corporation likewise require some formal process before they come into existence.[5] The principal exception

---

§ 1.2

1. The incorporator is the individual responsible for signing the articles and delivering them to the secretary of state. If the articles do not name the initial members of the board of directors, the incorporator also holds an organizational meeting to elect the initial directors and to adopt bylaws. There are several special service corporations that will act as incorporators.

2. A few states impose additional formalities over and above filing the articles of incorporation. About a dozen require filing of the articles with county, as well as state, agencies. About half that number require publication of the articles in addition to filing.

3. In most corporations, the board of directors does not run the corporation on a day-to-day basis. Instead, responsibility for most management decisions is delegated to the corporation's employees. Senior employees are referred to as managers (known collectively as the corporation's management). Officers are the most senior managers. A corporation's officers typically include its president (or chief executive officer), one or more vice-presidents, a treasurer or chief financial officer, and a secretary.

4. See § 2.3.

5. As to limited partnerships, both the ULPA and RULPA require compliance with certain statutory formalities, including filing a limited partnership certificate with the appropriate state official. In states that retain the ULPA, these formalities are espe-

is the general partnership: Under both the UPA (1914) and UPA (1997), forming a partnership involves none of the formalities required in the corporate context. All that is required is an agreement, explicit or implicit, between two or more people to act as co-owners of a business for profit.

C. Legal personality

As a legal matter, the corporation is an entity wholly separate from the people who own it and work for it. For most purposes the corporation is treated as though it were a legal person, having most of the rights and obligations of real people, and having an identity wholly apart from its constituents. Corporate law statutes, for example, typically give a corporation "the same powers as an individual to do all things necessary or convenient to carry out its business and affairs."[6]

Although the corporation's legal personality obviously is a fiction, it is a very useful one. Consider a large forestry company, owning forest land in many states. If the company were required to list all of its owners—i.e., every shareholder—on every deed recorded in every county in which it owned property, and also had to amend those filings every time a shareholder sold stock, there would be an intolerable burden not only on the firm but also on government agencies that deal with the firm.[7]

cially burdensome because of the substantial amount of information required in the certificate and the resulting need for frequent amendments to update the certificate. The RULPA retains the filing requirement, but the amount of information that must be contained in the certificate is considerably reduced. In addition, a limited partnership interest may be deemed to be a security and thus be subject to the extensive disclosure and filing requirements of the federal and state securities laws.

In most states, filing articles of organization with the appropriate state official creates a LLC. The articles of organization are comparable to corporate articles of incorporation and are treated as such by the statute with respect to such questions as amendment and filing. In addition, the LLC may adopt an operating agreement, which fulfills many of the same functions as a partnership agreement or corporate bylaws. As is also true of corporations and limited partnerships, the LLC must comply with various additional formalities, such as maintaining a registered office and keeping certain records.

6. MBCA § 3.02. As a legal person, a corporation has most of the constitutional rights possessed by natural persons. See, e.g., First Nat'l Bank of Boston v. Bellotti, 435 U.S. 765, 784 (1978) (corporation has

First Amendment right of free speech); Hale v. Henkel, 201 U.S. 43 (1906) (corporation gets Fourth Amendment protection against unreasonable searches and seizures but not protected by Fifth Amendment privilege against self-incrimination); Blake v. McClung, 172 U.S. 239 (1898) (corporation not covered by the privileges and immunities clause of the Fourteenth Amendment or of the comity clause of Article IV); Minneapolis & St. Louis Ry. Co. v. Beckwith, 129 U.S. 26, 28 (1889) (corporation entitled to due process of law under the Fifth and Fourteenth Amendments); Santa Clara County v. Southern Pacific Railroad Co., 118 U.S. 394, 416 (1886) (corporation entitled to equal protection of the law under the Fourteenth Amendment).

7. Like the corporation, a LLC is a legal person. In contrast, a theoretical debate raged for many years over whether a partnership is an entity separate from the partners or merely an aggregation of the partners. The answer to that question has a number of practical consequences. For example, if the partnership is an entity it can sue and be sued in its own name. If it is an aggregation of individuals, then each and every partner must be joined to a lawsuit involving the partnership. Numerous other examples could be cited, such as the names

An even more useful feature of the corporation's legal personality, however, is that it allows partitioning of business assets from the personal assets of shareholders, managers, and other corporate constituents.[8] This partitioning has two important aspects. On the one hand, asset partitioning creates a distinct pool of assets belonging to the firm on which the firm's creditors have a claim that is prior to the claims of personal creditors of the corporation's constituencies. By eliminating the risk that the firm will be affected by the financial difficulties of its constituencies, asset partitioning reduces the risks borne by creditors and thus enables the firm to raise capital at a lower cost. On the other hand, asset partitioning also protects the personal assets of the corporation's constituencies from the vicissitudes of corporate life. The doctrine of limited liability means that creditors of the firm may not reach the personal assets of shareholders or other corporate constituents.

Despite the utility of the fiction of corporate legal personhood, it is critical to remember that treating the corporation as an entity separate from the people making it up bears no relation to economic reality. In recognition of these facts, many legal scholars adopt the "nexus of contracts theory" of the corporation. According to the nexus of contracts theory, the corporation is not an entity but an aggregate of various inputs acting together to produce goods or services. In other words, the corporation is not a thing, but rather a web of explicit and implicit contracts establishing rights and obligations among the various parties making up the firm. Nexus of contracts theory has pervasive implications, both descriptively and normatively, for our understanding of the corporation.

D.   Separation of ownership and control

Corporations differ from most other forms of business organizations in that ownership of the firm is formally separated from its control.[9]

---

in which partnership property must be registered on a deed or certificate of title. The UPA (1914) does not come down squarely on one side or the other of this debate, instead treating the partnership as an entity for some purposes and as an aggregate for others. Knowing the circumstances under which each approach will be taken by statute or a court (and the implications of that approach) is an important, if mundane, aspect of practicing this branch of organization law. As a practical matter, however, most states have adopted separate statutes treating the partnership as a separate legal entity in most situations in which the partnership's status matters. The UPA (1997) codifies this result by declaring the partnership to be a legal entity separate from its partners.

8. See Henry Hansmann and Reinier Kraakman, The Essential Role of Organiza-

tional Law, 110 Yale L.J. 387 (2000), on which the following discussion draws.

9. Under both the UPA (1914) and UPA (1997), absent contrary agreement, all partners have an equal right to participate in the partnership's management on a one-person/one-vote basis, with most decisions being made by majority vote of the partners. UPA (1914) § 18; UPA (1997) § 401. The rules governing limited partnerships are somewhat more complex. Under the ULPA, limited partners do not participate in firm management and decision-making. A limited partner must give up the principal advantage of being a limited partner—limited liability—if "he takes part in the control of the business." ULPA § 7. Instead, the general partner has almost unfettered control over the operation of the business. The RULPA gives limited partners some voting and management rights, but

Although shareholders nominally "own" the corporation, they have virtually no decisionmaking powers—just the right to elect the firm's directors and to vote on an exceedingly limited—albeit not unimportant—number of corporate actions. Rather, management of the firm is vested by statute in the hands of the board of directors, who in turn delegate the day-to-day running of the firm to its officers, who in turn delegate some responsibilities to the company's employees.[10] The conflicts of interest created by this separation of ownership and control drive much of corporate law, especially the fiduciary obligations of officers and directors.

Although the separation of ownership and control is one of the corporation's essential attributes, it is also one of its most controversial ones. This controversy began taking its modern shape in what still may be the most influential book ever written about corporations, Berle and Means' *The Modern Corporation and Private Property*.[11] They identified three types of public corporations, classified according to the nature of share ownership within the firm:

- *Majority control*: a corporation having a dominant shareholder (or group of shareholders acting together) who owns more than 50% of the outstanding voting shares. Majority controlled corporations exhibit a partial separation of ownership and control: minority shareholders share in the corporation's ownership, but not in its control.

- *Minority control*: a corporation having a dominant shareholder (or group of shareholders acting together) who owns less than 50% of the outstanding voting shares, but is nevertheless able to exercise effective voting control. Minority controlled corporations also exhibit partial separation of ownership and control.

control of the firm basically remains vested in the general partner. RULPA § 303.

As for LLCs, the rules are even more complex, albeit highly flexible. Management of the LLC is vested in its members. Unlike the partnership's one-person/one-vote rule, the number of votes cast by each member of a LLC is determined by his proportional share in the book value of the membership interests. These rules are subject to any contrary provisions of the articles of organization and operating agreement. The LLC thus provides substantial flexibility in structuring the firm's decisionmaking processes. If the articles of organization so provide, the members may elect a manager to whom substantial authority may be delegated. Unless the articles provide to the contrary, the LLC's members lose control over areas delegated to the manager. Alternatively, one can have multiple managers, which allows committee management or even a corporate-like board of managers. The flexibility provided by the LLC statute is achieved at the cost of specificity. If the LLC's decisionmaking structure is to vary from the standard form contract, detailed contractual provisions are thus essential if later disputes are to be avoided.

10. Close corporations may differ. To be sure, the statutory separation of ownership and control applies to closely held corporations. Vesting formal decisionmaking power in the board of directors of a close corporation, however, is often unacceptable to the shareholders of such a firm. In this respect, a close corporation often closely resembles a partnership that for some business reason has been organized as a corporation. Under special statutory provisions, close corporations can be set up to give shareholders extensive management powers resembling those of partners.

11. Adolf A. Berle, Jr. and Gardiner C. Means, The Modern Corporation and Private Property (1932).

● *Managerial control*: a corporation in which no one shareholder (or group of shareholders acting together) owns sufficient stock to give him working control of the firm. Managerial controlled corporations exhibit complete separation of ownership and control.

The growth of managerial control occurred, according to Berle and Means, because stock ownership was dispersed amongst many shareholders, no one of whom owned enough shares to affect materially the corporation's management. In turn, Berle and Means believed that dispersed ownership was inherent in the corporate system. Important technological changes during the decades preceding publication of their work, especially the development of modern mass production techniques, gave great advantages to firms large enough to achieve economics of scale, which gave rise to giant industrial corporations. These firms required enormous amounts of capital, far exceeding the resources of most individuals or families. They were financed by aggregating many small investments, which was accomplished by selling shares to many investors, each of whom owned only a tiny fraction of the firm's stock.

Separation of ownership and control thus proved an essential prerequisite to corporate success. This conclusion is premised on two observations: (a) most investors in corporations prefer to be passive holders of stock; and (b) separating ownership and control results in various efficiencies in making decisions. Vesting decisionmaking power in the corporation's board of directors and managers allows shareholders to remain passive, while also preventing the chaos that would result from shareholder involvement in day-to-day decisionmaking.

While separation of ownership and control facilitated the growth of large industrial corporations, Berle and Means recognized that that separation created the potential for shareholder and managerial interests to diverge. As the residual claimants on the corporation's assets and earnings, the shareholders are entitled to the corporation's profits. But it is the firm's management, not the shareholders, which decides how the firm's earnings are to be spent. Thus, there is a risk that management will expend firm earnings on projects which benefit management, rather than shareholders. Suppose the President of Acme, Inc., is musing over the following question: "I can either spend $100 million on a new corporate jet or I can distribute the $100 million to the shareholders by increasing the size of the dividend." Can you doubt that some (most?) managers will buy the jet?

Corporate law has tried three policy responses to the potential divergence of shareholder and managerial interests created by the separation of ownership and control: (1) Some corporate laws try to reunite ownership and control, giving shareholders more control over the firm. The federal proxy rules are an example of such rules. Some legal scholars also believe that institutional investors will become more actively involved in corporate governance, at least partially reuniting ownership and control.[12] Whether this will prove true remains to be seen. (2) Some laws target the supposed lack of managerial accountability that purportedly is the basic problem caused by separating ownership and control. Because shareholders do not control the corporation, shareholders cannot discipline managers who put their self-interest ahead of the shareholders' interests. Corporate governance therefore provides alternative mechanisms—some legal, but some market—for disciplining managers who abuse their positions. Examples of this approach include judicial review under the duties of care and loyalty and hostile corporate takeovers. (3) Some laws try to align management and shareholder interests. Examples of this approach include tax provisions encouraging management to own a larger percentage of the firm's shares.

E. Indefinite duration

A corporation commonly is said to have a perpetual duration. In actuality, the corporation has an indefinite legal existence terminable only in rare circumstances: a vote of the shareholders to dissolve the company, an involuntary dissolution suit, or a merger or consolidation with another corporation.

F. Transferability

One of the great advantages of the corporate form is that shares of stock are freely transferable. Absent special contractual restrictions, shareholders are free to sell their shares to anybody at any price. A transfer of stock has no effect on the corporation, except that there is now a new voter of those shares. For public corporations, this process is facilitated greatly by the secondary trading markets.

None of the corporation's principal alternatives offer this degree of free transferability off-the-rack. Under both the UPA (1914) and UPA (1997), for example, no one can become a partner without the unanimous consent of all other partners.[13] A partner thus is effectively barred from selling his membership in the firm. A partner may assign his interest in the partnership to another party, but that interest consists only of the right to receive his share of partnership profits and losses. As a result, the assignee does not become a partner of the firm and has no rights vis-à-vis the firm other than the right to receive whatever profits are owed to the assignor partner.[14] These rules significantly impede transferability of a partner's rights in the business, although they do not wholly preclude transfers.[15]

---

12. For a critical analysis of this literature, see Stephen M. Bainbridge, The Politics of Corporate Governance, 18 Harv. J. L. & Pub. Pol'y 671 (1995).

13. UPA (1914) § 18(g); UPA (1997) § 401(i).

14. UPA (1914) § 27; UPA (1997) § 503.

15. LLCs and limited partnerships are subject to comparable rules, although determining the rights of the assignee is more complicated in the limited partnership setting then in the general partnership con-

As already noted, close corporations in some respects resemble partnerships more than other corporations. This is true of stock transferability, as well. Although shares of stock in a closely held corporation are freely transferable in theory, the lack of a readily available secondary trading market for such shares means they seldom are easily transferable in practice. Moreover, investors in a closely held corporation often prefer to restrict transferability. Like any other personal relationship, the success or failure of a small business often depends upon maintaining a rather delicate balance between the owners. Free transferability of ownership interests threatens that balance. In closely held corporations, shareholders therefore often agree to special contractual restrictions on the alienability of shares.

G. Limited liability

The limited liability doctrine holds that shareholders of a corporation are not personally liable for corporate obligations and thus put at risk only the amount of money that they invested in buying their shares. Suppose, for example, an employee of Acme, Inc., commits a tort against Paula Plaintiff. Under the tort and agency law doctrine of vicarious liability, Acme is held liable to Plaintiff for $10 million in damages resulting from the employee's tortious conduct. Acme has only $1 million in assets. The limited liability doctrine bars Plaintiff from seeking to recover the unsatisfied $9 million remainder of her claim from Acme's shareholders. The shareholders' investment in Acme stock may be worthless if Acme becomes bankrupt as a result of Plaintiff's lawsuit, but the shareholders will have lost only that portion of their wealth they invested in Acme.[16]

Members of a LLC and the limited partners (but not the general partners) in limited partnerships, like shareholders of a corporation, are not personally liable for the firm's obligations.[17] In contrast, partnership

---

text. Under ULPA § 19, the assignee of a limited partnership interest may become a limited partner if (a) the limited partnership certificate authorizes transfers of membership or (b) all other partners consent. RULPA § 704 is essentially identical. Under ULPA § 19(5) transferring a limited partnership interests is somewhat burdensome because it requires filing an amendment to the partnership certificate. The RULPA eliminates that requirement, making limited partnership interests somewhat more liquid.

16. In rare circumstances, courts may invoke an equitable exception to the limited liability rule called "piercing the corporate veil." If invoked, the veil piercing remedy allows shareholders to be held personally liable for the corporation's obligations. In the preceding example, if Paula Plaintiff successfully invokes the veil piercing doc-

trine, the court will allow her to recover the unsatisfied portion of her claim from Acme's shareholders. See § 4.3.

17. Some LLC statutes provide that a LLC member shall be held personally liable for the firm's obligations "to the extent that a shareholder of a business corporation is liable in analogous circumstances," which invites courts to extend the corporate veil piercing rules to the LLC context. Even in the absence of such statutes, it seems likely that courts will develop an analogous veil piercing rule for LLCs.

The liability of the general partner of a limited partnership is the same as that of a partner in a regular partnership. General partners thus remain subject to unlimited liability for the business' obligations. Limited partners, however, get the benefit of limited liability. As long as the formalities are properly observed, the limited partner

law provides no limitation on the potential liability partners face for obligations of the firm. Under the UPA (1914), each partner is jointly and severally liable for a tort or breach of trust committed by another partner if committed within the scope of the firm's business. In addition, each partner is jointly liable for all other partnership debts and obligations.[18] The UPA (1997) rules are the same, except that partners are jointly and severally liable for both types of obligations.[19] This problem is further compounded by the fact that each and every partner is an agent of the partnership with respect to its business and thus can enter into contracts binding the entire partnership.[20] Finally, because the partnership can be held liable for the acts of its nonpartner agents, so too can the individual partners. All of these potential sources of liability are unlimited, so that each partner could be forced to pay his share of a partnership obligation to the full extent of his personal assets. This rule may be the single most important deterrent to doing business in the partnership form.[21]

§ 1.3   Sources of corporate law

Corporate law differs in two important respects from the common law courses taken by most law students during the first year of law school. First, statutes are far more important in corporate law than is the case in most of the so-called common law courses. When faced with a corporate law issue, the first place one always looks is the corporation statute of the state of incorporation.[1] Second, as far as public corporations are concerned, federal law is much more important in corporate law than is the case in common law subjects. Indeed, publicly held corporations can be said to function in a dual regulatory scheme: federal securities law and state corporate law.

has fully paid any amounts required to purchase his interest, and the limited partner does not participate in management, the limited partner cannot be held liable to the firm's creditors. Thus, the limited partner only puts at risk the amount of his capital contribution to the firm.

18. UPA (1914) § 15.

19. UPA (1997) § 306.

20. UPA (1914) § 9; UPA (1997) § 301. About half the states have now created a variant on the general partnership called the limited liability partnership (LLP). The LLP essentially is a general partnership except that it provides limited liability for all partners (in most states for tort claims only).

21. To be sure, the importance of limited liability is easily overstated. On the one hand, the limited liability doctrine often fails to provide complete protection. Many contract creditors, for example, insist that shareholders of a closely-held corporation or members of a LLC guarantee the firm's debts. In addition, the common law doctrine of veil piercing enables courts to impose personal liability on shareholders (and members of a LLC) in appropriate cases. On the other hand, adequate capital reserves and insurance can provide partners with substantial protection despite their nominally unlimited liability.

§ 1.3

1. Although one must pay careful attention to the applicable state corporation statute, judicial opinions remain quite important in corporate law. Corporation statutes almost never rise to the level of detail found in, say, the federal tax code. Many provisions of corporation statutes are quite vague. Worse yet, corporation statutes often fail to address important issues. Courts have filled the resulting gaps through a process far more closely resembling common law adjudication than statutory interpretation. The fiduciary duties of directors and officers are especially prominent examples of this process, but they are hardly the only ones.

A. State corporate law

Virtually all U.S. corporations are formed ("incorporated") under the laws of a single state by filing articles of incorporation with the appropriate state official. (A very few exceptions are formed under federal law.) The state in which the articles of incorporation are filed is known as the "state of incorporation." Selecting a state of incorporation has important consequences, because of the so-called "internal affairs doctrine"—a conflicts of law rule holding that corporate governance matters are controlled by the law of the state of incorporation. Virtually all U.S. jurisdictions follow the internal affairs doctrine, even if the corporation in question has virtually no ties to the state of incorporation other than the mere fact of incorporation.

Suppose, for example, that Acme, Inc., is incorporated in Delaware, but all of Acme's assets are located in Illinois. All of Acme's shareholders, directors, and employees reside in Illinois. Acme's sole place of business is located in Illinois. An Acme shareholder brings suit against the board of directors, alleging that its members violated their fiduciary duty of care. The law suit is filed in an Illinois court. Despite all these Illinois ties, the Illinois court nevertheless will apply Delaware law.[2]

The internal affairs doctrine takes on particular transactional significance when considered in conjunction with the constitutional restrictions on a state's ability to exclude foreign corporations.[3] With rare exceptions, states have always allowed foreign and pseudo-foreign corporations to do business within their borders. As early as 1839, for example, the U.S. Supreme Court held that federal courts should presume a state would recognize foreign corporations in the absence of an express statement to the contrary by the legislature.[4] A subsequent Supreme Court decision implied that states could not exclude foreign corporations from doing business within the state provided that the business constituted interstate commerce under the Commerce Clause of the U.S. Constitution.[5] These decisions effectively created a common market for corporate charters. If Illinois, for example, adopts a restrictive corporation law, its businesses are free to incorporate in a less

---

2. See, e.g., Paulman v. Kritzer, 219 N.E.2d 541, 543 (Ill.App.1966), aff'd, 230 N.E.2d 262 (Ill.1967) (applying Delaware fiduciary duties to the directors of a Delaware corporation).

3. A foreign corporation is one incorporated either by a state or nation other than the state in question. A pseudo-foreign corporation that has most of its ties to the state in question rather than to the state of incorporation. Many Delaware corporations are pseudo-foreign corporations. They are incorporated in Delaware, but most of their operations are located in one or more other states. In most states, there is no significant legal difference between a foreign and a pseudo-foreign corporation, and the internal affairs doctrine will be applied to invoke the law of the state of the incorporation. California and New York are the principal exceptions to this rule. Both states purport to apply parts of their corporate laws to pseudo-foreign corporations formed in other states but having substantial contacts with California or New York. See, e.g., Cal. Corp. Code § 2115; N.Y. Bus. Corp. L. §§ 1317–20.

4. Bank of Augusta v. Earle, 38 U.S. 519, 597 (1839).

5. Paul v. Virginia, 75 U.S. 168 (1868).

restrictive state, such as Delaware, while continuing to conduct business within Illinois.

Throughout the nineteenth century state corporation laws gradually moved in the direction of increased liberality, making the incorporation process simpler on the one hand, while at the same time abandoning any effort to regulate the substantive conduct of corporations through the chartering process. In later years, this process became known as the "race to the bottom."[6] Corporate and social reformers believed that the states competed in granting corporate charters. After all, the more charters (certificates of incorporation) the state grants, the more franchise and other taxes it collects. According to this view, because it is corporate managers who decide on the state of incorporation, states compete by adopting statutes allowing corporate managers to exploit shareholders.

Many legal scholars reject the race to the bottom hypothesis.[7] According to a standard account, investors will not purchase, or at least not pay as much for, securities of firms incorporated in states that cater too excessively to management. Lenders will not make loans to such firms without compensation for the risks posed by management's lack of accountability. As a result, those firms' cost of capital will rise, while their earnings will fall. Among other things, such firms thereby become more vulnerable to a hostile takeover and subsequent management purges. Corporate managers therefore have strong incentives to incorporate the business in a state offering rules preferred by investors. Competition for corporate charters thus should deter states from adopting excessively pro-management statutes. The empirical research appears to bear out this view of state competition, suggesting that efficient solutions to corporate law problems win out over time.[8]

---

6. See generally William L. Cary, Federalism and Corporate Law: Reflections Upon Delaware, 83 Yale L.J. 663 (1974) (classic statement of race to the bottom hypothesis); see also Lucian Ayre Bebchuk, Federalism and the Corporation: The Desirable Limits on State Competition in Corporate Law, 105 Harv. L. Rev. 1437 (1992).

7. See Ralph K. Winter, Jr., State Law, Shareholder Protection, and the Theory of the Corporation, 6 J. Legal Stud. 251 (1977) (the seminal response to Cary); see also William J. Carney, The Political Economy of Competition for Corporate Charters, 26 J. Legal Stud. 303 (1997); Frank H. Easterbrook, Managers' Discretion and Investors' Welfare: Theories and Evidence, 9 Del. J. Corp. L. 540, 654–71 (1984); Daniel R. Fischel, The "Race to the Bottom" Revisited: Reflections on Recent Developments in Delaware's Corporation Law, 76 Nw. U. L. Rev. 913 (1982); Roberta Romano, The State Competition Debate in Corporate Law, 8 Cardozo L. Rev. 709 (1987); cf. Jonathan R. Macey and Geoffrey P. Miller, To-

ward an Interest Group Theory of Delaware Corporate Law, 65 Tex. L. Rev. 469 (1987) (public choice-based theory of state competition).

8. See Roberta Romano, The Genius of American Corporate Law (1993) (setting forth both an empirical analysis and theoretical arguments challenging race to the bottom hypothesis). As even many advocates of the race to the top hypothesis concede, however, state regulation of corporate takeovers appears to be an exception to the rule that efficient solutions tend to win out. See, e.g., Roberta Romano, Competition for Corporate Charters and the Lesson of Takeover Statutes, 61 Fordham L. Rev. 843 (1993); Ralph K. Winter, The "Race for the Top" Revisited: A Comment on Eisenberg, 89 Colum. L. Rev. 1526 (1989); see also Lucian Ayre Bebchuk and Allen Ferrell, Federalism and Corporate Law: The Race to Protect Managers from Takeovers, 99 Colum. L. Rev. 1168 (1999) (contending that the race to the bottom in takeover regulation may be a general phenomenon).

Whether state competition is a race to the bottom or the top, there is no question that Delaware is the runaway winner in this competition. More than half of the corporations listed for trading on the New York Stock Exchange and nearly 60% of the Fortune 500 corporations are incorporated in Delaware. Proponents of the race to the bottom hypothesis argue that Delaware is dominant because its corporate law is more pro-management than that of other states. Those who reject the race to the bottom theory ascribe Delaware's dominance to a number of other factors: There is a considerable body of case law interpreting the Delaware corporate statute (DGCL), which allows legal questions to be answered with confidence. Delaware has a separate court, the Court of Chancery, devoted largely to corporate law cases. The Chancellors have great expertise in corporate law matters, making their court a highly sophisticated forum for resolving disputes. They also tend to render decisions quite quickly, facilitating transactions that are often time sensitive.[9]

The most important alternative to Delaware law is the American Bar Association's Model Business Corporation Act (MBCA). The 1969 MBCA was adopted in whole or in large part by about 35 states. The 1984 MBCA has been adopted in whole by 24 states and in part by many others. Delaware, California, and New York remain the commercially most important holdouts. Each has preserved a largely unique corporate statute, although each also has adopted some elements of the MBCA.

An important nonstatutory source of corporate law is the American Law Institute's *Principles of Corporate Governance*, promulgated in 1992 after over ten years of work and considerable controversy.[10] The ALI PRINCIPLES resemble the ALI's well-known restatements of the law; each section sets forth some black letter rule of law, followed by explanatory comments and notes. Critics argue that the ALI PRINCIPLES do not restate existing law, but rather propose important changes in the law. In fairness, however, while initial drafts of the ALI PRINCIPLES frequently proposed quite radical reforms, most sections of the ALI PRINCIPLES, as finally adopted, ended up quite close to existing law. Although the ALI PRINCIPLES remain controversial, they provide a compact repository of corporate law doctrines. As such, they are likely to prove quite influential in jurisdictions lacking a well-developed body of corporate law.

B. Federal law

The issuance and trading of stocks and other corporate securities was largely unregulated until the passage of the first state "blue sky law" by Kansas in 1911. These laws were a response to widespread fraud in the sale of securities. Indeed, the name supposedly refers to unscrupu-

---

9. See generally Jill E. Fisch, The Peculiar Role of the Delaware Courts in the Competition for Corporate Charters, 68 U. Cin. L. Rev. 1061 (2000).

10. For the history of the controversy and speculation on its causes, see Stephen M. Bainbridge, Independent Directors and the ALI Corporate Governance Project, 61 Geo. Wash. L. Rev. 1034 (1993).

lous promoters who would sell building lots in the clear blue sky. State regulation proved largely ineffective, however, because the statutes had a limited jurisdictional reach, many statutes contained numerous special interest exemptions, and states had limited enforcement resources.[11]

In the aftermath of the Great Stock Market Crash of 1929 and the subsequent Great Depression, there was widespread agreement that the time had come for federal regulation of the securities markets. Between 1933 and 1940 Congress passed 7 statutes regulating various aspects of the industry, which have been amended on various subsequent occasions and joined by a few other highly specialized statutes.

The most important of these statutes for our purposes are the Securities Act of 1933 and the Securities Exchange Act of 1934. The Securities Act regulates primary market sales of securities by issuing corporations. The Securities Exchange Act regulates a host of matters, but is generally concerned with trading of corporate securities on securities exchanges and other secondary markets.[12]

The New Deal Congress considered three models for regulating the securities markets: the fraud model, which would simply prohibit fraud in the sale of securities; the disclosure model, which would allow issuers to sell very risky or even unsound securities, provided they gave buyers enough information to make an informed investment decision; and the merit review model, which would require some government agency to review the merits of a security and to prohibit the sale of investments that were unsound or excessively risky. Although merit review was a common feature of state blue sky laws, Congress rejected that approach. Instead, it combined the fraud and disclosure models.

Accordingly, while the two statutes are concerned with different transactions, they have the same basic purposes. The first is requiring corporations and other issuers of securities to provide full disclosure to ensure that investors have all the information they need to make informed decisions about buying, selling, or voting securities. The second is to punish fraud committed in connection with securities transactions.

The Securities Act follows a transactional disclosure model; i.e., it focuses attention on getting information concerning certain transactions from the issuer to investors. Accordingly, that act applies only when an

---

11. In Securities Act § 18 and Securities Exchange Act § 28(a), Congress expressly protected state blue sky laws from being preempted by those Acts. Amendments to those provisions in 1996 and 1998, however, created a complex preemption scheme that substantially limited the scope of the blue sky laws' potential application. Accordingly, while the blue sky laws remain on the books, the federal securities laws are now far more important in most situations. See generally David M. Levine & Adam C. Pritchard, The Securities Litigation Uniform Standards Act of 1998: The Sun Sets on California's Blue Sky Laws, 54 Bus. Law. 1 (1998); Richard W. Painter, Responding to a False Alarm: Federal Preemption of State Securities Fraud Causes of Action, 84 Cornell L. Rev. 1 (1998).

12. Subject to certain exemptions, all corporations that sell securities to the public are subject to the Securities Act. In contrast, the Securities Exchange Act applies to a narrower range of businesses. Although the Act has a complex set of rules for deciding which provisions apply to which corporations, as a general rule of thumb it applies only to publicly held corporations.

issuer is actually selling securities. As long as a company can raise funds by other means, the Securities Act does not require it to provide any disclosures whatsoever. Obviously, this leaves a significant gap in the disclosure requirements. The Securities Exchange Act addresses this problem by imposing a periodic disclosure system on certain issuers. It focuses attention on regularly and routinely getting information from the issuer to the market. In addition, the Securities Exchange Act includes a hodge-podge of other provisions, concerned with regulating secondary market trading and preventing fraud.

The Securities Exchange Act is also notable because it created the Securities and Exchange Commission (SEC), the primary federal agency charged with administering the various securities laws. The agency is headed by five Commissioners, who must be confirmed by the Senate. No more than three can belong to the same political party. Most of the agency's work, of course, is done not by the Commissioners but by the professional staff. The agency staff is organized into Divisions and Offices having various specialized responsibilities. The professional staff is comprised mainly of lawyers, although it also includes a number of accountants and economists. The staff has three primary functions: it provides interpretative guidance to private parties raising questions about the application of the securities laws to a particular transaction; it advises the Commission as to new rules or revisions of existing rules; and it investigates and prosecutes violations of the securities laws.

The U.S. Supreme Court has held repeatedly that the federal securities laws do not preempt state corporate law, but instead place only a limited gloss on the broader body of state law.[13] A fair rule of thumb is that state law is concerned with the substance of corporate governance, while federal law is concerned with disclosure and a limited number of procedural aspects of corporate governance (such as the solicitation of proxies and the conduct of a tender offer).[14] In certain areas, the dividing line between the federal and state role remains controversial. The two most important disputes concern shareholder voting rights and state regulation of takeovers.

§ 1.4 Law and economics

At least insofar as corporate law is concerned, law and economics has proven by far the most form of interdisciplinary scholarship. Law and economics, of course, is the school of jurisprudence in which the tools of microeconomic analysis are used to study law. Those tools are an increasingly common feature of the corporate lawyer's toolkit. The law journals are filled with increasingly sophisticated economically-oriented

13. See, e.g., CTS Corp. v. Dynamics Corp. of Am., 481 U.S. 69 (1987); Burks v. Lasker, 441 U.S. 471 (1979); Santa Fe Indus. v. Green, 430 U.S. 462 (1977).

14. See, e.g., Business Roundtable v. SEC, 905 F.2d 406 (D.C.Cir.1990); see generally Robert B. Thompson, Preemption and Federalism in Corporate Governance: Protecting Shareholder Rights to Vote, Sell, and Sue, 62 Law & Contemp. Probs. 215 (1999); Stephen M. Bainbridge, The Short Life and Resurrection of SEC Rule 19c–4, 69 Wash. U. L.Q. 565 (1991).

corporate law scholarship. It has begun filtering into judicial opinions.[1] Even those corporate law scholars critical of economic analysis necessarily spend considerable time and effort responding to those of us who practice it.

Those who practice economic analysis have a deceptively simple task. They translate some legal doctrine into economic terms. They then apply a few basic tools of neoclassical microeconomics—cost-benefit analysis, collective action theory, decisionmaking under uncertainty, risk aversion, and the like—to the problem. Finally, they translate the result back into legal terms.

Law and economics radically transformed legal thinking. Traditional forms of legal scholarship were mostly backward-looking. One reasoned from old precedents to decide a present case, seemingly without much concern (at least explicitly) for the effect today's decision would have on future behavior. Yet, law is necessarily forward-looking. To be sure, a major function of our legal system is to resolve present disputes, but law's principal function is to regulate future behavior. The law and economics movement succeeded because it recognized that judges cannot administer justice solely retrospectively. They must also consider what rules their decisions will create to guide the behavior of other actors in the future. The genius of law and economics was giving judges a systematic mechanism for predicting how rules will affect behavior.

A. Positive v. normative law and economics

At the outset, it is important to distinguish between positive and normative uses of economic analysis. At the risk of being too simplistic, positive law and economics asks whether the law is efficient; normative law and economics commands that the law ought to be efficient.[2] The point of positive economic analysis of law is to determine how people are likely to behave under a given legal regime. In trying to make behavioral predictions, positive law and economics does nothing more than to apply modern microeconomic tools to legal rules.

As corporate lawyers, much of what we do with economic analysis is positive rather than normative. The utility of positive economic analysis

---

§ 1.4

1. See, e.g., Basic Inc. v. Levinson, 485 U.S. 224 (1988); Edgar v. MITE Corp., 457 U.S. 624 (1982); Amanda Acquisition Corp. v. Universal Foods Corp., 877 F.2d 496 (7th Cir.1989); Credit Lyonnais Bank Nederland, N.V. v. Pathe Communications Corp., 1991 WL 277613 (Del.Ch.1991).

2. Economists differentiate between two forms of efficiency: A transaction is said to be efficient in the Pareto superiority sense if it makes at least one person better off and no one worse off. In contrast, Kaldor–Hicks efficiency does not require that no one be made worse off by a reallocation of resources. Instead, it requires only that the resulting increase in wealth be sufficient to compensate the losers. Note that there does not need to be any actual compensation—compensation simply must be possible. The validity of Kaldor–Hicks efficiency as a guide to public policy is sharply disputed. See Richard A. Posner, The Economics of Justice 91–94 (1981); Bruce Chapman, Trust, Economic Rationality, and the Corporate Fiduciary Obligation, 43 U. Toronto L. Rev. 547, 554–55 (1993).

should be obvious. Economics is generally quite good at predicting how people respond to changes in prices.[3] If we think of legal sanctions as the cost of engaging in certain activities, changing a legal rule is no different than any other change in prices. The former is just as subject to analysis under price theory and game theory as the latter. Imposing a more onerous legal sanction on the use of illegal drugs, for example, is the functional equivalent of charging more for tobacco. Just as people respond to higher prices by consuming less of the good (here tobacco), they should respond to enhanced legal sanctions by engaging in less of the regulated activity (here consuming illegal drugs). Hence, positive economics provides a mechanism for separating the wheat from the chaff—figuring out which facts are the really significant ones, by identifying those facts most relevant to behavior.

It is law and economics' normative claims that arouse the most controversy. In its normative guise, law and economics claims that society should make efficient decisions—put another way, society should make decisions that maximize social wealth. Normative economic analysis rests on two critical assumptions: wealth maximization and rational choice. We take them up in that order.

B. The wealth maximization norm

As a normative principle, wealth maximization seeks to increase social wealth, as measured by the dollar equivalents of everything in society.[4] In a society governed by such a norm, the only preferences that matter are those that are backed up by money. There is a vast (and, frankly, often quite dreary) literature on the wealth maximization norm. But while both the objections to and defenses of wealth maximization are getting a little shop-worn, it remains the essential starting point for any evaluation of law and economics.

At first blush, the wealth maximization norm strikes many people as unpalatable, at best. Is not "the love of money a root of all evil"? Do not most ethical systems teach us that there are many things more important than wealth? Practitioners of law and economics typically respond to these charges with one (or both) of the following moves: concede part of the objection, while seeking to preserve some role for economic analysis; or rise in defense of wealth maximization.

---

3. The positive claims of economic analysis are subject to the caveat that validity of the economic description of human behavior—the so-called rational choice model—has come under increasing fire in recent years. As we shall see, however, rational choice is still a decent first order approximation of human behavior.

4. Wealth maximization is a variation of Jeremy Bentham's famous assertion that people rationally strive to maximize their utility—i.e., whatever gave them the greatest happiness in all areas of life. The inability to conduct interpersonal comparisons of subjective utility is a principal reason many economists prefer to rely on wealth maximization rather than utility itself.

1. Evasive maneuvers

There are a couple of moves by which the lawyer-economist[5] can pull the teeth from objections to the wealth maximization norm. Changing the terminology is one of the easiest. Wealth maximization is a poor choice of words. It implies a normative principle calling for society to squeeze the maximum possible wealth out of every opportunity for profit. A better term might be wealth optimization, which takes a longer-term view. As a societal norm, wealth optimization would consider many factors besides immediate wealth maximization. Indeed, wealth optimization might even take into account preferences having no knowable monetary value.

Robert Cooter scored with a slightly more aggressive evasive tactic. Cooter focused not on wealth maximization, but on efficiency, which he defined as acting "without wasting money."[6] The wealth maximization norm thus transforms into the more palatable proposition that, as we move towards whatever goals society chooses, we should do so without wasting money. This was a brilliant debater's move: (1) it shifted the burden of proof to opponents of the norm and (2) left them the unpalatable task of advocating rules that waste money.

2. The partial concession gambit

When law and economics was a young academic discipline, its hard core practitioners rejected the notion that wealth maximization could be trumped by distributional considerations or other values. Contrary to what many believed, these scholars did not ignore the humanitarian considerations that underlie distributional claims. They asserted, however, that strict adherence to the wealth maximization norm was a more effective means of accomplishing altruistic goals. This view was most strongly articulated by Judge Richard Posner, who long was the foremost defender of using wealth maximization as society's basic decisionmaking norm. In an early article, he argued that "a society which aims at maximizing wealth ... will produce an ethically attractive combination of happiness, of rights (to liberty and property), and of sharing with the less fortunate members of society."[7]

Almost from the beginning, however, important law and economics scholars asserted that the wealth maximization norm could be trumped by what Guido Calabresi famously referred to as "other justice" norms.[8] The latter position now largely prevails in the law and economics community. Even Judge Posner now concedes (albeit with qualifications)

---

5. The term "lawyer-economist" is used not necessarily to refer to someone who has both a J.D. and a Ph.D. in economics, but as a short hand for the more cumbersome phrase "practitioner of law and economics."

6. See Robert D. Cooter, The Best Right Laws: Value Foundations of the Economic Analysis of Law, 64 Notre Dame L. Rev. 817 (1989).

7. Richard A. Posner, The Ethical and Political Basis of the Efficiency Norm in Common Law Adjudication, 8 Hofstra L. Rev. 487 (1980).

8. Guido Calabresi, About Law and Economics: A Letter to Ronald Dworkin, 8 Hofstra L. Rev. 553, 559 (1980).

that economic analysis can be trumped by moral values and other noneconomic concerns.[9] Posner continues to assert, however, that "[t]he great power of wealth maximization, and of economics generally, is in clarifying the costs and the benefits of a proposed course of action, eliminating or at least reducing the element of factual uncertainty, and in that way minimizing, the area of genuine irreducible moral debate."[10]

Although some variant on this position is now widely accepted by lawyer-economists, many remain skeptical of specific claims that wealth maximization should be trumped by "other justice" norms in any given setting. Note that this argument does not depend on a claim that wealth maximization is an ethically superior norm by which to guide societal decisionmaking. Instead, the argument rests on two prudential considerations: First, those who favor distributional concerns over wealth maximization often give short shrift to the positive social effects of wealth maximization. Second, many lawyer-economists believe that legal institutions are more likely to be effective when they seek to promote wealth maximization than when they seek to promote distributional justice.

Many lawyer-economists find much merit in the old adage "a rising tide lifts all boats." Although distributional concerns are relevant to analysis, lawyer-economists caution that care should be taken to address them in a manner that does no harm (or minimal harm) to wealth creation. Critics of neoclassical economics often fail to take into account the secondary unintended effects of economic regulation. Because the secondary effects of regulation readily can run counter to, and even be larger than, the primary intended effects, social legislation easily can make matters worse, not better. This is so, even if the public choice arguments made below are discounted, because the law of unintended consequences inevitably follows from the bounded rationality of human minds.

The second major prong of the law and economics argument rests on the inevitability of disagreement and the inadequacies of decisionmaking institutions staffed by fallible humans. In our society, questions of distributive justice have been taken out of the hands of individuals and reserved for the government. In particular, distributive justice is usually a matter for the legislative branch. Common law judges normally take the initial distribution of wealth as a given. Indeed, there is a considerable body of literature supporting the proposition that the common law has what Judge Posner calls an "implicit economic logic."[11]

In contrast, economic analysis of the legislative process offers a robust, yet disheartening perspective on legislative solutions to distributive problems. Public choice is the branch of law and economics relevant here. Public choice's basic tenet is that well-defined, politically influential interest groups use their influence with lawmakers to obtain legal

---

9. See, e.g., Richard A. Posner, The Economics of Justice 376–80 (1981).

10. Richard A. Posner, Rebuttal to Malloy, 24 Valpariso L. Rev. 183, 184 (1990).

11. Richard A. Posner, Economic Analysis of Law 251 (4th ed. 1992).

rules that benefit themselves at the expense of larger, more diffuse groups. In other words, legislative decisions are not driven by distributive justice, but by interest group pressures.

Obviously, not all legislative choices are driven solely by naked self-interest. Public choice theory has enormous explanatory power, but it has difficulty accounting for ideological politicians like Senator Kennedy, President Reagan, or Lady Thatcher. Any sensible account of modern politics must take into not only naked self-interest, but also the possibility that ideology and morality matter, even in the halls of Congress. Lawyer-economists merely claim that we need to be suspicious of legislators who claim to be acting in the name of distributive justice. Ideology and morality often serve as cover for self-interest. Worse yet, "human nature may incline even one acting in subjective good faith to rationalize as right that which is merely personally beneficial."[12] Before concluding that a wealth maximizing outcome is socially undesirable, one ought to ensure that reversing that outcome does not lead to an even more undesirable result.

C. Rational choice

As with any model claiming predictive power, law and economics rests on a theory of human behavior. Specifically, neoclassical economics is premised on rational choice theory, which posits an autonomous individual who makes rational choices that maximize his satisfactions.

To clear up one frequent misconception at the outset, rational choice does not claim that humans are driven solely by pecuniary incentives. To be sure, a rational actor's behavior is completely determined by incentives; human rationality in this sense is no different from that of a pigeon or a rat. But those incentives need not be pecuniary in nature. Instead, the theory of rational choice encompasses all incentives to which humans respond, including such things as risk aversion and even a generalized sense of fairness.

Another misconception about rational choice arises out of a failure to understand the role of assumptions and models in economic theory. Many people object that because rationality assumes both an autonomous individual and a pure rational calculator, the economic model of human behavior fails to account either for the importance of mediating institutions or of virtue. Their argument overlooks the fact that rationality is simply an abstraction developed as a useful model of predicting the behavior of large numbers of people—it does not purport to describe real people embedded in a real social order. But so what? A theory is properly judged by its predictive power with respect to the phenomena it purports to explain, not by whether it is a valid description of an objective reality. Indeed, important and significant hypotheses often will be found to have assumptions that are wildly inaccurate descriptive representations of

---

12. City Capital Assocs. Ltd. Partnership v. Interco Inc., 551 A.2d 787, 796 (Del. Ch.) (emphasis deleted), appeal dismissed, 556 A.2d 1070 (Del.1988).

reality. As such, the relevant question to ask about the assumptions of a theory is not whether they are descriptively realistic, for they never are, but whether they are sufficiently good approximations for the purpose in hand.[13] Empirical research confirms that the rational choice model of human behavior is a good first approximation of how large numbers of people are likely to behave in exchange transactions.[14]

The foregoing assertion is subject to two significant caveats. The first, bounded rationality, is provided by the New Institutional Economics (NIE) school of economic analysis. Both economists and lawyer-economists all too often narrowly focus on markets and contracts across markets. Such an approach, however, impedes understanding of the corporation, because it treats the firm as a mere production function—a black box—acting within a market, without paying attention to the internal workings of the firm as an institution. In contrast, NIE begins with the fundamental premise that an understanding of institutions is at least as important as that of markets.[15] Hence, NIE emphasizes close study of the internal governance of institutions. The relevance of such an approach to our study of corporate governance should be readily apparent—as corporate lawyers we likewise are just as concerned with the internal governance of corporations as we are with the external activities of our corporate clients as market actors.

At the core of NIE lie three basic concepts: (1) Property rights, which are the institutional arrangements governing the use of assets.[16] (2) Contract, which is the process by which property rights are created, assigned, and transferred. (3) Transaction costs, which are the economic equivalent of friction—the set of constraints and limitations on the contracting process.

Among the most important transaction costs recognized by NIE is the limited cognitive power of human decisionmakers. Unlike the Chicago School of law and economics, which posits the traditional concept of rational choice, NIE asserts that rationality is bounded. Put another way, NIE assumes that economic actors seek to maximize their expected utility, but also that the limitations of human cognition often result in

---

13. See generally Milton Friedman, The Methodology of Positive Economics, in Essays in Positive Economics 3, 23 (1953).

14. For a useful summary of rational choice theory, see Thomas S. Ulen, Rational Choice and the Economic Analysis of Law, 19 Law & Soc. Inquiry 487 (1994).

15. See generally Nicholas Mercuro and Steven G. Medema, Economics and the Law: From Posner to Post–Modernism 130–56 (1997); Oliver E. Williamson, The Economic Institutions of Capitalism 15–42 (1985). "The new institutionalists . . . study not 'the market' but the concrete institutions that enable markets to work—for example, the rules of the Chicago Board of Trade . . . or the governance structure of

conglomerate corporations. . . ." Richard A. Posner, Overcoming Law 429 (1995).

16. Some NIE scholars distinguish between the institutional environment, which is the set of rules providing the framework within which exchange and/or production occurs, and institutional arrangements, which are the mechanisms by which production and/or exchange are governed. The institutional environment constrains the choice of institutional arrangements, by limiting the opportunity set of viable alternatives. In this sense, our analysis of corporate governance law can be seen as the study of the institutional environment in which the corporation's institutional arrangements function.

decisions that fail to maximize utility. Decisionmakers inherently have limited memories, computational skills, and other mental tools, which in turn limit their ability to gather and process information.

This phenomenon, known as bounded rationality,[17] becomes a particular problem in the face of complex decisions. A problem may be complex either because it involves many options or because a limited number of initial options cascade into a decision tree with many branches. A closely related problem is that of ambiguity, which exists when decisionmakers are uncertain about the content of the alternatives available to them or otherwise lack the information necessary to make an optimizing choice. Under conditions of uncertainty and complexity, bounded rationality implies that decisionmakers will not be able to devise a fully specified solution to the problem at hand or fully assess the probable outcomes of their action.

Bounded rationality has pervasive implications for our analysis of corporate law. "If mind is the scarce resource, then economizing on claims against it is plainly warranted."[18] An actor can economize on limited cognitive resources in two ways. First, by adopting institutional governance structures designed to promote more efficient decisionmaking. Second, by invoking heuristic problem-solving decisionmaking processes. We shall frequently see both types of adaptations in this text.

The other major caveat to rational choice theory comes from the emerging school of behavioral economics. Drawing on experimental economics and cognitive psychology, this literature asserts that one can identify systematic departures from rational decisionmaking, even in market settings.[19] Put another way, behavioral economics claims that humans tend to make decisions in ways that systematically depart from the predictions of rational choice. The extent to which behavioral economics calls into question more traditional modes of economic analysis remains sharply contested. At the very least, however, it seems clear that attention must be paid to the possibility that a behavioral economics analysis might shed light on legal problems.[20]

---

17. The term bounded rationality was coined by Herbert Simon. See Herbert A. Simon, Rational Choice and the Structure of the Environment, in Models of Man 261, 271 (1957). For an especially detailed taxonomy of the various forms bounded rationality takes, with special emphasis on the theory's relevance with respect to the organization for firms, see Roy Radner, Bounded Rationality, Indeterminacy, and the Theory of the Firm, 106 Econ. J. 1360, 1362–68 (1996).

18. Oliver E. Williamson, The Economic Institutions of Capitalism 46 (1985) (citation omitted).

19. For descriptions of the principal decisionmaking biases identified in behavioral economics and overviews of their potential implications for legal scholarship, see Chris-tine Jolls et al., A Behavioral Approach to Law and Economics, 50 Stan L. Rev. 1471 (1998); Russell B. Korobkin and Thomas S. Ulen, Law and Behavioral Science: Removing the Rationality Assumption from Law and Economics, 88 Cal. L. Rev. 1051 (2000); Donald C. Langevoort, Behavioral Theories of Judgment and Decision Making in Legal Scholarship: A Literature Review, 51 Vand. L. Rev. 1499 (1998); Thomas S. Ulen, The Growing Pains of Behavioral Law and Economics, 51 Vand. L. Rev. 1747 (1998).

20. See generally Stephen M. Bainbridge, Mandatory Disclosure: A Behavioral Analysis, 68 U. Cin. L. Rev. 1023 (2000) (applying behavioral economics to securities regulation issues). A related body of literature is that in which law and economics scholars have begun to focus on the role of

Acknowledging these caveats, in any case, by admitting that rational choice is only a partial explanation of human behavior is by no means fatal to the law and economics project. We can usefully contrast economic analysis to Newtonian physics.[21] Both capture an important part of the phenomena they seek to explain, but neither is fully explanatory. Just as Newtonian physics adequately models the behavior of a falling rock, economics adequately explains the behavior of large masses of people engaged in exchange.

§ 1.5   Economic models of the business firm

The theory of the firm is the sub-branch of law and economics most directly relevant to courses in corporate law. The modern literature on the theory of the firm arguably stems from a single article by Nobel Prize laureate Ronald Coase, *The Nature of the Firm.*[1] Since Coase's article appeared more than six decades ago, economic analysis has taken on ever-increasing importance within corporate law. Indeed, it is fair to say that the economic theory of the firm is now the dominant paradigm in corporate law.[2] Not only legal scholars, but also judges and lawyers are becoming adept at using economic analysis.[3] Hence, even those who reject economic analysis must respond to those who practice it.

The economic theory that will inform our approach to corporate finance and governance is a variant of New Institutional Economics, which we described in the preceding section. The model used here has three major components:

- The nexus of contracts theory or the contractarian model of the firm, which describes the firm as a set of explicit and implicit contracts. The firm is neither an entity nor a thing capable of being owned. It is simply a legal fiction that encompasses a set of contractual relations.

- An emphasis on transaction costs. We can analogize transaction costs to friction: they are dead weight losses that reduce efficien-

---

nonlegal norms in regulating behavior. See, e.g., Robert C. Ellickson, Order without Law: How Neighbors Settle Disputes (1991). The core thesis of that literature is that behavior is regulated by both law and social norms. Melvin A. Eisenberg, Corporate Law and Social Norms, 99 Colum. L. Rev. 1253 (1999). For this purpose, we can roughly define a social norm as a social attitude specifying the behavior an actor ought to exhibit in a given situation. Deviation from that norm has no legal consequences, but may result in a variety of social sanctions. A standard example of the distinction between the law and norms is that leaving a tip after one eats in a restaurant is a social norm, while paying for one's food is a legal requirement.

21. See Richard A. Posner, The Problems of Jurisprudence 366 (1990).

§ 1.5

1. Ronald Coase, The Nature of the Firm, 4 Economica (n.s.) 386 (1937).

2. This verdict has been rendered by no less an authority than former Delaware Chancellor William Allen. See William T. Allen, Contracts and Communities in Corporation Law, 50 Wash. & Lee L. Rev. 1395, 1399 (1993).

3. Examples of judicial opinions in which economic reasoning figured prominently include: Basic Inc. v. Levinson, 485 U.S. 224 (1988); Edgar v. MITE Corp., 457 U.S. 624 (1982) (White, J.); Amanda Acquisition Corp. v. Universal Foods Corp., 877 F.2d 496 (7th Cir.1989); Credit Lyonnais Bank Nederland, N.V. v. Pathe Communications Corp., 1991 WL 277613 (Del.Ch. 1991).

cy. They make transactions more costly and less likely to occur. Although there are many sources and types of transaction costs, the three most important for our purposes are uncertainty, complexity, and opportunism. At the policy level, transaction cost analysis is highly relevant to setting legal rules. Suppose a steam locomotive drives by a field of wheat. Sparks from the engine set crops on fire. Should the railroad company be liable? In a world of zero transaction costs, the initial assignment of rights is irrelevant. If the legal rule we choose is inefficient, the parties can bargain around it. In a world of transaction costs, however, the parties may not be able to bargain. This is likely to be true in our example. The railroad travels past the property of many landowners, who put their property to differing uses and put differing values on those uses. Negotiating an optimal solution will all of those owners would be, at best, time consuming and onerous. Hence, choosing the right rule—which is typically the rule the parties would have chosen if they were able to bargain (the so-called hypothetical bargain)—becomes quite important. At the practical level, much of what transactional lawyers do is figure out ways to minimize transaction costs.

- Agency costs, which are defined as the sum of monitoring costs incurred by the principal, plus bonding costs incurred by the agent, plus the residual loss that inevitably falls through the cracks. Because agents have an incentive to shirk, and principals have an incentive to prevent shirking, much of corporate law necessarily is concerned with constraining agency costs.

Most of this text is devoted to developing these themes across a number of doctrinal fronts.

A. The corporation as nexus of contracts

Contractarians model the firm not as an entity, but as an aggregate of various inputs acting together to produce goods or services. Employees provide labor. Creditors provide debt capital. Shareholders initially provide equity capital and subsequently bear the risk of losses and monitor the performance of management. Management monitors the performance of employees and coordinates the activities of all the firm's inputs. The firm is a legal fiction representing the complex set of contractual relationships between these inputs. In other words, the firm is not a thing, but rather a nexus or web of explicit and implicit contracts establishing rights and obligations among the various inputs making up the firm.

The name "nexus of contracts," by the way, is somewhat unfortunate. For lawyers, the term carries with it all of the baggage learned in Contracts class during the first year of law school. Among that baggage are two particularly problematic features. First, the focus on legal notions such as consideration and mutuality. Second, the paradigm seems to be transactions on spot markets that are thick and relatively untroubled by asymmetric information.[4] Neither of which has much to do with the internal governance of corporations.

As used by contractarians, however, the term is not limited to those relationships that constitute legal contracts. Instead, recall that New Institutional Economics uses the word contract to refer to any process by which property rights to assets are created, modified, or transferred. Perhaps even more important, contractarians are concerned with long-term relationships characterized by asymmetric information, bilateral monopoly, and opportunism. The relationship between shareholders and creditors of a corporation is contractual in this sense, even though there is no single document we could identify as a legally binding contract through which they are in privity.

1. *Implications of the contractarian model*

The nexus of contracts model has important implications for a range of corporate law topics, the most obvious of which is the debate over the proper role of mandatory legal rules. As a positive matter, contractarians contend that corporate law in fact is generally comprised of default rules, from which the parties to the set of contracts making up the corporation are free to depart, rather than mandatory rules. As a normative matter, contractarians argue that this is just as it should be.

Contractarianism also has implications for the way in which we think about intra-corporate relationships. Take, for example, the commonly held assumption that shareholders own the corporation. Under traditional theories, the corporation is a thing, so it can be owned. In other words, traditionalists reify the corporation: they treat the firm as an entity separate from its various constituents. Nexus of contracts theory rejects this basic proposition. Because shareholders are simply one of the inputs bound together by this web of voluntary agreements, ownership is not a meaningful concept in nexus of contracts theory. Someone owns each input, but no one owns the totality. Instead, the corporation is an aggregation of people bound together by a complex web of contractual relationships. (The validity of this insight becomes apparent when one recognizes that buying a few shares of IBM stock does not entitle me to trespass on IBM's property—I do not own the land or even have any ownership-like right to enter its land.)

The implications of the foregoing may not seem as staggering as they actually are. Consider, for example, the traditional corporate law principle of shareholder wealth maximization. According to a significant line of corporate precedents, the principal obligation of corporate di-

---

4. A spot market is one where products and services are exchanged by autonomous market actors who may deal with one another only once. Contracts in such markets typically are executed simultaneously with the exchange and do not have on-going features. Commodities exchanges, such as those for livestock or grain, are good examples of spot markets. So are day laborer employment halls.

A thick market is one in which there are many buyers and sellers, typically characterized by goods for which there are ready substitutes.

rectors is to increase the value of the residual claim—i.e., to increase shareholder wealth.[5] In its traditional guise, this shareholder primacy norm derives from a conception of the corporation as a thing capable of being owned. The shareholders own the corporation, while directors are merely stewards of the shareholders' property.

The nexus of contracts model squarely rejects this conception of the corporation. As such, the shareholder wealth maximization norm is transformed from a right incident to private property into a mere bargained-for contract term. The contractarian account of this norm thus rests not on an outmoded reification of the corporation, but on the presumption of validity a free market society accords voluntary contracts.

Taken to its logical extreme, this insight allows us to transform the traditional notion of shareholder primacy into one of director primacy. The latter perspective regards the corporation as a vehicle by which directors hire capital from shareholders and creditors. The implications of this shift will affect our analysis of a host of issues, such as the allocation of decisionmaking authority within the corporation and the proper scope of fiduciary obligation. Indeed, director primacy figures as the central organizing principle of this treatise.

2.   *Choosing default rules: The hypothetical bargain*

In the nexus of contracts model, corporations statutes and judicial opinions can be thought of as a standard form contract voluntarily adopted—perhaps with modifications—by the parties. The point of a standard form contract, of course, is to reduce bargaining costs. Parties for whom the default rules are a good fit can take the default rules off the rack, without having to bargain over them. Parties for whom the default rules are inappropriate, in contrast, are free to bargain out of the default rules.

If transaction costs are zero, the default rules—whether contained in a statute or a private standard form contract—do not matter very much.[6] In the face of positive transaction costs, however, the default rule begins to matter very much. Indeed, if transaction costs are very high, bargaining around the rule becomes wholly impractical, forcing the parties to live with an inefficient rule. In such settings, we cannot depend on private contracting to achieve efficient outcomes. Instead, statutes must function as a substitute for private bargaining. The public corporation—with its thousands of shareholders, managers, employees, and creditors, each with different interests and asymmetrical information—is a very high transaction cost environment indeed.[7]

---

5.   See, e.g., Revlon, Inc. v. MacAndrews & Forbes Holdings, Inc., 506 A.2d 173 (Del. 1985); Dodge v. Ford Motor Co., 170 N.W. 668 (Mich.1919).

6.   This is simply a straight-forward application of the famous Coase Theorem, which asserts that, in the absence of trans-

action costs, the initial assignment of a property right will not determine its ultimate use. R. H. Coase, The Problem of Social Cost, 3 J. L. & Econ. 1 (1960).

7.   It should be apparent that the hypothetical bargain methodology is useful even in a relatively low transaction cost environ-

Identifying the party for whom getting its way has the highest value thus becomes the critical question. In effect, we must perform a thought experiment: "If the parties could costlessly bargain over the question, which rule would they adopt?" In other words, we mentally play out the following scenario: Sit all interested parties down around a conference table before organizing the corporation. Ask the prospective shareholders, employees, contract creditors, tort victims, and the like to bargain over what rules they would want to govern their relationships. Adopt that bargain as the corporate law default rule. Doing so reduces transaction costs and therefore makes it more efficient to run a business. Of course, you cannot really do this; but you can draw on your experience and economic analysis to predict what the parties would do in such a situation.

The basic thesis of the hypothetical bargain methodology is that by providing the rule to which the parties would agree if they could bargain (the so-called "majoritarian default"), society facilitates private ordering. In an important series of articles, however, Ian Ayres and his collaborators argued that majoritarian defaults are not always desirable, even if a potentially dominant one can be identified.[8] Among the alternative, nonmajoritarian defaults they identify, the most relevant for our purposes are: (1) Tailored defaults, which purport to fill gaps in the contract at bar by giving the litigants precisely the rule for which those litigants (as opposed to the hypothetical majority) would have bargained if they had thought to do so. (2) Muddy defaults, which make contractual obligations contingent on the circumstances in which the parties find themselves by asking the court to apply a rule that is fair or reasonable under those circumstances. Any rule authorizing judges to fill in gaps in incomplete contracts by supplying terms that are reasonable under the circumstances is an example of a muddy default. (3) Penalty defaults, which are designed to impose a penalty on at least one of the parties if they fail to bargain out of the default rule, thereby giving at least the party subject to the penalty an incentive to negotiate a contractual alternative to the penalty default. They force the parties to choose affirmatively the contract provision they prefer. Penalty defaults are appropriate where it is costly for courts to determine what the parties would have wanted. In such cases, it may be more efficient for the parties to negotiate a term ex ante than for courts to determine ex post what the parties would have wanted.[9]

ment like a small partnership or close corporation. Although partners can bargain amongst themselves, they cannot do so costlessly. Accordingly, providing partners a standard form contract comprised of the default rules that most parties would select should reduce transaction costs.

8. See, e.g., Ian Ayres, Making a Difference: The Contractual Contributions of Easterbrook and Fischel, 59 U. Chi. L. Rev. 1391 (1992); Ian Ayres and Robert Gertner, Filling Gaps in Incomplete Contracts: An

Economic Theory of Default Rules, 99 Yale L.J. 87 (1989); Ian Ayres and Eric Talley, Solomonic Bargaining: Dividing a Legal Entitlement to Facilitate Coasean Trade, 104 Yale L.J. 1027 (1995).

9. The penalty, or bargain-forcing, default flips the majoritarian default concept on its head—the terms imposed by bargain-forcing rules are designed to be contrary to those to which the parties likely would agree if they in fact bargained over the issue, thereby forcing them to choose

For our purposes, tailored defaults are the most important. Much of our attention will be devoted to fiduciary obligations within corporations. While it will often be the case that some form of fiduciary obligation would be the majoritarian default in a particular setting, those defaults are almost always tailored in the sense that fiduciary obligations are stated not as bright-line rules but as rather vague standards.[10] As a result, judges deciding fiduciary obligation cases typically have substantial discretion to tailor the result to the parties and circumstances at bar.

3. *Criticisms of the contractarian model*

As a matter of intellectual interest, the debate over the contractual nature of the firm is over. This is not to say that the contractarian view has pre-empted the field, as an important group of scholars continues to reject it,[11] but only to say that the debate has been fully played out. Contractarians and noncontractarians no longer have much of interest to say to one another; indeed, they barely speak the same language. To shift metaphors, those who adhere to the nexus of contracts model pass those who do not like two ships in the night, with only an occasional exchange of broadsides to enliven the proceedings. The real action now for contractarians is not in developing the paradigm, but rather in using

---

affirmatively the contract provision they prefer. Choosing between majoritarian and penalty defaults requires one to take into account the lessons of behavioral economics, especially the status quo bias. This aspect of behavioral economics posits a systematic decisionmaking bias pursuant to which people favor maintaining the status quo rather than switching to some alternative state. Selecting a default rule makes it part of the status quo, altering preferences with respect to contract terms by making parties favor the chosen default and, accordingly, making them less likely to bargain out of that default. A series of experiments using law students provides strong empirical support for that thesis. See generally Russell Korobkin, The Status Quo Bias and Contract Default Rules, 83 Cornell L. Rev. 608 (1998) (describing experiment and analyzing results). If this result can be generalized, it argues in favor of majoritarian defaults and against the use of penalty defaults. Default rules will tend to be sticky even in low transaction cost settings. Accordingly, penalty defaults will not lead to parties selecting an optimal rule through private ordering. Instead, provided we redefine the concept of majoritarian default as the rule most parties would select in the absence of any controlling legal authority if they could bargain costlessly, lawmakers should strive to provide socially efficient majoritarian defaults.

10. It is now conventional to distinguish between standards and rules. A requirement that automobile drivers use reason-

able care is a standard. A speed limit forbidding drivers to go faster than 30 miles an hour is a rule. In the former case, the court will have substantial discretion to decide whether the driver's conduct was reasonable, balancing competing policies and concerns. In the latter, the driver either was speeding or not.

11. See, e.g., William W. Bratton, Jr., The "Nexus of Contracts" Corporation: A Critical Appraisal, 74 Cornell L. Rev. 407 (1989); Melvin A. Eisenberg, The Conception That the Corporation is a Nexus of Contracts and the Dual Nature of the Firm, 24 J. Corp. L. 819 (1999); Melvin A. Eisenberg, Contractarianism Without Contracts: A Response to Professor McChesney, 90 Colum. L. Rev. 1321 (1990). For ripostes from contractarian scholars, see, e.g., Stephen M. Bainbridge, Community and Statism: A Conservative Contractarian Critique of Progressive Corporate Law Scholarship, 82 Cornell L. Rev. 856 (1997); Henry N. Butler and Larry Ribstein, Opting Out of Fiduciary Duties: A Response to the Anti-Contractarians, 65 Wash. L. Rev. 1 (1990); Fred S. McChesney, Contractarianism Without Contracts? Yet Another Critique of Eisenberg, 90 Colum. L. Rev. 1332 (1990); Fred S. McChesney, Economics, Law, and Science in the Corporate Field: A Critique of Eisenberg, 89 Colum. L. Rev. 1530 (1989).

it as a heuristic for exploring the nooks and crannies of corporate law. In the interests of completeness, however, we consider a few of the most common criticisms of the nexus of contracts theory of the firm.

The mandatory rules red herring. Some reject the positive contractarian story on grounds that corporate law is pervaded by mandatory rules.[12] But this objection is far from fatal. In the first instance, many mandatory corporate law rules are in fact trivial, in the sense that they are subject to evasion through choice of form or jurisdiction, or to the extent that some rules appear across the spectrum of possible organizational forms, they are rules almost everyone would reach in the event of actual bargaining.[13]

In the second, most contractarians probably regard the normative story as being the more important of the two. As such, we cheerfully concede the existence of mandatory rules, while deploring that unfortunate fact. Contractarians assume that default rules are preferable to mandatory rules in most settings.[14] So long as the default rule is properly chosen, of course, most parties will be spared the need to reach a private agreement on the issue in question. Default rules in this sense provide cost savings comparable to those provided by standard form contracts, because both can be accepted without the need for costly negotiation. At the same time, however, because the default rule can be modified by contrary agreement, idiosyncratic parties wishing a different rule can be accommodated. Given these advantages, a fairly compelling case ought to be required before we impose a mandatory rule.[15] Mandatory rules are justifiable only if a default rule would demonstrably create significant negative externalities or, perhaps, if one of the contracting parties is demonstrably unable to protect itself through bargaining.

12. See, e.g., Douglas M. Branson, The Death of Contractarianism and the Vindication of Structure and Authority in Corporate Governance and Corporate Law, in Progressive Corporate Law 93, 94–95 (Lawrence E. Mitchell ed. 1995).

13. Bernard S. Black, Is Corporate Law Trivial?: A Political and Economic Analysis, 84 Nw. U. L. Rev. 542 (1990).

14. Probably the best introduction to this debate is Symposium, Contractual Freedom in Corporate Law, 89 Colum. L. Rev. 1395 (1989). See also Robert B. Thompson, The Law's Limits on Contracts in a Corporation, 15 J. Corp. L. 377 (1990). In conjunction with the mid–1990s revisions to the Uniform Partnership Act, there was also a considerable blossoming of contractarian and anti-contractarian scholarship dealing with the central question of the extent to which freedom of contract trumped fiduciary obligation. See, e.g., J. Dennis Hynes, Fiduciary Duties and UPA (1997): An Inquiry Into Freedom of Con-

tract, 58 Law & Contemp. Probs. 29 (1995); Larry Ribstein, Fiduciary Duty Contracts in Unincorporated Firms, 54 Wash. & Lee L. Rev. 537 (1997); Allan W. Vestal, Advancing the Search for a Compromise: A Response to Professor Hynes, 58 Law & Contemp. Probs. 55 (1995); Allan W. Vestal, The Disclosure Obligations of Partners inter se under the Revised Uniform Partnership Act of 1994: Is the Contractarian Revolution Failing?, 36 Wm. & Mary L. Rev. 1559 (1995); Allan W. Vestal, Fundamental Contractarian Error in the Revised Uniform Partnership Act of 1992, 73 B.U. L. Rev. 523 (1993); see also Larry Ribstein, Unlimited Contracting in the Delaware Limited Partnership and its Implications for Corporate Law, 16 J. Corp. L. 299 (1991).

15. Cf. In re Pace Photographers, Ltd., 525 N.E.2d 713, 718 (N.Y.1988) ("Participants in business ventures are free to express their understandings in written agreements, and such consensual arrangements are generally favored and upheld by the courts.").

Lack of bargaining. As already noted, contractarians contend that corporate law consists mainly of default rules. Put another way, in the nexus of contracts model, corporate statutes and decisions amount to a standard form contract voluntarily adopted—perhaps with modifications—by the corporation's various constituencies. Some reject this argument on grounds that the corporation's constituencies do not and cannot actually bargain.

Part of the answer to this criticism derives from the distinction between actual and hypothetical bargaining. Contractarians concede (or at least should do so) that actual bargaining over corporate law rules is precluded by transaction cost barriers, but contend that this is precisely why corporate statutes provide a set of off-the-rack rules amounting to a standard-form contract. Put another way, legal rules function as a substitute for private bargaining.

A related point has to do with the distinction between outcome and process bargaining. A bargain can be understood in two distinct ways: as a process or as an outcome. There is no bargaining process between a shareholder and the public corporations in which he invests, but there is an outcome—the set of organic rules contained in the articles and bylaws as drafted by the corporation's founders or directors—that fairly can be described as a bargain. A bargain involving only an outcome is just as much a contract as a bargain involving both a process and an outcome.

Summation. Despite these and other objections by the nexus of contracts model's critics, there is no doubt that contractarianism is today the dominant theory of the firm in the legal academy. It is also steadily working its way into judicial decisionmaking. Delaware supreme court Chief Justice Veasey, for example, opines: "Although the contract analogy is imperfect, it comes reasonably close to a working hypothesis. I think courts might consider using as a point of departure—but not necessarily a controlling principle—what they perceive to be the investors' reasonable contractual expectations."[16]

B. Transaction costs

As already noted, transaction costs are the economic equivalent of friction—dead weight losses that increase the cost of transacting and, hence, reduce the number of transactions. Transaction costs are pervasive and, hence, drive the analysis both of market transactions and intrafirm governance. At present, however, the transaction costs most relevant for our purposes are those that explain the emergence and success of the corporation as an economic institution. As we shall see throughout this text, it is those costs that necessarily provide the framework for our analysis.

Why then do firms exist? In capitalist economic systems, there are two basic coordinating mechanisms: markets, in which resources are

---

16. E. Norman Veasey, An Economic Rationale for Judicial Decisionmaking in   Corporate Law, 53 Bus. Law. 681 (1998).

allocated by the price system, and firms, in which resources are allocated by authoritative direction. This was Ronald Coase's fundamental insight: If a workman moves from department Y to department X he does so not because of change in relative prices, but because he is ordered to do so. Accordingly, Coase opined, firms come into existence when the costs of bargaining are higher than the costs of command-and-control.[17]

Organizing economic activity within a firm, for example, may lower search and other transaction costs associated with bargaining. Consider Adam Smith's classic example: the manufacturing of pins in eighteenth century England.[18] Smith observed that making a pin involves eighteen distinct operations. A substantial synergistic effect resulted when a team was organized in which each operation was conducted by a separate individual: the team was able to produce thousands of pins a day, while an individual working alone might produce one pin a day at best. In theory, the team could be organized through a decentralized price mechanism; indeed, there are a few historical examples of quasi-assembly line production processes involving independent craftsmen transacting across a small local market. In normal practice, however, team production requires personnel interactions that are too complex to be handled through a price mechanism. The firm solves that problem by acting as a centralized contracting party—some team member is charged with seeking out the necessary inputs and bringing them together for productive labor.

Organizing production within a firm can also lower costs associated with uncertainty, opportunism, and complexity. Uncertainty arises because it is difficult to predict the future. Opportunism arises because parties to a contract are inevitably tempted to pursue their own self-interest at the expense of the collective good, which in market transactions leads to contract breaches requiring resort to costly enforcement mechanisms.[19] Complexity arises when the parties attempt to contractually specify how they will respond to a given situation. As the relationship's term lengthens, it necessarily becomes more difficult to foresee the needs and threats of the future, which in turn presents an ever-growing myriad of contingencies to be dealt with. The more contingencies to be accounted for, and the greater the degree of uncertainty that is present, the more difficult it becomes for the parties to draft completely specified contracts. Indeed, the phenomenon of bounded rationality implies that making complete contracts is costly, at best, and often impossible. Given the limits on cognitive competence implied by bounded rationality, incomplete contracts are the inevitable result of uncertainty and complexity, which in turn leave greater room for opportunistic behavior, and

17. Ronald Coase, The Nature of the Firm, 4 Economica (n.s.) 386 (1937).

18. Adam Smith, The Wealth of Nations 4–5 (Modern Library ed. 1937).

19. The transaction cost economics concept of opportunism or strategic behavior is closely related to agency cost economics, which is described in the next section. The two approaches are complementary rather than competing—indeed, agency costs can be thought of as a subset of transaction costs so important that they deserve separate consideration.

thus inexorably lead to the need for coordination. According to the Coasean theory of the firm, firms arise when it is possible to lower these costs by delegating to a team member the power to direct how the various inputs will be utilized by the firm; in effect, allowing one team member to constantly and, more important, unilaterally rewrite certain terms of the contract between the firm and its various constituents.

Centralized decisionmaking thus emerges as the defining characteristic of the Coasean firm. At first blush, there may appear to be an inconsistency between Coase's command-and-control theory of the firm and the contractarian model embraced above. In a classic article, Armen Alchian and Harold Demsetz rejected Coase's argument that the power of direction was the factor distinguishing firms from markets.[20] They argued that a firm has no power of fiat; instead, an employer's power to direct its employees does not differ from a consumer's power to direct his grocer. Just as a firm can fire a lousy worker, a consumer can "fire" a lousy grocer by patronizing a different store.

Coase may well have erred in treating the firm as a nonmarket institution in which prices and contracts are of relatively little consequence, but there also is something of a disconnect between Alchian and Demsetz's argument and the real world of work. Command-and-control is the norm in most workplaces. In any case, there is no necessary contradiction between a theory of the firm characterized by command-and-control decisionmaking and the contractarian model. The set of contracts making up the firm consists in very large measure of implicit agreements, which by definition are both incomplete and unenforceable. As we have just seen, under conditions of uncertainty and complexity, employees and employers cannot execute a complete contract, so that many decisions must be left for later contractual rewrites imposed by employer fiat. It is precisely the lack of enforceability of implicit corporate contracts that makes it possible for the central decisionmaker to rewrite them more-or-less freely. The parties to the corporate contract presumably accept this consequence of relying on implicit contracts because the resulting reduction in transaction costs benefits them all. It is thus possible to harmonize the Coasean and contractarian models without having to reject a theory of the firm in which management has the power to direct its workers or in which the corporation is characterized by bureaucratic hierarchies. Instead, the firm's employees voluntarily enter into a relationship in which they agree to obey managerial commands, while reserving the right to disassociate from the firm.

C. Agency costs

Organizing production within a firm creates certain costs, of which the class known as agency costs is the most important for our purposes. Agency costs are defined as the sum of the monitoring and bonding

---

20. Armen A. Alchian and Harold Demsetz, Production, Information Costs, and Economic Organization, 62 Am. Econ. Rev. 777 (1972).

costs, plus any residual loss, incurred to prevent shirking by agents.[21] In turn, shirking is defined to include any action by a member of a production team that diverges from the interests of the team as a whole. As such, shirking includes not only culpable cheating, but also negligence, oversight, incapacity, and even honest mistakes. In other words, shirking is simply the inevitable consequence of bounded rationality and opportunism within agency relationships.[22]

A sole proprietorship with no agents will internalize all costs of shirking, because the proprietor's optimal trade-off between labor and leisure is, by definition, the same as the firm's optimal trade-off. Agents of a firm, however, will not internalize all of the costs of shirking: the principal reaps part of the value of hard work by the agent, but the agent receives all of the value of shirking. In a classic article, Professors Alchian and Demsetz offered the useful example of two workers who jointly lift heavy boxes into a truck.[23] The marginal productivity of each worker is difficult to measure and their joint output cannot be separated easily into individual components. In such situations, obtaining information about a team member's productivity and appropriately rewarding each team member are very difficult and costly. In the absence of such information, however, the disutility of labor gives each team member an incentive to shirk because the individual's reward is unlikely to be closely related to conscientiousness.

Although agents ex post have strong incentives to shirk, ex ante they have equally strong incentives to agree to a corporate contract containing terms designed to prevent shirking. Bounded rationality, however, precludes firms and agents from entering into the complete contract necessary to prevent shirking by the latter. Instead, there must be some system of ex post governance: some mechanism for detecting and punishing shirking. Accordingly, an essential economic function of management is monitoring the various inputs into the team effort: management meters the marginal productivity of each team member and

---

21. Michael C. Jensen and William H. Meckling, Theory of the Firm: Managerial Behavior, Agency Costs and Ownership Structure, 3 J. Fin. Econ. 305 (1976).

22. A simple example of the agency cost problem is provided by the bail upon which alleged criminals are released from jail while they await trial. The defendant promises to appear for trial. But that promise is not very credible. The defendant will be tempted to flee the country. The court could keep track of the defendant—monitor him—by keeping him in jail or perhaps by means of some electronic device permanently attached to the defendant's person. Yet, such monitoring efforts are not free—indeed, keeping someone in jail is quite expensive (food, guards, building the jail, etc.). Alternatively, the defendant could give his promise credibility by bonding it,

which is exactly what bail does. The defendant puts up a sum of money that he will forfeit if he fails to appear for trial. (Notice that the common use of bail bonds and the employment of bounty hunters to track fugitives further enhances the credibility of bail as a deterrent against flight.) Of course, despite these precautions, some defendants will escape jail and/or jump bail. Hence, there will always be some residual loss in the form of defendants who escape punishment. Notice, by the way, that this example illustrates how economic analysis can be extended beyond the traditional agency relationship.

23. Armen A. Alchian and Harold Demsetz, Production, Information Costs, and Economic Organization, 62 Am. Econ. Rev. 777 (1972).

then takes steps to reduce shirking. (No implication is intended that ex post governance structures are noncontractual.)

The process just described, of course, raises a new question: who will monitor the monitors? In any organization, one must have some ultimate monitor who has sufficient incentives to ensure firm productivity without himself having to be monitored. Otherwise, one ends up with a never ending series of monitors monitoring lower level monitors. Alchian and Demsetz solved this dilemma by consolidating the roles of ultimate monitor and residual claimant. According to Alchian and Demsetz, if the constituent entitled to the firm's residual income is given final monitoring authority, he is encouraged to detect and punish shirking by the firm's other inputs because his reward will vary exactly with his success as a monitor.

Unfortunately, this elegant theory breaks down precisely where it would be most useful. Because of the separation of ownership and control, it simply does not describe the modern publicly held corporation. As the corporation's residual claimants, the shareholders should act as the firm's ultimate monitors. But while the law provides shareholders with some enforcement and electoral rights, these are reserved for fairly extraordinary situations. In general, shareholders of public corporation have neither the legal right, the practical ability, nor the desire to exercise the kind of control necessary for meaningful monitoring of the corporation's agents.

The apparent lack of managerial accountability inherent in the modern corporate structure has troubled legal commentators since at least Adolf Berle's time.[24] To be sure, agency costs are an important component of any viable theory of the firm. A narrow focus on agency costs, however, easily can distort one's understanding of the firm. Corporate managers operate within a pervasive web of accountability mechanisms that substitute for monitoring by residual claimants. Important constraints are provided by a variety of market forces. The capital and product markets, the internal and external employment markets, and the market for corporate control all constrain shirking by firm agents. In addition, the legal system evolved various adaptive responses to the ineffectiveness of shareholder monitoring, establishing alternative accountability structures to punish and deter wrongdoing by firm agents, such as the board of directors.

An even more important consideration, however, is that agency costs are the inevitable consequence of vesting discretion in someone other than the residual claimant. We could substantially reduce, if not eliminate, agency costs by eliminating discretion; that we do not do so suggests that discretion has substantial virtues. A complete theory of the

---

24. Adolf A. Berle, Jr. and Gardiner C. Means, The Modern Corporation and Private Property 6 (1932) ("The separation of ownership from control produces a condition where the interests of owner and of ultimate manager may, and often do, diverge, and where many of the checks which formerly operated to limit the use of power disappear.").

firm thus requires one to balance the virtues of discretion against the need to require that discretion be used responsibly. Neither discretion nor accountability can be ignored, because both promote values essential to the survival of business organizations. Unfortunately, they are ultimately antithetical: one cannot have more of one without also having less of the other. Managers cannot be made more accountable without undermining their discretionary authority. Establishing the proper mix of discretion and accountability thus emerges as the central corporate governance question,[25] and the one around which this text is largely centered.

D. Summation

Although each of the foregoing theories offers a useful heuristic, none is a complete theory of the firm. Corporations are astonishingly complex institutions, whose reality cannot be captured in a single, necessarily simplified, model. That we lack a unified single theory of the firm neither is disheartening nor calls into question the validity of any of the theories. No one expects a carpenter to use a hammer when a saw is the right tool. Just as the carpenter's toolbox has many different tools, each useful for its own task, the lawyer-economist has a number of different situation-specific theories upon which to draw. The task in any given case is to identify the tool most useful for the situation at hand, to use it properly, and to be prepared to defend both the choice of tool and the analytical result.

25. See generally Michael P. Dooley, Two Models of Corporate Governance, 47 Bus. Law. 461 (1992) (upon which the preceding discussion draws).

Chapter 2

FORMING THE CORPORATION

Analysis

---

§ 2.1 Introduction

Until fairly recently, governments regarded business corporations with considerable suspicion and therefore closely regulated them. Over the last century, however, much of this regulatory regime has faded away. Modern regulation of corporations tends to involve general welfare laws, such as environmental laws, rather than corporate law. Yet, some aspects of that earlier regime linger.

Barriers to forming a corporation were one consequence of legislative suspicion of the corporate form. Until the middle of the nineteenth century, incorporating a business required one to persuade the state legislature to pass a special law granting the company a corporate charter. The steadily increasing number of corporations caused an increase in applications for a charter and for amendments to existing charters, however, which constituted a considerable legislative burden. The process also invited corruption, because influential legislators frequently received under the table payments for their support.

As the nineteenth century progressed, states began adopting so-called enabling corporate laws. These statutes created the modern process of incorporating a business. Under the enabling laws, a corporation was formed simply by jumping through certain statutory hoops, the most important of which were preparing articles of incorporation conforming to the statute's requirements and filing them with the appropriate state official. Today, all states have enabling statutes and creating a corporation has become a straightforward process.

§ 2.2   Forming the corporation

Incorporating a business in a MBCA state is an astonishingly simple process. Articles of incorporation meeting certain minimal statutory requirements are drafted. One or more incorporators sign the articles and deliver them to the state of incorporation's secretary of state's office, along with a check for any applicable fees or taxes. The secretary of state retains the original articles and returns a copy to the incorporator with a receipt for the fee. Unless the articles provide to the contrary, the corporation comes into existence at the moment the secretary of state's office accepts the articles for filing.[1]

After the articles of incorporation are filed with the secretary of state, an organizational meeting is held. If the articles name the initial directors, the incorporator's role is finished and the directors will run the organizational meeting. At the organizational meeting, the directors appoint officers, adopt bylaws, and carry out any other business necessary to complete the organization of the corporation.[2] If the articles do not name the initial directors, the incorporator runs the organizational meeting. The incorporator may elect a board of directors, appoint officers, adopt bylaws, and otherwise complete the corporation's organization. Alternatively, the incorporator may simply elect a board of directors and leave those tasks to the new board.[3] The option of using the incorporator to conduct the organizational meeting permits one to avoid naming the initial directors in the articles in cases where confidentiality is important.[4]

---

§ 2.2

1. Some states impose additional requirements, usually additional filings. Some require filing of the articles with the county in which the corporation's registered office or principal place of business is located. A few require newspaper publication of the articles or a notice of incorporation. Several require newly formed corporations to receive payment for shares meeting some minimum amount of capital (typically $1,000) before transacting business or incurring debt. For an up to date listing, see MBCA § 2.03 cmt.

2.   MBCA § 2.05(a)(1).

3.   MBCA § 2.05(a)(2).

4. Minutes of the organizational meeting and, indeed, of all board and shareholder meetings should be kept. The minutes serve three purposes: (1) they are one of the formalities relevant to ensuring that the corporation's shareholders will get the benefit of limited liability; (2) the minutes provide a record of actions authorized by the board of directors (such a record is sometimes needed as proof that a corporate agent is authorized to enter into a contract); and (3) a director who disagrees with some proposed corporate action, and causes his dissent to be recorded in the minutes, may not be held personally liable in connection with the action. MBCA § 8.24(d).

§ 2.3   Drafting the organic documents

A corporation's articles and bylaws set out the firm's basic internal organization and governance rules.

A.   Articles of incorporation

Modern articles of incorporation usually are bare-bones documents, containing little more than the statutorily mandated terms. MBCA § 2.02(a), for example, requires the articles to contain only four items:

- *Name.* A corporation's name may not be the same or confusingly similar to that of another corporation incorporated or qualified to do business in the state of incorporation. The name must also include some word or abbreviation indicating that the business is incorporated, such as corporation, company, "Inc." or the like.

- *Authorized shares.* The articles must state the maximum number of shares the corporation is authorized to issue.

- *Registered agent.* The articles must state the name of the corporation's registered agent and the address of its registered office. The registered office must be located within the state of incorporation. The registered agent receives service of process when the corporation is sued.

- *Incorporators.* The articles must state the name and address of each incorporator.

Under MBCA § 2.02(b), the articles of incorporation also may contain a host of optional provisions. Some of these options alternatively may be included in the bylaws, but many must be included in the articles of incorporation in order to be effective. Some of the more common and important optional provisions include:

- *Statement of purpose.* The articles may state the nature of the corporation's business or the purposes for which it was formed.[1]

- *Classes and series of shares.* Corporate stock may be separated into multiple classes and series. If the corporation wishes to do so, the articles must identify the different classes and state the number of shares of each class the corporation is authorized to issue. Where one or more classes of shares have certain preferential rights over other classes, those rights must be spelled out in this part of the articles.

- *Director and officer indemnification and liability limitation.* We will see many situations throughout this text in which directors or officers of a corporation may be held liable for misconduct. Most

---

§ 2.3

1. At one time purpose and power clauses had considerable importance because of the ultra vires doctrine, but the erosion of that doctrine has rendered such clauses mere formalities. A number of states, prominently including Delaware, nevertheless still require that the articles contain a statement of corporate purpose. It is sufficient, however, to state that "the purpose of the corporation is to engage in any lawful act or activity...." DGCL § 102(a)(3).

corporate statutes now permit the articles to include provisions limiting the scope of a director's liability and/or permitting indemnification of directors.

The articles of incorporation may be amended at any time. A three-step process is normally involved. First, the board of directors must recommend the amendment to the shareholders. Second, the shareholders must approve the amendment.[2] Finally, the amendment must be filed with the secretary of state's office.[3]

The vote necessary to approve an amendment is the principal state-by-state variation on these basic themes. Under the MBCA, the quorum for a vote on amending the articles is a majority of the shares entitled to vote. If that quorum is present, the amendment is approved if more shares are voted affirmatively than voted negatively.[4] Under an earlier version of the MBCA, still in force in some states, amendments that trigger appraisal rights require approval by a majority of the shares entitled to vote,[5] while other amendments to the articles are approved if more shareholders vote affirmatively than vote negatively.[6] In Delaware, by contrast, amendments to the articles must be approved by a majority of the shares eligible to vote.[7]

Suppose, for example, that Acme, Inc. has 1,000 voting shares outstanding. Shareholders owning 600 shares are present at the annual meeting of the shareholders. At that meeting, the board of directors recommends two amendments to the articles. The first changes Acme's name to "Ajax, Inc." 250 shares are voted yes, 100 are voted no, the remainder abstain. If Acme is incorporated in a MBCA state, the amendment passes. The amendment only needs to receive more affirmative votes than negative votes. The second amendment abolishes the shares' preemptive rights.[8] The vote on this amendment is 450 yes, 125 no, 25 abstained. Under the MBCA as recently revised, this amendment also passes. The substantive content of the amendment is irrelevant—it

---

2. MBCA § 10.03(b).

3. MBCA § 10.06.

4. MBCA § 10.03(e). If the corporation has multiple classes or series of stock, certain amendments must be approved both by the shareholders as a whole and by the affected class. See MBCA § 10.04.

5. MBCA § 10.03(e)(1) (1984). Corporations generally operate by majority rule. Minority shareholders disappointed by some corporate action usually have no recourse except to sell their shares. A few corporate actions, however, are so important that the statute authorizes so-called appraisal rights (known in some states as dissenters' rights). If available, appraisal rights entitle the shareholder to demand the corporation buy his shares at some judicially determined fair price. Under prior MBCA § 13.02(a)(4), five types of amendments to the articles trigger appraisal

rights: (1) alteration or abolition of preferential rights; (2) changing redemption rights; (3) alteration or abolition of preemptive rights; (4) limitation of voting rights; and (5) a reverse stock split that reduces the number of shares owned by a shareholder to a fraction of a share. In each case, the amendment must "materially and adversely" affect the shareholder's rights. Note that under Delaware law, appraisal rights are not available in connection with any amendment to the articles of incorporation.

6. MBCA §§ 7.25(c) and 10.03(e)(2) (1984).

7. DGCL § 242(b)(1).

8. Preemptive rights give current shareholders the right to maintain their proportionate interest in the corporation by purchasing a pro rata share of any newly issued shares of stock.

need only receive more affirmative votes than negative votes. Under the prior version of the MBCA, however, this amendment fails. Because this is one of the five types of amendments that triggers appraisal rights, it must be approved by a majority of the outstanding shares entitled to vote, which requires a minimum affirmative vote of 501 shares on these facts. Both amendments would fail under Delaware law, because neither was approved by a majority of the outstanding shares entitled to vote (i.e., at least 501 affirmative votes). Note that abstentions are ignored under the MBCA, while they effectively count as negative votes under Delaware law.

B. Bylaws

Bylaws are the rules a corporation adopts to govern its internal affairs. Bylaws tend to be far more detailed than the articles of incorporation, for three reasons: (1) bylaws need not be filed with the state government, which means they are not part of any public record; (2) bylaws are more easily amended than articles of incorporation (see below); and (3) officers and directors tend to be more familiar with bylaws than with the articles, which makes them a ready repository of organizational rules. In the event of a conflict between a bylaw and the articles, the latter controls.

The bylaws typically deal with such matters as number and qualifications of directors, board vacancies, board committees, quorum and notice requirement for shareholder and board meetings, procedures for calling special shareholder and board meetings, any special voting procedures, any limits on the transferability of shares, and titles and duties of the corporation's officers.

1. *Adoption and amendment*

The corporation's initial bylaws are adopted by the incorporator or the initial directors at the corporation's organizational meeting. At early common law, only shareholders had the power to amend the bylaws. Many states thereafter adopted statutes allowing shareholders to delegate the power to amend the bylaws to the board of directors. DGCL § 109(a) typifies this approach: It provides that only shareholders have the power to amend bylaws, unless the articles of incorporation expressly confer that power on the board of directors. An article provision authorizing the board to amend the bylaws, moreover, does not divest the shareholders of their residual power to amend the bylaws.

In contrast, the MBCA reflects a modern trend of vesting the power to amend the bylaws in both the directors and the shareholders. MBCA § 10.20(b) allows the directors to amend the bylaws unless (1) the articles of incorporation give that power solely to the shareholders or (2) the shareholders amend the bylaw in question and provide that the directors cannot thereafter further amend the bylaw. By implication, MBCA § 10.20(a) authorizes the shareholders to amend the bylaws even though the directors also have that power. Notice that amendment of the bylaws is one of the few corporate actions the shareholders are entitled to initiate. Unlike the articles of incorporation, where an amendment must first be recommended by the board, no prior board action is required on a bylaw amendment.[9]

The concurrent power of both shareholders and boards to amend the bylaws raises the prospect of cycling amendments and counter-amendments. Suppose the shareholders adopted a bylaw limiting the number of terms a board member can serve. Disliking that limitation, the board repeals the new bylaw provision using its concurrent power to amend the bylaws. The MBCA allows the shareholders to forestall such an event. As noted, MBCA § 10.20(b)(2) authorizes the board to adopt, amend, and repeal bylaws unless "the shareholders in amending, repealing, or adopting a bylaw expressly provide that the board of directors may not amend, repeal, or reinstate that bylaw." In the absence of such a restriction, however, the board apparently retains its power to amend or even repeal the bylaw. If the board does so, the shareholders' remedies presumably are limited to readopting the term limit amendment, this time incorporating the necessary restriction, and/or electing a more compliant board.

Delaware § 109 is more problematic, as it lacks any comparable grant of power to the shareholders. Worse yet, because the board only has power to adopt or amend bylaws if that power is granted to it in the articles of incorporation, a bylaw prohibiting board amendment would be inconsistent with the articles and, therefore, invalid. In *American Int'l Rent a Car, Inc. v. Cross*,[10] the Delaware chancery court suggested that, as part of a bylaw amendment, the shareholders "could remove from the Board the power to further amend the provision in question." Dicta in several other Delaware precedents, however, is to the contrary. In *General DataComm Industries, Inc. v. State of Wisconsin Investment Board*,[11] for example, Vice Chancellor Strine noted the "significant legal uncertainty" as to "whether, in the absence of an explicitly controlling statute, a stockholder-adopted bylaw can be made immune from repeal or modification by the board of directors." In *Centaur Partners, IV v. National Intergroup, Inc.*,[12] the Delaware supreme court addressed a shareholder-proposed bylaw limiting the number of directors. As proposed, the bylaw contained a provision prohibiting the board from amending or repealing it. Noting that the corporation's articles gave the board authority to fix the number of directors through adoption of bylaws, the supreme court opined that the proposed by law "would be a nullity if adopted." Consequently, it seems doubtful that restrictions on the board's power over the bylaws will pass muster in Delaware or other states likewise lacking a MBCA-style provision.

---

9. As a practical matter, however, in public corporations, shareholders must rely on SEC Rule 14a–8, which authorizes inclusion of shareholder-initiated proposals in the company's proxy statement, to effect a bylaw amendment.

10. 1984 WL 8204 (Del.Ch.1984).

11. 731 A.2d 818, 821 n. 1 (Del.Ch. 1999).

12. 582 A.2d 923, 929 (Del.1990).

On the other hand, board amendments to bylaws adopted by the shareholders may run afoul of the Delaware supreme court's famous holding in *Schnell v. Chris–Craft Industries, Inc.,*[13] that "inequitable action does not become permissible merely because it is legally possible." To be sure, *Schnell* dealt with a slightly different problem. The board had amended the bylaws to change the date of the corporation's annual meeting, which was a legally permissible amendment, for the equitably impermissible purpose of defeating a proxy contest in which insurgent shareholders sought to oust the incumbent board. Yet, many courts have applied the principle in a variety of contexts. Under *Schnell*, a court thus likely would examine the purpose for which the board amended or repealed the shareholder-adopted bylaw. If the board did so to disenfranchise shareholders and/or entrench itself in office, for example, the action likely would not pass muster.[14]

2. Legality

DGCL § 109(b) imposes an important limitation on the otherwise sweeping scope of permissible bylaws:

> The bylaws may contain any provision, *not inconsistent with law or with the certificate of incorporation*, relating to the business of the corporation, the conduct of its affairs, and its rights or powers or the rights or powers of its stockholders, directors, officers or employees.

MBCA § 2.06(b) contains a comparable limitation.

Clear conflicts between the statute or articles and the bylaws present little difficulty. What if the bylaw nominally complies with the letter of the law, but conflicts with its spirit, however? As noted in the preceding section, Delaware courts not infrequently invoke the equitable doctrine that legally permissible actions nevertheless can be barred if undertaken for improper purposes. In a variety of settings, Delaware courts therefore have reviewed bylaws to determine whether they have a permissible purpose.[15]

---

13.   285 A.2d 437, 439 (Del.1971).

14.   Cf. Blasius Industries, Inc. v. Atlas Corp., 564 A.2d 651 (Del.Ch.1988) (invalidating board action undertaken "for the primary purpose of preventing the effectiveness of a shareholder vote"). See also Coalition to Advocate Public Utility Responsibility, Inc. v. Engels, 364 F.Supp. 1202 (D.Minn.1973) (holding that otherwise lawful board action becomes impermissible if undertaken in the midst of an election campaign for the purpose of obstructing a legitimate effort by dissident shareholders to obtain board representation).

15.   See generally Allen v. Prime Computer, Inc., 540 A.2d 417 (Del.1988) (holding that court may review reasonableness of a bylaw); In re Osteopathic Hospital Ass'n, 191 A.2d 333 (Del.Ch.1963) (holding with respect to nonprofit corporation that "a by-

law which is unreasonable, unlawful, or contrary to public policy may be declared void though adopted by legitimate procedures"); see, e.g., Allen v. Prime Computer, Inc., 540 A.2d 417 (Del.1988) (invalidating bylaw intended to impede use of written consents by shareholders); Frantz Manufacturing Co. v. EAC Industries, 501 A.2d 401 (Del.1985) (upholding shareholder-adopted bylaws intended to prevent disenfranchisement of majority shareholder); Datapoint Corp. v. Plaza Securities Co., 496 A.2d 1031 (Del.1985) (invalidating board-adopted bylaw intended to impede use of written consents by shareholders); Phillips v. Insituform of North America, Inc., 1987 WL 16285 (Del.Ch.1987) (granting preliminarily injunction against board-adopted bylaws intended to prevent one class of shareholders from controlling corporation); see also AHI

A critical issue here is whether shareholder-adopted bylaws may limit the board of directors' discretionary power to manage the corporation. There is an odd circularity in the Delaware code with respect to this issue. On the one hand, DGCL § 141(a) provides that "[t]he business and affairs of every corporation organized under this chapter shall be managed by or under the direction of a board of directors." A bylaw that restricts the board's managerial authority thus seems to run afoul of DGCL § 109(b)'s prohibition of bylaws that are "inconsistent with law." On the other hand, DGCL § 141(a) also provides that the board's management powers are plenary "except as may be otherwise provided in this chapter." Does an otherwise valid bylaw adopted pursuant to § 109 squeeze through that loophole?

In *Teamsters v. Fleming Companies*,[16] the Oklahoma supreme court upheld a bylaw limiting the board of directors' power to adopt a poison pill (a type of corporate takeover defense). The bylaw provided:

> The Corporation *shall* not adopt or maintain a poison pill, shareholder rights plan, rights agreement or any other form of 'poison pill' which is designed to or has the effect of making acquisition of large holdings of the Corporation's shares of stock more difficult or expensive ... unless such plan is first approved by a majority shareholder vote. The Company *shall* redeem any such rights now in effect.

The board argued that shareholders could not adopt a bylaw imposing such mandatory limitations on the board's discretion. The court rejected that argument. Absent a contrary provision in the articles of incorporation, shareholders therefore may use the bylaws to limit the board's managerial discretion.

Although the relevant Oklahoma and Delaware statutes are quite similar, dicta in at least one Delaware chancery court opinion is inconsistent with *Fleming*. In *General DataComm Industries, Inc. v. State of Wisconsin Investment Board*,[17] Vice Chancellor Strine observed:

> [W]hile stockholders have unquestioned power to adopt bylaws covering a broad range of subjects, it is also well established in corporate law that stockholders may not directly manage the business and affairs of the corporation, at least without specific authorization either by statute or in the certificate or articles of incorporation. There is an obvious zone of conflict between these precepts: in at least some respects, attempts by stockholders to adopt bylaws limiting or influencing director authority inevitably offend the no-

Metnall, L.P. v. J.C. Nichols Co., 891 F.Supp. 1352 (W.D.Mo.1995) (granting a preliminary injunction to plaintiffs who argued that a board-adopted bylaw imposing a 20% share ownership requirement for proposing board candidates or other business at a shareholder meeting was an unreasonable response to a pending takeover bid); Coalition to Advocate Public Utility Responsibility, Inc. v. Engels, 364 F.Supp. 1202 (D.Minn.1973) (invalidating board-adopted bylaws intended to block election of minority director).

16. International Broth. of Teamsters General Fund v. Fleming Companies, Inc., 975 P.2d 907 (Okla.1999).

17. 731 A.2d 818, 821 n. 2 (Del.Ch. 1999).

tion of management by the board of directors. However, neither the courts, the legislators, the SEC, nor legal scholars have clearly articulated the means of resolving this conflict and determining whether a stockholder-adopted bylaw provision that constrains director managerial authority is legally effective.

The Vice Chancellor is doubtless correct that there is no clear doctrinal answer under Delaware law. Yet, the relevant policy considerations are quite straightforward. Complete exposition of those policies would anticipate material to be covered in subsequent chapters, but a brief summary here seems useful.

Analysis must begin with the basic precepts of the contractarian model. Shareholders do not own the corporation. Instead, they are merely one of many corporate constituencies bound together by a complex web of explicit and implicit contracts. As such, the normative claims associated with ownership and private property are inapt in the corporate context.

In this model, the directors thus are not agents of the shareholders subject to the control of the shareholders. To be sure, shareholders elect the board and exercise certain other control rights through the franchise. Yet, shareholder voting is not an integral part of the corporate decisionmaking apparatus. Although corporate law grants shareholders exclusive electoral rights, those rights are quite limited. Instead, shareholder voting is merely one accountability mechanism among many—and one to be used sparingly at that. Put another way, the board of directors functions as a sort of Platonic guardian—a *sui generis* body that serves as the nexus for the various contracts making up the corporation. The board's powers flow from that set of contracts in its totality and not just from shareholders. The board's exercise of its discretionary authority therefore may not be unilaterally limited by any corporate constituency, including the shareholders.

This model is not inconsistent with the spirit of Delaware corporate law. As the Delaware supreme court recently opined:

> One of the most basic tenets of Delaware corporate law is that the board of directors has the ultimate responsibility for managing the business and affairs of a corporation. Section 141(a) requires that any limitation on the board's authority be set out in the certificate of incorporation.[18]

Note that, read literally, this dictum clearly precludes the result reached in *Fleming*.

The board's primacy has a compelling economic justification. The separation of ownership and control mandated by corporate law is a highly efficient solution to the decisionmaking problems faced by large corporations. Recall that because collective decisionmaking is impracticable in such firms, they are characterized by authority-based decisionmak-

---

18. Quickturn Design Systems, Inc. v. Shapiro, 721 A.2d 1281, 1291 (Del.1998).

ing structures in which a central agency (the board) is empowered to make decisions binding on the firm as a whole.

To be sure, this separation of "ownership" and control results in agency costs. Those costs, however, are the inevitable consequence of vesting discretion in someone other than the residual claimant. We could substantially reduce, if not eliminate, agency costs by eliminating discretion; that we do not do so confirms that discretion has substantial virtues. Given those virtues, one ought not lightly interfere with management or the board's decisionmaking authority in the name of accountability. Preservation of managerial discretion should always be the null hypothesis.

This line of argument explains much of corporate law. It is the principle behind such diverse doctrines as the business judgment rule, the limits on shareholder derivative litigation, the limits on shareholder voting rights, and the board's power to resist unsolicited corporate takeovers. Here it justifies strong skepticism as to the validity of shareholder-adopted bylaws that restrict management discretion. Indeed, absent an express statutory command to the contrary, courts should invalidate such bylaws.[19]

All of these problems would go away if state corporation codes treated bylaws the same way as articles of incorporation or, for that matter, virtually every other corporate action. The shareholder power to initiate bylaw amendments without prior board action is unique. It is also a historical anachronism states unthinkingly codified from old common law principles lacking either rhyme or reason. There simply is no good reason to treat bylaws differently than articles of incorporation.

§ 2.4 Preincorporation transactions by promoters

A corporation does not exist until its articles of incorporation are filed with the secretary of state's office. As a practical matter, however, the company's promoter often begins planning and preparing for the business long before undertaking the formal step of filing the articles.[1] If the promoter enters into contracts on behalf of the corporation before the articles are filed, three legal questions may arise: (1) Once the articles are filed, does the corporation become a party to the contract? (2) Once the articles are filed, is the promoter liable if the corporation

---

19. A useful analogy may be drawn to shareholder agreements that restrict board discretion. At one point, such agreements were *per se* invalid. See, e.g., McQuade v. Stoneham, 189 N.E. 234 (N.Y.1934). The modern trend is to allow such agreements, but only in close corporations. See, e.g., MBCA § 7.32; Galler v. Galler, 203 N.E.2d 577 (Ill.1964).

§ 2.4

1. In the broadest sense, the promoters are those individuals actively involved in organizing the corporation. In the present context, the term is used in a narrower sense to refer to persons who purport to act as agents of the business prior to its incorporation. Passive investors who do not act on the business' behalf during the pre-incorporation phase generally are not regarded as promoters. Instead, their potential liability is taken up under the defective incorporation doctrine discussed below.

breaches the contract? (3) If the articles are not filed, is the promoter liable on the contract?

A. Corporation as party

In agency law, a principal is not bound by contracts entered into by his agent unless the agent had authority to make the contract. If the principal ratifies an unauthorized contract, however, the principal is bound just as though the contract had been authorized from the outset. How do these rules apply when the principal is a newly formed corporation and the agent is a promoter who transacted business on the firm's behalf before it was formed?

The prevailing corporate law doctrine is that a corporation may not ratify acts that took place before it came into existence. The corporation may, however, adopt them.[2] The difference is largely semantic, but may be important for purposes of the statute of frauds.[3]

If the board adopts the contract, the corporation may enforce the contract, but is also liable if it subsequently breaches the contract.[4] The corporation may have third party beneficiary rights under the contract, moreover, even if it does not adopt it. Likewise, the other party to the contract may be able to assert quasi-contract or estoppel claims against the corporation even if the board of directors fails to adopt the contract.[5]

B. Promoter's liability after the corporation is formed

Absent an agreement to the contrary, the promoter remains liable on the contract even after the corporation comes into existence. This is true even if the corporation adopts the contract.[6] In order for the promoter to avoid liability on the contract, the other party must agree to excuse the promoter once the corporation comes into existence. If the contract explicitly releases the promoter, there is no difficulty, but many contracts are either ambiguous or silent with respect to the promoter's post-incorporation liability. If so, the court must infer whether the

---

2. See, e.g., Stolmeier v. Beck, 441 N.W.2d 888 (Neb.1989).

3. See, e.g., McArthur v. Times Printing Co., 51 N.W. 216 (Minn.1892) (corporation may adopt pre-incorporation contract; if the corporation does so, the contract is deemed made as of the date of its adoption for purposes of the statute of frauds).

4. Jacobson v. Stern, 605 P.2d 198 (Nev. 1980). When the board of directors passes a resolution expressly adopting the contract, there is no difficulty in holding the corporation to the contract. In the absence of an express action by the board, however, the court still may imply an adoption from the corporation's conduct. In McArthur v. Times Printing Co., 51 N.W. 216 (Minn.

1892), for example, plaintiff was given a one-year employment contract by the promoter of a publishing corporation. After the corporation was formed, the directors failed to formally adopt the contract. All of the directors knew of the contract, however, and allowed the corporation to accept the benefits of plaintiff's employment. The court held that the corporation had implicitly adopted the contract by acquiescence. The knowing receipt of the benefits of the contract constituted an implied adoption.

5. See, e.g., Clifton v. Tomb, 21 F.2d 893 (4th Cir.1927).

6. Jacobson v. Stern, 605 P.2d 198 (Nev. 1980).

parties intended to release the promoter from liability on the contract. In doing so, the court will consider a number of factors, including:

- *Form of signature:* Did the promoter sign the corporation in his individual capacity or as an agent of the corporation? If the form of signature explicitly designates the promoter as an agent of the corporation, this may demonstrate an intent that only the corporation would be bound by the contract.

- *Partial performance:* Has the promoter partially performed on the contract? Partial performance is deemed evidence of an intent to be personally bound by the contract.

- *Other party's knowledge and conduct:* Did the other party know that the business was to be incorporated? Did the other party do anything else that indicates an intent to look solely to the corporation for performance? If so, that may indicate an intent to release the promoter.

In *Quaker Hill, Inc. v. Parr,*[7] for example, plaintiff sold a large quantity of nursery stock (plants) to Denver Memorial Nursery, Inc. The contract was signed by "E.D. Parr, Pres." An accompanying promissory note was signed: "Denver Memorial Nursery, Inc./E.D. Parr, Pres./James P. Presba, Sc'y.-Treas." Plaintiff knew that the corporation had not been formed at the time the contract was made, but one of plaintiff's agents nevertheless urged defendants to make the contract in the corporation's name. Defendants eventually formed a corporation under a different name, but the corporation failed to perform. Plaintiff therefore sued defendants, seeking to hold them personally liable on the contract. The court acknowledged that, as general rule, promoters are personally liable on contracts made on behalf of a corporation before its incorporation. An exception to the general rule, however, is made for cases in which the contract is made on behalf of the corporation and the other party intended to look to the corporation and not to the promoters for payment. On these facts, the court held, the exception applied, and the defendant promoters were not personally liable. The key fact was that plaintiff's agent actually urged defendant to make the contract in the corporation's name, from which the court inferred that plaintiff intended to look solely to the corporation for payment.

MBCA § 2.04 provides: "All persons purporting to act as or on behalf of a corporation, knowing there was no incorporation under [the MBCA], are jointly and severally liable for all liabilities created while so acting." On its face, this statutory language is inconsistent with the holding in *Quaker Hill.* The official comment to § 2.04, however, opines that the statute does not foreclose application of an estoppel doctrine to appropriate facts. Under this formulation, someone who knows the corporation does not exist, but nevertheless urges the defendants to transact business in the corporation's name, may be estopped from seeking to hold the defendants personally liable.

---

7.   364 P.2d 1056 (Colo.1961).

The MBCA approach thus can be squared with the common law. Indeed, an estoppel-based theory seems the best explanation for the result in *Quaker Hill*. In a subsequent case, *Goodman v. Darden, Doman & Stafford Assoc.*,[8] for example, DDS entered into a contract with Goodman to repair an apartment building. The named parties were DDS and "Building Design and Development, Inc. (In Formation)/John A. Goodman, President." DDS knew Building Design and Development did not exist when the contract was made. DDS also knew that Goodman intended to form a corporation for the very purpose of limiting his liability. Finally, DDS made some payments in Building Design and Development's name. The court nonetheless held the promoter personally liable on the contract. In doing so, it distinguished *Quaker Hill* on grounds that DDS did not urge Goodman to make the contract in the corporation's name or even suggest incorporation to him. Accordingly, the requisite grounds for estoppel were not present. Absent the unusual facts of *Quaker Hill*, accordingly, promoters normally will be held liable for breach of pre-incorporation contracts.

C. Promoter's liability in the event the corporation never comes into existence

Absent an agreement to the contrary, the promoter remains liable on the contract if the corporation never comes into existence. The rules of contract interpretation for determining the parties' intent discussed in the preceding section apply to this situation, as well.

D. Analysis

If all of this strikes the reader as dry and formalistic, that is because it is dry and formalistic. A modest degree of ex ante planning and attention to contract language will solve a multitude of problems. A competently drafted preincorporation contract will specify the status of the enterprise, the intentions of the parties with respect to formation of the business, and the rights of the various parties.

Unfortunately, many small start-up businesses try to wing it without legal advice. In such cases, the estoppel-based interpretation of *Quaker Hill* gets it about right. In general, the promoter is the cheapest cost avoider—the promoter controls the incorporation process and ought to have an incentive to ensure that that process is carried through promptly and with due regard to creditor interests. The incorporation process has become so simple that promoters ought not get the benefit of limited liability until the corporation is validly formed. A general presumption that promoters are liable on preincorporation contrasts, such as that provided by MBCA § 2.04, gives the promoter an incentive to carry through the incorporation process and, moreover, to ensure that the contract is carried out. On the other hand, where the creditor knew

----

8.   670 P.2d 648 (Wash.1983).

the corporation did not yet exist, but nevertheless urged the promoter to transact business in the corporation's name, allowing the creditor to hold the promoter personally liable would give the former a windfall and encourage creditors to mislead promoters as to the latter's rights.

§ 2.5 Defective incorporation

The preceding section dealt with pre-incorporation transactions in which the promoter and, perhaps, the third party knew the corporation had not been formed as of the date of the transaction. This section deals with a slightly different variant of the problem: pre-incorporation transactions by a promoter who erroneously believes that the corporation exists as of the date of the transaction.

Defective incorporation was a fairly serious problem decades ago when incorporating a business involved far more technicalities than it does today. Older corporation statutes required compliance with substantial procedural formalities as a condition of incorporation. Multiple local filings, notice by publication, minimum capital requirements, and the like abounded. It was easy for some minor glitch in the incorporation process, such as failing to file all the requisite documents or failing to do so in all the requisite offices, to prevent the corporation from coming into existence as a legal entity.

Defective incorporation was a concern for promoters and other investors because limited liability attached only to validly formed corporations.[1] A defectively incorporated business could be viewed as a partnership or sole proprietorship, neither of which confer limited liability on their owners, rather than a corporation. Common law courts worked out two responses to the defective incorporation problem: the de facto corporation and the corporation by estoppel.[2]

A. De facto corporation

If the promoter failed to form a legal corporation because of some technical defect in the incorporation process, a court may nevertheless treat the business as a de facto corporation.[3] The rationale seems to be a

---

§ 2.5

1. Limited liability companies and limited liability partnerships are modern exceptions to this rule, which themselves require formal creation through filing of documents with the secretary of state.

2. Modern lawyers are far more likely to encounter a defective incorporation problem on a law school or bar exam than in their subsequent careers. In most states, the modern incorporation process is so straightforward that it is almost impossible to incorporate a firm defectively. There remain two situations, however, in which defective incorporation problems occasionally still arise. First, in some states, it is possi-

ble to file the articles of incorporation by mail. The promoter sometimes begins transacting business almost as soon as the articles are mailed. If the articles are lost in the mail or rejected by the secretary of state, a defective incorporation problem may arise. Second, promoters often rely on an attorney or service company to incorporate the business. If the attorney or service company fails promptly to file the articles of incorporation, the promoter may transact business in the mistaken belief that the corporation has been formed.

3. A de jure corporation is a true corporation: A legal entity that has been validly formed by complying with all statutory re-

concern that imposing full personal liability on the promoter may amount to a windfall for the other party to the transaction, which probably believed it was dealing with a corporation having limited liability. If so, the rule makes good economic sense.[4] As long as the creditor thought it was dealing with a de jure corporation, the firm's defective incorporation is irrelevant. Personal liability would constitute a windfall the creditor did not expect and has done nothing to earn. Put another way, giving a second bite at the apple to people who could have cheaply protected themselves creates perverse incentives, promotes litigation, and discourages investment.

The basic standard for invoking the de facto corporation doctrine is whether (1) there was a good faith effort to incorporate the business and (2) the putative shareholders carried on the business as though it were a corporation, especially with respect to the transaction in question.[5] Some jurisdictions use an alternative three-part test: (1) a statute must exist under which incorporation was legally possible; (2) there was a "colorable" (a.k.a. "bona fide") attempt to incorporate the business; and (3) there was an actual use or exercise of corporate powers and privileges.[6] The difference between the two tests is largely semantic. Both tend to collapse into the question of whether there was a good faith effort to incorporate the business.

The de facto corporation doctrine does not forbid the state from contesting the corporation's existence in a quo warranto proceeding brought to terminate the putative corporation's existence.[7] It simply holds that private parties who transact business with a de facto corporation may not hold the firm's promoters or investors personally liable for the firm's obligations.[8] In other words, investors in a de facto corporation

---

quirements. The term is also sometimes used for corporations that substantially complied with the statutory requirements for incorporation, but failed to comply with some very minor technical requirement. In the latter case, neither the state nor nonstate parties may contest the corporation's existence. If a defect in the incorporation process prevents the business from being treated as a de jure corporation, but the promoter made a good faith effort to incorporate the business, and carried on the business as though it were a corporation, some courts treat the firm as a de facto corporation. The state may contest the existence of the corporation, but nonstate parties who transact business with a de facto corporation may not hold the firm's promoters or investors personally liable for the firm's obligations.

4. The economic argument for not allowing creditors of a de facto corporation to hold shareholders personally liable is essentially the same as that for granting limited liability to shareholders of de jure corporations. For an analysis of the economics of

limited liability, see Stephen M. Bainbridge, Abolishing Veil Piercing, 26 J. Corp. L. 479 (2001).

5. See, e.g., Cantor v. Sunshine Greenery, Inc., 398 A.2d 571 (N.J.App.Div.1979).

6. Fred S. McChesney, Doctrinal Analysis and Statistical Modeling in Law: The Case of Defective Incorporation, 71 Wash. U.L.Q. 493, 498–99 (1993).

7. If the defect in the incorporation is minor, the court may treat the business as a de jure corporation. If so, the business' corporate existence may not even be challenged by the state.

8. In Cantor v. Sunshine Greenery, Inc., 398 A.2d 571 (N.J.App.Div.1979), for example, the promoter mailed articles of incorporation to the secretary of state's office. The articles were officially filed only after some unexplained delay. In the meanwhile, assuming that the articles had been filed and that the corporation existed, the promoter entered into a lease on the corporation's behalf. The lessor had considerable business experience, but did not require the promot-

get the benefit of limited liability, just as though the business were a de jure corporation.[9]

B.   Corporation by estoppel

Cases occasionally arise in which the promoter made no good faith effort to incorporate the business. This failure precludes one from invoking the de facto corporation doctrine. As noted, however, imposing full personal liability on the firm's would-be shareholders gives the other party to the transaction a windfall. Courts developed the corporation by estoppel doctrine to deal with such cases. The corporation by estoppel doctrine differs from the more familiar concept of equitable estoppel. There is no requirement of a misrepresentation, of reasonable reliance, or of a change in position. Instead, someone who deals with the firm as though it were a corporation is estopped later to deny the corporation's existence.[10]

er to guarantee the lease personally. Instead, the lessor knew and expected that the corporation would be responsible for the lease. When the corporation failed to perform, lessor sought to hold the promoter personally liable. The court held that, because of the delay in filing the articles, the business was not a legal corporation at the time the lease was made. The promoter's execution of articles of incorporation, the good faith effort to file them, and the carrying on of business in the corporation's name, however, justified treating the firm as a de facto corporation. The promoter therefore could not be held personally liable. Id.

9.   The case against imposing personal liability on shareholders of a defectively incorporated business is stronger yet when the third party seeks to hold liable participants other than the promoter. Courts have been willing to invoke the de facto corporation doctrine to protect an investor who actively participates in the firm's business in the honest and reasonable belief that the firm was properly incorporated. Inactive investors present an even stronger case for invoking the de facto corporation doctrine and are rarely held personally liable for the firm's obligations. See, e.g., Flanagan v. Jackson Wholesale Bldg. Supply Co., 461 So.2d 761, 765 (Miss.1984) (declining to hold inactive investor personally liable).

10.   A leading example of the doctrine in action is Cranson v. International Business Machines Corp., 200 A.2d 33 (Md.1964), in which the defendant was asked to invest in a corporation that was about to be created. Defendant was advised by an attorney that the business had been incorporated. Defen-

dant bought shares, received a stock certificate, was shown the corporation's seal and minute book. Defendant was elected an officer and director of the corporation. The firm operated as though it were a corporation and conducted business in its corporate name. Due to an oversight by the attorney, of which defendant was unaware, the firm was not incorporated until about seven months after Defendant invested in the firm. During that period the corporation entered into a contract to purchase typewriters from a supplier. The supplier dealt with the firm as though it were a corporation, and dealt with Defendant as an agent of the firm. When the corporation defaulted, the supplier sought to hold Defendant personally liable. The court held that the supplier was estopped to deny the corporation's existence and, accordingly, could not hold Defendant personally liable.

In *Cranson*, the Maryland Court of Appeals distinguished the corporation by estoppel doctrine from the de facto corporation doctrine by holding that the latter could be invoked only if articles of incorporation were filed. A corporation by estoppel, however, could be found because the third party had dealt with the firm as though it were a corporation and relied on the firm, not the individual defendant, for performance. While there is general agreement that the de facto corporation doctrine requires a good faith effort to incorporate, opinion is divided as to whether *Cranson* correctly held that a failure to file articles of incorporation—standing alone—precludes application of the de facto corporation doctrine.

C.   Statutory efforts to abolish the common law doctrines

Over the years, the MBCA's drafters have repeatedly tried to dispose of the common law rules on defective incorporation. Section 50 of the 1950 MBCA provided that a corporation comes into existence when the secretary of state issues a certificate of incorporation and that the certificate constituted conclusive evidence thereof. Section 139 stated: "All persons who assume to act as a corporation without authority so to do shall be jointly and severally liable for all" obligations of the firm. Nothing in the 1950 statute appeared to contemplate either common law doctrine; to the contrary, § 139 appeared to impose full personal liability unless a de jure corporation existed, while § 50 appeared to require a certificate of incorporation be issued in order for a de jure corporation to exist. A good faith effort to comply with the statute was simply irrelevant.[11] The 1969 MBCA explicitly embraced this interpretation, stating in the drafters' comments that § 50 was intended to abolish the de facto corporation doctrine.

Even in MBCA states, however, some courts nevertheless persisted in using the common law defective incorporation doctrines. Some continued to apply the corporation by estoppel doctrine when there was no attempt to incorporate.[12] Others held that the phrase "assume to act" in MBCA § 139 limited liability to active participants in the business— inactive investors of a defectively incorporated business would not be held personally liable.[13]

The 1984 MBCA's drafters recognized that courts were resisting their predecessors' attempt to abolish the de facto corporation and corporation by estoppel doctrines. Accordingly, the drafters chose to relax the statutory standard slightly. MBCA § 2.04 now provides: "All persons purporting to act as or on behalf of a corporation, knowing there was no incorporation under [the MBCA], are jointly and severally liable for all liabilities created while so acting." By negative inference, neither inactive investors nor active investors who are unaware of the defective incorporation may be held personally liable. The MBCA approach thus should lead to the same result as the common law doctrines in most cases, but (arguably) provides a clearer rule allowing for greater predictability.

The MBCA's drafters contend that the incorporation process has become so simple that allowing promoters to avoid personal liability by conducting business in a corporate name would "undermine the incorporation process."[14] On the other hand, at least insofar as the bargain

---

11. See, e.g., Robertson v. Levy, 197 A.2d 443 (D.C.App.1964).

12. See, e.g., Sherwood & Roberts–Oregon, Inc. v. Alexander, 525 P.2d 135 (Or. 1974).

13. Timberline Equip. Co. v. Davenport, 514 P.2d 1109 (Or.1973).

14. MBCA § 2.04 cmt. For a critique of the argument that the availability of limited liability ought to depend on formal incorporation through the filing process, see Larry E. Ribstein, Limited Liability and Theories of the Corporation, 50 Md. L. Rev. 80 (1991).

setting is concerned, a creditor who does business with a firm that purports to be incorporated knows (or should know) that the shareholders (and agents) of a corporation are not personally liable for the firm's obligations. The creditor could protect itself by demanding that the shareholders personally guarantee the debt or contract. A creditor who fails to do so arguably ought not get a second bite at the apple simply because of a minor defect in the incorporation process.

The issue here is analogous to that posed by preincorporation contracts. Do we want to maximize the incentive for promoters promptly and accurately to complete the incorporation process? Or do we want to give creditors who deal with a corporation (or what they think is a corporation) an incentive to protect themselves through devices such as personal guarantees? The MBCA's drafters tried to split that baby by (1) limiting liability to active participants—persons who act on the purported firm's behalf—who know no corporation exists and (2) admitting the possibility of estoppel for preincorporation contracts in which the creditor urged the promoter to use the putative corporation's name despite the creditor's knowledge that no corporation had been formed. If the MBCA's solution is not exactly Solomonic in its wisdom, the statute does seem get it about right. In case (1), the risk of liability gives the parties who control the incorporation process an incentive to carry out that process promptly, validly, and with due regard to creditor interests. In case (2), however, the MBCA denies a windfall to creditors who not only fail to protect themselves but affirmatively go out of their way to induce a contract from those who may be reluctant to transact business in their own names.

§ 2.6 Promoter's fiduciary duties

A corporation's promoter often controls assets that would be useful to the business. This is especially likely where a promoter incorporates a pre-existing business previously operated as a partnership or sole proprietorship. The conflict of interest presented by transactions between the promoter and the corporation should be readily apparent: The promoter is on both sides of the transaction, representing both himself and the corporation. On the one hand, the promoter is an agent of the corporation, charged with a fiduciary duty to get the best possible deal for the corporation. On the other hand, the promoter has a natural selfish interest to get the best possible deal for himself.

In this situation, courts impose a fiduciary duty of loyalty on promoters analogous to that imposed in connection with interested director transactions: If the transaction is later challenged, the promoter has the burden of proving that he dealt fairly with the corporation. If the promoter fails to do so, the corporation may void the transaction and/or recover any secret profits earned by the promoter.

Two issues are critical in determining whether the promoter breached his fiduciary duty to the corporation. First, was the promoter on both sides of the transaction or was the corporation represented by independent parties? In negotiations with the promoter, the corporation should be represented by independent directors who are neither dominated nor controlled by the promoter. Second, did the promoter provide full disclosure of the conflict and of the facts of the transaction?

In *Frick v. Howard*, for example, the promoter bought a parcel of land for $240,000. Shortly thereafter the promoter transferred the property to the corporation for $350,000, taking a mortgage. At the time of the transaction, the promoter was the sole stockholder and dominated the board of directors. The promoter also signed the mortgage on the corporation's behalf. The corporation later defaulted on the mortgage and the promoter attempted to foreclose on the mortgage. Because the promoter dominated the board at the time the sale took place, he had a fiduciary duty to give the corporation the benefit of his bargain. In other words, he could not earn a profit on the transaction without violating his fiduciary duty to the corporation. The mortgage was void for lack of consideration and foreclosure was not allowed.[1]

Frick's holding is absurd. It illustrates the mindless attachment some courts have to the notion that the corporation is a separate legal person. At the time the transaction occurred, the promoter and the corporation were economically one and the same. If he wanted to move an asset from his promoter pocket to his corporate pocket, that is no different than if he had shifted his change between his pants pockets. The law ought to be concerned only if the transaction somehow injured investors who became shareholders between the time the transaction occurred and the time promoter sought to foreclose on the mortgage.

Courts disagree as to whether promoters owe fiduciary duties to persons who become shareholders of the corporation after the transaction between the promoter and the corporation took place. The majority view (the so-called "Massachusetts rule") is that such a duty exists if, at the time of the transaction between the corporation, the promoter planned to bring in additional shareholders.[2] The minority view is that the promoter owes no fiduciary duty to subsequent investors.[3]

Suppose, for example, that Acme Mining Corporation is formed in December, at which time Promoter and Co-promoter are the sole shareholders. In return for 2,500 shares of Acme stock, Promoter sells 49 acres of land to Acme. In early January, the sale is approved by Promoter and Co-promoter in their capacity as shareholders of the company. The following April, Plaintiff buys 1000 Acme shares. Plaintiff later sues, alleging that Acme paid too high a price for Promoter's land. Under the minority view, Plaintiff may not prevail because he owned no

---

§ 2.6

1. Frick v. Howard, 126 N.W.2d 619 (Wis.1964). In *Frick*, the promoter's fiduciary duty ran to the corporation. The promoter also owes fiduciary duties to his co-promoters. See, e.g., Glassell v. Prentiss, 346 P.2d 895 (Cal.App.1959).

2. See, e.g., Old Dominion Copper Mining & Smelting Co. v. Bigelow, 89 N.E. 193 (Mass.1909); Northridge Co-op. Section No. 1, Inc. v. 32nd Ave. Constr. Corp., 141 N.E.2d 802 (N.Y.1957).

3. See, e.g., Old Dominion Copper Mining & Smelting Co. v. Lewisohn, 210 U.S. 206 (1908).

shares at the time of the challenged transaction. Under the majority view, Plaintiff may not prevail because there was no plan, at the time of the challenged transaction, to sell stock to additional shareholders.

The majority rule is almost as absurd as *Frick*. The relevant consideration ought not to be the existence of a plan to bring in additional investors, but whether such investors got full disclosure of relevant facts before investing. In *Frick*, if subsequent investors were told the material facts of the property sale and mortgage, they should have no claim against the promoter. Ditto in the preceding example. In both cases, provided there was disclosure, the price investors should pay for the corporation's shares ought to reflect the effect of the self-dealing transaction on the firm's value. Allowing them subsequently to sue for breach of fiduciary duty gives them a windfall. In any case, investing in a corporation is voluntary. Investors who make an informed decision to buy shares following a self-dealing transaction by a promoter have made their bed and ought to lie in it—even if that turns out to be uncomfortable or even unwise.

§ 2.7 Corporate powers and purposes: Herein of ultra vires

During the 19th century, state corporation codes typically required that the articles of incorporation set forth the purposes for which the corporation was organized. At that time, this requirement had considerable substantive importance because of the ultra vires doctrine. Most states have sharply emasculated this doctrine in recent years, however, so that ultra vires now is largely a dead letter. Hence, it is another one of those issues modern lawyers most likely encounter only in law school and on bar exams.

To put the ultra vires doctrine in its proper historical context, recall that corporations were long regarded as a source of potential mischief and evil. As a result, governments closely regulated corporations. As this suspicion faded, states started adopting general enabling corporate laws. Under these statutes, all one had to do to form a corporation was to jump correctly through certain statutory hoops. Traces of the traditional suspicion of corporations lingered for some time thereafter, however, taking the form of restrictions on the purposes for which corporations could be organized and the powers corporations were authorized to exercise. In addition, these statutes required that the articles of incorporation specify which of the permissible purposes the corporation was organized to achieve and which of the statutory powers it would exercise.

If a corporation exceeded the powers and purposes set forth in the statutes or the firm's articles, it was said to be acting "ultra vires." Suppose that neither the corporate statute nor the firm's articles gave it the power to make loans. If the firm lent money, no matter how small an amount, that action was ultra vires. An ultra vires act was illegal and, accordingly, null and void.

The ultra vires doctrine was frequently asserted as a defense in contract suits involving corporations. On the one hand, if the other party breached the contract, the corporation could not enforce an ultra vires contract against it. On the other hand, if the corporation breached the contract, it could assert the ultra vires doctrine as a defense against a breach of contract suit brought by the other party. The ultra vires doctrine also could be asserted affirmatively in a shareholder suit against officers and directors who caused the firm to commit an ultra vires act. The responsible officers and directors could be held personally liable for any losses resulting from the action.

In the leading case of *Jacksonville, M., P. Railway & Navigation Co. v. Hooper*,[1] for example, the plaintiffs leased a resort hotel to the defendant railroad corporation. The hotel was located near the railroad's seaside terminal. The lease required the railroad corporation to insure the hotel, but the corporation failed to do so. The hotel burnt down during the lease term. When plaintiffs sued the railroad for breach of the lease, the railroad defended on grounds that the lease was ultra vires. The railroad's powers included the right to "erect and maintain all convenient buildings . . . for the accommodation and use of [its] passengers." The railroad argued that operating a resort hotel was not within the scope of this grant of power. The U.S. Supreme Court (no less!) held that the corporate powers clause was sufficiently broad to encompass operation of a resort hotel located near one of its terminals. As a result, the action was not ultra vires, and the corporation was liable for breaching the lease.

The ultra vires doctrine frequently had inefficient (not to mention harsh and unfair) results. If one of the parties to an ultra vires contract later regretted its bargain, it could breach the agreement with impunity, even if the transaction had been completed. The doctrine was even less attractive in tort cases, where it was sometimes invoked as a defense against tort suits brought by those injured by corporate agents committing an ultra vires act.

To avoid such outcomes, courts began eviscerating the doctrine. Some courts limited the doctrine's impact by broadly construing the corporation's purpose and powers clause to encompass the transaction in question.[2] Other courts enforced completed transactions by invoking such equitable doctrines as estoppel, quasi-contract, and waiver.

Moving the story forward towards the present, recall that state corporation laws gradually became more liberal, making the incorporation process much simpler. At about the same time, states began abandoning any effort to regulate the substantive conduct of corporations through the incorporation process. Several statutory reforms had a direct impact on the importance of the ultra vires doctrine, reducing it to its present non-issue status.

First, states have abandoned the effort to limit corporate powers and purposes. MBCA § 3.01(a) provides that every corporation shall have the

§ 2.7
1. 160 U.S. 514 (1896).

2. See, e.g., Jacksonville M., P. Ry. & Nav. Co. v. Hooper, 160 U.S. 514 (1896).

purpose of engaging in any lawful business,[3] unless the articles set forth a more limited purpose. Section 3.02 says that every corporation shall have "the same powers as an individual to do all things necessary or convenient to carry out its business and affairs," including a list of specified powers. Section 2.02(b)(2) makes optional the inclusion of a purpose clause in the articles. Taken together, these provisions make it essentially impossible for an act to be ultra vires: if the corporation can pursue any lawful purpose and use any lawful power in so doing, no action can be said to be ultra vires, because no corporate act can involve an impermissible power or purpose.[4]

Second, states have enacted statutory limits on standing to challenge ultra vires acts. It is difficult to imagine a situation in which a transaction planner would choose to put limits on a corporation's purposes or powers in the articles of incorporation. But even if the articles include some such limitation, MBCA § 3.04(a) provides that the validity of a corporation's act may not be challenged on the ground that it lacks the power to so act.[5] In one fell swoop, this provision de facto eliminates the ultra vires doctrine. Because the validity of the act cannot be challenged, neither the corporation nor the other party to the transaction can raise the ultra vires doctrine as a defense to a breach of contract or tort claim.

3. The MBCA position that a corporation may engage in any lawful activity and exercise any lawful power implicitly suggests that a corporation exceeds its lawful powers, and thus commits an ultra vires act, by engaging in illegal conduct. Although courts sometimes refer to illegal corporate acts as ultra vires, corporate law scholars disfavor this usage. As with natural persons, corporations have the power to break the law, but not the right to do so.

4. DGCL § 102(a)(3) retains a requirement that the articles include a purpose clause, but allows the drafter simply to state that the corporation's purpose is to engage in any lawful business. The substantive effect is the same as the MBCA approach.

5. MBCA § 3.04(b) contains three limited exceptions under which the ultra vires doctrine has some lingering validity: (1) a shareholder may bring suit to enjoin an ultra vires act; (2) the corporation may bring suit against an officer or director who commits an ultra vires act; and (3) the state may bring an involuntary dissolution suit against the corporation for abusing its authority. An interesting example of these provisions at work is provided by Inter-

Continental Corp. v. Moody, 411 S.W.2d 578 (Tex.Civ.App.1966). Corporation guaranteed a note given by its president to Lender. When Lender brought suit against Corporation to enforce the guarantee, Corporation raised the ultra vires defense. In addition, a shareholder intervened to enjoin performance of the guarantee on ultra vires grounds. The court held that Texas' ultra vires statute, comparable to MBCA § 3.04, bars the corporation from raising the ultra vires defense even if the other party knew the transaction exceeded the corporation's powers or purposes. The court further held that the statute permits a shareholder to intervene to enjoin the contract, however, even if the corporation solicited him to do so. Only if the shareholder was acting as the corporation's agent would the shareholder be denied standing. Interestingly, the shareholder would not become the corporation's agent even where the corporation notified the shareholder of the suit and suggested the shareholder intervene. If the corporation paid the shareholder's attorney's fees, however, an agency could be found. Perhaps surprisingly, uncompensated collusion between the defendant corporation and one of its shareholders thus seems possible.

Chapter 3

FINANCING THE CORPORATION

Analysis

§ 3.1   Introduction

It is difficult to imagine how a modern economy could function without something like our present corporate finance system. The numerous technological changes wrought by the Industrial Revolution, especially the development of modern mass production techniques in the nineteenth century, gave great advantages to firms large enough to achieve economics of scale. In turn, those advantages gave rise to giant industrial corporations. These firms required enormous amounts of capital, far exceeding the resources of any single individual or family. They could be financed only by aggregating many small investments, which was accomplished by selling stock or bonds to many investors— each of whom held only a tiny fraction of the firm's total capital.

Capital markets facilitated this process in at least two respects. First, the primary market gave issuers access to a large and ever-growing pool of potential investors. Second, the secondary markets for corporate stocks and bonds gave investors essential liquidity and, accordingly, encouraged investment. In a liquid market, investors can freely sell their securities without involving the firm. Liquidity, in turn, makes it easier and cheaper for the company subsequently to raise capital in the primary market, because investors generally prefer (and will be willing to pay more) for liquid securities.

Corporate lawyers are one of three basic categories of advisors who play a critical role in virtually all corporate finance transactions (the others being accountants and investment bankers). Why? The reason people hire litigators is obvious—either they are being sued or they want to sue somebody else. Unauthorized practice of law statutes and bar admission rules give lawyers a near-total monopoly on litigation. The rationale for hiring transactional lawyers, by contrast, is less obvious. Much of the work of transactional lawyers entails giving advice that could be given by other professionals. Accordingly, it seems fair to ask: why does anybody hire transactional lawyers?

Two competing hypotheses suggest themselves.[1] The first might be termed the "Pie Division Role." In this version of the transactional lawyer story, lawyers strive to capture value—maximizing their client's gains from the deal. Although there are doubtless pie division situations in transactional practice, this explanation of the lawyer's role is flawed.

---

§ 3.1

1. See generally Ronald J. Gilson and Bernard S. Black, The Law and Finance of Corporate Acquisitions 5–11 (2d ed. 1995); Ronald Gilson, Value Creation by Lawyers: Legal Skills and Asset Pricing, 94 Yale L.J. 239 (1984); see also Charles R.T. O'Kelley, Delaware Corporation Law and Transaction Cost Engineering, 34 Ga. L. Rev. 929 (2000); Peter C. Kostant, Exit, Voice, and Loyalty in the Course of Corporate Governance and Counsel's Changing Role, 28 J. Socio–Econ. 203 (1999); Donald C. Langevoort, The Epistemology of Corporate–Securities Lawyering: Beliefs, Biases, and Organizational Behavior, 63 Brook. L. Rev. 629 (1997).

Pie division assumes a zero sum game in which any gains for one side come from the other side's share. Assume two sophisticated clients with multiple advisers, including competent counsel. Is there any reason to think that one side's lawyer will be able to extract significant gains from the other? No. A homely example may be helpful: You and a friend go out to eat. You decide to share a pizza, so you need to agree on its division. Would you hire somebody to negotiate a division of the pizza? Especially if they were going to take one of your slices as their fee?

The second hypothesis might be termed the "Pie Expansion Role." In this version of the story, people hire transactional lawyers because they add value to the deal. This conception of the lawyer's role rejects the zero sum game mentality. Instead, it claims that the lawyer makes everybody better off by increasing the size of the pie.

The emphasis herein on the pie expansion model is consistent with our concomitant emphasis on transaction costs economics. For the most part, lawyers increase the size of the pie by reducing transaction costs. One way of lowering transaction cost is through regulatory arbitrage. The law frequently provides multiple ways of effecting a given transaction, all of which will have various advantages and disadvantages. By selecting the most advantageous structure for a given transaction, and ensuring that courts and regulators will respect that choice, the transactional lawyer reduces the cost of complying with the law and allows the parties to keep more of their gains.

An example may be helpful. Acme Corporation wants to acquire Ajax, Inc., using stock as the form of consideration to be paid Ajax shareholders. Acme is concerned about the availability of appraisal rights to shareholders of the two corporations.[2] Presumably Acme doesn't care about the legal niceties of doing the deal—Acme just wants to buy Ajax at the lowest possible cost and, by hypothesis, with the minimal possible cash flow. In other words, the client cares about the economic substance of the deal, not the legal form it takes. As Acme's transactional lawyer, you know that corporate law often elevates form over substance—and that the law provides multiple ways of acquiring another company. A solution thus suggests itself: Delaware law only permits shareholders to exercise appraisal rights in connection with mergers. Appraisal rights are not allowed in connection with an acquisition structured as a sale of assets. Hence, while there is no substantive economic difference between an asset sale and a merger, there is a significant legal difference. By selecting one form over another, the transactional lawyer ensures that the deal is done at the lowest possible cost.

Parties would experience some transaction costs even in the absence of regulation, however. Reducing those nonregulatory costs is another function of the transactional lawyer. Information asymmetries are a good example. A corporation selling securities to an investor has consid-

---

2. Appraisal rights permit shareholders to demand that their stock be bought for cash at a judicially-determined fair price.

erably greater information about the firm than does the prospective buyer. The wise potential investor knows about this information asymmetry and, as a result, takes precautions. Worse yet, what if the seller lies? Or shades the truth? Or is itself uninformed? The wise investor also knows there is a risk of opportunistic withholding or manipulation of asymmetrically held information. Note that this is a species of the agency cost problem. One response to agency costs is monitoring, which in this context takes the form of investigation—due diligence—by the buyer. Another response to agency costs is bonding by seller, which in this context would take the form of disclosures including representations and warranties. In either case, by finding ways for the seller to credibly convey information to the investor, the transactional lawyer helps eliminate the information asymmetry between them. In turn, a variety of other transaction costs will fall. There is less uncertainty, less opportunity for strategic behavior, and less need to take costly precautions.

§ 3.2 Corporate securities

A. Overview

A corporation's capital structure consists of the permanent and long-term contingent claims on the corporation's assets and future earnings issued pursuant to formal contractual instruments called securities. There are two basic types of securities: debt and equity. In most cases, of course, the funds needed to finance the corporation will largely come from bank loans or retained earnings, not through selling debt or equity securities. Bank loans and retained earnings are not regarded as being part of the corporation's capital structure, however, because neither involves a securitized investment in the firm.

Equity securities are issued in the form of shares, which represent "the units into which the proprietary interests in a corporation are divided."[1] As this statutory definition suggests, the law traditionally regards a corporation as being owned by the holders of its equity securities.[2] Holders of debt securities are not in any sense owners of the corporation; rather, they are creditors of the corporation. In contractarian terms, of course, the concept of "ownership" is not particularly meaningful in the corporate context. Instead, equity and debt are simply two different types of financial interests represented by contractual claims on the firm.

A principal distinction between debt and equity securities is their respective risk exposure. All else being equal, equity securities are riskier

---

§ 3.2

1. MBCA § 1.40(22).

2. The law's conception of equity security holders as the corporation's owners has the important consequence that corporate officers and directors owe fiduciary duties to the equity security holders. In contrast, the relationship between the corporation and its debt security holders is essentially contractual. Directors and officers normally owe no fiduciary duties to debt security holders. See, e.g., Metropolitan Life Ins. Co. v. RJR Nabisco, Inc., 716 F.Supp. 1504 (S.D.N.Y.1989); Simons v. Cogan, 549 A.2d 300 (Del.1988); Katz v. Oak Indus., 508 A.2d 873 (Del.Ch.1986).

than debt securities issued by the same corporation. Equity securities represent the "residual claim," which means their holders are entitled to whatever funds are left after all other claims on the corporation's assets and earnings have been satisfied. In contrast, debt securities represent a fixed claim on the corporation's assets and earnings superior to that of the equity. Because debt securityholders are entitled to be paid before the equity securityholders, they are less likely to be hurt by sub-par corporate performance.

Another important distinction between debt and equity is their respective duration. Although equity securities often change hands, the securities themselves represent permanent claims on the corporation. In contrast, debt securities usually are limited in duration. At some contractually specified date, the debt security will mature and the corporation will pay off the principal.

B. Equity securities

Many corporations divide their equity securities into multiple classes of stock, of which common and preferred stock are the basic forms. As with other corporation statutes, the MBCA requires the articles of incorporation to authorize one or more classes of stock together having unlimited voting rights and one or more classes that together are entitled to receive the assets of the corporation upon dissolution.[3] They need not be the same class, however, which gives transaction planners considerable flexibility.

1. Terminology

Authorized shares: All states require that the articles of incorporation specify the number and classes of shares the corporation is authorized to issue. A corporation may not sell more shares of a class than the number of authorized shares. If the board of directors wishes to issue a greater number of shares than the articles authorize, it must ask the shareholders to amend the articles to increase the number of authorized shares.

Outstanding shares: The number of shares the corporation has sold and not repurchased. Only outstanding shares have the voting and economic rights associated with stock.

Authorized but unissued shares: Shares that are authorized by the articles of incorporation but have not been sold. Example: The articles authorize the corporation to issue up to 20,000 common shares. It has 20,000 authorized shares. The firm sells 4,000 shares to investors. At that point, it has 4,000 outstanding shares and 16,000 authorized but unissued shares.

Treasury shares: Shares that were once issued and outstanding, but have been repurchased by the corporation. Example: If the corporation

---

3.　MBCA § 6.01(b).

described in the preceding example repurchased 1,000 of its outstanding shares, it would now have 3,000 outstanding shares, 16,000 authorized but unissued shares and 1,000 treasury shares. The MBCA has eliminated the concept of treasury shares (which had importance mainly for purposes of certain accounting conventions), so that reacquired shares under the MBCA are simply classified as authorized but unissued shares. Thus, if the preceding example took place in a state which has adopted the MBCA, after the firm bought back the 1,000 shares it would simply have 3,000 outstanding shares and 17,000 authorized but unissued shares.

Classes of shares: A class of shares is a type or category of stock all shares of which have the same basic characteristics. Thus, common stock is considered to be a class of stock. Preferred stock would be a second class of shares. Multiple classes must be authorized by the articles, which must set forth the number of shares of the class the corporation is authorized to issue and the class' basic rights.

Series of shares: A series of shares is a subclass of stock. All series within a class will have the same basic characteristics, but each series may also have slightly different rights. Corporations with a class of preferred shares often divide that class into series. All members of the class will have some preference over the common stock, but each series will have different rights and preferences from the others. Multiple series may or may not be identified in the articles of incorporation.

2. Common stock

In practice, the common stock traditionally is a bundle of two basic rights, voting and economic, both of which are subject to being unbundled and sold separately. As to voting rights, holders of common stock have a limited right to participate in corporate decisionmaking by electing directors and voting on major corporate decisions. The number of votes which can be cast by any one shareholder are determined by the number of shares owned, usually on a one-vote per share basis.

As to economic rights, holders of common stock possess the residual claim on the corporation's assets. In other words, each share of common stock has an equal right to participate in distributions of the firm's earnings in the form of dividends and, in the event the corporation is liquidated, to share equally in the firm's assets remaining after all prior claims have been satisfied.

3. Preferred stock

Preferred stock is an odd beast, neither wholly fish nor wholly fowl. Like convertible debt, preferred stock lies on the boundary between debt and equity. As the name implies, preferred stock is given certain rights superior to those of common stock. (Remember that the claims of creditors always come before the claims of shareholders, regardless of the type of stock in question.) Specifically, preferred stock may have a preference over common stock with respect to dividends and/or liquidation. If the corporation is liquidated, preferred stock with a liquidation preference has a right to be paid a specified portion of the corporation's assets before any portion thereof is distributed to the common shareholders.[4]

Preferred stock with a dividend preference will receive dividends before any are paid to the common stock. Dividends differ significantly from interest payable on a bond. The corporation must pay the required interest on its debt securities or it will be deemed to be in default. In the event of a default, creditors have various rights under the bankruptcy laws to force a liquidation or reorganization of the firm. In contrast, the corporation is not required to pay dividends to the preferred stock. Its obligation merely is to pay the stated dividend to the preferred shareholders before any dividend is paid to the common stock. Most corporations, however, voluntarily assume certain additional obligations to give the preferred shareholders some assurance they will receive the stated dividend.

The preferred stock's right to dividends is usually cumulative; i.e., if the corporation fails to pay a dividend, the missed dividends accumulate and all missed dividends must be paid before any dividend is paid to the common. Suppose the preferred shares are entitled to a $1 dividend in each calendar quarter and the corporation has failed to pay any dividends for the four preceding quarters. In this situation, the corporation would have to pay the dividend for the current quarter ($1) plus the four missed dividends ($4, for a total payment of $5 per share) before it could pay dividends to the common stock. Alternatively, although preferred stock usually has no voting rights, many corporations give preferred shareholders the right to elect some or all directors in the event a specified number of dividends are missed.

The preferences and other rights of preferred stock are spelled out in the articles of incorporation. MBCA § 6.02, however, allows the corporation to create so-called "blank check" preferred stock. If blank check preferred is authorized, the rights and preferences of the preferred stock will not be contained in the articles. Instead, the articles will empower the board of directors to specify those rights and preferences at the time the shares are issued. An amendment to the articles, creating the shares and detailing their rights and preferences, must be filed with the secretary of state's office before the shares are issued, but this amendment does not require shareholder approval.

Blank check preferred has obvious advantages. If the articles authorize blank check preferred, the board can respond quickly and flexibly to changing market conditions. The ability to precisely tailor dividend rates and other provisions for prevailing market conditions lowers the corporation's cost of capital and thus benefits the shareholders.

---

4. Because of the differing rights of preferred and common stock, their interests sometimes clash. When this happens, the board of director's ultimate fiduciary duty is to the common shareholders. The board must perform their obligations to the preferred, but those obligations are regarded as contractual rather than fiduciary in nature. See, e.g., Wood v. Coastal States Gas Corp., 401 A.2d 932 (Del.1979).

On the other hand, blank check preferred has even more obvious disadvantages. The name says it all: would you give someone a blank check? There is some risk that the board of directors will abuse their power to set the terms of the blank check preferred. Early defenses against hostile takeovers, for example, often involved the use of blank check preferred.

C. Debt securities

Debt securities come in three basic flavors: (1) bonds, which are unsecured long-term instruments; (2) debentures, which are secured long-term instruments; and (3) notes, which are short-term instruments that usually are unsecured.[5] Although the dividing line between bonds and debentures on the one hand and notes on the other is not always precise, a good rule of thumb is that notes are obligations having a maturity of nine months or less. For purposes of semantic convenience, all debt securities are referred to as bonds in this text unless the context requires otherwise.

Bonds typically consist of two distinct rights. First, the bondholder is entitled to receive a stream of payments in the form of interest over a period of years. Second, at the end of the bond's prescribed term (i.e., at maturity), the bondholder is entitled to the return of the principal—the amount paid to purchase the bond. (There are certain other types of bonds, such as zero-coupon bonds and asset-backed securities, having somewhat different characteristics, but we will ignore them.)

1. Bond value and interest rates

Bonds are typically issued in $1,000 denominations with a coupon rate expressed as some percentage of the face value of the bond. A $1,000 bond with an 8% coupon rate, for example, pays $80 per year in interest. The value of a bond at any time prior to maturity is not determined by its denomination (or face value), but by the price the bond would command if sold in the market. A bond's secondary market price is a function of the bond's coupon rate and current market interest rates for bonds with similar risks. The relationship between current price and yield is an inverse one: if market rates have risen since the bond was issued, its current price will fall. In converse, if market rates have fallen, the bond's current price will rise.

The current value of a bond varies inversely with market interest rates because the coupon rate does not change when market rates do. If you bought a ten year $1,000 bond with a coupon rate equal to prevailing market rates of 6%, you purchased (among other things) the right to receive $60 per year in interest for ten years. If market rates fall to 5%, a newly issued $1,000 bond with a coupon rate equal to the market rate

---

5. For a useful discussion of more eso-teric types of corporate securities, see Kenneth A. Carow et al., A Survey of U.S. Corporate Financing Innovations: 1970–1997, 12 J. Applied. Corp. Fin. 55 (1999).

carries only the right to get $50 per year in interest. All other things being equal, it should be obvious that the previously-issued bond paying $60 per year is worth more than the subsequently-issued bond paying $50: if you would rather receive $60 per year than $50 per year, you would be willing to pay more for a bond that pays $60 per year.

2. *The indenture*

Bonds are issued pursuant to complex contracts called indentures. In general, however, all of the indenture's myriad terms are designed to accomplish a single task: protecting the bondholder's right to interest and return of principal.

One of the more important parts of the indenture is the statement of what actions will constitute a default by the issuer. If a default occurs, the bondholders are entitled to accelerate the maturity of the bonds: they become immediately due and payable. Thus, if the bond is scheduled to mature on January 1, 2030, the issuer normally would not be required to pay back the principal until that date. If a default occurs today, however, the bondholders will be entitled to immediate return of their investment. Failure to pay interest when owed is the most obvious event of default, but many indentures will specify certain other violations of the indenture to be events of default.

The indenture typically contains a variety of restrictions, whose violation will either constitute an event of default or which may mature into an event of default if not cured. Restrictions on the corporation's ability to pay dividends are common. While most indentures permit the payment of some reasonable level of dividends, indentures by particularly risky companies may prohibit the payment of any dividends during the life of the bonds. The goal of such provisions is to retain earnings within the firm, so they are available to the bondholders in the event of a default. Another common restriction is the negative pledge covenant, which restricts the corporation's ability to issue debt senior to the bonds covered by the indenture.

Call provisions allow the issuer to repay the principal before maturity.[6] A related provision is the sinking fund, which requires the issuer to pay back the principal in installments throughout the life of the bond.

In a corporation having hundreds or thousands of bondholders, it obviously would be very difficult for the issuer to bargain with all of the bondholders or for the bondholders to effectively enforce the indenture agreement. Instead, two intermediaries act on behalf of the bondholders. One is the underwriter: the investment banking firm that sells the bonds to the public. The underwriter negotiates the terms of the indenture with the issuer. The other intermediary is the indenture trustee. The indenture trustee's job is an enforcer: if the issuer defaults, it is the indenture trustee who takes action (such as bringing suit) on behalf of the bondholders to enforce their rights under the indenture.

---

6. See generally William A. Klein et al., The Call Provision of Corporate Bonds: A Standard Form in Need of Change, 18 J. Corp. L. 653 (1993).

D. Convertible securities

A corporation may issue securities that are convertible into another form of the corporation's securities. Convertible bonds and convertible preferred stock are the most common types of convertibles. Solely for purposes of convenience, the following discussion refers only to convertible bonds. In general, the principles discussed apply equally to convertible preferred.

A convertible bond essentially combines two different types of securities into a single instrument.[7] One half of the package is a traditional bond, with the usual right to periodic interest and ultimate repayment of principal. The other half is a warrant, which is a type of option issued by the corporation. The warrant's holder receives a right to purchase securities of the corporation (usually common stock) at the price and on those conditions specified by the warrant.

In order to exercise the conversion feature, the holder of a convertible bond surrenders it to the corporation, which thereupon issues the number of shares of common stock specified in the indenture. The so-called "conversion ratio" is the number of shares the bondholder will receive when the bond is surrendered. The conversion price is the per share cost of those shares to the shareholder. If the conversion ratio is known, the conversion price may be determined by dividing the face value of the bond by the conversion ratio. Conversely, if the conversion price is known, the conversion ratio may be determined by dividing the face value of the bond by the conversion price. The indenture typically states the conversion price, rather than the conversion ratio.

As an example, assume Acme, Inc., issues convertible bonds having a face value of $1,000 and a coupon rate of 8%. The indenture states that upon surrender of the bond the holder will receive 1 share for every $25 of the bond's face value. The conversion price thus is $25, which gives us a conversion ratio of 40 shares per bond ($1,000 divided by $25).

The conversion price tells us the minimum price the corporation's stock must reach before it makes economic sense for the holder to convert the bond into stock. The issuer will normally set the conversion price 10—30% above the stock market price prevailing when the bonds are issued. Only if the stock's market price subsequently rises towards and past the conversion price, will the holder profit by converting. Suppose that in the preceding example the market price of the corporation's stock was $20 when the bond was sold. If the holder bought the bond for $1,000 (face value) and immediately exercised the conversion right, he would receive 40 shares worth $20 on the market. The holder would lose money on the deal, because he would surrender a bond worth $1,000 to receive shares worth $800. If the stock price subsequently rises

---

7. See generally George W. Dent, Jr., The Role of Convertible Securities in Corporate Finance, 21 J. Corp. L. 241 (1996); William A. Klein, The Convertible Bond: A Peculiar Package, 123 U. Pa. L. Rev. 547 (1975).

to $30, however, the holder could profit by exercising the conversion feature. Now he would surrender a bond with a face value of $1,000 to receive stock worth $1,200.

Until quite recently, most corporate law statutes permitted only down-stream conversion. In other words, a security could be convertible only into junior securities. Bonds could be converted into common stock, but stock could not be converted into bonds. MBCA § 6.01(c)(2) permits up-stream conversion, but few companies appear to have availed themselves of this option.

E. Asset backed securities

In an asset securitization transaction, a company sells some assets (typically accounts receivable) to a so-called "bankruptcy remote vehicle" (BRV), which pays for those assets with the proceeds of an offering of fixed income securities. Like traditional factoring, which it somewhat resembles, asset securitization creates value in several ways.

The type of debt issued by a firm affects its debt capacity. Most mature firms issue claims on their general cash flows and assets. These claims depend on the firm's going-concern value. Determining this value for growth firms is difficult, due to information asymmetries and valuation discrepancies. Consequently, capital providers apply a significant uncertainty discount when they advance funds to such firms. One way for growth firms to access the debt market is through asset securitization, which does not rely on the value of the firm as a going concern. They are instead tied to specific, easier-to-measure asset values. Growth firms thus can use asset-based borrowings to enhance an otherwise constrained balance sheet.

Securitization also creates value by increasing liquidity. It turns illiquid raw assets into securities that can be bought and sold much more easily.

Finally, securitization creates value by dividing the risks associated with a particular lending arrangement and selling the risks off to the investors most able (or willing) to bear that particular type of risk. Put another way, securitization generally takes the different characteristics of the raw asset and puts them into separate classes, which can be sold separately rather than bundled. Accordingly, each risk characteristic can be sold to the buyer who is best able to bear that risk. Credit risk can be sold to those who best understand credit risk or who are hedged against credit risk, for example, without obliging the buyer to bear other risks they understand less well or for which they are not the best bearer.[8]

---

8. Financial theory generally contends that dividing up the risks of a particular business into multiple classes does not add value because it does not change the total risk and thus does not change the total return the business must pay. But that assumption does not hold true when the investor pool is heterogeneous. Asset securitization assumes investor heterogeneity.

F.   Is there an optimal capital structure?

Do changes in a corporation's capital structure—i.e., its debt to equity ratio—have predictable effects on the corporation's value? The traditional view was that a judicious use of debt, by virtue of the leverage phenomenon and tax advantages, enhanced firm values.[9] Nobel prize laureates Modigliani and Miller, however, made an elaborate proof that there is no such thing as an optimal debt-equity ratio.[10] Consider the following example: Assume two firms (A and B) identical in all respects save capital structure.[11] Firm A has no debt and earns a return of 15 percent on equity of $66,667 (i.e., $10,000). Firm B has debt of $30,000 carrying a 12 percent interest rate and equity of $40,000 on which it earns a 16 percent return (i.e., $6,400). Assume Shareholder owns 1 percent of Firm B (400 shares) on which she earns $64 per year. She could replicate Firm B's leverage by borrowing $300 at 12 percent interest and selling her Firm B shares for $400 (remember she holds 1 percent of the equity). She could then buy 1 percent of Firm A for $667. Shareholder earns $100 (15 percent of $667 per year) and pays $36 in interest, for a total return of $64. In other words, by using home made leverage she can earn the same rate of return but has an extra $33 ($400 sale proceeds minus $367 cash payment) in her pocket.

Such a situation should not persist. The price differential between the two firms creates an opportunity for arbitrage. Arbitrage is the attempt to profit from price differentials between perfect substitutes selling in the same market. Arbitragers buy the relatively under-priced security—here, Firm A—and sell the relatively over-priced security—here, Firm B. This process will continue until there is no further opportunity to reduce their investment outlay while achieving the same dollar return. Hence, the price of Firm A stock should rise and the price of Firm B stock should fall until the returns equilibrate. Arbitrage thus makes debt-equity ratios irrelevant to the question of firm value. All other things being equal, firms with the same net earnings will end up with the same value regardless of how their capital structure is divided between debt and equity.[12]

9. See, e.g., Benjamin Graham et al., Security Analysis 539–43 (4th ed. 1962).

10. Franco Modigliani and Merton Miller, The Cost of Capital, Corporation Finance and the Theory of Investment, 48 Am. Econ. Rev. 261 (1958). See generally G. Mitu Gulati et al., Connected Contracts, 47 UCLA L. Rev. 887 (2000).

11. The example is taken from Lawrence E. Mitchell et al., Corporate Finance and Governance 1031–32 (2d ed. 1996).

12. The capital asset pricing model, discussed below, provides an intuitive basis for this proposition: namely, value depends on risk and return. Two firms that are identical in all respects, except for capital structure, should have the same overall level of systematic risk (assuming that capital structure changes do not affect systematic risk). You can divide up capital into low systematic risk claims (debt) and high systematic risk claims (equity). Low risk claims will require a lower market rate of return; high risk claims will require a higher rate of return. The more low risk debt a company has, the more risk is concentrated on the high risk equity, and the higher the required rate of return on that equity. But the total risk is the same, no matter how that risk is divided up.

If the Modigliani and Miller hypothesis is correct, we ought to observe a wide range of debt-equity ratios. Yet, in the real world, there does seem to be an upper limit on the amount of debt incurred by firms: we don't see firms with very high percentages of their capital in the form of debt. Why not?

Once we relax the assumptions made by Modigliani and Miller, it becomes clear that while there may not be a single optimal capital structure, there are nonoptimal capital structures. Modigliani and Miller ignored the tax and bankruptcy consequences of choosing between debt and equity, assumed zero transaction costs, and assumed that individuals and corporations can borrow at the same rates. Yet, these factors are clearly relevant. The tax laws provide some incentive to use debt rather than equity, because the interest payments on debt are deductible. Conversely, however, high debt increases the risk of bankruptcy. Arbitrage does have transaction costs, although they are relatively low. Some corporations can obtain lower interest rates than individuals, although the disparity is usually minor.

Modigliani and Miller also failed to take into account the possibility that management can use changes in the firm's debt-equity ratio to send signals to the market about the firm's health and future income. Suppose the board of directors believes that the firm is prospering, but has not been able to persuade the market of that fact. Perhaps the board lacks credibility with market analysts or is unable to disclose some of the basis for its optimism. The board might respond by causing the corporation to borrow and use the proceeds to repurchase some of the firm's outstanding shares. In order to satisfy the new interest obligations, the board must expect higher earnings in the future. Otherwise the board would either have to reduce reinvestment, due to the fall in retained earnings, or cut the dividend. This course of action sends a particularly strong signal because greater debt necessarily implies a greater risk of default and firm failure. Given that managers are often the heaviest losers from firm failure, the leveraged repurchase program implies a high degree of confidence. The signal is even stronger, of course, if the recapitalization results in management owning a higher percentage of the firm's equity.

Probably the most important constraint on debt-equity ratios, however, results from an agency cost problem. Recall that whenever you have two or more individuals working together to achieve a collective goal, all team members have an incentive to shirk unless their individual reward is closely related to their personal conscientiousness. The principal can minimize the losses from shirking by monitoring the marginal productivity of each team member. This requires that the principal be given the power to observe the performance of the various workers, be the central party to all contracts with the workers, and have the power to alter or discontinue those contracts so as to punish and thereby deter shirking. Alternatively, agents may expend resources in order to guarantee that they will not take actions that injure the principal: in other words, the agents may incur bonding costs to provide assurances to the principal that the agents will not shirk their duties.

Treat bondholders as the principal and shareholders as the agent. The rate of return demanded by principals will reflect the amount of monitoring expenses they expect to incur and the amount of the residual loss they anticipate. Thus, the agents may try to reduce the rate of return they must pay by engaging in bonding. Bear in mind that the bondholders get paid first out of the firm's income, while shareholders get whatever is left over. Shareholders thus have an incentive to make the firm invest in projects that offer potentially high rate of returns, so there will be something left over after the bondholders get paid. But high return projects usually involve high levels of risk.

Bondholders might respond by increasing the extent to which they monitor the firm's behavior, so as to prevent the firm from engaging in high risk projects. Such monitoring efforts are costly, however, so the bondholders will demand a higher rate of interest. As a result, less of the firm's income will be left over for the shareholders. In such a firm, the shareholders therefore have an incentive to prefer very high risk, high return projects. In turn, bondholders will step up the extent to which they monitor the firm and raise their interest demands. A high level of debt thus becomes a vicious cycle—you get a spiral of increasingly risky projects and ever increasing interest burdens. It is that vicious cycle that puts an upper limit on the level of debt that a firm can manage. A low level of debt, consequently, is a form of bonding by shareholders. It represents a commitment by the shareholders that they will not engage in excessively risky projects.

An alternative agency cost story looks at a more traditional agency relationship—i.e., the relationship between managers and shareholders. Under this "free cash flow" model,[13] managers with too much cash and too few good investments will divert cash flow into management perquisites and/or find bad investments. Creating a capital structure with lots of debt forces managers to pay out free cash flows as interest. Dividends are optional and flexible, while debt payments are mandatory and inflexible. Debt forces managers to disgorge earnings instead of plowing cash back into a mature business that has few positive net present value investments available. In a sense, high debt is a way of sopping up free cash flow.

The free cash flow model offers a plausible theory that some debt does increase firm value. Coupled with the preference for debt created by the tax system, it seems that there was something to the traditional argument that debt is good and judicious increases in debt may be even better. Yet, free cash flow does not suggest that there is a single optimal capital structure. As is so often true, one size does not fit all.

---

13. Free cash flow is that portion of the firm's earnings in excess of that needed to fund all available positive net present value investments. Michael C. Jensen, Agency Costs of Free Cash Flow, Corporate Finance, and Takeovers, 76 Am. Econ. Rev. 323 (1986).

What is the legal policy implication of this analysis? In brief, laissez-faire. Government regulation of capital structure is no more likely to "get it right" than is private ordering. The choice of an appropriate debt-equity ratio should be vested in the board of directors and the business judgment rule ought to insulate that decision from review by both judges and regulators.

§ 3.3 Issuance of securities: The business context

The vast majority of U.S. corporations are closely-held. These corporations rarely sell securities. Any sales they do make are effected through private placements to small numbers of investors. No public secondary market exists on which their shares are traded. If such a corporation decides to "go public," it does so by conducting an initial public offering of its securities.[1]

A. Offering terminology

Some of the following terms have highly technical legal meanings under the federal securities laws, but those statutory definitions are essentially irrelevant for present purposes. The definitions given below thus are the meanings used in common parlance.

Issuer: The corporation that sold the securities.

Underwriter: An investment bank that specializes in selling securities to investors on behalf of their issuers.

Best efforts underwriting: An offering in which the underwriter acts as broker—i.e., an agent for the issuer/seller—to distribute the securities, with the issuer paying a commission of 1–2% on sales. This form of underwriting is predominately used for new, speculative equity securities or below investment grade debt offerings. About 5% of public offerings fall into this category.

Firm commitment underwriting: An offering in which the underwriter acts as a dealer (a principal). The underwriter purchases securities from the issuer and then resells them to the public. Firm commitment underwriting accounts for about 90% of all public offerings.

Lead underwriter: The issuer selects a lead underwriter who is generally responsible for conducting the offering. The issuer and lead underwriter jointly settle on the type, form and nature of the offering. The basic terms of their agreement are set forth in a nonbinding letter of intent. The two parties then prepare and file the initial registration statement. Once the registration statement is about to become effective the issuer and the lead underwriter enter into an underwriting agreement setting forth the final, binding terms of the transaction. The final

---

§ 3.3

1. The dividing line between public offerings and private placements is far from clear. As a general rule of thumb, however, a private placement involves an unadver-tised sale to a small number of investors, while a public offering involves a sale to a substantial portion of the investing public at large.

offering price is set on the day before the registration statement becomes effective.

Underwriting syndicate: While the registration statement is being prepared, the lead underwriter assembles an underwriting syndicate of other investment banking firms. The members of the syndicate become parties to the agreement among underwriters, which sets forth the terms of their relationship. Part of the offering will be sold directly to the public by syndicate members. The remainder will be sold to retail securities dealers who join the so-called selling group and who in turn resell the securities to their customers.

B. The going public decision

Going public has a number of significant advantages. It necessarily creates a public secondary market when the initial shareholders (or bondholders) begin trading the corporation's securities with other investors. The availability of a secondary market makes the corporation's securities liquid, which means investors can freely sell their securities without involving the firm. Liquidity, in turn, makes it easier and cheaper to subsequently raise capital in the primary market, because investors generally prefer (and will be willing to pay more) for liquid securities. A secondary market also permits the firm to utilize stock-based forms of management compensation. Finally, banks may charge lower interest rates to public firms, because changes in stock prices are a good barometer of the firm's condition. This same factor also means that the issuer can often offer a lower interest rate in subsequent private placements of debt securities with institutional investors.

On the other hand, there are some significant disadvantages associated with going public. A public corporation is subject to unsolicited changes of control through hostile tender offers and proxy contests. A public corporation also must provide far greater disclosure to investors, which results in reduced privacy on sensitive issues like executive compensation and research.

Once a corporation decides to raise funds through a primary market offering, it next must decide whether to utilize the services of an underwriter or to sell the securities itself in a direct offering. Direct offerings by issuers are very rare. Typically, only well-established firms making a private placement of debt securities to institutional investors use direct offerings.

Once they go public, established corporations rarely return to the primary market for further public offerings. If an established corporation needs primary market financing, it normally relies on private placements of debt securities. Because the regulatory burden faced by issuers is significantly reduced in the private placement context, private placements are faster and much less expensive than underwritten public offerings.

§ 3.4 Issuance of securities: Corporate law aspects

Most regulatory burdens on issuing securities today are imposed by federal law. Several state corporate law doctrines, however, continue to affect the issuance process. Four seem especially worthy of note: (1) the respective roles of the board of directors and the shareholders; (2) the legal capital rules; (3) the law governing subscription agreements; and (4) preemptive rights.

A. The respective roles of the board and shareholders

State law empowers the board of directors to cause the corporation to issue debt securities, at any time and for any valid purpose, without shareholder action or approval. The board thus essentially has unfettered discretion to issue debt, subject to its fiduciary duties and any pre-existing contractual restrictions on the issuance of additional debt.

The board's authority with respect to issuing additional stock is slightly less sweeping. In general, the board has wide discretion to issue additional shares of stock, so long as there is a valid purpose for doing so and the corporation receives adequate consideration for the shares. In three situations, however, the board must obtain shareholder approval before issuing additional stock.

If the corporation wishes to issue additional shares in excess of the number of authorized shares, shareholder approval of an amendment increasing the number of authorized shares is required. Suppose, for example, that Acme Corporation's articles of incorporation authorize 30,000 shares of common stock, 10,000 of which are already outstanding. The board could authorize the sale of up to 20,000 shares without shareholder approval, but the board wishes to sell 40,000 shares. Because Acme's articles presently authorize only 30,000 shares, the board must ask the shareholders to approve an amendment increasing the number of authorized shares of common stock from 30,000 to at least 50,000. In real life, this is fairly rare. The articles normally set an authorized number of shares exceeding the number of shares the corporation would expect to issue in the near term.

If the board of directors wishes to issue a new class of shares not authorized in the articles, it must ask the shareholders to approve an amendment authorizing the new class. In the preceding example, the articles authorized only common stock. If the board wishes to sell preferred stock, it must first ask the shareholders to approve an amendment creating a class of preferred stock and setting the number of authorized shares of the new class.

Finally, the Model Act requires shareholder approval of an issuance of shares (or convertible securities) if (1) the shares are issued for noncash consideration and (2) the issued shares represent more than 20 percent of the voting power of the shares outstanding prior to the issuance.[1] The major stock exchanges and NASDAQ have similar requirements in their listing standards.

§ 3.4

1. MBCA § 6.21(f).

B. Legal capital

At one time, all stock was required to have a "par value," which was stated in the articles of incorporation. The par value represented the price at which the corporation initially sold shares to the public. A firm could not sell shares for less than par value and, at least in its initial offering, usually did not sell shares for more than par value. If the firm issued stock for less than the par value, the shares were called "watered stock." Shareholders who purchased watered stock could be held liable to creditors for the amount of any water.

A vast and arcane body of law grew up to implement these so-called legal capital requirements. Today, however, most of that law has fallen into decrepitude. Virtually all states allow one to sell stock with low or even no par value. To the extent legal capital restrictions still matter, they do so mainly as part of the statutory apparatus regulating payment of dividends.

C. Subscription agreements

A subscription agreement is a contract pursuant to which an investor agrees to buy corporate stock. If the subscription agreement is entered into by an investor and an existing corporation, ordinary contract law rules govern. If the subscription agreement is signed before the business is incorporated, however, a more complex body of corporate law applies.

At one time, promoters commonly used subscription agreements to measure investor interest in the proposed corporate venture. The promoter solicited investors to subscribe for shares. If enough investors agreed to buy stock in the venture, the promoter went forward with the incorporation. After incorporation, the firm made "calls" for payment on the investors. A number of legal problems arose in connection with subscription agreements, the most important of which was the question of whether the subscription agreement constituted a binding contract.

Recall that a corporation cannot make contracts until it comes into de jure existence. The majority common law view therefore treated subscription agreements as a continuing offer, rather than a binding contract. An investor therefore could revoke the subscription agreement at any time before the firm was incorporated or, in some states, before the corporation issued the call for payment.[2]

Most modern corporation statutes reject the common law approach. MBCA § 6.20(a) is typical. It provides that a subscription agreement is irrevocable for six months after it is signed, unless the agreement states to the contrary or all subscribers agree to a revocation.

2. See, e.g., Hudson Real Estate Co. v. Tower, 30 N.E. 465 (Mass.1892); cf. Minneapolis Threshing Machine Co. v. Davis, 41 N.W. 1026 (Minn.1889) (pre-incorporation subscription agreement constituted a continuing offer to the corporation, but also constituted a binding contract among the subscribers).

D. Preemptive rights

When a corporation issues additional shares, the proportional financial interests and voting rights of existing shareholders are reduced. Preemptive rights were developed to provide a mechanism for preserving the proportional interests of existing shareholders. Preemptive rights give the shareholder the right to purchase a pro rata share of any new issues at the new issue price.

Suppose Susan Shareholder owns 200 of Acme, Inc.'s 1,000 outstanding shares. Assume the corporation's book value is $12,000—or $12 per share. Acme plans to issue 400 additional shares at $10 per share. Before that dilutive transaction, Susan's stock gave her 20% of the corporation's voting power. Afterwards, Susan will only have about 14% of the voting power. Worse yet, after the dilutive transaction, the book value of Susan's stock will have declined to $11.42 (the corporation received an additional $4,000 in assets, raising its value to $16,000, but that value is now divided by 1,400 shares).

If Acme's stock is subject to preemptive rights, Shareholder is entitled to buy enough new shares to maintain her proportional interest in the corporation. Before any additional shares are issued, Susan owns 20% of the outstanding shares. She is therefore entitled to buy 80 of the 400 additional shares when they are issued. If she does so, she will still own a 20% interest in the corporation (she will own 280 out of 1,400 shares, which is 20%). Shareholder must pay the price asked by the corporation, which is $10 on these facts.

At early common law, shareholders possessed an "inherent right" to purchase a pro rata share of newly issued common stock.[3] Modern statutes reject the notion of preemptive rights as an inherent attribute of common stock. Under MBCA § 6.30, for example, shareholders of a corporation are entitled to preemptive rights only if the articles of incorporation explicitly provide for them. About two-thirds of the states follow the MBCA's "opt in" approach, most notably including Delaware. Most of the rest follow an "opt out" approach, under which shareholders are entitled to preemptive rights unless the articles of incorporation provide to the contrary. Virtually all public corporations have chosen to eliminate preemptive rights, because of the complications they create when the corporation wishes to issue new stock.

In any event, because shareholders must make an additional investment in order to exercise their preemptive rights, those rights provide only limited protection for shareholders who wish to maintain their

---

3. See, e.g., Stokes v. Continental Trust Co., 78 N.E. 1090 (N.Y.App.1906). Even today, courts may still intervene even if the shareholder challenging a stock issuance is not entitled to preemptive rights. For instance, courts may interdict a stock issuance that is designed to preserve the board of directors' authority, or that is made at an unfairly low price. This practice is sometimes referred to as a "quasi-preemptive right." See, e.g., Sheppard v. Wilcox, 26 Cal. Rptr. 412, 417 (Cal.Ct.App.1962); see also Condec Corp. v. Lunkenheimer Co., 230 A.2d 769 (Del.Ch.1967).

existing proportional interest in the corporation.[4] Indeed, preemptive rights are useless if the shareholder lacks sufficient funds to purchase her pro rata share of the newly-issued stock.

§ 3.5   Issuance of shares: Federal law

State corporate law imposes few meaningful restrictions on a corporation's ability to issue equity or debt securities. A corporation proposing to issue securities, however, does face significant regulatory hurdles from federal securities law. The Securities Act of 1933 is the main federal statute regulating primary market transactions. The Securities Act has two principal goals: assuring adequate disclosure of material information to investors and preventing fraud. As to the former, the Act follows a transactional disclosure model; i.e., the Act focuses on getting information concerning certain transactions from the issuer to investors. As to the latter, the Act imposes both civil and criminal liability on those who use fraud in the sale of securities.

A.   Definition of security

Stocks and bonds issued by a corporation are deemed a security and, as such, regulated by the federal securities laws. Because business lawyers not infrequently face clients who sell (or buy) more esoteric investment vehicles, however, it seems worthwhile to devote some atten-

---

4. In Katzowitz v. Sidler, 301 N.Y.S.2d 470 (1969), the court granted relief to a complaining shareholder despite his failure to exercise extant preemptive rights. Sulburn Holding Corp. had three shareholders, each of whom also served as a director: Isador Katzowitz, Jacob Sidler, and Max Lasker. Each owned five shares of Sulburn common stock. By the time of the dispute, Sulburn's per share book value was $1,800. Sidler and Lasker voted, over Katzowitz's objection, to cause the corporation to issue up to 75 additional shares at their par value of $100 per share. Katzowitz did not exercise his preemptive rights. Sidler and Lasker each purchased 25 shares. Sulburn dissolved shortly thereafter. Upon liquidation of the corporation, each shareholder received a liquidating dividend of approximately $630 per share. As a result of the recent stock issuance, Sidler and Lasker each received $18,885.52, while Katzowitz received only $3,147.59. Per Judge Keating, the court held that a challenged issuance of shares by a closely-held corporation was subject to judicial scrutiny if two conditions are met: (1) the issuing price is shown to be substantially below the shares' book value and (2) the defendant shareholder-directors benefited from the issuance. If these conditions are met, as they were on these facts, the defendant shareholder-directors must show there was a valid business reason for issuing the shares at that price. Because the defendants failed to make such a showing, Katzowitz was entitled to a pro rata share of the firm's assets based on his pre-stock issuance proportional interest less the amount Sidler and Lasker paid to purchase their new shares. Book value is a very poor measurement of stock value. As such, testing the validity of a stock issuance by comparing the issuance price to book value is like comparing apples and oranges. Indeed, the board of directors may often have a legitimate business purpose for issuing shares at below book value. This will clearly be the case when the stock's fair value is lower than book value. It might also be the case if the corporation is failing, requires additional capital, and must give a prospective investor a discount as an inducement for making the necessary investment. Unfortunately for Messrs. Sidler and Lasker they failed to prove any such necessity. In fact, because Sidler and Lasker knew that Katzowitz did not wish to buy any more shares, it appears they ganged up on Katzowitz, using their voting control of the company to benefit themselves at the latter's expense. On the other hand, Katzowitz could have protected himself by exercising his preemptive rights. Some courts therefore have rejected claims by persons in Katzowitz's position. See, e.g., Hyman v. Velsicol Corp., 97 N.E.2d 122 (Ill.App.1951).

tion to the statutory definition of a security. Indeed, investments in worm farms, orange groves, and a host of even more exotic investments have been deemed securities. Conversely, some investments labeled as "stock" or "notes" have been excluded from the definition of security.

Oddly, Securities Act § 2(1) does not really define the term "security." Instead, it contains a long list of specific instruments deemed securities. Among these are "stock," "bond," and "note." At the end of this list is a set of catch-all phrases, of which "investment contract" is the most important. If an instrument is specifically listed in Section 2(1), the definitional task usually is straightforward. If you are dealing with an investment that is not listed in the statute, such as limited partnership interests or orange groves, however, the definitional task is more complex. The basic question is whether one of the catch-all clauses applies, which usually becomes an inquiry into whether the instrument is an "investment contract."

An investment contract is (1) a contract, transaction or scheme whereby a person invests money, (2) in a common enterprise, (3) and is led to expect profits solely from the efforts of the promoter or a third party. In the leading *Howey* decision, a Florida corporation owned large tracts of citrus groves. The groves were divided into long narrow tracts and the tracts were sold to investors. Each prospective investor was offered both a land sales contract and a service contract. The latter agreement provided that the defendants would cultivate the groves and harvest and market the crop. The purchasers were mainly nonFlorida residents lacking the skill, knowledge, and equipment necessary to cultivate their tracts. The Supreme Court held that an investment contract and, thus, a security was present. Purchasers invested money. A common enterprise was present, because profits from the defendants' operations were pooled and then divided amongst the investors. Because investors expected the defendants to run the operation, and to do so profitably, the third condition was also met.[1]

Now let's flip the situation around to examine investment vehicles denominated "stocks" or "notes" that are excluded from the statutory definition of a security. In general, stock is always a security, unless the instrument in question really is not stock, in which case the instrument might still be a security if it is an investment contract. All of which may sound sort of silly, but actually is a fair description of the current state of the law.

As noted above, stock is one of the terms specifically listed in Section 2(1)'s definition of a security. The very first sentence of Section 2, however, provides that terms used in the Securities Act have the meaning set forth in the various subsections of Section 2 "unless the context otherwise requires." This so-called "context" clause offers courts an escape hatch. It allows courts to hold that although an instrument

§ 3.5

1. SEC v. W.J. Howey Co., 328 U.S. 293 (1946).

appears to fall within one of the listed types of securities, the instrument shall not be deemed a security because "the context otherwise requires."

In the leading *United Housing* decision,[2] residents of a cooperative apartment complex purchased their home not by buying a fee interest in their apartment, but rather purchasing shares of "stock" in the housing cooperative. Plaintiffs in *United Housing* were disappointed purchasers of cooperative shares. They brought suit under the securities laws' antifraud provisions. The issue presented to the Supreme Court was whether the cooperative shares were securities.

Plaintiffs first argued that the instruments they purchased were called stock. Section 2(1) includes stock in the definition of a security. Q.E.D. The Supreme Court rejected this argument. The majority found the cooperative shares had none of the characteristics of true corporate stock: they were nonnegotiable, had no voting rights, and could not appreciate in value. Accordingly, even though the instruments are called stock, they were not stock as that term is used in Section 2(1).

Plaintiffs next argued the cooperative shares were investment contracts. The majority also rejected this argument. One must look at the economic realities of the transaction in order to decide whether a security is present. Plaintiffs had no expectation of profit from the efforts of others. Indeed, the cooperative in question was subsidized public housing and plaintiffs could not sell either the apartment or their shares. Plaintiffs therefore had no expectation of profits at all. To the contrary, they were simply buying a place to live.

The Supreme Court, however, subsequently limited the extent to which the economic realities standard controls. After *United Housing*, some lower courts extended Supreme Court's emphasis therein on economic realities to sales of a business. Sales of closely-held corporations are often effected by a sale of all of the corporation's outstanding shares. According to the lower courts, even though such a sale may involve a transfer of stock, the economic reality of the transaction is that purchaser is buying a business, just as the *United Housing* plaintiffs were buying a residence.[3] The Supreme Court rejected this line of cases, holding that a sale of a corporation by means of a sale of stock involves a security.[4] The "economic realities" question is directed at the attributes of the instrument, not those of the transaction. If the instrument in question has the attributes of stock, as all corporate common stock does, it is a security.

As with bonds and some other debt securities, notes are one of the specifically listed instruments within Section 2(1)'s definition of a security. Many notes, however, have no investment character whatsoever. Promissory notes evidencing a bank loan are a good example of such a

---

2. United Housing Foundation, Inc. v. Forman, 421 U.S. 837 (1975).

3. See, e.g., Sutter v. Groen, 687 F.2d 197 (7th Cir.1982); Frederiksen v. Poloway, 637 F.2d 1147 (7th Cir.1981).

4. Landreth Timber Co. v. Landreth, 471 U.S. 681 (1985).

note. In recognition of this fact, the Supreme Court has adopted a multi-prong test for determining whether a note constitutes a security.[5] The party asserting that a note is not a security has the burden of showing that the context requires that the note not be treated as a security. Certain notes are presumed not to be securities, such as: consumer financing obligations, home mortgages, notes evidencing a bank loan, short-term notes secured by an assignment of accounts receivable, or notes formalizing an open account debt incurred in the ordinary course of business (such as a note on a brokerage account). The foregoing list of notes excluded from the definition of a security is not exclusive. A four part test is applied to decide whether a note not on the list should be treated as a security: (1) was the motivation for the transaction investment or commercial; (2) was the plan of distribution such that notes would be sold to a broad class of the public; (3) would the public reasonably perceive the note to be a security; and (4) are there other factors, such as presence of an alternative regulatory scheme, that render application of the Act unnecessary.

In *Reves v. Ernst & Young*,[6] a farmer's cooperative issued demand notes to both members and nonmembers. Advertising for the notes emphasized the investment nature of the notes and their safety. When the cooperative went bankrupt, the disappointed purchasers sued the cooperative's accountants under the antifraud provisions of the securities laws. The Supreme Court held the demand note was not on the list of notes presumed not to be securities, nor did the note resemble them under the four factor test: (1) the notes were sold as an investment to raise capital for issuer; (2) they were widely distributed; (3) the advertising probably led the public to think of the notes as securities; and (4) the notes were unregulated and uninsured. Ergo, the note was a security.

B. The registration process

Securities Act § 5(a) makes it unlawful to sell a security unless a registration statement is in effect with respect to the securities. In other words, unless an exemption is available, the prospective issuer must file a registration statement with the SEC and wait for the registration statement to become effective before selling securities.[7] Oddly, as the

---

5. Reves v. Ernst & Young, 494 U.S. 56 (1990). In *Reves*, a farmer's cooperative issued demand notes to both members and nonmembers. The advertising emphasized the investment nature of the notes and their safety. When the cooperative went bankrupt, the disappointed purchasers sued the cooperative's accountants under the antifraud provisions of the securities laws. The Supreme Court held the demand note was not on the list of notes presumed not to be securities, nor did the note resemble them under the four factor test: (1) the notes were sold as an investment to raise capital for issuer; (2) they were widely dis-

tributed; (3) the advertising probably led the public to think of the notes as securities; and (4) the notes were unregulated and uninsured. Ergo, the note was a security.

6. 494 U.S. 56 (1990).

7. Securities Act § 5 effectively divides the registration process into three periods: the pre-filing period, which is the period before the registration statement is filed; the waiting period, which is the period between the date the registration statement is filed with the SEC and the date it becomes effective; and the post-effective period,

registration process evolved, practice departed substantially from the statutory theory.

Securities Act Section 8(a) provides that a registration statement becomes effective 20 days after it is filed with the SEC, unless the SEC permits an earlier effective date. Filing an amendment to the registration statement starts a new 20 day period. As adopted, the Securities Act thus contemplated that the SEC would engage in a thorough review of the registration statement during the 20 day period and, if the registration statement complied with the statute's requirements, the offering would commence at the end of the 20 day period.

The statute gave the SEC two vehicles for preventing a registration statement from becoming effective. Under § 8(b), the SEC may issue a refusal order preventing the registration statement from becoming effective. A refusal order proceeding must begin within 10 days after the registration statement is filed. In addition, the statute only authorizes a refusal order where a problem is apparent on the face of the registration statement. Under § 8(d), a stop order can be imposed whenever the registration statement contains an untrue statement of a material fact or omits material facts. The stop order proceeding has several obvious advantages over the refusal order. First, the problem need not be apparent, so the SEC can catch things that only turn up after detailed examination. More important, the SEC can institute a stop order proceeding at "any time," even after the registration statement has become effective. Thus, the ten day limit applicable to refusal orders simply doesn't apply to stop order proceedings.

In practice, the SEC has never made significant use of its § 8(b) or § 8(d) powers. The large volume of registration statements filed with the SEC and its limited resources have meant that by the time the SEC gets around to prosecuting most violations, the offering is long since over. The SEC therefore usually relies on other civil and criminal sanctions to punish violators. Indeed, the SEC cannot even make a detailed examination of all of the registration statements that are filed with it. A two-tier system of review has thus evolved. A full-blown SEC review normally is undertaken only with respect to initial public offerings and with respect to filings by financially troubled companies. Other filings typically only receive cursory review.

Even full blown review doesn't work the way one might think based on reading the statute. The theory that one could move from initially filing the registration statement to selling securities within a 20 day period simply hasn't proven true. After the registration statement is filed, it goes to a SEC staff member in the Division of Corporate Finance. The staff member reviews the registration statement for accuracy and content under the disclosure standards discussed in the next section.

which is the period after the effective date. Under § 5(a), no sales of a security may take place until the post-effective period. Some limited selling activities may take place during the waiting period. Only minimal preparation may take place during the pre-filing period.

The staff member also makes sure that it complies with the various format rules under Regulation S–K. The staff member will then send that issuer a deficiency letter, spelling out certain changes, deletions or additions the SEC wants in the registration statement. These comments often are not limited to specific disclosure items, but also can refer to readability and the ease with which disclosures can be understood by investors.

At the same time, or even before, the staff member will ask the issuer to file a delaying amendment to the registration statement. Since any amendment (no matter how trivial) starts a new 20 day period, the delaying amendment keeps the registration statement from becoming effective while the issuer responds to the staff's comments. The issuer typically files the delaying amendment immediately and then later submits a revised registration statement reflecting the staff's position. This process may be repeated several times, and in particularly difficult situations may include face to face negotiations.

In virtually all cases the issuer cravenly goes along with this system. It meekly files its delaying amendments when requested. In fact, many issuers now file a permanent delaying amendment under Rule 473 at the same time as they file the original registration statement. This effectively permits the SEC to take as long as it wants in reviewing the registration statement—a process easily taking months, although the staff does make an effort to get the initial comment letter out within one month after the registration statement is first filed.

Why do issuers go along with this perversion of the statutory scheme and the extensive delays it entails? The current review process hinges on the SEC's power under § 8(a) to permit a registration statement to become effective before the 20 day waiting period ends. Consider the following: the registration statement must disclose the price at which securities are to be offered. Underwriters and issuers obviously do not want to be held to a price set 20 days earlier. Accordingly, the registration statement is filed without price information. Instead, an amendment containing price dependent information is filed on the day or at the earliest on the day before the underwriters want to start selling securities. Unfortunately, the so-called "price amendment" starts a new 20 day period. The issuer will ask the SEC to accelerate the effective date, so that the registration statement becomes effective when the price amendment is filed.

The SEC's broad discretion to accelerate the effective date gives the SEC enormous power.[8] The agency has used its acceleration power in two ways. First, the acceleration power has been used as a club to force issuers to accept a much longer review process than § 8(a) envisioned.

---

8. This power is somewhat less effective in the case of best efforts underwriting, auction offerings, and first time issuers. Even in those cases, however, full-blown SEC review provides a valuable insurance policy for issuers. Moreover, issuers and underwriters have generally feared that failure to cooperate will lead to SEC reprisals in other ways.

Second, the acceleration power also has been used by the SEC as a means of forcing issuers to comply with certain SEC policies. For example, Rules 460 and 461 condition acceleration on the issuer taking reasonable steps to distribute a preliminary prospectus during the waiting period. In passing upon an acceleration request, the SEC wants to make sure there has been adequate distribution of the preliminary prospectus so as to ensure complete and adequate disclosure.[9]

C.   Registration statement disclosures

As originally adopted, the Securities Act and the Securities Exchange Act established two separate disclosure systems. The Securities Act imposed transactional disclosure obligations, requiring disclosure in connection with particular transactions. In contrast, the Securities Exchange Act imposed a system of periodic disclosures on certain companies.[10] This created a certain amount of overlap and duplication. In the early 1980s, the SEC adopted a program of integrated disclosure, which partially combined the two systems. Under the integrated disclosure system, an issuer planning a registered offering follows a three-step procedure. It first looks to the various registration statement forms to determine which form it is eligible to use. The issuer then looks to Regulation S–K for the substantive disclosure requirements. Regulation S–K adopted uniform disclosure standards for both Acts, so that virtually all filings are now prepared under identical instructions. As a result, the style and content of disclosure documents under both Acts are now essentially identical. Finally, Regulation C provides the procedural rules which must be followed.

The registration statement forms and Regulation S–K spell out in great detail the information that must be contained in the registration statement. But their requirements do not tell the complete story. The registration statement must not only contain the information specifically required by the forms, but also must contain any additional material

---

9. SEC critics charge that the SEC also denies acceleration based upon certain policies which are almost wholly unrelated to disclosure. For example, Item 512(i) of Regulation S–K conditions acceleration on the issuer disclosing any arrangement to indemnify officers or directors against liabilities arising under the securities laws. The disclosure also must state that the SEC believes that such arrangements are void as being contrary to public policy. This is perhaps the best example of a situation in which the SEC used its acceleration power as a means of achieving a substantive policy, here the policy being a prohibition of indemnification arrangements. Whether the issuer has agreed to indemnify officers and directors against Securities Act liabilities really has nothing to do with the decision to accelerate the registration statement's ef-

fectiveness. Critics charge that the SEC is using its discretionary power not to ensure that potential investors are informed, but rather to advance its own views on fairness, which is not what the regulatory scheme envisions. These criticisms have largely been ignored by the SEC.

10. A significant question is the extent to which the judicially created "duty to update" corporate disclosures and various aggressive SEC rulemaking actions have converted the system of periodic disclosure into one of "continuous disclosure." See Dale Arthur Oesterle, The Inexorable March Toward a Continuous Disclosure Requirement for Publicly Traded Corporations: "Are We There Yet?," 20 Cardozo L. Rev. 135 (1998).

information which is necessary to give investors a clear picture of the company and the securities it is offering.[11] The SEC recently required that portions of the prospectus be written in "plain English," a requirement whose utility remains controverted.

D.   Exemptions from registration

Issuers have several good reasons to avoid registration when selling securities. First, a registered public offering is a very expensive proposition. Lawyers, accountants, and printers are required, none of whom come cheap. Underwriters and dealers take substantial commissions. Second, a registered public offering subjects the issuer to on-going disclosure obligations under the Securities Exchange Act. Third, a registered public offering easily can take months to complete. Finally, some important liability provisions attach only to registered public offerings.

On the other hand, the consequences of failing to register securities before selling them are severe. The SEC may seek civil fines and other sanctions. In egregious cases, such as where the failure to register is coupled with fraudulent practices, the SEC may refer the matter to the Justice Department for criminal prosecution. Purchasers of unlawfully unregistered securities may seek rescission of the sale under Securities Act § 12(a)(1).[12]

Many issuers therefore seek to structure the transaction so as to qualify for one of the several exemptions that permit unregistered sales.[13] In this context, the exemption's provisions drive the planning process. Exemptions from registration are also important where the issuer and its counsel (if any) fail to realize that registration is required or deliberately ignore the registration requirements. In this context, the availability of an exemption determines the outcome of the resulting litigation.

The party claiming an exemption always has the burden of proving that the exemption was available in connection with the transaction in question. In other words, exemptions are an affirmative defense to a § 5 charge. As a planning matter, it is critical that the issuer's lawyers

---

11. See, e.g., In re Universal Camera Corp., 19 S.E.C. 648 (1945).

12. Securities Act § 12(a)(1) imposes strict liability for offers or sales made in violation of Section 5. Under Section 12(a)(1), only the seller of a security can be held liable. The principal remedy is rescission: the buyer can recover the consideration paid for the security, plus interest, less income received on the security. If the buyer no longer owns the securities, he can recover damages comparable to those which would be provided by rescission.

13. We are mainly concerned here with transactional exemptions. If A sells a non-exempt security to B in an exempt transaction, B is not automatically free to resell that security. B must either register it or utilize another exempt transaction. In contrast, exempt securities are always exempt from the registration requirements. Thus, the initial sale need not be registered. Nor is the registration requirement applicable to subsequent transactions. Both types of exemptions relieve only the issuer from the registration requirements. Most civil liability provisions continue to apply, even if one of the exemptions is available.

create a full paper trail of the transaction so that every element of the exemption may be proved.

1. *Private placements*

Securities Act § 4(2) exempts "transactions by an issuer not involving any public offering." This is the so-called "private placement" exemption. Significant private placements were rare when the Securities Act was adopted. Yet § 4(2) has become the most important exemption from registration, with more securities sold under it than are sold through the registration process.

Section 4(2) has almost no legislative history. As a result, the private placement exemption's elements were worked out in a series of SEC and judicial decisions. Unfortunately, the SEC and the courts have not done a particularly good job of it, creating considerable uncertainty as to the circumstances under which the exemption is available.

In the seminal *Ralston Purina* decision, the issuer sold unregistered common stock to its "key" employees. Hundreds of workers qualified as "key" employees, including loading dock workers and secretaries. When the SEC sued the issuer for allegedly violating § 5 by selling unregistered securities, the issuer defended by claiming the offering was a private placement exempt from registration pursuant to § 4(2). The Supreme Court held that the large number of offerees and their relative lack of knowledge and sophistication precluded the transaction from qualifying for the private placement exemption. One must look at the personal characteristics of the investors to determine whether they need the protections provided by registration. Many of these investors had limited access to information about the issuer and limited investment sophistication.[14]

If nothing else, *Ralston Purina* proved that easy cases make bad law too. It would be difficult to imagine a worse set of facts for using the private placement exemption. Unfortunately, the case was so easy that the Supreme Court failed to address the parameters of the exemption in any detail. Since *Ralston Purina*, lower courts have struggled to define the exemption in more concrete terms. Although the tests used vary somewhat from court to court, most look at some or all of the following factors: (1) A small number of offerees should be involved. (2) The issuer should not use mass solicitations or general advertising. (3) Investors should be knowledgeable, sophisticated, and experienced. (4) Investors should be given access to the same kind of information as would be provided by a registration statement. (5) The issuer should take steps to prevent resales by the purchasers.[15]

---

14. SEC v. Ralston Purina Co., 346 U.S. 119 (1953).

15. See, e.g., Doran v. Petroleum Management Corp., 545 F.2d 893 (5th Cir.1977) (setting forth four factors: number of offerees and their relationship to each other and the issuer; number of units offered; size of the offering; manner of the offering); see also American Bar Association, Section 4(2) and Statutory Law—A Position Paper of the Federal Regulation of Securities Committee, 31 Bus. Law. 485 (1975) (setting out

2. Reg D

Securities Act § 3(b) authorizes the SEC to adopt rules exempting transactions where registration is not necessary in light of the relatively small amount of money involved. Regulation D is most recent but also the most important of the "limited offering" exemptions adopted under § 3(b).[16] "Reg D," as it is known, is comprised of 11 rules, Rules 501 to 508 and 701 to 703, and two forms, Form D and Form 701. Rules 501 to 503 set forth certain general provisions that apply to the entire regulation, while 504 to 506 and 701 contain the various exemptions. Rule 701 provides a safe harbor for employee benefit plans of nonreporting companies[17] and will not be discussed herein.

Rule 501 defines various terms used in the Regulation, the most important of which deals with accredited investors. The accredited investor concept is critical for a number of reasons. First, it is relevant to the permissible number of purchasers. The Rule 505 and Rule 506 exemptions are only available for offerings in which there are 35 or fewer purchasers. Accredited investors do not count against the 35 purchaser maximum, however, so that issuers may sell securities to an unlimited number of accredited investors under these rules. Second, the issuer need not provide any disclosures to accredited investors. Finally, accredited investors are presumed to meet Rule 506's sophistication requirement.

Rule 501(a) provides several different ways in which an investor may qualify as accredited. Among those who qualify are: most institutional investors (501(a)(1) and 501(a)(2)), charities with assets greater than $5 million (501(a) (3)), certain insiders of the issuer (501(a)(4)), any purchaser whose net worth is greater than $1 million (501(a)(5)), and any purchaser who made at least $200,000 in each of the last two years (or had $300,000 in combination with a spouse) and expects to make at least $200,000 in the current year (501(a)(6)).

Turning to the substantive aspects of Reg D, Rule 504 permits issuers to sell up to $1 million worth of securities in any twelve-month period. There are no limits on the number of offerees or purchasers. There is no requirement that offerees or purchasers be sophisticated. There is no disclosure requirement. (On the other hand, many 504 offerings are subject to state regulation.) Reporting companies may not use the Rule 504 exemption.

---

four attributes of an exempt offering: offeree qualification as a knowledgeable and sophisticated investor; access to information; manner of offering; and absence of resales).

16. Regulation A is the other limited offering exemption adopted by the SEC under Section 3(b). Regulation A offerings are limited to no more than $5 million worth of securities in any 12–month period. Only nonreporting companies may use Regulation A. The mechanics of complying with Regulation A are very cumbersome. A Reg-ulation A offering is more closely akin to a mini-registered offering than to an exemption from registration. Instead of a registration statement, the issuer files a so-called "Offering Statement" with the SEC. Instead of a prospectus, the issuer distributes an "Offering Circular" to investors.

17. Reporting companies is a term of art for those firms that must file Securities Exchange Act periodic reports with the SEC.

Rule 505 permits an issuer to sell up to $5,000,000 in any twelve-month period to any number of accredited investors and up to 35 nonaccredited investors. Unlike § 4(2) private placements, Rule 505 does not require that the 35 nonaccredited investors meet any knowledge or sophistication requirement.

Rule 506 permits an issuer to sell an unlimited amount of securities to any number of accredited investors and up to 35 nonaccredited investors. Unlike Rules 504 and 505, Rule 506 was not adopted under Section 3(b). Instead, it replaced old Rule 146 as a safe harbor provision under Section 4(2). As a practical matter, the major import of this distinction is that offerings under 506 do not count towards the dollar limits under Rules 504 and 505. Another consequence of the adoption of Rule 506 pursuant to § 4(2) is the imposition of a knowledge and sophistication requirement. Accredited investors are assumed to satisfy the knowledge and sophistication requirement. nonaccredited investors must have sufficient knowledge and experience to be capable of evaluating the merits and risks of the investment or be represented by someone with such knowledge and experience.

There are two important procedural restrictions on Rule 505 and 506 offerings. First, Rule 502(c) requires that such offerings not involve any general advertising or solicitation efforts. Second, Rule 502(d) limits resales by purchasers. Recently these restrictions were extended to most 504 offerings, as well, excepting those 504 offerings registered under state law.

If all purchasers are accredited, issuers making an offering pursuant to either Rule 505 or 506 are not subject to any disclosure requirement. If there are any nonaccredited purchasers, however, those investors must receive a disclosure statement. The precise amount of information that must be provided depends on the size of the offering, but it is always less than would be required in a full-fledged registration statement.

3. *Intrastate Offerings*

The Securities Act applies only to sales or purchases of securities made by the "use of any means or instruments of transportation or communication in interstate commerce or of the mails."[18] Because of the sweeping modern definition given interstate commerce, very few transactions escape capture by this jurisdictional nexus. When the Act was adopted Congress believed there should be a specific exemption for offerings that satisfy the jurisdictional nexus, but nevertheless are made by issuers with localized operations as part of a plan to raise local financing. Section 3(a)(11), the intrastate offering exemption, resulted.

Section 3(a)(11) exempts from registration "any security which is part of an issue offered and sold only to persons resident within a single State or Territory, where the issuer of such security is a person resident

---

18. Securities Act § 5(a)(1).

and doing business within or, if a corporation, incorporated by and doing business within, such State or Territory." So long as these requirements are met, the issuer may use selling devices falling within the sphere of interstate commerce, such as telephone contacts, general advertisements, airline travel, and out-of-state dealers or underwriters.

On its face, § 3(a)(11) appears to create a class of exempt securities. The legislative history, however, shows that § 3(a)(11) was meant to exempt only the intrastate offering. Accordingly, courts treat § 3(a)(11) as one of the transactional exemptions.[19] The Securities Act's antifraud provisions remain fully applicable to intrastate offerings that satisfy the jurisdictional nexus.

Once the issuer sells the securities to the investing public, there is some risk that they will be resold to out-of-state investors. Resales of securities sold under § 3(a)(11) do not automatically destroy the exemption. The relevant question is whether the offering was complete at the time of the sale; in other words, whether the securities had come to rest in the hands of resident investors. The initial in-state purchasers must hold their shares long enough to establish that the offering has come to an end before they may resell them. The SEC generally suggests that a one-year holding period suffices for this purpose, although courts have allowed holding periods as short as seven months.[20] In addition, the issuer must impose restrictions on resales (such as legends on the securities) to ensure that the entire offering comes to rest in the state.

Where the issuer is a corporation, securities may be sold in reliance on § 3(a)(11) only in the state of incorporation. In addition, the issuer must be "doing business within" the state in which the offering is made. The income producing activities into which the proceeds of the offering are invested must be located within the state in which the offering was made.[21]

The SEC takes the position that all offerees must be domiciles of the state in which the offering is made.[22] Offers therefore may not be made to people living in the state temporarily, such as college students and military personnel. In theory, a single offer to one nonresident destroys the exemption as to the entire offering.

In 1974, the SEC promulgated a safe harbor rule under § 3(a)(11): Rule 147. Rule 147 states several conditions that, if met, will qualify an offering under Section 3(a)(11). In particular, Rule 147 codifies and elaborates upon several definitions and concepts which developed in the common law exemption.

19. See Securities Act Release No. 4434 (Dec. 6, 1961).

20. See, e.g., Busch v. Carpenter, 827 F.2d 653 (10th Cir.1987).

21. See, e.g., Chapman v. Dunn, 414 F.2d 153 (6th Cir.1969); SEC v. McDonald Inv. Co., 343 F.Supp. 343 (D.Minn.1972);

SEC v. Truckee Showboat, Inc., 157 F.Supp. 824 (S.D.Cal.1957).

22. See Securities Act Release No. 4434 (Dec. 6, 1961); see also SEC v. Spence & Green Chemical Co., 612 F.2d 896 (5th Cir. 1980)

Rule 147 sets forth several objective tests to determine whether the issuer meets the "doing business" requirement: 80% of the issuer's gross revenues must come from within the state; 80% of the issuer's assets must be located in the state; the issuer must intend to use (and actually use) 80% of the proceeds in the state; and the issuer's principal office must be in the state.

Rule 147 requires that all offerees have their principal residence within the state. This formulation again excludes college students and military personnel residing temporarily within the state.

Rule 147 clarifies the resale issue by establishing a specific holding period, which ends nine months after the last sale by the issuer. During this holding period resales must be limited to residents of the state. After the nine-month period, resales can be made to anyone, irrespective of residency. In order to assure that the 9 month holding period is compiled with, Rule 147(f) requires the issuer to take certain steps designed to prevent resales out of state during the holding period. The prescribed measures include marking the securities with a notice of the nine-month holding period, registering stop-transfer orders with transfer agents, and securing written representations from each purchaser as to his residence. Under both the statutory exemption and Rule 147, advertisements should note that only residents of the state are being offered the securities, and the issuer should be sure that underwriters and dealers understand the restricted nature of the offering.

The intrastate offering exemption's utility is obviously limited somewhat by the rather restrictive conditions which must be satisfied in order for it to be available. If those conditions can be satisfied, however, the exemption offers several significant advantages over those described above. Neither § 3(a)(11) nor Rule 147 limits the number of permissible offerees or purchasers. Nor is there any limit on the amount of funds that can be raised under the exemption. In addition, funds raised under § 3(a)(11) or Rule 147 are not counted against the dollar limits on the Regulation D offerings.

E. Civil liabilities for securities fraud and other violations

Before the Securities Act's adoption, securities fraud was solely the province of state common law—under which it was treated just like any other kind of fraud. Plaintiff had to prove that the defendant had misrepresented a material fact. Plaintiff also had to prove all of the other elements of common law fraud: reliance, causation, scienter, and injury. Finally, plaintiff's recovery was limited to the amount of loss: the difference between what he paid and what the securities were truly worth. In light of these limitations, the common law was almost incapable of dealing with securities fraud. Many securities cases, for example, involve omissions—i.e., failures to speak. How does a plaintiff show reliance on silence? As a result, prior to the Securities Act, securities fraud cases were rare and even more rarely successful. To achieve its goal of attacking fraud in securities transactions Congress therefore adopted civil and criminal liability provisions far more liberal than those available at common law.

A person who violates the securities laws faces three possible antagonists. First, the SEC. Securities Act § 20(a) gives the SEC broad power to investigate violations of the Act or the SEC rules adopted under the Act. Section 20(b) gives the SEC the power to bring a civil action in US District Court seeking an injunction against on-going or future violations. A number of other sanctions are potentially available under other statutes. For example, the SEC can suspend or bar a professional underwriter, broker or dealer from working in the securities industry. The SEC may also impose a variety of administrative penalties on violators.

Second, the Justice Department. Section 20(b) authorizes the SEC to refer securities violations to the Attorney General who may then institute criminal proceedings against the violator. We shall largely ignore criminal liabilities herein.

Finally, the plaintiff's bar. Many plaintiffs' lawyers handle securities cases on an occasional basis. In addition, however, there is a small, but active and very capable, group of plaintiffs' lawyers who specialize in securities litigation under the civil liability provisions discussed below. Our focus herein will be on the civil liability provisions available in private party securities fraud litigation.

The Securities Act contains two express private causes of action for securities law violations.[23] Section 11 imposes civil liability for fraudulent registration statements. Not only is § 11 restricted to securities sold through the use of a registration statement, but the misrepresentation or omission must be in the registration statement. In contrast, § 12(a)(2) is the general civil liability under the Securities Act for fraud and misrepresentation. Although it overlaps somewhat with § 11, § 12(a)(2) is a broader remedy. Liability under § 12(a)(2) arises not only in connection with material misrepresentations or omissions in a registration statement, but also in connection with misrepresentations or omissions made in other writings or oral statements used in connection with any public offering.

---

23. Where Congress was silent as to whether there is a private right of action under a particular statutory provision, courts have sometimes implied a private right of action. Whether such an implied cause of action exists under Securities Act § 17(a) is currently the subject of much disagreement. Section 17(a) prohibits fraud in the interstate offer or sale of securities. Section 17(a) clearly gives the SEC authority to bring civil actions against those who commit securities fraud. Some courts have said that there also is an implied private right of action under § 17(a), but many courts disagree. The current trend is strongly towards rejecting an implied private right of action under Section 17. See, e.g., Sears v. Likens, 912 F.2d 889 (7th Cir.1990); Krause v. Perryman, 827 F.2d 346 (8th Cir.1987); In re Washington Public Power Supply System Securities Litigation, 823 F.2d 1349 (9th Cir.1987).

An implied private right of action unquestionably exists under Securities Exchange Act Rule 10b–5. Much of the conduct giving rise to liability under Securities Act §§ 11, 12(a)(2), and 17(a) is also actionable under Rule 10b–5.

1. Securities Act § 11

Section 11 provides an private right for purchasers of securities sold by means of a registration statement containing a material misrepresentation or omission. A misrepresentation or omission is deemed material if there is a substantial likelihood that a reasonable investor would consider it important in deciding whether to invest.[24] Because the misrepresentation or omission must be contained in the registration statement,[25] § 11 does not reach fraudulent oral communications or other written communications.

As originally adopted, § 11 did not require plaintiff to show reliance. In 1934, an amendment to § 11(a) introduced a very limited reliance requirement. In the first year after the registration statement has become effective, plaintiff need not prove he relied on the misstatement or omission. A very minimal reliance requirement kicks in thereafter. In order for reliance to be required, several conditions must be satisfied. First, at least 12 months must have passed since the effective date. Second, the issuer must have sent out an earnings statement covering a period of at least 12 months after the effective date. The annual report to shareholders will suffice, as long as it covers a period of at least 12 months following the effective date. Third, plaintiff must have acquired the securities after the one year period has passed.

Just as with reliance, proof of causation was not required by the original version of § 11 but was mandated by the 1934 amendment. At common law, there were two forms of causation: transaction causation, pursuant to which plaintiff must show that but for the misrepresentation he would not have invested; and loss causation, pursuant to which plaintiff must show that the misrepresentation caused his loss. Section 11(e) looks solely to loss causation: did the misrepresentation cause the loss? In addition, plaintiff does not bear the burden of proving causation. Instead, defendant has the burden of proving noncausation with respect to damages. Under § 11(e), a defendant can reduce the amount of damages if he is able to prove that the reduction in value of plaintiff's shares was caused by some factor other than the misrepresentation or omission. Causation thus is not a complete defense, but rather one of mitigation.

There is an extensive but exhaustive list of possible defendants under § 11(a): (1) Anyone who signed who signed the registration statement can be held liable. Section 6(a) requires the registration statement to be signed by the issuer, the issuer's principal executive officers, the issuer's chief financial officer, the issuer's principal accounting officer, and a majority of the issuer's directors. (2) Plaintiff may also sue every director of the issuer at the time the registration statement

---

24. Akerman v. Oryx Communications, Inc., 609 F.Supp. 363 (S.D.N.Y.1984), aff'd, 810 F.2d 336 (2d Cir.1987).

25. Plaintiff must be able to trace his shares to the registered offering affected by the fraudulent registration statement. See Barnes v. Osofsky, 373 F.2d 269 (2d Cir. 1967); see generally Hillary A. Sale, Disappearing Without a Trace: Sections 11 and 12(a)(2) of the 1933 Securities Act, 75 Wash. L. Rev. 429 (2000)

became effective, every person named in the registration statement as someone about to become a director is a defendant, every expert named as having prepared or certified any part of the registration statement, and every underwriter involved in the distribution. Most courts hold that this list is exclusive and, consequently, that there is no aiding and abetting liability under § 11.[26]

State of mind is not an element of plaintiff's case under § 11, but some defendants have a state of mind defense. The issuer is strictly liable under § 11. Pursuant to § 11(b)(3), however, other defendants may escape § 11 liability if they prove they used due diligence in preparing and reviewing the registration statement. The defendant's burden depends on whether the fraudulent portion of the registration statement was prepared by an expert (such as financial statements prepared by an accountant).[27]

Under § 11(b)(3)(A), a nonexpert has a three part burden of proof with respect to nonexpertised parts of the registration statement: First, he actually believed that the registration statement was accurate and complete. Second, his belief was reasonable. Third, he conducted a reasonable investigation into the facts on which the registration statement was based.

Under § 11(b)(3)(C), a nonexpert has a two part burden of proof with respect to expertised parts of the registration statement: First, he did not believe the registration statement was inaccurate or incomplete. Second, he had no reasonable grounds to so believe. Notice that there is no requirement of a reasonable investigation. nonexperts are thus entitled to rely on statements made by experts; no investigation need be made by the nonexpert. On the other hand, a duty to inquire may arise if there are obvious problems with the expertised portion of the registration statement.[28]

Under § 11(b)(3)(B), an expert only has liability for misrepresentations or omissions contained in the portion of the registration statement he expertised. As to that portion, he has a three part burden of proof to make out his due diligence defense: First, he actually believed that the statements made in the expertised portion were accurate and complete. Second, he had reasonable grounds for that belief. Finally, he made a reasonable investigation into the factual basis for the statements.

As a practical matter, due diligence is delegated to lawyers. The issuer's directors and officers rely on the corporation's counsel to conduct a due diligence investigation. The underwriter relies on its counsel to conduct such an investigation. Only experts normally conduct their own due diligence. If the lawyer's conduct satisfies the standards set

---

26. Marc I. Steinberg, Understanding Securities Law 147 (2d ed. 1996).

27. An expertised portion of the registration statement is one prepared by an expert. All other portions of the registration statement are "non-expertised."

28. See, e.g., Escott v. BarChris Construction Corp., 283 F.Supp. 643 (S.D.N.Y. 1968).

forth above, the parties who relied on the lawyer get the benefit of the due diligence defense. If not, all parties who relied on the lawyer lose their defense, but may have a malpractice action against the lawyer. This makes conducting a due diligence investigation one of the most nerve-wracking assignments a young corporate lawyer faces.

In addition to the causation and due diligence defenses already mentioned, at least three other defenses may be available. (1) Per § 11(a), plaintiffs who knew of the alleged misrepresentations or omissions when they bought the securities may not recover. (2) Securities Act § 13 time bars any Section 11 action that is not brought within one year after discovery of the untrue statement or omission, or after discovery should have been made by reasonable diligence, or that is not brought within 3 years after the securities were first sold to the public. (3) *In pari delicto* apparently is a defense to all securities law claims,[29] including those arising under § 11. The Supreme Court has set forth a two pronged test for deciding whether or not the *in pari delicto* defense is available:[30] First, the defendant must show that the plaintiff was at least equally responsible for the actions that render the transaction illegal. Second, allowing the defense must not frustrate relevant statutory policies. The relevant policy in most securities cases will be the goal of full and fair disclosure to investors. According to the Supreme Court, one must look at the plaintiff's role in the transaction. If plaintiff was acting mainly as an investor, the equal fault defense is unavailable, even if the plaintiff was an active participant in the illegal transaction. If plaintiff was acting as a promoter, however, the defense is available.

2. Securities Act § 12(a)(2)

Section 12(a)(2) imposes private civil liability on any person who offers or sells a security in interstate commerce, who makes material misrepresentation or omission in connection with the offer or sale, and cannot prove he did not know of the misrepresentation or omission and could not have known even with the exercise of reasonable care. Plaintiff's prima facie case has six elements: (1) the sale of a security; (2) through instruments of interstate commerce or the mails; (3) by means of a prospectus or oral communication; (4) containing an untrue statement or omission of a material fact; (5) by a defendant who offered or sold the security; and (6) which defendant knew or should have known of the untrue statement (if plaintiff pleads defendant's knowledge, the burden of proving otherwise shifts to the defendant). Notice that plaintiff need not prove reliance. Unlike § 11, in fact, reliance is not even a defense under § 12(a)(2).[31]

A key issue in § 12(a)(2) litigation is the question of who is a seller. This is significant because the class of permissible defendants under

29. See, e.g., Bateman Eichler, Hill Richards, Inc. v. Berner, 472 U.S. 299 (1985).

30. Pinter v. Dahl, 486 U.S. 622 (1988).

31. Cf. Sanders v. John Nuveen & Co., Inc., 619 F.2d 1222, 1226 (7th Cir.1980), cert. denied, 450 U.S. 1005 (1981) (plaintiff need not prove that he ever received the misleading prospectus").

§ 12(a) is narrower than under any of the other major anti-fraud provisions: only sellers can be held liable. In *Pinter v. Dahl*, the Supreme Court held that persons in contractual privity with the plaintiff are sellers for purposes of Section 12(a). In addition, the Court held that someone not in contractual privity with the plaintiff may still be deemed a seller if he "successfully solicits the purchase, motivated at least in part by a desire to serve his own financial interests or those of the securities owner."[32] Brokers or other agents who assist the issuer in soliciting sales thus face liability. On the other hand, the privity requirement sharply limits the scope of secondary liability, so that participants in the offering who do not engage in soliciting or selling activities—such as accountants and lawyers—generally cannot be held liable.[33]

Until the Supreme Court's decision in *Gustafson v. Alloyd Co.*,[34] most lawyers assumed that § 12(a)(2)'s scope was considerably broader than that of § 11. It was assumed to apply not only to fraudulent registration statements, but also to fraudulent selling materials and oral communications. It was assumed to apply to exempt offerings, whereas § 11 is limited to registered offerings. Finally, most lawyers assumed that § 12(a)(2) reached secondary market transactions. In *Gustafson*, however, the Supreme Court held that liability arises under § 12(a)(2) only with respect to material misrepresentations or omissions made in written documents or oral communications used in connection with public offerings. Although the concept of public offering seems to include some unregistered offerings, the Court's opinion makes clear that liability under Section 12(a)(2) at a minimum does not arise in secondary market transactions or private placements.[35]

Five defenses are available in § 12(a)(2) cases. (1) Section 13 again provides a statute of limitations, such that no Section 12(a)(2) action may be maintained if it is not brought within one year after the discovery of the untrue statement or omission, or within one year after discovery should have been made by reasonable diligence, or within three years after the issuer offered the securities to the public. (2) Plaintiff's knowledge is a defense, but a plaintiff has no obligation to conduct due diligence or use reasonable care in purchasing the securities. (3) *In pari*

---

32. Pinter v. Dahl, 486 U.S. 622 (1988). Although Pinter was decided under § 12(a)(1), courts have uniformly held its definition of seller applicable to § 12(a)(2). See, e.g., Ackerman v. Schwartz, 947 F.2d 841, 844–45 (7th Cir.1991); Moore v. Kayport Package Express, Inc., 885 F.2d 531 (9th Cir.1989); Wilson v. Saintine Exploration and Drilling Corp., 872 F.2d 1124 (2d Cir.1989).

33. See, e.g., Ackerman v. Schwartz, 947 F.2d 841, 844–45 (7th Cir.1991) (attorney); Wilson v. Saintine Exploration and Drilling Corp., 872 F.2d 1124 (2d Cir.1989) (attorney).

34. 513 U.S. 561 (1995). See generally Stephen M. Bainbridge, Securities Act Section 12(2) After the *Gustafson* Debacle, 50 Bus. Law. 1231 (1995); Edmund W. Kitch, *Gustafson v. Alloyd Co.*: An Opinion that did not Write, 1995 Sup. Ct. Rev. 99; Therese Maynard, A Requiem: Reflections on *Gustafson*, 57 Ohio St. L.J. 1327 (1996); Elliot J. Weiss, Securities Act Section 12(2) After *Gustafson v. Alloyd Co.*: What Questions Remain?, 50 Bus. Law. 1209 (1995).

35. See Vannest v. Sage, Rutty & Co., 960 F.Supp. 651 (W.D.N.Y.1997); see generally Stephen M. Bainbridge, Securities Act Section 12(2) After the *Gustafson* Debacle, 50 Bus. Law. 1231, 1260–70 (1995) (criticizing that outcome).

delicto, as described above. (4) A defendant is not liable if he proves that he did not know, and in exercise of reasonable care could not have known, of the misrepresentation or omission.[36] In other words, defendant's state of mind is not an element of plaintiff's case, but defendant's nonnegligence is an affirmative defense. (5) Section 12(b) provides that loss causation is a defense of mitigation—to the extent that the defendant can prove that some or all of the damages suffered by plaintiff were caused by factors other than the fraud, such as a general market decline, such portion is not recoverable. Loss causation is further discussed in the next section.

3. Securities Exchange Act § 10(b) and Rule 10b–5

We now turn to Rule 10b–5—easily the most famous, and arguably the most important, of all the SEC's many rules:

It shall be unlawful for any person, directly or indirectly, by the use of any means or instrumentality of interstate commerce, or of the mails or of any facility of any national securities exchange,

(a) To employ any device, scheme, or artifice to defraud,

(b) To make any untrue statement of a material fact or to omit to state a material fact necessary in order to make the statements made, in the light of the circumstances under which they were made, not misleading, or

(c) To engage in any act, practice, or course of business which operates or would operate as a fraud or deceit upon any person,

in connection with the purchase or sale of any security.

The central theme of the Rule's history is one of repeated judicial glosses on this relatively innocuous text. As Justice Rehnquist has observed, Rule 10b–5 is now "a judicial oak which has grown from little more than a legislative acorn."[37] In effect, we are dealing here with a species of federal common law only loosely tied to the statutory text.

On its face, the rule does not tell us very much other than that fraud in connection with securities transactions is a bad thing. What elements does one have to prove in order to show a violation of the rule? Who has standing to sue violators? What remedies can they seek? Few of these questions are answered by the plain text of the rule (or the statute, for that matter).[38] Instead, these issues have been worked out in a long

---

36. On the scope of the reasonable care defense, see Ambrosino v. Rodman & Renshaw, Inc., 972 F.2d 776 (7th Cir.1992) (holding that the degree of care required varies with the facts of the case, such as the nature of the instrument being sold); Sanders v. John Nuveen & Co., 524 F.2d 1064 (7th Cir.1975), vacated, 425 U.S. 929 (1976) (holding under the factual circumstances that reasonable care required an investigation under standards arguably converging with the due diligence obligation under

§ 11); Franklin Savings Bank of N.Y. v. Levy, 551 F.2d 521 (2d Cir.1977) (defendant must have conducted an investigation providing an adequate basis in fact for the statements and opinions made).

37. Blue Chip Stamps v. Manor Drug Stores, 421 U.S. 723, 737 (1975).

38. Both the statute and the rule plainly require a jurisdictional nexus: there must be a use of a means or instrumentality of interstate commerce, the mails, or any facil-

series of decisions, including a number of important Supreme Court decisions.

Standing. Both the United States Justice Department (typically acting through local U.S. Attorney's offices) and the SEC clearly have standing to sue those who violate Rule 10b–5. The more interesting question is whether private parties have standing to sue under the rule. Nothing in either the rule or the statute explicitly authorizes such a private party cause of action. Lower federal courts recognized an implied right of action under Rule 10b–5 as early as 1946,[39] however, and the Supreme Court followed suit in 1971.[40] Today, of course, judicial implication of private rights of action is highly controversial and the current Supreme Court seems less inclined to create or preserve such rights of action than any of its recent predecessors.[41] The private right of action under Rule 10b–5 nevertheless remains quite firmly established. As former Justice Thurgood Marshall once observed, the "existence of this implied remedy is simply beyond peradventure."[42]

Although the Supreme Court has confirmed the implied right of action under Rule 10b–5, it has limited private party standing to persons who actually buy or sell a security.[43] This may seem trivial or obvious, but in fact it is not. Suppose the executives of a company wanted to drive down the price of the firm's stock so that they could buy it for themselves. They put out false bad news about the company. You were considering buying stock in the company but were dissuaded by the bad news put out by the executives. If you later try to sue, arguing that but for the executives' misconduct you would have bought some of the company's stock, the Supreme Court's standing rules will bar you from bringing suit.

Although one must have either purchased or sold a security in order to have standing to sue under Rule 10b–5, one need not have purchased or sold in order to be a proper party defendant. In the seminal insider trading case, *SEC v. Texas Gulf Sulphur Co.*,[44] the defendant corporation issued a misleading press release. Because the corporation had neither

---

ity of a national securities exchange in order for the statute to be applicable. In most cases, this requirement is easily satisfied: basically, if the defendant made a phone call or sent a letter in connection with the fraud, § 10(b) can apply. Section 10(b) will also apply if the defendant takes either of those steps indirectly; for example, if the defendant orders his broker to sell shares, and the broker uses the phone or the mails, the statute is triggered.

39. Kardon v. National Gypsum Co., 69 F.Supp. 512 (E.D.Pa.1946).

40. Superintendent of Insurance v. Bankers Life & Cas. Co., 404 U.S. 6, 13 n. 9 (1971).

41. See generally Marc I. Steinberg, The Ramifications of Recent U.S. Supreme Court Decisions on Federal and State Secu-

rities Regulation, 70 Notre Dame L. Rev. 489 (1995).

42. Herman & MacLean v. Huddleston, 459 U.S. 375, 380 (1983). For an intriguing and provocative argument that the SEC could (and should) destroy the implied private right of action under Rule 10b–5, see Joseph Grundfest, Disimplying Private Rights of Action Under the Federal Securities Laws: The Commission's Authority, 107 Harv. L. Rev. 963 (1994).

43. Blue Chip Stamps v. Manor Drug Stores, 421 U.S. 723 (1975).

44. 401 F.2d 833 (2d Cir.1968), cert. denied, 394 U.S. 976 (1969).

bought nor sold any securities during the relevant time period, it argued that it could not be held liable under Rule 10b–5. The court rejected this argument, observing that Rule 10b–5 on its face prohibits fraud "in connection with the purchase or sale of any security." The court interpreted this language as requiring "only that the device employed, whatever it might be, be of a sort that would cause reasonable investors to rely thereon, and, in connection therewith, so relying, cause them to purchase or sell a corporation's securities."

Application to Omission Cases. Rule 10b–5 applies to both affirmative misrepresentations and passive omissions. Two aspects of Rule 10b–5, as applied to omission cases, are especially important. First, not all omissions give rise to liability. Instead, liability can be imposed only if the defendant had a duty to speak. Second, reliance and transaction causation are presumed in omission cases. In private party litigation under Rule 10b–5, plaintiffs generally must prove that they reasonably relied upon the defendant's fraudulent words or conduct.[45] Plaintiffs also must prove both transaction causation and loss causation.[46] The former is analogous to but for causation in tort law—it is a showing that defendant's words or conduct caused plaintiff to engage in the transaction in question.[47] Loss causation is somewhat analogous to the tort law concept of proximate causation—it involves showing that the defendant's words or conduct caused plaintiff's economic loss.[48] In omission cases, both transaction causation and reliance generally are presumed so long as plaintiffs can show defendant had a duty to disclose and failed to do so.[49]

Materiality. Under Rule 10b–5, only material misrepresentations or omissions are actionable. Materiality is determined by asking whether there is a substantial likelihood that a reasonable investor would consid-

---

45. In some misrepresentation cases, reliance and transaction causation may be presumed under the so-called "fraud on the market" theory. A rebuttable presumption arises under this theory if plaintiff can prove defendant made material public misrepresentations, the security was traded on an efficient market, and plaintiff traded in the security between the time the misrepresentations were made and the truth was revealed. Basic Inc. v. Levinson, 485 U.S. 224 (1988).

46. See, e.g., Grace v. Rosenstock, 228 F.3d 40 (2d Cir.2000); Robin v. Arthur Young & Co., 915 F.2d 1120 (7th Cir.1990), cert. denied, 499 U.S. 923 (1991); Wilson v. Ruffa & Hanover, P.C., 844 F.2d 81 (2d Cir.1988), vacated, 872 F.2d 1124 (2d Cir. 1989); Currie v. Cayman Resources Corp., 835 F.2d 780 (11th Cir.1988).

47. LHLC Corp. v. Cluett, Peabody & Co., Inc., 842 F.2d 928, 931 (7th Cir.), cert. denied, 488 U.S. 926 (1988) ("'transaction causation' means that the investor would not have engaged in the transaction had the other party made truthful statements at the time required").

48. LHLC Corp. v. Cluett, Peabody & Co., Inc., 842 F.2d 928, 931 (7th Cir.), cert. denied, 488 U.S. 926 (1988) ("'Loss causation' means that the investor would not have suffered a loss if the facts were what he believed them to be"). See also Bastian v. Petren Resources Corp., 892 F.2d 680, 685 (7th Cir.1990) (loss causation reflects "the standard rule of tort law that the plaintiff must allege and prove that, for the defendant's wrongdoing, the plaintiff would not have incurred the harm of which he complains"). On the relationship between loss causation and the various presumptions of reliance and transaction causation, see Litton Industries, Inc. v. Lehman Bros. Kuhn Loeb Inc., 967 F.2d 742 (2d Cir.1992) (loss causation a required element of Rule 10b–5 claim and may not be presumed).

49. Affiliated Ute Citizens v. United States, 406 U.S. 128 (1972).

er the information important in deciding how to act.[50] When one is dealing with speculative or contingent facts, of course, this test can be hard to apply. In *Basic Inc. v. Levinson*,[51] the Supreme Court adopted what it called "a highly fact-dependent probability/magnitude balancing approach" to materiality in the context of contingent facts. Although Basic in fact was secretly negotiating a possible merger with another company, it issued three public denials that any such negotiations were underway. When the merger was finally announced, a class action was brought on behalf of those investors who had sold Basic stock during the period between the false denials and the merger announcement. The plaintiff class allegedly received a lower price for their shares than would have been the case if Basic had told the truth.

The core issue was whether the denials were material. When the denials were made, it had not been certain that the merger would go through. The probability/magnitude balancing test was thus appropriate. As to the probability part of the equation, the court looked to "indicia of interest in the transaction at the highest corporate levels." Evidence such as "board resolutions, instructions to investment bankers, and actual negotiations between principals or their intermediaries may serve as indicia of interest." As to magnitude, the court deemed it quite high, opining that a merger is "the most important event that can occur in a small corporation's life, to wit, its death...." Notice, however, that magnitude appears to have both a relative and an absolute component. A merger of a small company into a large company, for example, is a big deal for the target, but may be insignificant from the acquirer's perspective.

Although the probability/magnitude language sounds technically sophisticated and precise, it is in fact inherently subjective and indeterminate. You may recall the famous Hand Formula from torts—multiply the probability of injury times the magnitude of the likely resulting injury; if the product exceeds the cost of precautions preventing the injury, liability for allegedly negligent conduct may be imposed.[52] At first glance, the *Basic* test sounds like the Hand formula, but on closer examination there is no magic product to serve as a threshold above which information becomes material. The court never tells us how high a probability nor how large a magnitude is necessary for information to be deemed material. One thus acts on the basis of speculative information knowing that a jury, acting with the benefit of hindsight, may reach a different conclusion about how probability and magnitude should be balanced than you did.

Scienter. One can easily mislead investors without intending to do so. Even an honest mistake might cause some to be misled. As such, it is not apparent that liability for securities fraud should be premised on intent. Tort law encourages drivers to drive more safely, because they

50. TSC Industries, Inc. v. Northway, Inc., 426 U.S. 438 (1976).

51. 485 U.S. 224 (1988).

52. See United States v. Carroll Towing Co., 159 F.2d 169 (2d Cir.1947).

can be held liable for negligent accidents. Tort law also encourages manufacturers to put out safer products by imposing strict liability for defective products. Should securities law be any less rigorous in encouraging accurate disclosure?

Liability in fact can be imposed for unintentional misrepresentations under some securities law provisions. Sections 11 and 12(a)(2) of the 1933 Securities Act, for example, require no evidence from plaintiff with respect to the defendant's state of mind. Instead, state of mind is at most an affirmative defense under these provisions. In order to make out the state of mind defense, moreover, defendants must show that they were nonnegligent.

Under Rule 10b–5, however, the Supreme Court has held that plaintiff's prima facie case must include proof defendant acted with scienter, which the court defined as a mental state embracing an intent to deceive, manipulate, or defraud.[53] Although this formulation clearly precludes Rule 10b–5 liability for those who are merely negligent, the Supreme Court left open the issue of whether recklessness alone met the scienter requirement. Subsequent lower court decisions have generally held that recklessness suffices.[54]

The Limits of Rule 10b–5: The Need for Deception. In *Santa Fe Industries, Inc. v. Green,*[55] Santa Fe effected a short-form merger with a subsidiary corporation. Minority shareholders of the subsidiary were dissatisfied with the consideration they were paid for their stock. Although plaintiffs had state law remedies, such as the statutory appraisal proceeding, they opted to sue under Rule 10b–5. Plaintiffs claimed that the merger violated 10b–5 because it was effected without prior notice to the minority shareholders and was done without any legitimate business purpose. They also claimed that their shares had been undervalued. Both claims raised, quite directly, the question of what conduct is covered by the rule. The Supreme Court held that plaintiffs had not stated a cause of action under Rule 10b–5.

Drawing on the plain text and legislative history of the rule, the court concluded that a 10b–5 cause of action arises only out of deception or manipulation. Deception requires a misrepresentation or omission. Because the *Santa Fe* plaintiffs received full disclosure, there was no misrepresentation or omission. In addition, neither of plaintiffs' claims went to disclosure violations; rather, both went to the substance of the transaction. Plaintiffs were not claiming that Santa Fe lied to them, but that the transaction was unfair. In other words, they were claiming that a breach of fiduciary duty gives rise to a cause of action under 10b–5.

53. Aaron v. SEC, 446 U.S. 680 (1980); Ernst & Ernst v. Hochfelder, 425 U.S. 185 (1976).

54. According to one recent count, 11 of the 12 circuits have adopted a recklessness standard. See Richard W. Jennings et al., Securities Regulation: Cases and Materials 1142–43 (8th ed. 1998) (citing cases).

55. 430 U.S. 462 (1977).

The Supreme Court held that a mere breach of duty will not give rise to liability under 10b–5.[56]

Manipulation is conduct intended to mislead investors by artificially affecting market activity. In other words, defendant must engage in conduct that creates artificial changes in the price of a security or artificially changes the volume of trading in a security. Again, Santa Fe was mainly being charged with a breach of the state law fiduciary duties a majority shareholder owes to minority shareholders. Nothing Santa Fe did constituted unlawful manipulation.

In addition to its textual arguments, the Supreme Court also relied on policy considerations grounded in federalism. The court clearly was concerned that allowing plaintiffs to go forward in this case would federalize much of state corporate law, in many cases overriding well-established state policies of corporate regulation. In the court's view, if the Santa Fe plaintiffs were allowed to sue, every breach of fiduciary duty case would give rise to a federal claim under Rule 10b–5. The court refused to give the Rule 10b–5 such an expansive reach, instead holding that it did not reach "transactions which constitute no more than internal corporate mismanagement."[57]

Santa Fe was a critical holding in Rule 10b–5's evolution, putting the substantive fairness of a transaction outside the rule's scope. The rule henceforth was limited to disclosure violations. *Santa Fe* also implied a second—and potentially even more significant—constraint on the rule by suggesting that misconduct covered by state corporate law should be left to state law.

The lower courts have frequently treated *Santa Fe* as something to be evaded, rather than followed. Some courts have permitted 10b–5 causes of action to lie where the nondisclosure led plaintiffs to forego pursuing an available state law remedy.[58] This approach has been subjected to substantial criticism.[59] It allows litigants to end-run *Santa Fe* by pointing to a nondisclosure or misrepresentation even though the bulk of their case goes to breach of fiduciary duty. While it might be argued that liability is being imposed because of the nondisclosure of the breach, rather than the breach itself, it has been held that failure to disclose a

---

56. See generally Stephen M. Bainbridge, Incorporating State Law Fiduciary Duties into the Federal Insider Trading Prohibition, 52 Wash. & Lee L. Rev. 1189, 1257–61 (1995) (discussing *Santa Fe* in the context of the federal insider trading regime, which requires a fiduciary relationship).

57. Santa Fe Industries, Inc. v. Green, 430 U.S. 462, 479 (1977). For discussion of federalism issues in the securities regulation context, see Stephen M. Bainbridge, Redirecting State Takeover Laws at Proxy Contests, 1992 Wis. L. Rev. 1071, 1120–44 (discussing line of Supreme Court cases refusing to preempt state corporate law gen-

erally and state takeover legislation specifically); Stephen M. Bainbridge, The Short Life and Resurrection of SEC Rule 19c–4, 69 Wash. U.L.Q. 565 (1991) (discussing legislative history of the Securities Exchange Act of 1934, which demonstrates that Congress did not intend to give the SEC regulatory power over corporate governance).

58. See, e.g., Healey v. Catalyst Recovery of Pa., Inc., 616 F.2d 641 (3d Cir.1980); Goldberg v. Meridor, 567 F.2d 209 (2d Cir. 1977), cert. denied, 434 U.S. 1069 (1978).

59. See, e.g., Healey v. Catalyst Recovery of Pa., Inc., 616 F.2d 641, 651–61 (3d Cir.1980) (Aldisert, J., dissenting).

breach of duty is not actionable under Rule 10b–5.[60] In any case, the lower court approach imposes liability for failing to disclose information relevant not to making investment decisions, the concern of the securities laws, but to making state law litigation decisions, a matter wholly outside the scope of the securities laws. Finally, and most troublingly, the lower court's chosen escape device ignores the thrust of *Santa Fe* by giving no deference to the strong policy reasons laid out by the Supreme Court for refraining from intruding federal law into a sphere traditionally left for state law.

In *Central Bank of Denver v. First Interstate Bank of Denver*,[61] which is discussed in the next section, the Supreme Court reaffirmed what it called the holding of *Santa Fe*—namely, that § 10(b) does not reach mere breaches of fiduciary duty. In a more recent insider trading decision under Rule 10b–5, however, the court dismissed *Santa Fe* as a mere disclosure case, asserting: "in *Santa Fe Industries*, all pertinent facts were disclosed by the persons charged with violating § 10(b) and Rule 10b–5; therefore, there was no deception through nondisclosure to which liability under those provisions could attach."[62] The court thus wholly ignored the important federalism concerns upon which *Santa Fe* rested and which are implicated by the federal insider trading prohibition.

Secondary Liability and the Plain Meaning Issue. In *Central Bank of Denver v. First Interstate Bank of Denver*,[63] the Supreme Court held that there was no implied private right of action against those who aid and abet violations of Rule 10b–5. *Central Bank* thus substantially limited the scope of secondary liability under the rule, at least insofar as private party causes of action are concerned. For our purposes, however, the case is more significant for its methodology than its holding.

Until quite recently, Rule 10b–5 was regarded as an example of interstitial lawmaking in which the courts used common-law adjudicatory methods to flesh out the text's bare bones. In *Central Bank*, however, the Court held the scope of conduct prohibited by § 10(b) (and thus the rule) is controlled by the text of the statute. Where the plain text does not resolve some aspect of the Rule 10b–5 cause of action, courts must "infer 'how the 1934 Congress would have addressed the issue had the 10b–5 action been included as an express provision in the 1934 Act.'" The court has elsewhere acknowledged this to be an "awkward task,"[64] but Justice Scalia has put it more colorfully: "We are imagining here."[65]

60. See, e.g., Biesenbach v. Guenther, 588 F.2d 400 (3d Cir.1978); In re Sears, Roebuck and Co. Sec. Litig., 792 F.Supp. 977 (E.D.Pa.1992); Merritt v. Colonial Foods, Inc., 499 F.Supp. 910, 913–14 (D.Del.1980).

61. 511 U.S. 164 (1994).

62. United States v. O'Hagan, 521 U.S. 642, 655 (1997). For a critical commentary on the impact of *O'Hagan* on *Santa Fe*, see Stephen M. Bainbridge, Insider Trading Regulation: The Path Dependent Choice be-

tween Property Rights and Securities Fraud, 52 SMU L. Rev. 1589, 1640–44 (1999).

63. 511 U.S. 164 (1994).

64. Lampf, Pleva, Lipkind, Prupis & Petigrow v. Gilbertson, 501 U.S. 350, 359 (1991).

65. Lampf, Pleva, Lipkind, Prupis & Petigrow v. Gilbertson, 501 U.S. 350, 366 (1991) (Scalia, J., dissenting).

Central Bank constrained this imaginative process by requiring courts to "use the express causes of action in the securities acts as the primary model for the § 10(b) action."[66]

To the extent *Central Bank* repudiates the notion that Rule 10b–5 has become a species of federal common law, the decision poses a significant threat to the further evolution of the Rule's jurisprudence. In at least some subsequent Supreme Court decisions, however, the interpretive methodology expounded in *Central Bank* has been essentially ignored.[67] One is therefore left to wonder whether the strict textualist approach taken by *Central Bank* was a one time aberration.[68]

F. Becoming a reporting company: Registration under the Securities Exchange Act

If a corporation is required to register under the Securities Exchange Act,[69] it becomes subject to the Act's periodic disclosure rules. In addition, the corporation also becomes subject to the proxy rules under § 14, the tender offer rules under §§ 13 and 14, and certain of the Act's anti-fraud provisions.

There are three basic categories of companies subject to the Securities Exchange Act's requirements. The first two are identified by §§ 12 and 13(a) of the Act. Section 13(a) requires periodic reports from any company registered with the SEC under Section 12 of the Act. In turn, § 12(a) requires that any class of securities listed and traded on a national securities exchange (such as the New York or American Stock Exchanges) must be registered under the Securities Exchange Act. In addition, § 12(g) and the rules there under require all other companies with assets exceeding $10 million and a class of equity securities held by 500 or more record shareholders to register that class of equity securities with the SEC. The third and final group of companies subject to the Securities Exchange Act is identified by § 15(d), which picks up any issuer that made a public offering of securities under the Securities Act. Issuers with less than 300 record shareholders, however, are not subject to this requirement except during the fiscal year in which they made the offering.

---

66. Central Bank of Denver v. First Interstate Bank of Denver, 511 U.S. 164, 178 (1994).

67. See Stephen M. Bainbridge, Insider Trading Regulation: The Path Dependent Choice between Property Rights and Securities Fraud, 52 SMU L. Rev. 1589, 1640–44 (1999) (arguing that the Supreme Court's decision in United States v. O'Hagan, 521 U.S. 642 (1997), improperly ignored and, indeed, undermined *Central Bank*).

68. For an interesting and provocative argument that *Central Bank* will prove less influential than one might have expected, see Donald C. Langevoort, Words From on High About Rule 10b–5: *Chiarella's* History, *Central Bank's* Future, 20 Del. J. Corp. L. 865 (1995).

69. It is sometimes said that the Securities Exchange Act registers companies, while the Securities Act registers securities. In fact, the former registers classes of securities, but the point is otherwise well-taken. A corporation that has registered a class of securities under the Securities Exchange Act must nevertheless register a particular offering of securities of that class under the Securities Act.

The periodic reports required by the Securities Exchange Act include: (1) Form 10, the initial Securities Exchange Act registration statement. It is only filed once with respect to a particular class of securities. It closely resembles a Securities Act registration statement. (2) Form 10–K, an annual report containing full audited financial statements and management's report of the previous year's activities. It usually incorporates the annual report sent to shareholders. (3) Form 10–Q, filed for each of first three quarters of the year. The issuer does not file a Form 10–Q for the last quarter of the year, which is covered by the Form 10–K. Form 10–Q contains unaudited financial statements and management's report of material recent developments. (4) Form 8–K, which must be filed within 15 days after certain important events affecting the corporation's operations or financial condition, such as bankruptcy, sales of significant assets, or a change in control of the company.

G. The boundary between state corporate and federal securities law

While there has been a long-standing debate over whether Congress, as a matter of sound policy, should adopt federal corporate governance standards, no one seriously doubts its ability to do so under the Commerce Clause.[70] To date, Congress has not done so explicitly. Despite occasional claims to the contrary, moreover, Congress did not do so implicitly in adopting the federal securities laws.

The key statute here is the Securities Exchange Act of 1934, which critics claimed was a federal attempt to usurp corporate governance powers. To be sure, The Exchange Act on its face says nothing about regulation of corporate governance. Instead, the Act's basic focus is trading of securities and securities pricing. Virtually all of its provisions are thus addressed to such matters as the production and distribution of information about issuers and their securities, the flow of funds in the market and the basic structure of the market.

This approach resulted from Congress' interpretation of the Great Crash and the subsequent Depression. Rightly or wrongly, many people believed that excessive stock market speculation and the collapse of the stock market had caused the Great Depression. The drafters of the Exchange Act were thus primarily concerned with preventing a recurrence of the speculative excesses that they believed had caused the market's collapse.[71]

---

70. There is a voluminous literature on the federal incorporation debate. For two useful, albeit somewhat dated, compilations of the major arguments, see Symposium, Current Issues in Corporate Governance, 45 Ohio St. L.J. 513 (1984); Symposium, An In–Depth Analysis of the Federal and State Roles in Regulating Corporate Management, 31 Bus. Law. 863 (1976).

71. See Securities Exchange Act, Pub. L. No. 73–291, § 2, 48 Stat. 881, 881–82 (1934); S. Rep. No. 792, 73d Cong., 2d Sess. 3 (1934) (need to control excessive stock market speculation that had "brought in its train social and economic evils which have affected the security and prosperity of the entire country."); 78 Cong. Rec. 7921–22 (1934) (Rep. Mapes) (the Act had two objec-

Disclosure was the chief vehicle by which the Act's drafters intended to regulate the markets. Indeed, it was widely acknowledged that allocating primary responsibility over corporate disclosure to the federal government was essential. Brandeis' famous dictum—"Sunlight is ... the best of disinfectants; electric light the most efficient policeman"[72]—was well accepted by the 1930s; indeed, it was the basic concept around which the federal securities laws were ultimately drafted.[73] However, the states faced serious obstacles in attempting to regulate corporate disclosure. Although the Supreme Court had upheld state blue sky laws against constitutional challenge,[74] the Commerce Clause limited the states' ability to apply those laws extraterritorially. As a result, most blue sky laws did not regulate out-of-state transactions. The problem was exacerbated by the difficulty of attaining uniformity and coordination among the states. Promoters could evade restrictive state laws simply by limiting their activities to more permissive jurisdictions. Because state securities laws thus could not effectively assure full disclosure, federal intervention was accepted as essential to maintaining the national capital markets.

Opponents of the legislation, however, quickly claimed that it went far beyond its stated purposes. According to Richard Whitney, President of the NYSE and a leading opponent of the bill, a number of provisions, including the predecessor to Section 19(c), collectively gave the Commission "powers ... so extensive that they might be used to control the management of all listed companies,"[75] a charge repeated by Congressional opponents of the bill.[76] Others acknowledged that early drafts of the legislation had justifiably raised such concerns, but argued the legislation had been redrafted so as to eliminate any legitimate fears on this score.[77]

The bill's supporters strenuously denied that they intended to regulate corporate management. The Senate Banking and Currency Committee went to the length of adding a proposed Section 13(d) to the bill, which provided: "[n]othing in this Act shall be construed as authorizing the Commission to interfere with the management of the affairs of an issuer."[78] The Conference Committee deleted the provision because it

tives: to prevent excessive speculation and to provide a fair and honest market for securities transactions); see also Dann v. Studebaker–Packard Corp., 288 F.2d 201, 207 (6th Cir.1961).

72. Louis D. Brandeis, Other People's Money 92 (1914).

73. Ernst & Ernst v. Hochfelder, 425 U.S. 185, 195 (1976); SEC v. Capital Gains Research Bureau, Inc., 375 U.S. 180, 186 (1963).

74. Hall v. Geiger–Jones Co., 242 U.S. 539 (1917); Caldwell v. Sioux Falls Stock Yards Co., 242 U.S. 559 (1917); Merrick v. N.W. Halsey & Co., 242 U.S. 568 (1917).

75. Letter from Richard Whitney to all NYSE members (Feb. 14, 1934), reprinted in 78 Cong. Rec. 2827 (Feb. 20, 1934).

76. E.g., 78 Cong. Rec. 8271 (1934) (Sen. Steiwer); id. at 8012 (Rep. McGugin); id. at 7937 (Rep. Bakewell); id. at 7710 (Rep. Britten); id. at 7691 (Rep. Crowther); id. at 7690 (Rep. Cooper).

77. E.g., 78 Cong. Rec. 7863 (1934) (Rep. Wolverton); id. at 7716–17 (Rep. Ford); id. at 7713 (Rep. Wadsworth).

78. S. 3420, 73d Cong., 2d Sess. § 13(d) (1934).

was seen "as unnecessary, since it is not believed that the bill is open to misconstruction in this respect."[79]

Admittedly, this debate need not be read as going to preemption of state corporate law. After all, interference with management might mean a variety of things. Perhaps the debate was really about charges of creeping socialism. Opposition to New Deal legislation typically included charges of radicalism and collectivism. The Exchange Act was no different. Even with this gloss, however, the legislative history still suggests that Congress' focus was mainly on regulating the securities industry, not listed companies. Moreover, the same Congress that insisted it was not trying to regiment industry also rejected explicit proposals for establishing a federal law of corporations.

During the New Deal era there were a number of efforts to grant the SEC authority over corporate governance. While the Exchange Act was being drafted, the Roosevelt administration considered developing a comprehensive federal corporation law. The Senate Banking and Currency Committee's report on stock exchange practices also suggested that the cure for the nation's "corporate ailments ... may lie in a national incorporation act."[80] In the late 1930s, then SEC Chairman William O. Douglas orchestrated yet another effort to replace state corporate law with a set of federal rules administered by the SEC. In this, he was anticipated and assisted by Senators Borah and O'Mahoney who introduced a series of bills designed to regulate corporate internal affairs.[81]

Proposals for a federal corporation statute did not stop when the New Deal ended.[82] In the 1970s, the SEC considered imposing a variety of corporate governance reforms, as a matter of federal law.[83] After vigorous objections that the Commission had exceeded its statutory authority, the rules were substantially modified before adoption.[84]

Consequently, none of these proposals ever came to fruition. Legislative inaction is inherently ambiguous, even when that inaction takes the form of rejecting a specific proposal. All that can be said with certainty is that Congress chose not to act. However, while the evidence admittedly is not conclusive, there is considerable reason to believe that the Seventy-third Congress did not intend for the SEC's powers to extend to

---

79. H.R. Conf. Rep. No. 1838, 73d Cong., 2d Sess. 35 (1934).

80. S. Rep. No. 1455, 73d Cong., 2d Sess. 391 (1934).

81. Joseph C. O'Mahoney, Federal Charters to Save Free Enterprise, 1949 Wis. L. Rev. 407. See generally Harris Berlack, Federal Incorporation and Securities Regulation, 49 Harv. L. Rev. 396 (1936); Winston S. Brown, Federal Legislation: The Federal Corporation Licensing Bill: Corporate Regulation, 27 Geo. L.J. 1092 (1939); Harold Gill Reuschlein, Federalization—Design for Corporate Reform in a National Economy, 91 U. Pa. L. Rev. 91 (1942).

82. E.g., Protection of Shareholders' Rights Act of 1980: Hearing before the Subcomm. on Securities of the Sen. Comm. on Banking, Housing, and Urban Affairs, 96th Cong., 2d Sess. (1980); The Role of the Shareholder in the Corporate World: Hearings before the Subcomm. on Citizens and Shareholders Rights and Remedies of the Sen. Comm. on the Judiciary, 95th Cong., 1st Sess. (1977).

83. Exchange Act Rel. No. 14,970 (July 18, 1978).

84. Exchange Act Release No. 15,384 (Dec. 6, 1978). See generally Homer Kripke, The SEC, Corporate Governance, and the Real Issues, 36 Bus. Law. 173 (1981).

matters of corporate governance. Granted Congress did not expressly state any such limitation. But Congress apparently did not believe it was necessary to do so. True, arguments based on rejections of proposed amendments must be taken with a grain of salt, especially those made after enactment of the original legislation. But surely the Congress that repeatedly denied any intent to regiment corporate management, and later repeatedly rejected proposals to federalize corporate law, did not intend to sneak those powers back into the bill through the back door by authorizing the SEC to adopt corporate governance rules.

Consistent with this clear congressional intent, the Supreme Court has routinely rejected efforts to preempt state law and create a de facto federal law of corporations. Because "state regulation of corporate governance is regulation of entities whose very existence and attributes are a product of state law," the court has consistently reaffirmed that: "It . . . is an accepted part of the business landscape in this country for states to create corporations, to prescribe their powers, and to define the rights that are acquired by purchasing their shares." Indeed, the Supreme Court opines that "[n]o principle of corporation law and practice is more firmly established than a State's authority to regulate domestic corporations."[85]

It is state law, for example, that determines the rights of shareholders, "including . . . the voting rights of shareholders." State law thus determines such questions as which matters may be authorized by the board of directors acting alone and which must be authorized by the shareholders. State law typically requires, for example, that certain control transactions, such as mergers or sales of substantially all corporate assets, be approved in advance by the shareholders and establishes the vote required (often a supermajority) for shareholder approval of such matters. State law likewise regulates the conduct of shareholder meetings, specifies who may call such meetings and prescribes whether, and the procedures by which, actions may be taken without a shareholder meeting.

The Supreme Court also has consistently recognized that state law governs the rights and duties of corporate directors: "As we have said in the past, the first place one must look to determine the powers of corporate directors is in the relevant State's corporation law. 'Corporations are creatures of state law' and it is state law which is the font of corporate directors' powers."[86] State law defines the directors' powers over the corporation, for example. State law establishes the vote required to elect directors. State law determines whether shareholders have the right to cumulative voting in the election of directors, whether the corporation's directors may have staggered terms of office, and whether shareholders have the right to remove directors prior to the expiration of their term of office.

85. CTS Corp. v. Dynamics Corp. of Am., 481 U.S. 69, 89 (1987).

86. Burks v. Lasker, 441 U.S. 471, 478 (1979) (citations omitted).

Does the Supreme Court's defense of what might be called "corporate federalism" make policy sense? Those who believe in the so-called "race to the bottom" hypothesis will argue that it does not, but the empirical evidence on that purported race, while mixed, tends to favor the competing race to the top hypothesis. In the absence of compelling evidence on the competing race hypotheses, we do well to consider the Supreme Court's argument that states have a number of legitimate interests in regulating such matters. The corporation is a creature of the state, "whose very existence and attributes are a product of state law."[87] States therefore were said to have an interest in overseeing the firms they create. States also have an interest in protecting the shareholders of their corporations. Finally, states have a legitimate "interest in promoting stable relationships among parties involved in the corporations it charters, as well as in ensuring that investors in such corporations have an effective voice in corporate affairs." If so, state regulation not only protects shareholders, but also protects investor and entrepreneurial confidence in the fairness and effectiveness of the state corporation law.[88]

The Supreme Court has suggested that the country as a whole benefits from state regulation in this area, as well. The markets that facilitate national and international participation in ownership of corporations are essential for providing capital not only for new enterprises but also for established companies that need to expand their businesses. This beneficial free market system depends at its core upon the fact that corporations generally are organized under, and governed by, the law of the state of their incorporation.[89]

This is so in large part because ousting the states from their traditional role as the primary regulators of corporate governance would eliminate a valuable opportunity for experimentation with alternative solutions to the many difficult regulatory problems that arise in corporate law. As Justice Brandeis pointed out many years ago, "It is one of the happy incidents of the federal system that a single courageous State may, if its citizens choose, serve as a laboratory; and try novel social and economic experiments without risk to the rest of country."[90] So long as state legislation is limited to regulation of firms incorporated within the state, as it generally is, there is no risk of conflicting rules applying to the same corporation. Experimentation thus does not result in confusion, but may well lead to more efficient corporate law rules.

---

87. CTS Corp. v. Dynamics Corp. of Am., 481 U.S. 69, 89 (1987).

88. Some argue that the state also has an interest in corporations that make a substantial contribution to the state. Corporations provide employment and a crucial tax base, sell and purchase goods and services, and supply support for community activities. This interest in any corporation will vary from case to case, but it is a real interest, deriving from the corporation's existence as a tangible economic entity created by state law. See Mark A. Sargent, Do the Second Generation State Takeover Statutes Violate the Commerce Clause?, 8 Corp. L. Rev. 3, 23 (1985).

89. CTS Corp. v. Dynamics Corp. of Am., 481 U.S. 69, 90 (1987).

90. New State Ice Co. v. Liebmann, 285 U.S. 262, 311 (1932) (Brandeis, J., dissenting).

Where then do we draw the line between the state and federal regulatory regimes? As a general rule of thumb, federal law appropriately is concerned mainly with disclosure obligations, as well as procedural and antifraud rules designed to make disclosure more effective. In contrast, regulating the substance of corporate governance standards is appropriately left to the states.

§ 3.6   Reading corporate financial statements

As discussed in the preceding section, financial statements are a key part of corporate disclosures under the federal securities laws. The two basic financial statements are the balance sheet and the income statement. The difference between these two statements is often analogized to that between a snapshot and a motion picture. The balance sheet provides a snap shot of the corporation's financial structure at a given point in time, while the income statement shows the corporation's profits or losses over a period of time. The following discussion focuses on the balance sheet, because it is the financial statement of greatest doctrinal importance in corporate law.

The following is a simplified balance sheet for the Acme Corporation at the end of its most recent fiscal year.

Assets		*Liabilities and Shareholder Equity*	
Cash	$4,550	Accounts payable	$27,000
Accounts receivable	$29,800	Loans outstanding	$33,500
Inventory	$4,150	Total liabilities	$60,500
Store/land	$34,500	Capital	$1,000
Total assets	$73,000	Surplus	$11,500
		Total shareholder equity	$12,500

The balance to which this statement's name refers is between assets on the left side and liabilities and shareholders' equity on the right side. A balance sheet is balanced when a corporation's total assets equal its total liabilities plus shareholders' equity.

Many of the terms used in the balance sheet are not only of accounting, but also of legal, importance. Definitions of the most important terms follow:

Assets: Tangible or intangible property owned by the corporation, expected to generate future economic benefits. Most assets are carried on their balance sheet at their historical cost (what the corporation paid to purchase them), less any accumulated depreciation. As such, the values reflected on the asset side of the balance sheet often bear no relationship whatsoever to the asset's actual fair market value.

Current assets: Assets expected to be converted into cash within the longer of one year or the company's operating cycle (the time it takes to create inventory, sell it, and collect cash from the sale). Includes cash, inventory, and other highly liquid assets.

Fixed assets: Illiquid assets, such as land or equipment.

Accounts receivable: Amounts owed to the corporation for goods or services.

Depreciation: An expense charged against fixed assets representing the asset's gradual wearing out. Because most fixed assets, except for land, wear out and lose value with the passage of time, accounting principles require the periodic conversion of a fixed asset's cost (carried on the balance sheet) into an expense (reported on the income statement) .

Goodwill: Because of name recognition, brand loyalty, and a host of other factors, a corporation is often worth far more as a going concern than the sum of its assets. In most cases, this additional value is not reflected on the company's balance sheet. If the company is sold as a going concern for more than the fair market value of its assets, however, the purchasing company will enter the difference on its own balance sheet as goodwill.

Liabilities: The corporation's debts and other obligations.

Current liabilities: Those liabilities, such as debts coming due within one year, that are expected to consume current assets.

Long-term liabilities: Those liabilities, such as debts not maturing for several years, that are not expected to consume current assets.

Shareholder's equity: The difference (hopefully positive) between the corporation's total assets and its total liabilities. As the corporation's residual claimants, shareholders are entitled to the proceeds of this account upon liquidation.

Capital: In its traditional form, the total par value of all outstanding shares.

Surplus: Shareholder equity over and above the corporation's capital.

§ 3.7 The economics of securities markets

Although the nexus of contracts model is the foundation for any economic analysis of corporate law, two economic theories relating to the behavior of securities markets are also important components of any such analysis. One is the efficient capital markets hypothesis. The other is portfolio theory (and its corollary, the capital asset pricing model).

A. Efficient capital markets

The efficient capital markets hypothesis (ECMH) is one of the most basic principles of modern corporate finance theory. Its influence on corporate law has been dramatic. ECMH, for example, has had an enormous impact on the SEC's disclosure rules and the elements of securities fraud. It also has been a crucial part of the debate over the desirability of insider trading prohibitions.

ECMH's fundamental thesis is that, in an efficient market, current prices always and fully reflect all relevant information about the commodities being traded.[1] In other words, in an efficient market, commodities are never over-or under-priced. The current price is an accurate reflection of the market's consensus as to the commodity's value. Of course, there is no real world condition like this, but the U.S. securities markets are widely believed to be close to this ideal.

Studies of the ECMH, as applied to the securities markets, have explored three forms of the theory.[2] Each tests a different level on which markets process information. The weak form posits that all information concerning historical prices is fully reflected in the current price. Put another way, the weak form predicts that price changes in securities are random.[3] Randomness does not mean that the stock market is like throwing darts at a dart board. Stock prices go up on good news and down on bad news. If a company announces a major oil find, all other things being equal, the stock price will go up. Randomness simply means that stock price movements are serially independent: future changes in price are independent of past changes. In other words, investors can not profit by using past prices to predict future prices.[4]

The ECMH's semi-strong form posits that current prices incorporate not only all historical information but also all current public information. This form predicts that investors can not expect to profit from studying publicly available information about particular firms because the market almost instantaneously incorporates information into the price of the firm's stock. In other words, the semi-strong form predicts that prices will change only in response to new information. If information was previously leaked or anticipated, the price will not change when it is formally disclosed.

The ECMH's strong form predicts that prices incorporate all information, whether publicly available or not. As such, the strong form also

---

§ 3.7

1. The classic (albeit somewhat dated) treatment of ECMH in the legal literature is Ronald J. Gilson and Reinier H. Kraakman, The Mechanisms of Market Efficiency, 70 Va. L. Rev. 549 (1984). For a highly accessible treatment of ECMH, see Burton G. Malkiel, A Random Walk Down Wall Street 137–221 (1996).

2. See Eugene F. Fama, Efficient Capital Markets: A Review of Theory and Empirical Work, 25 J. Fin. 383 (1970) (setting out three forms).

3. Eugene F. Fama, The Behavior of Stock Market Prices, 38 J. Bus. 34 (1965); Paul Samuelson, Proof that Properly Antic-

ipated Prices Fluctuate Randomly, 6 Indus. Mgmt. Rev. 41 (1965).

4. If the weak form of the hypothesis is true, charting—the attempt to predict future prices by looking at the past history of stock prices—can not be a profitable trading strategy over time. And, indeed, empirical studies have demonstrated that securities prices do move randomly and, moreover, have shown that charting is not a long-term profitable trading strategy. See Burton G. Malkiel, A Random Walk Down Wall Street 196–204 (1996) (critiquing recent studies purporting to find violations of the weak form hypothesis).

predicts that no identifiable group can systematically earn positive abnormal returns from trading in securities. In other words, over time nobody outperforms the market. To some extent, this is true. The empirical evidence suggests that the vast majority of mutual funds that outperform the market in a given year falter in future years. Once adjustment is made for risks, it seems reasonably certain that most mutual funds do not systematically outperform the market over long periods.

In general, however, the ECMH's strongest form makes no intuitive sense. How can prices reflect information that only one person knows? In fact, empirical research suggests that strong form has only limited validity. There is good empirical evidence that corporate insiders, who have access to information not available to anyone else, consistently out perform the market.[5]

In an efficient stock market, the price of a share of corporate stock thus represents the consensus of all market participants as to the present discounted value of the future dividend stream in light of all currently available public information. In general, it is therefore meaningless to talk about the "intrinsic value" of corporate stock. As a marketable commodity, a share of stock has no value other than what someone else is willing to pay for it. In an efficient market, idiosyncratic valuations tend to wash out, and market price becomes the only meaningful value one can put on a share of stock.

The market thus builds consensus through trading. When new information is released, investors with high estimates of the firm's new net present value will buy, while those with lower estimates will sell. An equilibrium price quickly results. This process necessarily assumes that investors are engaging in precisely the behavior the ECMH predicts they should eschew, namely searching out new information and seeking to capitalize on the information's value through stock trading. Accordingly, some suggest that there is a paradox behind the ECMH: markets may be efficient only if large numbers of investors do not believe in market efficiency. If everyone believed the ECMH, no one would engage in securities analysis to find "undervalued" or "overvalued" stocks. Only because a large number of investors engage in precisely this activity are the markets efficient.

More sophisticated analysis eliminates the apparent paradox behind the ECMH. The first analyst to correctly interpret new information can profit by being the first to buy or sell. Full-time professional investors capture enough of the value of new information to make the game one worth playing. It is trading by these investors that moves a stock's price to a new equilibrium in response to changed information. These investors thus set the price at which other investors trade.

5. See, e.g., Dan Givoly and Dan Palmon, Insider Trading and the Exploitation of Inside Information: Some Empirical Evidence, 58 J. Bus. 69 (1985).

The ECMH is widely regarded as one of the most well-established propositions in the social sciences.[6] Three important caveats to the ECMH are worth bearing in mind, however. First, most of the tests of the ECMH have been internal to the stock markets. In other words, researchers focused on whether the stock market is efficient in pricing stocks relative to one another. There is little good evidence with respect to whether the stock markets are efficient in an absolute sense. In other words, we do not know whether the stock market accurately measures the value of stocks relative to that of other commodities. The stock market could be efficient in this sense only if it were fundamentally efficient, which means that the market in fact accurately estimates the discounted present value of all future corporate dividends. There is some evidence that the market is not efficient in this sense.[7]

Noise theory purportedly offers additional evidence that the stock market is not fundamentally efficient.[8] Markets are made of human actors, who bring to bear their own individual foibles. Idiosyncratic valuations generate noise that may skew the market's valuation of stock prices. (Just as it is hard to carry on an accurate conversation in a noisy room, it is hard to accurately value stocks in a noisy market.) Research in cognitive psychology suggests that investor idiosyncrasies do not always cancel one another out.[9] Instead, investors sometimes act like a herd all running in the same direction, which can produce pricing errors. Large speculative bubbles that appear out of nowhere and crash without apparent reason are the most visible form of this phenomenon.

Finally, U.S. stock markets exhibit some anomalous behaviors that are hard to explain in ECMH terms. Stocks tend to suffer abnormally large losses in December and on Mondays. Stocks with low price/earnings ratios tend to outperform the market, as do stocks of the smallest public corporations. Various explanations for these anomalies have been advanced, with varying degrees of persuasiveness.

---

6. As Michael Jensen famously claimed, "there is no other proposition in economics which has more solid empirical evidence supporting it than the Efficient Market Hypothesis." Michael C. Jensen, Some Anomalous Evidence Regarding Market Efficiency, 6 J. Fin. Econ. 95 (1978). During the 1990s there was something of a cottage industry of attacks on ECMH in the legal literature, the best examples of which include Lawrence A. Cunningham, From Random Walks to Chaotic Crashes: The Linear Genealogy of the Efficient Capital Market Hypothesis, 62 Geo. Wash. L. Rev. 546 (1994); Donald C. Langevoort, Theories, Assumptions, and Securities Regulation: Market Efficiency Revisited, 140 U. Pa. L. Rev. 851 (1992); Lynn A. Stout, How Efficient Markets Undervalue Stocks: CAPM and ECMH Under Conditions of Uncertainty and Disagreement, 19 Cardozo L. Rev. 475 (1997);

Lynn A. Stout, The Unimportance of Being Efficient: An Economic Analysis of Stock Market Pricing and Securities Regulation, 87 Mich. L. Rev. 613 (1988).

7. Ronald J. Gilson and Bernard S. Black, The Law and Finance of Corporate Acquisitions 138–39 (2d ed. 1995).

8. See, e.g., Fischer Black, Noise, 41 J. Fin. 529 (1986); Andrei Shleifer and Lawrence H. Summers, The Noise Trader Approach to Finance, 4 J. Econ. Persp. 19 (1990). But see Eugene F. Fama, Efficient Capital Markets: II, 46 J. Fin. 1575 (1991) (criticizing early noise theory studies).

9. See generally Stephen M. Bainbridge, Mandatory Disclosure: A Behavioral Analysis, 68 U. Cin. L. Rev. 1023 (2000) (discussing cognitive psychology in capital markets).

The ECMH is often brought to bear on politically charged policy disputes, such as mandatory corporate disclosure and insider trading. Those who are troubled by the ECMH's implications in these areas find comfort in the foregoing caveats, asserting that these caveats argue against using the ECMH as a public policy tool. Many of those who support the ECMH's use in public policy admit the caveats, but deny their force. According to this view, it takes a theory to beat a theory, and no theory does a better job of explaining the vast bulk of stock market phenomena than the ECMH. At the moment, the fairest comment one can make probably is that the debate is likely to continue.

B. Portfolio theory

Risk and return are positively correlated. A corporation seeking to sell risky securities therefore must pay a correspondingly high rate of return on that investment. The question addressed by portfolio theory is whether investors must be compensated for all risks that might effect a share of stock's value or only for certain risks. Modern portfolio theory claims that investors need to be compensated only for bearing certain risks.

In economic terms, risk is simply the probability that the actual outcome of an event will diverge from the expected outcome. As it becomes more likely that the actual and expected outcomes will differ, and as the spread of possible outcomes becomes wider, the riskiness of the event increases. Putting $1,000 in a federally-insured one year bank certificate of deposit, for example, is not a very risky investment. The expected outcome of this investment is the return of your principal plus any accrued interest. It is highly unlikely that the actual outcome of this investment will differ from this expected outcome. If you had invested $1,000 in the stock market, however, that would be a very risky investment. Although you may expect to earn a certain return on your investment, there is a very high probability that the actual return will be different from what you expect. In addition, the breadth of possible outcomes is quite wide. At the end of one year, your investment might be worth much more than $1,000 or much less.

Attitudes towards risk vary considerably. Someone who is risk averse would rather have a sure thing than take a gamble, even if they have the same expected outcome. A risk preferrer would rather take the gamble than the sure thing, even if they have the same expected outcome. A risk neutral person would be indifferent between a sure thing and a gamble with the same expected outcome.[10]

10. Suppose, for example, that a gambler offers three people the following deal: "I'll give you a choice: you can have a dollar outright or we can flip a coin. Heads, you win $2; tails, you win nothing." Notice that the expected outcome of the sure thing and the gamble are the same, one dollar, because in the gamble there is a 50% probability of winning $2. The risk averse person will take the dollar outright, the risk preferrer will flip the coin, and the risk neutral person will be indifferent between the two.

Attitudes towards risk change over time as a person ages: When young, a person is less likely to be risk averse, but as they get older there comes a time when they become truly conscious of their own mortality and then their risk attitude begins to shift towards risk aversion. Attitudes towards risk also vary depending on the degree of risk present. Many people are risk preferrers with respect to small sums (witness state lotteries) but risk averse with respect to large sums (witness life insurance). Finally, risk aversion may also depend on whether you're gambling with your own money or somebody else's. As a general rule, however, most people are risk averse most of the time.

The proposition that most people are risk averse most of the time has very important implications for corporate finance, most notably in the relationship between risk and return. The idea that risk and return are positively correlated should not be controversial. We see examples all around us: Christmas club accounts at federally insured banks pay a lower interest rate than junk bonds issued by companies on the verge of insolvency.[11] This phenomenon is a direct consequence of risk aversion: because people prefer low risk to high risk, they must be compensated for bearing risk. The more risk you ask them to bear, the more compensation you must pay. Hence, risk and return are positively correlated. Issuers, however, only need compensate investors for certain types of risk—namely, systematic risks.

Unsystematic risk can be thought of as firm-specific risk. The risk that the CEO will have a heart attack, the firm's workers will go out on strike, or the plant will burn down are all firm-specific risks. In contrast, systematic risk might be regarded as market risk. Systematic risks affect all firms to one degree or another: changes in market interest rates; election results; recessions; and so forth. Portfolio theory acknowledges that risk and return are related: investors will demand a higher rate of return from riskier investments. In other words, a corporation issuing junk bonds must pay a higher rate of return than a company issuing investment grade bonds. Yet, portfolio theory claims that issuers of securities need not compensate investors for unsystematic risk. In other words, investors will not demand a risk premium to reflect firm-specific risks.

Investors can eliminate unsystematic risk by diversifying their portfolio. Diversification eliminates unsystematic risk, because things tend to come out in the wash. One firm's plant burns down, but another hits oil. A well-chosen portfolio of 20 stocks can virtually eliminate unsystematic risk.[12] Thus, even though the actual rate of return earned on a particular investment is likely to diverge from the expected return, the actual return on a well-diversified portfolio is less likely to diverge from the expected return. A well-diversified investor thus need not be concerned with unsystematic risk and therefore will not demand to be compensated

11. On junk bonds, see generally William A. Klein, High–Yield ("Junk") Bonds as Investments and as Financial Tools, 19 Cardozo L. Rev. 505 (1997).

12. Burton G. Malkiel, A Random Walk Down Wall Street 245 (1996).

for that risk. Systematic risk by definition cannot be eliminated by diversification, because it effects all stocks. Ergo investors will demand to be compensated for bearing systematic risk.

Although all stocks are affected by systematic risk, not all companies have the same exposure to systematic risk. A recession hurts almost all firms, for example, but it hurts cyclical manufacturing firms more than it hurts tobacco companies. If it were not so, of course, all stocks would pay identical rates of return. The capital asset pricing model (CAPM) was developed to quantify the relationship between systematic risk and return.[13]

CAPM was designed to answer a very specific question: what rate of return can we expect from an investment whose response to systematic risks differs from that of the market as whole? In other words, suppose the market rate of return is 10%. Investment A is known to be more sensitive to systematic risk than the market as a whole: if the market goes up, Investment A goes up faster and higher; if the market goes down; Investment A goes down faster and lower. Because investors want to be compensated for systematic risk, they will want a higher rate of return for Investment A than the market rate. CAPM gives us a mathematical basis for figuring out how much higher Investment A's rate of return must be to compensate investors for bearing this additional risk.

The beta coefficient is the heart of the CAPM. Beta is simply a measurement of the investment's sensitivity to systematic risk. A beta of 1 shows that the firm tends to pay the same rate of return as the market as a whole. A beta greater than one suggests that the firm is more sensitive to systematic risk than is the market on average, so the firm will tend to pay higher rates of return. Beta thus gives us a way of comparing the riskiness of two securities by giving us a measure of each stock's sensitivity to systematic risk. Beta also gives us a way of measuring the impact of a proposed new investment on our portfolio. You can measure the beta of your portfolio by taking the weighted average of the betas of all the securities therein. By comparing that figure to the beta of the proposed investment, you know whether the investment would make your portfolio more or less risky.

Beta is calculated graphically by plotting market return on the X-axis and the firm's return on the Y-axis. After enough data points are assembled, you draw a regression line that fits the data best. The slope of that line is beta. Calculating beta thus involves lots of math, but we need not attempt it. Brokerage houses and investment advisors typically publish a stock's beta as part of their investor advising services.

Once beta is determined, one can use it to estimate the expected return on the asset in question using the following formula:

$$r = r_{rf} + [\beta \times (r_m - r_{rf})]$$

13. Franco Modigliani and Gerald A. Pogue, An Introduction to Risk and Return: Concepts and Evidence, Fin. Analysts J., May–June 1974, at 69.

where r_{rf} is the risk free rate (usually measured by the current interest rate paid on short-term U.S. Treasury obligations), and r_m is the stock market's current rate of return (usually measured by reference to some market index, such as the S & P 500). As an example, assume the corporation's beta is 1.5, the market rate of return is 10%, and the risk-free rate of return is 5%. The company should pay a rate of return of 12.5%:

$$0.05 + 1.5(0.10-0.05) =$$
$$0.05 + 0.075 = 12.5\%$$

Beta and CAPM have been quite controversial in the financial economics literature. Critics contend that beta is not a complete measure of the risks that are priced by securities markets—in other words, that the market compensates investors for bearing some nonsystematic risks.[14] Various alternatives to CAPM have been proposed, most notably the Arbitrage Pricing Theory developed by Richard Roll and Stephen Ross.[15] As yet, however, CAPM remains state of the art in the legal literature. CAPM is still very widely used, for example, in valuing businesses for purposes of the statutory appraisal proceeding.[16]

C. Securities law implications: Integrated and mandatory disclosure

Recall that the Securities Act and the Securities Exchange Act originally established two separate disclosure systems. Further recall that the Securities Act requires disclosures with respect to particular transactions, such as new issues of stocks or bonds to the public. In contrast, the Securities Exchange Act imposes a system of periodic disclosures on reporting companies. For publicly-traded reporting companies, there long was a substantial amount of overlap and duplication between the Securities Exchange Act reports it files and the Securities Act registration statement disclosures.

---

14. See, e.g., Eugene F. Fama and Kenneth R. French, The Cross–Section of Expected Stock Returns, 47 J. Fin 427 (1992).

15. See, e.g., Richard Roll and Stephen A. Ross, An Empirical Investigation of the Arbitrage Pricing Theory, 35 J. Fin. 1073 (1980).

16. See, e.g., Cede & Co. v. Technicolor, Inc., 1990 WL 161084 (Del.Ch.1990), rev'd on other grounds, 684 A.2d 289 (Del.1996); see also Hintmann v. Fred Weber, Inc., 1998 WL 83052 (Del.Ch.1998), modified, 1999 WL 182577 (Del.Ch.1999), modified, 2000 WL 376379 (Del.Ch.2000) (using CAPM to determine cost of equity); Le Beau v. M. G. Bancorporation, Inc., 1998 WL 44993 (Del.Ch.1998), aff'd, 737 A.2d 513 (Del.1999) (using CAPM to determine discount rate); Gilbert v. MPM Enters., Inc., 709 A.2d 663 (Del.Ch.1997), modified, 1998 WL 229439 (Del.Ch.1998), aff'd, 731 A.2d 790 (Del.1999) (using CAPM to determine cost of equity); Ryan v. Tad's Enters., Inc., 709 A.2d 682 (Del.Ch.1996), aff'd, 693 A.2d. 1082 (Del.1997) (using CAPM to determine discount rate); TV58 Ltd. Partnership v. Weigel Broad. Co., 1993 WL 285850 (Del.Ch.1993) (using CAPM to determine discount rate); MacLane Gas Co. Ltd. Partnership v. Enserch Corp., 1992 WL 368614 (Del.Ch.1992), aff'd, 633 A.2d 369 (Del. 1993) (using CAPM to determine discount rate); Hodas v. Spectrum Tech., Inc., 1992 WL 364682 (Del.Ch.1992) (using CAPM to determine discount rate); In re Radiology Assocs., Inc. Litig., 611 A.2d 485 (Del.Ch. 1991) (using CAPM to determine discount rate); In re Appraisal of Shell Oil Co., 1990 WL 201390 (Del.Ch.1990), aff'd, 607 A.2d 1213 (Del.1992) (using CAPM to determine discount rate).

If markets are efficient, however, this duplication of effort was not only expensive, but unnecessary. According to the efficient capital markets hypothesis, an issuer only needs to disclose information once. If ECMH is valid, accordingly, all of the information released in the firm's regular Securities Exchange Act disclosure statements will be digested by securities analysts and investors and reflected in the firm's market price. And because virtually all securities offerings by established companies are made either at the current market price of its securities or at a slight discount from market price, there is no need to reiterate all of the Securities Exchange Act information in a Securities Act filing. The market has already gotten the information and accounted for it.

The SEC eventually saw ECMH as providing a way out of the box— a way of eliminating the complex and expensive dual disclosure system. It therefore adopted the so-called "Integrated Disclosure System," one of the truly major changes in its history. As we've seen, under the integrated disclosure system, an issuer planning a registered offering under the '33 Act follows a three-step procedure. It first looks to the various registration statement forms to determine which form it is eligible to use. The forms then cross-reference to Regulation S–K for the substantive disclosure requirements. Regulation S–K adopted uniform disclosure standards for both Acts, so that virtually all '33 and '34 Act filings are now prepared under identical instructions. As a result, the style and content of disclosure documents under both Acts are now essentially identical. Thus, for example, the annual 10–K report contains information that can be directly transferred into a registration statement.

Certain issuers in fact are entitled to do just that. The basic registration statement form requires disclosure of both information about the transaction and information about the issuer (a.k.a. registrant). Most reporting companies, however, are eligible to use an alternative form that basically requires disclosure about only the transaction. Information about the registrant is incorporated by reference from the last 10–K and other Securities Exchange Act disclosure documents. The basic idea is that reporting companies regularly provide disclosure to the market and, moreover, their securities are traded in an efficient market that impounds the disclosed information into price quickly. Given these criteria, the SEC concluded (based on the ECMH) that disclosure of registrant-related information by such issuers would be unnecessarily duplicative.

Although law and economics scholars generally support integrated disclosure, subject to the occasional quibble that the SEC should be even more liberal in permitting incorporation by reference, many such scholars remain fundamentally unconvinced of the basic premise of the federal securities laws; namely, that issuers should be required to disclose. The debate over mandatory disclosure has raged for a long time, largely inconclusively.

Being cognizant of the pitfalls awaiting anyone who attempts to briefly summarize a lengthy and voluminous debate, not least of which is failing to cite any number of classic works, [17] our goal for this section is to do no more than summarize a complex and nuanced literature.

Start with the perfectly plausible assumptions that investors value disclosure and that corporations desire to minimize their cost of capital. Or, more precisely, assume that the marginal benefit of an additional unit of disclosure (however measured) declines as more is produced, while the marginal social cost of producing additional units rises as more are produced. If investors in fact value disclosure, an issuer's voluntary disclosure will reduce its cost of capital. Investors will be willing to pay more (i.e., demand a lower return) for securities of companies that make voluntary disclosure. Put another way, the information asymmetry between firms and investors increases the latter's risk and therefore manifests itself in reduced liquidity. To overcome investor reluctance to hold risky, illiquid shares, firms must issue capital at a discount, which leads to a higher cost of capital. In turn, the corporate managers who actually make disclosure decisions frequently have large and nondiversified investments in firm-specific human capital. Suboptimal disclosure practices thus put management at risk.

Further assume that at $t=0$ the capital markets are in a disequilibrium state in which the marginal benefit of additional disclosure to investors exceeds the marginal cost to a firm of providing such disclosure. Under those conditions, potential gains from trade exist. Both investors and the firm will be better off if the latter provides additional disclosure. Absent some market failure, neoclassical economics predicts that the firm will voluntarily provide additional disclosures until an equilibrium is reached in which the marginal social benefit of providing an additional unit of disclosure equals the marginal social cost of producing that additional unit.

A basic premise of welfare economics is that a market failure is a necessary (but not sufficient) justification for government intervention. Hence, the mandatory disclosure debate has generally focused on identifying market failures that would prevent achievement of a Pareto optimal equilibrium within a regime of voluntary disclosure.[18] Welfare economics classically recognizes four basic sources of market failures:

---

17. For useful reviews of the disclosure system, which offer trenchant critiques of its foundational normative premises, see Edmund W. Kitch, The Theory and Practice of Securities Disclosure, 61 Brooklyn L. Rev. 763 (1995); Alan R. Palmiter, Toward Disclosure Choice in Securities Offerings, 1999 Colum. Bus. L. Rev. 1, 10–29.

18. Various other justifications for the mandatory disclosure system have been offered, as well. One of the more common is that mandatory disclosure is necessary to prevent fraud. While essentially wrong, this argument does play some role in the analysis that follows. Another is that disclosure fosters good corporate practices; hence, the sobriquet "therapeutic disclosure." Still others include vague notions of investor protection and the maintenance of investor confidence. These and other similar justifications are canvassed (and mostly rebutted) in Frank H. Easterbrook and Daniel R. Fischel, The Economic Structure of Corporate Law 296–300 (1991). Finally, issuers might rationally prefer a mandatory disclosure regime specifying which disclosures must and must not be made as a safe harbor against the risk that a jury, acting with the benefit of hindsight, might determine that the issuer's voluntary disclosures omitted material facts and, thus, constituted securities fraud.

producer monopoly; the good to be produced is a public good; externalities; and informational asymmetry between producer and consumer. The latter three have all been invoked to justify mandatory disclosure, although each remains highly contested.

The Public Goods-based Market Failure Story: Professor John Coffee argues that "because information has many characteristics of a public good, securities research tends to be underprovided.... A mandatory disclosure system can thus be seen as a desirable cost reduction strategy through which society ... secure[s] both a greater quantity of information and a better testing of its accuracy."[19] Although it is conventional to treat information as a public good, slapping the public good label on securities-related information is not enough to justify government intervention. It must first be shown that firms in fact will not voluntarily disclose optimally and that government mandates will lead to efficient levels of disclosure. Those points are still controverted.

The Externalities-based Market Failure Story: Several third party effects—externalities—have been identified as potential sources of capital market failure. In most cases, effective disclosure requires not only historical information about the firm, but also its future plans, as well as comparative data about its competitors and its industry in general. An individual firm will resist producing the latter types of information, because competitors might free ride on its general disclosures about the industry and might use information about future plans to their own competitive advantage. Hence, such information will tend to be underproduced.

Some scholars also argue that a mandatory disclosure system offers positive network externalities.[20] Standardized modes of disclosure clearly facilitate investor analysis by creating economies of scale. Investors and managers only need learn how to deal with a single set of disclosure standards. Comparisons across companies are facilitated. The lawyers and accountants who assist firms to prepare disclosures will develop expertise that can be applied across many firms, lowering costs. Individual firms, however, may lack incentives to develop or comply with such standards.

The Information Asymmetry-based Market Failure Story: While there is an obvious information asymmetry between issuers and investors, it is a fallacy to assume that if some disclosure is useful, more is always better. In light of management's incentives to voluntarily disclose up to the point at which marginal cost equals marginal benefits, the question is whether a system of voluntary disclosure induced by competitive market pressures will optimally ameliorate the asymmetry of information between investors and issuers. At its simplest level, the information asymmetry argument is that, "in the absence of a compulsory

19. John C. Coffee, Jr., Market Failure and the Economic Case for a Mandatory Disclosure System, 70 Va. L. Rev. 717, 722 (1984).

20. Frank H. Easterbrook and Daniel R. Fischel, The Economic Structure of Corporate Law 291–92 (1991).

corporate disclosure system some issuers will conceal or misrepresent information material to investment decisions."[21]

No one disputes the importance of a steady flow of truthful information to both the primary and secondary capital markets. If the market can efficiently price securities, the market will also efficiently allocate capital investment. Capital will flow in the directions indicated by changes in market prices. In order to efficiently price securities, investors must have a constant flow of complete and accurate information. If management misrepresents or omits to disclose material information, both investors and society thus suffer. To be sure, management has incentives to provide *ex ante* assurances that it will provide a steady stream of truthful information. Basic principles of agency cost economics, however, predict that managers sometimes break those promises. In particular, managers will often have an incentive to withhold bad news.[22]

Under a regime of voluntary disclosure, if management wants to lower the firm's cost of capital, its promises must have credibility. Investors will not be willing to pay more for securities unless management provides a credible promise—a bond—that guarantees that it will disclose bad information just as promptly as good information. Law can facilitate private ordering by providing such a bond. Query, however, whether one needs the full panoply of disclosure and procedural rules imposed by U.S. securities law in order to provide such a bond? A credible commitment-based disclosure regime requires an antifraud rule like present Rule 10b–5, perhaps with somewhat expanded liability for nondisclosures, such as affirmative duties to update or disclose soft information. Less obvious is the necessity for the detailed disclosures specified by Regulation S–K or the various ancillary features of the present mandatory disclosure regime, such as the proxy and tender offer rules, in order to make a credible commitment to investors.

In any case, a mandatory disclosure system laying out detailed required disclosures will not prevent issuers from fraudulently violating their commitments. Issuers who are going to commit fraud still will make fraudulent disclosures—they will simply use the approved form to do so. Hence, rigorously enforced proscriptions of fraud seem far more important than the mandatory disclosure system, insofar as one is concerned about bonding the credibility of managerial disclosure promises.

Conclusions. Although even most critics of the mandatory disclosure regime concede that the debate has not reached closure, there may be growing evidence that there is no persistent market failure in U.S.

21. Joel Seligman, The Historical Need for a Mandatory Corporate Disclosure System, 9 J. Corp. L. 1, 9 (1983).

22. See Mitu Gulati, When Corporate Managers Fear a Good Thing is Coming to an End: The Case of Interim Nondisclosure, 46 UCLA L. Rev. 675, 732–39 (1999); see also Jennifer H. Arlen and William J. Car-

ney, Vicarious Liability for Fraud on Securities Markets: Theory and Evidence, 1992 U. Ill. L. Rev. 691 (an analysis of securities fraud litigation finding that managers typically committed fraud in order to conceal bad news, such as an earnings decline, that might have placed their jobs in jeopardy).

capital market disclosure practices. Consider, first, domestic issuer behavior in private placements: In response to investor demand and insistence by reputational intermediaries such as underwriters, issuers making private placements provide disclosures comparable to those made in registered public offerings subject to the mandatory disclosure system. The behavior of international issuers also tends to disprove the existence of a market failure. Foreign issuers with securities traded on U.S. secondary markets often provide greater disclosure than U.S. law requires of such issuers. Even more strikingly, many international issuers have voluntarily adopted U.S.-style accounting standards that promote transparency.[23]

Assume, however, that U.S. capital markets would fail to produce optimal disclosure through voluntary corporate action. The mere existence of such a market failure does not—standing alone—justify legal intervention. In addition to the standard prudential arguments in favor of limited government, which counsel caution in concluding that any purported market failure requires government correction, a regulatory regime is unlikely to peg prices at the equilibrium point at which marginal cost and marginal benefit are equal. As with price controls, for example, the mandatory disclosure regime thus is likely to be under- and/or over-inclusive. Under-inclusive disclosure rules harm investors by denying them information they need. Over-inclusive rules harm investors by requiring the firm to spend money on unnecessary disclosures, which essentially comes out of the investors' pockets. Investors presumably do not want management to engage in disclosure that produces diminishing returns; i.e., investors will not want management to spend a dollar on disclosure unless that expenditure produces at least a dollar's worth of benefit to the shareholders. Under a regime of voluntary disclosure, management has an incentive to provide disclosure until it achieves that equilibrium. Because management's wealth is closely tied to the firm's financial well-being, it has an incentive to achieve an efficient trade-off between lowering the cost of capital and spending money on disclosure. The government has no comparable incentive. Moreover, different firms are likely to achieve equilibrium at different levels of disclosure. Consequently, government regulation by definition will be both over-and under-inclusive. To be sure, government could address the problem of under-inclusiveness by requiring issuers to disclose any additional information necessary to make the mandated disclosures intelligible and understandable. In determining the cost of disclosure, however, managers would have to factor in the possibility of liability for fraud if they failed to disclose information a court, acting with the benefit of hindsight, thought should have been disclosed.[24] Hence, management might tend to over-invest in disclosure. In any case,

---

23. Alan R. Palmiter, Toward Disclosure Choice in Securities Offerings, 1999 Colum. Bus. L. Rev. 1, 21–22.

24. The hindsight bias is a well-established component of behavioral economics, positing that decisionmakers tend to assign an erroneously high probability of occurrence to a probabilistic event simply because it ended up occurring.

there is no way for the government to avoid the problem of over-inclusiveness.

As a practical matter, legislators and regulators necessarily have less information about the needs of a particular firm than do that firm's managers and directors. A fortiori, legislatures will make poorer decisions than the firm's directors. Put another way, legislators and regulators are no less subject to bounded rationality and other cognitive biases than any other decisionmakers.

Public choice theory provides still another reason market failure is not a sufficient justification for government intervention. A welfare economics model that posits legal intervention as a solution to market failure ignores the fact that regulators are themselves actors with their own self-interested motivations. The capital, product, and labor markets give corporate directors incentives to attract capital at the lowest possible cost. Voluntary disclosure thus should be designed to meet specific firm needs relating to monitoring and information transmission. In contrast, the incentives of legislators and regulators are driven by rent-seeking and interest group politics, which have no necessary correlation to corporate profit-maximization.[25] Accordingly, mandatory disclosure is likely to be driven by the political concerns of the governmental actors drafting the mandates.

25. See Jonathan R. Macey, Corporate Law and Corporate Governance: A Contractual Perspective, 18 J. Corp. L. 185, 205 (1993) ("there is no reason to believe that politicians and bureaucrats are any more benign, selfless, and impartial than the corporate managers, directors, and controlling shareholders whose authority would be displaced in a legal regime governed by mandatory rules").

Chapter 4

LIMITED LIABILITY

Analysis

---

§ 4.1 Introduction

Limited liability means that shareholders of a corporation are not personally liable for debts incurred or torts committed by the firm. If the firm fails, shareholders' losses thus are limited to the amount the shareholders invested in the firm—i.e., the amount the shareholders initially paid to purchase their stock.

MBCA § 6.22(b) offers a typical statutory formulation of the doctrine: "Unless otherwise provided in the articles of incorporation, a shareholder of a corporation is not personally liable for the acts or debts of the corporation except that he may become personally liable by reason of his own acts or conduct." Notice that § 6.22(b) contains two provisos. First, the articles of incorporation may provide for personal liability. This is nothing more than an example of the familiar principle that most corporate law rules are default rules—i.e., off-the-rack principles that may be modified by contract. Second, personal "liability may be assumed voluntarily or otherwise."[1] A shareholder, for example, voluntarily may assume liability through a personal guaranty. A guaranty is a contract by which the guarantor is bound to perform in the event of a breach of contract by the party whose performance is guaranteed. Contract creditors of close corporations often require controlling shareholders to personally guarantee the firm's debts.

Alternatively, personal liability may be involuntarily thrust upon a shareholder under the equitable remedy known as "piercing the corporate veil."[2] As a seminal 1912 law review article put it, "When the conception of corporate entity is employed to defraud creditors, to evade an existing obligation, to circumvent a statute, to achieve or perpetuate monopoly, or to protect knavery or crime, the courts will draw aside the web [i.e., veil] of entity, will regard the corporate company as an association of live, up-and-doing, men and women shareholders, and will do justice between real persons."[3] The veil piercing terminology is, admittedly, curious. Think, by way of analogy, of the scene in the *Wizard of Oz* in which Toto pulls aside the curtain to reveal the charlatan. Just as the curtain prevented Dorothy from seeing the Wizard's true nature, the corporate veil prevents the creditor from seizing the personal assets of the shareholders.

Obviously, veil piercing is where much of the action is for lawyers. From a litigation standpoint, veil piercing allows creditors to satisfy their claims out of the personal assets of shareholders. From a transactional planning perspective, the risk of veil piercing requires lawyers to exercise some care in forming the corporation and advising the client as to its conduct.

§ 4.1

1. MBCA § 6.22 cmt.

2. Although the better view is that veil piercing is an equitable remedy, there is substantial disagreement on that question in the literature. The significance of the issue, of course, is that equitable remedies need not be tried before a jury but parties subject to legal remedies generally are entitled to trial by jury. Compare U.S. v. Golden Acres, Inc., 684 F.Supp. 96, 103 (D.Del. 1988) (veil piercing is equitable remedy and affords no right to jury trial); Dow Jones Co. v. Avenel, 198 Cal.Rptr. 457, 460 (Cal. App.1984) (same) with Bower v. Bunker Hill Co., 675 F.Supp. 1254, 1261–62 (E.D.Wash.1986) (veil piercing is a legal remedy because it seeks a money judgment and thus a right to jury trial exists). See also Wm. Passalacqua Builders, Inc. v. Res-nick Developers South, Inc., 933 F.2d 131, 136 (2d Cir.1991) (veil piercing has roots in both law and equity, so it was proper for trial court to submit issue to jury); American Protein Corp. v. AB Volvo, 844 F.2d 56, 59 (2d Cir.1988) (veil piercing is an equitable remedy but issue is normally submitted to a jury).

3. I. Maurice Wormser, Piercing the Veil of Corporate Entity, 12 Colum. L. Rev. 496, 517 (1912). Shareholders may also face personal liability in connection with watered stock or unlawful dividends. In some states, special statutory provisions impose personal liability on shareholders with respect to certain corporate debts. New York and Wisconsin, for example, do so with respect to employee wages. See, e.g., N.Y. Bus. Corp. L. § 630.

Having said that, it is critical to stress that veil piercing is the exception, not the rule. The law permits incorporation of a business for the very purpose of avoiding personal liability.[4] The equitable exception obviously could easily swallow the legal rule unless courts are careful to permit veil piercing only in certain egregious cases. Accordingly, many decisions in this area state that courts will pierce the veil only reluctantly.[5]

Note: Our analysis of veil piercing will focus on cases in which a creditor seeks to pierce the veil of a close corporation to hold liable for the corporation's acts or debts the natural person who is the controlling shareholder. Unfortunately, veil piercing terminology often is also used to allocate liabilities within corporate groups.[6] Suppose Ajax Corporation is a wholly owned subsidiary of Parent Inc., which is a public corporation. Agents of Ajax cause a mass tort. The resulting plaintiff class brings claims that far exceed Ajax's value and, accordingly, seeks to reach Parent's assets and those of its shareholders. The claim against Parent's shareholders will fail. Shareholders of public corporations are effectively immune from veil piercing claims. Insofar as the liability of natural persons is concerned, veil piercing is really an issue only for the very smallest close corporations.

But what of Parent itself? In many cases nominally characterized as veil piercing, the defendant is not an individual but rather a second corporation. Where a plaintiff seeks to hold a parent or other affiliated corporation liable for the acts of another member of a corporate group, courts generally apply the same standards applicable to individual defendants. Holding a parent corporation liable for the acts of a subsidiary nevertheless presents a conceptually different problem than holding an individual shareholder liable. One useful reform of veil piercing law would be to stop thinking of the parent-subsidiary problem in veil piercing terms. Instead, this chapter argues that parent-subsidiary liability is more appropriately treated as a variant of the related doctrine of enterprise liability. Once that reform is effected, the case for preserving enterprise liability within corporate groups is far stronger than the case for preserving veil piercing.

§ 4.2 Thinking about limited liability

A. The classic case: Walkovszky v. Carlton

An example is always helpful, so we begin with one of corporate law's hoariest chestnuts—*Walkovszky v. Carlton*.[1] Plaintiff Walkovszky

---

4. See, e.g., Bartle v. Home Owners Coop., 127 N.E.2d 832, 833 (N.Y.1955).

5. See, e.g., DeWitt Truck Brokers v. W. Ray Flemming Fruit Co., 540 F.2d 681, 683 (4th Cir.1976).

6. See generally Phillip I. Blumberg, Limited Liability and Corporate Groups, J. Corp. L. 573 (1986); Christopher W. Frost, Organizational Form, Misappropriation Risk, and the Substantive Consolidation of Corporate Groups, 44 Hastings L.J. 449 (1993); Robert B. Thompson, Piercing the Veil Within Corporate Groups: Corporate Shareholders as Mere Investors, 13 Conn. J. Int'l L. 379 (1999).

§ 4.2

1. 223 N.E.2d 6 (N.Y.1966).

was a pedestrian struck by a New York City taxi cab operated by the Seon Cab Corp. In turn, Seon was one of 10 taxi cab corporations controlled by defendant-shareholder Carlton. Each corporation carried only the minimum liability insurance required by law ($10,000). Each corporation also owned two taxis, doubtless beat-up hacks worth little, but was otherwise judgment proof. Seon's assets, accordingly, were hopelessly inadequate to satisfy Walkovszky's claimed $500,000 damages. Indeed, the combined assets of all 10 cab companies probably would not have sufficed, even if Walkovszky had been able to reach them.

If Walkovszky could have held Carlton personally liable, Carlton's individual assets might well have satisfied his claim. Unfortunately for Walkovszky, Seon's corporate status meant that the limited liability doctrine insulated Carlton from personal liability for a tort committed by one of Seon's agents. In order to circumvent that obstacle, Walkovszky invoked the equitable doctrine of piercing the corporate veil.

Walkovszky first complained that none of the ten corporations had a separate identity; instead, each was part of a single enterprise through which Carlton operated the taxi cab business. The court rejected this theory. The mere fact that a corporation is part of a larger enterprise is insufficient to justify veil piercing, or so the court opined. Splitting a single business up into many different corporate components thus will not result in the controlling shareholder being held personally liable for the obligations of one of the corporate entities. At most, only the larger corporate combine, taken as a whole, could be held liable.

Alternatively, Walkovszky contended that Carlton's multiple corporate structure constituted an unlawful fraud on the public. The court rejected this theory, as well. Fraud can justify veil piercing in appropriate cases, suggested the court, but Carlton committed no fraud. There is nothing intrinsically fraudulent about deciding to incorporate or about dividing a single enterprise into multiple corporations, even when done solely to get the benefit of limited liability. Both possibilities are an unavoidable consequence of the statutory grant of limited liability to all corporations.

Although the Court of Appeals affirmed the lower court's dismissal of Walkovszky's complaint, the court did not deprive Walkovszky of all hope of reaching Carlton's personal assets. The court not only remanded the case with leave for Walkovszky to file an amended complaint, it went so far as to suggest a theory under which it believed the corporate veil could be pierced on the facts of the case—the alter ego doctrine.

According to the *Walkovszky* court, a shareholder may be held personally liable for the corporation's acts and debts on a principal-agent theory if the shareholder uses his control of the corporation to further his own, rather than the corporation's, interests. The corporation is treated as the agent of the shareholder-principal and liability is imposed on the shareholder under the familiar tort/agency law doctrine of vicarious liability. On remand, Walkovszky (not surprisingly) amended his complaint to allege that Carlton was conducting the business in his individual capacity. The amended complaint was held to state a cause of action,[2] after which the parties reportedly settled.

B.   Limited liability and the contractarian model

Walkovszky's version of the alter ego doctrine treats limited liability as an expression of agency principles. As the story goes, the corporation is the principal of its employee-agents and, accordingly, incurs contractual or tort obligations because of its agents' actions. As with any other principal, the corporation may be held vicariously liable for the actions of its agents. Because the law generally does not regard a corporation as the agent of its shareholders, however, those shareholders may not be held vicariously liable for the firm's torts or debts. Why not? The answer one usually gets is quite formalistic, treating limited liability as a corollary of the corporation's status as a separate legal person. In the eyes of the law, it is the corporation that incurs the debt or commits the tort and the corporation which must bear the responsibility for its actions. Where the shareholders treat the corporation as their "alter ego," however, the firm is treated as their agent and the shareholders may be held vicariously liable for the corporation's actions.

Walkovszky's alter ego approach is partly right, but mostly wrong. As we shall see, it introduces a number of unfortunate doctrinal complications and, indeed, errors into limited liability law. From a policy perspective, it reflects the unfortunate lingering effects of the traditional notions that the corporation is a thing capable of being owned and that the shareholders are the corporation's owners. Under *Walkovszky*, limited liability is premised on the mindlessly formalistic notion that the corporation is a real entity distinct from its owners. In turn, the imposition of personal liability through the alter ego doctrine assumes both (1) that shareholders sometimes blur the supposed distinction between themselves and the business and (2) that there is something wrong with doing so.

Thinking coherently about limited liability, as with so much else of corporate law, requires us to toss out this out-dated reification of the corporation. Recall that the nexus of contract model treats corporate law as doing little more than providing a standardized form contract. In other words, corporate law exists mainly to provide default rules that facilitate private ordering. So long as the default rules are properly chosen, most parties will be spared the need to reach a private agreement on the issue in question. Corporate law thus serves to reduce bargaining costs, just as a standard form contract does, because most people will accept the default rules without undertaking costly negotia-

2. Walkovszky v. Carlton, 287 N.Y.S.2d   (N.Y.1968).
546 (N.Y.App.Div.), aff'd, 244 N.E.2d 55

tions. At the same time, however, because the default rules can be modified by contrary agreement, idiosyncratic parties wishing different rules can be accommodated.

The correct approach to limited liability thus treats it as one of the many terms in the set of contracts making up the corporation.[3] Refusing to hold shareholders personally liable for firm debts thus is the precise equivalent of enforcing a standard form sales contract. Nothing more and nothing less.

Viewed from this contractarian perspective, the interesting questions are: (1) why would creditors agree to insulate the corporation's residual claimants from personal liability—especially given that the partnership's residual claimants are denied that benefit; and (2) what restrictions would creditors place on the limited liability term of the contract. In other words, limited liability becomes another problem to be analyzed within the hypothetical bargain methodology.

The substance of a default rule does not matter very much as long as transaction costs are low, because the parties can simply contract around the rule. When transaction costs are high, however, the default rule's substantive content begins to matter very much. If the law imposes full personal liability on shareholders, but limited liability is the efficient outcome, the parties must incur substantial and, worse yet, unnecessary bargaining costs to contractually override the legal rule. Indeed, when transaction costs are very high, bargaining around the rule becomes wholly impractical, forcing the parties to live with an inefficient rule. In such settings, we cannot depend on private contracting to achieve efficient outcomes. Instead, legal rules must function as a substitute for private bargaining. We thus perform a thought experiment: "If the shareholders and creditors could costlessly bargain over the question, would they adopt a rule of limited or unlimited personal liability?"

Although the utility of the hypothetical bargain methodology seems self-evident with respect to voluntary creditors, it may seem odd to speak of involuntary creditors agreeing to anything. Yet, remember that this is a hypothetical bargaining session. The thought experiment is to ask what the parties would have agreed to if they *could* have bargained ex ante. The claim made on behalf of the methodology is that the answer to that question is instructive, even though there will never be a real world bargaining session of its ilk.

Figure 1 presents a simplified matrix summarizing these transaction costs of bargaining over a rule like limited liability. One side of the matrix is defined by the nature of the creditor's claim. Bargain settings, such as negotiated contracts, generally entail lower transaction costs than nonbargain settings, such as tort claims.[4] The other side differentiates firms by whether they are publicly or closely held.

3. See Larry E. Ribstein, Limited Liability and Theories of the Corporation, 50 Md. L. Rev. 80, 82 (1991) ("Limited liability can be regarded as a term of the contract among shareholders and creditors. . . .").

4. In this Chapter, we use the terms "contract creditor" to encompass all classes

Figure 1. Transaction Cost Matrix

	Bargain Setting (e.g., contract creditor)	Non-bargain setting (e.g., tort creditor)
Public corporation	Ex ante bargaining prohibitively costly	Ex ante bargaining effectively impossible
Close corporation	Ex ante bargaining relatively low cost	Ex ante bargaining effectively impossible

It should be apparent that bargaining between a public corporation's shareholders and its contract creditors takes place in a prohibitively high transaction cost setting.[5] Ditto ex ante "bargaining" between any corporation (public or close) and its tort creditors. How could Walkovszky have bargained ex ante with Carlton? In contrast, however, the transaction costs of bargaining between contract creditors and shareholders of a close corporation often are low, which would permit actual bargaining, a point potentially of considerable significance in the analysis that follows.

C.   Justifying limited liability

At the risk of over-generalizing and/or over-simplifying, we can use the matrix in Figure 1 to apply the hypothetical bargain methodology to limited liability in four steps, progressing from the easiest case to justify limited liability to the hardest: contract creditors of public corporations; tort creditors of public corporations; contract creditors of close corporations; and tort creditors of close corporations.

1.   *Contract creditors of public corporations*

Admittedly, the idea that creditors would agree to limited liability seems counter-intuitive. Limited liability entails negative externalities— it allows shareholders to externalize part of the costs of their investment onto other corporate constituencies and, in a sense, to society at large.[6]

of voluntary creditors and "tort creditor" to encompass all classes of involuntary creditors.

5. Obviously, contract creditors bargain with public corporations all the time. Here is another instance, however, where reification of the corporation easily can lead one astray. When we say that a creditor bargains with a public corporation, we are really saying that agents of the creditor are bargaining with agents of the corporation. Such bargains take place in a relatively low transaction cost environment. A corporation's agents, however, lack authority to enter into contracts purporting to hold the corporation's shareholders personally liable. Hence, a creditor wishing to hold shareholders of a public corporation liable must bargain directly with the individual share-

holders. In addition to the potential for hold-out, free-rider, and other collective action problems in such settings, the sheer number of shareholders in public corporations makes such bargaining prohibitively costly.

6. Externalities are a very important concept in welfare economics. Suppose Acme built a factory that spewed toxic fumes into the air. If those fumes injured the health and property of Acme's neighbors, the damage they suffered would be an externality—a cost that Acme's actions had imposed upon its neighbors without their consent. Where one reaps the full benefits of an activity, but only internalizes part of the costs, one is likely to engage in more of the activity than is socially desirable. Assume Acme's profit from running the facto-

Yet, on closer examination, it seems clear that limited liability is the majoritarian default in this setting.

Let's begin by examining how limited liability allows shareholders to externalize risk onto creditors. Suppose a corporation borrowed $2,000 from a bank to invest. There are two available investments: A and B, each of which has three possible pay-offs: best case, worst case, and break even.[7]

Investment A

	Probability	Nominal Value	Expected Value
Best-case	10%	$3,000	$ 300
Break-even	80%	$2,000	$1,600
Worst-case	10%	$1,000	$ 100
Expected Value			$2,000

Investment B

	Probability	Nominal Value	Expected Value
Best-case	20%	$5,000	$1,000
Break-even	60%	$2,000	$1,200
Worst Case	20%	$ 0	$ 0
Expected Value			$2,200

Investment B is the more risky of the two options. Both default risk (the risk that the company won't be able to pay back its debt) and volatility risk (the likelihood of an outcome other than the break-even scenario) are much higher in Investment B.

ry is $80 per month, while the costs borne by its neighbors are $100 per month. Acme will keep operating the factory because it is making a profit, even though from a societal perspective it would be better if the factory shut down.

Externalities sometimes justify government intervention. The damage to Acme's neighbors is part of the overall social cost of running the factory. Because Acme doesn't bear that portion of the cost, however, it has no incentive to reduce the pollution the factory generates. By adopting appropriate regulations, the government can force Acme to internalize the cost of pollution, which is a fancy way of saying that the government can force Acme to take that cost into account when it makes decisions.

The mere existence of an externality does not justify legislation. In a free society, characterized by limited government and respect for private property rights, at least two conditions must be satisfied before government intervention is warranted. First, Acme's actions must in fact produce external costs. Second, there must be a market

failure; that is, people must be unable to solve the problem without government help.

7. The example is a modified version of one used in Michael P. Dooley, Fundamentals of Corporation Law 33–34 (1995), which in turn drew on William A. Klein and John C. Coffee, Jr., Business Organization and Finance 228–229 (5th ed. 1992). The example introduces the important distinction between nominal and expected value. Consider a state lottery with a pay-off of $10,000 but a 1 in 10,000 chance of winning. The nominal value of a lottery ticket is the amount the players will win if their tickets win; here $10,000. The players shouldn't count their chickens before they hatch, however, because the players only have a 1 in 10,000 chance of winning. The expected value of the lottery ticket is the probability of winning times the nominal value: $10,000 times .0001 = $1. Where a contingent event has multiple possible outcomes, we calculate the expected value associated with each outcome and then sum them to determine the expected value of the event (here an investment) as a whole.

In a world of zero transaction costs and unlimited liability—i.e., one in shareholders are personally liable for corporate debts—the bank would be indifferent as to which investment the company made. If the company fails, the bank can simply collect from the shareholder. In a world of limited liability—i.e., one in which the shareholders have no liability for the corporation's contract debts—the bank will prefer Investment A. Even in the worst case scenario, the bank will get half its money back, plus there's a 90% probability the bank will be repaid in full. The bank will not be impressed that Investment B offers a higher expected return, because the bank has no claims on the residual. Anything over $2,000 goes to the shareholders, not the bank (ignoring interest).

Conversely, shareholders will strongly prefer Investment B. Because creditors (like the bank) have a prior claim on the firm's assets and earnings, they get paid first; shareholders get the residual—whatever is left over. Shareholders thus prefer projects offering potentially high rate of returns, so there will be something left over after the creditors get paid.

The problem, of course, is that high return projects usually involve high levels of risk. The greater the risk, the more likely it becomes that the project will be unsuccessful. In that event, it becomes more likely that the firm's income will not suffice to pay the creditors, let alone leave anything over for the shareholders. Shareholders will not care about Investment B's greater risk, however, because the doctrine of limited liability means their personal assets are not at risk. Limited liability thus generates negative externalities by creating incentives for shareholders to cause the company to invest in higher risk projects than would the firm's creditors. Because shareholders do not put their personal assets at jeopardy, they effectively externalize some portion of the risk associated with such investments to creditors.[8]

It seems self-evident that shareholders would want (even insist upon) a rule of limited liability. But why? The obvious answer is that the shareholders want to protect their personal assets and limit their risk exposure. Unfortunately, the obvious answer has to be wrong.[9] If it is

---

8. Michael C. Jensen and Clifford W. Smith, Stockholder, Manager, and Creditor Interests: Applications of Agency Theory, in Recent Advances in Corporate Finance 93 (1985). To be sure, creditors could protect themselves ex ante either by negotiating contractual limitations on corporate behavior, such as restrictions on the types of projects in which the firm may invest, or by negotiated for a share of the up-side, such as through the use of convertible debt securities. The utility of such devices, however, depends on preventing ex post opportunism by the shareholders. Alternatively, creditors can force shareholders to internalize those risks by charging a higher interest rate that compensates the creditor for the higher risk of default. Indeed, the distinguishing characteristic of voluntary creditors (as opposed

to involuntary creditors) is that they can allow for the risk of default in the initial contract with the corporation. Lenders, for example, factor in the risk of default in calculating the interest rate. Thus, it matters little to the lender if an individual corporation goes bankrupt (assuming diversification of risk). While the lender will sustain a loss as a result of the transaction with the bankrupt corporation, it will recoup that loss through the interest rate it receives from other borrowers. In this way, voluntary creditors pass on the risk of default to the shareholders, even in a system of limited liability.

9. Or, at least partially wrong. Shareholder loss aversion does seem to be relevant to the analysis.

true, why is the default rule in partnerships one of unlimited personal liability?[10] Do not partners also want to protect their assets? Something more subtle must be going on.

One approach to the problem focuses on the perverse incentives unlimited liability creates for shareholders of large corporations. Most people whose entire personal estate is subject to claims arising out of the conduct of a business would want, at the bare minimum, to know how that business was being conducted and, more likely, also would want to have a proportionate voice in deciding how the business was to be conducted.[11] Because investor participation in firm decisionmaking is generally appropriate in the small firm setting, the default partnership law rule is that all partners have "equal rights in the management and conduct of the partnership business."[12] Partners thus are given an equal voice in decisions that expose them to potentially unlimited personal liability. In a firm the size of General Motors, say, with millions of shareholders, however, investor participation in firm decisionmaking would result in chaos. A regime of unlimited personal liability thus would directly conflict with the efficient centralized decisionmaking apparatus that is the hallmark of modern corporations.

In addition to the costs it would impose on the firm, a regime of unlimited personal liability would also directly raise the cost to shareholders of investing. With limited liability, shareholders are free to diversify and refrain from monitoring portfolio firms. This is desirable, because most investors are rationally apathetic. Because monitoring efforts are hardly free, but typical shareholders are engaged in a full time job unrelated to their investments, they are not going to put in the time and effort required to engage in active monitoring. Under conditions of limited liability and diversification, shareholder passivity is possible because the shareholders stand to lose only a small portion of their individual wealth in the event one of their portfolio firms goes bankrupt. Indeed, if the bankruptcy of Firm A redounds to the benefit of competitor Firm B, diversified shareholders who own stock in both

10. Under the UPA (1914), each partner is jointly and severally liable for a tort or breach of trust committed by another partner if committed within the scope of the firm's business. In addition, each partner is jointly liable for all other partnership debts and obligations. UPA (1914) § 15. The UPA (1996) rules are the same, except that partners are jointly and severally liable for both types of obligations. UPA (1996) § 306. All of these potential sources of liability are unlimited, so that every partner can be forced to pay their share of a partnership obligation to the full extent of their personal assets. The problems posed for partners by the firm's lack of limited liability are further compounded by the fact that each partner is an agent of the partnership with respect to its business and thus can enter into contracts binding the entire partnership. UPA (1914) § 9; UPA (1996) § 301. Because the partnership can be held liable for the acts of its nonpartner agents, moreover, so too can the individual partners. Contrary to the implications in the text, however, Larry Ribstein has argued that unlimited liability in partnership law "has survived because of regulation and tax law, and not because of the preferences of individual contracting parties." Robert W. Hamilton & Larry E. Ribstein, Limited Liability and the Real World, 54 Wash. & Lee. L. Rev. 687, 693 (1997).

11. Paul Halpern et al., An Economic Analysis of Limited Liability in Corporation Law, 30 U. Toronto L. Rev. 117, 125 (1980) (summarizing argument).

12. UPA (1996) § 401(f).

might even be better off. If the shareholders are personally liable for damages, however, they will want to monitor not only how the corporation conducts its business, but also the creditworthiness of their fellow investors.[13] At least as to the former, creditors likely have a comparative advantage over passive shareholders.[14]

A rule of personal liability thus would decrease shareholders' ability to invest in a diverse portfolio of investments. The greater the degree of monitoring of each investment required, the fewer investments will be made. Given the importance of diversification as a means of reducing the risk associated with investments, a regime of personal liability would have a significant adverse effect on investors.[15] In turn, that adverse effect would be felt by issuers in the form of higher costs of capital, which in turn would harm society by inhibiting economic growth.

Alternatively, but equally undesirably, a regime of unlimited personal liability might result in substantial free riding by shareholders. Free riding can occur whenever it is necessary to extract contributions from a group of individuals in order to carry out collective goals. Free riders assume that they need not contribute because others will contribute enough resources to ensure that the goal will be achieved. Thus the free riders anticipate receiving the benefits of the collective activity without having to expend any personal resources. Under a regime of unlimited personal liability, each shareholder has incentive to free ride: only a fraction of the gains expected from effective monitoring will go to the monitor, the rest of the gains will go to all shareholders—whether or not they were active monitors of the firm. We therefore would expect to see many free riders. Many shareholders will assume that other shareholders will expend resources in monitoring the corporation and will try to free ride on the efforts of those shareholders. But if there are too many free riders, there will not be an appropriate level of monitoring and losses become likely.

---

13. Again, the analogy to partnership law seems helpful. UPA (1996) § 403(b) entitles a partner to access to the firm's books and records. Section 403(c) further entitles a partner to any information concerning the partnership's business and affairs. Although there are various reasons why such broad access rights are desirable in the partnership context, the unlimited liability of partners and the consequent need to monitor the firm's business doubtless is a highly significant consideration. We are assuming joint and several liability here, however. The analysis would change if shareholders were only subject to pro rata liability (e.g., a shareholder who owned 10% of the stock could be held liable for no more than 10% of the debt).

14. Robert B. Thompson, Unpacking Limited Liability: Direct and Vicarious Liability of Corporate Participants for Torts of the Enterprise, 47 Vand. L. Rev. 1, 13 (1994).

15. In addition to discouraging diversification, a rule of unlimited liability would also reduce liquidity. Judge Posner posits that "without limited liability a shareholder would not even be allowed to sell his shares without the other shareholders' consent, since if he sold them to someone poorer than he, the risk to the other shareholders would be increased." Richard A. Posner, Economic Analysis of Law 394 (4th ed. 1992). The validity of this observation is confirmed by the default rules of partnership law, under which unanimous consent is required for admission of a new partner and a partner's ability to transfer his interest in the firm is limited to the right to assign his share of profits to an outsider. See UPA (1914) §§ 18(g), 27.

If it seems self-evident that shareholders will want limited liability, it admittedly seems less plausible that creditors would be willing to concede such protections. Yet, in the public corporation context, it would be prohibitively costly for the creditor of a corporation to bring individual suits against thousands of geographically diverse investors. At least insofar as the liability phase is concerned, a creditor perhaps could try the case as a class action with the shareholders as a defendant class, which is theoretically possible but practically difficult, but the creditor likely would still have to bring numerous individual suits to collect any judgment.

Even if a creditor were willing to shoulder that burden, moreover, various legal rules would impede its efforts to do so. First, there is a choice of law problem. Does the law of the state of incorporation govern such suits, as it does most corporate governance matters? If so, might not some states become incorporation havens by offering limited liability?[16] Second, can the forum state in which the underlying tort claim was brought constitutionally obtain personal jurisdiction over out-of-state shareholders?

In a world of personal, rather than limited liability, creditors would rely on the ability of each shareholder to repay at least some portion of the debt. Accordingly, creditors would be obliged to assess and continually monitor the creditworthiness of all shareholders. Doing so would be burdensome, if not prohibitively costly, for the creditor. Limited liability eliminates the need for doing this; the creditor only need concern itself with the creditworthiness of the debtor corporation. To the extent that the creditor is concerned about the corporation's creditworthiness it can simply raise the interest rate it charges to reflect the risk that the firm will not repay the obligation.

To be sure, joint and several liability (if applicable) might solve some of these problems for some creditors. They could simply collect from the wealthiest shareholders. Yet, it is not clear that a regime of unlimited personal liability necessarily would be one of joint and several liability. California law imposed personal liability on shareholders until as recently as 1931, but each shareholder was only liable for a pro rata share of the obligation.[17] The UPA (1914) likewise imposed joint liability on partners for many firm obligations.

While creditors might prefer joint and several liability, it is not clear the state should accommodate them. From society's perspective, personal liability merely shifts enforcement costs to the named defendant shareholders who (presumably) will seek contribution from their fellow shareholders. Hence, limited liability prevents the unfairness of allowing the

---

16. During the early 1800s Massachusetts corporations did not get the benefit of limited liability but Maine and New Hampshire corporations did. In Massachusetts a public debate over limited liability broke out during the 1820s, in which "Jacksonian liberals" contended that capital was fleeing Massachusetts for those neighboring states. Herbert Hovenkamp, Enterprise and American Law: 1836–1937 50 (1991).

17. Harold Marsh, Jr. & R. Roy Finkle, Marsh's California Corporation Law 274 (3d ed. 1990).

creditor to pick and choose among shareholders and reduces the potential enforcement costs incurred by society. A distinct social cost arises because joint and several liability would reduce (if not eliminate) the efficiency of secondary trading markets—corporate shares would no longer be fungible, because the value of specific shares under a regime of personal liability would be a function not only of business cash flows but also the wealth of the shareholder who owned them.[18]

To be sure, given that the stated goal of the hypothetical bargain methodology is determining what rule the *parties* would choose if they could bargain, it may seem incongruous to consider social costs in this analysis. Yet, just as Don Corleone was wont to make competitors an "offer they can't refuse," setting legal policy requires one to consider not only the needs of the parties to the regulated transaction, but also the totality of social costs created by a given legal regime.[19] In deciding whether to set up the majoritarian default as the governing rule, society appropriately considers the full social cost of the proposed rule. Those costs are not merely the transaction costs incurred by parties seeking to bargain around the rule, but also the costs of administering the rule (such as running a judicial system) and externalities imposed by parties acting in accord with the rule. Properly understood, contractarianism merely claims that society is generally better off when law facilitates private ordering; contractarianism does not claim that private ordering trumps all other considerations.

In sum, assuming the option of joint and several liability is denied them, one feels confident predicting that contract creditors of large corporations would be willing to accept limited liability for corporate shareholders.[20] If our hypothetical bargain took place, those creditors presumably would be willing to trade limited liability for something they valued more highly, such as the prior claim on the corporation's assets. As such, limited liability ought to be the majoritarian default.

2. *Tort creditors of public corporations*

Modern industrial enterprises can do harm on a vast scale. At the same time, the emergence of mass tort litigation means that such enterprises face unprecedented potential liability. In recent years, numerous public corporations have been hit with multi-billion dollar lawsuits, which forced some of them into bankruptcy. Claims have ranged from products liability, such as those at issue in the Dalkon Shield and breast implant litigation, to environmental, such as those portrayed in *A Civil Action*,[21] to class action discrimination suits. Yet, even though many

18. William J. Carney, Limited Liability, in III Encyclopedia of Law and Economics: The Regulation of Contracts 659, 671 (2000).

19. See Guido Calabresi, The Costs of Accidents 225–26 (1970).

20. Indeed, creditors of joint stock associations (which lacked limited liability) often entered into express nonrecourse contracts pursuant to which they agreed to look only to the firm's assets. William J. Carney, Limited Liability, in III Encyclopedia of Law and Economics: The Regulation of Contracts 659, 666 (2000).

21. Jonathan Harr, A Civil Action (1995) (describing litigation against a chemical company charged with contaminating the water table in Woburn, Ma.).

of the firms involved went through bankruptcy reorganizations, in none of these cases were their shareholders held personally liable for the firm's tortious conduct.

A number of commentators have complained that limited liability permits investors to externalize the risks of modern industrial enterprise. Professor Ronald M. Green, for example, has argued that limited liability rule is a privilege conferred by society and that, in light of the externalities created by that privilege, society is therefore entitled to demand socially responsible corporate behavior:

> In a host of industries, including pharmaceuticals, chemicals, energy, and transport, the misuse of corporate property and technologies can kill or maim hundreds or thousands of people and cause damages in the tens of billions of dollars. The record of the past two decades is littered with disasters of this magnitude: A.H. Robins and the Dalkon Shield; Union Carbide and Bhopal; Johns–Manville and asbestos; Exxon and the Valdez oil spill; and, most recently, Dow–Corning and silicone breast implants.

> . . . Thanks to limited liability, shareholders can fund the activities of large corporations, receive dividends and capital gains on their investments, and yet remain immune to some of the costs of misconduct or misjudgment by their corporate agents. . . .

> . . . The Bhopal disaster provides a good example. Senior managers at Union Carbide and at Union Carbide's Indian affiliate, Union Carbide India Limited, were apprised of the poor maintenance conditions and general disrepair of the company's Bhopal facility. It may well be that failure to correct these problems resulted only from miscommunication and the kinds of confusion that can occur in a large international organization. But Union Carbide's failure to invest heavily in the Bhopal plant can also be seen as the outcome of a chain of business reasoning predicated on the shareholder [wealth maximization] model. To begin with, the chances of an accident were relatively slight and these had to be weighed against the major outlays needed to bring the Indian facility up to United States' standards. Because the Bhopal plant had been losing money for several years and had no prospects of turning around, it would have been hard for any senior manager concerned with quarterly results to justify such costs. . . . For one thing, there was substantial likelihood from Union Carbide's perspective that liability could be confined to its Indian affiliate. Sheltered behind international legal boundaries and the rule of limited liability, Union Carbide's American and Indian shareholders might well be financially better off if managers gambled against safety. Furthermore, even if the almost unimaginable worst case scenario became reality—the two thousand deaths and thousands of injuries that actually occurred—the very low economic value of Indian lives made reduced attention to safety a reasonable gamble from Union Carbide's perspective. . . . Within the traditional model of fiduciary responsibilities these managers

would be in the difficult position of arguing that slight risks to human life and health justify incurring relatively high and unreasonable costs. [22]

Hence, Green argues, the fiduciary duties of managers should allow them to consider the impact of corporate decisions on nonshareholder constituencies. We are not concerned here with the fiduciary duties of managers, of course; instead, for our purposes, the interesting questions posed by Green's analysis are (1) whether limited liability should be seen as a privilege granted by society and (2) whether the externalities created by limited liability mandate some policy response.

Green's privilege argument is a variant of the old concession theory, pursuant to which the corporation was regarded as a quasi-state actor exercising powers delegated by the state. It has been over half-a-century since corporate legal theory, of any political or economic stripe, took the concession theory seriously.[23] In particular, concession theory is plainly inconsistent with the contractarian model of the firm, which treats corporate law as nothing more than a set of standard form contract terms provided by the state to facilitate private ordering.

The notion that the alleged privilege of limited liability amounts to a social subsidy in return for which society may demand certain forms of corporate behavior is also flawed. Limited liability is properly regarded as a subsidy only if it constitutes a wealth transfer from one segment of society to another. As Professor Herbert Hovenkamp concludes: "It is hard to make such a showing about limited liability."[24] To the contrary, society benefits in a variety of ways from limited liability. Indeed, there is a widely shared view that limited liability was, and remains, essential to attracting the enormous amount of investment capital necessary for industrial corporations to arise and flourish. "One of the great advantages of the large corporate system is that it allows individuals to use small fractions of their savings for various purposes, without risking a disastrous loss if any corporation in which they have invested becomes insolvent."[25] By allowing the public corporation to develop, limited liability thus was in large measure responsible for the development of our modern economic system.

But what about those pesky externalities? Even if Green is wrong about limited liability being a privilege, shouldn't society do something to force investors to internalize the tort risks their firms create? In a provocative article, Professors Henry Hansmann and Reinier Kraakman

---

22. Ronald M. Green, Shareholders as Stakeholders: Changing Metaphors of Corporate Governance, 50 Wash. & Lee L. Rev. 1409, 1414–15 and 1419–20 (1993).

23. William W. Bratton, Jr., The "Nexus of Contracts" Corporation: A Critical Appraisal, 74 Cornell L. Rev. 407, 433–36 (1989); Paul G. Mahoney, Contract or Concession? An Essay on the History of Corporate Law, 34 Ga. L. Rev. 873 (2000).

24. Herbert Hovenkamp, Enterprise and American Law: 1836–1937 54 (1991).

25. Henry G. Manne, Our Two Corporation Systems: Law and Economics, 53 Va. L. Rev. 259, 262 (1967). "Limited liability is probably an essential aspect of a large corporate system with widespread public participation." Id.

argued society should eliminate limited liability with respect to tort claims precisely so as to force investors to internalize those risks. Their argument is premised on the purported ability limited liability gives corporations to externalize mass tort risk: "Changes in technology, knowledge, liability rules, and procedures for mass tort litigation have for the first time raised the prospect of tort claims that exceed the net worth of even very large corporations."[26] (Query whether this is an argument for tort reform rather than for abolishing limited liability?)

One widely accepted reason for limited liability even as to tort claimants is that, just as with contract creditors, such claimants would face prohibitively high collection costs.[27] Hansmann and Kraakman purport to solve the administrative problem by proposing a rule of pro rata, rather than joint and several, liability. As we have seen, pro rata liability doubtless is preferable to joint and several, but their argument that it is also preferable to limited liability is not persuasive. They justify it by noting that bankruptcy trustees routinely collect accounts receivable from numerous debtors of bankrupt firms. Unless we assume that all tort claims will be pursued in the context of a bankruptcy proceeding, however, their proposal will require setting up a new legal infrastructure to process such claims.

As Janet Cooper Alexander has pointed out, moreover, unlimited liability for public corporation shareholders faces nearly insurmountable constitutional and procedural hurdles. As to claims arising under state law, neither state nor federal courts (sitting in diversity) could obtain personal jurisdiction over most out-of-state shareholders.[28] As a result, tort creditors would have to bring collection suits in many different forums, which would result in high costs. Many such collection suits would not be worth pursuing, because the shareholders will hold such a small share of the firm's stock—or be otherwise so judgment proof—that the costs of collecting against them will substantially erode the prospective recovery. Perhaps these concerns could be addressed by imposing unlimited liability as a matter of federal law and creating a mechanism (analogous to bankruptcy courts) for handling such suits in a single forum. Even so, as Joseph Grundfest has demonstrated, our increasingly global capital markets could undercut a regime of unlimited liability by creating a cadre of off-shore investors who would be effectively judgment

26. Henry Hansmann & Reinier Kraakman, Toward Unlimited Liability for Corporate Torts, 100 Yale L.J. 1879, 1880 (1991). Hansmann and Kraakman also note that firms have sought to evade tort liability through business reorganizations, such as putting hazardous activities in separate subsidiaries. Id. at 1881. To the extent this is a problem, however, it is better addressed through proper application of the enterprise liability remedy than through general abolition of limited liability.

27. See, e.g., David W. Leebron, Limited Liability, Tort Victims, and Creditors, 91 Colum. L. Rev. 1565, 1611 (1991).

28. Janet Cooper Alexander, Unlimited Shareholder Liability Through a Procedural Lens, 106 Harv. L. Rev. 387 (1992). Where the claim is pursued in a bankruptcy proceeding, however, the availability of nationwide service of process creates a form of nationwide jurisdiction. See Lynn LoPucki, Strategies for Creditors in Bankruptcy Proceedings § 3.03[D] (3d ed. 1997).

proof.[29]

A related source of administrative costs for both tort creditors and society-at-large arises out of the difficulty of deciding which investors are liable on particular claims. Because the liquidity of capital markets means that the composition of a given firm's shareholder pool changes constantly, under Hansmann and Kraakman's unlimited liability regime it becomes essential to define when liability attaches. If liability attaches when the injury occurs, there is no chance for shareholders to avoid liability. Such a rule may be impossible to administer, however, as claimants would have to determine who owned shares at the time of injury, even when the judgment came years later. A rule attaching liability at the time of judgment is easier to administer (although by no means easy), but would lead to mass dumping of the stock when suit was filed and every time the market got spooked by an impending judgment. Attaching liability at the time the claim is filed does not solve the problem either. Where claims are made gradually, or an event becomes public before claims are filed, shareholders still have an opportunity to evade liability. Hansmann and Kraakman propose a claims-made rule attaching liability at the earliest of either (1) when the claims are filed, (2) when corporate management becomes aware "with a high probability" that claims will be filed, or (3) when the corporation is dissolved. While this rule at least partially solves the shareholder exodus problem, it seems cumbersome (and expensive) to apply in practice. The question of when management became aware that the claim would be filed, in particular, could be a fertile ground of litigation. On the other hand, while the tort creditors represented by plaintiffs' lawyers operating on a contingent fee basis will get adequate legal representation, what mechanism is there for ensuring that small shareholders will be adequately represented with respect to litigating such issues? Many such shareholders may be forced to forego legitimate defenses for lack of funds. All of which makes an unlimited liability regime expensive to enforce and a likely drag on the liquidity of corporate equity.

Limited liability also can be justified on grounds that it increases the size of the pie out of which the tort creditors' claims may be satisfied, by encouraging equity investment in corporations. Tort creditors are dependent on corporations having a substantial equity cushion, because under current bankruptcy law tort claims are subordinate to those of secured creditors and share pro rata with general creditors. Under a rule of personal liability, however, few people would be willing to become shareholders. In such a world, large-scale businesses would be conducted by highly-leveraged firms having a very small amount of equity capital and a very large amount of secured debt. The mass tort plaintiffs with whom Hansmann and Kraakman are concerned, in particular, would have a very difficult time satisfying their claims against such a firm. By

---

29. Joseph A. Grundfest, The Limited Future of Unlimited Liability: A Capital Markets Perspective, 102 Yale L.J. 387 (1992).

encouraging equity investment, the limited liability doctrine thus actually makes it easier for all creditors to be compensated.

Hansmann and Kraakman do not deny that their proposal would raise the costs of equity investment: "Indeed, the purpose of unlimited liability is to make share prices reflect tort costs."[30] Yet, they deny that their proposal would lead investors to abandon the equity market in favor of debt or other nonequity investments because, inter alia, such behavior would be irrational. But behavioral economics is teaching us that one cannot dismiss otherwise plausible behavior patterns simply because they are inconsistent with the predictions of neoclassical economics' rational choice model. Loss aversion is the cognitive bias relevant here. Behavioral economists have demonstrated that people evaluate the utility of a decision by measuring the change effected by the decision relative to a neutral reference point. Changes framed in a way that makes things worse (losses) loom larger in the decisionmaking process than changes framed as making things better (gains) even if the expected value of the two decisions is the same. Hence, a loss averse person (as are most people) will be more perturbed by the prospect of losing $100 than pleased by that of gaining $100.[31] To be sure, loss aversion primarily affects owners of goods bought for consumption rather than investment. Yet, it seems plausible that prospective investors will tend to overstate the risks associated with equity investments under an unlimited liability regime.

One of the curious features of Hansmann and Kraakman's proposal is its limitation to shareholders. (The same might be said of veil piercing generally, of course.) Recall that the nexus of contracts model treats the corporation not as an entity but as an aggregate of various inputs linked by a web of explicit and implicit contracts. Shareholders are simply one of numerous different sets of inputs. Given that conception of the firm, why should not other corporate constituents—such as creditors, employees, or managers—be liable for the corporation's torts as well?[32] Indeed, the case for imposing liability on the managers who make decisions that lead to mass torts seems far stronger than the case for imposing liability on passive shareholders.

The fact that shareholders hold an equity stake in the corporation is no answer to that question. As we shall emphasize at several points, because shareholders are simply one of the inputs bound together by the web of voluntary agreements making up the firm, ownership is not a meaningful concept in nexus of contracts theory. Someone owns each

30. Henry Hansmann & Reinier Kraakman, Toward Unlimited Liability for Corporate Torts, 100 Yale L.J. 1879 (1991).

31. Richard H. Thaler, The Winner's Curse: Paradoxes and Anomalies of Economic Life 70–72 (1992).

32. "From the perspective of the connected contracts model, it is interesting and surprising that no one seems to have considered the possibility of applying the arguments for shareholder personal liability to other participants such as creditors, suppliers, customers, directors, officers, and employees. From that perspective, at first blush, all of these other participants might be fair game." G. Mitu Gulati et al., Connected Contracts, 47 UCLA L. Rev. 887, 930 (2000).

input, but no one owns the totality. Even if shareholders properly could be deemed to own the corporation, moreover, personal liability would not necessarily follow. In California, for example, purchase money home mortgages are effectively nonrecourse.[33] Accordingly, home owners put at risk only the money invested in their homes—as to the home owners' other assets, they effectively have a form of limited liability.[34]

Another difficulty with Hansmann and Kraakman's argument is the assumption that sound social policy mandates internalization of tort risk. In many instances, society tolerates (even encourages) actors who externalize risks. Consider automobile driving, which produces manifold tort and environmental externalities. We could eliminate those externalities by banning driving. Yet, we do not. To the contrary, we facilitate driving (and, thus, its externalities) by expending public resources on roads and the other infrastructure necessary to support an automobile-based culture. Presumptively, the benefits of driving outweigh the social costs thereof.[35] Corporations likewise generate positive as well as negative externalities. Although it is admittedly difficult to measure either with precision, there is general agreement, Hansmann and Kraakman excepted, that the social benefits of limited liability likewise exceed its costs.

Even if the consensus is wrong, moreover, it is not clear that much would be gained by eliminating limited liability. The core argument for doing so must be that shareholder monitoring of managers will reduce the risk of mass torts. Hansmann and Kraakman thus claim that the "marginal increase" in monitoring necessitated by their proposal "would not differ in kind from what shareholders already do."[36] Yet, shareholders are rationally apathetic—they do not engage in much, if any, monitoring of their corporations. The great virtue of limited liability, in fact, is that it facilitates passive investing. Accordingly, shareholders of public corporations do not have—and do not want—actual control over the corporate policies, activities, or employee practices. As such, shareholders are poorly suited to assume the risk of corporate activities. To force them to internalize such risks would either reduce their inclination to invest, and thus decrease the liquidity of the market, or simply lead to widespread free riding. Moreover, as Hansmann and Kraakman acknowledge, their proposal would reduce monitoring of agency costs on the part of corporate managers by discouraging investors from assembling control blocks of stock and thus impeding the working of the market for corporate control.

33. Grant S. Nelson & Dale A. Whitman, Real Estate Finance Law § 8.3 (3d ed.1994).

34. Another good example is that of principals in agency law, who are not personally liable for torts committed by independent contractors. In effect, the principal who employs such an agent gets a form of limited liability. Larry E. Ribstein, Limited Liability and Theories of the Corporation, 50 Md. L. Rev. 80, 128 (1991).

35. Or the political costs of banning driving are too high, which likely is also true of abolishing limited liability.

36. Henry Hansmann & Reinier Kraakman, Toward Unlimited Liability for Corporate Torts, 100 Yale L.J. 1879, 1906 (1991).

A related point was made by Michael Dooley, who observed that "many corporations—probably most, unless we are nearing Doomsday—produce goods and services that are entirely benign from a health standpoint and restrict their 'risk-taking' to the financial variety."[37] In other words, a proposal to abolish limited liability grounded on concerns over mass torts would allow the tail to wag the dog. Given that tort creditors are protected by the incentives a corporation's managers have to insure the firm even under a rule of limited liability, there seems no reason to affect such a radical change in the law.[38]

The point needs no further belaboring. Suffice it to say that, in the years since Hansmann and Kraakman's article was published, no state has repealed limited liability for mass torts or, indeed, torts of any kind. The availability of limited liability in related contexts, such as environmental clean up duties under CERCLA, likewise has been reaffirmed.[39] Indeed, states have been busily expanding the scope of limited liability through the creation of such new enterprise forms as limited liability companies and limited liability partnerships.

3. *Contract creditors of a close corporation*

When we turn to the close corporation setting, the contract creditor's incentives to consent to limited liability fall away. (As do the incentives of the state to make such creditors the proverbial offer they can't refuse.) First, it becomes significantly more likely that shareholders will cause the corporation to act in ways that in fact externalize risk onto creditors. In the public corporation context, the separation of ownership and control means that shareholders cannot cause the corporation to do anything. Decisions about risk bearing are made by managers who likely are substantially more risk averse than diversified shareholders. In contrast, in the close corporation, shareholders and managers frequently are one and the same. Shareholder-managers in fact can cause the corporation to externalize risk and have strong incentives to do so.

Second, because of the small number of shareholders typical of close corporations, the creditor faces relatively low monitoring and collection

---

37. Michael P. Dooley, Fundamentals of Corporation Law 56 (1995). Put another way, relatively few public corporations suffer tort judgments in excess of their shareholder equity. If there are few social costs associated with limited liability, why adopt a radical reform? Hansmann and Kraakman contend that under limited liability there is a strong incentive for claimants to settle for less than the corporation is worth, thus skewing the data. Yet, because most cases settle, pointing to a high settlement rate in the corporate context is speculative.

38. By virtue of their nondiversifiable investment in firm specific human capital, corporate managers are far more adversely affected by a corporate bankruptcy than are diversified shareholders. As such, managers of a public corporation have strong incentives to fully insure against tort liability. See Frank H. Easterbrook & Daniel R. Fischel, The Economic Structure of Corporate Law 52–53 (1991). Indeed, while Hansmann and Kraakman speculate that their proposal would lead to managers adopting a higher standard of care and purchasing greater insurance, they hardly can be said to have proven the point that current managerial incentives are inadequate.

39. U.S. v. Bestfoods, 524 U.S. 51 (1998).

costs. Obtaining personal jurisdiction and enforcing a judgment become far easier. The costs of adjudicating a case involving claims against both the corporation and a handful of shareholders differ but little from those of adjudicating a claim against the corporation alone.

Hence, it is hardly surprising that creditors often circumvent the corporation's limited liability by requiring that the shareholders sign a guarantee pursuant to which they put their personal assets at risk. Yet, the default rule remains one of limited liability—the parties are obliged to bargain around it. Why? After all, if we are trying to reduce transaction costs, why not give the parties the rule for which we think they would bargain?

An obvious answer is the line drawing problem. Most people might agree to do away with limited liability in the case of a one shareholder firm. But what about a corporation with 10 shareholders, or 100, or 1000? Where do you draw the line? Parties to a real bargain can draw a line that best suits their needs, but it would be very difficult for the law to try to draw a general line based on firm size. That difficulty, doubtless, explains why the rule looks to form rather than size. It seems more expeditious for the legal system to create a general default rule, which says everybody dealing with corporations must expect that limited liability is the rule, and let them plan their affairs accordingly. The limited liability rule thus creates an efficient general presumption about the allocation of risks between shareholders and creditors.

Put another way, basing the availability of limited liability on the legal form assumed by the business (partnership or corporation) rather than on, say, the size of the business is admittedly arbitrary. Yet, any attempt to base the availability of limited liability on the size of the business or number of passive shareholders would be just as arbitrary— and, hence, just as under-and over-inclusive—as the current form-based approach.

Another answer is suggested by the adage, "you made your bed, now you must lie in it." As noted, contract creditors can protect themselves by bargaining with the controlling shareholder and obtaining a modification of the default rule. To the extent contract creditors fail to do so, and accordingly fail to adequately protect their own interests, there seems little reason for the law to protect them.[40] Put another way, the creditor ought to lose because it assumed the risk of doing business with an individual who chose incorporation.

The economic rationale under-girding this approach is the "cheapest cost avoider" concept. Where some activity generates losses, society wants to reduce the size of those losses in the cheapest possible way. It makes no sense, after all, to expend $2 on precautions against a loss if doing so only reduces those losses by $1. In many situations, it thus

---

40. See U.S. v. Jon–T Chemicals, Inc., 768 F.2d 686, 693 (5th Cir.1985) ("Unless the [corporation] misrepresents its financial condition to the creditor, the creditor should be bound by its decision to deal with the [corporation]; it should not be able to complain later that the [corporation] is unsound.").

makes sense to impose liability on the cheapest cost avoider—the party who could have most cheaply taken precautions against the loss. Doing so gives that party an incentive to take precautions, while minimizing the cost of those precautions.

It would be expensive for a shareholder to figure out whether a given creditor needs a personal guarantee. By contrast, the contract creditor is able at low cost to determine whether it needs the added assurance of a personal guarantee. A contract creditor who could have prevented its loss by demanding a personal guarantee, yet failed to do so, appropriately is left without a remedy against the shareholder.

In other words, at least in this context, limited liability functions as a penalty default. As we have seen, the hypothetical bargain methodology typically focuses on the search for a majoritarian default—i.e., the rule most parties would have bargained for in the absence of transaction costs. A number of scholars, however, most notably Ian Ayres, argue that nonmajoritarian defaults sometimes may be preferable.[41] Among the alternative, nonmajoritarian defaults they identify, the most relevant for present purposes is the so-called penalty default, which is designed to impose a penalty on at least one of the parties if they fail to bargain out of the default rule, thereby giving at least the party subject to the penalty an incentive to negotiate a contractual alternative to the penalty default. The penalty, or bargain forcing default, flips the majoritarian default concept on its head—the terms imposed by bargain-forcing rules are designed to be contrary to those to which the parties likely would agree of they in fact bargained over the issue, thereby forcing them to choose affirmatively the contract provision they prefer. Penalty defaults thus are most appropriate where it is more costly for courts to determine what the parties would have wanted than for the parties to bargain ex ante. The across-the-board applicability of the penalty default concept has been called into question by recent empirical work in the behavioral economics literature, but in this context it has considerable utility.

Limited liability functions as a bargain forcing rule in this context.[42] If the creditor does not protect itself by extracting a personal guarantee from the shareholder, it is penalized by having its recovery limited to the corporation's assets. To be sure, the penalty is one-sided. One-sided penalty defaults are appropriate where the parties to the contract have

---

41. See, e.g., Ian Ayres and Robert Gertner, Filling Gaps in Incomplete Contracts: An Economic Theory of Default Rules, 99 Yale L.J. 87 (1989); Ian Ayres and Eric Talley, Solomonic Bargaining: Dividing a Legal Entitlement to Facilitate Coasean Trade, 104 Yale L.J. 1027 (1995).

42. Cf. Ian Ayres, Making a Difference: The Contractual Contributions of Easterbrook and Fischel, 59 U. Chi. L. Rev. 1391, 1398 (1992), in which Professor Ayres identifies as a penalty default the "rule which allows even voluntary creditors to pierce the veil of limited liability if the firm is undercapitalized." Unfortunately, there is no such rule. At most, there is a standard in which undercapitalization is a relevant but not dispositive factor. See § 4.3.B. In any case, Ayres' implication that limited liability is generally to be understood as a penalty default overstates the case. Only in the narrow setting of contract creditors of a close corporation are transaction costs sufficiently low, and the likelihood of actual bargaining function sufficiently great, for limited liability to have a bargain forcing effect.

asymmetrical information, however, because they force the better-informed party to disclose information. If we are correct that contract creditors possess the most relevant information, which is unavailable to the shareholders, the penalty aspects of the limited liability default appear to be efficient.

Given this analysis, of course, there is a fact pattern in which we would expect to see the corporate veil pierced when the claim sounds in contract; namely, misrepresentation cases. If the shareholder in some way deceived the creditor into believing that the corporation had adequate assets to cover its obligations and the creditor, relying on that misstatement, failed to demand a personal guarantee, the shareholder ought to end up being held liable.

Note on the purportedly special problem of trade creditors. Some scholars contend that trade creditors of a close corporation cannot protect themselves by bargaining and, accordingly, posit that the rule of limited liability should be relaxed with respect to them.[43] Their concerns are misplaced. Trade creditors concerned about limited liability should simply raise their interest rates or refuse to transact except on a cash basis. If limited liability increases the risk of default, the lender is fully compensated for that risk by the higher interest rate.[44] In any event, the transaction costs of differentiating between incorporated and unincorporated businesses may well not be worth it for trade creditors, as evidenced by the widespread use of standardized prices and terms by such creditors.[45]

4. *Tort creditors of close corporations*

We come at last to the tort creditor of the close corporation. This is the hardest case in which to justify limited liability. As for shareholder incentives, the shareholders of a close corporation frequently are actively engaged in the business on a full-time basis. Intra-firm monitoring costs will be far lower, although still nonzero. Hence, concerns that unlimited liability would deter diversification and encourage active shareholder decisionmaking are far less significant in this context.

Conversely, while in the public corporation context externalization of tort risk is simply a by-product of the corporation's business and affairs, in the close corporation setting externalizing such risks likely is the very purpose of incorporating. Let's go back to *Walkovszky*: Carlton

---

43. See, e.g., William P. Hackney and Tracey G. Benson, Shareholder Liability for Inadequate Capital, 43 U. Pitt. L. Rev. 837, 860–64 (1982).

44. The argument in the text admittedly is somewhat simplified. Creditors cannot always solve the problems created by limited liability simply by increasing the interest rate they charge because the increase in the interest rate itself alters the behavior of the other party. The borrowers' level of care itself is a function of the interest rate.

Hence, a higher interest rate might cause the borrower to take more risks (so that the project will pay a higher return so that the borrower can pay off the high interest). An increase in interest rates works, therefore, only if the risk (or variance) can be held constant.

45. Jonathan M. Landers, Another Word on Parents, Subsidiaries and Affiliates in Bankruptcy, 43 U. Chi. L. Rev. 527, 530 (1976).

could have set his business up as a sole proprietorship, but presumably opted for corporate status so as to avoid personal liability. Having done so, he further limited the business' potential liability by: (1) splitting the enterprise into multiple corporations, each of which owned only a small part of the business' assets;[46] (2) undercapitalizing the corporations at their inception, so that only minimal assets would be available to creditors; and (3) draining all income out of the corporations for the same purpose. As the dissent explained, all this doubtless was done "for the purpose of avoiding responsibility for acts which were bound to arise as a result of the operation of a large taxi fleet having cars out on the street 24 hours a day and engaged in public transportation."[47] In other words, although the taxicab is "capable of causing severe and costly injuries when not operated in the proper manner," Carlton had devised a business structure that externalized most of those risks onto the public.

Walkovszky is further instructive because it reminds us that there typically is no relationship between the parties until after the injury has occurred and, as such, the tort creditor has no ability to bargain out of the default rule. As is often the case, moreover, Carlton almost certainly was the cheapest cost avoider. Carlton could have used his control to cause the corporation to carry an adequate amount of insurance and/or to prevent the loss in the first instance by adequately monitoring his employee's behavior. Finally, given that there apparently was only one shareholder (or, at least, only one of any import) tort creditors like Walkovszky face relatively low enforcement costs.

Why then does the default rule remain one of limited liability in the tort context? Again, the line drawing problem may be the most plausible answer. As with tort claims against public corporations, moreover, it may be socially undesirable to force close corporation shareholders to internalize all tort risks generated by their firm's activities. In the first place, limited liability does not allow investors to get off scot-free. If the firm is bankrupted by a tort claim, the shareholders will lose all funds invested in the venture and, most likely, their livelihood. Reputational considerations may also provide incentives for people to pay their debts. This especially true in small close knit business communities. As such, the shareholders are not without incentives to insure and take precautions. (Recall that Carlton's severing his business into multiple firms can be dealt with through enterprise liability and thus is irrelevant to the policy debate over limited liability.) In the second place, contract creditors frequently demand that the corporation retain substantial unen-

---

46. Walkovszky v. Carlton, 223 N.E.2d 6, 7 (N.Y.1966).

47. Walkovszky v. Carlton, 223 N.E.2d 6, 11 (N.Y.1966) (Keating, J., dissenting). Put more generally, limited liability for torts in close corporations has at least two undesirable effects. First, it may encourage over-investment in hazardous activities. Because the shareholder can externalize some part of the risks associated with such activities, those activities could have a positive value for the investor even though they have negative net social costs. Second, the incentive to minimize investment in the firm so as to limit potential tort losses may induce socially undesirable under-investment.

cumbered assets. Tort creditors thus effectively free ride on the contract creditors' monitoring of the corporation.

In light of such considerations, few commentators support abolishing limited liability for close corporations even with respect to tort claims. Instead, the usual move in the academic literature goes something like this: (1) as a general matter, shareholders ought to internalize tort risk; (2) the social costs of forcing public corporation shareholders to internalize tort risk outweigh the benefits of doing so, hence limited liability is appropriate in that context; (3) in the close corporation context, however, courts ought to pierce the veil in order to force shareholders to internalize tort risk.[48]

Unfortunately, this line of argument hardly gets going before it starts bumping into some messy facts. Based on our analysis thus far one would expect to find fewer contract than tort cases and, moreover, that the rate at which courts pierce the corporate veil would be lower in contract than tort cases. Neither turns out to be true. Tort creditors of close corporations do not routinely pierce the corporate veil; to the contrary, their attempts to do so are only successful about one-third of the time.[49] In fact, veil piercing claims by contract creditors not only are more frequent than by tort creditors, but also are more likely to succeed.[50]

Although these results are exactly opposite of that theory predicts, the data nonetheless do not wholly disprove the theory. In the first instance, the data set in question consisted of reported judicial opinions in the Westlaw system through 1985, which suggests the potential for selection bias.[51] It may be that only contract creditors who correctly believe their case has an unusually high probability of success press their claims vigorously enough to result in a reported opinion. In the second, the data also reveal that courts imposed personal liability in 94% of cases involving misrepresentation, but declined to impose personal liability in 92% of the cases in which there was a specific finding that there was no misrepresentation,[52] which is consistent with the emphasis our analysis

48. "Finally, the doctrine of piercing the corporate veil allows courts to impose liability on shareholders in appropriate cases, notwithstanding the limited-liability rule.... As a practical matter, therefore, the piercing doctrine may act as a safety valve that takes some of the pressure off the limited liability rule in cases where the rule is most dubious." William L. Cary and Melvin Aron Eisenberg, Corporations: Cases and Materials 191 (7th ed. unabr. 1995). See also Frank H. Easterbrook and Daniel R. Fischel, The Economic Structure of Corporate Law 55–56 and 58–59 (1991) (opining courts ought to be more willing to pierce in cases involving close corporations and tort creditors).

49. Robert B. Thompson, Piercing the Corporate Veil: An Empirical Study, 76

Cornell L. Rev. 1036, 1058 (1991) (tort creditor success rate of 31%).

50. Id. (finding 779 contract veil piercing cases versus only 226 tort claims; contract creditor success rate of 42%).

51. Id. at 1046. An additional source of selection bias may be that settlement practices may differ in contract and tort cases, especially in light of the substantial role insurance companies play in the latter context. Robert W. Hamilton and Larry E. Ribstein, Limited Liability and the Real World, 54 Wash. & Lee. L. Rev. 687, 699 (1997) (stating Hamilton's views).

52. Robert B. Thompson, Piercing the Corporate Veil: An Empirical Study, 76 Cornell L. Rev. 1036, 1063–65 (1991).

places on the importance of misrepresentation in contract cases. At the very least, however, the data presents us with a significant problem in trying to square theory with practice.

Professor Stephen Presser looked to the history of limited liability to explain such findings, contending that limited liability was an outgrowth of populist democratic theory. The 19th century legislators who first adopted limited liability as a central feature of corporate law did so, Presser contends, to encourage small and impecunious entrepreneurs to start and grow new businesses.[53] Without the shield of limited liability, only very wealthy persons would incorporate their businesses. It seems probable that such considerations, coupled with a closely-related desire to promote capital formation and economic growth, drove (and still drive) the political support for limited liability. In contrast to the usual academic move, this leads Presser to conclude that preserving limited liability is most important with respect to close corporations. Yet, he fails to tell us how that concern ought to be balanced against the concern that limited liability allow shareholders to externalize risks, leaving that task to courts under the veil piercing doctrine.

In sum, our analysis of limited liability suggests that the veil piercing doctrine has a most difficult task. On the one hand, it must identify situations in which shareholders have externalized risk. On the other hand, as we have seen, limited liability remains the appropriate default rule. As such, the law will not oblige shareholders to internalize all risks. Accordingly, the veil piercing doctrine must not only identify externalized risks, but must also differentiate those risks shareholders ought to be forced to internalized from those that they should be allowed to externalize. In doing so, the law must take into account such considerations as compensation of victims of corporate wrongdoing, capital formation, economic growth, and perhaps even populist notions of economic democracy. Is the doctrine up to this seemingly Herculean set of tasks? In short, no. Let's see why.

§ 4.3 Veil piercing and related doctrines

Courts have given various names to the veil piercing rule set out in *Walkovszky*. Some veil pierce when the corporation is the controlling shareholder's "alter ego," others when the firm is the controlling shareholder's "corporate dummy," and still others when it is his "instrumentality." No matter which of these names the court chooses, you will not find a bright-line standard. As then-New York Court of Appeals Judge Benjamin Cardozo observed over six decades ago, veil piercing is a doctrine "enveloped in the mists of metaphor,"[1] a complaint that remains true today. Veil piercing cases are highly fact-specific.[2] Successful

---

53. Stephen B. Presser, Thwarting the Killing of the Corporation: Limited Liability, Democracy, and Economics, 87 Nw. U. L. Rev. 148 (1992).

§ 4.3

1. Berkey v. Third Ave. Ry. Co., 155 N.E. 58, 61 (N.Y.1926).

2. Courts treat veil piercing claims as pure questions of fact. Whether the trier of

veil piercing claims differ only in degree, but not in kind, from unsuccessful claims. It is therefore very hard to make sweeping generalizations in this area. What follows is thus somewhat of an exercise in futility—an attempt to impose doctrinal coherence and clarity on an area all too often characterized by ambiguity, unpredictability, and even a seeming degree of randomness. Having said that, however, we can at least identify those factors that point towards veil piercing and those that point against it.

A. Standards

Control is the common (if sometimes implicit) feature of all the concepts used to describe cases in which veil piercing is appropriate. Minority shareholders who do not actively participate in the corporation's business or management are rarely held liable on a veil piercing theory. Hence, it seems clear that control is an essential prerequisite for holding a shareholder liable.

The more difficult question is whether control, standing alone, suffices. It is at this point in the analysis that thinking about the limited liability in agency terms can lead one astray. In setting out its alter ego theory, the *Walkovszky* court embraced an agency-based approach to the problem. How does one show that the corporation was the defendant shareholder's agent? Recall that the agency relationship is defined as one in which (1) the principal consents that the agent act on the principal's behalf and subject to the principal's control and (2) the agent consents so to act. Consensual control over someone acting on your behalf thus suffices to establish an agency relationship.

Given its agency-based approach to the problem, accordingly, the *Walkovszky* court implied that Carlton faced personal liability merely upon a showing that he dominated and controlled Seon. But that cannot be right. If domination and control suffices, courts would be obliged to veil pierce far more often than they in fact do.

Here is the problem: As is true of most veil piercing cases, *Walkovszky* involved a close corporation with a single dominant shareholder. Such a shareholder's ability to elect the board of directors by definition gives him control of the corporation. In exercising that control, such a shareholder's decisions naturally are based on his own best interests. The corporation thus has no interests other than the interests of the dominant shareholder. Hence, it begs the question to describe a corporation, as the *Walkovszky* court did, as "a 'dummy' for its individual shareholders who are in reality carrying on the business in their personal capacities for purely personal rather than corporate ends."[3] The close

fact will be the judge or jury depends on whether the jurisdiction treats veil piercing as an equitable remedy. In either case, however, appellate courts generally defer to the trier of fact and reverse only for abuse of discretion. Stark v. Coker, 129 P.2d 390, 394 (Cal.1942). As the California Supreme Court acknowledged, this standard means that appellate opinions typically provide only "general rules" for guidance. Id.

3. Walkovszky v. Carlton, 223 N.E.2d 6, 8 (N.Y.1966).

corporation with a single dominant shareholder has no "corporate ends" separate from those of its owner. In apparent recognition of this fact, courts generally require plaintiff to show something more than mere control.[4]

Interpreting New York law, the Second Circuit held that the corporate veil may be pierced either "to prevent a fraud or other wrong, or where a parent [corporation] dominates and controls a subsidiary [corporation]."[5] Admittedly, this standard appears to endorse a reading of *Walkovszky* that permits veil piercing simply by a showing of control. In fact, however, even the Second Circuit requires something more than a mere showing of control. Instead, in order to show domination by the controlling shareholder, it appears that plaintiff must prove some fraud or misuse of the corporate form, typically by invoking the same sort of factors described in the next section.[6]

Courts applying the so-called instrumentality rule require plaintiffs to show: (1) control of the corporation by defendant that is so complete as to amount to total domination of finances, policy, and business practices such that the controlled corporation has no separate mind, will or existence; (2) such control is used to commit a fraud, wrong or other violation of plaintiff's rights; and (3) the control and breach of duty owed to plaintiff was a proximate cause of the injury.[7] Note that this standard clearly rejects any implication that control, standing alone, suffices.

While the instrumentality rule on its face requires something more than control and domination, courts have sometimes been rather sloppy in applying it. In *Zaist v. Olson*,[8] for example, defendant owned and controlled two corporations, East Haven and Olson, Inc. Acting for East Haven, Olson hired plaintiff to do construction work. Before full payment could be made, East Haven went bankrupt. Plaintiff sought to recover from Olson personally. Applying the instrumentality rule, the court found Olson personally liable. The majority opinion emphasized that the firms had the same office, all of the work went to benefit Olson—not East Haven, corporate formalities were ignored, and East Haven was undercapitalized and had no separate financial identity. But so what? Many of these facts seem irrelevant to the applicable standard. Who cares if the firms had the same office, after all? At most, some of these facts tend to establish that Olson controlled East Haven and, accordingly, that the first prong of the instrumentality test might be

---

4. Luis v. Orcutt Town Water Co., 22 Cal. Rptr. 389 (Cal.App.1962) ("It is not true that any wholly-owned subsidiary is necessarily the alter ego of the parent corporation."); Shafford v. Otto Sales Co., 260 P.2d 269, 277 (Cal.App.1953) ("complete stock ownership and actual one-man control will not alone be sufficient").

5. Carte Blanche Singapore Pte., Ltd. v. Diners Club Int'l, Inc., 2 F.3d 24, 26 (2d Cir.1993).

6. See, e.g., Wm. Passalacqua Builders, Inc. v. Resnick Developers South, Inc., 933 F.2d 131, 139 (2d Cir.1991).

7. See, e.g., Zaist v. Olson, 227 A.2d 552, 558 (Conn.1967); Collet v. American Nat'l Stores, Inc., 708 S.W.2d 273, 284 (Mo.Ct. App.1986).

8. 227 A.2d 552 (Conn.1967).

satisfied. Unfortunately, as one of the dissenting judges pointed out, plaintiff failed to show—and the majority did not require it to show—that the other two elements of the instrumentality standard were met: "I do not agree that the facts found by the referee support a conclusion that the control which [Olson] undoubtedly did exercise over The East Haven Homes, Inc., was used by [Olson] 'to commit fraud or wrong, to perpetrate the violation of a statutory or other positive legal duty, or a dishonest and unjust act in contravention of' the plaintiffs' legal rights."[9] To which the dissent fairly could have had added that the majority also failed to require plaintiff to show that Olson's misconduct was the proximate cause of plaintiff's injury. If the requirement that plaintiff must show something more than mere control is to have teeth, the dissent's position seems unassailable.

California and Illinois courts use a slightly different test, which requires plaintiff to meet two requirements: (1) the corporation was the controlling shareholder's alter ego; and (2) adherence to the limited liability rule would "sanction a fraud or promote injustice."[10] Under this standard, the prospect of an unsatisfied claim is not enough to meet the latter prong of the test.[11] After all, why would a plaintiff invoke the doctrine if the corporation had enough assets to satisfy the claim? If an unsatisfied claim sufficed, the veil would be pierced in every case. As in *Walkovszky*, accordingly, incorporating a business to avoid personal liability neither promotes injustice nor sanctions a fraud. Instead, there must be some element of unjust enrichment.[12] Of course, unjust enrichment itself is a pretty ambiguous standard, which further illustrates the broad discretion courts have in veil piercing cases.

A third set of courts uses a test superficially similar to, but subtly different than, the California/Illinois standard. Under Virginia law, for example, a court must find (1) undue domination and control of the corporation by the defendant and (2) that the corporation was a device or sham used to disguise wrongs, perpetuate fraud, or conceal crime.[13] Again, the mere existence of an unsatisfied claim should not suffice; nor should the mere fact of control.

The first prong of both the California/Illinois and Virginia standards resembles the *Walkovszky* standard—both initially look to whether the shareholder treated the corporation as his alter ego. Both, however, reject the notion that control, standing alone, suffices. Both add a second

---

9. Zaist v. Olson, 227 A.2d 552, 560 (Conn.1967) (House, J., dissenting). The other dissenting judge agreed that the majority's conclusion was "not warranted by the record," but dissented mainly on the grounds that contract creditors who choose to deal with a close corporation without demanding a personal guarantee from the dominant shareholder do so at their own risk. Id. at 561 (Cotter, J., dissenting).

10. Van Dorn Co. v. Future Chemical and Oil Corp., 753 F.2d 565, 570 (7th Cir.

1985); Minifie v. Rowley, 202 P. 673, 676 (Cal.1921).

11. Associated Vendors, Inc. v. Oakland Meat Co., 26 Cal. Rptr. 806, 816 (Cal.App. 1962) ("it is not sufficient to merely show that a creditor will remain unsatisfied if the corporate veil is not pierced").

12. Sea-Land Services, Inc. v. Pepper Source, 941 F.2d 519 (7th Cir.1991).

13. See, e.g., Perpetual Real Estate Services, Inc. v. Michaelson Properties, Inc., 974 F.2d 545, 548 (4th Cir.1992).

factor asking for something beyond mere control. As between the two, the Virginia standard appears to contemplate more egregious misconduct by the defendant shareholder; in particular, the Virginia standard appears to look for some element of active and intentional misconduct by the shareholder-defendant. Yet, neither seems any more useful than *Walkovszky* as an ex ante guide to planning the capital structure and operation of a newly-formed corporation. As the leading treatise on California corporate law opines of its standard, "it merely measures the rule by the length of the Chancellor's foot. The generalized phrases, 'sanction a fraud or promote injustice,' are useless in predicting the outcome of a particular case."[14]

B.   Critical factors in any veil piercing case

As is readily apparent from the nature of the tests just outlined, none provide a bright-line standard. One can identify a number of factors, however, which courts applying those tests commonly cite to justify veil piercing.

1.   *Nature of the claim*

Contract v. Tort. As we have seen, there are sound theoretical reasons for thinking that courts ought to be far less willing to pierce the corporate veil in contract cases than in tort cases. Contract creditors can protect their interests by demanding a personal guaranty from the firm's controlling shareholders. According to this view, if contract creditors fail to protect themselves, there is no reason for the law to do so.[15]

Although the contract/tort distinction makes so much sense as to seem unassailable, it has received a surprisingly mixed reception from courts. On the one hand, a substantial number of courts correctly have accepted the proposition that they ought not pierce on behalf of contract creditors in the absence of fraud or other unusual circumstances.[16] Indeed, at least one state (Texas), has even enshrined the distinction in statute.[17] On the other hand, an older but still widely cited opinion by the D.C. Circuit expressly rejected the "position of some commentators" that contract creditors should not be allowed to pierce the veil.[18] In

---

14. Harold Marsh, Jr. and R. Roy Finkle, Marsh's California Corporation Law § 16.16 at 1392. (3d ed. 1990).

15. See, e.g., Perpetual Real Estate Services, Inc. v. Michaelson Properties, Inc., 974 F.2d 545 (4th Cir.1992); Brunswick Corp. v. Waxman, 459 F.Supp. 1222 (E.D.N.Y.1978), aff'd, 599 F.2d 34 (2d Cir. 1979).

16. See, e.g., Secon Serv. System, Inc. v. St. Joseph Bank and Trust Co., 855 F.2d 406, 415–16 (7th Cir.1988); Perpetual Real Estate Services, Inc. v. Michaelson Properties, Inc., 974 F.2d 545 (4th Cir.1992); U.S. v. Jon–T Chemicals, Inc., 768 F.2d 686, 693

(5th Cir.1985); Laya v. Erin Homes, Inc., 352 S.E.2d 93, 100 (W.Va.1986).

17. Tex. Bus. Corp. Act § 2.21A(2).

18. Labadie Coal Co. v. Black, 672 F.2d 92, 100 (D.C.Cir.1982). See also Kinney Shoe Corp. v. Polan, 939 F.2d 209 (4th Cir.1991); Consumer's Co–op. v. Olsen, 419 N.W.2d 211 (Wis.1988). Recall that some legal scholars argue that courts should be more receptive to veil piercing claims brought by trade creditors and purportedly unsophisticated creditors, who are said to be unable to protect themselves through bargaining. This view has been accepted by some courts, as well. See, e.g., Consumer's

practice, moreover, as we have seen, courts in fact tend to pierce more often in contract than in tort cases.

If veil piercing is disfavored in contract cases because the complaining creditor should have protected itself through bargaining, the logic of this presumption does not hold in cases in which the shareholder caused the creditor's failure to protect itself. Hence, for example, the veil should be pierced in contract cases if the corporation or the controlling shareholder misrepresented the firm's financial condition to a prospective creditor.[19] Indeed, if it was the controlling shareholder who misled the creditor, it may be unnecessary to invoke the veil piercing doctrine. Recall that the MBCA's section on limited liability contains a proviso under which a shareholder "may become personally liable by reason of his own acts or conduct." MBCA § 6.22(b). Misleading a prospective creditor seems like just the sort of conduct this provision was intended to capture.

Note on statutory claims. We are concerned here solely with the equitable veil piercing remedy available under state law. In a growing category of cases nominally categorized as veil piercing, however, both the liability and/or the remedy arise out of some specific statute. Environmental liabilities under CERCLA, for example, have become a common source of veil piercing-like claims.[20] Although veil piercing principles are sometimes invoked in these cases, they are more properly regarded as *sui generis*. Most such statutes contain language that creates a separate basis for imposing personal liability on shareholders.

2. *The nature of the defendant*

To this point, our analysis of veil piercing has focused on cases like *Walkovszky*—i.e., those in which a creditor seeks to pierce the veil of a close corporation to hold a natural person, such as Carlton, who is the controlling shareholder, liable for the corporation's acts or debts. Our analysis will continue to focus on cases of that ilk, but it is important to note three alternative settings in which veil piercing is potentially at issue. As we shall see, none is an appropriate case in which to invoke the veil piercing remedy.

Co–op. v. Olsen, 419 N.W.2d 211 (Wis. 1988); Laya v. Erin Homes, Inc., 352 S.E.2d 93 (W.Va.1986). As we saw above, however, the trade creditor has a very simple alternative just as good as bargaining—it can raise the interest rate it charges (or refuse to transact on a basis other than cash in hand) to reflect the risks imposed on it by dealing with a corporation possessing limited liability. The presumption against veil piercing in contract cases therefore ought to extend to trade creditors.

19. Browning-Ferris Indus. Ill., Inc. v. Ter Maat, 195 F.3d 953, 959–60 (7th Cir.

1999); Perpetual Real Estate Services, Inc. v. Michaelson Properties, Inc., 974 F.2d 545, 550 (4th Cir.1992); United States v. Jon–T Chemicals, Inc., 768 F.2d 686, 693 (5th Cir.1985).

20. See George W. Dent, Jr., Limited Liability in Environmental Law, 26 Wake Forest L. Rev. 151 (1991); Harvey Gelb, CERCLA versus Corporate Limited Liability, 48 U. Kan. L. Rev. 111 (1999); Catherine Ann Hilbert, Comment, United States v. Bestfoods: Parent Corporation Liability under CERCLA, 24 Del. J. Corp. L. 919 (1999).

Passive shareholders of a close corporation. Shareholders who neither control the corporation nor are actively involved in its management are unlikely to be held liable on a veil piercing theory. Instead, it is shareholders like Carlton—the dominant controlling investor—who are most at risk. This result follows naturally from the phrasing of the relevant standards, all of which require some element of control before the veil will be pierced.

Shareholders of a public corporation. Consistent with the theoretical justification for treating close and public corporations differently for veil piercing purposes, shareholders of the latter are almost never subjected to a veil piercing claim. Indeed, about two-thirds of such suits brought against individual defendants involved corporations having three or fewer shareholders.[21] Hence, veil piercing is really an issue only for the very smallest close corporations.

Parent-subsidiary or sibling corporations. In many cases nominally characterized as veil piercing, the defendant is not an individual but rather a second corporation. Where a plaintiff seeks to hold a parent or other affiliated corporation liable for the acts of another member of a corporate group, courts generally apply the same standards applicable to individual defendants. Some scholars argue that courts should be more willing to pierce the corporate veil in the parent-subsidiary context than with respect to an individual shareholder, but there seems to be little support in the case law for that proposition.[22]

Holding a parent corporation liable for the acts of a subsidiary nevertheless presents a conceptually different problem than holding an individual shareholder liable. Among other things, the likelihood is far greater in the former context that significant risks will be externalized. One useful reform of veil piercing law would be to stop thinking of the parent-subsidiary problem in veil piercing terms. Instead, as we shall see below, parent-subsidiary liability is more appropriately treated as a variant of the related doctrine of enterprise liability.

3. *The laundry list*

At some point in most veil piercing opinions, the court will set out a long list of factors against which the facts of the case at bar are then compared. The precise content of the list varies considerably across jurisdictions, but the following example from a California decision exhaustively canvasses the factors likely to be cited as relevant to veil piercing:

A review of the cases which have discussed the problem discloses the consideration of a variety of factors which were pertinent to the trial

---

21. Robert B. Thompson, The Limits of Liability in the New Limited Liability Entities, 32 Wake Forest L. Rev. 1, 9 n.48 (1997) ("Piercing occurs only within corporate groups or in close corporations with fewer than 10 shareholders.").

22. See U.S. v. Bestfoods, 524 U.S. 51, 61–62 (1998) (citing numerous authorities for the "bedrock" proposition that parents generally are not liable for a subsidiary's acts or debts).

court's determination under the particular circumstances of each case. Among these are the following: [1] Commingling of funds and other assets, failure to segregate funds of the separate entities, and the unauthorized diversion of corporate funds or assets to other than corporate uses; [2] the treatment by an individual of the assets of the corporation as his own; [3] the failure to obtain authority to issue stock or to subscribe to or issue the same; [4] the holding out by an individual that he is personally liable for the debts of the corporation; [5] the failure to maintain minutes or adequate corporate records, and the confusion of the records of the separate entities; [6] the identical equitable ownership in the two entities; [7] the identification of the equitable owners thereof with the domination and control of the two entities; [8] identification of the directors and officers of the two entities in the responsible supervision and management; [9] sole ownership of all of the stock in a corporation by one individual or the members of a family; [10] the use of the same office or business location; [11] the employment of the same employees and/or attorney; [12] the failure to adequately capitalize a corporation; [13] the total absence of corporate assets and undercapitalization; [14] the use of a corporation as a mere shell, instrumentality or conduit for a single venture or the business of an individual or another corporation; [15] the concealment and misrepresentation of the identity of the responsible ownership, management and financial interest, or concealment of personal business activities; [16] the disregard of legal formalities and the failure to maintain arm's length relationships among related entities; [17] the use of the corporate entity to procure labor, services or merchandise for another person or entity; [18] the diversion of assets from a corporation by or to a stockholder or other person or entity, to the detriment of creditors, or the manipulation of assets and liabilities between entities so as to concentrate the assets in one and the liabilities in another; [19] the contracting with another with intent to avoid performance by use of a corporate entity as a shield against personal liability, or the use of a corporation as a subterfuge of illegal transactions; [20] and the formation and use of a corporation to transfer to it the existing liability of another person or entity.[23]

No fewer than 20 separate (albeit overlapping) factors, many of which have multiple sub-factors! Most of which, moreover, are wholly unrelated to the policy concerns presented by limited liability. Where is the concern for externalization of risk? Or the effect of the decision on capital formation? Or on populist notions of economic democracy? Worse yet, at least from a doctrinal perspective, the court fails to give any guidance as to how the factors should be weighted or balanced. It contented itself with merely observing that in all prior California cases

---

23. Associated Vendors, Inc. v. Oakland Meat Co., 26 Cal.Rptr. 806, 813–15 (Cal. App.1962) (citations omitted).

in which the veil had been pierced "several of the factors mentioned were present." How very helpful!

As an example of the laundry list in action, consider the Seventh Circuit Court of Appeals' opinion *Sea-Land Services, Inc. v. Pepper Source*:

> The first and most striking feature that emerges from our examination of the record is that these corporate defendants are, indeed, little but Marchese's playthings. [Gerald J.] Marchese is the sole shareholder of [Pepper Source], Caribe Crown, Jamar, and Salescaster. He is one of the two shareholders of Tie–Net. Except for Tie–Net, none of the corporations ever held a single corporate meeting. (At the handful of Tie–Net meetings held ..., no minutes were taken.) During his deposition, Marchese did not remember any of these corporations ever passing articles of incorporation, bylaws, or other agreements. As for physical facilities, Marchese runs all of these corporations (including Tie–Net) out of the same, single office, with the same phone line, the same expense accounts, and the like. And how he does "run" the expense accounts! When he fancies to, Marchese "borrows" substantial sums of money from these corporations—interest free, of course. The corporations also "borrow" money from each other when need be, which left at least [Pepper Source] completely out of capital when the Sea–Land bills came due. What's more, Marchese has used the bank accounts of these corporations to pay all kinds of personal expenses, including alimony and child support payments to his ex-wife, education expenses for his children, maintenance of his personal automobiles, health care for his pet—the list goes on and on. Marchese did not even have a personal bank account! (With "corporate" accounts like these, who needs one?)[24]

All of which makes for unusually entertaining reading, but so what? What should we learn to guide clients or even to litigate future cases? Perhaps the clearest lesson is that controlling shareholders should maintain some distance between their personal life and their business. Yet, are we really surprised that the single shareholder of a corporate enterprise fails to draw a sharp distinction between his personal and business life?[25]

The court's criticism of Marchese's disregard for corporate formalities seems especially puzzling. Disregard for corporate formalities typi-

---

24. Sea-Land Services, Inc. v. Pepper Source, 941 F.2d 519, 521 (7th Cir.1991). Pepper Source was the debtor corporation, having defaulted on debts owed Sea–Land. The other named entities were nominally separate corporations also controlled by Marchese. Sea–Land sought to pierce the corporate veil in order to hold Marchese liable.

25. In the court's defense, it went on to hold that Marchese's cited misconduct only established his domination and control of Pepper Source and the affiliated enterprises. Sea–Land was also obliged to show that "honoring the separate corporate existences of the defendants 'would sanction a fraud or promote injustice.'" Sea–Land Services, Inc. v. Pepper Source, 941 F.2d 519, 522 (7th Cir.1991) (quoting Van Dorn Co. v. Future Chemical and Oil Corp., 753 F.2d 565, 570 (7th Cir.1985)). In other words, the court (correctly) held that control is not enough to justify piercing the veil.

cally is said to include such significant blunders as: (a) failure to keep separate corporate books and records; (b) failure to hold periodic meetings of the board of directors and of the shareholders; (c) failure to appoint a board of directors; or (d) failure to formally issue stock to the shareholders in the form of share certificates. Although it will strike many clients as unduly picayune, the competent transactional lawyer will encourage the client to carefully comply with these seemingly technical formalities. But while a controlling shareholder's failure to observe these and similar corporate formalities is often cited with great fanfare in opinions ordering veil piercing, it fairly might be asked why this fact is considered relevant. Recall that we worry about limited liability mainly because it permits shareholders to externalize risk. If so, what on earth does Marchese's failure to hold corporate meetings have to do with anything? Setting aside the rare cases in which failure to observe corporate formalities misleads a creditor into believing it is dealing with an individual rather than a corporation, there simply is no causal link between the creditor's injury and the shareholder's misconduct. Perhaps courts believe a failure to observe the requisite corporate formalities inferentially indicates a potential disregard for creditors' interests—if you play fast and lose with formalities, maybe courts suspect that you are likely to play fast and loose with your bills, as well. But even that explanation seems tenuous, at best.[26]

Relying on the shareholder's disregard for corporate formalities as a justification for veil piercing seems especially problematic on *Sea-Land*'s facts because this was a contract case. As we have seen, contract creditors like Sea–Land generally should not get relief. As another court explained in a case focusing on the undercapitalization factor:

> When, under the circumstances, it would be reasonable for [a creditor] entering into a contract with the corporation ... to conduct an investigation of the credit of the corporation prior to entering into the contract, such party will be charged with the knowledge that a reasonable credit investigation would disclose. If such an investigation would disclose that the corporation is grossly undercapitalized, based upon the nature and the magnitude of the corporate undertaking, such party will be deemed to have assumed the risk of the gross undercapitalization and will not be permitted to pierce the corporate veil.[27]

26. In many states, a closely held corporation may be formed under a separate statute distinct from the state's general business corporation law. A notation in the corporation's articles will identify the corporation as having opted to be incorporated under the close corporation statute. Hence, such firms are known as "statutory close corporations." In general, the drafters of these statutes recognized that disregard for corporate formalities seems a trivial basis for piercing the corporate veil. Section 25 of the Model Statutory Close Corporation Supplement, for example, provides that "failure ... to observe the usual corporate formalities ... is not a ground for imposing personal liability on the shareholders for liabilities of the corporation."

27. Laya v. Erin Homes, Inc., 352 S.E.2d 93, 100 (W.Va.1986).

It is hard to see why the same logic should not apply to nonfinancial factors, such as disregard for corporate formalities.[28] Yet, the corporate formalities clearly matter. Disregard of corporate formalities does not always lead to veil piercing, but the empirical data shows that courts do pierce in two-thirds of those cases in which they explicitly state that the defendant had failed to comply with those formalities. Conversely, courts decline to pierce in over 90% of cases in which they explicitly note that the defendant complied with the corporate formalities.[29]

In sum, the laundry list approach found in many opinions seems wholly nonexplanatory. The laundry list is simply an *ex post* rationalization of a conclusion reached on grounds that are often unarticulated. Not surprisingly, the most commonly cited judicial justifications for veil piercing are mere conclusory statements, such as "domination or control," "alter ego," and the like.

4.   Is undercapitalization, standing alone, enough?

In *Walkovszky v. Carlton*, Judge Keating dissented on grounds that Carlton's corporations were undercapitalized. When forming his corporations, Carlton put into each only the minimum amount of capital required to purchase the taxis. The corporations carried the minimum amount of liability insurance permitted by statute. Carlton drained all income out of the corporations. These actions, taken together, meant that Carlton's taxi cab companies lacked sufficient assets to meet their potential personal injury liability. According to Keating's dissent, the attempt to carry on a business in corporate form without providing a sufficient financial base was an abuse of the corporate process justifying a piercing of the corporate veil:

> What I would merely hold is that a participating shareholder of a corporation vested with a public interest, organized with capital insufficient to meet liabilities which are certain to arise in the ordinary course of the corporation's business, may be held personally responsible for such liabilities. Where corporate income is not sufficient to cover the cost of insurance premiums above the statutory minimum or where initially adequate finances dwindle under the pressure of competition, bad times or extraordinary and unexpected liability, obviously the shareholder will not be held liable.[30]

As Keating's dissent implies, undercapitalization can be understood in either of two senses: (a) the funds put into the corporation at the outset

28.   To be clear, the point is not that corporate formalities are wholly irrelevant. In some cases, a failure to observe corporate formalities may be suggestive of other faults with the defendant's conduct. Evidence that the defendant failed to observe the corporate formalities might tend to buttress evidence that the shareholder never intended to use the corporation for any purpose other than to perpetuate a fraud on creditors, for example. The point here thus is simply that a single-minded emphasis on formalities tends to lead the adjudicator down the wrong path by obscuring the real issues.

29.   Robert B. Thompson, Piercing the Corporate Veil: An Empirical Study, 76 Cornell L. Rev. 1036, 1064–65 n.141 and 1067 (1991).

30.   Walkovszky v. Carlton, 223 N.E.2d 6, 13 (N.Y.1966) (Keating, J., dissenting).

were clearly insufficient to satisfy existing contractual and likely tort obligations; or (b) all profits are drained out of the firm in the form of dividends or salaries paid to the controlling shareholders, leaving it with insufficient reserves to meet its likely obligations. In some cases, such as *Walkovszky*, the firm may be undercapitalized in both senses of the word.

Keating's proposed rule sounds sensible enough at first blush, but quickly crumbles once one begins to think about operationalizing it. Suppose prospective shareholders of a close corporation come to you for advice in setting up their corporation. Consider the questions you have to answer in order to ensure that they will get the benefit of limited liability under Keating's standard. Is their corporation "vested with a public interest"? How do you decide? What liabilities are "certain" to arise in the ordinary course of their business? And how much capital/insurance is necessary to safeguard against them? What are "extraordinary and unexpected liabilities"? Would jurors, operating with the benefit of hindsight, be tempted to use the plaintiff's damages as a rough guide to the amount of necessary capital? The jurors might well look at the damage claim, compare it to the amount of capital, and if damages exceed capital, conclude the firm was undercapitalized. Keating's standard thus makes ex ante transaction planning less certain, while increasing litigation costs by introducing some inherently ambiguous considerations into the analysis.

It also seems noteworthy that there is no statutory basis for treating either form of undercapitalization as grounds for piercing the veil. In most states, the corporation statute neither requires any initial capital contribution nor mandates the maintenance of any minimum capital. In the few states with minimum capital requirements, the amounts involved are nominal—typically $1,000.

Perhaps these sort of concerns have motivated the courts' well-nigh universal refusal to treat undercapitalization, standing alone, as dispositive. To be sure, undercapitalization is one of the factor courts commonly consider, which may result in personal liability, when taken in conjunction with the factors we discussed earlier, but it is not enough standing alone to pierce the corporate veil.[31] Put another way, "some 'wrong' beyond a creditor's inability to collect" must be shown before the veil will be pierced.[32]

The case usually cited for the proposition that undercapitalization alone suffices, *Minton v. Cavaney*,[33] arguably does not in fact stand for that proposition and, in any event, probably is no longer good law even in its home jurisdiction. In *Minton*, plaintiffs' child drowned in a swim-

31. See, e.g., Browning–Ferris Indus. Ill., Inc. v. Ter Maat, 195 F.3d 953, 959–60 (7th Cir.1999); Gartner v. Snyder, 607 F.2d 582, 588 (2d Cir.1979) ("Although Enterprises was thinly capitalized, that alone is not a sufficient ground for disregarding the corporate form. We know of no New York authority that disregards corporate form solely because of inadequate capitalization.").

32. Sea–Land Services, Inc. v. Pepper Source, 941 F.2d 519, 524 (7th Cir.1991).

33. 364 P.2d 473 (Cal.1961).

ming pool operated by the Seminole Hot Springs Corporation. Plaintiffs won a judgment of $10,000 against the corporation, but could not collect because the corporation had no assets. Plaintiffs then brought a veil piercing suit against Cavaney, who was the corporation's lawyer, a shareholder, and a director. In the course of his opinion for the California Supreme Court, Chief Justice Traynor stated that a shareholder can be held liable if the firm is undercapitalized and the shareholder was actively involved in the business. At first blush, *Minton* thus appears to be consistent with Judge Keating's Walkovszky dissent. Both purport to regard undercapitalization standing alone as sufficient to pierce the corporate veil. On closer examination, however, *Minton* proves more complicated than Traynor acknowledged.

Cavaney admittedly served in various corporate capacities, but only temporarily and as an accommodation to his client. Cavaney was to receive one of three shares but no shares were ever issued. Indeed, the state commissioner of corporations refused to allow the corporation to issue stock. The corporation never had any substantial assets and "never functioned as a corporation." Arguably, the pool business never was a proper corporation at all. If so, Cavaney was the co-owner of a business for profit—in other words, a partnership. Under partnership law, Cavaney would be fully and personally liable for firm obligations. Hence, the real issue in *Minton* is not whether the business was undercapitalized but rather what legal form the business took.

In any event, *Minton*'s importance is often over-stated. Justice Traynor was an activist judge who viewed the tort system primarily as a compensation scheme.[34] *Minton*, arguably, is just another example of his pro-plaintiff stance. If so, it can be dismissed as a sport. Tellingly, subsequent California cases have not followed *Minton*. Instead, they follow the mainstream in treating undercapitalization as merely a relevant, but not dispositive, factor.[35] At least one subsequent California decision thus squarely refused to hold "that, per se, inadequate capitalization renders the shareholders ... liable for the obligations of the corporation."[36]

5. *The take-home lesson: Operationalizing veil piercing*

Those who like tidy doctrines that admit of easy application will not care for veil piercing law. Judicial opinions in this area tend to open with vague generalities and close with conclusory statements, with little or no concrete analysis in between. There simply are no bright-line rules for deciding when courts will pierce the corporate veil. This makes life hard for litigators, of course, but who really cares? What matters is that it also makes life hard on those of us who work as transactional lawyers. Our job is to keep our client out of court in the first place. In this context,

---

34. See G. Edward White, Tort Law in America: An Intellectual History 181 (1980).

35. See, e.g., Arnold v. Browne, 103 Cal. Rptr. 775, 783 (Cal.App.1972).

36. Harris v. Curtis, 87 Cal.Rptr. 614, 617 (Cal.App.1970).

that means our job is to help our clients set up their business so as to insure that they will get the benefit of limited liability.

Once again, let's use *Walkovszky v. Carlton* as our model. Suppose you were Carlton's lawyer. Carlton comes by your office and asks, "how do I avoid losing these cases in the future?" What do you tell him? Telling him not to use the corporation as his alter ego, dummy or instrumentality will not be very helpful, even though those are the precise things the court said he should avoid. You need to operationalize those vague standards.

Assuming Carlton wants to stay in charge, you can't do much about the control-based aspects of the relevant standards. Instead, it is the second prong of those standards that give you some flexibility. Yet, those standards don't provide much in the way of guidance either. Telling Carlton to avoid disguising wrongs, perpetuating frauds, or concealing crimes isn't going to get you very far.

Here then is where the laundry list of factors comes into play. From a transactional planning perspective, you want to set up the business so as few of the relevant factors are present. Hence, using the *Associated Vendors* list as a template, one might advise Carlton as follows: Do not commingle personal and corporate funds. Issue stock certificates. Adopt and comply with articles of incorporation and bylaws. Appoint a board of directors. Hold regular board and shareholder meetings. Keep minutes of those meetings. Keep corporate financial books and records, which are kept separate from personal effects. Comply with any statutory capital and/or insurance requirements. Take funds out of the corporation in the form of salary and/or dividends paid on a regular basis, being careful not to draw funds out haphazardly or as needed for personal matters.

None of these precautionary actions have very much to do with the real policy concerns at issue in this area. Which of them, if any, would make Walkovszky feel better about his uncompensated injuries? Which of them would help sort out risks that ought to be internalized from those that appropriately may be externalized? Which of them promote capital formation? Which of them promote populist notions of economic democracy? None. Yet, if Carlton had taken such precautions, on what principled basis could the court have pierced the veil under the relevant standards? None.

C. What law applies?

In contrast to most other areas of corporate law, in which Delaware law is well-developed and highly prominent, Delaware's veil piercing doctrine is comparatively underdeveloped.[37] Presumably this is because Delaware's dominance is largely a public corporation phenomenon, while

---

37. David L Cohen, Theories of the Corporation and the Limited Liability Company: How Should Courts and Legislatures Articulate Rules for Piercing the Veil, Fiduciary Responsibility and Securities Regulation for the Limited Liability Company?, 51 Okla. L. Rev. 427, 480 (1998).

veil piercing is a close corporation phenomenon. In any case, the question of what law applies takes on greater prominence in this context than in most others with which we are concerned.

New York law is instructive on this score, not least because that state seems to generate more veil piercing cases than any other. New York relies on a choice of law rule known as the paramount interest test, under which "the law of the jurisdiction having the greatest interest in the litigation will be applied and ... the facts or contacts which obtain significance are those which relate to the purpose of the particular law in conflict."[38] A number of federal decisions applying the New York standard have held that the state of incorporation (of the corporation whose veil is to be pierced) has the paramount interest with respect to veil piercing claims and, accordingly, applied that state's law.[39] The state of incorporation's interest derives from the fact that it is that state whose law confers limited liability on the enterprise in the first place.[40]

Surprisingly, Delaware courts do not always apply the law of the state of incorporation. Where a Delaware parent corporation is to be held liable for the acts of a non-Delaware subsidiary (i.e., the subsidiary's corporate veil is to be pierced), Delaware courts have applied Delaware law.[41] On the other hand, where it is a Delaware corporation whose veil is to be pierced, Delaware courts do apply their state's law.[42] Maybe the Delaware rule is just to apply Delaware law!

D. Related doctrines

1. Reverse veil piercing

Reverse piercing of the corporate veil is a rare and controversial variant of the basic doctrine. If invoked, it permits a shareholder to disregard the corporation's separate identity, just as "forward" veil piercing permits a creditor to do so. Suppose, for example, that Frank Farmer is the controlling shareholder of Family Farms, Inc. In addition to 800 acres of prime Minnesota farmland, Family Farms owns a farmhouse that Frank uses as his personal residence. All of Family Farms' profits are paid out to Frank as salary or dividends. Although separate corporate books are maintained and both director and share-

---

38. Intercontinental Planning, Ltd. v. Daystrom, 248 N.E.2d 576, 582 (N.Y.1969) (internal quotation marks omitted).

39. See, e.g., Fletcher v. Atex, Inc., 68 F.3d 1451, 1456 (2d Cir.1995); Soviet Pan Am Travel Effort v. Travel Committee, Inc., 756 F.Supp. 126, 131 (S.D.N.Y.1991). An interesting wrinkle on the choice of law problem is presented when the veil piercing claim arises under a federal statute. In U.S. v. Bestfoods, 524 U.S. 51 (1998), the Supreme Court noted the "significant disagreement among courts and commentators over whether, in enforcing CERCLA's indirect liability, courts should borrow state law, or instead apply a federal common law of veil piercing." Id. at 63 n.9. Unfortunately for those who like doctrinal closure, the court declined to resolve that disagreement. Id.

40. Soviet Pan Am Travel Effort v. Travel Committee, Inc., 756 F.Supp. 126, 131 (S.D.N.Y.1991).

41. Japan Petroleum Co. (Nigeria) Ltd. v. Ashland Oil, Inc., 456 F.Supp. 831, 840 n. 17 (D.Del.1978).

42. Mobil Oil Corp. v. Linear Films, Inc., 718 F.Supp. 260, 267 (D.Del.1989).

holder meetings are held, other corporate formalities are ignored. Two years ago Family Farms borrowed $1 million from the First National Bank of St. Paul, giving the bank a mortgage on the land and farmhouse. Family Farms defaulted on the loan last month. First National is now seeking to foreclose on the farm and the house. Under Minnesota's Farm Homestead Act, up to 80 acres of farmland owned by an individual is exempt from foreclosure. The Act does not preclude foreclosure on corporate-owned property. Frank seeks reverse veil piercing, so that the farmhouse and 80 acres of land will be deemed his personal assets and thus a homestead exempt from foreclosure. On facts very much like these, Minnesota courts have allowed reverse veil piercing. They concluded that the farm corporation was the farmer's alter ego and that allowing reverse veil piercing would work no injustice against the farm's creditors.[43]

A shareholder seeking reverse veil piercing must make the same sort of factual showing required of creditors in a forward veil piercing case. In other words, one way of determining whether a court should allow reverse veil piercing in the preceding hypothetical is to flip the situation around, asking: If First National had sought to hold Frank personally liable on the mortgage, would a court permit forward veil piercing on the facts of this case? On the one hand, a number of our laundry list of factors are present: (1) use of corporate assets for personal purposes (the farmhouse); (2) draining of funds; and (3) disregard of some corporate formalities. On the other hand, a strong argument could be made against forward veil piercing in this case, because First National's claim sounds in contract.

The precedents are roughly evenly divided between those that accept reverse veil piercing and those that reject the doctrine.[44] Quite frankly, however, the doctrine should be firmly rejected. Conventional veil piercing is a seriously flawed doctrine for all the reasons developed in this chapter, but reverse veil piercing is even worse. All too often, reverse veil piercing is imposed to effect the judge's personal policy preferences with respect to sympathetic plaintiffs. Indeed, predicting how any given court will come out in a particular case probably depends more on understanding the policy issues at stake than applying some formulaic standard. In *State Bank v. Euerle Farms, Inc.*,[45] which accepted the doctrine, the court emphasized Minnesota's strong policy of protecting family farm homesteads from foreclosure. In contrast, *Kiehl v. Action Manufacturing*

---

43. See, e.g., Cargill, Inc. v. Hedge, 375 N.W.2d 477 (Minn.1985); State Bank v. Euerle Farms, Inc., 441 N.W.2d 121 (Minn. App.1989); see generally Gregory S. Crespi, The Reverse Pierce Doctrine: Applying Appropriate Standards, 16 J. Corp. L. 33 (1990); Michael J. Gaertner, Note, Reverse Piercing the Corporate Veil: Should Corporation Owners Have it Both Ways?, 30 Wm. and Mary L. Rev. 667 (1989).

44. Compare, e.g., Hogan v. Mayor & Aldermen of Savannah, 320 S.E.2d 555 (Ga. App.1984) (rejecting reverse veil piercing) and Kiehl v. Action Manufacturing Co., 535 A.2d 571 (Pa.1987) (same) with Crum v. Krol, 425 N.E.2d 1081 (Ill.App.1981) (accepting doctrine) and State Bank v. Euerle Farms, Inc., 441 N.W.2d 121 (Minn.Ct.App. 1989) (same).

45. 441 N.W.2d 121 (Minn.Ct.App. 1989).

Co.,[46] which rejected the doctrine, involved a shareholder seeking to avoid obligations under the state's Workmen's Compensation Act. Similarly, in *Aladdin Oil Corp. v. Perluss*, the shareholders sought to ignore the corporation's existence so as to evade paying state unemployment insurance taxes. In rejecting that effort, the court opined:

> Parties who determine to avail themselves of the right to do business by means of the establishment of a corporate entity must assume the burdens thereof as well as the privileges. The alter ego doctrine is applied to avoid inequitable results not to eliminate the consequences of corporate operations.[47]

Determining the direction in which relevant policy considerations cut, accordingly, serves as a useful basis for predicting the outcome.

One court's view of appropriate social policy, of course, may differ radically from that of another. Consider, for example, the contrast between *Wodogaza v. H & R Terminals, Inc.,*[48] and *Woodson v. Rowland.*[49] Both cases involved suits arising out of workplace accidents and, accordingly, put in issue the state's worker's compensation statute. In *Wodogaza,* plaintiff was employed by a trucking company. He was injured while working at a site owned by one of the company's subsidiaries and operating a forklift owned by a second subsidiary. The defendant corporations invoked reverse veil piercing in hopes of being treated as a single entity. Because the state worker's compensation statute provides the exclusive remedy in cases brought by an injured employee against his employer, plaintiff would not be allowed to sue the subsidiaries in tort if they were treated as part of single entity by which he was employed. The court declined to invoke reverse veil piercing. In contrast, *Woodson* involved a wrongful death suit brought against both the deceased worker's corporate employer and its sole shareholder. Again, defendant invoked the reverse veil piercing doctrine so that the shareholder would be treated as an employer for purposes of the state worker's compensation statute. Holding that to refuse reverse veil piercing would effectively negate the exclusivity provisions of that statute, because the shareholder would otherwise be vulnerable to a tort action, the court deemed the corporation to be the shareholder's alter ego.

So-called "outsider reverse piercing" presents yet another wrinkle on limited liability. In this situation, a personal creditor of the shareholder seeks to disregard the corporation's separate legal existence. Unlike regular veil piercing, in which a creditor of the corporation is trying to reach the personal assets of a shareholder, in this situation a creditor of the shareholder wants to reach the assets of the corporation in order to satisfy the creditor's claims against the shareholder. A few courts have recognized such a cause of action.[50]

---

46. 535 A.2d 571 (Pa.1987).

47. Aladdin Oil Corp. v. Perluss, 41 Cal. Rptr. 239, 246 (Cal.App.1964).

48. 411 N.W.2d 848 (Mich.App.1987).

49. 373 S.E.2d 674 (N.C.App.1988).

50. See, e.g., C.F. Trust, Inc. v. First Flight Ltd. Partnership, 111 F.Supp.2d 734 (E.D.Va.2000).

The problem presented by outsider reverse veil piercing is reminiscent of the issues raised by the old "jingle rule" of partnership law. Section 40 of the UPA (1914) provides that personal creditors of a partner have priority with respect to the partner's personal assets and creditors of the partnership have priority with respect to partnership assets. The "jingle rule," however, has been superseded for all practical purposes by Section 723 of the federal Bankruptcy Code. That section provides that the firm's creditors will be paid out of firm assets and then have equal rights to participate with personal creditors in dividing up personal assets. The rationale for this change seems to have been that prospective creditors of the partnership rely on the creditworthiness of the individual partners in making lending and contracting decisions. In response to he federal law, UPA (1996) § 807 de facto repealed the jingle rule.

To the extent that outsider reverse veil piercing effectively gives priority to personal creditors in the corporate setting, it likewise seems problematic, albeit for slightly different reasons. As with the jingle rule question, the issue is whose creditors shall have priority with respect to which assets? Outsider reverse veil piercing effectively bypasses the usual method of collecting a judgment against a corporate shareholder, in which the creditor attaches the debtor's shares in the corporation and not assets of the corporation.[51] Unsecured creditors who relied on firm assets in lending to the corporation are thus disadvantaged. Similarly, if there are other shareholders, their interests are adversely affected if the corporation's assets can be directly attached by the personal creditor of one shareholder.[52]

2. *Enterprise liability*

In *Walkovszky v. Carlton*, plaintiff Walkovszky complained that Seon and its sister corporations had no separate existence, but rather were components of Carlton's single business enterprise. Recall that the court rejected this theory, holding that the corporate veil may not pierced simply because the defendant corporation is part of a larger enterprise. The mere fact that a corporation is part of a larger enterprise is insufficient to justify veil piercing. Splitting a single business up into many different corporate components thus will not result in the control-

---

51. In partnership law, UPA (1996) does not allow a personal creditor of a partner direct access to partnership assets. Section 502 limits the partner's "transferable interest" in the firm to "the partner's share of the profits and losses of the partnership and the partner's right to receive distributions." Section 504 then allows a "judgment creditor" of a partner to "charge the transferable interest of the judgment debtor to satisfy the judgment." In effect, the creditor thus gets a lien on the partner's interest. Although a creditor who has foreclosed on that lien may seek judicial dissolution of the partnership, a court will only grant dissolution if "it is equitable to wind up the partnership business." UPA (1996) § 801(6). Corporate law does not contain comparable provisions, but essentially the same result obtains through application of the standard judgment collection rules. Courts that accept outsider reverse veil piercing, however, disrupt this scheme by allowing personal creditors of a shareholder direct access to corporate assets.

52. See Cascade Energy and Metals Corp. v. Banks, 896 F.2d 1557, 1577 (10th Cir.1990) (rejecting reverse veil piercing on these grounds).

ling shareholder being held personally liable for the obligations of one of the corporate entities. At most, only the larger corporate combine as a whole could be held liable.

The distinction between veil piercing and enterprise liability is subtle, especially when one is dealing solely with corporate groups rather than individual shareholders. Properly understood, veil piercing is a vertical form of liability—it provides a mechanism for holding a shareholder personally liable for the corporation's obligations. Enterprise liability provides a horizontal form of liability—it offers a vehicle for holding the entire business enterprise liable.

While the single business enterprise theory thus will not allow one to reach a shareholder's personal assets, enterprise liability can be a useful remedy in some settings. If correctly (and successfully) invoked, enterprise liability does permit a creditor to reach the collective assets of all of the corporations making up the enterprise. Suppose, for example, that one of Carlton's other corporations was better capitalized than Seon, having sufficient assets to satisfy Walkovszky's claim. Enterprise liability would allow Walkovszky to reach the assets of that other corporation. In fact, an enterprise liability theory would permit plaintiff to recover from all ten of Carlton's corporations, although—I again stress—not from Carlton individually. Obviously, this theory is most useful when the responsible corporation is insolvent, but the enterprise as a whole has sufficient assets to satisfy the creditor's claim.

Gartner v. Snyder is a useful real world example of enterprise liability in action. A real estate developer used three corporate entities to develop a housing project in New York. The three corporations acted as one: all documents were kept in a single file; all financial records were kept in a single account book; letters purportedly being sent on behalf of one entity were typed on another's letterhead; offices were shared; no separate corporate formalities were observed. On these facts, the Second Circuit opined that enterprise liability would be appropriate, but that the controlling shareholder could not be held personally liable.[53]

A California appellate court similarly imposed enterprise liability in *Pan Pacific Sash & Door Co. v. Greendale Park, Inc.*,[54] in which the promoters of a real estate venture split the business into two corporations: one that owned the land and one that was to provide construction services. The land corporation had all the assets, while the construction company incurred all the debts. Plaintiff was a supplier who sold building materials to the construction corporation. When the debt was not paid, he attempted to reach the assets of the land corporation. The court allowed plaintiff to do so, holding that the land corporation was the alter ego of the construction company. Hence, the court used a *Walkovsz-*

---

53. Gartner v. Snyder, 607 F.2d 582, 588 (2d Cir.1979) (dictum). Hence, if plaintiff Walkovszky had wished to invoke enterprise liability, he would have been obliged to show that Carlton did not respect the separate identities of the corporations, as,

for example, in the assignment of drivers, in the use of bank accounts, in the ordering of supplies, etc.

54. 333 P.2d 802 (Cal.App.1958).

ky-like alter ego doctrine to achieve an enterprise liability result. Among the grounds cited for imposing liability in this case were: (1) both corporations were half of a single venture; (2) they had the same shareholders, directors, and officers; (3) they occupied the same premises; (4) they had common employees; and (5) neither was adequately capitalized.

Under *Pan Pacific*, the basic standard for invoking enterprise liability requires a two-pronged showing: (1) such a high degree of unity of interest between the two entities that their separate existence had de facto ceased and (2) that treating the two entities as separate would promote injustice.[55] The observant reader will note substantial overlap between the factors considered in enterprise liability cases, such as *Gartner* and *Pan Pacific*, and the veil piercing cases. Indeed, while the remedies are conceptually distinct, in practice the line between them tends to blur. In many cases, much the same set of facts could be invoked to justify either or both remedies. Yet, comparing cases like *Pan Pacific* to, say, *Walkovszky* is like comparing apples to oranges. As we shall see, one useful reform in this area would be to more clearly distinguish the two remedies. Veil piercing ought to be limited to holding natural persons liable for the debts and obligations of the corporations of which they are shareholders. Enterprise liability ought to be invoked whenever one is attempting to hold an entire corporate group liable, whether one is nominally dealing with affiliated corporations or a parent and subsidiary. The current practice of trying to use the same doctrine— i.e., veil piercing—to deal both with the liability of natural persons (such as that of Carlton in *Walkovszky*) and that of parent corporations for the acts of their subsidiaries has been the source of much doctrinal and theoretical confusion.

As to the first prong of the *Pan Pacific* test, common ownership is an important—if not essential—consideration.[56] Yet, at the same time, common ownership, standing alone, is not enough. In *Macrodyne Indus., Inc. v. State Board of Equalization*, the court held that (albeit for tax purposes) a parent corporation's ownership all of the stock of the subsidiary corporation did not "establish the identity of the corporations."[57] Neither did the fact that the two had common management and direction. As long as the two behaved "as separate entities," the court would treat them as such. Because the principals had respected the separate corporate existence of the two entities and they had independent business purposes, the court treated the two as separate entities.

Merely showing control, moreover, in the absence of an intent to defraud or promote injustice, is insufficient to overcome the presumption in favor of respecting the separate corporate existence of the various

---

55. See Las Palmas Assoc. v. Las Palmas Center Assoc., 235 Cal.App.3d 1220, 1250 (1991) (adopting *Pan Pacific* standard in an explicitly enterprise liability theory case).

56. See, e.g., Associated Vendors, Inc. v. Oakland Meat Co., 210 Cal. App.2d 825, 839 (1962).

57. Macrodyne Indus., Inc. v. State Board of Equalization, 192 Cal. App.3d 579, 581 (1987).

enterprises. As we have seen, there must be some injustice that would result from respecting the separate corporate existence of the various entities. What sorts of misconduct would or would not meet that standard? The prospect of an unsatisfied claim is not enough to meet the latter prong of the test.[58] After all, why would a plaintiff invoke the doctrine if the corporation had enough assets to satisfy the claim?

Conversely, at least by negative implication, where the assets of the corporation whose alleged misconduct purportedly was the proximate cause of plaintiff's injury suffice to satisfy the plaintiff's claims, the court should not disregard the separate existence of any affiliated corporations.[59] If the court will not treat the affiliated corporations as a single business enterprise (or pierce the corporate veil, for that matter) to ensure that a tort or contract creditor's claims will be satisfied, the court certainly should not do so where those claims can be satisfied out of the assets of the principal defendant.

The mere fact that one divided one's business activities into multiple corporations likewise fails to satisfy the second prong. As the New York court held in *Walkovszky*, incorporating a business to avoid personal liability neither promotes injustice nor sanctions a fraud. Walkovszky contended that Carlton's multiple corporate structure constituted an unlawful fraud on the public. The court rejected this theory. There is nothing intrinsically fraudulent about deciding to incorporate or about dividing a single enterprise into multiple corporations, even when done solely to get the benefit of limited liability. Both possibilities are an unavoidable consequence of the statutory grant of limited liability to all corporations. As a California court observed: "It is well recognized that the law permits the incorporation of businesses for the very purpose of isolating liabilities among several entities."[60] Instead, presumably, there must be some element of unjust enrichment.[61]

§ 4.4   Rethinking veil piercing

If our review of veil piercing law teaches anything, it is that Judge Cardozo understated the case when he described it as an enigmatic doctrine caught "in the mists of metaphor."[1] It is aptly said that corporate law's main goals ought to be certainty and predictability.[2]

---

58. Cf. Associated Vendors, Inc. v. Oakland Meat Co., 210 Cal.App.2d 825, 842 (1962) ("it is not sufficient to merely show that a creditor will remain unsatisfied if the corporate veil is not pierced").

59. In California, plaintiffs frequently invoke enterprise liability where the principal defendant is solvent so as to expand the size of the enterprise so as to support a larger punitive damage claim. In Walker v. Signal Cos., Inc., 84 Cal.App.3d 982 (1978), the court held that: "the sole basis for holding [the parent] liable would be to enable the plaintiffs to obtain an increased award of punitive damages because of the substantial net worth of the parent. There

is no factual justification to do so." Id. at 1001.

60. Pacific Landmark Hotel, Ltd. v. Marriott Hotels, Inc., 19 Cal.App.4th 615, 628 (1993).

61. Cf. Sea–Land Services, Inc. v. Pepper Source, 941 F.2d 519 (7th Cir.1991) (Illinois law).

§ 4.4

1. Berkey v. Third Ave. Ry. Co., 155 N.E. 58, 61 (N.Y.1926).

2. See, e.g., Harff v. Kerkorian, 324 A.2d 215 (Del.Ch.1974) ("It is obviously important that the Delaware corporate law have stability and predictability.").

Uncertainty about the contours and content of a legal rule imposes substantial costs. When litigation risks cannot be confidently predicted, parties can be deterred from engaging in socially desirable activities or, at the least, will take excessive (and costly) precautions.[3]

Veil piercing abjectly fails this test. The doctrine's vague standards, such as "sanction fraud or promote injustice," give judges little guidance but wide discretion.[4] As a result, judges frequently seem to be concerned more with the equities of the specific case at bar than with the implications of personal shareholder liability for society at large. If we may mix anatomical metaphors, this likely is why the "Chancellor's foot" rears its ugly head so often. The present state of veil piercing doctrine allows judges to impose their own brand of rough justice without being overly concerned with precedent or appellate review.

This assessment of the state of the veil piercing doctrine is consistent with the widespread use of conclusory announcements of result. Courts likely have a vague intuitive sense of what constitutes a fair outcome, but which they cannot easily articulate. Instead of reasoned analysis, courts typically fall back on vague labels such as "alter ego" or "lack of separation," which has been variously characterized as analysis by epithet and reasoning by pejorative.[5]

If the point needs further elaboration, consider the absurd internal inconsistency in *DeWitt Truck Brokers, Inc. v. W. Ray Fleming Fruit Co.*[6] The opinion opens with the observation that courts pierce the veil "reluctantly" and "cautiously." Two pages later, however, we learn that courts "have experienced 'little difficulty' and have shown no hesitancy" in piercing the veil of close corporations. Which is it? The answer matters a lot to transaction planners, but the court leaves uncertain whether veil piercing is supposed to be the norm or the exception.

All of this, obviously, is inconsistent with the goals of certainty and predictability. At the same time, however, it may be doubted whether veil piercing contributes much to any plausible conception of either efficiency or equity. Yes, limited liability allows shareholders to externalize certain risks. Yet, veil piercing cannot be shown to cause investors to internalize risks appropriately. To the contrary, veil piercing "seems to happen freakishly. Like lightning, it is rare, severe, and unprincipled."[7] Finally, because the veil piercing remedy is limited to shareholders, it is inconsistent with the contractarian model of the firm. As we have seen,

3. See generally John Calfee & Richard Craswell, Some Effects of Uncertainty on Compliance with Legal Standards, 70 Va. L. Rev. 965 (1984).

4. "A trial court's ruling on such questions will be regarded as presumptively correct and will not be overturned on appeal unless clearly erroneous." Cheatle v. Rudd's Swimming Pool Supply Co., Inc., 360 S.E.2d 828, 831 (Va.1987).

5. Phillip I. Blumberg, The Law of Corporate Groups: Procedural Law 8 (1983) ("metaphor or epithet"); Franklin A. Gevurtz, Piercing Piercing: An Attempt to Lift the Veil of Confusion Surrounding the Doctrine of Piercing the Corporate Veil, 76 Or. L. Rev. 853, 855 (1997) ("pejorative").

6. 540 F.2d 681 (4th Cir.1976).

7. Frank H. Easterbrook and Daniel R. Fischel, Limited Liability and the Corporation, 52 U. Chi. L. Rev. 89 (1985).

when shareholders are regarded as simply one constituency within the web of contracts making up the firm, there is no theoretical justification for holding them personally liable while bestowing *de facto* limited liability on all other corporate constituencies.

What then ought we to make of this area of law? In short, the case for limited liability seems unassailable. To be sure, a few commentators have argued against limited liability. Yet, this is hardly surprising. Academics are rewarded for developing novel ideas, without much regard to those ideas' validity or viability as law reform. The question is who gets to define the null hypothesis. As least in this instance, the status quo deserves to be the null hypothesis. Limited liability has been known in American law since the eighteenth century and has been common since at least the middle of the nineteenth. It has antecedents stretching back at least to Roman law.[8] Because the individual is foolish but the species is wise, we tamper with such long-standing conventions at our peril. If nothing else, the law of unintended consequences must be given its due. The prudent legislator is hesitant to promulgate reforms that may give rise to new and unforeseen abuses worse than the evil to be cured.

On the other hand, reasoned change is essential if society is to progress. While limited liability seems to have stood the test of time, the same cannot be said of veil piercing. Hence, our analysis of these doctrines ends with an admittedly radical proposal; namely, to abolish the doctrine of piercing the corporate veil insofar as individual shareholders (i.e., natural persons) are concerned. (Whether some form of veil piercing ought to be preserved with respect to corporate shareholders is a conceptually distinct question, which we shall defer until the next section.)

In most states, abolishing veil piercing would not require statutory change. Recall the MBCA's phrasing: "Unless otherwise provided in the articles of incorporation, a shareholder of a corporation is not personally liable for the acts or debts of the corporation except that *he may become personally liable by reason of his own acts or conduct.*"[9] This statutory formulation precisely captures limited liability as it ought to work: shareholders are not vicariously liable for corporate acts or debts, but shareholders may be held directly liable for their own misconduct.[10] In other words, the appropriate question is not whether the shareholders used the corporation as their alter ego, but whether the shareholders personally engaged in conduct for which they ought to be held directly liable.

---

8. Robert W. Hillman, Limited Liability in Historical Perspective, 54 Wash. & Lee L. Rev. 615 (1997).

9. MBCA § 6.22(b) (emphasis supplied).

10. Having gotten it right in the text, the MBCA's drafters then wimped out in the historical background section of the statutory commentary by legitimating the "common law doctrine of 'piercing the corporate veil.'" MBCA § 6.22 cmt. 2.

In many nominally piercing cases, the plaintiff in fact could have brought a direct action against the shareholder.[11] Often, for example, the individual defendant said or did something that misled the creditor. In others, the individual defendant could be held liable either as a joint tortfeasor with the corporate defendant or on a vicarious liability theory. Because these examples capture the cases in which limited liability seems most problematic—namely, misrepresentation in connection with contract claims and deliberate externalization of unreasonable risks in tort cases—abolishing veil piercing would not leave deserving creditors without a remedy.

If we are to replace the vicarious liability of veil piercing with the direct liability of a personal misconduct standard, it must be shown that direct liability offers a more workable standard. Given veil piercing's demonstrated dysfunctionality, however, this should not prove too onerous a task. In the first place, note that focusing the inquiry on the personal conduct of shareholders effectively incorporates the important distinction between public and close corporations. Given that public corporation shareholders typically are passive investors, it will rarely be the case that they will expose themselves to liability. Instead, the cases in which shareholder liability will be in play are those involving the conduct of a controlling shareholder of a closely held corporation who is actively involved in the management of the firm, such as Carlton in *Walkovszky*, which is precisely the class of cases with which this area of the law traditionally has been concerned.

A. Contract creditors and other bargain settings

As we have seen, contract creditors can require shareholders of a close corporation to provide a personal guarantee of corporate debts. Where a contract creditor fails to bargain around the limited liability default rule, there is no justification for giving it a second bite at the apple through a veil piercing remedy. Although the empirical evidence shows that courts pierce frequently in contract cases, this does not invalidate the contract/tort distinction, as many contract cases likely involve active misconduct by the shareholder affording grounds for direct liability.

In light of this analysis, there are only two classes of cases in which personal liability ought to be in play: (1) where the creditor was misled by the shareholder and, as a result of that misrepresentation, forewent the protections of a personal guarantee; (2) where the shareholder has siphoned funds out of the firm, so that it is ex post undercapitalized.

1. Commercial misrepresentation

The tort of fraud or misrepresentation is, of course, well-established. It requires plaintiff to prove five things: (1) a false representation or an

---

11. See Robert W. Hamilton, The Corporate Entity, 49 Tex. L. Rev. 979, 983   (1971).

omission where there was a duty to speak; (2) scienter; (3) intent to induce plaintiff to act or refrain from acting; (4) justifiable reliance by plaintiff; and (5) damage to plaintiff.[12] If a lender showed that it loaned money to the corporation as a result of the shareholder's misrepresentations, for example, the lender will be entitled to direct damages (measured by the amount lent) plus such special or consequential damages as the plaintiff is able to prove.

An example may be helpful. In *Perpetual Real Estate Services, Inc. v. Michaelson Properties, Inc.*,[13] one Aaron Michaelson was the president and sole shareholder of Michaelson Properties, Inc. ("Properties"), a real estate venture capital firm. Properties formed a pair of partnerships with Perpetual Real Estate Services, Inc. ("Perpetual") to convert apartment complexes into condominiums. In the course of their relationship, Perpetual extracted several personal guarantees from Michaelson of various loans and other arrangements. At the end of their relationship, one of the partnerships was sued for breach of contract (on matters outside the Perpetual–Michaelson relationship) by several condominium purchasers. Perpetual paid the settlement and then sought contribution from Properties and Michaelson.

Under the applicable Virginia veil piercing standard, Perpetual was entitled to hold Michaelson personally liable only if it showed "that the corporate entity was the alter ego, alias, stooge, or dummy of [Michaelson] and that the corporation was a device or sham used to disguise wrongs, obscure fraud, or conceal crime."[14] At trial, the jury found for Perpetual and the trial judge rejected Michaelson's motion for jnov. The appellate court reversed on grounds that there was no evidence to support a jury finding for Perpetual on the second prong of the Virginia standard. While this doubtless was the correct result, neither the jury nor the trial judge managed to reach it. Instead, they focused solely on the first prong of the test, emphasizing those facts tending to show that Michaelson dominated Properties.

In contrast, had Perpetual been forced to bring an action for fraud rather than veil piercing, the weakness of its case would have been self-evident. Perpetual and Properties had a longstanding business relationship. Perpetual had full knowledge of Properties' corporate and capital structure. Perpetual had several times extracted personal guarantees from Michaelson, although not in connection with the final disbursement of funds at issue in the litigation. In sum, there was no evidence that

---

12. W. Page Keeton et al., Prosser and Keeton on Torts § 105 at 728 (5th ed. 1984).

13. 974 F.2d 545 (4th Cir.1992). As another example, consider a case in which "a retailer has dealt with and received credit from a supplier over a number of years and then, without notice to the supplier, incorporates his business but continues to deal with the supplier without clearly indicating the fact of incorporation...." Paul Halpern et al., An Economic Analysis of Limited Liability in Corporation Law, 30 U. Toronto L. Rev. 117, 121 (1980). A Canadian court pierced on such facts, id., but could just as well have held the shareholder directly liable for misrepresentation.

14. Cheatle v. Rudd's Swimming Pool Supply Co., Inc., 360 S.E.2d 828, 830 (Va. 1987).

Michaelson committed any misrepresentation intended to induce Perpetual to act. Even if there had been such a misrepresentation, moreover, there was no evidence that Perpetual could have justifiably relied on such a misrepresentation. Perpetual had made its bed, so it ought to lie in it. Whether Michaelson, *inter alia*, respected the corporate formalities necessary to preclude veil piercing is simply irrelevant. Yet, because the veil piercing doctrine encouraged the jury and trial judge to focus on such irrelevancies, Michaelson had a narrow (and presumably expensive) escape:

> The jury verdict stripped Michaelson of the protections against personal liability to which he was entitled under the settled corporate law of Virginia. It awarded to [Perpetual] a new contract—one that bestowed on [Perpetual] a personal guarantee on the part of Michaelson that [Perpetual] had been unable to obtain at the bargaining table....[15]

Unfortunately, given the vagaries of veil piercing law, not all shareholders make such an escape. In *Kinney Shoe Corp. v. Polan*, for example, Kinney sublet property to Industrial Realty Company. When Industrial defaulted, Kinney sought to hold Industrial's sole shareholder, one Lincoln Polan, liable. The trial court found that Polan dominated Industrial, he had failed to observe corporate formalities, and that Industrial was undercapitalized. Yet, because the relationship was contractual, the trial court held that Kinney was not entitled to pierce the veil. Without much in the way of reasoned analysis, the appellate court reversed.[16] In doing so, it focused solely on Industrial's lack of capital and Polan's failure to observe corporate formalities. This result makes no sense whatsoever, a point that would have been abundantly clear if the court had been forced to look at the case as an action for fraud rather than for veil piercing. Polan could have avoided veil piercing liability by following "the simple formalities of maintaining the corporation," such as buying stock, making a capital contribution, keeping minutes, and electing officers. Yet, what good would those steps have done Kinney?

As far as we know from the reported decision, Kinney entered into the lease with full knowledge of Industrial's corporate status and finances. There are no facts presented to indicate that Polan in any way misled Kinney. Kinney could have negotiated a lease that included a recourse provision—i.e., one holding Polan liable if Industrial failed to perform. Kinney failed to do so, but the appellate court gave it a second bite at the apple. This potentially gives firms in Kinney's position a windfall. They can negotiate a nonrecourse lease, which presumably will carry a higher rent so as to compensate the lessor for the added risk, but

---

15. Perpetual Real Estate Services, Inc. v. Michaelson Properties, Inc., 974 F.2d 545, 551 (4th Cir.1992).

16. Kinney Shoe Corp. v. Polan, 939 F.2d 209, 213 (4th Cir.1991) ("When nothing is invested in the corporation, the corporation provides no protection to its owner; noting in, nothing out, no protection.").

then pierce the corporate veil to recover personally from the investor if that risk materializes.

In sum, veil piercing in this context easily can lead to arbitrary and erroneous results. The questions veil piercing asks are the wrong ones, encouraging decisionmakers to focus on side issues. In contrast, a standard of direct liability premised on fraud and misrepresentation asks the right questions and seems far more likely to lead to correct outcomes.

2. *Ex post undercapitalization*

In the absence of misrepresentation, ex ante undercapitalization is irrelevant. In *Kinney*, for example, Industrial was grossly undercapitalized from the outset. Indeed, it appears that Polan never put any money into Industrial and it had neither assets nor income. But so what? Kinney knew or should have known that Industrial was an undercapitalized shell, yet it nevertheless entered into a nonrecourse lease. Only by persuading the appellate court to invoke veil piercing to rewrite the contract did Kinney prevail. The availability of piercing gave Kinney a second bite at the apple, by which it reaped a windfall for which it had not bargained.

In contrast, there may be a class of cases in which ex post undercapitalization is potentially troubling. We might refer to these situations as siphoning cases: the firm was adequately capitalized when the contract was made, so the creditor forewent a personal guarantee, but the shareholder has subsequently drained the firm of funds through dividends, loans, and/or large salaries. One answer to the siphoning problem would be to ask why the creditor did not bargain for contractual protections against such shareholder conduct, but such provisions can be difficult to draft and enforce. Recall that bounded rationality means that all contracts are to some extent incomplete. An unscrupulous shareholder might well take advantage of any loopholes the contract affords.

The legitimacy of concern with siphoning, however, does not legitimate veil piercing. The law affords creditors two powerful tools to deal with siphoning: fraudulent transfer law and bankruptcy preferences. In addition, where dividends are the siphon, state legal capital rules will be available (albeit not very efficacious).

The law governing fraudulent transfers is complex,[17] but has the virtue of being more squarely focused on the problematic behavior than

---

17. For an excellent overview, see Charles Jordan Tabb, The Law of Bankruptcy 412–57 (1997). Dean Robert Clark pioneered the overlap between fraudulent transfer law and veil piercing, contending that fraudulent conveyance principles shed valuable light on veil piercing. Robert C. Clark, The Duties of the Corporate Debtor to its Creditors, 90 Harv. L. Rev. 505 (1977). At the same time, however, he noted that the vague veil piercing standards make it "easier for plaintiff to prove their cases" and give "judges more flexibility and discretion." Id. at 85. In contrast, our argument is that it is precisely those aspects of veil piercing law that justify its abolition, while leaving plaintiffs fraudulent transfer law as a remedy. For a newer treatment of the relationship between limited liability and fraudulent transfer law, which is also more favorable towards veil piercing than our

is veil piercing. Fraudulent transfer law does not ask whether the shareholder took minutes of board meetings. Instead, the actual fraud variant of fraudulent transfer law asks whether the debtor transferred property with the intent to hinder the creditor by putting collateral beyond reach. The constructive fraud variant asks whether the debtor received less than reasonably equivalent value for the property transferred and was insolvent at the time of the transfer or rendered insolvent by the transfer. Admittedly, these are not bright-line standards, but at least both ask the right questions. In contrast, most of the factors considered in veil piercing cases are "singularly lacking in *direct* relevance to the question of the existence, and the amount, of harm caused the outside creditor by the misbehavior of the controlling shareholder."[18]

Recall how the *Sea-Land* court applied the laundry list of veil piercing factors. Here is the sole context in which its otherwise puzzling emphasis on corporate formalities might make sense. Marchese's commingling of corporate and personal assets, his use of corporate accounts to pay personal debts, his swapping funds amongst the various corporate entities, and his failure to keep good financial records all suggest some fraudulent transfers may have occurred. If so, his creditors may well have suffered an injury for which they deserved legal recompense. Yet, because veil piercing does not force the court to squarely address that issue, we do not know. If veil piercing were abolished, forcing plaintiffs to rely on fraudulent transfer law, courts would be obliged to determine whether the creditors were in fact injured.

If the corporation is bankrupt, siphoning also can be redressed through the trustee's avoidance powers with respect to preferences. Bankruptcy Code § 547 allows the trustee to recover property of the corporate debtor transferred to or for the benefit of a controlling shareholder (or other insider) within one year prior to the bankruptcy. The transfer must be for or on account of an antecedent debt, made while the corporate debtor was insolvent, and enable the insider to receive more than it would have received in a hypothetical Chapter 7 liquidation.

Franklin Gevurtz notes the availability of these alternatives, but justifies the survival of piercing on grounds of deterrence and putting the burden of uncertainty about the import of any siphoning on the shareholder. The survival of piercing, however, given the availability of these alternative remedies, is better explained by the fact that they require careful review of specific transactions. This is especially true of fraudulent transfer law: "What did the corporation transfer [to the shareholder]? What is the defendant's justification for the transfer? How does this measure up against the specific tests of fairness or solvency imposed by the relevant statute or judicial doctrine?"[19] In contrast, veil piercing merely requires analysis by epithet.

analysis, see Frederick Tung, Limited Liability and Creditors' Rights: The Limits of Risk Shifting to Creditors, 34 Ga. L. Rev. 547 (2000).

18. Robert C. Clark, Corporate Law 85 (1986).

19. Franklin A. Gevurtz, Piercing Piercing: An Attempt to Lift the Veil of Confusion Surrounding the Doctrine of Piercing

Assume judges are boundedly rational and (sometimes) shirk—the basic assumptions about human nature upon which New Institutional Economics is built. The inherent cognitive limitations implied by bounded rationality are reinforced by significant institutional constraints providing further incentives for judges to minimize effort. All judges function under severe time and resource constraints. Worse yet, state court judges (outside Delaware) rarely come to the bench with significant corporate law expertise. One further (plausibly) assumes that state judges do not have much interest in developing substantial expertise in this area after they arrive or incentive to do so, because (outside Delaware) corporate law cases are handled by courts of general civil jurisdiction whose judges must decide corporate law issues only episodically. Under such conditions, bounded rationality, the institutional constraints on judicial decisionmaking, and the incentives to shirk familiar from agency cost theory, all argue for finding ways of deciding these cases with minimal effort. A basic way of economizing on limited cognitive resources is to invoke shortcuts; i.e., heuristic problem-solving decisionmaking processes. On the one hand, the shortcut allows the judge to dispose of the case summarily without dealing with time-and-resource-consuming complexities. On the other hand, provided the shortcut is well-accepted, it provides a doctrinally plausible ground for dismissing the case, so the judge is insulated from injury to his reputation or self-esteem. Slapping the requisite veil piercing epithet on a case is just such a shortcut, and doing so is far more consistent with judicial incentives than puzzling through the complexities of fraudulent transfer law. Abolishing veil piercing thus is a necessary step towards redirecting judicial incentives towards the correct set of solutions to the problem.

There is something of a chicken and the egg problem here, of course. Why would boundedly rational judicial agents abolish such a useful doctrine? Yet, one need not persuade all trial judges to give up this useful shortcut, since abolition can be effected on a top-down basis. Abolition could be effected simply by persuading one court—typically, the state supreme court—or the legislature to act.

The prospects of the reform proposals put forward herein perhaps could be enhanced by slightly less aggressive packaging. Courts may well be reluctant to abolish long-standing doctrines, but they frequently "fix" creaky doctrines and find ways to reform them by clarifying the analysis. An appellate advocate pressing these reforms thus might not argue that veil piercing should be abolished, but rather that veil piercing should be improved by refocusing the analysis to eliminate irrelevancies and by rearticulating the standard to tie the doctrine more closely to the policy purposes it is intended to effectuate.

B. Tort creditors

When we turn to veil piercing in tort cases, framing becomes critical. Banish from your mind the specter of large-scale industrial actions going

the Corporate Veil, 76 Or. L. Rev. 853, 878 (1997). As we have seen, a deterrence rationale is problematic due to the rarity of successful veil piercing and the unprincipled way in which the law is applied.

uncompensated. Mass torts and veil piercing simply do not coincide. Outside the parent-subsidiary corporation setting, which the next section contends is more appropriately dealt with as a species of enterprise liability, the appropriate mental picture is not Union Carbide's Bhopal disaster, but rather Walkovszky's injury at the hands of Carlton's driver.

Properly framing the issues greatly facilitates cost-benefit analysis. Veil piercing has real costs. Ex ante, investors are denied certainty and predictability. Some investors will over-invest in expensive precautions, while others will under-invest in insurance and risk reduction. Ex post, the vague veil piercing standards lead to expensive litigation and, not infrequently, erroneous results. Again, it is critical to remember that the social costs of legal rules include not only the costs they impose upon the parties, but also the costs the legal system incurs in enforcing those rules. As we have seen, the vagueness and vagaries of veil piercing entails substantial enforcement costs both for creditors and, as a result, for the judicial system as well.

Conversely, the benefits seem low. Veil piercing is not going to prevent industrial holocausts—at best it may induce the Carltons of the world to buy somewhat larger insurance policies. Yet, given the seemingly arbitrary way veil piercing functions, query whether it leads close corporation investors to optimally internalize risks. There are hundreds of thousands of closely held corporations in the United States. According to one survey, however, there were only 226 tort cases reported in Westlaw's various databases through 1985.[20] In only 70 of those did the court pierce the veil. The Carltons of the world have a far greater chance of being struck by lightning than being held personally liable. Whether viewed as a device for compensating tort victims or inducing investors to internalize risk, veil piercing fails the test.

Worse yet, the doctrine asks the wrong questions. Why would a tort creditor care, after all, if the firm followed corporate formalities? Again, all the tort creditor wants is for the firm to have enough assets to satisfy the claim. If it does not, the tort victim is unlikely to be assuaged by the knowledge that the corporation had regular board meetings of which they kept minutes.

From an ex ante perspective, veil piercing functions either as tax on entrepreneurs or as trap for the unwary. Shareholders with competent counsel will spend time, effort, and resources to ensure that their business is conducted in ways that limit veil piercing risk. Hence, veil piercing is a tax on such clients for the benefit of legal counsel. On the other hand, unwary shareholders without the benefit of competent counsel may be trapped by piercing without regard to whether their

---

20. Robert B. Thompson, Piercing the Corporate Veil: An Empirical Study, 76 Cornell L. Rev. 1036, 1058 (1991).

conduct is really culpable or socially undesirable. From an ex post perspective, veil piercing can be an expensive doctrine to litigate, but one that seems unlikely to result in socially optimal outcomes.

The basic problem is that veil piercing brings a shotgun approach to a context in which more carefully targeted solutions are preferred. Abolishing veil piercing would not eliminate direct liability, so that shareholders who participate in tortious conduct can (and should) be held personally liable. Abolishing veil piercing would not eliminate the various constraints, noted in the preceding section, on siphoning of funds by shareholders. Recall that, according to Judge Keating's dissent, *Walkovszky* was a siphoning case. The cab corporation had been thinly capitalized and all income had been drained out. As with contract creditors, tort creditors ought to be able to use fraudulent transfer law and bankruptcy preferences to redress siphoning in such cases.

Commentators have suggested a variety of legislative reforms designed to induce shareholders of close corporations to optimally internalize tort risk. Some would mandate a statutory minimum amount of capital. Others would require the corporation to post a bond equal to its likely liabilities.[21] Others would mandate that corporations carry a minimum level of liability insurance. A different take on the problem would give tort creditors higher priority in bankruptcy.[22] Finally, some suggest creating a tort-based duty of adequate capitalization.[23]

Oddly, commentators often ignore the use of general welfare laws designed to deter specific corporate conduct through criminal and civil sanctions imposed on the corporation, its directors, and its senior officers. If taxi drivers are endangering pedestrians, regulate taxi companies. Such targeted regulation doubtless is superior to any of the options offered by commentators.

When proposed as sweeping reforms applicable to all corporations, after all, most of the commentator's proposed approaches are seriously flawed. If the statute specifies a minimum amount of capital (or bond or insurance), for example, that amount will either be too large or too small. One size does not fit all. One could solve that problem by requiring the firm to have sufficient capital (or insurance) to meet those liabilities certain to arise in the ordinary course of business. That approach, however, suffers from the same flaws as Judge Keating's attempt to judicially impose such a requirement in his *Walkovszky* dissent. Only with hindsight can one determine accurately how much capital or insurance will be necessary for any given corporation.

Yet, if general welfare laws are thought inadequate to the task, one perhaps could implement versions of the commentators' proposals on a piecemeal basis. Consider *Walkovszky*: It ought to be possible for the

---

21. See, e.g., Richard A. Posner, Economic Analysis of Law 406 (4th ed. 1992).

22. David W. Leebron, Limited Liability, Tort Victims, and Creditors, 91 Colum. L. Rev. 1565 (1991).

23. See, e.g., Douglas C. Michael, To Know a Veil, 26 J. Corp. L. 41 (2000).

legislature to gather statistics on the frequency of taxi accidents and the severity of the injuries that result. With such data in hand, the legislature could determine the minimum desirable level of insurance and condition the grant of a taxi license on the operator carrying at least that much insurance.

There are a number of precedents for such an approach. In *Walkovszky* itself, the New York legislature had already mandated minimum insurance levels. To be sure, it appears that the specified minimum was set far too low. Yet, as the court pointed out, "if the insurance coverage required by statute 'is inadequate for the protection of the public, the remedy lies not with the courts but with the Legislature.' "[24] Similarly, minimum capital requirements are widespread in banking and a number of other regulated industries.

Workers' rights are another example of the piecemeal approach. A corporation's workers are strongly affected by limited liability.[25] As the principal victims of industrial accidents they make up a significant set of potential tort creditors. With respect to salary and benefits, workers comprise an important set of contract creditors. Instead of resolving workers' claims through veil piercing, however, their rights have been established through various legislative schemes. Worker's compensation bypassed limited liability by shifting the employer's tort liability out of the corporate law area. Wage claims are given priority in bankruptcy proceedings. New York and several other states allow shareholder liability for certain wage claims.

As a final example of successful piecemeal solutions to the problem, consider the various approaches states have taken to limited liability for professional corporations. Professionals, such as doctors and lawyers, traditionally were not allowed to incorporate their businesses. In the 1960s, however, states began to pass special professional corporation statutes, which allow certain regulated professionals to incorporate so as to take advantage of favorable tax treatment.[26] Some states gave shareholders of professional corporations the same limited liability as those of ordinary corporations, sometimes modified to permit imposition of vicarious liability for the acts of those who operate under the shareholder's direct supervision. A few states imposed partnership-like unlimited liability on professional corporations. A third group of states, however, allowed professional corporations limited liability provided they posted a bond or purchased an insurance policy to meet their potential liabilities.

To be sure, public choice analysis of the legislative process tells us that such legislation easily could be held up by affected interest groups. On the other hand, it is precisely the availability of veil piercing that lets

24. Walkovszky v. Carlton, 223 N.E.2d 6, 9 (N.Y.1966).

25. Henry G. Manne, Our Two Corporation Systems: Law and Economics, 53 Va. L. Rev. 259, 263 (1967). See also Dana M. Muir and Cindy A. Schipani, The Intersec-tion of State Corporation Law and Employee Compensation Programs: Is It Curtains for Veil Piercing?, 1996 U. Ill. L. Rev. 1059.

26. Michael P. Dooley, Fundamentals of Corporation Law 51–52 (1995).

the legislatures off the hook. Judicial abolition of veil piercing thus might well be a useful (if not necessary) first step towards prompting legislative action.

C.   Enterprise liability and parent-subsidiary corporations

The analysis thus far has focused on the use of veil piercing to hold natural persons, such as Carlton, personally liable for the debts and torts of the corporations of which they are shareholders. As we have seen, however, veil piercing-like issues also are frequently presented in cases involving groups of affiliated corporations, such as parent and subsidiary corporations. Do the considerations arguing for elimination of veil piercing as applied to individual shareholders likewise apply to corporate shareholders? Although this is a close question, on balance the better answer seems to be no.

The preliminary step in the analysis is to recognize that the liability of corporate shareholders is more appropriately regarded as a question of enterprise liability rather than of veil piercing. Much confusion has arisen because we have tried to squeeze wildly disparate cases, such as *Walkovszky* and *In re Silicone Gel Breast Implants Products Liability Litigation*,[27] within a single doctrine. As is so often the case, one size does not fit all.

To be sure, as we have seen, the line between veil piercing and enterprise liability becomes especially blurry when one is dealing with a corporate shareholder. To say that Subsidiary is Parent's alter ego and that Parent is therefore liable for Subsidiary's obligations differs only semantically from saying that Parent and Subsidiary are a single business enterprise. In either case, a successful plaintiff will be able to reach the combined assets of Parent and Subsidiary.[28] Put another way, in the corporate group context, what has been labeled "veil piercing" has been, in substance, enterprise liability all along. That being the case, courts ought to shed the misleading label and call the analysis by its true name.

In general, the law makes no distinction between the parent-subsidiary context and the *Walkovszky v. Carlton* setting. Generally, absent fraud or bad faith, a corporation will not be held liable for the acts of its subsidiaries.[29] There is a presumption of separateness the plaintiff must overcome to establish liability by showing that the parent is employing the subsidiary to perpetrate a fraud and that this was the proximate

27. 887 F.Supp. 1447 (N.D.Ala.1995) (whether parent corporation could be liable for acts of a subsidiary that manufactured such implants).

28. A distinction may arise at the judgment stage of the proceeding, however. Under enterprise liability, a judgment would be enforceable against the single business enterprise; under veil piercing, the judgment could be separately enforced against either firm. In the latter case, moreover, a settlement by one presumably would not foreclose collection of the judgment against the other. See Fletcher Cyc. Corp. § 43 at 727.

29. See, e.g., Pacific Landmark Hotel, Ltd. v. Marriott Hotels, Inc., 19 Cal.App.4th 615 (1993) (trial court erred in failing to treat subsidiary as separate from its parent).

cause of the plaintiff's injury.[30] In other words, the same enterprise liability standards applicable to affiliated corporations controlled by one or more individual shareholders apply to the situation of corporate groups controlled by an incorporated parent.

Yet, from a policy perspective, the considerations justifying limited liability insofar as individual shareholders are concerned seem far less powerful when applied to corporate shareholders.[31] Consider the following hypothetical: Acme Corp. is a wholly owned subsidiary of Parent Inc. In turn, Parent is a publicly held corporation with thousands of shareholders. An agent of Acme injures Plaintiff, who seeks to hold Parent liable for Acme's resulting obligations on a veil piercing theory. Plaintiff also seeks to hold Parent's shareholders liable on a veil piercing theory. The considerations militating against the latter lawsuit seem less pertinent to the former.

Recall, for example, that one justification of limited liability is encouraging shareholders to diversify. So long as the parent's limited liability insulates the parent's individual shareholders, their potential losses remain limited to the amount they invested in the parent. Hence, holding the parent liable for the subsidiary's conduct would not discourage investor diversification. For similar reasons, holding Parent liable for Acme's debts would not encourage Parent's shareholders to seek a more active role in firm management. The fact that a subsidiary might get into financial difficulty differs but little from the risk that one of Parent's internal lines of business might do so; in either case, that is an operational risk passive shareholders will be willing to leave to management.

Conversely, the ability to allocate business activities between a parent and various subsidiaries facilitates the externalization of risk. Professor Lynn LoPucki posits a model in which a single business enterprise is divided into two pieces symbiotically linked through contracts: the owning entity, which holds title to enterprise assets and undertakes any necessary contract liabilities, and the operating entity, which runs the actual hazardous activities and thus has any prospective tort liability.[32] Due to limited liability and the formalistic separation of the two entities, tort creditors are left without a remedy. The operating entity, which has the tort liability, has no assets, while limited liability

---

30. Fletcher Cyc. Corp. § 43 at 713–16.

31. Jonathan Landers has argued that subsidiaries are run for the benefit of their parent corporations, "not with a view to ensuring that the subsidiary will function as a viable corporate entity." Jonathan M. Landers, A Unified Approach to the Parent, Subsidiary, and Affiliate Question in Bankruptcy, 42 U. Chi. L. Rev. 589, 599 (1975). Hence, he criticizes courts for treating enterprise liability "as an offshoot of the problem of piercing the corporate veil." Id. at 633. But see Richard A. Posner, The Rights

of Creditors of Affiliated Corporations, 43 U. Chi. L. Rev. 499 (1976) (criticizing Landers). Courts continue to routinely hold that corporate parents ought to get the benefit of limited liability. Robert B. Thompson, Piercing the Veil Within Corporate Groups: Corporate Shareholders as Mere Investors, 13 Conn. J. Int'l L. 379, 388–89 (1999).

32. Lynn LoPucki, The Essential Structure of Judgment Proofing, 51 Stanford L. Rev. 147 (1998).

bars tort plaintiffs from reaching the owning entity's assets. In effect, the enterprise is judgment proof.

LoPucki contends that such an enterprise structure will not interfere unduly with corporate operations. The owning and operating entities can enter into a contractual relationship whereby the owning entity guarantees payment of the operating entity's voluntary debts, but does not assume liability for tort claims. In this way, contract creditors are satisfied that the operating entity will meet its obligations, but tort creditors are left with no recourse.

Suppose a major oil corporation concluded from the Exxon Valdez incident, in which an Exxon oil tanker ran aground resulting in major tort and environmental liabilities, that its oil shipping activities presented too great a risk. The oil corporation could separate its shipping from its nonshipping assets by dividing them among multiple corporations. The shipping end of the business then could be subdivided into an owning entity and an operations entity. The former would own the oil tankers and lease them to the operating entity, which in turn would actually conduct the shipping operations. If an oil tanker ran aground, it would be the fault of the operating entity's agent and, hence, that entity's legal responsibility. Yet, because the operating entity does not own any significant assets, the resulting creditors will have no recourse. To be sure, they can bankrupt the operating entity, but who cares? The owning entity will still have all the relevant assets, which the operating entity's creditors cannot touch. The owning entity can simply find or create a new operating entity and carry on as before. LoPucki contends that these sorts of liability avoidance strategies will become increasingly common because the development of asset securitization has made the financial aspects of the structure practicable, while the burgeoning information economy has created systems to handle the operational details.[33]

The core premise of LoPucki's judgment proofing analysis is that the purely contractual links between the operating and owning entity will not entitle tort creditors to get at the assets of the owning entity. As we have seen, enterprise liability provides a vehicle for doing so, but LoPucki is pessimistic as to the prospects for such litigation:

> The search for the boundaries of the "enterprise" will fail. It is an effort to distinguish the substance of the business organization from its form, but in substance there are no sharp boundaries among businesses. Firms in independent ownership link to one another through formal contract, informal business relationship, or some combination of the two. The firms themselves are often composed of numerous legal entities which may be completely or partially owned by one another. These contractual webs extend throughout the economy. To hold the entity that commits the tort and all contractu-

33. Lynn M. LoPucki, The Death of Liability, 106 Yale L.J. 1 (1996).

ally related entities liable would be to hold the entire American economy liable.[34]

LoPucki no doubt overstates the case—courts can and do apply enterprise liability without having to hold the entire economy liable. The *Pan Pacific* case discussed above, for example, involved a corporate structure almost identical to LoPucki's model.

Yet, LoPucki's basic insight is doubtless correct. Enterprise liability is an imperfect constraint on judgment proofing. The vagaries and inadequacies of veil piercing law carry over into full force to the enterprise liability context. As such, division into operating and owning entities does give the enterprise a substantial chance to essentially judgment proof itself. Given that courts only pierce about 37% of the time when corporate groups are involved,[35] the odds such a strategy will succeed are pretty good. (Note that the ability to judgment proof an enterprise in this way would pull the teeth out of Hansmann and Kraakman's unlimited liability regime, because the tort creditor would be obliged to overcome the legal separation of the judgment proof operating entity and the owning entity.)

How should the legal system respond to the judgment proofing problem and the consequent potential for corporate groups to externalize vast risks? Although there are a host of potential regulatory solutions to the problem, we focus here on only those relating to limited liability as such. In that context, three possible solutions suggest themselves. At one extreme, we could eliminate limited liability in parent-subsidiary and other affiliated corporation groups. At the other extreme, we could simply throw up our hands, say there is nothing to be done, and abolish the enterprise liability doctrine so as to allow corporations to judgment proof themselves freely. (Note that LoPucki's pessimism about enterprise liability is consistent with this alternative.) Somewhere in the middle, we could retain both limited liability as a basic principle and enterprise liability as an exception to deal with cases in which it seems appropriate to hold the entire corporate group liable. In evaluating these options, it is useful to keep in mind the theory of the second best. It posits that, in a complex and interdependent system, inefficiencies in one part of the system should be tolerated if "fixing" them might create even greater inefficiencies elsewhere in the system as a whole.

Proposals to eliminate limited liability as to corporate shareholders almost certainly would prove political nonstarters, just as Hansmann and Kraakman's more sweeping proposal did. Such proposals, moreover, are also undesirable from a theoretical perspective. One difficulty with them is deciding when corporations are sufficiently affiliated with one another that the veil of limited liability would be lost. Presumably only controlling corporate shareholders should lose the protection of limited

34. Lynn LoPucki, The Essential Structure of Judgment Proofing, 51 Stanford L. Rev. 147, 158 (1998).

35. Robert B. Thompson, Piercing the Corporate Veil: An Empirical Study, 76 Cornell L. Rev. 1036, 1055 (1991).

liability or we risk, among other things, interfering with the important role of financial intermediaries such as banks and mutual funds that own much corporate stock. Determining whether one corporation controls another is easy when a parent owns all of the stock of a subsidiary, but what about cases in which the alleged parent owns, say, 25% of the subsidiary's stock. To be sure, in a variety of contexts, courts have developed standards to determine which investors should be deemed to control the corporation.[36] Yet, those standards are vague and operate best by hindsight. As such, ex ante predictability and certainty would be lost.

Eliminating limited liability as to controlling corporations, moreover, would give such corporations a variety of undesirable incentives. They might, for example, spin-off high risk subsidiaries to individual shareholders, which would not improve the likelihood that victims of mass torts would be compensated but would probably result in less efficient management and operation of such firms. Conversely, doing so might encourage such corporations to reduce their unsystematic risk through parent-level diversification—i.e., becoming a conglomerate holding a portfolio of subsidiaries engaged in widely diverse lines of business. There is a general consensus that diversification by individuals is desirable, but that intra-corporate diversification is undesirable, a view that finds strong empirical support in the demise of conglomerate corporations.[37] Once again, a key rationale for preserving the limited liability of formally separate entities thus may be that society's cost-benefit analysis favors allowing enterprises to externalize risk: "Since society recognizes the benefits of allowing persons and organizations to limit their business risks through incorporation, sound public policy dictates that disregard of those separate corporate entities be approached with caution."[38]

Another consideration is the many legitimate reasons for enterprises to split assets among multiple corporate entities. In some cases, doing so is compelled by the nature of the business and or applicable regulations. Mutual fund companies, for example, typically have a separate management company that operates the funds. Bank holding companies segregate banking assets from nonbanking assets through the use of multiple subsidiaries. In other cases, an enterprise may be separated into multiple entities as a means of regulatory arbitrage. Many regulated professionals, such as doctors and lawyers, are prohibited from entering into partnerships with unlicensed persons. These restrictions can be bypassed

---

36. See, e.g., Harrison v. Dean Witter Reynolds, Inc., 974 F.2d 873 (7th Cir.1992) (defining control for purposes of controlling person liability under Securities Exchange Act § 20(a)); Pennaluna & Co. v. SEC, 410 F.2d 861 (9th Cir.1969) (defining control for purposes of the definition of an underwriter under Securities Act § 2(11)); see generally Rutherford B. Campbell, Jr., Defining Control in Secondary Distributions, 18 B.C. Indus. & Com. L. Rev. 37 (1976) (discussing various definitions of control).

37. See William J. Carney, Limited Liability, in III Encyclopedia of Law and Economics: The Regulation of Contracts 659, 671 (2000).

38. Pacific Landmark Hotel, Ltd. v. Marriott Hotels, Inc., 19 Cal.App.4th 615, 628 (1993).

by setting up affiliated entities in which the unlicensed persons may be partners or shareholders.

More generally, a basic principle of New Institutional Economics is that institutional design matters—it can create value.[39] Separation of an enterprise into multiple entities allows firms, inter alia, to benefit from efficiencies of specialization, avoid various market risks, and allocate and capture tax benefits such as depreciation. One of LoPucki's examples involves a fast food franchise restaurant that has lost an $80 million judgment for food poisoning, but essentially owns nothing and thus is judgment proof.[40] The land is leased from a real estate investment trust (REIT), the equipment is leased from another vendor, and the going concern value—the trademark and business system—are essentially leased from the franchisor. Yet, the judgment proof-nature of business likely is simply a serendipitous effect of concerns unrelated to avoiding tort liability. If the franchisee has a limited amount of capital, he will invest in operations rather than long-term assets such as land. He does this not to externalize tort liability, but rather because the lender is a more efficient bearer of certain business risks—such as fluctuation of property values. REITs solely own and manage real property. They thus develop industry-specific capital—i.e. efficiency in the ownership and management of property—and offer benefits to business in the form of lower leasing rates from efficiencies and from capture of depreciation. In addition, REITs are largely a creation of the tax code, such that leasing the land from a REIT has tax benefits. (Similarly, businesses often lease equipment not only to minimize some risks of ownership but also because tax rules make it difficult for small businesses to fully capture the depreciation benefits of owning capital equipment.)

Sorting out legitimate uses of multiple entities from those serving solely as a vehicle for judgment proofing is a nontrivial task. Even in cases in which judgment proofing might have been a motivating factor, moreover, the market already constrains the use of such schemes. Absent a demonstrated market failure, therefore, the dramatic step of eliminating limited liability with respect to corporate shareholders seems unwarranted.

One market constraint on splitting a single business enterprise into owning and operating entities is provided by reputational considerations. The enterprise's reputation may be harmed substantially if it escapes tort or environmental liability using this evasive scheme. Absent a cultural shift, the costs of alienating key constituencies, such as consumers, regulators, legislators, and shareholders may be greater in the long run than the costs of bearing liability. Undesirable attention by regulators, in particular, may be a significant disincentive.

---

39. Larry E. Ribstein, Limited Liability Unlimited, 24 Del. J. Corp. L. 407, 439 (1999).

40. Lynn LoPucki, The Essential Structure of Judgment Proofing, 51 Stanford L. Rev. 147, 157–58 (1998).

The ever-present risk of opportunism is a second cost of splitting a single business enterprise. As with any contract, the contract between the operating and owning entities will be drafted under the constraint of bounded rationality, which in turn implies that the contract is likely to be incomplete. As such, the necessity to rely on contract to create the symbiotic relationship between the two entities leaves the relationship open to opportunism by the operating entity.[41] Moreover, the owning entity has no real economic recourse against the operating entity because the latter, by definition, holds no assets. Put another way, dividing a single business enterprise into multiple entities creates agency costs. In order to prevent opportunism, the parties will expend considerable resources on monitoring one another and/or bonding their conduct. Because the operating entity will need the owning entity to extend guarantees to the former's contract creditors (such as suppliers), for example, the owning entity will have leverage to ensure access to the operating entity's books, records, etc. The downside is that monitoring for opportunistic behavior is costly. Because no monitoring scheme is perfect, moreover, there will always be some residual loss from strategic behavior that slips through the net.

A third market constraint exists whenever the operating entity is run by different managers than the owning entity.[42] Whether or not the firm has assets, managers make substantial investments in firm-specific human capital that, by its very nature, is nondiversifiable. The need to protect that investment, which would be lost if the operating entity fails, give the operating entity's managers an incentive to insure against tort liabilities that could threaten their employer's solvency. In turn, this reduces the extent to which splitting enterprise into multiple firms generates externalities. As a contract creditor, the insurer can set its premiums to account for the riskiness of the firm. Hence, to reduce insurance premiums, managers of the operating entity will limit the riskiness of their activities.

---

41. In Preferred Physicians Mutual Management Group v. Preferred Physicians Mutual Risk Retention, 918 S.W.2d 805 (Mo.Ct.App.1996), for example, the founders of an insurance company simultaneously set up a management company to operate the former. One of the shareholders/employees of the management company induced the board of directors of the insurer to terminate the contract with the management company and hire him to operate the insurer. Despite the significant overlap in ownership and employees between the two companies, the court allowed the management company to bring suit against both the insurer and the traitorous employee. By implication then, the court acknowledged the separateness of the two entities. Yet, it was precisely that separateness that allowed the traitor's opportunism to prosper in the first instance.

42. LoPucki acknowledges that the incentives of operating company managers are inconsistent with judgment proofing. To get the full benefit of judgment proofing, he asserts, large businesses periodically will need to sweep away their liabilities in Chapter 11 reorganizations. Lynn M. LoPucki, The Death of Liability, 106 Yale L.J. 1, 42 (1996). In such reorganizations, top managers will typically lose their jobs. Hence, he contends, this conflict of interest will need to be resolved in ways that facilitate judgment proofing. Id. at 43. Yet, solving the conflict of interest between the operating entity's managers and shareholders will not resolve the problem posed by the incentives of operating entity management.

The point is not that LoPucki erred in asserting that firms can judgment proof themselves by splitting a single business enterprise into multiple legal entities. He was quite correct—they can do so and more are likely to do so in the future. The point is only that the risk of judgment proofing does not justify the elimination of limited liability with respect to corporate shareholders.

In light of these considerations, and despite LoPucki's pessimism about the viability of enterprise liability, the case for preserving both limited liability and a veil piercing-like remedy with respect to parent and subsidiary corporations is far stronger than is the case for preserving that remedy with respect to individual shareholders. We are not writing on a blank slate: enterprise liability is on the books and the question is whether it should stay there. Given that preserving enterprise liability seems unlikely to change the incentives of corporate groups to judgment proof themselves (or otherwise externalize additional risks), and that repealing enterprise liability might encourage such conduct, enterprise liability should not be abolished. (If there is a "can't hurt, might help" quality to the argument, so be it.)

Analytical clarity would be furthered, however, by treating the former class of cases as a variant of enterprise liability rather than as a species of veil piercing. First, doing so would acknowledge the important conceptual distinctions between holding an individual liable and holding a larger corporate enterprise liable. Second, it would recognize that the issue in the parent-subsidiary context is whether the firm has split up a single business enterprise into multiple corporations with the goal of externalizing specific risks. Finally, it will allow us to abolish veil piercing with respect to individual shareholders without confusing the issue with parent-subsidiary questions.

Chapter 5

DIRECTOR PRIMACY: THE FORMAL STRUCTURES OF CORPORATE GOVERNANCE

Analysis

§ 5.1 An overview of corporate governance

Any organization needs a governance system that facilitates efficient decisionmaking. Although firms can choose amongst a wide array of options, most decisionmaking structures fall into one of two categories: "consensus" and "authority."[1] Consensus is utilized where each member of the organization has comparable information and interests. Under such conditions, assuming no serious collective action problems, decisionmaker preferences can be aggregated at low cost. In contrast, authority-based decisionmaking structures arise where team members have different interests and amounts of information. Such structures are characterized by the existence of a central agency to which all relevant information is transmitted and which is empowered to make decisions binding on the whole.

American business law allows one to choose between off-the-rack governance systems ranging from an almost purely consensus-based model to an almost purely authority-based model. (Recall that the nexus of contract model views law as a sort of standard form contract.) At one extreme, the decisionmaking structure provided by partnership law is largely a consensus model. Partners, for example, have equal rights to participate in management of the firm on a one-vote per partner basis.[2] This outcome is predictable because all partners are also entitled to share equally in profits and losses,[3] giving them essentially identical interests (namely higher profits), and are entitled to equal access to information,[4] giving them essentially identical levels of information. In addition, the small size characteristic of most partnerships means that collective action problems generally are not serious in this setting. (Large multi-jurisdiction law firms are a prominent exception to this rule, which explains why many such firms have created corporation-like governance structures in their partnership agreement.)

At the other extreme, a publicly held corporation's decisionmaking structure is principally an authority-based one. As a practical matter, most public corporations are marked by a separation of ownership and control.[5] Shareholders, who are said to "own" the firm, have virtually no power to control either its day-to-day operation or its long-term policies. In contrast, the board of directors and senior management, whose equity stake often is small, effectively controls both. As a doctrinal matter, moreover, corporate law essentially carves this separation into stone. Under all corporation statutes, the board of directors is the key player in

§ 5.1

1. Kenneth J. Arrow, The Limits of Organization 68–70 (1974).

2. As with most partnership rules, the off-the-rack rule is subject to contrary agreement among the parties. UPA (1914) § 18(e).

3. UPA (1914) § 18(a).

4. UPA (1914) §§ 19 and 20.

5. Adolf A. Berle & Gardiner C. Means, The Modern Corporation and Private Property 84–89 (1932).

the formal decisionmaking structure. As the Delaware code puts it, for example, the corporation's business and affairs "shall be managed by or under the direction of a board of directors."[6]

The vast majority of corporate decisions thus are assigned by statute to the board of directors. Having said that, however, several qualifications must be introduced immediately. First, we will use "decision" as a shorthand for a process that often is much less discrete in practice. Most board of director activity "does not consist of taking affirmative action on individual matters; it is instead a continuing flow of supervisory process, punctuated only occasionally by a discrete transactional decision."[7]

Second, operational decisions are normally delegated by the board to subordinate employees. The board, however, retains the power to hire and fire firm employees and to define the limits of their authority. Moreover, certain extraordinary acts may not be delegated, but are instead reserved for the board's exclusive determination.

In any case, the statutory separation of ownership and control means that shareholders have essentially no power to initiate corporate action and, moreover, are entitled to approve or disapprove only a very few board actions.[8] The statutory decisionmaking model thus is one in which the board acts and shareholders, at most, react.[9] One of the fundamental tenets of this text, in fact, is that shareholder voting rights are not an integral part of the corporate governance scheme. Instead, shareholder voting rights should be regarded as merely one mechanism of board accountability among many.

6. DGCL § 141(a).

7. Bayless Manning, The Business Judgment Rule and the Director's Duty of Attention: Time for Reality, 39 Bus. Law. 1477, 1494 (1984).

8. Under the Delaware code, for example, shareholder voting rights are essentially limited to the election of directors and approval of charter or bylaw amendments, mergers, sales of substantially all of the corporation's assets, and voluntary dissolution. As a formal matter, only the election of directors and amending the bylaws do not require board approval before shareholder action is possible. See DGCL §§ 109 and 211. In practice, of course, even the election of directors (absent a proxy contest) is predetermined by the existing board nominating the next year's board.

9. To be sure, the shareholders' right to elect the board of directors can give the former de facto control even though the statute assigns de jure control to the latter. Consequently, we can speak of a "control block," i.e., shares held by one or more shareholders whose stock ownership gives them effective control. In their classic study, Berle and Means in fact found that relatively small blocks of stock could give their owners effective control of the enterprise. Berle and Means identified such firms as minority controlled corporations. These firms exhibit a partial separation of ownership and control. The dominant shareholder controls the firm, despite owning less than 50% of the outstanding voting shares, leaving the minority shareholders without significant control power. Adolf A. Berle & Gardiner C. Means, The Modern Corporation and Private Property 80–84 (1932). Majority controlled firms, in which a dominant shareholder (or group of shareholders acting together) owns more than 50% of the outstanding voting shares, likewise exhibit a partial separation of ownership and control. Id. at 70–72. Where no such control block exists, however, Berle and Means found that control passes from the firm's shareholders to its managers. Although shareholders of such firms retain the right to elect directors, management controls the election process, and thus the firm. Id. at 86–87. At the time they wrote, about half of the 200 largest U.S. corporations exhibited total separation of ownership and control. Id. at 94.

In sum, the formal model of corporate governance contemplates a pyramidal hierarchy surmounted not by an individual arbiter but by a small collaborative body.[10] This model raises a number of questions: Why are corporate decisions made through the exercise of authority rather than by consensus? Why is corporate authority exercised hierarchically? Put another way, what survival advantage does a large corporation gain by being structured as a bureaucratic hierarchy? Why is the firm's ultimate decisionmaker a collective rather than an individual? Why do only shareholders, among all the corporation's constituencies, elect the board? Our answers to these questions build on all three components of the economic theory of the firm.

§ 5.2 The allocation of corporate decisionmaking power

As noted above, the formal statutory model contemplates a corporation run by its board of directors: "All corporate powers shall be exercised by or under the authority of, and the business and affairs of the corporation managed by or under the direction of, its board of directors...."[1] How well does the statutory model match up to the real world? In practice, most corporate actions are actually taken by corporate officers and subordinate employees pursuant to delegated authority. Yet, even a board that has been thoroughly captured by senior management typically retains at least some formal functions.

In any case, it is possible to identify several basic roles that most boards perform most of the time. First, and foremost, the board monitors and disciplines senior management. Second, while boards almost never get involved in making day-to-day operational decisionmaking, most boards have some managerial functions. Broad policymaking is commonly a board prerogative, for example.[2] Even more commonly, however, individual board members provide advice and guidance to senior managers with respect to operational and/or policy decisions. Finally, the board provides access to a network of contacts useful in gathering resources and/or obtaining business.[3]

10. Alfred D. Chandler, Jr., The Visible Hand: The Managerial Revolution in American Business 8 (1977) (over time, corporate hierarchies have proven to possess "a permanence beyond that of any individual or group of individuals who worked in them"); Peter F. Drucker, Concept of the Corporation 141 (rev. ed. 1972) ("the corporation must be organized on hierarchical lines").

§ 5.2

1. MBCA § 8.01(b).

2. The RJR Nabisco anecdote recounted below suggests that policymaking remains an important board function, albeit one that is closely related to the board's primary oversight role. Indeed, the board is often involved in "strategic and important

policy decisions affecting the future development of the company." Kenneth R. Andrews, Rigid Rules Will Not Make Good Boards, Harv. Bus. Rev., Nov.-Dec. 1982, at 35, 44. Although "it remains clear that the management directs operations," "the board's participation in strategic planning can enhance the quality of strategic decisions and empower the board better to understand and evaluate management performance." Id. See also George W. Dent, Jr., The Revolution in Corporate Governance, the Monitoring Board, and the Director's Duty of Care, 61 B.U. L. Rev. 623 (1981).

3. Lynne L. Dallas, The Relational Board: Three Theories of Corporate Boards of Directors, 22 J. Corp. L. 1, 10–16 (1996).

Among these functions, however, the board's monitoring role reigns supreme. To be sure, at one time, corporation statutes affirmatively required the board to manage the corporation. Delaware's statute, for example, formerly provided: "The business and affairs of every corporation organized under this chapter shall be managed by a board of directors."[4] It was only when the legislature added the phrase "or under the direction of" that the statute expressly contemplated the delegation of managerial functions to corporate officers.

Query, however, whether boards of large public corporations ever really managed firms in the sense of day-to-day operational decisionmaking? To the contrary, that they have never done so is suggested by the very antiquity of complaints that boards fail to actively manage their firms.[5] Instead, the emergence of large public corporations in the 19th century (such as the railroads) both necessitated and facilitated the concomitant emergence of a class of professional managers. Oversight of such managers long has been the board's primary function.

In practice, of course, the old statutory formulation did not preclude the board from delegating management responsibility. Indeed, as early as 1922, the Delaware Chancery Court held that the directors' role was one of supervision and control, with the detailed conduct of the business being a matter that properly could be delegated to subordinate employees.[6] The modern statutory formulation that the firm shall be "managed by or under the direction of" the board of directors simply codifies this understanding.

§ 5.3　Director primacy: Herein of the separation of ownership and control

The 1932 publication of Adolf Berle and Gardiner Means' THE MODERN CORPORATION AND PRIVATE PROPERTY began the modern era of corporate governance scholarship. Berle and Means demonstrated that public corporations were characterized by a separation of ownership and control—the firm's nominal owners, the shareholders, exercised virtually no control over either day to day operations or long-term policy. Instead, control was vested in the hands of professional managers, who typically owned only a small portion of the firm's shares. Separation of ownership and control occurred, according to Berle and Means, because stock ownership was dispersed amongst many shareholders, no one of whom owned enough shares to materially affect the corporation's management. Berle and Means believed that this separation of ownership and control was both a departure from historical norms and a serious economic problem.[1] They were wrong on both scores.

---

4. Delaware General Corporation Law § 141(a), quoted in Ernest L. Folk III, The Delaware General Corporation Law: A Commentary and Analysis 50 (1972).

5. See, e.g., William O. Douglas, Directors Who Do Not Direct, 47 Harv. L. Rev. 1305 (1934).

6. Cahall v. Lofland, 114 A. 224, 229 (Del.Ch.1921), aff'd, 118 A. 1 (Del.1922).

§ 5.3

1. Adolf A. Berle & Gardiner C. Means, The Modern Corporation and Private Property 6–7 (1932).

A. The separation of ownership and control in historical perspective

According to Berle and Means' version of economic history, dispersed ownership arose as a consequence of the development of large capital-intensive industrial corporations during the late–19th century. These firms required investments far larger than a single entrepreneur or family could provide, which could be obtained only by attracting funds from many investors. Because small investors needed diversification, even very wealthy individuals limited the amount they would put at risk in any particular firm, further fragmenting share ownership. The modern separation of ownership and control was the direct result of these forces, or so the story goes.

Professor Walter Werner aptly referred to Berle and Means account as the "erosion doctrine." According to the erosion version of history, there was a time when the corporation behaved as it was supposed to:

> The shareholders who owned the corporation controlled it. They elected a board of directors to whom they delegated management powers, but they retained residual control, uniting control and ownership. In the nation's early years the states created corporations sparingly and regulated them strictly. The first corporations, run by their proprietors and constrained by law, exercised state-granted privileges to further the public interest. The states then curtailed regulation ..., and this Eden ended. The corporation expanded into a huge concentrate of resources. Its operation vitally affected society, but it was run by managers who were accountable only to themselves and could blink at obligations to shareholders and society.[2]

The erosion doctrine, however, rested on a false account of the history of corporations. Werner explained that economic separation of ownership and control in fact was a feature of American corporations almost from the beginning of the nation: "Banks, and the other public-issue corporations of the [antebellum] period, contained the essential elements of big corporations today: a tripartite internal government structure, a share market that dispersed shareholdings and divided ownership and control, and tendencies to centralize management in full-time administrators and to diminish participation of outside directors in management."

In contrast to Berle and Means' account, which rests on technological changes during the nineteenth century, this alternative account rests on the early development of secondary trading markets. Such markets existed in New York and Philadelphia by the beginning of the 19th century. The resulting liquidity of corporate stock made it an especially attractive investment, which in turn made selling stock to the public an

---

2. Walter Werner, Corporation Law in   1611, 1612 (1981).
Search of its Future, 81 Colum. L. Rev.

attractive financing mechanism. Stocks were purchased by a diversified and dispersed clientele,[3] including both institutions and individuals. The national taste for speculation also played a part in the early growth of the secondary trading markets and, in turn, to dispersal of stock ownership. As a result of these economic forces, ownership and control separated not at the end of the nineteenth century, but at its beginning.

If this version of history is correct, there never was a time in which unity of control and ownership was a central feature of U.S. corporations. To the contrary, it appears that ownership and control separated at a very early date. In turn, this analysis suggests that the separation of ownership and control may be an essential economic characteristic of such corporations.

B. The separation of ownership and control in economic perspective

The chief criteria for any model of the corporation must be the model's ability to explain the separation of ownership and control, the institutional governance structures following from their separation, and the legal rules responsive to their separation. Over the years, legal scholars have developed numerous theories of the firm that purport to satisfy that standard. Although these theories can be classified in various ways, and some defy classification, two basic systems of classification capture most of the competing theories. (See Figure 1.) Along one axis (call it the "control axis"), theories of the firm are plotted according to whether they emphasize managerial or shareholder primacy. Theories at the shareholder primacy end of the spectrum traditionally claimed that shareholders own the corporation and, accordingly, that directors and officers are mere stewards of the shareholders' interests. A more recent variation of the shareholder primacy model, which arguably is the dominant model in today's scholarship, melds the nexus of contracts theory with agency cost economics. Scholars relying on this model purport to deny the relevance of ownership, treating shareholders as mere contractual claimants. Yet, shareholders retain a privileged position under this model because their contract with the firm has ownership-like features, including the right to vote and the fiduciary obligations of directors and officers.

---

3. A slightly different version of this story is told by Herbert Hovenkamp, who argues that separation of ownership and control is less a function of firm size than of firm complexity. Under this model, neither technological change nor corporate financing was the dispositive factor. Rather, ownership and control separated when, because of a high degree of vertical integration, firms became sufficiently complex to re-quire professional managers. Herbert Hovenkamp, Enterprise and American Law: 1836–1937 357–60 (1991). Notice the close fit between this interpretation and the economic model advanced in this Chapter. Under both, the unique attribute of modern public corporations is the hierarchical decisionmaking structure adopted as an adaptive response to organizational complexity.

Figure 1
Plotting the Theories of the Firm

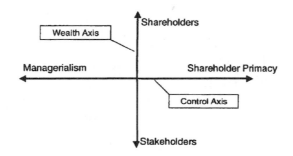

At the other end of the control axis lies managerialism. Managerialism conceives the corporation as a bureaucratic hierarchy dominated by professional managers. Directors are figureheads, while shareholders are nonentities. Managers are thus autonomous actors free to pursue whatever interests they choose. Variants of managerialism long dominated corporate law scholarship and remain influential in some other disciplines, but they no longer have much traction in the legal academy.

Along the other axis (call it the "wealth axis"), theories of the firm can be plotted according to the interests the corporation serves. At one end of the spectrum are those who contend corporations should be run so as to maximize shareholder wealth. At the other end are those who argue that directors and managers should consider the interests of all corporate constituencies in making corporate decisions.

At bottom, all of these models must answer two basic questions: (1) Who decides? When push comes to shove, who ultimately is in control? (2) Whose interests prevail? When the ultimate decisionmaker is presented with a zero sum game, in which it must prefer the interests of one constituency class over those of all others, which constituency wins? Any model that can command the loyalty of one or more generations of scholars doubtless has more than a grain of truth. Yet, none of the standard models is fully satisfactory. Shareholder primacy models assume that shareholders both control the corporation, at least in some ultimate fashion, and are the appropriate beneficiaries of director fiduciary duties. Managerialist models assume that top management control the corporation, but differ as to the interests managers should pursue. Stakeholderist models rarely focus on control issues, instead emphasizing the argument that shareholders should not be the sole beneficiaries of director and officer fiduciary duties.

In contrast, this text propounds a model that might be called "director primacy." As to the control axis, director primacy asserts that neither end of the spectrum gets it right. Neither shareholders nor managers control corporations—boards of directors do. As to the wealth axis, director primacy claims that shareholders are the appropriate beneficiary of director fiduciary duties. Hence, director accountability for maximizing shareholder wealth remains an important component of director primacy.

Prevailing models of the firm in legal scholarship all too often pay insufficient attention to the power of fiat exercised by the board. Some go so far as to claim that fiat does not exist. Still others acknowledge the board's discretionary powers, but treat those powers mainly as a source of agency costs to be constrained by market and/or legal forces. In doing so, however, they have allowed the tail to wag the dog. To be sure, deterrence and punishment of misconduct by the board is necessary. Accountability standing alone, however, is an inadequate normative account of corporate law. Fiat exists—and fiat matters. A fully specified account of corporate law therefore must incorporate the value of authority—i.e., the need to develop a set of rules and procedures that provides the most efficient decisionmaking system.[4]

At the core of the director primacy model therefore lies the normative claim that the virtues of fiat, in terms of corporate decisionmaking efficiency, can be ensured only by preserving the board's decisionmaking authority from being trumped by either shareholders or courts. Achieving an appropriate mix between authority and accountability is a daunting task, but a necessary one. Ultimately, authority and accountability cannot be reconciled. At some point, greater accountability necessarily makes the decisionmaking process less efficient, while highly efficient decisionmaking structures necessarily entail nonreviewable discretion.

The predictive power of director primacy is demonstrated in the host of legal doctrines and governance structures that resolve the tension between authority and accountability in the favor of the former. Because only shareholders are entitled to elect directors, for example, boards of public corporations are insulated from pressure by nonshareholder corporate constituencies, such as employees or creditors. At the same time, the diffuse nature of U.S. stock ownership and regulatory impediments to investor activism insulate directors from shareholder pressure. As such, the board has virtually unconstrained freedom to exercise business judgment. Preservation of this largely unfettered discretion is—and should always be—the null hypothesis. Hence, the term director primacy, which reflects the board's sovereignty.

1.　The contractarian foundations of director primacy

The dominant model of the corporation in legal scholarship is the so-called nexus of contracts theory. Recall that the term "contract," as used in this context, is not limited to relationships constituting legal contracts. Instead, contractarians use the word contract to refer generally to long-term relationships characterized by asymmetric information, bilateral monopoly, and opportunism. The relationship between shareholders

---

4. See, e.g., Michael P. Dooley, Two Models of Corporate Governance, 42 Bus. Law. 461 (1992), which builds on Kenneth J. Arrow, The Limits of Organization (1974).

and creditors of a corporation is contractual in this sense, even though there is no single document we could identify as a legally binding contract through which they are in privity.

In a sense, the corporation *is* the nexus of the various contracts among the factors of production comprising the firm. (See Figure 2.) This standard account has a considerable virtue—it emphasizes that the firm is not an entity but rather a set explicit and implicit contracts establishing rights and obligations among various factors of production. Yet, the standard account fails to capture the more important sense in which the corporation *has* a nexus. Put another way, the standard account understates the role of fiat in corporate governance.

The corporation is a nexus. Corporate constituents contract not with each other, but with the corporation. A bond indenture thus is a contract between the corporation and its creditors,[5] an employment agreement is a contract between the corporation and its workers,[6] and a collective bargaining agreement is a contract between the corporation and the union representing its workers.[7] If the contract is breached on the corporate side, it will be the entity that is sued in most cases, rather than the individuals who decided not to perform. If the entity loses, damages typically will be paid out of its assets and earnings rather than out of those individuals' pockets.

Figure 2
The standard contractarian account
The firm *is* a nexus

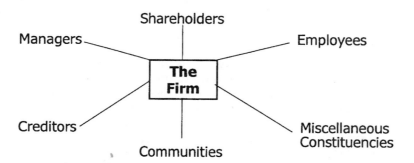

5. See, e.g., Lorenz v. CSX Corp., 1 F.3d 1406, 1417 (3d Cir.1993) (stating "It is well-established that a corporation does not have a fiduciary relationship with its debt security holders, as with its shareholders. The relationship between a corporation and its debentureholders is contractual in nature."); Simons v. Cogan, 549 A.2d 300, 303 (Del.1988) (holding that "a convertible debenture represents a contractual entitlement to the repayment of a debt").

6. See, e.g., Berman v. Physical Med. Assocs., 225 F.3d 429, 433 (4th Cir.2000) (holding that, "as to Berman's claims under the employment agreement and severance benefit agreement, only the corporation owed Berman a contractual duty").

7. See John Wiley & Sons, Inc. v. Livingston, 376 U.S. 543, 546 (1964) (asking "whether the arbitration provisions of the collective bargaining agreement survived the Wiley–Interscience merger, so as to be operative against" successor corporation).

One cannot dismiss all of this as mere reification, as some have done. If there were no nexus, employment contracts would cascade—looking rather like a standard hierarchical organization chart—with each employee contracting with his superior. (Debt contracts would be even more complex.) Such a cascade would be costly to assemble, if not impossible.[8] Indeed, most corporate constituents lack any mechanism for communicating with other constituencies of the firm—let alone contract with one another. Instead, each constituency contracts with a central nexus. Accordingly, constituencies must be (and are) linked to the nexus and not each other.

The corporation has a nexus. Economists Armen Alchian and Harold Demsetz famously claimed that the firm "has no power of fiat, no authority, no disciplinary action any different in the slightest degree from ordinary market contracting between any two people."[9] Hence, Alchian and Demsetz argued, an employer's control over its employees differs not all from the power of a consumer over the grocer with whom the consumer does business.

If they are right and fiat is not an essential attribute of "firm-ishness," the firm would be just a legal fiction describing the space within which the set of contracts are worked out. Power exists within firms, however, and it matters. The corporation has a nexus—and that nexus wields a power of fiat different from that of a consumer over a grocer. Indeed, fiat is the chief characteristic that distinguishes firms from markets. As economist Ronald Coase explained long ago, firms emerge when it is efficient to substitute entrepreneurial fiat for the price mechanisms of the market.[10] One team member is empowered to constantly and, more important, unilaterally rewrite certain terms of the contract between the firm and its various constituents. By creating a central decisionmaker—a nexus—with the power of fiat, the firm thus substitutes ex post governance for ex ante contract.

Coordination need not imply fiat, as illustrated by the democratic decisionmaking processes of many partnerships and other small firms. In the public corporation, however, fiat is essential. All organizations must have some mechanism for aggregating the preferences of the organization's constituencies and converting them into collective decisions. Recall that such mechanisms fall out on a spectrum between "consensus" and "authority." Further recall that authority-based decisionmaking structures—characterized by the existence of a central office empowered to make decisions binding on the firm as a whole—arise where the firm's constituencies have different interests and access to information. The necessity of a literal nexus—a center of power capable of exercising

8. Such a cascade also would be subject to opportunistic disassembly threats in which one or more of the contracting parties seeks to hold up the others.

9. Armen A. Alchian & Harold Demsetz, Production, Information Costs, and Economic Organization, 62 Am. Econ. Rev. 777, 777 (1972).

10. Ronald Coase, The Nature of the Firm, 4 Economica (n.s.) 386 (1937).

fiat—within the corporation thus follows as a matter of course from the asymmetries of information and interests among the corporation's various constituencies. Shareholders care about the value of the residual claim on the corporation. Customers care about the quality and quantity of the goods produced by the corporation. Workers care about salary and conditions of employment. And so on. Under such conditions, efficient decisionmaking demands an authority-based governance structure.

Consider the problems faced by shareholders, who are conventionally assumed to be the corporate constituency with the best claim on control of the decisionmaking apparatus. At the most basic level, the mechanical difficulties of achieving consensus amongst thousands of decisionmakers impede shareholders from taking an active role. Put another way, in large corporations, authority-based decisionmaking structures are desirable because of the potential for division and specialization of labor. Bounded rationality and complexity, as well as the practical costs of losing time when one shifts jobs, make it efficient for corporate constituents to specialize. Directors and managers specialize in the efficient coordination of other specialists. In order to reap the benefits of specialization, all other corporate constituents should prefer to specialize in functions unrelated to decisionmaking, such as risk-bearing (shareholders) or labor (employees), delegating decisionmaking to the board and senior management. This natural division of labor, however, requires that the chosen directors and officers be vested with discretion to make binding decisions. Separating ownership and control by vesting decisionmaking authority in a centralized nexus distinct from the shareholders and all other constituents is what makes the large public corporation feasible.

Even if one could overcome the seemingly intractable collective action problems plaguing shareholder decisionmaking, active shareholder participation in corporate decisionmaking would still be precluded by the shareholders' widely divergent interests and distinctly different levels of information. Although neoclassical economics assumes that shareholders come to the corporation with wealth maximization as their goal, and most presumably do so, once uncertainty is introduced it would be surprising if shareholder opinions did not differ on which course will maximize share value. More prosaically, shareholder investment time horizons are likely to vary from short-term speculation to long-term buy-and-hold strategies, which in turn is likely to result in disagreements about corporate strategy. Even more prosaically, shareholders in different tax brackets are likely to disagree about such matters as dividend policy, as are shareholders who disagree about the merits of allowing management to invest the firm's free cash flow in new projects.

As to Arrow's information condition, shareholders lack incentives to gather the information necessary to actively participate in decisionmaking. A rational shareholder will expend the effort necessary to make informed decisions only if the expected benefits of doing so outweigh its costs. Given the length and complexity of corporate disclosure documents, the opportunity cost entailed in making informed decisions is both high and apparent. In contrast, the expected benefits of becoming informed are quite low, as most shareholders' holdings are too small to have significant effect on the vote's outcome. Corporate shareholders thus are rationally apathetic. Instead of exercising their voting rights, disgruntled shareholders typically adopt the so-called Wall Street Rule— it's easier to switch than fight—and sell out.

The efficient capital markets hypothesis provides yet another reason for shareholders to eschew active participation in the governance process. If the market is a reliable indicator of performance, as the efficient capital markets hypothesis claims, investors can easily check the performance of companies in which they hold shares and compare their current holdings with alternative investment positions. An occasional glance at the stock market listings in the newspaper is all that is required. Because it is so much easier to switch to an new investment than to fight incumbent managers, a rational shareholder will not even care why a firm's performance is faltering. With the expenditure of much less energy than is needed to read corporate disclosure statements, he will simply sell his holdings in the struggling firm and move on to other investments.[11]

Consequently, it is hardly surprising that the modern public corporation's decisionmaking structure precisely fits Arrow's model of an authority-based decisionmaking system. Overcoming the collective action problems that prevent meaningful shareholder involvement would be difficult and costly, of course. Even if one could do so, moreover, shareholders lack both the information and the incentives necessary to make sound decisions on either operational or policy questions.[12] Under these conditions, it is "cheaper and more efficient to transmit all the pieces of information to a central place" and to have the central office "make the collective choice and transmit it rather than retransmit all the information on which the decision is based."[13] Accordingly, shareholders will prefer to irrevocably delegate decisionmaking authority to some smaller group.

2. *Locating the nexus*

Under conditions of asset specificity, bounded rationality, and opportunism, the ability to adapt becomes the central problem of organization.

---

11. Finally, portfolio theory offers yet another justification for separating ownership and control. By virtue of their nondiversified investment in firm specific human capital, managers bear part of the risk of firm failure. As the firm's residual claimants, however, shareholders also bear a portion of the risk associated with firm failure. Portfolio theory tells us that individual shareholders can minimize that risk through diversification, which managers cannot do with respect to their human capital. Separating ownership and control thus unbundles the risks associated with the firm and allocates each of those risks to the party who can bear it at the lowest cost. We regard this explanation as somewhat problematic, however, due to its managerialist overtones.

12. Similar analyses apply to other corporate constituents on whose behalf claims to control of the decisionmaking apparatus might be made, such as employees or creditors.

13. Kenneth J. Arrow, The Limits of Organization 68–69 (1974).

In large public corporations, adaptation is effected by fiat. Obviously, fiat within firms has limits. Some choices are barred by contract, such as negative pledge covenants in bond indentures. Other choices may be barred by regulation or statute. Still other choices may be unattractive for business reasons, such as those with potentially adverse reputational consequences. Within such bounds, however, adaptation effected through fiat is the distinguishing characteristic of the firm.

A central decisionmaker with largely unreviewable authority thus is an essential attribute of firms in general and the modern public corporation in particular. It is for this reason that the firm must have a nexus—a central coordinator that is a party to the set of contracts we call the firm and that has the power to effect adaptive responses to changed conditions by fiat.

If the corporation has a nexus, however, where is it located? The Delaware code, like the corporate law of virtually every other state, gives us a clear answer: the corporation's "business and affairs ... shall be managed by or under the direction of the board of directors."[14] Put simply, the board is the nexus. (See Figure 3.)

Figure 3
Director Primacy:
The firm *has* a nexus

Indeed, we can think of the corporation as a vehicle by which the board of directors hires capital by selling equity and debt securities to risk bearers with varying tastes for risk. The board of directors thus can be seen as a sort of Platonic guardian—a sui generis body serving as the nexus for the various contracts making up the corporation and whose powers flow not from shareholders alone but from the complete set of contracts constituting the firm. As a early New York decision put it, the board's powers are "original and undelegated."[15]

---

14. Del. Code Ann., tit. 8, § 141(a) (2000). For a summary of comparable state corporation code provisions, see Mod. Bus. Corp. Act. Ann. § 8.01 at 8–10 (1997 supp.).

15. Manson v. Curtis, 119 N.E. 559, 562 (N.Y.1918).

3. *Director primacy v. managerialism*

Director primacy should not be confused with what might be termed "contractarian managerialism." Although managerialist theories are now passe, there was a time when the leading corporate law theorists embraced such models. In Adolf Berle and E. Merrick Dodd's famous debate over corporate social responsibility, for example, both started with an assumption of managerial discretion. Berle opined that corporate managers were akin to "princes and ministers."[16] Dodd similarly believed that managers were "free from any substantial supervision by stockholders."[17] They differed only in their policy prescriptions. Berle thought the law should emphasize managers' fiduciary duty to maximize shareholder wealth.[18] In contrast, Dodd argued that corporations have a "social service as well as a profit-making function." The corporate social responsibility debate lives on as the progeny of these arguments.

Of present import, however, is the point that both Berle and Dodd erred by failing to distinguish between directors and officers. The board of directors must not be confused with a mere executive committee. Unlike the executive committee of a large law firm partnership, for example, the board of directors is not principally an instrument by which some managers control others. Those who control large unincorporated firms commonly retain both day-to-day operating control and a significant equity stake in the enterprise, even though the flexible governance rules of partnership and limited liability company law permit such firms to draft operating agreements effecting a substantial separation of ownership and control. In contrast, a unique attribute of the modern public corporation is the ever-increasing use of independent board members who typically lack both day-to-day management power and any significant equity stake in the corporation. These characteristics highlight the unique nature of the corporation and its board-based governance system.

To be sure, the extent to which boards actually monitor management and effectively discipline sub-par performance has been the subject of considerable dispute. Conventional wisdom asserts that, in the real world, boards commonly are captured by a dominant CEO. According to this view, senior "managers dominate their boards by using their de facto power to select and compensate directors and by exploiting personal ties with them."[19] The board capture phenomenon seems less valid today, however, than it used to be. Modern CEOs are constrained both from below, by other members of the top management team, and from above, by the board.

16. Adolf Berle, For Whom Corporate Managers Are Trustees, 45 Harv. L. Rev. 1365, 1366 (1932).

17. E. Merrick Dodd, Jr., For Whom Are Corporate Managers Trustees?, 45 Harv. L. Rev. 1145, 1147 (1932).

18. Adolf Berle, Corporate Powers as Powers in Trust, 44 Harv. L. Rev. 1049, 1049 (1931).

19. Barry Baysinger & Robert E. Hoskisson, The Composition of Boards of Directors and Strategic Control: Effects on Corporate Strategy, 15 Acad. Mgmt. Rev. 72, 72–73 (1990).

During the 1980s and '90s, several trends coalesced to encourage more active and effective board oversight. Much director compensation is now paid in stock, for example, which helps align director and shareholder interests.[20] Courts have made clear that effective board processes and oversight are essential if board decisions are to receive the deference traditionally accorded them under the business judgment rule, especially insofar as structural decisions are concerned (such as those relating to corporate acquisitions).[21] Third, director conduct is constrained by an active market for corporate control, ever-rising rates of shareholder litigation, and, some say, activist shareholders.[22] In sum, modern boards of directors are smaller than their antecedents, meet more often, are more independent from management, own more stock, and have better access to information. All of which culminated in a series of high-profile board revolts against incumbent managers at such iconic American corporations as General Motors, Westinghouse, and American Express.[23] More recently, the firing of "Chainsaw Al" Dunlap by Sunbeam's board provided additional anecdotal evidence of board activism.[24]

In any event, the institutional structure created by corporate law allows but does not contemplate one-man rule. If it comes to overt conflict between board and top management, the former's authority prevails as a matter of law, if not always in practice. Indeed, it is the necessity for retaining dismissal of senior management as a potential sanction that explains why the board is at the apex of the corporate hierarchy rather than functioning as an advisory committee off to the side of the corporate organizational chart. One can imagine a structure of corporate authority identical to current norms except that the board acts as a mere advisory body to a single autocratic CEO. On the face of it, such a structure seemingly would preserve most advantages of the current structure. Consequently, it is the board's power to hire and fire senior management that explains their position at the apex of the corporate hierarchy. Hence, our emphasis on director rather than managerial primacy.

20. See Charles M. Elson, Director Compensation and the Management–Captured Board: The History of a Symptom and a Cure, 50 SMU L. Rev. 127 (1996).

21. See Stephen M. Bainbridge, Independent Directors and the ALI Corporate Governance Project, 61 Geo. Wash. L. Rev. 1034, 1068–81 (1993) (describing how judicial review of management buyouts and other conflict of interest transactions focuses on role of independent directors).

22. Daniel P. Forbes & Frances J. Milliken, Cognition and Corporate Governance: Understanding Boards of Directors as Strategic Decision-making Groups, 24 Acad. Mgmt. Rev. 489 (1999). For a review of the literature on the corporate governance role of institutional investors generally and board reform specifically, see Jonathan L. Johnson et al., Boards of Directors: A Review and Research Agenda, 22 J. Mgmt. 409, 414–16 (1996). For skepticism as to the merits and likely sustainability of institutional investor activism, see Stephen M. Bainbridge, The Politics of Corporate Governance, 18 Harv. J. L. & Pub. Pol'y 671 (1995).

23. See Ira M. Millstein, The Evolution of the Certifying Board, 48 Bus. Law. 1485, 1489–90 (1993).

24. In most cases, of course, board oversight tends to be both less dramatic and more informal. Individual directors pass concerns onto the CEO, who in turn bounces ideas off board members. Rather than struggling to overcome the collective action problems that impede firing a CEO, an individual director tries to obtain better performance through a private reprimand.

C. Consequences of the separation of ownership and control

Modern scholars refer to the consequences of separating ownership and control as agency costs,[25] but Berle and Means had identified the basic problem over forty years before the current terminology was invented: "The separation of ownership from control produces a condition where the interests of owner and of ultimate manager may, and often do, diverge."[26] Will the board of directors use its control of the corporation to further the selfish interest of the board members rather than the best interests of the corporation's shareholders and other constituencies? To ask the question is to answer it. Given human nature, it would be surprising indeed if directors did not sometimes shirk or self-deal. Consequently, much of corporate law is best understood as a mechanism for constraining agency costs.

A narrow focus on agency costs, however, easily can distort one's understanding. In the first instance, corporate managers operate within a pervasive web of accountability mechanisms that substitute for monitoring by residual claimants. The capital and product markets, the internal and external employment markets, and the market for corporate control all constrain shirking by firm agents.

In the second, agency costs are the inescapable result of placing ultimate decisionmaking authority in the hands of someone other than the residual claimant. Because we could substantially reduce agency costs by eliminating discretion, but do not do so, one infers that discretion has substantial virtues. In a complete theory of the firm, neither discretion nor accountability can be ignored, because both promote values essential to the survival of business organizations.[27] At the same time, however, the power to hold to account is ultimately the power to decide.[28] Managers cannot be made more accountable without undermining their discretionary authority. Establishing the proper mix of discretion and accountability thus emerges as the central corporate governance question.

25. Michael C. Jensen & William H. Meckling, Theory of the Firm: Managerial Behavior, Agency Costs, and Ownership Structure, 3 J. Fin. Econ. 305 (1976). Recall that agency costs are defined as the sum of the monitoring and bonding costs, plus any residual loss, incurred to prevent shirking by agents. See generally Bernard S. Black, Agents Watching Agents: The Promise of Institutional Investor Voice, 39 UCLA L. Rev. 811 (1992); Brian R. Cheffins, Current Trends in Corporate Governance: Going from London to Milan via Toronto, 10 Duke J. Comp. & Int'l L. 5, 13–17 (2000); Lynne L. Dallas, Two Models of Corporate Governance: Beyond Berle and Means, 22 U. Mich. J.L. Reform, 19 (1988); Harold Demsetz, The Structure of Ownership and the Theory of the Firm, 26 J. L. & Econ. 375 (1983); Frank H. Easterbrook, Two Agency Cost Explanations of Dividends, 74 Am. Econ. Rev. 650 (1984); Frank H. Easterbrook, Managers' Discretion and Investors' Welfare: Theories and Evidence, 9 Del. J. Corp. L. 540 (1984); Ronald J. Gilson, A Structural Approach to Corporations: The Case Against Defensive Tactics in Tender Offers, 33 Stan. L. Rev. 819, 833–44 (1981).

26. Adolf A. Berle & Gardiner C. Means, The Modern Corporation and Private Property 6 (1932).

27. Michael P. Dooley, Two Models of Corporate Governance, 47 Bus. Law. 461 (1992).

28. Kenneth J. Arrow, The Limits of Organization 78 (1974).

The tension between authority and accountability is a theme to which we will often return, most notably in connection with the business judgment rule and shareholder voting rights. Suffice it for now to note that, given the significant virtues of discretion, one ought not lightly interfere with management or the board's decisionmaking authority in the name of accountability. Indeed, the claim should be put even more strongly: Preservation of managerial discretion should always be the null hypothesis. Because the separation of ownership and control mandated by U.S. corporate law has precisely that effect, by constraining shareholders both from reviewing most board decisions and from substituting their judgment for that of the board, that separation has a strong efficiency justification.

§ 5.4 The board as collective

A. Why a board?

At the apex of the corporate hierarchy stands not a single individual but a collective—the board of directors. The legal rules governing the board of directors, moreover, put considerable emphasis on the need for collective rather than individual action.[1] As the Restatement (Second) of Agency puts it, for example, a director "has no power of his own to act on the corporation's behalf, but only as one of a body of directors acting as a board."[2] Why this emphasis on collective action? Put another way, why not vest the ultimate power of fiat in an individual autocrat rather than a collegial group?

The commentary to the MBCA's provisions on board meetings provides one answer:

> A well-established principle of corporate common law accepted by implication in the Model Act is that directors may act only at a meeting unless otherwise expressly authorized by statute. The underlying theory is that the consultation and exchange of views is an integral part of the functioning of the board.[3]

The drafters' argument runs afoul of the old joke that a camel is a horse designed by a committee, yet their "underlying theory" is pervasively reflected in the statutory rules governing corporate boards.[4] The implicit

---

§ 5.4

1. At one time, many states in fact required that the board have at least three members, although most have eliminated that requirement. MBCA § 8.03(a) cmt.

2. Agency Restatement § 14 C cmt.

3. MBCA § 8.20 cmt. An alternative explanation is suggested by Jeffrey Gordon's persuasive demonstration that voting within a corporation is subject to Arrow's impossibility theorem, in the sense that voting on most matters of day-to-day policy would result in cyclical majorities. Although we will rely more heavily on information-and-

incentive-based arguments for the board's authority than does Gordon, he does present a convincing argument that corporate law's authority-based board of directors system is explicable in very large measure as a device for avoiding the cycling problem by restricting owner voice. Jeffrey Gordon, Shareholder Initiative and Delegation: A Social Choice and Game Theoretic Approach to Corporate Law, 60 U. Cin. L. Rev. 347 (1991).

4. Many of these housekeeping rules doubtless seem formalistic or even a little silly, but the requirement that the board

preference for group decisionmaking also finds support in two of the basic economic principles that have guided our analysis: bounded rationality and agency costs.[5]

1. *The board as an adaptive response to bounded rationality*

Vesting decisionmaking authority in a group rather than a single individual is a high value-added adaptive response to the problem of bounded rationality. Decisionmaking requires the use of scarce resources for four purposes: (1) observation, or the gathering of information; (2) memory, or the storage of information; (3) computation, or the manipulation of information; and (4) communication, or the transmission of information.[6] How do groups minimize these transaction costs vis-à-vis individual decisionmakers? Multiple sources of information may make it less costly to gather information, but it seems unlikely that directors qua directors do much to facilitate the observation process. Any such savings,

act only after meeting as a collective body actually has a sound economic basis. Work by experimental psychologists has found that group decisionmaking, under certain circumstances, can be superior to decisionmaking by individuals. Where evaluation of complex problems requiring the exercise of critical judgment is concerned, the evidence is clear that the performance of a group will be superior to that of the group's average member. This result has been confirmed by experiments requiring performance of a wide variety of tasks. See, e.g., Larry K. Michaelsen et al., A Realistic Test of Individual Versus Group Consensus Decision Making, 74 J. App. Psych. 834 (1989) (test taking in team learning settings); Marjorie E. Shaw, A Comparison of Individuals and Small Groups in the Rational Solution of Complex Problems, 44 Am. J. Psych. 491 (1932) (puzzle solving); see generally Gayle W. Hill, Group Versus Individual Performance: Are N + 1 Heads Better than One?, 91 Psych. Bull. 517 (1982). For a detailed review of the evidence on group decisionmaking, with applications to corporate law, see Stephen M. Bainbridge, Why a Board? Group Decision Making in Corporate Governance, 55 Vanderbilt L. Rev. 1 (2001).

5. There may also be a behavioral explanation for the board. Research in behavioral economics has identified a number of pervasive cognitive errors that bias decisionmaking. Several of the identified decisionmaking biases seem especially pertinent to managerial decisionmaking, especially the so-called overconfidence bias. The old joke about the camel being a horse designed by a committee captures the valid empirical observation that individuals are often superior to groups when it comes to matters requiring creativity. Research on brainstorming as a decisionmaking process, for example, confirms that individuals working alone generate a greater number of ideas than do groups, especially when the assigned task is "fanciful" rather than "realistic." Gayle W. Hill, Group Versus Individual Performance: Are N + 1 Heads Better than One?, 91 Psych. Bull. 517, 527 (1982). Individuals often become wedded to their ideas, however, and fail to recognize flaws that others might identify. Peter M. Blau & W. Richard Scott, Formal Organizations 116–21 (1962). In contrast, there is a widely-shared view that groups are superior at evaluative tasks. Group decisionmaking presumably checks individual overconfidence by providing critical assessment and alternative viewpoints, which is consistent with the standard account of the board's function. Recall that our taxonomy identified three basic board roles: monitoring, service, and resource gathering. At the core of the board's service role is providing advice and counsel to the senior management team, especially the CEO. At the intersection of the board's service and monitoring roles is the provision of alternative points of view. Put another way, most of what boards do requires the exercise of critical evaluative judgment but not creativity. Even the board's policymaking role entails judgment more than creativity, as the board is usually selecting between a range of options presented by subordinates. The board serves to constrain subordinates who have become wedded to their plans and ideas, rather than developing such plans in the first instance.

6. Roy Radner, Bounded Rationality, Indeterminacy, and the Theory of the Firm, 106 Econ. J. 1360, 1363 (1996).

moreover, likely are off-set by increased communication costs. By decentralizing both access to information and decisionmaking power, group decisionmaking requires additional resources and imposes additional delays on the decisionmaking process.

The relevant advantages of group decisionmaking therefore likely arise with respect to either memory and/or computation. As to the former, groups develop a sort of collective memory that consists not only of the sum of individual memories, but also an awareness of who knows what. Consequently, institutional memory is superior when the organization is structured as a set of teams rather than as a mere aggregate of individuals. There is some laboratory evidence, moreover, that the collective memory of groups leads to higher quality output.[7] Group members, for example, seem to specialize in memorizing specific aspects of complex repetitive tasks.

As to the relationship between group decisionmaking and computation-based costs, an actor can economize limited cognitive resources in two ways. First, by adopting institutional governance structures designed to promote more efficient decisionmaking. Second, by invoking shortcuts; i.e., heuristic problem-solving decisionmaking processes. Here we focus on the former approach, positing that group decisionmaking provides a mechanism for aggregating the inputs of multiple individuals with differing knowledge, interests, and skills. Numerous studies suggest that groups benefit from both by pooling of information and from providing opportunities for one member to correct another's errors.[8] In the corporate context, the board of directors thus may have emerged as an institutional governance mechanism to constrain the deleterious effect of bounded rationality on the organizational decisionmaking process.

2. *The board as a constraint on agency costs*

Individuals are subject to the temptations to shirk or self-deal. The internal dynamics of group governance, however, constrain self-dealing and shirking by individual team members. In this regard, group decisionmaking has a bi-directional structure. In the vertical dimension, a group may be superior to an individual autocrat as a monitor of subordinates in the corporate hierarchy. In the horizontal dimension, intra-group governance structures help constrain shirking and self-dealing at the apex of the hierarchy.

Vertical monitoring. Suppose the corporate hierarchy was capped by an individual autocrat rather than a board of directors. Under such circumstances, a bilateral vertical monitoring problem arises. On the one hand, the autocrat must monitor his/her subordinates. On the other hand, someone must monitor the autocrat.

---

7. Susan G. Cohen & Diane E. Bailey, What Makes Teams Work: Group Effectiveness Research from the Shop Floor to the Executive Suite, 23 J. Mgmt. 239, 259 (1997).

8. See Gayle W. Hill, Group Versus Individual Performance: Are N + 1 Heads Better than One?, 91 Psych. Bull. 517, 533 (1982).

In theory, if corporate law vested ultimate decisionmaking authority in individual autocrats, chief executives could be monitored by their subordinates. Economist Eugene Fama contends, for example, that lower level managers monitor more senior managers.[9] It seems unlikely, however, that such up-stream monitoring happens often or in a sufficiently systematic way to provide a meaningful constraint on upper management. In any case, this monitoring mechanism does not take full advantage of specialization. Fama and Jensen elsewhere point out that one response to agency costs is to separate "decision management"—initiating and implementing decisions—from "decision control"—ratifying and monitoring decisions.[10] Such separation is a defining characteristic of the central office typical of M-form corporations. The monitoring mechanisms described herein could be accomplished through a simple pyramidal hierarchy of the sort found in U-form corporations. The M-form corporation adds to this structure a rationalization of decisionmaking authority in which the central office has certain tasks and the operating units have others, which allows for more effective monitoring through specialization, sharper definition of purpose, and savings in informational costs.[11] In particular, the central office's key decisionmakers—the board of directors and top management—specialize in decision control. Because low-and mid-level managers specialize in decision management, expecting them to monitor more senior managers thus requires them to perform a task for which they are poorly-suited.

A different critique of Fama's hypothesis is suggested by evidence with respect to meeting behavior. In mixed status groups, higher status persons talk more than lower status members. Managers, for example, talk more than subordinates in business meetings.[12] Such disparities result in higher status group members being more inclined to propound initiatives and wielding greater influence over the group's ultimate decision. Consequently, a core board function is providing a set of status equals for top managers.[13] As such, corporate law's insistence on the formal superiority of the board to management begins to make sense. To the extent law shapes social norms, admittedly a contested proposition,[14] corporate law empowers the board to more effectively constrain top management by creating a de jure status relationship favoring the board.

Horizontal monitoring. Who watches the watchers? Because all members of the corporate hierarchy—including our hypothetical autoc-

9. See, e.g., Eugene F. Fama, Agency Problems and the Theory of the Firm, 88 J. Pol. Econ. 288, 293 (1980).

10. Eugene F. Fama & Michael C. Jensen, Separation of Ownership and Control, 26 J. L. & Econ. 301, 315 (1983).

11. Oliver E. Williamson, The Economic Institutions of Capitalism 320 (1985).

12. Sara Kiesler & Lee Sproull, Group Decision Making and Communication Technology, 52 Org. Behav. & Human Decision Processes 96, 109–110 (1992).

13. Robert J. Haft, The Effect of Insider Trading Rules on the Internal Efficiency of the Large Corporation, 80 Mich. L. Rev. 1051, 1061 (1982) (describing the board as "a peer group—a collegial body of equals, with the chief executive as the prima inter pares").

14. See Stephen M. Bainbridge, Mandatory Disclosure: A Behavioral Analysis, 68 U. Cin. L. Rev. 1023, 1052–53 (2000) (describing debate).

rat—are themselves agents of the firm with incentives to shirk, a mechanism to monitor their productivity and reduce their incentive to shirk must also be created or one ends up with a never ending series of monitors monitoring lower level monitors. Economists Armen Alchian and Harold Demsetz famously solved this dilemma by requiring that the monitor be given the residual income left after all other workers have been paid.[15] This arrangement encourages the monitor to promote the most efficient use of the other inputs and to reduce shirking because his reward will depend upon the efficacy of his monitoring efforts. Unfortunately, their otherwise quite useful model has limited relevance to the public corporation. Although common stockholders are the corporation's residual claimants, they also are the corporate constituency perhaps least able to meaningfully monitor management behavior.

Consequently, corporate law and governance must provide alternatives to monitoring by the residual claimants. A hierarchy of individuals whose governance structures contemplate only vertical monitoring, such as that hypothesized above, cannot resolve the problem of who watches the watchers. By adding the dimension of horizontal monitoring, however, placing a group at the apex of the hierarchy provides a solution to that problem. Where an individual autocrat would have substantial freedom to shirk or self-deal, the internal dynamics of group governance constrain self-dealing and shirking by individual team members and, perhaps, even by the group as a whole. Within a production team, for example, mutual monitoring and peer pressure provide a coercive backstop for a set of interpersonal relationships founded on trust and other noncontractual social norms. Of particular relevance here are effort and cooperation norms.[16]

While the old adage opines "familiarity breeds contempt," personal proximity to others in fact deeply affects behavior. As people become closer, their behavior tends to improve: "something in us makes it all but impossible to justify our acts as mere self-interest whenever those acts are seen by others as violating a moral principle"; rather, "[w]e want our actions to be seen by others—and by ourselves—as arising out of appropriate motives."[17] Small groups strengthen this instinct in several ways. First, they provide a network of reputational and other social sanctions that shape incentives. Because membership in close knit groups satisfies the human need for belongingness, the threat of expulsion gives the group a strong sanction by which to enforce compliance with group norms. Because close knit groups involve a continuing relationship, the threat of punishment in future interactions deters the

---

15. Armen A. Alchian & Harold Demsetz, Production, Information Costs, and Economic Organization, 62 Am. Econ. Rev. 777 (1972).

16. Social norms are relevant to other aspects of decisionmaking besides agency costs. Group norms of reciprocity, for example, facilitate the process of achieving consensus within groups.

17. James Q. Wilson, What is Moral and How do we Know It?, Commentary, June 1993, at 37, 39. See also Kenneth L. Bettenhausen, Five Years of Groups Research: What have we Learned and What Needs to be Addressed?, 17 J. Mgmt. 345, 348 (1991).

sort of cheating possible in one-time transactions.[18] Second, because people care about how they are perceived by those close to them, communal life provides a cloud of witnesses whose good opinion we value. We hesitate to disappoint those people and thus strive to comport ourselves in accordance with communal norms. Effort norms will thus tend to discourage board members from simply going through the motions, but instead to devote greater cognitive effort to their tasks. Finally, there is a transaction costs economics explanation for the importance of closeness in trust relationships. Close knit groups know a lot about one another, which reduces monitoring costs and thus further encourages compliance with group norms. Members of close-knit groups therefore tend to internalize group norms.

Taken together, these factors suggest that group decisionmaking is a potentially powerful constraint on agency costs. It creates a set of high-powered incentives to comply with both effort and cooperation norms. This analysis thus goes a long way towards explaining the formalistic rules of state corporate law governing board decisionmaking.[19]

B. Implications: Board of directors housekeeping rules

1.   The requirement that boards act collectively by meeting

The board of directors is a collegial body that, for the most part, makes decisions by consensus. Accordingly, an individual director acting

18. See generally Oliver E. Williamson, The Economic Institutions of Capitalism 48 (1985) ("Informal peer group pressures can be mobilized to check malingering. . . . The most casual involves cajoling or ribbing. If this fails, rational appeals to persuade the deviant to conform are employed. The group then resorts to penalties by withdrawing the social benefits that affiliation affords. Finally, overt coercion and ostracism are resorted to.")

19. The case should not be overstated. Cohesive groups are subject to inherent cognitive biases that limit their effectiveness. A widely-cited example is the so-called risky shift phenomenon. There seems to be a polarizing effect in group decisionmaking, so that post-discussion consensus is more extreme than the individual pre-test results. See Norbert L. Kerr, Group Decision Making at a Multialternative Task: Extremity, Interfaction Distance, Pluralities, and Issue Importance, 52 Org. Behav. and Human Decision Processes 64 (1992). The most significant group bias for our purposes, however, is the "group think" phenomenon. Highly cohesive groups with strong civility and cooperation norms value consensus more greatly than they do a realistic appraisal of alternatives. Irving Janis, Victims of Groupthink (1972). In such groups, groupthink is an adaptive response to the stresses generated by challenges to group solidarity. To avoid those stresses, groups may strive for unanimity even at the expense of quality decisionmaking. To the extent groupthink promotes the development of social norms, it facilitates the board's monitoring function (see the next section). It may also be relevant to other board functions, such as resource acquisition, to the extent that it promotes a sort of esprit de corps. Yet, the downside is an erosion in the quality of decisionmaking. The desire to maintain group cohesion trumps the exercise of critical judgment. Adverse consequences of groupthink thus include not examining alternatives, being selective in gathering information, and failing to be either self-critical or evaluative of others. Studies of meeting behavior, for example, conclude that people tend to prefer options that have obvious popularity. Sara Kiesler & Lee Sproull, Group Decision Making and Communication Technology, 52 Org. Behav. & Human Decision Processes 96 (1992). In the corporate setting, board culture often encourages groupthink. Boards emphasize politeness and courtesy at the expense of oversight. CEOs can foster and channel groupthink through their power to control information flows, reward consensus, and discourage reelection of troublemakers. The groupthink phenomenon therefore demands close attention with respect to a variety of corporate governance issues, but is most directly relevant to the board composition debate discussed below.

alone generally has neither rights nor powers.[20] Instead, unless otherwise authorized by statute, only collective decisions taken at a meeting of the board at which a quorum is present are binding on the corporation.[21] This common law principle is reflected, albeit by negative implication, in DGCL § 141(b)'s statement that "[t]he vote of the majority of the directors present at a meeting at which a quorum is present *shall be the act of the board of directors* . . . ."[22]

2. *Board size*

Corporate statutes historically required that boards consist of at least three members, who had to be shareholders of the corporation and, under some statutes, residents of the state of incorporation.[23] Today these requirements have largely disappeared. DGCL § 141(b) authorizes boards to have one or more members and mandates no qualifications for board membership. MBCA §§ 8.02 and 8.03 are comparable. As a default rule, allowing single member boards probably makes sense. It gives promoters maximum flexibility, while allowing the creation of multi-member boards at low cost. In light of the apparent advantages of group decisionmaking, however, it is hardly surprising that multi-member boards are the norm for corporations of any significant size.[24]

Is there an optimal board size? One meta-analysis found a statistically significant correlation between increased board size and improved financial performance.[25] Given the potential influence of moderating variables, however, it does not seem safe to draw firm conclusions from that survey. Other studies, moreover, are to the contrary.[26]

---

20. This general statement is subject to the caveat that individual directors do have rights to inspect corporate books and records. See, e.g., Cohen v. Cocoline Products, Inc., 150 N.Y.S.2d 815 (1956).

21. See e.g., Greenberg v. Harrison, 124 A.2d 216 (Conn.1956) (directors cannot vote by proxy); Baldwin v. Canfield, 1 N.W. 261 (Minn.1879) (corporation not bound by a sale of land where the board never met to vote, even though all directors individually executed the deed). But see, e.g., Myhre v. Myhre, 554 P.2d 276 (Mont.1976) (board could act informally in a close corporation in which all shareholders were also directors); Gerard v. Empire Square Realty Co., 187 N.Y.S. 306 (N.Y.App.Div.1921) (informal approval of a contract by the board of a close corporation, all of whose shareholders were represented on the board, and all of whom had consented, was binding on the corporation); Remillong v. Schneider, 185 N.W.2d 493 (N.D.1971) (close corporation board with long-standing practice of acting informally could bind corporation by informal act); Baker v. Smith, 102 A. 721 (R.I.1918) (same).

22. DGCL § 141(b) (emphasis supplied). MBCA § 8.21 and DGCL § 141(f) authorize boards to act without a meeting by means of written consents, but require unanimity.

23. MBCA § 8.03(a) cmt.

24. Board sizes vary widely. A 1999 survey found that slightly less than half of had 7 to 9 members, with the remaining boards scattered evenly on either side of that range. National Association of Corporate Directors, Public Company Governance Survey 1999–2000 7 (Oct. 2000) (44 percent between 7 and 9).

25. Dan R. Dalton, Number of Directors and Financial Performance: A Meta–Analysis, 42 Acad. Mgmt. J. 674, 676 (1999).

26. See, e.g., Theodore Eisenberg et al., Larger Board Size and Decreasing Firm Value in Small Firms, 48 J. Fin. Econ. 35 (1998) (finding a significant negative correlation between board size and firm profitability in small and medium Finnish firms); see generally Sanjai Bhagat & Bernard Black, The Uncertain Relationship Between Board Composition and Firm Performance,

In theory, larger boards may facilitate the board's resource-gathering function by providing interlocking relationships with potential customers, suppliers, and other strategic partners. Large boards also provide more opportunities to create insurgent coalitions that constrain agency costs with respect to senior management. On the other hand, however, large boards likely will be contentious and fragmented, which reduces their ability to collectively monitor and discipline senior management. In such cases, the senior managers can affirmatively take advantage of the board through coalition building, selective channeling of information, and dividing and conquering. In sum, the question of whether there is an optimum board size lacks a parsimonious answer. As is so often the case, one size likely will not fit all.

3. *Electronic participation in board meetings*

Modern statutes typically provide that directors may participate in board meetings by conference call or speakerphone, provided that all participants can hear one another.[27] The requirement that members be able to "hear" one another seems quaint in an era of electronic mail, instant messaging, and so forth. Interestingly, however, research on decisionmaking has found that groups linked by computer make fewer remarks and take longer to reach decisions than do groups meeting face to face.[28]

As with other aspects of the rules governing board meetings, accordingly, there seems to be a legitimate basis for otherwise formalistic rules. Electronic communication takes place mostly through text-based mediums. Reading and typing, for many people, are slower and require greater effort than verbal communication. Text-based communication also deprives participants of social cues, such as body language and tone of voice, that may be important signals. Social norms constraining behavior apparently function less well in text-based communication, as demonstrated by the flaming phenomenon in Usenet discussion groups.

4. *Notice of board meetings*

Unless the articles of incorporation require otherwise, no notice of regularly scheduled board meetings is required.[29] Special meetings require at least two days notice.[30] As a matter of statutory law, the requisite notice need not announce the purpose of the meeting. Because the directors' duty of care requires them to make an informed decision, however, it is advisable to provide directors of advance notice of the reason for calling a meeting and any relevant documentation.[31] Notice

---

54 Bus. Law. 921, 941–42 (1999) (summarizing studies).

27. See, e.g., DGCL § 141(i); MBCA § 8.20(b).

28. Starr Roxanne Hiltz et al., Experiments in Group Decision Making: Communication Process and Outcome in Face-to-Face versus Computerized Conferences, 13 Human Communication Research 225, 243–44 (1986); Jane Siegel et al., Group Processes in Computer–Mediated Communication, 37 Org. Behavior & Human Decision Processes 157 (1986).

29. MBCA § 8.22(a).

30. MBCA § 8.22(b).

31. See, e.g., Smith v. Van Gorkom, 488 A.2d 858 (Del.1985), in which the court held that the board breached its fiduciary

may be waived in writing, either before or after the meeting.[32] Attendance at a meeting also constitutes waiver of notice, unless the director objects to the lack of notice at the beginning of the meeting and thereafter refrains from voting.[33] Any party may challenge the adequacy of notice in any context in which the validity of the board's actions are challenged.[34] As with other requirements relating to board meetings, the notice rules are intended to ensure that the board functions as a collegial body, all of whose members participate and get the benefit of the participation by all other members.

5.   *Quorum and voting*

The statutory default for a quorum is a majority of the directors, although the articles or bylaws may provide for either a greater or lesser number.[35] As for voting, the statute further provides: "If a quorum is present when a vote is taken, the affirmative vote of a majority of directors present is the act of the board of directors unless the articles of incorporation or bylaws require the vote of a greater number of directors."[36] Note that the effectively treats abstentions as no votes, because abstaining directors are "present." By negative implication, this provision also ensures "that the board of directors may act only when a quorum is present."[37] If the quorum is broken by departing directors, the board may not act. Directors who are present at the meeting are deemed to assent to any actions taken unless they, inter alia, ensure that their dissent is noted on the minutes of the meeting.[38] This provision reinforces the notion of the board as a collegial body, "forcefully bringing the position of the dissenting member to the attention of the balance of the board of directors."[39]

6.   *Board term limits*

Corporate law statutes generally limit directors to one year terms of office, although the Delaware code provides that directors shall serve

---

duty of care by "approving the 'sale' of the Company upon two hours' consideration, without prior notice, and without the exigency of a crisis or emergency." Id. at 874. The court went on to note: "None of the directors, other than Van Gorkom and Chelberg [two insiders], had any prior knowledge that the purpose of the meeting was to propose a cash-out merger of Trans Union.... Without any documents before them concerning the proposed transaction, the members of the Board were required to rely entirely upon Van Gorkom's 20–minute oral presentation of the proposal." Id. See also Gimbel v. Signal Companies, Inc., 316 A.2d 599 (Del.Ch.), aff'd per curiam, 316 A.2d 619 (Del.1974), in which the court criticized the facts that (1) the "board meeting was called on only one-and-a-half days' notice" and (2) that the company's "outside directors were not notified of the

meeting's purpose," which were cited as factors in the court's determination that the company's management had failed to give the board "the opportunity to make a reasonable and reasoned decision." Id. at 615.

32.   MBCA § 8.23(a).

33.   MBCA § 8.23(b).

34.   Schroder v. Scotten, Dillon Co., 299 A.2d 431 (Del.Ch.1972).

35.   See, e.g., DGCL § 141(b) (providing a minimum quorum of 1/3 of the directors); MBCA § 8.24(b) (same).

36.   MBCA § 8.24(c).

37.   MBCA § 8.24 cmt.

38.   MBCA § 8.24(d).

39.   MBCA § 8.24 cmt.

until their successor is elected and qualified.[40] Where the corporation has adopted a classified board, the directors' term of office is either two or three years, depending on whether the board was divided into two or three classes respectively. In any case, the statutes are silent as to the number of terms a director may serve. Because corporation statutes broadly authorize corporations to adopt articles of incorporation specifying director qualifications, however, corporations may adopt charter provisions limiting the number of times someone may serve as a director.

Director term limits remain rare, but are becoming more common. In 1999, 19% of surveyed boards had some restriction on board tenure, although the maximum tenure varied widely.[41] Are they a good idea? On the one hand, a high degree of turnover among board members may be healthy because a skeptical outsider perspective helps prevent groupthink. On the other hand, however, high turnover discourages individual board members from investing in firm-specific human capital. As such, high turnover rates undermine both the board's ability to effectively monitor and its role as a source of institutional memory. High turnover rates also interfere with group cohesiveness, with potentially adverse effects on the role of social norms as a mechanism of team governance. The prescriptive lesson is that one size will not fit all and firms should be allowed to determine whether director term limits are in their individual interest.

§ 5.5   Board composition

A.   Formalities: Herein of board qualifications

Corporate statutes historically required that directors be shareholders of the corporation and, under some statutes, residents of the state of incorporation. Today these requirements have largely disappeared. DGCL § 141(b) mandates no qualifications for board membership, nor does MBCA § 8.02. Interestingly, however, requiring directors to own stock in the corporation has come back into vogue in recent years. Although neither the MBCA nor the DGCL require corporations to impose any qualifications on board membership, both permit corporations to do so in their articles of incorporation. Many public corporations now require directors to own stock and, moreover, compensate directors in stock rather than cash.

B.   Proposals for reform: Herein of independent directors

Critics of state corporate law complain that it is both descriptively and normatively deficient, because state corporate codes do little to define either the composition or function of the board, its committees, and its subordinates. Proposals to reform the board of directors

---

40. DGCL § 141(b).

41. National Association of Corporate Directors, Public Company Governance Survey 1999–2000 15 (Oct. 2000).

abound—either to bring its composition and functions into line with the board's alleged real world role or, even more commonly, into line with some purported ideal.[1] The most ambitious reform effort to date remains the ALI PRINCIPLES. Virtually every proposal made by the ALI PRINCIPLES was controversial to some degree. Among the most hotly debated, however, was the basic issue of what role the board of directors, especially the independent members of the board, should play in corporate governance.

When the idea of an ALI restatement of corporate law emerged in the 1970s, corporate law was under attack from many directions. In TAMING THE GIANT CORPORATION,[2] for example, Ralph Nader claimed that pollution, workplace hazards, discrimination, unsafe products, corporate crime, and a host of other antisocial corporate social behaviors all were attributable to lack of management accountability. Accordingly, Nader called for a federal corporation law, displacing state law, which would be structured to make management more accountable to shareholders and to society.

In his attack on corporate boards, Nader compared directors to "cuckolds," who are "often the last to know when [their] dominant partner—management—has done something illicit." To redress this situation, Nader called for the institution of full-time professional directors. Incumbent managers could neither sit on the board nor nominate candidates for the board. Once elected, by way of cumulative voting, the board members would serve on a full-time basis, with no outside employment, and for no more than 4 two-year terms. Board members would be provided with staffs and full access to corporate information. Each board member would be responsible for some specified aspect of the business, such as employee welfare or law compliance.

Reform proposals from more traditional scholars were modest only by comparison. Professor Melvin Eisenberg, for example, argued that corporate statutes required the board to manage the corporation, but in the real world the board was essentially passive, with most of its functions being performed by senior executives. Arguing that the board's principal remaining function was the selection and monitoring of the firm's chief executive, Eisenberg claimed that most boards failed to adequately perform even that residual task.[3] In response, Eisenberg set

---

§ 5.5

1. See generally Victor Brudney, The Independent Director—Heavenly City or Potemkin Village?, 95 Harv. L. Rev. 597 (1982); Jill E. Fisch, Taking Boards Seriously, 19 Cardozo L. Rev. 265 (1997); Ronald J. Gilson & Reinier Kraakman, Reinventing the Outside Director: An Agenda for Institutional Investors, 43 Stan. L. Rev. 863 (1991); Ira M. Millstein & Paul W. MacAvoy, The Active Board of Directors and Performance of the Large Publicly Traded Corporation, 98 Colum. L. Rev. 1283 (1998); James M. Tobin, The Squeeze

on Directors—Inside is Out, 49 Bus. Law. 1707 (1994).

2. Ralph Nader et al., Taming the Giant Corporation 17–32 (1976).

3. Melvin A. Eisenberg, The Structure of the Corporation 139–41, 162–72 (1976). See also Alfred F. Conard, Corporations in Perspective 349 (1976); Myles L. Mace, Directors: Myth and Reality 184–90 (1971); Harold M. Williams, Corporate Accountability and Corporate Power, in Power and Accountability: The Changing Role of the Corporate Board of Directors 13–14 (1979).

forth a set of reform proposals that foreshadowed in large measure the provisions of the early Tentative Drafts of the ALI PRINCIPLES.

1. *Defining our terms: Who is an independent director?*

In common parlance, a director is viewed as independent if he is neither employed by the corporation nor controlled by insiders. In contrast, the ALI PRINCIPLES use an elaborate standard for determining whether a director is independent. Indeed, the ALI PRINCIPLES generally do not even use the term "independent director." Rather, they look to whether the director has a "significant relationship" with the corporation's senior executives. Significant relationship includes employment by the corporation, prior employment within the two preceding years, family relationships, and various economic relationships.[4] The term "senior executive" picks up the chief executive, operating, financial, legal, and accounting officers, as well as the chairman of the board of directors, the president, treasurer, secretary, and vice-chairmen or vice-presidents having major policymaking functions.[5]

The NYSE has adopted stock exchange listing standards providing that a director will not be deemed independent if, inter alia, (1) the director was employed by the corporation or its affiliates in the past three years, (2) the director has an immediate family member who, during the past three years, was employed by the corporation or its affiliates as an executive officer, (3) the director has a direct business relationship with the company,[6] and (4) the director is a partner, controlling shareholder, or executive officer of an organization that has a business relationship with the corporation, unless the corporation's board determines in its business judgment that the relationship does not interfere with the director's exercise of independent judgment.[7]

2. *Independent directors under the ALI PRINCIPLES*

In Part III of Tentative Draft No. 1, the drafters proposed scrapping state corporate law's traditionally minimalist approach in favor of a new "monitoring model." In prescribing both the board's composition and function, the drafters' main goal was to explicitly separate the task of managing large publicly held corporations from that of monitoring those who do the managing.[8] The corporation's officers were to carry out the

---

4. ALI PRINCIPLES at § 3A.01.

5. ALI PRINCIPLES at §§ 1.27(a), 1.33.

6. For this purpose, the requisite business relationships include commercial, banking, consulting, legal, and accounting relationships.

7. New York Stock Exchange, Listed Company Manual § 303.01 (2000).

8. The ALI PRINCIPLES divide corporations into three categories. "Large publicly held corporation" means a corporation having two thousand or more record stockholders and $100 million in total assets. ALI PRINCIPLES at § 1.24. "Publicly held corporation" is defined as a corporation having five hundred or more record stockholders and $5 million in total assets. Id. at § 1.31. The term "small publicly held corporation" is used in the ALI PRINCIPLES to describe those companies that fall within the definition of publicly held corporation, but do not qualify as a large publicly held corporation. Id. at § 1.35. In general, the mandatory provisions contained in part III of Tentative Draft No. 1 applied only to large publicly held corporations. For small publicly held corporations, these provisions generally

former set of responsibilities, while the board was charged with the latter.[9] To promote managerial accountability, great emphasis was laid on the use of independent directors.

Tentative Draft No. 1 required that independent directors comprise a majority of the board of directors of a large publicly held corporation.[10] This was intended to ensure objective board evaluation of management's performance. The same concern led the drafters to urge that, as a matter of good corporate practice, the independent directors should not have outside employment or other commitments that would interfere with their performance of their duties. Likewise, provisions allowing the independent directors to call upon corporate employees for assistance, to retain separate council or other experts on special issues, and to inspect corporate records and interview corporate personnel, were intended to allow the independent directors to bypass the company's senior executives when gathering information.

Tentative Draft No. 1 also laid great stress on the role of three oversight committees, comprised primarily of independent directors. Specifically, Tentative Draft No. 1 mandated audit and nominating committees for large publicly held corporations and recommended the establishment of a compensation committee. Because financial data is the basic means by which management performance is measured, the audit committee was intended to provide a forum for independent directors to discuss the firm's financial results outside of management's presence. It was therefore to be comprised exclusively of independent directors. The committee was to select the corporation's independent auditor and, among other things, review the corporation's financial results in consultation with the auditor.

The nominating committee was to be comprised exclusively of outside directors, including at least a majority of independent directors (i.e., directors lacking a "significant relationship" with the corporation), and was charged with, among other things, recommending candidates for director positions.[11] The exclusion of officers or employees from member-

---

were recommended as rules of good corporate practice. See, e.g., American Law Inst., Principles of Corporate Governance and Structure: Restatement and Recommendations 89 (Tentative Draft No. 1, 1982) (audit committees).

9. The ALI PRINCIPLES overstated the distinction between monitoring and managing. To take but a single anecdotal example, during the 1970s and '80s, RJR Nabisco's management spent millions of dollars to develop a smokeless cigarette. See Bryan Burrough & John Helyar, Barbarians at the Gate: The Fall of RJR Nabisco 74–77 (1990). When the board was finally informed, many directors were reportedly angered by management's failure to consult with them beforehand. Their anger was wholly justified, for the smokeless cigarette

flopped. Those responsible resigned to avoid being fired. The corporation probably would have been better served if the board had rejected the smokeless cigarette early in its development. But would this be monitoring or managing? Monitoring the performance of senior executives is the board's major function, but that necessarily involves activities that can best be described as managing the corporation.

10. American Law Inst., Principles of Corporate Governance and Structure: Restatement and Recommendations § 3.03(a) (Tentative Draft No. 1, 1982).

11. American Law Inst., Principles of Corporate Governance and Structure: Restatement and Recommendations § 3.06 (Tentative Draft No. 1, 1982).The drafters

ship on the nominating committee was intended to ensure that senior executives did not play a significant role in the selection of board members. The same concern is further reflected in the rule allowing the nominating committee to consider candidates proposed by the senior executives, but giving only the committee the power to recommend such candidates to the board or shareholders.

The recommended compensation committee, like the nominating committee, was to be comprised solely of outside directors, including at least a majority of independent directors.[12] As the name suggests, it was to review and approve (or recommend to the full board) the compensation of senior executives and generally oversee the corporation's compensation policies. A separate compensation committee was recommended because of concerns that inside directors, even if recused from considering their own compensation, would not be able to objectively evaluate the compensation of other senior executives in light of the close relationship between one executive's compensation and that of another.

In response to the sharp criticism to which Tentative Draft No. 1 was subjected,[13] subsequent drafts were revised in a number of respects. Some of the changes were merely cosmetic. For example, while the word monitoring no long appears in the final version's description of the board's function, the basic division between monitoring and management functions was retained under new terminology.[14] The ALI PRINCI-PLES thus still urge that the company be managed by its principal senior executives,[15] as well as arguing that the selection and oversight of those executives is the board's basic function.

likely expected that a nominating committee comprised of independent directors would screen out individuals who nominally meet the ALI PRINCIPLES' definition of an independent director but in fact are biased towards the incumbent senior executives. See Melvin Aron Eisenberg, The Modernization of Corporate Law: An Essay for Bill Cary, 37 U. Miami L. Rev. 187, 205 (1983).

12. American Law Inst., Principles of Corporate Governance and Structure: Restatement and Recommendations § 3.07 (Tentative Draft No. 1, 1982).

13. For discussion of the ALI PRINCIPLES' controversial origin and evolution, see Stephen M. Bainbridge, Independent Directors and the ALI Corporate Governance Project, 61 Geo. Wash. L. Rev. 1034 (1993); William J. Carney, The ALI's Corporate Governance Project: The Death of Property Rights?, 61 Geo. Wash. L. Rev. 898 (1993); see also Joseph F. Johnston, Social Affairs Unit Research Report 33—An American Lesson for European Company Directors: The Emerging Consensus in Corporate Governance 13–15 (2000).

14. Among the many striking stylistic changes introduced in Tentative Draft No. 2 was the new name given the project. Having begun life as "Principles of Corporate Governance: Restatement and Recommendations," the project became (and remains) "Principles of Corporate Governance: Analysis and Recommendations." This change made clear that the project was not merely a restatement of existing law, but in fact often recommended changes in existing law. See American Law Inst., Principles of Corporate Governance: Analysis and Recommendations (Tentative Draft No. 2, 1983). Second, recommendations concerning corporate practice were eliminated from the black letter sections; in addition, the phraseology used was changed from "good corporate practice" to mere "corporate practice." Id. at viii. Finally, the second draft made explicit that recommendations concerning corporate practice were "not intended as legal rules, noncompliance with which would impose liability." Id. at 83. As adopted, the ALI PRINCIPLES retain these stylistic points.

15. ALI PRINCIPLES at § 3.01.

Perhaps the most meaningful change was the conversion of virtually all of the proposed mandatory board composition and function rules into mere recommendations of corporate practice.[16] Where Tentative Draft No. 1 prohibited the board of a large publicly held corporation from managing the firm on a regular basis, for example, the ALI PRINCIPLES, as adopted, restored the board's traditional power to do so.[17] Where Tentative Draft No. 1 required that independent directors make up a majority of a large publicly held corporation's board, the final version merely recommends such a composition as a matter of corporate practice.[18]

The provisions on oversight committees were similarly watered down. While the final version retains the requirement that large publicly held corporation have an audit committee,[19] for example, its composition has been broadened and its functions have been sharply limited. Where the audit committee once was to be comprised solely of independent directors, such directors now need comprise only a majority of the committee.[20] Where the audit committee was once at the heart of the board's monitoring role, the audit committee's role is now limited to reviewing the corporation's auditing systems and the independence of the outside auditor.[21]

3. Stock exchange listing standards

Although no state has implemented the ALI PRINCIPLES' proposals in this area, a number of comparable provisions have been incorporated into stock exchange listing standards. The NYSE, for example, requires that all listed companies have an audit committee comprised solely of independent directors. The committee must have at least three members, all of whom must be "financially literate." At least one committee member must have expertise in accounting or financial management.[22]

The SEC put additional teeth into the exchanges' audit committee requirements by mandating that corporate proxy statements include a report from that committee containing a variety of disclosures. The report, for example, must state whether the committee reviewed and discussed the company's audited financial statements with management and the firm's independent auditors. The report must disclose whether

16. Tentative Draft No. 4 announced that the project's recommendations with respect to board composition and the oversight committees would be moved into a new Part III–A, to more clearly distinguish them from the provisions of Part III having legal effect. This approach was retained in the Principles as adopted.

17. ALI PRINCIPLES at § 3.02(b)(6).

18. ALI PRINCIPLES at § 3A.01(a).

19. ALI PRINCIPLES at § 3.05. A nominating committee now is merely recommended and its functions have been likewise scaled back. Id. at § 3A.04.

20. ALI PRINCIPLES at § 3.05. All committee members, however, must be outside directors. Id.

21. Id. (the audit committee is to periodically review "the corporation's processes for producing financial data, its internal controls, and the independence of the corporation's external auditor"). On the other hand, § 3A.03 recommends as a matter of corporate practice that the audit committee recommend the firm to be employed as the corporation's external auditor and review the results of the audit and the corporation's financial results.

22. New York Stock Exchange, Listed Company Manual § 303.01 (2000).

the board of directors has adopted a written charter for the committee; if so, the company must include a copy of that charter in its proxy statement at least once every three years. Finally, the report must state whether the audit committee's members are independent as defined in the relevant stock exchange listing standards and, if not, why not.[23]

One can but infer from these moves that the Commission has gotten back into the therapeutic disclosure business. In other words, the Commission is using disclosure requirements not to inform shareholders, but to affect substantive corporate behavior. In this case, to change how corporations use their audit committees.

Therapeutic disclosure requirements undoubtedly affect corporate behavior. If the company must report bribes paid to foreign officials, for example, those disclosures will be picked up by the media. The fear of negative publicity thus discourages bribery. So too does the fear of litigation.

Therapeutic disclosure, however, is problematic because seeking to effect substantive goals through disclosure requirements violates the putative Congressional intent behind the federal securities laws. When the New Deal era Congresses adopted the Securities Act and the Securities Exchange Act, there were three possible statutory approaches under consideration: (1) the fraud model, which would simply prohibit fraud in the sale of securities; (2) the disclosure model, which would allow issuers to sell very risky or even unsound securities, provided they gave buyers enough information to make an informed investment decision; and (3) the blue sky model, pursuant to which the Commission would engage in merit review of a security and its issuer. The federal securities laws adopted a mixture of the first two approaches, but explicitly rejected federal merit review. As such, the substantive behavior of corporate issuers is not within the SEC's regulatory purview.

4. *Do corporations really need independent directors?*

Should a board of directors include any independent directors? They are such an ingrained part of the corporate landscape that it seems odd even to ask the question. Yet, it is still worth asking. Two functions of independence seem especially plausible sources of an affirmative answer to that question: providing interlocks and constraining agency costs.

Interlocks and decisionmaking. Putting outside directors on the board creates interlocks with a variety of potential strategic partners. This is relevant not only to the board's resource gathering function, but also to its monitoring and service functions. Complex business decisions require knowledge in such areas as accounting, finance, management, and law. Providing access to such knowledge can be seen as part of the board's resource gathering function. Board members may either possess such knowledge themselves or have access to credible external sources thereof. Specialization of this sort is a rational response to bounded

---

23. Exchange Act Rel. No. 42,266 (Dec. 22, 1999).

rationality. The expert in a field makes the most of his limited capacity to absorb and master information by limiting the amount of information that must be processed by limiting the breadth of the field in which the expert specializes. As applied to the corporate context, more diverse boards likely contain more specialists, and therefore should get greater benefits from specialization.[24]

Having said that, however, a full-time senior employee has other informational advantages over outsiders who devote but a small portion of their time and effort to the firm. At the minimum, the presence of outsiders on the board increases decisionmaking costs simply because the process takes longer. Outsiders by definition need more information and are likely to take longer to persuade than are insiders.[25] More subtly, and perhaps more importantly, long-term employees make significant investments in firm-specific human capital. Any employee who advances to senior management levels necessarily invests considerable time and effort in learning how to do his job more effectively. Much of this knowledge will be specific to the firm for which he works, such as when other firms do not do comparable work or his firm has a unique corporate culture. In either case, the longer he works for the firm, the more firm-specific his human capital becomes. Such an employee is likely to make better decisions for the firm than an outsider, even assuming equal levels of information relating to the decision at hand. The insider can put the decision in a broader context, seeing the relationships and connections it has to the firm as whole.

This analysis implicates our argument that the board of directors is best understood as a collegial body using consensus-based decisionmaking. Recall that Arrow demonstrated that consensus works only where team members have equal information and comparable interests. Insiders are more likely to have comparable access to information and similar interests than are disparate outsiders. Boards meet relatively rarely and, qua boards, often have little information. Insiders have lots of informal contacts, which promotes team formation, and better access to informa-

---

24. Conversely, however, note that, because their decisions are publicly observable, board members have a strong incentive to defer to expert opinion. Because even a good decision maker is subject to the proverbial "act of God," the market for reputation evaluates decisionmakers by looking at both the outcome and the action before forming a judgment. If a bad outcome occurs, but the action was consistent with approved expert opinion, the hit to the decisionmaker's reputation is reduced. In effect, by deferring to specialists, a decisionmaker operating under conditions of bounded rationality is buying insurance against a bad outcome. In a collegial, multi-actor setting, the potential for log-rolling further encourages deference. A specialist in a given field is far more likely to have strong feelings about the outcome of a particular case than a nonexpert. By deferring to the specialist, the nonexpert may win the specialist's vote in other cases as to which the nonexpert has a stronger stake. Such log-rolling need not be explicit, although it doubtless is at least sometimes, but rather can be a form of the tit-for-tat cooperative game. In board decisionmaking, deference thus invokes a norm of reciprocation that allows the non-expert to count on the specialist's vote on other matters.

25. Michael P. Dooley & E. Norman Veasey, The Role of the Board in Derivative Litigation: Delaware Law and the Current ALI Proposals Compared, 44 Bus. Law. 503, 533 (1989).

tion. Hence, in Arrow's model, consensus decisionmaking should work best in insider dominated boards.

Independence and agency costs. The conventional justification for director independence is grounded in agency cost economics. Recall, however, that the very centralization of management making possible the large corporation also introduces the potential for agency costs. Corporate law therefore provides a series of accountability mechanisms designed to constrain agency costs. Chief among them is the board of directors, especially the independent directors. To be sure, outsiders have neither the time nor the information necessary to be involved in the minutiae of day-to-day firm management. What outsiders can do, however, is to monitor senior managers and replace those whose performance is sub-par. Hence, for example, the emphasis in the ALI PRINCI-PLES on the board's monitoring function.

If independent directors effectively constrain agency costs, however, there should be an identifiable correlation between the presence of outsiders on the board and firm performance. Yet, the empirical data on this issue is decidedly mixed. Some early studies found such correlations. Rosenstein and Wyatt, for example, found that shareholder wealth increased when independent directors are appointed by management.[26] Weisbach studied board decisions to remove a CEO, finding that boards comprised mainly of independent directors were more likely to base the removal decision on poor performance, as well as being more likely to remove an under-performing CEO, than were insider dominated boards. He also found that CEO removals by outsider dominated boards added to firm value, while CEO removals by insider dominated boards did not.[27] Baysinger and Butler found that corporate financial performance tends to increase (up to a point) as the percentage of independent directors increases.[28] Cotter et al. found that boards dominated by outsiders generate higher shareholder gains from tender offers.[29]

Other studies, however, such as that by MacAvoy, found that board composition had no effect on profitability.[30] Klein likewise found little evidence of a general association between firm performance and board composition, but found a positive correlation between the presence of

26. Stuart Rosenstein & Jeffrey G. Wyatt, Outside Directors, Board Independence, and Shareholder Wealth, 26 J. Fin. Econ. 175 (1990).

27. Michael S. Weisbach, Outside Directors and CEO Turnover, 20 J. Fin Econ. 431 (1988).

28. Barry D. Baysinger & Henry N. Butler, Revolution Versus Evolution in Corporation Law: The ALI's Project and the Independent Director, 52 Geo. Wash. L. Rev. 557, 572 (1984).

29. James F. Cotter et al., Do Independent Directors Enhance Target Shareholder Wealth During Tender Offers?, 43 J. Fin. Econ. 195 (1997). See also Bernard S.

Black, The Value of Institutional Investor Monitoring: The Empirical Evidence, 39 UCLA L. Rev. 895, 900 (1992) (asserting that boards with a majority of independent directors make better acquisition decisions, citing an unpublished study by John Byrd and Kent Hickman).

30. Paul MacAvoy, et al., ALI Proposals for Increased Control of the Corporation by the Board of Directors, in Statement of the Business Roundtable on the American Law Institute's Proposed "Principles of Corporate Governance and Structure: Restatement and Recommendations" C–1 (Feb. 1983).

insiders on board finance and investment committees and firm performance.[31] Rosenstein and Wyatt found that the stock market experienced a significantly positive price reaction to announcements that insiders had been appointed to the board when insiders owned more than 5% of the firm's stock.[32] A meta-analysis of numerous studies in this area concluded that there was no convincing evidence that firms with a majority of independent directors outperform other firms. It further concluded that there is some evidence that a "moderate number" of insiders correlates with higher performance.[33] Another recent meta-analysis likewise found no evidence that board composition affects financial performance.[34]

A recent literature review by Wagner et al. further complicated the empirical landscape by effectively splitting the baby.[35] Their meta-analysis of 63 correlations found that, on average, increasing the number of outsiders on the board is positively associated with higher firm performance. On the other hand, increasing the number of insiders on the board had the same effect. A second meta-analysis confirmed that greater board homogeneity was positively associated with higher firm performance, which is not what standard theory would predict.

If independent directors are not effective monitors of senior management, why might that be the case? One obvious answer is that shirking is an endemic problem. Monitoring the performance of the firm's officers and employees is hard, time-consuming work. Moreover, most outside directors have full-time employment elsewhere, which commands the bulk of their attention and provides the bulk of their pecuniary and psychic income. Independent directors therefore may prefer leisure or working on their primary vocation to monitoring management. As Adam Smith observed three centuries ago,

---

31. April Klein, Firm Performance and Board Committee Structure, 41 J. L. & Econ. 275 (1998).

32. Stuart Rosenstein & Jeffrey G. Wyatt, Outside Directors, Board Independence, and Shareholder Wealth, 26 J. Fin. Econ. 175 (1990). In another study of the relationship between director stock ownership and firm performance, Bhagat, Carey, and Elson found a significant positive correlation between stock ownership by nominally independent directors and a variety of firm performance measures. They also found that as the dollar value of such holdings increased so did the probability that poorly performing firms would fire their CEO. Sanjai Bhagat et al., Director Ownership, Corporate Performance, and Management Turnover, 54 Bus. Law. 885 (1999). As already noted, modern corporation statutes do not mandate any specific qualifications for board membership. Interestingly, however, requiring directors to own stock in the corporation has come back into vogue

in recent years. Both the MBCA and DGCL allow the corporation to impose qualifications on board membership in the articles of incorporation. Many public corporations now require directors to own stock and, moreover, compensate directors in stock rather than cash. Charles M. Elson, Director Ownership, Corporate Performance, and Management Turnover, Corporate Governance Advisor, Sept./Oct. 1999.

33. Sanjai Bhagat & Bernard Black, The Uncertain Relationship Between Board Composition and Firm Performance, 54 Bus. Law. 921, 922 (1999).

34. Dan R. Dalton et al., Meta–Analytic Reviews of Board Composition, Leadership Structure, and Financial Performance, 19 Strategic Mgmt. J. 269 (1998).

35. John A. Wagner et al., Board Composition and Organizational Performance: Two Studies of Insider/Outsider Effects, 35 J. Mgmt. Stud. 655 (1998).

The directors of [joint stock] companies, however, being the managers rather of other people's money than of their own, it cannot well be expected, that they should watch over it with the same anxious vigilance with which the partners in a private co-partnery frequently watch over their own. Like the stewards of a rich man, they are apt to consider attention to small matters as not for their master's honour, and very easily give themselves a dispensation from having it. Negligence and profusion, therefore, must always prevail, more or less, in the management of the affairs of such a company.[36]

Other factors impede an independent director from monitoring management, even if he wishes to do so. Board meetings are few and short. According to one survey, directors in large manufacturing companies average a total of 14 board and committee meetings per year, with the average board meeting lasting only three hours.[37] Moreover, outside directors are generally dependent upon management for information.[38]

Worse yet, nominally independent directors may be effectively controlled by the insiders. It has long been common practice, for example, for a corporation's outside directors to include lawyers and bankers (of both the investment and commercial varieties) who are currently providing services to the corporation or may wish to provide services in the future. University faculty or administrators, to take another common example, may be beholden to insiders who control corporate donations to their home institutions. None of these outsiders are likely to bite the hand that feeds them.

Even if the independent directors are not actually biased in favor of the insiders, they often are predisposed to favor the latter. Most of the learning on this phenomenon, known as structural bias, arises out of the use of special litigation committees to terminate shareholder derivative litigation against officers or directors. Outside directors tend to be corporate officers or retirees who share the same views and values as the insiders.[39] A sense of "there but for the grace of God go I" therefore is

---

36. Adam Smith, The Wealth of Nations 700 (Modern Library ed. 1937). A 1911 British decision described the selection of a rubber corporation's board thusly:

The directors of the company, Sir Arthur Aylmer Bart., Henry William Tugwell, Edward Barber and Edward Henry Hancock were all induced to become directors by Harboard or persons acting with him in the promotion of the company. Sir Arthur Aylmer was absolutely ignorant of business. He only consented to act because he was told the office would give him a little pleasant employment without his incurring any responsibility. H.W. Tugwell was partner in a firm of bankers in a good position in Bath; he was seventy-five years of age and very deaf; he was induced to join the board by representations made to him in January, 1906. Bar-

ber was a rubber broker and was told that all he would have to do would be to give an opinion as to the value of rubber when it arrived in England. Hancock was a man of business who said he was induced to join by seeing the names of Tugwell and Barber, whom he considered good men.

In re Brazilian Rubber Plantations & Estates Ltd., [1911] 1 Ch. 425.

37. The Conference Board, Membership and Organization of Corporate Boards 25 (1990).

38. See Charles N. Waldo, Boards of Directors: Their Changing Roles, Structure, and Information Needs 95–118 (1985).

39. See Joy v. North, 692 F.2d 880, 888 (2d Cir.1982); George W. Dent, Jr., The Power of Directors to Terminate Sharehold-

said to be a likely response to litigation against fellow directors.[40]

Concern over structural bias was an important driving force behind the restrictive rules on special litigation committees in Tentative Draft No. 1.[41] Query, however, whether the derivative litigation context is really all that special. All outside directors—not just those who serve on SLCs—are nominated by the incumbent board members and passively elected by the shareholders, which supposedly biases the selection process towards directors whose cooperation and support the incumbents can count on. As such, if purportedly independent directors are likely to favor their fellow directors when the latter are sued, they are equally likely to do so in any conflict of interest situation. Consider, for example, the hostile takeover context. According to a survey taken during the "merger mania" days of the 1980s, over 50 percent of responding companies believed they were possible takeover targets, 45 percent had been the subject of takeover rumors, and 36 percent had experienced unusual or unexplained trading activity.[42] Where a nominally independent director's principal occupation is serving as an officer of another corporation, the "there but for the grace of God go I" syndrome again rears its head. Despite being an outsider, fears for his own firm may often render an independent director sympathetic to insiders' job security concerns when a hostile takeover threatens the firm.[43]

To be sure, the potential for shirking and bias easily can be overstated. Not all directors are biased—actually or structurally—and the annals of corporate law are replete with instances in which seemingly biased directors nevertheless did the right thing. Better still, independent directors have affirmative incentives to actively monitor management and to discipline poor managers. If the company fails on their watch, for example, the independent directors' reputation and thus their future employability is likely to suffer.[44]

Indeed, one can also overstate the argument that there is something problematic about protection of insider interests. Economist Oliver Williamson in fact suggests that one of the board's functions is to "safeguard the contractual relation between the firm and its management."[45] Insider board representation may be necessary to carry out that function. Many adverse firm outcomes are beyond management's control. If the board is limited to monitoring management, and especially if it is

er Litigation: The Death of the Derivative Suit, 75 Nw. U. L. Rev. 96, 111–13 (1980).

40. See, e.g., Zapata Corp. v. Maldonado, 430 A.2d 779, 787 (Del.1981).

41. TD No. 1 at 314.

42. S. Rep. No. 265, 100th Cong., 1st Sess. 79 (1987) (additional views of Sens. Sasser, Sanford & Chaffee).

43. See Dynamics Corp. v. CTS Corp., 794 F.2d 250, 256 (7th Cir.1986), rev'd on other grounds, 481 U.S. 69 (1987); see generally Michael P. Dooley & E. Norman Veasey, The Role of the Board in Derivative Litigation: Delaware Law and the Current

ALI Proposals Compared, 44 Bus. Law. 503, 534 (1989) ("the structural bias argument has no logical terminus").

44. Eugene F. Fama & Michael C. Jensen, Separation of Ownership and Control, 26 J. L. & Econ. 301, 315 (1983) ("outside directors will monitor the management that chooses them because outside directors have incentives to develop reputations as experts in decision control").

45. Oliver E. Williamson, The Economic Institutions of Capitalism 298 (1985).

limited to objective measures of performance, however, the board may be unable to differentiate between acts of god, bad luck, ineptitude, and self-dealing. Insiders' greater knowledge and firm-specific human capital would help draw such distinctions. Under such conditions, a variety of adverse outcomes may result. Risk averse managers may demand a higher return, for example. Alternatively, managers may reduce the extent of their investments in firm-specific human capital, so as to minimize nondiversifiable employment risk.

Insider representation on the board, in turn, will encourage learned trust between insiders and outsiders. Insider representation on the board thus provides the board with a credible source of information necessary to accurate subjective assessment of managerial performance. In addition, however, it also serves as a bond between the firm and the top management team. Insider directors presumably will look out for their own interests and those of their fellow managers. Board representation thus offers some protection against dismissal for adverse outcomes outside management's control.

Such considerations likely explain the finding by Klein of a positive correlation between the presence of insiders on board committees and firm performance.[46] They also help explain the finding by Wagner et al. that increasing the number of insiders on the board is positively correlated with firm performance.[47]

In sum, one size does not fit all. This result should not be surprising. On one side of the equation, firms do not have uniform needs for managerial accountability mechanisms. The need for accountability is determined by the likelihood of shirking, which in turn is determined by management's tastes, which in turn is determined by each firm's unique culture, traditions, and competitive environment. We all know managers whose preferences include a penchant for hard, faithful work. Firms where that sort of manager dominates the corporate culture have less need for outside accountability mechanisms.

On the other side of the equation, firms have a wide range of accountability mechanisms from which to choose. Independent directors are not the sole mechanism by which management's performance is monitored. Rather, a variety of forces work together to constrain management's incentive to shirk: the capital and product markets within which the firm functions; the internal and external markets for managerial services; the market for corporate control; incentive compensation systems; auditing by outside accountants; and many others. The importance of the independent directors' monitoring role in a given firm depends in large measure on the extent to which these other forces are allowed to function. For example, managers of a firm with strong takeover defenses are less subject to the constraining influence of the

46. See April Klein, Firm Performance and Board Committee Structure, 41 J. L. & Econ. 275 (1998).

47. See John A. Wagner et al., Board Composition and Organizational Performance: Two Studies of Insider/Outsider Effects, 35 J. Mgmt. Stud. 655 (1998).

market for corporate control than are those of a firm with no takeover defenses. The former needs a strong independent board more than the latter does.

The critical mass of independent directors needed to provide optimal levels of accountability also will vary depending upon the types of outsiders chosen. Strong, active independent directors with little tolerance for negligence or culpable conduct do exist. A board having a few such directors is more likely to act as a faithful monitor than is a board having many nominally independent directors who shirk their monitoring obligations.

§ 5.6   Removal and vacancies

Modern statutes generally allow the shareholders to remove directors with or without cause, unless the articles of incorporation specify that directors may be removed only for cause.[1] Removal is accomplished by the affirmative vote of a majority of the shares cast at a meeting at which a quorum is present. The board has no right to remove one of its members,[2] although the board obviously could recommend that shareholders remove one of its members and call a special meeting of the shareholders for that purpose. Grounds to remove a director for cause include "fraud, criminal conduct, gross abuse of office amounting to a breach of trust, or similar conduct."[3]

At early common law, the reservation to shareholders of the power to elect directors was interpreted to mean that the board could not fill vacancies. In contrast, modern statutes typically provide that vacancies in the board, whether the result of removal, resignation, death, expansion of the board, or what have you, may be filled either by the board or by the shareholders.[4]

§ 5.7   Board committees

Virtually all states allow the board to establish committees to which some board powers may be delegated, although a number do so only on an opt-in basis pursuant to which committee formation must be authorized by the articles of incorporation or bylaws. DGCL § 141(c)(2), for example, provides that the board may set up one or more committees consisting of one or more members. The jurisdiction and powers of the committee must be specified either in the bylaws or in the board resolution creating the committee. All of the powers and authority of the board may be delegated to such committees, except that board committees are barred from acting on matters requiring shareholder approval or changes to the bylaws. MBCA § 8.25 is comparable, except that it requires committees have 2 members and lists 8 specific acts that the board may not delegate to committees. Among the tasks forbidden to

§ 5.6

1. See, e.g., MBCA § 8.08(a).

2. Dillon v. Berg, 326 F.Supp. 1214 (D.Del.), aff'd, 453 F.2d 876 (3d Cir.1971);

Bruch v. National Guarantee Credit Corp., 116 A. 738 (Del.Ch.1922).

3. MBCA § 8.08 cmt.

4. See, e.g., MBCA § 8.10(a).

committees are: proposing any act requiring shareholder approval, changing the bylaws, authorizing distributions, or approving a plan of merger that does not require shareholder action.

§ 5.8   Officers

A.   Delegation of corporate powers to officers

Assume a public corporation incorporated in a Model Business Corporation Act state. The Company's Chief Executive Officer just retired. Who will select the CEO's replacement? In all probability, the board of directors. Recall that under MBCA § 8.01(b) all corporate powers are exercised by or under the board's authority—which includes the power to hire and fire. A significant personnel decision, such as the one in question, almost certainly would be made by the board. On the other hand, one would scarcely expect the board of directors of a public corporation to make minor personnel decisions, such as hiring a shop foreman.

Put bluntly, the modern public corporation is just too big for the directors to manage on anything resembling a day-to-day basis. Many directors of large corporations are outsiders, moreover, who have full time jobs elsewhere and therefore can devote relatively little time to the running of the business for which they act as directors. MBCA § 8.01(b) reflects these basic truisms in two respects. First, the statute provides that the "business and affairs of the corporation" shall be "managed by or under the direction of" the board. This formulation is intended to make clear that the board's role is to formulate broad policy and oversee the subordinates who actually conduct the business day-to-day. Second, the statute also provides that corporate powers may be exercised "under the [board's] authority," which allows (but does not require) the board to delegate decisionmaking authority to corporate officers.[1] In turn, corporate officers may delegate some of their responsibilities to less senior employees, and so forth down the organizational chart.

B.   The economics of hierarchy

Hierarchy has gotten a bad rap in many quarters. Over time, however, corporate hierarchies have proven to possess a permanence beyond that of any individual or group of individuals who worked in them. Despite the flattening of corporate hierarchies in recent years due

---

§ 5.8

1. Older corporation statutes required corporations to have specified officers. MBCA (1969) § 50 required a president, one or more vice presidents, a secretary, and a treasurer. Modern statutes allow the corporation to designate in its bylaws such officers as it wishes to have and allow officers to hold multiple offices. See, e.g., MBCA § 8.40. Being an officer, as opposed to a nonofficer employee, has legal significance for a couple of limited purposes. First, the scope of an officer's implied or apparent authority is probably broader than that of a nonofficer employee. Second, officers are subject to the short-swing profit liability provision in Securities Act Section 16(b).

to corporate down-sizing and the widespread adoption of employee involvement programs (such as quality circles),[2] moreover, most workplaces are still highly bureaucratic.

Put into contractarian terms, the hierarchical structures established by the corporate contract persisted as the parties to those contracts changed because such structures are a high survival value adaptive response to the transaction costs associated with organizing production within a firm. One role hierarchy plays relates to the transaction costs of gathering, transmitting, and processing information within a firm. A second entails the agency costs that follow from the human tendency towards opportunism.

1. *Hierarchy and information*

Every organization needs a transaction cost economizing mechanism for providing information to those with the power to make decisions. Efficient flows of information are especially critical to the success of authority-based decisionmaking structures. As a scarce good, however, information is costly to produce and transmit, which has implications for decisionmaking. For effective management, a low cost mechanism must be created to ensure that those with the power to make decisions have the necessary information, which must not be distorted by others' subjective interpretations, but does not overload the decisionmakers with unnecessary, distracting information.

Viewing the management process from this perspective, we can treat the hierarchical structure as nothing more than an efficient mechanism for information development and transmittal. Put another way, hierarchy is an adaptive response to the phenomenon of bounded rationality. Recall that bounded rationality claims that decisionmakers are rational actors with limited cognitive powers. Among other things, bounded rationality implies that decisionmakers can only gather so much information from so many inputs before being overloaded. In the corporate context, bounded rationality thus specifically implies that an individual manager can gather information about the productivity and capacities of only a limited number of inputs and, consequently, that no supervisor should receive such information from more than a few subordinates.

Branching hierarchies are a highly efficient adaptation to bounded rationality. They limit the span of control over which any individual manager has supervision to a small number of subordinates. Specifically, branching hierarchies put people into small groups, each member of which reports information to the same supervisor. That supervisor is likewise a member of a small group that reports to a superior and so on up to the top.[3] Such an organizational system gets reliable information to

---

2. On these phenomena and their relationship to the economics of hierarchy, see Stephen M. Bainbridge, Privately Ordered Participatory Management: An Organizational Failures Analysis, 23 Del. J. Corp. L. 979 (1998).

3. No implication is intended that information is always funneled to the top of the hierarchy or that all decisions are made there. To the contrary, all corporate hierarchies are characterized by a degree of

the right decisionmaker more efficiently than any other organizational system. Not surprisingly, some form of branching hierarchy therefore tends to be found in most public corporations: they could not make decisions without it.

Other features commonly associated with hierarchical organizations enhance the transaction cost economizing effect of hierarchy. Information processing and decisionmaking skills are neither widely nor equally distributed, which has significant implications for hierarchical decisionmaking. Top-level decisions have ripple effects throughout the chain-of-command. As a result, the cream must be allowed to rise to the top—control must be vested in the most capable decisionmakers. Hence, the widely observed phenomena of ports of entry and internal promotion ladders. New members generally enter a hierarchy at low level positions—ports of entry—with higher level positions being filled by internal promotion. This practice has several functions, one of which appears to be an adaptive response to bounded rationality. By giving firms a form of experience-rating, it allows them to ensure that top-level decisions are in fact made by those with the fewest limits on their cognitive powers.

2. Hierarchy and agency costs

Organizing production within a firm creates certain costs, of which the class known as agency costs is the most important for our purposes. Recall that a sole proprietorship with no agents will internalize all costs of shirking, because the proprietor's optimal trade-off between labor and leisure is, by definition, the same as the firm's optimal trade-off. Agents of a firm, however, will not internalize all of the costs of shirking: the principal reaps part of the value of hard work by the agent, but the agent receives all of the value of shirking.

Although agents ex post have strong incentives to shirk, ex ante they have equally strong incentives to agree to a corporate contract containing terms designed to prevent shirking. In any organization, however, the familiar triad of contracting problems—uncertainty, complexity, and opportunism—precludes the organization and its agents from entering into the complete contract necessary to prevent shirking by the latter. In large organizations, these transaction cost barriers to contracting are compounded by the equally familiar litany of collective action problems associated with bargaining in large number contexts. Accordingly, organizations rely not on ex ante contracting but on ex post governance—creating mechanisms for detecting and punishing shirking. Specifically, managers of such organizations are tasked with monitoring the organization's members: management meters the marginal productivity of each member and responds as necessary to prevent shirking.

decentralization of decisionmaking, with numerous decisionmakers at various levels within the hierarchy being tasked with particular areas of responsibility. Indeed, firms most appropriately might be described as a set of many overlapping hierarchies. Roy Radner, Hierarchy: The Economics of Managing, 30 J. Econ. Lit. 1382, 1412 (1992). The point is only that branching hierarchies are an efficient means of ensuring that information flows to the correct supervisor.

Just as hierarchy emerged as an essential component of the information processing aspects of managing large organizations, it also plays an equally essential role in the monitoring component of the managerial function. This is especially evident in the most important form of business organization: the M-form corporation. Such firms have two defining characteristics: many distinct operating units and management by a hierarchy of salaried executives. The board of directors delegates responsibility to senior management and monitors their performance. The senior managers in the firm's central office delegate responsibility to managers of operating units. In turn, the managers of each operating unit are responsible for monitoring the productivity of their unit. The process continues down to the foreman on the shop floor. Creating such a branching hierarchy addresses the problems of uncertainty, bounded rationality, and shirking faced by monitors by breaking the firm team into discrete segments, each of which is more readily monitored than the whole. At each hierarchical level, the responsible monitor is responsible for supervising only a few individuals, which usefully limits and focuses his task.

Hierarchical monitoring systems are especially important in large organizations due to the phenomenon known as "social loafing."[4] A famous 1913 study of pulling on a rope (think tug-of-war), for example, found members of two-person teams pulled to only 93% of their individual capacity, members of trios pulled to only 85%, and members of groups of 8 pulled to only 49% of capacity.[5] This phenomenon is attributable partially to the difficulty of coordinating group effort as size increases. Social loafing is also attributable, however, to the difficulty of motivating members of a group where identification and/or measurement of individual productivity is difficult. Because the conditions that give rise to social loafing are to be found in virtually all corporations of any significant size, hierarchical subdivision and monitoring of the workforce seems essential.

C. Officer powers: Herein of agency authority in the corporate setting

Suppose a newly appointed CEO wishes to hire an Administrative Assistant. If the CEO signs an employment contract with a prospective assistant, purporting to act on behalf of the corporation, will that contract be binding on the firm? The answer to that question depends on whether the CEO has authority as that term of art is used in agency law. Accordingly, we must (briefly) digress into agency law and the authority of agents.

---

4. Bibb Latané et al., Many Hands Make Light the Work: The Causes and Consequences of Social Loafing, 37 J. Personality & Soc. Psych. 822 (1979).

5. David A. Kravitz & Barbara Martin, Ringelmann Rediscovered: The Original Article, 50 J. Personality & Soc. Psych. 936 (1986).

1. The agency relationship defined

The agency relationship, in its broadest sense, includes any relationship in which one person (the agent) is authorized to act on behalf of another person (the principal). More specifically, an agency relationship arises when there is a manifestation of consent by the principal that the agent act on the principal's behalf and subject to the principal's control, and the agent consents to so act.[6] The requisite manifestation of consent can be implied from the circumstances, which makes it possible for the parties to have formed a legally effective agency relationship without realizing they had done so. Corporate employees, especially officers, are generally regarded as agents of the corporation.[7]

Curiously, neither an individual director nor even the board as a whole are regarded as agents of the corporation.[8] In a sense, when the board acts collectively, it functions as a principal in agency law terms. Unless shareholder approval is required, after all, the act of the board is the act of the corporation. As to the individual director, recall that he "has no power of his own to act on the corporation's behalf, but only as one of the body of directors acting as a board."[9]

2. Authority of agents

An agent may have either actual, apparent, or inherent authority to enter into contracts on behalf of the corporate principal. Likewise, in some settings, the corporation may be estopped from denying the authority of its employees. Determining whether an agent had the requisite authority in any given situation can be challenging. The differences between the various categories of authority are complex and subtle. In addition, many of the categories overlap—it is not at all uncommon for more than one type of authority to be present in a single transaction. Finally, the courts are not always precise when using labels. For example, estoppel and inherent authority are often called apparent authority. For our purposes, however, it is critical for you to understand that the legal consequences of an agent's actions do not depend on the type of authority at hand. For purposes of determining whether or not the corporate principal is bound by the contract vis-à-vis the third party to the transaction, authority is authority and the different types of authority are essentially irrelevant.

Why then does the law distinguish between different categories of authority? A former student of your author claimed that it was a deliberate attempt to confuse people, which called to mind the old joke— "just because you're paranoid doesn't mean you aren't being followed." As Justice Holmes once observed, albeit in a different context, "common sense is opposed to the fundamental theory of agency."[10]

---

6. Agency Restatement § 1.
7. Agency Restatement § 14 C cmt. a.
8. Agency Restatement § 14 C.

9. Agency Restatement § 14 C cmt. b.
10. Oliver Wendell Holmes, Jr., Agency II, 5 Harv. L. Rev. 1, 14 (1891).

It will be helpful to focus for a moment on the two basic types of authority: "actual authority" and "apparent authority." Consider the following hypothetical: Pam owns Whiteacre. Alan is her real estate broker and, indisputably, her agent. Ted is an outsider who claims that Alan entered into a contract on Pam's behalf to sell Whiteacre. Suppose Ted seeks to prove the existence of authority by evidence relating to communications between Pam and Alan, such as a letter from Pam to Allen in which Pam directed Alan to sell Whiteacre. In this instance, Ted is attempting to establish the existence of actual authority. In contrast, suppose Ted seeks to establish authority by evidence relating to communications from Pam to Ted. Suppose Pam sent Ted a letter in which she said that she had ordered Alan to sell Whiteacre. In this case, Ted is trying to establish apparent authority. Importantly, the contract will be no less binding if Ted proves apparent authority rather than actual. The difference between actual and apparent authority thus arises out of the way in which Ted seeks to prove that Alan was authorized to enter into the contract. In other words, the different categories of authority really are ways of classifying the proof the plaintiff must offer to bind the principal to the contract.

Actual authority exists when the agent reasonably believes the principal has consented to a particular course of conduct.[11] Actual authority can be express, as where the principal instructs the agent to "sell Whiteacre on my behalf." In the corporate context, express actual authority is usually vested in officers by a resolution of the board and/or a description of the officer's duties set forth in the bylaws.[12] Actual authority can also be implied, however, if the principal's acts or conduct are such the agent can reasonably infer the requisite consent. An agent has incidental actual authority, for example, to use all means reasonably necessary to carry out a particular result expressly mandated by the principal. A pattern of acquiescence by the board in a course of conduct may also give rise to implied actual authority to enter into similar contracts in the future.[13]

A contract entered into by an agent, purportedly on the principal's behalf, can be binding even if the agent lacks actual authority. Apparent authority exists where words or conduct of the principal lead the third party to reasonably believe that the agent has authority to make the contract.[14] Of particular importance with respect to the authority of corporate officers is the concept of apparent authority implied by custom. Suppose the board of directors instructed the CEO not to hire an

---

11. Agency Restatement §§ 7 & 26.

12. Compare Musulin v. Woodtek, Inc., 491 P.2d 1173 (Or.1971) (unless authorized by the bylaws or board resolution, corporate officers lacked authority to execute a promissory note on the corporation's behalf); Daniel Webster Council, Inc. v. St. James Ass'n, Inc., 533 A.2d 329 (N.H.1987) (officers have only such actual authority as provided in the bylaws or board resolutions)

with King World Prod., Inc. v. Financial News Network, Inc., 660 F.Supp. 1381 (S.D.N.Y.1987) (corporate officer had actual authority to execute a lease based, *inter alia*, on the job description in his employee contract).

13. Agency Restatement § 7 cmt. c & § 26 cmt. d.

14. Agency Restatement § 27.

assistant. The CEO thus lacked actual authority. The CEO nonetheless signs a prospective assistant to an employment contract that purports to be binding on the corporation. Is it binding? If the assistant (the third party) knew that that the corporation had placed the CEO in that position and its was customary for CEOs to have authority to hire assistants, the CEO will have apparent authority by virtue of that custom and the contract will be binding.[15] The economic rationale for this rule should be self-evident—it is the basic concept of the cheaper cost avoider. Sound social policy dictates that the loss be put on the party who could have most cheaply avoided it. Here the corporation's position, by definition, is idiosyncratic. Most firms let their CEOs hire assistants. It's cheaper for the few idiosyncratic principals to take precautions than for all job applicants to be obliged to take precautions.

3. *Authority of corporate officers*

Most of the case law on the apparent authority of corporate officers relates to the powers of presidents. Corporate presidents are regarded as general agents of the corporation vested with considerable managerial powers. Accordingly, contracts that are executed by the president on the corporation's behalf and arise out of the ordinary course of business matters are binding on the corporation.[16]

Cases dealing with the authority of subordinate officers are much rarer. As to vice presidents, a number of (mostly older) cases hold they have little or no implied or apparent authority to bind the corporation. Accordingly, they have only such authority as is expressly conferred on them in the bylaws or by board resolution.[17] The corporate secretary is

15. Agency Restatement § 27 cmt. d. Because apparent authority requires a manifestation by the principal, some connection between the third party and the principal is necessary. You must always look at how the third party learned of the agent's alleged authority and ask whether the principal reasonably can be said to have been the source of that knowledge. The act of placing the agent in a position customarily carrying certain powers, however, is deemed an adequate manifestation of consent by the principal. Id. Apparent authority by virtue of custom and inherent authority are most clearly different in cases where there is an undisclosed principal (i.e., the situation in which the third party is unaware that a principal exists). Where the third party knows that the principal exists and has placed the agent in a position carrying certain customary powers, there has been the requisite manifestation by the principal. Inherent authority does not require such a holding out and, hence, can exist even as to an undisclosed principal. Id., § 195.

16. See, e.g., Buxton v. Diversified Res. Corp., 634 F.2d 1313 (10th Cir.1980) (president had authority to sign audit statements in the ordinary course of his job); Evanston Bank v. Conticommodity Servs., Inc., 623 F.Supp. 1014 (N.D.Ill.1985) (president's inherent authority extended only to ordinary matters); Belcher v. Birmingham Trust Nat'l Bank, 348 F.Supp. 61 (N.D.Ala.1968) (president has power to bind corporation in ordinary course of business); Custer Channel Wing Corp. v. Frazer, 181 F.Supp. 197 (S.D.N.Y.1959) (president had authority to bring suit on the corporation's behalf because doing so was incidental to the ordinary business of the firm); Western Am. Life Ins. Co. v. Hicks, 217 S.E.2d 323 (Ga. App.1975) (president has power to act in ordinary course of business); Quigley v. W. N. Macqueen & Co., 151 N.E. 487 (Ill.1926) (by virtue of his office, president has power to bind the corporation to contracts made in the ordinary course of business).

17. See, e.g., Interstate Nat'l Bank v. Koster, 292 P. 805 (Kan.1930); James F. Monaghan, Inc. v. M. Lowenstein & Sons, 195 N.E. 101 (Mass.1935); Musulin v. Woodtek, 491 P.2d 1173 (Or.1971).

assumed to be the custodian of the corporation's books and records. Accordingly, the secretary has actual authority to certify those records. Otherwise, however, the secretary has no authority other than that conferred on him by the bylaws or board resolutions.[18]

An important line of cases limits the implied and apparent authority of corporate officers to matters arising in the ordinary course of business. In the leading decision of *Lee v. Jenkins Bros.*, the Second Circuit held:

> The rule most widely cited is that the president only has authority to bind his company by acts arising in the usual and regular course of business but not for contracts of an "extraordinary" nature....
>
> Apparent authority is essentially a question of fact. It depends not only on the nature of the contract involved, but the officer negotiating it, the corporation's usual manner of conducting business, the size of the corporation and the number of its stockholders, the circumstances that give rise to the contract, the reasonableness of the contract, the amounts involved, and who the contracting third party is, to list a few but not all of the relevant factors. In certain instances a given contract may be so important to the welfare of the corporation that outsiders would naturally suppose that only the board of directors (or even the shareholders) could properly handle it. It is in this light that the "ordinary course of business" rule should be given its content.[19]

As *Lee* suggests, there is no bright line between ordinary and extraordinary acts. It seems reasonable to assume, however, that acts consigned by statute to the board of directors will be deemed extraordinary.[20] Consequently, for example, the eight acts specified in MBCA § 8.25(e) that a board of directors may not delegate to a committee doubtless are extraordinary in nature. (Of course, once the board has made its decision with respect to an extraordinary matter, implementation of that decision can be delegated to officers.)

---

18. See, e.g., In re Drive–In Development Corp., 371 F.2d 215 (7th Cir.1966) (corporation estopped to deny validity of board resolutions certified by corporate secretary); Meyer v. Glenmoor Homes, Inc., 54 Cal.Rptr. 786 (Cal.App.1966) (secretary had power to affix corporate seal to documents but no authority re contracts of indebtedness); Blair v. Brownstone Oil & Refining Co., 120 P. 41 (Cal.App.1911) (no authority to execute release); Ideal Foods, Inc. v. Action Leasing Corp., 413 So.2d 416 (Fla.App. 1982) (secretary is a ministerial position with no authority to conduct business); Shunga Plaza, Inc. v. American Employer's Ins. Co., 465 P.2d 987 (Kan.1970) (corporate secretary has no power to bind the corporation unless the board has entrusted him with management of the business); Easter Oil Corp. v. Strauss, 52 S.W.2d 336 (Tex.Civ.App.1932) (secretary had no authority to execute promissory note)

19. Lee v. Jenkins Bros., 268 F.2d 357, 365–70 (2d Cir.), cert. denied, 361 U.S. 913 (1959). See also In re Mulco Products, Inc., 123 A.2d 95 (Del.Super.Ct.1956); Lucey v. Hero Int'l Corp., 281 N.E.2d 266 (Mass. 1972).

20. See, e.g., Plant v. White River Lumber Co., 76 F.2d 155 (8th Cir.1935) (sale of all or substantially all corporate assets).

In general, when one must decide a particular action is ordinary or extraordinary, the following factors seem especially pertinent:[21] How much of the firm's assets or earnings are involved? Suppose a corporation running a video tape rental store has $10,000 in cash available. A decision to spend $50 to buy a new tape would be ordinary, a decision to spend $5,000 to establish a line of compact discs for rent probably would be regarded as extraordinary. How much risk is involved? A decision to buy one tape is not very risky and would be an ordinary action, while a decision to open a new store might be very risky and therefore extraordinary. A decision to buy tapes on installment where the purchase price is paid off in three months probably would be seen as ordinary. A decision to take out a thirty year loan probably would be seen as extraordinary. How long will the action have an effect on the corporation? How much would it cost to reverse the decision? A decision to open a new store might be very expensive to reverse, as the corporation might not be able to get out of the lease if things went bad. Such a decision thus would be extraordinary.

As to most matters falling in the gray area between ordinary and extraordinary, a small host of decisions could be cited on either side.[22] There is relatively little consistency of outcome in this area. Courts are divided, for example, as to whether such basic matters as filing a lawsuit[23] or executing a guarantee of another corporation's debts are

---

21. ALI PRINCIPLES § 3.01 rptr. note.

22. For cases holding particular acts to be "ordinary," see, e.g., Lee v. Jenkins Bros., 268 F.2d 357 (2d Cir.), cert. denied, 361 U.S. 913 (1959) (hiring or firing employees and fixing their compensation and benefits); United Producers and Consumers Coop. v. Held, 225 F.2d 615 (9th Cir.1955) (same); Custer Channel Wing Corp. v. Frazer, 181 F.Supp. 197 (S.D.N.Y.1959) (initiating lawsuit); Memorial Hosp. Ass'n of Stanislaus County v. Pacific Grape Products Co., 290 P.2d 481 (Cal.1955) (making charitable pledge); In re Mulco Products, Inc., 123 A.2d 95 (Del.Super.Ct.1956) (executing promissory note); Quigley v. W. N. Macqueen & Co., 151 N.E. 487 (Ill.1926) (corporation would repurchase stock from shareholder at latter's option); Sperti Products, Inc. v. Container Corp., 481 S.W.2d 43 (Ky. App.1972) (executing guarantee of another firm's debts); Emperee v. Meyers, 269 A.2d 731 (Pa.1970) (executing note for benefit of prospective employee).

For cases holding particular acts to be extraordinary, see, e.g., In re Lee Ready Mix & Supply Co., 437 F.2d 497 (6th Cir. 1971) (mortgaging assets); Maple Island Farm, Inc. v. Bitterling, 209 F.2d 867 (8th Cir.1954) (lifetime employment contract); Abraham Lincoln Life Ins. Co. v. Hopwood, 81 F.2d 284 (6th Cir.1936); (contract to effectuate a merger); Computer Maint. Corp. v. Tilley, 322 S.E.2d 533 (Ga.App. 1984) (shareholder buy-sell agreement); First Nat'l Bank v. Cement Products Co., 227 N.W. 908 (Iowa 1929) (guaranteeing debt of another firm); Ney v. Eastern Iowa Tel. Co., 144 N.W. 383 (Iowa 1913) (initiating a lawsuit against the corporation's largest shareholder); Chesapeake & Potomac Tel. Co. v. Murray, 84 A.2d 870 (Md.1951) (lifetime employment contract); Daniel Webster Council, Inc. v. St. James Ass'n, Inc., 533 A.2d 329 (N.H.1987) (land sales contract); Myrtle Ave. Corp. v. Mt. Prospect Bldg. & Loan Ass'n, 169 A. 707 (N.J.1934) (postponing mortgage foreclosure); Burlington Indus., Inc. v. Foil, 202 S.E.2d 591 (N.C.1974) (guaranteeing another firm's debts); Brown v. Grayson Enter., Inc., 401 S.W.2d 653 (Tex.Civ.App.1966) (making lifetime employment contract); Lloydona Peters Enterprises, Inc. v. Dorius, 658 P.2d 1209 (Utah 1983) (initiating litigation).

23. Compare Custer Channel Wing Corp. v. Frazer, 181 F.Supp. 197 (S.D.N.Y. 1959) (president had authority to do so) with Lloydona Peters Enter., Inc. v. Dorius, 658 P.2d 1209 (Utah 1983) (no authority to do so); Ney v. Eastern Iowa Tel. Co., 144 N.W. 383 (Iowa 1913) (no authority to do so with respect to the corporation's largest shareholder).

ordinary or extraordinary.[24] One is tempted to remind the courts that Emerson's famous dictum against a fetish for consistency holds only that a *"foolish* consistency is the hobgoblin of little minds."

How should cases falling between the extremes be resolved? Put bluntly, the authority of corporate officers should be regarded as virtually plenary. Only matters expressly reserved to the board by statute, the articles of incorporation, or the bylaws should be deemed "extraordinary" and, consequently, beyond the scope of senior officers' authority.

One rationale for this position is suggested by simple statutory interpretation. recall that both the MBCA and Delaware law provide that the business of the corporation "shall be managed by or under the direction of a board of directors."[25] The use of the disjunctive prior to the phrase "under the direction of" suggests that the statute's drafters anticipated that the corporation would be managed by its officers with the board mainly exercising oversight authority. Unless a decision is expressly reserved to the board, the statutory language thus contemplates that a corporation may act through its officers subject to review by the board.

This reading of the statute comports with modern board practice. The de facto role of the board in most large public corporations consists of providing informal advice to senior management (especially the CEO) and episodic oversight. An extensive definition of extraordinary acts thus seems a needless formality.

An alternative justification for the proposed rule rests on the costs the existing rule imposes on third parties. Persons who do business with a corporation do so at some peril of discovering that their transaction will be deemed to implicate an extraordinary act and, accordingly, required express board action. An expansive definition of extraordinary matters increases this risk. Transaction costs thus increase in several respects. An expansive variant of the rule creates uncertainty, obliging third parties to take costly precautions. They may insist, for example, on seeing an express authorization from the board. Uncertainty about the outer perimeters of the rule also encourages opportunism by the corporation. If contracts dealing with extraordinary matters are voidable, the corporation effectively has a put with respect to the transaction. Uncertainty as to the enforceability of a contract gives the board leverage to extract a favorable settlement of the third party's claims.

---

24. Compare Sperti Products, Inc. v. Container Corp. of Am., 481 S.W.2d 43 (Ky. App.1972) (president had authority) with First Nat'l Bank v. Cement Products Co., 227 N.W. 908 (Iowa 1929) (no authority to do so); Burlington Indus., Inc. v. Foil, 202 S.E.2d 591 (N.C.1974) (president lacked authority, inter alia, because making such guarantees was not part of the corporations' ordinary business).

25. DGCL § 141(a); see also MBCA § 8.01.

Chapter 6

THE DUTY OF CARE AND THE BUSINESS JUDGMENT RULE

Analysis

---

§ 6.1   Authority and accountability

The business judgment rule is corporate law's central doctrine. It pervades every aspect of the state law of corporate governance, from negligence by directors to self-dealing transactions to termination of shareholder litigation and so on.[1] Yet, in many ways, it remains poorly understood. In part, this is because the doctrine is neither straightforward nor even, in some respects, well-developed. In part, however, the problem is attributable to the lack of a coherent and unified theory explaining why the rule exists and where its limits should be placed.

Admittedly, the business judgment rule is a curious doctrine. On the one hand, the duty of care tells directors to exercise reasonable care in making corporate decisions. On the other hand, the business judgment rule says that courts must defer to the board of directors' judgment absent highly unusual exceptions. Compare the liability of physicians, who are also held to a duty of care, but whose medical judgment gets no such deference. Why are directors of an incorporated business entitled to deference that physicians are denied?

Our analysis proceeds from the premise that the business judgment rule, like all of corporate law, reflects an inherent tension between two competing values: the need to preserve the board of directors' decision-making discretion and the need to hold the board accountable for its decisions.[2] Courts and commentators frequently focus almost solely on the latter value, emphasizing the need to deter and remedy misconduct by the firm's decisionmakers and agents. While the separation of ownership and control in modern public corporations indisputably implicates important accountability concerns, accountability standing alone is an inadequate normative account of corporate law. A fully specified account of corporate law must incorporate the value of authority—i.e., the need to develop a set of rules and procedures that provides the most efficient decisionmaking system. As it turns out, corporate decisionmaking efficiency can be ensured only by preserving the board's decisionmaking authority from being trumped by courts under the guise of judicial review.

Achieving an appropriate mix between these competing models of corporate governance is a daunting—but necessary—task. Ultimately, authority and accountability cannot be reconciled. At some point, greater accountability necessarily makes the decisionmaking process less efficient, while highly efficient decisionmaking structures necessarily involve reduced levels of accountability. Making corporate law thus requires a careful balancing of these competing values. Nowhere has this proven more challenging than with respect to the business judgment rule.

§ 6.2   A substantive standard or a rule of abstention?

The duty of care requires corporate directors to exercise "that amount of care which ordinarily careful and prudent men would use in

---

§ 6.1

1. See, e.g., Sinclair Oil Corp. v. Levien, 280 A.2d 717 (Del.1971) (fiduciary duties of controlling shareholder); Shlensky v. Wrigley, 237 N.E.2d 776 (Ill.App.1968) (operational decision); Auerbach v. Bennett, 393 N.E.2d 994 (N.Y.1979) (dismissal of derivative litigation).

2. See generally Michael P. Dooley, Two Models of Corporate Governance, 47 Bus. Law. 461 (1992).

similar circumstances.''[1] Because the corporate duty of care thus resembles the tort law concept of reasonable care, one might assume the duty of care is violated when directors act negligently. Yet, the one thing about the business judgment rule on which everyone agrees is that it insulates directors from liability for negligence: "While it is often stated that corporate directors and officers will be liable for negligence in carrying out their corporate duties, all seem agreed that such a statement is misleading.... Whatever the terminology, the fact is that liability is rarely imposed upon corporate directors or officers simply for bad judgment and this reluctance to impose liability for unsuccessful business decisions has been doctrinally labeled the business judgment rule."[2]

Beyond this point, however, agreement ceases. Two basic conceptions of the business judgment rule compete in the case law. One treats the rule as a standard of review. In effect, if not in doctrine, the rule simply raises the liability bar from mere negligence to, say, gross negligence or recklessness. The other treats the rule as an abstention doctrine that creates a presumption against judicial review of duty of care claims. The court will abstain from reviewing the substantive merits of the directors' conduct unless the plaintiff can rebut the business judgment rule by showing that one or more of its preconditions are lacking.

A. *Shlensky* and abstention

In the wonderful case of *Shlensky v. Wrigley*, plaintiff Shlensky challenged Philip Wrigley's famous refusal to install lights in Wrigley Field.[3] Shlensky was a minority shareholder in the corporation that owned the Chicago Cubs and operated Wrigley Field. Wrigley was the majority stockholder (owning 80% of the stock) and president of the company. In the relevant period, 1961–1965, the Cubs consistently lost money. Shlensky alleged that the losses were attributable to their poor home attendance. In turn, Shlensky alleged that the low attendance was attributable to Wrigley's refusal to permit installation of lights and night baseball. Shlensky contended Wrigley refused to institute night baseball because the latter believed (1) that baseball was a day-time sport and (2) that night baseball might have a negative impact on the neighborhood

---

§ 6.2

1. See, e.g., Graham v. Allis–Chalmers Mfg. Co., 188 A.2d 125, 130 (Del.1963).

2. Joy v. North, 692 F.2d 880, 885 (2d Cir.), cert. denied, 460 U.S. 1051 (1983).

3. Shlensky v. Wrigley, 237 N.E.2d 776, 777–78 (Ill.App.1968). The court also found Shlensky's claim defective for failure to allege damages. This is mainly an issue of causation. To be sure, the Cubs' poor attendance probably contributed to the firm's losses, but was poor home attendance attributable to the lack of night baseball or to the Cubs' performance? During the relevant time period, the Cubs were pretty consistent losers. In any event, this portion of the court's opinion is dicta. Once the court decided the business judgment rule was applicable, the inquiry could have (and should have) ended.

surrounding Wrigley Field. The other defendant directors allegedly were so dominated by Wrigley that they acquiesced in his policy of day-only baseball, which allegedly violated their duty of care.

The defendants moved to dismiss for failure to state a claim, asserting a strong abstention version of the business judgment rule: "defendants argue that the courts will not step in and interfere with honest business judgment of the directors unless there is a showing of fraud, illegality or conflict of interest." The court's analysis of that claim opened by extracting "certain ground rules" from prior precedents:

- "[C]ourts of equity will not undertake to control the policy or business methods of a corporation although it may be seen that a wiser policy might be adopted and the business more successful if other methods were pursued."

- "We have then a conflict in view between the responsible managers of a corporation and an overwhelming majority of its stockholders on the one hand and a dissenting minority on the other— a conflict touching matters of business policy, such as has occasioned innumerable applications to courts to intervene and determine which of the two conflicting views should prevail. The response which courts make to such applications is that it is not their function to resolve for corporations questions of policy and business management. The directors are chosen to pass upon such questions and their judgment unless shown to be tainted with fraud is accepted as final."

- "In a purely business corporation ... the authority of the directors in the conduct of the business of the corporation must be regarded as absolute when they act within the law, and the court is without authority to substitute its judgment for that of the directors."

Collectively, these "ground rules" describe the business judgment rule in action. From them, moreover, we can distill a basic statement of that rule: absent a showing of fraud, illegality, or conflict of interest, the court must abstain from reviewing the directors' decision.

The *Shlensky* court thus could have (and, perhaps, should have) dismissed plaintiff's claim without touching on the substantive merits of the defendants' decision or the motivation behind that decision. Curiously, however, the court took some pains to posit legitimate business reasons for that decision. The court opined, for example, that "the effect on the surrounding neighborhood might well be considered by a director." Likewise, the court asserted that "the long run interest" of the firm "might demand" consideration of the effect night baseball would have on the neighborhood. Does this mean that courts will examine the substantive merits of a board decision? No. The court did not require defendants to show either that such considerations motivated their decisions or that the decision in fact benefited the corporation. To the contrary, the court acknowledged that its speculations in this regard were irrelevant dicta:

> By these thoughts we do not mean to say that we have decided that the decision of the directors was a correct one. That is beyond our jurisdiction and ability. We are merely saying that the decision is one properly before directors and the motives alleged in the amended complaint showed no fraud, illegality or conflict of interest in their making of that decision.[4]

In sum, if we may invoke an appropriate metaphor, the Illinois court did not even allow Shlensky to get up to bat.

Although *Shlensky* is a particularly explicit example of the abstention version of the business judgment rule, it is far from unique. In *Kamin v. American Express Co.*,[5] for example, plaintiff challenged the board's decision to declare an in-kind dividend of shares in a second corporation. The court dismissed for failure to state a claim, opining: "The directors' room rather than the courtroom is the appropriate forum for thrashing out purely business questions which will have an impact on profits, market prices, competitive situations, or tax advantages." Hence, absent "fraud, dishonesty, or nonfeasance," the court would not substitute its judgment for that of the directors.

Abstention does not mean courts simply rubberstamp the board's decision. Both *Shlensky* and *Kamin* make clear that the business judgment rule has no application when fraud and/or self-dealing are present. Both cases also imply various prerequisites must be satisfied before the rule may be invoked. *Kamin*'s reference to "non-feasance" suggests, for example, that the business judgment rule may only be invoked where the board has made a conscious business decision—a point that becomes especially significant with respect to the burgeoning class of board oversight cases.[6] The good faith and disinterested independence of the directors also are often identified as conditions on which the rule is predicated.[7] Finally, albeit controversially, some courts and commenta-

---

4. The principle so announced is a very old one, indeed. See, e.g., Dodge v. Ford Motor Co., 170 N.W. 668, 682 (Mich.1919) (quoting authorities); Leslie v. Lorillard, 18 N.E. 363, 365 (N.Y.1888) (opining that "courts will not interfere unless the [directors'] powers have been illegally or unconscientiously executed; or unless it be made to appear that the acts were fraudulent or collusive, and destructive of the rights of the stockholders. Mere errors of judgment are not sufficient. . . .").

5. 383 N.Y.S.2d 807 (Sup.Ct.1976), aff'd, 387 N.Y.S.2d 993 (App.Div.1976). See also Norlin Corp. v. Rooney, Pace Inc., 744 F.2d 255, 264 (2d Cir.1984) (holding that New York's business judgment rule "bars judicial inquiry into actions of corporate directors taken in good faith and in the exercise of honest judgment in the lawful and legitimate furtherance of corporate purposes"); Gearhart Indus., Inc. v. Smith Int'l Inc., 741 F.2d 707 (5th Cir.1984) (under Texas law only fraud, self-dealing, or ultra vires conduct rebuts business judgment rule's protection).

6. See, e.g., Aronson v. Lewis, 473 A.2d 805, 813 (Del.1984) (stating that the business judgment rule is inapplicable "where directors have either abdicated their functions, or absent a conscious decision, failed to act").

7. See, e.g., Auerbach v. Bennett, 393 N.E.2d 994, 999 (N.Y.1979) (so long as directors were disinterested and acted in good faith, the business judgment rule required court to defer to board committee's recommendation to dismiss a shareholder derivative suit).

tors contend that the business judgment rule does not protect an irrational decision.[8] If these preconditions are satisfied, however, the abstention cases hold that the inquiry must end. There will be no judicial review of the substantive merits of the board's decision—whether those merits are measured in terms of fairness, reasonableness, wisdom, care, or what have you.

B. *Technicolor* and substantive review

In sharp contrast to *Shlensky* and its ilk, the Delaware supreme court's decision in *Cede & Co. v. Technicolor, Inc.*[9] embraced a conception of the business judgment potentially allowing far more intrusive judicial review. In late 1982, the board of Technicolor approved a merger of the company into a subsidiary of MacAndrews and Forbes Group, Inc. (MAF), for a cash consideration of $23 per share. Plaintiff Cinerama, Inc., the beneficial owner of 4.4% of Technicolor stock, dissented from the merger and brought suit. As the unusually convoluted litigation evolved, Cinerama eventually settled on a theory of the case positing that Technicolor's board violated its duty of care when it approved the merger.[10]

Cinerama's claim requires a brief digression on the Delaware Supreme Court's earlier decision in *Smith v. Van Gorkom*.[11] As with *Technicolor*, the *Van Gorkom* decision arose out of a shareholder's duty of care-based challenge to a board of directors' decision to approve a merger. In concluding that the business judgment rule did not entitle the directors to protection in that case, the court focused on the process by which the board made its decision, exhaustively detailing its many purported process failures. *Van Gorkom* thus established a requirement of what might be called procedural or process due care as a prerequisite for invoking the business judgment rule.[12] Put another way, directors

---

8. See, e.g., Brehm v. Eisner, 746 A.2d 244, 264 (Del.2000) ("Irrationality is the outer limit of the business judgment rule."); cf. ALI PRINCIPLES § 4.01(c)(3) (director must rationally believe action to be in corporation's best interest). For criticism of this requirement, which grapples at some length with the problems inherent in positing rationality as a predicate for invoking the business judgment rule, see Michael P. Dooley, Two Models of Corporate Governance, 47 Bus. Law. 461, 478–81 (1992).

9. 634 A.2d 345 (Del.1993).

10. The suit was originally filed as an appraisal proceeding. During the discovery phase of that proceeding, Cinerama uncovered evidence of an apparent procedural error in the merger approval process. Technicolor's organic documents contained an unusual provision mandating unanimous board approval of mergers, but, according

to Cinerama, one director had opposed the merger. Cinerama then filed a separate nonappraisal action to challenge the alleged procedural error, while also continuing to pursue its appraisal remedy. In its initial decision, the Supreme Court held that Cinerama need not elect between its appraisal remedy and the action for equitable or legal relief. Cede & Co. v. Technicolor, Inc., 542 A.2d 1182 (Del.1988). On remand, Cinerama was unable to prove the alleged procedural irregularity entitled it to relief, and was relegated to its duty of care claim.

11. 488 A.2d 858 (Del.1985).

12. Cf. Brehm v. Eisner, 746 A.2d 244, 262–64 (Del.2000) (rejecting plaintiff shareholder's contention that the business judgment rule includes an element of "substantive due care" and holding that the business judgment rule requires only "process due care").

who fail "to act in an informed and deliberate manner" may not assert the business judgment rule as a defense to care claims.[13]

In assessing Cinerama's breach of fiduciary duty claim, Chancellor Allen expressed "grave doubts" that Technicolor's board had discharged its *Van Gorkom* duties. He found it unnecessary to resolve those doubts, however, because he believed Cinerama could not prove damages: Allen had already determined the fair value of Technicolor at the time of the merger to be $21.60 per share, but the merger paid them $23.

On appeal, Justice Horsey's opinion for the supreme court began with a fairly standard statement of the board of directors' authority to manage the business and affairs of the corporation. The justice immediately went off the rails, however, by describing the business judgment rule as being intended "to preclude a court from imposing itself *unreasonably* on the business and affairs of a corporation." Compare that formulation to *Van Gorkom*'s statement that the rule's purpose is to "protect and promote the full and free exercise of the managerial power granted to Delaware directors." The striking contrast between these formulations strongly implies that the board's decision will no longer get much in the way of deference. Instead of preserving the board's decision-making authority, the *Technicolor* version of the business judgment rule apparently allows courts to second-guess board decisions if it is "reasonable" to do so.

Justice Horsey's willingness to second-guess board decisions is further suggested by his treatment of Chancellor Allen's duty of care analysis. Recall that Allen expressed "grave doubts" as to whether Technicolor's board satisfied its *Van Gorkom* duties. On appeal, Justice Horsey transformed the Chancellor's "grave doubts" into five "presumed findings" of gross negligence on the board's part: (1) the board had failed to make a "prudent search for alternatives" before approving the agreement; (2) once the merger agreement was signed, the board had no reasonable basis for believing that competing bids might be made; (3) most directors had little information about the merger and its terms before the meeting at which they approved it; (4) MAF locked up the transaction through stock options granted by the corporation and the two principal shareholders; and (5) the board was not "adequately informed" before approving the agreement. In sum, he concluded, "Cinerama clearly met its burden of proof for the purpose of rebutting the rule's presumption by showing that the defendant directors of Technicolor failed to inform themselves fully concerning all material information reasonably available prior to approving the merger agreement."

Yet, it gets worse. To be sure, Justice Horsey described the business judgment rule as "a powerful presumption" against judicial interference with board decisionmaking. But he then proceeded to gut the rule:

> Thus, a shareholder plaintiff challenging a board decision has the
> burden at the outset to rebut the rule's presumption. *To rebut the*

---

13. Smith v. Van Gorkom, 488 A.2d 858, 873 (Del.1985).

rule, a shareholder plaintiff assumes the burden of providing evidence that directors, in reaching their challenged decision, breached any one of the triads of their fiduciary duty—good faith, loyalty or due care. If a shareholder plaintiff fails to meet this evidentiary burden, the business judgment rule attaches to protect corporate officers and directors and the decisions they make, and our courts will not second-guess these business judgments. If the rule is rebutted, the burden shifts to the defendant directors, the proponents of the challenged transaction, to prove to the trier of fact the "entire fairness" of the transaction to the shareholder plaintiff.[14]

Notice how the justice puts the cart before the horse. Directors who violate their duty of care do not get the protections of the business judgment rule; indeed, the rule is rebutted by a showing that the directors violated their fiduciary duty of "due care." But this is exactly backwards. Under the abstention theory of the business judgment rule, the rule's core purpose is to prevent precisely what *Technicolor* requires. Recall that the rule prevented Shlensky from even getting up to bat with his care claims. The business judgment rule thus precludes courts from asking the question of—let alone deciding—whether the directors violated their duty of care. In contrast, under *Technicolor* the business judgment rule's primary function is the procedural task of assigning burdens of proof. In that limited guise, moreover, the rule merely assigns to plaintiff the burden of establishing a prima facie case—the same burden plaintiff bears in all civil litigation.[15] If plaintiff fails to carry that burden, the business judgment rule requires the court to dismiss the lawsuit without inquiry into the merits of the decision. But so what? Under this conception, the business judgment rule is nothing more than a restatement of the basic principle that the defendant is entitled to summary judgment whenever plaintiff fails to state a prima facie case. At best, *Technicolor* thus trivializes the rule.

By opening the courthouse door to care questions at the outset of the litigation, however, *Technicolor* went beyond merely trivializing the rule to gutting it. Arguably, *Technicolor* broadened the scope of judicial review of board decisionmaking to reach not just the process by which the decision was made but also the substance of the directors' decision. Significant consequences follow from this distortion of the business judgment rule. It is commonly held, for example, that mere allegations of director impropriety do not entitle plaintiff to discovery.[16] Yet, one can plausibly read *Technicolor* as authorizing precisely the sort of fishing expeditions the business judgment rule was intended to prevent.

---

14. Cede & Co. v. Technicolor, Inc., 634 A.2d 345, 361 (Del.1993) (emphasis supplied).

15. Granted, *Technicolor* does not mandate liability in the event that plaintiff carries its burden of showing a breach of fiduciary duty. Instead, per *Technicolor*, that showing merely shifts the burden to the defendant to show the entire fairness of the challenged transaction. Cede & Co. v. Technicolor, Inc., 634 A.2d 345, 361 (Del.1993). Yet, the court's importation of the entire fairness standard into duty of care litigation is itself a highly problematic feature of the opinion.

16. See, e.g., Stoner v. Walsh, 772 F.Supp. 790, 800 (S.D.N.Y.1991).

Technicolor can be reconciled with the mainstream of business judgment rule analysis only by interpreting the duty of "due care" as being limited to the adequacy of the decisionmaking process. At several points in the opinion, Justice Horsey in fact so characterized that duty.[17] In addition, numerous Delaware precedents interpret the requirement of due care as being limited to questions of process.[18] Yet, nothing in *Technicolor* explicitly limits its references to the duty of care to the decisionmaking process. Arguably, the cart remains before the horse.

C.   Where is Delaware now?

In view of Delaware's prominence in corporate jurisprudence, the importance of knowing where Delaware stands on such a fundamental question should be apparent. Unfortunately, Delaware law on this score remains ambiguous.[19] In *Brehm v. Eisner,*[20] for example, the Delaware supreme court failed even to cite *Technicolor.* More significantly, Chief Justice Veasey's opinion for the court explicitly rejected, as "foreign to the business judgment rule," plaintiffs' argument that the rule could be rebutted by a showing that the directors failed to exercise "substantive due care":

> Courts do not measure, weigh or quantify directors' judgments. We do not even decide if they are reasonable in this context. Due care in the decisionmaking context is *process* due care only . . . .

> . . . Thus, directors' decisions will be respected by courts unless the directors are interested or lack independence relative to the decision, do not act in good faith, act in a manner that cannot be attributed to a rational business purpose or reach their decision by a grossly

---

17. See, e.g., Cede & Co. v. Technicolor, Inc., 634 A.2d 345, 367 (Del.1993) (duty of care requires that directors "act on an informed basis").

18. See, e.g., Brehm v. Eisner, 746 A.2d 244, 264 (Del.2000) ("Due care in the decisionmaking context is *process* due care only."; emphasis in original); Citron v. Fairchild Camera & Instrument Corp., 569 A.2d 53, 66 (Del.1989) ("our due care examination has focused on a board's decision-making process").

19. Delaware courts often have not been as clear as they might be about the effect of the business judgment rule. In Warshaw v. Calhoun, 221 A.2d 487 (Del.1966), for example, the Delaware supreme court held that the business judgment rule precluded judicial interference with the board's decision absent a showing of bad faith or "gross abuse of discretion." Id. at 492–93. In Sinclair Oil Corp. v. Levien, 280 A.2d 717 (Del.1971), the court held that so long as the board's decision could be attributed to

any rational business purpose the business judgment rule precluded the court from substituting its judgment as to the merits of the decision for those of the board. Among other claims at issue therein, the plaintiff minority shareholder of a Sinclair subsidiary claimed that Sinclair had used its majority stock ownership to direct opportunities for expansion away from the subsidiary. After concluding that Sinclair had not engaged in self-dealing, the court held that the firm's expansion policy was a business decision entrusted to the board with which the court could not interfere absent "gross and palpable overreaching." Id. at 720. Both the "gross abuse of discretion" and the "gross and palpable overreaching" arguably contemplate some judicial review of the substantive merits of a board decision, but the latter standard seems far more deferential. Indeed, overreaching by definition seems to contemplate some element of fraud or unfair dealing beyond mere negligence.

20. 746 A.2d 244 (Del.2000).

negligent process that includes the failure to consider all material facts reasonably available.

If *Brehm* is not as an pure abstention decision as was *Shlensky*, it is close enough for government work. None of the preconditions to the rule's application stated by *Brehm* contemplate substantive review of the merits of the decision. Even the chief justice's reference to a rational business purpose requires only the possibility that the decision was actuated by a legitimate business reason, not that directors must prove the existence of such a reason. Absent self-dealing or other conflicted interests, or truly egregious process failures, the court will abstain.

On the other hand, in *McMullin v. Beran*, the Delaware supreme court reaffirmed the *Technicolor* approach. Per Justice Holland, the court explained that:

> The business judgment rule "operates as both a procedural guide for litigants and a substantive rule of law." Procedurally, the initial burden is on the shareholder plaintiff to rebut the presumption of the business judgment rule. To meet that burden, the shareholder plaintiff must effectively provide evidence that the defendant board of directors, in reaching its challenged decision, breached any *one* of its "triad of fiduciary duties, loyalty, good faith or due care." Substantively, "if the shareholder plaintiff fails to meet that evidentiary burden, the business judgment rule attaches" and operates to protect the individual director-defendants from personal liability for making the board decision at issue.[21]

Once again, the business judgment rule is treated as a standard of review rather than an abstention doctrine. Unlike poor old Shlensky, who was not even allowed up to bat, litigants suing under *McMullin* get to present evidence that the board failed to exercise due care. This distinction has important procedural consequences. In *Shlensky*, plaintiff could not survive a motion to dismiss, while plaintiff in *McMullin* was able to do so. Does that matter? Of course. As the probability increases that a cause of action will survive a motion to dismiss, both the probability that more such actions will be brought and the settlement value of such actions also increase.

Professor David Skeel contends that Delaware corporate decisional law cycles between competing doctrinal approaches to the same problem.[22] Skeel attributes this phenomenon to the Delaware supreme court's norm of unanimous decisionmaking. Although the Delaware supreme court has five members, most cases are heard by three judge panels. By tradition, the court strongly prefers to issue unanimous decisions. As a result of these factors, the membership of the panel that hears the case

21. McMullin v. Beran, 765 A.2d 910, 916–17 (Del.2000) (footnotes omitted). Accord Emerald Partners v. Berlin, 726 A.2d 1215, 1221 (Del.1999) (opining that "a breach of any one of the board of directors' triad of fiduciary duties, loyalty, good faith, or due care, sufficiently rebuts the business judgment presumption and permits a challenge to the board's action under the entire fairness standard").

22. David A. Skeel, Jr., The Unanimity Norm in Delaware Corporate Law, 83 Va. L. Rev. 127 (1997).

and the identity of the justice to whom the opinion is assigned matter a lot. The contrast between *Brehm* and *McMullin* provides rather compelling evidence for this hypothesis. Cases assigned to Chief Justice Veasey and like-minded members of the court will take an abstention-based approach. Cases assigned to justices of the same ilk as former Justice Horsey presumably will incline towards *Technicolor*. About all one can say with confidence, therefore, is that we probably have not heard the last word on this subject.

§ 6.3   The business judgment rule within a theory of the firm

Shlensky and *Technicolor* offer radically differing conceptions of the business judgment rule. Deciding between these competing conceptions requires us to situate the business judgment rule within a theory of the firm having analytical coherency and economic validity. We begin with first principles, starting with a brief review of the economic theory of the firm.

A.   First principles

Because only shareholders are entitled to elect directors, boards of U.S. public corporations are substantially insulated from pressure by nonshareholder corporate constituencies, such as employees or creditors. At the same time, the diffuse nature of U.S. stock ownership and regulatory impediments to investor activism substantially insulates directors from shareholder pressure. As such, the separation of ownership and control vests the board with virtually unconstrained freedom to exercise business judgment. In our theory of the firm, of course, this freedom is viewed as an essential attribute of efficient corporate governance.

The business judgment rule is an inevitable corollary of our explanation for the separation of ownership and control.[1] To review as briefly as possible, for the benefit of those who came in late, due to the limits on cognitive competence implied by bounded rationality, and the uncertainty and complexity inherent in long-term business relationships, incomplete contracts are inevitable, which in turn leaves greater room for opportunistic behavior, and thus inexorably leads to the need for coordination.[2] According to the Coasean theory of the firm, firms arise when it

---

§ 6.3

1. Recall that contractarians view the phrase "separation of ownership and control" as misleading. Shareholders do not own the corporation, they are just one of many constituencies bound together by a web of voluntary agreements. This understanding of the corporation liberates us from much of the baggage associated with earlier conceptions, especially those that treat the corporation as a thing capable of being owned. Under such models, stock ownership is no different than any other form of private property. From that erroneous premise follows the equally flawed cor-

ollary that the corporation's directors are merely stewards of shareholder interests. If directors are mere stewards of the shareholders, after all, it seems hard to justify the business judgment rule. Why should stewards be allowed to escape the consequences of their negligence? In contrast, under the nexus of contracts model, the duties directors owe shareholders differ only in degree and not in kind from the duties any party to a long-term contracts owes the other parties thereto.

2. See generally Oliver D. Hart, Incomplete Contracts and the Theory of the Firm, 4 J. L. Econ. & Org. 119, 121–25 (1988)

is possible to reduce transactions costs by delegating to a central agency the power to direct how the various inputs will be utilized by the firm; in effect, allowing the central agency to constantly and, more important, unilaterally rewrite certain terms of the contract between the firm and its various constituents. Centralized decisionmaking thus emerges as the defining characteristic of the Coasean firm. The board of directors and its subordinate top management team serve as the central decisionmaking agency for corporations.[3]

Contrary to what some have argued, this separation of ownership and control is a highly efficient solution to the decisionmaking problems faced by large corporations. Recall that authority-based decisionmaking structures arise where team members have different interests and amounts of information. Because collective decisionmaking is impracticable in such settings, authority-based structures are characterized by the existence of a central agency to which all relevant information is transmitted and which is empowered to make decisions binding on the whole. The modern public corporation is a classic example of an authority-based decisionmaking structure. Neither shareholders nor any other constituency have the information or the incentives necessary to make sound decisions on either operational or policy questions. Overcoming the collective action problems that prevent meaningful shareholder involvement would be difficult and costly. Rather, shareholders will prefer to irrevocably delegate decisionmaking authority to some smaller group. Separating ownership and control by vesting decisionmaking authority in a centralized entity distinct from the shareholders is what makes the large public corporation feasible.

To be sure, this separation results in agency costs. A narrow focus on agency costs, however, can lead one astray. Corporate managers operate within a pervasive web of accountability mechanisms that substitute for monitoring by residual claimants. Important constraints are provided by a variety of market forces. The capital and product markets, the internal and external employment markets, and the market for corporate control all constrain shirking by firm agents. In addition, the legal system has evolved various adaptive responses to the ineffectiveness of shareholder monitoring, establishing alternative accountability structures to punish and deter wrongdoing by firm agents, such as the board of directors.

An even more important consideration, however, is that agency costs are the inevitable consequence of vesting discretion in someone other than the residual claimant. We could substantially reduce, if not eliminate, agency costs by eliminating discretion; that we do not do so

(arguing that transaction costs are pervasive and large, which leads to a theory of the firm premised on transaction cost minimization).

3. Consistent with the importance of agency cost economics to our theory of the firm, we also saw that monitoring of management is one of the board's core functions. Put another way, a central part of the ex post governance structure must be some mechanism for detecting and punishing shirking by the firm's agents. The board of directors' monitoring function provides just such a mechanism.

suggests that discretion has substantial virtues. A complete theory of the firm thus requires one to balance the virtues of discretion against the need to require that discretion be used responsibly.[4] Neither discretion nor accountability can be ignored, because both promote values essential to the survival of business organizations. Unfortunately, they are ultimately antithetical: one cannot have more of one without also having less of the other. As Kenneth Arrow has observed, the power to hold to account is ultimately the power to decide.[5] The board thus cannot be made more accountable without shifting some of its decisionmaking authority to shareholders or judges.[6] To be clear, this is not an argument for unfettered board authority. In some cases, accountability concerns become so pronounced as to trump the general need for deference to the board's authority. Establishing the proper mix of deference and accountability thus emerges as the central problem in applying the business judgment rule to particular situations.

Given the significant virtues of discretion, however, one must not lightly interfere with management or the board's decisionmaking authority in the name of accountability. Preservation of managerial discretion should always be the null hypothesis. The separation of ownership and control mandated by U.S. corporate law has precisely that effect. Likewise, the business judgment rule exists because judicial review threatens the board's authority.[7]

B.　Defending deference to board authority

Critics of our approach might concede that judicial review shifts some power to decide to judges but nevertheless contend that that observation is normatively insufficient. To be sure, they might posit, centralized decisionmaking is an essential feature of the corporation. Judicial review could serve as a redundant control on board decisionmaking, however, without displacing the board as the primary decisionmaker.[8] An analogy to engineering concepts may be useful. If a mechanical

---

4. Michael P. Dooley, Two Models of Corporate Governance, 47 Bus. Law. 461, 464–71 (1992).

5. Kenneth J. Arrow, The Limits of Organization 78 (1974).

6. "To recognize in courts a residual power to review the substance of business decisions for 'fairness' or 'reasonableness' or 'rationality' where those decisions are made by truly disinterested directors in good faith and with appropriate care is to make of courts super-directors." In re RJR Nabisco, Inc. Shareholders Litig., 1989 WL 7036 *13 n. 13 (Del.Ch.1989).

7. See Michael P. Dooley, Two Models of Corporate Governance, 47 Bus. Law. 461, 469–76 (1992); see also Bayer v. Beran, 49 N.Y.S.2d 2, 6 (Sup.Ct.1944) ("To encourage freedom of action on the part of directors,

or to put it another way, to discourage interference with the exercise of their free and independent judgment, there has grown up what is known as the 'business judgment rule.' ").

8. Ronald Gilson argues that where markets constrain management's behavior one would not expect courts "to provide redundant controls." Ronald J. Gilson, A Structural Approach to Corporations: The Case Against Defensive Tactics in Tender Offers, 33 Stan. L. Rev. 819, 839 (1981). The business judgment rule thus "operates to bar courts from providing additional, and unnecessary, constraints on management discretion through judicial review of operating decisions." Id. As discussed in the text, however, the question of redundant controls turns out to be more complicated than Gilson acknowledged.

system is likely to fail, and its failure likely to entail high costs, basic engineering theory calls for redundant controls to prevent failure. It would be naive to assume that markets fully constrain director behavior. Why then is judicial review not an appropriate redundant control? Just as tort liability for negligence encourages people to be careful,[9] judicial review of board decisions would likewise help reduce the residual loss left by market failures by encouraging directors to be careful. If we further assume that corporate law is generally efficient, the losses tolerated by judicial abstention must be outweighed by benefits elsewhere in the system. This section speculates as to the likely source of those benefits.

1. *Judges are not business experts, but so what?*

The business judgment rule's traditional justification is that courts are not business experts.[10] It is probably true that most judges do not have much expertise in business law matters. A survey of judicial decisions in the consumer credit area, for example, strongly suggested that the judges involved did not understand the basic concept of present value.[11] Although we are sympathetic to the behavioral assumptions underlying this analysis, we regard it as an inadequate normative account of the business judgment rule. Moreover, business law is not the only context in which judges are called upon to review complex issues arising under conditions of uncertainty. Reviewing a baseball team's board of directors' refusal to play games at night, for example, seems no more technically demanding than reviewing medical or product design decisions. Yet, no "medical judgment" or "design judgment" rule precludes judicial review of malpractice or product liability cases. Having said that, however, perhaps we can construct a more sophisticated version of this rationale by building on the burgeoning insights for legal analysis of cognitive psychology and behavioral economics.

Is the business judgment rule an excuse for judicial shirking? Cognitive power is a scarce resource that boundedly rational decision-makers will try to allocate as efficiently as possible in light of their limited mental tools. Consistent with that prediction, there is evidence that actors attempt to minimize effort in the face of complexity and ambiguity.[12] As applied to judicial decisionmaking, the inherent cognitive

---

9. The rhetorical power of the analogy to tort liability fails, of course, if the threat of tort liability does not in fact encourage optimal care taking. Given cognitive biases in how actors assess the risk of liability and juries determine liability, plus the availability of both first-and third-person insurance, the assumption that tort liability encourages due care seems quite heroic. See Robert Cooter & Thomas Ulen, Law and Economics 296–98 (2d ed. 1997) (discussing implications of cognitive biases and insurance for efficiency of tort system and tentatively concluding that tort system may nonetheless be efficient).

10. See, e.g., Dodge v. Ford Motor Co., 170 N.W. 668, 684 (Mich.1919).

11. Jeffrey E. Allen & Robert J. Staaf, The Nexus between Usury, "Time Price," and Unconscionability in Installment Sales, 14 UCC L.J. 219 (1982).

12. See Russell B. Korobkin & Thomas S. Ulen, Law and Behavioral Science: Removing the Rationality Assumption from Law and Economics, 88 Cal. L. Rev. 1051, 1078 (2000) (citing studies).

limitations implied by bounded rationality are reinforced both by the incentive structures familiar from agency cost economics and institutional constraints on adjudication.[13] Under such conditions, judges will shirk—i.e., look for ways of deciding cases with minimal effort. One well-established way of doing so is to invoke shortcuts—heuristic problem-solving decisionmaking processes. Is the business judgment rule an example of this tactic at work? When one considers the ease with which the *Shlensky* court disposed of plaintiff's claims, the idea seems plausible.

On closer examination, however, this analysis seems less plausible. The analysis overlooks both the pervasive role Delaware plays in business judgment rule jurisprudence and the unique incentive structure in which Delaware courts function. As is true of everyone, the rationality of Delaware chancellors is bounded. As with all judges, Delaware chancellors are time-and resource-constrained. Yet, Delaware chancellors also have considerable incentives to develop specialized expertise in dealing with complex corporate law issues arising in the context of sophisticated financial transactions. The Delaware courts are "the center of the corporate law universe."[14] In contrast to judges in other jurisdictions who decide corporate cases only episodically, Delaware chancellors must decide many such cases and must do so on an on-going basis, which makes it rational for them to devote effort to mastering both doctrine and the business environment in which the doctrine works.[15]

Delaware chancellors also face a different agency cost schedule than do judges in other jurisdictions. Delaware chancellors typically come to the bench as experienced corporate practitioners. Once on the bench, there is a substantial pay-off for Delaware chancellors who continue to master corporate law. Sitting without juries in a court of equity, Delaware chancellors put their reputation on the line whenever they make a decision. Because so many major corporations are incorporated in Delaware, chancery court decisions are frequently high-profile and, as such,

---

13. Put another way, bounded rationality and information asymmetries counsel judicial reticence in reviewing board decisions. Business decisions are frequently complex and made under conditions of uncertainty. Judges likely have less general business expertise than directors. They also have less information about the specifics of the particular firm in question. Consider the *Shlensky* court's discussion of possible effects of putting lights in Wrigley Field, which can be read as an acknowledgment of the limits of the court's knowledge. See Shlensky v. Wrigley, 237 N.E.2d 776, 780 (Ill.App.1968) (acknowledging that deciding whether the board made the right decision was "beyond our jurisdiction and *ability*"; emphasis supplied). Finally, most judges only rarely face business judgment issues. Many judges arrive on the bench with little expertise in corporate law and, moreover, have little incentive to develop substantial institutional expertise in this area after they arrive. Because the legal and business issues are complex, and because judges are as subject as anyone to the cognitive limitations implied by bounded rationality, they have an incentive to duck these cases.

14. D. Gordon Smith, Chancellor Allen and the Fundamental Question, 21 Seattle U. L. Rev. 577, 578 (1998).

15. Cf. Kent Greenfield & John E. Nilsson, Gradgrind's Education: Using Dickens and Aristotle to Understand (and Replace?) the Business Judgment Rule, 63 Brooklyn L. Rev. 799, 825 (1997) ("the Delaware Supreme Court displays a marked ability to address business decisions in a very detailed way. This ability undermines the notion . . . that courts are incapable of such analysis.").

subject to scrutiny by the media, academics, and practitioners. The reputation of a Delaware chancellor thus depends mostly on his ability to decide corporate law matters quickly, thoroughly, and accurately.

In sum, there may well be some doctrines that are best explained by a model in which judges are both boundedly rational and agents with an incentive to shirk. Veil piercing, for example, is probably an instance of this phenomenon.[16] Given Delaware's prominence as a generator of corporate law and especially of business judgment rule jurisprudence, and the resulting incentives Delaware judges and chancellors have to become "business experts," however, something else must be going on as well.

Decisionmaker incentives. Justice Jackson famously observed of the U.S. Supreme Court: "We are not final because we are infallible, but we are infallible only because we are final."[17] Neither courts nor board or directors are infallible, but someone must be final. Otherwise we end up with a never ending process of appellate review. The question then is a simple one: Who is better suited to be vested with the mantle of infallibility that comes by virtue of being final—directors or judges?

Judges necessarily have less information about the needs of a particular firm than do that firm's directors. A fortiori, judges will make poorer decisions than the firm's board:

> [C]ourts recognize that after-the-fact litigation is a most imperfect device to evaluate corporate business decisions. The circumstances surrounding a corporate decision are not easily reconstructed in a courtroom years later, since business imperatives often call for quick decisions, inevitably based on less than perfect information. The entrepreneur's function is to encounter risks and to confront uncertainty, and a reasoned decision at the time made may seem a wild hunch viewed years later against a background of perfect knowledge.[18]

Put another way, judges are no less subject to bounded rationality than any other decisionmakers. Just as the limits on cognitive competence impede the ability of market actors to write complete contracts, those

---

16. See Stephen M. Bainbridge, Abolishing Veil Piercing, 26 J. Corp. L. 479 (2001) (making that argument).

17. Brown v. Allen, 344 U.S. 443, 540 (1953) (Jackson, J., concurring). Justice Jackson's point implicates the principle of subsidiarity, which posits the social primacy of the smallest units in society. In turn, subsidiarity provides both moral and instrumental justification for the business judgment rule:

> [Subsidiarity] suggests that people closest to the problem at hand are the ones with the strongest moral claim to finding a solution. To empower higher authorities as anything but second-best solutions or even last resorts endangers the rights

and liberties of those who are most affected. The subsidiarity principle also embodies the practical point that those closest to the problem have the strongest interest in seeing that the problem is solved most competently.

Robert A. Sirico, Subsidiarity, Society, and Entitlements: Understanding and Application, 11 Notre Dame J. L. Ethics & Pub. Pol'y 549, 552 (1997). Because boards are closer to the problem than courts, subsidiarity posits that they should have decision-making primacy.

18. Joy v. North, 692 F.2d 880, 886 (2d Cir.1982), cert. denied, 460 U.S. 1051 (1983).

same limits necessarily impede judicial review. Only with the benefit of hindsight will judges be able to make better decisions than boards, but we have already seen that hindsight review is problematic. While market forces work a sort of Darwinian selection on corporate decisionmakers, moreover, no such forces constrain erring judges.[19] As such, rational shareholders might prefer the risk of managerial error to that of judicial error.

The posited preference for managerial error, however, only extends to decisions motivated by a desire to maximize shareholder wealth. Given that market forces encourage directors to make such decisions carefully, such a preference makes sense. Where the directors' decision was motivated by considerations other than shareholder wealth, as where the directors engaged in self-dealing or sought to defraud the shareholders, however, the question is no longer one of honest error but of intentional misconduct. Despite the limitations of judicial review, rational shareholders would prefer judicial intervention with respect to board decisions so tainted. As Delaware Chief Justice Veasey observes, "investors do not want self-dealing directors or those bent on entrenchment in office. . . . Trust of directors is the key because of the self-governing nature of corporate law. Yet the law is strong enough to rein in directors who would flirt with an abuse of that trust."[20] The affirmative case for disregarding honest errors thus simply does not apply to intentional misconduct. To the contrary, given the heightened potential for self-dealing in an organization characterized by a separation of ownership and control, the risk of legal liability may be a necessary deterrent against such misconduct.

>   2.   *Corporate decisions affect nonshareholder constituencies, but so what?*

In rejecting the business judgment rule's traditional explanation, we observed that judges are unlikely to be medical or engineering experts, yet no "medical judgment rule" nor "designer judgment rule" insulates doctors from malpractice claims or manufacturing firms from product liability claims. We further implied that judicial review of business decisions would not differ from judicial review of medical or product design decisions. In terms of the technical complexity of the decisions at bar, that assertion is doubtless true. Yet, business decisions do differ in an important way from those other sorts of claims.

Imagine an automobile manufacturer whose cars have a defective gas tank. Fixing the design problem would cost the manufacturer $50 per car. Injuries caused by the defective product average $75 per car. Suppose that under a negligence-based tort liability regime, the manu-

19. Frank H. Easterbrook & Daniel R. Fischel, The Economic Structure of Corporate Law 100 (1991).

20. E. Norman Veasey, An Economic Rationale for Judicial Decisionmaking in Corporate Law, 53 Bus. Law. 681, 694 (1998). Note the Chief Justice's emphasis on the "self-governing" aspect of corporate law, which is consistent with the argument that judicial review of director decisions inappropriately degrades the board's decisionmaking authority.

facturer would be held liable for an average of only $25 per car. Because such a negligence-based regime does not cause the manufacturer to fully internalize the social costs of its conduct, it would be economically irrational for the manufacturer to fix the defect. A socially sub-optimal outcome thus results. An important justification for the strict liability-based products liability regime thus is that it is more likely to lead manufacturers to internalize the costs of their activities than is a negligence-based regime.[21]

As a society, we probably want manufacturers and physicians to fully internalize the costs of their activities. Tort liability arguably is a reasonably efficient way of accomplishing that desirable outcome. While we also likely want directors to internalize the social costs of their decisions, however, corporate law in general and fiduciary obligation in particular is not an appropriate vehicle achieving that result.

The point is not that director decisionmaking has no externalities. It does. Board decisions can adversely affect not only true outsiders to the corporation but also nonshareholder constituencies. The interests of such parties are more appropriately dealt with by contract and general welfare legislation, however. Corporate law, especially fiduciary obligation, should be concerned solely with the relationship between shareholders and directors. As explained in Chapter 9, moreover, the obligation arising out of that relationship should be one of maximizing shareholder wealth.

Because no other interests are at stake with respect to the law of fiduciary obligation, society should specify as the default rule that regime most shareholders would prefer.[22] If a regime of judicial deference to board decisionmaking is more likely to maximize shareholder wealth than is a regime of judicial review, shareholders will prefer the former and it should be the default. The remaining question therefore is whether a deference-based regime is wealth maximizing. We shall see that it is.

---

21. Cf. Robert Cooter & Thomas Ulen, Law and Economics 319 (2d ed. 1997).

22. Recall that the nexus of contracts model treats corporate law as a set of default rules provided by the state. Viewed ex ante, fiduciary duties are a species of muddy defaults. Put differently, fiduciary duties are gap-fillers by which judges complete incomplete contracts. As with any other rule under which judges fill gaps in incomplete contracts by supplying reasonable terms, fiduciary duties are necessarily somewhat ambiguous. From an ex ante perspective, muddy defaults can encourage parties to provide their own clarity through private ordering. If the parties are not sure what rules the court will impose, they have an incentive to draft a contract incorporating the rules they prefer. Viewed from an ex post perspective, of course, fiduciary duties are a species of tailored defaults. The ambiguity of fiduciary obligation necessarily gives courts a certain flexibility. Courts thus can use fiduciary duties to fill gaps in the contract at bar by giving the litigants the rule for which those litigants (as opposed to the hypothetical majority) would have bargained if they had thought to do so. Ultimately, however, both the duty of care and the business judgment rule also likely qualify as majoritarian defaults. Insofar as public corporations are concerned, bargaining over the scope and content of fiduciary obligation is rare. Almost all parties live with the off the rack rules. Consequently, neither doctrine would have survived for so long if they were seriously inefficient at their core.

3. *Encouraging optimal risk-taking*

In its *Principles of Corporate Governance*, the American Law Institute justified the business judgment rule on grounds that it encourages directors to take risks. According to the ALI, the rule protects "directors and officers from the risks inherent in hindsight reviews of their unsuccessful decisions" and avoids "the risk of stifling innovation and venturesome business activity."[23] The ALI's explanation is valid but incomplete. The prospect of duty of care litigation, after all, probably does far less to stifle innovation and business risk-taking than does product liability and securities fraud litigation.

At the outset, we need a story explaining why hindsight review of business decisions is inconsistent with shareholder interests. One lies readily to hand. As the firm's residual claimants, shareholders do not get a return on their investment until all other claims on the corporation have been satisfied. All else equal, shareholders therefore prefer high return projects. Because risk and return are directly proportional, however, implementing that preference necessarily entails choosing risky projects. All of which should be familiar concepts by now.

Rational shareholders will have a high tolerance for such risks, however. First, the doctrine of limited liability substantially insulates shareholders from the downside risks of corporate activity. Limited liability, of course, means that shareholders of a corporation are not personally liable for debts incurred or torts committed by the firm. If the firm fails, a shareholder's losses thus are limited to the amount the shareholder has invested in the firm—i.e., the amount the shareholder initially paid to purchase his stock. Put another way, because shareholders do not put their personal assets at jeopardy, they effectively externalize some portion of the business' total risk exposure to creditors.

Second, portfolio theory teaches that shareholders can eliminate firm-specific risk by holding a diversified portfolio. Investors, on average, are risk averse. Accordingly, they must be compensated—paid a higher return—for bearing risk. Hence, we speak of a risk premium, which is the difference in the rate of return paid on a risky investment and the rate of return on a risk-free investment. The risk premium, however, will only reflect certain risks. Investors can eliminate unsystematic risk by diversifying their portfolio, but diversification cannot eliminate systematic risk. Ergo, portfolio theory claims, investors must be compensated for bearing systematic risk but need not be compensated for bearing unsystematic risk.

Given limited liability and diversification, shareholders will be indifferent to corporate policies that affect unsystematic risks, but will prefer policies that portend a higher return by increasing the firm's beta. In contrast, management will be risk averse with respect to such policies. Corporate managers frequently have substantial firm-specific human capital, which constitutes an investment upon which the managers can

---

23. ALI Principles § 4.01 cmt. d at 141.

earn a return only so long as they remain with that firm. Managers obviously cannot diversify their human capital among a number of different firms and thus commit their principal source of wealth to the fortunes of a single firm. If pursuing a risky course of action fails to pay off, management may suffer far greater losses than do their diversified shareholders. As such, managers will be averse to risks shareholders are perfectly happy to tolerate.

The diversion of interests as between shareholders and managers will be compounded if managers face the risk of legal liability, on top of economic loss, in the event a risky decision turns out badly. Board decisions rarely involve black-and-white issues, instead they typically involve prudential judgments among a number of plausible alternatives. Given the vagaries of business, moreover, even carefully made choices among such alternatives may turn out badly.

At this point, the well-known hindsight bias comes into play. Decisionmakers tend to assign an erroneously high probability of occurrence to a probabilistic event simply because it ended up occurring.[24] Knowledge that an injury occurred, for example, biases jurors to impose negligence liability even though there was a very low probability of such an injury and, if viewed ex ante, precautions against such an injury were not cost effective. Knowing with the benefit of hindsight that a business decision turned out badly likewise could bias judges or juries towards finding a breach of the duty of care.

In other words, both shareholders and judges will find it difficult to distinguish between competent and negligent management. By virtue of the hindsight bias, bad outcomes are often regarded, ex post, as foreseeable ex ante. If bad outcomes result in liability, however, managers will be discouraged from taking risks:

> Corporate directors of public companies typically have a very small proportionate ownership interest in their corporations and little or no incentive compensation. Thus, they enjoy (as residual owners) only a very small proportion of any "upside" gains earned by the corporation on risky investment projects. If, however, corporate directors were to be found liable for a corporate loss from a risky project on the ground that the investment was too risky ... their liability would be joint and several for the whole loss (with I suppose a right of contribution). Given the scale of operation of modern public corporations, this stupefying disjunction between risk and reward for corporate directors threatens undesirable effects. Given this disjunction, only a very small probability of director liability based on "negligence", "inattention," "waste," etc., could induce a board to avoid authorizing risky investment projects to any extent! Obviously, it is in the shareholders' economic interest to offer

24. Christine Jolls et al., A Behavioral Approach to Law and Economics, 50 Stan L. Rev. 1471, 1523–27 (1998). For a discussion relating the hindsight bias to the business judgment rule, see Hal R. Arkes & Cindy A. Schipani, Medical Malpractice v. the Business Judgment Rule: Differences in Hindsight Bias, 73 Ore. L. Rev. 587 (1994).

sufficient protection to directors from liability for negligence, etc., to allow directors to conclude that, as a practical matter, there is no risk that, if they act in good faith and meet minimal proceduralist standards of attention, they can face liability as a result of a business loss.[25]

Put another way, if judicial decisionmaking could flawlessly sort out sound decisions with unfortunate outcomes from poor decisions, and directors were confident that there was no risk of hindsight-based liability, the case for the business judgment rule would be substantially weaker. As long as there is some nonzero probability of erroneous second-guessing by judges, however, the threat of liability will skew director decisionmaking away from optimal risk-taking. That this result will occur even if the risk of judicial error is quite small is suggested by the work of behavioral economists on loss aversion and regret avoidance. Behavioral economists have demonstrated that people evaluate the utility of a decision by measuring the change effected by the decision relative to a neutral reference point.[26] Changes framed in a way that makes things worse (losses) loom larger in the decisionmaking process than changes framed as making things better (gains) even if the expected value of the two decisions is the same. Hence, a loss averse person (as are most people) will be more perturbed by the prospect of losing $100 than pleased by that of gaining $100. A bias against risk-taking is a natural result of loss aversion, because the decisionmaker will give the disadvantages of a change greater weight than its potential advantages. Hence, the so-called status quo bias. Closely related to the loss aversion phenomenon, and a possible explanation for it, is the psychological concept of regret avoidance. Decisionmakers experience greater regret when undesirable consequences follow from action than from inaction.[27] As a result, decisionmakers tend towards inertia. Because the effect of these cognitive biases is considerably greater than traditional rational choice theory predicts, even a small risk of liability can be expected to have a large deterrent effect.

Rational shareholders therefore should prefer a regime that encourages managerial risk-taking by, inter alia, pre-committing to a policy of not litigating the reasonableness of managerial business decisions. Obviously, however, the practicalities of running a large corporation with fluid stock ownership preclude effecting such a policy by contract. The business judgment rule thus can be seen as providing a default (off the rack) rule that both shareholders and managers would prefer, as Judge Ralph Winter opined in *Joy v. North*:

25. Gagliardi v. TriFoods Int'l, Inc., 683 A.2d 1049, 1052 (Del.Ch.1996).

26. Richard H. Thaler, The Winner's Curse: Paradoxes and Anomalies of Economic Life 68–70 (1992).

27. See Russell Korobkin, The Status Quo Bias and Contract Default Rules, 83 Cornell L. Rev. 608, 657–59 (1998); (positing regret avoidance as an explanation of the status quo bias); Russell Korobkin, Inertia and Preference in Contract Negotiation: The Psychological Power of Default Rules and Form Terms, 51 Vand. L. Rev. 1583, 1619–20 (1998) (same).

Although the rule has suffered under academic criticism, it is not without rational basis.... [S]hareholders to a very real degree voluntarily undertake the risk of bad business judgment. Investors need not buy stock, for investment markets offer an array of opportunities less vulnerable to mistakes in judgment by corporate officers. Nor need investors buy stock in particular corporations. In the exercise of what is genuinely a free choice, the quality of a firm's management is often decisive and information is available from professional advisors. Since shareholders can and do select among investments partly on the basis of management, the business judgment rule merely recognizes a certain voluntariness in undertaking the risk of bad business decisions.[28]

Judge Winter further explained:

[B]ecause potential profit often corresponds to the potential risk, it is very much in the interest of shareholders that the law not create incentives for overly cautious corporate decisions. Some opportunities offer great profits at the risk of very substantial losses, while the alternatives offer less risk of loss but also less potential profit. Shareholders can reduce the volatility of risk by diversifying their holdings. In the case of the diversified shareholder, the seemingly more risky alternatives may well be the best choice since great losses in some stocks will over time be offset by even greater gains in others. Given mutual funds and similar forms of diversified investment, courts need not bend over backwards to give special protection to shareholders who refuse to reduce the volatility of risk by not diversifying. A rule which penalizes the choice of seemingly riskier alternatives thus may not be in the interest of shareholders generally.[29]

Note that Winter's portfolio theory-based justification for the business judgment rule implicitly identifies an important distinction between the function of liability rules in tort and corporate law. A basic function of tort liability is loss spreading. By encouraging potential tortfeasors (such as automobile drivers) to purchase insurance, the tort system encourages the process by which the risk of loss is shifted from specific victims to a larger pool.[30] In contrast, if directors were routinely held liable, losses

---

28. Joy v. North, 692 F.2d 880, 885 (2d Cir.1982), cert. denied, 460 U.S. 1051 (1983).

29. Joy v. North, 692 F.2d 880, 886 (2d Cir.1982), cert. denied, 460 U.S. 1051 (1983). Or, as Chancellor Allen similarly observed:

Shareholders can diversify the risks of their corporate investments. Thus, it is in their economic interest for the corporation to accept in rank order all positive net present value investment projects available to the corporation, starting with the *highest risk adjusted rate of return first*. Shareholders don't want (or

shouldn't rationally want) directors to be risk averse. Shareholders' investment interests, across the full range of their diversifiable equity investments, will be maximized if corporate directors and managers honestly assess risk and reward and accept for the corporation the highest risk adjusted returns available that are above the firm's cost of capital.

Gagliardi v. TriFoods Int'l, Inc., 683 A.2d 1049, 1052 (Del.Ch.1996) (emphasis in original).

30. Kenneth B. Davis, Jr., Once More, the Business Judgment Rule, 2000 Wis. L. Rev. 573, 575.

would be shifted from the larger pool of residual claimants to a small group of specific individuals. Because that larger pool can reduce the risk of loss by holding a diversified pool of investments, however, the insulation provided directors by the business judgment rule can be seen as a form of corporate self-insurance. Hence, the analogy between tort and corporate liability fails because the imposition of liability in those contexts has differing effects with respect to an important social policy.

Yet, Winter's explanation is incomplete in important respects. If Winter's argument is correct, for example, negligence by corporate directors must be a form of unsystematic risk. Otherwise, it could not be diversified away. If so, however, why is not fraud or illegality on the part of such directors also a form of unsystematic risk? Just as a shareholder could protect herself against bad decisions, so could a shareholder protect herself against fraudulent decisions. Yet, the business judgment rule has never protected directors who commit fraud.[31]

Second, Winter's explanation of the business judgment rule conflates the roles of corporate officers and directors. In contrast, we shall repeatedly see that the Delaware courts take the board's distinct role quite seriously, especially with respect to its independent members. Compared to managers, outside directors make relatively small investments in firm-specific human capital. At the same time, it has become very common for public corporations to require that newly appointed directors purchase substantial blocks of the corporation's shares and/or compensate directors in the corporation's stock, which in practice has been empirically linked to improved corporate performance.[32] As a result, it seems unlikely that directors will be as risk averse as officers. Indeed, to the contrary, director incentives may well be more in line with shareholder preferences than with those of managers.

Finally, encouraging risk-taking must be deemed an incomplete explanation because it fails to account for many of the rule's applications. Consider, for example, the business decision made in *Shlensky*. Was Wrigley an innovator making a venturesome business decision or an eccentric coot who was just behind the times? How can we know when the business judgment rule precluded Shlensky from even getting up to bat?[33] In sum, something else must be going on as well.

31. Alternatively, it might be objected that portfolio theory is not even relevant to the analysis. In financial economics, risk is defined by reference to the variance of return. Management misconduct—whether of the misfeasance or malfeasance variety—arguably does not affect the variance of return but rather merely erodes the expected return. If so, neither type of management misconduct is a diversifiable risk.

32. See generally Sanjai Bhagat et al., Director Ownership, Corporate Performance, and Management Turnover, 54 Bus. Law. 885 (1999) (discussing trends in director stock ownership); Charles M. Elson, Director Compensation and the Management–Captured Board: The History of a Symptom and a Cure, 50 SMU L. Rev. 127 (1996) (same).

33. Alternatively, consider the business judgment rule's role in precluding shareholder derivative litigation. Although some scholars regard decisions about pursuing specific litigation as being more appropriate for judicial review than ordinary business decisions, the business judgment rule substantially insulates such decisions from judicial review. See, e.g., John C. Coffee & Donald Schwartz, The Survival of the Derivative Suit: An Evaluation and a Proposal

4. *The board as a consensus-based team*

The final piece in the puzzle is provided by our distinction between consensus-and authority-based governance structures. The governance of a modern public corporation is almost purely authority-based, of course. Information flows up a branching hierarchy to a central office and binding decisions flow back down. Yet, at the apex of that decisionmaking pyramid is not a single hierarch but rather a team—a multi-member body—that usually functions by consensus. Indeed, the board of directors is a good example of what new institutional economics guru Oliver Williamson refers to as a "relational team."[34] Such teams arise when (1) team members make large investments in firm-specific human capital and (2) their productivity is costly to measure because of task nonseparability. Both conditions are satisfied by board membership.

Surprisingly, however, corporate law scholarship rarely focuses on the board as a team production problem, which turns out to be a significant oversight. Team governance is an important part of the business judgment rule's justification. In many settings, teams make superior decisions than do individuals acting alone.[35] Individuals are subject to the constraints of bounded rationality and the temptations to shirk or self-deal. Group decisionmaking responds to bounded rationality by creating a system for aggregating the inputs of multiple individuals with differing knowledge, interests, and skills. In addition, the internal dynamics of team governance constrain self-dealing and shirking by individual team members.

Although teams can be a highly effective decisionmaking mechanism, they are hard to monitor. Team production typically results in nonseparable outputs. Accordingly, the productivity of individual team members cannot be measured on an output basis. Yet, at the same time, individual productivity also may be quite costly to measure from an input perspective. The monitoring problem is especially severe when assessing individual productivity requires something more than mere effort measurement. Measuring individual productivity of board members might require, for example, assessing whether the director cooperates with other team members in responding to changed circumstances or emergencies.

At best, the board can be monitored only in terms of its joint output. Unlike a manufacturing team, where one can measure the quantity and quality of goods produced, however, the joint output of the board can be assessed only in terms of the quality of its decisionmaking. Not only is that assessment inherently subjective, it is also likely to be tainted by the hindsight bias discussed above.

Relational teams are not only hard to monitor, they are also hard to discipline. Members of such a team often develop idiosyncratic working

for Legislative Reform, 81 Colum. L. Rev. 261, 280–83 (1981).

34. Oliver E. Williamson, The Economic Institutions of Capitalism 246–47 (1985).

35. See Stephen M. Bainbridge, Why a Board? Group Decision Making in Corporate Governance, 55 Vand. L. Rev. 1 (2002).

relationships with one another. In a sense, members of a relational team develop not only firm-specific human capital but also team-specific human capital. The existence of such internal relationships limits the array of sanctions that can be effectively applied to misbehaving teams. Dismissal becomes a sanction of last resort, for example, because no member of the team can be replaced without having a highly disruptive effect on the entire team. Because relational teams can become insular, moreover, even external sanctions falling short of dismissal may have ripple effects throughout the team. We know, for instance, that insular workplace teams often fail to deal effectively with outsiders and even expend resources on power struggles with other teams.[36] Relational teams thus respond to external monitoring efforts by "circling the wagons" around the intended subject of sanctions.

Because external monitoring of relational teams is so difficult, agency costs within such teams tend to be constrained by internal governance mechanisms rather than by external review procedures. Specifically, monitoring of such teams is most efficiently effected through mutual motivation, peer pressure, and internal monitoring. Members of a production team interact over an extended period of time and develop relationships with one another that are important in determining their conduct. This process leads to a group dynamic that functions as one of the team's important internal governance structures. With respect to the relationship between management and the board for example, well-functioning group dynamics of this sort will discourage insiders from presenting a proposal to the board that the latter will perceive as self-dealing by the former. In turn, when the board deliberates on management's proposal, the same sorts of internal group dynamics should preclude the board from approving a deal tainted by self-dealing.

In theory, external review could serve as a backstop reinforcing the network of social sanctions that shape incentives within teams. Judges are a poor substitute, however, for the norm inculcating power of close knit groups. While courts cannot make citizens virtuous, they can destroy the intermediary institutions that do inculcate virtue: "Communities can be destroyed from without, but they cannot be created from without; they must be built from within."[37] The "every man for himself" phenomenon that so often arises in litigation is but one way in which judicial review might well destroy the interpersonal relationships that foster internal team governance.[38]

36. Stephen M. Bainbridge, Privately Ordered Participatory Management: An Organizational Failures Analysis, 23 Del. J. Corp. L. 979, 1044 (1998).

37. Richard A. Epstein, Simple Rules for a Complex World 324 (1995).

38. To the extent that external review undermines mutual trust within a board, it adversely affects not only the board's monitoring role but also its service functions. Trust arises out of two primary sources. "Affinity trust" exists ex ante. It is based mostly on shared values and is most likely to exist where there is ethnic and/or religious affinity. "Learned trust" arises out of repeat transactions in which the players prove consistently trustworthy. In a small but heterogeneous community, such as most boards, learned trust dominates. Trust counteracts the fear of embarrass-

A related but slightly different concern is the multiplicative effect that external review of team decisionmaking may have on the firm as a whole. Because "the efficiency of organization is affected by the degree to which individuals assent to orders, denying the authority of an organization communication is a threat to the interests of all individuals who derive a net advantage from their connection with the organization...."[39] Put another way, by calling into question the legitimacy of the central decisionmaking body's authority, external review may reduce the incentive for subordinates to assent to that body's decisions and thereby undermines the efficient functioning of the entire firm.

Finally, as noted above, one significant advantage of group decisionmaking is its ability to ameliorate the problem of individual bounded rationality. If external review adversely affects internal team functioning, however, that advantage is lost. There is considerable evidence that external review in fact has undesirable effects on the efficiency of corporate decisionmaking. Shareholder litigation encourages directors to be risk averse. In turn, risk averse directors take excessive precautions and avoid risky decisions. If the risk of shareholder litigation causes some members of the team to exercise more care than is optimal, moreover, the team must now monitor not only the quality of the decisionmaking inputs coming from each member, but also the risk that any given member is unusually risk averse and thus especially subject to having his/her inputs into the team processes skewed by the fear of liability.

In sum, internal team governance structures provide a strong set of constraints on misconduct by the board. In contrast, external review can undermine the internal team governance structures that regulate team behavior. Accordingly, courts should be reluctant to interfere with board decisionmaking, which is precisely what the business judgment rule commands. It cannot be said often enough that the business judgment rule, properly understood, really is an abstention doctrine. Courts will abstain from reviewing the substantive merits of the directors' conduct unless the plaintiff can rebut the business judgment rule's presumption of good faith.

Note that this approach explains a number of aspects of the business judgment rule left unexplained by alternative theories. The fact that the business judgment rule does not insulate director fraud or self-dealing, for example, makes good sense. The decisions to which duty of care litigation is addressed are typically collective actions by the board as a whole. Management teams are constrained to exercise reasonable care in decisionmaking by a combination of external market forces and internal team governance structures. When an individual director decides to

---

ment that induces reticence. In an environment of trust, board members are willing to present ideas that seem "half-baked," which promotes earlier and more extensive discussion of alternatives. Daniel P. Forbes & Frances J. Milliken, Cognition and Cor-

porate Governance: Understanding Boards of Directors as Strategic Decision-making Groups, 24 Acad. Mgmt. Rev. 489, 496 (1999).

39. Chester I. Barnard, The Functions of the Executive 169 (2d ed. 1962).

pursue a course of self-dealing, however, he has already committed to betraying internal team relationships.[40] Courts appropriately are less concerned about destroying internal team relationships when the defendant director's misconduct has already destroyed them. Conversely, by providing a set of external sanctions against self-dealing, the law encourages directors to refrain from such betrayals.

5. *Summary*

Our justification for the business judgment rule can be reconciled with Delaware law, *Technicolor* and its progeny notwithstanding. In a passage from *Van Gorkom* that has received less attention than it deserves, the Delaware supreme court opined:

> Under Delaware law, the business judgment rule is the offspring of the fundamental principle, codified in [DGCL] § 141(a), that the business and affairs of a Delaware corporation are managed by or under its board of directors.... The business judgment rule exists to protect and promote the full and free exercise of the managerial power granted to Delaware directors.[41]

In other words, the rule ensures that the null hypothesis is deference to the board's authority as the corporation's central and final decisionmaker.

To be clear, our argument is not for judicial abnegation but only for judicial abstention. The distinction is a significant one. Abstention contemplates judicial reticence, but leaves open the possibility of intervention in appropriate circumstances. Yet again, economist Kenneth Arrow is instructive:

> [Accountability mechanisms] must be capable of correcting errors but should not be such as to destroy the genuine values of authority. Clearly, a sufficiently strict and continuous organ of [accountability] can easily amount to a denial of authority. If every decision of A is to be reviewed by B, then all we have really is a shift in the locus of authority from A to B and hence no solution to the original problem.

> To maintain the value of authority, it would appear that [accountability] must be intermittent. This could be periodic; it could take the form of what is termed "management by exception," in which authority and its decisions are reviewed only when performance is sufficiently degraded from expectations....[42]

---

40. Cf. Robert J. Haft, The Effect of Insider Trading Rules on the Internal Efficiency of the Large Corporation, 80 Mich. L. Rev. 1051, 1062–63 (1982) (describing the deleterious effects on board effectiveness of director self-dealing).

41. Smith v. Van Gorkom, 488 A.2d 858, 872 (Del.1985). See also Nahikian v. Mattingly, 251 N.W. 421, 423 (Mich.1933)

("It is a well-settled rule of law that the authority of the directors is absolute when they act within the law, and that questions of policy and internal management are, in the absence of nonfeasance, misfeasance or malfeasance, left wholly to their decision....").

42. Kenneth J. Arrow, The Limits of Organization 78 (1974).

The problem then is to identify the circumstances in which intervention is necessary. Put another way, the task is to define the conditions under which accountability concerns ought to trump preservation of the board's authority.

If the business judgment rule is treated as a substantive standard of review, judicial intervention all too easily could become the norm rather than the exception. How one frames the question matters a lot. In polling, for example, both the order in which questions are asked and the way in which they are phrased can affect the outcome.[43] The same is true of legal standards.[44] This is why *Technicolor* is so troubling. Under the decision's cart before the horse formulation, the business judgment rule does not preclude judicial review of cases in which the board failed to exercise reasonable care. Yet, if the business judgment rule is to have teeth, it is precisely those cases in which it is especially important for courts to abstain.[45] No matter how gingerly courts apply a substantive standard, trying to measure the "quantity" of negligence is a task best left untried.[46] Courts will find it difficult to resist the temptation to tweak the standard so as to sanction honest decisions that, with the benefit of hindsight, proved unfortunate and/or appear inept. All of the adverse effects of judicial review outlined in the preceding sections are implicated, however, whether or not the board exercised reasonable care.

43. See, e.g., Brad Edmondson, How to Spot a Bogus Poll, Am. Demographics, Oct. 1996, at 10.

44. These effects follow, in part, from the phenomena known in behavioral economics as framing and anchoring. Framing refers to the process by which people code decisions as involving potential gains or losses. People tend to be risk averse with respect to potential gains, but risk preferring with respect to potential losses. Consequently, people will prefer a certain $100 gain to a 50% chance of gaining $200, but prefer a 50% chance of losing $200 to a certain loss of $100, even though the expected outcomes are the same in both cases. Anchoring refers to the effect initial reference points have on subsequent decisionmaking. Actors presented with a decision framed with an initial reference demonstrably allow that reference point to affect their decisionmaking processes. Marcel Kahan & Michael Klausner, Path Dependence in Corporate Contracting: Increasing Returns, Herd Behavior, and Cognitive Biases, 74 Wash. U.L.Q. 347, 362 (1996) (citing studies). One study asked professional accountants to estimate the prevalence of management fraud. One group of subjects was asked whether they believed management fraud occurred in more than 10 out of each 1000 companies audited, while a second group was asked whether they believed fraud occurred in more than 200 of every 1000 companies. Both groups were then asked to estimate the actual number of fraud cases per 1000 companies. Accountants in the latter group gave a significantly higher response to the second question than accountants in the former, showing that the subjects failed to adequately adjust their estimate of the incidence of fraud from the initial reference point to which they were exposed. Russell B. Korobkin & Thomas S. Ulen, Law and Behavioral Science: Removing the Rationality Assumption from Law and Economics, 88 Cal. L. Rev. 1051, 1100–02 (2000). Although tests of the anchoring phenomenon have concentrated on the effect of numbers as reference points, it seems plausible that verbal cues—like the phrasing of a legal standard—will have a similar effect. The framing and anchoring phenomena help explain why we regard *Technicolor* as so problematic. There is evidence that judges are subject to both types of cognitive error. Chris Guthrie et al., Inside the Judicial Mind, 86 Cornell L. Rev. 777 (2001). Consequently, both the phrasing of the legal standard and the ordering of the questions it asks are likely to effect outcomes.

45. Lyman Johnson, The Modest Business Judgment Rule, 55 Bus. Law. 625, 633 (2000).

46. Henry G. Manne, Our Two Corporation Systems: Law and Economics, 53 Va. L. Rev. 259, 271 (1967).

Unfortunately, *Technicolor* and its ilk threaten to nullify this essential aspect of the business judgment rule.

If the business judgment rule is framed as an abstention doctrine, however, judicial review is more likely to be the exception rather than the rule. Starting from an abstention perspective, the court will begin with a presumption against review. It will then review the facts to determine not the quality of the decision, but rather whether the decisionmaking process was tainted by self-dealing and the like. The requisite questions to be asked are objective and straightforward: Did the board commit fraud? Did the board commit an illegal act? Did the board self-deal? Whether or not the board exercised reasonable care is irrelevant, as well it should be. The business judgment rule thus builds a prophylactic barrier by which courts pre-commit to resisting the temptation to review the merits of the board's decision.

§ 6.4　The law of business judgment

To review, the duty of care requires directors to exercise the same care that "ordinarily careful and prudent men would use in similar circumstances."[1] The business judgment rule, however, provides that courts will abstain from reviewing board decisions unless those decisions are tainted by fraud, illegality, or self-dealing.[2] Operationalizing those vague statements requires some heavy lifting. Because the order in which one takes up questions matters, we focus on the business judgment rule in this section. Since courts should only reach duty of care questions after determining that the business judgment rule does not apply to the case at bar, analysis of that duty is deferred to the following section.

A.　The nature of the rule

Courts often refer to the business judgment rule as "a presumption" that the directors or officers of a corporation acted on an informed basis, in good faith, and in the honest belief that the action taken was in the best interests of the company.[3] This phraseology is unfortunate, at best. The business judgment rule is not a presumption "in the strict evidentiary sense of the term."[4] Instead, it is more in the nature of an

---

§ 6.4

1. See, e.g., Graham v. Allis–Chalmers Mfg. Co., 188 A.2d 125, 130 (Del.1963).

2. See, e.g., Mills Acquisition Co. v. Macmillan, Inc., 559 A.2d 1261, 1279 (Del. 1989); Smith v. Van Gorkom, 488 A.2d 858, 872–73 (Del.1985); Aronson v. Lewis, 473 A.2d 805, 812 (Del.1984); Sinclair Oil v. Levien, 280 A.2d 717, 720 (Del.1971); Shlensky v. Wrigley, 237 N.E.2d 776, 778 (Ill.App.1968).

3. See, e.g., Panter v. Marshall Field & Co., 646 F.2d 271, 293 (7th Cir.), cert. de-nied, 454 U.S. 1092 (1981); Treadway Cos., Inc. v. Care Corp., 638 F.2d 357, 382 (2d Cir.1980); Johnson v. Trueblood, 629 F.2d 287, 292 (3d Cir.1980), cert. denied, 450 U.S. 999 (1981); Unocal Corp. v. Mesa Petroleum Co., 493 A.2d 946, 954 (Del.1985); Aronson v. Lewis, 473 A.2d 805, 812 (Del. 1984); Auerbach v. Bennett, 393 N.E.2d 994 (N.Y.1979).

4. See, e.g., R. Franklin Balotti & James J. Hanks, Jr., Rejudging the Business Judgment Rule, 48 Bus. Law. 1337, 1345 (1993).

assumption; namely, courts assume they should not review director decisions absent fraud, illegality, or self-dealing. In any event, these disputes over terminology are largely inconsequential. The bottom line is that even clear mistakes of judgment rarely result in personal liability on the part of corporate directors.

B. Preconditions

The business judgment rule reflects a balance pursuant to which directors are given substantial discretion, but are not allowed to put their own interests ahead of those of the shareholders. In other words, we give them carte blanche to make decisions that might turn out badly, but no discretion to make selfish decisions. This balance is reflected in the various preconditions courts have identified that must be satisfied before directors may avail themselves of the rule's protection.

1. An exercise of judgment

The business judgment rule is relevant only where directors have actually exercised business judgment. A decision to refrain from action is protected just as much as a decision to act, but there is no protection where directors have made no decision at all.[5] Instead, the consequences of inaction are subject to review under the duty of care.[6]

This seemingly innocuous requirement actually is quite problematic. In discussing the board's corporate governance role, we have been using the term "decision" as a shorthand for a process that often is less clear-cut. It is again useful to note Bayless Manning's observation that boards rarely take affirmative action on specific matters. Instead, their role is "a continuing flow of supervisory process, punctuated only occasionally by a discrete transactional decision."[7] Accordingly, the business judgment rule is rendered inapplicable as to a very large swath of board activity. As described below, however, the problem can be ameliorated through proper application of the duty of care.

2. Disinterested and independent decisionmakers

The business judgment rule "presupposes that the directors have no conflict of interest."[8] Hence, self-dealing is one of the classic triad of ways in which the business judgment rule's presumptions are rebutted.[9] "A director is interested if he will be materially affected, either to his

---

5. See, e.g., Aronson v. Lewis, 473 A.2d 805, 813 (Del.1984) ("the business judgment rule operates only in the context of director action"); ALI Principles § 4.01(c) cmt. c; see also Rosenblatt v. Getty Oil Co., 493 A.2d 929, 943 (Del.1985) (holding that "an informed decision to delegate a task is as much an exercise of business judgment as any other").

6. See, e.g., Graham v. Allis–Chalmers Mfg. Co., 188 A.2d 125 (Del.1963); In re

Caremark Int'l Inc. Deriv. Litig., 698 A.2d 959 (Del.Ch.1996).

7. Bayless Manning, The Business Judgment Rule and the Director's Duty of Attention: Time for Reality, 39 Bus. Law. 1477, 1494 (1984).

8. Lewis v. S. L. & E., Inc., 629 F.2d 764, 769 (2d Cir.1980).

9. Shlensky v. Wrigley, 237 N.E.2d 776, 778 (Ill.App.1968).

benefit or detriment, by a decision of the board, in a manner not shared by the corporation and the shareholders."[10] Consequently, for example, a director who sells or leases property to or from the corporation is interested in that transaction.[11] Similarly, a director who contracts to provide services to the corporation is interested in that transaction.[12]

Directors also can be interested in a transaction by virtue of indirect connections. In *Bayer v. Beran*,[13] for example, the corporation hired the wife of its president. Their spousal relationship gave the president an indirect interest in the transaction. Similarly, in *Globe Woolen Co. v. Utica Gas & Electric Co.*,[14] a director of the defendant was also the president and chief stockholder of the plaintiff. By virtue of those business relationships, he was deemed interested in the transaction even though he was not a party to the contract.

In addition to lacking a personal interest in the transaction in question, a director must be independent.[15] "A director is independent if he can base his decision 'on the corporate merits of the subject before the board rather than extraneous considerations or influences.' "[16] In particular, a director who is beholden to, or under the influence of an interested party, lacks the requisite independence.[17]

Where the board has acted collectively, it is not enough to show that a single director was interested or lacked independence. The business judgment rule will still insulate the board's decision from judicial review unless plaintiff can show that a majority of the board was interested and/or lacked independence.[18] In order to prove that the directors were not independent, plaintiff must establish personal or business relationships by which the directors are either beholden to or controlled by the interested party.[19]

10. Seminaris v. Landa, 662 A.2d 1350, 1354 (Del.1995). See also In re RJR Nabisco, Inc. Shareholders Litig., 1989 WL 7036 at *14 (Del.Ch.1989) (a disqualifying interest "is a financial interest in the transaction adverse to that of the corporation or its shareholders").

11. See, e.g., Lewis v. S. L. & E., Inc., 629 F.2d 764 (2d Cir.1980).

12. See, e.g., Talbot v. James, 190 S.E.2d 759 (S.C.1972).

13. 49 N.Y.S.2d 2 (Sup.Ct.1944).

14. 121 N.E. 378 (N.Y.1918). Consequently, directors are deemed to be interested when they "stand in a dual relation which prevents an unprejudiced exercise of judgment." Stoner v. Walsh, 772 F.Supp. 790, 802 (S.D.N.Y.1991) (quoting United Copper Sec. Co. v. Amalgamated Copper Co., 244 U.S. 261, 264 (1917)).

15. See, e.g., Rales v. Blasband, 634 A.2d 927, 935 (Del.1993) ("the board must be able to act free of personal financial interest and improper extraneous influences").

16. Seminaris v. Landa, 662 A.2d 1350, 1354 (Del.1995) (quoting Aronson v. Lewis, 473 A.2d 805, 816 (Del.1984)).

17. See In re MAXXAM, Inc., 659 A.2d 760, 773 (Del.Ch.1995) ("To be considered independent a director must not be 'dominated or otherwise controlled by an individual or entity interested in the transaction.' ").

18. See Odyssey Partners, L.P. v. Fleming Cos., Inc., 735 A.2d 386, 407 (Del.Ch. 1999).

19. See Aronson v. Lewis, 473 A.2d 805, 815 (Del.1984); see also Odyssey Partners, L.P. v. Fleming Cos., Inc., 735 A.2d 386, 407 (Del.Ch.1999). In Kahn v. Tremont Corp., 694 A.2d 422 (Del.1997), a committee of nominally independent directors approved a corporate acquisition. Two of the three directors were wholly passive, acquiescing in the decisions of the committee chairman, who had a significant financial

3. *Absence of fraud or illegality*

The business judgment rule will not insulate from judicial review decisions tainted by fraud or illegality.[20] The key issue in this context is whether the board has a duty to act lawfully.[21] In the oft-cited *Miller v. American Telephone & Telegraph Co.* decision, the Third Circuit held that directors have such a duty. AT & T failed to collect a debt owed it by the Democratic National Committee for telecommunications services provided during the 1968 Democrat Party's convention. Several AT & T shareholders brought a derivative suit against AT & T's directors, alleging that the failure to collect the debt violated both federal telecommunications and campaign finance laws. Ordinarily, a board decision not to collect a debt would be protected by the business judgment rule.[22] Citing a 1909 New York precedent,[23] however, the Third Circuit held that the business judgment rule did not insulate defendant directors from liability for illegal acts "even though committed to benefit the corporation."[24]

Assuming a duty to act lawfully exists, operationalizing it is a nontrivial task. Should there be a de minimis exception?[25] If a package delivery firm told its drivers to illegally double-park, so as to speed up the delivery process, for example, it is hardly clear that liability should follow. Should the business judgment rule be set aside only where the board ordered violations of criminal statutes or should it also be set aside where the board authorized violation of some civil regulation? The criminal law long has distinguished between crimes that are malum in se and those that are merely malum prohibitum. The latter are acts that are criminal merely because they are prohibited by statute, not because they violate natural law. It is said that "misdemeanors such as jaywalking and running a stoplight are mala prohibita, as are most *securities-law* violations."[26] Individuals routinely make cost-benefit analyses before deciding to comply with some malum prohibitum law, such as when deciding to violate the speed limit. Is it self-evident that directors of a

relationship with a controlling shareholder. The directors' decision was not protected by the business judgment rule.

20. See, e.g., Shlensky v. Wrigley, 237 N.E.2d 776, 778 (Ill.App.1968); see also Cottle v. Storer Communication, Inc., 849 F.2d 570, 575 (11th Cir.1988) (holding that the business judgment rule protects directors "from liability absent a clear showing of fraud, bad faith or abuse of discretion").

21. Note that the issue here is distinct from the problem of board oversight discussed below. In oversight cases, corporate employees have committed some criminal act and the board is charged with having failed to prevent those acts. Here we ask a different question; namely, what happens when the board affirmatively instructs its subordinates to violate the law?

22. Miller v. AT & T Co., 507 F.2d 759, 762 (3d Cir.1974) (diversity case arising under New York corporation law).

23. Roth v. Robertson, 118 N.Y.S. 351 (Sup.Ct.1909).

24. Miller v. AT & T Co., 507 F.2d 759, 762 (3d Cir.1974). See also Abrams v. Allen, 74 N.E.2d 305 (N.Y.1947) (directors can be sued where they used corporate property to commit "an unlawful or immoral act"); Di Tomasso v. Loverro, 12 N.E.2d 570 (N.Y.App.1937) (directors liable for entering into a contract that was an illegal restraint of trade).

25. Cf. ALI Principles § 2.01 cmt. g (acknowledging that the "de minimis principle" applies to corporate law compliance "as elsewhere in the law").

26. Black's Law Dictionary 401 (pocket ed. 1996) (emphasis supplied).

corporation should be barred from engaging in similar cost-benefit analyses?[27]

And, yet, still more questions must be answered if a duty to act lawfully is to be imposed. If neither the corporation nor the board was convicted or even indicted, for example, should plaintiff have to make out the elements of the criminal charge?[28] If so, to what extent does the criminal law concept of reasonable doubt come into play? Is a knowing violation of criminal law a per se violation of the duty of care unprotected by the business judgment rule?[29] How are damages to be measured and is causation an issue?[30] And so on.

The point is not that corporations should be allowed to break the law. They should not. If a corporation breaks the law, criminal sanctions should follow for the entity and/or the responsible individuals.[31] The point is only that fiduciary obligation and the duty to act lawfully make a bad fit. If the question is one of reconciling authority and accountability, it is not self-evident that corporate law should hold directors accountable simply for deciding that the corporation's interests are served by violating a particular statute. After all, "[a] business corporation is organized and carried on primarily for the profit of the stockholders. The powers of the directors are to be employed for that end."[32]

Put another way, the point of the business judgment rule is that shareholders should not be allowed to recover monetary damages simply because the directors made the wrong decision. Allowing shareholders to sue over a decision made with the intent of maximizing corporate profits is nothing less than double-dipping, even if the decision proves misguided. This claim is further supported by the realities of shareholder litigation. Shareholder lawsuits alleging that directors violated the purported duty to act lawfully will be brought as derivative actions. The real party in interest in derivative litigation is the plaintiff's attorney, not the nominal shareholder-plaintiff. In most cases, the bulk of any monetary benefits go to the plaintiffs' lawyers rather than the corporation or its shareholders. In practice, such litigation is more likely to be a mere

---

27. But cf. ALI Principles § 2.01 cmt. g ("With few exceptions, dollar liability is not a 'price' that can properly be paid for the privilege of engaging in legally wrongful conduct.").

28. *Miller* answered that question in the affirmative. Miller v. American Telephone & Telegraph Co., 507 F.2d 759, 763–64 (3d Cir.1974). Accord ALI Principles § 4.01(a) cmt. d.

29. That question is answered in the negative by ALI Principles § 4.01(a) cmt. d.

30. Under the so-called net loss rule, directors cannot be held monetarily liable if the overall gains to the corporation from the violation exceed the losses directly attributable thereto, such as fines or legal expenses. See James D. Cox, Compensation, Deterrence, and the Market as Boundaries for Derivative Suit Procedures, 52 Geo. Wash. L. Rev. 745, 765 (1984).

31. There is an active debate over the appropriateness of corporate criminal liability, but that debate is beyond the scope of this text. For recent commentary on that issue, see, e.g., Norwood P. Beveridge, Does the Corporate Director Have a Duty Always to Obey the Law?, 45 DePaul L. Rev. 729 (1996); V.S. Khanna, Corporate Criminal Liability: What Purpose Does It Serve?, 109 Harv. L. Rev. 1477 (1996); William S. Laufer, Corporate Liability, Risk Shifting, and the Paradox of Compliance, 52 Vand. L. Rev. 1343 (1999).

32. Dodge v. Ford Motor Co., 170 N.W. 668, 684 (Mich.1919).

wealth transfer from corporations and their managers to the plaintiff bar than a significant deterrent to corporate criminality. Accordingly, the illegality of a board decision—standing alone—should not deprive the directors of the protection of the business judgment rule.

4. *Rationality*

In *Sinclair Oil Corp. v. Levien,* the Delaware supreme court held that so long as the board's decision could be attributed to any rational business purpose the business judgment rule precluded the court from substituting its judgment as to the merits of the decision for those of the board.[33] Similarly, in *Brehm v. Eisner*, the court held that the business judgment rule does not apply when the board has "act[ed] in a manner that cannot be attributed to a rational business purpose."[34]

The reference to a "rational business purpose," properly understood, does not contemplate substantive review of the decision's merits. As Professor Michael Dooley observes, "*Sinclair*'s use of [the word] rational is to be equated with conceivable or imaginable and means only that the court will not even look at the board's judgment if there is any possibility that it was actuated by a legitimate business reason. It clearly does not mean, and cannot legitimately be cited for the proposition, that individual directors must have, and be prepared to put forth, proof of rational reasons for their decisions."[35] Consequently, as Chancellor Allen has stated:

> [W]hether a judge or jury considering the matter after the fact, believes a decision substantively wrong, or degrees of wrong extending through "stupid" to "egregious" or "irrational", provides no ground for director liability, so long as the court determines that the process employed was either rational or employed in a *good faith* effort to advance corporate interests. To employ a different rule— one that permitted an "objective" evaluation of the decision—would expose directors to substantive second guessing by ill-equipped judges or juries, which would, in the long-run, be injurious to investor interests.[36]

Instead, as Chancellor Allen observed elsewhere, "such limited substantive review as the rule contemplates (i.e., is the judgment under review 'egregious' or 'irrational' or 'so beyond reason,' etc.) really is a way of inferring bad faith."[37]

Put another way, inquiry into the rationality of a decision is a proxy for an inquiry into whether the decision was tainted by self-interest. In *Parnes v. Bally Entertainment Corp.*, for example, the Delaware supreme

---

33. Sinclair Oil Corp. v. Levien, 280 A.2d 717, 720 (Del.1971).

34. Brehm v. Eisner, 746 A.2d 244, 264 n. 66 (Del.2000).

35. Michael P. Dooley, Two Models of Corporate Governance, 47 Bus. Law. 461, 478–79 n.58 (1992).

36. In re Caremark International Inc. Derivative Litig., 698 A.2d 959, 967 (Del. Ch.1996) (emphasis in original).

37. In re RJR Nabisco, Inc. Shareholders Litig., 1989 WL 7036 at *13 n. 13 (Del. Ch.1989).

court stated that: "The presumptive validity of a business judgment is rebutted in those rare cases where the decision under attack is 'so far beyond the bounds of reasonable judgment that it seems essentially inexplicable on any ground other than bad faith.' "[38] In that case, Bally's CEO allegedly demanded bribes from prospective takeover bidders and, moreover, allegedly received such a bribe from the successful bidder. In holding that the plaintiff shareholder had stated a cause of action, the court observed that "it is inexplicable that independent directors, acting in good faith, could approve the deal" when it was so tainted.

Litwin v. Allen is often cited as an exception to the foregoing proposition.[39] Put another way, *Litwin* supposedly creates an "incredible stupidity" exception to the business judgment rule. Under this reading of the opinion, it stands as an example of a board decision so irrational as to not deserve the protection of the business judgment rule. One problem with this analysis is that *Litwin* involved the directors of a bank, who are typically held to a higher standard of accountability than directors of other corporations. Another is that *Litwin* is a sport—a case that falls well outside the norm. It is cited so often, because it stands alone as plausible precedential support for the irrationality exception to the business judgment rule. Finally, consistent with our hypothesis that courts use rationality as a code word for self-dealing, the *Litwin* court found the transaction in question to be "so improvident, so risky, so unusual, and unnecessary as to be contrary to fundamental conceptions of prudent banking practice." Although the court expressly declined to find a violation of the duty of loyalty, it seems fair to ask whether "we have reason to disbelieve the protestations of good faith by directors who reach 'irrational' conclusions?"[40]

In sum, it may be that there are some board decisions that are so dumb that the business judgment rule will not insulate them from judicial review.[41] Even if the set of such decisions is not an empty one, however, the tail ought not wag the dog. Because a prerequisite of rationality easily can erode into a prerequisite of reasonableness, courts must tread warily here. If they want to persist in requiring that there be a rational business purpose, at least they can ensure that that requirement lacks teeth.

---

38. 722 A.2d 1243, 1246 (Del.1999) (quoting In re J.P. Stevens & Co., Inc., 542 A.2d 770, 780–81 (Del.Ch.1988)).

39. Litwin v. Allen, 25 N.Y.S.2d 667 (Sup.Ct.1940). Delaware Justice Henry Horsey, *Technicolor*'s author, asserts that *Litwin* articulates a *Technicolor*-like formulation of the business judgment rule under which, "for the rule of judicial deference to be invoked, directors of a board must be found to have met not only their duty of loyalty but also their duty of care." Henry Ridgely Horsey, The Duty of Care Component of the Delaware Business Judgment Rule, 19 Del. J. Corp. L. 971, 976 (1994). As described in the text, however, we regard *Litwin* as being even less defensible than *Technicolor*.

40. Michael P. Dooley, Fundamentals of Corporation Law 263 (1995).

41. See Gagliardi v. TriFoods Int'l, Inc., 683 A.2d 1049, 1051–52 (Del.Ch.1996) ("There is a *theoretical* exception ... that holds that some decisions may be so 'egregious' that liability for losses they cause may follow even in the absence of proof of conflict of interest or improper motivation. The exception, however, has resulted in no awards of money judgments. . . ."; emphasis supplied).

5. An informed decision (a.k.a. process due care)

It is frequently said that the exercise of "reasonable diligence and care" is a precondition for the business judgment rule's application.[42] This phraseology is most unfortunate. It implies the necessity to inquire into the care exercised by the board, which in turn easily slides into the *Technicolor* error of treating compliance with the duty of care as an essential prerequisite for invoking the rule.[43] The problem reduces to one of mere semantics, however, if we understand the requirement of "reasonable diligence and care" as being limited to the process by which the decision was made. Numerous Delaware decisions confirm that judicial references to a requirement of due care really go to the adequacy of the decisionmaking process—what the court has begun calling "process due care."[44] It would be better to follow the lead of those decisions and simply stop talking about whether the board exercised "reasonable diligence and care." Instead, the requisite precondition would be better stated as a rational and good faith decisionmaking process.

Smith v. Van Gorkom[45] was the seminal process case. In 1980, Trans Union's CEO and chairman, Van Gorkom, negotiated a merger between Trans Union and an entity controlled by financier Pritzker. Trans

---

42. See, e.g., S. Samuel Arsht, The Business Judgment Rule Revisited, 8 Hofstra L. Rev. 93, 100 (1979).

43. Another way of looking at the problem is the distinction between standards of review and standards of conduct, which is discussed below. If that distinction is to have teeth, failure to comply with the standard of conduct should not lead to liability. Instead, that standard should be largely exhortatory. The "reasonable diligence and care" formulation undermines the necessary dichotomy between these standards by conflating them. It conditions the lenient standard of review on compliance with the more exacting (but largely aspirational) standard of conduct.

44. Brehm v. Eisner, 746 A.2d 244, 264 (Del.2000) ("Due care in the decisionmaking context is *process* due care only."; emphasis in original); Citron v. Fairchild Camera & Instrument Corp., 569 A.2d 53, 66 (Del.1989) ("our due care examination has focused on a board's decision-making process"); In re Caremark Int'l Inc. Deriv. Litig., 698 A.2d 959, 967 (Del.Ch.1996) ("compliance with a director's duty of care can never appropriately be judicially determined by reference to *the content of the board decision* that leads to a corporate loss, apart from consideration of the good faith *or* rationality of the process employed"; emphasis in original). Gimbel v. Signal Cos., Inc., 316 A.2d 599 (Del.Ch. 1974), aff'd, 316 A.2d 619 (Del.1974), is sometimes cited as an example of a Delaware court engaging in substantive review

of a board's decision. Plaintiff Gimbel represents a shareholder group holding about 12% of Signal. They brought suit to prevent Signal from selling Signal Oil (a Signal subsidiary) to Burmah Oil. The sale price was set at $480 million, but Gimbel argued that, under a more correct set of valuation assumptions, the actual value of Signal Oil was around $760 million. The court acknowledged that there was no evidence of fraud or self-dealing. It held, however, that the business judgment rule did not protect directors who acted recklessly in accepting a "grossly inadequate" price. The court expressly grounded its opinion on the substance of the board's decision rather than the process by which that decision was reached, holding that the ultimate question was one of value and not method. But while the court was unwilling to hold that the directors had acted in an uninformed manner, it was clearly troubled by the haste in which the decision was made and, in particular, the failure of management to give prior notice to the board of the deal's progress. On balance, the court seemingly was concerned that management had railroaded the sale through the board. It is hard to imagine that the court would have held for plaintiff if the decisionmaking process had been less thoroughly flawed. In any event, Chancellor Allen later dismissed *Gimbel* as a "dubious holding." Gagliardi v. TriFoods Int'l, Inc., 683 A.2d 1049, 1052 (Del.Ch. 1996).

45. 488 A.2d 858 (Del.1985).

Union's board and shareholders approved the deal. Plaintiff-shareholder Smith sued, alleging that the board's approval of the deal merger violated the Trans Union directors' duty of care. The defendant directors contended that their decision to sell the company should be protected by the business judgment rule.

The court began its analysis by noting that the business judgment rule provides a presumption that in making a decision the directors acted on an informed basis, in good faith and in the honest belief that the decision was in the firm's best interests. None of the usual triad of exceptions to the rule—i.e., fraud, illegality, or self-dealing—were present in this case, as the court acknowledged.[46] The protection provided by the business judgment rule is unavailable, however, if the directors failed to inform themselves of all material information reasonably available to them. In the course of its opinion, the court focused closely on issues of board process. Indeed, one can plausibly read *Van Gorkom* as providing a procedural roadmap by which corporate decisions, at least of this magnitude, ought to be made. Accordingly, it seems appropriate to identify those aspects of the Trans Union board's conduct by which the court was troubled.

Consultations. During his negotiations with Pritzker, Van Gorkom consulted only with Trans Union's controller (Peterson). Worse yet, once he told other senior managers about the impending deal, their initial reaction was strongly negative. In particular, Romans (Trans Union's CFO) objected that the price was too low, the transaction would have adverse tax consequences for some shareholders, and an option given Pritzker to buy Trans Union shares amounted to a "lock-up" that would inhibit competing offers. Such evidence likely proved quite damning in the court's own decisionmaking process. Having evidence in the record of these types of internal disagreements obviously raised questions about the fairness of the transaction. The take-away lesson is that deal-makers should, early in the process, consult with senior management and get them "on board." In addition, Van Gorkom would have been well-advised to consult in advance with the board of directors and kept them informed as to the progress of the negotiations.

Setting the price. When selling an entire business, whether the sale is nominally structured as a merger or not, the board of directors "must focus on one primary objective—to secure the transaction offering the best value reasonably available for all stockholders."[47] In his negotiations

---

46. One could perhaps construct a self-dealing argument by focusing on the fact that Van Gorkom was very close to the mandatory retirement age and owned 75,000 shares of Trans Union stock. At $55 per share, those shares would be worth over $4 million; on the stock market, the shares had recently traded in a range of $30 to $39 per share. Even at the high end of that range, those shares were worth less than $3 million. One thus could argue that Van Gorkom's large stockholdings and his immi-

nent mandatory retirement meant that he had an incentive to sell the company. If so, however, his incentive clearly is to get the best possible price. The more money for which Trans Union was sold, the more money Van Gorkom would have in retirement. Consequently, his self-interest was directly in-line with the interests of the shareholders, who presumably also would want the best possible price.

47. McMullin v. Beran, 765 A.2d 910, 918 (Del.2000).

with Pritzker, it was Van Gorkom who proposed the price of $55. In evaluating the potential for a management-sponsored leveraged buyout, Romans had earlier determined that such a buyout would be easy at a price of $50 but very difficult at a price of $60. Van Gorkom then seemingly split the difference, picking $55 out of the air as a price he would accept for his shares.

The court emphasized that the price thus was based on an evaluation of the feasibility with which a leveraged deal could be financed, rather than the Trans Union's value.[48] To the extent the court's analysis rests on the idea that a company has some intrinsic value, the decision is seriously flawed. As with any other asset, a company is worth only what somebody is willing to pay for it. Although the company's only value thus is its market value, an asset can have different values in different markets. (Otherwise, arbitrage would never be profitable.) Two distinct markets are implicated in this setting. On the one hand, there is the ordinary stock market in which Trans Union's shares trade. On the other, however, there is the market for corporate control. Prices in the latter market typically exceed those in the former. Hence, we speak of a "control premium" that is paid when someone buys all of the shares of a company's stock.[49]

Trans Union's board made no effort to determine what control was worth to Pritzker, such as by ordering a valuation study, and in the absence of such a determination had no basis for deciding whether the price was a fair one. Put another way, the real issue, which is not well-framed in the majority opinion, is what the firm was worth to Pritzker and, accordingly, whether the board of directors did a good job in capturing that value on behalf of their shareholders. Trans Union's own estimate suggested that a price of up to $60 per share feasibly could be financed, albeit with some difficulty.[50] The feasibility study, moreover, was prepared internally by an officer who presumably did not do such studies for a living. Although the court explicitly stated that boards are

---

48. See, e.g., Smith v. Van Gorkom, 488 A.2d 858, 874 (Del.1985) (noting that the directors "were uninformed as to the intrinsic value of the Company").

49. Some scholars contend that the control premium is also attributable to a purportedly downward sloping demand curve for corporate stock. See, e.g., Richard A. Booth, The Efficient Market, Portfolio Theory, and the Downward Sloping Demand Hypothesis, 68 N.Y.U L. Rev. 1187 (1993); Lynn A. Stout, How Efficient Markets Undervalue Stocks: CAPM and ECMH Under Conditions of Uncertainty and Disagreement, 19 Cardozo L. Rev. 475 (1997); Lynn A. Stout, Are Takeover Premiums Really Premiums? Market Price, Fair Value, and Corporate Law, 99 Yale L.J. 1235 (1990). The existence of a control premium, however, is not inconsistent with efficient capital markets theory. Stock consists of two rights: economic and voting. A single share of stock gives the owner little control over the company. The market price of a single share of stock thus reflects nothing more than the estimated present value of the future stream of dividends payable on that share. Someone buying all, or even just a majority, of the stock, however, obviously gets significant control through his ability to elect the board of directors. Hence, their willingness to pay a control premium. They can use their control either to extract personal benefits from the corporation and/or tweak corporate policies in ways they believe will make the firm more profitable.

50. The difference between $60 and the $55 Pritzker agreed to pay is only $5 per share, but $5 per share times roughly 12.5 million outstanding shares works out to about $63 million, which is not chump change.

not obliged to hire outside financial experts, investment bankers in fact do valuation and feasibility studies for a living. The well-advised board thus obtains a fairness opinion that, at least in theory, gives them some basis for evaluating what the prospective buyer could afford, and would be willing, to pay. Not surprisingly, *Van Gorkom* is sometimes referred to as the "Investment Bankers' Full Employment Act."[51]

Negotiations. Van Gorkom's negotiations with Pritzker appear to have been less than demanding. Van Gorkom asked for a meeting, at which he basically said "if you'll pay $55, here's how you can finance the deal." Pritzker counter-offered with $50 per share, which Van Gorkom rejected. Pritzker then agreed to $55. Pritzker's quick acceptance of the price suggests that he thought he was getting a bargain, which enhances our questions about the adequacy of the price.

Time pressures. Pritzker imposed a tight time deadline in order to prevent leaks and the increased stock price that usually follows such leaks. As a result, the process went quite quickly and many decisions were made under significant time constraints. All of which evidently troubled the court, as it several times noted that there was no crisis or emergency justifying such speed. Does *Van Gorkom* thus imply that the board can never make quick decisions? Probably not. The speed with which the decision was made likely would have been unobjectionable if the process was otherwise adequate. A cautionary note is sounded, however, by the Delaware supreme court's recent observation that: "History has demonstrated boards 'that have failed to exercise due care are frequently boards that have been rushed.' "[52]

Information and process. The central issue in *Van Gorkom* was the board's failure to make an informed decision. The legal standard that emerges from the decision is straightforward—directors must inform themselves of all material information reasonably available to them.[53] This standard seemingly requires an in-depth study of the problem. The board must be informed of the company's value to the bidder, the course of the negotiations, the terms of the offer and their fairness, and the like.

This standard is too demanding. Information is costly and shareholders will only want managers to invest an additional dollar in gathering information where there is an additional dollar generated from better decision making. By requiring directors to have all information

51. See, e.g., Park McGinty, The Twilight of Fiduciary Duties: On the Need For Shareholder Self–Help in an Age of Formalistic Proceduralism, 46 Emory L.J. 163, 193 n.42 (1997); see also William J. Carney, Fairness Opinions: How Fair Are They and Why We Should Do Nothing About It, 70 Wash. U. L.Q. 523, 527 (1992) (opining that *Van Gorkom* "could be called the Investment Bankers' Civil Relief Act of 1985").

52. McMullin v. Beran, 765 A.2d 910, 922 (Del.2000).

53. Smith v. Van Gorkom, 488 A.2d 858, 872 (Del.1985). See also Washington Bancorporation v. Said, 812 F.Supp. 1256, 1269 (D.D.C.1993); Estate of Detwiler v. Offenbecher, 728 F.Supp. 103, 150 (S.D.N.Y.1989). The Delaware supreme court subsequently defined the term "material" in this context as "relevant and of a magnitude to be important to directors in carrying out their fiduciary duty of care in decisionmaking." Brehm v. Eisner, 746 A.2d 244, 259 n. 49 (Del.2000).

"reasonably available" to them the *Van Gorkom* court required the directors to over-invest in information.[54] In contrast, the ALI PRINCIPLES only require directors to be informed to the extent that they reasonably believe to be appropriate under the circumstances.[55] Unlike the Delaware standard, at least as read literally, the ALI standard permits directors to make decisions on less than all reasonable available information, provided they reasonably believe doing so is appropriate given the situation. The time available to make the decision may require that the directors take risks to secure what appears to be a good outcome, which includes the risk that they do not have all of the relevant facts. A decision to accept that risk in order to secure the benefits of a proposed transaction will be appropriate under some circumstances.

In practice, of course, there are significant limitations on the board's ability to gather primary sources of information. Nobody seriously expects boards to read merger agreements cover to cover—not even the *Van Gorkom* court.[56] Reading long and boring legal documents is what boards pay their lawyers and subordinates to do. Under the circumstances, however, Trans Union's directors had a duty of inquiry. Considering the haste and other circumstances surrounding the decision, they should have pressed Van Gorkom with regard to the details of the deal. Instead, the board blindly relied on Van Gorkom's assertion that the price was fair. Van Gorkom failed to disclose, and the board failed to make sufficient inquiry to discover, key facts suggesting that the deal was not as attractive as it might seem on first blush.[57]

Qualitative studies of board processes have found wide variances. Some boards simply go through the motions of showing up and voting, without having done their homework.[58] The Delaware supreme court concluded that the Trans Union directors were just such a board—the board was "grossly negligent in approving the 'sale' of the Company upon two hours' consideration, without prior notice, and without the exigency of a crisis or emergency." Other boards, however, exhibit far greater diligence. Such boards research issues, participate actively in discussion, and exercise critical judgment.[59]

---

54. Cf. In re RJR Nabisco, Inc. Shareholders Litig., 1989 WL 7036 (Del.Ch.1989), in which Chancellor Allen observed that "information has costs." Id at *19. He further opined "that the amount of information that it is prudent to have before a decision is made is itself a business judgment of the very type that courts are institutionally poorly equipped to make." Id.

55. ALI Principles § 4.01(c)(2).

56. Smith v. Van Gorkom, 488 A.2d 858, 883 n. 25 (Del.1985) ("We do not suggest that a board must read *in haec verba* every contract or legal document which it approves....").

57. In other words, the formal structure of the corporate governance system vests most decisionmaking power in the board of directors, especially with regard to major corporate changes such as a merger. Facts tending to suggest that senior officers are trying to railroad a decision through the board therefore are inconsistent with that model. Unfortunately for Trans Union's directors, the *Van Gorkom* record was rife with such facts.

58. Daniel P. Forbes & Frances J. Milliken, Cognition and Corporate Governance: Understanding Boards of Directors as Strategic Decision-making Groups, 24 Acad. Mgmt. Rev. 489, 494 (1999).

59. As for sorting out which type of board predominates, it seems noteworthy that about two-thirds of surveyed boards now have at least some control over their

How should corporate law encourage boards to exercise due diligence in the decisionmaking process? Should the corporate statute specify board procedures, for example? In general, corporation codes do not mandate detailed rules of board process or procedure. How the board sets its agenda, whether formal voting rules are observed, and other matters of parliamentary procedure are left to the board's discretion. Yet, there are lots of theoretical reasons—such as Arrow's Impossibility Theorem[60]—to think that the procedural rules for aggregating individual preferences have outcome determinative effects. Laboratory experiments on group decisionmaking, such as studies of mock juries, confirm that procedural matters such as the taking of straw votes and the setting of agendas do affect outcomes.[61] To be sure, it is doubtful whether ex ante legislative solutions would be viable given the complexities and uncertainties of life. Ex post judicial review of board process may be beneficial, however.

Consistent with that hypothesis, *Van Gorkom* rests not on failure to comply with some judicially imposed decisionmaking model but on the absence of a sufficient record of any deliberative process. Put differently, if the decisionmaking process is adequate, the court will continue to defer to the decision that emerges from that process. The basic thrust of the opinion then is that the board must provide some credible, contemporary evidence that it knew what it was doing. If such evidence exists, the court will not impose liability—even if the decision proves to have been the wrong one.

By so focusing its opinion, the *Van Gorkom* court arguably created a set of incentives consistent with the teaching of the literature on group decisionmaking. The decision disfavors agenda control by senior management. The decision penalizes boards that simply go through the motions. The decision encourages inquiry, deliberation, care, and process. The decision strongly encourages boards to seek outside counsel and financial advice, which is consistent with evidence groupthink can be prevented by

agenda. National Association of Corporate Directors, Public Company Governance Survey 1999–2000 12 (Oct. 2000) (58% in 1997 and 69% in 1999).

60. According to Arrow's Theorem, there is no consistent method of making a fair choice among three or more options. As a result, when individual preferences differ, the outcome of a decisionmaking process will be determined by the process itself.

61. Mock juries reviewing the same evidence, for example, regularly reach differing verdicts. See James H. Davis, Some Compelling Intuitions about Group Consensus Decisions, Theoretical and Empirical Research, and Interpersonal Aggregation Phenomena: Selected Examples, 1950–1990, 52 Org. Behav. & Human Decision Processes 3, 23–33 (1992) (summarizing studies);

see also Robert C. Erffmeyer & Irving M. Lane, Quality and Acceptance of an Evaluative Task: The Effects of Four Group Decision–Making Formats, 9 Group & Org. Stud. 509 (1984) (decisionmaking formats have predictable effects on quality of decision). One possible explanation for such divergences is the effect of agenda control. A well known study, for example, concluded that setting a specific agenda affected an airplane club's decision as to which plane to buy. Charles R. Plott & Michael E. Levine, A Model of Agenda Influence on Committee Decisions, 68 Am. Econ. Rev. 146 (1978); Michael E. Levine & Charles R. Plott, Agenda Influence and its Implications, 63 Va. L. Rev. 561 (1977). Such agenda research confirms that both the way the decision is cast and the sequence in which issues are taken up affect the outcomes of such decisions.

outside expert advice and evaluations.[62] Even the court's criticism of the board's willingness to take action after a single meeting is consistent with suggestions that a "second-chance meeting" also helps prevent groupthink.

Summation. While the substantial criticism to which *Van Gorkom* has been subjected is not wholly unmerited,[63] ultimately the decision is not inconsistent with our model. Even at the time *Van Gorkom* was decided, the more exaggerated fears of judicial intervention into board decisionmaking processes were clearly overstated. Strict adherence to the court's decisionmaking model likely is not a prerequisite for the business judgment rule to be applicable. On the facts of the case before it, however, the court concluded that the board had abdicated its responsibility and allowed itself to be railroaded by management to so great an extent that deference became inappropriate. In addition, the decision at issue related to a major transaction having final period consequences. Accountability thus appropriately trumped authority.

In closing, however, it should be noted that *Van Gorkom* probably has resulted in many board decisions being over-processed. In many cases, even relatively minor board decisions are subjected to exhaustive review, with detailed presentations by experts. Why? The answer lies in the incentive structures of the relevant players. Who pays the bill if the director is found liable for breaching the duty of care? The director.[64] Who pays the bill for hiring lawyers and investment bankers to advise the board? The corporation and, ultimately, the shareholders. Suppose you were faced with potentially catastrophic losses, for which somebody offered to sell you an insurance policy. Better still, you don't have to pay the premiums, someone else will do so. Buying the policy therefore doesn't cost you anything. Would not you buy it?

It's also important to consider the incentives of the lawyers who advise corporations. Deciding how much time and effort to spend on making decisions is itself a business decision. Because that decision is driven by liability concerns, however, legal advice is usually critical to the making of the decision. Why might lawyers have an incentive to encourage boards to over-invest in the decisionmaking process? The cynical answer is that a more complicated decisionmaking process, which is driven by liability concerns, is likely to result in higher fees. A less cynical explanation is that the law is full of sports, mutants, and mistakes. Clients often lack the information or willingness to recognize that their situation was one of the exceptions that proves the rule.

62. See generally Irving Janis, L. Groupthink (2d ed. 1982) (discussing solutions for groupthink).

63. For a trenchant doctrinal critique of *Van Gorkom*, which contends that the majority misused precedent, and which also summarizes criticisms made by other commentators, see William T. Quillen, Trans Union, Business Judgment, and Neutral Principles, 10 Del. J. Corp. L. 465 (1985).

64. Note that this assumes that neither indemnification or insurance is available. Given the ready availability of indemnification under Delaware law and the reasonable availability of D & O insurance, the caution often seen in board decisionmaking is truly puzzling.

Instead, clients tend to blame the lawyer for an adverse outcome even if the lawyer did nothing wrong. Because the lawyers will be blamed even if losing the case was an act of god equivalent to a 100–year flood, lawyers are often conservative in giving advice. (The term conservative here is not used in its political sense, but rather in the sense of being cautious.) In economic terms, lawyers are risk averse. In a risky situation, the best thing for the lawyer to do is to point the client towards strategies whose outcome is certain.

In sum, the incentives of both sellers and buyers of legal advice are congruent. Lawyers have strong incentives to encourage clients to expend a lot of time, energy, and money on the decisionmaking process, while corporate boards of directors have strong incentives to take that advice. All of which goes to show that otherwise puzzling things become readily explicable if one understands the economic incentives at play.

C.   The contextual business judgment rule

The business judgment rule is badly misnamed. In the legal literature, it is conventional to distinguish between standards and rules. Rules say, "drive 55 mph," while standards say, "drive reasonably." So defined, the business judgment rule is not a rule but a standard. The question is not whether the directors violated some bright-line precept, but whether their conduct satisfied some standard for judicial abstention.

The greater flexibility inherent in standards frequently comes into play in business judgment rule jurisprudence, as courts fine tune the doctrine's application to the facts at bar.[65] Much of that fine tuning is explicable as a (probably unconscious) attempt to strike an appropriate balance between authority and accountability under specific factual circumstances. As we have frequently observed, authority and accountability are in constant tension. Seeking to hold directors accountable for their decisions necessarily reduces the efficiency of corporate decisionmaking. Conversely, deference to the board's authority necessarily entails a risk of opportunism and even plain carelessness. In applying the business judgment rule, courts ought to be more explicit both about the fact that they are balancing these competing concerns and why they believe the balance struck in a particular case is the appropriate one.

Delaware courts have moved somewhat in this direction by recognizing that the fiduciary responsibilities of directors, and thus the appropriate degree of judicial review, depend "upon the specific context that gives occasion to the board's exercise of its business judgment."[66] Although the partition admittedly is somewhat artificial, a useful first cut at striking the necessary balance between authority and accountability is

---

65. Cf. Stahl v. Apple Bancorp, Inc., 579 A.2d 1115, 1125 (Del.Ch.1990) (Chancellor Allen opined that "inquiries concerning fiduciary duties are inherently particularized and contextual").

66. McMullin v. Beran, 765 A.2d 910, 918 (Del.2000).

provided by the distinction between operational issues, such as whether to install lighting in a baseball park, and structural choices, especially those creating a final period situation, such as takeovers.[67] This Chapter focuses on the business judgment rule as it relates to operational decisions. Omitted from this Chapter thus are such matters as:

- The role of the business judgment rule in conflict of interest transactions, which is discussed in Chapter 7.

- The extent to which the business judgment rule controls board efforts to terminate shareholder derivative litigation, which is discussed in Chapter 8.

- The relationship between the business judgment rule and the shareholder wealth maximization norm, which is discussed in Chapter 9.

- The conditional business judgment rule governing management resistance to takeover bids, which is discussed in Chapter 12.

Taken together with the cases discussed in this Chapter, these omitted applications suggest that three distinct versions of the business judgment rule can be identified. One is the traditional business judgment rule under which courts essentially decline to review decisions made by the board. A second, arguably more intrusive, variant of the business judgment rule is applied in cases such as *Van Gorkom* or *Technicolor*, which involve the sale of the business. The third variant, which might be called a conditional business judgment rule, is applied to takeover defenses per *Unocal* and its progeny.

As illustrated by the dichotomy between *Shlensky* and *Technicolor*, operational decisions typically (and appropriately) receive much less probing review than do the structural ones covered by the latter two variants of the rule. The principle is sufficiently well-established that a few examples will suffice. In *Shlensky*, the court declined to overrule the board's decision not to install lights in Wrigley Field.[68] In *Dodge v. Ford Motor Co.*,[69] the court refused to enjoin the board's decision to expand its factories, despite evidence that the decision was motivated by concerns other than shareholder wealth maximization. In *Theodora Holding Corp. v. Henderson*,[70] and *Ella M. Kelly & Wyndham, Inc. v. Bell*,[71] the business judgment rule insulated corporate charitable giving from judicial review. In *Kamin v. American Express Co.*,[72] the business judgment rule precluded review of a spin-off transaction. In *Weiss v. Samsonite Corp.*,[73] Vice Chancellor Jacobs held that the rule protected a board's

---

67. See E. Norman Veasey, The Defining Tension in Corporate Governance in America, 52 Bus. Law. 393, 394 (1997) (drawing a similar distinction between "enterprise" and "ownership" decisions).

68. Shlensky v. Wrigley, 237 N.E.2d 776 (Ill.App.1968).

69. 170 N.W. 668 (Mich.1919).

70. 257 A.2d 398 (Del.Ch.1969).

71. 266 A.2d 878 (Del.1970).

72. 383 N.Y.S.2d 807 (Sup.Ct.), aff'd, 387 N.Y.S.2d 993 (1976).

73. 741 A.2d 366 (Del.Ch.), aff'd. 746 A.2d 277 (Del.1999).

decision to take on considerable additional debt as part of a leveraged recapitalization. And the beat goes on.

Such results are tolerable because most operational decisions do not pose much of a conflict between the interests of directors and shareholders. Granting, for example, that Wrigley appears to have preferred the neighborhood's interests to those of his shareholders, what selfish interests was he advancing? Perhaps he was simply trying to comply with what he saw as appropriate business ethics. Or, as we have already suggested, maybe he had eccentric ideas about how baseball was to be played. At worst, he might have reaped some psychological benefits from implementing his attitudes. Even assuming arguendo that these sort of psychological benefits implicate the kinds of self-dealing concerns that justify setting aside the business judgment rule, it is not clear that Wrigley's "self-interest" conflicted with the interests of their shareholders. With their theoretically perpetual duration, corporations must plan for the long-term.[74] As the *Shlensky* court's dictum suggested, it is plausible that Wrigley's opposition to lights was in the shareholders' best long-term interest. Drunken fans reveling in the darkness might have a deleterious effect on the neighborhood. If so, attendance might decline as the neighborhood declined.

We doubt whether Wrigley made the right decision. But so what? Operational decisions are a species of what economists refer to as repeat transactions. Where parties expect to have repeated transactions, the risk of self-dealing by one party is constrained by the threat that the other party will punish the cheating party in future transactions. To be sure, shareholder discipline is not a very important check on directorial self-dealing. Yet, as we have seen, it is just one of an array of extrajudicial constraints that, in totality, give directors incentives to exercise reasonable care in decisionmaking. True, these constraining forces do not eliminate the possibility of director error. The directors will still err from time to time. That is precisely the sort of error, however, that the courts traditionally—and appropriately—eschew reviewing.

D. Application to officers

It is reasonably well-settled that officers owe a duty of care to the corporation.[75] It is less well-settled that officers get the benefit of the business judgment rule. Under the ALI PRINCIPLES, the rule applies to both directors and officers.[76] Judicial precedents are divided, however.[77]

---

74. Accordingly, directors may pursue plans that are in the corporation's "best interests without regard to a fixed investment horizon." Paramount Communications, Inc. v. Time Inc., 571 A.2d 1140, 1150 (Del.1989). See also In re Reading Co., 711 F.2d 509 (3d Cir.1983) (corporate pricing and dividend policies that failed to maximize short-term profits nevertheless could rationally be seen as in corporation's long-term interest).

75. See ALI Principles § 4.01 cmt. a; see, e.g., MBCA § 8.42(a)(2) (requiring that officers exercise the "care that a person in a like position would reasonably exercise under similar circumstances").

76. ALI Principles § 4.01.

77. Compare Galef v. Alexander, 615 F.2d 51, 57 n. 13 (2d Cir.1980) (holding that the business judgment rule "generally applies to decisions of executive officers as

Most of the theoretical justifications for the business judgment rule extend from the boardroom to corporate officers. Many corporate decisions are made by officers, for example, who are likely to be even more risk averse than directors. Accordingly, insulation from liability may be necessary to encourage optimal levels of risk-taking by officers. Just as the board of directors is properly regarded as a production team, so is the so-called top management team.[78] Accordingly, internal team governance may be preferable to external review. In sum, the better view is that officers are eligible for the protections of the business judgment rule.

§ 6.5 The duty of care

Because the business judgment rule is so pervasive, the underlying duty of care remains poorly developed. Recent statutory developments, however, shed important new light both on the duty of care and its sometimes tenuous relationship with the business judgment rule.

A. Is the duty of care a negligence standard?

As we have seen, Delaware law requires directors to exercise "that amount of care which ordinarily careful and prudent men would use in similar circumstances."[1] The ALI PRINCIPLES similarly require directors to use "the care that an ordinarily prudent person would reasonably be expected to exercise in a like position and under similar circumstances."[2] Until recently, the MBCA likewise required that directors discharge their duties "with the care an ordinarily prudent person would exercise under similar circumstances."[3] All of these statements sound like negligence standards.[4] Yet, as Professor Bishop famously observed: "The search for cases in which directors of industrial corporations have been held liable in derivative suits for negligence uncomplicated by self-dealing is a search for a very small number of needles in a very large haystack."[5] A more recent survey found only twelve cases imposing

well as those of directors"); FDIC v. Stahl, 854 F.Supp. 1565, 1570 n. 8 (S.D.Fla.1994) (holding that the rule "applies equally to both officers and directors") with Platt v. Richardson, 1989 WL 159584 at *2 (M.D.Pa.1989) (holding that the rule "applies only to directors of a corporation and not to officers."). At least one court claims that the former view is the majority position, rejecting an argument that "the business judgment rule applies only to the conduct of corporate directors and not to the conduct of corporate officers" on grounds that it was "clearly contrary to the substantial body of corporate case law which has developed on this issue." Selcke v. Bove, 629 N.E.2d 747, 750 (Ill.App.1994).

78. See Susan G. Cohen & Diane E. Bailey, What Makes Teams Work: Group Effectiveness Research from the Shop Floor to the Executive Suite, 23 J. Mgmt. 239, 265–76 (1997) (describing research on top management teams).

§ 6.5

1. See, e.g., Graham v. Allis–Chalmers Mfg. Co., 188 A.2d 125, 130 (Del.1963).

2. ALI Principles § 4.01(a).

3. MBCA § 8.30 cmt.

4. Delaware tort law defines negligence as "the want of due care or want of such care as a reasonably prudent and careful person would exercise under similar circumstances." Orsini v. K–Mart Corp., 1997 WL 528034 at *3 (Del.Super.1997).

5. Joseph W. Bishop, Jr., Sitting Ducks and Decoy Ducks: New Trends in the Indemnification of Corporate Directors and

liability on directors for negligence in the absence of a concurrent breach of the duty of loyalty or other conflict of interest.[6]

The paucity of such cases doubtless owes much to the business judgment rule. Yet, it also reflects a fundamental disagreement as to whether negligence is the appropriate standard of review in the corporate context. Precedents in several jurisdictions adopt ordinary negligence as the relevant standard of review in duty of care cases.[7] In contrast, the Delaware courts have adopted gross negligence as the relevant standard,[8] which they define as "reckless indifference to or a deliberate disregard of the stockholders" or conduct outside the "bounds of reason."[9]

B. Causation

Whether the standard of review is one of gross negligence or just ordinary negligence, the negligence-like phrasing of the duty of care might reasonably lead one to assume that liability should be imposed only where all the elements of the negligence cause of action are made out. In tort law, liability for negligence requires not just a breach of the duty of care but also a showing of causation and damages. An early opinion by famed jurist Learned Hand confirmed that just such a showing is required in the corporate duty of care context. In *Barnes v.*

Officers, 77 Yale L.J. 1078, 1099 (1968). See also Bayer v. Beran, 49 N.Y.S.2d 2, 6 (Sup. Ct.1944) (stating that "although the concept of 'responsibility' is firmly fixed in the law, it is only in a most unusual and extraordinary case that directors are held liable for negligence in the absence of fraud, or improper motive, or personal interest").

6. 1 Dennis J. Block et al., The Business Judgment Rule: Fiduciary Duties of Corporate Directors 167–72 (5th ed. 1998).

7. See, e.g., FDIC v. Stahl, 89 F.3d 1510 (11th Cir.1996) (Florida law); Theriot v. Bourg, 691 So.2d 213 (La.App.1997) (rejecting gross negligence standard in favor of a "reasonable care" standard); Litwin v. Allen, 25 N.Y.S.2d 667, 699 (Sup.Ct.1940) (stating that liability must be imposed on facts of that case if "the doctrine that directors of a bank are liable for negligence" is to be preserved).

8. See, e.g., McMullin v. Beran, 765 A.2d 910 (Del.2000) ("Director liability for breaching the duty of care 'is predicated upon concepts of gross negligence.'"); Smith v. Van Gorkom, 488 A.2d 858, 873 (Del.1985) (gross negligence is the proper standard for determining whether a business judgment was an informed one); In re RJR Nabisco, Inc. Shareholders Litig., 1989 WL 7036 at *18 (Del.Ch.1989) (plaintiff

must show "the directors were grossly negligent"); Rabkin v. Philip A. Hunt Chemical Corp., 547 A.2d 963, 970 (Del.Ch.1986) ("Gross negligence is the standard to be applied in deciding first, whether the directors' decisions were informed, and, if so, whether the directors may be held liable for reaching the wrong decision."); see also McCall v. Scott, 250 F.3d 997, 999 (6th Cir.2001) (asserting that the Delaware standard is one of gross negligence). Oddly, in Aronson v. Lewis, 473 A.2d 805 (Del.1984), the supreme court conflated the gross negligence standard and the business judgment rule: "While the Delaware cases use a variety of terms to describe the applicable standard of care, our analysis satisfies us that under the business judgment rule director liability is predicated upon concepts of gross negligence." Id. at 812. To the extent *Aronson* thus contemplates substantive review of board decisions, rather than review of the board's decisionmaking process, it is inconsistent with those Delaware precedents embracing the abstention version of the rule.

9. Rabkin v. Philip A. Hunt Chemical Corp., 547 A.2d 963, 970 (Del.Ch.1986). The *Rabkin* court further suggested that that standard created a higher threshold of liability than the usual tort concept of gross negligence. Id.

Andrews,[10] one Maynard set up a corporation to make starters for Ford Motors. Defendant Andrews purchased shares and agreed to serve as a director. The business was unable to get production going due to the incompetence of the factory manager and interpersonal conflicts between key employees. Andrews resigned in June 1920. In the spring of 1921, the company went bankrupt. The bankruptcy receiver sued Andrews for breaching the duty of care, charging that Andrews failed to give adequate attention to the company's business.

Judge Hand concluded that Andrews had breached his duty of care. Having accepted the post as director, Andrews had a duty to be informed as to whether the company was moving towards production and, if not, whether anything could be done to resolve the problem.[11] Consequently three of the key elements of a negligence cause of action were satisfied: there was a duty, a breach of that duty, and an injury (the company went under). Yet, Andrews escaped liability. Judge Hand held that plaintiff must show not only a breach, but also that the performance of the director's duties would have avoided a loss. In other words, plaintiff must prove causation. On these facts, plaintiff could not do so. Andrews was only one person and there was nothing a single director could have done to made the company successful.[12]

All of which seemed reasonably well-settled until our old friend *Technicolor* got into the act.[13] At one point in that long-running saga, Chancellor Allen ruled that plaintiff Cinerama could not prevail on its duty of care claims because it had failed to prove a financial injury caused by the Technicolor board's alleged misfeasances. In so holding, Allen relied on *Barnes*. The supreme court reversed, opining it to be "a 'mystery' how the [chancery] court discovered the *Barnes* case and then based its decision on *Barnes*."[14] Perhaps Chancellor Allen found the *Barnes* case by glancing at virtually any major corporate law text. If so, such a glance would have demonstrated that *Barnes* was (and still is) routinely cited as the leading authority for the well-accepted proposition that "the undoubted negligence of directors may not result in liability if the plaintiff cannot show that the negligence proximately caused dam-

---

10. 298 F. 614 (S.D.N.Y.1924).

11. Judge Hand acknowledged that Andrews was not obliged to single-handedly solve the problem. An individual director can only counsel and advise the officers, but Andrews did have a duty to keep himself informed and to offer such advice.

12. Part of the problem is that the receiver sued only Andrews. If he had sued all the directors, as was done in *Van Gorkom*, he might have been more successful. If all of the directors had acted as Andrews did, the receiver could have argued that, acting collectively, the board could have stepped in and required that the incompetent employees be fired. On the other hand, Judge Hand opined that it was not clear that the company would have been successful even if

a substitute had been brought in for the incompetents. Consequently, plaintiff still might not have been able to prove the amount of loss that could have been avoided.

13. For post-*Barnes* precedents assuming that plaintiff must prove causation, see Miller v. AT & T Co., 507 F.2d 759, 763 n. 5 (3d Cir.1974) (New York law); Pierce v. Lyman, 3 Cal.Rptr.2d 236, 240 (Cal.App. 1991); Rabkin v. Philip A. Hunt Chemical Corp., 1987 WL 28436 at *4 (Del.Ch.1987); Shlensky v. Wrigley, 237 N.E.2d 776, 780–81 (Ill.App.1968); Francis v. United Jersey Bank, 432 A.2d 814, 829 (N.J.1981).

14. Cede & Co. v. Technicolor, Inc., 634 A.2d 345, 370 (Del.1993).

ages to the corporation."[15] Even the Emanuel's law outline in print at the time cited *Barnes* for the proposition that "the traditional tort notions of cause in fact and proximate cause apply in [the duty of care] context"![16] Ditto the corporation law nutshell in print at the time *Technicolor* was decided, which likewise cited Barnes as "the leading case" for this proposition.[17] The true mystery thus is how the Delaware supreme court failed to discover *Barnes'* well-established status in corporate law jurisprudence. To be sure, the *Barnes* issue does not come up very often, but that is only because duty of care cases that reach the damages phase of litigation are so few and far between.

Technicolor's rejection of *Barnes* has troubling systemic implications. Under *Technicolor*, once plaintiff rebuts the business judgment rule by proving a breach of the duty of care (which you will recall itself puts the cart before the horse), the defendants have the burden of establishing "entire fairness." The court thus conflated the duties of loyalty and of care, which Delaware courts previously had been careful to keep separate.[18] Corporate law's "sweeping grant of authority to the board is, of course, subject to the overarching normative constraint that the directors exercise their authority with the intention of benefiting the shareholders and not themselves."[19] Where directors have conflicted interests, accountability necessarily trumps the principle of deference to board decisions. Consequently, courts review loyalty claims under a most exacting standard. In the classic case of *Weinberger v. UOP, Inc.*,[20] for example, the court described the entire fairness standard as placing on the defendant directors the burden of proving, subject to "careful scrutiny by the courts," "their utmost good faith and the most scrupulous inherent fairness of the bargain." This exacting burden is justified, inter alia, because knowledge of facts necessary to prove the nature and extent of self-dealing typically are peculiarly within the possession of the defendants.

The concept of entire fairness, however, has little relevance to a duty of care case like *Van Gorkom* or *Technicolor*. In the first place, the relevant factual issues go not to fairness but to negligence and errors of judgment, which are precisely the sorts of issues the business judgment rule was intended to prevent courts from addressing. In the second place, invocation of entire fairness carries with it important remedial implications. In *Weinberger*, the court had authorized the use of "any form of equitable or monetary relief as may be appropriate, including rescissory

---

15. Robert C. Clark, Corporate Law 126 (1986).

16. Steven Emanuel, Corporations 128 (1989).

17. Robert W. Hamilton, The Law of Corporations (3d ed. 1991).

18. See generally Michael P. Dooley, Fundamentals of Corporation Law 249–54 (1995). For a careful demonstration that *Technicolor*'s importation of entire fairness into the duty of care was a doctrinal novel-

ty, see Lyman Johnson, Rethinking Judicial Review of Director Care, 24 Del. J. Corp. L. 787, 799–801 (1999). Johnson correctly concludes there is "no clear and reasoned prior authority" supporting *Technicolor* in this respect. Id. at 801.

19. Michael P. Dooley, Fundamentals of Corporation Law 250 (1995).

20. 457 A.2d 701 (Del.1983).

damages" in loyalty cases. By conflating the loyalty and care analyses, *Technicolor* extends this broad grant of remedial authority to care claims, with potentially catastrophic consequences. Rescissory damages make sense in a loyalty case like *Weinberger*, because the wrongdoer was also the beneficiary of the wrongdoing.[21] In a care case like *Technicolor*, however, an award of rescissory damages would have the effect of ordering the defendant directors to return a benefit that they never received. As a practical matter, moreover, rescissory damages threaten to be so astronomical as to substantially chill the decisionmaking process. The threat of substantial liability is appropriate in loyalty cases. It ensures that the wrongdoer retains neither its ill-gotten gains nor their tainted fruits. By increasing the size of the nominal sanction, it also enhances the deterrent effect of loyalty litigation. But such enormous liability makes no sense in care litigation. By definition there are no ill-gotten gains to be recouped. More important, by increasing the deterrent effect of judicial review, coupled with its expansion of the scope of review, *Technicolor* substantially undermines the board's decisionmaking authority. Where legal standards are vague and the potential liability exposure is substantial, rational actors will not pursue a course of action that takes them into legal gray areas. Sensible directors thus will focus on making a defensible decision, rather than on making the best decision.

C. Reliance on officers

Wholly separate from the business judgment rule, both the Delaware code and the MBCA provide statutory safe harbors for directors who rely in good faith on information and reports from their subordinates. DGCL § 141(e) provides:

> A member of the board of directors, or a member of any committee designated by the board of directors, shall, in the performance of such member's duties, be fully protected in relying in good faith upon the records of the corporation and upon such information, opinions, reports or statements presented to the corporation by any of the corporation's officers or employees, or committees of the board of directors, or by any other person as to matters the member reasonably believes are within such other person's professional or expert competence and who has been selected with reasonable care by or on behalf of the corporation.

MBCA § 8.30(e) is similar.

In *Smith v. Van Gorkom*,[22] Trans Union's directors sought the safe harbor provided by § 141(e), but were denied admittance. To be sure, Van Gorkom had made a presentation to the board, albeit of only 20 minutes duration. Van Gorkom's oral presentation was based principally on his understanding of the relevant documents, but he had neither seen

21. Michael P. Dooley, Fundamentals of Corporation Law 256 (1995).

22. 488 A.2d 858, 875 (Del.1985).

nor been briefed on the terms of the documents. His oral presentation thus did not qualify as a "report" for purposes of § 141(e) because Van Gorkom himself was uninformed as to the details of the plan.

It is unlikely, of course, that the chairman and directors of a major corporation are going to parse through lengthy merger agreements with a fine tooth comb. Doing so is what they pay lawyers and investment bankers to do. If Van Gorkom had been briefed by the company's legal counsel, such that Van Gorkom could accurately relate the details to the board, that should have sufficed to qualify his presentation as a "report."

That the board receives a report is not enough, of course. The board's reliance on such a report must be in good faith, which on these facts imposed a duty of inquiry. Considering the haste and other circumstances surrounding the decision, the board should have pressed Van Gorkom with regard to the details on which his presentation was based. Instead, the board blindly relied on Van Gorkom's assertion that the price was fair.[23]

D. Oversight cases

Monitoring management is one of the board's three principal functions, of course, and, arguably, *prima inter pares*. Oddly, however, the business judgment rule rarely will insulate the directors from liability in connection with that function. The rule applies only where the board has exercised business judgment, while most oversight cases arise precisely because the board has failed to act.

It is well-settled that the duty of care requires directors to pay ongoing attention to the business and affairs of the corporation. In the leading case of *Francis v. United Jersey Bank*,[24] defendant Pritchard was the widow of the company's former president. She was also the company's largest shareholder and a director. Her sons Charles and William were also shareholders, officers, and directors of the company. Despite her husband's warning that Charles "would take the shirt off my back," Pritchard paid no attention to the business. Meanwhile, her nefarious sons had systematically robbed the company by causing the corporation to make purported loans to themselves in excess of any reasonable salary or dividends.[25]

---

23. Smith v. Van Gorkom, 488 A.2d 858, 875 (Del.1985). See also Hanson Trust PLC v. ML SCM Acquisition, Inc., 781 F.2d 264 (2d Cir.1986) (directors have a duty of inquiry with respect to conclusory statements of advisers).

24. 432 A.2d 814 (N.J.1981). Pritchard had died before case was brought and, technically, the defendant was her estate. We shall ignore that complication, which is irrelevant to the analysis.

25. Structuring their scheme as loans was actually quite clever. From a tax perspective, salary and dividends are taxable to the recipient, but the proceeds of a loan is not taxable income. From an accounting perspective, loans are corporate assets, so the money in a sense stays on the books, making it appear that the firm is solvent, while salary and dividends must be deducted from assets, which would have made it obvious that the company was in the red.

As the court bluntly put it, Pritchard "was old, was grief-stricken at the loss of her husband, sometimes consumed too much alcohol, and was psychologically overborne by her sons." None of which excused her failure to pay attention to the corporation's business:

> Directors are under a continuing obligation to keep informed about the activities of the corporation.... Directors may not shut their eyes to corporate misconduct and then claim that because they did not see the misconduct, they did not have a duty to look. The sentinel asleep at his post contributes nothing to the enterprise he is charged to protect.[26]

Maybe she never should have become a director, but having done so she had a duty to be informed and to take action to prevent the loss.[27]

Courts do not expect super-human performance. Directors are not expected to know, in minute detail, everything that happens on a day-to-day basis.[28] At the very least, however, a director should have a rudimentary understanding of the firm's business and how it works, keep informed about the firm's activities, engage in a general monitoring of corporate affairs, attend board meetings regularly, and routinely review financial statements. In doing so, if the director's suspicions are aroused, she should make inquiries into doubtful matters, raise objections to apparently illegal or questionable behavior, and resign if corrections aren't made. All of which Pritchard failed to do.

Pritchard's conduct was actionable because she failed over an extended period of time to pay attention to misconduct occurring right under her nose. *Francis* thus leaves open the extent to which the duty of care requires directors to proactively monitor the conduct of corporate subordinates. This question is especially controversial with respect to the board's duty, if any, affirmatively to ensure that the corporation complies with the law.

The Delaware supreme court first took this issue up in *Graham v. Allis–Chalmers Mfg. Co.*[29] In 1937, Allis–Chalmers had entered into two consent decrees with the FTC in connection with alleged antitrust violations. In the 1950s, the firm settled unrelated federal antitrust charges of price fixing by mid-level employees. After the 1950s settlement, a shareholder sued the board of directors of for having failed to install a law compliance program to prevent antitrust violations. Because plaintiff's claim was based on an alleged failure to act, the business

---

26. Francis v. United Jersey Bank, 432 A.2d 814 (N.J.1981). Accord Theriot v. Bourg, 691 So.2d 213, 224 (La.App.1997) (holding that "advanced age" does not lessen "the standard of care required of a director of a corporation").

27. It might be asked how one reconciles *Francis* with Barnes v. Andrews, 298 F. 614 (S.D.N.Y.1924). The two cases are similar in that both Pritchard and Andrews were charged with not keeping themselves informed about the business. In *Francis*,

however, Pritchard could have taken effective action. Simply by reading the financial statements she could have determined that there was wrongdoing and, probably, put a stop to it by telling her sons to cease and desist. Moreover, the loss can be quantified by the amount of the illegal loans the sons took from the company.

28. Rabkin v. Philip A. Hunt Chemical Corp., 1987 WL 28436 *2 (Del.Ch.1987).

29. 188 A.2d 125 (Del.1963).

judgment rule did not apply, and the supreme court proceeded to determine whether the directors had satisfied their duty of care.

Plaintiffs argued that the directors knew or were on notice of the 1950s price fixing violations. The court rejected that argument, however, because there was no credible evidence any of the directors actually knew of the 1950s-era violations until the federal government commenced grand jury proceedings. Plaintiffs then argued that, by virtue of the 1937 consent decrees, the directors were on notice that they had to take steps to prevent future violations and that they had failed to do so. Again, the court rejected that argument. Only a few of the inside directors had actual knowledge of the 1930s consent decrees. Moreover, the few directors who did know of them had reviewed the consent decrees and reasonably concluded that the corporation had done nothing wrong in the 1930s. The company had settled the case simply to avoid litigation. Accordingly, the court held that the directors were not on notice of the possibility of future illegal price fixing. The final theory, and the one on which the case turned, was that the directors were liable for failing to undertake a law compliance program to detect and prevent this type of wrongdoing.

The court also rejected plaintiff's lack of oversight claim. The *Graham* court held that directors are entitled to rely on the honesty of their subordinates until something occurs to put them on notice that illegal conduct is taking place. If they are put on notice and then fail to act, or if they recklessly repose confidence in an obviously untrustworthy employee, liability may follow.[30] But there is no duty to install a law compliance program from the outset, absent such red flags.

Graham is routinely criticized these days. The Delaware supreme court itself, in *Technicolor*, described it as "quite confusing and unhelpful."[31] Some commentators have suggested that firms should be required to maintain law compliance programs designed to prevent wrongdoing by employees, a position embraced by the ALI PRINCIPLES.[32]

Yet, there is method behind *Graham*'s supposed madness. Consider the old saying: "every dog gets one bite." This saying was based on the

---

30. Recall that Delaware law generally invokes gross negligence as the standard of review in duty of care cases. Oddly, it is not entirely clear whether the *Graham* court reviewed plaintiffs' claims under an ordinary or gross negligence standard. On the one hand, the court suggested directors could make "themselves liable for failure to exercise proper control" over the company's employees "by neglect." On the other hand, the court also used such terms as "recklessly" and "neglected cavalierly," both of which suggest a standard higher than ordinary negligence. Some chancery court opinions have used the gross negligence standard in similar cases. See, e.g., Seminaris v. Landa, 662 A.2d 1350, 1355 (Del.Ch.1995)

("In order to hold the directors liable, plaintiff will have to demonstrate that they were grossly negligent in failing to supervise these subordinates."). In the *Rabkin* decision, however, the chancery court split the baby, holding that the gross negligence standard is limited to situations in which the board has rendered a decision, but that ordinary negligence is the appropriate standard when directors fail to act. Rabkin v. Philip A. Hunt Chemical Corp., 1987 WL 28436 *2 (Del.Ch.1987).

31. Cede & Co. v. Technicolor, Inc., 634 A.2d 345, 364 n. 31 (Del.1993). See also ALI Principles § 4.01(a)(1) cmt. c.

32. See ALI PRINCIPLES § 4.01(a) cmt. d.

common law principle that a dog's master was only liable for bites if the master knew or had reason to know the dog had a propensity to bite.[33] Such knowledge could be based either on the breed's inherently violent propensities or a prior bite. The economic rátionale for such a rule is simple—monitoring costs. Keeping an eye on your dog requires costly precautions, such as leashes, fences, and the like. Why require such expenditures if Fido is as gentle as a lamb?

The analogy to *Graham* should be self-evident, but let's beat the dead horse anyway. Just as a dog owner does not have liability unless the owner knows the dog has a propensity to bite, directors are liable only if they are on notice that their employees have a propensity for crime. Just as a dog owner is put on such notice by a prior bite, prior criminal violations can put directors on notice. Just as owners have an affirmative duty to control dogs of an inherently vicious breed, directors may not recklessly fail to monitor an obviously untrustworthy employee.

As with the dog bite rule, *Graham* implicitly rests on a cost-benefit analysis. Law compliance programs are not free. At the very least, a law compliance program requires preparation of a company manual telling employees not to fix prices. It probably also requires training of employees. Beyond that, the firm probably should send lawyers out to do compliance audits from time to time. Programs with real teeth require substantial high-level commitment and review, frequent and meaningful communication to employees, serious monitoring and auditing, and appropriate discipline where violations are discovered. By analogy to the dog bite cases, one reasonably would expect a firm to go through all this only when on notice of a past violation.[34]

Contrast this result to *Francis v. United Jersey Bank*.[35] Why did Pritchard have a duty to be attentive and inquire, while the *Allis-Chalmers* defendants did not? In *Francis*, any attention at all by Ms. Pritchard would have discovered the improper loans. Recall that the loans would appear on the company's books, so a cursory glance at the financial statement would have revealed them. In this sense, she was like a person who doesn't even bother to check to see whether she owns a dog. Worse yet, and this is really too precious, recall that Pritchard's husband had warned her that Charles would "take the shirt off my back." So she knew her dog had a propensity to bite. In *Allis-Chalmers*, by contrast, the directors were not on notice of any wrongdoing, and could not readily have detected the wrongdoing. Consequently, they need not have done anything.[36]

33. See, e.g., Hyun Na Seo v. Yozgadlian, 726 A.2d 972 (N.J.App.Div.1999).

34. Where the relevant statute or regulation imposes strict liability, law compliance programs create a substantial dilemma. To the extent that the corporation's compliance program is effective, it will be required to report violations that will subject it to significant penalties. Under the federal sentencing guidelines, this problem is mitigated by provisions that reduce corporate penalties where the corporation has adopted appropriate compliance measures. See Jennifer Arlen, The Potentially Perverse Effects of Corporate Criminal Liability, 23 J. Leg. Stud. 833 (1994).

35. 432 A.2d 814 (N.J.1981).

36. To be sure, in some areas the law has long required that directors maintain internal controls to guard against wrongdo-

Unfortunately, Delaware probably no longer adheres to *Graham*. In the most recent judicial analysis of this problem, *In re Caremark International Inc. Derivative Litigation*,[37] Chancellor Allen outlined an obligation for directors to take some affirmative law compliance measures. Caremark was a health industry concern that provided a variety of managed care services. Much of Caremark's revenue came from federal government health programs. Under the federal Anti–Referral Payments Law (ARPL), Caremark was prohibited from paying doctors to refer patients to it. Caremark could, however, legally hire doctors under consulting agreements and research grants.

In 1994, the federal government prosecuted Caremark for criminal violations of the ARPL. The government argued that some of Caremark's consulting agreements and research grants with doctors were disguised kickbacks for patient referrals. In 1995, Caremark settled, paying fines and reimbursement of about $250 million. A group of shareholders thereafter filed derivative suits against Caremark directors. Those suits were settled pursuant to an agreement under which the directors paid nothing, Caremark agreed to make some cosmetic changes in the way it ran its business, and the plaintiffs' attorneys collected a fee of $1 million from Caremark. As with all derivative suit settlements, the agreement required judicial approval. Chancellor Allen approved the settlement, although he cut plaintiffs' attorneys fee to a mere $870,000. Because of the procedural posture, the case dealt only indirectly with the real issue of whether Caremark's directors had an obligation to create a working law compliance program. According to extensive dicta in Allen's opinion, however, the duty of care may require such programs.

Allen's analysis begins by distinguishing two scenarios in which directors might be sued with respect to the firm's law compliance. First, where the directors made an ill-advised decision, the business judgment rule will insulate that decision from judicial review "assuming the decision made was the product of a process that was either deliberately considered in good faith or was otherwise rational." (Note, once again, that the business judgment rule inquiry focuses on issues of process.)

Alternatively, however, liability issues also arise where the board failed to act. Allen acknowledged that much of what the corporation does never comes to the board's attention. Allen contended, however, that decisions made deep in the interior of the corporation by relatively junior employees can have devastating consequences. Allen also noted two concurrent regulatory trends. On one hand, federal law increasingly uses criminal sanctions to ensure corporate compliance with various regulatory regimes. On the other, the federal criminal sentencing guidelines mitigate sanctions where the corporate defendant had law compliance

ing. In particular, directors have an obligation to ensure that basic accounting practices are followed in preparing and auditing the firm's financial records. See, e.g., Atherton v. Anderson, 99 F.2d 883 (6th Cir.1938). In those contexts, it is relatively inexpensive to do so. The company already may hire outside accountants to prepare the books, so it is relatively inexpensive to also require them to report on their procedures and findings to the board.

37.   698 A.2d 959 (Del.Ch.1996).

programs in place. In light of these considerations, Allen held that *Graham* could no longer be interpreted as meaning that a corporate board has no obligation to create information gathering and monitoring mechanisms designed to ensure corporate law compliance.

As a matter of sound policy, Allen undoubtedly is correct that decisions made by subordinates can have substantial and often multiplicative effects throughout the corporation. Yet, *Caremark* threatens to open the door to expansive directorial liability. Because the board's exercise of its oversight function so often falls outside the business judgment rule, most of what directors actually do becomes subject to second-guessing by courts. Consequently, courts should return to those halcyon days when *Graham* replicated the dog bite rule.

Caremark leaves open a lot of hard questions, moreover. Suppose, for example, that the board considered the issue and then affirmatively decided not to adopt a law compliance program. Would it be liable if that decision resulted in corporate losses? In theory, a decision not to act does not differ from a decision to take action. Chancellor Allen said, moreover, that directors who act in good faith through proper procedures are not liable even if, in retrospect, they made the wrong decision. The business judgment rule, as typically formulated, would seem to protect directors who rationally adopt either a minimal compliance program or even no program at all after weighing the costs against the benefits.[38]

The MBCA's new director liability provisions, discussed in the next section, codify a standard closer to *Graham* than *Caremark*. Under MBCA § 8.31(a)(2)(iv), a director may be held liable for sustained inattention but only when "particular facts and circumstances materialize that" would put "a reasonably attentive director" on notice of the need for further inquiry. Under this provision, it would seem, proactive vigilance is not required.[39] Consequently, while the statute would not have allowed Pritchard to escape liability in *Francis*, it would not have resulted in liability in either *Graham* or *Caremark*. All of which is just as it should be.

E. Shareholder ratification

In *Smith v. Van Gorkom*,[40] the Trans Union director defendants argued that shareholder approval of the challenged merger cured their alleged duty of care violations. Even the plaintiffs conceded that a transaction tainted by director care violations was merely voidable, rather than void. As with other voidable corporate actions, such a

---

38. Cf. Rabkin v. Philip A. Hunt Chemical Corp., 1987 WL 28436 *3 (Del.Ch.1987) (holding that "a conscious decision as to the types of information provided to the directors would fall within the protection of the business judgment rule as a general matter").

39. See MBCA § 8.01(a) cmt. 1(f); see also MBCA § 8.01 cmt. ("directors should not be held personally responsible for actions or omissions of officers, employees, or agents of the corporation so long as the directors have relied reasonably upon these officers, employees, or agents").

40. 488 A.2d 858, 889–90 (Del.1985).

transaction therefore could be ratified by majority vote of the shareholders. On the facts of *Van Gorkom*, however, shareholder approval was unavailing. Only a fully informed vote of the shareholders could protect the directors from liability. Because they had failed to disclose various material facts, notably including the "fact that the Board had no reasonably adequate information indicative of the intrinsic value of the Company," the shareholder vote was uninformed.

In a leading opinion on the effect of shareholder ratification under Delaware law, Vice Chancellor Jacobs confirmed that a fully informed shareholder vote extinguishes duty of care claims.[41] Because litigated care claims frequently involve transactions requiring shareholder approval, such as mergers and the like, this is a significant additional protection for directors. The sticking point, of course, will be the adequacy of disclosure. It is hard to imagine a board disclosure along the lines of: "we're very sorry but we violated the duty of care in the following particulars, which we shall now describe at great length." As in *Van Gorkom*, if the court believes the directors violated their duty of care, it likely will find material nondisclosures as well.

F.   The new MBCA provisions

Some scholars have sought to reconcile the duty of care and the business judgment rule by distinguishing between standards of conduct and standards of review.[42] According to this conception, the duty of care is a standard of conduct, which specifies how directors should conduct themselves. In contrast, the business judgment rule is a standard of review, which sets forth the test courts will use in determining whether the directors' conduct gives rise to liability.[43] Unlike typical negligence tort cases, in which the standard of review and the standard of conduct are identical, in corporate law they purportedly diverge. The function of the business judgment rule thus is to create a less demanding standard of review than the (largely aspirational) standard of conduct created by the duty of care. But what is the standard? It may be mere subjective good faith, it may be a requirement of rationality, it may be gross negligence. No one seems to know for sure. The key point for our purposes, however, is the basic claim that, as a substantive standard of review, the business judgment rule entails "some objective review of the

41. In re Wheelabrator Technologies Shareholders Litig., 663 A.2d 1194, 1200 (Del.Ch.1995).

42. See, e.g., Melvin Aron Eisenberg, The Divergence of Standards of Conduct and Standards of Review in Corporate Law, 62 Fordham L. Rev. 437 (1993). For a critique of Eisenberg's position, as well as the new MBCA provisions, see D. Gordon Smith, A Proposal to Eliminate Director Standards from the Model Business Corporation Act, 67 U. Cin. L. Rev. 1201 (1999).

43. A somewhat similar conception of the rule is captured by the purported distinction between the business judgment rule, which is said to shield corporate officers and directors from personal liability in connection with business decisions, and the business judgment doctrine, which shields the decision itself from review. See Revlon, Inc. v. MacAndrews & Forbes Holdings, Inc., 506 A.2d 173, 180 n. 10 (Del.1985). The Delaware Supreme Court has recognized, but not adopted, that distinction. Id.

quality of the [board's] decision, however limited."[44] Accordingly, as articulated by most of its proponents, this dual standards interpretation is inconsistent with our argument that the business judgment rule should be deemed an abstention doctrine.

The MBCA recently adopted a different version of the dual standards approach, which ends up much closer to our abstention interpretation. New MBCA § 8.30 sets forth the standards of conduct for directors. Analogously to those Delaware decisions describing the duty of care as process oriented, § 8.30 focuses on the manner in which the board carried out its duties, not the correctness or reasonableness of its decisions.[45] Under § 8.30(a) the director must act in good faith and in a manner the director reasonably believes to be in the corporation's best interest. Note the absence of any reference to due or reasonable care. Those references appear only in § 8.30(b), which relates solely to the directors' duty to make informed decisions. When "becoming informed" the board is to exercise "the care that a person in a like position would reasonably believe appropriate under similar circumstances." There is a striking contrast with the *Van Gorkom* obligation to gather all materially information reasonably available to the board. Under the MBCA, directors can act on less than all available information, provided doing so satisfies the reasonable person standard.[46]

Conduct that satisfies the requirements of § 8.30 cannot result in liability. Conduct falling short of those aspirational goals can only result in liability if it violates the standards of director liability set forth in MBCA § 8.31.[47] Specifically, under § 8.31(a)(2), liability can be imposed where the director acted in bad faith, did not reasonably believe the action to be in the corporation's best interest, was not informed to the extent the director reasonably believed appropriate under the circumstances, was interested in the transaction, was not independent, engaged in self-dealing, or failed to exercise oversight over a sustained period.[48]

44. William L. Cary and Melvin Aron Eisenberg, Corporations 603 (7th ed. 1995). Notice that *Technicolor* went further even than Cary and Eisenberg's conception of the business judgment rule as a standard of review. Recall that under this alternative to the abstention view, the rule is said to provide a standard of review more lenient than the standard of conduct imposed by the duty of care. Under *Technicolor*, in contrast, the board must prove that it satisfied the more exacting standard of conduct before the business judgment rule standard of review can be invoked. Cede & Co. v. Technicolor, Inc., 634 A.2d 345, 361 (Del.1993). If so, however, what function remains for the rule?

45. MBCA § 8.30 cmt.

46. Consistent with our analysis of the board as a collegial body, § 8.30 stresses evaluation of the board's collective decision-making process. Defaults by a single di-

rector are irrelevant to the judicial evaluation. Instead, courts are to focus on the conduct of the board as a whole.

47. As implied by the basic dichotomy between standards of conduct and review, the statute thus contemplates a level of director conduct that falls short of the statutory ideal but for which the directors will not be liable. Courts will need to be vigilant to preserve a reasonable breadth for the resulting no man's land.

48. MBCA § 8.31(b). Unlike *Technicolor*, there is no hint in § 8.31 that courts can review the merits of board decisions. Also unlike *Technicolor*, § 8.31(b) treats causation as an element of the care claim. In order to recover monetary damages, plaintiff must prove both that harm resulted to the corporation and that that harm was proximately caused by the defendant director's misconduct.

Although the drafters deny any intent to codify the business judgment rule,[49] MBCA § 8.31(a)(2) effectively codifies a fairly aggressive version of the abstention approach to judicial review advocated by our interpretation of the business judgment rule.[50] Unlike *Van Gorkom*, for example, under which a court asks whether the director gathered all material information reasonably available, a court under § 8.31 asks only whether the director was informed to the extent the director reasonably believed appropriate under the circumstances, a much more deferential standard. Unlike *Caremark*, director misfeasance with respect to oversight results in liability under the MBCA only where there has been a "sustained failure" or the director failed to timely take action after being put on notice of potential problems.[51] The MBCA thus comes close to codifying *Graham*'s position on oversight duties.

§ 6.6   Statutory responses to *Van Gorkom* and the "D & O liability crisis"

It is often said that, absent the protections of the business judgment rule, no rational person would agree to serve as a director. Especially with respect to large public corporations, the potential liability of directors takes on catastrophic dimensions.[1] After *Smith v. Van Gorkom*, director and officer liability insurance became very hard to get.[2] Delaware and many other states responded to this purported crisis by adopting limitations on director liability and/or amending their existing indemnification statutes.

A.   Liability limitation statutes

DGCL § 102(b)(7) provides that a corporation's articles of incorporation may (but need not) contain:

> A provision eliminating or limiting the personal liability of a director to the corporation or its stockholders for monetary damages for breach of fiduciary duty as a director, provided that such provision

---

49. Neither § 8.30 nor 8.31 attempts to codify the business judgment rule. Nor do they purport to displace it. Courts in MBCA states apparently remain free to continue common law development of the rule. At the same time, however, the statute establishes a floor for director liability. Courts cannot reinterpret the rule so as to bypass the statute and impose liability.

50. MBCA § 8.31(a) provides that the standard of review applies to both affirmative decisions (whether it be a decision to act or refrain from acting) *and* a failure to act. Note the contrast with the business judgment rule, which gives no protection to directors who fail to exercise business judgment.

51. MBCA § 8.31(a)(2)(iv).

§ 6.6

1. No less a jurist than Learned Hand endorsed this concern. See Barnes v. Andrews, 298 F. 614, 617 (S.D.N.Y.1924) ("No men of sense would take the office, if the law imposed upon them a guaranty of the general success of their companies as a penalty for any negligence."); see also Solimine v. Hollander, 19 A.2d 344, 348 (N.J.Ch. 1941) (indemnification of expenses required so as to encourage responsible persons to serve). This view, however, seems inconsistent with the notion that a sufficiently high return will induce even risk averse persons to take on a risky job.

2. See generally Roberta Romano, What Went Wrong with Directors' and Officers' Liability Insurance?, 14 Del. J. Corp. L. 1 (1989).

shall not eliminate or limit the liability of a director: (i) For any breach of the director's duty of loyalty to the corporation or its stockholders; (ii) for acts or omissions not in good faith or which involve intentional misconduct or a knowing violation of law; (iii) under § 174 of this title [relating to liability for unlawful dividends]; or (iv) for any transaction from which the director derived an improper personal benefit.

MBCA § 2.02(b)(4) is similar. Virtually all states now have some such statute. Most public corporations have amended their charters to include such provisions.

Several aspects of the Delaware statute seem especially noteworthy.[3] First, it applies only to directors. Although officers also are subject to a duty of care, they are denied exculpation by charter provision. In *Arnold v. Society for Savings Bancorp, Inc.*,[4] the supreme court held that, as to a defendant who is both a director and an officer, an exculpatory § 102(b)(7) provision applies only to actions taken solely in his capacity as a director.

Second, the statute limits only the monetary liability of directors. Equitable remedies are still available. Because the real party in interest in many shareholder suits is the plaintiff's attorney rather than the shareholders, and because attorneys' fees can be recovered in connection with equitable remedies, § 102(b)(7) does not eliminate the incentive to bring shareholder litigation.

Third, the Delaware supreme court held in *Emerald Partners* that a § 102(b)(7) provision is an affirmative defense.[5] Defendant directors thus have the burden of proving that they are entitled to exculpation under the statute. If aggressively applied, *Emerald Partners* could mean that a § 102(b)(7) provision rarely will entitle directors to a dismissal on grounds that plaintiff's complaint fails to state a cause of action. Consequently, plaintiffs will be entitled to discovery, which some might call a fishing expedition, and the settlement value of such claims will go up. Thus far, however, the chancery court has continued to hold a § 102(b)(7)-based motion to dismiss is appropriate pre-discovery where plaintiff solely alleged violations of the duty of care.[6]

---

3. For commentary on § 102(b)(7) and comparable statutes, see Deborah A. DeMott, Limiting Directors' Liability, 66 Wash. U. L.Q. 295 (1988); Harvey Gelb, Director Due Care Liability: An Assessment of the New Statutes, 61 Temple L. Rev. 13 (1988); Thomas C. Lee, Comment, Limiting Corporate Directors' Liability: Delaware's Section 102(b)(7) and the Erosion of the Directors' Duty of Care, 136 U. Pa. L. Rev. 239 (1987); Marc I. Steinberg, The Evisceration of the Duty of Care, 42 Sw. L.J. 919 (1988).

4. 650 A.2d 1270 (Del.1994).

5. Emerald Partners v. Berlin, 726 A.2d 1215, 1223–24 (Del.1999). See also McMullin v. Beran, 765 A.2d 910, 926 (Del.2000).

6. See, e.g., McMillan v. Intercargo Corp., 768 A.2d 492 (Del.Ch.2000); In re Lukens Inc. Shareholders Litig., 757 A.2d 720 (Del.Ch.1999). The Delaware supreme court's most recent decision in the on-going *Emerald Partners* litigation confirms this approach, while emphasizing that limited discovery is available where plaintiff has adequately alleged a violation of the duty of loyalty or of good faith. Emerald Partners v. Berlin, 787 A.2d 85 (Del.2001).

Most importantly, however, notice that the statute apparently distinguishes self-dealing ("improper personal benefit") from the duty of care. Given *Technicolor*'s conflation of loyalty and care causes of action, plaintiffs can end-run § 102(b)(7) provisions by characterizing their claim as a loyalty violation. Interestingly, Chancellor Allen has suggested that *Van Gorkom* itself can be interpreted as a loyalty case.[7] Similarly, the Delaware supreme court has opined that *Van Gorkom* included a disclosure violation and implied that such violations have a loyalty component.[8] Ironically, a § 102(b)(7) provision thus might not have insulated the directors from liability in the very transaction that motivated the statute's adoption.

B. Indemnification statutes

At common law, corporate employees were entitled to indemnification for expenses incurred on the job, including certain legal liabilities, but directors were not.[9] Today, however, all states have statutory provisions authorizing director indemnification to some degree.[10] As usual, we will focus on the Delaware statute.

DGCL § 145 distinguishes in the first instance between direct suits against a director or officer by a shareholder or other third party and derivative suits brought against a director or officer "by or in the right of the corporation." As to the former, § 145(a) authorizes the corporation to indemnify the director or officer for expenses plus "judgments, fines, and amounts paid in settlement" of both civil and criminal proceedings. In contrast, as to derivative litigation, § 145(b) authorizes indemnification only for expenses, albeit including attorney's expenses. If the director or officer was held liable to the corporation, moreover, he may only be indemnified with court approval.

Section 145 also distinguishes between mandatory and permissive indemnification. Under § 145(c), the corporation must indemnify a director or officer who "has been successful on the merits or otherwise." As for directors and officers who are unsuccessful, indemnification is permissive, so long as it is not precluded by statute.

---

7. Gagliardi v. TriFoods Int'l, Inc., 683 A.2d 1049, 1052 n. 4 (Del.Ch.1996) ("I see it as reflecting a concern with the Trans Union board's independence and loyalty to the company's shareholders").

8. Cinerama, Inc. v. Technicolor, Inc., 663 A.2d 1156, 1166 n. 18 (Del.1995) ("In *Van Gorkom*, it was unnecessary for this Court to state whether the disclosure violation constituted a breach of the duty of care or loyalty or was a combined breach of both since 8 Del.C. § 102(b)(7) had not yet been enacted."). In addition, according to the Sixth Circuit, a § 102(b)(7) liability limitation provision may not insulate directors from duty of care claims based on intentional or reckless misconduct. McCall v. Scott, 250 F.3d 997, 1000–01 (6th Cir.2001).

9. See, e.g., New York Dock Co. v. McCollom, 16 N.Y.S.2d 844 (Sup.Ct.1939).

10. See generally James J. Hanks, Jr. & Larry P. Scriggins, Protecting Directors and Officers From Liability—The Influence of the Model Business Corporation Act, 56 Bus. Law. 3 (2000); Mae Kuykendall, A Neglected Policy Option: Indemnification of Directors for Amounts Paid to Settle Derivative Suits—Looking Past "Circularity" to Context and Reform, 32 San Diego L. Rev. 1063 (1995).

Because of the long delays inherent in litigation, indemnification may be of little assistance to a director or officer who has been bankrupted by legal or other costs in the meanwhile. Under § 145(e), the corporation may advance expenses to the officer or director provided the latter undertakes to repay any such amount if it turns out he is not entitled to indemnification.

Section 145(f) authorizes the corporation to enter into written indemnification agreements with officers and directors that go beyond the statute. Unfortunately, the plain text of the statute is, at best, ambiguous. Section 145(f) merely provides that statutory indemnification rights "shall not be deemed exclusive of any other rights" to indemnification created by "bylaw, agreement, vote of the stockholders or disinterested directors or otherwise." It seems clear that the statute authorizes indemnification agreements mandating payment of expenses that the statute merely permits. Indeed, most "public corporations have extended indemnification guarantees via bylaw to cases where indemnification is typically only permissive [by statute]."[11] In addition, an indemnification agreement properly may mandate advancement of expenses even though such advancement is merely permissive under § 145(e).[12] Finally, § 145(f) likely allows indemnification of certain expenses not contemplated by the statute. In *Mayer v. Executive Telecard*,[13] the plaintiff sought indemnification for expenses incurred in successfully defending federal securities antifraud claims. Mayer prevailed in his initial lawsuit seeking indemnification. Mayer then sued again, claiming he was entitled to reimbursement for his legal expenses in the first lawsuit. Vice Chancellor Jacobs referred to this as seeking "fees for fees," which Jacobs held § 145(a) did not allow. The statute authorizes only "the indemnification of fees incurred in the underlying action, not fees for fees." In dictum, however, Jacobs went on to opine that § 145(f) "arguably" authorizes indemnification agreements covering fees for fees.

Does § 145(f), however, allow the corporation to indemnify directors or officers where statutory indemnification is not permitted? In *Waltuch v. Conticommodity Services*,[14] the Second Circuit answered that question in the negative. Along the way, the court proffered several other noteworthy interpretations of open issues under § 145.

Waltuch was the silver trader for Conticommodity, a commodities trading firm. In 1979, the silver market famously went nuts after the Hunt brothers tried to corner the market. Silver prices spiked upwards but then crashed. Waltuch and Conticommodity were sued for fraud and market manipulation by their clients and, in a separate enforcement proceeding, the Commodity Futures Trading Commission (CFTC). Conticommodity paid $35 million to settle the private party litigation. Waltuch was dismissed from that litigation without having to make any monetary

11. VonFeldt v. Stifel Fin. Corp., 714 A.2d 79, 81, n. 5 (Del.1998).

12. See, e.g., Citadel Holding Corp. v. Roven, 603 A.2d 818 (Del.1992).

13. Mayer v. Executive Telecard, Ltd., 705 A.2d 220 (Del.Ch.1997).

14. Waltuch v. Conticommodity Services, Inc., 88 F.3d 87 (2d Cir.1996).

payment. He incurred $1.2 million in legal expenses in connection the private party litigation. Waltuch settled the CFTC litigation. To do so, he paid a $100,000 fine and agreed to a six month ban on trading. He spent an additional $1 million in legal fees in that proceeding.

Waltuch sued Conticommodity under § 145 and the indemnification provisions of Conticommodity's articles on incorporation. Article Nine thereof provided:

> The Corporation shall indemnify and hold harmless each of its incumbent or former directors, officers, employees and agents ... against expenses actually and necessarily incurred by him in connection with the defense of any action, suit or proceeding threatened, pending or completed, in which he is made a party, by reason of his serving in or having held such position or capacity, except in relation to matters as to which he shall be adjudged in such action, suit or proceeding to be liable for negligence or misconduct in the performance of duty.

Section 145(a) only authorizes indemnification of expenses incurred by a director or officer who "acted in good faith." Conticommodity claimed that Article Nine therefore was invalid, because it implicitly mandated indemnification of bad faith actions. Waltuch claimed that § 145(f) authorized the article without the need for any good faith limitation.

The court more or less split the baby down the middle. The standard adopted charitably can be described as elusive, although slippery probably fits the bill even better: "indemnification rights may be broader than those set out in the statute, but they cannot be inconsistent with the 'scope' of the corporation's power to indemnify, as delineated in the statute's substantive provisions." Where the statute requires good faith, as it does in both subsections (a) and (b), an agreement that purports even by implication to authorize indemnification for non-good faith conduct is inconsistent with the scope of the statute and therefore invalid.[15] Accordingly, Conticommodity need not (indeed, may not) indemnify Waltuch for his legal expenses in connection with the CFTC proceeding. By settling the CFTC case, Waltuch voluntarily gave up his opportunity to prove that he had acted in good faith.[16]

As to the private litigation, however, Waltuch arguably had been "successful." Recall that § 145(c) mandates indemnification where the defendant was "successful on the merits *or otherwise*." Waltuch claimed he was "successful" because he was dismissed from the private party cases without having to contribute to the settlement. Conticommodity claimed Waltuch was dismissed as a direct result of its $35 million settlement. The court adopts a no questions asked approach to § 145(c):

---

15. In *Mayer*, Vice Chancellor Jacobs concurred that "a Delaware corporation lacks the power [under § 145(a)] to indemnify a party who did not act in good faith." Mayer v. Executive Telecard, Ltd., 705 A.2d 220, 224 n. 6 (Del.Ch.1997).

16. Interpreting California law, the federal Fourth Circuit has held that a director or officer who intentionally participates in illegal activity cannot be deemed to have acted in good faith even if the conduct benefits the corporation. In re Landmark Land Co., 76 F.3d 553 (4th Cir.1996).

"the only question a court may ask is what the result [of the underlying litigation] was, not why it was."[17] Unlike subsections (a) and (b), there is no good faith limitation under § 145(c). Accordingly, opined the Second Circuit, success for purposes of subsection (c) does not require "moral exoneration."[18] It only requires escape. Waltuch satisfied that standard and thus was entitled to mandatory indemnification for his expenses in the private party litigation.[19]

Why did the legislature omit a requirement of good faith from the mandatory indemnification provision in Section 145(c)? The omission may have been intended to avoid collateral litigation. Suppose a director succeeds on the merits, but in a way that does not resolve the issue of his good faith—e.g., avoiding conviction in a criminal case. In seeking indemnification, the issue of good faith thus would not be subject to any form of collateral estoppel and would have to be litigated. Not only does this add collateral litigation, it also raises the specter of suits for "fees for fees," as Vice Chancellor Jacobs so aptly put it. Omitting a requirement of good faith forecloses these risks.

Second, the legislature may have intended to permit indemnification of directors who act in bad faith but nonetheless prevail. Why? Here are some possibilities: (1) Do not chill directors from taking risks. The good faith clause of § 145(a) includes a requirement that the party seeking indemnification had no "reasonable cause to believe that [his] conduct was illegal." Perhaps the director thought the conduct was illegal, but thought it was worth taking the risk (e.g., bribes to get a contract). Perhaps the legislature thought such a director should be indemnified if taking that risk was vindicated by an acquittal at trial. (Note that such an acquittal would not constitute an adjudication of the director's good faith.) Suppose he had gone ahead in the face of a warning from corporate counsel that there was a "strong possibility" the conduct would violate a criminal statute? (2) Encourage people to serve as directors of Delaware corporations, and thereby also encourage incorporators to incorporate in Delaware, by providing them with maximum protection.

17. Waltuch v. Conticommodity Services, Inc., 88 F.3d 87, 96 (2d Cir.1996). Where a case was dismissed without prejudice because the same issues were being litigated in a different proceeding, however, the Delaware federal district court has denied mandatory indemnification under § 145(c). Galdi v. Berg, 359 F.Supp. 698 (D.Del.1973).

18. Avoiding indictment or successfully plea bargaining away criminal charges, for example, constitutes "success on the merits or otherwise." See, e.g., Merritt–Chapman & Scott Corp. v. Wolfson, 321 A.2d 138 (Del.Super.1974) (indictment dismissed pursuant to plea bargain); Stewart v. Continental Copper & Steel Indus., Inc., 414 N.Y.S.2d 910 (App.Div.1979) (indictment avoided; interpreting Delaware law).

19. Interpreting a California statute limiting mandatory indemnification to situations in which the defendant prevailed "on the merits," a California appeals court held that a judicial determination of the merits of the defense was required. American Nat'l Bank & Trust Co. v. Schigur, 148 Cal.Rptr. 116 (Cal.App.1978).

Chapter 7

THE DUTY OF LOYALTY

Analysis

§ 7.1 Authority and accountability revisited

It is well-settled that directors have a duty to maximize shareholder wealth. As the Michigan supreme court famously observed in *Dodge v. Ford Motor Co.*: "A business corporation is organized and carried on primarily for the profit of the stockholders."[1] To be sure, in many settings, the business judgment rule will preclude judges from evaluating the shareholder wealth effects of board decisions. It is also well-settled, however, that the business judgment rule does not preclude judicial review of self-dealing transactions.

From an agency cost-based economic perspective, negligence and self-dealing differ in degree but not in kind. Both reduce shareholder wealth. Both are forms of shirking, at least in the broad sense that term is used by agency cost economists. At first blush, the differing legal treatment of care and loyalty thus seems puzzling.

On closer examination, however, loyalty does differ in kind, not just in degree, from care. As explained in Chapter 6, there is a compelling economic justification for insulating allegedly negligent board decisions from judicial review. Few components of that justification carry over to self-dealing. Indeed, the affirmative case for disregarding honest errors simply does not apply to intentional misconduct. Decisions implicating the duty of care typically are collective actions of the board as a whole. In making such decisions, the board is constrained to exercise reasonable care in decisionmaking by a combination of external market forces and internal team governance structures. Judicial review thus is at best redundant and may, in fact, have deleterious consequences for the efficiency of decisionmaking.

In contrast, self-dealing typically is more difficult to detect than is negligence. Self-dealing transactions rarely implicate the entire board. To the contrary, they often involve misconduct by a single director. Those who intentionally self-deal, moreover, likely will also actively seek to conceal their defalcations. Given the potential gains of self-dealing in an organization characterized by a separation of ownership and control, legal liability thus may be a necessary deterrent against such misconduct. When an individual director engages in self-dealing, moreover, he has already betrayed the internal team relationships that characterize boards.[2] Courts appropriately are less concerned about destroying internal team relationships in such cases.

§ 7.1

1. Dodge v. Ford Motor Co., 170 N.W. 668, 684 (Mich.1919). See generally Chapter 9.

2. Cf. Robert J. Haft, The Effect of Insider Trading Rules on the Internal Efficiency of the Large Corporation, 80 Mich. L. Rev. 1051, 1062–63 (1982) (describing the deleterious effects on board effectiveness of director self-dealing).

Yet, the intensity of judicial rhetoric in loyalty cases suggests something else is going on as well. Judge Cardozo's famous dictum on the duties of a partner, holding them to "something stricter than the morals of the market place,"[3] has provided a model for countless decisions excoriating those who self-deal. In part, this rhetoric likely rests on an assessment of self-dealing as reflecting greater moral culpability than does mere negligence. In part, however, judicial rhetoric in this area also likely reflects an attempt by judges to inculcate desirable social norms of honesty and trustworthiness.

Whatever the reasons for doing so, it remains clear that courts tilt the balance between authority and accountability in the latter direction when the conduct involves self-dealing. In this chapter, we will analyze the varying ways in which corporate law operationalizes the majoritarian default proscribing self-dealing. Pay especially close attention to one question that frequently recurs; namely, to what extent does approval of a conflicted interest transaction by the board of directors or shareholders insulate that transaction from the exacting scrutiny usually applied to self-dealing?

§ 7.2   Conflicted interest transactions

Directors and officers frequently contract with or otherwise transact business with their corporations. Such transactions range from routine and pervasive, such as employment and compensation agreements, to unusual one-time events, such as a sale of real property. In either case, the director has an obvious conflict of interest.[1] On the one hand, the director is acting in his own self-interest, with an incentive to get the best possible deal. On the other hand, the director is a fiduciary with an obligation to maximize shareholder wealth.

Conflicted interest transactions take two forms. In a direct transaction, the director is dealing directly with the firm, such as where a director sells property to the firm. In an indirect transaction, a person or entity in which the director has an interest is dealing with the firm. Both types potentially create a conflict of interest. Indirect conflicted interest transactions, however, present greater problems in several respects. On the one hand, they are more likely to escape ex ante notice, whether because of deliberate concealment or mere inadvertence. On the other hand, as the director's interest becomes more attenuated, an indirect transaction may not rise to the level of a legitimate conflict of interest.[2]

---

3. Meinhard v. Salmon, 164 N.E. 545, 546 (N.Y.1928).

§ 7.2

1. For semantic convenience, we shall refer solely to directors in this section. Unless otherwise indicated, however, the same legal principles also apply to conflicted interest transactions between an officer and the corporation.

2. In Beneville v. York, 769 A.2d 80 (Del.Ch.2000), Vice Chancellor Strine observed that a director is deemed interested for purposes of DGCL § 144 if the director would be deemed interested for purposes of excusing demand in a shareholder derivative suit and vice-versa. Id. at 84 n.4. He cited the Delaware supreme court's demand excusal decision in Rales v. Blasband, 634 A.2d 927 (Del.1993), which considered a director to be "interested where he or she

In an era of two career professional couples, for example, is a director interested in a transaction in which his spouse's employer enters into a contract with the corporation? What if the contract involves the director's ex-spouse?[3]

At early common law, conflicted interest transactions were per se voidable by the corporation without regard to whether they were fair to the corporation or had been approved by the board or shareholders, or so most authorities opine.[4] At an abstract level, prohibiting conflicted interest transactions fails to give due deference to the principles of party autonomy and freedom of contract, which are important values both in themselves and because they promote efficient transactions. At a practical level, many transactions between the corporation and a director prove beneficial to both sides. If a director owns a valuable piece of property, which would be useful to the corporation, should not the director be allowed to sell it to the firm? Yet, what rational director would do so under the early common law rule? A rule that makes conflicted interest contracts voidable at the corporation's option in effect gives the firm a put option in the underlying transaction. If the deal goes sour, the corporation can walk away from it, which will deter directors from making such contracts in the first place. Accordingly, consistent with the general modern corporate law trend of policing conflicts of interest rather than prohibiting them, the law gradually moved towards permitting interested director transactions subject to judicial review. Modern statutes have even further liberalized this area.

A. Common law evolution

In 1918, the New York court of appeals decided the oft-cited case of *Globe Woolen Co. v. Utica Gas & Electric Co.*[5] John F. Maynard was the

will receive a personal financial benefit from a transaction that is not equally shared by the stockholders." Absent classic self-dealing, in which the director stands on both sides of the transaction, however, other Delaware precedents suggest that the requisite benefit must be material or even "substantial." See Cinerama, Inc. v. Technicolor, Inc., 663 A.2d 1156, 1169 (Del. 1995) (distinguishing "classic self-dealing from incidental director interest. To be disqualifying, the nature of the director interest must be substantial."); see also HMG/Courtland Properties, Inc. v. Gray, 749 A.2d 94, 113–14 (Del.Ch.1999).

3. See, e.g., Rocket Mining Corp. v. Gill, 483 P.2d 897, 899 (Utah 1971) (directors having a family relationship with an interested party were not "interested" for purposes of conflict of interest statute). MBCA § 8.60(3) defines the term "related person" to include spouses, children, parents, grandparents, siblings, and persons sharing the same home as the director, as well as certain related trusts or estates. In turn, § 8.60(1)(i) states that a director has a conflicting interest if the director knows that

he or a related person is a party to the transaction or has such a significant financial interest that it "would reasonably be expected to exert an influence on the director's judgment" if the matter were put to a vote.

4. See, e.g., Cuthbert v. McNeill, 142 A. 819, 820 (N.J.Ch.1928) ("a director of a corporation cannot deal with the corporation which he represents. It does not matter how much good faith may have been exercised on his part, his contracts with his corporation are voidable at the instance of the corporation—they will not stand if repudiated as contracts" by the corporation); see generally Harold Marsh, Jr., Are Directors Trustees? Conflict of Interest and Corporate Morality, 22 Bus. Law. 35, 36–43 (1966) (tracing history of common law rule). But see Norwood P. Beveridge, Jr., The Corporate Director's Fiduciary Duty of Loyalty: Understanding the Self–Interested Director Transaction, 41 DePaul L. Rev. 655, 659–62 (1992) (arguing that the common law did not treat conflicted interest transactions as voidable per se).

major shareholder, president, and a board member of Globe, a textile manufacturer. Maynard also was a director of Utica, a utility. Globe had long considered converting its mills to electrical power; but Maynard had insisted on a guaranty that electricity would be cheaper than the plants' existing steam-generated power. An Utica employee, Greenidge, presented to Maynard the results of a study claiming such a conversion would generate considerable savings for Globe. Based on that study, Maynard and Greenidge prepared a contract for Utica to supply power to Globe, which included a guarantee that Globe would realize savings of $300 per month. The contract was brought before the Utica board of directors' executive committee for approval. At the meeting, one director asked whether the deal was a profitable contract for Utica, to which Greenidge responded affirmatively. A resolution was then moved and carried that the directors approve the contract. A subsequent contract further obligated Utica with respect to any expansion of the mills. It also provided that, in the case of a shortage of power, Globe would get preference over every other customer except the city. These changes were not disclosed to the board, which was told that the second contract was practically identical to the first. Again the contract was ratified by the board.

As to both contracts, Maynard presided over the meeting, but did not vote. The contracts proved unprofitable for Utica. It is not clear why. The problems may have resulted from a a change in the mills' operations, which required additional power, or because steam may have been more efficient since excess steam was used for heating. In any event, by the time things came to a head, Utica never had been paid a dime for the power it supplied. To the contrary, Utica owed Globe about $12,000 under the guaranty. Utica sought to void the contract.

In an opinion by Judge Cardozo, the court first held that the transaction would have been voidable if Maynard had voted for it. Because Maynard did not vote, however, the transaction received a presumption of propriety. Yet, even so, the director remains subject to "the duty of constant and unqualified fidelity." In order for a conflicted interest transaction to stand as valid, it must be ratified by a fully informed and disinterested majority of the board and be fair to the corporation. "There must be candor and equity in the transaction, and some reasonable proportion between benefits and burdens." The contract at bar failed both prongs of this conjunctive standard. Maynard failed to disclose material facts about planned changes in Globe's business that rendered the contract a loser for Utica. As to fairness, no matter what changes Globe made in the mills' operations, Utica was still held to its guarantee. As a result, Utica supplied power for free—indeed, it had to pay for the privilege.

5. 121 N.E. 378 (N.Y.1918).

Because *Globe Woolen* phrased the disclosure and fairness standards in the conjunctive, and per se voided the contract if the director failed to abstain from voting, entering into conflicted interest transactions remained a risky proposition. As the 20th Century wore on, however, the law continued to liberalize. In the New York supreme court's subsequent *Bayer v. Beran* decision, for example, the court evaluated an indirect interested director transaction implicating the president of Celanese Corporation.[6] The firm sold a type of rayon fabric under the trade name "Celanese." In order to appeal to an up-scale clientele, the firm invested a good deal of effort in convincing consumers that Celanese was not really rayon, a project that eventually ran afoul of Federal Trade Commission fair advertising rules. After the FTC in 1937 required that the firm's product be marketed under the name "celanese rayon," the corporation began a new advertising campaign directed at up-scale consumers. As part of that campaign, the corporation in 1941 started sponsoring a classical music radio program.

A conflict of interest arose when Jean Tennyson, wife of the corporation's president, Camille Dreyfus, was hired to sing on the program. The board of directors did not formally vote to approve Tennyson's contract and, in fact, were unaware of her participation in the project until after the project as a whole had been approved. Indeed, the project itself had been approved only informally.

Failure to obtain formal approval by a disinterested majority following full disclosure would have damned the contract under *Globe Woolen*. Yet, the court declined to impose liability on Dreyfus or his fellow directors. Because of the conflict of interest, the business judgment rule did not apply. Instead, Dreyfus and the other directors bore the burden of proving the fairness of the transaction. After "careful scrutiny," however, the court deemed the contract to be fair. Tennyson's compensation was reasonable, the program was not designed to further her career, and the company got its money's worth from the radio campaign.[7] As a result, a fair transaction would be upheld even if it was not approved by the board, which made transacting business with one's corporation a much less risky proposition.

B. Interested director statutes

Conflicted interest transactions today are governed by so-called interested director statutes, of which DGCL § 144 is typical. Section 144(a) states that an conflicted interest transaction shall not be "void or voidable solely" because of the director's conflict or "solely because the director or officer is present at or participates in the meeting of the board or committee which authorizes the contract or transaction, or solely because any such director's or officer's votes are counted for such

6. Bayer v. Beran, 49 N.Y.S.2d 2 (Sup. Ct.1944).

7. ALI Principles § 5.08 adopts a new rule prohibiting directors from knowingly advancing the pecuniary interests of their associates, a term that includes spouses.

purpose," provided at least one of three conditions are satisfied. Subsection (a)(1) shields transactions approved by "a majority of the disinterested directors" provided there has been full disclosure of the material facts relating both to the transaction and to the director's conflict of interest. Subsection (a)(2) shields transactions "specifically approved in good faith by vote of the shareholders," again following full disclosure. Subsection (a)(3) shields a transaction that is "fair as to the corporation as of the time it is authorized, approved or ratified, by the board of directors, a committee or the shareholders."[8] The three subsections are in the disjunctive, so satisfying any one will invoke the statute's protection for the challenged transaction.

1. Approval of conflicted interest transactions by a disinterested board majority

Under DGCL § 144(b), an interested director may be counted towards the quorum necessary for board action.[9] Subsection (a) rejects common law cases like *Globe Woolen* that invalidate a conflicted interest transaction solely because the interested director voted on the transaction. Subsection (a) also rejects common law cases invalidating transactions in which a majority of the board is interested. So long as the transaction is approved by a majority of disinterested directors, even if they be less than a quorum, the transaction is not void or voidable solely on any of those grounds.

There is surprisingly little case law on the effect of approval by the disinterested directors. The leading Delaware case remains the decades-old *Puma v. Marriott* decision,[10] in which a disgruntled Marriott Corporation shareholder challenged the corporation's purchase of six other companies from the Marriott family. At the time of the transaction, the

---

8. In Marciano v. Nakash, 535 A.2d 400 (Del.1987), the Delaware supreme court rejected a claim that § 144 is the sole means of validating conflicted interest transactions under Delaware law. Section 144 did not preempt the common law, but instead simply overturned those common law cases deeming conflicted interest transactions voidable per se. Modern Delaware common law does not purport to invalidate conflicted interest transactions solely by virtue of the director's interest. Instead, such a transaction will be upheld, so long as the director proves it was fair to the corporation. Id. at 404.

9. There is an interesting dichotomy between the general director voting rule set out in DGCL § 141(b) and that of § 144(a)(1). The former looks to whether the proposed action was approved by a "majority of the directors present at a meeting at which a quorum is present." The latter requires the "affirmative votes of a majority of the disinterested directors." Note the absence of the qualifying word "present" in the latter. Suppose the corporation has 5 directors, one of whom is interested in the transaction. Two of the four disinterested directors attend the board meeting at which the transaction is to be approved. Because the interested director counts towards a quorum, they can proceed to vote. Assume both disinterested directors vote to approve the transaction, while the interested director abstains. A majority of the directors present at the meeting voted for the transaction, so it is properly approved for purposes of § 141(b). Yet, two out of four disinterested directors is not a majority and, as such, the transaction seemingly has not been approved for purposes of § 144(a)(1). Cf. Beneville v. York, 769 A.2d 80, 82 (Del.Ch.2000) (noting that under "traditional rules of board governance" a motion on which the board is evenly divided fails). Presumably the transaction therefore would have to pass muster under § 144(a)(3).

10. Puma v. Marriott, 283 A.2d 693 (Del.Ch.1971).

Marriott family collectively owned 44% of Marriott Corporation's stock. Four of the nine directors were Marriott family members. The acquisition was unanimously approved by the five disinterested directors. Without reference to § 144, the court held that one those facts the business judgment rule was the applicable standard of review.

Some commentators contend the same rule applies to transactions reviewed under § 144(a)(1).[11] Dicta in at least one Delaware supreme court decision seemingly supports this view.[12] It also is supported by a few decisions from other jurisdictions interpreting comparable statutes.[13] This view also is consistent with case law on the effect of shareholder approval under § 144(a)(2). Finally, this interpretation of § 144(a)(1) is consistent with the economic justification for the business judgment rule as developed in Chapter 6. If the disinterested directors have approved the transaction, courts should defer to their judgment, just as they would with respect to any other business decision. All of the economic arguments in favor of the rule of judicial abstention apply here, just as they do to any other business decision made by impartial directors.

2. *Approval of conflicted interest transactions by shareholders*

DGCL § 144 is an oddly drafted statute. Recall that it provides that a conflicted interest transaction shall not be "void or voidable solely" by virtue of the director's conflict or for the other specified reasons. As such, the statute does not fully validate such transactions, but rather only shields them from per se invalidation. The distinction may seem only semantic, but in fact is critical because it fails to preclude judicial review of a properly approved transaction.

In *Fliegler v. Lawrence*,[14] the Delaware supreme court laid down both holdings and dicta that have been pivotal in the interpretation of DGCL § 144, especially with respect to the shareholder approval provision of subsection (a)(2). John C. Lawrence was president of Agau Mines, Inc., a gold and silver mining corporation. Lawrence had individually acquired some antimony properties, which he offered to Agau. In consultation with Lawrence, the Agau board declined on grounds that the corporation's legal and financial position did not allow it to undertake the venture. Lawrence then formed the United States Antimony Co.

---

11. See, e.g., Michael P. Dooley, Two Models of Corporate Governance, 47 Bus. Law. 461, 490 (1992); Charles Hansen et al., The Role of Disinterested Directors in "Conflict" Transactions: The ALI Corporate Governance Project and Existing Law, 45 Bus. Law. 2083, 2093–94 (1990). But see Melvin Aron Eisenberg, Self–Interested Transactions in Corporate Law, 13 J. Corp. L. 997, 1005 (1988) (contending that "approval by disinterested directors should not insulate a self-interested transaction from judicial review for fairness").

12. Marciano v. Nakash, 535 A.2d 400, 405 n. 3 (Del.1987) (opining that "approval by fully-informed disinterested directors

under section 144(a)(1) . . . permits invocation of the business judgment rule and limits judicial review to issues of gift or waste with the burden of proof upon the party attacking the transaction").

13. See, e.g., Cohen v. Ayers, 596 F.2d 733, 740 (7th Cir.1979) (under New York law, after approval by the disinterested directors, "the business judgment rule is again applicable [to an interested director transaction] and the plaintiff can succeed only by meeting the burden applicable to challenges of any corporate transaction").

14. 361 A.2d 218 (Del.1976).

(USAC), to which the properties were transferred. USAC granted Agau an option to acquire USAC in exchange for Agau stock, which Agau eventually exercised. The decision to exercise the option was approved by the shareholders. Dissenting Agau shareholders then sued.

Defendants relied on DGCL § 144(a)(2) in arguing that shareholder approval relieved defendants of the common law obligation to prove the transaction's fairness. The court agreed that shareholder ratification of a conflicted interest transaction shifted the burden of proof from the defendants to the objecting shareholders. On the facts of this case, however, the burden would not shift. A majority of the shares voted in favor of the transaction had been cast by the interested defendants in their capacities as Agau shareholders. Only approval by disinterested shareholders has the desirable burden-shifting effect.

The court's reading of § 144 is inconsistent with a plain-meaning approach to statutory construction. Section 144(a)(1) requires approval by "a majority of the disinterested directors," but § 144(a)(2) requires only approval by a "vote of the shareholders." The statute's drafters thus inserted a requirement of disinterest in (a)(1) but not in (a)(2). Accordingly, on the face of the statute, shareholder approval ought to be effective even if the shareholders are not disinterested.

Although the court was not faithful to the statutory language, its interpretation does appeal to common sense. Cases arising under these statutes confront courts with issues of ethics and morality, principles of fiduciary obligation, and situations in which the facts are all important. Consequently, the courts tend to treat the precise language of these provisions somewhat cavalierly.

Assuming disinterested shareholder approval were to be obtained, what effect would such approval have on judicial review of the transaction? In broad dicta, the Delaware supreme court rejected a defense argument that shareholder approval precluded judicial review of the transaction:

> We do not read the statute as providing the broad immunity for which defendants contend. It merely removes an "interested director" cloud when its terms are met and provides against invalidation of an agreement "solely" because such a director or officer is involved. Nothing in the statute sanctions unfairness to Agau or removes the transaction from judicial scrutiny.[15]

After an extended analysis of the transaction's history and terms, the court concluded the deal was fair to Agau and held for defendants.

Under *Fliegler*, disinterested shareholder approval thus does not preclude judicial review. Shareholder approval or ratification of a conflicted interest transaction, however, does not simply shift the burden of

---

15. Fliegler v. Lawrence, 361 A.2d 218, 222 (Del.1976). See also Lewis v. S.L. & E., Inc., 629 F.2d 764, 769 (2d Cir.1980) (interpreting New York's conflicted interest statute as allowing judicial scrutiny of the transaction's fairness); Remillard v. Remillard–Dandini Co., 241 P.2d 66, 73 (Cal.App. 1952) ("Even though the requirements of § 820 [California's conflicted interest transaction statute] are technically met, transactions that are unfair and unreasonable to the corporation may be avoided.").

proof with respect to the fairness of a transaction. An objecting share-holder cannot prevail simply by showing that a properly approved transaction is unfair. Fairness was the standard of review in *Fliegler* because § 144(a)(2), as interpreted by the court, had not been satisfied. If § 144(a)(2) had been satisfied, the burden of proof would have shifted to the objecting shareholders to "demonstrate that the terms are so unequal as to amount to a gift or waste of corporate assets." Put another way, as Vice Chancellor Jacobs subsequently observed in a scholarly and comprehensive overview of the effect of shareholder approval on various conflicts of interest under Delaware corporate law: "Approval by fully informed, disinterested shareholders pursuant to § 144(a)(2) invokes 'the business judgment rule and limits judicial review to issues of gift or waste with the burden of proof upon the party attacking the transaction.' "[16]

3. *A brief digression on the meaning of waste*

Under the Delaware precedents outlined in the preceding sections, valid approval by disinterested decisionmakers both changes the stan-

---

16. In re Wheelabrator Tech., Inc., Shareholders Litig., 663 A.2d 1194, 1203 (Del.Ch.1995) (quoting Marciano v. Nakash, 535 A.2d 400, 405 n. 3 (Del.1987)). See also Cede & Co. v. Technicolor, Inc., 634 A.2d 345, 366 n. 34 (Del.1993) ("approval of an interested transaction by either a fully-informed disinterested board of directors, 8 Del.C. § 144(a)(1), or the disinterested shareholders, 8 Del.C. § 144(a)(2), provides business judgment protection"). In Cooke v. Oolie, 1997 WL 367034 at *9 (Del.Ch.1997), however, then Vice Chancellor Chandler held: "Compliance with section 144 merely shifts the burden to the plaintiffs to demonstrate that the transaction was unfair." As support for that proposition, Chandler cited Chancellor Allen's opinion in Cinerama, Inc. v. Technicolor, Inc., 663 A.2d 1134, 1154 (Del.Ch.1994). Because Allen concluded in *Cinerama* that § 144 did not apply to the transaction at bar, the statement upon which Chandler relied was mere dicta. As support for that dicta, moreover, Allen cited the Delaware supreme court's decision in Kahn v. Lynch Communication Systems, 638 A.2d 1110 (Del.1994). *Kahn* was not an interested director transaction, but rather a freeze-out merger effected by a controlling shareholder. As Vice Chancellor Jacobs observed in *Wheelabrator*, shareholder ratification of transactions by a controlling shareholder is treated differently than shareholder (or board) approval of § 144 transactions. See *Wheelabrator*, 663 A.2d at 1203 (distinguishing the two types of transaction and identifying disparate standards of review applicable to each). Finally, in affirming Allen's *Technicolor* decision, the Delaware supreme court opined that "ap-

proval of a transaction by a board of which a majority of directors is disinterested and independent 'bring[s] it within the scope of the business judgment rule.' " Cinerama, Inc. v. Technicolor, Inc., 663 A.2d 1156, 1170 (Del.1995) (quoting Oberly v. Kirby, 592 A.2d 445, 466 (Del.1991)). As such, Chandler's *Coolie* opinion was an erroneous interpretation of Delaware law. In a subsequent opinion arising out of the same lawsuit, Chancellor Chandler attributed his 1997 holding to his having "inadvertently assumed" that the defendants were controlling shareholders. Cooke v. Oolie, 2000 WL 710199 at *13 n. 41 (Del.Ch.2000). With that assumption corrected, the Chancellor articulated a standard consistent with that of *Wheelabrator*: "this Court will apply the business judgment rule to the actions of an interested director, who is not the majority shareholder, if the interested director fully discloses his interest and a majority of the disinterested directors ratify the interested transaction." Id. at *13. See also Solomon v. Armstrong, 747 A.2d 1098, 1115 (Del.Ch. 1999) (Chandler, C.) ("in a classic self-dealing transaction the effect of a fully-informed shareholder vote in favor of that particular transaction is to maintain the business judgment rule's presumptions"), aff'd without op., 746 A.2d 277 (Del.2000); In re Walt Disney Co. Derivative Litigation, 731 A.2d 342, 369 (Del.Ch.1998) (Chandler, C.) ("ratification under § 144(a)(2) cloaks the board's decision with the protection of the business judgment rule"), rev'd on other grounds, 746 A.2d 244 (Del.2000).

dard of review and shifts the burden of proof. Instead of the defendant being obliged to prove the transaction's fairness, the plaintiff must prove waste. But what is waste?

As a standard of review, waste requires proof that the consideration received is so clearly inadequate that the transaction effectively amounts to a gift of corporate assets serving no corporate purpose.[17] In other words, the court will dismiss a waste claim so long as any reasonable person might conclude that the deal made sense. Because courts correctly regard the waste doctrine as setting out a very stringent standard of review, successful waste claims are quite rare.[18]

4. *Fairness absent valid approval or ratification*

DGCL § 144(a)(3) shields from voidability those transactions that are fair to the corporation "as of the time" they are approved or ratified by the board or shareholders. Section 144(a)(3) thus covers situations in which board or shareholder approval was obtained but in a manner inadequate for purposes of subsections (a)(1) or (a)(2). Subsection (a)(3) applies, for example, where the interested director failed to disclose material facts.[19] Alternatively, it would also apply where the approval was effected by the vote of interested parties.

The interested director bears the burden of proving the transaction's fairness.[20] What are the hallmarks of a fair transaction? One might plausibly determine fairness by asking whether the terms of the transaction are within the range of terms to which disinterested parties bargaining at arms-length might have agreed. In *HMG/Courtland Properties v. Gray*,[21] however, Vice Chancellor Strine rejected that interpretation on the grounds that failure to disclose material facts is highly relevant to a determination of fairness. If undisclosed facts had been known to the corporation, it might have insisted on terms at the low end of the range of fair value or refused to transact at all.

---

17. See, e.g., Grobow v. Perot, 539 A.2d 180, 189 (Del.1988) ("what the corporation has received is so inadequate in value that no person of ordinary, sound business judgment would deem it worth that which the corporation has paid"); Michelson v. Duncan, 407 A.2d 211, 224 (Del.1979) ("no person of ordinary, sound business judgment would say that the consideration received for the options was a fair exchange for the options granted"); Because reasonable corporate charitable donations are deemed to serve a legitimate corporate purpose, they are rarely invalidated as waste.

18. See Steiner v. Meyerson, 1995 WL 441999 at *5 (Del.Ch.1995) ("rarest of all—and indeed, like Nessie, possibly non-existent—would be the case of disinterested business people making non-fraudulent

deals (non-negligently) that meet the legal standard of waste!").

19. Cede & Co. v. Technicolor, Inc., 634 A.2d 345, 366 n. 34 (Del.1993) ("a nondisclosing interested director can remove the taint of interestedness by proving the entire fairness of the challenged transaction").

20. Marciano v. Nakash, 535 A.2d 400, 405 n. 3 (Del.1987).

21. HMG/Courtland Properties, Inc. v. Gray, 749 A.2d 94 (Del.Ch.1999). See also U.S. v. Lemire, 720 F.2d 1327, 1336 n. 10 (D.C.Cir.1983) ("where an official of the corporation does not disclose his personal interest in a transaction, the transaction is merely voidable and the company may choose to go ahead with the transaction . . . as long as the transaction is fair to the corporation").

Under *HMG/Courtland Properties*, a transaction is not unfair solely because there are undisclosed material facts. Such an interpretation would be inconsistent with the clear thrust of § 144(a)(3), which contemplates that transactions may be deemed fair even though the requisite board or shareholder approval was tainted by nondisclosures. Indeed, such an interpretation would essentially negate subsection (a)(3) as to the class of transactions as to which it is most likely to apply. Instead, *HMG/Courtland Properties* simply requires nondisclosing defendants to show that (1) the terms of the deal were within the range of fair value and (2) the corporation would not have gotten a materially better deal if the defendants had "come clean."

Finally, suppose the corporation's CEO approved a contract with a director without referring the transaction to the board or shareholders. Absent the director's conflict of interest, such a transaction normally would be binding. As an agent of the corporation, its CEO has expansive actual and apparent authority to enter into contracts on behalf of the corporation. As for the conflict of interest issue, however, DGCL § 144(a)(3) is inapplicable, because the transaction received neither board nor shareholder approval. Recall, however, that § 144 is not the only means of validating conflicted interest transactions under Delaware law. If the director proves the transaction was fair to the corporation, no liability will result.[22]

5.   *The ALI alternative*

During their decade-long evolution, the ALI Principles' substantive provisions traced a predictable pattern. Early drafts focused on the need for management accountability and relied on judicial review as the primary mechanism for accomplishing that goal. The early drafts therefore increased the likelihood of a corporate decision undergoing judicial review and the concomitant risk of liability for directors and officers. Under pressure from corporate lawyers whose clients generally opposed the ALI Principles, later drafts commonly retreated towards a position more or less resembling existing law.

This pattern is well exemplified by the ALI Principles' treatment of conflicted interest transactions.[23] When a shareholder challenges an interested-director transaction, the lawsuit usually must be brought as a derivative cause of action. If Tentative Draft No. 1 of the Principles had become law,[24] it would have authorized the use of special litigation committees, comprising newly appointed independent directors, to represent the corporation's interests in the litigation.[25] Courts, however, were

---

22. Marciano v. Nakash, 535 A.2d 400, 403 (Del.1987).

23. For an interest group analysis of the ALI Principles, see Stephen M. Bainbridge, Independent Directors and the ALI Corporate Governance Project, 61 Geo. Wash. L. Rev. 1034, 1044–52 (1993).

24. It is worth remembering that the ALI Principles are not themselves law and, moreover, do not even purport to restate existing law.

25. American Law Inst., Principles of Corporate Governance and Structure: Restatement and Recommendations § 7.03 (Tentative Draft No. 1, 1982).

not to defer to a committee recommendation to terminate the lawsuit. Instead, the PRINCIPLES would have required the court to determine whether the business justification advanced by the committee warranted dismissal of the action. In addition, the court was to make an independent judgment whether the committee's proffered justification was advanced in good faith, was outweighed by the probable recovery or other relief likely to result from the litigation, or frustrated any authoritatively established public policy.

Assuming that a shareholder successfully passed the special litigation committee hurdle, which seemed likely,[26] the substantive rule also would have been quite favorable to plaintiffs. Valid approval of an interested-director transaction by the independent directors would have shifted the burden of proof from the defendant to the plaintiff, but the transaction still would have been set aside if the challenging shareholder proved that the independent directors could not have reasonably believed the transaction to be fair.[27] Because this rule was intended to create a range of reasonableness within which the transaction had to fall in order to withstand scrutiny, courts presumably were to exercise some degree of independent judgment as to the reasonableness of the transaction's terms.[28]

In contrast, under existing state law, an interested-director transaction is much less likely to result in liability. Where Tentative Draft No. 3's safe harbor would have been available only in the case of ex ante board approval, for example, most state interested-director statutes allow ex post ratification.[29] Where Tentative Draft No. 3 would have permitted judicial scrutiny of the transaction's fairness, existing law limits further judicial review to the confines of the business judgment rule if there has been a determination by a disinterested and independent board that the transaction is fair.

In the face of substantial opposition to the approach of Tentative Draft No. 3, the drafters of the PRINCIPLES steadily backed down. The compromises that were ultimately reached generally reduced the likelihood of director and officer liability. In particular, the procedures gov-

---

26. See Business Roundtable, Statement of the Business Roundtable on the American Law Institute's Proposed "Principles of Corporate Governance and Structure: Restatement and Recommendations" 52 (1983) ("many of the provisions in Part VII are unabashedly designed to facilitate derivative litigation").

27. American Law Inst., Principles of Corporate Governance: Analysis and Recommendations § 5.08(a)(2)(A) (Tentative Draft No. 3, 1984).

28. In addition to the factors identified in the text, approval by the independent directors shifted the burden of proof from the defendant director to the plaintiff shareholder only if such approval was obtained before the transaction took place.

This approach seemingly was premised on the assumption that the board would treat interested-director transactions as faits accompli rather than give them a hard look. Finally, if the transaction was validly approved by the disinterested shareholders, the plaintiff would have to show that the transaction amounted to a waste of corporate assets. American Law Inst., Principles of Corporate Governance: Analysis and Recommendations § 5.08(a)(2)(B) (Tentative Draft No. 3, 1984).

29. Compare American Law Inst., Principles of Corporate Governance: Analysis and Recommendations § 5.08(a)(2)(A) (Tentative Draft No. 3, 1984) with MBCA § 8.61(b)(1).

erning derivative suits gradually moved toward the Delaware position, as did the substantive provisions governing interested-director transactions. Perhaps as a mere incidental byproduct, these changes also introduced a greater degree of deference to decisions made by independent directors. For example, while the initial draft looked to whether the transaction fell within a range of reasonableness, the final draft's commentary looks to whether the terms are clearly outside the range of reasonableness. This reformulation of the standard should insulate more board decisions from judicial intervention.

6. MBCA subchapter F

Former MBCA § 8.31 largely tracked DGCL § 144, although there were a few key differences. MBCA § 8.31(a)(1) allowed directors to approve or ratify a conflicted interest transaction, while DGCL § 144(a)(1) speaks only of authorization. MBCA § 8.31(a)(3) ambiguously referred to transactions that are "fair to the corporation," while DGCL § 144(a)(3) is limited to transactions that are fair to the corporation "as of the time" they are approved or ratified by the board of shareholders. Note how this distinction implicated not only timing issues, but also the validity of transactions that are unapproved by either board or shareholders. Although former MBCA § 8.31 remains on the books in many states, in the Model Act it has been superseded by new subchapter F.

A striking difference between subchapter F and its predecessor—or DGCL § 144, for that matter—is the sheer level of complexity.[30] Section 8.60 opens with a purportedly bright-line definition of "conflicted interest" transactions. Such transactions include not those effected or proposed to be effected by the corporation, but also those by a subsidiary of the corporation or any other entity which the corporation controls. In order for the transaction to be a conflicted one, however, the director must know when the deals is made that the director or "a related person" is a party to the transaction.[31] The director also must know that he or a related person has a beneficial financial interest in the transaction or is so closely linked to the transaction that the interest would reasonably be expected to exert an influence on the director's judgment if the director were called upon to vote on the transaction.[32] Note that the foregoing definition encompasses mainly classic self-dealing of the sort defined as direct interests. MBCA § 8.60(1)(ii) addresses indirect interests, deeming such interests conflicting when the director knows that the other party is an entity of which the director is an owner, employee, or an affiliate of such an entity.

---

30. Another difference is that subchapter F applies only to directors, not officers. Conflicts of interest on the part of officers, as well as nonofficer employees, are left to agency law.

31. Related person is defined by § 8.60(3) to include "the spouse (or a par-

ent or sibling thereof) of the director, or a child, grandchild, sibling, parent (or spouse of any thereof) of the director, or an individual having the same home as the director," plus specified trusts and estates.

32. MBCA § 8.60(1)(i).

Subsection 8.61(a) then preempts the field of conflicted interest transactions. Unlike DGCL § 144, which does not preempt the common law, MBCA subchapter F is intended to do so. If a transaction does not satisfy the statutory definition of a conflicted interest transaction, no liability or equitable relief may be granted on grounds that the director had an interest in the transaction. Suppose a corporation enters into a contract with the cousin of a director. Cousins are not related persons as defined by the statute. The contract thus is not a conflicted interest transaction, as defined by the statute, and a court has no authority to set it aside or otherwise grant relief. Similarly, where the director's allegedly conflicted interest arises out of nonfinancial considerations, such as the desire to join a country club, the court lacks authority to intervene.[33]

As to transactions falling within the statutory definition of a conflicted interest transaction, subsection 8.61(b) creates three safe harbors. If any of the three is satisfied, a court may neither enjoin or set aside the transaction nor impose liability in connection with it on grounds that the director had an interest in the transaction. Approval by a fully informed majority of disinterested directors (who must number at least two) suffices.[34] So does approval by fully informed shareholders.[35] Alternatively, absent the requisite approvals, a transaction is validated if fair to the corporation.[36]

The third safe harbor obviously contemplates judicial review of the transaction's merits. As with Delaware law, moreover, the concept of fairness embraces both the terms of the deal and the course of dealing by the interested party. If the interested director failed to disclose material information, for example, the court may treat the transaction as voidable or even impose monetary damages.[37]

The first two safe harbors purportedly limit judicial review to oversight of the approval process. On the face of the statute, the court may only determine that the defendant jumped through the proper procedural hoops. Closer examination, however, suggests some ambiguities. The drafter's commentary on § 8.61(b) states "that the board's action must comply with the care, best interests and good faith criteria prescribed in section 8.30(a) for all directors' actions."[38] The commentary further opines that "manifestly unfavorable" terms would be evidence of lack of good faith. Some contend these comments permit judicial review of the merits of the transaction, even if it was approved by the directors, at least to the extent of determining whether the deal was "manifestly unfavorable."[39] Yet, MBCA § 8.30(a) merely sets forth a

---

33.　MBCA § 8.31 cmt. 1.

34.　MBCA §§ 8.61(b)(1) and 8.62.

35.　MBCA §§ 8.61(b)(2) and 8.63. MBCA § 8.60(d) specifies the disclosure required by the interested director to include the existence and nature of the conflict and all facts known to the director "that an ordinarily prudent person would reasonably believe to be material to a judgment about

whether or not to proceed with the transaction."

36.　MBCA § 8.61(b)(3).

37.　MBCA § 8.61 cmt.

38.　MBCA § 8.61 cmt. 2.

39.　See, e.g., 1 ALI Principles at 244 (so asserting).

standard of conduct. Director liability is governed by § 8.31(a), which sets out two relevant criteria. To be sure, § 8.31(a)(2) allows for imposition of liability where board actions are not taken in good faith, but only if the safe harbor provision of § 8.61(b)(1) is unavailable.[40] The commentary to § 8.31 purports to resolve the apparent circularity in favor of the safe harbor, which is deemed "self-executing," but there is still an ambiguity. The drafters assert that absent "any of the valid bases for contesting the availability of the liability shelter" of § 8.61(b)(1), "the individual director's exoneration from liability is automatic."[41] Given that good faith is a "critically important predicate condition" for § 8.61(b)(1) to apply,[42] however, would not lack of good faith constitute a "valid basis" for setting aside the safe harbor. If all of this seems unnecessarily confusing and circular, that is probably because it is unnecessarily confusing and circular. Read in context and taken as a whole, the statute's thrust is to preclude judicial review provided basic prophylactic procedures are followed.[43] Reportedly, the problem will be fixed by future amendments to the relevant commentary intended to more clearly confirm that basic thrust.

In sum, the model act's safe harbors differ but little from Delaware law. Both contemplate limited judicial review of conflicted interest transactions validated by a disinterested majority of the board or shareholders. As we have seen, this approach is fully consistent with our standard economic model. As always, the task is to strike an appropriate balance between authority and accountability. Obviously, significant accountability concerns are present when interested parties approve their own self-dealing. Where the transaction has passed muster by independent and disinterested reviewers, however, those concerns are vitiated. Given the significant advantages of preserving the board's authority, and the limited benefits of accountability through judicial review, courts should abstain from reviewing a transaction approved by disinterested decisionmakers. And that is what both the MBCA and DGCL accomplish.

C. Executive compensation

Although executive compensation long has been a subject of intense controversy in both the popular and academic literature, it presents few

---

40. The statute specifically provides: "A director shall not be liable . . . unless the party asserting liability . . . establishes that: (1) . . . the protection afforded by section 8.61 for action taken in compliance with section 8.62 or 8.63, if interposed as a bar to the proceeding by the director, does not preclude liability; and (2) the challenged conduct consisted or was the result of: (i) action not in good faith. . . ." Because the two prongs are stated in the conjunctive, both must be satisfied.

41. MBCA § 8.31 cmt. 1.

42. MBCA § 8.61 cmt. 2.

43. The Model Act's current reporter, for example, refers to the "limited review of internal corporate procedures contemplated by subsections [8.61](1) and (2)." Michael P. Dooley and Michael D. Goldman, Some Comparisons Between the Model Business Corporation Act and the Delaware General Corporation Law, 56 Bus. Law. 737, 744 n.37 (2001) (Dooley is the act's reporter; Goldman is a member of the ABA committee that oversees the statute).

doctrinal complexities.[44] A compensation contract between the corporation and one of its officers does not differ in kind from any other conflicted interest transaction covered by the statutes considered in this section. If the disinterested directors, following full disclosure, approve the contract in good faith, the transaction will receive the protection of the business judgment rule.[45] Accordingly, many public corporations have established compensation committees staffed by independent directors to review and approve executive compensation.

As a result, successful shareholder challenges to executive compensation typically involve close corporations in which disinterested director approval was not (or could not) be obtained. In such cases, the burden of proof remains on the defendant executive to prove that the compensation was fair to the corporation. In *Wilderman v. Wilderman*,[46] for example, the Delaware chancery court identified a number of factors to be considered: (1) whether the Internal Revenue Service allowed the corporation to take a deduction for the challenged compensation (unreasonable compensation may not be deducted); (2) the value of the challenged compensation relative to that paid other employees; (3) the ability of the executive; (4) the executive's salary history; (5) and whether the salary is reasonable in relation to the corporation's success.

§ 7.3 Corporate opportunities

The doctrine generically known as "organizational opportunities" deals with situations in which an agent usurps a business opportunity that rightfully belongs to the principal. In doing so, the agent has violated his fiduciary duty to the principal by usurping this opportunity for his own gain. This prohibition of against usurping organizational opportunities is found in agency law, partnership law, and, in its most developed form, corporate law.[1]

---

44. For a small sampling of the extensive literature, see Charles M. Elson, Executive Overcompensation—A Board–Based Solution, 34 B.C. L. Rev 937 (1993); Mark J. Loewenstein, Reflections on Executive Compensation and a Modest Proposal for (Further) Reform, 50 SMU L. Rev. 201 (1996); Kevin J. Murphy, Politics, Economics, and Executive Compensation, 63 U. Cin. L. Rev. 713 (1995); Susan J. Stabile, Viewing Corporate Executive Compensation through a Partnership Lens, 35 Wake Forest L. Rev. 153 (2000); Charles M. Yablon, Bonus Questions—Executive Compensation in the Era of Pay for Performance, 75 Notre Dame L. Rev. 271 (1999).

45. See, e.g., Zupnick v. Goizueta, 698 A.2d 384 (Del.Ch.1997) (after holding that approval of a stock option-based compensation plan by the disinterested directors shifted the burden of proof to plaintiff to show waste, the court further held: "To state a cognizable claim for waste where there is no contention that the directors were interested or that shareholder ratification was improperly obtained, the well-pleaded allegations of the complaint must support the conclusion that 'no person of ordinary, sound business judgment would say that the consideration received for the options was a fair exchange for the options granted.' ").

46.   315 A.2d 610 (Del.Ch.1974).

§ 7.3

1. See generally Victor Brudney & Robert C. Clark, A New Look at Corporate Opportunities, 94 Harv. L. Rev. 997 (1981); Kenneth B. Davis, Jr., Corporate Opportunity and Comparative Advantage, 84 Iowa L. Rev. 211 (1998); Richard A. Epstein, Contract and Trust in Corporate Law: The Case of Corporate Opportunity, 21 Del. J. Corp. L. 5 (1996); Harvey Gelb, The Corporate Opportunity Doctrine—Recent Cases and the Elusive Goal of Clarity, 31 U. Richmond L. Rev. 371 (1997); Eric L. Talley,

A prohibition of some sort against usurping organizational opportunities is almost certainly a majoritarian default. Consider the most famous fiduciary obligation cases, *Meinhard v. Salmon.*[2] Meinhard and Salmon formed a joint venture to lease an office building. Shortly before expiration of the lease, Salmon began secret negotiations with the lessor, as a result of which Salmon's real estate corporation was able to lease the building and several adjoining lots. Salmon planned to eventually replace the existing building with a new and considerably more profitable facility. Meinhard did not learn of Salmon's new arrangement until after the new lease was finalized. At that time he demanded that the new lease be held in trust for the joint venture. Salmon refused and the lawsuit ensued.

If partners can withhold new information—such as the discovery of a new business opportunity—from each other, then each has an incentive to drive the other out so as to take full advantage of the information. As each incurs costs to exclude the other, or to take precautions against being excluded, the value of the firm declines. A legal rule vesting the firm with a property right to the information and requiring disclosure is more efficient than forcing the partners to draft disclosure agreements and monitor one another's behavior. Note that this rule does not discourage the production of new information, because the partners still have incentives to produce information because they share in its value to the firm. As no one will withhold information, however, the firm's productivity is maximized.[3] As a result, we can confidently predict that the partners would agree ex ante to bar any one partner from taking an organizational opportunity for his personal gain.

While some such prohibition thus emerges from our hypothetical bargain as a majoritarian default, the form such a prohibition ought to take is less obvious. Does it matter if one partner is actively managing the business (as was Salmon) while the other is passive (as was Meinhard)? Should all outside business ventures be proscribed or only some? If the latter, how do we decide which are proscribed? Should we adopt a bright-line rule or a flexible standard? What should be the remedy?

In a justly famous passage, Judge Cardozo adopted a wonderfully vague standard to govern these problems:

> Joint adventurers, like copartners, owe to one another, while the enterprise continues, the duty of the finest loyalty. Many forms of conduct permissible in a workaday world for those acting at arm's length, are forbidden to those bound by fiduciary ties. A trustee is held to something stricter than the morals of the market place. Not honesty alone, but the punctilio of an honor the most sensitive, is then the standard of behavior. As to this there has developed a tradition that is unbending and inveterate. Uncompromising rigidity

Turning Servile Opportunities to Gold: A Strategic Analysis of the Corporate Opportunities Doctrine, 108 Yale L.J. 277 (1998).

2. 164 N.E. 545 (N.Y.1928).

3. Michael P. Dooley, Enforcement of Insider Trading Restrictions, 66 Va. L. Rev. 1, 64–66 (1980).

has been the attitude of courts of equity when petitioned to undermine the rule of undivided loyalty by the "disintegrating erosion" of particular exceptions. Only thus has the level of conduct for fiduciaries been kept at a level higher than that trodden by the crowd. It will not consciously be lowered by any judgment of this court.[4]

In applying this standard, Cardozo focused closely on the specific circumstances of the case. As such, he converted the vague majoritarian default into one specifically tailored for the parties at bar. Hence, Cardozo emphasized that Salmon was "in control with exclusive powers of direction...."[5] Salmon "was much more than a coadventurer. He was a managing coadventurer."[6] Cardozo further acknowledged that:

> A different question would be here if there were lacking any nexus of relation between the business conducted by the manager and the opportunity brought to him as an incident of management.... For this problem, as for most, there are distinctions of degree. If Salmon had received from Gerry a proposition to lease a building at a location far removed, he might have held for himself the privilege thus acquired, or so we shall assume. Here the subject-matter of the new lease was an extension and enlargement of the subject-matter of the old one. A managing coadventurer appropriating the benefit of such a lease without warning to his partner might fairly expect to be reproached with conduct that was underhand, or lacking, to say the least, in reasonable candor, if the partner were to surprise him in the act of signing the new instrument. Conduct subject to that reproach does not receive from equity a healing benediction.[7]

Whether a "different question" also have been presented if the entity in question had been a corporation rather than a partnership is the subject of this section.

A. Delaware's standard

Guth v. Loft, Inc. remains Delaware's classic statement of the corporate opportunity doctrine.[8] Loft was a manufacturer and retailer of candy, syrups, drinks and food. It did not manufacture a cola syrup, instead selling Coke in its retail outlets. Charles Guth was the president and a director of Loft. To greatly simplify a complex set of facts, Guth obtained effective control of the then-struggling Pepsi–Cola Corporation. Guth then began a clandestine program of using Loft funds, facilities, and employees to get Pepsi off the ground. Loft later sued Guth on the grounds that the chance to acquire Pepsi was a corporate opportunity. In other words, Loft alleged that Guth had a duty to give Loft an informed chance to acquire Pepsi before doing so himself. Put yet another way, Loft essentially claimed that Guth had to give Loft a right of first refusal to acquire Pepsi.

---

4. Meinhard v. Salmon, 164 N.E. 545, 546 (N.Y.1928) (citations omitted).

5. Id. at 547.

6. Id. at 548.

7. Id.

8. Guth v. Loft, Inc., 5 A.2d 503 (Del. 1939).

At that time, there were three common law tests used by the courts to determine whether or not something was a corporate opportunity. The *Guth* court invoked all three: First, it identified what is now known as the line of business test. Is the business venture in question intimately or closely associated with the existing or prospective businesses of the corporation? On that score, the court held Pepsi was squarely within Loft's lines of business. As noted, Loft was both a manufacturer and purchaser of soft drink syrups. Although it was not presently in the business of making cola syrups, the court held that the line of business test had to allow for future development or expansion of the firm. Making cola syrups was within Loft's reasonable future business. Loft had a continuing business need for cola syrups to supply its retail outlets. Then, as now, cola-flavored syrups were the major soft drink product. Indeed, because Guth had used the powers of his position as president to terminate Loft's contract with Coca–Cola, that on-going need had been greatly exacerbated.[9] Loft also had the knowledge, experience and resources necessary to exploit the Pepsi opportunity. The combination of the need and the ability brought the Pepsi opportunity within Loft's line of business.

Second, the court asked whether Loft had a prior interest or expectancy in the opportunity. Arguably, one could distinguish between an interest and an expectancy. A director or officer takes the corporation's "interest" if he takes something to which the firm has a better right. The director or officer takes an "expectancy" if he takes something which, in the ordinary course of things, would come to the corporation—i.e., something the corporation could expect to receive. If an officer bought land to which the corporation had a contractual right, for example, the officer took an "interest." If the officer took the renewal rights to a lease the corporation had, the officer took an "expectancy."

As a practical matter, however, courts do not make such fine distinctions.[10] When Guth discontinued Loft's contract with Coca–Cola, for example, it became a matter of business necessity that Loft acquire an alternative source of cola syrups. Because Guth's actions created the need, the court opined, Loft had an equitable interest in the opportunity

---

9. In his capacity as Loft's president, Guth terminated the supply contract with Coca–Cola. Guth then caused Loft to enter into a supply contract with Pepsi. Note that Guth's conduct thus also implicated the conflict of interest transaction doctrine discussed in the preceding section. A corporate officer or director may only compete with the corporation if the competition involves no breach of duty. Here there was a clear cut breach of duty because of Guth's self-dealing. He controlled Loft and thus could force it to buy syrup from Pepsi; he controlled Pepsi and thus could set the terms on which the syrup would be supplied. By being on both sides of the transaction he had a rather pronounced conflict of interest.

10. See, e.g., Southeast Consultants, Inc. v. McCrary Engineering Corp., 273 S.E.2d 112, 117 (Ga.1980) (asking whether the corporation had a " 'beachhead' in the sense of an equitable expectancy growing out of a pre-existing relationship"); Shapiro v. Greenfield, 764 A.2d 270, 278 (Md.App. 2000) (noting that Maryland uses the interest or expectancy standard, which it said is focused "on whether the corporation could realistically expect to seize and develop the opportunity").

to buy Pepsi. Loft also had an equitable interest in Pepsi because of the way in which Guth handled the transaction. Guth's use of corporate funds and facilities to operate Pepsi for his own personal profit amounted to stealing from the company, giving the company an equitable right to the fruits of his theft.

Finally, the court looked to the capacity in which Guth discovered the opportunity. Pepsi's prior owner had not approached Guth in his personal capacity, but rather as Loft's president. If it had been the other way around, however, Guth might have been allowed to take the opportunity. The capacity standard is highly problematic. Every director or officer will claim that the opportunity was presented to him in his individual capacity. Courts therefore should ignore the form of the transaction, on the assumption that the deal was structured to create an appearance of individual capacity, and put a heavy burden of proof on the director to show that it was presented to him as an individual. Where the sole evidence is the director's word, the court should presume that the opportunity was presented to him in his capacity as a director or officer.

Guth, of course, is an easy case. Not only did Guth appropriate an opportunity that Loft could have exploited, but he also engaged in a massive campaign of self-dealing and outright theft. Analysis by platitude more than sufficed. Subsequent cases involving less egregious conduct therefore have helped flesh out the doctrine.

In *Broz v. Cellular Information Systems, Inc.,*[11] Robert Broz was the sole shareholder and President of RFB Cellular, Inc., a small cell phone company. Broz was also a member of the board of Cellular Information Systems, Inc., which also provided cell phone service. David Rhodes, a broker, informed Broz of an opportunity to acquire a cellular telephone service license called Michigan–2, which would entitle the buyer to provide cell phone service to an area in rural Michigan. RFB Cellular already owned and operated a similar license known as Michigan–4.

Broz bought Michigan–2 for RFB Cellular without formally offering it to Cellular Information Systems. Before doing so, Broz did mention the opportunity informally to Richard Treibick, Cellular Information Systems' CEO and to Peter Schiff, a Cellular Information Systems board member, both of whom expressed a lack of interest on Cellular Information Systems' behalf. During the relevant time period, Cellular Information Systems was in financial difficulty and was in the process of being acquired by PriCellular, Inc., yet another cell phone operator. PriCellular was bidding on the Michigan–2 license, a fact of which Treibick was well aware. Broz outbid ProCellular. Because of financing difficulties, PriCellular's acquisition of Cellular Information Systems was not completed until shortly after RFB Cellular's successful bid for the license. Once PriCellular completed its acquisition of Cellular Information Systems, it

11. 673 A.2d 148 (Del.1996).

caused Cellular Information Systems to sue Broz for breach of fiduciary duty, claiming that Broz had usurped the Michigan–2 opportunity.

The Delaware supreme court held Broz had not violated his fiduciary obligation to Cellular Information Systems by failing to formally offer the Michigan–2 license to Cellular Information Systems. The court identified four relevant considerations: (1) Is the corporation financially able to take the opportunity? (2) Is the opportunity in the corporation's line of business? (3) Does the corporation have an interest or expectancy in the opportunity? (4) Does an officer or director create a conflict between his self-interest and that of the corporation by taking the opportunity for himself?

The line of business factor obviously was satisfied. Cellular Information Systems was in the business of operating cellular phone franchises. Michigan–2 was a cellular phone franchise. Yet, Cellular Information Systems' stated business plans did not contemplate further expansion of its cellular phone business. To the contrary, Cellular Information Systems was divesting some of its existing licenses. Accordingly, Cellular Information Systems had no interest or expectancy in the license. The court further emphasized that Cellular Information Systems lacked the financial capacity to acquire the Michigan–2 license. Cellular Information Systems had only recently emerged from a bankruptcy reorganization and remained in a precarious financial position. Finally, just as Guth was clearly a bad guy, Broz was a good guy. The court took pains to stress that formal processes were not required. Broz did not have to formally present the opportunity to Cellular Information Systems' board, not did that board have to formally reject the opportunity, before Broz was free to take it. Formal processes may create a safe harbor, but they are not required.

The standard that emerges from cases like *Guth* and *Broz* is not very precise. The lists of relevant considerations differ not just in number but also in substantive content. In *Guth*, the capacity in which the director or officer learned of the opportunity is one of the relevant factors. In *Broz*, the court merely "note[s] at the outset" that Broz learned of the Michigan–2 opportunity in his individual capacity and, moreover, emphasizes that "this fact is not dispositive."

The listed considerations also seems somewhat arbitrary. One could readily construct a longer laundry list of factors that seem at least as relevant as those on which the *Guth* and *Broz* courts relied. For example, one might readily consider such facts as: (1) Were there prior negotiations with the firm about the opportunity? (2) Did the director conceal the opportunity from the firm? (3) Did the director make use of corporate funds or property in exploiting the opportunity? (4) Will the opportunity involve competition with the firm or otherwise thwart firm policy? (5) Did the corporation have a substantial need that the opportunity would have filled? (6) Did the corporation have the necessary technical resources to exploit the opportunity? (7) Is the director an insider.

Additional imprecision follows from the court's insistence that the listed considerations are factors not elements. Put another way, the court evaluates the director or officer's conduct under the totality of the circumstances.[12] From a transactional planning standpoint, the lack of clear guidance places considerable value on obtaining a safe harbor. Formal presentment of the opportunity to the board may not be required by Delaware law, but it is surely the prudent course of action.

B. Alternatives to Delaware

1. A proposal

If the corporation is best described as the nexus of a set of relational contracts between various corporate constituencies, our analysis of corporate law appropriately is informed by the contract law principles applicable to relational contracts. In a classic article on such contracts, Professors Robert Scott and Charles Goetz argued that relational contracts should be interpreted using a "joint maximization model."[13] Their model requires an agent to use best efforts on behalf of the principal. The best efforts standard does not require the agent to advance the principal's interests at the agent's expense (contra Cardozo). Instead, the agent must seek to maximize the joint interests of the agent and the principal. Using this insight, one can propose a four-step test for how corporate opportunity cases should be analyzed:

(1) Was this venture an "opportunity"? Delaware law does not clearly bifurcate definitional issues from conduct issues. Bifurcating the two, however, would lead to greater clarity. A bright-line definition would enable the officer or director to more readily determine whether the venture is legally problematic. At the same time, however, a director or officer would not be liable merely for taking a venture that falls within the definition of a corporate opportunity. Instead, liability results only if the director usurped—wrongfully took—the opportunity.

(2) Did the officer or director disclose the opportunity to the corporation? (a) If not, the director is liable for his failure to do so, with liability being measured by the traditional common law constructive trust rules. (b) If disclosure was made, go on to step 3.

(3) Did the corporation accept or reject the offered opportunity? (a) If the corporation chose to accept the opportunity, the director may not personally exploit it. If he does so, a constructive trust

---

12. See Broz v. Cellular Information Systems, Inc., 673 A.2d 148 (Del.1996) ("the totality of the circumstances indicates that Broz did not usurp an opportunity that properly belonged to CIS"); see also Schreiber v. Bryan, 396 A.2d 512 (Del.Ch. 1978) ("a claim that a corporate opportunity has been wrongfully taken is wholly de-pendent upon the facts presented. . . . The application of these principles depends on the facts.").

13. Charles J. Goetz & Robert E. Scott, Principles of Relational Contracts, 67 Va. L. Rev. 1089 (1981).

can be imposed on his ill-gotten gains. (b) If the corporation rejected the opportunity, the director is free to personally exploit it, subject to the requirements of Step 4.

(4) Does the manner in which the director or officer exploited the opportunity work to the detriment or to the benefit of the corporation? (a) If the opportunity works to the firm's detriment, then the director or officer may be liable for damages for breach of the agency law duty not to compete with the firm. (b) If the opportunity benefits the corporation, no liability.

This disclosure and consent rule has a number of advantages. First, it encourages competition and discourages costly opportunism within the firm. If directors were able to freely compete with the firm their would be a strong incentive to pursue their self-interest at the expense of the firm—perhaps even to sabotage the firm as Guth did. In other words, this proposal treats the problem as one of allocating property rights to information generated by agents of a corporation. Corporate agents generate lots of information. It is hard sometimes to figure out whether the information belongs to the corporation. Consequently, a prophylactic rule of disclosure seems appropriate. It removes the incentive for agents to divert potential opportunities to their own use.

Second, disclosure may encourage joint maximization. Presumably, firms will consent to the director or officer exploiting the opportunity when it is in both parties interest. To be sure, the rule arguably requires too much disclosure, especially if we embrace a broad definition of corporate opportunity. One might, for example, require an officer or director to disclose all outside profit-making ventures in which the officer or director has an interest, including indirect interests such as being an officer, director or large shareholder of an entity exploiting the opportunity. On balance, however, the benefits of a disclosure based approach likely outweigh the costs of repetitive disclosure.

Arguably the disclosure and consent test does a better job than do the courts' stated rationales at explaining and justifying results in *Guth* and *Broz*. What really bothered the court in *Guth*, probably, was the fact that Guth did not offer Loft a right of first refusal to buy Pepsi, but instead went behind Loft's back to purchase Pepsi for himself. In contrast, in *Broz* the director fully disclosing the opportunity to the firm and gave it a fair opportunity to compete.

2. *The Miller two-step*

A widely discussed alternative to the Delaware standard was announced by the Minnesota supreme court in *Miller v. Miller*.[14] Joseph Miller founded a corporation—Miller Waste Mills, Inc.—that made lubri-

---

14. 222 N.W.2d 71 (Minn.1974). Cases following *Miller* include: Regal–Beloit Corp. v. Drecoll, 955 F.Supp. 849 (N.D.Ill.1996) (applying Wisconsin law); Southeast Consultants, Inc. v. McCrary Engineering Corporation, 273 S.E.2d 112 (1980); Racine v. Weisflog, 477 N.W.2d 326 (Wis.App.1991). Cases rejecting *Miller* in whole or part include: Northeast Harbor Golf Club, Inc. v. Harris, 661 A.2d 1146 (Me.1995); Klinicki v. Lundgren, 695 P.2d 906 (Or.1985).

cating products for heavy industry. When Joseph Miller retired, control of the business passed to his sons Rudolph and Benjamin. For some reason, Oscar—a third son—did not participate in the firm's management. Indeed, Oscar did not receive any shares of stock in Miller Waste until both his parents died.

Rudolph and Benjamin, both individually and jointly with their wives, formed a series of separate companies, at least one of which directly competed with Miller Waste. However, all of those companies used Miller Waste as a source of raw materials and all of the companies, including Miller Waste, profited. Oscar challenged the formation of these separate companies, arguing that Rudolph and Benjamin had appropriated to themselves corporate opportunities rightfully belonging to Miller Waste.

Noting the "often-expressed criticism that the [corporate opportunity] doctrine is vague and subjects today's corporate management to the danger of unpredictable liability," the court offered a purportedly superior standard affectionately known (at least to line dancers) as the *Miller* two-step. As with the proposal outlined in the preceding section, the court advocated bifurcating the definitional and conduct inquiries.

On the definitional prong, the court advocated a variation on the standard line of business test. Under the totality of the circumstances, the court will consider such factors as: (1) Does the corporation have existing contract rights in the opportunity? (2) Is the business essential to the firm? (3) Does the opportunity represent an area into which the firm would readily or logically seek to expand? (4) Would competition between the firm and the director taking advantage of the opportunity be harmful to the firm? (5) Does the firm have the financial and technical ability to exploit the opportunity? The more of these questions receiving affirmative answers, the more likely it becomes that the prospective venture is a "corporate opportunity."

Where it is clear that under no circumstances could the opportunity be said to belong to the firm (presumably cases in which all of the relevant questions get no answers), the inquiry ends and the director is not liable. Where reasonable people could differ (presumably cases in which some of the questions get yes answers and some get no answers), the court proceeds to the second step. The director should not be held liable "if the evidence establishes that his acquisition [of the venture] did not violate his fiduciary duties of loyalty, good faith, and fair dealing toward the corporation."[15] Unlike the purely disclosure-oriented approach of the proposal advanced above, the *Miller* court advocated yet another totality of the circumstances standard. In this second step, the burden of proof shifts to the director or officer. Relevant factors to be

15. *Miller*'s second step builds on the fairness test proposed by the Massachusetts supreme judicial court in Durfee v. Durfee & Canning, Inc., 80 N.E.2d 522 (Mass.1948), which contends that it is unfair for a director to take advantage of an opportunity for personal profit. To determine whether the director acted improperly, the fairness standard requires "application of ethical standards of what is fair and equitable ... [in] particular sets of facts." Id. at 529.

considered include: (1) In what capacity did the director or officer learn of the opportunity? (2) What is the director's or officer's relationship with the firm? (Presumably, inside directors and officers are held to a stricter standard than outside directors.) (3) To what extent, if any, did the director or officer disclose the venture to the board? (4) To what extent, if any, did the director or officer make use of corporate funds or facilities to exploit the opportunity for personal gain? Liability can be imposed on the director only if both steps of the test are satisfied, so not only must the opportunity properly belong to the firm, but also the director's conduct must constitute a breach of the duty of loyalty and fair dealing.

Applying these factors the court determined that Rudolph and Benjamin had not wrongfully appropriated any opportunities rightfully belonging to Miller Waste. To be sure, at least one of their separate businesses presumably was within Miller Waste's line of business, because it was engaged in competition with Miller Waste. No corporate facilities were used in creating or running the separate business, there was full disclosure of their separate activities, and their separate business had the effect of turning Miller Waste into a very profitable business because they used Miller Waste as the sole source of the raw materials they needed. Accordingly, the creation of the separate businesses did not give rise to liability for breach of the corporate opportunity doctrine.

Guth was an easy case, because Guth acted in such a clearly unfair manner. But *Miller* was an easy case, as well. Rudolph and Benjamin never stole anything from Miller Waste. To the contrary, their operation of a separate set of businesses directly contributed to Miller Waste's continued viability and success. Moreover, they never hid anything, all of their actions were fully disclosed to the directors and shareholders of Miller Waste and, apparently, ratified by the other shareholders. Finally, they never agreed to work full time for Miller Waste—the relationship between them and the firm suggested that they were free to pursue outside business interests. That in doing so they benefited Miller Waste merely redounds to their credit. As a result, while the *Miller* court sought to provide greater clarity, its analysis—like *Guth*'s—scarcely rises above the level of platitude.

Because both steps rely on a totality of the circumstances approach in which numerous factors are relevant but no one is dispositive, *Miller* does not really provide any greater certainty than does the Delaware standard.[16] *Miller*'s second step seems especially problematic. Query why fairness is relevant, especially if the real issue is allocation of property rights? We don't ask whether a thief acted fairly, after all. If certainty is the goal, the first step ought to be a bright line definition. If the venture meets that bright-line standard, the property right to information relat-

---

16. See, e.g., Northeast Harbor Golf Club, Inc. v. Harris, 661 A.2d 1146, 1150 (Me.1995) ("the test adopted in *Miller* merely piles the uncertainty and vagueness of the fairness test on top of the weaknesses in the line of business test").

ing to the venture should be allocated to the corporation. In the second step, we therefore ought to ask whether the director or officer disclosed the venture and received permission to take it for personal gain.

3. The ALI approach

ALI PRINCIPLES § 5.05 bifurcates the definitional and conduct inquiries, requiring the court to ask two distinct questions: (1) Was the business venture was a corporate opportunity within the definition of § 5.05(b)? (2) If so, was the venture properly rejected by the appropriate decisionmaker per § 5.05(a).[17] As with the proposal outlined above, the ALI PRINCIPLES thus focus on disclosure and rejection by the corporation.

ALI PRINCIPLES § 5.05(b) identifies four distinct ways in which a venture might be deemed a corporate opportunity. Note that the four definitions are phrased in the disjunctive, such that the venture will be deemed a corporate opportunity if any of the four is satisfied:

- A business venture of which a director or senior executive becomes aware in connection with the performance of his functions as a director or senior executive. (§ 5.05(b)(1)(A))

- A business venture of which a director or senior executive becomes aware under circumstances that should reasonably lead the director or senior executive to believe that the person offering the opportunity expects it to be offered to the corporation. (§ 5.05(b)(1)(A))

- A business venture of which a director or senior executive becomes aware through the use of corporation information or property and which the director or senior executive reasonably should be expected to believe would be of interest to the corporation. (§ 5.05(b)(1)(B))

- Any business venture of which a senior executive becomes aware and knows is closely related to a business in which the corporation is engaged or expects to engage. (§ 5.05(b)(2))

Note that the fourth definition, which resembles the common law line of business standard, applies only to senior executives. Outside directors thus have greater freedom to engage in business ventures that fall within the firm's line of business.

Suppose the Delaware supreme court had adopted this approach. Would *Broz* have been decided any differently? Probably not. Michigan–2 likely would be deemed a corporate opportunity under § 5.05(b)(2), but that section applies only to senior executives. As for the other three categories, the *Broz* facts do not fall within any of them. Broz learned of

---

17. Courts in several jurisdictions have adopted ALI PRINCIPLES § 5.05. See, e.g., Northeast Harbor Golf Club v. Harris, 661 A.2d 1146 (Me.1995); Derouen v. Murray, 604 So.2d 1086 (Miss.1992); see also Klinicki v. Lundgren, 695 P.2d 906 (Or.1985) (adopting the earlier version set out in Tentative Draft number 3 of the ALI PRINCIPLES); see also Demoulas v. Demoulas Super Mkts., 677 N.E.2d 159 (Mass.1997) (doctrinal statement claimed to be consistent with ALI approach). Cases rejecting the ALI approach include: Ostrowski v. Avery, 703 A.2d 117 (Conn.1997).

the opportunity in his individual capacity, not while performing corporate functions. The broker who brought the venture to Broz's attention specifically avoided offering it to the firm. Broz made no use of corporate property or assets.

If a venture is deemed a corporate opportunity, § 5.05(a) generally requires disclosure and rejection by a proper corporate decisionmaker. As for the disclosure prong of the standard, there must be full disclosure of both the venture and the resulting conflict of interest. Per ALI PRINCIPLES § 5.05(d), good faith but defective disclosure may be cured by corrective disclosure followed by ratification of the decision by the corporate decisionmaker who initially made the decision to reject it.

As for the rejection prong, a post-disclosure rejection of the opportunity by an appropriate corporate decisionmaker does not foreclose judicial review but does affect the standard of review. The disinterested shareholders may either reject the venture before the director or senior executive takes it or ratify a prior taking. If there is valid shareholder action, judicial review is limited to determining whether the decision amounts to a waste of corporate assets, with the burden of proof on the plaintiff.[18] The disinterested directors may reject a venture before it is taken by a director, but may not ratify a taking ex post.[19] In the case of a senior executive who is not a director, the venture may be rejected in advance—but not ratified—by a disinterested superior. In either of the latter cases, the business judgment rule provides the standard of review. Finally, if none of those conditions are satisfied, a director or senior executive can also avoid liability by showing that the transaction was fair to the corporation.[20]

Note that all of these provisions require an affirmative rejection of the opportunity by some decisionmaker acting on the corporation's behalf. Is a director or officer per se liable for taking an opportunity without first presenting it to the board? Not per se, but the odds of escaping liability are slim. If the only reason the officer or director did not offer the opportunity to the corporation was a good faith belief that the business venture was not a corporate opportunity, § 5.05(e) is applicable. This section permits ex post ratification under those circumstances. When § 5.05(e) is read together with § 5.05(a), however, it appears that only ex post ratification by the disinterested shareholders will be availing. Consequently, the fairness of the defendant's conduct standing alone is not a defense under § 5.05. This seemingly harsh rule is justified by the need for certainty and the need to encourage directors and senior executives to resolve close cases in favor of disclosure.

C. Defenses

1. Capacity

Those charged with usurping a corporate opportunity frequently defend their conduct by claiming they learned of the opportunity in their

---

18. ALI PRINCIPLES § 5.05(a)(3)(C).

19. ALI PRINCIPLES § 5.05(a)(3)(B).

20. ALI PRINCIPLES § 5.05(a)(3)(A).

individual—rather than corporate—capacity. Under Delaware law, the capacity in which the defendant learned of the opportunity is a relevant, but not dispositive, consideration.[21] Under the ALI approach, capacity is relevant to determining whether the business venture meets the definition of a corporate opportunity. On the one hand, if the director or senior executive learns of the venture while performing corporate functions, the venture is a corporate opportunity.[22] On the other hand, where a senior executive is concerned, a venture that falls within the corporation's line of business will be deemed a corporate opportunity without regard to the capacity in which the executive learned of the venture. Capacity thus is not a complete defense under either Delaware law or ALI approach.

2. *Financial or technical inability*

In many cases, the defendant will argue that the corporation lacked the money and/or the technical ability to exploit the opportunity. In *General Automotive Manufacturing Co. v. Singer*,[23] for example, defendant Singer was a key managerial employee of General Automotive, a small firm engaged in the business of machine shop jobbing. Singer's employment contract called for him to devote his "entire time, skill, labor and attention" to the job, and to work 5 1/2 days per week. When customers sent business to Singer that he believed General Automotive could not handle, Singer sent the work out to other shops, taking a finder's fee from the customer. Singer took the position that he was running a separate brokering business with respect to orders that General Automotive could not handle. Singer made a profit of $64,088 on his side business, which General Automotive sued to recover. Applying agency law principles analogous to the corporate opportunity doctrine, the court held that Singer had a duty to "exercise good faith by disclosing to Automotive all the facts regarding this matter."

Assume Singer sincerely believed that General Automotive could not handle the work. Assume Singer also sincerely believed that his own reputation might be impaired if General Automotive tried and failed. Even so, Singer should not make this decision on his own in light of his conflicting interest. Put another way, what is the harm in disclosure? On questions of an agent's duty to disclose, it is almost always decisive to ask: "Why didn't you tell me?"

The financial inability defense is even more problematic than the technical incapacity defense proffered by Singer. A director or officer frequently is involved in raising funds for the firm. Consequently, the financial inability defense creates an incentive for directors and officers to fail to use their best efforts to help the firm raise the necessary funds. Put another way, if the defendant director or officer could finance the venture, why should we not assume that the firm likely could have done

---

21. Broz v. Cellular Information Systems, Inc., 673 A.2d 148, 155 (Del.1996).

22. ALI Principles § 5.05(b)(1)(A).

23. 120 N.W.2d 659 (Wis.1963).

so?[24] Conversely, if the defendant director or officer could finance the venture, but the corporation could not, why should we not encourage the director or officer to make his resources available to the corporation at a fair rate of return? As Judge Cardozo put it in *Meinhard v. Salmon*, after all, a fiduciary must renounce thought of self.[25]

Curiously, however, the Delaware supreme court allowed a variant of the financial inability defense in *Broz*. More precisely, the court identified the corporation's financial ability to effectively exploit the business venture as one of the considerations relevant in deciding whether the venture is a corporate opportunity.[26] Worse yet, a number of courts have held that financial and/or technical inability properly can be raised as affirmative defenses.[27]

If the corporation's financial or technical inability to exploit the venture must be considered either as a relevant consideration or an affirmative defense, a position we deplore in light of the perverse incentives it creates, courts still should be sensitive to the conflicted interests at issue in this setting. Consequently, courts should apply a stringent standard to determining financial or technical inability. Delaware Chancellor Chandler, for example, suggests the corporation must be practically defunct before the financial incapacity defense will be given weight. Technical insolvency, such as inability to pay current bills when due or inability to secure credit, is not enough—the corporation must be on the way down the tubes.[28]

3. *Refusal to deal*

In *Energy Resources Corp. v. Porter*,[29] defendant James Porter was a vice-president and head scientist of plaintiff ERCO. Before joining

---

24. A showing that the director or officer failed to use his best efforts to raise the necessary funds will vitiate a financial ability defense. See, e.g., Banks v. Bryant, 497 So.2d 460, 462 (Ala.1986).

25. See Meinhard v. Salmon, 164 N.E. 545, 550 (N.Y.1928). But see Anderson v. Clemens Mobile Homes, Inc., 333 N.W.2d 900, 905 (Neb.1983) (director has no duty "to use or pledge his personal funds to enable the corporation to take advantage of a business opportunity").

26. Broz v. Cellular Information Sys., Inc., 673 A.2d 148, 155–56 (Del.1996). See also Miller v. Miller, 222 N.W.2d 71, 81 (Minn.1974); Hannerty v. Standard Theater Co., 19 S.W. 82, 84 (Mo.1892); Anderson v. Clemens Mobile Homes, Inc., 333 N.W.2d 900, 905 (Neb.1983). In Lussier v. Mau–Van Dev., Inc., 667 P.2d 804 (Hawaii App.1983), the court held that there was no corporate opportunity if the corporation was unable to exploit the venture and the director disclosed it. Id. at 813. Given the benefits of disclosure, this approach seems preferable.

27. See, e.g., Katz Corp. v. T.H. Canty & Co., 362 A.2d 975, 980 (Conn.1975); CST,

Inc. v. Mark, 520 A.2d 469, 471 (Pa.Super.Ct.1987). Cases rejecting financial inability as a defense include: W.H. Elliott & Sons Co. v. Gotthardt, 305 F.2d 544, 546–47 (1st Cir.1962); Irving Trust Co. v. Deutsch, 73 F.2d 121, 124 (2d Cir.1934); Electronic Dev. Co. v. Robson, 28 N.W.2d 130, 138 (Neb.1947).

28. Stephanis v. Yiannatsis, 1993 WL 437487 at *4 (Del.Ch.1993) (quoting 18B Am. Jur. 2d Corporations § 1790 at 642–43 (1985)), aff'd on other grounds, 653 A.2d 275 (Del.1995). See also Jasper v. Appalachian Gas Co., 153 S.W. 50, 55 (Ky.1913); Electronic Dev. Co. v. Robson, 28 N.W.2d 130, 138 (Neb.1947); Klinicki v. Lundgren, 695 P.2d 906, 915 (Or.1985); Nicholson v. Evans, 642 P.2d 727, 732 (Utah 1982). But see Borden v. Sinskey, 530 F.2d 478 (3d Cir.1976); Katz Corp. v. T.H. Canty & Co., 362 A.2d 975 (Conn.1975); Daloisio v. Peninsula Land Co., 127 A.2d 885, 892 (N.J.Super.Ct.App.Div.1956).

29. 438 N.E.2d 391 (Mass.App.1982).

ERCO, Porter had taught chemical engineering at MIT, where he apparently developed professional relationships with two Howard University professors named Cannon and Jackson. The three scientists developed a joint proposal to the Department of Energy for a research grant. Howard University was designated the lead applicant, with ERCO acting as a subcontractor. Porter, Cannon, and Jackson are all African–Americans. Howard University is a historically black college. Jackson subsequently decided that he did not want to serve as a front "for white firms getting minority money." Accordingly, Jackson persuaded Porter to leave ERCO and start his own firm (called EEE in the opinion). Jackson and Porter eliminated ERCO from the application, substituting EEE as the subcontractor. Porter misled ERCO management as to both the status of the application and his reasons for quitting. After Jackson and Porter won the government grant, ERCO sued Porter for usurping a corporate opportunity.

Porter relied on the so-called "refusal to deal" defense. Porter argued—and the trial court agreed—that Jackson's refusal to deal with ERCO relieved Porter of his obligations to ERCO. The appeals court reversed, holding that a refusal to deal must be disclosed to the corporation before an officer or director may take the opportunity for personal gain. The result should be noncontroversial. A contrary result would encourage officers or directors to avoid the corporate opportunity doctrine simply by finding an intransigent partner willing to make the requisite objections. At the very least, Porter owed ERCO the chance to call Jackson's bluff—and perhaps to submit a rival application if Jackson was adamant in his refusal to deal.

§ 7.4   Fiduciary duties of controlling shareholders

A.   Introduction

As the corporation's nexus of contracts, the board of directors hires the various factors of production necessary for the firm to conduct its affairs. Hence, for example, the board hires equity capital by selling stock to investors. As explained in Chapter 9, the contract by which the board hires equity capital imposes fiduciary duties on the board for the benefit of the shareholders. Because investors are assumed to buy stock with the goal of maximizing their own wealth, however, shareholders stand in a fundamentally different position in relation to each other than directors stand in relation to shareholders. One thus would not expect that the fiduciary standards would be the same.

At early common law, it was well-settled that a shareholder acting as a shareholder was entitled to vote his shares without regard to the interests of other shareholders.[1] As a general matter, it remains the law

§ 7.4

1. See, e.g., Haldeman v. Haldeman, 197 S.W. 376, 381 (Ky.1917) ("A stockholder may in a stockholders' meeting vote with the view of his own benefit; he represents himself only.").

that shareholders qua shareholders are allowed to act selfishly in deciding how to vote their shares.[2] Conversely, where a shareholder is elected
to the board of directors, and acts in his capacity as a director, the
shareholder-director naturally assumes fiduciary obligations towards the
other shareholders.[3]

Falling between those two extremes is the case of a shareholder with
voting control. Absent cumulative voting, such a shareholder's voting
power will suffice to elect the entire board of directors. Recognizing that
such a board may not act independently of the controlling shareholder,
courts early began to extend the board's fiduciary duties to the controlling shareholder.[4] Agency concepts provide a useful way of looking at the
problem. Under familiar principles of vicarious liability, the controlling
shareholder can be held liable (as principal) for the acts of the directors
(as its agents). In other words, it is not necessary to disturb the notion
that shareholders as such are independent of the corporation and of each
other. Instead, the controlling shareholder is derivatively liable for the
misconduct of its agents.[5] To be sure, courts do not require proof of an
agency relationship between the controlling shareholder and the board.
Instead, they ask whether the shareholder controlled the corporation
and whether the board lacked independence.

B. Identifying controlling shareholders

In the federal securities laws, there is a presumption that a shareholder who owns ten percent or more of the voting stock has control.[6]
ALI PRINCIPLES § 1.10(b) likewise presumes a shareholder who owns
more than 25 percent of the voting stock has control. It is certainly true
that a shareholder who owns relatively small amounts of stock nevertheless can exercise effective control. John D. Rockefeller, for example,
succeeded in his famous struggle to oust the chairman of the board of
Standard Oil of Indiana despite controlling only 14.9 percent of Standard
Oil's stock. A bright-line presumption of control, however, is inappropri-

---

2. See, e.g., Thorpe v. CERBCO, Inc.,
1993 WL 443406 at *5 (Del.Ch.1993); Gabhart v. Gabhart, 370 N.E.2d 345, 355 (Ind.
1977).

3. Zahn v. Transamerica Corp., 162
F.2d 36, 45 (3d Cir.1947) ("there is a radical difference when a stockholder is voting
strictly as a stockholder and when voting as
a director; that when voting as a stockholder he may have the legal right to vote with
a view of his own benefits and to represent
himself only; but that when he votes as a
director he represents all the stockholders
in the capacity of a trustee for them and
cannot use his office as a director for his
personal benefit at the expense of the stockholders.").

4. See, e.g., Southern Pac. Co. v. Bogert,
250 U.S. 483, 487–88 (1919) ("The majority

[shareholder] has the right to control; but
when it does so, it occupies a fiduciary
relation toward the minority, as much so as
the corporation itself or its officers and
directors."). The standard citation for this
proposition remains Pepper v. Litton, 308
U.S. 295 (1939), in which Justice Douglas
famously opined: "A director is a fiduciary.
So is a dominant or controlling stockholder
or group of stockholders." Id. at 306 (citations omitted).

5. Cf. Summa Corp. v. Trans World Air-
lines, Inc., 540 A.2d 403 (Del.1988) (imposing liability on controlling shareholder
where "no independent board" would have
taken the challenged action).

6. A.A. Sommer, Jr., Who's "In Control"?—SEC, 21 Bus. Law. 559, 568 (1966).

ate in this setting. The basis for imposing fiduciary obligations on a controlling shareholder is not mere ownership of a specified amount of stock, but rather the creation of a de facto agency relationship between the shareholder and the board of directors. In other words, the question is whether a majority of the board lacks independence from the allegedly controlling shareholder.[7] Determining whether such a relationship exists necessarily must be done on a case by case basis. Any bright-line rule inevitably will be set arbitrarily and therefore prove simultaneously over-and under-inclusive.

Under Delaware law, a shareholder is deemed to have control if the shareholder either owns a majority of the voting stock or exercises control over corporate decisionmaking.[8] If the shareholder owns less than 50 percent of the voting stock, plaintiff must show evidence of actual control of corporate conduct.[9] Consequently, for example, the Delaware supreme court in *Kahn v. Lynch Communication Systems, Inc.*,[10] held that a 43.3 percent shareholder exercised control, not based on the number of shares it owned, but because the board of directors deferred to the shareholder's wishes.

Kahn's emphasis on board domination carried over into the standard of review applicable to alleged misconduct by a controlling shareholder. In *Kahn*, the controlling shareholder attempted to freezeout the

7. See Odyssey Partners, L.P. v. Fleming Companies, Inc., 735 A.2d 386, 407 (Del.Ch.1999) ("A party alleging domination and control of the majority of a company's board of directors, and thus the company itself, bears the burden of proving such control by showing a lack of independence on the part of a majority of the directors."). Put another way, as Delaware Vice Chancellor Jack Jacobs accurately observed, the concern in this context is "the potential for process manipulation by the controlling stockholder, and the concern that the controlling stockholder's continued presence might influence even a fully informed shareholder vote." In re Wheelabrator Technologies, Inc. Shareholders Litigation, 663 A.2d 1194, 1205 (Del.Ch.1995). If the shareholder lacks the power to so manipulate the process, there is no justification for departing from the traditional view that shareholders are entitled to act in their own self-interest.

8. See, e.g., Ivanhoe Partners v. Newmont Mining Corp., 535 A.2d 1334, 1344 (Del.1987) ("a shareholder owes a fiduciary duty only if it owns a majority interest in or exercises control over the business affairs of the corporation"); Solomon v. Armstrong, 747 A.2d 1098, 1116 n. 53 (Del.Ch.1999) ("Under Delaware law, the notion of a 'controlling' stockholder includes both *de jure* control and *de facto* control."). Conversely, where corporate action requires a superma-

jority shareholder vote and the majority shareholder's holdings are below the super-majority threshold, actual control may not exist. Cf. Gould v. Ruefenacht, 471 U.S. 701, 705 (1985) (federal securities law opinion noting that control may not exist where a supermajority clause is present).

9. See, e.g., Emerald Partners v. Berlin, 726 A.2d 1215, 1221 n. 8 (Del.1999); Kahn v. Lynch Communication Sys., 638 A.2d 1110 (Del.1994); Citron v. Fairchild Camera & Instrument Corp., 569 A.2d 53, 70 (Del. 1989). Similar standards have been adopted in other jurisdictions, as well. See, e.g., Locati v. Johnson, 980 P.2d 173, 176 (Or.App. 1999) ("In order to be a controlling shareholder who owes fiduciary duties a shareholder must either be (1) an individual who owns a majority of the shares or who, for other reasons, has domination or control of the corporation or (2) a member of a small group of shareholders who collectively own a majority of shares or otherwise have that domination or control."); cf. Essex Universal Corp. v. Yates, 305 F.2d 572 (2d Cir. 1962) (putting burden on 28.3 percent stockholder to rebut presumption of control by showing that another block could outvote the 38.3 percent stockholder or other circumstances would lead shareholders to band together to oppose the 28.3 percent stockholder).

10. 638 A.2d 1110 (Del.1994).

minority shareholders via a merger. In such a transaction, the controlling shareholder bears the burden or proving the transaction's "entire fairness." If the transaction has been approved by a committee of independent directors or by a fully informed majority of the minority shareholders, however, the burden of proof shifts to the plaintiff on the issue of fairness. In general, disinterested director approval of a controlling shareholder transaction thus will provide a significant layer of protection against challenges by minority shareholders.

C. Parent-subsidiary transactions

One of corporation law's central legal fictions is the idea that a corporation is a legal person possessing most of the rights and powers of a natural person. One of the resulting powers with which corporations are endowed is that of owning stock in another corporation. Consequently, one corporation may own all or part of the stock of a second corporation. If Corporation A owns 100 percent of the stock of Corporation B, for example, we refer to Corporation A as the parent and Corporation B as a wholly-owned subsidiary. If Corporation A owns only 51 percent of Corporation B's voting stock, Corporation A still would be called the parent, but Corporation B now would be called a majority-owned subsidiary. This nomenclature change reflects an important change in the ownership structure of Corporation B. Corporation A is still the principal stockholder, but now there are outsiders who own a minority interest in the firm. Logically enough, these outsiders are termed minority shareholders. (If Corporation A controls Corporation B, while owning less than a majority of the stock, Corporation B would be referred to as a minority-controlled subsidiary.)

Transactions between parent companies and wholly-owned subsidiaries rarely raise corporate law concerns, beyond whatever ministerial requirements the statutes may impose. In contrast, transactions between parent corporations and their majority-owned or minority-controlled subsidiaries have been a fertile field for litigation. Understandably, minority shareholders often feel that the parent company is using its voting control of the subsidiary to benefit itself at their expense. In such cases, the minority asserts that the parent company should owe them a duty of loyalty comparable to that owed by directors.

1. The canonical Sinclair Oil opinion

The canonical parent-subsidiary case remains the Delaware supreme court's opinion in *Sinclair Oil v. Levien*.[11] Sinclair Oil owned 97 percent of the stock of a subsidiary, the Sinclair Venezuelan Oil Company (Sinven), with the remaining 3 percent being held by minority shareholders. A minority shareholder challenged three transactions between Sinclair Oil and Sinven: (1) Payment of large cash dividends by Sinven; (2) Sinclair Oil's use of other (wholly-owned) subsidiaries to develop oil

---

11. Sinclair Oil Corp. v. Levien, 280 A.2d 717 (Del.1971).

fields located outside of Venezuela; and (3) Sinclair Oil's actions with respect to a contract between Sinven and another Sinclair Oil subsidiary.

What standard of review should a court apply to such disputes? The Delaware supreme court identified two standards potentially applicable in such situations: the business judgment rule and the intrinsic fairness rule. Under the business judgment rule, the directors of Sinven get the benefit of a rebuttable presumption of good faith. Under the intrinsic fairness test, the burden of proof is on the directors to show, subject to close scrutiny, that the transactions were objectively fair to Sinven. In this case, as in most, it mattered quite a lot which standard applied. As is often the case, the party bearing the burden of proof on a given dispute lost.

Under Sinclair Oil, a court will apply the intrinsic fairness standard, as opposed to the business judgment rule, when the parent has received a benefit "to the exclusion and at the expense of the subsidiary."[12] In other words, the fiduciary obligations owed by a parent corporation are limited to self-dealing. The more exacting intrinsic fairness standard comes into play only when the parent is on both sides of the transaction and, moreover, used its position to extract nonpro rata benefits from a transaction to the minority shareholders' detriment.

The *Sinclair Oil* opinion began with a summary of the court's prior decision in *Getty Oil Co. v. Skelly Oil Co.*[13] In that case, a regulatory agency overseeing oil imports concluded that Skelly was controlled by Getty. As a result, the agency further determined that Skelly was no longer entitled to a separate allocation of imported crude oil. Skelly sued Getty, contending that it was entitled to a share of Getty's allocation. The court upheld Getty's refusal to share its allocation with Skelly, applying the business judgment rule. Intrinsic fairness was inapplicable, because Getty had not received a benefit at the expense of Skelly. Getty gained nothing to which it was not already entitled. Accordingly, no self-dealing, no intrinsic fairness review, and no liability.

The *Sinclair Oil* opinion then turned to whether Sinven's dividend payment policy violated Sinclair's fiduciary duties. Sinven had paid out large amounts of dividends during the applicable period—dividends that in fact exceeded its earnings. Plaintiff contended that the dividends resulted from an improper motive; namely, Sinclair's need for cash. The court applied the business judgment rule to this dispute. Because the minority shareholders had received a pro rata share of the dividends, Sinclair did not receive a nonpro rata benefit at their expense. The dividends were within the limits proscribed by the relevant legal capital statute and were not so large as to amount to a waste of corporate assets. Accordingly, plaintiff was unable to rebut the business judgment rule's presumption of good faith. In dicta, the court suggested that the

12. Sinclair Oil Corp. v. Levien, 280 A.2d 717, 720 (Del.1971). See also Case v. New York Central Railroad Co., 204 N.E.2d 643 (N.Y.1965) (applying business judgment rule because parent had not benefited at minority's expense).

13. 267 A.2d 883 (Del.1970).

intrinsic fairness test would be applied to dividend decisions in which there are two classes of stock and dividends are paid on the class owned by the parent but not on the class owned by the minority. This example implicates the conflict of classes discussed in the next section.

The court next took up plaintiff's claim that Sinclair Oil had prevented Sinven from expanding. The Chancellor had applied the intrinsic fairness standard to this issue, concluding that Sinclair had improperly and unfairly denied Sinven opportunities to expand its operations outside of Venezuela. On appeal, the Delaware supreme court reversed, identifying the business judgment rule as the proper standard of review. Plaintiff could point to no opportunities that Sinclair had usurped from Sinven. Absent the taking of a corporate opportunity properly belonging to Sinven, the decision of which subsidiary would be allowed to act outside of Venezuela was a business judgment for Sinclair Oil to make.[14] Again, the key consideration was that Sinclair Oil did not take anything away from Sinven that belonged to Sinven.

Finally, the court turned to a contract between another Sinclair Oil subsidiary and Sinven. Sinclair Oil had used its power to cause Sinven to enter into a contract to exclusively sell oil to a wholly-owned Sinclair Oil subsidiary. When that subsidiary breached the contract, Sinclair Oil prevented Sinven from suing to enforce its contract rights. According to the court, this issue properly was reviewed under the intrinsic fairness standard. Forcing Sinven to contract with a Sinclair Oil entity was itself self-dealing. Because the contract was breached and not enforced, moreover, Sinclair Oil had gotten a nonpro rata benefit from the contract at the expense of the minority. Accordingly, Sinclair Oil had to show that its failure to enforce the contract was intrinsically fair to Sinven, which it could not do.

2. Zahn v. Transamerica and conflicts between classes of stock

It is instructive to compare *Sinclair Oil* with the Third Circuit's decision in *Zahn v. Transamerica Corp.*[15] At first blush, *Zahn* seems to present the same sort of issues discussed in *Sinclair Oil*—a majority shareholder who benefited itself at the minority's expense. On closer examination, however, there are some interesting complications. In particular, *Zahn* posed the question: What obligations does the board of directors have when there is more than a single class of stock?

Plaintiff was a minority shareholder of Axton–Fisher Tobacco Co., a Kentucky corporation. Plaintiff challenged a decision by Axton–Fisher's board to redeem a class of Axton–Fisher shares prior to liquidation of the firm. It is important to understand the capital and ownership structure of Axton–Fisher in order to understand the case and the holding. Axton–Fisher had 3 class of shares: (1) Preferred shares with a par value of $100, a cumulative dividend preference of $6 per year, and a liquidation

---

14. See David J. Greene & Co. v. Dunhill Int'l, Inc., 249 A.2d 427 (Del.Ch.1968) (invoking corporate opportunity doctrine to hold parent liable for usurping an opportunity from a majority-owned subsidiary).

15. 162 F.2d 36 (3d Cir.1947).

preference of $105 plus accrued dividends; (2) Class A common stock; and (3) Class B common stock. In the case at bar, only the latter two classes were in play. The rights of those two classes differed in five significant areas:

- The Class A stock had an annual cumulative dividend of $3.20, while the Class B stock had a $1.60 annual dividend. If dividends above the specified minimums were paid, such dividends were shared equally by the two classes.

- The Class A could be called (a mandatory redemption) by the firm on 60 days notice at $60 per share plus accrued dividends. The Class B could not be called.

- If the firm was liquidated, the Class A was entitled to receive twice as much per share as the Class B (e.g., if Class B was to get $50 per share on liquidation, Class A would be entitled to $100).

- Class A shares were convertible into Class B shares at the option of the holder at any time on a share for share basis.

- The Class A stock had no voting rights, unless there were four successive failures to pay quarterly dividends, in which case it would receive equal voting rights with the Class B. As of the time of this dispute, Class A had such voting rights. The Class B had full voting rights.

Transamerica owned almost all of the Class B shares and about two-thirds of the Class A stock. Most members of the board were officers or agents of Transamerica.

Axton–Fisher's main asset was leaf tobacco. Because of rationing and shortages caused by the Second World War, the value of its tobacco inventory had risen from about $6 million to about $20 million. Plaintiff alleged that Transamerica devised a scheme to appropriate to itself most of that increase in value. The scheme called for Axton–Fisher's board to call the Class A shares at a price of about $80. Following the redemption, the firm was to be liquidated with the remaining assets being distributed to the Class B shareholders—thus, mainly to Transamerica. If the Class A shares had not been redeemed, they would have received around $240 upon liquidation of the firm.

Once a decision was made to liquidate the firm, the directors had three options: (1) Redeem the Class A shares without disclosing the extent of the appreciation of the inventory and without disclosing their intent to liquidate the firm. (2) Disclose the firm's true value and the liquidation plan, give notice of intent to redeem the Class A stock, then liquidate. (3) Decline to redeem the Class A shares and simply liquidate the company, thereby giving the Class A shareholders twice as much as the Class B shareholders. The issue in this case, put simply, was whether the directors breached their fiduciary duty to the minority shareholders by selecting the first option.

The court held that there was a breach of fiduciary duty. The Class A redemption was effected at the direction of the principal Class B shareholder in order to benefit the Class B stock in preference to the Class A. The *Sinclair Oil* court doubtless would have reached the same result. The directors took an action intended to extract a nonpro rata benefit for the parent at the expense of the minority.

Does this result mean that a similarly placed board is obliged to choose the third option? Put another way, would the result have changed if the directors had selected option 2, disclosed all material facts, and then called the Class A shares for redemption? There is some broad language in the opinion implying that the directors had a fiduciary duty to select option 3—i.e., to liquidate without redemption. But that dictum makes no sense.

Suppose the board had selected option 2. After the board announced its plans, rational Class A shareholders would exercise their conversion rights and become Class B shareholders, sharing equally in the redemption. Option 2 thus gives the minority shareholders a chance to participate equally through exercise of their conversion rights. In such a case, the parent would not be getting anything at the expense of the minority.

There is an even more fundamental reason why the directors should be permitted to follow option 2. Under the nexus of contracts model, the rights of the various classes amount to a contract between the shareholders and the corporation. The contracts governing the Class A shares' rights included a provision giving the firm the option of redeeming their shares at a fixed price if the board saw fit to do so. This term allocated risk between the two classes. The Class A stock had certain dividend and liquidation preferences over the Class B, and thus was a safer stock to be holding if things went badly for the firm. In contrast, the Class B was designed to take second place in many respects, but was to garner the lion's share of the profits if the company was successful. As a result, the Class A stock is more akin to preferred stock than to true common stock.

One purpose of the redemption provisions of the Class A stock was to enable the Class B stock to buy out the former if things went well. If you give someone an option to buy shares at a fixed price, you can hardly complain if that person exercises the option if the shares go up in value. Management's primary duty is to the residual claimants—here, the Class B shareholders. Management had a duty to fulfill its contractual obligations to the Class A holders, including giving them an option to convert their shares, but its primary duty was to maximize the value of the Class B shares. It could balance its obligations to all parties by selecting option 2. The fact that a majority shareholder is in the mix does not change that analysis. In a subsequent decision on damages, the Third Circuit in fact affirmed that what we have called option 2 would be consistent with the board's fiduciary duties.[16]

16. Speed v. Transamerica Corp., 235 F.2d 369, 373 (3d Cir.1956).

D. Sales of control

Suppose a parent corporation or other controlling shareholder wishes to sell its stock in the subsidiary to an outsider. In all probability, this "control block" will sell at a price substantially higher than the market price for the stock. Or, in the case of a close corporation without an active market for its stock, at a price higher than that which minority shares would command. Can the selling shareholder be held liable for failing to share the control premium with the minority?

We can imagine at least 3 possible standards that might be applied to such transactions: (1) A sharing rule, under which every holder of the class of stock in question is entitled to an equal opportunity to sell the holder's shares on a pro rata basis. (2) A no sharing rule, pursuant to which the controlling shareholder is free to sell at the highest price offered by a willing buyer. (3) A fiduciary duty-based rule, which asks whether the sale harms the minority shareholders.

Does our choice of standard depend on the reason the buyer is willing to pay a control premium? Recall that stock consists of two rights: economic and voting. A single share of stock gives the owner little control over the company. The market price of a share of stock thus reflects nothing more than the estimated present value of the future stream of dividends payable on that share. Someone buying a control block of stock, however, obtains significant control through the ability to elect the board of directors. Such control might be valuable if the purchaser believes it can use its position to extract nonpro rata special benefits from the corporation, such as generous salaries, perquisites, and the like. Note that such a sale does not necessarily leave the minority shareholders any worse off. The selling shareholder may well have been doing the same thing. Alternatively, the purchaser may believe that the shares will be worth more in its hands than in those of the incumbent. Perhaps the incumbent is a poor manager. If the stock price is depressed due to poor management, replacing the incumbents with more competent managers should raise the stock price and enable the purchaser to profit.[17] The problem, of course, is that motive can be difficult to

---

17. If so, of course, one must wonder why the purchaser did not attempt to acquire all of the outstanding shares by making an any-and-all offer—i.e., one open to all shareholders pursuant to which the buyer will purchase any and all shares tendered to it. Assume, for example, that the corporation has 100 outstanding shares, currently trading at $10 per share, of which the present controlling shareholder owns 40. The prospective buyer correctly believes that under its management the firm's shares would be worth $20. If the buyer successfully purchases the control block for $19 per share, its stock will produce a $40 profit when the stock price rises to reflect

the company's value under its management. All the other shareholders, however, will also automatically receive a pro rata share of those gains. There is nothing the buyer lawfully can do to capture a nonpro rata share of the gains. As a result, the buyer confers a $600 benefit on the other shareholders. In contrast, if the buyer is able to purchase all the outstanding shares, at any price below $19 per share, its profit will exceed $100. To do so, moreover, it need not persuade all of the other shareholders to sell. As long as the holders of at least 51 shares are willing to sell at a price below $19 per share, our hypothetical buyer will

determine and, moreover, mixed motives often will be present. At the very least, however, the potential for improper motives suggests a need to police sales of control.

1. The general rule

As a general rule, shareholders—controlling or not—are free to dispose of their stock as they see fit and on such terms as a willing buyer offers.[18] One of the risks incident to owning a minority interest in a corporation is that the majority may decide to sell—or decide not to sell—without consulting the minority. The cases setting out the general rule, however, typically go on to identify a number of exceptions. The laundry list usually includes such misconduct as a sale under circumstances indicating that the purchasers intend to loot or mismanage the corporation, the sale involves fraud or misuse of confidential information, the sale amounts to a wrongful appropriation of corporate assets that properly belong to the corporation, or the sale includes a premium for the sale of office.

2. Sale to a looter

Suppose that Susan Stockholder, the controlling shareholder of Acme Inc., sells her control block to Lorraine Looter. Looter then proceeds to loot Acme—she liquidates all the assets, steals the cash from the bank account, and absconds to some Pacific island where she sets up a satellite dish and spends her ill-gotten gains in general debauchery. Looter then dies from one of those nasty diseases to which debauchery so often leads. After casting about for a deep pocket to sue, the minority shareholders sue Susan Stockholder. Liability?

There are not a lot of true sale to looter cases. In the leading *DeBaun v. First Western Bank and Trust Co.* decision, the controlling shareholder was aware of considerable information that should have alerted it to potential problems. A credit report on the prospective buyer indicated a large number of business failures. The purchase price was so high that the buyer would have to tap corporate assets in order to make the required payments. The selling shareholder had obtained but not collected a fraud judgment against the buyer. "Armed with knowledge of these facts," the seller knew or should have known that a sale would be detrimental to the minority shareholders' interests.[19] So, as a general rule, there is no duty to investigate. Where the controlling shareholder is

---

obtain voting control. It may then freeze out the remaining minority shareholders in a subsequent merger at approximately the same price. The most plausible good faith reason a buyer might be unwilling to make an any-and-all offer are risk aversion—a reluctance to put too many of the buyer's eggs into one basket—or a shortage of funds.

    18. For statements of the general rule, see Treadway Companies, Inc. v. Care

Corp., 638 F.2d 357, 375 (2d Cir.1980); Clagett v. Hutchison, 583 F.2d 1259, 1262 (4th Cir.1978); Zetlin v. Hanson Holdings, Inc., 397 N.E.2d 387, 388 (N.Y.1979); Tryon v. Smith, 229 P.2d 251, 254 (Or.1951); Glass v. Glass, 321 S.E.2d 69, 74 (Va.1984).

    19. DeBaun v. First Western Bank and Trust Co., 120 Cal.Rptr. 354, 360 (Cal.App. 1975).

presented with a suspicious character and/or a suspiciously high price, however, the controlling shareholder has a duty to reasonably investigate the buyer's plans.[20]

3. *Sale of office*

Suppose Lorraine Looter agrees to purchase a control block of stock from Susan Stockholder. As part of their agreement, Stockholder promises to transfer control of the board to new directors of Looter's choosing. They effect the transfer through sequential resignations. Assume there are three directors: Stockholder, Frank Flunky, and Corrine Crony. Flunky resigns, which he may do at any time under DGCL § 141(b). Per DGCL § 223(a)(1), vacancies may be filled by majority of remaining directors. Acting pursuant to that statutory grant of authority, Stockholder and Crony then appoint Looter to the board. Crony then resigns, creating a vacancy to be filled by Stockholder and Looter. And so on, until Looter and her nominees hold all board spots. The new board then appoints Looter and her cronies as officers and day-to-day control has changed hands without a formal shareholder vote. Liability?

As a general rule, sales of corporate office are voidable as contrary to public policy. Any portion of the control premium attributable to the sale of office must be forfeited to the minority shareholders.[21] But suppose the buyer acquired a majority of the voting stock. The buyer then waits until the next annual meeting of the shareholders. Absent cumulative voting, the buyer's holdings suffice to elect the entire board. Yet, the minority shareholders would have no cause for complaint. Alternatively, the shareholder could call a special meeting to remove the existing board and elect replacements. Assuming the board may be removed without cause, or is willing to resign en masse, the minority again would have no cause for complaint. Imposing liability on a majority block seller and/or buyer who accomplish the same result by sequential resignations simply elevates form over substance and thus makes little policy sense. But what if the control block is less than a majority of the shares? At least in theory, if the issue were put before them at a meeting, the other shareholders could do something silly—like voting for other directors. In that case, perhaps liability should be imposed where sequential resignations are used to transfer control without a shareholder vote.

In the leading decision, *Essex Universal Corp. v. Yates*,[22] a high-powered three judge panel of the Second Circuit splintered three differ-

---

20. See, e.g., Harris v. Carter, 582 A.2d 222, 235 (Del.Ch.1990) (although the seller is "not a surety for his buyer, when the circumstances would alert a reasonably prudent person to a risk that his buyer is dishonest or in some material respect not truthful, a duty devolves upon the seller to make such inquiry as a reasonably prudent person would make"); see also Gerdes v. Reynolds, 28 N.Y.S.2d 622 (Sup.Ct.1941) (gross inadequacy of price could put seller on inquiry notice); but see Clagett v. Hutch-

ison, 583 F.2d 1259, 1262 (4th Cir.1978) ($34.75 per share price for stock trading at $7.50 to $10 "cannot be said to be so unreasonable as to place [the seller] on notice of the likelihood of fraud on the corporation or the remaining shareholders").

21. See, e.g., Brecher v. Gregg, 392 N.Y.S.2d 776 (Sup.Ct.1975); Gerdes v. Reynolds, 28 N.Y.S.2d 622 (Sup.Ct.1941).

22. 305 F.2d 572 (2d Cir.1962).

ent ways on this question. Chief Judge Lumbard said there should be no liability if the buyer purchased more than 50 percent of the voting stock, because the buyer would eventually get control of the board anyway. If the buyer purchased less than 50 percent, however, liability for sale of office should be imposed unless the buyer "would as a practical certainty have been guaranteed of the stock voting power to choose a majority of the directors." Because the 28.3 percent block acquired by the purchaser is "usually tantamount to majority control" Chief Judge Lumbard would put the burden of proof on the challenger. In contrast, Judge Friendly would hold a sequential resignation plan voidable as contrary to public policy except "when it was entirely plain that a new election would be a mere formality—i.e., when the seller owned more than 50% of the stock." Where the buyer purchases less than 50 percent of the shares, after all, it is not certain that its slate would in fact be elected. Finally, Judge Clark thought such arrangements are not per se unlawful. Instead, their legality was a question of fact to be determined at trial. Query: How?

4.   *Usurping a corporate opportunity*

We come at last to one of corporate law's hoariest chestnuts: *Perlman v. Feldmann*.[23] Newport Steel Corporation, as its name suggests, was a steel manufacturer. During the Korean War demand for steel was very high relative to the available supply of steel. Basic economics tells us that the price of steel should have risen substantially. It did not, however, because the Truman administration had imposed price controls on steel. Newport Steel's dominant shareholder, one C. Russell Feldmann, devised the so-called Feldmann plan, pursuant to which steel purchasers were obliged to extend interest free loans to Newport Steel. The effective price Newport Steel received thus included both the nominal purchase price and the present value of the interest charges it avoided. This was a legal—but somewhat shady—way of getting around the price controls on steel.

A consortium of manufacturers decided to ensure their access to steel by purchasing a steel company. One way to do so, of course, would be to acquire a steel company by means of a merger or tender offer in which all shareholders of the target steel manufacturer would share equally in any premium the consortium was willing to pay. Instead, the consortium formed the Wilport Company, a Delaware corporation, which then purchased Feldman's controlling block of Newport Steel shares at a substantial premium over market. The minority shareholders got nothing and sued. On those facts, the court held for the minority, opining that "siphoning off for personal gain corporate advantages to be derived from a favorable market situation" violated Feldmann's fiduciary duties to the minority.

A simplified example may be helpful. Assume there are 10 Newport Steel shares outstanding, of which Feldmann owns 3. Each year for the

---

23.   219 F.2d 173 (2d Cir.1955).

next ten years Newport Steel is expecting to sell $120 worth of steel. Ignoring expenses, assume projected annual earnings of $120 or $12 per share, $10 per share of which represents the sale of steel at the controlled price, and $2 per share of which represents cash flows generated by the Feldmann Plan. How much is one share of stock worth? In the real world, we would have to take into account the time value of money and risk by projecting the cash flow into the future and discounting the anticipated cash flows back to present value. To keep the problem simple, we will ignore that complication and assume each share of stock is worth $120 ($12 earnings per year per shore times ten years). If Wilport obtains control by purchasing Feldman's stock, it will get to decide who may purchase Newport Steel's output. Presumably, Wilport will force Newport Steel to sell all of its output to Wilport, a fact of which the court made much. But so what? As long as Newport is operating at full capacity and Wilport pays the maximum controlled price, the minority are no worse off under Wilport than they were under Feldmann. The kicker therefore is that Wilport also gets to decide whether or not to keep the Feldmann plan in place. If Wilport buys Newport and keeps the plan in place, it will pay $120 per year for steel. If Wilport buys Newport and cancels the plan, it will only pay $100 per year for Steel. Suppose Wilport pays Feldmann $150 per share ($450) for his stock and then cancels the Feldmann plan. Feldmann received $30 more than the stock is worth on a per share basis—a control premium. Everybody else now has stock that is worth only $100 ($10 earnings per year per shore, reflecting loss of Feldmann plan revenues, times ten years). Wilport thus paid $450 for stock that is only worth $300, but Wilport will save $20 per year on the price it pays for Steel, which translates into $200 over the ten year period for which we are projecting earnings. So Wilport is better off by a net of $50. The decline of $150 in the value of its Newport shares is off-set by the $200 it saves in costs.

Perlman v. Feldmann thus presented a very unique set of facts: (1) A unique profit making opportunity was available to the corporation only because of the government price controls. (2) The value of that profit making opportunity could be capitalized and divided between the purchaser and seller of the control block. (3) The minority shareholders thus lost significant sums that otherwise would have come to them in the ordinary course. So understood, *Perlman* is a very simple case. *Perlman* does not stand for the proposition that a controlling shareholder must give all other shareholders an equal opportunity to sell their stock on a pro rata basis. Instead, it simply stands for the proposition that a controlling shareholder may not usurp an opportunity that should be available to all shareholders. One could have reached the very same result under a *Sinclair Oil*-style analysis. The controlling shareholder received a benefit "to the exclusion and at the expense" of the minority. Not only were the minority excluded from the opportunity to sell at a premium, they were left worse off as a result.

Beyond *Perlman*'s unique facts, where are corporate opportunity issues most likely to arise? Probably in connection with structuring of acquisitions. Suppose Lorraine Looter approaches Susan Stockholder with an offer to buy Stockholder's control block at a premium. Should there be liability? Not if we adopt the *Sinclair Oil* analogy. The majority shareholder can do whatever she wants as long as she does not deprive the minority shareholders of something to which they are entitled. On these facts, there is no corporate opportunity to be usurped. But suppose Looter approached Stockholder with a slightly different proposal, under which Acme would be merged into a corporation owned by Looter. Stockholder rejects the merger proposal, but offers to sell Looter her control block at a premium. On these facts, the *Perlman* court likely would impose liability. The *Perlman* court found that Feldmann breached his fiduciary duty to the minority shareholders by arranging the transaction so that only Feldmann and his cronies shared in the premium. Susan Stockholder has done essentially the same thing. The original offer was a merger in which all shareholders would have a chance to participate. But the controlling shareholder refused to go along, effectively saying: "if you don't buy me out at a premium over what everybody else gets—no deal." Looter had no choice but to go along, thereby denying the minority shareholders an opportunity to share in the control premium. Stockholder abused her position to usurp an opportunity available to all shareholders.

5.   *Building a better approach to sales of control*

Courts have not imposed a general obligation for controlling shareholders to share a control premium with the minority. The conventional explanation given by the courts is that it is not per se wrong for a controlling shareholder to sell at a price significantly higher than that available to noncontrolling shareholders. It becomes wrong only under special circumstances, such as sale to a looter, sale of office, or taking of a corporate opportunity. In contrast, many scholars have argued for some sort of sharing or equal opportunity rule.[24] Should we adopt such a rule? In short, no.

One of the risks minority shareholders assume when they acquire stock in a corporation with a controlling shareholder is that the latter may sell at a premium without giving the minority an opportunity to participate. If the control block existed when the minority shareholder invested, the minority shareholder presumably paid a lower per share price than he would have paid in the absence of a controlling shareholder. In other words, assuming full disclosure, the minority became shareholders having accepted as adequate whatever trade-off was offered in recompense. Even if the control block was assembled after the minority shareholder invested, moreover, the possibility that such a block would

---

24. Compare William D. Andrews, The Stockholder's Right to Equal Opportunity in the Sale of Shares, 78 Harv. L. Rev. 505, 506 (1965) (shareholders should have an "equal opportunity to participate ratably" on substantially the same terms) with Frank Easterbrook & Daniel Fischel, Corporate Control Transactions, 91 Yale L.J. 698 (1982) ("those who produce a gain should be allowed to keep it, subject to the constraint that other parties to the transaction be at least as well off as before the transaction").

be assembled is one of those risks of which a rational shareholder should be aware in making pricing decisions.

Bounded rationality and other transaction cost obstacles to complete contracting, of course, somewhat weaken the foregoing argument's force. Even if the pricing mechanism does not adequately protect minority shareholders, however, there are still efficiency arguments in favor of a no sharing rule. If we believe corporate takeovers promote economic efficiency by displacing inefficient incumbent managers, for example, controlling shareholders generally should be allowed to keep their premiums. Unequal distribution lowers the cost of doing takeovers, because the new controlling shareholder only needs to buy the control block, which should result in more takeovers. Giving the controlling shareholders a special premium, moreover, essentially bribes them to quit. Consequently, a no sharing rule should facilitate replacement of inefficient incumbents.

The *Sinclair Oil* analogy provides the right default rule. As long as the controlling shareholder does nothing to leave the minority worse off, it should be allowed to sell on whatever terms the market will bear. Doing so is consistent with the reasonable expectations of minority shareholders and promotes efficient changes in control. If controlling shareholders could engage in transactions that affirmatively injure the minority, however, the latter doubtless would take precautions to prevent such transactions. By providing a coercive backstop preventing such transactions, the *Sinclair Oil*-based default rule minimizes bargaining and enforcement costs.

6. *Refusals to sell*

Courts make cases like *Sinclair Oil* or *Perlman* unnecessarily difficult by blurring the distinction between director and shareholder fiduciary duties. Consider the sale of office cases: The real problem in these cases is not the sale of a control block, but rather the directors' abdication of their duty to make an informed business judgment. Instead of exercising their best individual business judgment, they mindlessly followed a contractual obligation.

Only rarely do you get cases that starkly presents the question of shareholder duties qua shareholder duties without any intervening issue of director duties. Delaware Chancellor Allen's decision in *Mendel v. Carroll* is about as clear an example of such a case as one can ever expect to get. The Carroll Family collectively controlled Katy Industries, Inc., owning at various times 48 to 52% of the stock. Even when they did not have an outright majority, their status as the largest shareholder ensured that they had effective control.

The Carroll family proposed a freezeout merger that would have cashed out the minority shareholders at about $26 per share.[25] The board set up a special committee comprised of independent directors to consid-

---

25. On freeze-out mergers, see § 7.4.E.

er the offer. A competing offer was made by a group organized by a fellow named Sanford Pensler at about $28 per share. The Carroll Family withdrew their merger proposal, but also announced they had no interest in selling their shares.[26] Their opposition to the Pensler proposal effectively precluded it from going forward. Minority shareholders sued, alleging both that the Carroll Family violated its fiduciary duties and that the board of directors violated its fiduciary duties.

If Carroll Family directors had voted on the proposal, the Carroll Family would have been on both sides of the deal. Because the board used a special committee of independent directors to make the decision, however, thereby keeping the Carroll Family out of the board's decision-making process, there are no complicating issues of whether any member of the Carroll Family had director duties. Instead, we have two distinct issues: (1) did the directors violate their fiduciary duties by failing to act against the majority shareholders' interests; (2) did the majority share-holder violate its fiduciary duty to the minority?

As to the board's duties, plaintiff argued that the originally proposed freezeout merger amounted to a shift in control. Under Delaware law governing corporate takeovers, where such a shift in control occurs the board of directors has a fiduciary duty to maximize immediate sharehold-er value.[27] The Carroll Family proposal was only $26, Pensler offered $28. The Pensler deal therefore was the better deal and the board had a duty to take it. The board responded by arguing that the Carroll Family would not sell their shares. If the family will not go along, a deal cannot be done. Consequently, the board's duty to the shareholders is limited to getting the best deal possible given the Carroll Family's intransigence. Plaintiff replied that the board was obligated under these circumstances to act against the majority shareholders' interest. Plaintiff suggested the board sell additional shares to the Pensler group, thereby diluting the Carroll Family holdings to the point at which they no longer had control.

Chancellor Allen left open the possibility that a board might some-times be required to act against the majority's interest. Because the board also owes fiduciary duties to the majority, however, he limited this possibility to cases in which the majority shareholder is overreaching and trying to injure the minority. On the facts, this was not such a case. Allen pointed out that the plaintiff's argument broke down at several points. First, because the Carroll Family already had effective control at all relevant times, nothing they did amounted to a shift of control, and the takeover precedents were irrelevant. Second, Allen also took issue with the proposition that $28 was a better deal for the shareholders than $26. The Carroll Family already had control. Their offer thus would not include a control premium. The Pensler group was trying to buy control.

26. As a business matter, why was the Carroll Family so adamant about not selling their shares? We can only speculate, of course, but one suspects the company had substantial free cash flow. The company was said to be "awash in capital." The board had enough money laying around to propose a $14 per share dividend.

27. See Revlon, Inc. v. MacAndrews & Forbes Holdings, Inc., 506 A.2d 173 (Del. 1985).

The fact that they were only willing to pay a $2 control premium suggests that they might be low-balling the shareholders. Of course, Allen did not need to decide whether $28 from Pensler was in fact better or worse for the shareholders than $26 from the Carroll Family. In the absence of a showing that the board acted from conflicted interests, he properly left that issue to the board.

Turning to the fiduciary duties of controlling shareholders, the majority opinion in *Perlman v. Feldmann* had analogized shareholders to partners, drawing special attention to the broad dicta Judge Cardozo's famous *Meinhard v. Salmon* opinion. If we take Cardozo literally, partners may not behave selfishly towards one another. If we take *Perlman* literally, neither may "corporate fiduciaries." If we apply *Meinhard* and *Perlman* to the facts of *Mendel*, surely we conclude that the Carroll Family was acting selfishly, probably motivated by their desire to retain control over the firm's free cash flow.

Allen touched on the sale of control cases in passing. On the one hand, he recognized the legitimacy of sales of control at a premium. At the same time, however, he noted that liability for sale of control at a premium over market could be imposed in the usual cases of sale to looters, sale of office, or usurpation of corporate opportunity. In any event, *Mendel* involved the reverse situation: where the controlling shareholder refused to sell and, by that refusal, prevented a takeover. In that context, Allen held that self-sacrifice is not required. The family had no obligation to sell.

In connection with the sale of control cases, we suggested that liability should be imposed where the minority shareholders are worse off after the transaction than before. Why should that rule not be extended to cases in which the controlling shareholder refuses to sell? One answer may be the well-established distinction in tort between action and inaction. Another is that such a rule would amount to a species of private eminent domain—the would-be buyer can effectively condemn the majority shareholders' interest and force them to sell. Finally, on the facts, it was not clear the minority was injured. The price they paid for their shares presumably impounded the risk of intransigence by the Carrolls.

E.   Freezeouts

In a freezeout transaction, the controlling shareholder buys out the minority shareholders, even if the minority object. The transaction typically is effected using a so-called triangular merger in which the corporation is merged with a wholly owned subsidiary of the controlling shareholder. A merger combines two corporations to form a single firm. After a merger, only one of the two companies will survive, but that survivor succeeds by operation of law to all of the assets, liabilities, rights, and obligations of the two constituent corporations. In addition, a merger also converts the shares of each constituent corporation into whatever consideration was specified in the merger agreement. Suppose the merger agreement provided that minority shareholders were to receive $50 per share in cash. After the merger takes place, their shares are transformed by operation of law into a mere IOU for the promised cash payment.

Corporate law originally required unanimous shareholder approval of mergers. The unanimity requirement created serious holdout problems, allowing dissenting minorities to block Kaldor–Hicks efficient transactions. In the 1800s, the necessary vote was reduced in most states to a majority of the outstanding shares. A few states have slightly higher vote requirements, such as two-thirds, but none retains the old unanimity requirement.

Taken together, these rules provide the controlling shareholder with a form of private eminent domain. Its shares standing alone may suffice to approve the merger, even if every other shareholder votes against it. Assuming the merger is approved, the minority shareholders will be forced to accept the consideration specified in the merger agreement.

Although minority shareholders have no power to block a freezeout merger, they are not wholly lacking in remedies. When states began moving away from the unanimity requirement, they also created the statutory appraisal proceeding. In brief, appraisal rights give dissenting shareholders the right to have the fair value of their shares determined and paid to them in cash, provided that the dissenting shareholder complies with specified procedures.[28] In practice, however, appraisal is not a very attractive remedy. Getting a shareholder to the point where the statutes permit exercise of the appraisal rights tends to be like working one's way through a labyrinth. There are many traps for the unwary—the most significant of which is the requirement that a shareholder perfect his appraisal rights by giving the corporation written notice of his intent to do so before the shareholder vote on the merger. Facts tending to show that the price was unfair often will not be discovered until after the shareholder vote. In addition, many jurisdictions do not permit the use of class actions in appraisal proceedings. Accordingly, it can be very expensive to exercise appraisal rights because each dissenting shareholder must hire his own lawyer. In contrast, if he can bring a fraud or fiduciary duty claim outside the appraisal statute he can do so via a class or derivative action. Finally, it also is possible that he will get greater relief in a cause of action for damages than under appraisal.

Because of the advantages class and derivative actions possess over appraisal proceedings, the exclusivity of such proceedings is the critical issue. Should appraisal be regarded as the exclusive remedy or should unhappy shareholders be allowed to challenge the merger even if they were not eligible to make use of the appraisal remedy? This issue tends to come up most often in going private or freezeout transactions where

28. See § 12.4.

the buyer is either management and/or a controlling shareholder. Plaintiffs claim that there has been a breach of fiduciary duty or fraud or what have you. The question then becomes whether they are entitled to a remedy outside the appraisal process.

Current Delaware law on these issues originated with the supreme court's decision in *Weinberger v. UOP*.[29] A conglomerate named The Signal Companies purchased 50.5% of UOP's stock. Sometime thereafter Signal decided to acquire the remaining 49.5% of UOP's shares at $21 per share through a freezeout merger between a wholly owned Signal subsidiary and UOP. Plaintiff challenged the fairness of the merger on a variety of grounds. In a far-reaching opinion, the court laid out a number of important principles. Although some of its pronouncements have undergone substantial subsequent modification, *Weinberger* remains the starting point for any discussion of freezeout mergers.

1. The business context: Why freezeout the minority?

After acquiring a majority block of UOP shares, Signal faced the same problem created by any successful tender offer. Where the acquirer obtains control of the target through a tender offer there will almost always be some holdout shareholders. Some target shareholders simply won't tender into the offer, either due to opposition or mere cluelessness, even if the offer is structured as a cash bid for any and all outstanding shares. Getting rid of the minority is fairly straight-forward—a triangular merger between the target corporation and a wholly owned subsidiary of the acquirer will do the trick.

The question remains however: why get rid of the minority? What is the cost-benefit analysis? On the cost side of the ledger, the principal factor is the price the controlling shareholder will have to pay minority shareholders in the freezeout merger. The main planning issue on this side of the ledger therefore is the extent to which the law precludes the controlling shareholder from paying a low-ball price.

On the benefit side of the ledger, there are costs that can be eliminated through a freeze-out merger. If the target is a public company, taking it private eliminates all of the costs associated with the proxy rules and the periodic disclosure filings required of public firms. Sole ownership also may give the controlling shareholder more flexibility to transfer assets from one subsidiary to another or to dispose of assets.

To what extent do the fiduciary duties owed to the minority justify effecting a freezeout merger? In other words, does complying with the rules set forth in the preceding section sufficiently complicate the controlling shareholder's life so as to justify the costs associated with eliminating the minority? To be sure, transactions between parent companies and their majority-owned subsidiaries are a fertile field for litigation. On balance, however, the controlling shareholder's liability

---

29. Weinberger v. UOP, Inc., 457 A.2d 701 (Del.1983).

exposure generally will not justify the expense (and litigation risk) associated with freezeout mergers.

Recall from *Sinclair Oil* that the Delaware Supreme Court identified two legal standards potentially applicable to transactions between the target and the controlling shareholder: (1) the business judgment rule; and (2) the intrinsic fairness standard.[30] A court will apply the intrinsic fairness test, as opposed to the business judgment rule, when the parent has received a benefit to the exclusion and at the expense of the minority shareholders of the subsidiary. The choice of which standard to apply matters because the burden of proof shifts depending on which standard is applied. Under the business judgment rule, the directors get the presumption of good faith and plaintiff must rebut that presumption. Under the intrinsic fairness test, the burden of proof is on the directors to show, subject to close scrutiny, that the transactions were objectively fair to the firm.

Although the fiduciary duties of a controlling shareholder seem like a significant limitation on its freedom to run the company, in practice they are not all that important. The situations in which majority shareholders have been held liable are fairly limited. Liability usually arises only where the minority shareholders have an expectancy in the challenged benefit and then fail to receive their pro rata share. As long as the controlling shareholder is willing to give the minority their pro rata share of any benefits, there should not be major liability concerns.

Why then do controlling shareholders so frequently insist on freezing out the minority? Two answers suggest themselves. On the one hand, perhaps the controlling shareholder plans to extract more than its pro rata share of some corporate benefit. On the other hand, perhaps the controlling shareholder is simply risk averse and wishes to avoid the potential for aberrational litigation outcomes. The extent to which one thinks courts should scrutinize these transactions depends in large part on which answer seems more plausible.

2. *The business purpose test*

In *Singer v. Magnavox*, shareholders of Magnavox challenged the corporation's agreement to be acquired by North American Philips in a reverse triangular merger.[31] Because North American indirectly owned 84.1% of Mangnavox's outstanding shares by virtue of a prior tender offer, the outcome of the shareholder vote on the merger proposal was a foregone conclusion. After the merger became effective, plaintiff shareholders sought an order nullifying the merger and awarding compensatory damages on the grounds that the merger was fraudulent and constituted a breach of duty by the defendant directors and by North American as the controlling shareholder.

In *Singer*, the challenged freezeout merger fully complied with the relevant Delaware merger statutes. The supreme court, however, held

---

30. Sinclair Oil Corp. v. Levien, 280 A.2d 717 (Del.1971).

31. Singer v. Magnavox Co., 380 A.2d 969 (Del.1977).

that compliance with the form of the statute did not end the inquiry: "inequitable action does not become permissible simply because it is legally possible." Accordingly, the court imposed certain limitations on the acquiring company's ability to freezeout minority shareholders. Among these was the so-called business purpose test, which held that a merger could not be effected for the "sole purpose of freezing out minority shareholders."

If the business purpose test is based solely on the target corporation's interests, effecting a freezeout merger becomes quite difficult. In many cases, the advantages of a going private transaction accrue mainly to the controlling shareholder. In subsequent decisions, however, the Delaware supreme court effectively eviscerated the business purpose test by requiring only that the merger serve some bona fide purpose of the parent corporation.[32] Because competent transaction planners easily could create a paper trail showing the merger promoted some business interest of the parent, the test was left as mere formalism. Recognizing that the business purpose test afforded minority shareholders no meaningful protections, the Delaware supreme court abandoned it in *Weinberger*.[33]

3. *Freezeouts and fairness*

Weinberger is an annoyingly difficult decision to parse. It reminds one of trying to finish a jigsaw puzzle when some of the pieces are missing and others came from an entirely different puzzle. The court overruled a number of precedents, creating an entirely new remedy for freezeout mergers, but declined to do so retrospectively. Portions of the opinion thus applied only to future cases, while other portions applied only to cases then pending. Worse yet, some of the prospective rules

---

32. See, e.g., Tanzer v. International General Industries, Inc., 379 A.2d 1121 (Del.1977).

33. Weinberger v. UOP, Inc., 457 A.2d 701, 715 (Del.1983). In Coggins v. New England Patriots Football Club, Inc., 492 N.E.2d 1112 (Mass.1986), the Massachusetts court declined to follow *Weinberger* in this regard. The Massachusetts court both retained the business purpose test and interpreted that test to require the merger serve some legitimate business interest of the target subsidiary. As is often the case, the challenged merger's benefits flowed to the controlling shareholder, which the court deemed improper. Even in *Coggins*-like jurisdictions, however, careful transaction planning often can create the requisite paper trail showing a purported interest of the target subsidiary served by the freezeout merger. See, e.g., Dower v. Mosser Industries, 648 F.2d 183 (3d Cir.1981) (merger enabled subsidiary to obtain a loan for expansion of its business); Grimes v. Don-aldson, Lufkin and Jenrette, Inc., 392 F.Supp. 1393 (N.D.Fla.1974), aff'd, 521 F.2d 812 (5th Cir.1975) (merger permitted transactions between related corporations that otherwise would have been deemed a conflict of interest); Teschner v. Chicago Title & Trust Co., 322 N.E.2d 54 (Ill.1974) (merger intended to reduce corporate expenses and simplify internal procedures); Alpert v. 28 Williams Street Corp., 483 N.Y.S.2d 667 (1984) (merger allowed firm to obtain additional capital from an investor who would not invest without elimination of minority interests); cf. Leader v. Hycor, Inc., 479 N.E.2d 173 (Mass.1985) (reverse stock split effected to take company private because costs of a public market for the stock was not justified by the poor market for that stock). Consequently, *Coggins* simply raises transaction costs, creates traps for the unwary, and provides employment for transactional lawyers.

announced by *Weinberger* have undergone significant subsequent modifications.

According to *Weinberger*, a freezeout merger must satisfy an "entire fairness" standard. In turn, entire fairness has two components: fair price and fair dealing. The controlling shareholder's obligation to pay a fair price raises valuation issues discussed in Chapter 12. Here we focus on the controlling shareholder's duty to deal fairly with the minority.

Even after acquiring a majority position in UOP, Signal still was sitting on a pile of excess cash for which it had been unable to find profitable uses. Illustrating the agency costs inherent in free cash flow, Signal's board failed to pay out the cash to the shareholders via a dividend or stock repurchase. Instead, after considering and rejecting many options, Signal turned its attention back to UOP. Signal's board ordered that a feasibility study be prepared relating to the possible acquisition by Signal of the remaining minority UOP shares. Messrs. Arledge and Chitiea prepared the study. They were both officers of Signal and also directors of both UOP and Signal. Using confidential UOP information, Arledge and Chitiea concluded that buying the remaining 49.5% of UOP's stock at any price up to $24 per share would be a good investment for Signal. After the feasibility study was completed, Signal's executive committee decided to effect a freezeout merger at $21 per share, which the committee purportedly believed would be a fair price.

Negotiations between Signal and UOP were conducted on the latter's behalf by one Crawford, who was UOP's president but also had been a long-time Signal employee. Indeed, the court described Crawford as "Signal's man at UOP." When the matter was laid before UOP's board, the UOP board members who had been nominated by Signal were present at the meeting in person or by telephone conference call. They left the meeting to permit free discussion by the non-Signal directors, but returned before the final vote. Although they did not vote, the record showed that they would have voted affirmatively.

The court concluded that this course of conduct violated the duty of fair dealing in at least three respects. First, the Arledge–Chitiea report was prepared using confidential UOP information. It is perfectly permissible for someone to be a director of two corporations simultaneously, even if those corporations are related as parent and subsidiary.[34] "But such common directors owe the same fidelity to both corporations."[35] Consequently, Arledge and Chitiea could not use their positions as UOP directors to benefit Signal.

Second, there was a lack of candor. As a controlling shareholder seeking to effect a freezeout transaction, Signal's fiduciary duties to the

34. See, e.g., Roberts v. Prisk, 284 P. 984, 987 (Cal.App.1930) ("There must be either fraud or a lack of good faith, or some breach of trust shown in addition to the fact of interlocking directorates" for liability to be imposed or to avoid a conflicted interest transaction).

35. San Diego, Old Town, and Pacific Beach R.R. Co. v. Pacific Beach Co., 44 P. 333, 334 (Cal.1896).

minority included an obligation to fully disclose all material facts.[36] The Arledge–Chitiea report was clearly material—the reasonable investor would consider both the information therein and the manner in which it was prepared to be important in deciding how to vote—but the report was not disclosed either to the independent UOP directors or to the minority shareholders.

Finally, there was a lack of arms-length bargaining. As a prudential matter, Crawford and the Signal-affiliated board members should have recused themselves from the negotiations. A special committee of UOP's independent directors then should have been appointed to study the offer and conduct any negotiations. As the court explained: "Although perfection is not possible, or expected, the result here could have been entirely different if UOP had appointed an independent negotiating committee of its outside directors to deal with Signal at arm's length."[37] Instructively, the court went on to equate "fairness in this context" to the conduct that might be expected from "a theoretical, wholly independent, board of directors acting upon the matter before them." Notice how this expectation squares with the authority/accountability dichotomy we have developed in connection with judicial oversight of board decisionmaking. Only where there is evidence of possible self-dealing do accountability concerns trump the null hypothesis of preserving the board's discretionary authority from judicial review. If independent and disinterested directors have conducted the transaction, accountability concerns are minimized, and the court appropriately will give more deference to the board's decisions.

Unlike some duty of loyalty settings, however, approval of a freeze-out merger by the disinterested directors (or shareholders for that matter) does not change the applicable standard of review to, say, the business judgment rule. As the Delaware court explained in *Kahn v. Lynch Communication Systems*,[38] "approval of the transaction by an independent committee of directors or an informed majority of minority shareholders shifts the burden of proof on the issue of fairness from the controlling or dominating shareholder to the challenging shareholder-plaintiff. Nevertheless, even when an interested cash-out merger transaction receives the informed approval of a majority of minority stockholders or an independent committee of disinterested directors, an entire fairness analysis is the only proper standard of judicial review." The court went on to emphasize that the burden shifts to plaintiff only if the majority shareholder does not dictate the terms of the merger and the independent committee has "real bargaining power that it can exercise with the majority shareholder on an arm length basis."

36. Cf. In re Wheelabrator Technologies, Inc. Shareholders Litigation, 663 A.2d 1194, 1198 (Del.Ch.1995) ("Delaware law imposes upon a board of directors the fiduciary duty to disclose fully and fairly all material facts within its control that would have a significant effect upon a stockholder vote.").

37. Weinberger v. UOP, Inc., 457 A.2d 701, 709 n. 7 (Del.1983).

38. 638 A.2d 1110, 1117 (Del.1994).

4. Freezeouts, fiduciary duties, and appraisal

Weinberger's basic requirement of entire fairness was not a novel development, although the emphasis on fair dealing constituted an important refinement of the standard.[39] What good is a fairness requirement, however, if there is no effective remedy? Under *Singer* and its pre-*Weinberger* progeny, the statutory appraisal proceeding was not the sole remedy available for mergers failing to satisfy the entire fairness test. Instead, aggrieved shareholders could bring a class action for money damages, even if they were not eligible for appraisal. This had the significant advantage of permitting shareholders who voted for the merger to change their minds and seek damages if they subsequently decided the merger was unfair.

In contrast, the *Weinberger* court ruled that any future challenges to a merger's fairness generally must be made by means of an appraisal proceeding. (Cases then pending were allowed to proceed as class actions.) As the court explained, "a plaintiff's monetary remedy ordinarily should be confined to the more liberalized appraisal proceeding herein established." The court acknowledged that appraisal might not be "adequate in certain cases, particularly where fraud, misrepresentation, self-dealing, deliberate waste of corporate assets, or gross and palpable overreaching are involved." But while the chancery court was authorized to provide alternative measures of damages in those cases, such as by granting rescissory damages,[40] the court was to do so within the confines of the appraisal process.[41]

Weinberger appeared to unequivocally leave appraisal as the exclusive remedy in freezeout mergers. If a minority shareholder thought a merger was unfair, his remedy was to bring an appraisal proceeding, which meant there would be no class action and the shareholder would have to perfect his appraisal rights. In its subsequent *Rabkin* opinion, however, the Delaware supreme court took it all back—or, at least, most of it.

39. See, e.g., Singer v. Magnavox Co., 380 A.2d 969, 980 (Del.1977) (requiring that freezeout mergers satisfy an "entire fairness" standard).

40. Rescissory damages give shareholders the value of their stock measured at the time of judgment, thereby giving the shareholders a share of the gains from the merger. This, at least in theory, was supposed to deter the practice of "low-balling," in which the bidder offered a price less than that which likely would be available in an appraisal proceeding on the theory that few if any shareholders would exercise their appraisal rights. In practice, however, it gives shareholders a put option. In other words, the dissenter can elect to be treated as though he had been a shareholder in the firm all along. This allows the dissenter to free ride on the majority shareholder's efforts to enhance share value. If the firm does worse than the market, however, he'll probably get at least the appraisal price plus interest. As a result, the availability of rescissory damages makes appraisal a no-risk proposition.

41. In light of the court's subsequent retreat from this position, it is worth quoting the relevant passage in full: "the provisions of 8 Del.C. § 262, as herein construed, respecting the scope of an appraisal and the means for perfecting the same, shall govern the financial remedy available to minority shareholders in a cash-out merger. Thus, we return to the well established principles of Stauffer v. Standard Brands, Inc., Del. Supr., 187 A.2d 78 (1962) and David J. Greene & Co. v. Schenley Industries, Inc., Del.Ch., 281 A.2d 30 (1971), mandating a stockholder's recourse to the basic remedy of an appraisal." Weinberger v. UOP, Inc., 457 A.2d 701, 715 (Del.1983).

On March 1, 1983, the Olin Corporation bought 63 percent of the outstanding stock of the Philip A. Hunt Chemical Corporation from a company called Turner & Newall. Olin paid Turner & Newall $25 per share. The parties agreed that, if Olin bought the remainder of Hunt stock within one year, Olin would pay the minority shareholders $25 as well. At the time, Olin stated it had "no present intention" to buy the remaining shares. The court observed, however, that "it is clear that Olin always anticipated owing 100 percent of Hunt." In any case, just over one year later, on March 23, 1984, Olin met with its investment banking firm to plan its purchase of the remaining stock at $20 per share. Within a short time, it had engineered a freezeout merger at $20.

Disgruntled shareholders plaintiffs rejected an appraisal and brought a class action challenging the merger as unfair. The defendants moved to dismiss on grounds that appraisal is the exclusive remedy. The chancery court agreed with the defendants and dismissed. The Delaware supreme court reversed, however, holding that the chancery court's view "render[ed] meaningless our extensive discussion of fair dealing" in *Weinberger*.[42] To be sure, *Weinberger* contemplated that the chancery court could take into account breaches of fiduciary duty when valuing stock in an appraisal proceeding. Ultimately, however, appraisal is concerned mainly with the adequacy of the price. If there is to be a successful collateral attack on the manner in which the controlling shareholder dealt with the minority, a class action for damages provides a far more effective tool. *Rabkin* implicitly recognized this truth, leaving appraisal a very limited scope of action. After *Rabkin*, appraisal apparently is exclusive only when plaintiff's claims go solely to the fairness of the price.[43] Although the court did not say so expressly, this conclusion follows inexorably from three aspects of the decision: (1) the supreme court's rejection of the chancery court's "narrow" interpretation of *Weinberger*; (2) the supreme court's emphasis that the case involved charges of "unfair dealing"; (3) the fact that plaintiff's allegation of unfair dealing was enough to defeat dismissal of the class action. In other words, Delaware has come full circle. In order to ensure that

---

42. Rabkin v. Philip A. Hunt Chemical Corp., 498 A.2d 1099, 1104 (Del.1985). There is something of a puzzle in the court's apparent belief that Olin had dealt unfairly with the minority shareholders of Hunt. Suppose that at the time Olin bought its majority stake in Hunt, Olin anticipated buying the minority interest at $20 per share as soon as possible. The law is that paying a premium for control, without more, is unobjectionable. All that is added here Turner & Newall's insistence that Olin wait at least a year before cashing out the minority at a price below $25. The court seems to interpret the one-year rule as some sort of effort by Turner & Newall to encourage Olin to pay $25 per share to the minority shareholders, and some sort of agreement by Olin to do so, when in fact it probably was just an attempt by Turner & Newall to avoid sale of control litigation. To be sure, *Rabkin* was an appeal from a grant of a motion to dismiss on the pleadings. Yet, by giving plaintiffs an opportunity to prove a contractual right to the $25, the court implicitly acknowledges at least the potential that such a contract right exists. If so, however, where did it come from? Is the court saying that the plaintiffs were third party beneficiaries of the contract between Turner & Newall and Olin? Admittedly, the court noted some possible defalcations by Hunt directors, but it also squarely stated that plaintiffs sought "to enforce a contractual right to receive $25 per share."

43. See Cede & Co. v. Technicolor, Inc., 542 A.2d 1182 (Del.1988).

minority shareholders have an effective remedy in freezeout mergers, the court has reopened the courthouse door to class and derivative actions.

In contrast, the Model Act has moved in just the opposite direction. Subject to two exceptions, MBCA § 13.02(d) states that a shareholder entitled to appraisal rights "may not challenge" a completed merger. One exception authorizes suit to remedy serious procedural errors in the decisionmaking process, such as a failure to obtain the required votes. The other permits a class action outside of appraisal where shareholder approval of the merger was procured by fraud. Note also the implicit exception for equitable relief sought prior to the merger's completion. Finally, the exclusivity principle does not preclude a class action for damages brought against directors for violating their duties of care and loyalty. Hence, a *Van Gorkom*-type suit is not barred.[44]

5. *Effect of shareholder ratification*

As with other duty of loyalty claims, shareholder approval and/or ratification is not claim preclusive. Instead, valid shareholder action shifts the burden of proof from defendants to plaintiffs. Given the outcome determinative potential of assigning the burden of proof, of course, this is a nontrivial benefit for the defendants.

In a freezeout merger, the controlling shareholder's conflict of interest is imputed to the target subsidiary's board. Accordingly, such a merger is treated as a type of self-dealing transaction and the burden of proof is on the defendant controlling shareholder and/or the controlled directors to prove that the transaction was fair to the minority. If a freezeout merger is approved by a majority of the disinterested share-holders—the so-called "majority of the minority," however, the burden of proof shifts to the plaintiff to show that the merger was unfair. The standard of review remains entire fairness, with its integral fair price and fair dealing components, but the burden is now on plaintiff to show lack of fairness on one or both grounds.[45]

---

44. Smith v. Van Gorkom, 488 A.2d 858 (Del.1985).

45. See In re Wheelabrator Technologies, Inc. Shareholders Litigation, 663 A.2d 1194, 1203 (Del.Ch.1995); see also Kahn v. Lynch Communication Sys., 638 A.2d 1110 (Del.1994); Rosenblatt v. Getty Oil Co., 493 A.2d 929 (Del.1985).

Chapter 8

SHAREHOLDER LITIGATION

Analysis

---

§ 8.1   Introduction

We have frequently described the corporation as the nexus of a web of interlocking constituencies bound together by a complex set of contracts. Within that web, two tensions predominate. One is the conflict between shareholders and creditors. The other is the conflict between shareholders and managers.

One way in which corporate law responds to the latter conflict is by imposing fiduciary duties on corporate management and the board of directors that supervises those managers. Fiduciary duties of officers and directors are generally owed to the corporation as an entity, rather than to individual shareholders. Accordingly, this Chapter focuses on the mechanism by which those duties frequently are enforced—the derivative suit.[1]

The law governing derivative litigation has many unfortunate complexities. Just as the Himalayas were thrown up by the collision between the Indian and Asiatic continental plates, the complexities of derivative litigation result from the collision of two basic principles. On the one hand, the derivative cause of action belongs to the corporation. The board of directors is charged with running the corporation and therefore ought to control corporate litigation. On the other hand, when it is the directors or their associates who are on trial, we may not trust them to make unbiased decisions. Consequently, like the substantive content of fiduciary duties, the law governing derivative litigation must balance the competing policies of deference to the board's decisionmaking authority and the need to ensure directorial accountability.

§ 8.2 Direct v. derivative litigation

"Direct" shareholder suits arise out of causes of action belonging to the shareholders in their individual capacity. It is typically premised on an injury directly affecting the shareholders and must be brought by the shareholders in their own name. In contrast, a "derivative" suit is one brought by the shareholder on behalf of the corporation. The cause of action belongs to the corporation as an entity and arises out of an injury done to the corporation as an entity. The shareholder is merely acting as the firm's representative.

Distinguishing direct and derivative suits is easier said than done. The basic tests are: (1) Who suffered the most immediate and direct injury? Note that it is not enough for a shareholder to allege that the challenged conduct resulted in a drop in the corporation's stock market price.[1] (2) To whom did the defendant's duty run?[2]

---

§ 8.1

1. In theory, of course, a derivative suit may be brought by any shareholder who meets the specified procedural requirements to redress any injury done the corporation by any party. As noted, however, its most important function is providing an by which breaches of fiduciary duty are remedied.

§ 8.2

1. See, e.g., Barth v. Barth, 659 N.E.2d 559, 560 (Ind.1995) (noting "the well-established general rule is that shareholders of a corporation may not maintain actions at law in their own names to redress an injury to the corporation even if the value of their stock is impaired as a result of the injury"); see also Lewis v. Chiles, 719 F.2d 1044,

1049 (9th Cir.1983); Rose v. Schantz, 201 N.W.2d 593 (Wis.1972). The ALI PRINCIPLES (§ 7.01(d)) and a few states have adopted a general rule that derivative litigation may be brought by shareholders of close corporations as though the suits were direct in nature. See, e.g., Richards v. Bryan, 879 P.2d 638 (Kan.App.1994); Crosby v. Beam, 548 N.E.2d 217 (Ohio 1989); see also Bagdon v. Bridgestone/Firestone, Inc., 916 F.2d 379 (7th Cir.1990), cert. denied, 500 U.S. 952 (1991) (criticizing that rule and concluding that Delaware would reject it); Landstrom v. Shaver, 561 N.W.2d 1 (S.D. 1997) (rejecting ALI PRINCIPLES' approach); Simmons v. Miller, 544 S.E.2d 666 (Va. 2001) (rejecting special exception for close corporations).

Assume, for example, Jones entered into a contract with ABC Corp. Jones has breached the contract, but ABC has not sued her for that breach. May a shareholder of ABC Corp sue Jones directly? No. Jones owed no duty to the shareholder as such and, moreover, her breach did not injure the shareholder directly. Instead, it was the corporate entity that was injured. Recovery by the entity, instead of by an individual shareholder, provides a remedy that redounds to the benefit of all shareholders. Consequently, the shareholder's suit against Jones must be brought as a derivative action.

When the defendants are corporate directors or officers, it is particularly important identify the party to whom the defendants owed the relevant duty, because they owe duties to both the corporation as an entity and the shareholders as individuals. Because of this dual loyalty, a particular course of conduct sometimes will violate two or more duties owed by the same defendant—one to the corporation and a different one owed to the shareholders as individuals. Insider trading, for example, can violate both a duty owed to the corporation as an entity and a separate duty owed to the shareholder who is selling the securities. In such a case, the shareholders may bring a direct action to redress their own injuries, while also bringing a derivative action to redress the injury to the corporation.[3]

Specific suits that have been characterized as derivative in nature include claims involving corporate rights arising out of tort or contract,[4] monetary damages based on corporate mismanagement,[5] executive compensation,[6] waste of corporate assets,[7] and the adequacy of consideration for issuance of corporate stock.[8] Suits that may be brought directly include claims involving oppression of minority shareholders,[9] a proposed

2. ALI PRINCIPLES § 7.01. See also Eisenberg v. Flying Tiger Line, Inc., 451 F.2d 267, 269–70 (2d Cir.1971); Grimes v. Donald, 673 A.2d 1207, 1213 (Del.1996); Bennett v. Breuil Petroleum Corp., 99 A.2d 236, 241 (Del.Ch.1953); G & N Aircraft, Inc. v. Boehm, 743 N.E.2d 227, 234 (Ind.2001). In diversity actions brought in federal court, state law controls whether a suit is direct or derivative. Sax v. World Wide Press, Inc., 809 F.2d 610, 613 (9th Cir.1987).

3. ALI PRINCIPLES 7.01(c).

4. See, e.g., Schaffer v. Universal Rundle Corp., 397 F.2d 893 (5th Cir.1968); Bruno v. Southeastern Servs., Inc., 385 So.2d 620 (Miss.1980); Hunter v. Knight, Vale & Gregory, 571 P.2d 212 (Wash.App.1977).

5. See, e.g., Sax v. World Wide Press, Inc., 809 F.2d 610 (9th Cir.1987); Hoffman v. Optima Sys., Inc., 683 F.Supp. 865 (D.Mass.1988); Palowsky v. Premier Bancorp, Inc., 597 So.2d 543 (La.App.1992). The famous case of Smith v. Van Gorkom, 488 A.2d 858 (Del.1985), in which plaintiffs sought monetary damages for violations of the duty of care, was brought as a direct

class action because the board's misconduct directly impacted the price paid for the shareholders' stock. See also Parnes v. Bally Entertainment Corp., 722 A.2d 1243 (Del.1999); Crescent/Mach I Partners, L.P. v. Turner, 2000 WL 1481002 (Del.Ch.2000). In general, however, corporate mismanagement injures the corporation in the first instance and the shareholders only indirectly.

6. Grimes v. Donald, 673 A.2d 1207 (Del.1996); Marx v. Akers, 644 N.Y.S.2d 121 (1996).

7. See, e.g., Lewis v. S. L. & E., Inc., 629 F.2d 764 (2d Cir.1980); Kramer v. Western Pacific Indus., Inc., 546 A.2d 348 (Del. 1988); Lincoln First Bank v. Sanford, 579 N.Y.S.2d 781 (App.Div.1991).

8. See, e.g., Bennett v. Breuil Petroleum Corp., 99 A.2d 236 (Del.Ch.1953).

9. See, e.g., Wilkes v. Springside Nursing Home, Inc., 353 N.E.2d 657 (Mass. 1976); see also Horton v. Benjamin, 1997 WL 778662 (Mass.Super.1997) (freezeout of minority shareholders).

reorganization favoring one class of shares over another,[10] compelling declaration of a dividend,[11] inspection of corporate books and records,[12] shareholder voting rights,[13] preemptive rights,[14] and injunctive relief where the board of directors improperly abdicated its authority to corporate officers.[15] Examples of conduct simultaneously giving rise both to derivative and direct causes of action include sale of corporate offices[16] and violations of the federal proxy rules.[17] In close cases, courts are often willing to accept a plaintiff's characterization of the suit as direct, provided plaintiff is seeking only injunctive or prospective relief.[18]

Why not just allow shareholders to sue whenever they are injured by corporate mismanagement or malfeasance, whether that injury is direct or indirect? A fair question, indeed. One commonly given answer is that to do so would result in a multiplicity of suits brought by numerous shareholders.[19] Today, of course, such concerns are substantially mitigated by the availability of class actions. In this sense, derivative litigation is a mere historical accident. The derivative suit was recognized by the U.S. Supreme Court as early as 1855, long before the modern class action procedure emerged.[20] Perhaps it survives today as a mere anachronism and out to be replaced by the class action.

An alternative justification for the separate derivative suit procedure is based on the corporation's legal personhood. According to this view, an injury to the corporation gives rise to a cause of action belonging to the corporation.[21] But so what? Besides being hyper-technical, this explana-

---

10. See, e.g., Lehrman v. Godchaux Sugars, Inc., 138 N.Y.S.2d 163 (Sup.Ct.1955).

11. See, e.g., Knapp v. Bankers Sec. Corp., 230 F.2d 717 (3d Cir.1956); Tankersley v. Albright, 80 F.R.D. 441 (N.D.Ill.1978). But see Gordon v. Elliman, 119 N.E.2d 331 (N.Y.1954) (legislatively overturned by adoption of New York Business Corporation Act § 626).

12. See, e.g., Kahn v. American Cone & Pretzel Co., 74 A.2d 160 (Pa.1950).

13. See, e.g., Eisenberg v. Flying Tiger Line, Inc., 451 F.2d 267 (2d Cir.1971); Reifsnyder v. Pittsburgh Outdoor Advertising Co., 173 A.2d 319 (Pa.1961).

14. See, e.g., See, e.g., Saigh v. Busch, 403 S.W.2d 559 (Mo.1966).

15. See, e.g., Grimes v. Donald, 673 A.2d 1207 (Del.1996).

16. See, e.g., Snyder v. Epstein, 290 F.Supp. 652, 655 (E.D.Wis.1968).

17. See, e.g., Studebaker Corp. v. Gittlin, 360 F.2d 692 (2d Cir.1966).

18. ALI PRINCIPLES § 7.01 cmt. d.

19. See, e.g., Watson v. Button, 235 F.2d 235, 237 (9th Cir.1956) ("the reasons behind the general rule are as follows: (1) to avoid a multiplicity of suits by each injured shareholder, (2) to protect the corporate

creditors, and (3) to protect all the stockholders since a corporate recovery benefits all equally"); Moll v. South Central Solar Sys., Inc., 419 N.E.2d 154, 161 (Ind.App. 1981) (noting potential for "multitudinous litigation"); Wells v. Dane, 63 A. 324, 325 (Me.1905) ("Any other rule would admit of as many suits against the wrongdoer as there were stockholders in the corporation."); Strasenburgh v. Straubmuller, 683 A.2d 818, 829 (N.J.1996) ("The policy reasons include maintaining the investment resources of the corporation, avoiding a multiplicity of suits, providing equal benefit for all shareholders and avoiding partial dividends or partial liquidation."). In addition, a double recovery might result if the defendant were potentially liable to both the corporation and the shareholders. ALI PRINCIPLES § 7.01 Reporter's Note 2.

20. See Ross v. Bernhard, 396 U.S. 531, 534–35 (1970) (citing Dodge v. Woolsey, 18 How. 331 (1856)).

21. See, e.g., Smith v. Bramwell, 31 P.2d 647, 648 (Or.1934) ("The wrong is against the corporation and the cause of action belongs to it."). A more plausible version of this story asserts that injuries to the corporation impinge not only on shareholders but also creditors. Because deriva-

tion runs afoul of our basic contractarian model. The corporation's separate legal personhood is a mere legal fiction. Consequently, to assert that principle as a bar to shareholder suits seems an inappropriate reification of the firm.

The most plausible justification for preserving the separate derivative suit is based on the fundamental dichotomy between authority and accountability. As we shall see, the derivative suit adds multiple layers of additional procedural obstacles to shareholder litigation. Just as the business judgment rule insulates board of director decisions from judicial review so as to ensure deference to board authority, requiring shareholders to proceed derivatively helps prevent judicial oversight of directors. Yet, this justification begs the question, "why have the derivative suit at all?" We revisit that issue at the end of this chapter.

§ 8.3 Attorneys fees: Herein of strike suits and their converse

In the derivative suit context, the usual tension between authority and accountability is confounded by a second set of conflicting incentives. The derivative litigation regime creates incentives for plaintiffs' attorneys to bring nonmeritorious lawsuits. Perversely, however, the regime also encourages plaintiffs' attorneys and managerial defendants to collusively settle meritorious cases.[1] These clashing incentives complicate an already byzantine set of doctrines.

The potential for abusive shareholder litigation has long been known. In 1949, the U.S. Supreme Court observed:

> This [derivative suit] remedy, born of stockholder helplessness, was long the chief regulator of corporate management and has afforded no small incentive to avoid at least grosser forms of betrayal of stockholders' interests.... Unfortunately, the remedy itself provided opportunity for abuse, which was not neglected. Suits sometimes were brought not to redress real wrongs, but to realize upon their nuisance value.... These litigations were aptly characterized in professional slang as "strike suits."[2]

As the Supreme Court elsewhere explained, strike suits are nonmeritorious actions brought "by people who might be interested in getting quick dollars by making charges without regard to their truth so as to coerce

---

tive litigation typically results in a recovery by the corporation, rather than by individual shareholders, maintaining a distinct derivative suit process is necessary for the protection of creditors. See Caswell v. Jordan, 362 S.E.2d 769, 773 (Ga.App.1987); W & W Equip. Co. v. Mink, 568 N.E.2d 564, 571 (Ind.App.1991).

§ 8.3

1. See generally Reinier Kraakman et al., When are Shareholder Suits in Share-

holder Interests?, 82 Geo. L.J. 1733 (1994); Jonathan R. Macey & Geoffrey P. Miller, The Plaintiffs' Attorney's Role in Class Action and Derivative Litigation: Economic Analysis and Recommendations for Reform, 58 U. Chi. L. Rev. 1 (1991).

2. Cohen v. Beneficial Indus. Loan Corp., 337 U.S. 541, 548 (1949).

corporate managers to settle worthless claims in order to get rid of them."[3]

The basic problem is that the real party in interest is the plaintiffs' attorney rather than the plaintiff-shareholders themselves. Because the derivative cause of action belongs to the corporation, any monetary recovery belongs to the corporation and normally will be paid into the corporate treasury. The sole benefit the representative shareholder-plaintiff receives is the increase in share price, if any, resulting from that recovery and/or from any improved management that results from the suit.

Why would a shareholder expend sizeable legal fees and other costs in an effort to achieve such an uncertain reward, especially given the obvious free rider problem?[4] It was early recognized that shareholders would not bring derivative suits if they were obliged to bear the legal costs of suit in all cases. As a result, both federal and state law provide for payment of the plaintiff's legal fees in derivative litigation.

The usual American Rule, of course, is that each party pays its own legal fees and other expenses. In the derivative suit context, however, the corporation may be ordered to pay the plaintiff-shareholder's fees and expenses if the litigation results in a monetary recovery or confers a substantial nonmonetary benefit on the corporation. Courts are quite generous in finding a substantial benefit, even in cases where the outcome clearly had little effect on the corporation's finances or stock price.

In re Caremark International Inc.,[5] forcefully illustrates the incentives provided plaintiffs' attorneys by the derivative suit regime. The government charged Caremark, a health services corporation, with violating the federal Anti–Referral Payments Law. Caremark settled, paying a fine of about $250 million. Several shareholders filed thereupon derivative suits against Caremark's board of directors, alleging duty of care violations. The shareholders' derivative lawsuits were settled pursu-

---

3. Surowitz v. Hilton Hotels Corp., 383 U.S. 363, 371 (1966). A federal district court put it even more colorfully: "Strike suits are a particularly repugnant species of blackmail. Such lawsuits are the base work of rapacious jackals whose declared concern for the corporate well-being camouflages their unwholesome appetite for corporate dollars." Brown v. Hart, Schaffner & Marx, 96 F.R.D. 64, 67 (N.D.Ill.1982).

4. Free riding is one of the more common forms of collective action problems. Where it is desirable for a group to produce some collective good, some members may decline to contribute to the good's production even though they expect to derive benefits from it. These free riders anticipate that others will make a sufficient contribution to ensure the good's production. Two conditions must be met for free riding to occur. First, there should be no sanctions for noncontribution. Second, the free riders must assume that no individual contribution will be decisive. Where free riding occurs, the collective good will tend to be under-produced. In the corporate context, the relevant collective good is monitoring corporate directors and managers. Because all shareholder can assume that there will be no sanction for failing to monitor and that their monitoring efforts would contribute only at the margins, they have an incentive to free ride. Under such conditions, shareholder monitoring of management will be sub-optimal.

5. In re Caremark International Inc. Derivative Litig., 698 A.2d 959 (Del.Ch. 1996).

ant to an agreement under which the directors paid nothing, Caremark promised to implement certain minor changes to its corporate governance procedures, and Caremark agreed to pay the plaintiffs' attorneys fees. In reviewing the proposed settlement, Chancellor Allen determined that the board had not intentionally broken the federal statute, and, moreover, had exercised due care. Concluding that the proposed settlement conferred "very modest benefits" on Caremark, Chancellor Allen cut the plaintiffs' requested legal fees from $1,025,000 to a mere $816,000, which reflected a 15% premium on the normal hourly rate, plus $53,000 in other expenses.[6] In other words, the defendants basically did nothing wrong, the shareholders got no significant improvements in corporate management, and the plaintiff-shareholders' lawyers still got fees of almost $1 million.

It is for this reason that the real party in interest—the party on the plaintiffs' side with the greatest personal interest in the outcome of the litigation—is the plaintiffs' attorney rather than the nominal shareholder-plaintiff. Consequently, those attorneys have little incentive to refrain from bringing strike suits. The fee regime encourages them to bring nuisance suits in the hope that management will settle just so that the case will go away, while the shareholders ultimately bear any expenses incurred in the settlement.

Conversely, however, the shareholder-plaintiffs' attorney may be too eager to settle a meritorious suit. Recall that all corporate statutes allow the corporation to indemnify management for expenses incurred in defending or settling suits brought against them in their official capacity.[7] The corporation, moreover, must indemnify managers who succeed "on the merits or otherwise."[8] A manager who is dismissed from the litigation, for whatever reason, without having to make a monetary payment is deemed to have "succeeded" for this purpose.[9] As a result, it may be in the interests of both the plaintiff-shareholders' attorney and the managerial defendants to settle meritorious litigation before trial. The settlement can be crafted in such a way as to exonerate the individual defendants, while still permitting payment of plaintiffs' legal fees. The individual defendants face no risk of personal liability or expense, because the firm will reimburse them, and plaintiffs' counsel is assured of some payment. In contrast, taking the case to trial significantly increases the uncertainty and, hence, the risks facing both sides. Plaintiff's counsel will get no fee if the trial does not result in some "substantial benefit," but defendants who lose at trial may have to pay a judgment without benefit of indemnification.

---

6. Id. at 972. Other cases commonly cited as involving large fees for seemingly minimal benefits include In re General Tire & Rubber Co. Securities Litig., 726 F.2d 1075 (6th Cir.1984) (approving fees of $500,000 where sole benefit was an agreement to appoint two independent directors); Lewis v. Anderson, 692 F.2d 1267 (9th Cir. 1982) (fees of $110,000 approved where sole benefit was a shareholder vote on stock option plan).

7. See § 6.6.

8. See, e.g., DGCL § 145(c).

9. See, e.g., Waltuch v. Conticommodity Servs., Inc., 88 F.3d 87 (2d Cir.1996).

The corporation and its shareholders lose under either settlement scenario. A rational shareholder would not bring strike suits, absent some sort of side payment or other nonpro rata benefit, because any expenses incurred by the corporation reduce the value of the residual claim and, accordingly, come out of the shareholder's pocket. Because the real party in interest is the plaintiffs' attorney, who will not own stock in the affected corporation and thus will lack any economic incentive to maintain the value of the residual claim, however, there is no disincentive to bringing nonmeritorious suits and plenty of incentive to do so. Conversely, rational shareholders would not want to settle meritorious suits for less than their (discounted) full value, but again the real parties in interest have incentives to do so.

Research by Professor Romano confirms such abuses exist.[10] Romano found that shareholders rarely prevail on the merits, suggesting that strike suits are a problem. In about half of settled cases, there is some monetary recovery by the corporation, but such recoveries are usually quite modest—mere pennies per share. Plaintiffs' attorneys fees were paid in almost all settlements, however, confirming that lawyers are the chief beneficiaries of derivative litigation. Many of the rules governing derivative litigation are best understood as a response to these abuses.

§ 8.4 Procedural aspects

A. FRCP 23.1

Derivative suits have some unique procedural aspects, most of which are nicely captured by Federal Rule of Civil Procedure 23.1:

> In a derivative action brought by one or more shareholders or members to enforce a right of a corporation or of an unincorporated association, the corporation or association having failed to enforce a right which may properly be asserted by it, the complaint shall be verified and shall allege (1) that the plaintiff was a shareholder or member at the time of the transaction of which the plaintiff complains or that the plaintiff's share or membership thereafter devolved on the plaintiff by operation of law, and (2) that the action is not a collusive one to confer jurisdiction on a court of the United States which it would not otherwise have. The complaint shall also allege with particularity the efforts, if any, made by the plaintiff to obtain the action the plaintiff desires from the directors or comparable authority and, if necessary, from the shareholders or members, and the reasons for the plaintiff's failure to obtain the action or for not making the effort. The derivative action may not be maintained if it appears that the plaintiff does not fairly and adequately repre-

---

10. Roberta Romano, The Shareholder Suit: Litigation Without Foundation?, 7 J. L. & Econ. 55 (1991). Research by Janet Cooper Alexander in the related area of securities fraud litigation confirms that set- tlements have little to do with the merits of the litigation. Janet Cooper Alexander, Do the Merits Matter? A Study of Settlements in Securities Class Actions, 43 Stan. L. Rev. 497 (1991).

sent the interests of the shareholders or members similarly situated in enforcing the right of the corporation or association. The action shall not be dismissed or compromised without the approval of the court, and notice of the proposed dismissal or compromise shall be given to shareholders or members in such manner as the court directs.

Many states, including Delaware, have comparable rules. The following sections break out the various elements of Rule 23.1, as well as describing some additional procedural rules imposed by various states. Because the seemingly trivial provision for demand on the board of directors has assumed great doctrinal significance, that requirement is deferred for separate consideration.

B.   Choice of law

As a preliminary matter, we must address the conflict of law and federalism issues posed by the intersection of Federal Rule 23.1 and substantive state corporate law. Consider, for example, the problems presented by *Cohen v. Beneficial Industrial Loan Corp.*[1] Cohen filed, in federal district court in New Jersey, a derivative action claiming that Beneficial's directors had committed various breaches of fiduciary duty. Because a breach of fiduciary duty implicates state rather than federal law, subject matter jurisdiction rested solely on diversity of citizenship. Under a New Jersey security for expenses statute, shareholder-plaintiffs who lost a derivative action were liable for the corporation's reasonable expenses and attorneys fees. In addition, the statute authorized defendants to require plaintiffs who owned less than $50,000 worth of stock to post a bond ensuring payment of such expenses. Federal Rule 23.1 lacks any such requirement, as does Delaware law—the state in which Beneficial was incorporated. Under standard choice of law rules, Delaware law provided the governing substantive law. But what about that pesky New Jersey security for expenses statute? Did it apply to Cohen's suit?

The Supreme Court held that under *Erie Railroad Co. v. Tompkins*,[2] in diversity actions, "mere rules of procedure" are governed by federal law but "rules of substantive law" are provided by state law. Consequently, for example, "questions of whether or not a stockholder may bring a derivative action are governed by state law."[3] As for the securities for expense statute, the Supreme Court deemed it to be substantive in nature for *Erie* purposes, because the statute created both a potential liability and a mechanism for recovering any such liability. In contrast, the various requirements set forth in Federal Rule 23.1 are procedural in nature. A federal court sitting in diversity therefore will apply Rule 23.1 rather than any inconsistent state rules.[4]

§ 8.4

1. 337 U.S. 541 (1949).

2. 304 U.S. 64 (1938).

3. Galef v. Alexander, 615 F.2d 51, 58 (2d Cir.1980).

4. See, e.g., Kona Enter., Inc. v. Bishop, 179 F.3d 767 (9th Cir.1999) (holding that

A different question is presented when federal subject matter jurisdiction over a derivative action is based on a federal cause of action. Suits involving federal questions, of course, are not subject to the *Erie* regime. Courts have thus held, for example, that state security for expenses statutes do not apply to such suits.[5] A choice of law problem nevertheless persists in derivative actions involving federal questions. In *Burks v. Lasker,*[6] a shareholder of a federally regulated investment company brought suit under the federal securities laws against the company's board of directors. The Supreme Court held that state law controls the board of directors' ability to use a special litigation committee to terminate the litigation. In *Kamen v. Kemper Financial Services, Inc.,*[7] the Court extended *Burks,* describing the federal law governing derivative suits brought under the Investment Company Act as a species of federal common law, and incorporating state law governing excusal of the demand requirement in such suits. Unless there is a clear inconsistency between the federal and state law, or the state law would frustrate relevant federal policies, state law thus controls most aspects of derivative litigation in federal question cases except for basic substantive issues of liability.

C. Verification

Federal Rule 23.1 and the corporation statutes of about 20 states require verification of the complaint. To verify the complaint, the plaintiff swears that the allegations in the complaint are true. The verification requirement's supposed purpose has been stated as follows: "The verification of the complaint in a shareholder derivative action may appear at first blush to be a purely technical requirement, but it serves the important purpose of ensuring 'that the plaintiff or some other person has investigated the charges and found them to have substance,' and thereby prevent the filing of strike suits."[8] On the other hand, courts have emphasized that the verification requirement is "not to be a general impediment to shareholder derivative actions."[9]

Courts routinely grant plaintiffs leave to replead and properly verify a deficient complaint.[10] Courts have likewise waived the verification

---

Federal Rule 23.1's continuous share ownership requirement is procedural for this purposes and therefore applies in diversity proceedings); Overberger v. BT Fin. Corp., 106 F.R.D. 438 (W.D.Pa.1985) (same); see generally Sax v. World Wide Press, Inc., 809 F.2d 610, 613 (9th Cir.1987) ("In federal courts, derivative suits are subject to the procedural requirements of Fed.R.Civ.P. 23.1.").

5. See, e.g., McClure v. Borne Chem. Co., 292 F.2d 824 (3d. Cir.), cert. denied, 368 U.S. 939 (1961). Such statutes will apply to any pendent state claims, however. See, e.g., Weisfeld v. Spartans Indus., Inc., 58 F.R.D. 570, 578 (S.D.N.Y.1972) (holding that "[t]he law is clear that state security requirements for shareholders' derivative actions should be enforced by the federal courts in both pendent and diversity jurisdiction cases but as to *State* causes of action only."); see also Haberman v. Tobin, 480 F.Supp. 425, 426 (S.D.N.Y.1979) (same).

6. 441 U.S. 471 (1979).

7. 500 U.S. 90 (1991).

8. Smachlo v. Birkelo, 576 F.Supp. 1439, 1442 (D.Del.1983).

9. See, e.g., Lewis v. Curtis, 671 F.2d 779, 787 (3d Cir.1982).

10. See, e.g., Smachlo v. Birkelo, 576 F.Supp. 1439, 1442 (D.Del.1983).

requirement when it was apparent from a plaintiff's deposition that he was sufficiently cognizant of the complaint's allegations.[11] Courts have also waived the requirement if plaintiff filed an affidavit verifying the complaint and further swearing the failure to properly verify the complaint was a mere oversight.[12] Finally, courts have held that plaintiffs' failure to comply with the verification requirement at the time the complaint was filed is not a jurisdictional defect, such that defendant waives the objection if it is not made on a timely basis.[13]

The U.S. Supreme Court arguably sounded the de facto death knell for the verification requirement when it deemed that requirement to be satisfied where plaintiff "verified the complaint, not on the basis of her own knowledge and understanding, but in the faith that her son-in-law had correctly advised her either that the statements in the complaint were true or to the best of his knowledge he believed them to be true."[14] As a result, the verifying plaintiff no longer need have detailed personal knowledge of the events that gave rise to the suit.[15] Instead, it suffices that "some person, party, attorney, advisor, or otherwise has responsibly investigated the allegations at the behest of the named plaintiff, who then stands behind the merits of the complaint."[16]

Given the verification requirement's substantial erosion, it now seems wholly pointless. The MBCA has eliminated its former verification requirement. The ALI PRINCIPLES substituted a requirement of attorney certification for that of verification by the plaintiff. ALI PRINCIPLES § 7.04(b) thus provides that counsel must certify that every pleading and motion is well grounded in fact and is warranted by existing law or by a good faith argument for the extension, modification, or reversal of existing law, and further that the filing is not made for any improper purpose, such as to cause unnecessary delay. As the commentary to § 7.04(b) indicates, this standard essentially tracks the sanction provisions of Federal Rule of Civil Procedure 11. If preventing strike suits is the goal, the ALI's approach seems a more effective solution than Federal Rule 23.1's verification requirement.

D.   Contemporaneous ownership

1.   *The basic requirement*

Federal Rule 23.1's contemporaneous ownership provision requires the verified complaint to allege that the plaintiff was a shareholder at

---

11. See, e.g., Deaktor v. Fox Grocery Co., 332 F.Supp. 536, 541 (W.D.Pa.1971).

12. See, e.g., Markowitz v. Brody, 90 F.R.D. 542, 549 n. 2 (S.D.N.Y.1981); Weisfeld v. Spartans Indus., Inc., 58 F.R.D. 570, 577–58 (S.D.N.Y.1972).

13. See, e.g., Alford v. Shaw, 398 S.E.2d 445, 447 (N.C.1990).

14. Surowitz v. Hilton Hotels Corp., 383 U.S. 363, 370–71 (1966).

15. Brown v. Hart, Schaffner & Marx, 96 F.R.D. 64, 67 (N.D.Ill.1982).

16. Rogosin v. Steadman, 65 F.R.D. 365, 367 (S.D.N.Y.1974). See also Porte v. Home Fed. Savings & Loan Ass'n of Chicago, 409 F.Supp. 752, 754 (N.D.Ill.1976) ("Before a court can proceed with a derivative suit, it must be assured that the plaintiff or some other person has investigated the charges and found them to have substance.").

the time of the challenged or event. MBCA § 7.41 elevates the contemporaneous ownership requirement into a rule of standing. Under it, shareholders may not "commence or maintain" a derivative suit unless they were shareholders "at the time of the act or omission complained of." The phrase "commence or maintain" codifies the long-standing common law rule that standing to sue derivatively is limited to those who are shareholders both at the time the cause of action was arose and when the suit was filed.[17] In some states, moreover, one must also be a shareholder when judgment is entered,[18] or even through the appeals process.[19]

Both Federal Rule 23.1 and MBCA § 7.41 provide limited exceptions to the contemporaneous ownership requirement. Both grant standing to shareholders who received their shares by operation of law—e.g., via bequest—from a contemporaneous shareholder.[20] In addition, both provide that plaintiff need not be a record owner of shares—beneficial ownership suffices.[21]

17. See, e.g., Hawes v. Oakland, 104 U.S. 450, 461 (1881); Werfel v. Kramarsky, 61 F.R.D. 674 (S.D.N.Y.1974); Green v. Bradley Const., Inc., 431 So.2d 1226 (Ala. 1983); see also Lewis v. Anderson, 477 A.2d 1040, 1046 (Del.1984) (noting that plaintiff "must not only be a stockholder at the time of the alleged wrong and at time of commencement of suit but that he must also maintain shareholder status throughout the litigation"). But cf. Bateson v. Magna Oil Corp., 414 F.2d 128 (5th Cir.1969), which held that a shareholder who inadvertently sold his stock but shortly thereafter reacquired stock for very purpose of filing a previously planned derivative suit had standing. Id. at 131.

18. See, e.g., Sorin v. Shahmoon Indus., Inc., 220 N.Y.S.2d 760, 781 (Sup.Ct.1961); see also ALI PRINCIPLES § 7.02(a). But see Alford v. Shaw, 398 S.E.2d 445, 449 (N.C. 1990) (holding "there is no requirement of continuing share ownership in order for an individual who is a shareholder at the time of the transaction about which he is complaining and at the time the action is filed, to proceed with a derivative action").

19. See Schilling v. Belcher, 582 F.2d 995 (5th Cir.1978), interpreting Florida law as providing that shareholder who sells his stock while an appeal from a favorable judgment is pending loses standing to further prosecute the case except to extent that the judgment runs personally to his favor. Id. at 996. This holding was rejected by ALI PRINCIPLES § 7.02(a)(2) and, in any event, would be inapplicable as to jurisdictions in which shareholders are not obliged to hold their stock through judgment.

20. See Phillips v. Bradford, 62 F.R.D. 681, 684 (S.D.N.Y.1974) (holding that "a devolution by will is as much a devolution 'by operation of law' as is a devolution by intestacy").

21. See, e.g., Schupack v. Covelli, 498 F.Supp. 704 (W.D.Pa.1980); Jones v. Taylor, 348 A.2d 188 (Del.Ch.1975) (contractually created legacy sufficient to provide standing); Brown v. Dolese, 154 A.2d 233 (Del. Ch.1959), aff'd, 157 A.2d 784 (Del.1960) (beneficiary of trust that owned stock had standing); Rosenthal v. Burry Biscuit Corp., 60 A.2d 106, 111–12 (Del.Ch.1948) (record ownership not required); Gustafson v. Gustafson, 734 P.2d 949 (Wash.App.1987) (pledgee of stock has standing). But see Pessin v. Chris–Craft Indus., Inc., 586 N.Y.S.2d 584 (App.Div.1992) (holding that shares acquired by a deliberate act, such as by gift or contract, did not "devolve by operation of law"). To the extent beneficial ownership exists solely by virtue of a conversion right, as where the holder of convertible bonds might be deemed the beneficial owner of the shares into which the bonds are convertible, the holder of such instruments lacks standing. See, e.g., MBCA § 7.41 cmt.; Harff v. Kerkorian, 324 A.2d 215 (Del.Ch.1974), rev'd in part on other grounds, 347 A.2d 133 (Del.1975); see ALI PRINCIPLES § 7.02(a) (record ownership not required, but mere creditor lacks standing).

Various common law exceptions to the contemporaneous ownership requirement also have been created. Some courts, for example, recognize a quasi-exemption to the requirement by allowing so-called double derivative suits in which a shareholder of a parent corporation sues on behalf of a wholly-owned subsidiary.[22] Both corporations must be made party to such a suit and demand must be made on both boards of directors.[23]

Some courts have also recognized a so-called continuing wrong exception to the contemporaneous ownership requirement.[24] The cases are all over the map, however, and many courts apply this exception quite conservatively. As Delaware Chancellor Allen once observed, "[t]he effects of an act can ripple through decades. But that fact does not mean that the act itself continues . . . so as to entitle later purchasers of the stock to sue on earlier wrongs."[25]

What if the would-be plaintiffs involuntarily lost their status as shareholders as a result of corporate action, perhaps even the action of which plaintiffs complain, as where the shareholders were forced out by a freezeout merger? Courts are divided here. In *Gaillard v. Natomas Co.*,[26] for example, a California appellate court held that such a shareholder retains standing. In *Lewis v. Anderson*,[27] however, the Delaware supreme court held that such a shareholder lacks standing.[28] It is hard to see any justification for the *Lewis* rule, other than the highly formalistic notion that the cause of action belongs to the corporation. The rule is "tantamount to paving the way for deliberate corporate pilfering by management and then for the immunization of the guilty officers from liability therefor by their arranging for a merger or consolidation of the corporation into or with another corporation."[29]

The continuous ownership requirement is sometimes justified as being necessary to ensure that the plaintiff will adequately represent interests of all shareholders. Because any recovery in derivative litigation normally is paid to the corporation, someone who is not now a

---

22. See, e.g., Brown v. Tenney, 532 N.E.2d 230 (Ill.1988); see also Shaev v. Wyly, 1998 WL 13858 (Del.Ch.), aff'd, 719 A.2d 490 (Del.1998) (plaintiff originally had standing to bring a double derivative action, but such standing was extinguished by a subsequent spin off of the subsidiary); cf. Pessin v. Chris–Craft Indus., Inc., 586 N.Y.S.2d 584 (App.Div.1992) (recognizing validity of double derivative suit, but holding that parent corporation must control subsidiary in order for would-be plaintiff to have standing).

23. Cochran v. Stifel Fin. Corp., 2000 WL 286722 (Del.Ch.); Flocco v. State Farm Mut. Auto. Ins. Co., 752 A.2d 147, 154 (D.C.2000) (interpreting Illinois law).

24. See, e.g., Valle v. North Jersey Auto. Club, 376 A.2d 1192 (N.J.1977).

25. Thorpe v. CERBCO, Inc., 1993 WL 35967 at *4 (Del.Ch.).

26. 219 Cal. Rptr. 74 (Cal.App.1985). See also Alford v. Shaw, 398 S.E.2d 445 (N.C.1990).

27. 477 A.2d 1040 (Del.1984). Cf. Professional Mgmt. Assoc., Inc. v. Coss, 598 N.W.2d 406 (Minn.App.1999) (shareholders had standing, *inter alia*, because merger agreement by its express terms gave them a continuing interest in the acquired firm).

28. Two exceptions recognized by Delaware to the *Lewis* rule are: "(1) where the merger itself is the subject of a claim of fraud; and (2) where the merger is in reality a reorganization which does not affect plaintiff's ownership." Lewis v. Anderson, 477 A.2d 1040, 1046 n. 10 (Del.1984).

29. Platt Corp. v. Platt, 249 N.Y.S.2d 75, 83 (App.Div.1964), aff'd mem., 256 N.Y.S.2d 335 (1965).

shareholder will not benefit from a successful suit. A former shareholder thus supposedly has an incentive to negotiate an inadequate settlement that confers some personal benefit on the shareholder. because it is the shareholder-plaintiff's lawyer who is the real party in interest, however, this justification for the rule has little merit.

The contemporaneous ownership requirement also is often justified as necessary to prevent courts from being used as a forum for purchased grievances or speculative suits.[30] Hence, for example, the rule prevents "an outsider from buying or acquiring shares for the purpose of seeking to upset an action that had been taken by the corporation at some previous time."[31] According to some courts, those who bring such suits would be unjustly enriched by a recovery under the circumstances.[32] As long as any recovery is paid into the corporate treasury, however, concerns over potential unjust enrichment seem misplaced. All current shareholders are benefited by such a recovery, without regard to when they acquired their shares. If the company is publicly held, moreover, the correct question is not when the challenged event occurred but when it became public knowledge. Because capital markets are not strong form efficient, prices will not adjust until wrongdoing is discovered. Because capital markets are semi-strong efficient, prices will adjust immediately after wrongdoing becomes public. Barring shareholders who acquired their stock in the interim from suing derivatively thus bars suit by persons who were doubtless injured.[33] ALI PRINCIPLES § 7.02(a)(1) correctly grants standing to persons who acquired their shares before the material facts were disclosed to the public or otherwise known by the purchaser.

2. *Bondholder standing to sue derivatively*

Federal Rule 23.1's contemporaneous ownership provision requires an allegation "that the plaintiff was a *shareholder*" at the requisite

---

30. Cohen v. Beneficial Industrial Loan Corp., 337 U.S. 541, 556 (1949). See also Bank of Santa Fe v. Petty, 867 P.2d 431 (N.M.App.1993) (noting that requirement is intended to prevent champerty).

31. Kaplus v. First Continental Corp., 711 So.2d 108, 112 (Fla.App.1998).

32. See Bangor Punta Operations, Inc. v. Bangor & Aroostook R.R., 417 U.S. 703, 711 (1974) (rule prevents a windfall).

33. One court opined:

When the prior mismanagement, fraud, or negligence has produced results that are obvious and substantial, those results should be reflected in the price of the corporation's stock—the price should drop due to the mismanagement or other fault. Theoretically, the shareholder then purchases the stock at a reduced price due to the negative results flowing from the mismanagement or other fault. The shareholder should not later be permitted to obtain double recovery by filing a law-

suit based on the events preceding his acquisition.

Bank of Santa Fe v. Petty, 867 P.2d 431, 434 (N.M.App.1993). The relevant price drop, of course, will only occur if the information is public. See also Bird v. Lida, Inc., 681 A.2d 399 (Del.Ch.1996), which held that "the fact that plaintiff acquired his stock ... at time when the [challenged transactions] were publicly and widely disclosed, would foreclose his maintenance of a derivative suit...." Id. at 406. "The justification for such a rule would be that the market priced what the buyer was buying, warts and all. It would be neither fair nor efficient to permit later complaints about a disclosed wart." Id. at 406 n.4. Cf. Rifkin v. Steele Platt, 824 P.2d 32, 34 (Colo.App. 1991) (remanding to trial court for determination of whether "the purchase price reflected the prior wrongdoings").

times. MBCA § 7.40 likewise refers solely to shareholders when discussing the right to sue derivatively. Do these seemingly procedural provisions imply a further standing limitation? Specifically, does the contemporaneous ownership requirement deny standing to bondholders?

Although the MBCA's statutory text does not speak directly to this issue, the statute's drafters assert that MBCA § 7.41 implicitly limits derivative standing to shareholders. Consequently, "creditors or holders of options, warrants, or conversion rights" lack standing to sue derivatively.[34] In *Harff v. Kerkorian*,[35] the Delaware chancery court likewise limited standing under its derivative litigation statute to shareholders.

In *Harff*, holders of MGM convertible bonds claimed that MGM's directors had breached their fiduciary duty to the corporation by paying an excessive dividend. Although suits to enforce a dividend right are treated as direct, this lawsuit was derivative because it involved claims that a dividend was paid improperly. Convertible bonds generally have a lower coupon rate than regular bonds. To the extent that the conversion feature has value to the debtholders, that value is part of the economic return on their investment. Accordingly, the debtholders will not demand as high a rate of interest as will the holder of a nonconvertible bond. The allegedly excessive dividend reduced the value of the common stock and, indirectly, injured the bondholders by reducing the value of their conversion feature.

Neither the corporation nor its directors owe any fiduciary duties to bondholders, at least so long as the corporation is solvent.[36] Why then did the *Harff* court need to reach this issue? The answer, of course, is that the question is a trick one. The claim involved fiduciary duties owed to the corporation by its officers and directors. The real question is whether the bondholders have the right to sue derivatively on behalf of the corporate enterprise. In any case, *Harff* squarely held that bondholders have no standing to sue derivatively, even if their bonds have a conversion feature. Even if the word "shareholder" in the relevant statutes is broadly interpreted to include holders of all equity securities, a convertible bond remains purely a debt security until such time as it is converted into stock.[37]

The leading case holding to the contrary is *Hoff v. Sprayregan*,[38] which involved a claim that the directors had wasted corporate assets by issuing stock for inadequate consideration to a person who thereby became a controlling shareholder. As with *Harff*, the transactions at

---

34. MBCA § 7.41 cmt.

35. 324 A.2d 215 (Del.Ch.1974), rev'd in part on other grounds, 347 A.2d 133 (Del. 1975).

36. See § 9.4.

37. In Simons v. Cogan, 549 A.2d 300 (Del.1988), the Delaware supreme court endorsed *Harff*. Additional cases holding that bondholders (convertible or otherwise) lack standing to sue derivatively include: Kusner

v. First Pa. Corp., 395 F.Supp. 276 (E.D.Pa. 1975), rev'd on other grounds, 531 F.2d 1234 (3d Cir.1976); Brooks v. Weiser, 57 F.R.D. 491 (S.D.N.Y.1972); In re Will of Migel, 336 N.Y.S.2d 376 (Surr.Ct.1972);

38. 52 F.R.D. 243 (S.D.N.Y.1971). See also Weitzen v. Kearns, 271 F.Supp. 616 (S.D.N.Y.1967) (allowing, without discussion, convertible bondholders to sue derivatively).

issue made exercising the conversion feature less attractive and thus reduced the value of that feature, reducing the return to investors. First, the transactions entailed creation of a new class of preferred stock with rights superior to the common into which the debentures were convertible. Second, the issuance of stock below market value had a dilutive effect, which lowered the value of the common. Finally, the transaction resulted in Sprayregan becoming the dominant shareholder of the firm.

Hoff held that holders of convertible bonds have standing to sue derivatively on behalf of the corporation. The *Hoff* court finessed the apparent standing limitation imposed by FRCP 23.1's reference to shareholders by defining that term to include holders of convertible bonds. The underlying cause of action was based on the federal Securities Exchange Act, which includes convertible bonds within its definition of equity securities.[39] It is not self-evident that the definitions of equity securities and shareholder are co-extensive, but without any real explanation or justification the court nevertheless equated them. Accordingly, the court held that the convertible bondholders had standing to sue derivatively.

Note that, even if it was correctly decided, *Hoff* thus does not grant standing to holders of nonconvertible bonds. One also could argue that *Hoff*'s analysis is mere dicta. As an alternative holding, the court noted that the convertible bondholders had exercised their conversion rights in July 1969. Certain aspects of the challenged transactions were not completed until August of that year. Invoking the continuing wrong principle, the court held that the former bondholders—who were now shareholders—were entitled to sue. In any event, the subsequent *Brooks v. Weiser* decision limited *Hoff* to its specific legal setting—i.e., a federal claim arising under a statute including convertible securities within the definition of equity securities. Where state corporate law provides the underlying substantive legal regime, standing before a federal court sitting in diversity is determined by reference to state law definitions of the term shareholder.[40]

Hoff and *Harff* raise two policy questions that are worth exploring. First, should bondholders be allowed to sue derivatively? Second, should convertible bondholders be treated as bondholders or shareholders for this purpose? Consider the following hypothetical, which is loosely based on the facts of *Harff*: Jane Doe is the controlling shareholder of Corporate Law, Inc. Doe needs cash for personal reasons. Doe uses her control to force the directors of Corporate Law to pay a large dividend. Although the dividend technically met the requirements of the applicable legal capital statute, the dividend was improvident under the company's financial circumstances.

An improvidently large dividend paid by directors who did not exercise independent business judgment, but instead simply followed the controlling shareholders' orders, likely violates the directors' duty of

---

39. Securities Exchange Act § 3(a)(11).

40. Brooks v. Weiser, 57 F.R.D. 491, 494 (S.D.N.Y.1972).

care. A shareholder would have standing to bring this claim derivative-ly,[41] assuming the shareholder met the continuity of ownership standards set forth in FRCP 23.1 and comparable state laws. Assuming the case got to the merits, however, the shareholder is unlikely to prevail. Under *Sinclair Oil v. Levien*,[42] a board decision to pay a lawful dividend is protected by the business judgment rule so long as the minority share-holders received their pro rata share of the dividend.

Given that the business judgment rule would preclude a shareholder from bringing this suit successfully, bondholders should not be allowed to do so either. The business judgment rule balances the competing policy goals of deference to the board's decisionmaking authority and ensuring accountability on the board's part. Allowing bondholders to sue, where shareholders may not, upsets that balance.

This analysis explains why bondholders should not be allowed to bring a derivative suit if the shareholders could not, but why not permit bondholders to bring suit if the shareholders could do so? One answer is that such bondholder suits are presumptively unnecessary, assuming a vigilant plaintiff's bar suing on behalf of shareholders. More importantly, however, where shareholder and bondholder interests are not congruent, shareholder interests prevail. To be sure, as the *Hoff* court argued, bondholders make a substantial investment in the firm that often exceeds that made by shareholders who have standing. Until they exercise their conversion feature, however, the nature of the bondhold-ers' interest remains a fixed claim. It is shareholders who hold the residual claim and thus bear greater risk. It is shareholder wealth that the board is obliged to maximize when the interests of bondholders and shareholders clash. It is for this reason, after all, that the directors' and officers' duties run to shareholders while bondholder rights are purely contractual. Accordingly, bondholders should not be allowed to sue to enforce a corporate cause of action when doing so is not in the share-holders' interest. Bondholders have alternative sources of protection, moreover, such as fraudulent conveyance law and/or enforcing the provi-sions of the bond indenture. Allowing them to sue derivatively would be a backdoor method of imposing fiduciary duties on the directors running to the bondholders.

The equity component of convertible securities does not justify treating them differently than nonconvertible bonds. So long as they remain creditors, convertible bondholders' interests can differ from those of shareholders. Indeed, until they convert, their interests are closer to those of bondholders than to those of shareholders. All of the arguments against allowing nonconvertible bondholders to sue derivatively thus apply in full force to convertible bondholders.

41. A lawsuit seeking to remedy the div-idend payment would be derivative in na-ture, as the directors' duty of care generally runs to the corporation and the injury is one to the corporation in the first instance.

42. 280 A.2d 717 (Del.1971).

3. *Director qua director standing*

Assume an injury to the corporation giving rise to a claim belonging to the corporation. Obviously, the board of directors, acting collectively, could authorize the corporation's agents to bring the lawsuit in question. Suppose, however, the board has not acted. An individual director who is also a shareholder obviously could bring a derivative cause of action in the latter capacity. But does a director qua director have standing? The logical answer is no, although that answer is based on the implications of several distinct principles rather than a single statement of doctrine. First, both MBCA § 7.41 and Federal Rule 23.1 speak only of shareholders. As we have seen, other corporate constituents (such as creditors) lack standing. Second, under AGENCY RESTATEMENT § 14 C, an individual director is not an agent of the corporation. Indeed, comment b to that section states that the individual director "has no power of his own to act on the corporation's behalf, but only as one of the body of directors acting as a board." Taken together, these principles logically suggest that a director acting alone has no standing to sue qua director.

A few states, most notably New York, confer standing by statute on individual directors to bring derivative proceedings.[43] A director may not initiate a derivative action after leaving office, but neither removal nor expiration of the director's term of office extinguishes the director's standing to continue a previously filed suit.[44] ALI PRINCIPLES § 7.02(c) adopted the same rule.

Although director standing remains very much the minority position, it has a certain attraction. Recall the basic tenet of this text; namely, that shareholders do not own the corporation. Instead, they are merely one of many corporate constituencies bound together by a complex web of explicit and implicit contracts. To be sure, by virtue of their contractual status as residual claimants, shareholders ought to have standing to pursue suits that lower the value of that claim. If we view the directors as the corporation's Platonic guardians, however, perhaps the directors ought to have prior standing to litigate injuries to the corporation. On the other hand, given the strong efficiency justifications for corporate law's emphasis on the board as a collective, perhaps we ought to discourage directors from acting as lone rangers.

E.   Collusive jurisdiction and realignment of parties

Federal courts worry incessantly that parties to a lawsuit will collusively manipulate their alignment so as to invoke federal diversity jurisdiction. Hence, Federal Rule 23.1's requirement that the plaintiff verify that the suit is "not a collusive one to confer jurisdiction on a court of the United States...." Whether or not this is a real problem and, if so, what to do about it, are questions best left to those who toil in the civil procedure vineyard.

---

43.   N.Y. Bus. Corp. Law § 720.   **44.**   2 ALI PRINCIPLES at 42 (citing cases).

For our purposes, the significant questions are (1) whether the corporation is a necessary party to the litigation and (2) whether the corporation should be aligned as a plaintiff or defendant. As to the former question, the corporation is deemed an indispensable party who must be joined to the litigation.[45] Accordingly, plaintiffs normally start out by naming the corporation as a defendant, so as to ensure it is joined to the litigation. In theory, courts then should realign the corporation as a plaintiff, because any recovery normally will be paid to the corporation. If the corporation's board of directors is actively opposing the shareholder-plaintiff, however, such that the corporation is "antagonistic" to the lawsuit, courts will align the corporation as a defendant.[46]

F.   Fair and adequate representation

Under both Federal Rule 23.1 and MBCA § 7.41(2), the named shareholder-plaintiff must be a fair and adequate representative. But of what? Under the Rule, the plaintiff must fairly and adequately represent the interests of similarly situated shareholders. Under MBCA § 7.41(2), the plaintiff must fairly and adequately represent the corporation's interests. Given that the derivative suit conceptually "belongs" to the corporation and not the shareholders, the latter approach seems preferable.

In practice, would-be plaintiffs are most commonly disqualified under the fairness and adequacy standard where they brought the derivative suit for strategic purposes relating to other disputes with the corporation or its management. In *Recchion v. Kirby*,[47] for example, the would-be plaintiff-shareholder owned only one share of stock, brought the suit six years after he learned of the allegedly wrongful conduct, was supported by no other shareholders, and had a pending personal lawsuit against the corporation. Concluding that the derivative action was brought for use as leverage in plaintiff's personal lawsuit, the court disqualified the plaintiff.

In several cases brought by shareholder-plaintiffs who were pursuing an attempted acquisition of the corporation, the would-be plaintiffs have been disqualified.[48] In contrast, courts have divided on whether

---

45. See, e.g., Liddy v. Urbanek, 707 F.2d 1222, 1224 (11th Cir.1983); Dean v. Kellogg, 292 N.W. 704, 707 (Mich.1940); but cf. Weinert v. Kinkel, 71 N.E.2d 445 (N.Y.1947) (dissolved corporation was not an indispensable party).

46. Smith v. Sperling, 354 U.S. 91, 95 (1957).

The question of whether to realign the corporation as a plaintiff or allow it to remain as a defendant is "a practical not a mechanical determination and is resolved by the pleadings and the nature of the dispute." Thus, if the complaint in a derivative action alleges that the controlling shareholders or dominant officials of the corporation are guilty of fraud or malfeasance, then antagonism is clearly evident and the corporation remains a defendant. On the other hand, if the individual plaintiff is the majority stockholder or a controlling officer, then the corporation cannot be deemed antagonistic to the suit and it should be realigned as a plaintiff.

Liddy v. Urbanek, 707 F.2d 1222, 1224–25 (11th Cir.1983) (citations omitted).

47. 637 F.Supp. 1309 (W.D.Pa.1986).

48. See, e.g., Nolen v. Shaw–Walker Co., 449 F.2d 506 (6th Cir.1971); Adiel v. Electronic Fin. Systems, Inc., 513 So.2d 1347 (Fla.App.1987).

shareholders who have tried to compel the corporation or its other shareholders to buy their shares at an above-market price should be disqualified.[49]

Plaintiffs also will be disqualified where they participated in, knowingly acquiesced in, or voted to ratify the challenged conduct. In *Recchion*, for example, the court held that plaintiff had unclean hands because he had participated in some of the alleged misconduct knowing that his actions were improper and inconsistent with generally accepted accounting practices. Plaintiff was therefore estopped to bring a derivative suit.[50]

Given that the real party in interest usually is the plaintiff's lawyer rather than the nominal shareholder-plaintiff, it is noteworthy that at least one court has disqualified a plaintiff on grounds that she possessed "little, if any, comprehension of the litigation" and "that total control as well as financing of the action rests with the lawyers."[51] Conversely, however, a named plaintiff who is not an attorney may not proceed pro se.[52] The apparent Catch–22 is solved by combining a knowledgeable named plaintiff with competent legal counsel.

In general, the adequacy of the named plaintiff is determined under the totality of the circumstances. In doing so, courts consider a number of factors: (1) economic or other conflicts between the named plaintiff and other shareholders; (2) evidence that the named plaintiff was not the driving force behind the litigation, especially with respect to the degree of control exercised by counsel; (3) plaintiff's lack of familiarity with the litigation; (4) pendency of other litigation between the named plaintiff and the individual defendants and/or the corporation; (5) evidence of personal vindictiveness toward the defendants; and (6) the support plaintiff receives from other shareholders, if any.[53]

---

49. Compare Vanderbilt v. Geo–Energy Ltd., 725 F.2d 204 (3d Cir.1983) (not disqualified) with Steinberg v. Steinberg, 434 N.Y.S.2d 877 (Sup.Ct.1980). In the latter decision, the court's finding that the would-be plaintiff's lawsuit was "so fraught with such conflict of interest as to be legally impermissible" doubtless was influenced by court's further finding that "the derivative action was deliberately instituted to obtain leverage in the matrimonial [divorce] proceeding" between the shareholder-plaintiff and her ex-husband, who was a shareholder and president of the corporation. Id. at 879.

50. Recchion v. Kirby, 637 F.Supp. 1309, 1316 (W.D.Pa.1986).

51. Mills v. Esmark, Inc., 573 F.Supp. 169, 176 (N.D.Ill.1983). Other courts have indicated that plaintiff's knowledge and the degree of control exercised by counsel are factors to be considered. See, e.g., Rothenberg v. Security Mgmt. Co., Inc., 667 F.2d 958, 961 (11th Cir.1982); Davis v. Comed, Inc., 619 F.2d 588, 593–94 (6th Cir.1980).

52. Pridgen v. Andresen, 113 F.3d 391, 393 (2d Cir.1997); In re Texaco Inc. Shareholder Derivative Litig., 123 F.Supp.2d 169, 172 (S.D.N.Y.2000). The explanation for this rule was remarkably formalistic: "Courts have repeatedly held that the substantive right in a stockholder's derivative suit is that of the corporation, and not that of the stockholders.... Since a corporation may not appear except through an attorney, likewise the representative shareholder cannot appear without an attorney." Phillips v. Tobin, 548 F.2d 408, 411 (2d Cir.1976). A better justification might be that lone rangers not represented by counsel should not be allowed to monkey about with claim preclusive litigation that can effect numerous other persons.

53. See, e.g., Rothenberg v. Security Mgmt. Co., Inc., 667 F.2d 958, 961 (11th Cir.1982); Davis v. Comed, Inc., 619 F.2d 588, 593–94 (6th Cir.1980).

G.   Judicial approval of settlements

Federal Rule 23.1 and MBCA § 7.45 require judicial approval before a derivative suit may be settled and notice of a proposed settlement must be given to the shareholders. To be approved, the settlement is supposed to be fair, reasonable and adequate.[54] The settlement must not be collusive, but rather the product of arm's length negotiations following adequate discovery. Courts purportedly consider a wide range of factors in deciding whether to approve a settlement, including: (1) the maximum and likely recovery; (2) the complexity, expense, and duration of continued litigation; (3) the probability of success; (4) the stage of the proceedings; (5) the ability of the defendants to pay a larger judgment; (6) the adequacy of the settlement terms; (7) whether the settlement vindicates important public policies; (8) whether the settlement was approved by disinterested directors; and (9) whether other shareholders have objected.[55] Cases in which objecting shareholders intervene to challenge a settlement likely get far more exacting scrutiny than those in which the other shareholders remain quiescent. If objecting shareholders are able to force a better deal, they are entitled to their own legal fees.[56]

The judicial approval requirement is especially significant in light of the claim preclusive effect of settlements.[57] In theory, judicial approval acts as a check on both the incentive to bring strike suits and the incentive to settle meritorious claims too cheaply. In practice, however, trial courts possess broad discretion to approve derivative suit settlements.[58] Settlements imposing minimal sanctions on individual defendants and conferring nominal benefits on the corporation, if any, but large legal fees for the plaintiffs' lawyers are routinely approved. The judicial approval requirement commonly seems all bark and no bite.

H.   Recovery

In general, any monetary recovery from a derivative lawsuit will be paid over to the corporation rather than either the named shareholder-plaintiff or the shareholders as a class. In many cases, of course, the individual defendant directors or officers will also be shareholders and therefore will benefit along with all other shareholders from the result-

---

54. See 2 ALI Principles at 188; cf. Desimone v. Indus. Bio–Test Labs., Inc., 83 F.R.D. 615, 618 (S.D.N.Y.1979) (discussing comparable rules governing settlement of class actions).

55. See, e.g., Shlensky v. Dorsey, 574 F.2d 131 (3d Cir.1978); Krasner v. Dreyfus Corp., 500 F.Supp. 36 (S.D.N.Y.1980); see also Polk v. Good, 507 A.2d 531, 536 (Del. 1986) (holding that the chancellor "exercises a form of business judgment to determine the overall reasonableness of the settlement"); see generally 2 ALI Principles at 188–90; cf. Desimone v. Indus. Bio–Test Labs., Inc., 83 F.R.D. 615, 619 (S.D.N.Y.

1979) (discussing factors to be considered with respect to settlement of shareholder class actions).

56. White v. Auerbach, 500 F.2d 822 (2d Cir.1974) (remanding for evidentiary hearing on issue).

57. Cf. Matsushita Elec. Indus. Co. v. Epstein, 516 U.S. 367 (1996) (giving full faith and credit to a state court settlement purporting to release both state and federal claims).

58. In re General Tire & Rubber Co. Sec. Litig., 726 F.2d 1075 (6th Cir.1984).

ing increase in value of the residual claim. Although it is often said that individual shareholder recovery is appropriate in derivative proceedings when necessary to prevent a wrongdoer from benefiting by a corporate recovery, in practice that fact alone rarely results in individual recovery.[59] Among other things, because corporate creditors have a prior claim on the firm's assets, individual recovery by shareholders would be inconsistent with the creditors' rights.

Courts have done a lousy job of specifying when individual recovery is appropriate. In *Perlman v. Feldmann*,[60] for example, in which defendant shareholders had bought a control block of stock from defendant former shareholders at a substantial premium over market, the court ordered individual recovery on the bare assertion that the defendants should not "share in any judgment which may be rendered." To which one might reasonably respond, why not? In trying to summarize the few and often conflicting cases, the ALI PRINCIPLES' drafters seemingly just threw up their hands, merely suggesting individual recovery should be ordered when it is "equitable in the circumstances and adequate provision has been made for the creditors of the corporation."[61]

Where individual recovery is ordered, it should be on a pro rata basis. In *Perlman v. Feldmann*, for example, the plaintiff-shareholders owned approximately 63% of the corporation's stock. Having determined defendant's potential liability to be just under $2,126,280.91, the trial court awarded the plaintiffs 63% thereof—$1,339,769.62—plus interest and costs.[62] Notice that corporate recovery thus would have subjected the defendants to greater total liability. Indeed, that fact formed part of the appellate court's sparse justification for the imposition of individual recovery.[63]

I. Security for expenses statutes

We touched on security for expenses statutes in our earlier discussion of the federalism and choice of law issues presented by derivative litigation. Only eight states still have such statutes, but that number includes the commercially important states of California and New York, so they deserve some attention. Both the New York and California statutes are intended to discourage strike suits by creating shareholder liability for the other side's reasonable legal fees and other expenses. They are also intended to ensure that a fund is available from which

59. See, e.g., Glenn v. Hoteltron Systems, Inc., 547 N.Y.S.2d 816 (1989).

60. 219 F.2d 173 (2d Cir.), cert. denied, 349 U.S. 952 (1955).

61. ALI PRINCIPLES § 7.18(e).

62. Perlman v. Feldmann, 154 F.Supp. 436 (D.Conn.1957). Similarly, in Lynch v. Patterson, 701 P.2d 1126 (Wyo.1985), plaintiff owned 30% of the corporation's stock, with the remaining 70% owned by the defendants. Having successfully established

that the defendants had paid themselves excess compensation in the amount of $266,000, plaintiff was awarded 30% of that amount.

63. Perlman v. Feldmann, 219 F.2d 173, 178 (2d Cir.), cert. denied, 349 U.S. 952 (1955) ("Defendants cannot well object to this form of recovery, since the only alternative, recovery for the corporation as a whole, would subject them to a greater total liability.").

those fees can be paid. Their solutions to these concerns differs rather dramatically, however.

New York requires security for expenses only if the shareholder-plaintiff's stock represents less than 5% of the outstanding shares or has a market value less than $50,000. The idea seems to be that any shareholder willing to make such a large investment in the corporation is unlikely to bring a strike suit involving it. If a security is required, it typically takes the form of a bond posted with the court. The bond's amount must correspond to the reasonable expenses likely to be incurred by the corporation directly or indirectly through indemnification of other defendants. Security is only required if requested by the defendants.[64]

In *Cohen v. Beneficial Industrial Loan Corp.*,[65] the Supreme Court upheld the New York statute against various constitutional challenges. Because the security for expenses statute only required payment of the corporation's reasonable expenses, it did not offend the Due Process Clause: "No type of litigation is more susceptible of regulation than that of a fiduciary nature. And it cannot seriously be said that a state makes such *unreasonable* use of its power as to violate the Constitution when it provides liability and security for payment of reasonable expenses if a litigation of this character is adjudged to be unsustainable." That the statute applied only to shareholder-plaintiffs who owned less than $50,000 worth of stock did not violate the Equal Protection Clause: "We do not think the state is forbidden to use the amount of one's financial interest, which measures his individual injury from the misconduct to be redressed, as some measure of the good faith and responsibility of one who seeks at his own election to act as custodian of the interests of all stockholders, and as an indication that he volunteers for the large burdens of the litigation from a real sense of grievance and is not putting forward a claim to capitalize personally on its harassment value."

California's code likewise allows the defendants to request that the shareholder-plaintiff to post a bond against their reasonable expenses. The bond may not exceed $50,000.[66] The bond may only be ordered if the court determines either that (1) there is no "reasonable possibility" the lawsuit will benefit the corporation or its shareholders or (2) the moving defendant, other than the corporation itself, did not participate in the challenged wrongdoing.[67] In other words, if the court believes the lawsuit probably will not succeed, but does not yet have a basis for dismissing the case, the court can require plaintiff to put up a bond, which seems a more sensible approach to the strike suit problem than does that of New York.

California's statute likewise has passed constitutional muster. In *Beyerbach v. Juno Oil Co.*,[68] plaintiff objected that the statute discriminated against poor shareholders who could not afford to post the bond.

---

64. N.Y. Bus. Corp. Law. § 627.

65. 337 U.S. 541 (1949).

66. Cal. Corp. Code § 800(e).

67. Cal. Corp. Code § 800(c).

68. 265 P.2d 1 (Cal.), appeal dismissed, 347 U.S. 985 (1954).

The court rejected this argument, comparing the security for expenses requirement to constitutionally permissible filing fees and other financial barriers to litigation. The court also emphasized that the shareholder-plaintiff was not enforcing a personal right but rather was acting in a fiduciary capacity on behalf of the corporation and its other shareholders. Consequently, it was permissible for the state to regulate such lawsuits to protect the interests of those parties. On similar grounds the court also rejected plaintiff's further argument that the statute unconstitutionally discriminated because it did not require the defendants to post a bond for their expenses.

Wherever one stands on the strike suit issue, there is a basic problem with security for expenses statutes: they don't work. In the first place, security for expenses statutes apply only to derivative actions. Given that many controversial board actions likely fall within the gray area between direct and derivative proceedings, careful pleading and/or a sympathetic bench can evade the statute simply by characterizing the action as direct.[69]

Assuming diversity jurisdiction can be invoked, plaintiffs frequently can evade such statutes by suing in a federal court located in a state lacking such a statute. Under *Klaxon Co. v. Stentor Electric Manufacturing Co.*,[70] a federal court sitting in diversity must apply the forum state's conflict of laws rules. According to most states' choice of law rules, procedural aspects of derivative litigation are governed by the law of the forum state, while substantive issues are governed by the state of incorporation's law.[71] For this purpose, a security for expenses statute is treated as a procedural rule.[72] Hence, New York's securities for expenses statute would not apply to a derivative action filed in a federal court in Delaware, even though the firm is incorporated in New York.[73]

Even if plaintiff ends up in a forum state having a security for expenses statute, the consequences may not be all that severe. In New

---

69. See, e.g., Eisenberg v. Flying Tiger Line, Inc., 451 F.2d 267 (2d Cir.1971) (acknowledging that the nature of the proceeding was ambiguous, but choosing to characterize it as direct and, thereby, allowing plaintiff to avoid compliance with New York's statute).

70. 313 U.S. 487 (1941).

71. See, e.g., Galef v. Alexander, 615 F.2d 51 (2d Cir.1980) (holding that New York would apply Ohio law to determine whether the board of directors of an Ohio corporation had the power to terminate derivative actions).

72. See, e.g., Berkwitz v. Humphrey, 130 F.Supp. 142 (N.D.Ohio 1955) (holding that Ohio state courts would not apply Pennsylvania security for expenses statute to a derivative proceeding brought in Ohio on behalf of a Pennsylvania corporation).

73. See, e.g., Eisenberg v. Flying Tiger Line, Inc., 451 F.2d 267 (2d Cir.1971); see also Pessin v. Chris–Craft Indus., Inc., 586 N.Y.S.2d 584 (App.Div.1992) (New York would not apply Delaware law with respect to contemporaneous ownership requirement). Note that a rule treated as substantive for *Erie* purposes thus may be treated as procedural for choice of law purposes. Assuming both personal and subject matter jurisdiction could be obtained, much the same result could be reached by suing in the state court of a jurisdiction lacking a security for expense statute. Alternatively, of course, if the claim involves a federal question, the statute will not apply, although it will to any pendent state claims. See, e.g., Haberman v. Tobin, 480 F.Supp. 425, 426 (S.D.N.Y.1979); Weisfeld v. Spartans Indus., Inc., 58 F.R.D. 570, 578 (S.D.N.Y.1972).

York, for example, plaintiffs may band together to satisfy the threshold stock ownership level necessary to defuse the statute. Plaintiffs are entitled to access to the shareholder list in order to solicit enough other shareholders to join the lawsuit, moreover, which is a right they routinely invoke.[74]

Since 1986, five states have repealed their security for expenses statutes.[75] Given the availability of sanctions for frivolous lawsuits, the substantial powers of the board to terminate nonmeritorious litigation, and the ineffectiveness of the statutes, the security for expenses statutes are mere historical anachronisms. Both MBCA § 7.46 and ALI PRINCIPLES § 7.04(b) have taken the lead by replacing security for expenses provisions with sanctions for frivolous filings. The remaining states with security for expenses statutes should follow suit.

J.   Jury trial

In *Ross v. Bernhard*,[76] the U.S. Supreme Court held that the Seventh Amendment right to jury trial potentially applied to derivative proceedings in federal court. The test is whether there would have been a right to trial by jury if the corporation had brought the suit. If so, the equitable nature of the derivative suit does not eliminate the constitutional requirement of trial by jury. State court decisions vary widely. New York recognizes a right to jury trial in derivative suits, for example, while California does not.[77]

§ 8.5   Demand and board control of derivative litigation

A.   The demand requirement

Because the derivative suit is premised on a cause of action belonging to the corporation, one might assume that the corporation would simply bring the lawsuit itself. Derivative suits in fact are relatively rare; most corporate lawsuits are brought by the entity, rather than its shareholders. The derivative suit, of course, was devised so as to permit shareholders to seek relief on behalf of the firm in those cases where the corporation's management for some reason elected not to pursue the claim. Logically, however, it would seem that the corporation should be given an opportunity to decide whether to bring suit before a shareholder is allowed to file a derivative suit.

Accordingly, Federal Rule 23.1 provides that shareholders may not bring suit unless they first make demand on the board of directors or

---

74. Note, Security for Expenses in Shareholders' Derivative Suits: 23 Years' Experience, 4 Colum. J.L. & Soc. Probs. 50 (1968).

75. 2 ALI PRINCIPLES at 95–96.

76. 396 U.S. 531 (1970).

77. Compare Fedoryszyn v. Weiss, 310 N.Y.S.2d 55 (Sup.Ct.1970) with Metcalf v. Shamel, 333 P.2d 857 (Cal.App.1959). See generally Jean E. Maess, Annot., Right to Jury Trial in Stockholder's Derivative Action, 32 A.L.R.4th 1111 (1984).

demand is excused.[1] The requisite demand can take any form, although most jurisdictions require that it be in writing. The demand need not be in the form of a pleading nor a detailed as a complaint, but rather simply must request that the board bring suit on the alleged cause of action. To be sure, the demand must be sufficiently specific as to apprise the board of the nature of the alleged cause of action and to evaluate its merits.[2] "At a minimum, a demand must identify the alleged wrongdoers, describe the factual basis of the wrongful acts and the harm caused to the corporation, and request remedial relief."[3]

Although the demand requirement looks like a mere procedural formality, it has evolved into the central substantive rule of derivative litigation.[4] The foundational question in derivative litigation is the extent to which the corporation, acting through the board of directors or a committee thereof, is permitted to prevent or terminate a derivative action. Put another way, who gets to control the litigation—the shareholder or the corporation's board of directors? Curiously, the answer to that question depends mainly on the procedural posture of the particular case with respect to the demand requirement.

We take up the substantive implications of the demand requirement below. In this section, we focus on the procedural issue of when a shareholder is required to make demand. In particular, we contrast the two leading approaches to the problem—those of New York and Delaware.

1. New York's demand futility standard

Demand is required in all cases, except those in which it is excused. Well, you ask, when is it excused? Demand is excused when it is futile. New York restated its demand futility standard in *Marx v. Akers*.[5] Plaintiff filed a derivative suit against IBM and its directors alleging that the directors had authorized excessive compensation both for themselves and IBM executives. The defendants moved to dismiss on the ground that plaintiff had failed to make demand. As to plaintiff's claim that the board had approved excessive executive salaries, the court agreed that

---

§ 8.5

1. Federal Rule 23.1 contemplates that demand may be made on shareholders in appropriate cases. A few jurisdictions require demand on shareholders, at least in some cases. See, e.g., Heilbrunn v. Hanover Equities Corp., 259 F.Supp. 936 (S.D.N.Y. 1966) (demand on shareholders excused where wrongdoers hold a majority of corporation's stock); Mayer v. Adams, 141 A.2d 458 (Del.Supr.1958) (demand on shareholders excused where alleged wrong could not be ratified by shareholders).

2. See, e.g., Shlensky v. Dorsey, 574 F.2d 131, 141 (3d Cir.1978) (demand must be made in writing, be addressed to the board, and provide sufficient specificity to "give the directors a fair opportunity to initiate the action").

3. Allison v. General Motors Corp., 604 F.Supp. 1106, 1117 (D.Del.), aff'd mem., 782 F.2d 1026 (3d Cir.1985).

4. See Levine v. Smith, 591 A.2d 194, 207 (Del.1991) ("The demand requirement is not a 'mere formalit[y] of litigation,' but rather an important 'stricture[ ] of substantive law.' "); see also Barr v. Wackman, 368 N.Y.S.2d 497, 505 (1975) ("demand is generally designed to weed out unnecessary or illegitimate shareholder derivative suits").

5. 644 N.Y.S.2d 121 (1996).

demand was required. As to the claim that the directors had approved excessive compensation for themselves, however, demand was excused.

In a commendably scholarly opinion, the court identified three bases on which demand is excused under New York law: First, the complaint alleges with particularity that a majority of the board of directors is interested in the challenged transaction. Director interest obviously is present where the directors have a personal self-interest in the challenged transaction. Directors who cause the corporation to enter into a transaction from which they financially benefit, for example, are clearly interested for this purpose.[6] Alternatively, however, director interest may be present where the director has no personal interest in a transaction but is dominated or controlled by a self-interested director.[7]

Second, demand is excused if the complaint alleges with particularity that the board of directors did not fully inform themselves about the challenged transaction to the extent reasonably appropriate under the circumstances. (Notice the implicit parallel to Delaware's decision in *Smith v. Van Gorkom*[8] that the business judgment rule does not protect directors who have made an uninformed judgment.) Consistent with corporate law's strong formal emphasis on the board's primacy, *Marx* makes clear that directors who "passively rubber-stamp" management decisions have not made an informed judgment.[9]

Finally, demand is excused where the complaint alleges with particularity that the challenged transaction was so egregious on its face that it could not have been the product of sound business judgment of the directors. Note the parallel to cases like *Litwin v. Allen*,[10] which supposedly withdraw the business judgment rule's protections from directors who have acted irrationally. Because a prerequisite of rationality easily can erode into a prerequisite of reasonableness, courts would do well to reserve this prong of *Marx* for the legal equivalent of a hundred year flood.

In *Marx*, the court acknowledged that its earlier decision in *Barr v. Wackman*[11] had been widely interpreted as creating a lenient standard for demand futility. Whether or not *Barr* had been read correctly, which the court denied, the court clearly raised the bar in *Marx*. It is not enough that one director is interested in the transaction or even if several directors are interested (or failed to inform themselves). Instead, demand is excused only when one of the three *Marx* prongs is satisfied with respect to a majority of the board.[12] The mere fact that a majority of the board is named as defendants does not make them interested for purposes of demand futility. Although being named as defendants may

6. Barr v. Wackman, 368 N.Y.S.2d 497 (1975).

7. Marx v. Akers, 644 N.Y.S.2d. 121, 128 (1996).

8. 488 A.2d 858 (Del.1985).

9. Marx v. Akers, 644 N.Y.S.2d. 121, 128 (1996).

10. 25 N.Y.S.2d 667 (Sup.Ct.1940).

11. 368 N.Y.S.2d 497 (1975).

12. Marx v. Akers, 644 N.Y.S.2d 121, 127–28 (1996).

give them a stake in the lawsuit, the requisite interest must be one in the underlying transaction or event. Finally, and perhaps most significantly in light of prior more lenient precedents to the contrary, the mere fact that a majority of the board acquiesced in or approved the transaction is insufficient.

As applied to the case at bar, demand was required with respect to the claim of excessive executive compensation. Only three of the 18 directors were executives and only they had a direct personal interest in such compensation. There was no showing that the 15 outsiders were dominated by interested parties and plaintiff's "conclusory allegations" that the board had used faulty procedures to calculate executive salaries did not suffice with respect to either of the latter two Marx prongs. With respect to the allegedly excessive director compensation, however, demand was excused. The court adopted a virtual per se rule that directors are interested in their own compensation. Defendants, however, had also moved to dismiss for failure to state a claim. Taking back with one hand what it had given with the other, the court agreed that plaintiff's "conclusory allegations" did not state a claim.

2. Delaware's demand futility standard

As with New York, Delaware requires demand in all cases except those in which it is excused on grounds of futility. In the seminal *Aronson v. Lewis* decision, the Delaware supreme court set forth the following test for demand futility:

> [T]he Court of Chancery in the proper exercise of its discretion must decide whether, under the particularized facts alleged, a reasonable doubt is created that: (1) the directors are disinterested and independent and (2) the challenged transaction was otherwise the product of a valid exercise of business judgment.[13]

Several aspects of this standard jump out at one. First, did the court really mean to phrase it in the conjunctive? Must plaintiff create a reasonable doubt as to both prongs? In its subsequent *Levine v. Smith* opinion, the court made clear that the test is in the disjunctive, such that satisfying either prong suffices.[14]

Second, and more significant, what is this business about "reasonable doubt"? This odd phrasing has been widely (and justly) criticized. As Judge (and former corporate law professor) Easterbrook complained:

> The reference to "reasonable doubt" summons up the standard applied in criminal law. It is a demanding standard, meaning at least a 90% likelihood that the defendant is guilty. If "reasonable doubt"

---

13. Aronson v. Lewis, 473 A.2d 805, 814 (Del.1984).

14. Levine v. Smith, 591 A.2d 194 (Del. 1991), stating without apologies or blushes that: "The premise of a shareholder claim of futility of demand is that a majority of the board of directors either has a financial interest in the challenged transaction *or* lacks independence *or* otherwise failed to exercise due care. On either showing, it may be inferred that the Board is incapable of exercising its power and authority to pursue the derivative claims directly." Id. at 205 (citations and emphasis in the original omitted; emphasis supplied).

in the *Aronson* formula means the same thing as "reasonable doubt" in criminal law, then demand is excused whenever there is a 10% chance that the original transaction is not protected by the business judgment rule. Why should demand be excused on such a slight showing? Surely not because courts want shareholders to file suit whenever there is an 11% likelihood that the business judgment rule will not protect a transaction. *Aronson* did not say, and later cases have not supplied the deficit. If "reasonable doubt" in corporate law means something different from "reasonable doubt" in criminal law, however, what is the difference?, and why use the same term for two different things?[15]

In its most recent defense of the reasonable doubt standard, the Delaware supreme court rather weakly countered that "the term is apt and achieves the proper balance."[16] Somewhat more helpfully, the court rephrased the test by reversing it: "the concept of reasonable doubt is akin to the concept that the stockholder has a 'reasonable belief' that the board lacks independence or that the transaction was not protected by the business judgment rule." As we shall see, however, the standard still needs further tweaking.

Let's start our analysis of the *Aronson* standard where the plaintiff begins—at the pleading stage. Because the relevant facts must be plead with particularity, prolix pastiches of conclusory allegations will not cut it.[17] If plaintiffs file without first making pre-suit demand, and defendant(s) move to dismiss for failure to do so, however, the issue of demand futility is decided on the pleadings—plaintiffs are not entitled to discovery.[18] What then is the plaintiff to do? For the most part, plaintiffs must rely on what the Delaware supreme court calls "the tools at hand";[19] i.e., external sources of information, such as media reports and corporate regulatory filings. In appropriate cases, shareholder-plaintiffs also may invoke their inspection rights to demand pre-suit access to corporate books and records.

We turn then to the substantive standard for demand futility. The confusing and somewhat problematic *Aronson* standard was helpfully restated in *Grimes v. Donald*:

> One ground for alleging with particularity that demand would be futile is that a "reasonable doubt" exists that the board is capable of making an independent decision to assert the claim if demand were made. The basis for claiming excusal would normally be that: (1) a majority of the board has a material financial or familial interest; (2) a majority of the board is incapable of acting independently for some

---

15. Starrels v. First Nat'l Bank of Chicago, 870 F.2d 1168, 1175 (7th Cir.1989) (Easterbrook, J., concurring) (citations omitted). See also Marx v. Akers, 644 N.Y.S.2d 121, 125 (1996); 2 ALI Principles at 57.

16. Grimes v. Donald, 673 A.2d 1207, 1217 (Del.1996).

17. Brehm v. Eisner, 746 A.2d 244, 249 (Del.2000).

18. Rales v. Blasband, 634 A.2d 927, 934 n. 10 (Del.1993); Levine v. Smith, 591 A.2d 194, 208–10 (Del.1991),

19. Brehm v. Eisner, 746 A.2d 244, 249 (Del.2000).

other reason such as domination or control; or (3) the underlying transaction is not the product of a valid exercise of business judgment. If the stockholder cannot plead such assertions consistent with Chancery Rule 11, after using the "tools at hand" to obtain the necessary information before filing a derivative action, then the stockholder must make a pre-suit demand on the board.[20]

As to the first prong, directors are interested if they have a personal financial stake in the challenged transaction or otherwise would be materially affected by the board's actions.[21] Consequently, for example, the chancery court excused demand on director interest grounds where five of nine directors approved a stock appreciation rights plan likely to benefit them.[22]

Under the second *Grimes* prong, the key doctrinal question is whether the directors can base their judgment on the merits rather than on extraneous considerations. Again, demand is not excused simply because the plaintiff has named a majority of the board as defendants.[23] Indeed, it is not enough even to allege that a majority of the board approved of, acquiesced in, or participated in the challenged transaction.[24] In other words, merely being named as defendants or participants

20. Grimes v. Donald, 673 A.2d 1207, 1216 (Del.1996). The term "majority" should be taken literally. In Kohls v. Duthie, 2000 WL 1041219 (Del.Ch.2000), for example, demand was excused even though half of the board was deemed capable of impartially assessing the litigation. Id. at *7.

21. See, e.g., Pogostin v. Rice, 480 A.2d 619, 624 (Del.1984) ("Directorial interest exists whenever divided loyalties are present, or a director either has received, or is entitled to receive, a personal financial benefit from the challenged transaction which is not equally shared by the stockholders."); Seminaris v. Landa, 662 A.2d 1350, 1354 (Del.Ch.1995) ("A director is interested if he will be materially affected, either to his benefit or detriment, by a decision of the board, in a manner not shared by the corporation and the stockholders.").

22. Bergstein v. Texas Int'l Co., 453 A.2d 467, 471 (Del.Ch.1982).

23. Grimes v. Donald, 673 A.2d 1207, 1216 n. 8 (Del.1996). See also Lewis v. Anderson, 615 F.2d 778, 783 (9th Cir. 1979), cert. denied, 449 U.S. 869 (1980) ("To allow one shareholder to incapacitate an entire board of directors merely by leveling charges against them gives too much leverage to dissident shareholders."). Recall that the same is true in New York. See Marx v. Akers, 644 N.Y.S.2d 121, 128 (1996). Likewise, directors are not interested for purposes of the first *Grimes* prong just because they are named as a defendant

in the derivative litigation. The "mere threat" of personal liability in connection with the litigation also is not enough, although a "substantial likelihood" of personal liability in connection therewith will excuse demand. Rales v. Blasband, 634 A.2d 927, 936 (Del.1993); Aronson v. Lewis, 473 A.2d 805, 815 (Del.1984); Seminaris v. Landa, 662 A.2d 1350, 1354–55 (Del.Ch. 1995). There are cases to the contrary outside Delaware. See, e.g., Abbey v. Control Data Corp., 603 F.2d 724, 727 (8th Cir. 1979) (directors "subject to personal liability in the action cannot be expected to determine impartially whether it is warranted"). Note that the analysis of this issue also tends to merge with the third *Grimes* prong, in which courts seek to determine whether the transaction involved misconduct sufficiently egregious that the business judgment rule is unlikely to shield the directors from liability. See, e.g., Kohls v. Duthie, 2000 WL 1041219 (Del.Ch.2000); Seminaris v. Landa, 662 A.2d 1350, 1354–55 (Del.Ch.1995).

24. Grimes v. Donald, 673 A.2d 1207, 1216 n. 8 (Del.1996). See also Aronson v. Lewis, 473 A.2d 805, 817 (Del.1984) ("In Delaware mere directorial approval of a transaction, absent particularized facts supporting a breach of fiduciary duty claim, or otherwise establishing the lack of independence or disinterestedness of a majority of the directors, is insufficient to excuse demand."). Again, recall that the same is true in New York. See Marx v. Akers, 644

does not render the board incapable, as a matter of law, of objectively evaluating a pre-suit demand and, accordingly, does not excuse such a demand. Instead, demand typically will be excused under this prong only if a majority of the board was dominated or controlled by someone with a personal financial stake in the transaction.[25] Directors whose independence is compromised by undue influences exerted by interested parties are presumed, as a matter of law, of being incapable of exercising valid business judgment.

The inquiry under the first two *Grimes* prongs, which collectively comprise the first *Aronson* prong, is a highly factual and contextual one. In *Cooper Companies,* for example, Vice Chancellor Jacobs held that three of ten directors were interested in the challenged transactions because they derived personal benefits from those transactions. A fourth director lacked the requisite independence due to a familial relationship with one of the principal wrongdoers. Two other directors were corporate officers and subordinates of a principal wrongdoer who exercised "considerable influence" over them. Consequently, demand was excused.[26] The third set of directors raised the most difficult questions. Although members of the board are nominally equals, there can be de facto hierarchies within the board. Where board members were nominated and/or elected by a controlling shareholder, for example, concerns over their independence seem legitimate. Likewise, insider board members may be dependent upon other board members for their continued employment. Neither fact standing alone suffices, however, as the Delaware supreme court made clear in *Aronson.* In that case, the chief alleged wrongdoer owned 47% of the corporation's stock and allegedly had personally selected each board member. The supreme court held that all of this did not render the board per se incapable of exercising independent judgment. Instead, plaintiff must "demonstrate that through personal or other relationships the directors are beholden to the controlling person."[27] Consequently, courts should not presume inside directors are subject to improper influence merely by virtue of their employment relationship with the firm.

Turning to the third *Grimes* prong, should one rephrase it to ask whether the business judgment rule applies to the underlying challenged

---

N.Y.S.2d 121, 128 (1996). There are contrary precedents in other jurisdictions, however. See, e.g., Galef v. Alexander, 615 F.2d 51 (2d Cir.1980) (opining that Ohio law might excuse demand where the directors simply authorized the underlying transaction); cf. Nussbacher v. Chase Manhattan Bank, 444 F.Supp. 973, 977 (S.D.N.Y.1977) (opining that it is "inconceivable that directors who participated in and allegedly approved of the transaction under attack can be said to have exercised unbiased business judgment in declining suit based on that very transaction").

25. See Aronson v. Lewis, 473 A.2d 805, 814 (Del.1984) ("where officers and di-

rectors are under an influence which sterilizes their discretion, they cannot be considered proper persons to conduct litigation on behalf of the corporation"); cf. Marx v. Akers, 644 N.Y.S.2d 121, 125 (1996) (describing Delaware law).

26. In re Cooper Cos., Inc. Shareholders Derivative Litigation, 2000 WL 1664167 at *7 (Del.Ch.2000).

27. Aronson v. Lewis, 473 A.2d 805, 815 (Del.1984). See also Polar Intern. Brokerage Corp. v. Reeve, 108 F.Supp.2d 225, 247 n. 38 (S.D.N.Y.2000).

transaction? Some cases have done so. In *Zupnick v. Goizueta*,[28] plaintiff conceded that the board was disinterested and independent. Under those circumstances, Vice Chancellor Jacobs properly phrased the test as whether the "particularized factual allegations of the complaint create a reason to doubt" that the board's decision "was entitled to the protection of the business judgment rule." In *Brehm* v. *Eisner*, the Delaware supreme court adopted a similar approach, emphasizing that the inquiry under this prong focuses on "the directors' decisionmaking process, *measured by concepts of gross negligence.*"[29]

In both *Zupnick* and *Brehm*, however, plaintiff's complaint challenged a specific board action; namely, allegedly excessive executive compensation. What about the important class of cases in which plaintiff alleges that the board failed to exercise proper oversight? Recall that the business judgment rule is inapplicable where the board did not exercise business judgment.[30] Is demand therefore automatically excused in oversight cases?

The Delaware supreme court first addressed this question in *Rales v. Blasband*. Plaintiff brought a double derivative suit on behalf of a parent corporation with respect to the sale of subordinated debentures by its wholly owned subsidiary. Because the derivative suit did not challenge a decision by the parent corporation's board, the court held that the *Aronson* standard did not apply:

> Instead, it is appropriate in these situations to examine whether the board that would be addressing the demand can impartially consider its merits without being influenced by improper considerations. Thus, a court must determine whether or not the particularized factual allegations of a derivative stockholder complaint create a reasonable doubt that, as of the time the complaint is filed, the board of directors could have properly exercised its independent and disinterested business judgment in responding to a demand. If the derivative plaintiff satisfies this burden, then demand will be excused as futile.[31]

The court noted three scenarios in which this test is to be used in lieu of the *Aronson* standard: (1) where a majority of the board that made the challenged transaction has been replaced by disinterested and independent members; (2) where the litigation arises out of some transaction or event not involving a business decision by the board; and (3) where the challenged decision was made by the board of a different corporation.

The *Rales* standard makes sense as applied to derivative suits brought to enforce corporate rights as against wrongdoers outside the corporation. If the shareholder-plaintiff sued a third party for breach of contract vis-à-vis the corporation, for example, the board obviously ought to have a chance to evaluate the suit before it goes forward. It is less

28. 698 A.2d 384 (Del.Ch.1997).

29. Brehm v. Eisner, 746 A.2d 244, 259 (Del.2000) (emphasis in original).

30. See § 6.5.

31. Rales v. Blasband, 634 A.2d 927, 934 (Del.1993).

obvious that *Rales* should apply where the shareholder-plaintiff alleges, for example, that the board failed to adequately supervise corporate employees. Yet, post-*Rales* decisions have applied its standard to such board oversight cases.[32]

Finally, we turn to appellate review of a chancery court decision on demand futility. Until quite recently, it was assumed that the chancery court's decision on demand futility was subject to review by the Delaware supreme court solely for abuse of discretion. Indeed, numerous supreme court opinions so stated, going back as far as *Aronson* itself.[33] In *Brehm v. Eisner*,[34] however, the Delaware supreme court disavowed all such statements as mere dicta. Because demand futility is decided on the pleadings, the *Brehm* court held, the chancery court's decision is subject to de novo review on appeal.

B. Board control of derivative litigation

It is curious that the seemingly technical requirement of demand on the board has become the critical issue in derivative litigation. If demand is required, the shareholder-plaintiff has very little prospect of success. If demand is excused, the shareholder-plaintiff's prospects improve—albeit not by much. Derivative litigation thus bifurcates at the demand stage. If demand is required, two questions arise: What happens if the board accepts the demand? Conversely, what happens if the demand is rejected? If demand is excused, the key issue is whether the board can wrest control of the litigation back from the shareholder-plaintiff .

1. Demand required cases

At least in Delaware, a plaintiff who makes demand is deemed to concede that demand was required.[35] Accordingly, due to the demand required/demand excused bifurcation of substantive standards, which make it very difficult for plaintiffs to prevail in the former, well-counseled plaintiffs almost never make demand. The initial issue in almost all derivative suits therefore is whether demand is required under the standards described in the preceding section.

If the court concludes that demand was required, what happens next? In theory, failure to make demand is grounds for dismissal with prejudice. In practice, however, the court likely will either stay further

---

32. See, e.g., Kohls v. Duthie, 2000 WL 1041219 at *4–5 (Del.Ch.2000); Seminaris v. Landa, 662 A.2d 1350, 1354 (Del.Ch. 1995).

33. See, e.g., Scattered Corp. v. Chicago Stock Exch., 701 A.2d 70, 72–73 (Del.1997); Grimes v. Donald, 673 A.2d 1207, 1217 n. 15 (Del.1996); Heineman v. Datapoint Corp., 611 A.2d 950, 952 (Del.1992); Levine v. Smith, 591 A.2d 194, 207 (Del.1991); Grobow v. Perot, 539 A.2d 180, 186 (Del. 1988); Pogostin v. Rice, 480 A.2d 619, 624–

25 (Del.1984); Aronson v. Lewis, 473 A.2d 805, 814 (Del.1984).

34. 746 A.2d 244, 254–54 (Del.2000).

35. Rales v. Blasband, 634 A.2d 927, 935 n. 12 (Del.1993); Spiegel v. Buntrock, 571 A.2d 767, 775 (Del.1990). Conversely, however, appointment by the board of a special committee to investigate the challenged transaction is not deemed a concession that demand would be futile. Seminaris v. Landa, 662 A.2d 1350, 1353 (Del.Ch. 1995).

proceedings or, at worst, dismiss without prejudice while plaintiff made the required demand.[36] The case would then go forward as described below.

Where the shareholder makes demand, either pre-suit or after a judicial determination that demand was required, the board is expected to undertake a two-step process.[37] The board must first inform itself of the relevant facts relating to the challenged transaction or other alleged wrongdoing, as well as the legal and business considerations attendant to resolving the matter. Any factual investigation must be reasonable and conducted in good faith, but within those parameters the board has great discretion.[38] Having done so, the board must elect amongst the three principal alternatives available to it: (1) accepting the demand and prosecuting the action; (2) resolving the matter internally without resort to litigation; or (3) refusing the demand.[39]

If the board accepts the demand and then attempts to resolve the matter through a settlement of the derivative claim with the shareholder-plaintiff, the parties must comply with the judicial approval requirement of Federal Rule 23.1 or its relevant state counterpart. Suppose, however, that the corporation resolves the matter through a settlement with the alleged wrongdoers. In that case, the judicial approval requirement under Federal Rule 23.1 and its state counterparts does not apply.[40] If the corporation gives the defendants a sweetheart deal, of course, the shareholder-plaintiff could initiate a new derivative suit for "fraud or waste in releasing corporate claims for inadequate payment."[41] Presumably the same would be true if the corporation accepted demand but then lost the case due to a failure to vigorously prosecute it.

---

36. See, e.g., Elfenbein v. Gulf & W. Indus., Inc., 590 F.2d 445, 450 (2d Cir.1978) (opining that dismissal with "leave to replead within a specified time period" is the preferable disposition); Brody v. Chemical Bank, 66 F.R.D. 87, 90 (S.D.N.Y.), aff'd, 517 F.2d 932 (2d Cir.1975) (dismissing derivative action, with leave to replead, for failure to comply with demand requirement); Markowitz v. Brody, 90 F.R.D. 542 (S.D.N.Y. 1981) (same); Brehm v. Eisner, 746 A.2d 244, 249 (Del.2000) (setting aside chancery court dismissal with prejudice, dismissing part of complaint without prejudice, and remanding remainder with instructions that chancery court permit plaintiff to file and amended complaint); Levine v. Smith, 591 A.2d 194, 201–03 (Del.1991) (holding that trial judge did not abuse his discretion by allowing plaintiffs to file a second amended complaint).

37. Rales v. Blasband, 634 A.2d 927, 935 (Del.1993).

38. Levine v. Smith, 591 A.2d 194, 213–14 (Del.1991).

39. See Weiss v. Temporary Inv. Fund, Inc., 692 F.2d 928, 941 (3d Cir.1982) (identifying alternatives), vacated on other grounds, 465 U.S. 1001 (1984). The Delaware supreme court has held that when a board of directors is confronted with a derivative action asserted on its behalf, the board cannot stand neutral. Kaplan v. Peat, Marwick, Mitchell & Co., 540 A.2d 726, 731 (Del.1988).

40. Wolf v. Barkes, 348 F.2d 994, 997 (2d Cir.), cert. denied, 382 U.S. 941 (1965). The ALI PRINCIPLES take the position that, once a derivative suit has been commenced, any settlement must receive judicial approval. ALI PRINCIPLES § 7.15 cmt. c. In addition, the drafters note that most corporations voluntarily seek judicial approval, id. Reporter's Note 1, presumably so as to obtain the maximum claim preclusive effect.

41. Wolf v. Barkes, 348 F.2d 994, 996 (2d Cir.), cert. denied, 382 U.S. 941 (1965).

Anecdotal evidence strongly suggests that the board's typical response, however, is to refuse the demand. If the board does so, the shareholder may seek judicial review of that refusal, but the plaintiff bears the burden of proving that the refusal was wrongful.[42] Worse yet, at least from plaintiff's perspective, the relevant standard of review is the business judgment rule.[43] Worst of all, again from plaintiff's perspective, plaintiff is not entitled to discovery.[44]

Some suggest that the wrongful refusal inquiry should be directed at the business judgment rule's applicability to the underlying challenged transaction where that transaction "was approved by the same directors who are reviewing the plaintiff's demand."[45] In *Grimes*, however, the Delaware supreme court made clear that the inquiry is directed to whether "the board in fact acted independently, disinterestedly, or with due care *in response to the demand.*"[46] Note the potential for a clear case of self-dealing, such as an interested director transaction, to be immune from challenge through a derivative suit. A disinterested and independent majority of the board is deemed capable of deciding whether to refuse demand, at least where the decision does not involve fraud, illegality or self-dealing on the part of a majority of the board. A demand refusal by such a board will be protected by the business judgment rule.

2. *Demand excused cases*

Anecdotal evidence suggests that boards generally settle demand excused cases. The incentives for both sides to settle before a decision on the merits are just too strong. Yet, a recalcitrant board intent upon resisting a derivative suit has a weapon by which it can regain control of the litigation even when demand is excused; namely, the so-called special litigation committee (SLC).

The SLC emerged in response to a sharp rise in derivative litigation during the 1970s. In demand excused cases, the board would appoint a committee to investigate the challenged transaction or event and make a recommendation to the court as to whether or not the litigation was in the firm's best interests. The committee members were specially chosen for their independence and disinterest (or so corporations said). Indeed, the committee typically was comprised of newly appointed board members chosen specifically to serve on the committee. The committee was vested with all of the board's powers for the limited purpose of deciding what position the corporation should take in connection with the litigation. The theory explained to the courts was that the committee could take over and prosecute meritorious suits, while seeking dismissal of

---

42. Allison v. General Motors Corp., 604 F.Supp. 1106, 1121 (D.Del.1985); Grimes v. Donald, 673 A.2d 1207, 1219 (Del.1996).

43. Spiegel v. Buntrock, 571 A.2d 767, 776 (Del.1990); Aronson v. Lewis, 473 A.2d 805, 813 (Del.1984); Zapata Corp. v. Maldonado, 430 A.2d 779, 784 n. 10 (Del.1981) (dicta).

44. Levine v. Smith, 591 A.2d 194, 208–10 (Del.1991).

45. Michael P. Dooley, Fundamentals of Corporation Law 334 (1995).

46. Grimes v. Donald, 673 A.2d 1207, 1219 (Del.1996) (emphasis supplied).

frivolous actions. The principal legal issue thus was whether the court should defer to a committee recommendation that the suit be dismissed.

New York law. New York's answer to that question was handed down in *Auerbach v. Bennett.*[47] Agents of GTE had paid out some $11 million in illegal bribes and kickbacks. Four of GTE's directors were personally involved in the misconduct. A GTE shareholder brought a derivative action against GTE, all of its directors, and its outside auditor for breach of fiduciary duty to the corporation. The board responded to the litigation by appointing a SLC, which concluded that none of the defendants had violated their statutory duty of care, none had profited personally from the incidents and that the claims were without merit. The committee therefore recommended that the court dismiss the suit. Noting that the business judgment doctrine generally bars judicial inquiry into actions of corporate directors taken in good faith and in the exercise of honest judgment in the lawful furtherance of corporate purposes, the court opined that analysis of the case at bar turned on whether the business judgment rule applied to such a recommendation by a SLC.

Judicial review of a SLC recommendation to terminate derivative litigation implicates a two-tiered set of questions. The first tier is the challenged transaction; here the illegal payments. The second tier is the committee's recommendation that the action be dismissed. The *Auerbach* defendants argued that the second tier action insulated the first tier from judicial review because the business judgment rule mandates judicial deference to the committee's recommendation. We might call this the Tootsie Pop defense—you cannot see the chewy center (the first tier wrongdoing) because the hard candy shell (the second tier committee recommendation) blocks your view.

The Court of Appeals agreed that the committee's ultimate substantive decision to dismiss the litigation is protected from review. Judicial

47. 419 N.Y.S.2d 920 (1979). Everyone involved seems to have assumed that *Auerbach* was properly viewed as a demand excused case. Query whether that would still be true today, following the subsequent decision in Marx v. Akers, 644 N.Y.S.2d 121 (1996). The first *Marx* prong asks whether a majority of the board of directors was interested in the challenged transaction. Director interest may either be self-interest in the transaction at issue, or because a director with no direct interest in a transaction is controlled by a self-interested director. In *Auerbach*, although all directors sued, only 4 were alleged to have participated in the challenged transaction. Merely being named as a defendant is not enough to render one interested for purposes of this prong of *Marx*. Under *Marx*'s second prong, demand will be excused where the complaint alleges that the board of directors did not fully inform themselves about the chal-

lenged transaction to the extent reasonably appropriate under the circumstances. Under the third prong, demand is excused where the complaint alleges that the challenged transaction was so egregious on its face that it could not have been the product of sound business judgment of the directors. How should we apply the latter two factors to a case in which a majority of the board was unaware of the alleged misconduct and, consequently, did not exercise business judgment? Under Rales v. Blasband, 634 A.2d 927 (Del.1993), Delaware would not regard the failure to exercise business judgment as grounds for excusing demand. If New York followed that precedent, demand would not be excused on *Auerbach*-like facts. For a still useful critique of *Auerbach*, see George W. Dent, Jr., The Power of Directors to Terminate Shareholder Litigation: The Death of the Derivative Suit?, 75 Nw. U. L. Rev. 96 (1980).

inquiry is permissible with respect to two aspects of the committee's work, however: (1) the committee's disinterested independence; and (2) the adequacy and appropriateness of the procedures by which the decision was made. It seems that plaintiff has the ultimate burden of proof with respect to the committee's independence and the adequacy of their procedures, although there is language in the opinion suggesting that the committee may have the initial burden of showing that its procedures were reasonable.

If the court is not satisfied as to either the SLC's disinterested independence or the adequacy of its procedures, the suit will not be dismissed and review of the first tier decision will not be foreclosed. If the court is satisfied on both scores, however, the case must be dismissed without reaching the merits. In *Auerbach*, accordingly, in which there apparently was no question that the payments were illegal, the challenged misconduct thus was not to be reviewed so long as the committee was independent and used proper procedures in reaching its decision. (Of course, if one thinks that directors and officers can violate the law without necessarily violating their fiduciary duties, this outcome will not seem problematic.)

On the facts before it, the court determined that the committee was independent. None of the committee members were members of the board when the illegal payments took place and none had any prior affiliation with the firm. The latter point—lack of prior affiliation—seems to be the key. As long as the committee members have no demonstrable contact with the corporation or the board, they likely will be deemed independent.

In examining the committee's procedures, *Auerbach* teaches that a reviewing court may explore whether the areas and subjects the committee investigated were reasonably complete. The court may also determine whether the inquiry was conducted in good faith. The court will be looking for proof that the investigation was restricted in scope, shallow in execution, pro forma or half-hearted. Relevant factors thus include such matters as the number of hours spent on the matter, whether the committee had independent legal counsel and other advisers, who was interviewed, and the like. On the other hand, the court may not consider the evidence the committee uncovered, the factors the committee considered, the relative weight accorded to those factors in the committee's decisionmaking process, or even whether the evidence supports the conclusion. The following analogy may be useful—the court may ensure all the proper papers are in the file, but is forbidden from reading the papers to see what they say.

Delaware law. The Delaware supreme court took a less deferential approach to this issue in *Zapata Corp. v. Maldonado.*[48] In *Zapata*, the Delaware supreme court specifically rejected *Auerbach*'s conclusion that

---

48. 430 A.2d 779 (Del.1981). In Alford v. Shaw, 358 S.E.2d 323 (N.C.1987), North Carolina adopted a *Zapata*-based standard for all derivative suits, without regard to whether demand is excused or required.

the business judgment rule applies to a SLC's recommendations. Instead, the court laid out a new set of procedures to be followed in such cases. After an "objective and thorough investigation," the committee may cause the corporation to file a motion to dismiss the derivative action. The motion should include a written record of the committee's investigation and its findings and recommendations. Each side is given a limited opportunity for discovery with respect to the court's mandated areas of inquiry.

In deciding whether to dismiss the action, the court is to apply a two-step test: (1) The court should inquire into the independence and good faith of the committee. The court also should inquire into the bases supporting the committee's recommendations. The corporation will have the burden of proving independence, good faith, and a reasonable investigation. (2) If the first step is satisfied, the court may but need not go on to apply its own business judgment to the issue of whether or not the case is to be dismissed.

The first step differs from *Auerbach* in that the Delaware court looks not only at the procedures used, but also at the reasonableness of the basis for the committee's decision—something *Auerbach* expressly forbids.[49] In other words, Delaware judges not only make sure all the papers are in the file, they also read the papers to see if the investigative results support the committee's conclusions.

The second step is intended to catch cases complying with the letter, but not the spirit, of the first step.[50] In other words, the court is saying that judges should not dismiss meritorious derivative suits merely because the board and its committee jumped through the correct procedural hoops. Unfortunately, *Zapata* gave no real standards by which judges should apply their own business judgment in the second-step. The supreme court simply opined that the trial court should consider such things as the corporation's interest in having the suit dismissed and "matters of law and public policy,"[51] which could mean everything under the sun. In its subsequent *Kaplan v. Wyatt* decision, moreover, the court made clear that the chancellors are not obliged to conduct the second step inquiry and that a refusal to do so was subject to review under the abuse of discretion standard.[52]

In *Joy v. North*,[53] a diversity case arising under Connecticut law, federal Circuit Judge Ralph Winter held that Connecticut courts would follow *Zapata*, rather than *Auerbach*, but thought it necessary to lay out more determinate guidelines for judicial review of SLC recommenda-

---

49. Several other states also require their courts to determine whether the committee's recommendation has a reasonable basis. See, e.g., Houle v. Low, 556 N.E.2d 51 (Mass.1990); Lewis v. Boyd, 838 S.W.2d 215 (Tenn.App.1992).

50. Cf. Johnson v. Hui, 811 F.Supp. 479, 490 (N.D.Cal.1991) (describing second step of *Zapata* as a "smell test").

51. Zapata Corp. v. Maldonado, 430 A.2d 779, 789 (Del.1981).

52. Kaplan v. Wyatt, 499 A.2d 1184, 1192 (Del.1985).

53. 692 F.2d 880 (2d Cir.1982), cert. denied, 460 U.S. 1051 (1983). As a diversity case applying the law of another state, of course, *Joy* is not binding on the Delaware courts.

tions. The central question under *Joy* is whether the litigation is in the best interests of the corporation. The burden is on the corporation to demonstrate that the litigation is more likely than not to be against its interests. The court will examine the underlying data developed by the committee, the adequacy of the committee's procedures, and whether there is a reasonable basis for the committee's recommendation. Again, note the difference from *Auerbach*. As in *Zapata*, Judge Winter looks behind the procedures to see what the committee actually found.

The break with *Zapata* came when Judge Winter articulated a methodology not unlike the Hand Formula familiar from tort law. If the cost of litigation to the corporation exceeds the product of the likely recoverable damages times the probability of liability, suit must be dismissed. The costs that may be considered include attorney's fees, out of pocket expenses, time spent by corporate personnel preparing for and participating in trial, and potential mandatory indemnification (discounted by the probability of liability). On the cost side, the court may not consider discretionary indemnification or insurance.[54] Where the likely recovery to the corporation is small in comparison to total shareholders' equity, the court may also consider two other factors: (1) the degree to which key personnel may be distracted from corporate business by the litigation and (2) the potential for lost business.

3. Judicial concern with structural bias

The significantly less deferential approach taken by *Zapata* and *Joy*, relative to *Auerbach*, resulted from the former courts' heightened sensitivity to the potential for bias on the part of SLC members. Because the members of the committee typically are appointed by the defendants to the derivative litigation, there is a natural concern that the persons selected will be biased in favor of the defendants. The requirements of independence and disinterest purportedly eliminate the risk of actual bias. Because the persons selected frequently are directors or senior officers of other corporations, however, there is a concern that the SLC's members will have excessive sympathy for colleagues facing personal liability. As the Delaware supreme court put it: "The question naturally arises whether a 'there but for the grace of God go I' empathy might not play a role."[55] The legitimacy of this concern is supported by the fact

---

54. Suppose plaintiff's claim is for $1 million. Defendant director has personal assets of $100,000, but is covered by a D & O liability policy that will pay up to $20 million per incident. Can the existence of that policy be considered by the court and, if so, for what purposes? Insurance is relevant to the likely recovery side of the equation, but not to the costs side of the formula. Thus, the court cannot consider either past premiums or future premium increases in its calculation of costs.

55. *Zapata Corp. v. Maldonado*, 430 A.2d 779, 787 (Del.1981). Or, as Judge Winter put it in *Joy*: "It is not cynical to expect that such committees will tend to view derivative actions against the other directors with skepticism. Indeed, if the involved directors expected any result other than a recommendation of termination at least as to them, they would probably never establish the committee." 692 F.2d 880, 888 (2d Cir.1982), cert. denied, 460 U.S. 1051 (1983).

that in only one of the first 20 reported SLC decisions did the committee determine that the suit should proceed.[56]

Despite the potential for actual or structural bias, neither *Auerbach*, *Zapata*, nor *Joy* accepted their respective plaintiffs' arguments that the defendant board of directors was per se disabled from appointing a SLC and delegating to that committee power to act on the corporation's behalf. In *Miller v. Register and Tribune Syndicate, Inc.*,[57] by way of contrast, the Iowa supreme court concluded that the structural bias purportedly inherent in the SLC process incapacitated directors charged with misconduct from appointing a SLC. Instead, the board may petition the court to appoint a special panel, to whose recommendations the court will defer.

4. Policy

The *Zapata* court correctly identified the basic issue: If the corporation can consistently defeat bona fide derivative actions through procedural devices, much of the derivative suit's supposed utility in punishing and deterring managerial misconduct will evaporate. On the other hand, the underlying cause of action belongs to the corporation and the corporation should be able to rid itself of nonmeritorious or even harmful litigation.[58] Subsequent decisions have recognized an even more serious concern: "the derivative action impinges on the managerial freedom of directors."[59] Due regard therefore must be given "the fundamental precept that directors manage the business and affairs of corporations."[60] In other words, shareholder derivative litigation presents the same tension between authority and accountability we have pervasively encountered throughout corporate law. Consequently, the question to be resolved is whether the derivative suit process deserves what the *Zapata* court referred to as its "generally recognized effectiveness as an intracorporate means of policing boards of directors."[61]

The significance of accountability concerns depends, at least in the first instance, on the nature of the defendant and of the claim. A board decision not to sue a supplier for breach of contract, for example, really is no different from a decision to enter into the contract in the first place. On the other hand, a board decision not to sue a fellow board member who has, for example, usurped a corporate opportunity is qualitatively different.

In supplier-type cases, accountability concerns have little traction. Consequently, it ought to be quite easy for the board to regain control over cases in which the shareholder-plaintiff sues some corporate outsider on a derivative basis. If the shareholder-plaintiff sues the board for

---

56. See James D. Cox, Searching for the Corporation's Voice in Derivative Suit Litigation: A Critique of *Zapata* and the ALI Project, 1982 Duke L.J. 959.

57. 336 N.W.2d 709 (Iowa 1983).

58. Zapata Corp. v. Maldonado, 430 A.2d 779, 786–87 (Del.1981).

59. Pogostin v. Rice, 480 A.2d 619, 624 (Del.1984).

60. Aronson v. Lewis, 473 A.2d 805, 812 (Del.1984).

61. Zapata Corp. v. Maldonado, 430 A.2d 779, 786 (Del.1981).

failing to enforce the contract, it likewise should be easy for the board to regain control over the litigation. If the board decided not to sue the supplier, there probably was a reasonable justification for that decision. Even if there was not, the policies against judicial second-guessing of board conduct underlying the business judgment rule remain compelling. Indeed, in light of those policies, one could plausibly argue that shareholders should have no standing to bring derivative suits based on such claims.

In cases in which a director allegedly violated the duty of loyalty, however, accountability concerns seem more pressing. But do those accountability concerns trump the authority-based justification for deferring to decisions by a disinterested and independent board majority or committee? In a well-known article, Professors Coffee and Schwartz argued that ordinary business decisions and decisions not to pursue litigation are distinguishable.[62] Accordingly, they contended, the business judgment rule is irrelevant to judicial review of a special litigation committee's decision to terminate a derivative suit. Rather, courts should aggressively review the merits of the case.

Coffee and Schwartz offered four principal justifications for their position. First, ordinary business decisions are made under time pressure and uncertainty. But so what? In our old friend, *Shlensky v. Wrigley*,[63] the board had something like 20 years in which to ponder its decision. Should the board therefore have been denied the protection of the business judgment rule? Given the time pressures associated with litigation, moreover, is there really that much difference between regular decisions and litigation decisions?

Second, Coffee and Schwartz argued, the business judgment rule's main purpose is to shield directors from liability for honest mistakes. Directors who decide to dismiss derivative suits do not need such a shield from personal liability—or so Coffee and Schwartz opined. After *Smith v. Van Gorkom*,[64] however, one can plausibly imagine a scenario in which the committee members could be held liable if they were grossly negligent in failing to gather all material information reasonably available to them with respect to the prospective litigation.

Third, Coffee and Schwartz contended that courts have greater expertise in assessing the merits of litigation than they do with respect to typical business decisions. One problem with this argument is that judicial expertise, or the lack thereof, is only a small part of the case for judicial deference to board decisions. It is far from clear, moreover, the judges really have superior judgment with respect to such matters as the impact of litigation on firm morale or the amount of time defendants are likely to spend reading their liability insurance policies instead of working.

62. John C. Coffee, Jr., and Donald E. Schwartz, The Survival of the Derivative Suit: An Evaluation and a Proposal for Legislative Reform, 81 Col. L. Rev. 261 (1981).

63. 237 N.E.2d 776 (Ill.App.1968).

64. 488 A.2d 858 (Del.1985).

Finally, Coffee and Schwartz pointed to the potential for structural bias. (As discussed in the preceding section, structural bias refers to the possibility that SLC members, by virtue of their typical background as business executives will be biased in favor of the defendants.) Here, of course, we come to the nub of the matter. As illustrated by *Zapata*'s concern that SLC members will have a "there but for the grace of God go I" empathy for the defendants, concerns about structural bias pervade the law in this area. If structural bias is the main concern, Delaware law seems to get at the problem more directly than, say, does New York. Under Delaware law, demand will be excused where a majority of the board is either interested in the transaction or otherwise failed to validly exercise business judgment. Once demand is excused, Delaware courts take a close look at the merits of allowing the litigation to go forward, while New York courts are barred from doing so.

To be sure, Delaware law in this area could stand a good tweaking. The *Aronson/Zapata* framework continues to rely unduly on bizarrely worded standards that often fail to grapple with the real issue. The Delaware courts would do well to adopt a simpler standard, which asks whether the board of directors is so clearly disabled by conflicted interests that its judgment cannot be trusted.[65] If so, the shareholder should be allowed to sue. If not, the shareholder should not.

Or maybe not. Perhaps the standard should be further tweaked to make it even easier for boards to terminate derivative suits. In the first place, concern over structural bias can be taken too far. Indeed, "the structural bias argument has no logical terminus."[66] If purportedly independent directors are likely to favor their fellow directors when the latter are sued, they are equally likely to do so in any conflict of interest situation. In the corporate takeover setting, for example, some commentators argue that nominally independent directors' fears for their owns firm can render those directors unduly sympathetic to insiders' job security concerns.[67] It is far from clear that structural bias can justify carving out special rules for derivative litigation, but not for other types of conflicted interest transactions.

In any event, one can concede both the importance of board accountability and the potential for structural bias without having to concede the utility—or even the legitimacy—of derivative litigation. In a seminal empirical study of derivative litigation, Professor Roberta Romano found

---

65. See Kohls v. Duthie, 2000 WL 1041219 (Del.Ch.2000), in which Vice Chancellor Lamb noted that the *Rales* standard arguably provides a simpler and more directly relevant test than the *Aronson* standard. Id. at *5. (Recall that under Rales v. Blasband, 634 A.2d 927, 934 (Del.1993), the standard is whether the board could have properly exercised disinterested and independent judgment in assessing the demand.) See also Starrels v. First Nat'l Bank of Chicago, 870 F.2d 1168 (7th Cir.1989), in which Judge Easterbrook extensively argued for a test under which courts inquire whether the board could make a valid business judgment in response to a demand. Id. at 1175 (Easterbrook, J., concurring).

66. Michael P. Dooley & E. Norman Veasey, The Role of the Board in Derivative Litigation: Delaware Law and the Current ALI Proposals Compared, 45 Bus. Law. 503, 534 (1989).

67. See Dynamics Corp. of Am. v. CTS Corp., 794 F.2d 250, 256 (7th Cir.1986), rev'd on other grounds, 481 U.S. 69 (1987).

that derivative litigation is relatively rare.[68] Of those cases that go to trial, shareholder-plaintiffs almost always lose. As is generally true of all litigation, however, most derivative suits settle. Only half of the settled derivative suits resulted in monetary recoveries, with an average recovery of about $6 million. In almost all cases, the legal fees collected by plaintiff counsel exceeded the monetary payments to shareholders. Romano further concluded that nonmonetary relief typically was inconsequential in nature.

Romano's empirical analysis is consistent with our analysis of the relevant players' incentives. A substantial percentage of derivative litigation likely consists of strike suits, which are settled for their nuisance value. Conversely, meritorious suits likely are settled too cheaply, albeit with inflated legal fees paid to plaintiff's counsel. Because settlements typically are structured so that both any monetary payment and any legal fees are paid out of the corporate treasury,[69] derivative litigation necessarily tends to reduce the value of the residual claim.

Derivative litigation mainly serves as a means of transferring wealth from investors to lawyers. At best, derivative suits take money out of the firm's residual value and return it to shareholders minus substantial legal fees. In many cases, moreover, little if any money is returned to the shareholders—but legal fees are almost always paid. Why would a diversified shareholder approve such a process?

If derivative litigation cannot be justified on compensatory grounds, can it still be justified as a useful deterrent against managerial shirking and self-dealing? In short, no. There is no compelling evidence that derivative litigation deters a substantial amount of managerial shirking and self-dealing. Certainly there is no evidence that litigation does a better job of deterring such misconduct than do markets. There is evidence that derivative suits do not have significant effects on the stock price of the subject corporations, however, which suggests that investors do not believe derivative suits deter misconduct.[70] There is also substantial evidence that adoption of a charter amendment limiting director liability has no significant effect on the price of the adopting corporation's stock, which suggests that investors do not believe that duty of care liability has beneficial deterrent effects.[71]

---

68. Roberta Romano, The Shareholder Suit: Litigation without Foundation?, 7 J. L. Econ. & Org. 55 (1991).

69. Some commentators assert that most out-of-pocket losses in derivative litigation are ultimately paid by liability insurers under D & O liability policies. See, e.g., Reinier Kraakman et al., When are Shareholder Suits in Shareholder Interests?, 82 Geo. L.J. 1733, 1745–46 (1994). If so, the cost of such suits still comes out of the residual claim in the form of insurance premiums.

70. See Daniel R. Fischel & Michael Bradley, The Role of Liability Rules and the Derivative Suit in Corporate Law: A Theoretical and Empirical Analysis, 71 Cornell L. Rev. 261 (1986).

71. See, e.g., Michael Bradley & Cindy A. Schipani, The Relevance of the Duty of Care Standard in Corporate Governance, 75 Iowa L. Rev. 1 (1989); Roberta Romano, Corporate Governance in the Aftermath of the Insurance Crisis, 39 Emory L.J. 1155 (1990).

A radical solution would be elimination of derivative litigation. For lawyers, the idea of a wrong without a legal remedy is so counter-intuitive that it scarcely can be contemplated. Yet, derivative litigation appears to have little if any beneficial accountability effects. On the other side of the equation, derivative litigation is a high cost constraint and infringement upon the board's authority. If making corporate law consists mainly of balancing the competing claims of accountability and authority, the balance arguably tips against derivative litigation. Note, moreover, that eliminating derivative litigation does not eliminate director accountability. Directors would remain subject to various forms of market discipline, including the important markets for corporate control and employment, proxy contests, and shareholder litigation where the challenged misconduct gives rise to a direct cause of action.

If eliminating derivative litigation seems too extreme, why not allow firms to opt out of the derivative suit process by charter amendment? Virtually all states now allow corporations to adopt charter provisions limiting director and officer liability.[72] If corporate law consists of a set of default rules the parties generally should be free to amend, as we claim, there seems little reason not to expand the liability limitation statutes to allow corporations to opt out of derivative litigation.

To be sure, it seems unlikely that courts or legislatures will eliminate derivative litigation any time soon. In the meanwhile, courts should use the tools at hand to discourage derivative litigation. As the *Marx* court put it, courts should be "reluctant to permit shareholder derivative suits."[73] Only cases in which a majority of the board is disabled by conflicted interests from making impartial decisions on the merits of prospective litigation should courts allow a shareholder derivative suit to go forward.

C. The ALI and MBCA universal demand alternatives

As noted above, the demand requirement is, at least in part, a corollary of the basic proposition that a derivative action is representative in nature. The demand requirement thus allows the corporation to take over the cause of action or to resist it, according to the judgment of the directors. Under both Delaware and New York law, however, the demand requirement has been charged with an additional task; namely, functioning as the principal sieve by which meritorious shareholder litigation is separated from the chaff. If the board of directors is so clearly disabled by conflicted interests that its judgment cannot be trusted, the shareholder should be permitted to go forward, absent intervention by a special litigation committee. If not, the board should be allowed to decide whether the litigation should proceed.

Although an inquiry into the board's ability to exercise disinterested judgment seems warranted, it is not at all clear that the demand

---

72. See, e.g., DGCL § 702(b)(7).

73. Marx v. Akers, 644 N.Y.S.2d 121, 124 (1996).

requirement is a necessary—or even appropriate—vehicle for undertaking said inquiry. Both the ALI PRINCIPLES and the Model Business Corporation Act have done away with the demand futility inquiry. In its place, both have imposed a universal demand requirement, while preserving, albeit in different forms, a sieve to identify cases in which the board's conflicted interests preclude deference to board decisions.

1. MBCA § 7.44

MBCA § 7.42 requires a written demand upon the board in all cases and, further, precludes a shareholder from bringing suit for 90 days after the demand is made unless irreparable injury would result or the board rejects demand. MBCA § 7.44 then takes over, providing two alternatives for internal corporate review of the demand: If the independent and disinterested directors constitute a quorum, the demand may be reviewed by the board. Whether or not the independent directors constitute a quorum, the independent directors may appoint by majority vote a committee of two or more independent directors.[74]

As under both New York and Delaware law, directors can be deemed independent even if they were nominated by the defendants, area named as a defendants, or they approved the challenged transaction. If either the board or committee "determined in good faith after conducting a reasonable inquiry upon which its conclusions are based that the maintenance of the derivative proceeding is not in the best interests of the corporation" the court "shall" dismiss the complaint.[75] If a majority of the board was independent at the time that determination was made, the burden of proof with respect to the board's independent disinterest and the adequacy of its investigation is on plaintiff; if a majority of the board was not independent, the burden of proof is on the defendant. The comments to § 7.44 make clear that the MBCA's drafters rejected *Zapata*: "Section 7.44 does not authorize the court to review the reasonableness of the determination" made by the board or committee. So long as the determination has "some support" in the findings of the inquiry, the standard is satisfied.

2. ALI PRINCIPLES Part VII

As for the ALI PRINCIPLES, years of controversy and repeated drafting efforts, including last-minute amendments from the floor, produced an astonishingly long and complex set of rules and commentary that basically tracks Delaware law, albeit adding (among other wrinkles) a universal demand requirement.[76] PRINCIPLES § 7.03(b) requires demand in

---

74. Interestingly, the MBCA partially followed the Iowa Supreme Court's *Miller* decision by providing a third alternative. Under MBCA § 7.44(f), upon motion by the corporation, the court may appoint a panel of one or more independent persons to determine whether the suit should go forward. If that panel recommends dismissal, the court shall dismiss the action unless plaintiff can prove the independent panel failed to act in good faith or failed to conduct a reasonable inquiry upon which its conclusions were based. Unlike *Miller*, however, this option is not exclusive of the SLC process.

75. MBCA § 7.44(a).

76. See generally Carol B. Swanson, *Juggling Shareholder Rights and Strike Suits in Derivative Litigation: The ALI*

all cases, excepting only those in which plaintiff demonstrates that irreparable injury to the corporation would result. In the following sections, covering well over 100 pages (counting commentary and reporters' notes), the PRINCIPLES distinguish and provide for judicial review of two basic categories of cases.

The first set of cases is comprised of proceedings against persons other than directors, senior executives, or controlling persons of the corporation. A board recommendation to dismiss a derivative suit against such non-insiders is reviewed under the business judgment rule.[77] The second set comprises suits against directors, senior executives, or controlling persons of the corporation. Judicial review of a derivative proceeding against such insiders is further bifurcated, with the scope of review effectively depending on whether the cause of action is premised on a breach of the duty of care or the duty of loyalty. In the former case, the court should apply the business judgment rule to a recommendation to dismiss made by the disinterested directors (acting either as the board or a committee thereof).[78] In the latter case, subject to a convoluted exception for certain cases in which defendants would retain an improper personal benefit, the court should dismiss the proceeding upon such a recommendation "if the court finds ... that the board or committee was adequately informed under the circumstances and reasonably determined that dismissal was in the best interests of the corporation, based on grounds that the court deems to warrant reliance."[79]

3. *Evaluating universal demand*

The demand futility inquiry mandated by both New York and Delaware law has been subjected to considerable criticism. Judge Frank Easterbrook contends, for example, that the demand futility inquiry produces "gobs of litigation" collateral to the merits. In a derivative proceeding under the federal Investment Company Act against fund directors, Easterbrook therefore fashioned a federal common law of derivative proceedings that included a universal demand requirement.[80] As Professor Michael Dooley notes, "the usually highly perceptive Judge Easterbrook [was led into this] reversible error" by a misunderstanding of the demand futility inquiry's function.[81]

Determining the scope of judicial review of any board of director decision requires one to make trade-offs between preserving the board's decisionmaking authority and ensuring that the board has not misused its authority for the personal benefit of board members. In the derivative litigation context, New York and Delaware have used the demand futility

Drops the Ball, 77 Minn. L. Rev. 1339 (1993). Pennsylvania has adopted the ALI approach *in toto*. Cuker v. Mikalauskas, 692 A.2d 1042 (Pa.1997).

77. ALI PRINCIPLES § 7.07(a)(1).

78. ALI PRINCIPLES §§ 7.07(a)(2) and 7.10(a)(1).

79. Id. at § 7.10(a)(2).

80. Kamen v. Kemper Fin. Servs., Inc., 908 F.2d 1338 (7th Cir.1990), rev'd, 500 U.S. 90 (1991).

81. Michael P. Dooley, Two Models of Corporate Governance, 47 Bus. Law. 461, 502 (1992).

inquiry as the vehicle by which those trade-offs are made. Replacing the demand futility inquiry with a universal demand requirement does not eliminate the need to separate out those cases in which conflicted interests have so tainted the board's decisionmaking processes as to preclude giving the resulting decisions the deference usually accorded them by corporate law. Instead, as the drafters of both the ALI PRINCIPLES and the MBCA appear to have recognized, it simply shifts the task of effecting such a separation to a different stage of the process.

The only justification for a universal demand therefore seems to be the claim that it conserves judicial resources. In its perceptive unanimous opinion reversing Judge Easterbrook, the Supreme Court explained that a universal demand requirement was unlikely to produce much in the way of judicial economy. In support of Easterbrook's universal demand rule, the defendants contended such a rule "would force would-be derivative suit plaintiffs to exhaust their intracorporate remedies before filing suit and would spare both the courts and the parties the expense associated with the often protracted threshold litigation that attends the collateral issue of demand futility." In rejecting defendants' argument, the Court first noted the federalism implications of creating universal demand requirement as a matter of federal common law. "Under KFS' proposal, federal courts would be obliged to develop a body of principles that would replicate the substantive effect of the State's demand futility doctrine but that would be applied *after* demand has been made and refused." Doing so would impinge on the states' power to regulate corporations, as well as subjecting corporations to conflicting standards in state and federal litigation. The court then turned to the purported judicial economies of a federal universal demand rule:

> Requiring demand in all cases, it is true, might marginally enhance the prospect that corporate disputes would be resolved without resort to litigation; however, nothing disables the directors from seeking an accommodation with a representative shareholder even after the shareholder files his complaint in an action in which demand is excused as futile. At the same time, the rule proposed by KFS is unlikely to avoid the high collateral litigation costs associated with the demand futility doctrine. So long as a federal court endeavors to reproduce through independent review standards the allocation of managerial power embodied in the demand futility doctrine, KFS' universal-demand rule will merely shift the focus of threshold litigation from the question whether demand is excused to the question whether the directors' decision to terminate the suit is entitled to deference under federal standards. Under these circumstances, we do not view the advantages associated with KFS' proposal to be sufficiently apparent to justify replacing "the entire corpus of state corporation law" relating to demand futility.[82]

Well said, indeed.

82. Kamen v. Kemper Fin. Servs., Inc., 500 U.S. 90, 106 (1991).

Chapter 9

THE LIMITS OF FIDUCIARY OBLIGATION

Analysis

---

§ 9.1   Introduction

Since Ronald Coase's justly famous article, *The Nature of the Firm*,[1] appeared over six decades ago, both economists and legal scholars have devoted considerable attention to the theory of the firm. As we saw in Chapter 5, two basic systems of classification capture most of the competing theories. Along the means axis of Chapter 5's Figure 1, theories of the firm run the spectrum from managerialism to shareholder primacy. Managerialism claims that managers are autonomous actors free to pursue whatever interests they choose (or society directs). In contrast, under the traditional conception of shareholder primacy, shareholders are said to own the corporation. Consequently, directors and officers are regarded as mere stewards of the shareholders' interests. The law and economics version of shareholder primacy, which is one of Coase's many progeny, argues that shareholders are merely one of many factors of production bound together in a complex web of explicit and implicit contracts. Influenced by agency cost economics, proponents of

§ 9.1

1. R.H. Coase, The Nature of the Firm,
4 Economica (n.s.) 386 (1937).

408

this variant continue to treat directors and officers as agents of the shareholders, with fiduciary obligations to maximize shareholder wealth. Shareholders therefore retain a privileged position among the corporation's various constituencies, enjoying a contract with the firm that possesses ownership-like features.

Along the ends axis of Chapter 5's Figure 1, models run the spectrum from shareholder wealth maximization to stakeholderism. are can be plotted according to the interests the corporation is said to serve. The former contend corporations should be run so as to maximize shareholder wealth.[2] The latter argue that directors and managers should consider the interests of all corporate constituencies in making corporate decisions.[3] Put another way, stakeholderists advocate what they call "corporate social responsibility." Hence, stakeholderists define the "socially responsible firm" as "one that becomes deeply involved in the solution of society's major problems."[4] In particular, they emphasize the corporation's obligation to consider the impact of its actions on nonshareholder corporate constituents, such as employees, customers, suppliers, and local communities.

The ends axis reflects the division in corporate law scholarship along public-private lines.[5] Proponents of shareholder wealth maximization

2. For an interesting argument that the correct norm is one obliging the board to maximize the value of all the claims the corporation has issued, see Thomas A. Smith, The Efficient Norm for Corporate Law: A Neotraditional Interpretation of Fiduciary Duty, 98 Mich. L. Rev. 214 (1999). Smith's argument is based in the first instance on an assumption that investors (and, presumably, managers) are rational. Id. at 239–42. To the extent one assumes rationality is bounded, however, a simpler norm—maximize share value rather than the aggregate value of all financial claims—may be desirable. Cf. Richard A. Booth, Stockholders, Stakeholders, and Bagholders (or How Investor Diversification Affects Fiduciary Duty), 53 Bus. Law. 429 (1998) (arguing that corporate fiduciary duties should not be defined by reference to rational diversified investors, in part because managers cannot know what policies such investors would prefer). In any case, Smith assumes that rational investors invest across a wide array of assets and therefore would prefer a rule requiring that "managers should make the choice that will maximize the value of rational investors' diversified portfolios." Smith, supra, at 242. Yet, to the extent we have evidence as to the preferences of actual investors, those investors appear to prefer a rule of share value maximization. The Council of Institutional Investor's corporate governance policy, for example, calls for "governance structures and practices" that "protect and enhance accountability to, and equal financial treat-

ment of, shareholders. An action should not be taken if its purpose is to reduce accountability to shareholders." Council of Institutional Investors, Corporate Governance Policies, available at http://www.cii.org/corp_governance.htm. Similarly, Lens Investment Management LLC's policy statement refers to its desire to "to maximize shareholder values." Lens Investment Management LLC, Statement of Policy, available at http://www.lens-inc.com/lenspolicy.html (emphasis supplied). Finally, Smith does not resolve the two masters problem. In other words, when managers are confronted with a zero-sum situation requiring them to make trade-offs between various claims, which claim do they prefer? Cf. Katz v. Oak Indus., Inc., 508 A.2d 873, 879 (Del.Ch. 1986) (holding that a corporation's board is obliged to maximize shareholder interests, even if doing so is adverse to the interests of debenture holders).

3. The term "stakeholders" reportedly originated in a 1963 Stanford Research Institute memorandum as a descriptive term for "those groups without whose support the organization would cease to exist." R. Edward Freeman & David L. Reed, Stockholders and Stakeholders: A New Perspective on Corporate Governance, 25 Cal. Mgmt. Rev. 88, 89 (1983).

4. Robert Hay and Ed Gray, Social Responsibilities of Business Managers, in Managing Corporate Social Responsibility 8, 11 (Archie B. Carroll ed. 1977).

5. See William W. Bratton, Berle and Means Reconsidered at the Century's Turn,

typically treat corporate governance as a species of private law, such that the separation of ownership and control does not in and of itself justify state intervention in corporate governance. In contrast, stakeholderists commonly treat corporate governance as a species of public law, such that the separation of ownership and control becomes principally a justification for regulating corporate governance so as to achieve social goals unrelated to corporate profitability.

At bottom, all of these models are ways of thinking about the means and ends of corporate governance. They strive to answer two basic sets of questions: (1) As to the means of corporate governance, who decides? In other words, when push comes to shove, who ultimately is in control? (2) As to the ends of corporate governance, whose interests prevail? When the ultimate decisionmaker is presented with a zero sum game, in which it must prefer the interests of one constituency class over those of all others, which constituency wins? We took up the first set of questions in Chapter 5, where we saw that the board of directors is the body ultimately in control. In this chapter, we take up the second set of questions. Lest we prolong the suspense unduly, we acknowledge up front our view that long-run shareholder wealth maximization is the only proper end of corporate governance.

§ 9.2 Shareholder wealth maximization in law and practice

A. The law of shareholder wealth maximization

In general, corporate law does not mandate corporate social responsibility. Instead, the question is whether the law even permits corporate social responsibility. Put another way, to what extent do the fiduciary duties of corporate directors permit them to consider nonshareholder interests when making corporate decisions?

1. Case law

Despite the obvious centrality of this problem to the operation of business corporations, there are surprisingly few authoritative precedents on point. The law's basic position on corporate social responsibility famously was articulated in *Dodge v. Ford Motor Co.*[1] In 1916, Henry

26 J. Corp. L. 737, 760–61 (2001) (noting public/private divide); Lawrence E. Mitchell, Private Law, Public Interest? The ALI Principles of Corporate Governance, 61 Geo. Wash. L. Rev. 871, 876 (1993) (noting debate as to "whether the modern corporation is essentially a matter of public or private concern").

§ 9.2

1. 170 N.W. 668 (Mich.1919). For an interesting reinterpretation of Dodge,

which argues that the shareholder wealth maximization norm originated as a means for resolving disputes among majority and minority shareholders in closely held corporations, see D. Gordon Smith, The Shareholder Primacy Norm, 23 J. Corp. L. 277 (1998). The *Dodge* court's analysis, however, is not expressly limited to close corporations. Smith places considerable emphasis on the sentence immediately preceding the court's statement of the shareholder wealth maximization norm. See id. at 319. In that sentence, the court draws a distinction be-

Ford owned 58% of the stock of Ford Motor Co. The Dodge brothers owned 10%. The remainder was owned by five other individuals. Beginning in 1908, Ford Motor paid a regular annual dividend of $1.2 million. Between 1911 and 1915 Ford Motor also regularly paid huge "special dividends," totaling over $40 million. In 1916, Henry Ford announced that the company would stop paying special dividends. Instead, the firm's financial resources would be devoted to expanding its business. Ford also continued the company's policy of lowering prices, while improving quality. The Dodge brothers sued, asking the court to order Ford Motor to resume paying the special dividends and to enjoin the proposed expansion of the firm's operations. At trial, Ford testified to his belief that the company made too much money and had an obligation to benefit the public and the firm's workers and customers.

The plaintiff Dodge brothers contended an improper altruism[2] towards his workers and customers motivated Ford. The court agreed, strongly rebuking Ford:

> A business corporation is organized and carried on primarily for the profit of the stockholders. The powers of the directors are to be employed for that end. The discretion of directors is to be exercised in the choice of means to attain that end, and does not extend to a change in the end itself, to the reduction of profits, or to the nondistribution of profits among stockholders in order to devote them to other purposes.[3]

Consequently, "it is not within the lawful powers of a board of directors to shape and conduct the affairs of a corporation for the merely incidental benefit of shareholders and for the primary purpose of benefiting others."

tween the duties Ford believed he and his fellow stockholders owed to the general public "and the duties which in law he and his codirectors owe to protesting, minority stockholders." *Dodge*, 170 N.W. at 684. On its face, the duty to which the court refers is that of a director rather than the duties of a majority shareholder. (Concededly, both the specific passage in question and the opinion in general are sufficiently ambiguous to permit Smith's interpretation.) In the second instance, whatever Dodge originally meant, the evolutionary processes of the common law have led to Dodge being interpreted as establishing a basic rule for boards of directors; namely, that the board has a duty to maximize shareholder wealth. As Smith concedes, his interpretation departs from the "consensus" of most corporate law scholars. Smith, supra, at 283.

2. The term altruism is used in this chapter to describe any decision motivated by considerations other than shareholder wealth maximization. It thus includes, but also is much broader than, the special case

of corporate philanthropy. As for the latter, see § 9.6.

3. Dodge v. Ford Motor Co., 170 N.W. 668, 684 (Mich.1919). Despite its strong emphasis on the board's obligation to pursue shareholder interests, the court recognized that, in many situations, ethical or humanitarian considerations are wholly consistent with long-term shareholder wealth maximization. Providing health care to employees costs money in the short-run, for example, but in the long-run healthy employees with high morale may be more productive. A board of directors thus may decide to incur such short-run costs in order to reap long-term gains without fear of liability: "The difference between an incidental humanitarian expenditure of corporate funds for the benefit of the employees, like the building of a hospital for their use and the employment of agencies for the betterment of their condition, and a general purpose and plan to benefit mankind at the expense of others, is obvious."

Despite its strong rhetoric, *Dodge* does not stand for the proposition that directors will be held liable for considering the social consequences of corporate actions. To be sure, having found that Ford had failed to pursue shareholder wealth maximization, the court ordered Ford Motor to resume paying its substantial special dividends. Invoking the business judgment rule, however, the *Dodge* court declined to interfere with Ford's plans for expansion and dismissed the bulk of plaintiff's complaint. Recall from Chapter 6 the distinction between standards of review and of conduct. The shareholder wealth maximization norm set forth in *Dodge* is a standard of conduct, but the business judgment rule remains the standard of review. Consequently, *Dodge* does not stand for the proposition that courts will closely supervise the conduct of corporate directors to ensure that every decision maximizes shareholder wealth. As the court's refusal to enjoin Ford Motor's proposed expansion illustrates, courts generally will not substitute their judgment for that of the board of directors. If a proposed course of action plausibly relates to long-term shareholder wealth maximization, courts will not intervene. Ford's proposed expansion plans did so, and thus were allowed to go forward. Ford's refusal to pay a special dividend, while simultaneously lowering prices, compounded by his anti-profitmaking trial testimony, did not. Accordingly, the court ordered him to pay the requested dividend. As always, authority and accountability are in tension. We have consistently argued that, absent self-dealing or other unusual circumstances, authority should prevail. Ford's conduct lay at the outer boundary of defensible exercises of authority and the court appropriately slapped his wrist.[4]

As the law evolved, corporate altruism began to be seen as proper so long as it was likely to provide direct benefits to the corporation and its shareholders. Applying the business judgment rule, moreover, many courts essentially presumed that an altruistic decision was in the corporation's best interests. Our old friend *Shlensky v. Wrigley*[5] exemplifies this approach. Recall that Shlensky, a minority shareholder in the Chicago Cubs, challenged the decision by Wrigley, the majority shareholder, not to install lights at Wrigley Field. Shlensky claimed the Cubs were persistent money losers, which he attributed to poor home attendance, which in turn he attributed to the board's refusal to install lights and play night baseball. According to Shlensky, Wrigley was indifferent

---

4. One can plausibly argue that Ford's seemingly altruistic conduct in fact was a shrewd and ruthless attempt to stifle competition. In addition to being shareholders of Ford Motor Co., the Dodge brothers were also competitors. They founded the business that is now the Dodge brand of DaimlerChrysler. Their likely goal for this litigation was not only restoration of the special dividends, which they needed to finance their competing business, but also to prevent Ford from expanding capacity. Ford's decisions effectively cut the Dodge Brothers off at the knees. The brothers had a large investment in Ford Motor Co. stock, which was producing minimal returns (absent the special dividends). Cancellation of those dividends would help fund expansion of the brothers' main competitor. If so, however, why didn't Ford explain all this to the court? Perhaps he feared antitrust litigation or perhaps he simply didn't want to look like a robber baron.

5. 237 N.E.2d 776 (Ill.App.1968), see § 6.2. Accord Ella M. Kelly & Wyndham, Inc. v. Bell, 266 A.2d 878, 879 (Del.1970); Union Pac. R.R. Co. v. Trustees, Inc., 329 P.2d 398, 401–02 (Utah 1958).

to the effect of his continued intransigence on the team's finances. Instead, Shlensky argued, Wrigley was motivated by his beliefs that baseball was a day-time sport and that night baseball might have a deteriorating effect on the neighborhood surrounding Wrigley Field.

Despite Shlensky's apparently uncontested evidence that Wrigley was more concerned with interests other than those of the shareholders, the court did not even allow him to get up to bat. Instead, the court presumed that Wrigley's decision was in the firm's best interests. Indeed, the court basically invented reasons why a director might have made an honest decision against night baseball. The court opined, for example, "the effect on the surrounding neighborhood might well be considered by a director."[6] Again, the court said: "the long run interest" of the firm "might demand" protection of the neighborhood. Accordingly, Shlensky's case was dismissed for failure to state a claim upon which relief could be granted.

The rhetorical emphasis shifted significantly between *Dodge* and *Shlensky*. Where *Dodge* emphasized the directors' duty to maximize profits, *Shlensky* emphasized the directors' authority and discretion. Ultimately, however, they are consistent. The Illinois Appellate Court did not reject the profit-maximizing norm laid down by *Dodge*, but rather followed *Dodge* in holding that the business judgment rule immunized the directors' decision from judicial review.

To be sure, a few cases posit that directors need not treat shareholder wealth maximization as their sole guiding star. *A. P. Smith Manufacturing Co. v. Barlow*, the most frequently cited example, upheld a corporate charitable donation on the ground, inter alia, that "modern conditions require that corporations acknowledge and discharge social as well as private responsibilities as members of the communities within which they operate."[7] Ultimately, however, the differences between *Barlow* and *Dodge* have little more than symbolic import. As the *Barlow* court recognized, shareholders' long-run interests are often served by decisions (such as charitable giving) that appear harmful in the short-run. Because the court acknowledged that the challenged contribution thus could be justified on profit-maximizing grounds, its broader language on corporate social responsibility is arguably mere dictum.

In any event, *Dodge*'s theory of shareholder wealth maximization has been widely accepted by courts over an extended period of time. Almost three quarters of a century after *Dodge*, the Delaware chancery court similarly opined: "It is the obligation of directors to attempt, within the law, to maximize the long-run interests of the corporation's stockholders."[8]

---

6. Shlensky v. Wrigley, 237 N.E.2d 776, 780 (Ill.App.1968).

7. A. P. Smith Mfg. Co. v. Barlow, 98 A.2d 581, 586 (N.J.1953). See also Theodora Holding Corp. v. Henderson, 257 A.2d 398,

404 (Del.Ch.1969) (opining that corporate social responsibility is a desirable goal).

8. Katz v. Oak Indus., Inc., 508 A.2d 873, 879 (Del.Ch.1986). In Long v. Norwood Hills Corp., 380 S.W.2d 451 (Mo.Ct.App. 1964), the court observed: "Plaintiff cites

In sum, the law governing operational decisions has a somewhat schizophrenic feel. In most jurisdictions, courts will exhort directors to use their best efforts to maximize shareholder wealth. In a few, courts may exhort directors to consider the corporation's social responsibility. In either case, however, the announced principle is no more than an exhortation. The court may hold forth on the primacy of shareholder interests, or may hold forth on the importance of socially responsible conduct, but ultimately it does not matter. Under either approach, directors who consider nonshareholder interests in making corporate decisions, like directors who do not, will be insulated from liability by the business judgment rule.[9]

The proposition that corporate directors generally should not be held liable for allegedly considering the effects of their decisions on nonshareholder constituencies and interests follows directly from our theory of the firm. As we have seen, authority and accountability are in constant tension. With respect to operational decisions, authority appropriately prevails. Sometimes consideration of nonshareholder interests is consistent with long-term shareholder interests, and sometimes it is not. In all operational cases, however, deciding whether nonshareholder interests are congruent with shareholder interests is a question for the board of directors. Courts therefore properly invoke the business judgment rule to insulate such decisions from review.

2.   Nonshareholder constituency statutes

Over thirty states have purported to address the corporate social responsibility debate by adopting so-called nonshareholder constituency statutes.[10] Typically, these statutes amend the existing statutory state-

---

many authorities [including *Dodge*] to show that the ultimate object of every ordinary trading corporation is the pecuniary gain of its stockholders and that it is for this purpose the capital has been advanced." Id. at 476. The court further stated that it had "no quarrel with plaintiff insofar as the rules of law stated therein govern the actions of majority stockholders and the boards of directors of corporations." Id.

9. The principal exception to this rule is where directors rely on nonshareholder interests to justify takeover defenses, which do not necessarily get business judgment rule protection. See, e.g., Revlon, Inc. v. MacAndrews & Forbes Holdings, Inc., 506 A.2d 173 (Del.1985).

10. For selected references from the extensive literature on these statutes, see ABA Committee on Corp. Laws, Other Constituencies Statutes: Potential for Confusion, 45 Bus. Law. 2253 (1990); Stephen M. Bainbridge, Interpreting Nonshareholder Constituency Statutes, 19 Pepperdine L. Rev. 971 (1992); William W. Bratton, Confronting the Ethical Case Against the Ethi-

cal Case for Constituency Rights, 50 Wash. & Lee L. Rev. 1449 (1993); William J. Carney, Does Defining Constituencies Matter?, 59 U. Cin. L. Rev. 385 (1990); Michael E. DeBow and Dwight R. Lee, Shareholders, Nonshareholders and Corporate Law: Communitarianism and Resource Allocation, 18 Del. J. Corp. L. 393 (1993); James J. Hanks, Jr., Playing with Fire: Nonshareholder Constituency Statutes in the 1990s, 21 Stetson L. Rev. 97 (1991); Charles Hansen, Other Constituency Statutes: A Search for Perspective, 46 Bus. Law. 1355 (1991); Morey W. McDaniel, Stockholders and Stakeholders, 21 Stetson L. Rev. 121 (1991); David Millon, Redefining Corporate Law, 24 Ind. L. Rev. 223 (1991); Lawrence E. Mitchell, A Theoretical and Practical Framework for Enforcing Corporate Constituency Statutes, 70 Tex. L. Rev. 579 (1992); Eric W. Orts, Beyond Shareholders: Interpreting Corporate Constituency Statutes, 61 Geo. Wash. L. Rev. 14 (1992); Roberta Romano, What is the Value of Other Constituency Statutes to Shareholders?, 43 U. Toronto L. Rev. 533 (1993); Mark E. Van Der Weide, Against

ment of the director's duty of care. They commonly authorize the board of directors, in discharging its duty of care, to consider the impact a decision will have on not only shareholders, but also on a list of other constituency groups, such as employees, suppliers, customers, creditors, and the local communities in which the firm does business. In addition to the laundry list of constituency factors, some statutes more generally authorize directors to consider both the long-and short-term effects of the decision.

Most nonshareholder constituency statutes are permissive. Directors "may," but need not, take nonshareholder interests into account. There are no express constraints on the directors' discretion in deciding whether to consider nonshareholder interests and, if they decide to do so, which constituency groups' interests to consider. As a result, the statutes should not be interpreted as creating new director fiduciary duties running to nonshareholder constituencies and the latter should not have standing under these statutes to seek judicial review of a director's decision.[11]

Beyond this, however, the nonshareholder constituency statutes uniformly are silent on many key issues. Among the issues left open by almost all statutes are such critical questions as: How should directors decide whether particular claimants fall into one of the protected constituent categories, some of which, such as customers and communities, are

---

Fiduciary Duties to Corporate Stakeholders, 21 Del. J. Corp. L. 27 (1996); Katherine Van Wezel Stone, Employees as Stakeholders under State Nonshareholder Constituency Statutes, 21 Stetson L. Rev. 45 (1991); Steven M.H. Wallman, The Proper Interpretation of Corporate Constituency Statutes and Formulation of Director Duties, 21 Stetson L. Rev. 163 (1991).

11. Although most statutes are silent on this point, the New York and Pennsylvania statutes explicitly state that they create no duties towards any party. N.Y. Bus. Corp. Law § 717(b); 15 Pa. Cons. Stat. § 1717. Some commentators assert that the nonshareholder constituency statutes are, or should be, enforceable by stakeholders; alternatively, some posit that the nonshareholder constituency statutes create, or may lead to the creation of, management fiduciary duties to the stakeholders. See, e.g., Morey W. McDaniel, Bondholders and Stockholders, 13 J. Corp. L. 205, 265–313 (1988); William R. Newlin & Jay A. Gilmer, The Pennsylvania Shareholder Protection Act: A New State Approach to Deflecting Corporate Takeover Bids, 40 Bus. Law. 111, 114 (1984); see generally Marleen A. O'Connor, Introduction to the Symposium on Corporate Malaise—Stakeholder Statutes: Cause or Cure?, 21 Stetson L. Rev. 3 (1991). Whatever the policy merits of creating fiduciary duties running from the directors to the

stakeholders, it is difficult to find such a duty in the statutory language. Even a leading proponent of creating fiduciary duties running to stakeholders has recognized this point: "Because these statutes do not mandate that directors consider nonshareholder constituents, these [stakeholder] groups probably do not have standing to enforce these statutes." Marleen A. O'Connor, Restructuring the Corporation's Nexus of Contracts: Recognizing a Fiduciary Duty to Protect Displaced Workers, 66 N.C. L. Rev. 1189, 1233–34 (1991). Given that the extrinsic information about legislative intent suggests that the legislatures saw the statutes as making only minor changes in the law, the legislative history likewise provides no basis for reading such a duty into the current statutes. See Stephen M. Bainbridge, Interpreting Nonshareholder Constituency Statutes, 19 Pepperdine L. Rev. 971, 992–93 (1992). Finally, it is important to note that at common law the board of directors has no duty to consider nonshareholder interests. See, e.g., Local 1330, United Steel Workers v. U.S. Steel Corp., 631 F.2d 1264, 1280–82 (6th Cir.1980). Accordingly, judicial creation of such a duty should require a clearer legislative statement. Put another way, proposals for stakeholder standing seem more appropriately addressed to legislatures than to courts interpreting the existing statutes.

very amorphous? What weight should directors assign to shareholder and nonshareholder interests? What should directors do when those interests cannot be reconciled? What should directors do when the interests of various nonshareholder constituencies conflict amongst themselves? What standards should courts use in reviewing a director's decision not to consider nonshareholder interests? What standards of review apply to director action claimed to be motivated by concern for nonshareholder constituents? Nor is there, as yet, any significant guidance from the courts. The statutes have rarely been cited outside the takeover setting, and even there they have not received authoritative interpretation. To the contrary, the decisions generally are limited to the not very startling observation that the statutes permit director consideration of stakeholder interests.[12] The waters thus remain quite murky.

Plausible interpretations of nonshareholder constituency statutes fall on a spectrum between two extremes. At one end of the spectrum is a reading that allows directors to ignore shareholder interests in making corporate decisions. At the other end is a reading under which the statutes simply codify the pre-existing common law, including an unmodified shareholder wealth maximization norm. Neither extreme seems likely to emerge as the prevailing interpretation. Instead, we will end up somewhere in the middle. But where?

At a minimum, if the statutes do anything beyond merely codifying present law, they presumably permit directors to select a plan that is second-best from the shareholders' perspective, but which alleviates the decision's impact on the firm's nonshareholder constituencies. In other words, the directors may balance a decision's effect on shareholders against its effect on stakeholders. If the decision would harm stakeholders, the directors may trade-off a reduction in shareholder gains for enhanced stakeholder welfare.

This interpretation is virtually compelled by the statutory language. What purpose is there in giving the directors the right to consider nonshareholder interests if the directors cannot protect those interests? Without the right to act on their deliberations, the right to include stakeholder interests in those deliberations is rendered nugatory. If the statutes are to have any meaning, they must permit directors to make some trade-offs between their various constituencies.

How then might these statutes change the outcome of specific cases, if at all? Assume the XYZ Company operates a manufacturing plant nearing obsolescence in an economically depressed area. XYZ's board of directors is considering three plans for the plant's future. Plan A will keep the plant open, which will preserve the jobs of two hundred fifty workers, but will reduce earnings per share by ten percent as long as the plant remains open. Plan B will close the plant immediately, which will put the two hundred fifty plant employees out of work in an area where manufacturing jobs are scarce, but will cause earnings per share to rise

---

12. See, e.g., Keyser v. Commonwealth Nat'l Fin. Corp., 675 F.Supp. 238, 265–66 (M.D.Pa.1987); Baron v. Strawbridge & Clothier, 646 F.Supp. 690, 697 (E.D.Pa.1986).

by ten percent. Plan C contemplates closing the plant, but implementing a job training and relocation program for its workers as a supplement to state-provided programs. Plan C will cause a ten percent reduction in earnings per share for one year.

A shareholder threatens to bring a derivative action against the directors charging breach of their duty of care if they pick any plan other than Plan B. Under traditional corporate law principles, as espoused by *Dodge*, XYZ's board is required to choose the plan that maximizes shareholder wealth: Plan B. However, because the statutes permit directors to balance shareholder and stakeholder interests, the board should be free to adopt either Plan A or Plan C without fear of liability if a shareholder challenges the board's decision.

As a practical matter, however, the result would be no different under traditional common law rules. The business judgment rule undoubtedly would preclude judicial review of the board's decision. In *Shlensky v. Wrigley,*[13] Wrigley's stubborn opposition to lights probably cost the shareholders money over the short term, but the business judgment rule prevented Shlensky's lawsuit from going forward. In *Dodge v. Ford Motor Co.,*[14] Ford's concern for his workers and customers likewise may have harmed the other shareholders, but again the business judgment rule shielded him from liability in connection with the plant expansion decision. Just so, the business judgment rule would shield our hypothetical XYZ board's decision from judicial review. In theory, of course, absent a nonshareholder constituency statute, a shareholder might be able to rebut the business judgment rule's presumption of good faith and hold directors liable for considering nonshareholder interests. In practice, however, cases in which the business judgment rule does not shield operational decisions from judicial review are so rare as to amount to little more than aberrations. In sum, the probability of holding directors liable for operational decisions was so low before the nonshareholder constituency statutes came along that the statutes could not further lower it.

B.   The shareholder wealth maximization norm in practice

Shareholder wealth maximization is not only the law, it is also a basic feature of corporate ideology. Although some claim that directors do not adhere to the shareholder wealth maximization norm, the weight of the evidence is to the contrary.[15] A 1995 National Association of Corporate Directors (NACD) report, for example, stated: "The primary objective of the corporation is to conduct business activities with a view to enhancing corporate profit and shareholder gain," albeit subject to the qualification that "long-term shareholder gain" may require "fair treat-

---

13.   237 N.E.2d 776 (Ill.App.1968).

14.   170 N.W. 668 (Mich.1919).

15.   See, e.g., Margaret M. Blair & Lynn A. Stout, A Team Production Theory of Corporate Law, 85 Va. L. Rev. 247, 286 (1999); D. Gordon Smith, The Shareholder Primacy Norm, 23 J. Corp. L. 277, 290–91 (1998).

ment'' of nonshareholder constituents.[16] A 1996 NACD report on director professionalism set out the same objective, without any qualifying language on nonshareholder constituencies.[17] A 1999 Conference Board survey found that directors of U.S. corporations generally define their role as running the company for the benefit of its shareholders.[18] The 2000 edition of Korn/Ferry International's well-known director survey found that when making corporate decisions directors consider shareholder interests most frequently, albeit also finding that a substantial number of directors feel some responsibility towards stakeholders.[19]

What people do arguably matters more than what they say. Director fidelity to shareholder interests has been enhanced in recent years by the market for corporate control and, some say, activism by institutional investors. Hence, for example, the widespread corporate restructurings of the 1990s are commonly attributed to director concern for shareholder wealth maximization.[20] In addition, changes in director compensation have created hostages ensuring director fidelity to shareholder interests.[21] Directors have long given shareholders reputational hostages. If the company fails on their watch, after all, the directors' reputation and thus their future employability is likely to suffer. In addition, it is becoming common to compensate outside directors in stock rather than cash and to establish minimum stock ownership requirements as a qualification for election. Tying up a proportion of directors' personal wealth in stock of the corporation creates another hostage, further aligning the directors' interests with those of shareholders.

§ 9.3 The corporate social responsibility debate

Every couple of decades the corporate social responsibility debate heats up again. While it is almost as old as the corporate form itself, the debate took its modern form in the 1930s in an exchange between Professors Adolf Berle and Merrick Dodd.[1] Recall that Berle showed that ownership and control had separated in the modern publicly-held corpo-

---

16. National Association of Corporate Directors, Report of the NACD Blue Ribbon Commission on Director Compensation: Purposes, Principles, and Best Practices 1 (1995).

17. See National Association of Corporate Directors, Report of the NACD Blue Ribbon Commission on Director Professionalism 1 (1996).

18. The Conference Board, Determining Board Effectiveness: A Handbook for Directors and Officers 7 (1999).

19. Korn/Ferry International, 27th Annual Board of Directors Study 33–34 (2000).

20. See, e.g., Michael Useem, Investor Capitalism: How Money Managers Are Changing the Face of Corporate America 137–67 (1996) (discussing corporate restructurings as a consequence of investor pressure).

21. Hostages—reciprocal transaction-specific investments—are a central concept in institutional economics. Giving and taking hostages is a mechanism for making credible commitments. I'll pay the ransom, because I know that you will kill the hostage if I do not.

§ 9.3

1. Compare A. A. Berle, Jr., Corporate Powers as Powers in Trust, 44 Harv. L. Rev. 1049 (1931) and A. A. Berle, Jr., For Whom Corporate Managers Are Trustees, 45 Harv. L. Rev. 1365 (1932) with E. Merrick Dodd, Jr., For Whom Are Corporate Managers Trustees?, 45 Harv. L. Rev. 1145 (1932) and E. Merrick Dodd, Jr., Is Effective Enforcement of the Fiduciary Duties of Corporate Managers Practicable?, 2 U. Chi. L. Rev. 194 (1935).

ration. Berle contended that, in light of this separation, the board of directors should operate the corporation for the sole benefit of the shareholders. Berle, and his fellow advocates of this position, argued that corporate concern for nonshareholder interests is appropriate only if shareholder interests are thereby advanced. Or, as Nobel laureate economist Milton Friedman once quipped, "the social responsibility of business is to increase its profits."[2] A fairly standard litany of supporting arguments evolved, ranging from concerns over management accountability to claims that a sole focus on maximizing shareholder wealth benefits all members of society.[3]

Dodd generally accepted the separation of ownership and control as describing public corporations, but rejected Berle's views on corporate social responsibility. Dodd, and his fellow proponents of this side of the debate, saw shareholders as absentee owners whose interests can be subjugated to those of other corporate constituencies and those of society at large. Again, a fairly standard litany of supporting arguments evolved, ranging from long-run shareholder self-interest to the very viability of capitalism.

As described in the preceding section, the law largely accords with the views advocated by Berle.[4] Yet, many commentators still echo Dodd in arguing that directors should have a duty to consider the effects of corporation actions on nonshareholder interests and constituencies. At the very least, holders of this view assert, directors' fiduciary duties should not preclude directors from considering such interests.

A.　Shareholder wealth maximization norm and the nexus of contracts model

A critical question is whether the concept of director accountability for shareholder wealth maximization can be squared with the contractarian account on which our approach to corporate law and governance is

2.　Milton Friedman, The Social Responsibility of Business Is to Increase Its Profits, N.Y. Times, Sept. 13, 1970, § 6 (Magazine), at 32.

3.　For useful summaries, see Keith Davis, The Case for and Against Business Assumption of Social Responsibilities, in Managing Corporate Social Responsibility 35, 40–44 (Archie B. Carroll ed. 1977); Lyman Johnson, Corporate Takeovers and Corporations: Who are They For?, 43 Wash. & Lee L. Rev. 781, 789–98 (1986).

4.　Berle's views were slightly more complex than the text acknowledges. Berle suggested a time might come when managers would "develop into a purely neutral technocracy, balancing a variety of claims by various groups in the community." Adolf Berle & Gardiner C. Means, The Modern Corporation and Private Property 356 (1933). Until that time, however, Berle thought it better to treat directors as trustees for the shareholders. Id. at 355. In a later work, published near the end of his career, Berle concluded that his debate with Dodd "ha[d] been settled (at least for the time being) squarely in favor of Professor Dodd's contention." Adolf A. Berle, Jr., The 20th Century Capitalist Revolution 169 (1954). This concession appears to have been motivated in large part by the New Jersey Supreme Court's decision in A.P. Smith Mfg. Co. v. Barlow, 98 A.2d 581 (N.J.), appeal dismissed, 346 U.S. 861 (1953), in which the court broadly endorsed the corporate social responsibility doctrine. As discussed above, however, *Barlow*'s result is not inconsistent with the profit maximization theory and, in any event, it remains in the minority among the decided cases.

based. Because ownership is not a meaningful concept in the contractarian model, contractarianism seems inconsistent with the traditional views espoused in cases like *Dodge* or by scholars like Friedman. Our director primacy variant of contractarianism, which treats the board of directors as a sort of Platonic guardian, whose power devolves from the set of contracts making up the corporation as a whole rather than solely from shareholders, looks especially like a stakeholderist model. Yet, contractarianism and shareholder wealth maximization are not inconsistent. One reconciles them by affirmatively answering the following question: Would a shareholder wealth maximization norm emerge from the hypothetical bargain as the majoritarian default?

1. *A quick review of the hypothetical bargain methodology*

If corporate law consists mainly of default rules, corporate statutes and decisions can be viewed as a standard form contract voluntarily adopted—perhaps with modifications—by the corporation's various constituencies. The point of a standard form contract, of course, is to reduce bargaining costs. Parties for whom the default rules are a good fit can take the default rules off the rack, without having to bargain over them. Parties for whom the default rules are inappropriate are free to bargain out of the default rules.

In selecting the appropriate default rule, we therefore perform a thought experiment: "If the parties could costlessly bargain over the question, which rule would they adopt?" To answer that question we draw on both experience and economic analysis. Once we figure out a plausible majoritarian default, we adopt that hypothetical bargain as the corporate law default rule. Doing so reduces transaction costs and therefore makes firms more efficient.

2. *Identifying the bargainers*

As a preliminary matter, we need to identify the relevant participants in the hypothetical bargain. Arguably, one could focus on a hypothetical bargain between shareholders and nonshareholder constituencies. Alternatively, one could focus on bargaining between shareholders and the entity as nexus. Because our model treats the corporation as a vehicle by which directors hire capital, however, the focus here is on bargaining between shareholders and the board of directors.

As discussed in the next section, directors and shareholders would strike a bargain in which directors pursue shareholder wealth maximization. Shareholders will insist on that norm when entering into their contract with the corporation or, at least, would be willing to pay more for stock protected by that norm. Because directors have an incentive to minimize the firm's cost of capital, they will agree to be bound by the norm.

This result does not change even if we introduce into the mix nonshareholder constituencies as a bargaining party. Director pursuit of shareholder wealth maximization often redounds to the benefit of nonshareholder constituencies. Even where shareholder and nonshareholder interests conflict, moreover, nonshareholders receive superior protection from contracts and both targeted and general welfare legislation. Because shareholders will place a higher value on being the beneficiaries of director fiduciary duties than will nonshareholder constituencies, gains from trade are available, and we would expect a bargain to be struck in which shareholder wealth maximization is the chosen norm.

3.   *The bargain over ends*

Given the substantial discretion vested in the board, directors could pursue their own personal self-interest. Alternatively, directors could pursue personal policy preferences, such as favoring the interests of employees over those of other corporate constituents. Yet, boards do not insist on unfettered discretion. Instead, boards voluntarily limit their discretion with respect to the proper ends of corporate governance by embracing the shareholder wealth maximization norm. Why?

Return is positively correlated with risk. If directors expose shareholders to greater risk, shareholders will demand a higher rate of return.[5] Greater risk thus translates directly into a higher corporate cost of capital. At the margins, a higher cost of capital increases the probability of firm failure or takeover. Given the reputational cost of firm failure, the board thus has an incentive to adopt the decisionmaking norm preferred by shareholders. To the extent the directors invest in firm specific human capital, which would be lost if they lost their positions following a firm failure or takeover, the board's incentives are further aligned to shareholder preferences.

Shareholders will view a director preference for other constituencies as a risk demanding compensatory returns. First, absent the shareholder wealth maximization norm, the board would lack a determinate metric for assessing options. Because stakeholder decisionmaking models necessarily create a two masters problem,[6] such models inevitably lead to indeterminate results. Recall the XYZ hypothetical from the preceding section, in which the board of directors is considering closing an obsolete plant. Assume the closing will harm the plant's workers and the local community, but will benefit shareholders, creditors, employees at a more modern plant to which the work previously performed at the old plant is transferred, and communities around the modern plant. Further assume that the latter groups cannot gain except at the former groups' expense. By what standard should the board make the decision? Shareholder wealth maximization provides a clear answer—close the plant. Once the directors are allowed to deviate from shareholder wealth maximization,

---

5. We are using the term "risk" here in its colloquial rather than its technical sense. In the strict sense in which the term is used in conventional finance lingo, director misconduct of the type described here does not create risk, because such misconduct does not affect the variation of returns. Instead, director misconduct erodes the expected shareholder return.

6. Cf. Matthew 6:24 (stating: "No one can serve two masters.").

however, they must inevitably turn to indeterminate balancing standards.

Second, any legal standards developed to review such decisions would operate mostly by virtue of hindsight. Such rules deprive directors of the critical ability to determine ex ante whether their behavior comports with the law's demands, raising the transaction costs of corporate governance. The conflict of interest rules governing the legal profession provide a useful analogy. Despite many years of refinement, these rules are still widely viewed as inadequate, vague, and inconsistent—hardly the stuff of which certainty and predictability are made.[7]

Finally, absent clear standards, directors will be tempted to pursue their own self-interest. One may celebrate the virtues of granting directors largely unfettered discretion to manage the business enterprise, as we have done throughout this text, without having to ignore the agency costs associated with such discretion. Discretion should not be allowed to camouflage self-interest.

Directors who are responsible to everyone are accountable to no one. In the foregoing hypothetical, for example, if the board's interests favor keeping the plant open, we can expect the board to at least lean in that direction. The plant likely will stay open, with the decision being justified by reference to the impact of a closing on the plant's workers and the local community. In contrast, if directors' interests are served by closing the plant, the plant will likely close, with the decision being justified by concern for the firm's shareholders, creditors, and other benefited constituencies.

At best, stakeholder models give directors a license to reallocate wealth from shareholders to nonshareholder constituencies. Would investors be willing to invest their retirement savings in corporate stock if that approach became law? Probably not. An investment in corporate stock must bring shareholders a rate of return commensurate with the risks they are taking. If it does not, they will divest stock in favor of other investments or, at least, monitor directors more closely. In either case, the cost of equity capital will rise under stakeholder models.

To be sure, the business judgment rule (appropriately) insulates directors from liability despite the potential for conflicted interests. The psychological effects of a switch to stakeholder models, however, should not be downplayed. Because the shareholder wealth maximization norm is central to director socialization, the norm provides a forceful reminder of where the director's loyalty lies. Even if the business judgment rule renders its rhetoric largely unenforceable, the shareholder wealth maximization norm is an ever present goad. By removing the psychological constraint that the shareholder wealth maximization norm provides, and

---

7. See Marc I. Steinberg & Timothy U. Sharpe, Attorney Conflicts of Interest: The Need for a Coherent Framework, 66 Notre Dame L. Rev. 1, 2 (1990); see generally Nancy J. Moore, Conflicts of Interest in the Simultaneous Representation of Multiple Clients: A Proposed Solution to the Current Confusion and Controversy, 61 Tex. L. Rev. 211 (1982).

simultaneously exacerbating the two masters problem, nonshareholder constituency statutes are less likely to encourage directors to pursue the collective interests of the firm's various constituents than to encourage directors to pursue their own self-interest.

The critical difference between the existing regime and the stakeholder models, moreover, emerges when we turn to those cases in which the business judgment rule does not apply with full force. Suppose, for example, that our hypothetical corporation receives a takeover bid from a bidder with a history of closing obsolete plants. The board rejects the bid, citing the bidder's history. All of the practical problems discussed above are present. More important, while an honest concern for the threatened workers may have motivated the directors' decision, so too might a concern for their own positions and perquisites. Indeed, corporate managers are much more likely to suffer losses as a result of takeovers than are other nonshareholder constituencies. Accordingly, it is not at all difficult to imagine a target board using nonshareholder interests as nothing more than a negotiating device to extract side payments from the bidder. Under current law, the business judgment rule would not protect the directors' decision unless they could show that it also benefited the shareholders.[8] Because stakeholder models permit managers to play one constituency off against another, however, the accountability provided by current law would be lost. Hence, such models are less likely to transfer wealth from shareholders to nonshareholder constituencies than they are to transfer wealth from both shareholders and nonshareholders to managers.

As compensation for bearing these risks, shareholders will demand a higher return on their investment. Whatever value unfettered discretion has for directors would be outweighed by the costs associated with the increased risk of error and opportunism that would follow from adoption of any decisionmaking principle other than shareholder wealth maximization. Accordingly, when directors use the corporation as a vehicle for hiring equity capital, they would include that norm as one of the terms of the deal. Society therefore appropriately adopts the shareholder wealth maximization norm as a governing principle—it is the majoritarian default that emerges from the hypothetical bargain.

4. Another perspective

Boards of directors sometimes face decisions in which it is possible to make at least one corporate constituent better off without leaving any constituency worse off. In economic terms, such a decision is Pareto efficient—it moves the firm from a Pareto inferior position to the Pareto

---

8. In Unocal Corp. v. Mesa Petroleum Co., 493 A.2d 946 (Del.1985), the Delaware supreme court opined that directors may consider the impact of takeover decisions on nonshareholder constituencies. Id. at 955. The court later held, however, that directors may only consider stakeholder interests if doing so would benefit shareholders and, further, that directors may not do so at all once the corporation is "for sale." Revlon, Inc. v. MacAndrews & Forbes Holdings, Inc., 506 A.2d 173, 182 (Del.1985).

frontier.[9] Other times, however, they face a decision that makes at least one constituency better off but leaves at least one worse off. The familiar concept of zero sum games is just the worst-case variation on this theme. Imagine a decision with a pay-off for one constituency of $150 that leaves another constituency worse off by $100. As a whole, the organization is better off by $50. In economic terms, this decision is Kaldor–Hicks efficient.[10] With this background in mind, the shareholder wealth maximization norm can be described as a bargained-for term of the board-shareholder contract by which the directors agree not to make Kaldor–Hicks efficient decisions that leave shareholders worse-off.

A commonly used justification for adopting Kaldor–Hicks efficiency as a decisionmaking norm is the claim that everything comes out in the wash. With respect to one decision, you may be in the constituency that loses, but next time you will be in the constituency that gains. If the decisionmaking apparatus is systematically biased against a particular constituency, however, that justification fails. If shareholders suspect that their constituency would be systematically saddled with losses, they will insist on contract terms precluding directors from making Kaldor–Hicks decisions that leave shareholders worse off. As explained in the next section, shareholders in fact are the constituency most vulnerable to board misconduct and, by extension, to being on the losing end of Kaldor–Hicks efficient decisions. Hence, they predictably will bargain for something like the shareholder wealth maximization norm.

B. Quasi-rents and fiduciary duties

One of the chief tenets of contractarianism is that the law ought to facilitate private ordering; hence, the preference of contractarians for default rules the parties are free to modify. So long as the default rule is properly chosen, most parties will be spared the need to reach a private agreement on the issue in question. Default rules in this sense provide cost savings comparable to those provided by standard form contracts, because both can be accepted without the need for costly negotiation. At the same time, however, because the default rule can be modified by contrary agreement, idiosyncratic parties wishing a different rule can be accommodated. Given these advantages, a fairly compelling case ought to be required before we impose a mandatory rule. Yet, the law should not always facilitate private ordering. Where there is a market failure, regulatory intervention may be appropriate. Welfare economics classically recognizes four basic sources of market failures: producer monopoly; the good to be produced is a public good; informational asymmetry between producer and consumer; and externalities. Of these, the latter is most pertinent for our purposes.

9. A Pareto superior transaction makes at least one person better off and no one worse off.

10. Kaldor-Hicks efficiency does not require that no one be made worse off by a reallocation of resources. Instead, it requires only that the resulting increase in wealth be sufficient to compensate the losers. Note that there does not need to be any actual compensation, compensation simply must be possible.

Corporate conduct doubtless generates negative externalities.[11] In appropriate cases, such externalities should be constrained through general welfare legislation, tort litigation, and other forms of regulation. The question here is whether the law should also seek to constrain them through the fiduciary duties of corporate directors.

In the contractarian model, fiduciary duties are gap-fillers by which courts resolve disputes falling through the cracks of incomplete contracts. More specifically, however, fiduciary duties prevent corporate directors and officers from appropriating quasi-rents through opportunistic conduct unanticipated when the firm was formed. Quasi-rents arise where investments in transaction specific assets create a surplus subject to expropriation by the contracting party with control over the assets.[12] A transaction specific asset is one whose value is appreciably lower in any other use than the transaction in question. Once a transaction specific investment has been made, it generates quasi-rents—i.e., returns in excess of that necessary to maintain the asset in its current use.[13] If such quasi-rents are appropriable by the party with control of the transaction specific asset, a hold up problem ensues. Investments in transaction specific assets therefore commonly are protected through specialized governance structures created by detailed contracts. As we have seen, however, under conditions of uncertainty and complexity, bounded rationality precludes complete contracting. Under such conditions, accordingly, fiduciary duties provide an alternative source of protection against opportunism.

The shareholder's investment in the firm is a transaction specific asset, because the whole of the investment is both at risk and turned over to someone else's control. In contrast, many corporate constituencies do not make firm specific investments in human capital (or otherwise). Many corporate employees, for example, lack significant firm specific human capital. For such employees, mobility is a sufficient defense against opportunistic conduct, because they can quit and be replaced without productive loss to either employee or employer. If the

---

11. It is for this reason that one cannot justify the shareholder wealth maximization norm by claiming that a rising tide lifts all boats. In many cases, this will be true. Nonshareholder constituencies have a claim on the corporation that is both fixed and prior to that of the shareholders. So long as general welfare laws prohibit the corporation from imposing negative externalities on those constituencies, the shareholder wealth maximization norm redounds to their benefit. In some cases, however, the rising tide argument is inapplicable because it fails to take into account the question of risk. Pursuing shareholder wealth maximization often requires one to make risky decisions, which disadvantages nonshareholder constituencies. The increased return associated with an increase in risk does not benefit nonshareholders, because their claim is fixed, whereas the simultaneous increase in the corporation's riskiness makes it less likely that nonshareholder claims will be satisfied. Hence, the rising tide argument cannot be a complete explanation for the shareholder wealth maximization norm.

12. See Benjamin Klein et al., Vertical Integration, Appropriable Rents and the Competitive Contracting Process, 21 J. L. & Econ. 297 (1978).

13. The asset may also generate true rents—i.e., returns exceeding that necessary to induce the investment in the first place—but the presence or absence of true rents is irrelevant to the opportunism problem.

employee's general human capital suffices for him to do his job at Firm A, it presumably would suffice for him to do a similar job at Firm B. Such an employee resembles an independent contractor who can shift from firm to firm at low cost to either employee or employer.[14] Because the relationship between such employees and the corporation does not create appropriable quasi-rents, opportunism by the board is not a concern.

Consequently, shareholders are more vulnerable to director misconduct than are most nonshareholder constituencies. Consider a classic case of self-dealing. Assume a solvent corporation able to pay its debts and other obligations (especially employee salaries) as they come due in the ordinary course of business. Further assume that the corporation has substantial free cash flow—i.e., cash flows in excess of the positive net present value investments available to the corporation. If the directors siphon some portion of the corporation's free cash flow into their own pockets, shareholders are clearly hurt, because the value of the residual claim has been impaired. Yet, in this case, there is no readily apparent injury to the value of the fixed claim of all other corporate constituents.

For the sake of argument, however, assume that appropriation of quasi-rents is an equally severe problem for both shareholders and nonshareholder constituencies. Many employees do invest in firm specific human capital. Creditors may also develop firm specific expertise, particularly in long-term relationships with a significant number of repeat transactions.

Relative to many nonshareholder constituencies, shareholders are poorly positioned to extract contractual protections.[15] Unlike bondholders, for example, whose term-limited relationship to the firm is subject to extensive negotiations and detailed contracts, shareholders have an indefinite relationship that is rarely the product of detailed negotiations. The dispersed nature of stockownership, moreover, makes bilateral negotiation of specialized safeguards especially difficult:

> Arrangements among a corporation, the underwriters of its debt, trustees under its indentures and sometimes ultimate investors are typically thoroughly negotiated and massively documented. The rights and obligations of the various parties are or should be spelled out in that documentation. The terms of the contractual relationship

---

14. This is not to say that exit is costless for either employees or firms. All employees are partially locked into their firm. Indeed, it must be so, or monitoring could not prevent shirking because disciplinary efforts would have no teeth. The question is one of relative costs.

15. The analysis herein applies mainly to voluntary constituencies of the firm, although the political process point is not wholly inapt with respect to involuntary constituencies. In any case, corporate law is an exceptionally blunt instrument with which to protect involuntary constituencies (and voluntary constituencies, as well, for that matter). Tort, contract, and property law, as well as a host of general welfare laws, provide them with a panoply of protections. See generally Jonathan R. Macey, An Economic Analysis of the Various Rationales for Making Shareholders the Exclusive Beneficiaries of Corporate Fiduciary Duties, 21 Stetson L. Rev. 23 (1991).

agreed to and not broad concepts such as fairness [therefore] define the corporation's obligation to its bondholders.[16]

Put another way, bond indentures necessarily are incomplete.[17] Even so, they still provide bondholders with far greater contractual protections than shareholders receive from the corporate contract as represented by the firm's organic documents. Accordingly, we can confidently predict the majoritarian default that would emerge from the hypothetical bargain. Shareholders will want the protections provided by fiduciary duties, while bondholders will be satisfied with the ability to enforce their contractual rights, which is precisely what the law provides.[18]

Like bondholders, employees regularly bargain with employers both individually and collectively. So do other stakeholders, such as local communities that bargain with existing or prospective employers, offering firms tax abatements and other inducements in return for which they could and should extract promises about the firm's conduct. In general, the interests of such constituents lend themselves to more concrete specification than do the open-ended claims of shareholders. Those nonshareholder constituencies that enter voluntary relationships with the corporation thus can protect themselves by adjusting the contract price to account for negative externalities imposed upon them by the firm.

Granted, the extent of negotiations between the corporation and nonshareholders is likely to vary widely. In many cases, such as hiring shop floor employees, the only negotiation will be a take it-or-leave it offer. But so what? Is a standard form contract any less of a contract just because it is offered on a take it-or-leave it basis? If the market is competitive, a party making a take it-or-leave it offer must set price and other terms that will lead to sales despite the absence of particularized negotiations. As long as the firm must attract inputs from nonshareholder constituencies in competitive markets, the firm similarly will have to offer those constituencies terms that compensate them for the risks they bear.

This point persistently eludes proponents of the stakeholder model, who ask: "Can it really be said that employees (or local communities or dependent suppliers) are really better able to 'negotiate' the terms of their relationship to the corporation than are shareholders?"[19] While

---

16. Katz v. Oak Indus. Inc., 508 A.2d 873, 879 (Del.Ch.1986).

17. See Thomas A. Smith, The Efficient Norm for Corporate Law: A Neotraditional Interpretation of Fiduciary Duty, 98 Mich. L. Rev. 214, 234 (1999) (stating that "[a]ll contracts have gaps"). The claim here is simply that the shareholder-corporation contract is especially "gappy." The ownership-like rights conferred by the shareholder's contract follow from this phenomenon.

18. See, e.g., Katz v. Oak Indus. Inc., 508 A.2d 873, 879 (Del.Ch.1986) (holding

that "the relationship between a corporation and the holders of its debt securities, even convertible debt securities, is contractual in nature"); see also Metropolitan Life Ins. Co. v. RJR Nabisco, Inc., 716 F.Supp. 1504, 1524–25 (S.D.N.Y.1989); Simons v. Cogan, 549 A.2d 300, 304 (Del.1988); Revlon, Inc. v. MacAndrews & Forbes, Inc., 506 A.2d 173, 182 (Del.1985).

19. Ronald M. Green, Shareholders as Stakeholders: Changing Metaphors of Corporate Governance, 50 Wash. & Lee L. Rev. 1409, 1418 (1993).

they presumably intend this to be a purely rhetorical question, in fact it has an answer and the answer is an affirmative one.

Shareholders have no meaningful voice in corporate decisionmaking. In effect, shareholders have but a single mechanism by which they can "negotiate" with the board: withholding capital. If shareholder interests are inadequately protected, they can refuse to invest. The nexus of contracts model, however, demonstrates that equity capital is but one of the inputs that a firm needs to succeed. Nonshareholder corporate constituencies can thus "negotiate" with the board in precisely the same fashion as do shareholders: by withholding their inputs. If the firm disregards employee interests, it will have greater difficulty finding workers. Similarly, if the firm disregards creditor interests, it will have greater difficulty attracting debt financing, and so on.

In fact, withholding one's inputs may often be a more effective tool for nonshareholder constituencies than it is for shareholders. Some firms go for years without seeking equity investments. If these firms' boards disregard shareholder interests, shareholders have little recourse other than to sell out at prices that will reflect the board's lack of concern for shareholder wealth. In contrast, few firms can survive for long without regular infusions of new employees and new debt financing. As a result, few boards can prosper for long while ignoring nonshareholder interests.

Let us assume, however, that nonshareholder constituencies are unable to protect themselves through contract. The right rule would still be director fiduciary duties incorporating the shareholder wealth maximization norm. Many nonshareholder constituencies have substantial power to protect themselves through the political process.[20] Public choice theory teaches that well-defined interest groups are able to benefit themselves at the expense of larger, loosely defined groups by extracting legal rules from lawmakers that appear to be general welfare laws but in fact redound mainly to the interest group's advantage. Absent a few self-appointed spokesmen, most of whom are either gadflies or promoting some service they sell, shareholders—especially individuals—have no meaningful political voice. In contrast, many nonshareholder constituencies are represented by cohesive, politically powerful interest groups. Consider the enormous political power wielded by unions, who played a major role in passing state anti-takeover laws. Because those laws temporarily helped kill off hostile takeovers, the unions helped slay the goose that laid golden eggs for shareholders. From the unions' perspective, however, hostile takeovers were inflicting considerable harm on workers. The unions were probably wrong on that score, but the point is

---

20. Where the board has been captured by senior management, nonshareholders also are indirectly protected because management's interests are more likely to be aligned with those of nonshareholder constituencies than with those of the shareholders. Salaried managers hold what amounts to a fixed claim on the corporation's assets and earnings, which is not too dissimilar from the claims of other nonshareholder constituencies. Moreover, much of corporate managers' wealth is tied up in nondiversified firm specific human capital. These factors tend to make them more concerned with ensuring the firm's survival than with taking risks that would maximize shareholder wealth.

that the unions used their political power to transfer wealth from shareholders to nonshareholder constituencies.

Collective bargaining obviously does not protect nonunionized workers, but they receive comparable protections from both legal and market forces. Various market mechanisms have evolved to protect employee investments in firm specific human capital, such as ports of entry, seniority systems, and promotion ladders. As private sector unions have declined, moreover, the federal government has intervened to provide through general welfare legislation many of the same protections for which unions might have bargained. The Family & Medical Leave Act grants unpaid leave for medical and other family problems.[21] The Occupational Safety & Health Administration (OSHA) mandates safe working conditions.[22] Plant closing laws require notice of layoffs.[23] Civil rights laws protect against discrimination of various sorts.[24] And so on.

Such targeted legislative approaches are a preferable solution to the externalities created by corporate conduct. General welfare laws designed to deter corporate conduct through criminal and civil sanctions imposed on the corporation, its directors, and its senior officers are more efficient than stakeholderist tweaking of director fiduciary duties. By virtue of their inherent ambiguity, fiduciary duties are a blunt instrument. There can be no assurance that specific social ills will be addressed by the boards of the specific corporations that are creating the problematic externalities.[25]

§ 9.4 Extra-contractual duties to bondholders

In the contractarian theory of the firm, corporate law is just a standard form contract provided by the state. Where actual corporate contracts are silent, the legal standards fill in the gaps. The fiduciary duties of care and loyalty owed to shareholders thus complete the contract between the corporation and its equity investors.

As with any long-term relational contract, bond indentures inevitably prove incomplete. In a world characterized by uncertainty, complexity, and bounded rationality, it cannot be otherwise. Where the bond indenture is silent, should the law invoke fiduciary duties or other extra-contractual rights as gap fillers?

21. 29 U.S.C. § 2612.

22. 29 U.S.C. § 651.

23. 29 U.S.C. §§ 2101(b)(1), 2102.

24. See, e.g., 42 U.S.C. § 2000e–2 (prohibiting employment discrimination on the basis of race, color, sex, or national origin); id. § 2000e–3 (prohibiting employment discrimination for the bringing of charges, testifying or other participation in law enforcement proceedings or for employer publication or advertisement of a preference for employees of a specific race, color, religion, sex, or national origin).

25. Targeted legislation becomes an even more attractive alternative to fiduciary-based norms of corporate social responsibility when one realizes that consideration of nonshareholder interests is a task for which corporate directors are poorly suited. The shareholder wealth maximization principle dominates both legal and managerial thinking about fiduciary duties. Given the socialization and training of modern U.S. corporate managers, shareholder wealth maximization is the norm most likely to prevail in any consensus-building process.

This debate is a sub-species of the larger controversy over corporate social responsibility, of course. If we may allude to the biblical injunction that no one can serve two masters, for example, fiduciary duties to bondholders would create a two masters problem. When shareholder and bondholder interests conflict, which interests do the directors pursue? A closely related concern is the potential that directors would camouflage self-interested decisions by aligning themselves with the affected group whose interests mirror their own.

In addition, the underwriting process ensures that the indenture will contain efficient protections for bondholders. Some argue that the underwriters have a pecuniary interest in pleasing the issuer, not the bondholders,[1] but the relationship between underwriters and bondholders is a classic repeat transaction phenomenon. Underwriters will not sully their reputation with bondholders for the sake of one issuer.[2] In a firm commitment underwriting, moreover, the underwriters buy the securities from the issuer. If the indenture does not provide adequate levels of protection, the underwriters will be unable to sell the bonds.[3]

Portfolio theory further suggests that bondholders are fully compensated for the risks posed by potential breaches of fiduciary duty. Arguably such risks are unsystematic in nature, so that the bondholders can eliminate them by holding a diversified portfolio. Even if such risks are characterized as systematic risks, moreover, the pricing mechanism will ensure a rate of interest that compensates the bondholders for those risks.

Consequently, the better view is that neither the corporation itself nor its officers and directors owe fiduciary duties to bondholders, as the leading cases hold.[4] Instead, "the relationship between a corporation and the holders of its debt securities, even convertible debt securities, is

---

§ 9.4

1. See, e.g., Lawrence E. Mitchell, The Fairness Rights of Corporate Bondholders, 65 N.Y.U. L. Rev. 1165, 1183 (1990); see also Dale B. Tauke, Should Bonds Have More Fun? A Reexamination of the Debate Over Corporate Bondholder Rights, 1989 Colum. Bus. L. Rev. 1, 24–26 (noting potential conflicts of interest on the part of underwriters). For an instructive critique of the contractarian position, see Eric W. Orts, Shirking and Sharking: A Legal Theory of the Firm, 16 Yale L. & Pol'y Rev. 265 (1998).

2. Marcel Kahan, The Qualified Case against Mandatory Terms in Bonds, 89 Nw. U. L. Rev. 565, 591–92 (1995).

3. The issuer's board and management has a strong self-interest in holding down the corporation's cost of capital—e.g., avoiding takeovers, maximizing personal wealth, and avoiding the adverse consequences of firm failure. Because directors and manag-

ers cannot diversify away the risk of firm failure, as shareholders may, they are more risk averse than shareholders with respect to conduct that could raise the firm's cost of debt capital. If directors and managers pursue shareholder wealth at the expense of bondholders, however, such conduct will come back to haunt management the next time it uses the bond market to raise capital. Coupled with the fact that their nondiversifiable interest in firm failure means that board and officer risk preferences typically are closer to those of creditors than of shareholders, their self-interest provides significant protections for bondholders.

4. See, e.g., Metropolitan Life Ins. Co. v. RJR Nabisco, Inc., 716 F.Supp. 1504, 1524–25 (S.D.N.Y.1989); Simons v. Cogan, 549 A.2d 300, 304 (Del.1988); Revlon, Inc. v. MacAndrews & Forbes Holdings, Inc., 506 A.2d 173, 182 (Del.1985).

contractual in nature."[5] The indenture thus both defines and confines the scope of the corporation's obligations to its bondholders.

To be sure, a few cases purportedly hold to the contrary. The leading precedents, however, relate to corporations in or near insolvency.[6] It makes sense to impose fiduciary duties to bondholders on the boards of such companies, because insolvency is a paradigmatic final period situation in which the market constraints characteristic of repeat transactions are inoperative. In addition, because a common outcome of bankruptcy reorganization is the effective elimination of existing shareholders and the issuance of equity in the post-reorganization firm to bondholders, the effect of insolvency is to render bondholders the de facto residual claimants.

Outside the insolvency setting, however, there is little support for fiduciary duties to bondholders. Most of the cases opining to the contrary involved fraudulent schemes or conveyances actionable outside the bounds of corporate fiduciary obligation.[7] Other cases in this genre involve recharacterization of nominal debt securities as equity.[8] Still others are mere dicta.[9]

The limited extra-contractual rights of bondholders are provided by the implied covenant of good faith found in all contracts. *Katz v. Oak Industries*, for example, held that the implied covenant is breached when it is clear from the express terms of the indenture that the parties would have prohibited the challenged act if they had thought to negotiate about it:

> [T]he appropriate legal test is not difficult to deduce. It is this: is it clear from what was expressly agreed upon that the parties who negotiated the express terms of the contract would have agreed to proscribe the act later complained of as a breach of the implied

5. Katz v. Oak Indus. Inc., 508 A.2d 873, 879 (Del.Ch.1986).

6. See, e.g., Credit Lyonnais Bank Nederland, N.V. v. Pathe Communications Corp., 1991 WL 277613 (Del.Ch.1991).

7. See Metropolitan Life Ins. Co. v. RJR Nabisco, Inc., 716 F.Supp. 1504, 1524 (S.D.N.Y.1989) (analyzing cases).

8. Cf. Eliasen v. Green Bay & W.R.R. Co., 569 F.Supp. 84 (E.D.Wis.1982) (discussing theory and cases). In *Eliasen*, the Class B debentures in question had economic rights more closely resembling those of common stock than normal debt. The Class B debentures had no right to regular payment of interest, but were paid interest only when the board chose and only after the nominal stockholders had been paid, and the debentures came last in a liquidation. The court nevertheless declined to treat the debentures as the equivalent of stock because the Class B debentures had no voting rights and, moreover, were originally issued in a reorganization of an insol-

vent debtor to creditors who would have been entitled to nothing in a liquidation. Id.

9. The classic example is Green v. Hamilton Int'l Corp., 437 F.Supp. 723 (S.D.N.Y. 1977), in which the court held that "[a]s holders of convertible debentures, plaintiffs were part of 'the entire community of interests in the corporation—creditors as well as stockholders' to whom the fiduciary duties of directors and controlling shareholders run." Id. at 729 n.4 (quoting Justice Douglas' famous dictum in Pepper v. Litton, 308 U.S. 295, 307 (1939)). The passage from *Green* is mere dicta because the court simply determined that plaintiff's claim of fraud under Securities Exchange Act Rule 10b–5 could survive a FRCP 12(b)(6) motion to dismiss. In addition, while *Green* purported to interpret Delaware law, the Delaware supreme court specifically disavowed *Green* in Simons v. Cogan, 549 A.2d 300, 303–04 (Del.1988).

covenant of good faith—had they thought to negotiate with respect to that matter. If the answer to this question is yes, then, in my opinion, a court is justified in concluding that such act constitutes a breach of the implied covenant of good faith.[10]

The oft-cited *Met Life* decision likewise invoked an implied covenant of good faith, although its treatment of that covenant differed somewhat from *Katz.*[11] In the latter, the chancery court suggested that an implied covenant of good faith is part of every contract. In *Met Life*, however, the court suggested that a covenant of good faith is implied only when necessary to ensure that neither side deprives the other side of the "fruits of the agreement." The court then seemingly limited the fruits of the bond indenture to regular payment of interest and ultimate repayment of principal. In any case, the court made clear that "the implied covenant will only aid and further the explicit terms of the agreement and will never impose an obligation which would be inconsistent with other terms of the contractual relationship." Consequently, the implied covenant will not give bondholders any extra-contractual rights inconsistent with those set out in the indenture.

Assuming the two tests are different, does the difference matter? *Katz* seems a bit broader, perhaps applying the covenant to conduct that does not directly threaten either the repayment of principal or regular payment of interest. In particular, *Katz* seemingly allows the covenant of good faith to address matters that affect the market price of the bonds. In order to do so, of course, the court would require express terms in the indenture addressing such matters, because only then could one draw the inferences necessitated by the decision's hypothetical bargain-like standard.

Despite this potential difference, however, the two cases are quite similar in a number of respects. In particular, both *Katz* and *Met Life*

---

10. Katz v. Oak Indus. Inc., 508 A.2d 873, 880 (Del.Ch.1986). *Katz* involved the common situation in which a debtor attempts to avoid bankruptcy through a workout including an exchange offer with bondholders. Oak undertook a drastic down-sizing and recapitalization involving the sale of a major part of its business to Allied–Signal. The buyer also agreed to purchase $15 million of newly issued common stock, but that obligation was conditioned on a restructuring of Oak's debt. Oak agreed to effect a series of exchange offers in which at least 85% of Oak's debt securities would get cash or stock worth substantially less than the principal amount of their present securities. Covenants in Oak's indentures prohibited both the recapitalization and the exchange offers. Accordingly, Oak had to obtain bondholder approval of appropriate amendments to the various indentures. To do so, Oak required the bondholders to consent to the requisite amend-

ments as a condition of participating in the exchange offer. Plaintiff objected to the transaction on the grounds that it was "coercive." Chancellor Allen framed the issue not as whether plaintiff was coerced, but as whether such coercion, if any, was "wrongful." Id. at 879–80.

11. Metropolitan Life Ins. Co. v. RJR Nabisco, Inc., 716 F.Supp. 1504 (S.D.N.Y. 1989). *Met Life* arose out of the leveraged buyout of RJR Nabisco by Kohlberg Kravis Roberts & Co. (KKR). The new RJR Nabisco debt issued to finance the LBO had the same bankruptcy priority as RJR Nabisco's pre-LBO debt. RJR Nabisco's equity cushion thus was substantially diminished and the value of the existing debt was substantially reduced. The pre-LBO bondholders claimed that their contract rights had been violated. Because the express terms of the contract had not been violated, the court focused on the implied covenant of good faith.

constrain the implied covenant of good faith by reference to the express terms of the contract. Taken together, the two decisions reflect a basic principle, which can be expressed colloquially as "you made your bed, now you have to lie in it."

§ 9.5 Extra-contractual duties to preferred shareholders

Unlike bondholders, who are creditors of the corporation, holders of preferred stock are nominally shareholders. In addition, while bond indentures tend to be lengthy and highly detailed, the organic documents governing preferred stock tend to be bare-bones affairs. To what extent are preferred stockholders therefore entitled to the benefits of fiduciary duties or other extra-contractual protections?

Jedwab v. MGM Grand Hotels, Inc.,[1] split the baby in an interesting way. A prospective buyer of MGM, Bally Manufacturing, made a total offer for the company, leaving to MGM's board the task of dividing the proceeds between the common and the preferred. The preferred shareholders objected to the division set by the board. Did the board owe the preferred shareholders fiduciary duties of care and loyalty with respect to division of the deal?

The chancery court's opinion acknowledged a number of prior Delaware decisions holding that "preferential rights are contractual in nature."[2] The chancellor rejected, however, the defendants' asserted corollary that all rights of preferred stock are contractual in nature. Instead, the chancellor drew a distinction between the preferential rights and special limitations associated with preferred stock, which are created by the articles of incorporation or other organic corporate documents, and rights that both the preferred and common shares possess by virtue of being stock. The former are contractual in nature and, as such, the board's sole obligation is to give the preferred their contract rights. The latter, however, may give rise to fiduciary obligations. The disputed merger implicated none of the relevant preferential rights or special limitations of MGM's preferred. Accordingly, the court identified three aspects of the preferred holders' complaint as implicating fiduciary duties: "(a) to a 'fair' allocation of the proceeds of the merger; (b) to have the defendants exercise appropriate care in negotiating the proposed merger; and (c) to be free of overreaching by Mr. Kerkorian [a controlling shareholder] . . . ."

Jedwab has a certain superficial plausibility, but proves unpersuasive on closer examination. First, a number of Delaware supreme court precedents in fact suggest that all of the rights of preferred stockholders are contractual in nature, not just those relating to their preferential rights and special limitations.[3] The supreme court's holding in *Wood v.*

§ 9.5

1. 509 A.2d 584 (Del.Ch.1986).

2. See, e.g., Rothschild Int'l Corp. v. Liggett Group, Inc., 474 A.2d 133, 136 (Del. 1984).

3. See, e.g., Judah v. Delaware Trust Co., 378 A.2d 624, 628 (Del.1977) ("Generally, the provisions of the certificate of incorporation govern the rights of preferred shareholders, the certificate . . . being inter-

Coastal States Gas Corp.[4] seems particularly problematic for *Jedwab's* viability. In *Coastal*, plaintiff-preferred shareholders challenged a spin-off transaction as violating the provision of Coastal's articles of incorporation governing conversion of their stock to common. Holding that its duty was to interpret the contract created by the conversion provision, the court concluded that the preferred stockholders' rights were not violated. To be sure, *Coastal* involved a preferential right and thus fell into the category of rights that even *Jedwab* acknowledges to be contractual in nature. The *Coastal* court, however, used very broad language in defining the rights of preferred stockholders: "For most purposes, the rights of the preferred shareholders as against the common shareholders are fixed by the contractual terms agreed upon when the class of preferred stock is created." The qualifier, "for most purposes," does not leave a lot of wiggle room for *Jedwab* to sneak through. Even more significantly, however, the *Coastal* court expressly rejected the plaintiff-preferred shareholders' claim that the spin-off unjustly enriched the common stockholders. In so holding, the court opined that whatever participation rights the preferred stockholders possessed must be created by the articles of incorporation. By thus rejecting an extra-contractual remedy, the *Coastal* court further confirmed the essentially contractual nature of preferred stockholders' rights.

Second, *Jedwab* depends on the proposition that preferred stock is granted certain rights by statute and common law even where the corporation's organic documents are silent. The chancellor cited two such examples: Where the contract is silent, preferred stock get the same voting rights as common stock. Where the contract is silent, preferred stock participates pro rata with the common in a liquidation.[5] Neither of these examples, however, rise to the same level as conferring the benefits of fiduciary obligation on preferred stockholders. Neither entails the sort of open-ended inquiry required by fiduciary obligation, nor does either entail the same risk of conflicting interests.

Finally, from a policy perspective, several objections to *Jedwab* can be noted. Once again, we observe a two masters issue. *Jedwab* does not eliminate potential conflicts of interest between the holders of preferred and common. Whose interests must the board maximize when those interests clash? On a related note, the *Jedwab* opinion makes clear that the preferred are not entitled to an equal share in the merger consideration—only to a fair share. Yet, how does the board decide what is fair ex ante? Even if the board makes a good faith effort to set a fair price, the indeterminacy of valuation means that reasonable people could differ. Conversely, if the prospective buyer proposed the division to be made between the common and the preferred, the board likely would escape liability. Among other things, the board could defend itself on causation grounds—i.e., whether or not the board breached its fiduciary duties,

---

preted in accordance with the law of contracts, with only those rights which are embodied in the certificate granted to preferred shareholders.").

4. 401 A.2d 932 (Del.1979).

5. Jedwab v. MGM Grand Hotels, Inc., 509 A.2d 584, 593–94 (Del.Ch.1986).

that breach was not the cause of plaintiff's injuries.[6] Finally, *Jedwab* implies that the preferred may have greater rights with respect to nonpreference issues than with respect to preferences, which seems odd at best.[7]

In fairness, *Jedwab* wrestled with a persistent problem in the preferred stock area. As noted, bond indentures are hundreds of pages long and deal with virtually every conceivable contingency. In contrast, preferred stock certificates of designation tend to be relatively short and to deal with only a few issues. Which leaves unresolved a nagging question; namely, how do you deal with issues that come up that the contract does not cover? The answer, by analogy to the bond setting, is to use an implied covenant of good faith rather than fiduciary duties.[8] In this context, such a covenant would preclude the board from taking action that deprives the preferred of the benefit of their bargain. To the extent that covenant fails to provide adequate protections, portfolio theory teaches that the preferred stockholders should engage in self-help by diversifying their portfolio.

§ 9.6   The "special" problem of corporate philanthropy

As we have seen, *A. P. Smith Manufacturing Co. v. Barlow*,[1] is often cited as a leading corporate social responsibility decision. Ironically, however, the specific question presented therein—the validity of corporate philanthropy—has been resolved in a more narrow way. Corporate charitable donations are subject to attack under two doctrines: ultra vires and breach of fiduciary duty. Neither is likely to succeed, so long as the amount in question is reasonable and some plausible corporate purpose may be asserted.

---

6. See, e.g., Dalton v. American Inv. Co., 490 A.2d 574 (Del.Ch.), aff'd, 501 A.2d 1238 (Del.1985) (declining to reach issue of fiduciary obligation to preferred stockholders as there was no causal link between alleged breach and alleged injury).

7. The Delaware chancery court continues to follow *Jedwab*. See, e.g., Jackson Nat'l Life Ins. Co. v. Kennedy, 741 A.2d 377, 386–87 (Del.Ch.1999) ("fiduciary duties as well may be owed to preferred stockholders in limited circumstances.... Whether a given claim asserted by preferred stockholders is governed by contract or fiduciary duty principles, then, depends on whether the dispute arises from rights and obligations created by contract or from a right or obligation that is not by virtue of a preference but is shared equally with the common") (footnotes and internal quotation marks omitted); see also Winston v. Mandor, 710 A.2d 835, 845 (Del.Ch.1997); Moore Business Forms, Inc. v. Cordant Holdings Corp., 1995 WL 662685 (Del.Ch. 1995). On the other hand, in RGC Intern.

Investors, LDC v. Greka Energy Corp., 2000 WL 1706728 (Del.Ch.2000), Vice Chancellor Strine favorably referred to a characterization of *Jedwab* as an exception to the general rule "that the rights of preferred stockholders are largely governed by contract law and that corporate directors do not owe preferred stockholders the broad fiduciary duties belonging to common stockholders." Id. at *16.

8. Cf. Gale v. Bershad, 1998 WL 118022 (Del.Ch.1998), in which Vice Chancellor Jacobs followed *Jedwab* in asking whether the right in question is "created not by virtue of any preference" but is "shared equally with the Common." Id. at *5. As to contractual rights arising out of the preferred stock's preferential rights or special limitations, however, Vice Chancellor Jacobs further noted that an implied covenant of good faith constrained the board's discretion. Id.

§ 9.6

1. 98 A.2d 581, 586 (N.J.1953).

Virtually all states have adopted statutes specifically granting corporations the power to make charitable donations,[2] which eliminates the ultra vires issue. Although these statutes typically contain no express limit on the size of permissible gifts, courts interpreting the statutes require corporate charitable donations to be reasonable both as to the amount and the purpose for which they are given.[3] The federal corporate income tax code's limits on the deductibility of corporate charitable giving are often used by analogy by courts seeking guidance on whether a gift was reasonable in amount.

As for breach of fiduciary duty claims, the principles announced in *Dodge v. Ford Motor Co.*[4] arguably require that corporate philanthropy redound to the corporation's benefit. As *Shlensky v. Wrigley*[5] suggests, however, reasonable corporate donations should be protected by the business judgment rule.[6] Consequently, *Barlow*'s discourse on corporate social responsibility properly is regarded as mere dicta.

Law professors worry a lot about corporate philanthropy—a small forest has died to print all the law review articles on the subject.[7] Yet, the corporate law rules governing this subject are perfectly consistent with our theory of the firm. To be sure, corporate philanthropy poses a classic agency cost problem. Just as corporate managers may divert resources to perquisites for themselves, they likewise may divert resources to philanthropic giving from which they derive psychic utility. This suspicion is confirmed by Warren Buffet's amusing anecdote:

> I have a friend who is the chief fundraiser for a philanthropy.... All he wants is to take some other big shot with him who will sort of nod affirmatively while he meets with the CEO. He has found that what many big shots love is what I call elephant bumping. I mean they like to go to the places where other elephants are, because it reaffirms the fact when they look around the room and they see all these other elephants that they must be an elephant too, or why

2. See, e.g., DGCL § 122(9); MBCA § 3.02(13).

3. See, e.g., Memorial Hospital Ass'n v. Pacific Grape Products Co., 290 P.2d 481 (Cal.1955); Kahn v. Sullivan, 594 A.2d 48 (Del.1991); Theodora Holding Corp. v. Henderson, 257 A.2d 398 (Del.Ch.1969); Union Pac. R. Co. v. Trustees, Inc., 329 P.2d 398 (Utah 1958).

4. 170 N.W. 668 (Mich.1919).

5. 237 N.E.2d 776 (Ill.App.1968).

6. See, e.g., Ella M. Kelly & Wyndham, Inc. v. Bell, 266 A.2d 878, 879 (Del.1970); Union Pac. R. Co. v. Trustees, Inc., 329 P.2d 398, 401–02 (Utah 1958).

7. See, e.g., Jayne W. Barnard, Corporate Philanthropy, Executives' Pet Charities and the Agency Problem, 41 N.Y. L. Sch. L. Rev. 1147 (1997); Margaret M. Blair, A Contractarian Defense of Corporate Philanthropy, 28 Stetson L. Rev. 27 (1998); Henry N. Butler & Fred S. McChesney, Why they Give at the Office: Shareholder Welfare and Corporate Philanthropy in the Contractual Theory Of The Corporation, 84 Cornell L. Rev. 1195 (1999); Melvin Aron Eisenberg, Corporate Conduct That Does Not Maximize Shareholder Gain: Legal Conduct, Ethical Conduct, the Penumbra Effect, Reciprocity, the Prisoner's Dilemma, Sheep's Clothing, Social Conduct, and Disclosure, 28 Stetson L. Rev. 1 (1998); Jill E. Fisch, Corporate Philanthropy is as American as Apple Pie, 84 Cornell L. Rev. 1282 (1999); Faith Stevelman Kahn, Pandora's Box: Managerial Discretion and the Problem of Corporate Philanthropy, 44 UCLA L. Rev. 579 (1997); Symposium, Corporate Philanthropy, 28 Stetson L. Rev. 1 (1998); Symposium, Corporate Philanthropy: Law, Culture, and Education and Politics, 41 N.Y.L. Sch. L. Rev. 753 (1997).

would they be there? ... So my friend always takes an elephant with him when he goes to call on another elephant. And the soliciting elephant, as my friend goes through his little pitch, nods and the receiving elephant listens attentively, and as long as the visiting elephant is appropriately large, my friend gets his money. And it's rather interesting, in the last five years he's raised about 8 million dollars. He's raised it from 60 corporations. It almost never fails if he has the right elephant. And in the process of raising this 8 million dollars from 60 corporations from people who nod and say it's a marvelous idea, it's pro-social, etc., not one CEO has reached in his pocket and pulled out 10 bucks of his own to give to this marvelous charity. They've given 8 million dollars collectively of other people's money.[8]

The identities of the typical beneficiaries of corporate philanthropy likewise confirm that it is driven more by managerial ego than corporate advantage. The charities supported by most corporations tend to be rich people's charities: art, music, public television, and the like. One can but question how big a bang a company gets for its advertising buck in giving to those charities.

One can concede the agency cost story, however, without conceding that the legal system ought to regulate corporate charitable giving. In the first place, it seems unlikely that corporate charitable giving even remotely approaches a level that materially injures shareholders. Although estimates vary widely, it seems unlikely that corporate charitable giving amounts to more than a couple of billion dollars annually, an infinitesimally small portion of total corporate earnings.

More important, deference to corporate philanthropic decisions is consistent with—indeed, mandated by—our overall theory of the firm. The case for judicial and regulatory deference was developed in detail in our discussion of the business judgment rule in Chapter 6. An abbreviated version is worth recalling here, however.

As noted, corporate charitable giving typically is defended on grounds that it produces good will and favorable publicity. In effect, charitable giving is simply another form of advertising. As such, it supposedly results in more business and higher profits. Who knows for sure if that is true? Maybe GM really does sell more luxury sport utility vehicles because it sponsors PBS programs—or maybe not. But that is not the right question. The right question is: who decides? The board of directors or the courts? That directors feel good about themselves for having made such a decision hardly seems like the kind of self-dealing that justifies heightened scrutiny.

Board discretion over issues like charitable giving is the inescapable side-effect of separating ownership and control. If there are good reasons for maintaining that separation, and there are, the board's discretionary

8. John C. Coffee, Jr. et al., Knights, Raiders, and Targets: The Impact of the   Hostile Takeover 14 (1988).

authority must be preserved. As we have repeatedly seen, holding directors accountable for their use of that discretionary authority inevitably limits that discretion. Consequently, deference to board decisions is always the appropriate null hypothesis.

There are cases where the board's abuse of its discretionary authority warrants regulatory or judicial intervention. Breaches of the duty of loyalty spring to mind as the clearest example. As already noted, it seems doubtful that corporate philanthropy poses the sort of conflict of interest necessary to justify limiting board discretion. Yet, even if corporate philanthropy involved material sums, deference would still be appropriate. The theory of the second best holds that inefficiencies in one part of the system should be tolerated if "fixing" them would create even greater inefficiencies elsewhere in the system as a whole. Even if we concede arguendo the case against board control over corporate giving, judicial oversight or regulatory intervention still would be inappropriate if it imposes costs in other parts of the corporate governance system. By restricting the board's authority in this context, the various academic proposals to "reform" corporate philanthropy impose just such costs by also restricting the board's authority with respect to the everyday decisions upon which shareholder wealth principally depends. Slippery slope arguments are usually the last resort of those with no better argument, but one nonetheless must beware eviscerating exceptions that could swallow the general rule of deference. Once regulation of corporate philanthropy allows the camel's nose in the tent, it becomes harder to justify resistance to further encroachments on board discretion.

Chapter 10

SHAREHOLDER VOTING

Analysis

---

§ 10.1   Introduction

Shareholder voting can serve three different purposes, depending upon the nature of the firm in question. Consider, as the first category, firms with a small number of shareholders all of whom have ready access to firm information and homogeneous preferences. In such a case, voting is effectively an exercise of managerial power. Both strategic and tactical business decisions can be made efficiently through voting, because in such a firm there is no need to incur the costs of retaining specialized managers. Accordingly, such a firm usually will lack the separation of ownership and control characteristic of public corporations.

A second category of firms include those that are more complex, but in which there are controlling shareholders. Such a firm displays partial separation of ownership and control. Controlling shareholders of such firms have substantial access to firm information and retain incentives to cast informed votes. Although the firm probably will have a professional managing body, the managers face a real possibility of being voted out of office by the controlling shareholder if their performance is sub-par. Hence, voting again has both managerial and oversight functions.

In the final category of cases, the firm is highly complex, the shareholders are numerous and have diverse preferences, and the shareholders lack both the knowledge and incentives necessary to exercise an informed vote. Such a firm displays complete separation of ownership and control. The modern public corporation is the best example of this type of firm.

Despite the separation of ownership and control in public corporations, many observers believe that shareholder voting is an integral component of corporate governance. Even sophisticated corporate law experts, such as those on the Delaware courts, say so: "The shareholder franchise is the ideological underpinning upon which the legitimacy of directorial power rests."[1] But this is error. Worse, it is pernicious. Much bad policy and doctrinal confusion have followed from it.

In public corporations, shareholder voting has very little to do with corporate decisionmaking, if anything. Recall that, under DGCL § 141, the corporation's business and affairs are "managed by or under the direction of a board of directors." The vast majority of corporate decisions accordingly are made by the board of directors acting alone, or by persons to whom the board has properly delegated authority. Shareholders have virtually no right to initiate corporate action and, moreover, are entitled to approve or disapprove only a very few board actions. The statutory decisionmaking model thus is one in which the board acts and shareholders, at most, react.

Shareholder voting thus is simply one of many corporate accountability mechanisms—and not a very important one at that. In theory, of course, shareholders could vote incompetent directors out of office. In the real world, however, so-called proxy contests are subject to numerous legal and practical impediments that render them largely untenable as a tool for disciplining managers. Accordingly, the product, capital, and employment markets are all far more important than voting as a constraint on agency costs. To the extent voting matters, it does so solely because it facilitates the market for corporate control. If agency costs get high enough, it will become profitable for some outsider to acquire a controlling block of shares and exercise their associated voting rights to oust the incumbent board.

The prevailing notion that shareholder voting rights matter likely follows from the even more pernicious and fundamental misconception that shareholders own the corporation. Since Berle and Means' day, for example, we have used the phrase "separation of ownership and control" to describe the predominant corporate governance system. In order for

§ 10.1

1. Blasius Indus., Inc. v. Atlas Corp., 564 A.2d 651, 659 (Del.Ch.1988).

shareholders to own the corporation, however, the corporation must be a thing capable of being owned. It is not. The corporation is just a legal fiction, albeit a highly useful one. Under the prevailing economic model, the corporation is a nexus of explicit and implicit contracts between a wide array of constituencies, of whom shareholders are but one among many. To be sure, shareholders own the residual claim on the corporation's assets and earnings. At bottom, the ownership of that claim is why the set of contracts making up the corporation treats the shareholders as the beneficiaries of director accountability. Yet, ownership of the residual claim is not the same as ownership of the firm itself. The corporation is simply a vehicle by which the board of directors hires capital by selling equity and debt securities to risk-bearers with varying tastes for risk. Ownership of the residual claim thus differs little from ownership of debt claims. The contractarian theory of the firm allows—nay, requires—us to rethink traditional conceptions of intra-corporate relationships. Insofar as decisionmaking is concerned, corporate governance is characterized by director rather than shareholder primacy. The board of directors functions as a sort of Platonic guardian—a sui generis body serving as the nexus for the various contracts making up the corporation. The board's powers flow from that set of contracts in its totality and not just from shareholders. Consequently, it would be surprising if shareholders had the right to overrule board decisions.

§ 10.2   State law

A.   Overview

Shareholders normally vote only at meetings, called (logically enough) shareholder meetings.[1] All statutes require that there be at least one shareholder meeting a year (called, logically enough, the annual meeting of shareholders). In addition, all statutes have some provision for so-called special meetings—i.e., meetings held between annual meetings to consider some extraordinary matter that cannot wait. Who is entitled to call a special meeting varies from state to state. Almost all state corporation laws allow the board to call a special meeting. Most allow a specified percentage of the shareholders acting together to call a special meeting. A few allow a specified corporate officer, such as the president or chairman of the board, to call a special meeting. MBCA § 7.02(a)(1) empowers the board of directors and any other person authorized by the articles or bylaws to call a special meeting. MBCA § 7.02(a)(2) empowers the holders of at least 10% of the voting shares to call a special meeting. The articles may specify a lower or higher percentage, but not to exceed, 25% of the voting power. In contrast, per DGCL § 211(d) special meetings may be called only by the board of directors and any other person authorized by the articles or bylaws.

---

§ 10.2

1. A majority of states allow shareholders to act without a meeting by unanimous written consent. See, e.g., MBCA § 7.04. A substantial minority, including Delaware, permit shareholders to act by written consent even if the shareholders are not unanimous. See, e.g., DGCL § 228.

Whether it is an annual or special meeting, most shareholders will not show up. Large corporations with thousands of shareholders frequently hold their shareholder meetings in small halls or even just a very large conference room. Most shareholders vote by proxy. (In a sense, proxy voting is the corporate law equivalent of absentee voting.) Since the 1930s, proxy voting has been extensively regulated by the federal securities laws. Hence, many of the mechanics of shareholder voting are governed by federal rather than state law. Generally speaking, state law governs substantive aspects of shareholder voting, such as how many votes a shareholder gets, when they get to vote, and the types of questions on which they get to vote. Federal law governs the procedures by which shareholders vote and the disclosures to which shareholders are entitled.

B. Notice, quorum, and votes required

Whether shareholders will vote in person or by proxy, statutory notice and quorum requirements must be satisfied if their action is to be valid. MBCA § 7.05(a), for example, requires no less than 10 but no more than 60 days notice for both annual and special meetings. Under MBCA § 7.05(b), notice of an annual meeting need not state the purposes for which the meeting is called, although the federal proxy rules mandate such notice. Under MBCA § 7.05(c), by contrast, only those matters specified in the notice may be taken up at a special meeting.

The Model Act's default quorum is a majority of the shares entitled to vote, although the articles of incorporation can specify either a higher or lower figure.[2] Although there is some case law to the contrary, the Model Act effectively precludes a shareholder from "breaking the quorum" by leaving the meeting. If a shareholder's stock is represented at the meeting in person or by proxy for any reason, that shareholder's stock is deemed to be present for quorum purposes for the remainder of the meeting.[3]

Subject to the special rules governing election of directors and group voting, which are discussed in subsequent sections, MBCA § 7.25(c) provides that "action on a matter ... is approved if the votes cast ... favoring the action exceed the votes cast opposing the action." In contrast, DGCL § 216 states that "the affirmative vote of the majority of shares present in person or represented by proxy at the meeting and entitled to vote on the subject matter shall be the act of the stockholders." The distinction between the two formulations is subtle but significant. Suppose there are 1000 shares entitled to vote, 800 of which are

---

2. MBCA § 7.25(a). Delaware law is similar, except it forbids the articles from setting a quorum of less than one-third the shares entitled to vote. DGCL § 216.

3. See MBCA § 7.25(b); but see, e.g., Levisa Oil Corp. v. Quigley, 234 S.E.2d 257 (Va.1977) (shareholder may break quorum by departing meeting); see also Textron, Inc. v. American Woolen Co., 122 F.Supp. 305 (D.Mass.1954) (shareholder present before a quorum is established may depart and, if so, may not be counted towards a quorum).

represented at the meeting either in person or by proxy, and which are voted as follows:

In Favor	399
Opposed	398
Abstain	3

Under the MBCA, the motion carries, as more shares were voted in favor of the motion than against it. Under the Delaware statute, however, a majority of the shares present at the meeting—401—must be voted in favor of the motion for it to carry, and this motion therefore fails. In effect, Delaware treats abstentions as no votes, while the MBCA ignores them.

The articles of incorporation may require a higher vote than the default statutory minimum, either across the board or on specified issues. State corporation laws also typically provide that certain extraordinary actions require approval by a higher vote. MBCA § 10.03 requires, for example, that amendments to the articles of incorporation be approved by a majority of the shares entitled to vote. Again, suppose there are 1000 shares entitled to vote, 800 of which are represented at the meeting either in person or by proxy. In order for the amendment to be adopted, 501 shares must be voted in favor. The same vote is required for approval of a merger (per § 11.04) or sale of all or substantially all the corporation's assets (per § 12.02). Delaware law is similar.

C. Election of directors

1. Cumulative voting

Under the standard voting rules, a majority shareholder can elect the entire board of directors. This is why prospective buyers place a higher value on control blocks vis-à-vis shares owned by noncontrolling shareholders. Cumulative voting provides an alternative mechanism for electing the board of directors that can assure board representation for the minority. An example will be helpful.

Assume ABC Corporation has 3 shareholders: A, who owns 250 shares; B, who owns 300 shares; C, who owns 650.[4] The bylaws specify a four member board of directors. Under standard voting procedures, directors are elected by a plurality of the votes cast at the meeting on a one share-one vote basis.[5] Suppose, for example, that each of A, B and C are supporting four different candidates for director. The following will result:

---

4. The example is taken from Michael P. Dooley, Fundamentals of Corporation Law 376 (1995).

5. See, e.g., MBCA § 7.28 (a). It might help if you think of director balloting as voting for a slate: Each share entitles its owner to cast one vote towards determining which slate will be elected. Alternatively, you can think of each director position as a seat that can be filled by only one person. Each share entitles its owner to cast one vote towards determining the occupant of that seat.

A–1: 250 for	B–1: 300 for	C–1: 650 for; elected
A–2: 250 for	B–2: 300 for	C–2: 650 for; elected
A–3: 250 for	B–3: 300 for	C–3: 650 for; elected
A–4: 250 for	B–4: 300 for	C–4: 650 for; elected

Consequently, C elects the entire board of directors. This is of vital importance, because directors make most corporate decisions. In this example, the board will be composed entirely of people nominated by C.

In cumulative voting, by contrast, the number of votes each shareholder may cast is determined by multiplying the number of shares owned by the number of director positions up for election. Each shareholder then may concentrate his votes by casting all of his votes for one candidate (or distributing his votes among two or more candidates).[6] The directors receiving the highest number of votes will be elected. In this example, A has 1000 votes available to be cast; B has 1200 votes; and C has 2600 votes. A and B each nominate themselves and cast all of their votes for themselves on their respective ballots. A receives 1000 votes. B receives 1200 votes. C nominates herself and her friends C–1, C–2, and C–3. But C cannot cast her votes so as to elect all four of her nominees. C might, for example, cast 1100 votes for herself and 1000 votes for C–1. Both C and C–1 will be elected. Unfortunately for C, however, she has only 500 votes left to divide between C–2 and C–3. Accordingly, they cannot be elected.

The following formula is used to determine the number of directors a given shareholder may elect under cumulative voting:

$$X = \frac{Y \times N_1}{N+1} + 1$$

where N is the total number of directors to be elected; N_1 is the number of directors a shareholder wishes to elect; Y is the total number of shares outstanding; and X is the number of shares needed to elect the desired number of directors (N_1). If you solve this equation for directors $N_1 = 4$; you will find that C needs 961 shares in order to elect all 4 directors. Notice that even if B and C cumulated their votes together, they could not prevent A from electing at least one director. If you work out all the permutations, you will find that in this hypothetical A can elect one director, B can elect one, and C can elect two. Unless all three agree, no combination of shareholders can elect all four directors.

Cumulative voting was very much in vogue in the late 1800s. A number of states adopted mandatory cumulative voting as part of their state constitutions. Others did the same by statute. During the last few decades, however, cumulative voting in public corporations has increasingly fallen out of favor. Opponents of cumulative voting argue it

6. See, e.g., MBCA § 7.28 (c).

produces an adversarial board and results in critical decisions being made in private meetings held by the majority faction before the formal board meeting. Today, only 8 states have mandatory cumulative voting.[7] The MBCA, Delaware, and most other states allow cumulative voting on an opt-in basis.[8] In other words, standard voting is the default rule in these states but the corporation may provide for cumulative voting in its articles of incorporation. In all states, of course, cumulative voting is limited to the election of directors—shareholders are not allowed to cumulate votes as to other types of shareholder decisions.

2. *Classified boards*

Typically, the entire board of directors is elected annually, whether by standard or cumulative voting, to a one-year term.[9] Alternatively, however, the articles of incorporation or bylaws may provide for a classified or staggered board of directors.[10] In this model, the board is divided into two or three classes. In a board with two classes of directors, the members serve two-year terms so that only half the board is up for election in any given year. In a board with three classes, directors serve three year terms and only a third of the board is up for election annually.

Classified boards have significant change of control implications and are often used as a defense against proxy contests and corporate take-overs. Under a staggered board with three classes, for example, the shareholders must wait two annual meeting cycles before they can replace a majority of the board. In order for the classified board to actually delay a change of control, of course, the classification scheme must be protected from the possibility that the shareholders will remove the directors without cause or pack the board with new appointments. Classified board provisions in articles of incorporation therefore typically are coupled with additional terms reserving to the board the sole right to determine the number of directors and to fill any vacancies. If permitted

---

7. MBCA § 7.28 stat. comp. ¶ 2 (listing Arizona, California, Hawaii, Kentucky, Nebraska, North Dakota, South Dakota, and West Virginia). The California Corporations Code provides for application of various code provisions to a foreign corporation if the firm does a majority of its business in California and if a majority of the record holders of their shares are California residents. In Wilson v. Louisiana–Pacific Res., Inc., 187 Cal.Rptr. 852 (Cal.App.1982), application of California's cumulative voting provisions to a Utah corporation meeting the foregoing test was upheld against a dormant commerce clause challenge. The court opined: "A corporation can do a majority of its business in only one state at a time; and it can have a majority of its shareholders resident in only one state at a time. If a corporation meets those requirements in this state, no other state is in a position to regulate the method of voting by shareholders on the basis of the same or similar criteria. It might also be said that no state could claim as great an interest in doing so." Id. at 860.

8. See DGCL § 214; MBCA § 7.28(b); see generally MBCA § 7.28 stat. comp. ¶ 3 (listing 30 states with opt-in cumulative voting and 12 with opt-out cumulative voting).

9. Under MBCA § 8.05(b), the directors' term in office technically expires at the next annual shareholders' meeting following their election. Under DGCL § 141(b), a director's term continues until his successor is elected.

10. See, e.g., DGCL § 141(d). Curiously, MBCA § 8.06 permits staggered boards only if there are nine or more directors.

by state law, drafters of a classified board scheme also limit or abolish the right of shareholders to call a special shareholders meeting or to remove directors without cause.

Notice that by decreasing the number of directors up for election in any given year classification of a board of directors can substantially increase the number of shares that must be cumulated to elect a director. This effect is nicely illustrated by *Coalition to Advocate Public Utility Responsibility, Inc. v. Engels*.[11] Northern States Power Company (NSP) had 14 directors, each elected annually for a one-year term by means of cumulative voting. In 1973, CAPUR (a coalition of consumer and environmental groups) sought to elect to the board a "public interest" candidate named Alpha Smaby (really).[12] Smaby promised that, if elected to the board, she would promote the "public interest" with special concern for environmental and consumer issues. NSP's board opposed Smaby's election and sought to prevent it by (1) reducing the number of directors to 12 and (2) classifying the board into three groups of four directors with staggered three-year terms. As a result, only four directors would be up for election in any given year. Under the old rules, Smaby needed the cumulated votes of just over 7% of the shares to be elected. The changes made by the board raised the number of shares needed to assure her election to about 20%.

Both changes were permitted by statute. Most corporate law codes give the board power to make unilateral changes in its size. Most likewise permit the corporation to have a staggered board. The trial court nonetheless granted a preliminary injunction against the board. Why? Basically because it is inequitable to change the rules in the middle of the game—or so the court opined. Consistent with well-established principles of Delaware law,[13] the court held that otherwise lawful actions can be enjoined as if they unfairly injure rights of minority shareholders. By implementing these changes in the middle of an election campaign, without disclosure, and for the purpose of defeating a minority candidate, the board breached its fiduciary duties. Although the election thus went forward under the old rules, Smaby ultimately did not receive a sufficient number of votes to be elected.[14] The case nevertheless reaffirms the principle that otherwise lawful board action becomes impermissible if undertaken in the midst of an election campaign for the purpose of obstructing a legitimate effort by dissident shareholders to obtain board representation. From the perspective of corporate counsel working with the incumbent directors, of course, the

11. 364 F.Supp. 1202 (D.Minn.1973).

12. Smaby's obituary does not relate whether Alpha was her original birth name, but does tell us that she was "a former Minnesota state lawmaker active in opposing the Vietnam War and in promoting liberal causes.... Smaby served two terms in the state House of Representatives. During the 1968 presidential campaign, she was a delegate to the Democratic National Convention and supported anti-war candidate Eugene McCarthy." Orlando Sentinel Trib., July 20, 1991, at A16.

13. See, e.g., Schnell v. Chris–Craft Indus., Inc., 285 A.2d 437 (Del.1971); Condec Corp. v. Lukenheimer, 230 A.2d 769 (Del. Ch.1967).

14. Michael P. Dooley, Fundamentals of Corporation Law 382–85 (1995).

transactional implication is that such changes should be undertaken in mid-year long before any insurgent shareholders begin making noise.

D. Group voting

Ordinarily all shares with voting rights vote as a single group. In some circumstances, however, the shareholders may be divided into two or more voting groups with each group consisting of one or more classes or series of stock. For example, where an amendment to the articles of incorporation or a proposed reorganization affects a particular class or series of stock, that class or series likely will have the right to vote on the proposed amendment as a separate group. Indeed, the group may be entitled to vote even if the class or series otherwise has no voting rights.

MBCA § 10.04(a) details eight distinct changes to the articles that trigger group voting: (1) an exchange or reclassification of all or part of the shares of the class into shares of another class; (2) an exchange or reclassification of all or part of the shares of another class into shares of the class; (3) a change in the rights, preferences, or limitations of all or part of the shares of the class; (4) changing the shares of all or part of the class into a different number of shares of the same class; (5) creating a new class of shares having rights or preferences with respect to distributions or to dissolution that are prior or superior to the shares of the class; (6) increasing the rights, preferences, or number of authorized shares of any class that, after giving effect to the amendment, will have rights or preferences with respect to distributions or to dissolution that are prior or superior to the shares of the class; (7) limiting or denying an existing preemptive right of all or part of the shares of the class; or (8) canceling or otherwise affecting rights to distributions that have accumulated but not yet been authorized on all or part of the shares of the class. Per § 10.04(b), if the amendment would affect a series of stock in one of the specified ways, the series is entitled to vote as a separate group. Conversely, per subsection (c), if an amendment that effects two or more classes or series in substantially similar ways, the affected classes or series must vote as a single group. Finally, subsection (d) grants voting rights to affected classes even though the articles of incorporation provide that the shares are nonvoting. MBCA § 11.04 similarly requires group voting on a merger if the plan of merger would affect one or more classes or series of stock in any of the foregoing ways.

In contrast, DGCL § 242(b)(2) only triggers group voting if the class is affected adversely. Specifically, the statute provides for group voting on an amendment to the articles "if the amendment would increase or decrease the aggregate number of authorized shares of such class, increase or decrease the par value of the shares of such class, or alter or change the powers, preferences, or special rights of the shares of such class so as to affect them adversely." The analysis does not change if the class lacks voting rights, as is often the case with preferred stock, because § 242(b) confers group voting rights even if the group is otherwise denied voting rights by the articles.

Delaware's "adversely affect" language is less determinate than the more specific MBCA formulations and, hence, more likely to produce litigation. In *Dalton v. American Investment Co.*,[15] for example, AIC was acquired by Leucadia, Inc. in a triangular merger between AIC and a wholly owned Leucadia subsidiary. AIC was the surviving entity. AIC's common shareholders were cashed out, but AIC's preferred shareholders were left in place. Certain of AIC preferred's holders sued. Because the plan of merger would amend AIC's articles of incorporation, the preferred claimed a right to vote on the plan of merger as a separate group. The pre-merger articles contained two relevant provisions: (1) The board was authorized to redeem—but not to call—the preferred. (2) If the board offered to buy back some (but not all) of the preferred shares, and the offer was over-subscribed, the shares to be redeemed were to be determined by lot. The plan of merger replaced these provisions with a sinking fund coupled with a call provision. Under the sinking fund provision, the board would retire 5% of the preferred annually for 20 years. To the extent that board repurchased preferred shares on the open market during a given year, those shares would count as a credit against the redemption obligation. The Chancellor determined that the amendment did not adversely affect the preferred and, accordingly, they were not entitled to vote as a separate group. To be sure, if the market price of the preferred was below the redemption price specified in the articles, the board could satisfy its obligation under the sinking fund by buying stock on the market. As a result, the apparent opportunity to get cashed out at a premium proved illusory. Yet, as the Chancellor pointed out, the amendment did not deprive the preferred of any rights they had previously possessed.

How then would the "adversely affect" phraseology impact other cases? Suppose the corporation's board of directors proposed an amendment that would cut the preferred stock's dividend from 8% to 5%. The amendment doubtless adversely affects the preferred and that class' holders would be entitled to vote as a separate group. Assume the requisite majority of the class of common stock votes yes, but that the proposed amendment is not approved by the requisite majority of the class of preferred. What happens? The amendment is not approved. Approval of this amendment requires approval by both classes.

Now suppose the corporation's board of directors proposed an amendment to create a new class of preferred stock with rights superior to those of the existing class of preferred. This amendment adversely affects the interests of the existing class of preferred, whose claims have been subordinated to a prior claimant, but the amendment does not "alter or change the powers, preferences, or special rights of the preferred." Although creation of a class with superior rights may redound to the economic detriment of both the existing common and the existing preferred, it does not "alter or change" the rights of either class. As an old Delaware case explained, "the relative position of one class of shares

15. 490 A.2d 574 (Del.Ch.), aff'd, 501 A.2d 1238 (Del.1985).

in the scheme of capitalization is not to be confused with rights incident to that class as compared with other classes of shares."[16] The amendment in question affects the former, rather than the latter, but only the latter is covered by the statute.

E. The one vote-one share norm and departures therefrom

Shares of common stock represent a bundle of ownership interests: a set of economic rights, such as the right to receive dividends declared by the board of directors; and a right to vote on certain corporate decisions. For over a century, those rights typically were packaged in a single class of common stock possessing equal economic rights and one vote per share. Yet, it was not always so, and even today state statutes allow corporations to derogate from the one vote-one share norm. Does it matter? And, if so, how should we regulate deviations from the norm?

1.   *A brief history of corporate voting rights*

One share-one vote may be the modern standard, but it was not the sole historical pattern. To the contrary, limitations on shareholder voting rights in fact are as old as the corporate form itself. Prior to the adoption of general incorporation statutes in the mid–1800s, the best evidence as to corporate voting rights is found in individual corporate charters granted by legislatures. Three distinct systems were used. A few charters adopted a one share-one vote rule.[17] Many charters went to the opposite extreme, providing one vote per shareholder without regard to the number of shares owned.[18] Most followed a middle path, limiting the voting rights of large shareholders. Some charters in the latter category simply imposed a maximum number of votes to which any individual shareholder was entitled. Others specified a complicated formula decreasing per share voting rights as the size of the investor's holdings increased. These charters also often imposed a cap on the number of votes any one shareholder could cast.[19]

16. Hartford Accident & Indemnity Co. v. W. S. Dickey Clay Mfg. Co., 24 A.2d 315, 318 (Del.1942).

17. See 4 Joseph S. Davis, Essays in the Earlier History of American Corporations 324 (1912); 1 William R. Scott, The Constitution and Finance of English, Scottish and Irish Joint–Stock Companies to 1720 228 (1912).

18. Samuel Williston, History of the Law of Business Corporations Before 1800 (Part II), 2 Harv. L. Rev. 149, 156 (1888). Taylor v. Griswold, 14 N.J.L. 222 (1834), is often cited for the proposition that the common law rule, in the absence of controlling statute or charter provisions, was one vote per shareholder. E.g., Jeffrey Kerbel, An Examination of Nonvoting and Limited Voting Common Stock—Their History, Legality and Validity, 15 Sec. Reg. L.J. 37, 47 (1987). But see David L. Ratner, The Government of Business Corporations: Critical Reflections on the Rule of "One Share, One Vote," 56 Cornell L. Rev. 1, 9–11 (1970) (arguing that the common law in fact had no fixed rule as to corporate voting rights).

19. For example, a Maryland charter, typical of the period 1784 to 1818, provided: "for one share, and not more than two shares, one vote; for every two shares above two, and not exceeding ten, one vote; for every four shares above ten, and not exceeding thirty, one vote; for every six shares above thirty, and not exceeding sixty, one vote; for every eight shares above sixty, and not exceeding one hundred, one vote; but no person, co-partnership or body politic shall be entitled to a greater number than thirty votes...." Joseph G. Blandi, Mary-

Gradually, however, a trend towards a one share-one vote standard emerged. Maryland's experience was typical of the pattern followed in most states, although the precise dates varied widely. Virtually all charters granted by the Maryland legislature between 1784 and 1818 used a weighted voting system. After 1819, however, most charters provided for one vote per share, although approximately 40 percent of the charters granted between 1819 and 1852 retained a maximum number of votes per shareholder. Finally, in 1852, Maryland's first general incorporation statute adopted the modern one vote per share standard.[20]

Legislative suspicion of the corporate form and fear of the concentrated economic power it represented probably motivated the early efforts to limit shareholder voting rights. A variety of factors, however, combined to drive the legal system towards the one share-one vote standard. Because reform efforts were almost invariably led by corporations, apparently under pressure from large shareholders, it may be assumed that one factor was a desire to encourage large scale capital investment. The ease with which restrictive voting rules could be evaded also undermined the more restrictive rules. Large shareholders simply transferred shares to straw-men, who thereupon voted the shares as the true owner directed.[21] Finally, while other factors also contributed, the most important factor probably was the fading of public prejudice towards corporations.

By 1900, the vast majority of U.S. corporations had moved to one vote per share.[22] Indeed, contrary to present practice, most preferred shares had voting rights equal to those of the common shares. State corporation statutes of the period, however, merely established the one share-one vote principle as a default rule.[23] Corporations were free to deviate from the statutory standard,[24] and during the first two decades of the 1900s the trend towards one share-one vote began to reverse.

land Business Corporations 1783–1852 66 (1934).

20. See generally Joseph G. Blandi, Maryland Business Corporations 1783–1852 (1934).

21. This practice is noted, for example, in the preamble to an English act of 1766. 7 Geo. III., ch. 48. Apparently, it was (or became) lawful. See, e.g., Moffatt v. Farquhar, 7 Ch.D. 591 (1878). The same practice arose in the United States, the Maryland legislature going so far as to require each voting shareholder to swear an oath that the shares he was voting were his property and had not been acquired with the intent of increasing the number of votes to which the shares were entitled. 1836 Md. Laws ch. 264. See also Annals of Cong. 923 (1819) (resolution proposing to prohibit transfers of stock made for the purpose of evading

the limits on voting rights of shares in the first Bank of the United States).

22. W.H.S. Stevens, Stockholders' Voting Rights and the Centralization of Voting Control, 40 Q.J. Econ. 353, 354 (1926).

23. New York's General Corporation Law of 1909, for example, entitled each shareholder to one vote per share "[u]nless otherwise provided in the certificate of incorporation." 1909 N.Y. Laws, ch. 28, § 23, reprinted in Joseph A. Arnold, New York Business Corporations 39 (4th ed. 1911).

24. E.g., St. Regis Candies v. Hovas, 3 S.W.2d 429 (Tex.Com.App.1928); General Inv. Co. v. Bethlehem Steel Corp., 100 A. 347 (N.J.Ch.1917); People ex rel. Browne v. Keonig, 118 N.Y.S. 136 (A.D.1909); Bartlett v. Fourton, 38 So. 882 (La.1905).

Two distinct deviations from the one share-one vote standard emerged in the years prior to the Great Crash of 1929. One involved elimination or substantial limitation of the voting rights of preferred stock. In particular, it became increasingly common to give preferred shares voting rights only in the event of certain contingencies (such as nonpayment of dividends). While controversial at the time, this practice is the modern norm.

The more important development for present purposes was the emergence of nonvoting common stock. One of the earliest examples was the International Silver Company, whose common stock (issued in 1898) had no voting rights until 1902 and then only received one vote for every two shares. After 1918, a growing number of corporations issued two classes of common stock: one having full voting rights on a one vote per share basis, the other having no voting rights (but sometimes having greater dividend rights). By issuing the former to insiders and the latter to the public, promoters could raise considerable sums without losing control of the enterprise.[25]

While disparate voting rights plans were gaining popularity with corporate managers in the 1920s, and investors showed a surprising willingness to purchase large amounts of nonvoting common stock, an increasingly vocal opposition also began emerging. William Z. Ripley, a Harvard professor of political economy, was the most prominent (or at least the most outspoken) proponent of equal voting rights. In a series of speeches and articles, eventually collected in a justly famous book, he argued that nonvoting stock was the "crowning infamy" in a series of developments designed to disenfranchise public investors.[26] (In essence, this was an early version of the conflict of interest argument made below: promoters were using nonvoting common stock as a way of maintaining voting control for themselves.)

The opposition to nonvoting common stock came to a head with the NYSE's 1925 decision to list Dodge Brothers, Inc. for trading. Dodge sold a total of $130 million worth of bonds, preferred stock and nonvoting common shares to the public. Dodge was controlled, however, by an investment banking firm, which had paid only $2.25 million for its voting common stock.[27] In January 1926, the NYSE responded to the resulting public outcry by announcing a new position: "Without at this time attempting to formulate a definite policy, attention should be drawn to the fact that in the future the [listing] committee, in considering applications for the listing of securities, will give careful thought to the matter of voting control." This policy gradually hardened, until the NYSE in 1940 formally announced a flat rule against listing nonvoting common stock. Although there were occasional exceptions, the most prominent being the 1956 listing of Ford Motor Company despite its dual

25. Adolf A. Berle & Gardiner C. Means, The Modern Corporation and Private Property 75–76 (1932).

26. William Z. Ripley, Main Street and Wall Street 77 (1927).

27. See Joel Seligman, Equal Protection in Shareholder Voting Rights: The One Common Share, One Vote Controversy, 54 Geo. Wash. L. Rev. 687, 694–97 (1986).

class capital structure, the basic policy remained in effect until the mid–1980s.

In the years between 1927 and 1932, at least 288 corporations issued nonvoting or limited voting rights shares (almost half the total number of such issuances between 1919 and 1932).[28] But the Great Depression, with an assist from the opposition led by Ripley and the NYSE's growing resistance, finally killed off most disparate voting rights plans. Not until the hostile takeover wave of the 1980s would they again play an important corporate finance role for most companies.

2. State law today

As it has long done, state law today generally provides corporations with considerable flexibility with respect to allocation of voting rights. Virtually all state corporate codes adopt one vote per common share as the default rule, but allow corporations to depart from the norm by adopting appropriate provisions in their organic documents. Likewise, dual class capital structures are routinely upheld by courts.[29]

A particularly telling example of state law laissez faire is provided by the well-known decision in *Stroh v. Blackhawk Holding Corp.*[30] At the time of the events in question, Illinois' state constitution prohibited nonvoting common stock. The defendant firm evaded this prohibition by issuing two classes of common stock: One (Class A) having both voting and economic, the other (Class B) possessing only voting rights. Virtually all of the Class B shares had been bought by management, at a tiny fraction of the price at which the Class A was sold, giving management effective voting control despite its minority economic interest. Plaintiffs sued to have the Class B shares invalidated. Plaintiffs relied on a statutory provision defining shares as the proprietary interests in the corporation. Proprietary, they argued, necessarily assumes an economic interest.

The court rejected plaintiffs' argument, holding that the Class B shares were valid. Citing a prior statutory definition of shares as the "units into which a shareholder's rights to participate in control of the corporation, in its surplus or earnings, or in the distribution of its assets, are divided," the court emphasized the disjunctive ("or") character of the definition. Hence, to be valid, a share apparently need only contain any of those three rights.

As a matter of statutory interpretation, the court's approach is somewhat problematic. The court's analysis seemingly validates nonvoting stock, which does possess two of the identified rights; yet, as noted, nonvoting stock was prohibited by the Illinois state constitution. If not

28. 1 Arthur S. Dewing, The Financial Policy of Corporations 161 (5th ed. 1953).

29. E.g., Groves v. Rosemound Improvement Ass'n, Inc., 413 So.2d 925, 927 (La. App.1982); Providence & Worcester Co. v. Baker, 378 A.2d 121, 122–24 (Del.1977); Hampton v. Tri–State Fin. Corp., 495 P.2d 566, 569 (Colo.App.1972); Shapiro v. Tropicana Lanes, Inc., 371 S.W.2d 237, 241–42 (Mo.1963): Deskins v. Lawrence County Fair & Dev. Corp., 321 S.W.2d 408, 409 (Ky.1959).

30. 272 N.E.2d 1 (Ill.1971).

conclusive, the constitutional prohibition of nonvoting common at least weakens the reliance on the disjunctive nature of the statute.

Why, after all, did the Illinois constitution prohibit nonvoting stock? Presumably the drafters were motivated by the same concerns that have always motivated critics of nonvoting common; namely, such stock allows the firm's promoters to retain voting control despite having made a relatively small equity investment. If so, although the court's opinion can be squared with the plain text of the constitution, the opinion creates a loophole by which promoters can end-run the constitutional prohibition. We leave it to the reader to decide whether adhering to the plain text of constitutional provisions should trump enforcement of the drafters' likely intent.[31]

3. The revival of dual class stock plans as a takeover defense

So-called dual class capital structures, also known as disparate voting rights plans, come in a wide variety of forms. An almost equally wide variety of techniques for implementing them have also been developed. Modern disparate voting rights plans, however, often share at least one common feature: they are usually motivated by a desire to make hostile takeovers harder by concentrating voting power in the hands of incumbent managers and their allies.

Although departures from the one share-one vote standard were well-known historically, dual class stock had largely fallen into disuse after the 1930s. One comprehensive survey, for example, found only 30 issuers with nonvoting or dual class common stock that had been traded on any U.S. secondary market between 1940 and 1978.[32] As hostile takeovers of large corporations became more common, however, dual class capital structures became much more popular with corporate managers. One survey found that 37 of 44 publicly-traded firms adopting disparate voting rights plans between 1962 and 1984 did so after January 1980.[33] According to yet another survey, 34 more corporations created dual class capital structures between March 1986 and May 1987 alone.[34] Most commentators believed this revival was motivated by

---

31. Note that on the facts of the case, the outcome is less troubling than it might otherwise seem. The Class A stock was issued in a public offering. In such an offering, management was obliged to disclose the control effects of the firm's capital structure. Public investors who did not want lesser voting rights stock simply would not buy Class A stock. Those who were willing to purchase it presumably were compensated by a lower per share price than full voting rights stock would have commanded.

32. Ronald C. Lease et al., The Market Value of Control in Publicly–Traded Corporations, 11 J. Fin. Econ. 439, 450–52 (1983). Even more strikingly, in no year during

that period were there more than 11 such issuers. Id. at 456 (table 2).

33. Megan Partch, The Creation of a Class of Limited Voting Common Stock and Shareholder Wealth, 18 J. Fin. Econ. 313, 314 (1987).

34. SEC Office of the Chief Economist, Update—The Effects of Dual–Class Recapitalizations on Shareholder Wealth: Including Evidence from 1986 and 1987 2 (July 16, 1987). An earlier study by the same authors found 65 dual class capital structures created between 1976 and 1986, three-quarters of which were adopted between 1983 and 1986. SEC Office of the Chief Economist, The Effects of Dual–Class

managerial fears of hostile takeovers.[35]

The basic dual class recapitalization provides a useful example of how dual class stock plans were used in the 1980s to defend against hostile takeovers. Shareholders were asked to approve a charter amendment creating two classes (typically referred to as Class A and Class B) of common stock. The Class A shares were essentially the preexisting common stock under a new name, retaining all of its former attributes, including the usual one vote per share. The Class B shares had all of the attributes of common stock, with three exceptions: (1) ownership of Class B stock was effectively nontransferable; (2) Class B shares could be converted into shares of Class A, however, which were freely transferable; and (3) the Class B stock had a larger number of votes, usually 10, per share. The Class B shares were then distributed to the shareholders as a stock dividend on their existing common shares.

As the Class B shares were not transferable, if a shareholder wished to sell his shares of Class B stock, he had to convert them into shares of Class A. Over time, as the normal process of shareholder turn-over proceeded, the number of outstanding Class B shares accordingly fell. In contrast, because incumbent managers were more likely to retain their Class B shares, the superior voting shares gradually concentrated in their hands. A dual class recapitalization thus eventually gave management voting control without requiring it to invest any additional equity in the firm.

A closely related alternative involved issuing the Class B shares, previously created by appropriate charter amendments, in an exchange offer. Shareholders were invited to exchange their existing Class A stock for the higher voting rights Class B shares. In these cases, however, the Class B shares were typically given lesser dividend rights and a concomitant lower dividend rate. Accordingly, it was expected that most public investors would not exchange their shares. If, in fact, only management and its allies acquired the higher voting right shares, an exchange offer dual class recapitalization could give management immediate voting control.

The effectiveness of such plans as anti-takeover devices is obvious. For managers of potential takeover targets, the surest takeover defense is possession of voting control. A hostile bidder by definition cannot oust incumbents who can outvote it. Even less than majority control may help managers fend off hostile takeovers, as by making it easier to obtain

Recapitalizations on the Wealth of Shareholders 11–12 (June 1, 1987).

35. See, e.g., Stephen M. Bainbridge, The Short Life and Resurrection of SEC Rule 19c–4, 69 Wash. U.L.Q. 565, 570–71 (1991); Richard M. Buxbaum, The Internal Division of Powers in Corporate Governance, 73 Cal. L. Rev. 1671, 1713–15 (1985); George W. Dent, Jr., Dual Class Capitalization: A Reply to Professor Seligman, 54 Geo. Wash. L. Rev. 725, 726 (1986); Jeffrey N. Gordon, Ties that Bond: Dual Class Common Stock and the Problem of Shareholder Choice, 76 Cal. L. Rev. 1, 4 (1988); Joel Seligman, The Transformation of Wall Street 10 (1982); Richard S. Ruback, Coercive Dual–Class Exchange Offers, 20 J. Fin. Econ. 153 (1988). But see Daniel R. Fischel, Organized Exchanges and the Regulation of Dual Class Common Stock, 54 U. Chi. L. Rev. 119, 149–51 (1987).

shareholder approval of other types of takeover defenses. Moreover, the plans' anti-takeover effects were immediate, even if management did not hold a majority of the superior voting rights shares, because the restrictions on transferability precluded an offeror from acquiring any of the Class B stock.

4. Do principles of corporate democracy justify a mandatory one share-one vote standard?

One of the most common arguments against dual class stock is based on notions of corporate democracy. Some argue that shareholder participation in corporate decisionmaking on a one-vote per share basis is desirable in and of itself. This notion makes for powerful rhetoric, but its premise is refuted both by history and modern practice. As the preceding sections demonstrated, deviations from the one share-one vote standard were historically commonplace. Moreover, the analogy between modern public corporations, even those with a single class of voting shares, and democratic institutions is simply inapt. As Delaware's Chancellor William Allen has observed, our "corporation law does not operate on the theory that directors, in exercising their powers to manage the firm, are obligated to follow the wishes of a majority of shares. In fact, directors, not shareholders, are charged with the duty to manage the firm."[36] Allen further recognized that the fact that many, "presumably most, shareholders" would have preferred the board to make a different decision "does not . . . afford a basis to interfere with the effectuation of the board's business judgment." In short, corporations are not New England town meetings.

5. Does the principle of director accountability justify a mandatory one share-one vote standard?

Some argue that equal voting rights help reduce agency costs by ensuring that management accountability to shareholders. This argument, however, proves unpersuasive on close examination. First, shareholder voting as such is a relatively inefficient accountability mechanism. The shareholders' incentives to be rationally apathetic, coupled with their relative powerlessness, renders them the corporate constituency perhaps least able to hold management accountable for misbehavior.

To be sure, voting rights enable shareholders to indirectly hold management's feet to the fire via a proxy contest or by selling their shares to a takeover bidder. From this perspective, dual class capital structures are problematic not because they deprive shareholders of voting rights, but because they shield management from exposure to the full force of these other accountability mechanisms. Having said that, however, the anti-takeover effects of dual class stock do not justify prohibiting such a capital structure. Proscribing dual class stock because of its takeover effects puts one on a very slippery slope indeed. Taken to

---

36. Paramount Communications Inc. v.   1989), aff'd, 571 A.2d 1140 (Del.1989).
Time Inc., 1989 WL 79880 at *30 (Del.Ch.

its logical extreme, the argument against dual class stock based on its anti-takeover effect would justify a sweeping prohibition of all effective takeover defenses, a solution that no court or legislature has been willing to adopt.

    6.   *Does the potential for shareholder injury justify a mandatory one share-one vote standard?*

Opponents of dual class stock commonly argue that it somehow harms shareholders. But the empirical evidence as to the effect of dual class stock on shareholder wealth is, at best, mixed. Lesser-voting rights shares typically sell at a slight discount to full-voting rights shares.[37] At a minimum, this differential suggests that the market anticipates a lower future stream of income from the lesser-voting shares. Surprisingly, however, studies find that dual class recapitalizations have no statistically significant effect on shareholder wealth (as measured by changes in the firm's stock price).[38] One study in fact found positive shareholder wealth effects in certain types of recapitalizations.[39]

The inconclusive nature of the empirical studies may be attributable to a variety of offsetting factors. The higher dividends often payable to the lesser-voting rights shares may offset any negative price effects. In addition, because an oft-stated rationale for adopting a disparate voting rights plan is the desire to raise new equity capital, while maintaining insider control, the recapitalization proposal is a signal that management believes profitable investment opportunities are available to the firm. This good news about the firm's future performance may mask any negative effects resulting from the recapitalization itself. Finally, many firms adopting a dual class capital structure exhibit substantial ownership by insiders prior to recapitalizing. The market previously will have discounted the firm's stock price to reflect its lower probability of a takeover in comparison to more diversely-held firms. Adoption of the plan thus will not significantly affect the market's evaluation of future payouts nor the firm's stock price.

    7.   *Do managerial conflicts of interest justify a mandatory one share-one vote standard?*

The strongest argument against dual class stock rests on conflict of interest grounds.[40] There is good reason to be suspicious of manage-

---

37. Ronald C. Lease, et al., The Market Value of Control in Publicly–Traded Corporations, 11 J. Fin. Econ. 439, 466 (1983).

38. See, e.g., SEC Office of the Chief Economist, The Effects of Dual–Class Recapitalizations on the Wealth of Shareholders 4 (June 1, 1987).

39. Megan Partch, The Creation of a Class of Limited Voting Common Stock and Shareholder Wealth, 18 J. Fin. Econ. 313, 332 (1987) (statistically significant positive price effect found in subsample of firms in

which insiders already owned sufficient shares to pass recapitalization plan over objection of all minority shareholders; Partch, however, questions the significance of this finding).

40. The following argument differs from the accountability argument discussed and rejected above largely in terms of timing. The accountability argument focuses on the ex post effects of a dual class recapitalization. The conflict of interest argument focuses on management's ex ante incentives. See generally Stephen M. Bainbridge, Re-

ment's motives and conduct in certain dual class recapitalizations. Dual class transactions motivated by their anti-takeover effects, like all take-over defenses, pose an obvious potential for conflicts of interest. If a hostile bidder succeeds, it is almost certain to remove many of the target's incumbent directors and officers. On the other hand, if the bidder is defeated by incumbent management, target shareholders are deprived of a substantial premium for their shares. A dual class capital structure, of course, effectively assures the latter outcome.

In addition to this general concern, a distinct source of potential conflict between managers' self-interest and the best interests of the shareholders arises in dual class recapitalizations. An analogy to man-agement-led leveraged buyouts ("MBOs") may be useful. In these trans-actions, management has a clear-cut conflict of interest. On the one hand, they are fiduciaries of the shareholders charged with getting the best price for the shareholders. On the other, as buyers, they have a strong self-interest in paying the lowest possible price.

In some dual class recapitalizations, management has essentially the same conflict of interest. Although they are fiduciaries charged with protecting the shareholders' interests, the disparate voting rights plan typically will give them voting control. The managers' temptation to act in their own self-interest is obvious. Yet, unlike MBOs, in a dual class recapitalization, management neither pays for voting control nor is its conduct subject to meaningful judicial review. As such, the conflict of interest posed by dual class recapitalizations is even more pronounced than that found in MBOs.

While management's conflict of interest may justify some restric-tions on some disparate voting rights plans, it hardly justifies a sweeping prohibition of dual class stock. First, not all such plans involve a conflict of interest. Dual class IPOs are the clearest case. Public investors who don't want lesser voting rights stock simply won't buy it. Those who are willing to purchase it presumably will be compensated by a lower per share price than full voting rights stock would command and/or by a higher dividend rate. In any event, assuming full disclosure, they become shareholders knowing that they will have lower voting rights than the insiders and having accepted as adequate whatever trade-off is offered by the firm in recompense. In effect, management's conflict of interest is thus constrained by a form of market review.

Another good example of a dual class transaction that fails to raise conflict of interest concerns is subsequent issuance of lesser-voting rights shares. Such an issuance does not disenfranchise existing shareholders, as they retain their existing voting rights. Nor are the purchasers of such shares harmed; as in an IPO, they take the shares knowing that the rights will be less than those of the existing shareholders. For the same

visiting the One–Share/One–Vote Contro-   Rights Policy, 22 Sec. Reg. L.J. 175 (1994).
versy: The Exchanges' Uniform Voting

reason, issuance of lesser-voting rights shares as consideration in a merger or other corporate acquisition should not be objectionable.

Second, even with respect to those disparate voting rights plans that do raise conflict of interest concerns, it must be recognized that there is only a potential conflict of interest. Despite the need for skepticism about management's motives, it is worth remembering that "having a 'conflict of interest' is not something one is 'guilty of'; it is simply a state of affairs."[41] That the board has a conflict of interest thus does not necessarily mean that the directors' conduct will be inconsistent with the best interests of any or all of the corporation's other constituents. The mere fact that a certain transaction poses a conflict of interest for management therefore does not justify a prohibition of that transaction. It simply means that the transaction needs to be policed to ensure that management pursues the shareholders' best interests rather than their own.

Why not regulate dual class stock the same way we regulate other conflict of interest transactions, such as two-tier tender offers, freeze-out mergers, and interested director transactions?[42] At the outset, we need to identify those dual class stock recapitalizations that actually entail a conflict of interest. Hence, for example, no safeguards over and above those already provided by state law are necessary with respect to dual class stock issued in an IPO, a subsequent offering or dividend of lesser-voting stock, or dual class stock issued in a bona fide acquisition. Nor are any additional safeguards necessary with respect to super-voting rights shares issued without transfer restrictions or in a lock-up.

Transactions involving more subtle conflicts require some additional safeguards. Among these are exchange offers and recapitalizations creating super-voting rights stock bearing transfer restrictions. In order to dissipate the conflicts of interest they raise, they should be permitted only if they are approved by the corporation's independent directors and disinterested shareholders.

Requiring approval by a committee of independent board members created to negotiate with management and/or the controlling shareholder is common in conflict of interest transactions. In the freeze-out merger context, the Delaware Supreme Court has made clear that this procedure is "strong evidence that the transaction meets the test of fairness."[43] Statutes governing interested director transactions and two-tier tender offers effectively presume that the transaction is fair if

---

41. Committee on Corporate Laws, Changes in the Model Business Corporation Act–Amendments Pertaining to Directors' Conflicting Interest Transactions, 44 Bus. Law. 1307, 1309 (1989).

42. Imposing a requirement that the disparate voting rights plan fully compensate shareholders for the loss of their voting rights is an alternative solution. Dual class stock would be unobjectionable if management provided such compensation. However, the difficulty of measuring the voting rights' value makes this solution impractical. One simply could not be confident that the plan fully compensated the minority.

43. Weinberger v. UOP, Inc., 457 A.2d 701, 709–10 n. 7 (Del.1983).

approved by the independent directors.[44] There is always, of course, some risk that purportedly independent directors will be biased in favor of their compatriots, but courts give greatest deference to independent directors in contexts like this one in which a market test of the transaction is impractical.[45] This is so in large part, of course, because the absence of a market test gives courts little option but to rely upon independent directors as the chief accountability mechanism. Yet, it is also so because courts know that independent directors are capable of serving as an effective accountability mechanism. Despite the potential for structural or actual bias, independent directors have affirmative incentives to actively monitor management and to discipline managers who prefer their own interests to those of shareholders. If the company suffers or even fails on their watch, for example, the independent directors' reputation and thus their future employability is likely to suffer. Guided by outside counsel and financial advisers and facing the risk of person liability for uninformed or biased decisions, disinterested directors therefore should be an effective check on unfairness in a dual class recapitalization.

If the board lacks independence or is otherwise disabled by conflicted interests, approval by a majority of the disinterested shares should also insulate the dual class recapitalization from judicial review.[46] Approval of a freeze-out merger or interested director transaction by a majority of the disinterested shareholders, for example, shifts the burden of proof with respect to fairness back to the complaining shareholder. Under so-called fair price statutes, the obligation to pay a statutorily defined fair price in the second-step of a two-tier offer will be waived if the transaction is approved by the disinterested shareholders. These rules give the shareholders a collective opportunity to reject unfair proposals, thereby helping to eliminate the pressure on individual shareholders to accept the offer. Shareholder approval of a dual class recapitalization should likewise vitiate conflict of interest and collective action concerns.[47]

Admittedly, neither approval by independent directors nor disinterested shareholders will perfectly eliminate the possibility of management self-dealing in connection with a dual class recapitalizations. But that is

---

44. See, e.g., Pogostin v. Rice, 480 A.2d 619 (Del.1984) (disinterested director approval of interested director transaction shifts burden of proof to plaintiff to show transaction amounts to waste).

45. Stephen M. Bainbridge, Exclusive Merger Agreements and Lock–Ups in Negotiated Acquisitions, 75 Minn. L. Rev. 239, 278–79 (1990).

46. Of course, the vote must be an informed one. Compare Lacos Land Co. v. Arden Group, Inc., 517 A.2d 271, 279–81 (Del.Ch.1986) (preliminary injunction granted where proxy statement failed to fully disclose consequences of dual class plan), with Weiss v. Rockwell Int'l Corp.,

1989 WL 80345 (Del.Ch.1989), aff'd without op., 574 A.2d 264 (Del.1990) (preliminary injunction denied where proxy statement made full disclosure of effect of dual class plan on voting control of firm).

47. In Weiss v. Rockwell Int'l Corp., 1989 WL 80345 (Del.Ch.1989), aff'd without op., 574 A.2d 264 (Del. 1990), plaintiff claimed that a disparate voting rights plan violated management's fiduciary duties. The Delaware Chancery Court held that informed shareholder approval of the plan constituted an effective ratification of the plan and thereby precluded judicial review of the fiduciary duty claim.

true of every conflict of interest transaction. As we have seen, the problems associated with dual class stock are no different than those associated with any other conflict of interest transaction. One therefore must again ask, why should dual class stock be singled out for special treatment? No good reason has been forthcoming. As has been the case with all other corporate conflicts of interest, the law should develop standards of review for dual class recapitalizations that are designed to prevent self-interested management behavior but not to proscribe all such transactions. But the law thus far has failed to do so.

F.   Shareholder inspection rights

An insurgent shareholder conducting a proxy contest typically wants to communicate directly with his fellow shareholders. In addition, the shareholder may want access to other corporate books and records, so as to gain information that might bolster his arguments. The federal proxy rules provide limited mailing rights for an insurgent, but no other inspection rights. Consequently, the insurgent must look to state law inspection rights.

State shareholder inspection rights statutes must balance two competing concerns. On the one hand, shareholders have a legitimate interest in using the proxy system to hold the board accountable. On the other hand, nobody wants a junk mail distributor to get access to the shareholder list or a competitor to get access to the corporation's trade secrets and other proprietary information.[48] DGCL § 220(b) balances these concerns by requiring a shareholder asserting inspection rights to make a written demand setting forth a "proper purpose" for the request. The statute further defines a "proper purpose" as one "reasonably related to such person's interest as a stockholder." If the corporation denies the shareholder access to its records, the shareholder may sue in the Chancery Court. Under subsection (c), where the shareholder only seeks access to the shareholder list or stock ledger, the burden of proof is on the corporation to show that the shareholder is doing so for an improper reason. Where the shareholder seeks access to other corporate records, however, the shareholder must prove that he is doing so for the requisite proper purpose.

The statutory framework poses several questions. First, what reasons for seeking access to a shareholder list constitute proper purposes? Attempts to investigate alleged corporate mismanagement are usually deemed proper, although the shareholder must have some factual basis for making the request and is not allowed to conduct a fishing expedition.[49] Collecting information relevant to valuing shares is a proper

---

48. Cf. Cooke v. Outland, 144 S.E.2d 835, 842 (N.C.1965) ("Considering the huge size of many modern corporations and the necessarily complicated nature of their bookkeeping, it is plain that to permit their thousands of stockholders to roam at will through their records would render impossible not only any attempt to keep their records efficiently, but the proper carrying on of their businesses.").

49. See, e.g., Nodana Petroleum Corp. v. State, 123 A.2d 243, 246 (Del.1956); Helms-

purpose.[50] A tender offeror stated a proper purpose in desiring to inform other shareholders of the pending offer and soliciting tenders from them.[51] Most pertinently for purposes of this Chapter, communicating with fellow shareholders in connection with a planned proxy contest is a proper purpose.[52] Improper purposes include attempting to discover proprietary business information for the benefit of a competitor, to secure prospects for personal business, to institute strike suits, and to pursue one's own social or political goals.[53]

The latter improper purpose—pursuit of noneconomic social or political goals—has proven an especially problematic subject for Delaware courts. In the well-known *State ex rel. Pillsbury v. Honeywell, Inc.* decision,[54] plaintiff belonged to an antiwar group trying to stop Honeywell from producing anti-personnel fragmentation bombs for the military. After buying some Honeywell stock, plaintiff requested access to Honeywell's shareholder list and to corporate records relating to production of such bombs. In denying plaintiff access to those records, the court emphasized that plaintiff's stated reasons were based on his pre-existing social and political views rather than any economic interest. Accordingly, the court carefully limited its holdings to the facts at bar: "We do not mean to imply that a shareholder with a bona fide investment interest could not bring this suit if motivated by concern with the long-or short-term economic effects on Honeywell resulting from the production of war munitions." The court further noted that the "suit might be appropriate when a shareholder has a bona fide concern about the adverse effects of abstention from profitable war contracts on his investment in Honeywell." As such, *Honeywell* puts more emphasis on proper phrasing of one's statement of purpose than on the validity of the purpose itself. So long as one's social agenda can be dressed up in the language of economic consequences, one gets access to the list.[55] Does this formalistic approach make sense? The Delaware chancery court seems to think not, as at least one chancery decision opines that Delaware law has de facto rejected *Honeywell*'s requirement that the shareholder's purpose must relate to the "enhancement of the economic value of the corporation."[56]

man Mgmt. Servs., Inc. v. A & S Consultants, Inc., 525 A.2d 160, 165 (Del.Ch. 1987); Skouras v. Admiralty Enters., Inc., 386 A.2d 674, 678 (Del.Ch.1978).

50. See, e.g., State ex rel. Nat'l Bank of Del. v. Jessup & Moore Paper Co., 88 A. 449 (Del.Super.Ct.1913).

51. Crane Co. v. Anaconda Co., 382 N.Y.S.2d 707 (N.Y.1976).

52. See, e.g., Hatleigh Corp. v. Lane Bryant, Inc., 428 A.2d 350 (Del.Ch.1981).

53. Tatko v. Tatko Bros. Slate Co., 569 N.Y.S.2d 783 (App.Div.1991).

54. 191 N.W.2d 406 (Minn.1971) (interpreting Delaware law).

55. See, e.g., Conservative Caucus Research, Analysis & Education Foundation, Inc. v. Chevron Corp., 525 A.2d 569 (Del. Ch.1987) (a political group successfully sought access to Chevron's shareholder list for the stated purpose of warning its fellow "stockholders about the allegedly dire economic consequences which will fall upon Chevron if it continues to do business in Angola").

56. Food & Allied Serv. Trades Dep't, AFL–CIO v. Wal–Mart Stores, Inc., 1992 WL 111285 at *4 (Del.Ch.1992).

Second, to what extent will the court scrutinize the shareholder's stated reasons? On the one hand, Delaware courts expressly retain the right to scrutinize the shareholder's stated purpose to determine whether it is the real reason for which he seeks access. On the other hand, Delaware courts have made clear that the existence of an improper secondary purpose is not enough to deny the shareholder access. Because "a shareholder will often have more than one purpose, [§ 220(b)] has been construed to mean that the shareholder's *primary* purpose must be proper; any *secondary* purpose, whether proper or not, is irrelevant."[57]

Finally, to which shareholder list is the plaintiff entitled? All corporations maintain a list of shareholders of record. When investors buy stock of public corporations through a broker, however, their shares typically are registered in so-called "street name." The broker places shares in the custody of depository firms, such as Depository Trust Co., which then uses a so-called "nominee" to register the shares with the issuer. The broker, of course, retains records identifying the beneficial owner of the shares. As a result, a public corporation's list of record shareholders will consists mostly of street names—i.e., the names of the nominees used by the various depository firms—not the names of the actual beneficial owners. A so-called CEDE list identifies the brokerage firms on whose behalf the depository institution's nominee holds shares.[58] A nonobjecting beneficial owner (NOBO) list pierces the street name by providing a list of the names and addresses of beneficial owners who have not objected to being identified as such.[59] Under New York state law, a shareholder is entitled to both the CEDE and NOBO lists. Indeed, if the corporation has not already compiled such lists, New York law entitles a shareholder to demand that the corporation do so.[60] In contrast, while Delaware law grants the shareholder access to pre-existing lists of both types, it does not require the issuer to compile a NOBO list on shareholder request.[61]

---

57. BBC Acquisition v. Durr–Fillauer Medical, 623 A.2d 85, 88 (Del.Ch.1992). On yet another hand, however, where the corporation is able to show an improper secondary purpose, the court may circumscribe the shareholder's access so as to protect legitimate corporate interests. Safecard Servs., Inc. v. Credit Card Serv. Corp., 1984 WL 8265 (Del.Ch.1984).

58. The list's name comes from the fact that the largest depository firm, Depository Trust Co., uses Cede & Co. as its nominee name.

59. SEC Exchange Act Rule 14b–1 requires brokers to assemble a NOBO list at the issuer's request. The question of whether a shareholder is entitled to demand that the issuer request the creation of such a list or to access to a pre-existing NOBO list, however, is left to state corporate law.

60. Sadler v. NCR Corp., 928 F.2d 48 (2d Cir.1991).

61. RB Assocs. of N.J., L.P. v. Gillette Co., 1988 WL 27731 (Del.Ch.1988). See also Luxottica Group S.p.A. v. U.S. Shoe Corp., 919 F.Supp. 1091, 1093 (S.D.Ohio 1995) (because Ohio statute only authorized inspection of records, "if any, on file with the corporation," the court declined to order issuer to compile a NOBO list for shareholder to inspect); Cenergy Corp. v. Bryson Oil & Gas P.L.C., 662 F.Supp. 1144 (D.Nev. 1987) (corporation is not obliged to produce information it did not possess).

§ 10.3   Why shareholders and only shareholders?

Is it curious that only shareholders get the vote? What about all of the corporation's other constituencies, such as employees, creditors, customers, suppliers, etc.? Why do they not get a voice in, say, the election of directors? The traditional answer is that shareholders own the corporation. Ownership typically connotes control, of course. Consequently, despite the separation of ownership and control characteristic of public corporations, shareholders' ownership of the corporation might be deemed to vest them with unique control rights. Recall that the nexus of contracts theory of the firm demonstrates that shareholders do not in fact "own" the corporation in any meaningful sense. By throwing the concept of ownership out the window, however, the contractarian model eliminates the obvious answer to our starting question—why are only shareholders given voting rights?

Our answer to that question relies on the analysis of organizational decisionmaking economist Kenneth Arrow set out in THE LIMITS OF ORGANIZATION.[1] Recall that Arrow identified two basic modes of decisionmaking: consensus and authority. Consensus requires that each member of the organization have identical information and interests so that preferences can be aggregated at low cost. In contrast, authority-based decisionmaking structures arise where group members have different interests and information.

The analysis that follows proceeds in three steps. First, why do corporations not rely on consensus-based decisionmaking? In answering that question, we begin by imagining an employee-owned firm with many thousands of employee-shareholders. (Employees are used solely for purposes of illustration—the analysis would extend to any other corporate constituency.) After demonstrating that Arrow's conditions cannot be satisfied in such a firm, we then turn to the more complex public firm in which employees and shareholders constitute separate constituencies to demonstrate that Arrow's conditions are even less likely to be met in this type of firm. Second, why do corporations not permit multiple constituencies to elect directors? Finally, why are shareholders the favored constituency?

A.   The necessity of authority

1. Information

Assume an employee-owned corporation with 5,000 employee-shareholders. Could such a firm function as a participatory democracy? Not if we hoped that each participant would make informed decisions. As a practical matter, of course, our employee-shareholders are not going to have access to the same sorts of information. Assuming at least some employees serve in managerial and supervisory roles, they will tend to have broader perspectives, with more general business information,

§ 10.3

1. Kenneth J. Arrow, The Limits of Organization 63–79 (1974).

while line workers will tend to have more specific information about particular aspects of the shop floor.

These information asymmetries will prove intractable. A rational decisionmaker expends effort to make informed decisions only if the expected benefits of doing so outweigh its costs. In a firm of the sort at bar, gathering information will be very costly. Efficient participatory democracy requires all decisionmakers to have equal information, which requires that each decisionmaker have a communication channel to every other decisionmaker. As the number of decisionmakers increases, the number of communication channels within the firm increases as the square of the number of decisionmakers.[2] Bounded rationality makes it doubtful that anyone in a firm of any substantial size could process the vast number of resulting information flows. Even if they were willing to try, moreover, members of such a firm could not credibly bind themselves to reveal information accurately and honestly or to follow prescribed decisionmaking rules. Under such conditions, Arrow's model predicts that the firm will tend towards authority-based decisionmaking. Accordingly, the corporation's employer-owners will prefer to irrevocably delegate decisionmaking authority to some central agency, such as a board of directors.

Now introduce the complication of separating capital and labor. Nothing about such a change economizes on the decisionmaking costs outlined above. Instead, as described below, labor and capital can have quite different interests, which increases decisionmaking costs by introducing the risk of opportunism. In particular, capital and labor may behave strategically by withholding information from one another.

2. Interests

Again, begin by assuming an employee-owned firm with 5,000 employee shareholders. Is it reasonable to expect the similarity of interest required for consensus to function in such a firm? Surely not. In some cases, employees would differ about the best way in which to achieve a common goal. In others, individual employees will be disparately affected by a proposed course of action. Although the problems created by divergent interests within the employee block are not insurmountable, such differences at least raise the cost of using consensus-based decisionmaking structures in employee-owned firms.

The existence of such divergent interests within the employee group is confirmed by the empirical evidence. Labor-managed firms tend to remain small, carefully screen members, limit the franchise to relatively

---

2. Oliver E. Williamson, Markets and Hierarchies: Analysis and Antitrust Implications 46 (1975). In addition to the transaction costs associated with making an informed decision, which by themselves are doubtless preclusive of participatory democracy in the large firm setting, the opportunity cost entailed in making informed decisions is also high and, even more important, readily apparent. In contrast, the expected benefits of becoming informed are quite low, as an individual decisionmaker's vote will not have a significant effect on the vote's outcome. Our employee-owners thus will be rationally apathetic.

homogeneous groups, and use agenda controls to prevent cycling and other public choice problems.[3] All of these characteristics are consistent with an attempt to minimize the likelihood and effect of divergent interests.

Now again complicate the analysis by separating capital and labor. Although employee and shareholder interests are often congruent, they can conflict. Consider, for example, the down-sizing phenomenon. Corporate restructurings typically result in substantial reductions in force, reduced job security, longer work weeks, more stress, and diminished morale.[4] From the shareholders' perspective, however, the market typically rewards restructurings with substantial stock price increases. The divergence of interest suggested by this example looms large as a bar to the use of consensus in capitalist firms.

B. The inefficiency of multiple constituencies

The analysis to this point merely demonstrates that corporate decisionmaking must be made on a representative, rather than on a participatory, basis. As yet, nothing in the analysis dictates the U.S. model in which only shareholders elect directors. One could plausibly imagine a board of directors on which multiple constituencies are represented. Indeed, imagination is not required, because the supervisory board component of German codetermination provides a real world example of just such a board.[5] Empirical evidence, however, suggests that codetermi-

---

3. Greg Dow & Louis Putterman, Why Capital (Usually) Hires Labor: An Assessment of Proposed Explanations, Brown Univ. Dep't of Econ. Working Paper 96–21 at 63–64 (Sep. 1996).

4. Michael Useem, Investor Capitalism 164–65 (1996).

5. In Germany alone, there are at least four different statutory models of participatory management. Some other member-states of the European Union also have some form of employee representation, and there have long been proposals to develop harmonized company laws or even a European Union-wide company law that would provide for employee representation. See generally Terence L. Blackburn, The Societas Europea: The Evolving European Corporation Statute, 61 Fordham L. Rev. 695, 743–55 (1993). Unless otherwise indicated, discussion of codetermination herein focuses on the 1976 German codetermination statute, which applies to corporations having more than 2,000 employees. Codetermination includes a dual board structure: a supervisory board that appoints a managing board, with the latter actively operating the firm. Workers are represented only on the former. The supervisory board concept is difficult to translate into terms familiar to those trained exclusively in U.S. forms of corporate governance. Its statutory mandate is primarily concerned with the appointment and supervision of the managing board. In theory, employees and shareholders are equally represented on the supervisory board. In practice, however, the board is often controlled either by the firm's managers or a dominant shareholder. One of the employee representatives must be from management, and shareholders are entitled to elect the chairman of the board, who has the power to break tie votes. If push comes to shove, which it reportedly rarely does, shareholders thus retain a slight but potentially critical edge.

Works councils are concerned with issues affecting individual plants, rather than the whole firm. In theory at least, works councils have considerable control over shop floor and other issues that affect the personnel of a particular plant. Depending on the nature of the issue at hand, the council may be entitled to provision of information, consultation with management, or codetermination. Their statutory mandate ranges from such minor issues as individual personnel grievances to such major concerns as the introduction of new technology or plant closings.

nation does not lead to efficiency or productivity gains.[6]

Why not? In Arrow's terminology, the board of directors serves as a consensus-based decisionmaking body at the top of an authority-based structure. Recall that for consensus to function, however, two conditions must be met: equivalent interests and information. Neither condition can be met when employee representatives are on the board.

The two factors are closely related, of course. Indeed, it is the potential divergence of shareholder and employee interests that ensures employee representatives will be deprived of the information necessary for them to function. Because of the board's position at the apex of the corporate hierarchy, employee representatives are inevitably exposed to a far greater amount of information about the firm than is normally provided to employees. As the European experience with codetermination teaches, this can result in corporate information leaking to the work force as a whole or even to outsiders. In the Netherlands, for example, the obligation of works council representatives to respect the confidentiality of firm information "has not always been kept, causing serious concerns among management which is required . . . to provide extensive 'sensitive' information to the councils."[7]

Given that providing board level information to employee representatives appears clearly contrary to shareholder interests,[8] we would expect managers loyal to shareholder interests to withhold information from the board of directors in order to deny it to employee representatives, which would seriously undermine the board's ability to carry out its essential corporate governance roles. This prediction is borne out by the German experience with codetermination. German managers sometimes deprive the supervisory board of information, because they do not want the supervisory board's employee members to learn it.[9] Alternatively, the board's real work may be done in committees or de facto rump caucuses from which employee representatives are excluded. As a result,

---

6. See generally Stephen M. Bainbridge, Participatory Management Within a Theory of the Firm, 21 J. Corp. L. 657 (1996) (summarizing studies).

7. Tom R. Ottervanger & Ralph M. Pais, Employee Participation in Corporate Decision Making: The Dutch Model, 15 Int'l Law. 393, 399 (1981).

8. One sure result of lost confidentiality will be worker demands for higher wages. This prediction is supported by an empirical study finding that provision of financial and other business information to employees of nonunionized firms had a negative effect on firm profitability, which was attributed to higher wages demanded by the informed employees. Morris M. Kleiner & Marvin L. Bouillon, Providing Business Information to Production Workers: Correlates of Compensation and Productivity, 41

Ind. & Lab. Rel. Rev. 605, 614–15 (1988). See also Stuart Ogden, The Limits to Employee Involvement: Profit Sharing and Disclosure of Information, 29 J. Mgmt Stud. 229 (1992) (stating that U.K. employers are reluctant to provide disclosure of financial information for fear of stimulating workers to make demands respecting pay and working conditions). In a unionized firm, moreover, management will be especially reluctant to inform union members on the board of information that might aid the union in collective bargaining.

9. Klaus J. Hopt, Labor Representation on Corporate Boards: Impacts and Problems for Corporate Governance and Economic Integration in Europe, 14 Int'l Rev. L. & Econ. 203, 206 (1994).

while codetermination raises the costs of decisionmaking, it may not have much effect on substantive decisionmaking.[10]

Although Arrow's equality of information criterion is important, in this context the critical element is the divergence of shareholder and employee interests. The interests of shareholders will inevitably differ as amongst themselves, as do those of employees, but individual constituents of the corporation nevertheless are more likely to share interests with members of the same constituency than with members of another constituency. Allowing board representation for employees thus tends only to compound the problem that gives rise to an authority-based hierarchical decisionmaking structure by bringing the differing interests of employees and shareholders directly into the board room.[11] The resulting conflicts of interest inevitably impede consensus-based decisionmaking within the board. Worker representatives on corporate boards tend to prefer greater labor advocacy than do traditional directors, no doubt in large part because workers evaluate their representatives on the basis of labor advocacy, which also results in role conflicts.[12] The problem with codetermination thus is not only that the conflict of employee and shareholder interests impedes the achievement of consensus, but also that it may result in a substantial increase in agency costs.[13]

10. Tove H. Hammer et al., Worker Representation on Boards of Directors: A Study of Competing Roles, 44 Indus. & Lab. Rel. Rev. 661, 663 (1991) (Scandinavian experience with codetermination shows it has little substantive effect on corporate decisionmaking).

11. The difficulty, of course, is not merely that the interests of employees and shareholders diverge, but also that different classes of employees have divergent interests. As we have seen, this seriously compounds the problem of aggregating constituency preferences.

12. John L. Cotton, Employee Involvement 128 (1993). This conflict is exacerbated in heavily unionized industries, as representatives of a single union might sit on the boards of multiple firms within the industry. In the extreme case, the demise of one firm might redound to the greater good of the greatest number by benefiting union members who work at competing corporations. This creates the potential for perverse incentives on the part of union representatives on the board.

13. The most obvious problem is the possibility that employee representation will permit management to pursue its own self-interest at the expense of both shareholders and employees by playing worker and shareholder representatives off against each other. Legal and market accountability mechanisms constrain this tendency, but because they are not perfect there remains the possibility that self-interested managers may throw their support behind the side of the board whose interests happen to coincide with those of management in the issue at hand. See William J. Carney, Does Defining Constituencies Matter?, 59 U. Cin. L. Rev. 385, 420–24 (1990).

This conflict is well-known, of course, but there is a more subtle problem that is often overlooked. Corporate employees have an incentive to shirk so long as their compensation does not perfectly align their incentives with those of the firm's shareholders. In turn, knowing of this phenomenon, the firm's shareholders should expect management to reduce the compensation of the firm's employees by the amount necessary to off-set the expected degree of employee shirking. Because ex ante wage adjustments rarely are fully compensatory, due to bounded rationality and the resulting use of incomplete contracts, the firm's shareholders should expect management to monitor the employees and punish ex post those who shirk. Benjamin Klein, Contracting Costs and Residual Claims: The Separation of Ownership and Control, 26 J. L. & Econ. 367, 368 n.2 (1983). Would it not seem odd that those who are to be monitored should be allowed to choose the monitors? One of the accountability mechanisms that aligns managerial and shareholder interests is

Although it is sometimes asserted that employee representation would benefit the board by promoting "discussion and consideration of alternative perspectives and arguments,"[14] the preceding analysis suggests that any such benefits would come at high cost. In addition, there is reason to doubt whether those benefits are very significant. Workers will be indifferent to most corporate decisions that do not bear directly on working conditions and benefits.[15] All of which tends to suggest that employee representatives add little except increased labor advocacy to the board.

C. Why only shareholders?

The analysis thus far demonstrates that public corporation decision-making must be conducted on a representative rather than participatory basis. It further demonstrates that only one constituency should be allowed to elect the board of directors. The remaining question is why shareholders are the chosen constituency, rather than employees. Answering that question is the task of this section.

The standard law and economics explanation for vesting voting rights in shareholders is that shareholders are the only corporate constituent with a residual, unfixed, ex post claim on corporate assets and earnings.[16] In contrast, the employees' claim is prior and largely fixed ex

---

monitoring by the board of directors. Allowing employee representation on the board necessarily reduces the likelihood that the board will be an effective monitoring device. Because shareholders "could seek profits by getting highly motivated managers who sweat the labor force," workers have an interest in supporting rules that free management from accountability to shareholders. Mark J. Roe, Strong Managers, Weak Owners: The Political Roots of American Corporate Finance 44 (1994). Managerial shirking of its monitoring responsibilities thus will often redound to the workers' benefit, which suggests that employee representatives on the board of directors are less likely to insist on disciplining lax managers than are shareholder representatives. If employees are entitled to voting representation on the board of directors, monitoring by the board and its subordinate managers will be less effective, which will cause agency costs to rise.

The validity of this prediction is confirmed by the German experience with codetermination. Conflicts of interest faced by employee representatives on the supervisory board remain a serious, but unresolved concern. Employee representation slows the finding of a consensus on the supervisory board and creates a built-in polarization problem. Not surprisingly, it is standard

practice for employee and shareholder representatives to have separate pre-meeting caucuses. Klaus J. Hopt, Labor Representation on Corporate Boards: Impacts and Problems for Corporate Governance and Economic Integration in Europe, 14 Int'l Rev. L. & Econ. 203, 206–08 (1994).

14.   Robert Howse & Michael J. Trebilcock, Protecting the Employment Bargain, 43 U. Tor. L. Rev. 751, 769 (1993).

15.   See Michael P. Dooley, European Proposals for Worker Information and Co-determination: An American Comment, in Harmonization of the Laws in the European Communities: Products Liability, Conflict of Laws, and Corporation Law 126, 129 (Peter E. Herzog ed. 1983) (opining: : "As to the majority of managerial policies concerning, for example, dividend and investment policies, product development, and the like, the typical employee has a much interest and as much to offer as the typical purchaser of light bulbs.").

16.   See, e.g., Frank H. Easterbrook and Daniel R. Fischel, The Economic Structure of Corporate Law 66–72 (1991). An alternative answer based on the model used herein returns to the divergence of interests within constituency groups. Although investors have somewhat different preferences on issues such as dividends and the like, they are generally united by a desire to maxim-

ante through agreed-upon compensation schedules. This distinction has two implications of present import. First, as noted above, employee interests are too parochial to justify board representation. In contrast, shareholders have the strongest economic incentive to care about the size of the residual claim, which means that they have the greatest incentive to elect directors committed to maximizing firm profitability.[17] Second, the nature of the employees' claim on the firm creates incentives to shirk. Vesting control rights in the employees would increase their incentive to shirk. In turn, the prospect of employee shirking lowers the value of the shareholders' residual claim.

At this point, it is useful to once again invoke the hypothetical bargain methodology. If the corporation's various constituencies could bargain over voting rights, to which constituency would they assign those rights? In light of their status as residual claimants and the adverse effects of employee representation, shareholders doubtless would bargain for control rights, so as to ensure a corporate decisionmaking system emphasizing monitoring mechanisms designed to prevent shirking by employees, and employees would be willing to concede such rights to shareholders.

Granted, collective action problems preclude the shareholders from exercising meaningful day-to-day or even year-to-year control over managerial decisions. Unlike the employees' claim, however, the shareholders' claim on the corporation is freely transferable. As such, if management fails to maximize the shareholders' residual claim, an outsider can profit by purchasing a majority of the shares and voting out the incumbent board of directors. Accordingly, vesting the right to vote solely in the hands of the firm's shareholders is what makes possible the market for corporate control and thus helps to minimize shirking. As the residual claimants, shareholders thus would bargain for sole voting control, in order to ensure that the value of their claim is maximized. In turn, because all corporate constituents have an ex ante interest in minimizing shirking by managers and other agents, the firm's employees have an incentive to agree to such rules.[18] The employees' lack of control rights

ize share value. Board consensus therefore will be more easily achieved if directors are beholden solely to shareholder interests, rather than to the more diverse set of interests represented by employees.

A related but perhaps more telling point is the problem of apportioning the vote. Financial capital is fungible, transferable, and quantifiable. Control rights based on financial capital are thus subject to low cost allocation and valuation. In contrast, the human capital of workers meets none of these criteria. While one-person/one-vote would be a low cost solution to the allocation problem, it appears highly inefficient given the unequal distribution of reasoning power and education. If the most competent people and/or those with the most at stake

should have the most votes, some more costly allocation device will be necessary.

17. The superiority of shareholder incentives is a relative matter. Shareholders may have better incentives than other constituencies, but the phenomenon of rational apathy nevertheless limits the extent to which shareholders can be expected to act on those incentives.

18. According to the Coase Theorem, rights will be acquired by those who value them most highly, which creates an incentive to discover and implement transaction cost minimizing governance forms. See Ronald H. Coase, The Problem of Social Cost, 3 J. L. & Econ. 1 (1960). Although shareholders and employees obviously do not bargain, a basic premise of the law and

thus can be seen as a way in which they bond their promise not to shirk. Their lack of control rights not only precludes them from double-dipping, but also facilitates disciplining employees who shirk. Accordingly, it is not surprising that the default rules of the standard form contract provided by all corporate statutes vest voting rights solely in the hands of common shareholders.

To be sure, the vote allows shareholders to allocate some risk to prior claimants. If a firm is in financial straits, directors and managers faithful to shareholder interests could protect the value of the shareholders' residual claim by, for example, financial and/or workforce restructurings that eliminate prior claimants. All of which raises the question of why employees do not get the vote to protect themselves against this risk. The answer is two-fold. First, as we have seen, multiple constituencies are inefficient. Second, as addressed below, employees have significant protections that do not rely on voting.

Suppose a firm behaves opportunistically towards it employees. What protections do the employees have? Some are protected by job mobility. The value of continued dealings with an employer to an employee whose work involves solely general human capital does not depend on the value of the firm because neither the employee nor the firm have an incentive to preserve such an employment relationships. If the employee's general human capital suffices for him to do his job at Firm A, it presumably would suffice for him to do a similar job at Firm B. Such an employee resembles an independent contractor who can shift from firm to firm at low cost to either employee or employer.[19] Mobility thus may be a sufficient defense against opportunistic conduct with respect to such employees, because they can quit and be replaced without productive loss to either employee or employer. Put another way, because there are no appropriable quasi-rents in this category of employment relationships, rent seeking by management is not a concern.

Corporate employees who make firm-specific investments in human capital arguably need greater protection against employer opportunism, but such protections need not include board representation. Indeed, various specialized governance structures have arisen to protect such workers. Among these are severance pay, grievance procedures, promotion ladders, collective bargaining, and the like.[20]

economics account is that corporate law provides them with a set of default rules reflecting the bargain they would strike if they were able to do so.

19. See generally Oliver Williamson, Corporate Governance, 93 Yale L.J. 1197 (1984). This is not to say that exit is costless for either employees or firms. All employees are partially locked into their firm. Indeed, it must be so, or monitoring could not prevent shirking because disciplinary efforts would have no teeth. The question is one of relative costs.

20. As private sector unions have declined, the federal government has intervened to provide through general welfare legislation many of the same protections for which unions might have bargained. The Family & Medical Leave Act grants unpaid leave for medical and other family problems. OSHA mandates safe working conditions. Plant closing laws require notice of layoffs. Civil rights laws protect against discrimination of various sorts. Even such matters as offensive horseplay have come within the purview of federal sexual harassment law.

In contrast, shareholders are poorly positioned to develop the kinds of specialized governance structures that protect employee interests. Unlike employees, whose relationship to the firm is subject to periodic renegotiation, shareholders have an indefinite relationship that is rarely renegotiated, if ever. The dispersed nature of stockownership also makes bilateral negotiation of specialized safeguards difficult. The board of directors thus is an essential governance mechanism for protecting shareholder interests.

If the foregoing analysis is correct, why do we nevertheless sometimes observe employee representation? An explanation consistent with our analysis lies close at hand. In the United States, employee representation on the board is typically found in firms that have undergone concessionary bargaining with unions. Concessionary bargaining, on average, results in increased share values of eight to ten percent.[21] The stock market apparently views union concessions as substantially improving the value of the residual claim, presumably by making firm failure less likely. While the firm's employees also benefit from a reduction in the firm's riskiness, they are likely to demand a quid pro quo for their contribution to shareholder wealth. One consideration given by shareholders (through management) may be greater access to information, sometimes through board representation. Put another way, board of director representation is a way of maximizing access to information and bonding its accuracy. The employee representatives will be able to verify that the original information about the firm's precarious financial situation was accurate. Employee representatives on the board also are well-positioned to determine whether the firm's prospects have improved sufficiently to justify an attempt to reverse prior concessions through a new round of bargaining.

§ 10.4 Federal regulation of proxies

A. Origins

Most shareholders attend neither the corporation's annual meeting nor any special meetings. Instead, they are represented—and vote—by proxy. Shareholders send in a card (called a proxy card) on which they have marked their vote. The card authorizes a proxy agent to vote the shareholder's stock as directed on the card. The proxy card may specify how the shares are to be voted or may simply give the proxy agent discretion to decide how the shares are to be voted. (Confusingly, older materials sometimes refer to both the proxy card and the proxy agent as a proxy without explanatory qualification.)

In 1934, when the federal Securities Exchange Act was first adopted, state corporate law was largely silent on the issue of corporate communi-

---

21. Brian E. Becker, Concession Bargaining: The Impact on Shareholders' Equi-   ty, 40 Indus. & Lab. Rel. Rev. 268 (1987).

cations with shareholders. Typical state statutes required only that the corporation send shareholders notice of a shareholders meeting, stating where and when the meeting would be held. Under most state laws, the notice merely was required to briefly identify the issues to be voted on— and some states did not even require that minimal disclosure in connection with annual meetings. (In most states, the corporation statute still does not require much more than this minimal notice.)

By 1934, however, we had already seen the development of large public corporations having thousands of shareholders and using the proxy system of voting. Congressional hearings on the Exchange Act presented numerous allegations that incumbent managers used the corporate shareholder list and corporate funds to solicit proxies in connection with a shareholder meeting. Obviously, because the incumbents were the ones asking for proxies, the proxy cards and soliciting materials were designed to encourage shareholders to vote as the incumbents desired. The proxy system thus allegedly helped incumbent directors and managers to perpetuate themselves in office.

Congress ultimately settled on disclosure as the principal vehicle by which the proxy system was to be regulated at the federal level. Incumbent corporate managers and directors were not to solicit proxies from shareholders without giving the shareholders enough information on which to make an informed voting decision. Comparable disclosures were to be required from insurgents soliciting proxies in opposition to the incumbents, as well.

After several legislative false starts, however, the Congress ultimately dumped the job of creating a disclosure-based proxy regime in the SEC's lap. As adopted, Exchange Act § 14(a) provides:

> It shall be unlawful for any person, by use of the mails or by any means or instrumentality of interstate commerce or of any facility of a national securities exchange or otherwise, in contravention of such rules and regulations as the Commission may prescribe as necessary or appropriate in the public interest or for the protection of investors, to solicit or to permit the use of his name to solicit any proxy or consent or authorization in respect of any security (other than an exempted security) registered pursuant to Section 12 of this title.

Notice that § 14(a) is not self-executing. It proscribed nothing until the SEC adopted implementing rules and regulations. Pursuant to this broad grant of authority, the SEC has created a complex regulatory scheme governing the manner in which proxies are solicited and, therefore, the manner in which shareholder decisions are made.

B.   The regulatory framework

Per Exchange Act § 14(a), federal proxy regulation extends only to corporations registered with the SEC under § 12 of that Act, which means that virtually all public corporations are picked up by this requirement, while most close corporations are exempt. Because § 14(a) simply states that it shall be unlawful to solicit proxies in contravention of such rules as the SEC may proscribe, however, the rest of the regulatory framework is provided not by statute but entirely by SEC rules.

1. What is a solicitation of proxies?

Given the wording of Exchange Act § 14(a), the definition of "solicit" is the linchpin of the entire regulatory structure. The standard judicial definition of "solicit" includes not only "direct requests to furnish, revoke or withhold proxies, but also ... communications which may indirectly accomplish such a result or constitute a step in a chain of communications designed ultimately to accomplish such a result."[1] The basic question is whether a communication is reasonably calculated to influence a shareholder's vote. If so, it is a proxy solicitation.

The expansive definition of solicitation long created major obstacles for prospective insurgents. In *Studebaker Corporation v. Gittlin*,[2] for example, defendant Gittlin was a disgruntled shareholder of plaintiff Studebaker. Gittlin and his associates requested changes in the board of directors and announced their intention of conducting a proxy contest if their demands were not met. When talks with the incumbent board broke down, Gittlin filed an action in New York state court seeking to inspect the corporation's shareholder list and other books and records. Under the applicable New York statute, only shareholders holding 5% or more of the corporation's stock are entitled to inspect such records. Because Gittlin owned only 5,000 shares, he gathered written authorizations from 42 other shareholders collectively holding an aggregate of more than 5% of the stock. Studebaker's incumbent board sued Gittlin under § 14(a), claiming that the process of gathering written authorizations was itself a solicitation of proxies.

Gittlin first argued that Studebaker lacked standing to sue for an alleged proxy violation. The court rejected this argument. As the court read the legislative history, Congress did not intend for incumbent directors to be a passive observer of proxy contests. In addition, the U.S. Supreme Court had characterized the individual shareholder's cause of action for violations of the proxy rules as being derivative in nature.[3] Accordingly, the *Gittlin* court reasoned, the cause of action really belongs

---

§ 10.4

1. Long Island Lighting Co. v. Barbash, 779 F.2d 793, 796 (2d Cir.1985). In *LILCO*, an environmentalist group ran newspaper and radio ads critical of the defendant electrical utility's management. The utility managers alleged that the group was acting in conjunction with an insurgent shareholder conducting a proxy contest. The incumbent managers sued the environmentalists, alleging that their ads constituted a proxy solicitation. Over a strong dissent by Judge Ralph Winter (a former professor of corporate law at Yale), the court declined to reach the obvious First Amendment issues posed by the case. Instead, having adopted the definition of a solicitation quoted in the text, the court remanded for a determination of whether the defendants had solicited proxies under that definition.

2. 360 F.2d 692 (2d Cir.1966).

3. See, e.g., J. I. Case Co. v. Borak, 377 U.S. 426 (1964).

to the firm, which therefore may bring actions in its own name.[4]

Turning to the definitional issue, the court noted § 14(a)'s broad application to solicitation of a "proxy, consent or authorization." Accordingly, the court opined, any communication with shareholders will be deemed a solicitation subject to the proxy rules if it is part of a continuous plan intended to end in a solicitation of proxies and to prepare the way for success in a proxy contest. Because gathering authorizations was part of such a plan, it therefore was a solicitation subject to the proxy rules, and Gittlin had violated the regulatory requirement to prepare and disseminate a proxy statement prior to soliciting proxies. Gittlin therefore had to start over by distributing a proxy statement to the 42 shareholders and resoliciting their authorizations.

The court rather summarily dismissed the "inconvenience to Gittlin in having to start over again." Consider, however, the decision's impact on Gittlin. Under SEC rules at the time, communications with up to 10 people were exempted from the definition of solicitation. In other words, Gittlin did not need to prepare, file, and distribute a proxy statement if he only talked to ten people. If Gittlin could access the shareholder list, he could use it to identify large holders. He could then communicate with the ten largest holders without having to give them a proxy statement. As a result of those communications, he could determine whether he could expect support in his proxy contest. This would assist him in determining whether it was worthwhile to go to the expense of a proxy contest. But the court required Gittlin to prepare a proxy statement just to get access to the list, because his talks with the group of 42 shareholders were part of a continuous plan intended to lead to a solicitation of proxies and, of course, he had to exceed the ten shareholder limit just to satisfy the statutory 5% threshold. The opinion thus required Gittlin to incur much of the expense of a proxy contest before he could determine whether it was worthwhile to conduct such a contest.

Fortunately for insurgents, subsequent regulatory developments have lessened *Gittlin*'s negative impact. SEC rules under Exchange Act § 13(d) now require that persons owning more than 5% of a public firm's stock must file reports of their holdings with the SEC. In addition, under § 13(f), most institutional investors (such as pension and mutual funds) must report all of their stock holdings, no matter how small. Because these reports are publicly available, shareholders in Gittlin's situation less often require early access to the shareholder list. Instead, the shareholders can now use the reports to identify large shareholders and then approach up to ten large shareholders to feel them out as to the merits of a proxy contest.

---

4. But cf. Diceon Elec., Inc. v. Calvary Partners, L.P., 772 F.Supp. 859 (D.Del. 1991) (holding that the issuer does not have standing to sue under § 14(a) for damages). As a practical matter, *Gittlin* thus gives incumbent directors yet another weapon with which to fend off insurgent shareholders.

Additionally, the SEC in 1992 liberalized the proxy rules to encourage greater communication between shareholders, in large part by exempting numerous communications from the definition of solicitation. Among the more important exemptions of general application are:

- Rule 14a–8(a)(1)(*l*) exempts public statements of how the shareholder intends to vote and its reasons for doing so.

- Rule 14a–8(b)(1), subject to numerous exceptions, exempts persons who do not seek "the power to act as proxy for a security holder" and do not furnish or solicit "a form of revocation, abstention, consent or authorization." Consequently, for example, a newspaper editorial advising a vote against incumbent managers is now definitively exempted.[5] Note that the Rule thus addresses—although hardly eliminates—the obvious First Amendment concerns implicated by regulating speech in connection with shareholder voting.

- Rule 14a–8(b)(2) preserves the long-standing exemption for solicitations of 10 or fewer persons.

- Rule 14a–8(b)(3) exempts the furnishing of proxy voting advice by someone with whom the shareholder has a business relationship. (A number of firms now provide such voting advice to institutional investors.)

Note, however, that most of these exemptions would not have helped Gittlin. Shareholders planning a proxy contest to oust the incumbent directors are still subject to the proxy rules in full force.

2. The proxy rules

Under SEC Rule 14a–3, the incumbent board of directors' first step in soliciting proxies must be the distribution to shareholders of the firm's annual report.[6] The annual report contains detailed financial statements and a discussion by management of the firm's business. It is intended to give shareholders up-to-date information about what the firm is doing and to give shareholders a basis on which to assess how well management is performing.

Once the annual report is in the shareholders' hands, the proxy solicitation process can begin. The solicitor's goal is to get the shareholder to sign and date a proxy card, voting his shares in the manner the solicitor desires. Because the end goal of this process is the proxy card, it may be helpful to focus initially on a simplified example of a proxy card that complies with the applicable rules. (See Figures 1 and 2. Obviously, the figures are not to scale.)

5. Note that all of the exemptions under Rule 14a8–2(b) are limited in that they do not exempt the communication from Rule14a–9's prohibition of fraudulent and misleading proxy solicitations.

6. The annual report may be sent to the shareholders before proxies are solicited or may be sent in the same package as the proxy solicitation materials. The main point is that the annual report must be in the shareholder's hands when they make voting decisions.

**Figure 1. Simplified sample proxy card
conforming to Rule 14a–4 (front)**

THIS PROXY IS SOLICITED ON BEHALF OF THE BOARD
OF DIRECTORS.

Alice Able, Bill Black, and Candice Charles and each of them, each with the power of substitution, are hereby authorized to represent and to vote the stock of the undersigned in ACME CORPORATION at the Annual Meeting of its stockholders to be held on April 29, 200X and any adjournments thereof.

MANAGEMENT RECOMMENDS AND WILL VOTE FOR THE ELECTION OF THE FOLLOWING AS DIRECTORS (UNLESS OTHERWISE DIRECTED):

1. Alice Able, Bill Black, Candice Charles, Delta Dawn, Eddie Eagle, and Fred MacFred.

To vote for all nominees, check this box. []

To withhold authority to vote for all nominees, check this box. []

To withhold authority to vote for any individual nominee while voting for the

remainder, write this nominee's name in the space following:

MANAGEMENT RECOMMENDS AND WILL VOTE FOR THE FOLLOWING (UNLESS OTHERWISE DIRECTED):

2. Appointment of Dewey Cheatem & Howe LLP as Independent Public Accountants.

FOR []   AGAINST []   ABSTAIN []

MANAGEMENT DOES NOT RECOMMEND AND WILL VOTE AGAINST THE FOLLOWING STOCKHOLDER PROPOSAL (UNLESS OTHERWISE DIRECTED):

3. Provide information about toxic chemicals.

FOR []   AGAINST []   ABSTAIN []

(OVER)

**Figure 2. Simplified sample proxy card
conforming to Rule 14a–4 (back)**

4. In their discretion, the Proxies are authorized to vote upon such other business as may properly come before the meeting.

You are encouraged to specify your choices by marking the appropriate boxes on the reverse side, but you need not mark any boxes. If you wish to vote in accordance with the board of directors recommendations, simply sign and date this form in the space below. The proxies cannot vote your shares unless you sign and return this card.

Signature: ＿＿＿＿＿＿＿

Date: ＿＿＿＿＿＿＿＿

The sample card has been designed to comply with the requirements of SEC Rule 14a–4, which governs the form of the proxy card. The first item of interest can be found at the top of Figure 1 (the card's front), where the card identifies the party soliciting the shareholder's proxy. In this case, it is the incumbent board of directors. This statement is mandated by SEC Rule 14a–4(a)(1), which requires that the proxy card clearly state whether or not is being solicited by the current board of directors.[7]

The second point to be noticed can be found in the paragraph just below that line. By signing the card, the shareholder appoints three people—Able, Black, and Charles—as proxies (i.e., proxy agents) and authorizes them to vote the shareholder's stock in accordance with the instructions on the card. Note that this proxy card is not a permanent delegation of authority—the proxy agents only have authority to vote the shares at the specified shareholder meeting.

Now look at the portion of the card relating to the election of directors (i.e., the first numbered paragraph in Figure 1). Under SEC Rule 14a–4(b), the solicitor must give shareholders three options: vote for all of the nominees for director, vote against all of them, and vote against certain of the directors by striking out their names. Note that provision need not be made for write-in candidates.

Now look at the next two numbered paragraphs. With respect to any other matters to be voted on at the meeting, the solicitor again must give shareholders three options. But this time the options are: vote for, vote against, or abstain.

Now look at Figure 2 (the back of the card). The first paragraph (numbered 4) gives the proxy agents authority to use their discretion to vote on any other business to come before the meeting. Under SEC Rule 14a–4(c), unless the proxy card contains an express statement like the one in this card, the shareholder's stock may not be voted on any matters other than the specific matters enumerated on the card. Discretionary authority can be very important. Suppose an insurgent shows up at the meeting and makes a motion to which the incumbent board objects. If the board has been granted the discretionary authority conveyed in numbered paragraph 4 of this card, all of the shares represented by those cards can be voted against the motion. If not, the board may have to scrounge up votes from those shareholders who attended in person. (If the party soliciting the proxies knew in advance that a particular issue would come before the meeting, however, the grant of discretionary authority will not be valid.)

The statement in the next paragraph tells shareholders how their stock will be voted if they return a signed card containing no instructions. This is to deal with the common problem of apathetic shareholders who simply sign the card and mail it back in, without ever indicating

---

7. In addition, SEC Rule 14a–9 provides that failure to clearly distinguish one party's proxy card from that of another party constitutes fraud. When a proxy contest occurs, for example, the two sides typically use different colored cards.

how their shares are to be voted. In such cases, a statement of this sort gives the proxy agents authority under SEC Rule 14a–4(e) to vote the shares in the indicated manner.

The signature block may seem purely ministerial, but even it has a substantive component. Proxies of the sort at issue here are revocable. Shareholders are free to change their minds and revoke previously granted proxies at any time up to the moment of the election. In practice, there are two ways shareholders revoke prior proxies: (1) by showing up at the shareholders' meeting and voting the shares in person; or (2) by giving a later dated proxy. Where the shareholder signs more than one proxy card, only the most recent card counts—all earlier cards are thereupon revoked. Hence, the significance of the date.

Along with the proxy card, the SEC requires that the solicitor provide solicited shareholders with a proxy statement containing mandated disclosures relating to the matters to be acted upon. The cover page of the proxy statement typically includes the state law-required notice of where and when the meeting is to be held, and will also state what issues are to be decided at the meeting. A proxy statement relating to an annual meeting, at which directors are being elected, will typically open with biographical information about the candidates. The proxy statement will also include disclosures about board of director committees, board and executive compensation (see the next section), relationships between the firm and its directors and senior officers, and a description of any other matters to come before the shareholders.

Per Rule 14a–6, a preliminary proxy card and statement must be filed with the SEC at least 10 calendar days before proxies are first solicited. Filing of preliminary materials is not required, however, with respect to an uncontested annual meeting at which only basic matters such as election of directors and appointment of an independent auditor are to be decided. In either case, definitive copies of the proxy card, proxy statement, and any other soliciting materials (such as letters to shareholders) must be filed with the SEC no later than the day they are first used.

In a proxy contest, a key factor will be the insurgent's ability to communicate directly with the shareholders. Towards that end, the insurgent will want access to the corporation's list of shareholders. SEC Rule 14a–7, however, does not require the incumbent board to provide a copy of the shareholder list to the insurgent. The incumbents are given an alternative: they can provide the shareholder list to the insurgent or they can require that the insurgent provide its proxy materials to the corporation, which is obligated to promptly mail those materials to the shareholders (at the insurgent's expense). The incumbents usually prefer the latter route, as it gives them greater control over the process by which proxies are solicited. Commonly, however, insurgents are able to circumvent this restriction by seeking access to the shareholder list under state law.

3. *Disclosure of director and executive compensation*

Proxy statements increasingly are dominated by disclosures relating to director and executive compensation. Under items 8 and 10 of Schedule 14A, disclosure is required not only when shareholders are asked to approve compensation plans but also whenever they are merely asked to elect directors. In effect, the proxy statement has become a vehicle for annual compensation disclosures. Per Item 402 of Regulation S–K, the extensive required disclosures include all compensation paid to the CEO and the next four most highly compensated executive officers. A table setting out total compensation must be supplemented by various other tables providing specific breakdowns of items such as option exercises.

The SEC argues that its rules provide shareholders with a clear and concise presentation of compensation paid officers, which supposedly gives shareholders greater opportunity to make their views known. Presumably, greater disclosure enables shareholders to complain to the board about excessively high compensation, challenge excessive compensation in derivative litigation, reject excessive compensation plans put to a shareholder vote, and vote out of office directors who approve excessive compensation. The theory of rational shareholder apathy, however, predicts that most shareholders prefer to be passive investors.[8] A rational shareholder will expend the effort to make an informed decision only if the expected benefits of doing so outweigh its costs. Given the length and complexity of SEC disclosure documents, the opportunity cost entailed in becoming informed before voting is quite high and very apparent. Moreover, most shareholders' holdings are too small to have any significant effect on the vote's outcome. Accordingly, shareholders assign a relatively low value to the expected benefits of careful consideration.

If shareholders are rationally apathetic, more comprehensible information will not lead to better decisions. Indeed, greater volumes of information will only make the situation worse. If the SEC's executive compensation disclosure rules thus increase the cost to companies of complying with their disclosure obligations, but do not lead to more informed shareholder decisionmaking, what then is their purpose? One can but infer that, in adopting these rules, the SEC got back into the therapeutic disclosure business. In other words, the Commission is using disclosure requirements not to inform shareholders, but to affect substantive corporate behavior. In this case, to put the brakes on executive compensation.

Therapeutic disclosure requirements undoubtedly affect corporate behavior. Therapeutic disclosure, however, is troubling on at least two

---

8. The SEC may believe that this shareholder passivity model no longer holds true in light of the growing importance of institutional investors. To be sure, institutional investors are an increasingly important force in the stock markets and, moreover, some institutions are playing a more active role in corporate governance. At the same time, however, the passivity model undoubtedly will remain applicable even to most institutional investors. See Stephen M. Bainbridge, The Politics of Corporate Governance, 18 Harv. J. L. & Pub. Pol'y 671 (1995).

levels. First, seeking to effect substantive goals through disclosure requirements violates the Congressional intent behind the federal securities laws. When the New Deal era Congresses adopted the Securities Act and the Securities Exchange Act, there were three possible statutory approaches under consideration: (1) the fraud model, which would simply prohibit fraud in the sale of securities; (2) the disclosure model, which would allow issuers to sell very risky or even unsound securities, provided they gave buyers enough information to make an informed investment decision; and (3) the blue sky model, pursuant to which the SEC would engage in merit review of a security and its issuer. The federal securities laws adopted a mixture of the first two approaches, but explicitly rejected federal merit review. As such, the substantive behavior of corporate issuers is not within the SEC's purview.

Second, and even more disturbing, in this case the SEC's rules overstep the boundaries between the federal and state regulatory spheres. The Commission contended that its rules bring shareholders into the compensation committee or board meeting room and thereby enable them to see specific decisions through the eyes of the directors. This goal, however, flies in the face of the separation of ownership and control created by state corporate law. Under state law, shareholders have no right to approve most board decisions, let alone to initiate corporate action. Of particular relevance in this context, shareholders have no right to participate in compensation decisions. In other words, they have no right to be brought within the meeting room.

4. *Disclosure of director misconduct*

The biographical information required of director candidates by the proxy rules includes such matters as bankruptcies, pending criminal charges and prior convictions, securities violations, and the like. To what extent must a director disclose other personal peccadilloes? Actual or potential conflicts of interest generally must be disclosed.[9] But what about matters that go not to the loyalty and honesty of the directors, but rather to simple mismanagement?

Where plaintiff complains of noncriminal conduct allegedly constituting mismanagement, courts have been unwilling to require disclosure. In *Amalgamated Clothing and Textile Workers Union, AFL–CIO v. J. P. Stevens & Co.,*[10] for example, plaintiffs argued that the board of directors had either knowingly violated the labor laws or, at least, failed to prevent management from doing so. According to plaintiffs, this alleged misconduct had harmed the corporation's reputation and exposed it to liability. The failure to disclose these purported facts in connection with the election of the directors allegedly constituted an omission of material facts. In rejecting plaintiff's argument, the court distinguished conflicts of interest from allegedly illegal conduct intended to benefit the corpora-

---

9. See, e.g., Maldonado v. Flynn, 597 F.2d 789 (2d Cir.1979).

10. 475 F.Supp. 328 (S.D.N.Y.1979).

tion. Only the former need be disclosed, as it would be "silly" to "require management to accuse itself of antisocial or illegal policies."[11]

A similar standard was set forth in *Gaines v. Haughton*.[12] Defendants were directors of Lockheed Corporation, a major aerospace and defense firm, who failed to disclose in their proxy solicitation materials that Lockheed had made over $30 million in foreign corrupt payments. Paying bribes to foreign officials so that the corporation can get contracts may be immoral or even illegal, the court opined, but such allegations are not material absent charges of self-dealing. In addition, the court stressed the lack of a causal nexus between the alleged misconduct and the matter put to the shareholders for a vote. Because the shareholders were asked only to elect the board, not to approve the allegedly improper bribes, the bribes did not need to be disclosed.

C. Proxy contests

In the usual case, only the incumbent board of directors solicits proxies and the board's recommendations usually get overwhelming support from the shareholders. Occasionally, however, an independent shareholder (often called an insurgent) may solicit proxies in opposition to management. Usually the insurgent is putting forward a slate of directors as an alternative to the slate proposed by management. Rarely, the insurgent may solicit proxies in opposition to some proposal made by management. In either case, the process is doubled. Both sides independently prepare proxy cards and proxy statements that are separately sent to the shareholders.

Law and economics scholar Henry Manne famously described proxy contests as "the most expensive, the most uncertain, and the least used of the various techniques" for acquiring corporate control.[13] Until the last few years, no one questioned his assessment. Insurgents contemplating a proxy battle face a host of legal and economic disincentives. In recent years, however, proxy contests have become somewhat more common as a new set of countervailing incentives favoring proxy contests have emerged.

1. Disincentives to proxy campaigns

A would-be insurgent's obstacles are legion. Various state statutes permit corporations to adopt measures—so-called shark repellents— making it more difficult for an insurgent to gain control of the board of directors via a proxy contest. Among the more important of these are classified boards, the elimination of cumulative voting, and dual class

---

11. If there has been a prior judicial determination that the directors in fact mismanaged the corporation, however, such a determination is a material fact that must be disclosed. See, e.g., Wilson v. Great American Industries, Inc., 855 F.2d 987 (2d Cir.1988).

12. 645 F.2d 761 (9th Cir.1981).

13. Henry G. Manne, Mergers and the Market for Corporate Control, 73 J. Pol. Econ. 110, 114 (1965).

stock plans. Other impediments include management's informational advantages and investor perceptions that proxy insurgents are not serious contenders for control. The two most important obstacles for a would-be insurgent, however, are probably the rules governing reimbursement of expenses and shareholder apathy.

2. *Reimbursement of expenses*

Proxy contests are enormously expensive. Any serious contest requires the services of lawyers, accountants, financial advisers, printers, and proxy solicitors. None of these folks come cheap. Even incidental costs, such as mailing expenses, mount up very quickly when one must communicate (usually several times) with the thousands of shareholders in the typical public corporation. As it is always more pleasant to spend someone else's money than it is to spend one's own, both incumbents and insurgents will want the corporation to pay their expenses.

In theory, incumbent directors do not have unbridled access to the corporate treasury. In practice, however, incumbents rarely pay their own expenses. Under state law, the board of directors may use corporate funds to pay for expenses incurred in opposing the insurgent, provided the amounts are reasonable and the contest involves policy questions rather than just a "purely personal power struggle."[14] Only the most poorly advised of incumbents find it difficult to meet this standard. The board merely needs have its lawyers parse the insurgent's proxy materials for policy questions on which they differ. Such a search is bound to be successful: if the insurgent agrees with all of management's policies, why is it trying to oust them?

In contrast, insurgents initially must bear their own costs. Insurgents have no right to reimbursement out of corporate funds. Rather, an insurgent will be reimbursed only if an appropriate resolution is approved by a majority of both the board of directors and the shareholders.[15] If the incumbents prevail, of course, they are unlikely to look kindly on an insurgent's request for reimbursement of expenses. In effect, the insurgent must win to have any hope of getting reimbursed.

The rules on reimbursement of expenses take on considerable importance when coupled with the rules on standing in proxy litigation. In *J. I. Case Co. v. Borak*,[16] the Supreme Court held that proxy claims under § 14(a) are both direct and derivative in nature. Consequently, *Borak* gives management standing to sue the insurgent in the corporation's name.[17] As a practical matter, the incumbent board thus has another weapon with which to fend off insurgent shareholders. If the Supreme Court had treated proxy litigation as direct in nature, only shareholders would have standing to sue for violations of the proxy rules.

---

14. E.g., Rosenfeld v. Fairchild Engine & Airplane Corp., 128 N.E.2d 291 (1955), reh'g denied, 130 N.E.2d 610 (1955).

15. E.g., Steinberg v. Adams, 90 F.Supp. 604 (S.D.N.Y.1950); Grodetsky v. McCrory Corp., 267 N.Y.S.2d 356 (Sup.Ct.1966).

16. 377 U.S. 426 (1964).

17. E.g., Studebaker Corp. v. Gittlin, 360 F.2d 692 (2d Cir.1966).

Although the board still could bring suit against the insurgent, it would have to do so in the directors' individual capacity as shareholders. As such, they could not use firm resources to finance the litigation. Because the firm is permitted to sue in its own name for violations of the proxy rules, however, the board can use the firm's deep pocket to pay for legal expenses incurred in such suits. In contrast, because of the rules on reimbursement of expenses, the insurgent's litigation costs come out of its own pocket.

3. *Shareholder apathy and related problems*

The insurgent's problems are said to be compounded by the other shareholders' rational apathy. As the theory goes, a rational shareholder will expend the effort to make an informed decision only if the expected benefits of doing so outweigh its costs. Given the length and complexity of proxy statements, especially in a proxy contest where the shareholder is receiving multiple communications from the contending parties, the opportunity cost entailed in reading the proxy statements before voting is quite high and very apparent. Shareholders also probably do not expect to discover grounds for opposing management from the proxy statements. Finally, most shareholders' holdings are too small to have any significant effect on the vote's outcome. Accordingly, shareholders can be expected to assign a relatively low value to the expected benefits of careful consideration. Shareholders are thus rationally apathetic. For the average shareholder, the necessary investment of time and effort in making informed voting decisions simply is not worthwhile.[18]

Instead of carefully considering the contending parties' arguments, shareholders typically adopt the so-called Wall Street Rule: it's easier to switch than fight. To the extent the shareholders are satisfied, they will vote for management. Disgruntled shareholders, in contrast, will have long since sold out. As a result, shareholders are likely to vote for management even where that is not the decision an informed shareholder would reach. The insurgent thus risks laying out considerable funds for no return on that investment.

4. *The proxy contest's (slight) resurgence*

In the last few years, various factors combined to make hostile tender offers a much less attractive, and proxy contests a much more attractive, acquisition technique than they were during most of the 1980s. Perhaps the most important factors in the proxy contest's resurgence were two supreme court decisions. *Paramount Communications, Inc. v. Time Inc.*,[19] by the Delaware Supreme Court, significantly weakened the standards by which target takeover defenses are measured.

---

18. Frank H. Easterbrook and Daniel R. Fischel, Voting in Corporate Law, 26 J. L. & Econ. 395, 402 (1983); Martin Lipton, Corporate Governance in the Age of Finance Corporatism, 136 U. Penn. L. Rev. 1, 66–67 (1987). The problem is compounded by the likelihood that a substantial number of shareholders will attempt to freeride on the efforts of the few informed shareholders.

19. 571 A.2d 1140 (Del.1989).

Under Delaware law, incumbent directors must show that the hostile offer poses a threat to corporate policy and that their response was reasonable in relation to the threat.[20] *Time* both recognized a much broader class of cognizable threats and weakened the proportionality requirement. As a result, effective management takeover defenses should pass muster more easily. Not only does this trend make hostile tender offers more difficult, it also encourages bidders to conduct a proxy contest before making a tender offer. If elected, the bidder's nominees often can lower the target's defenses and thereby permit the tender offer to go forward.

In *CTS Corp. v. Dynamics Corp.*,[21] the U.S. Supreme Court for the first time upheld a state takeover law against constitutional challenge. Since *CTS*, state takeover laws have routinely withstood constitutional scrutiny. By erecting new barriers to hostile tender offerors, they make tender offers less attractive. Because most permit the target's board of directors to waive their application to a particular bid, they also encourage pre-offer proxy contests.

Proxy contests probably will never become commonplace. They remain expensive and risky. Yet, they remain an essential part of the market for corporate control. So long as outsiders want to buy companies whose incumbent directors and officers want to remain independent, proxy contests will be part of the buyer's toolkit.

D. Proxy litigation

There are many ways to violate the proxy rules, because there are so many technical rules that must be complied with, but the likeliest source of liability is an illegal proxy solicitation. It is illegal to solicit proxies until the solicitor has delivered a proxy statement to the shareholders. It also is illegal to solicit proxies using materials that have not been filed with the SEC. Finally, it is illegal to solicit proxies using false or misleading soliciting materials. In examining these issues, we focus on several questions: (1) Does a cause of action exist for violations of the proxy rules and, if so, who has standing to bring such an action? (2) What must the plaintiff show in order to prevail in such a cause of action? (3) What remedies are available to injured parties?

1. *The implied private right of action*

No matter how closely one scrutinizes Securities Exchange Act § 14(a), one will not find anything relating to a private party cause of action under the statute or rules. In *J. I. Case Co. v. Borak*,[22] however, the Supreme Court implied a private right of action from the statute. Case proposed to merge with American Tractor Co. Borak owned around 2000 shares of Case stock and sought to enjoin the merger on the grounds, inter alia, that the company's proxy materials were false and

---

20. See Unocal Corp. v. Mesa Petroleum Co., 493 A.2d 946 (Del.1985).

21. 481 U.S. 69 (1987).

22. 377 U.S. 426 (1964).

misleading. Borak claimed that the merger was approved by a small margin and would not have been approved but for the false and misleading statements. Case argued that Borak had no standing to sue, as the federal proxy rules provided no private party cause of action.

Despite the lack of any statutory authorization for a private party cause of action, Justice Clark's opinion for the Court found that such an action in fact existed. As a fig leaf to cover the otherwise naked exercise of judicial activism, Justice Clark purported to find a statutory basis for the cause of action in Exchange Act § 27. Noting that § 27 gives district courts jurisdiction over "all suits in equity and actions at law brought to enforce any liability or duty" under the Act, Justice Clark contended that "[t] he power to enforce implies the power to make effective the right of recovery afforded by the Act. And the power to make the right of recovery effective implies the power to utilize any of the procedures or actions normally available to the litigant...." His argument, however, is spurious. Section 27 speaks of liabilities imposed by the Act, but nothing in § 14(a) or the rules thereunder creates such liabilities vis-à-vis shareholders.

Borak is better understood as an exercise of judicial fiat. A private right of action exists not because Congress intended it, but because a majority of the Supreme Court said so. The general legitimacy of implied private rights of action is beyond our purview, however.[23] Instead, we are concerned solely with Justice Clark's policy justification for this particular cause of action.

Justice Clark was quite above-board as to his motivation—he wanted to deter fraud and other proxy violations. According to Justice Clark, private enforcement provides "a necessary supplement" to SEC efforts. He implied that shareholders are in a better position than the SEC to detect proxy violations—they have fewer proxy statements to review and presumably are better informed about the company. Again, however, the argument is spurious. Most shareholders do not carefully review proxy materials. Instead, they are rationally apathetic. They lack both the desire and the incentive to closely monitor the firm. Justice Clark doubtless knew that individual shareholders were unlikely to emerge as champions of corporate truth and justice. Instead, it seems probable that he was trying to provide incentives for the plaintiffs' bar to become more active in proxy litigation.

---

23. For analyses with application to securities law, see Joseph A. Grundfest, Disimplying Private Rights of Action Under the Federal Securities Laws: The Commission's Authority, 107 Harv. L. Rev. 963 (1994); Michael J. Kaufman, A Little "Right" *Musick*: The Unconstitutional Judicial Creation of Private Rights of Action Under Section 10(b) of the Securities Exchange Act, 72 Wash. U. L.Q. 287 (1994); Marc I. Steinberg and William A. Reece, The Supreme Court, Implied Rights of Action, and Proxy Regulation, 54 Ohio St. L.J.

67 (1993). Noting that the Supreme Court's standards for creating implied private rights of action have stiffened in recent years, some lower courts have questioned whether *Borak* would be decided the same way today and even whether its reasoning remains valid. See, e.g., Reschini v. First Fed. Sav. & Loan Ass'n of Ind., 46 F.3d 246, 255 (3d Cir.1995) (opining that *Borak* "is still good law as a construction of the 1934 Act and Rule 14a–9. However, it is not clear that *Borak*, if it arose for the first time today, would be decided the same way.").

At this point, we must digress briefly to discuss the economics of deterrence. Following Jeremy Bentham, many modern deterrence theorists assume that man is a rational calculator of costs and benefits. A rational calculator will not violate the law if the costs of illegal activity exceed the benefits to be derived from it. To be sure, the idea that criminals are rational calculators seems improbable, but there is some evidence that criminals behave as though they were rational calculators, especially with respect to economic crimes like securities fraud.[24] The economic theory of deterrence therefore argues that the number of offenses reflects the expected benefits and sanctions associated with crime. Where potential offenders perceive that the potential gains from the activity are greater than the potential penalties, offenses will increase. In contrast, offenses will be reduced when the expected sanction exceeds the expected benefit. The expected benefit depends on the probability of success and the likely gain. Similarly, the expected sanction is a function of the nominal penalty and the probability of conviction or settlement.[25]

The express nominal sanctions for violations of the proxy rules are fairly severe. Violations can be referred to the Justice Department for criminal prosecutions, the SEC can bring an action to enjoin violations or to enjoin actions taken because of the violations (such as a merger based on false proxy materials), and the SEC can institute administrative proceedings to require compliance with its rules. However, as Justice Clark pointed out, the SEC has limited resources. The chances that the SEC will detect and successfully prosecute proxy violations are rather small. Because the expected sanction is a multiple of the nominal sanction and the probability of conviction, the expected sanction for violations of the proxy rules is relatively low. Accordingly, we would not expect SEC enforcement to provide an adequate level of deterrence.

The various forms of equitable and monetary relief made available by creating a private right action would increase the level of the nominal

---

24. Richard A. Posner, Economic Analysis of Law 223–224 (4th ed. 1992).

25. Put more precisely, deterrence seeks to minimize the social loss associated with crime, which can be viewed as a function of the loss created by the activity itself (activity loss), the cost of enforcing a prohibition against the activity (enforcement loss), and the cost of imposing sanctions against the activity (penalty loss). Activity loss is a function of the number of offenses and of the loss resulting from each offense. Enforcement and penalty losses are distinguished primarily by the stage of the deterrence process where they occur. Enforcement loss is the cost to society of detecting and convicting wrongdoers. Penalty loss is the cost of subsequent punishment. The sum of the costs to society and to the individual resulting from the imposition of the sanction and from any externalities created

is the net penalty loss to society. Any attempt to minimize social loss must attempt to minimize the sum of all three factors, and not merely activity losses. If activity losses were the only factor in determining social loss, the social loss could be minimized simply by increasing the nominal sanction or the probability of conviction until the expected sanctions far outweigh the expected benefits. An increase in enforcement activity, however, requires increased enforcement expenditures and increases the enforcement loss to society. Similarly, an increase in nominal sanctions increases the externalities associated with imposing the sanction—such as deterrence of beneficial activities—thereby increasing the penalty loss to society. See generally Gary S. Becker, Crime and Punishment: An Economic Approach, 76 J. Pol. Econ. 169 (1968).

sanction. More important, however, if the plaintiffs' bar could be encouraged to act as so-called "private attorneys general," the probability of detection and conviction would increase substantially.

That Justice Clark was concerned with creating incentives for the plaintiffs' bar is suggested by his characterization of the implied private right of action as being both direct and derivative in nature. (Strikingly, he did so over Borak's strong argument that the suit was only direct in nature.) At the time *Borak* was decided, the modern federal class action procedure had not yet been adopted. If proxy actions were allowed to proceed only directly, and plaintiffs' lawyers were limited to representing individual shareholders, the contingent fees generated by proxy litigation would be insufficient to attract quality lawyers. (The situation would be even worse in cases like *Borak*, where plaintiff sought only equitable relief.) Because the implied cause of action had a derivative element, however, a plaintiffs' lawyer could effectively sue on behalf of all shareholders, by nominally suing in the corporation's name, generating larger damage claims and bigger contingent fees.

The Supreme Court's emphasis on promoting private attorneys general became even more pronounced in its next major proxy decision, *Mills v. Electric Auto–Lite Co.*[26] Mergenthaler Linotype Company owned over 50% of Auto–Lite's stock. About one-third of Mergenthaler's voting stock, in turn, was owned by American Manufacturing Co. American had voting control of Mergenthaler and through it Auto–Lite. Auto–Lite and Mergenthaler agreed to merge. The merger agreement required approval by two-thirds of Auto–Lite's outstanding shares, which therefore required affirmative votes from at least some of the minority shareholders. Plaintiffs alleged that the proxy materials used to solicit those votes were false and misleading and sued to enjoin the shareholder vote.

In the portion of its opinion dealing with remedies, the Supreme Court created a strong incentive for members of the plaintiffs' bar to act as private attorneys general. The Court opined that shareholder-plaintiffs "who have established a violation of the securities laws by their corporation and its officials, should be reimbursed by the corporation or its survivor for the costs of establishing the violation." Note carefully that plaintiffs' counsel was entitled to attorney's fees simply for finding a violation—there was no requirement that the plaintiff ultimately prevail in the sense of recovering damages. Indeed, in *Mills*, the shareholders ultimately recovered nothing, but the plaintiffs' attorneys' fees were still paid by the corporation.[27] *Mills* thus created a powerful economic incentive for lawyers to sue even in cases where it was clear that no injury had been caused by the violation.

The sweeping mandate in *Mills* to plaintiff's attorneys to go forth and uncover proxy rule violations was somewhat pared back by later

26.　396 U.S. 375 (1970).

27.　Mills v. Eltra Corp., 663 F.2d 760 (7th Cir.1981); Mills v. Electric Auto–Lite Co., 552 F.2d 1239 (7th Cir.1977).

Supreme Court decisions.[28] Today, the case law requires that the plaintiff's cause of action must create either a common fund from recovered damages or some substantial nonmonetary benefit in order for fees to be awarded.[29] Because injunctive relief likely satisfies the "substantial benefit" standard, however, there is still an incentive to sue even where it seems unlikely that monetary damages ultimately will be forthcoming.

2. *Key elements of the proxy cause of action*

When proxy litigation is grounded on an allegation of fraud, four key elements must be considered: (1) the materiality of the alleged misrepresentation or omission; (2) causation; (3) reliance; and (4) the defendant's state of mind. We consider these elements seriatim in the sections that follow.

3. *Materiality*

Recall that in *Mills v. Electric Auto–Lite Co.*,[30] the plaintiffs were shareholders of Auto–Lite, which was controlled by Mergenthaler Linotype Company, which in turn was controlled by American Manufacturing Co. Plaintiffs alleged that the proxy materials used in connection with the shareholder vote on a proposed merger between Auto–Lite and Mergenthaler were false and misleading because they failed to disclose that all of Auto–Lite's directors were Mergenthaler nominees.

Under *Mills*, a statement or omission is material when "it might have been considered important by a reasonable shareholder who was in the process of deciding how to vote." In other words, the statement or omission must have "a significant propensity to affect the voting process." Today, it is still the case that materiality is an essential element of the cause of action, but the definition of materiality has changed. In the *TSC Industries* case, the Supreme Court adopted a uniform standard of materiality under the securities laws: whether "there is a substantial likelihood that a reasonable shareholder would consider it important in deciding how to vote."[31]

Query whether the *Mills* omission would have been material under today's standard? On the one hand, the proxy statement did inform shareholders that Mergenthaler owned over 50% of Auto–Lite and that the boards of both companies had approved the merger. Arguably, reasonable shareholders should have been able to figure out for themselves that all of Auto–Lite's directors were elected by Mergenthaler. On the other hand, facts tending to show that the merger was approved by a board subject to a conflict of interest likely would be considered impor-

28. See, e.g., Alyeska Pipeline Service Co. v. Wilderness Society, 421 U.S. 240 (1975) (holding that absent statutory authorization, courts should not award attorneys fees to a plaintiff simply because plaintiff he served as a private attorney general).

29. See, e.g., Goldberger v. Integrated Resources, Inc., 209 F.3d 43 (2d Cir.2000);

Amalgamated Clothing and Textile Workers Union v. Wal–Mart Stores, Inc., 54 F.3d 69 (2d Cir.1995); Smillie v. Park Chemical Co., 710 F.2d 271 (6th Cir.1983).

30. 396 U.S. 375 (1970).

31. TSC Indus., Inc. v. Northway, Inc., 426 U.S. 438, 449 (1976).

tant by a reasonable shareholder. If the proxy statement had highlighted the fact that all of Auto–Lite's directors were Mergenthaler nominees, the conflict of interest would have been flagged, and the shareholders might have assessed the merger more carefully. (Note that in assessing materiality of disclosures, courts ignore the fact that most shareholders are rationally apathetic.)

In *Virginia Bankshares, Inc. v. Sandberg,*[32] the Supreme Court further refined the materiality standard by addressing its application to statements of belief or opinion. First American Bancshares (FABI) owned 100 percent of Virginia Bankshares (VBI). In turn, VBI owned 85 percent of First American Bank of Virginia (Bank). VBI merged Bank into itself, and paid Bank shareholders $42 per share. Under Virginia law (the applicable standard), the merger required a two-thirds vote. Because VBI owned 85 percent of the voting stock, a proxy solicitation was unnecessary to effect the transaction. Nevertheless, VBI solicited proxies from the other shareholders. In pertinent part, the proxy statement opined: "The Plan of Merger has been approved by the Board of Directors because it provides an opportunity for the Bank's public shareholders to achieve a high value for their shares." Plaintiff Sandberg (a minority shareholder) claimed that the shares were worth $60, that the directors knew $42 was a low price, and that the directors nevertheless went along with a low-priced merger because they hoped not to lose their seats on the board. Justice Souter's majority opinion concluded that the statement was material, but only after an astonishingly tortuous analysis. Justice Scalia's concurring opinion summed up the resulting rule of law far more succinctly:

> As I understand the Court's opinion, the statement "In the opinion of the Directors, this is a high value for the shares" would produce liability if in fact it was not a high value and the directors knew that. It would not produce liability if in fact it was not a high value but the directors honestly believed otherwise. The statement "The Directors voted to accept the proposal because they believe it offers a high value" would not produce liability if in fact the directors' genuine motive was quite different—except that it would produce liability if the proposal in fact did not offer a high value and the Directors knew that.

Judge Scalia went on to caution, however:

> [N]ot every sentence that has the word "opinion" in it, or that refers to motivation for directors' actions, leads us into this psychic thicket. Sometimes such a sentence actually represents facts as facts rather than opinions—and in that event no more need be done than apply the normal rules for § 14(a) liability. I think that is the situation here. In my view, the statement at issue in this case is most fairly read as affirming *separately* both the fact of the Di-

---

32.　501 U.S. 1083 (1991).

rectors' opinion *and* the accuracy of the facts upon which the opinion was assertedly based.

4. Causation

The law is well-settled that a proxy litigation plaintiff seeking monetary damages must show that the violation caused an injury to the shareholders—but it is a funny kind of causation. In *Mills*, the Supreme Court held that a plaintiff proves causation by showing that the proxy solicitation itself (as opposed to the defect) was an "essential link" in the accomplishment of the transaction.[33] Note that under this standard almost any violation "causes" an injury. In most transactions requiring shareholder approval, the proxy solicitation will be an essential link in accomplishing the transaction, because the solicitation was necessary to obtain the requisite shareholder vote.

In *Mills*, the Supreme Court left open the question of "whether causation could be shown where the management controls a sufficient number of shares to approve the transaction without any votes from the minority." In *Virginia Bankshares*, whose facts were recounted in the preceding section, the Supreme Court concluded that the requisite causation could not be shown in that situation.[34] Plaintiff advanced two explanations for VBI's decision to solicit proxies, both of which plaintiff argued supported a finding of causation. First, plaintiff argued that FABI wanted minority shareholder approval for reasons of goodwill, an explanation the court deemed too speculative to provide the requisite causation. Second, and far more significantly, plaintiff argued that VBI sought shareholder ratification to insulate the transaction from challenge under state law fiduciary duty rules. On the facts at bar, the Court also rejected this argument. Under Virginia law, VBI would be immunized from breach of fiduciary duty claims only if the transaction was approved by a majority of the minority shareholders after full disclosure. If VBI lied in the proxy material, there could be no valid approval. Absent valid approval, VBI gets no protection from the shareholder vote, and the proxy solicitation could not have been an essential step in the merger. Absent that showing, plaintiff cannot prove causation.[35]

5. Reliance

According to the prevailing view, reliance is not an essential element of the plaintiff's cause of action under the proxy rules.[36] At one time, however, the Ninth Circuit held that "shareholders who do not rely on allegedly misleading or deceptive proxy solicitations lack standing to

---

33. Mills v. Elec. Auto–Lite Co., 396 U.S. 375, 385 (1970).

34. Virginia Bankshares, Inc. v. Sandberg, 501 U.S. 1083 (1991).

35. If VBI had been honest, there might have been ratification and the proxy might have been an essential step, but because there would not have been a misleading statement, the plaintiff would still lose. Cf.

Howing Co. v. Nationwide Corp., 972 F.2d 700 (6th Cir.1992) (upon remand by the Supreme Court for reconsideration in light of *Virginia Bankshares*, holding that loss of a state law appraisal remedy in a freezeout merger satisfies the causation requirement).

36. See, e.g., Cowin v. Bresler, 741 F.2d 410 (D.C.Cir.1984).

assert direct (as opposed to derivative) equitable actions under § 14(a)."[37] The court subsequently qualified that rule, granting standing to sure directly to a shareholder who did not rely on the alleged misrepresentations, provided suit was brought before the shareholder vote occurred. The court explained that otherwise "a shareholder who learns of a material omission in a proxy statement before an election could never sue directly, because a shareholder aware of the omission will not rely on the proxy statement when voting. Further, no shareholder could sue before the election, because those shareholders satisfying [the reliance] requirement ... would be precisely those who were ignorant of the information necessary to sue until after they voted."[38]

In *Stahl v. Gibraltar Financial Corp.*,[39] the Ninth Circuit disavowed any remaining reliance requirement. Gibraltar Financial's board of directors proposed an amendment to the articles of incorporation to immunize its directors from monetary liability for certain breach of fiduciary duty claims. In the proxy solicitation materials, the board stated that it was unaware of any relevant pending litigation. Shareholder Stahl, however, was personally involved in just such a lawsuit. Knowing the solicitation material was false, he sued to enjoin the vote, but failed to obtain a preliminary injunction. At the meeting, Stahl voted against the amendment. After the amendment nevertheless passed, Stahl filed an amended complaint seeking to overturn the result. The district court held that Stahl lacked standing to sue, because he obviously could not have relied on the misleading statement. Believing "it is somewhat incongruous to deny standing to those shareholders who ferret out the misstatements but grant it to those who were beguiled," the Ninth Circuit reversed. Accordingly, even those "who do not vote their proxies in reliance on the alleged misstatements have standing to sue under section 14(a)—both before and after the vote is taken."

Although the court's policy analysis seems sensible at first blush, it proves misguided on closer examination. The Ninth Circuit's pre-*Stahl* regime was problematic only when viewed ex post. From an ex ante perspective, however, that regime did a better job of setting the right incentives. If a shareholder received proxy solicitation material that he knew to be misleading, the old regime required the shareholder to act immediately. If the shareholder promptly sued, the court had a chance to resolve the matter before the shareholder vote. If the court found material misrepresentations or omissions, the court could order corrective disclosures. As such, shareholders have an opportunity to make an informed decision. If the shareholder waits until after the meeting, however, much greater cost and difficulty may be incurred in undoing the corporate action. As a way to give shareholders an incentive to sue

37. Gaines v. Haughton, 645 F.2d 761, 774 (9th Cir.1981).

38. Western Dist. Council v. Louisiana Pac. Corp., 892 F.2d 1412, 1415–16 (9th Cir.1989).

39. 967 F.2d 335 (9th Cir.1992).

while the annual meeting can still resolve the questions at issue, the old rule thus made eminently good sense.

In addition its misunderstanding of the policies at stake, the Ninth Circuit also botched its analysis of precedent. In deciding that plaintiff had standing, the court relied on the Supreme Court's decision in *Virginia Bankshares.* Reliance was not an issue in *Virginia Bankshares.* On the facts of *Virginia Bankshares,* however, it is clear that the plaintiff had not been misled. Hence, plaintiff could not have satisfied the reliance requirement. The Ninth Circuit opined: "Because standing to sue is jurisdictional . . . we take the Supreme Court's consideration of Sandberg's § 14(a) action to mean that a plaintiff may bring a direct action after the complained-of proxy vote even where he has not himself relied on the challenged misstatements." But this is error.[40]

Although standing and merits issues are often intertwined, the issue of standing mainly has to do with questions such as that of "injury in fact." We can plausibly assume that Stahl was injured, probably by a decrease in the value of his stock. The proper issue thus is not whether Stahl has standing, but whether reliance is an element of the 14(a) cause of action. Why then did the Ninth Circuit treat this as a standing issue? If reliance is an element of the cause of action, Stahl might have standing but (a) would not be an adequate representative of the class of shareholders and (b) would not himself have a cause of action because he cannot prove an essential element of the claim. If reliance is an element of the cause of action, moreover, the fact that Sandberg did not rely on the misrepresentation at issue in *Virginia Bankshares* loses jurisprudential significance. Unlike issues of standing, which courts are supposed to consider sua sponte, failure to plead and prove an element of the cause of action and the Supreme Court's subsequent failure to address Sandberg's lack of reliance would not have any precedential implications. If one had a policy goal of encouraging private attorneys general, however, Stahl is exactly the sort of person one would want to encourage. He knows the company lied and is motivated to litigate the issue. Accordingly, one would structure the issue to ensure that Stahl is able to bring the cause of action. Which is exactly what the Ninth Circuit did. The curious thing is that the Supreme Court, led in large part by its more conservative justices, has been hacking away at the private attorneys general concept for many years. Yet, here we have an opinion by one of the most conservative 9th Circuit judges (Kozinski) that makes sense only as being intended to promote the use of private attorneys general. It is all quite odd.

---

40. In addition, the Ninth Circuit gave the Supreme Court far too much credit. One doubts that anyone on the Supreme Court even thought about this issue when deciding *Virginia Bankshares.* In applying Supreme Court decisions in the securities arena, one generally should not assume that the justices knew what they were doing. See Stephen M. Bainbridge & Mitu Gulati, How do Judges Maximize? (The Same Way Everybody Else Does–Boundedly): Rules of Thumb in Securities Fraud Opinions, ___ Emory L.J. ___ (2002).

6. *State of mind*

In both *Virginia Bankshares* and *TSC Industries*, the Supreme Court declined to decide whether the defendant must have acted with scienter or merely negligently in order to be held liable for fraud in a § 14(a) action.[41] As to issuer liability, and that of officers and directors, courts generally hold that negligence suffices.[42] As to collateral participants, such as accountants who certify financial statements contained in a proxy statement (as is done when a merger is to be voted on), at least one court has held that plaintiff must prove scienter.[43]

7. *Remedies*

Probably the most common remedy in proxy litigation is some form of prospective relief, such as an ex ante injunction against the shareholder vote. The court typically forbids the company from going forward with the shareholder meeting until the party soliciting proxies provides a new proxy statement, correcting whatever violation has been identified, and resolicits the proxies. Retrospective monetary relief, however, is available in appropriate cases. Damages must be shown, which means that plaintiff must establish a monetary injury. Because the violation itself is not an injury, plaintiff must show some sort of actual loss or harm resulting from the violation.

The most drastic option, at least from the firm's perspective, is a setting aside of the transaction. In *Mills*, for example, the merger could be undone and the two firms restored to their prior position as separate entities. This option is chosen very rarely. Courts tend to look at mergers and similar transactions the way a cook looks at an omelet: once the eggs have been scrambled, you can't put them back in the shells. When a merger takes place, all sorts of commingling takes place. Employees are fired or transferred, assets (such as bank accounts) are mixed up and reallocated, operating procedures are changed, and the like. The courts are very aware of this commingling process and therefore will set aside a merger only where it is possible to do so without harming the overall value of the firms and no other remedy can make the injured parties whole.

§ 10.5   Shareholder proposals under Rule 14a–8

The phenomenon of rational shareholder apathy suggests that most shareholders will have little interest in exercising a greater voice in

---

41. Note that the *Virginia Bankshares* approach to opinions and statements of belief makes the state of mind issue—why the board voted in favor of the merger—irrelevant with respect to such opinions. The question in such cases becomes simply: did the board knowingly misstate the underlying facts? If VBI's stock is worth $60 and the board members announce that it is worth $42 when they know it is worth $60, the plaintiff can sue.

42. See, e.g., Wilson v. Great American Indus., Inc., 855 F.2d 987 (2d Cir.1988); Gerstle v. Gamble–Skogmo, 478 F.2d 1281 (2d Cir.1973); see also Shidler v. All American Life & Fin. Corp., 775 F.2d 917 (8th Cir.1985) (rejecting an argument that strict liability was the standard).

43. Adams v. Standard Knitting Mills, 623 F.2d 422 (6th Cir.1980).

corporate decisionmaking via the proxy process. In the name of share-holder democracy, however, the SEC nevertheless periodically tries to encourage shareholder participation in corporate policymaking. One of the SEC's chief vehicles in this endeavor is the shareholder proposal rule—Rule 14a–8.

Absent Rule 14a–8, there would be no vehicle for shareholders to put proposals on the firm's proxy statement. Shareholders' only practicable alternative would be to conduct a proxy contest in favor of whatever proposal they wished to put forward. The chief advantage of the shareholder proposal rule, from the perspective of the proponent, thus is that it is cheap. The proponent need not pay any of the printing and mailing costs, all of which must be paid by the corporation, or otherwise comply with the expensive panoply of regulatory requirements.

Shareholder proposals traditionally were used mainly by social activists. Prior to the end of apartheid in South Africa, for example, many proposals favored divestment from South Africa. The rule is still widely used by social activists, but the rule also is increasingly being used by institutional investors to press matters more closely related to corporate governance. For example, proposals in recent years have included such topics as repealing takeover defenses, confidential proxy voting, regulating executive compensation, and the like.

Not all shareholder proposals must be included in the proxy statement. Rule 14a–8 lays out various eligibility requirements, which a shareholder must satisfy in order to be eligible to use the rule. The rule also lays out various procedural hurdles the shareholder must clear. Finally, the Rule identifies a number of substantive bases for excluding a proposal.

A. SEC review

The SEC referees the shareholder proposal process, albeit sometimes reluctantly. If the subject corporation's management believes the proposal can be excluded from the proxy statement, management must notify the SEC that the firm intends to exclude the proposal. A copy of the notice must also be sent to the proponent.[1] Management's notice must be accompanied by an opinion of counsel if any of the stated grounds entail legal issues, such as when management claims the proposal is improper under state corporate law. Although the rule does not require the proponent to reply, the SEC staff will consider any arguments the proponent may wish to make in support of the resolution's eligibility for inclusion in management's proxy statement.

If the SEC staff agrees that the proposal can be excluded, it issues a so-called no action letter, which states that the staff will not recommend

---

§ 10.5

1. Rule 14a–8(j). Under Rule 14a–8(f)(1), if the alleged defect is potentially remediable, the company must reply within 14 calendar days after receiving the proposal. If the proponent can remedy the alleged deficiency, it must do so within 14 calendar days. This process is separate from the procedure under which management notifies the SEC of its intent to exclude the proposal.

that the Commission bring an enforcement proceeding against the issuer if the proposal is excluded.[2] On the other hand, if the staff determines that the proposal should be included in management's proxy statement, the staff notifies the issuer that the SEC may bring an enforcement action if the proposal is excluded. The SEC staff can also take an intermediate position; in effect, it says to the proponent: "As your proposal or your supporting statement are presently drafted, they can be excluded under Rule 14a–8. However, if you revise them as follows, we believe that management must include the proposal." Whichever side loses at the staff level can ask the Commissioners to review the staff's decision. After review by the Commissioners, the losing party can seek judicial review by the United States Circuit Court of Appeals for the District of Columbia. These reviews are very rare. If management is the losing party, it typically acquiesces in the staff's decision. If the shareholder proponent loses, he typically seeks injunctive relief in federal district court.[3]

B. Eligibility

Under Rule 14a–8(b)(1), a shareholder-proponent must have owned at least 1% or $2,000 (whichever is less) of the issuer's voting securities for at least one year prior to the date on which the proposal is submitted. What happens if the individual shareholder can not satisfy these requirements? (1) Suppose three shareholders want to jointly support a proposal: A, who has owned $800 in stock for 2 years; B, who has owned $900 in stock for 18 months; and C, who has owned $500 in stock for 13 months. (2) D and E want to sponsor a separate proposal. D has owned $1200 in stock for two years; E has owned $1200 in stock for two months.

The SEC permits aggregation of shareholdings for purposes of meeting the dollar limit but not the time limit. In case 1 above, A, B, and C satisfy the eligibility standard because they jointly own more than $2000 in stock and have all held stock for more than one year. In case 2, however, D and E would not meet the eligibility test. Although they collectively satisfy the $2,000 requirement, they can not satisfy the time

---

2. On no action letters, see generally Donna M. Nagy, Judicial Reliance on Regulatory Interpretations in SEC No-action Letters: Current Problems and a Proposed Framework, 83 Cornell L. Rev. 921 (1998).

3. Although the proxy solicitation process itself is quite expensive, the marginal cost of any one proposal is small. Why then do corporate officials waste time and money fighting these proposals? One suspects part of the reason is managerial dislike for people they regard as pests, paranoids, bubbleheads, self-righteous protectors of the public morality, and self-appointed shareholder spokesmen. Another reason may be mana-

gerial suspicion that proponents are using proposals for purposes unrelated to the merits of the proposal, as where union pension funds make corporate governance proposals. Finally, some proposals can negatively impact the corporation, even if only indirectly. As the result of an anti-affirmative action shareholder proposal put forward by a white supremacist group, for example, AT & T received considerable negative attention and ultimately felt obliged to issue a statement deploring "hate-filled proposals." Social Activists Fighting Gag Rule—SEC Seeks Limits On Proxy Issues, The Record, May 17, 1992, at B1.

period requirement because E has held stock for less than a year. In order for their proposal to be included, they would have to find a third shareholder who has held at least $800 in stock for at least one year.

C. Procedural issues

1. Number of submissions

Per Rule 14a–8(c), the proponent may only submit one proposal per corporation per year. There is no limit to the number of companies to which a proponent can submit proposals in a given year, however. As long as the proponent meets the eligibility requirements for each firm, an activist thus may press the same proposal at multiple firms.

2. Prior submissions

The proponent may continue to submit the same proposal to the same firm year after year in the hopes that it will eventually be adopted by the shareholders, provided the proposal annually receives a specified level of support. A resubmitted proposal (or a substantially similar one) must be included if it was submitted: (i) once during the preceding five years and received 3% or more of the vote; (ii) twice in the preceding five years and received 6% or more of the vote the last time it was submitted; or (iii) 3 or more times in the preceding five years and received 10% or more of the vote the last time it was submitted.[4]

3. Showing up

Although the proxy system generally is designed to facilitate participation by shareholders who choose not to attend the shareholders' meeting, the shareholder proposal rule requires the proponent to present the proposal in person at the meeting. If the proponent fails to show up, Rule 14a–8(h) bars the proponent from using the rule at that company for the following two years.

4. Timing

The proposal must be submitted to the corporation at least 120 days before the date on which proxy materials were mailed for the previous year's annual shareholder's meeting.[5] For example, if the firm mailed its proxy materials on May 1, 2010, one counts back 120 days from May 1 to determine when a proposal must be submitted to be included in the 2011 proxy statement, which works out to January 2, 2011. The SEC is surprisingly strict in enforcing this requirement.

5. Length

Under Rule 14a–8(d), a proposal and any accompanying supporting statement may not exceed 500 words in length. (There is no length restriction on rebuttal statements by management.) In the past, a

---

4. Rule 14a–8(i)(12)　　　　　　　　**5.** Rule 14a–8(e)

shareholder who wished to make a more expansive case for his proposal thus was required to conduct a full-fledged proxy solicitation, with all the expense and regulatory burden associated therewith.

In 1998, a shareholder of Templeton Dragon Fund, a closed-end mutual fund,[6] came up with an interesting end-run around Rule 14a–8(d). The shareholder, Newgate LLP, proposed a precatory resolution recommending that the board convert the Fund to an open-end fund. The supporting statement read, in pertinent part: "We are limited by Federal law to a 500 word statement. Accordingly, we hope that shareholders will carefully review the 4 points set forth below. Additional historical performance data on this Fund can be accessed on Newgate's Internet site at [web address]." Templeton Dragon sought to exclude the proposal on grounds, inter alia, that the reference to Newgate's web site "circumvented the spirit, if not the letter," of Rule 14a–8(d)'s 500 word limit. Although the SEC staff did not permit Templeton Dragon to exclude the entire proposal, it did permit the fund to omit the reference to Newgate's web site.[7]

Analyzing the issues presented by the Templeton Dragon no action letter requires one to divine the purpose behind Rule 14a–8(d)'s 500 word limit. Is the rule solely intended to limit the cost Rule 14a–8 imposes on issuers? If so, the SEC's position seems indefensible. Issuer cost saving, however, is not the sole purpose of Rule 14a–8(d). The shareholder proposal rule permits shareholders to put proposals before their fellow shareholders without going to the expense of a full-blown proxy solicitation. In a sense, the rule is analogous to the various exceptions in Rule 14a–2 to the definition of a solicitation subject to the proxy rules. As with those exceptions, Rule 14a–8 must be narrowly construed to prevent it from swallowing the general requirement that those wishing to affect shareholder voting must solicit proxies in a fashion complying with the SEC's disclosure, filing, and dissemination rules. The material contained in Newgate's web site presumably was intended to affect the outcome of the vote on its proposal. As such, the web site constituted a solicitation of proxies.[8] Because the material on

---

6. A mutual fund is an investment company, which sells units (called shares) to investors and then invests the proceeds in a diversified portfolio of securities. An open-end fund continually sells new shares to investors and redeems those tendered by shareholders. The daily price of an open-end fund's shares is determined by the fund's per share net asset value, which is calculated by adding up all of the fund's assets (mainly cash and securities), subtracting any liabilities, and dividing the result by the number of outstanding shares. A closed-end fund issues a limited number of shares in an initial public offering, which are typically listed for trading on a major stock exchange. The value of a closed-end fund's shares depends not just on the

fund's net asset value but also on other stock market factors, such as the supply and demand for the fund's stock. Closed-end funds commonly trade at a discount to the net asset value, which sometimes can be quite substantial. When a closed-end fund trades at a substantial discount to its net asset value, converting the fund to an open-end form allows the fund's investors to capture the difference.

7. In re Templeton Dragon Fund, Inc., SEC No Action Letter (June 15, 1998), 1998 WL 337469.

8. See, e.g., Long Island Lighting Co. v. Barbash, 779 F.2d 793, 796 (2d Cir.1985) (any communication is a solicitation if it, "seen in the totality of the circumstances, is

the web site had not been filed with the SEC, could be readily and constantly modified by Newgate, and did not comply with the disclosure requirements, Templeton Dragon contended—and the SEC agreed—that its inclusion in the proposal would constitute an impermissible end run around the proxy rules.

The SEC recently reversed the position taken in the Templeton Dragon no action letter.[9] In doing so, the SEC implicitly accepted the proponent's argument that censoring of web addresses impinged on free speech rights by impeding the dissemination of investment information. Yet, all proxy regulation impinges upon speech rights. Assuming the proxy regulatory regime is constitutional despite its impact on corporate and shareholder speech, it is not clear why the web page of a proponent should not also be deemed a solicitation of proxies.[10]

D. Substantive grounds for excluding a proposal

1. *Proper subjects for shareholder action*

If you closely examine a large number of shareholder proposals, you will notice that most are phrased as recommendations. The use of precatory language follows from Rule 14a–8(i)(1), which provides that a shareholder proposal must be a proper subject of action for security holders under the law of the state of incorporation. Recall that under state law, all corporate powers shall be exercised by or under the authority of the board.[11] Consequently, state corporate law commits most powers of initiation to the board of directors—the shareholders may not initiate corporate actions, they may only approve or disapprove of corporate actions placed before them for a vote. The SEC's explanatory note to Rule 14a–8(i)(1) recognizes this aspect of state law by explaining that mandatory proposals may be improper. The note goes on, however, to explain the SEC's belief that a shareholder proposal is proper if phrased as a request or recommendation to the board.

'reasonably calculated' to influence the shareholders' votes").

9. In re Electronic Data Systems Corp., SEC No Action Letter (March 24, 2000), 2000 WL 354383. See also In re The Gillette Company, SEC No Action Letter (February 1, 2001), 2001 WL 121998.

10. An issue not addressed in the Templeton Dragon no action letter is whether Newgate could design the web site to comply with the exemption provided by Rule 14a–1(*l*)(2)(iv) for communications by shareholders who do not otherwise solicit proxies and who simply make a public statement of how they intend to vote and the "reasons therefor." The key difficulty here is Rule 14a–1(*l*)(2)(iv)(A), which requires that the statement be "made by means of speeches in public forums, press releases, published or broadcast opinions,

statements, or advertisements appearing in a broadcast media, or newspaper, magazine or other bona fide publication disseminated on a regular basis." Internet web sites were relatively unimportant when the rule was adopted in 1992 and it will be interesting to see if the SEC amends the rule to include them. One argument against doing so is that the exemption appears to be directed towards relatively transitory statements. In contrast to a brief and ephemeral newspaper ad, which a shareholder may see once but then discard, a web site is constantly available and may contain considerable detail. In any event, with internet proxy voting becoming more widespread, the concomitant issue of internet proxy solicitations is likely to remain an area of intense regulatory activity.

11. See, e.g., DGCL § 141(a).

If a precatory proposal passes, the board is not obligated to implement it. Indeed, a board decision not to do so should be protected by the business judgment rule. On the other hand, the risk of adverse publicity and poor shareholder relations may encourage a board to implement an approved precatory proposal even where the board opposes the proposal on the merits.

Shareholder amendments to the bylaws may constitute an exception to the general rule that proposals cannot mandate board action. A bylaw that relates only to a specific business decision probably is invalid, as an improper intrusion on the board's exclusive power to make ordinary business decisions. Broader, more fundamental bylaws, especially ones that impose constraints rather than order the board to take action, however, pose a more difficult set of problems. The legality of such bylaws under state corporate law is sharply contested.[12] Where lawful, however, a mandatory shareholder proposal to adopt such a bylaw presumably could not be excluded under Rule 14a–8(i)(1).

2.   *False or misleading proposals*

Rule 14a–8(c)(3) provides that a proposal may be omitted if it violates any of the proxy rules, including Rule 14a–9 which prohibits false or misleading statements. Consequently, the issuer may exclude proposals containing misrepresentations or groundless assertions. For example, SEC explanatory note (b) to Rule 14a–9 provides that material impugning character or personal reputation violates Rule 14a–9 if made without factual foundation. Where the proposal impugns management's character, the SEC staff usually will require that the proposal can be included in the proxy statement if the proponent agrees to drop the offensive language or is able to factually demonstrate that it is true. If the proponent fails to provide the requisite factual basis for his assertion, and also refuses to revise the supporting statement, the whole proposal can be excluded.

3.   *Not otherwise significant*

Rule 14a–8(i)(5) provides that a proposal relating to operations accounting for less than 5 percent of the firm's assets, earnings or sales, and that is not otherwise significantly related to the firm's business, may be omitted from the proxy statement. The principal problem here is deciding whether a proposal falling short of the various 5% thresholds is "otherwise significantly related to the firm's business." The classic case is *Lovenheim v. Iroquois Brands, Ltd.*[13] The defendant imported various food stuffs into the United States, including pâté de foie gras from France. Lovenheim suspected that Iroquois Brands' French suppliers forced fed their geese, which produces larger livers, and which Loven-

---

12. Conversely, it seems clear that a corporate bylaw cannot trump the federal securities laws. Hence, bylaws that impede shareholders from making use of Rule 14a–8 appear to be invalid. See SEC v. Trans- america Corp., 163 F.2d 511, 518 (3d Cir. 1947) (holding that the SEC's regulatory powers "cannot be frustrated by a corporate bylaw").

13. 618 F.Supp. 554 (D.D.C.1985).

heim believed was a form of animal cruelty. Lovenheim proposed that Iroquois Brands form a committee to investigate the methods used by the firm's suppliers in producing pâté and report its findings to the shareholders.

Iroquois Brands pâté operations clearly did not satisfy Rule 14a–8(i)(5)'s five percent threshold tests. Pâté sales constituted a mere $79,000 per year, on which Iroquois Brands lost money, relative to annual revenues of $141 million and profits of $6 million. The result therefore turned on whether the pâté operations were "otherwise significantly related" to its business.[14] Iroquois Brands contended that the phrase related to economic significance. Lovenheim contended that noneconomic tests of a proposal's significance were appropriate.

The court agreed with Lovenheim, holding that while the proposal related "to a matter of little economic significance,"[15] the term "otherwise significantly related" is not limited to economic significance. Rather, matters of ethical and social significance also can be considered. The court articulated four rationales for its interpretation: (1) the rule itself was ambiguous; (2) the SEC previously had required inclusion of important social policy questions even where less than 1% of the firm's assets or earnings were implicated by the question; (3) in adopting the present 5% threshold tests, the SEC said proposals falling short of the thresholds still must be included if their significance appeared on the face of the proposal; (4) the earlier Medical Committee decision implied that proposals involving general political and social concerns were acceptable.[16]

As evidence that Lovenheim's proposal "ethical or social" significance, the court observed that humane treatment of animals was one of the foundations of western civilization, citing various old and new statutes, ranging from the Seven Laws of Noah to the Massachusetts

---

14. Courts have not always applied the 5% standards as precisely as they should. In New York City Employees' Retirement System v. Dole Food Co., Inc., 795 F.Supp. 95 (S.D.N.Y.1992), for example, the New York City employees' pension fund petitioned Dole to include a proposal recommending that Dole form a committee to study the impact of various national health care reform proposals would have on Dole.

The district court ordered Dole to include the proposal in the proxy statement. In rejecting Dole's arguments under Rule 14a–8(i)(5), the court held that health care reform had economic significance because health insurance and care imposed large financial costs on Dole. Specifically, the court opined: "It is substantially likely that Dole's health insurance outlays constitute more than five percent of its income." The opinion does not set out be any evidence as to Dole's health insurance expenses. Query whether courts ought simply assume away a critical element of the standard. In any

event, the court also misconstrued Rule 14a–8(i)(5). The rule does not speak of expenses that represent more than 5 percent of income. The Rule talks about operations—lines of business—that represent 5 percent of the company's total business, measured in various ways, none of which include expenditures. Despite the court's flawed reasoning, however, the result is probably right. Employee health benefits (or the decision not to provide such benefits) are a matter of considerable economic significance. Federal changes to the health insurance system doubtless would have had a major economic impact on employers. Accordingly, the proposal arguably had economic significance even though it did not satisfy any of the 5% thresholds.

15. Lovenheim v. Iroquois Brands, Ltd., 618 F.Supp. 554, 559 (D.D.C.1985).

16. See Medical Comm. for Human Rights v. SEC, 432 F.2d 659, 680 (D.C.Cir. 1970), vacated as moot, 404 U.S. 403 (1972).

Bay Colony's animal protection statute of 1641 to modern federal and state humane laws. Additional support came from the fact that "leading organizations in the field of animal care" supported measures aimed at eliminating force feeding.

Query whether we want federal bureaucrats or even federal judges deciding whether a politically-charged proposal has enough ethical or social significance to justify its inclusion in the proxy statement. Think about your least favorite political cause. Under *Lovenheim*, can the firm omit a shareholder proposal about that cause? If so, on what basis can you justify omitting that proposal and requiring inclusion of the *Lovenheim* proposal? The issue is particularly troubling because many proposals have less to do with a company's economic performance than with providing a soap-box for the proponent's pet political cause. In *Lovenheim*, for example, plaintiff knew that his proposal had little economic significance. Instead, he wanted to make a political statement about animal cruelty.

Here is a plausible alternative to the *Lovenheim* approach: Courts should ask whether a reasonable shareholder of this issuer would regard the proposal as having material economic importance for the value of his shares. This standard is based on the well-established securities law principle of materiality. It is intended to exclude proposals made primarily for the purpose of promoting general social and political causes, while requiring inclusion of proposals a reasonable investor would believe are relevant to the value of his investment. Such a test seems desirable so as to ensure that an adopted proposal redounds to the benefit of all shareholders, not just those who share the political and social views of the proponent. Absent such a standard, the shareholder proposal rule becomes nothing less than a species of private eminent domain by which the federal government allows a small minority to appropriate someone else's property—the company is a legal person, after all, and it is the company's proxy statement at issue—for use as a soap-box to disseminate their views. Because the shareholders hold the residual claim, and all corporate expenditures thus come out of their pocket, it is not entirely clear why other shareholders should have to subsidize speech by a small minority.

4.   Ordinary business

Rule 14a–8(i)(7) allows the issuer to exclude so-called "ordinary business matters." The question here is whether a proposal is an ordinary matter for the board or an extraordinary matter on which shareholder input is appropriate. The answer hinges on whether the proposal involves significant policy questions. As for deciding whether a policy question is significant, most courts assume that *Lovenheim*-style ethical or social significance suffices.

The SEC's policy on enforcing Rule 14a–8(i)(7) with respect to shareholder proposals concerned mainly with social—rather than economic—issues has fluctuated over the years. The SEC long handled such proposals on a case-by-case basis. In 1992, however, it departed from that practice and adopted a bright-line position that for the first time effectively excluded an entire category of social issue proposals. Cracker Barrel Old Country Stores attempted to exclude a shareholder proposal calling on the board of directors to include sexual orientation in its anti-discrimination policy. In a no action letter issued by the SEC's Division of Corporation Finance, the Commission took the position that all employment-related shareholder proposals raising social policy issues could be excluded under the "ordinary business" exclusion.

Subsequent litigation developed two issues. First, if a shareholder proponent sued a company whose management relied on *Cracker Barrel* to justify excluding an employment-related proposal from the proxy statement, should the reviewing court defer to the SEC's position? In *Amalgamated Clothing and Textile Workers Union v. Wal–Mart Stores, Inc.*,[17] a federal district court held that deference was not required and, moreover, that proposals relating to a company's affirmative action policies were not per se excludible as ordinary business under Rule 14a–8(i)(7).

Second, was the SEC's *Cracker Barrel* position valid? In other words, could the SEC properly apply the *Cracker Barrel* interpretation in internal agency processes, such as when issuing a no action letter? In *New York City Employees' Retirement System v. SEC*, the district court ruled that the SEC's *Cracker Barrel* position was itself invalid because the SEC had failed to comply with federal administrative procedures in promulgating the position. The Second Circuit reversed, thereby allowing the SEC to apply *Cracker Barrel* internally, but in doing so concurred with the trial court's view that *Cracker Barrel* was not binding on courts.[18]

In 1998, the SEC adopted amendments to Rule 14a–8 that, among other things, reversed its *Cracker Barrel* position.[19] In promulgating this change, the SEC emphasized that employment discrimination was a consistent topic of public debate, thereby highlighting the on-going importance of *Lovenheim*-style social and ethical considerations. Indeed, the SEC explicitly noted its belief that the Rule 14a–8(i)(7) exception did not justify excluding proposals that raise significant social policy issues.

Reversal of the *Cracker Barrel* position returned the SEC to its prior case-by-case approach. Specific management decisions relating to employment, such as hiring, promotion, and termination of employees, as well as other business decisions, such as product lines and quality, remain excludable. The SEC does not want shareholders to "micromanage" the company. Proposals broadly relating to such matters but

17. 821 F.Supp. 877 (S.D.N.Y.1993).

18. New York City Employees' Retirement Sys. v. SEC, 45 F.3d 7 (2d Cir.1995).

19. Amendments To Rules On Shareholder Proposals, Exchange Act Release No. 40018 (May 21, 1998).

focusing on significant social policy issues, such as affirmative action and other employment discrimination matters, generally are not excludable.[20]

We are thus returned to the frustratingly ambiguous task of deciding whether a particular proposal is "significant." On this issue, the federal district court decision in *Austin v. Consolidated Edison Company of New York, Inc.*[21] is both instructive and troubling. The plaintiffs put forward a proposal that the issuer provide more generous pension benefits to its employees. The court authorized the issuer to exclude the proposal as impinging on an ordinary business matter. Acknowledging that shareholder proposals relating to senior executive compensation were not excludable, the court observed that the issue of "enhanced pension rights" for workers "has not yet captured public attention and concern as has the issue of senior executive compensation." Does this mean that the significance of a proposal turns on whether its subject matter has become a routine story for CNBC or CNN?

The result in *Austin*—exclusion—doubtless was correct. The proposal was put forward by shareholders who were also officials of a union that represented company employees.[22] The proposal mandated a specific change in company pension policy; namely, to allow employees to retire with full benefits after 30 years of service regardless of age. This was precisely the sort of (self-interested) micro-management that even the SEC agrees ought not be allowed. Yet, we need a better test. Here we advocate the same standard proposed with respect to Rule 14a–8(i)(5)'s "otherwise significantly related" prong; namely, whether a reasonable shareholder of this issuer would regard the proposal as having material economic importance for the value of his shares. Again, this standard would lead to exclusion of proposals made primarily for the purpose of promoting general social and political causes, while requiring inclusion of proposals a reasonable investor would believe are relevant to the value of his investment.

§ 10.6 The boundary between federal proxy regulation and state corporate law

Recall that the corporate norm is one-vote per share. State law permits deviations from the norm, however, authorizing corporations to adopt various forms of dual class voting schemes. In the late 1980s, dual class stock provided the setting for the principal test to date of federal

---

20. See, e.g., New York City Employees' Retirement Sys. v. Dole Food Co., 795 F.Supp. 95 (S.D.N.Y.1992), in which the proponent offered a proposal requesting Dole to study the potential impact on the company of various pending national health care reform proposals. Dole relied on Rule 14a–8(i)(7) to exclude the proposal, among other provisions. The court rejected Dole's argument. Although employee benefits generally are an ordinary business matter, "a significant strategic decision" as to employee benefits fell outside the scope of ordinary business matters.

21. 788 F.Supp. 192 (S.D.N.Y.1992).

22. The issuer argued these facts entitled it to exclude the proposal as under Rule 14a–8(i)(4). Under that provision, an issuer may exclude proposals designed to redress a private grievance or further a private interest of the proponent not shared with the shareholders at large. The court declined to reach that issue.

regulatory power over shareholder voting rights. The story illustrates not only the limits of the SEC's regulatory purview, but also the SEC's ability to evade those limits.

A. SEC rule 19c–4 and the *Business Roundtable* decision

As we saw above, the NYSE long refused to list issuers having either a class of nonvoting common outstanding or multiple classes of common stock with disparate voting rights.[1] The AMEX likewise refused to list nonvoting common stock, but its policy with respect to disparate voting rights plans was more flexible. Issuers adopting such plans would be listed as long as the plan satisfied certain guidelines designed to create a minimum level of participation to which the lesser voting rights class was entitled. In contrast, the NASD imposed no voting rights listing standards in either the over-the-counter market or the NASDAQ system.

With the renewal of corporate interest in dual class stock during the 1980s, however, issuers began pressuring the NYSE to adopt a more flexible listing standard. In 1988, the SEC responded by adopting Rule 19c–4, which effectively amended the rules of all the exchanges (and the NASD) to prohibit them from listing an issuer's equity securities if the company issued securities or took other corporate action nullifying, restricting, or disparately reducing the voting rights of existing shareholders.[2] As such, Rule 19c–4 was the SEC's first direct attempt to regulate substantively a matter of corporate governance applicable to all public corporations. The Business Roundtable challenged the Rule, arguing that corporate governance regulation is primarily a matter for state law and that the SEC therefore had no authority to adopt rules affecting substantive aspects of corporate voting rights. The D.C. Circuit agreed, striking down the rule as beyond the Commission's regulatory authority.[3]

The Commission based its authority to adopt Rule 19c–4 on its powers under Securities Exchange Act § 19(c), which permits it to amend exchange rules provided that the Commission's action furthers the Act's purposes. Rule 19c–4 fell because the D.C. Circuit determined that its attempt to regulate corporate voting rights furthered none of the Exchange Act's purposes. In defending Rule 19c–4, the SEC trotted out its long-standing view that § 14(a) was intended to promote corporate democracy. In striking down the Rule, however, the D.C. Circuit adopted a much narrower view of § 14(a)'s purposes. According to the court, federal proxy regulation has two principal goals. First, and foremost, it regulates the disclosures shareholders receive when they are asked to vote. Second, it regulates the procedures by which proxy solicitations are

§ 10.6

1. See § 10.2.

2. For a detailed treatment of Rule 19c–4 and the surrounding legal issues, see Stephen M. Bainbridge, The Short Life and Resurrection of SEC Rule 19c–4, 69 Wash. U. L.Q. 565 (1991).

3. Business Roundtable v. SEC, 905 F.2d 406 (D.C.Cir.1990).

conducted. Section 14(a)'s purposes thus do not include regulating substantive aspects of shareholder voting.[4]

Although § 14(a)'s legislative history is relatively sparse, it tends to support the D.C. Circuit's interpretation. In defending Rule 19c–4, the SEC placed great weight on a House Committee Report statement that "[f]air corporate suffrage is an important right that should attach to every equity security bought on a public exchange."[5] While it is indisputable that Congress intended § 14(a) to give the SEC broad powers over corporate proxy solicitations, there is reason to believe that Congress had in mind an entirely different set of issues than those raised by nonvoting stock when it referred to fair corporate suffrage.

The controversy over federal proxy regulation was resolved early in the legislative process. As originally introduced, the proxy provision mandated substantial disclosures and gave the SEC authority to adopt additional disclosure requirements. The proposal met with substantial criticism. For example, AT & T pointed out that the bill required the

---

4. In Chevron USA, Inc. v. Natural Res. Def. Council, Inc., 467 U.S. 837 (1984), the Supreme Court opined that where Congress has "left a gap for the agency to fill," the agency's regulations will be "given controlling weight unless they are arbitrary, capricious, or manifestly contrary to the statute." Id. at 843–44. The D.C. Circuit questioned whether *Chevron* even applied to the Rule 19c–4 litigation, since the Business Roundtable's challenge "might be characterized as involving a limit on the SEC's jurisdiction" as to which deference may be inappropriate. Although the D.C. Circuit nonetheless assumed that the SEC was entitled to deference, it held that the Rule was contrary to the clearly expressed will of Congress and thus invalid even under *Chevron*. Business Roundtable v. SEC, 905 F.2d 406, 408 (D.C.Cir.1990).

5. H.R. Rep. No. 1383, 73d Cong., 2d Sess. 13 (1934). In addition to arguing from the legislative history and prior administrative practices, the SEC pointed to some loose language in a few cases suggesting a broad reading of the Congressional intent for § 14(a). Of course, prior to the D.C. Circuit's decision to invalidate Rule 19c–4 there were no judicial interpretations of the Act squarely on point. Moreover, when the cases upon which the SEC relied are read in context, they too support the conclusion that § 14(a) was narrowly drawn to deal with disclosure and procedural abuses. The Commission, for example, placed great emphasis on a prior D.C. Circuit decision describing the principal purpose of § 14 as assuring "to corporate shareholders the ability to exercise their right—some would say their duty—to control the important decisions which affect them in their capaci-

ty as stockholders and owners of the corporation." Medical Committee for Human Rights v. SEC, 432 F.2d 659, 680–81 (D.C.Cir.1970) (citations omitted), vacated as moot, 404 U.S. 403 (1972). This comment, however, was made in the rather different context of applying the shareholder proposal rule. Notice, moreover, the court's emphasis on the ability to exercise voting rights, which seems consistent with the interpretation that § 14 was intended solely to assure that shareholders could make effective use of whatever voting rights state law provides. As the Supreme Court once put it: "The purpose of § 14(a) is to prevent management or others from obtaining authorization for corporate action by means of deceptive or inadequate disclosure in proxy solicitation." J. I. Case Co. v. Borak, 377 U.S. 426, 431 (1964). Other judicial interpretations of § 14 are also consistent with the notion that it was directed at assuring full disclosure and a fair opportunity to exercise corporate voting rights (of course, these decisions were rendered in cases where it was those aspects of the rules that were at issue). E.g., Mills v. Electric Auto–Lite Co., 396 U.S. 375, 381 (1970); Greater Iowa Corp. v. McLendon, 378 F.2d 783, 795 (8th Cir.1967); Dann v. Studebaker–Packard Corp., 288 F.2d 201, 208 (6th Cir.1961); SEC v. Transamerica Corp., 163 F.2d 511, 518 (3d Cir.1947), cert. denied, 332 U.S. 847 (1948); NUI Corp. v. Kimmelman, 593 F.Supp. 1457, 1469 (D.N.J.1984); Freedman v. Barrow, 427 F.Supp. 1129, 1147 (S.D.N.Y.1976); Leighton v. American Telephone & Telegraph Co., 397 F.Supp. 133, 138 (S.D.N.Y.1975); Studebaker Corp. v. Allied Products Corp., 256 F.Supp. 173, 188–89 (W.D.Mich.1966).

proxy statement to include a list of all shareholders being solicited, which would force AT & T to prepare three large volumes, at a total cost of $950,000, every time proxies were solicited. Section 14(a) was redrafted in response to these criticisms. In doing so, Congress did what it often does when it has a tough problem to solve: it told somebody else to solve it. In effect, the Act simply made it unlawful to solicit proxies "in contravention of such rules and regulations as the Commission may prescribe as necessary or appropriate in the public interest or for the protection of investors."[6]

In implementing § 14(a), the SEC has affected corporate governance to a greater extent than under any other provision of the Exchange Act. Rule 14a–4 restricts management's use of discretionary power to cast votes obtained by a proxy solicitation. Rule 14a–7 requires management cooperation in transmitting an insurgent's proxy materials to shareholders. Rule 14a–8 requires management to include qualified shareholder proposals in the corporation's proxy statement at the firm's expense. Although these sorts of intrusions into internal corporate affairs were anticipated by some opponents of the legislation, § 14(a)'s impact on corporate governance in fact is rather narrow. Most of the SEC's proxy rules relate to disclosure. Full disclosure of matters to come before a shareholder meeting, for example, was the original justification for the shareholder proposal rule.[7] While the Commission's authority under § 14(a) is not limited to disclosure issues, its other proxy rules relate to the procedures by which the proxies are to be prepared, solicited, and used.

The limited scope of proxy regulation is consistent with a proper interpretation of the phrase "fair corporate suffrage." In using that term, Congress did not mean to address the substantive question of how many votes per share to which a stockholder is entitled. Instead, as the D.C. Circuit recognized in *Business Roundtable*, Congress was talking about an entirely different concern: the need for full disclosure and fair solicitation procedures.[8] The House Committee, for example, contended

6. Securities Exchange Act, Pub. L. No. 73–291, § 14(a), 48 Stat. 881, 895 (1934). As originally adopted, § 14(a) applied only to securities registered on a national securities exchange. In 1964, it was amended to apply to over-the-counter issuers as well. Otherwise, it remains largely intact.

7. Medical Comm. for Human Rights v. SEC, 432 F.2d 659, 677 (D.C.Cir.1970), vacated as moot, 404 U.S. 403 (1972).

8. The historical context in which § 14(a) was adopted supports this interpretation. When the Exchange Act was first being considered, state corporate law was largely silent on the issue of corporate communications with shareholders. It only required that the corporation send shareholders a notice of a shareholders meeting, stating where and when the meeting would

be held and briefly stating the issues to come before the meeting. By that time, of course, the proxy system of voting was well-established. So too were complaints about its operation. One common concern was that corporate managers were soliciting proxies from shareholders without giving shareholders enough information on which to make an informed voting decision. Another was that management used its control of the proxy process to ensure that only those directors who were acceptable to management were elected. In 1932, for example, Berle and Means complained that the proxy machinery had "become one of the principal instruments not by which a stockholder exercises power over the management of the enterprise, but by which his power is separated from him." Adolf A.

that management should not be able to perpetuate itself in office through "misuse" of corporate proxies.[9] It noted that insiders were using the proxy system to retain control "without adequate disclosure." It protested that insiders were soliciting proxies "without fairly informing" shareholders of the purpose of the solicitation. The passage concludes by stating that in light of these abuses § 14(a) gives the "Commission power to control the conditions under which proxies may be solicited...." In sum, the passage says nothing about the substance of the shareholders' voting rights. Instead, the focus is solely on enabling shareholders to make effective use of whatever voting rights they possess. Other references to proxy solicitations elsewhere in the legislative history likewise focus on disclosure concerns.[10]

B. Implications of *Business Roundtable* for SEC regulation of proxies

In sum, the D.C. Circuit correctly confirmed that the SEC has extensive authority to adopt rules assuring full disclosure and fair solicitation procedures. However, the court also drew a critical distinction between substantive and procedural regulation of shareholder voting. As to the former, the SEC has little, if any, authority. This holding has important implications for the SEC's scheme of proxy regulation. As we have seen, the SEC's existing proxy rules affect corporate governance in a variety of ways. Among these are the restrictions on the form of proxies and the use of discretionary voting authority, the requirement of management cooperation in disseminating an insurgent's proxy materials, and the obligation to include shareholder proposals in the company's proxy statement.

The SEC's authority to adopt some of these rules, especially the

---

Berle & Gardiner C. Means, The Modern Corporation and Private Property 139 (1932). While it is thus true that concerns were raised about management perpetuating itself in office, those concerns were phrased in terms of abuses of the process by which proxies were solicited. Indeed, commentators of the time were sharply critical of allegedly widespread procedural abuses. For example, proxy cards often failed to give shareholders the option of voting against a proposal. If the shareholder did not wish to support the proposal, his only option was to refrain from returning the proxy. Congress was made aware of these concerns in some detail. Thomas Corcoran, for example, told the House Committee that "[p]roxies, as solicitations are made now, are a joke." Stock Exchange Regulation: Hearings before the House Interstate and Foreign Commerce Comm., 73d Cong., 2d Sess. 140 (1934). He testified at length about the lack of disclosure provided to shareholders and abuses of the

proxy solicitation process. In answer to a question as to how these abuses could be prevented, he referred solely to the need for better disclosures. Similarly, in a brief supporting the Exchange Act's constitutionality, Corcoran and Benjamin Cohen stated that the proxy provisions were "designed to make available to the investor reasonable information regarding the possibility of control of the corporation...." Other favorable references to § 14 in the hearings are to like effect.

9. H.R. Rep. No. 1383, 73d Cong., 2d Sess. 13 (1934).

10. For detailed treatment of § 14(a)'s legislative history, and relevant subsequent legislative nonevents, see Stephen M. Bainbridge, Redirecting State Takeover Laws at Proxy Contests, 1992 Wis. L. Rev. 1071; Stephen M. Bainbridge, The Short Life and Resurrection of SEC Rule 19c–4, 69 Was. U. L.Q. 565 (1991)

shareholder proposal provision, has been questioned.[11] The *Business Roundtable* decision provides some support for these arguments. The opinion requires courts to determine whether a challenged rule is substantive or procedural. As the court recognized, there is "a murky area between substance and procedure," which may resist classification.[12] Nonetheless, the opinion offers a few signposts by which future cases can be resolved. In particular, consider the distinction the court drew between Rule 19c–4 and Rule 14a–4(b)(2)'s requirement that proxies give shareholders an opportunity to withhold authority to vote for individual director nominees. In the court's view, the latter "bars a kind of electoral tying arrangement, and may be supportable as a control over management's power to set the voting agenda, or, slightly more broadly, voting procedures," while "Rule 19c–4 much more directly interferes with the substance of what shareholders may enact."

Rules addressing unfair solicitation procedures thus should pass muster. The rules on the form of a proxy card, discretionary authority and mailing of insurgent materials, for example, plausibly can be said to relate to the Congressional goal of assuring procedural fairness in proxy contests. Each prevents management from using its control of the proxy solicitation process to manipulate the result of shareholder elections. As a means of preventing management coercion of voters, a confidential voting rule might pass muster as relating to the same sort of procedural unfairness.

The case for the shareholder proposal rule is less compelling. Even though full disclosure of all matters to come before a shareholders meeting was its original justification, at first blush the rule does not seem to have very much to do with either purpose of § 14(a). However, absent the rule, shareholders have no practical means of holding management accountable through the voting process or even affecting the agenda. As such, it may be supportable—just barely—"as a control over management's power to set the voting agenda."

C. The troubling epilogue

Slippery slope arguments are often the last refuge of those with no better case, but Rule 19c–4 was indeed the proverbial camel's nose. There simply was no firebreak between substantive federal regulation of dual class stock and a host of other corporate voting issues raising similar concerns. Nor did laws affecting shareholder voting rights differ in principle or theory from any other corporate governance rules. Having once entered the field of corporate governance regulation, the SEC would have been hard-pressed to justify stopping with dual class stock. Creeping federalization of corporate law was a plausible outcome. The D.C. Circuit quite properly foreclosed this possibility.

---

11. See, e.g., George W. Dent, Jr., SEC Rule 14a–8: A Study in Regulatory Failure, 30 N.Y.L. Sch. L. Rev. 1 (1985); Susan W. Liebeler, A Proposal to Rescind the Share-holder Proposal Rule, 18 Ga. L. Rev. 425 (1984).

12. Business Roundtable v. SEC, 905 F.2d 406 (D.C.Cir.1990).

The SEC could have sought Supreme Court review of the *Business Roundtable* decision, but did not. The SEC could have sought appropriate countervailing legislation from Congress, but did not. Instead, the Commission made use of what has been aptly called its "raised eyebrow" powers.[13] By virtue of the unique relationship between the SEC and the exchanges, the Commission naturally has considerable informal influence over exchange rulemaking. When the D.C. Circuit invalidated Rule 19c–4, SEC Chairman Arthur Levitt encouraged the three principal domestic securities exchanges—NYSE, AMEX, and NASDAQ—to adopt a uniform voting rights policy essentially tracking Rule 19c–4.[14]

The SEC's use of its "raised eyebrow" powers in this context is troubling on two grounds. First, as a regulatory agency with prosecutorial authority, the Commission routinely punishes those who seek to evade the law. Unfortunately, rather than obeying the law applicable to it, the Commission chose to end-run *Business Roundtable* by pressuring the exchanges to adopt "voluntary" listing standards modeled on Rule 19c–4. A fine example that sets. How can the Commission justly order enforcement proceedings against those who seek to evade the securities laws when it put so much time, talent, and effort into evading the rules applicable to it?[15]

Second, there are important federalism reasons for placing limits on the SEC's regulatory authority over questions of corporate governance. Through use of its "raised eyebrow" powers over exchange listing standards, the SEC may finally have found a way to end-run both Congress and the Supreme Court and create uniform, national corporate governance standards whenever it chooses to do so. As *Business Roundtable* confirmed, the SEC lacked authority to directly regulate dual class stock. Suspecting that the front door was locked, the Commission tried using Rule 19c–4 to sneak federal regulation through the back door. In *Business Roundtable*, however, the court squarely barred the Commission from doing indirectly what it could not do directly. Finding the back door to be locked as well, the SEC therefore sneaked through the cellar window. In doing so, it ran roughshod over the clear Congressional intent that the SEC was not to regulate corporate governance generally or the substance of shareholder voting rights in particular.

13. Donald E. Schwartz, Federalism and Corporate Governance, 45 Ohio St. L.J. 545, 571 (1984).

14. For a more detailed treatment of the post-*Business Roundtable* developments, see Stephen M. Bainbridge, Revisiting the One–Share/One–Vote Controversy: The Exchanges' Uniform Voting Rights Policy, 22 Sec. Reg. L.J. 175 (1994). See generally Roberta S. Karmel, The Future of Corporate Governance Listing Requirements, 54 SMU L. Rev. 325 (2001).

15. While it also was disappointing to see the major exchanges so willingly collaborating with the SEC's lawless behavior, it is important to note that we are not questioning the exchanges' well-established right and power to create corporate governance listing standards. Our quarrel is not with the exchanges, but rather with the Commission. The point thus is not that corporate governance listing standards infringe on the right of states to regulate corporate governance, but that the Commission's use of its "raised eyebrow" powers to force creation of such listing standards is an inappropriate intrusion of federal regulatory power into a sphere that both Congress and the courts have left to the states.

§ 10.7 Why not shareholder democracy?

As Berle and Means famously demonstrated, U.S. public corporations are characterized by a separation of ownership and control. The firm's nominal owners, the shareholders, exercise virtually no control over either day to day operations or long-term policy. Instead, control is vested in the directors and their subordinate professional managers, who typically own only a small portion of the firm's shares.[1]

A. Disincentives to shareholder activism

The separation of ownership and control is enforced both directly and indirectly. Direct limitations on shareholder control are created by the statutory assignment of decisionmaking authority to the board. Shareholders essentially have no power to initiate corporate action and, moreover, are entitled to approve or disapprove only a very few board actions.

These direct restrictions on shareholder power are supplemented by a host of other rules that indirectly prevent shareholders from exercising significant influence over corporate decisionmaking. Three sets of statutes are especially important: (1) disclosure requirements pertaining to large holders; (2) shareholder voting and communication rules; (3) insider trading and short swing profits rules. These laws affect shareholders in two respects. First, they discourage the formation of large stock blocks.[2] Second, they discourage communication and coordination among shareholders.

1. Disclosure requirements relating to large holders

Securities Exchange Act § 13(d) requires that any person who acquires beneficial ownership of more than 5 percent of the outstanding shares of any class of equity stock in a given issuer must file a report within 10 days of such acquisition with the SEC, the issuer, and the exchanges on which the stock is traded. Persons required to file a Schedule 13D must provide extensive disclosure. Those disclosures impinge substantially on investor privacy and thus may discourage some investors from holding blocks greater than 4.9% of a company's stock. Section 13(d) also discourages collaboration by groups of investors because it applies the disclosure obligation to two or more persons act as a

---

§ 10.7

1. Adolf A. Berle & Gardiner C. Means, The Modern Corporation and Private Property (1932).

2. Large block formation may also be discouraged by state corporate law rules governing minority shareholder protections. Under Delaware law, a controlling shareholder has fiduciary obligations to the minority. See, e.g., Zahn v. Transamerica Corp., 162 F.2d 36 (3d Cir.1947). A controlling shareholder who uses its power to force

the corporation to enter into contracts with the shareholder or its affiliates on unfair terms can be held liable for the resulting injury to the minority. See, e.g., Sinclair Oil Corp. v. Levien, 280 A.2d 717 (Del.1971). A controlling shareholder who uses its influence to effect a freeze-out merger in which the minority shareholders are bought out at an unfairly low price likewise faces liability. See, e.g., Weinberger v. UOP, Inc., 457 A.2d 701 (Del.1983).

group for the purpose of acquiring, holding or disposing of stock whose aggregate holdings exceed the 5% threshold. Institutional investors frequently cite § 13(d)'s application to groups and the consequent risk of liability for failing to provide adequate disclosures as an explanation for the general lack of shareholder activism on their part.

2. *Shareholder communication rules*

Because of the separation of ownership and control mandated by U.S. corporate law, even quite large shareholders are relatively powerless. Instead, to the extent they exercise any control over the corporation, they do so only through control of the board of directors. As such, it is the shareholder's ability to affect the election of directors that determines the degree of influence it will hold over the corporation. The proxy regime not only discourages large shareholders from seeking to replace incumbent directors with their own nominees, but also discourages shareholders from communicating with one another. Anyone who solicits a proxy must go to the expense of preparing and disseminating both a proxy card and a proxy statement. The definition of solicitation for this purpose is quite broad. The federal proxy rules "apply not only to direct requests to furnish, revoke or withhold proxies, but also to communications which may indirectly accomplish such a result or constitute a step in a chain of communications designed ultimately to accomplish such a result."[3] Hence, shareholders who communicate with one another run some risk of being deemed to have solicited proxies. The risk of liability and being put to the expense of conducting a proxy solicitation doubtless chills shareholder communication. To be sure, the SEC's 1992 amendments to the proxy rules modestly liberalized the proxy regime with the avowed intention of allowing greater shareholder activism. Experience teaches that these changes, however, were far too modest to have any significant effect.[4] The barriers to collective action by institutional investors and other large shareholders remained high enough to substantially deter shareholder activism in the electoral arena.[5]

3. *Insider trading rules*

Full treatment of the complex federal securities laws governing insider trading is well beyond the scope of this section. Yet, it is important to acknowledge that those laws substantially impinge the ability of shareholders holding large blocks to affect corporate policy and governance. Large block holders frequently get greater access to nonpublic information than do other investors. Where the large shareholder has board representation, this will inevitably be true. Even where the large

---

3. Long Island Lighting Co. v. Barbash, 779 F.2d 793 (2d Cir.1985).

4. See, e.g., Stephen Choi, Proxy Issue Proposals: Impact of the 1992 SEC Proxy Reforms, 16 J.L. Econ. & Org. 233 (2000).

5. In lieu of conducting a full-blown proxy contest (or engaging in conduct that might be deemed a proxy solicitation), institutional investors sometimes avail themselves of the option provided by SEC Rule 14a–8 to place a shareholder proposal on the company's proxy statement. As a governance device, however, the shareholder proposal rule is a relatively weak instrument.

holder lacks formal board representation, however, it may often benefit from selective disclosures by management. In either case, disclosure of information to large block shareholders raises serious insider trading concerns.

In addition, the short swing profits provision of Securities Exchange Act § 16(b) provide a substantial deterrent to holding large blocks of stock. An institutional investor (or any other shareholder) who owns more than 10% of a public corporation's stock will find its liquidity substantially reduced. If market developments make it desirable to sell some or all of the investor's holdings, the investor may lose some or even all of its gains on that sale. Because reduced liquidity equates to enhanced risk, investors are discouraged from holding blocks greater than 9.9%.

4. Net effect: The "Wall Street" rule

Many institutional investors, in particular, rationally prefer liquidity to activism. For fully-diversified institutions even the total failure of a particular firm will not have a significant effect on their portfolio, and may indeed benefit them to the extent they also hold stock in competing firms. Such investors prove less likely to join an insurgent coalition than to simply use an activist's call for action as a signal to follow the so-called Wall Street Rule (its easier to switch than fight—a play on an old cigarette advertisement) and switch to a different investment before conditions further deteriorate.

B. Shareholder activism and agency costs

Do the restrictions on shareholder activism matter? In the 1990s, a number of academics began arguing that shareholder activism could become an important constraint on agency costs within the firm.[6] Acknowledging that the rational apathy phenomenon would largely preclude small individual shareholders from playing an active role in corporate governance, even if the various legal impediments to shareholder activism were removed, these scholars focused their attention on institutional investors, such as pension and mutual funds. Institutional investors, at least potentially, may behave quite differently than dispersed individual investors. Because they own large blocks, and have an incentive to develop specialized expertise in making and monitoring investments, they could play a far more active role in corporate governance than dispersed shareholders. Institutional investors holding large blocks

6. See, e.g., Mark J. Roe, Strong Managers, Weak Owners: The Political Roots of American Corporate Finance (1994); Bernard S. Black, Shareholder Passivity Reexamined, 89 Mich. L. Rev. 520 (1990). For more skeptical analyses, see Stephen M. Bainbridge, The Politics of Corporate Governance, 18 Harv. J. L. & Pub. Pol'y 671 (1995); Edward B. Rock, The Logic and (Uncertain) Significance of Institutional Shareholder Activism, 79 Geo. L.J. 445 (1991); Roberta Romano, Public Pension Fund Activism in Corporate Governance Reconsidered, 93 Colum. L. Rev. 795 (1993); Robert D. Rosenbaum, Foundations of Sand: The Weak Premises Underlying the Current Push for Proxy Rule Changes, 17 J. Corp. L. 163 (1991).

have more power to hold management accountable for actions that do not promote shareholder welfare. Their greater access to firm information, coupled with their concentrated voting power, will enable them to more actively monitor the firm's performance and to make changes in the board's composition when performance lagged. Corporations with large blocks of stock held by institutional investors thus might reunite ownership of the residual claim and ultimate control of the enterprise. As a result, concentrated ownership in the hands of institutional investors might lead to a reduction in shirking and, hence, a reduction in agency costs. Or so the story went.

In the early 1990s, institutional investors did increasingly dominate U.S. equity securities markets. They also were beginning to play a somewhat more active role in corporate governance than they had in earlier periods. Institutions were taking their voting rights more seriously and using the proxy system to defend their interests. They began voting against takeover defenses proposed by management and in favor of shareholder proposals recommending removal of existing defenses. Many institutions also no longer routinely voted to reelect incumbent directors. Less visibly, institutions influenced business policy and board composition through negotiations with management. But while there seemed little doubt that institutional investor activism could have effects at the margins, the question remained whether the impact would be more than merely marginal.

Today, there is relatively little evidence that shareholder activism has mattered. Even the most active institutional investors spend only trifling amounts on corporate governance activism. Institutions devote little effort to monitoring management; to the contrary, they typically disclaim the ability or desire to decide company-specific policy questions. They rarely conduct proxy solicitations or put forward shareholder proposals. They tend not to try to elect representatives to boards of directors. They rarely coordinate their activities. Most importantly, empirical studies of U.S. institutional investor activism have found "no strong evidence of a correlation between firm performance and percentage of shares owned by institutions."[7]

C. The costs of shareholder activism

Let us assume that legal change could promote institutional investor activism.[8] Would such reforms be desirable? Perhaps not, as the agency

---

7. Bernard S. Black, Shareholder Activism and Corporate Governance in the United States, in The New Palgrave Dictionary of Economics and the Law 459, 462 (1998). Due to a resurgence of direct individual investment in the stock market, motivated at least in part by the day trading phenomenon and technology stock bubble, the trend towards institutional domination has stagnated. Large blocks held by a single investor also remain rare. Few U.S. corporations have any institutional shareholders who own more than 5–10% of their stock.

8. In the unlikely event that shareholder activism ever became a major feature of U.S. corporate governance, it seems probable that state legislatures would act to insulate corporate managers from activist shareholders. In the late 1980s there was an apparent rise in the frequency of proxy

cost-reducing benefits of institutional control may come at too high a cost. There is evidence, for example, that bank control of the securities markets has harmed that Japanese and German economies by impeding the development of new businesses.[9] Increased institutionalization of the capital markets thus might impede the active venture capital market that helps drive the U.S. economy.

Because we are concerned with the internal governance of corporations, however, our attention focuses on a different concern: namely, the risk that institutional investors may abuse their control by self-dealing and other forms of over-reaching. The interests of large and small investors often differ. As management becomes more beholden to the interests of large shareholders, it may become less concerned with the welfare of smaller investors.

Institutional investors with substantial decisionmaking influence will be tempted to use their position to self-deal; i.e., to take a nonpro rata share of the firms assets and earnings. Let us make the heroic assumption, however, that institutional investors are entirely selfless. Institutional investor activism would still be undesirable if the separation of ownership and control mandated by U.S. law has substantial efficiency benefits. Questions of whether differing corporate law regimes confer comparative advantages on national economies are sharply debated, and the relative merits of the various national models vigorously disputed even among those who think that corporate law matters insofar as national productivity and competitiveness are concerned. Yet, while the matter undoubtedly remains unproven, there are sound reasons to suspect that the U.S. model has significant advantages. In particular, our analysis of the separation of ownership and control strongly suggests that vesting decisionmaking authority in a centralized entity distinct from the shareholders—i.e., the board—is what makes the large public corporation feasible.

The root economic argument against shareholder activism thus becomes apparent.[10] Large-scale institutional involvement in corporate

contests as a takeover vehicle, which was partially attributable to a marginal increase in institutional investor activism. Several states responded to the prospect that shareholders might begin routinely voting out incumbent directors by passing legislation designed to deter proxy contests. Stephen M. Bainbridge, Redirecting State Takeover Laws at Proxy Contests, 1992 Wisconsin Law Review 1071.

9. See generally Bernard S. Black & Ronald J. Gilson, Venture Capital and the Structure of Capital Markets: Banks Versus Stock Markets, 47 J. Fin. Econ. 243 (1998); Curtis J. Milhaupt, The Market for Innovation in the United States and Japan: Venture Capital and the Comparative Corporate Governance Debate, 91 Nw. U. L. Rev. 865 (1997). It is conventional to bifurcate

corporate governance systems between a market-oriented model with an active capital market and diffuse ownership and a bank-oriented model with a less active capital market and highly concentrated ownership (mainly by banks). The U.S. falls well within the first model, while Germany is a good example of the bank-centered model. Gustavo Visentini, Compatibility and Competition between European and American Corporate Governance: Which Model of Capitalism?, 23 Brooklyn J. Int'l L. 833 (1998).

10. Attentive readers of the text in its entirety will note that the economic argument against shareholder democracy largely tracks the justification advanced in Chapter 6 for the business judgment rule. Indeed, given the greater collective action problems

decisionmaking seems likely to disrupt the very mechanism that makes the Berle–Means corporation practicable; namely, the centralization of essentially nonreviewable decisionmaking authority in the board of directors. The chief economic virtue of the Berle–Means corporation is not that it permits the aggregation of large capital pools, as some have suggested, but rather that it provides a hierarchical decisionmaking structure well-suited to the problem of operating a large business enterprise with numerous employees, managers, shareholders, creditors, and other inputs. In such a firm, someone must be in charge: "Under conditions of widely dispersed information and the need for speed in decisions, authoritative control at the tactical level is essential for success."[11] Shareholder activism necessarily contemplates that institutions will review management decisions, step in when management performance falters, and exercise voting control to effect a change in policy or personnel. In a very real sense, giving institutions this power of review differs little from giving them the power to make management decisions in the first place. As economist Kenneth Arrow observed, "If every decision of A is to be reviewed by B, then all we have really is a shift in the locus of authority from A to B and hence no solution to the original problem" of allocating control under conditions of divergent interests and differing levels of information. Even though institutional investors probably would not micromanage portfolio corporations, vesting them with the power to review major decisions inevitably shifts some portion of the board's authority to them. Given the significant virtues of discretion, preservation of board discretion should always be the null hypothesis. The separation of ownership and control mandated by U.S. corporate law has precisely that effect.

---

inherent in shareholder oversight of board decisionmaking, the case against shareholder democracy is even stronger than the case against judicial oversight.

11. Kenneth J. Arrow, The Limits of Organization 69 (1974).

Chapter 11

INSIDER TRADING

Analysis

---

§ 11.1 Introduction

Generally speaking, insider trading is trading in securities while in possession of material nonpublic information. Since the 1960s insider trading has been regarded mainly as a problem of federal securities laws. A principal thesis of this Chapter, however, is that insider trading is more closely akin to the fiduciary duty issues treated in the preceding chapters than it is to the sorts of securities frauds discussed in Chapter 3.

Someone violates the federal insider trading prohibition only if his trading activity breached a fiduciary duty owed either to the investor with whom he trades or to the source of the information.[1] From a securities law perspective, the federal prohibition thus is an empty shell. It has no force or substance until it has been filled with fiduciary duty concepts. Despite the centrality of the fiduciary duty element to the federal prohibition, however, that element has received relatively little attention. On close examination, however, requiring a breach of fiduciary

---

§ 11.1

1. This is true insofar as the core federal prohibition under Securities and Exchange Commission (SEC) Rule 10b–5, 17 C.F.R. § 240.10b–5, is concerned. Breach of fiduciary duty is not required for liability to arise under the narrower provisions of SEC Rule 14e–3, 17 C.F.R. § 240.14e–3. See U.S. v. O'Hagan, 521 U.S. 642 (1997). There is a voluminous academic literature on insider trading. For a comprehensive bibliography, see Stephen M. Bainbridge, Insider Trading, in III Encyc. of L. & Econ. 772, 798–811 (2000).

duty as a prerequisite for insider trading liability raises two interesting questions: What is the precise fiduciary duty at issue? Is the source of that duty federal or state law? The failure to resolve these issues has robbed the federal insider trading prohibition of coherence and predictability.

This Chapter argues that insider trading liability is premised not on the mere existence of a fiduciary relationship, but rather on the breach of a specific fiduciary duty—namely, the duty to refrain from self dealing in confidential information owned by another party. Put another way, the law of insider trading is one of the vehicles used by society to allocate the property rights to information produced by a firm. If true, the argument suggests that insider trading differs but little from other duty of loyalty problems, such as usurpation of corporate opportunities, in which the officer or director used proprietary information or other corporate assets for personal gain. In turn, the argument thus raises the interesting question of why insider trading is a matter of federal concern.

§ 11.2 Origins of the insider trading prohibition

Although we now take it for granted that regulating insider trading is a job for the SEC under federal law, it was not always so. Until quite recently, insider trading was handled as a matter of state corporate law. To be sure, the federal prohibition has largely eclipsed state law in this area, but the older state rules are still worth studying. The historical evolution of the insider trading prohibition is not only relevant to understanding current doctrine, but also is highly relevant to understanding the on-going policy debate over the merits of insider trading regulation.

A. State common law

Prior to 1900 it was treatise law that "[t]he doctrine that officers and directors [of corporations] are trustees of the stockholders ... does not extend to their private dealings with stockholders or others, though in such dealings they take advantage of knowledge gained through their official position."[1] Under this so-called "majority" or "no duty" rule, liability was based solely on actual fraud, such as misrepresentation or fraudulent concealment of a material fact. As one court explained, liability arose only where the defendant said or did something "to divert or prevent, and which did divert or prevent, the plaintiff from looking into, or making inquiry, or further inquiries, as to the affairs or condition of the company and its prospects for dividends...."[2]

§ 11.2

1. H. L. Wilgus, Purchase of Shares of a Corporation by a Director from a Shareholder, 8 Mich. L. Rev. 267, 267 (1910).

2. Carpenter v. Danforth, 52 Barb. 581, 589 (N.Y.Sup.Ct.1868). See also Grant v.

Attrill, 11 F. 469 (S.D.N.Y.1882) (holding that a sale of stock induced by the levy of an assessment was not so tainted with fraud as to render it void); Board of Comm'rs v. Reynolds, 44 Ind. 509 (1873) (holding over a strong dissent that there

1. Face to face transactions

The modern prohibition began taking shape in *Oliver v. Oliver*,[3] a 1903 decision in which the Georgia Supreme Court announced the so-called "minority" or "duty to disclose" rule. After 1900 most courts continued to reject any fiduciary duty on the part of corporate officers and directors in their private dealings with shareholders.[4] In *Oliver*, however, the court held that the shareholder had a right to disclosure, stating that "[w]here the director obtains the information giving added value to the stock by virtue of his official position, he holds the information in trust for the benefit of [the shareholders]." Other courts soon followed suit.[5] Under *Oliver* and its progeny, directors therefore had a quite modern fiduciary obligation to disclose material nonpublic information to shareholders before trading with them.

In *Strong v. Repide*,[6] the U.S. Supreme Court offered a third approach to the insider trading problem. The court acknowledged the majority rule, but declined to follow it. Instead, the court held that, under the particular factual circumstances of the case at bar, "the law would indeed be impotent if the sale could not be set aside or the defendant cast in damages for his fraud." Thus was born the so-called "special facts" or "special circumstances" rule, which holds that although directors generally owe no duty to disclose material facts when trading with shareholders, such a duty can arise in "special circumstances." What facts were sufficiently "special" for a court to invoke the rule? *Strong v. Repide* identified the two most important fact patterns:

was no trustee relationship because directors did not have control, power, or dominion over the shares); Crowell v. Jackson, 23 A. 426 (N.J.1891) (liability only for active misrepresentation, no general duty of disclosure); Krumbhaar v. Griffiths, 25 A. 64 (Pa.1892) (shareholder cannot rescind sale of stock to secretary of corporation who discloses all information he has and conceals neither the condition of the corporation nor the value of the stock); Fisher v. Budlong, 10 R.I. 525 (1873) (liability solely because director was acting as an agent for the shareholder in the sale of the stock and abused that relationship to obtain the shares for himself at a price lower than their actual value); Deaderick v. Wilson, 67 Tenn. 108 (1874) (directors are free to purchase stock from a shareholder in the corporation on the same terms as others unless prohibited by legislative action); Hume v. Steele, 59 S.W. 812 (Tex.Civ.App.1900) (liability based only on actual fraud); Haarstick v. Fox, 33 P. 251 (Utah 1893) (no duty of disclosure absent active misrepresentation). For contemporary academic commentary on the state common law of insider trading, see A.A. Berle, Jr., Publicity of Accounts and Directors' Purchases of Stock,

25 Mich. L. Rev. 827 (1927); Clarence D. Layline, The Duty of a Director Purchasing Shares of Stock, 27 Yale L.J. 731 (1918); Roberts Walker, The Duty of Disclosure by a Director Purchasing Stock from his Stockholders, 32 Yale L.J. 637 (1923).

3.   45 S.E. 232 (Ga.1903).

4.   See, e.g., Hooker v. Midland Steel Co., 74 N.E. 445 (Ill.1905); Walsh v. Goulden, 90 N.W. 406 (Mich.1902).

5.   See, e.g., Stewart v. Harris, 77 P. 277, 279 (Kan.1904); cf. Von Au v. Magenheimer, 110 N.Y.S. 629 (N.Y.App.Div.1908) (stockholder in nonpublic corporation who was induced to sell shares by misrepresentation on the part of management has action for damages). In Steinfeld v. Nielsen, 100 P. 1094 (Ariz.1909), rev'd, 224 U.S. 534 (1912), the lower court followed Oliver and Stewart but found no liability because the plaintiff had equal access to the information. On remand, the court appeared to follow Strong v. Repide, 213 U.S. 419 (1909), discussed below, but found no special circumstances justifying a duty of disclosure. Steinfeld v. Nielsen, 139 P. 879 (Ariz.1913).

6.   213 U.S. 419 (1909).

Concealment of identity by the defendant and failure to disclose significant facts having a dramatic impact on the stock price.

As state law evolved in the early 1900s, both the special circumstances and minority rules rapidly gained adherents.[7] Every court faced with the issue during this period felt obliged to discuss all three rules. While many courts adhered to the majority no-duty rule, they typically went out of their way to demonstrate that the case at bar in fact did not involve any special facts. Even more strikingly, during this period no court deciding the issue as a matter of first impression adopted the old majority rule. As a result, by the late 1930s, a head count of cases indicated that the special circumstances rule prevailed in a plurality of states, the older no duty rule no longer commanded a majority, and the duty to disclose rule had been adopted in a substantial number—albeit, still a minority—of states.[8]

2. Do selling directors owe a fiduciary duty to their nonshareholder purchasers?

Given that both the special circumstances and minority rules were based on the director or officer's fiduciary duties, a problem arose: What happened when a director sold shares, rather than buying them? A director who buys shares is trading with someone who is already a shareholder of the corporation and, as such, someone to whom the director has fiduciary obligations. A director who sells shares, however, likely is dealing with a stranger, someone not yet a shareholder and, as such, not yet someone to whom the director owes any duties. Assuming *arguendo* that the director's fiduciary duties to shareholders proscribe buying shares from them on the basis of undisclosed material information, the logic of that rule does not necessarily extend to cases in which the director sells to an outsider. As with most questions of state law in this area, the issue is not solely of historical or academic interest. As we shall see, the modern federal insider trading prohibition is also premised on a violation of fiduciary duty, Unfortunately, while the federal prohibition indisputably applies both to insiders who buy and those who sell,[9] state law remains uncertain.

---

7. A 1921 article identified 13 cases dealing with the duty to disclose inside information. Eight of these cases imposed liability for failure to disclose. Six cases, following the *Strong* special circumstances rule, found special facts justifying liability. The other two cases followed *Oliver*'s fiduciary duty approach. Of the five cases finding no liability, three cases said they would follow the older no duty rule, but went out of their way to demonstrate that there were no special circumstances on the facts of the case. The other two cases refused to adopt the older rule, but found no special circumstances justifying imposing a duty of disclosure. Harold R. Smith, Purchase of Shares of a Corporation by a Director from a Shareholder, 19 Mich. L. Rev. 698, 712–13 (1921).

8. I. Beverly Lake, The Use for Personal Profit of Knowledge Gained While a Director, 9 Miss. L.J. 427, 448–49 (1937).

9. See, e.g., SEC v. Texas Gulf Sulphur Co., 401 F.2d 833 (2d Cir.1968), cert. denied, 394 U.S. 976 (1969) (where insiders purchased stock on inside information); SEC v. Adler, 137 F.3d 1325 (11th Cir.1998) (where defendant sold shares of stock based on his possession of material nonpublic information).

3. *Stock market transactions*

Both the special circumstances and minority rules were more limited in scope than may appear at first blush.[10] Most of the cases in which plaintiffs succeeded involved some form of active fraud, not just a failure to disclose. More important, all of these cases involved face-to-face transactions. The vast majority of stock transactions, both then and now, take place on impersonal stock exchanges. In order to be economically significant, an insider trading prohibition must apply to such transactions as well as face-to-face ones.

The leading state case in this area remains *Goodwin v. Agassiz.*[11] Defendants were directors and senior officers of a mining corporation. A geologist working for the company advanced a theory suggesting there might be substantial copper deposits in northern Michigan. The company thought the theory had merit and began securing mineral rights on the relevant tracts of land. Meanwhile, the defendants began buying shares on the market. Plaintiff was a former stockholder who had sold his shares on the stock market. The defendants apparently had bought the shares, although neither side knew the identity of the other party to the transaction until much later. When the true facts became known, plaintiff sued the directors, arguing that he would not have sold if the geologist's theory had been disclosed. The court rejected plaintiff's claim, concluding that defendants had no duty to disclose the theory before trading.

Goodwin is commonly read as standing for the proposition that directors and officers trading on an impersonal stock exchange owe no duty of disclosure to the persons with whom they trade. Although that reading is correct as a bottom line matter, it ignores some potentially important doctrinal complications. The Massachusetts Supreme Judicial Court's analysis begins with a nod to the old majority rule, opining that directors generally do not "occupy the position of trustee toward individual stockholders in the corporation." The court went on, however, to note that "circumstances may exist ... [such] that an equitable responsibility arises to communicate facts," which sounds like the special circumstances rule. Indeed, the court made clear that Massachusetts would apply the special circumstances rule to face-to-face transactions: "where a director personally seeks a stockholder for the purpose of buying his shares without making disclosure of material facts within his peculiar knowledge and not within reach of the stockholder, the transaction will be closely scrutinized and relief may be granted in appropriate instances." Was the court likewise applying the special circumstances rule to stock market transactions? Perhaps. The court took pains to carefully analyze the nature of the information in question, concluding that it was "at most a hope," and was careful to say that there was no affirmative duty to disclose under the circumstances at bar. At the same

---

10. See generally Michael Conant, Duties of Disclosure of Corporate Insiders Who Purchase Shares, 46 Cornell L.Q. 53 (1960).

11. 186 N.E. 659 (Mass.1933).

time, however, the dispositive special circumstance clearly was the stock market context. As to transactions effected on an impersonal exchange, no duty to disclose would be imposed.

Given that federal law later imposed just such a duty, it is instructive to carefully examine the court's explanation for its holding:

> Purchases and sales of stock dealt in on the stock exchange are commonly impersonal affairs. An honest director would be in a difficult situation if he could neither buy nor sell on the stock exchange shares of stock in his corporation without first seeking out the other actual ultimate party to the transaction and disclosing to him everything which a court or jury might later find that he then knew affecting the real or speculative value of such shares. Business of that nature is a matter to be governed by practical rules. Fiduciary obligations of directors ought not to be made so onerous that men of experience and ability will be deterred from accepting such office. Law in its sanctions is not coextensive with morality. It cannot undertake to put all parties to every contract on an equality as to knowledge, experience, skill and shrewdness. It cannot undertake to relieve against hard bargains made between competent parties without fraud.

Defenders of the insider trading prohibition find much that is contestable in the court's rationale. Two observations suffice for present purposes: First, notice the strongly normative (and strongly laissez faire) tone of the quoted passage. Why can't the law undertake to ensure that all parties to stock market transaction have at least roughly equal access to information? This question turns out to be one of insider trading jurisprudence's recurring issues. Second, consider the "difficult situation" the court claims an insider trading prohibition would create for "honest directors." Even at its most expansive, the federal insider trading prohibition never required directors to individually seek out those with whom they trade and personally make disclosure of "everything" they know about the company. A workable insider trading prohibition simply requires directors to publicly disclose all material facts in their possession before trading or, if they are not able to do so, to refrain from trading. Corporate policies could be developed to limit director and officer trading to windows of time in which there is unlikely to be significant undisclosed information, such as those following dissemination of periodic corporate disclosures. An inconvenience for all concerned, to be sure, but hardly enough to keep able people from serving as directors of publicly traded corporations. Not surprisingly, this aspect of the court's rationale has gotten short shrift from later courts.

B. Origins of the federal prohibition

The modern federal insider trading prohibition has its statutory basis in the federal securities laws—principally the Securities Exchange Act of 1934. As with the other New Deal-era securities laws, the

Exchange Act was a response to the 1929 stock market crash and the subsequent depression. Like its fellow securities laws, the Exchange Act had two basic purposes: protecting investors engaged in securities transactions and assuring public confidence in the integrity of the securities markets. As the Supreme Court has put it, the fundamental aim was "to substitute a philosophy of full disclosure for the philosophy of *caveat emptor* and thus to achieve a high standard of business ethics in the securities industry."[12] Towards that end, prohibitions of fraud and manipulation in connection with the purchase or sale of securities buttressed the Exchange Act's disclosure requirements.

Is insider trading a breach of the disclosure obligations created by the Exchange Act? If not, is it otherwise captured by the Exchange Act's prohibition of fraud and manipulation? The United States Supreme Court, among others, thinks so: "A significant purpose of the Exchange Act was to eliminate the idea that use of inside information for personal advantage was a normal emolument of corporate office."[13] Careful examination of the relevant legislative history, however, suggests that regulating insider trading was not one of the Exchange Act's original purposes.[14]

A cautionary note: Change is one of the key distinguishing characteristics of the federal insider trading prohibition. Although the prohibition is only about three decades old, already it has seen more shifts in doctrine than most corporate law rules have seen in the last century. Exploring this rich history is a useful exercise—in many respects you cannot understand today's issues without the historical background—but is also fraught with danger: you must draw clear distinctions between what was the law and what is the law. One point requiring particular attention is the evolution of new theories on which insider trading liability can be based. We shall see two very important cases in which the Supreme Court restricted the scope of the traditional disclose or abstain rule. In response to those cases, the SEC and the lower courts developed two new theories on which liability could be imposed. As we move through this material, pay close attention to which theory is under discussion at any given moment.

1. *The statutory background and its legislative history*

The core of the modern federal insider trading prohibition derives its statutory authority from § 10(b) of the Exchange Act, which provides in pertinent part that:

> It shall be unlawful for any person, directly or indirectly, by the use of any means or instrumentality of interstate commerce or of the mails, or of any facility of any national securities exchange—

12. SEC v. Capital Gains Research Bureau, Inc., 375 U.S. 180, 186 (1963).

13. Dirks v. SEC, 463 U.S. 646, 653 n. 10 (1983).

14. See generally Stephen M. Bainbridge, Incorporating State Law Fiduciary Duties into the Federal Insider Trading Prohibition, 52 Wash & Lee L. Rev. 1189, 1228–1237 (1995); Michael P. Dooley, Enforcement of Insider Trading Restrictions, 66 Va. L. Rev. 1, 55–69 (1980); Frank H. Easterbrook, Insider Trading, Secret Agents, Evidentiary Privileges, and the Production of Information, 1981 Sup. Ct. Rev. 309, 317–20.

(b) To use or employ, in connection with the purchase or sale of any security registered on a national securities exchange or any security not so registered, any manipulative or deceptive device or contrivance in contravention of such rules and regulations as the Commission may prescribe as necessary or appropriate in the public interest or for the protection of investors.[15]

Notice two things about this text. First, it is not self-executing. Section 10(b) gives the SEC authority to prohibit "any manipulative or deceptive device or contrivance" and then makes the use of such proscribed devices illegal. Until the SEC exercises its rulemaking authority, however, the statute is unavailing.

The second point to be noticed is the absence of the word "insider." Nothing in § 10(b) explicitly proscribes insider trading. To be sure, § 10(b) often is described as a catchall intended to capture various types of securities fraud not expressly covered by more specific provisions of the Exchange Act.[16] What the SEC catches under § 10(b), however, must not only be fraud, but also within the scope of the authority delegated to it by Congress.[17] Section 10(b) received little attention during the hearings on the Exchange Act and apparently was seen simply as a grant of authority to the SEC to prohibit manipulative devices not covered by § 9. As Thomas Corcoran, a prominent member of President Roosevelt's administration and leader of the Exchange Act's supporters, put it: § 10(b) was intended to prohibit the invention of "any other cunning devices" besides those prohibited by other sections.[18] Only a single passage, albeit an oft-cited one, in the Exchange Act's voluminous legislative history directly indicates insider trading was one of those cunning devices: "Among the most vicious practices unearthed at the hearings ... was the flagrant betrayal of their fiduciary duties by directors and officers of corporations who used their positions of trust and the confidential information which came to them in such positions, to aid them in their market activities."[19] In context, however, this passage does not deal with insider trading as we understand the term today, but rather with manipulation of stock prices by pools of insiders and speculators through cross sales, wash sales, and similar "cunning" methods. Nothing else in the legislative history suggests that Congress intended § 10(b) to create a sweeping prohibition of insider trading.

To the extent the 1934 Congress addressed insider trading, it did so not through § 10(b), but rather through § 16(b), which permits the

---

15. 15 U.S.C. § 78j(b).

16. Chiarella v. United States, 445 U.S. 222, 234–35 (1980).

17. See Ernst & Ernst v. Hochfelder, 425 U.S. 185, 213–14 (1976) ("The rule-making power granted to an administrative agency ... is not the power to make law. Rather, it is 'the power to adopt regulations to carry into effect the will of Congress as expressed by the statute.'"); cf. Business Roundtable v. SEC, 905 F.2d 406 (D.C.Cir.

1990) (invalidating SEC Rule 19c–4 as exceeding scope of SEC's authority under Exchange Act §§ 14(a) and 19(c)).

18. Stock Exchange Regulation: Hearing on H.R. 7852 and H.R. 8720 Before the House Comm. on Interstate and Foreign Commerce, 73d Cong., 2d Sess. 115 (1934).

19. S. Rep. No. 1455, 73d Cong., 2d Sess. 55 (1934).

issuer of affected securities to recover insider short-swing profits.[20] As we will see below, § 16(b) imposes quite limited restrictions on insider trading. It does not reach transactions occurring more than six months apart, nor does it apply to persons other than those named in the statute or to transactions in securities not registered under § 12. Indeed, some have argued that § 16(b) was not even intended to deal with insider trading, but rather with manipulation.[21] In any event, given that Congress could have struck at insider trading both more directly and forcefully, and given that Congress chose not to do so,[22] § 16(b) offers no statutory justification for the more sweeping prohibition under § 10(b).

If Congress had intended in 1934 that the SEC use § 10(b) to craft a sweeping prohibition on insider trading, moreover, the SEC was quite dilatory in doing so. Rule 10b–5, the foundation on which the modern insider trading prohibition rests, was not promulgated until 1942, eight years after Congress passed the Exchange Act. The Rule provides:

> It shall be unlawful for any person, directly or indirectly, by the use of any means or instrumentality of interstate commerce, or of the mails or of any facility of any national securities exchange,
>
>   (a) To employ any device, scheme, or artifice to defraud,
>
>   (b) To make any untrue statement of a material fact or to omit to state a material fact necessary in order to make the statements made, in the light of the circumstances under which they were made, not misleading, or
>
>   (c) To engage in any act, practice, or course of business which operates or would operate as a fraud or deceit upon any person,
>
> in connection with the purchase or sale of any security.[23]

Note that, as with § 10(b) itself, the rule on its face does not prohibit (or even speak to) insider trading. Nor was Rule 10b–5 initially used against insider trading on public secondary trading markets. Instead, like state common law, the initial Rule 10b–5 cases were limited to face-to-face and/or control transactions.[24] Not until 1961 did the SEC finally conclude that insider trading on an impersonal stock exchange violated Rule 10b–

---

20.   15 U.S.C. § 78p(b).

21.   Michael P. Dooley, Enforcement of Insider Trading Restrictions, 66 Va. L. Rev. 1, 56–58 (1980).

22.   The first version of § 16 (§ 15 in draft) permitted corporate recovery of both insider and tippee short-swing profits and prohibited the tipping of confidential information by insiders. Stock Exchange Regulation: Hearings on H.R. 7852 and H.R. 8720 Before the House Comm. on Interstate and Foreign Commerce, 73d Cong., 2d Sess. 9–10 (1934). The House deleted both provisions, but the restriction on insider short-swing profits was restored in conference. S. Doc. No. 185, 73d Cong., 2d Sess. 16–17 (1934).

23.   17 CFR § 240.10b–5.

24.   See, e.g., Speed v. Transamerica Corp., 99 F.Supp. 808 (D.Del.1951) (omissions in connection with what amounted to tender offer); Kardon v. National Gypsum Co., 73 F.Supp. 798 (E.D.Pa.1947) (sale of control negotiated face to face); In re Ward La France Truck Corp., 13 S.E.C. 373 (1943) (same). Interestingly, in a pre-TGS case arising under Rule 10b–5, the Seventh Circuit applied the special circumstances rule to a face-to-face transaction, which confirms that there was no general bar on insider trading prior to TGS. Kohler v. Kohler Co., 319 F.2d 634 (7th Cir.1963).

5.[25] Only then did the modern federal insider trading prohibition at last begin to take shape.

In sum, the modern prohibition is a creature of SEC administrative actions and judicial opinions, only loosely tied to the statutory language and its legislative history. U.S. Supreme Court Chief Justice William Rehnquist famously observed that Rule 10b–5 is "a judicial oak which has grown from little more than a legislative acorn."[26] Nowhere in Rule 10b–5 jurisprudence is this truer than where the insider trading prohibition is concerned, given the tiny (even nonexistent) legislative acorn on which it rests.

2.   Cady, Roberts

The modern federal insider trading prohibition fairly can be said to have begun with *In re Cady, Roberts & Co.,*[27] an SEC enforcement action. Curtiss–Wright Corporation's board of directors decided to reduce the company's quarterly dividend. One of the directors, J. Cheever Cowdin, was also a partner in Cady, Roberts & Co., a stock brokerage firm. Before the news was announced, Cowdin informed one of his partners, Robert M. Gintel, of the impending dividend cut. Gintel then sold several thousand shares of Curtiss–Wright stock held in customer accounts over which he had discretionary trading authority. When the dividend cut was announced, Curtiss–Wright's stock price fell several dollars per share. Gintel's customers thus avoided substantial losses.

Cady, Roberts involved what is now known as tipping: an insider (the tipper) who knows confidential information does not himself trade, but rather informs (tips) someone else (the tippee) who does trade. It also involved trading on an impersonal stock exchange, instead of a face-to-face transaction. As the SEC acknowledged, this made *Cady, Roberts* a case of first impression. Prior 10b–5 cases in which inside information was used for personal gain had involved issues of tortious fraudulent concealment little different from the sorts of cases with which the state common law had dealt. Notwithstanding that limitation, the SEC held that Gintel had violated Rule 10b–5. In so doing, it articulated what became known as the "disclose or abstain" rule: An insider in possession of material nonpublic information must disclose such information before trading or, if disclosure is impossible or improper, abstain from trading.

3.   Texas Gulf Sulphur

It was not immediately clear what precedential value *Cady, Roberts* would have. It was an administrative ruling by the SEC, not a judicial opinion. It involved a regulated industry closely supervised by the SEC. There was the long line of precedent, represented by *Goodwin v. Agassiz,*

---

25.   In re Cady, Roberts & Co., 40 S.E.C. 907 (1961).

26.   Blue Chip Stamps v. Manor Drug Stores, 421 U.S. 723, 737 (1975).

27.   40 S.E.C. 907 (1961).

to the contrary. In short order, however, the basic *Cady, Roberts* principles became the law of the land.

In March of 1959, agents of Texas Gulf Sulphur Co. (TGS) found evidence of an ore deposit near Timmins, Ontario.[28] In October 1963, Texas Gulf Sulphur began ground surveys of the area. In early November, a drilling rig took core samples from depths of several hundred feet. Visual examination of the samples suggested commercially significant deposits of copper and zinc. TGS's president ordered the exploration group to maintain strict confidentiality, even to the point of withholding the news from other TGS directors and employees. In early December, a chemical assay confirmed the presence of copper, zinc, and silver. At the subsequent trial, several expert witnesses testified that they had never heard of any other initial exploratory drill hole showing comparable results. Over the next several months, TGS acquired the rights to the land under which this remarkable ore deposit lay. In March and early April 1964, further drilling confirmed that TGS had made a significant ore discovery. After denying several rumors about the find, TGS finally announced its discovery in a press conference on April 16, 1964.

Throughout the fall of 1963 and spring of 1964, a number of TGS insiders bought stock and/or options on company stock. Others tipped off outsiders. Still others accepted stock options authorized by the company's board of directors without informing the directors of the discovery. Between November 1963 and March 1964, the insiders were able to buy at prices that were slowly rising, albeit with fluctuations, from just under $18 per share to $25 per share. As rumors began circulating in late March and early April, the price jumped to about $30 per share. On April 16th, the stock opened at $31, but quickly jumped to $37 per share. By May 15, 1964, TGS's stock was trading at over $58 per share—a 222% rise over the previous November's price. Any joy the insiders may taken from their profits was short-lived, however, as the SEC sued them for violating Rule 10b–5.

Texas Gulf Sulphur is the first of the truly seminal insider trading cases. It is still widely taught, in large part because it presents such a stark and classic fact pattern. In examining *Texas Gulf Sulphur*, however, it is critical to distinguish between what the law *was* and what the law *is*—although much of what was said in that opinion is still valid, the core insider trading holding is no longer good law.

The Second Circuit Court of Appeals held that when an insider has material nonpublic information the insider must either disclose such information before trading or abstain from trading until the information has been disclosed. Thus was born what is now known as the "disclose or abstain" rule. The name is something of a misnomer, of course. The court presumably phrased the rule in terms of disclosure because this was an omissions case under Rule 10b–5. In such cases, the defendant

28. SEC v. Texas Gulf Sulphur Co., 401   U.S. 976 (1969).
F.2d 833 (2d Cir.1968), cert. denied, 394

must owe a duty of disclosure to some investor in order for liability to be imposed.[29] As a practical matter, however, disclosure will rarely be an option.

During the relevant time period, TGS had no affirmative duty to disclose the ore strike. As the Second Circuit correctly noted, the timing of disclosure is a matter for the business judgment of corporate managers, subject to any affirmative disclosure requirements imposed by the stock exchanges or the SEC.[30] In this case, moreover, a valuable corporate purpose was served by delaying disclosure: confidentiality prevented competitors from buying up the mineral rights and kept down the price landowners would charge for them. The company therefore had no duty to disclose the discovery, at least up until the time that the land acquisition program was completed.

Given that the corporation had no duty to disclose, and had decided not to disclose the information, the insiders' fiduciary duties to the corporation would preclude them disclosing it for personal gain. In this case, the company's president had specifically instructed insiders in the know to keep the information confidential, but such an instruction was not technically necessary. Agency law precludes a firm's agents from disclosing confidential information that belongs to their corporate principal, as all information relating to the ore strike clearly did.[31]

Disclosure by an insider who wishes to trade thus is only feasible if there is no legitimate corporate purpose for maintaining secrecy. These situations, however, presumably will be relatively rare—it is hard to imagine many business developments that can be disclosed immediately without working some harm to the corporation. In most cases, the disclose or abstain rule really does not provide the insider with a disclosure option: generally the duty will be one of complete abstention.

The policy foundation on which the Second Circuit erected the disclose or abstain rule was equality of access to information. The court contended that the federal insider trading prohibition was intended to assure that "all investors trading on impersonal exchanges have relatively equal access to material information." Put another way, the majority thought Congress intended "that all members of the investing public should be subject to identical market risks."[32]

---

29. See e.g., Chiarella v. United States, 445 U.S. 222, 230 (1980) (stating that liability for nondisclosure "is premised upon a duty to disclose arising from a relationship of trust and confidence between parties to a transaction"); see also Dirks v. SEC, 463 U.S. 646, 654 (1983) (stating that there is no general duty to disclose and the duty to disclose must arise from a fiduciary relationship); SEC v. Switzer, 590 F.Supp. 756, 766 (W.D.Okla.1984) (holding that overhearing inadvertently revealed inside information does not create a duty to disclose before trading because for a fiduciary duty

to run to a tippee, the inside information must be disclosed for an improper purpose).

30. SEC v. Texas Gulf Sulphur Co., 401 F.2d 833, 850–51 & n. 12 (2d Cir.1968), cert. denied, 394 U.S. 976 (1969).

31. Restatement (Second) of Agency § 395 (1958).

32. SEC v. Texas Gulf Sulphur Co., 401 F.2d 833, 852 (2d Cir.1968), cert. denied, 394 U.S. 976 (1969). For a defense of the equal access standard, see Victor Brudney, Insiders, Outsiders, and Information Advantages Under the Federal Securities

The equality of access principle admittedly has some intuitive appeal. As we shall see, the SEC consistently has tried to maintain it as the basis of insider trading liability. Many commentators still endorse it, typically on fairness grounds.[33] The implications of the equal access principle, however, become troubling when we start dealing with attenuated circumstances, especially with respect to market information. Suppose a representative of TGS had approached a landowner in the Timmins area to negotiate purchasing the mineral rights to the land. TGS' agent does not disclose the ore strike, but the landowner turns out to be pretty smart. She knows TGS has been drilling in the area and has heard rumors that it has been buying up a lot of mineral rights. She puts two and two together, reaches the obvious conclusion, and buys some TGS stock. Under a literal reading of *Texas Gulf Sulphur*, has our landowner committed illegal insider trading?

The surprising answer is "probably." The *Texas Gulf Sulphur* court stated that the insider trading prohibition applies to "anyone in possession of material inside information," because § 10(b) was intended to assure that "all investors trading on impersonal exchanges have relatively equal access to material information."[34] The court further stated that the prohibition applies to any persons who have "access, directly or *indirectly*" to confidential information (here is the sticking point) if they know that the information is unavailable to the investing public. The only issue thus perhaps would be a factual one turning on the landowner's state of mind: Did she know she was dealing with confidential information? If so, the equal access policy would seem to justify imposing a duty on her. Query whether the insider trading prohibition should stretch quite that far? Ultimately, the Supreme Court concluded that it should not.

§ 11.3 The modern federal insider trading prohibition emerges: The disclose or abstain rule and the Supreme Court

Texas Gulf Sulphur sent the insider trading prohibition down a path on which insider trading was deemed a form of securities fraud and, accordingly, within the SEC's regulatory jurisdiction. There was nothing inevitable about that choice, however. State corporate law had been regulating insider trading for decades before *Texas Gulf Sulphur* was decided. Well-established state precedents treated the problem as one implicating not concepts of deceit or manipulation, but rather the fiduciary duties of corporate officers and directors. To be sure, many

Laws, 93 Harv. L. Rev. 322 (1979). To be clear, Brudney does not claim that investors may not take advantage of inequalities arising out of superior intelligence or diligence. His claim is only that investors who have monopolistic access to material nonpublic information should not be allowed to use it for profit. Id.

33. See, e.g., Donald C. Langevoort, Words From on High About Rule 10b–5:

Chiarella's History, Central Bank's Future, 20 Del. J. Corp. L. 865, 883 (1995) (expressing a preference for an insider trading prohibition grounded on a duty to disclose to the market).

34. SEC v. Texas Gulf Sulphur Co., 401 F.2d 833, 848 (2d Cir.1968), cert. denied, 394 U.S. 976 (1969).

states held that insider trading did not violate those duties, especially with respect to stock market transactions, but so what? In light of those precedents, the Second Circuit could have held that insider trading was not within Rule 10b–5's regulatory purview. If it had done so, the prohibition would have evolved along a far different path than the one it actually followed.

A. *Chiarella*

1. *The facts*

Vincent Chiarella was an employee of Pandick Press, a financial printer that prepared tender offer disclosure materials, among other documents.[1] In preparing those materials Pandick used codes to conceal the names of the companies involved, but Chiarella broke the codes. He purchased target company shares before the bid was announced, then sold the shares for considerable profits after announcement of the bid. He was caught and indicted for illegal insider trading. He was thereafter convicted of violating Rule 10b–5 by trading on the basis of material nonpublic information. The Second Circuit affirmed his conviction, applying the same equality of access to information-based disclose or abstain rule it had created in Texas Gulf Sulphur.

Chiarella was one of the first of a series of high profile takeover-related insider trading cases during the 1980s. Obviously, one can significantly increase takeover profits if one knows in advance that a takeover will be forthcoming. If you know of an impending bid prior to its announcement, you can buy up stock at the low pre-announcement price and sell or tender at the higher post-announcement price. The earlier one knows of the bid, of course, the greater the spread between your purchase and sale prices and the greater the resulting profit. By using options, rather than actually buying target stock, you can further increase your profits, because options permit one to control larger blocks of stock for the same investment.[2] During the 1980s, a number of Wall Street takeover players—among whom Dennis Levine, Ivan Boesky, and Michael Milken are the best-known—allegedly added millions of illegally gained insider trading dollars to the already vast fortunes they realized from more legitimate takeover activity.[3]

§ 11.3

1. Chiarella v. United States, 445 U.S. 222 (1980).

2. See William K. S. Wang, A Cause of Action for Option Traders Against Insider Option Traders, 101 Harv. L. Rev. 1056 (1988).

3. See generally Robert D. Rosenbaum and Stephen M. Bainbridge, The Corporate Takeover Game and Recent Legislative Attempts to Define Insider Trading, 26 Am.

Crim. L. Rev. 229 (1988). The volatile mix of takeovers and insider trading is depicted in Oliver Stone's movie Wall Street (1987). For a fascinating popular history of the 1980s insider trading scandals, see James B. Stewart, Den of Thieves (1991). For a spirited defense of Milken and his ilk, see Daniel R. Fischel, Payback: The Conspiracy to Destroy Michael Milken and His Financial Revolution (1995).

2. *A digression on the difference between inside and market information*

Nonpublic information, for purposes of Rule 10b–5, takes two principal forms: "inside information" and "market information." Inside information typically comes from internal corporate sources and involves events or developments affecting the issuer's assets or earnings. Market information typically originates from sources other than the issuer and involves events or circumstances concerning or affecting the price or market for the issuer's securities and does not concern the issuer's assets or earning power. The information at issue in *Chiarella* thus was a type of market information. This distinction is unimportant for our purposes because insider trading liability can be imposed on those who trade while in possession of either type.[4]

3. *The holding*

Relative to some of those who followed him into federal court, Vincent Chiarella was small fry. But his case produced the first landmark Supreme Court insider trading ruling since *Strong v. Repide.*[5] As noted, in affirming Chiarella's conviction the Second Circuit had invoked *Texas Gulf Sulphur*'s equality of access to information-based disclose or abstain rule. Under the equal access-based standard, Chiarella clearly loses: he had greater access to information than those with whom he traded. But notice: Chiarella was not an employee, officer, or director of any of the companies in whose stock he traded. He worked solely for Pandick Press, which in turn was not an agent of any of those companies. Pandick worked for acquiring companies—not the takeover targets in whose stock Chiarella traded.

Chiarella's conviction demonstrated how far the federal insider trading prohibition had departed from its state common law predecessors. Recall that state common law had required, where it imposed liability at all, a fiduciary relationship between buyer and seller. The mere fact that one party had more information than the other was not grounds for setting aside the transaction or imposing damages. Yet, it was for that reason alone that the Second Circuit upheld Chiarella's conviction.

The Supreme Court reversed.[6] In doing so, the court squarely rejected the notion that § 10(b) was intended to assure all investors equal access to information. The Court said it could not affirm Chiarella's conviction without recognizing a general duty between all participants in market transactions to forego trades based on material, nonpublic information, and it refused to impose such a duty.

Chiarella thus made clear that the disclose or abstain rule is not triggered merely because the trader possesses material nonpublic infor-

---

4. Stephen M. Bainbridge, Note, A Critique of the Insider Trading Sanctions Act of 1984, 71 Va. L. Rev. 455, 477 n.177 (1985).

5. 213 U.S. 419 (1909).

6. Chiarella v. United States, 445 U.S. 222 (1980).

mation. When a 10b–5 action is based upon nondisclosure, "there can be no fraud absent a duty to speak," and no such duty arises from the mere possession of nonpublic information. Instead, the disclose or abstain theory of liability for insider trading was now premised on the inside trader being subject to a duty to disclose to the party on the other side of the transaction that arose from a relationship of trust and confidence between the parties thereto.

Chiarella radically limited the scope of the insider trading prohibition as it had been defined in *Texas Gulf Sulphur*. Consider the landowner hypothetical discussed above: Under an equal access to information-based standard, she is liable for insider trading because she had material information unavailable to those with whom she traded. Under *Chiarella*, however, she cannot be held liable. She is (by hypothesis) not the agent or fiduciary of TGS shareholders and, presumably, has no other special relationship of trust and confidence with them. Accordingly, she is free to trade on the basis of what she knows without fear of liability. The policy conundrum is now flipped, of course: after *Texas Gulf Sulphur*, the question was how large a net should the prohibition cast; after *Chiarella*, the question was how broad should be the scope of immunity created by the new fiduciary relationship requirement.

B. *Dirks*

The Supreme Court tackled that question three years later in *Dirks v. SEC*.[7] Raymond Dirks was a securities analyst who uncovered the massive Equity Funding of America fraud. Dirks first began investigating Equity Funding after receiving allegations from Ronald Secrist, a former officer of Equity Funding, that the corporation was engaged in widespread fraudulent corporate practices. Dirks passed the results of his investigation to the SEC and the Wall Street Journal, but also discussed his findings with various clients. A number of those clients sold their holdings of Equity Funding securities before any public disclosure of the fraud, thereby avoiding substantial losses. After the fraud was made public and Equity Funding went into receivership, the SEC began an investigation of Dirk's role in exposing the fraud. One might think Dirks deserved a medal (certainly Mr. Dirks seems to have felt that way), but one would be wrong. The SEC censured Dirks for violating the federal insider trading prohibition by repeating the allegations of fraud to his clients.

Under the *Texas Gulf Sulphur* equal access to information standard, tipping of the sort at issue in *Dirks* presented no conceptual problems. The tippee had access to information unavailable to those with whom he traded and, as such, was liable. After *Chiarella*, however, the tipping problem was more complex. Neither Dirks nor any of his customers were agents, officers, or directors of Equity Funding. Nor did they have any

7. 463 U.S. 646 (1983).

other form of special relationship of trust and confidence with those with whom they traded.

In reversing Dirk's censure, the Supreme Court expressly reaffirmed its rejection of the equal access standard and its requirement of a breach of fiduciary duty in order for liability to be imposed:

> We were explicit in *Chiarella* in saying that there can be no duty to disclose where the person who has traded on inside information "was not [the corporation's] agent, . . . was not a fiduciary, [or] was not a person in whom the sellers [of the securities] had placed their trust and confidence." Not to require such a fiduciary relationship, we recognized, would "[depart] radically from the established doctrine that duty arises from a specific relationship between two parties" and would amount to "recognizing a general duty between all participants in market transactions to forgo actions based on material, nonpublic information."

Recognizing that this formulation posed problems for tipping cases, the court held that a tippee's liability is derivative of that of the tipper, "arising from [the tippee's] role as a participant after the fact in the insider's breach of a fiduciary duty." A tippee therefore can be held liable only when the tipper breached a fiduciary duty by disclosing information to the tippee, and the tippee knows or has reason to know of the breach of duty.

On the *Dirks* facts, this formulation precluded imposition of liability. To be sure, Secrist was an employee and, hence, a fiduciary of Equity Funding. But the mere fact that an insider tips nonpublic information is not enough under *Dirks*. What *Dirks* proscribes is not merely a breach of confidentiality by the insider, but rather the breach of a fiduciary duty of loyalty to refrain from profiting on information entrusted to the tipper. Looking at objective criteria, courts must determine whether the insider-tipper personally benefited, directly or indirectly, from his disclosure. Secrist tipped off Dirks in order to bring Equity Funding's misconduct to light, not for any personal gain. Absent the requisite personal benefit, liability could not be imposed.

In *Dirks*, the Supreme Court identified several situations in which the requisite personal benefit could be found. The most obvious is the quid pro quo setting, in which the tipper receives some form of pecuniary gain. Nonpecuniary gain can also qualify, however. Suppose a corporate CEO discloses information to a wealthy investor not for any legitimate corporate purpose, but solely to enhance her own reputation. *Dirks* would find a personal benefit on those facts. Finally, *Dirks* indicated that liability could be imposed where the tip is a gift. A gift satisfies the breach element because it is analogous to the situation in which the tipper trades on the basis of the information and then gives the tippee the profits.

1. *Selective disclosure and Regulation FD*

The SEC long has been concerned that selective disclosure to analysts undermines public confidence in the integrity of the stock markets:

> [M]any issuers are disclosing important nonpublic information, such as advance warnings of earnings results, to securities analysts or selected institutional investors or both, before making full disclosure of the same information to the general public. Where this has happened, those who were privy to the information beforehand were able to make a profit or avoid a loss at the expense of those kept in the dark.

> We believe that the practice of selective disclosure leads to a loss of investor confidence in the integrity of our capital markets. Investors who see a security's price change dramatically and only later are given access to the information responsible for that move rightly question whether they are on a level playing field with market insiders.[8]

Unfortunately for the SEC, the *Dirks'* tipping regime was an inadequate constraint on the selective disclosure practice because, inter alia, it can be difficult to prove that the tipper received a personal benefit in connection with a disclosure. In 2000, the SEC adopted Regulation FD to create a noninsider trading-based mechanism for restricting selective disclosure.[9] If someone acting on behalf of a public corporation discloses material nonpublic information to securities market professionals or "holders of the issuer's securities who may well trade on the basis of the information," the issuer must also disclose that information to the public. Where the issuer intentionally provides such disclosure, it must simultaneously disclose the information in a manner designed to convey it to the general public. Hence, for example, if the issuer holds a briefing for selected analysts, it must simultaneously announce the same information through, say, a press release to "a widely disseminated news or wire service." The SEC encouraged issuers to make use of the Internet and other new information technologies, such as by webcasting conference calls with analysts. Where the disclosure was not intentional, as where a corporate officer "let something slip," the issuer must make public disclosure "promptly" after a senior officer learns of the disclosure.

2. *Tipping chains*

At least in theory, it is possible for a tipper to be liable even if the tippee is not liable. The breach of duty is enough to render the tipper

---

8. Exchange Act Rel. No. 43,154 (Aug. 15, 2000). On the relationship between investment analysis and insider trading, see Daniel R. Fischel, Insider Trading and Investment Analysts: An Economic Analysis of Dirks v. SEC, 13 Hofstra L. Rev. 127 (1984); Donald C. Langevoort, Investment Analysts and the Law of Insider Trading, 76 Va. L. Rev. 1023 (1990).

9. See generally Marc I. Steinberg, Insider Trading, Selective Disclosure, and Prompt Disclosure: A Comparative Analysis, 22 U. Penn. J. Int'l Econ. L. 635 (2001).

liable, but the tippee must know of the breach in order to be held liable. Notice also that it is possible to have chains of tipping liability: Tipper tells Tippee #1 who tells Tippee #2 who trades. Tippee #2 can be held liable, so long as she knew or had reason to know that the ultimate source of the information had breached his fiduciary duties by disclosing it.

§ 11.4   The prohibition evolves: The misappropriation theory and rule 14e–3 emerge as post-*Chiarella* gap-fillers

Chiarella created a variety of significant gaps in the insider trading prohibition's coverage. Consider this standard law school hypothetical: A law firm is hired by Raider Corporation to represent it in connection with a planned takeover bid for Target Company. Ann Associate is one of the lawyers assigned to the project. Before Raider publicly discloses its intentions, Associate purchases a substantial block of Target stock. Under the disclose or abstain rule, she has not violated the insider trading prohibition. Whatever the scope of the duties she owed Raider, she owed no duty to the shareholders of Target. Accordingly, the requisite breach of fiduciary duty is not present in her transaction. Rule 14e–3 and the misappropriation theory were created to fill this gap.

A.   Rule 14e–3

Rule 14e–3 was the SEC's immediate response to *Chiarella*.[1] The Rule was specifically intended to reach the wave of insider trading activity associated with the increase in merger and acquisition activity during the 1980s. The rule prohibits insiders of the bidder and target from divulging confidential information about a tender offer to persons that are likely to violate the rule by trading on the basis of that information. This provision (Rule 14e–3(d)(1)) does not prohibit the bidder from buying target shares or from telling its legal and financial advisers about its plans. What the rule prohibits is tipping of information to persons who are likely to buy target shares for their own account. In particular, the rule was intended to strike at the practice known as warehousing. Anecdotal evidence suggests that before Rule 14e–3 was on the books bidders frequently tipped their intentions to friendly parties. Warehousing increased the odds a hostile takeover bid would succeed by increasing the number of shares likely to support the bidder's proposal.

Rule 14e–3 also, with certain narrow and well-defined exceptions, prohibits any person that possesses material information relating to a tender offer by another person from trading in target company securities if the bidder has commenced or has taken substantial steps towards commencement of the bid. The requisite "substantial step" can be found

---

§ 11.4

1.   17 C.F.R. § 240.14e–3. In fact, Rule 14e–3 was pending at the time *Chiarella* was decided, see Chiarella v. United States, 445 U.S. 222, 234 n. 18 (1980), almost as though the Commission knew that its attempts to reach warehousing of takeover securities under Rule 10b–5 were of questionable validity.

even if formal announcement of a tender offer has not yet occurred and, perhaps, even if a tender offer never takes place. Substantial steps include such things as voting on a resolution by the offering person's board of directors relating to the tender offer; the formulation of a plan or proposal to make a tender offer by the offering person; activities which substantially facilitate the tender offer, such as arranging financing for a tender offer, or preparing or directing or authorizing the preparation of tender offer materials.[2] The trader must know or have reason to know that the information is nonpublic. The trader also must know or have reason to know the information was acquired from the bidder or the target company or agents of either.

Unlike both the disclose or abstain rule and the misappropriation theory under Rule 10b–5, Rule 14e–3 liability is not premised on breach of a fiduciary duty. There is no need for a showing that the trading party or tipper was subject to any duty of confidentiality, and no need to show that a tipper personally benefited from the tip. In light of the well-established fiduciary duty requirement under Rule 10b–5, however, the rule arguably ran afoul of *Schreiber v. Burlington Northern, Inc.*,[3] in which the Supreme Court held that § 14(e) was modeled on § 10(b) and, like that section, requires a showing of misrepresentation or nondisclosure. If the two sections are to be interpreted in pari materia, as *Shreiber* indicated, and § 10(b) requires a showing of a breach of a duty in order for liability to arise, the SEC appeared to have exceeded its statutory authority by adopting a rule that makes illegal a variety of trading practices that do not involve any breach of duty. In *United States v. O'Hagan*,[4] however, the Supreme Court upheld Rule 14e–3 as a valid exercise of the SEC's rulemaking authority despite the absence of a fiduciary duty element.

While Rule 14e–3 thus escapes the fiduciary-duty based restrictions of the *Chiarella/Dirks* regime, the Rule nevertheless is quite limited in scope. One prong of the rule (the prohibition on trading while in possession of material nonpublic information) does not apply until the offeror has taken substantial steps towards making the offer. More important, both prongs of the rule are limited to information relating to a tender offer. As a result, most types of inside information remain subject to the duty-based analysis of *Chiarella* and its progeny.

Although most lawsuits under 14e–3 have been brought by the SEC, it seems likely that a private right of action exists under the rule and is

---

2. SEC Release No. 34–17,120 (1980). See, e.g., SEC v. Maio, 51 F.3d 623 (7th Cir.1995) (signing a confidentiality agreement constituted a substantial step where one of the corporate parties had earlier solicited a tender offer); SEC v. Musella, 578 F.Supp. 425 (S.D.N.Y.1984) (retaining law firm to advise on an impending offer constituted a substantial step); Camelot Indus. Corp. v. Vista Resources, Inc., 535 F.Supp. 1174 (S.D.N.Y.1982) (meeting between target managers, prospective acquiror, and an investment banker deemed a substantial step); O'Connor & Assoc. v. Dean Witter Reynolds, Inc., 529 F.Supp. 1179 (S.D.N.Y.1981) (Rule 14e–3 can be violated even if offer never becomes effective).

3. 472 U.S. 1 (1985).

4. 521 U.S. 642, 666–76 (1997).

available to investors trading in the target's securities at the same time as the persons who violated the rule.[5]

B. Misappropriation

In response to the set-backs it suffered in *Chiarella* and *Dirks*, the SEC began advocating a new theory of insider trading liability: the misappropriation theory. Unlike Rule 14e–3, the SEC did not intend for the misappropriation theory to be limited to tender offer cases (although many misappropriation decisions have in fact involved takeovers). Accordingly, the Commission posited misappropriation as a new theory of liability under Rule 10b–5. Which meant, in turn, that the SEC had to find a way of finessing the fiduciary duty requirement imposed by *Chiarella* and *Dirks*.

1. Origins

The misappropriation theory is commonly (but incorrectly) traced to Chief Justice Burger's *Chiarella* dissent. Burger contended that the way in which the inside trader acquires the nonpublic information on which he trades could itself be a material circumstance that must be disclosed to the market before trading. Accordingly, Burger argued, "a person who has misappropriated nonpublic information has an absolute duty [to the persons with whom he trades] to disclose that information or to refrain from trading."[6] The majority did not address the merits of this theory; instead rejecting it solely on the ground that the theory had not been presented to the jury and thus could not sustain a criminal conviction.

Consequently, the way was left open for the SEC to urge, and the lower courts to adopt, the misappropriation theory as an alternative basis of insider trading liability.[7] The Second Circuit swiftly moved to take advantage of that opportunity. In *United States v. Newman*,[8] employees of an investment bank misappropriated confidential information concerning proposed mergers involving clients of the firm. As was true of Vincent Chiarella, the Newman defendants' employer worked for prospective acquiring companies, while the trading took place in target

---

5. See, e.g., O'Connor & Assoc. v. Dean Witter Reynolds, Inc., 529 F.Supp. 1179 (S.D.N.Y.1981).

6. Chiarella v. United States, 445 U.S. 222, 240 (1980) (Burger, C.J., dissenting).

7. On the post-*Chiarella* definition of insider trading, see generally Douglas Branson, Discourse on the Supreme Court Approach to SEC Rule 10b–5 and Insider Trading, 30 Emory L.J. 263 (1981); James D. Cox, Choices: Paving the Road Toward a Definition of Insider Trading, 39 Ala. L. Rev. 381 (1988); Jill E. Fisch, Start Making Sense: An Analysis and Proposal for Insider Trading Regulation, 26 Ga. L. Rev. 179 (1991); Donald C. Langevoort, Insider Trading and the Fiduciary Principle: A Post-Chiarella Restatement, 70 California Law Review 1 (1982); Jonathan R. Macey, From Judicial Solutions to Political Solutions: The New, New Direction of the Rules Against Insider Trading, 39 Ala. L. Rev. 355 (1988); Lawrence E. Mitchell, The Jurisprudence of the Misappropriation Theory and the New Insider Trading Legislation: From Fairness to Efficiency and Back, 52 Albany L. Rev. 775 (1988); William K. S. Wang, Post–Chiarella Developments in Rule 10b–5, 15 Rev. Sec. Reg. 956 (1982); William K. S. Wang, Recent Developments in the Federal Law Regulating Stock Market Inside Trading, 6 Corp. L. Rev. 291 (1983).

8. 664 F.2d 12 (2d Cir.1981).

company securities. As such, the Newman defendants owed no fiduciary duties to the investors with whom they traded. Moreover, neither the investment bank nor its clients traded in the target companies' shares contemporaneously with the defendants.

Unlike Chief Justice Burger's *Chiarella* dissent, the Second Circuit did not assert that the Newman defendants owed any duty of disclosure to the investors with whom they traded or had defrauded. Instead, the court held that by misappropriating confidential information for personal gain, the defendants had defrauded their employer and its clients, and this fraud sufficed to impose insider trading liability on the defendants with whom they traded.[9] As eventually refined, the (pre-*O'Hagan*) misappropriation theory thus imposed liability on anyone who: (1) misappropriated material nonpublic information; (2) thereby breaching a fiduciary duty or a duty arising out of a similar relationship of trust and confidence; and (3) used that information in a securities transaction, regardless of whether he owed any duties to the shareholders of the company in whose stock he traded.[10]

Like the traditional disclose or abstain rule, the misappropriation theory thus required a breach of fiduciary duty before trading on inside information became unlawful.[11] The fiduciary relationship in question, however, was a quite different one. Under the misappropriation theory, the defendant did not need to owe a fiduciary duty to the investor with whom he traded, nor did he need to owe a fiduciary duty to the issuer of the securities that were traded. Instead, the misappropriation theory applied when the inside trader violated a fiduciary duty owed to the source of the information.[12] Had the misappropriation theory been available against Chiarella, for example, his conviction could have been upheld even though he owed no duties to those with whom he had traded. Instead, the breach of the duty he owed to Pandick Press would have sufficed.

The misappropriation theory should be seen as the vehicle by which the SEC sought to recapture as much as possible the ground it had lost in *Chiarella* and *Dirks*. In the years following those decisions, the SEC (and the lower courts) seemed to view the fiduciary duty element as a mere inconvenience that should not stand in the way of expansive insider trading liability. They consistently sought to evade the spirit of the fiduciary duty requirement, while complying with its letter. Even a former SEC Commissioner admitted as much, acknowledging that the misappropriation theory was "merely a pretext for enforcing equal

---

9. See U.S. v. Newman, 664 F.2d 12, 17 (2d Cir.1981); see also United States v. Carpenter, 791 F.2d 1024 (2d Cir.1986), aff'd on other grounds, 484 U.S. 19 (1987); SEC v. Materia, 745 F.2d 197 (2d Cir.1984), cert. denied, 471 U.S. 1053 (1985).

10. See United States v. Bryan, 58 F.3d 933, 945 (4th Cir.1995).

11. See SEC v. Switzer, 590 F.Supp. 756, 766 (W.D.Okla.1984) (stating that it is not unlawful to trade on the basis of inadvertently overheard information).

12. See, e.g., United States v. Carpenter, 791 F.2d 1024, 1028–29 (2d Cir.1986) (applying misappropriation theory to a journalist who breaches his duty of confidentiality to his employer).

opportunity in information."[13] Put another way, the SEC used the misappropriation theory as a means of redirecting the prohibition back towards the direction in which *Texas Gulf Sulphur* had initially set it.[14]

2.   O'Hagan and Bryan: The misappropriation theory is called into question

The Supreme Court first took up the misappropriation theory in *Carpenter v. United States*,[15] in which a Wall Street Journal reporter and his confederates misappropriated information belonging to the Journal. The Supreme Court upheld the resulting convictions under the mail and wire fraud statutes, holding that confidential business information is property protected by those statutes from being taken by trick, deceit, or chicanery.[16] As to the defendants' securities fraud convictions, however, the court split 4–4. Following the long-standing tradition governing evenly divided Supreme Court decisions, the lower court ruling was affirmed without opinion, but that ruling had no precedential or stare decisis value.

The way was thus left open for lower courts to reject the misappropriation theory, which the Fourth and Eighth Circuits subsequently did in, respectively, *United States v. Bryan*[17] and *United States v. O'Hagan*.[18] These courts held that Rule 10b–5 imposed liability only where there has been deception upon the purchaser or seller of securities, or upon some other person intimately linked with or affected by a securities transaction. Because the misappropriation theory involves no such deception, but rather simply a breach of fiduciary duty owed to the source of the information, the theory could not stand. The Supreme Court took cert in *United States v. O'Hagan* to resolve the resulting split between these

---

13. Charles C. Cox & Kevin S. Fogarty, Bases of Insider Trading Law, 49 Ohio St. L.J. 353, 366 (1988).

14. One of the more puzzling features of the federal insider trading prohibition is the willingness of courts to aid and abet the Commission's efforts. Although the SEC's incentive to erect a broad insider trading prohibition seems easily explainable as a matter of political economy, it is far less clear why courts would be willing to go along. Yet they have consistently done so. The *Cady, Roberts* power grab was validated by *Texas Gulf Sulphur Co.*. The reversal suffered in *Chiarella* was followed by *Newman*. The SEC's most recent reversals in *O'Hagan* and *Bryan* were swept aside by the Supreme Court. At every turn, judges have aided and abetted the SEC. For an attempt to explain this course of judicial conduct, see Stephen M. Bainbridge, Insider Trading Regulation: The Path Dependent Choice between Property Rights and Securities Fraud, 52 SMU L. Rev. 1589, 1635–40 (1999).

15. 484 U.S. 19 (1987).

16. The federal mail and wire fraud statutes, 18 U.S.C. §§ 1341 and 1343, respectively prohibit the use of the mails and "wire, radio, or television communication" for the purpose of executing any "scheme or artifice to defraud." The mail and wire fraud statutes protect only property rights, McNally v. United States, 483, U.S. 350 (1987), but confidential business information is deemed to be property for purposes of those statutes. Carpenter v. United States, 484 U.S. 19, 25 (1987). Hence, the Supreme Court held, the Wall Street Journal owned the information used by Winans and his co-conspirators and, moreover, that their use of the mails and wire communications to trade on the basis of that information constituted the requisite scheme to defraud. Arguably, after *Carpenter* and *O'Hagan*, if there is a Rule 10b–5 violation there will also be a mail and wire fraud violation and vice-versa.

17. 58 F.3d 933 (4th Cir.1995).

18. 92 F.3d 612 (8th Cir.1996), rev'd, 521 U.S. 642 (1997).

circuits and the prior Second Circuit holdings validating the misappropriation theory.

3. O'Hagan: Facts

James O'Hagan was a partner in the Minneapolis law firm of Dorsey & Whitney. In July 1988, Grand Metropolitan PLC (Grand Met), retained Dorsey & Whitney in connection with its planned takeover of Pillsbury Company. Although O'Hagan was not one of the lawyers on the Grand Met project, he learned of their intentions and began buying Pillsbury stock and call options on Pillsbury stock. When Grand Met announced its tender offer in October, the price of Pillsbury stock nearly doubled, allowing O'Hagan to reap a profit of more than $4.3 million.

O'Hagan was charged with violating 1934 Act § 10(b) and Rule 10b–5 by trading on misappropriated nonpublic information. As with Chiarella and the *Newman* defendants, O'Hagan could not be held liable under the disclose or abstain rule because he worked for the bidder but traded in target company stock. He was neither a classic insider nor a constructive insider of the issuer of the securities in which he traded.[19]

4. O'Hagan: Issues

Both § 10(b) and Rule 10b–5 sweep broadly, capturing "any" fraudulent or manipulative conduct "in connection with" the purchase or sale of "any" security. Despite the almost breath-taking expanse of regulatory authority Congress thereby delegated to the Commission, the Supreme Court has warned against expanding the concept of securities fraud beyond that which the words of the statute will reasonably bear.[20] The validity of the misappropriation theory thus depends upon whether (1) the deceit, if any, worked by the misappropriator on the source of the information constitutes deception as the term is used in § 10(b) and Rule 10b–5 and (2) any such deceit is deemed to have occurred "in connection with" the purchase or sale of a security.

Deceit on the source of the information; herein of Santa Fe. In *Bryan*, the Fourth Circuit defined fraud—as the term is used in § 10(b) and Rule 10b–5—"as the making of a material misrepresentation or the nondisclosure of material information in violation of a duty to dis-

---

19. O'Hagan was also indicted for violations of Rule 14e–3, which proscribes insider trading in connection with tender offers, and the federal mail fraud and money laundering statutes. The Eighth Circuit overturned O'Hagan's convictions under those provisions. As to Rule 14e–3, the court held that the SEC lacked authority to adopt a prohibition of insider trading that does not require a breach of fiduciary duty. U.S. v. O'Hagan, 92 F.3d 612, 622–27 (8th Cir. 1996), rev'd, 521 U.S. 642 (1997). As to O'Hagan's mail fraud and money laundering convictions, the Eighth Circuit also reversed them on grounds that the indict-

ment was structured so as to premise the charges under those provisions on the primary securities fraud violations. Id. at 627–28. Accordingly, in view of the court's reversal of the securities fraud convictions, the latter counts could not stand either. The Supreme Court reversed on all points, reinstating O'Hagan's convictions under all of the statutory violations charged in the indictment. United States v. O'Hagan, 521 U.S. 642 (1997).

20. Central Bank of Denver v. First Interstate Bank, 511 U.S. 164, 174 (1994).

close.''[21] So defined, fraud is present in a misappropriation case only in a technical and highly formalistic sense. Although a misappropriator arguably deceives the source of the information, any such deception is quite inconsequential. The source of the information presumably is injured, if at all, not by the deception, but by the conversion of the information by the misappropriator for his own profit. Hence, it is theft—and any concomitant breach of fiduciary duty—by the misappropriator that is truly objectionable. Any deception on the source of the information is purely incidental to the theft. Accordingly, the Fourth Circuit held, the misappropriation theory runs afoul of the Supreme Court's holding in *Santa Fe* that a mere breach of duty cannot give rise to Rule 10b–5 liability.[22]

Recall from Chapter 3 that Santa Fe had attempted to freeze out minority shareholders of one of its subsidiaries by means of a statutory short-form merger. While plaintiff-shareholders had a state law remedy available in the statutory appraisal rights provision, they sought redress under Rule 10b–5 instead. They claimed that the merger violated Rule 10b–5 because the deal was effected without prior notice to the minority shareholders and was done without any legitimate business purpose. They also claimed that their shares had been fraudulently under-valued. In holding that plaintiffs had failed to state a cause of action under Rule 10b–5, the Supreme Court opined that § 10(b) and Rule 10b–5 were only intended to reach deception and manipulation—neither of which was present in the case at bar.

Santa Fe's requirement that conduct involve deception in order to fall within Rule 10b–5's scope featured prominently in the reasoning of those circuit courts that rejected the misappropriation theory. In *Bryan*, for example, the Fourth Circuit opined that "the misappropriation theory does not even require deception, but rather allows the imposition of liability upon the mere breach of fiduciary relationship or similar relationship of trust and confidence."[23] And, as such, ran afoul of *Santa Fe*.

Of even greater potential relevance to the problem at hand, however, is the *Santa Fe* Court's concern that a decision in favor of the

21. U.S. v. Bryan, 58 F.3d 933, 946 (4th Cir.1995).

22. See Santa Fe Industries, Inc. v. Green, 430 U.S. 462, 476 (1977). See generally Stephen M. Bainbridge, Incorporating State Law Fiduciary Duties into the Federal Insider Trading Prohibition, 52 Wash & Lee L. Rev. 1189, 1258–61 (1995) (discussing the federalism implications of insider trading regulations); Richard W. Painter et al., Don't Ask, Just Tell: Insider Trading after United States v. O'Hagan, 84 Va. L. Rev. 153, 174–86 (1998) (same); Larry E. Ribstein, Federalism and Insider Trading, 6 Sup. Ct. Econ. Rev. 123, 149–54 (1998) (same).

23. U.S. v. Bryan, 58 F.3d 933, 949 (4th Cir.1995). This interpretation of the misappropriation theory is clearly incorrect post-*O'Hagan*, in light of the Supreme Court's requirement that the source of the information be deceived, and arguably misreads the pre-*O'Hagan* circuit court decisions endorsing the theory. Although courts adopting the misappropriation theory recognized that Rule 10b–5 only encompasses fraud and manipulation, they held that the deception the misappropriator works on the source of the information suffices to impose liability on him. See, e.g., United States v. Chestman, 947 F.2d 551, 566 (2d Cir.1991).

plaintiffs would result in federalizing much of state corporate law.[24] *Santa Fe* is part of a long line of securities law cases in which the Supreme Court came down on the states side of federalism disputes. For example, the Court has emphasized that "state regulation of corporate governance is regulation of entities whose very existence and attributes are a product of state law,"[25] from which the Court extrapolated the proposition that "it . . . is an accepted part of the business landscape in this country for States to create corporations, to prescribe their powers, and to define the rights that are acquired by purchasing their shares." In keeping with that principle, the Court emphasized that state law governs the rights and duties of corporate directors: "As we have said in the past, the first place one must look to determine the powers of corporate directors is in the relevant State's corporation law.... 'Corporations are creatures of state law' . . . and it is state law which is the font of corporate directors' powers."[26]

The insider trading prohibition co-exists uneasily with these principles, at best. In *Santa Fe*, for example, the Court held that Rule 10b–5 did not reach claims "in which the essence of the complaint is that shareholders were treated unfairly by a fiduciary."[27] Yet, this is the very essence of the complaint made in insider trading cases. The Court also held that extension of Rule 10b–5 to breaches of fiduciary duty was unjustified in light of the state law remedies available to plaintiffs. Likewise, insider trading plaintiffs have available state law remedies. Granted, these remedies vary from state to state and are likely to prove unavailing in many cases. The same was true, however, of the state law remedy at issue in *Santa Fe*. Finally, the Court expressed reluctance "to federalize the substantial portion of the law of corporations that deals with transactions in securities, particularly where established state policies of corporate regulation would be overridden." But this is precisely what the federal insider trading prohibition did.

Santa Fe thus loomed as a substantial obstacle for proponents of an insider trading prohibition grounded in securities fraud. As the Fourth Circuit put it: "the misappropriation theory transforms Section 10(b) from a rule intended to govern and protect relations among market participants who are owed duties under the securities laws into a federal common law governing and protecting any and all trust relationships."[28] It thus amounts to "the effective federalization of [fiduciary] relationships historically regulated by the states," which is precisely what *Santa Fe* was intended to prevent.

The "in connection with" requirement; herein of Central Bank. According to the Eighth Circuit's *O'Hagan* opinion, "the misappropriation theory does not require 'deception,' and, even assuming that it does,

---

24. See Santa Fe Industries, Inc. v. Green, 430 U.S. 462, 478–79 (1977).

25. CTS Corp. v. Dynamics Corp., 481 U.S. 69, 89 (1987).

26. Burks v. Lasker, 441 U.S. 471, 478 (1979) (citations omitted).

27. Santa Fe Industries, Inc. v. Green, 430 U.S. 462, 477 (1977).

28. See U.S. v. Bryan, 58 F.3d 933, 950 (4th Cir.1995).

it renders nugatory the requirement that the 'deception' be 'in connection with the purchase or sale of any security,' " as required by the text of § 10(b).[29] As such, the Eighth Circuit held that the theory ran afoul of the Supreme Court's *Central Bank*[30] decision.

Recall from Chapter 3 that *Central Bank* held the text of § 10(b) to be dispositive with respect to the scope of conduct regulated by that section. The Eighth Circuit interpreted the statutory prohibition of fraud created by § 10(b) narrowly to exclude conduct constituting a "mere breach of a fiduciary duty," but rather to capture only conduct constituting a material misrepresentation or the nondisclosure of material information in violation of the duty to disclose. Insofar as the misappropriation theory permits the imposition of § 10(b) liability based upon a breach of fiduciary duty without any such deception, the Eighth Circuit held that the theory was inconsistent with the plain statutory text of § 10(b) and, accordingly, invalid as per *Central Bank*.

The Eighth Circuit's principal rationale for rejecting the misappropriation theory, however, was based on the statutory limitation that the fraud be committed "in connection with" a securities transaction. Again relying upon the Supreme Court's *Central Bank* decision, the *O'Hagan* court gave this provision a narrow interpretation. Specifically, the court held that § 10(b) reaches "only a breach of a duty to parties to the securities transaction or, at the most, to other market participants such as investors."[31] Absent such a limitation, the court opined, § 10(b) would be transformed "into an expansive 'general fraud-on-the-source theory' which seemingly would apply infinite number of trust relationships." Such an expansive theory of liability, the court further opined, could not be justified by the text of statute.

In the typical misappropriation case, of course, the source of the information is not the affected purchaser or seller. Often the source is not even a contemporaneous purchaser or seller and frequently has no stake in any affected securities transaction. In *Carpenter*, for example, the Wall Street Journal was neither a purchaser nor seller of the affected securities, nor did it have any financial stake in any of the affected transactions. Similarly, in *Bryan*, the state of West Virginia was not a purchaser or seller, and had no direct stake in Bryan's securities transactions. In neither case did the defendant fail to disclose material information to a market participant to whom he owed a duty of disclosure. One thus must stretch the phrase "in connection with" pretty far in order to bring a misappropriator's alleged fraud within the statute's ambit, even assuming the misappropriator has deceived the source of the information . As the Fourth Circuit put it: "The misappropriation of information

29. U.S. v. O'Hagan, 92 F.3d 612, 617 (8th Cir.1996), rev'd, 521 U.S. 642 (1997).

30. Central Bank of Denver v. First Interstate Bank, 511 U.S. 164 (1994).

31. U.S. v. O'Hagan, 92 F.3d 612, 618 (8th Cir.1996), rev'd, 521 U.S. 642 (1997). In *Bryan*, the Fourth Circuit similarly opined § 10(b) is primarily concerned with deception of purchasers and sellers of securities, and at most extends to fraud committed against other persons closely linked to, and with a stake in, a securities transaction. U.S. v. Bryan, 58 F.3d 933, 946 (4th Cir.1995).

from an individual who is in no way connected to, or even interested in, securities is simply not the kind of conduct with which the securities laws, as presently written, are concerned."[32]

The Eighth and Fourth Circuits' interpretation of § 10(b) has much to commend it. The courts carefully considered the Supreme Court's relevant precedents, especially *Santa Fe* and *Central Bank*. Insofar as the misappropriation theory imposes liability solely on the basis of a breach of fiduciary duty to the source of the information, without any requirement that the alleged perpetrator have deceived the persons with whom he traded or other market participants, it arguably ran afoul of those precedents. As the Eighth Circuit opined, the lower court decisions endorsing the misappropriation theory had generally failed to conduct a rigorous analysis of § 10(b)'s text or the pertinent Supreme Court decisions. Indeed, in a telling passage of his partial dissent to a leading Second Circuit opinion endorsing and fleshing out the misappropriation theory, Judge Winter (a former corporate law professor at Yale) stated the misappropriation theory lacked "any obvious relationship" to the statutory text of § 10(b) because "theft rather than fraud or deceit" had become "the gravamen of the prohibition."[33] In light of these considerations, reconciling the insider trading prohibition with *Central Bank* loomed as one of the major doctrinal problems facing the Supreme Court in *O'Hagan*.

5. *O'Hagan: Holding*

In *O'Hagan*, a majority of the Supreme Court upheld the misappropriation theory as a valid basis on which to impose insider trading liability. A fiduciary's undisclosed use of information belonging to his principal, without disclosure of such use to the principal, for personal gain constitutes fraud in connection with the purchase or sale of a security, the majority (per Justice Ginsburg) opined, and thus violates Rule 10b–5.[34]

The court acknowledged that misappropriators such as O'Hagan have no disclosure obligation running to the persons with whom they trade. Instead, it grounded liability under the misappropriation theory on deception of the source of the information. As the majority interpreted the theory, it addresses the use of "confidential information for securities trading purposes, in breach of a duty owed to the source of the information." Under this theory, the majority explained, "a fiduciary's undisclosed, self serving use of a principal's information to purchase or sell securities, in breach of a duty of loyalty and confidentiality, defrauds the principal of the exclusive use of that information." So defined, the majority held, the misappropriation theory satisfies § 10(b)'s require-

---

32. U.S. v. Bryan, 58 F.3d 933, 950 (4th Cir.1995).

33. United States v. Chestman, 947 F.2d 551, 578 (2d Cir.1991) (Winter, J., concurring in part and dissenting in part).

34. United States v. O'Hagan, 521 U.S. 642 (1997). See generally Donna Nagy, Reframing the Misappropriation Theory of Insider Trading Liability: A Post-*O'Hagan* Suggestion, 59 Ohio St. L.J. 1223 (1998).

ment that there be a "deceptive device or contrivance" used "in connection with" a securities transaction.[35]

Status of Central Bank: As we have just seen, the tension between *Central Bank* and the insider trading prohibition was a major doctrinal issue facing the court in *O'Hagan*. Surprisingly, however, the majority essentially punted on this issue. The majority ignored the statutory text, except for some rather glib assertions about the meaning of the phrases "deception" and "in connection with." The Supreme Court also ignored the cogent arguments advanced by both the Eighth and Fourth Circuits with respect to the implications of *Central Bank* for the misappropriation theory. To the extent the majority discussed *Central Bank*'s implications for the problem at hand, it focused solely on the Eighth Circuit's argument that *Central Bank* limited Rule 10b–5's regulatory purview to purchasers and sellers. The interpretive methodology expounded in *Central Bank* was essentially ignored. One is therefore left to wonder whether the strict textualist approach taken by *Central Bank* was a one time aberration.

The majority's failure to more carefully evaluate *Central Bank*'s implications for the phrase "in connection with," as used in § 10(b), is especially troubling. By virtue of the majority's holding that deception on the source of the information satisfies the "in connection with" requirement, fraudulent conduct having only tenuous connections to a securities transaction is brought within Rule 10b–5's scope. There has long been a risk that Rule 10b–5 will become a universal solvent, encompassing not only virtually the entire universe of securities fraud, but also much of state corporate law. The minimal contacts *O'Hagan* requires between the fraudulent act and a securities transaction substantially exacerbate that risk. In addition to the risk that much of state corporate law may be preempted by federal developments under Rule 10b–5, the uncertainty created as to Rule 10b–5's parameters fairly raises vagueness and related due process issues,[36] despite the majority's rather glib dismissal of such concerns.

Status of Santa Fe: The majority opinion treated *Santa Fe* as a mere disclosure case, asserting: "in *Santa Fe Industries*, all pertinent facts were disclosed by the persons charged with violating § 10(b) and Rule 10b–5; therefore, there was no deception through nondisclosure to which liability under those provisions could attach." The court thus wholly ignored the important federalism concerns upon which *Santa Fe* rested and which are implicated by the misappropriation theory (indeed, by the insider trading prohibition as a whole).

---

35. The Supreme Court thus rejected Chief Justice Burger's argument in *Chiarella* that the misappropriation theory created disclosure obligation running to those with whom the misappropriator trades. United States v. O'Hagan, 521 U.S. 642, 655 n. 6 (1997). Instead, it is the failure to disclose one's intentions to the source of the information that constitutes the requisite disclosure violation under the *O'Hagan* version of the misappropriation theory. Id. at 653–55.

36. See Richard W. Painter et al., Don't Ask, Just Tell: Insider Trading after United States v. O'Hagan, 84 Va. L. Rev. 153, 196–200 (1998).

6. Open questions

In many respects, *O'Hagan* posed more new questions than it answered old ones. Here are some of the more interesting and important issues it left open:

Liability for brazen misappropriators? The *O'Hagan* majority made clear that disclosure to the source of the information is all that is required under Rule 10b–5. If a brazen misappropriator discloses his trading plans to the source, and then trades on that information, Rule 10b–5 is not violated, even if the source of the information refused permission to trade and objected vigorously.[37] If this rule seems odd, so did the majority's justification for it.

According to the majority, "investors likely would hesitate to venture their capital in a market where trading based on misappropriated nonpublic information is unchecked by law," because they suffer from "a disadvantage that cannot be overcome with research or skill." As such, the majority claimed, the misappropriation theory advances "an animating purpose of the Exchange Act: to ensure honest securities markets and thereby promote investor confidence."

The difficulties with this argument should be readily apparent. Investors who trade with a brazen misappropriator presumably will not feel any greater confidence in the integrity of the securities market if they later find out that the misappropriator had disclosed his intentions to the source of the information. Worse yet, both the phraseology and the substance of the majority's argument plausibly could be interpreted as resurrecting the long-discredited equal access test.[38] If the goal of insider trading law in fact is to insulate investors from information asymmetries that cannot be overcome by research or skill, the equal access test is far better suited to doing so than the current test.

Merely requiring the prospective misappropriator to disclose his intentions before trading also provides only weak protection of the source of the information's property rights therein. To be sure, because of the disclosure requirement concerns about detecting improper trading are alleviated. As the majority pointed out, moreover, the source may have state law claims against the misappropriator. In particular, the agency law prohibition on the use of confidential information for personal gain will often provide a remedy to the source. In some jurisdictions, however, it is far from clear whether inside trading by a fiduciary violates state law. Even where state law proscribes such trading, the Supreme Court's approach means that in brazen misappropriator cases we lose the comparative advantage the SEC has in litigating insider

---

37. United States v. O'Hagan, 521 U.S. 642, 655 (1997) ("full disclosure forecloses liability under the misappropriation theory ... if the fiduciary discloses to the source that he plans to trade on the nonpublic information, there is no 'deceptive device' and thus no § 10(b) violation").

38. For an argument that *O'Hagan* is premised on equal access-related concerns, see Elliott J. Weiss, United States v. O'Hagan: Pragmatism returns to the Law of Insider Trading, 23 J. Corp. L. 395 (1998).

trading cases and, moreover, also lose the comparative advantage provided by the well-developed and relatively liberal remedy under Rule 10b–5.

Liability for authorized trading? Suppose a takeover bidder authorized an arbitrageur to trade in a target company's stock on the basis of material nonpublic information about the prospective bidder's intentions. Warehousing of this sort is proscribed by Rule 14e–3, but only insofar as the information relates to a prospective tender offer. Whether such trading in a nontender offer context violated Rule 10b–5 was unclear before *O'Hagan*.

The *O'Hagan* majority at least implicitly validated authorized trading. It approvingly quoted, for example, the statement of the government's counsel that "to satisfy the common law rule that a trustee may not use the property that [has] been entrusted [to] him, there would have to be consent."[39] On the facts of *O'Hagan*, as the majority indicated, insiders would need approval from both Dorsey & Whitney and Grand Met in order to escape Rule 10b–5 liability. Is it plausible that Grand Met would have given such approval? Maybe. Warehousing of takeover stocks and tipping acquisition plans to friendly parties were once common—hence the need for Rule 14e–3—and probably still occurs.

Notice the interesting question presented by the requirement that O'Hagan disclose his intentions to Dorsey & Whitney. Given that O'Hagan was a partner in Dorsey & Whitney, query whether his knowledge of his intentions would be imputed to the firm. As a practical matter, of course, O'Hagan should have informed the lawyer with the principal responsibility for the Grand Met transaction and/or the firm's managing partner.

The authorized trading dictum has significant, but as yet little-noticed, implications. Query, for example, whether it applies to all insider trading cases or just to misappropriation cases. Suppose that in a classic disclose or abstain case, such as *Texas Gulf Sulphur*, the issuer's board of directors adopted a policy of allowing insider trading by managers. If they did so, the corporation has consented to any such inside trading, which under Justice Ginsburg's analysis appears to vitiate any deception. The corporate policy itself presumably would have to be disclosed, just as broad disclosure respecting executive compensation is already required, but the implication is that authorized trading should not result in 10b–5 liability under either misappropriation or disclose or abstain theory of liability.

On the other hand, the two theories can be distinguished in ways that undermine application of the authorized trading dictum to disclose or abstain cases. In a misappropriation case, such as *Carpenter*, liability is premised on fraud on the source of the information. In *Carpenter*, acting through appropriate decision making processes, the Journal could authorize inside trading by its agents. By contrast, however, *Chiarella* focused the classic disclose or abstain rule on fraud perpetrated on the

---

39. United States v. O'Hagan, 521 U.S. 642, 654 (1997).

specific investors with whom the insiders trade. Authorization of inside trading by the issuer's board of directors, or even a majority of the shareholders, does not constitute consent by the specific investors with whom the insider trades. Nothing in *O'Hagan* explicitly suggests an intent to undermine the *Chiarella* interpretation of the traditional disclose or abstain rule. To the contrary, Justice Ginsburg expressly states that the two theories are "complementary." Because the disclose or abstain rule thus remains conceptually distinct from the misappropriation theory, the authorized trading dictum can be plausibly limited to the latter context.

The fiduciary relationship requirement. Does a duty to disclose to the source of the information arise before trading in all fiduciary relationships? Consider ABA Model Rule of Professional Conduct 1.8(b), which states: "A lawyer shall not use information relating to representation of a client to the disadvantage of the client unless the client consents after consultation. . . ." Does a lawyer's use of confidential client information for insider trading purposes always operate to the client's disadvantage? If not, and assuming the Model Rule accurately states the lawyer's fiduciary obligation, O'Hagan did not violate § 10(b).

The *O'Hagan* majority, however, failed to inquire into the nature of O'Hagan's duties, if any, to Grand Met. Instead, the majority assumed that lawyers are fiduciaries, all fiduciaries are subject to a duty to refrain from self dealing in confidential information, and, accordingly, that the misappropriation theory applies to lawyers and all other fiduciaries. The majority's approach, of course, begs the question—how do we know O'Hagan is a fiduciary?

Criminal or civil? In rejecting the Eighth Circuit's argument that Rule 10b–5 is primarily concerned with deception of market participants, the majority noted that the discussion in *Central Bank* upon which the Eighth Circuit relied dealt only with private civil litigation under § 10(b). The court then went on to discuss its holding in *Blue Chip Stamps*[40] that only actual purchasers or sellers of securities have standing to bring private causes of action under Rule 10b–5. The court concluded: "Criminal prosecutions do not present the dangers the Court addressed in *Blue Chip Stamps*, so that decision is 'inapplicable' to indictments for violations of § 10(b) and Rule 10b–5."[41]

This passage opens the door for misappropriators to argue that *O'Hagan* should be limited to criminal prosecutions, because the majority acknowledged the limitations imposed by *Central Bank* and *Blue Chip Stamps* on private party litigation. Such a limitation on private party litigation, however, seems unlikely. Although the majority declined to address the significance of the 1988 statute and its legislative history for the validity of the misappropriation theory, interpreting *O'Hagan* as validating the misappropriation theory only as to criminal actions would

40. Blue Chip Stamps v. Manor Drug Stores, 421 U.S. 723 (1975).

41. United States v. O'Hagan, 521 U.S. 642, 665 (1997).

render the private party cause of action created by Exchange Act § 20A nugatory.

§ 11.5   Elements of the modern prohibition

A.   Material nonpublic information

1.   *Materiality*

In cases arising under § 10(b) and Rule 10b–5, liability arises only with respect to the misuse of material information. Materiality is defined for this purpose as whether there is a substantial likelihood that a reasonable investor would consider the omitted fact important in deciding whether to buy or sell securities.[1] Where a fact is contingent or speculative, such as was the case in *Texas Gulf Sulphur*, materiality is determined by balancing the indicated probability that the event will occur and the anticipated magnitude of the event in light of the totality of the company's activity.

In a case like *Texas Gulf Sulphur*, it is just as important to determine when the information in question became material as it is to determine whether the information was material. Consider how the materiality standard would apply at two critical dates: November 12, when the visual assay indicated a potentially significant ore strike, and April 7, when the results of additional test holes confirmed that mining would be commercially viable.

Under these standards, the ore discovery was certainly material as of April 7. The additional test holes had confirmed that the initial core sample was not an aberration—TGS really had a major find on its hands. After April 7, the critical issue is not whether the strike will pay off, but when. The balancing test thus is not at issue, because we are no longer dealing with a contingent fact. Given the size of the discovery, this was certainly information any reasonable investor would consider significant.

It is less clear that the information known on November 12th would be regarded as material as of that date. Before April there was only one core sample. While that sample was remarkable, only a highly trained geologist would be able to draw conclusions from it. Since it would take a highly sophisticated investor with considerable expertise in mining operations to understand the relevance of the find, perhaps the hypothetical reasonable investor would not consider it important. On the other hand, however, there was testimony from a stock broker that one good test hole was a signal to buy mining stock.[2]

One might also consider the response of the company and the insiders. The firm's decision to acquire options on the surrounding land tends to point towards a finding of materiality. According to the court, so

§ 11.5

1. Basic Inc. v. Levinson, 485 U.S. 224, 231–32 (1988).

2. SEC v. Texas Gulf Sulphur Co., 401 F.2d 833, 850–51 (2d Cir.1968), cert. denied, 394 U.S. 976 (1969).

did the insiders' own trading conduct, although this is a somewhat dubious proposition in view of the resulting bootstrapping effect.

2. *Nonpublic information: When can insiders trade?*

When can insiders start trading in their company's securities, if ever? The simple answer is that insiders who do not possess (or, perhaps, use) material nonpublic information may trade freely. Timing questions arise, however, when an insiders trade contemporaneously with public disclosure of the material nonpublic information in their possession. In such cases, insiders may only trade after the information in question has been made public. The difficulty, of course, is knowing whether or not the information in question has entered the public domain. Because insiders with access to confidential information trade at their own risk, this timing issue is a critical question.

Texas Gulf Sulphur again is instructive.[3] The ore strike was first announced by a press release to the Canadian news media disseminated at 9:40 a.m. on April 16, 1964. A news conference with the American media followed at 10 a.m. on the same day. The news appeared on the Dow Jones ticker tape at 10:54 a.m. that day. Defendant Crawford had telephoned his stockbroker at midnight on the 15th with instructions to buy TGS stock when the Midwest Stock Exchange opened the next morning. Defendant Coates left the April 16th news conference to call his stockbroker shortly before 10:20 a.m. In addition to executing Coates' order, the broker ordered an additional 1500 TGS shares for himself and other customers. Crawford and Coates conceded that they traded while in possession of material information, but claimed that the information had been effectively disseminated to the public (and thus had lost its nonpublic character) before their trades were executed.

The court disagreed, holding that before insiders may act upon material information, the information must have been disclosed in a manner that ensures its availability to the investing public. Merely waiting until a press release has been read to reporters, as Coates did, is not enough. The information must have been widely disseminated and public investors must have an opportunity to act on it. At a minimum, the court opined, insiders therefore must wait until the news could reasonably be expected to appear over the Dow Jones ticker tape—the news service that transmits investment news to brokers and investment professionals.

Unlike other aspects of *Texas Gulf Sulphur*, this rule is still good law today. It also makes good policy sense. The efficient capital markets hypothesis tells us that all currently available public information about a corporation is reflected in the market price of its securities. However, the hypothesis depends on the ability of investment professionals to adjust their selling and offering prices to reflect that information. By

---

3. SEC v. Texas Gulf Sulphur Co., 401   U.S. 976 (1969).
F.2d 833 (2d Cir.1968), cert. denied, 394

requiring that insiders wait until the news has gone out over the Dow Jones wire, the court assured that brokers would have the information before trading; in other words, the price should have already started rising (or falling, as the case may be) to reflect the new information.

While the *Texas Gulf Sulphur* standard works well for the sort of dramatic, one-time event news at issue there, it works less well for the more mundane sorts of nonpublic information to which insiders routinely have access. A corporation always has undisclosed information about numerous different aspects of its business. By the time all of that information has been disseminated publicly, moreover, new undisclosed information doubtless will have been developed. In response to this concern, many firms have developed policies pursuant to which insiders may only trade during a specified window of time after the corporation has issued its quarterly and annual reports. Per SEC regulations, public corporations must send an annual report to the shareholders and also file a Form 10–Q after each of the first three quarters of their fiscal year and a Form 10–K after year's end. Because of the substantial and wide-ranging disclosures required in these reports, which are publicly available, there is a relatively low probability that an insider who trades during the time immediately following their dissemination will be deemed to have traded on material nonpublic information. As *Texas Gulf Sulphur* suggests, however, the insider may not trade the moment the report goes in the mail. Instead, the insider must wait until the market has had time to digest the report. In any event, of course, an insider who knows that he possesses material information that was not disclosed in the report must refrain from trading at all times—whether or not the corporation has released a periodic disclosure report.

B. The requisite fiduciary relationship

After *Chiarella*, liability for insider trading could be imposed only on persons who owe fiduciary duties to those with whom they trade: agents, fiduciaries, persons in whom the investors had placed their trust and confidence.[4] Unfortunately, the Supreme Court has failed to do a very good job of fleshing out this requirement. Is it enough that a fiduciary relationship exist, without any breach of the duties arising out of it? If a breach is required, which duty must be breached? What law determines whether the requisite fiduciary relationship and/or breach of duty is present in a particular fact pattern? Under state law, for example, corporate officers and directors generally owe no fiduciary duty to bondholders. Can insiders therefore inside trade in debt securities with impunity? Although corporate officers and directors owe fiduciary duties

---

4. "When an allegation of fraud is based upon nondisclosure, there can be no fraud absent a duty to speak," and no such duty arises "from the mere possession of non-public market information." Chiarella v. United States, 445 U.S. 222, 235 (1980). Thus, there can be no duty to disclose where the person who has traded on or tipped inside information "was not [the corporation's] agent, . . . was not a fiduciary, [or] was not a person in whom the sellers [of the securities] had placed their trust and confidence." Id. at 232; accord Dirks v. SEC, 463 U.S. 646, 653–55 (1983).

to their shareholders, we've seen that in many states insider trading does not breach those duties. Can insiders of firms incorporated in those states inside trade with impunity?

1. *Defining the fiduciary duty requirement*

In both *Chiarella* and *Dirks*, the Supreme Court frequently spoke of the need to show the existence of a "fiduciary relationship" as a predicate to liability.[5] Yet, surely that is not enough. As Justice Frankfurter put it, albeit in a different context, "to say that a man is a fiduciary only begins analysis; it gives direction to further inquiry. To whom is he a fiduciary? What obligations does he owe as a fiduciary? In what respect has he failed to discharge those obligations?"[6] In other words, it should not be enough to establish the existence of a fiduciary relationship. Before liability can be imposed one must also establish that the defendant violated a fiduciary duty arising out of the fiduciary relationship in question.[7]

In any fiduciary relationship, however, a variety of duties may arise. Which is the duty whose violation triggers insider trading liability? Again, the Court has not been very precise on this score. It has spoken mainly of a duty to disclose before trading. While so describing the duty perhaps sufficed for purposes of applying the disclose or abstain rule to trading insiders, it created analytical problems when the insider tipped information rather than trading on it. The duty to disclose phraseology created even greater problems when the misappropriation theory was created. Given that Chiarella owed no fiduciary duties to the investors with whom he traded, for example, he plainly owed those investors no duty to disclose nonpublic information before trading.

Faced with these problems, some lower courts switched the inquiry to whether the defendant was subject to a duty of confidentiality.[8] Using a duty of confidentiality as the requisite fiduciary duty, however, makes little sense in the insider trading context. Unlike most types of tangible property, the same piece of information can be used by more than one person at the same time; an insider's use of the information, moreover, does not necessarily lower its value to its owner. When an executive that has just negotiated a major contract for his employer thereafter inside

---

5. E.g., Dirks v. SEC, 463 U.S. 646, 654 (1983); Chiarella v. United States, 445 U.S. 222, 232 (1980).

6. SEC v. Chenery Corp., 318 U.S. 80, 85–86 (1943).

7. This conclusion is supported by the Supreme Court's treatment of tippee liability. It is not enough to show that the tipper was party to a fiduciary relationship with the source of the information. As we have seen, there must also be a breach of the tipper's fiduciary duty before tippee liability can result. That this requirement extends to insider trading liability generally seems reasonably clear from *Dirks'* discussion of

Chiarella. See Dirks v. SEC, 463 U.S. 646, 653–54 (1983).

8. See, e.g., United States v. Libera, 989 F.2d 596 (2d Cir.1993), cert. denied, 510 U.S. 976 (1993); United States v. Carpenter, 791 F.2d 1024, 1034 (2d Cir.1986), aff'd on other grounds, 484 U.S. 19 (1987). Note that these cases arose in the employment context, in which it is thought that an implicit duty to refrain from self dealing is created by agency law. Those courts thus did not have to face, let alone resolve, the potential disparity between a duty of confidentiality and a duty to refrain from self dealing.

trades in the employer's stock, for example, the value of the contract to the employer has not been lowered nor, absent some act of disclosure, has the executive violated his duty of confidentiality. Using nonpublic information for personal gain thus is not inconsistent with a duty of confidentiality, unless one's trades somehow reveal the information.

The fiduciary duty requirement therefore should be satisfied only by a duty to refrain from self dealing in nonpublic information. This conclusion finds considerably greater support in *Dirks* than does the duty of confidentiality approach. Justice Powell, for example, described the elements of an insider trading violation as: "(i) the existence of a relationship affording access to inside information intended to be available only for a corporate purpose, and (ii) the unfairness of allowing a corporate insider to take advantage of that information by trading without disclosure." Another passage likewise described insider trading liability as arising from "the 'inherent unfairness involved where one takes advantage' of 'information intended to be available only for a corporate purpose and not for the personal benefit of anyone.'" Yet another noted that insiders are "forbidden by their fiduciary relationship from personally using undisclosed corporate information to their advantage." The focus in each instance is on the duty to refrain from self dealing.

The emphasis on self dealing, rather than confidentiality, is further confirmed by the result in *Dirks*. Secrist violated his duty of confidentiality by disclosing the information to Dirks. Yet, the fact of the tip alone did not suffice for liability to be imposed. Rather, as we have seen, the court held that liability could be imposed only if Secrist had made the tip for personal gain, in other words, only if the tip involved self dealing. Hence, mere violation of the duty of confidentiality is not enough. Rather, a duty to disclose before trading arises only if trading would violate a duty to refrain from self dealing in confidential information owed by the trader to the owner of that information.

2.   A state or federal duty?

Having identified the requisite fiduciary duty, a question remains: Whence comes that duty? Courts and commentators uniformly treat the *Chiarella* fiduciary duty as a species of federal law. True enough, in the sense that the underlying cause of action arises under federal law. But while the prohibition is tied to a federal statute and the regulations there under, we have seen that there is nothing in either the text or legislative history of Exchange Act § 10(b) or Rule 10b–5 to support the modern substantive definition of insider trading. Instead, it is wholly a judicial creation. Like the rest of modern Rule 10b–5 jurisprudence, the definition of insider trading is "a judicial oak which has grown from little more than a legislative acorn."[9] The federal insider trading prohibi-

---

9. Blue Chip Stamps v. Manor Drug Stores, 421 U.S. 723, 737 (1975). Even a former SEC solicitor admits that "modern development of the law of insider trading is a classic example of common law in the federal courts. No statute defines insider

tion thus is best classified within the genus of federal common law. It is an example of interstitial lawmaking in which the courts are using common-law adjudicatory methods to flesh out the bare statutory bones.[10]

Once the problem is seen as one to be solved by application of federal common law, a choice of law question arises. Federal common law often is influenced by, and not infrequently incorporates, state law. In *Burks v. Lasker*,[11] for example, a shareholder of a federally regulated investment company brought suit under the federal securities laws against the company's board of directors. The Supreme Court held that state law controls the board of directors' ability to use a special litigation committee to terminate the litigation. In *Kamen v. Kemper Financial Services, Inc.*,[12] the Court extended *Burks*, describing the federal law governing derivative suits brought under the Investment Company Act as a species of federal common law, and incorporating state law governing excusal of the demand requirement in such suits. Until quite recently, for another example, the federal courts applied state statutes of limitation to private party lawsuits under Rule 10b–5. Although the Supreme Court adopted a unique federal limitations period in *Lampf, Pleva, Lipkind, Prupis & Petigrow v. Gilbertson*,[13] the Court indicated that it would continue to borrow state statutes of limitations in appropriate cases.

To be sure, while many of these examples involve the use of state common law to fill the interstices of the federal securities laws, and thus suggest that state law could appropriately play a role in insider trading prohibition as well, none directly addresses the use of state common law to define the elements of a federal claim. This too is possible, however. In *De Sylva v. Ballentine*,[14] for example, the court looked to the state law definition of "children" for purposes of interpreting a federal statute.

In light of these precedents, the question is not whether state law is relevant to the task of defining insider trading, but rather the extent to which it should be incorporated into the federal prohibition. In particular, the question at hand is the extent to which state law fiduciary duty concepts should be incorporated into the fiduciary duty requirement established by *Chiarella* and its progeny. In answering that question, courts have two options. First, they may create a unique rule of federal common law that applies uniformly throughout the nation. The courts

trading; no statute expressly makes it unlawful." Paul Gonson & David E. Butler, In Wake of *'Dirks,'* Courts Debate Definition of 'Insider,' Legal Times, Apr. 2, 1984, at 16.

10. Pre-*O'Hagan*, it appeared that this conclusion would run afoul of *Central Bank* and other recent Supreme Court decisions in which the Court adopted a narrow approach to interpreting Rule 10b–5 that purports to focus on the text of the rule and Section 10(b). See Stephen M. Bainbridge,

Incorporating State Law Fiduciary Duties into the Federal Insider Trading Prohibition, 52 Wash & Lee L. Rev. 1189, 1201–07 (1995). As we have seen, however, *O'Hagan* blithely ignored those doctrinal complications.

11.   441 U.S. 471 (1979).

12.   500 U.S. 90 (1991).

13.   501 U.S. 350 (1991).

14.   351 U.S. 570 (1956).

could draw on state law by analogy in doing so, but the rule would remain wholly federal. Second, they may adopt state law as the federal rule. If this option is selected, the substantive content of the federal rule will vary depending on which state's law controls.

Yet again, this is a question the Supreme Court failed to answer with clarity. On the one hand, the *Dirks* court contended "that '[a] significant purpose of the Exchange Act was to eliminate the idea that use of inside information for personal advantage was a normal emolument of corporate office.' "[15] If so, one would assume that the fiduciary duty arises out of federal law. As we have seen, however, this contention is at best an overstatement.

The Court's repeated references to a *"Cady, Roberts* duty" may also point towards a federal source for the requisite duty. There is at least the implication that *Cady, Roberts* created a federal duty to refrain from self dealing in confidential information, which has become part of the overall bundle of fiduciary duties to which insiders are subject. This analysis, however, suffers from two flaws. First, it reads an awful lot into some vague passages of both *Dirks* and *Cady, Roberts*. Second, as we shall see, creation of such a duty is inconsistent with the Court's holding in *Santa Fe*.

On the other hand, the *Dirks* Court also implied that the requisite duty arose out of state common law:

> In the seminal case of In re Cady, Roberts & Co., the SEC recognized that the common law in some jurisdictions imposes on "corporate 'insiders,' particularly officers, directors, or controlling shareholders" an "affirmative duty of disclosure ... when dealing in securities." The SEC found that ... breach of this common law duty also establish[ed] the elements of a Rule 10b–5 violation. . . .

In other words, the federal securities laws are violated only upon breach of this purported state common-law duty.[16] This interpretation of *Dirks* also would seem to be supported by the misappropriation theory: The focus in most misappropriation cases is on violation of duties arising out of the employment relationship, which in turn implicates agency law and thus points towards a state law source for the requisite duty.

How then should courts choose between these options? Unfortunately, the standards governing that choice are not particularly well-developed. The basic test, however, is the impact incorporation of state law would have on the relevant federal statutory policies. In *Lampf*, for example, the Court created a unique federal statute of limitations for implied federal rights of action because borrowing a state limitations

---

15. Dirks v. SEC, 463 U.S. 646, 653 n. 10 (1983) (quoting In re Cady, Roberts & Co., 40 S.E.C. 907, 912 n. 15 (1961)).

16. In a noninsider trading case, the Seventh Circuit interpreted *Dirks* as hold-

ing that "the existence of a requirement to speak [under Rule 10b–5] ... is itself based on state law...." Jordan v. Duff & Phelps, Inc., 815 F.2d 429, 436 (7th Cir.1987), cert. dismissed, 485 U.S. 901 (1988).

rule would frustrate the purpose of the underlying federal statute.[17] In *Burks*, the Court used state law to fill the interstices of a federal statute affecting the powers of directors because doing so did not permit acts prohibited by the federal statute and was otherwise not inconsistent with the statutory policy.[18] In *Kemper Financial Services*, the Court reaffirmed what it termed "the basic teaching of Burks v. Lasker: Where a gap in the federal securities laws must be bridged by a rule that bears on the allocation of governing powers within the corporation, federal courts should incorporate state law into federal common law unless the particular state law in question is inconsistent with the policies underlying the federal statute."[19] The bottom line then is whether there are important federal interests that would be adversely affected by adopting state law fiduciary duty principles as the federal rule of decision.[20]

What federal interests might be adversely affected by incorporation of state common law as the source of the requisite fiduciary duties?[21] Here are some possibilities:

- Some contend that Congress intended to prohibit insider trading. If so, and if incorporation of state law would make it harder to prosecute inside traders, the requisite federal interest might exist. As we have seen, however, the evidence of legislative intent is scanty, at best.

- Some contend that a prohibition of insider trading is necessary to protect the federal mandatory disclosure system, but this argument proves unpersuasive upon examination.

- Some contend that a prohibition of insider trading is necessary to protect investors from harm and/or to preserve their confidence in the integrity of the markets. These arguments also prove unpersuasive, however.

17. Lampf, Pleva, Lipkind, Prupis & Petigrow v. Gilbertson, 501 U.S. 350, 356 (1991).

18. Burks v. Lasker, 441 U.S. 471, 479 (1979).

19. Kamen v. Kemper Fin. Servs., Inc., 500 U.S. 90, 108 (1991).

20. This interpretation is consistent with the test laid out in the leading case of United States v. Kimbell Foods, 440 U.S. 715 (1979), in which the Supreme Court laid out the following criteria for deciding when state law should be incorporated into federal common-law rules:

Undoubtedly, federal programs that "by their nature are and must be uniform in character throughout the nation" necessitate formulation of controlling federal rules. Conversely, when there is little need for a nationally uniform body of law, state law may be incorporated as the federal rule of decision. Apart from considerations of uniformity, we must also determine whether application of state law would frustrate specific objectives of the federal programs. If so, we must fashion special rules solicitous of those federal interests. Finally, our choice-of-law inquiry must consider the extent to which application of a federal rule would disrupt commercial relationships predicated on state law.

Id. at 728–29. To be sure, *Kimbell Foods* is not squarely on point because the occasion for creating federal common law arose in that case because the United States was a party to the litigation rather than because the claim arose under federal law. It does confirm, however, the importance of determining whether incorporating state law would adversely affect some federal policy.

21. See generally Stephen M. Bainbridge, Incorporating State Law Fiduciary Duties into the Federal Insider Trading Prohibition, 52 Wash & Lee L. Rev. 1189, 1228–45 (1995).

- Some contend that a federal prohibition of insider trading is necessary to protect property rights in information, which is true but also does not justify a unique federal rule.

In sum, there is no compelling federal interest at stake that would justify creating a unique federal fiduciary duty respecting insider trading.

Indeed, to the contrary, creation of such a unique federal duty is inconsistent with the Supreme Court's Rule 10b–5 jurisprudence. In *Santa Fe Industries, Inc. v. Green*,[22] the Supreme Court held that creation of corporate fiduciary duties is a task that must be left to state law. If so, why is insider trading be singled out for special treatment? As we have seen, *Dirks* and *Chiarella* simply ignored the doctrinal tension between their fiduciary duty-based regime and *Santa Fe*. In *O'Hagan*, Justice Ginsburg's majority opinion at least recognized that *Santa Fe* presented a problem for the federal insider trading prohibition, but her purported solution is quite unconvincing. Justice Ginsburg correctly described *Santa Fe* as "underscoring that § 10(b) is not an all-purpose breach of fiduciary duty ban; rather it trains on conduct involving manipulation or deception."[23] Instead of acknowledging that insider trading is mainly a fiduciary duty issue, however, she treated it as solely a disclosure issue. It is thus the failure to disclose that one is about to inside trade that is the problem, not the trade itself: "A fiduciary who '[pretends] loyalty to the principal while secretly converting the principal's information for personal gain' . . . 'dupes' or defrauds the principal." As Justice Ginsburg acknowledged, this approach means that full disclosure must preclude liability. If the prospective inside trader informs the persons with whom he is about to trade that "he plans to trade on the nonpublic information, there is no 'deceptive device' and thus no § 10(b) violation."

Justice Ginsburg's approach fails to solve the problem. Granted, insider trading involves deception in the sense that the defendant by definition failed to disclose nonpublic information before trading. Persons subject to the disclose or abstain theory, however, often are also subject to a state law-based fiduciary duty of confidentiality, which precludes them from disclosing the information. As to them, the insider trading prohibition collapses into a requirement to abstain from trading on material nonpublic information. As such, it really is their failure to abstain from trading, rather than their nondisclosure, which is the basis for imposing liability. A former SEC Commissioner more or less admitted as much: "Unlike much securities regulation, insider trading rules probably do not result in more information coming into the market: The 'abstain or disclose' rule for those entrusted with confidential information usually is observed by abstention."[24] Yet, *Santa Fe* clearly precludes the creation of such duties.

---

22. 430 U.S. 462 (1977).

23. United States v. O'Hagan, 521 U.S. 642, 655 (1997).

24. Charles C. Cox & Kevin S. Fogarty, Bases of Insider Trading Law, 49 Ohio St. L.J. 353 (1988).

In any event, Justice Ginsburg's solution also is essentially circular. Failure to disclose material nonpublic information before trading does not always violate Rule 10b–5. In omission cases, which include all insider trading on impersonal stock exchanges, liability can be imposed only if the defendant had a duty to disclose before trading. If Rule 10b–5 itself creates the requisite duty, however, this requirement is effectively negated. As such, the requisite duty must come from outside the securities laws. Indeed, given *Santa Fe*, it must come from outside federal law. Yet, as we have seen, the *Dirks/O'Hagan* framework appears to violate this requirement through circularity—creating a federal disclosure obligation arising out of Rule 10b–5.

Repealing the federal prohibition in fact would be the simplest means of resolving the tension between *Dirks/O'Hagan* and *Santa Fe*. The simplest approach, however, is not always the best. As we shall see, there are sound pragmatic reasons to retain a federal prohibition of insider trading. None of those reasons, however, necessitates the creation of a unique federal fiduciary duty against insider trading. Nor do any of them resolve the doctrinal tension between *Dirks/O'Hagan* and *Santa Fe*. Rather, that tension is best resolved by adopting state law standards as the requisite fiduciary duty. This approach strikes an appropriate balance between the federalism concerns expressed by *Santa Fe* and the policies that favor federalizing the prohibition.

The Court's decision in *Burks v. Lasker* is especially supportive of this approach. In *Burks*, the Court applied state law governing termination of derivative litigation to a case arising under the federal Investment Company Act. Although the cause of action clearly arose under federal law, the Court applied state law because state law "is the font of corporate directors' powers" and because application of state law did not pose a "significant threat to any identifiable federal policy or interest."[25] Burks thus strongly argues in favor of using state law to supply the fiduciary duty element of the federal insider trading prohibition. State law is the "font" of corporate fiduciary duties, while we have seen that incorporation of state law poses no threat to "any identifiable federal policy or interest."

Although the Supreme Court's decision in *De Sylva v. Ballentine*[26] arose outside the securities law area, it is also quite instructive. In that case the Supreme Court considered what familial relationships were encompassed by the term "children" as used in a federal statute. The Court looked to state law for a definition of the term. It did so in large measure because there is no federal law of domestic relations:

> The scope of a federal right is, of course, a federal question, but that does not mean that its content is not to be determined by state, rather than federal law. This is especially true where a statute deals with a familial relationship; there is no federal law of domestic relations, which is primarily a matter of state concern.

25. Burks v. Lasker, 441 U.S. 471, 477–78 (1979).

26. 351 U.S. 570 (1956).

De Sylva is an especially apt precedent for the insider trading prohibition. Just as there was no general body of federal domestic relations law, *Santa Fe* teaches that there is no general federal law of fiduciary duty. Just as the Court incorporated state law in *De Sylva,* it thus should incorporate state law here.

C. Who is an insider?

The term insider trading is something of a misnomer. It conjures up images of corporate directors or officers using secret information to buy stock from (or sell it to) unsuspecting investors. To be sure, the modern federal insider trading prohibition proscribes a corporation's officers and directors from trading on the basis of material nonpublic information about their firm, but it also casts a far broader net. Consider the following people who have been convicted of insider trading:

- A partner in a law firm representing the acquiring company in a hostile takeover bid who traded in target company stock.[27]

- A Wall Street Journal columnist who traded prior to publication of his column in the stock of companies he wrote about.[28]

- A psychiatrist who traded on the basis of information learned from a patient.[29]

- A financial printer who traded in the stock of companies about which he was preparing disclosure documents.[30]

Consequently, the phrase insider trading thus includes a wide range of individuals who trade in a corporation's stock on the basis of material information unknown by the investing public at large.

It seems reasonably clear that the principal task in this area is to determine whether a fiduciary relationship exists between the inside trader and the person with whom he trades. Whether that determination is made as a matter of state or federal law, unfortunately, remains unclear. *O'Hagan* confirms that the attorney-client relationship is a fiduciary one.[31] Dictum in all three Supreme Court precedents tells us that corporate officers and directors are fiduciaries of their shareholders. Beyond these two categories we must make educated guesses. Until a majority of the Supreme Court has held that a particular relationship is fiduciary in nature, however, we cannot know for sure.

1. Classic insiders

At common law, the insider trading prohibition focused on corporate officers and directors. The short-swing profit insider trading restrictions

---

27. U.S. v. O'Hagan, 521 U.S. 642 (1997).

28. United States v. Carpenter, 791 F.2d 1024 (2d Cir.1986), aff'd on other grounds, 484 U.S. 19 (1987).

29. United States v. Willis, 737 F.Supp. 269 (S.D.N.Y.1990).

30. Chiarella v. United States, 445 U.S. 222 (1980).

31. Although one could plausibly argue to the contrary. See Stephen M. Bainbridge, Insider Trading under the Restatement of the Law Governing Lawyers, 19 J. Corp. L. 1 (1993).

provided by § 16(b) similarly are limited to officers, directors, and shareholders owning more than 10 percent of the company's stock. One of the many issues first addressed in the seminal *Texas Gulf Sulphur* case was whether § 10(b) was restricted to that class of persons. Some of the *Texas Gulf Sulphur* defendants were middle managers and field workers. The *Texas Gulf Sulphur* court had little difficulty finding that such mid-level corporate employees were insiders for purposes of § 10(b). But that holding followed directly from the court's equal access test: "Insiders, as directors or management officers are, of course, by this Rule, precluded from [insider] dealing, but the Rule is also applicable to one possessing [nonpublic] information who may not be strictly termed an 'insider' within the meaning of [section] 16(b) of the Act."[32] *Chiarella*'s rejection of the equal access test thus reopened the question of how far down the corporate ladder Rule 10b–5 extended.

Recall that the Supreme Court had said Chiarella could not be held liable under Rule 10b–5 because, as to the target companies' shareholders, "he was not their agent, he was not a fiduciary, [and] he was not a person in whom the sellers had placed their trust and confidence."[33] Were the TGS geologists who discovered the ore deposit persons in whom TGS' shareholders placed their trust and confidence? Presumably not, because TGS' shareholders likely did not even know of their existence. On the other hand, the geologists were agents of TGS and, as such, likely would be deemed fiduciaries of TGS' shareholders for purposes of Rule 10b–5. Although the question of whether all corporate employees will be deemed insiders remains open, there seems little doubt that the insider trading prohibition includes not only directors and officers, but also at least those key employees who have been given access to confidential information for corporate purposes. In *Chiarella*, the majority opinion implied that the duty to disclose or abstain applies to anyone in "a relationship [with the issuer] affording access to inside information intended to be available only for a corporate purpose." The Second Circuit likewise has stated that: "it is well settled that traditional corporate 'insiders'—directors, officers and persons who have access to confidential corporate information—must preserve the confidentiality of nonpublic information that belongs to and emanates from the corporation."[34]

Suppose, however, that the TGS geologists had written a memo to their supervisor describing the ore discovery. A TGS janitor discovered a draft of the memo in the trash and bought a few shares. Although the janitor may be an agent of TGS, the janitor is not a key employee given access to confidential information for a corporate purpose. It is therefore doubtful whether the janitor should be regarded as an insider for Rule 10b–5 purposes.

32. SEC v. Texas Gulf Sulphur Co., 401 F.2d 833, 848 (2d Cir.1968), cert denied, 394 U.S. 976 (1969).

33. Chiarella v. United States, 445 U.S. 222, 232 (1980).

34. Moss v. Morgan Stanley Inc., 719 F.2d 5, 10 (2d Cir.1983), cert. denied, 465 U.S. 1025 (1984).

2. *Constructive insiders*

In *Dirks*, the Supreme Court made clear that the disclose or abstain rule picks up a variety of nominal outsiders whose relationship to the issuer is sufficiently close to justify treating them as "constructive insiders":

> Under certain circumstances, such as where corporate information is revealed legitimately to an underwriter, accountant, lawyer, or consultant working for the corporation, these outsiders may become fiduciaries of the shareholders. The basis for recognizing this fiduciary duty is not simply that such persons acquired nonpublic corporate information, but rather that they have entered into a special confidential relationship in the conduct of the business of the enterprise and are given access to information solely for corporate purposes.... For such a duty to be imposed, however, the corporation must expect the outsider to keep the disclosed nonpublic information confidential, and the relationship at least must imply such a duty.[35]

A firm's outside legal counsel are widely assumed to be paradigmatic constructive insiders.[36] Yet, there still must be a relationship with the issuer. In *O'Hagan*, for example, the defendant could not be held liable under the disclose or abstain rule as a constructive insider because he worked for the bidder but traded in target company stock.

Although *Dirks* clearly requires that the recipient of the information in some way agree to keep it confidential, courts have sometimes overlooked that requirement. In *SEC v. Lund*,[37] for example, Lund and another businessman discussed a proposed joint venture between their respective companies. In those discussions, Lund received confidential information about the other's firm. Lund thereafter bought stock in the other's company. The court determined that by virtue of their close personal and professional relationship, and because of the business context of the discussion, Lund was a constructive insider of the issuer. In doing so, however, the court focused almost solely on the issuer's expectation of confidentiality. It failed to inquire into whether Lund had agreed to keep the information confidential.

Lund is usefully contrasted with *Walton v. Morgan Stanley & Co.*[38] Morgan Stanley represented a company considering acquiring Olinkraft Corporation in a friendly merger. During exploratory negotiations Olinkraft gave Morgan confidential information. Morgan's client ultimately decided not to pursue the merger, but Morgan allegedly later passed the acquired information to another client planning a tender offer for Olinkraft. In addition, Morgan's arbitrage department made purchases of Olinkraft stock for its own account. The Second Circuit held that Morgan was not a fiduciary of Olinkraft: "Put bluntly, although, accord-

---

35. Dirks v. SEC, 463 U.S. 646, 655 n. 14 (1983).

36. See, e.g., United States v. Elliott, 711 F.Supp. 425, 432 (N.D.Ill.1989).

37. 570 F.Supp. 1397 (C.D.Cal.1983).

38. 623 F.2d 796 (2d Cir.1980).

ing to the complaint, Olinkraft's management placed its confidence in Morgan Stanley not to disclose the information, Morgan owed no duty to observe that confidence." Although *Walton* was decided under state law, it has been cited approvingly in a number of federal insider trading opinions and is generally regarded as a more accurate statement of the law than *Lund*.[39] Indeed, a subsequent case from the same district court as *Lund* essentially acknowledged that it had been wrongly decided:

> What the Court seems to be saying in *Lund* is that anytime a person is given information by an issuer with an expectation of confidentiality or limited use, he becomes an insider of the issuer. But under *Dirks*, that is not enough; the individual must have expressly or impliedly entered into a fiduciary relationship with the issuer.[40]

Even this statement does not go far enough, however, because it does not acknowledge the additional requirement of an affirmative assumption of the duty of confidentiality.

3. *Tippers and tippees*

Recall that under *Dirks* tippees are only liable if two conditions are met: (1) the tipper breached a fiduciary duty to the corporation by making the tip and (2) the tippee knew or had reason to know of the breach. The requirement that the tip constitute a breach of duty on the tipper's part eliminates many cases in which an insider discloses information to an outsider. Hence, the SEC's decision to adopt Regulation FD as a mechanism for proscribing selective disclosure without reliance on the *Dirks* formulation.

Indeed, not every disclosure made in violation of a fiduciary duty constitutes an illegal tip. What *Dirks* proscribes is not just a breach of duty, however, but a breach of the duty of loyalty forbidding fiduciaries to personally benefit from the disclosure. An instructive case is *SEC v. Switzer*,[41] which involved Barry Switzer, the well-known former coach of the Oklahoma Sooners and Dallas Cowboys football teams. Phoenix Resources Company was an oil and gas company. One fine day in 1981, Phoenix's CEO, one George Platt, and his wife attended a track meet to watch their son compete. Coach Switzer was also at the meet, watching his son. Platt and Switzer had known each other for some time. Platt had Oklahoma season tickets and his company had sponsored Switzer's television show. Sometime in the afternoon Switzer laid down on a row of bleachers behind the Platts to sunbathe. Platt, purportedly unaware of Switzer's presence, began telling his wife about a recent business trip to New York. In that conversation, Platt mentioned his desire to dispose of or liquidate Phoenix. Platt further talked about several companies bidding on Phoenix. Platt also mentioned that an announcement of a

39. See, e.g., Dirks v. SEC, 463 U.S. 646, 662 n. 22 (1983); United States v. Chestman, 947 F.2d 551, 567–68 (2d Cir. 1991), cert. denied, 503 U.S. 1004 (1992); Moss v. Morgan Stanley Inc., 719 F.2d 5 (2d Cir.1983), cert. denied, 465 U.S. 1025 (1984).

40. SEC v. Ingram, 694 F.Supp. 1437, 1440 n. 3 (C.D.Cal.1988).

41. 590 F.Supp. 756 (W.D.Okla.1984).

"possible" liquidation of Phoenix might occur the following Thursday. Switzer overheard this conversation and shortly thereafter bought a substantial number of Phoenix shares and tipped off a number of his friends. Because Switzer was neither an insider or constructive insider of Phoenix, the main issue was whether Platt had illegally tipped Switzer.

Per *Dirks*, the initial issue was whether Platt had violated his fiduciary duty by obtaining an improper personal benefit: "Absent some personal gain, there has been no breach of duty to stockholders. And absent a breach by the insider [to his stockholders], there is no derivative breach [by the tippee]." The court found that Platt did not obtain any improper benefit. The court further found that the information was inadvertently (and unbeknownst to Platt) overheard by Switzer. Chatting about business with one's spouse in a public place may be careless, but it is not a breach of one's duty of loyalty.

The next issue is whether Switzer knew or should have known of the breach. Given that there was no breach by Platt, of course, this prong of the *Dirks* test by definition could not be met. But it is instructive that the court went on to explicitly hold that "Rule 10b–5 does not bar trading on the basis of information inadvertently revealed by an insider."

4. *Nontraditional relationships*

Once we get outside the traditional categories of Rule 10b–5 defendants—insiders, constructive insiders, and their tippees—things get much more complicated. Suppose a doctor learned confidential information from a patient, upon which she then traded? Is she an insider? As the Second Circuit observed in *United States v. Chestman*:

> [F]iduciary duties are circumscribed with some clarity in the context of shareholder relations but lack definition in other contexts. Tethered to the field of shareholder relations, fiduciary obligations arise within a narrow, principled sphere. The existence of fiduciary duties in other common law settings, however, is anything but clear. Our Rule 10b–5 precedents ..., moreover, provide little guidance with respect to the question of fiduciary breach, because they involved egregious fiduciary breaches arising solely in the context of employer/employee associations.[42]

At issue in that case was inside trading by a member of the Waldbaum family in stock of a corporation controlled by that family. Ira Waldbaum was the president and controlling shareholder of Waldbaum, Inc., a publicly-traded supermarket chain. Ira decided to sell Waldbaum to A & P at $50 per share, a 100% premium over the prevailing market price. Ira informed his sister Shirley of the forthcoming transaction. Shirley told her daughter Susan Loeb, who in turn told her husband Keith Loeb. Each person in the chain told the next to keep the information confiden-

---

42. 947 F.2d 551, 567 (2d Cir.1991) (ci-   (1992).
tations omitted), cert. denied, 503 U.S. 1004

tial. Keith passed an edited version of the information to his stockbroker, one Robert Chestman, who then bought Waldbaum stock for his own account and the accounts of other clients. Chestman was accused of violating Rule 10b–5. According to the Government's theory of the case, Keith Loeb owed fiduciary duties to his wife Susan, which he violated by trading and tipping Chestman.

The Second Circuit held that in the absence of any evidence that Keith regularly participated in confidential business discussions, the familial relationship standing alone did not create a fiduciary relationship between Keith and Susan or any members of her family. Accordingly, Loeb's actions did not give rise to the requisite breach of fiduciary duty.

In reaching that conclusion, the court laid out a general framework for dealing with nontraditional relationships. The court began by identifying two factors that did not, standing alone, justify finding a fiduciary relationship between Keith and Susan. First, unilaterally entrusting someone with confidential information does not by itself create a fiduciary relationship.[43] This is true even if the disclosure is accompanied by an admonition such as "don't tell," which Susan's statements to Keith included. Second, familial relationships are not fiduciary in nature without some additional element.

Turning to factors that could justify finding a fiduciary relationship on these facts, the court first identified a list of "inherently fiduciary" associations:

> Counted among these hornbook fiduciary relations are those existing between attorney and client, executor and heir, guardian and ward, principal and agent, trustee and trust beneficiary, and senior corporate official and shareholder. While this list is by no means exhaustive, it is clear that the relationships involved in this case—those between Keith and Susan Loeb and between Keith Loeb and the Waldbaum family—were not traditional fiduciary relationships.

A rather serious problem with the *Chestman* court's glib assertion that the specified relationships are "inherently fiduciary" is the resulting failure to seriously evaluate whether any duty arising out of such relationships was violated by the defendant's conduct. In *United States v. Willis*,[44] for example, the court determined that a psychiatrist violated the prohibition by trading on information learned from a patient. In determining that the requisite breach of fiduciary duty had occurred, the court relied in large measure on the Hippocratic Oath. In relevant part, the Oath reads: "Whatsoever things I see or hear concerning the life of men, in my attendance on the sick or even apart therefrom, which ought

---

43. Repeated disclosures of business secrets, however, could substitute for a factual finding of dependence and influence and, accordingly, sustain a finding that a fiduciary relationship existed in the case at bar. U.S. v. Chestman, 947 F.2d 551, 569 (2d Cir.1991), cert. denied, 503 U.S. 1004 (1992). Hence, the court's emphasis on the absence of such repeated disclosures as between Keith and Susan or her family.

44. 737 F.Supp. 269 (S.D.N.Y.1990).

not to be noised abroad, I will keep silence thereon, counting such things to be as sacred secrets." While the Oath thus imposes a duty of confidentiality on those who take it, it does not forbid them from self dealing in information learned from patients so long as the information is not thereby disclosed. As such, it is not at all clear that the requisite breach of duty was present in *Willis*. Unfortunately, as *Willis* illustrates, these issues routinely are swept under the rug.

In any event, once one moves beyond the class of "hornbook" fiduciary relationships, *Chestman* held that the requisite relationship will be found where one party acts on the other's behalf and "great trust and confidence" exists between the parties:

> A fiduciary relationship involves discretionary authority and dependency: One person depends on another—the fiduciary—to serve his interests. In relying on a fiduciary to act for his benefit, the beneficiary of the relation may entrust the fiduciary with custody over property of one sort or another. Because the fiduciary obtains access to this property to serve the ends of the fiduciary relationship, he becomes duty-bound not to appropriate the property for his own use.[45]

In the insider trading context, of course, the relevant property is confidential information belonging to the principal. Because the relationship between Keith and Susan did not involve either discretionary authority or dependency of this sort, their relationship was not fiduciary in character.[46]

In 2000, the SEC addressed the *Chestman* problem by adopting Rule 10b5–2, which provides "a nonexclusive list of three situations in which a person has a duty of trust or confidence for purposes of the 'misappropriation' theory...."[47] First, such a duty exists whenever someone agrees to maintain information in confidence. Second, such a duty exists between two people who have a pattern or practice of sharing confidences such that the recipient of the information knows or reasonably should know that the speaker expects the recipient to maintain the information's confidentiality. Third, such a duty exists when someone receives or obtains material nonpublic information from a spouse, parent, child, or sibling. On the facts of *Chestman*, accordingly, Rule 10b5–2 would result in the imposition of liability because Keith received the

---

45. U.S. v. Chestman, 947 F.2d 551, 569 (2d Cir.1991), cert. denied, 503 U.S. 1004 (1992).

46. The *Chestman* framework is yet another area in which the federalism concerns raised by *Santa Fe* ought to have figured more prominently than they did. As we have seen, the requisite fiduciary duty cannot be derived from Rule 10b–5 itself without making the rule incoherently circular and, moreover, violating *Santa Fe*. Unfortunately, the *Chestman* court simply ignored this problem. The court created a generic framework for deciding whether a fiduciary

relationship is present, which purports to take its "cues as to what is required to create the requisite relationship from the securities fraud precedents and the common law." U.S. v. Chestman, 947 F.2d 551, 568 (2d Cir.1991), cert. denied, 503 U.S. 1004 (1992). The court thus mixed both federal and state law sources without much regard either for potential circularity or federalism.

47. Exchange Act Rel. No. 43,154 (Aug. 15, 2000).

information from his spouse who, in turn, had received it from her parent.

5. *What does "other relationship of trust and confidence" mean?*

In *Chiarella*, the Supreme Court referred to a disclosure obligation arising out of a relationship of trust and confidence.[48] In *Chestman*, the Second Circuit juxtaposed that phrase with the related concept of fiduciary relationships. Consequently, the court observed, the requisite relationship could be satisfied either by a fiduciary relationship or by a "similar relationship of trust and confidence."[49]

So expanding the class of relationships that can give rise to liability may lead to a results-oriented approach. If a court wishes to impose liability, it need simply conclude that the relationship in question involves trust and confidence, even though the relationship bears no resemblance to those in which fiduciary-like duties are normally imposed. Accordingly, courts should be loath to use this phraseology as a mechanism for expanding the scope of liability. The *Chestman* court was sensitive to this possibility, holding that a relationship of trust and confidence must be "the functional equivalent of a fiduciary relationship" before liability can be imposed. *Chestman* also indicates that regardless of which type of relationship is present the defendant must be shown to have been subject to a duty (incorrectly described by the court as one of confidentiality) and to have breached that duty. Finally, the court indicated that at least as to criminal cases, it would not expand the class of relationships from which liability might arise to encompass those outside the traditional core of fiduciary obligation. Accordingly, for most purposes it should be safe to disregard any possible distinction between fiduciary relationships and other relationships of "trust and confidence."

D. Possession or use?

The SEC long has argued that trading while in knowing possession of material nonpublic information satisfies Rule 10b–5's scienter requirement. In *United States v. Teicher*,[50] the Second Circuit agreed, albeit in a passage that appears to be dictum. An attorney tipped stock market speculators about transactions involving clients of his firm. On appeal, defendants objected to a jury instruction pursuant to which they could be found guilty of securities fraud based upon the mere possession of fraudulently obtained material nonpublic information without regard to whether that information was the actual cause of their transactions. The Second Circuit held that any error in the instruction was harmless, but

48. Chiarella v. United States, 445 U.S. 222, 230 (1980).

49. U.S. v. Chestman, 947 F.2d 551, 568 (2d Cir.1991), cert. denied, 503 U.S. 1004 (1992).

50. 987 F.2d 112 (2d Cir.1993). See generally Allan Horwich, Possession Versus Use: Is there a Causation Element in the Prohibition on Insider Trading? 52 Bus. Law. 1235 (1997); Donna M. Nagy, The "Possession vs. Use" Debate in the Context of Securities Trading by Traditional Insiders: Why Silence Can Never Be Golden, 67 U. Cin. L. Rev. 1129 (1999).

went on to opine in favor of a knowing possession test. The court interpreted *Chiarella* as comporting with "the oft-quoted maxim that one with a fiduciary or similar duty to hold material nonpublic information in confidence must either 'disclose or abstain' with regard to trading." The court also favored the possession standard because it "recognizes that one who trades while knowingly possessing material inside information has an informational advantage over other traders." The difficulties with the court's reasoning should be apparent. In the first place, a mere possession test is inconsistent with Rule 10b–5's scienter requirement, which requires fraudulent intent (or, at least, recklessness). In the second, contrary to the court's view, *Chiarella* simply did not address the distinction between a knowing possession and a use standard. Finally, the court's reliance on the trader's informational advantage is inconsistent with *Chiarella*'s rejection of the equal access test.

In *SEC v. Adler*,[51] the Eleventh Circuit rejected *Teicher* in favor of a use standard. Under *Adler*, "when an insider trades while in possession of material nonpublic information, a strong inference arises that such information was used by the insider in trading. The insider can attempt to rebut the inference by adducing evidence that there was no causal connection between the information and the trade—i.e., that the information was not used." Although defendant Pegram apparently possessed material nonpublic information at the time he traded, he introduced strong evidence that he had a plan to sell company stock and that that plan predated his acquisition of the information in question. If proven at trial, evidence of such a pre-existing plan would rebut the inference of use and justify an acquittal on grounds that he lacked the requisite scienter.

The choice between *Adler* and *Teicher* is difficult. On the one hand, in adopting the Insider Trading Sanctions Act of 1984, Congress imposed treble money civil fines on those who illegally trade "while in possession" of material nonpublic information. In addition, a use standard significantly complicates the government's burden in insider trading cases, because motivation is always harder to establish than possession, although the inference of use permitted by *Adler* substantially alleviates this concern. On the other hand, a number of decisions have acknowledged that a pre-existing plan and/or prior trading pattern can be introduced as an affirmative defense in insider trading cases, as such evidence tends to disprove that defendant acted with the requisite scienter. Dictum in each of the Supreme Court's insider trading opinions also appears to endorse the use standard. In light of the Circuit split that now exists between *Teicher* and *Adler*, the Supreme Court may eventually have to resolve the conflict.

51. 137 F.3d 1325 (11th Cir.1998). The Ninth Circuit subsequently agreed with *Adler* that proof of use, not mere possession, is required. The Ninth Circuit further held that in criminal cases no presumption of use should be drawn from the fact of possession—the government must affirmatively prove use of nonpublic information. United States v. Smith, 155 F.3d 1051 (9th Cir.1998).

Or, perhaps not. In 2000, the SEC addressed this issue by adopting Rule 10b5–1, which states that Rule 10b–5's prohibition of insider trading is violated whenever someone trades "on the basis of" material nonpublic information.[52] Because one is deemed, subject to certain narrow exceptions, to have traded "on the basis of" material nonpublic information if one was aware of such information at the time of the trade, Rule 10b5–1 formally rejects the *Adler* position. In practice, however, the difference between *Adler* and Rule 10b5–1 may prove insignificant. On the one hand, *Adler* created a presumption of use when the insider was aware of material nonpublic information. Conversely, Rule 10b5–1 provides affirmative defenses for insiders who trade pursuant to a pre-existing plan, contract, or instructions. As a result, the two approaches should lead to comparable outcomes in most cases.

E.   Is there liability for trading in debt securities?

One of the areas in which the Supreme Court's failure to specify the source and nature of the fiduciary obligation underlying the disclose or abstain rule has proven especially problematic is insider trading in debt securities. Yet, the prohibition's application to debt securities has received surprisingly little judicial attention. One court has held that insider trading in convertible debentures violates Rule 10b–5,[53] but this case is clearly distinguishable from nonconvertible debt securities. Because they are convertible into common stock at the option of the holder, both the market price and interest rate paid on such instruments are affected by the market price of the underlying common stock. Federal securities law recognizes the close relationship of convertibles to common stock by defining the former as equity securities. As such, the status of nonconvertible debt remains unresolved. A strong argument can be made, however, that the prohibition should not extend to trading in nonconvertible debt.

In most states, neither the corporation nor its officers and directors have fiduciary duties to debtholders. Instead, debtholders' rights are limited to the express terms of the contract and an implied covenant of good faith.[54] Cases in a few jurisdictions purport to recognize fiduciary duties running to holders of debt securities, but the duties imposed in these cases are more accurately characterized as the same implied covenant of good faith found in most other jurisdictions.[55]

---

52. Exchange Act Rel. No. 43,154 (Aug. 15, 2000).

53. In re Worlds of Wonder Securities Litigation, [1990–1991 Trans. Binder] Fed. Sec. L. Rep. (CCH) ¶ 95,689, 1990 WL 260675 (N.D.Cal.1990).

54. See, e.g., Metropolitan Life Ins. Co. v. RJR Nabisco, Inc., 716 F.Supp. 1504 (S.D.N.Y.1989); Katz v. Oak Indus., 508 A.2d 873 (Del.Ch.1986).

55. See, e.g., Broad v. Rockwell Int'l Corp., 642 F.2d 929 (5th Cir.), cert. denied, 454 U.S. 965 (1981); Gardner & Florence Call Cowles Found. v. Empire, Inc., 589 F.Supp. 669 (S.D.N.Y.1984), vacated, 754 F.2d 478 (2d Cir.1985); Fox v. MGM Grand Hotels, Inc., 187 Cal.Rptr. 141 (Cal.Ct.App. 1982).

The distinction between this implied covenant and a fiduciary duty is an important one for our purposes. An implied covenant of good faith arises from the express terms of a contract and is used to fulfill the parties' mutual intent. In contrast, a fiduciary duty has little to do with the parties' intent. Instead, courts use fiduciary duties to protect the interests of the duty's beneficiary. Accordingly, a fiduciary duty requires the party subject to the duty to put the interests of the beneficiary of the duty ahead of his own, while an implied duty of good faith merely requires both parties to respect their bargain.

A two-step move thus will be required if courts are to impose liability under the disclose or abstain rule on those who inside trade in debt securities. First, the clear holdings of *Chiarella* and *Dirks* must be set aside so that the requisite relationship can be expanded to include purely contractual arrangements and the requisite duty expanded to include mere contractual covenants. Second, the implied covenant of good faith must be interpreted as barring self dealing in nonpublic information by corporate agents. In that regard, consider the leading *Met Life* decision, which indicates that a covenant of good faith will be implied only when necessary to ensure that neither side deprives the other of the fruits of the agreement.[56] The fruits of the agreement are limited to regular payment of interest and ultimate repayment of principal. Because insider trading rarely affects either of these fruits, it does not violate the covenant of good faith.[57]

To be sure, the courts could simply ignore state law. Yet, the Supreme Court has consistently held that insider trading liability requires an agency or fiduciary relationship. As to common stock, *Dirks* created what appears to be a federal fiduciary obligation, but recall that that obligation was extrapolated from state common law. It seems unlikely that the courts will treat the state law status of debtholders as irrelevant.

F.   Remedies and penalties

Woe unto those who violate the insider trading prohibition, for the penalties are many, cumulative, and severe. The Justice Department may pursue criminal charges. The SEC may pursue a variety of civil penalties. Private party litigants may bring damage actions under both federal and state law.

The SEC has no authority to prosecute criminal actions against inside traders, but it is authorized by Exchange Act § 21(d)(1) to ask the

---

56. Metropolitan Life Ins. Co. v. RJR Nabisco, Inc., 716 F.Supp. 1504, 1517 (S.D.N.Y.1989).

57. Various alternative theories of liability may come into play in this context. In particular, the misappropriation theory might apply. Suppose a corporate officer traded in the firm's debt securities using material nonpublic information belonging to the corporation. As the argument would go, even though the officer owes no fiduciary duties to the bondholders, he owes fiduciary duties to the corporation. The violation of those duties might suffice for liability under the misappropriation theory. The misappropriation theory clearly would not reach trading by an issuer in its own debt securities, which would come under the disclose or abstain rule.

Justice Department to initiate a criminal prosecution. In addition, the Justice Department may bring such a prosecution on its own initiative. Under § 32(a), a willful violation of Rule 10b–5 or 14e–3 is a felony that can be punished by a $1 million fine ($2.5 in the case of corporations) and up to 10 years in jail. Since the mid–1980s insider trading scandals, criminal prosecutions have become fairly common in this area.

The SEC long has had the authority to pursue various civil penalties in insider trading cases. Under Exchange Act § 21(d), the SEC may seek a permanent or temporary injunction whenever "it shall appear to the Commission that any person is engaged or is about to engage in any acts or practices constituting a violation" of the Act or any rules promulgated thereunder. Courts have made it quite easy for the SEC to obtain injunctions under § 21(d). The SEC must make a "proper showing," but that merely requires the SEC to demonstrate a violation of the securities laws occurred and there is a reasonable likelihood of future violations.[58] The SEC is not required to meet traditional requirements for equitable relief, such as irreparable harm.[59] The SEC is not required to identify particular individuals who were wronged by the conduct, moreover, but only that the violation occurred.

"Once the equity jurisdiction of the district court has been properly invoked by a showing of a securities law violation, the court possesses the necessary power to fashion an appropriate remedy."[60] Thus, in addition to or in place of injunctive relief, the SEC may seek disgorgement of profits, correction of misleading statements, disclosure of material information, or other special remedies. Of these, disgorgement of profits to the government is the most commonly used enforcement tool.

The SEC may also punish insider trading by regulated market professionals through administrative proceedings. Under § 15(b)(4) of the 1934 Act, the SEC may censure, limit the activities of, suspend, or revoke the registration of a broker or dealer who willfully violates the insider trading prohibition. Similar sanctions may be imposed on those associated with the broker or dealer in such activities. The SEC may issue a report of its investigation of the incident even if it decides not to pursue judicial or administrative proceedings, which may lead to private litigation.

During the 1980s, Congress significantly expanded the civil sanctions available to the SEC for use against inside traders. The Insider Trading Sanctions Act of 1984 created a civil monetary penalty of up to three times the profit gained or loss avoided by a person who violates rules 10b–5 or 14e–3 "by purchasing or selling a security while in the

---

58. See SEC v. Commonwealth Chem. Sec., Inc., 574 F.2d 90, 99–100 (2d Cir. 1978). But cf. SEC v. Lund, 570 F.Supp. 1397, 1404 (C.D.Cal.1983) (court denied an injunction on the grounds that the defendant's action was "an isolated occurrence" and that his "profession [was] not likely to lead him into future violations").

59. See SEC v. Management Dynamics, Inc., 515 F.2d 801 (2d Cir.1975); SEC v. Manor Nursing Centers, Inc., 458 F.2d 1082 (2d Cir.1972).

60. SEC v. Manor Nursing Centers, 458 F.2d 1082, 1103 (2d Cir.1972).

possession of material nonpublic information." An action to impose such a penalty may be brought in addition to or in lieu of any other actions that the SEC or Justice Department is entitled to bring. Because the SEC thus may seek both disgorgement and treble damages, an inside trader faces potential civil liability of up to four times the profit gained.

In the Insider Trading and Securities Fraud Act of 1988 (ITSFEA), Congress made a number of further changes designed to augment the enforcement resources and penalties available to the SEC. Among other things, it authorized the SEC to pay a bounty to informers of up to 10 percent of any penalty collected by the SEC. The treble money fine was extended to controlling persons, so as to provide brokerage houses, for example, with greater incentives to monitor the activities of their employees.[61]

Although it has long been clear that persons who traded contemporaneously with an inside trader have a private cause of action under Rule 10b–5 (and perhaps Rule 14e–3), and may also have state law claims, private party litigation against inside traders has been rare and usually parasitic on SEC enforcement actions. Private party actions were further discouraged by the Second Circuit's decision in *Moss v. Morgan Stanley, Inc.*,[62] which held that contemporaneous traders could not bring private causes of actions under the misappropriation theory. ITSFEA attempted to encourage private actions by overruling *Moss*. Under Exchange Act § 20A, contemporaneous traders can sue to recover up to the amount of profit gained or loss avoided. Tippers and tippees are jointly and severally liable. The amount recoverable is reduced by any amounts disgorged to the Commission. As yet, however, it does not appear that plaintiffs have made very frequent use of § 20A.

§ 11.6   Insider trading under state corporate law today

Although the federal securities laws did not preempt state corporate law, federal regulation has essentially superseded them insofar as insider trading is concerned. State law is not just a historical footnote, however. Some cases still fall though the federal cracks, being left for state law to decide. Plaintiffs still sometimes include a state law-based count in their complaints. Most important, as we have seen, state law ought to provide the basic analytical framework within which the federal regime operates. Having said that, however, it must be admitted that the post-*TGS* focus on federal law aborted the evolution of state common law in this area. With one important exception, discussed below, we are still more or less where we were in the late 1930s.

A.   Do directors have a state law fiduciary duty prohibiting insider trading today?

The special circumstances and minority rules continued to pick up adherents during the decades after 1930.[1] Perhaps surprisingly, however,

---

61.   On control person liability, see Marc I. Steinberg and John Fletcher, Compliance Programs for Insider Trading, 47 S.M.U. L. Rev. 1783 (1994).

62.   719 F.2d 5 (2d Cir.1983).

§ 11.6

1.   See, e.g., Broffe v. Horton, 172 F.2d 489 (2d Cir.1949) (diversity case); Childs v. RIC Group, Inc., 331 F.Supp. 1078, 1081

a number of states continue to adhere to the no duty rule.[2] Insofar as stock market transactions are concerned, moreover, *Goodwin v. Agassiz*[3] apparently remains the prevailing view.[4]

At least insofar as trading on secondary markets is concerned, the SEC thus seriously erred when it asserted in *Cady, Roberts & Co.* that state common law imposed fiduciary duties on corporate insiders that trade with shareholders.[5] As we have seen, the law varied substantially from state to state, and even in the jurisdictions where the requisite duty existed, it was arguably limited to face-to-face transactions involving unusual fact situations. *Dirks'* invocation of the *Cady, Roberts* duty as the basis for imposing federal insider trading liability was thus something of a stretch.[6]

B. Derivative liability for insider trading under state corporate law

Although *Goodwin* rejected the argument that directors "occupy the position of trustee towards individual stockholders,"[7] it also recognized that directors are fiduciaries of the corporate enterprise. Holdings barring shareholders from seeking direct relief thus do not necessarily prohibit corporate actions against insider traders. Granted, a leading case did not emerge until the 1960s but lawyers eventually stumbled on the possibility of derivative litigation against inside traders.

(N.D.Ga.1970), aff'd, 447 F.2d 1407 (5th Cir.1971) (diversity case); Hobart v. Hobart Estate Co., 159 P.2d 958 (Cal.1945); Hotchkiss v. Fischer, 16 P.2d 531 (Kan.1932); Jacobson v. Yaschik, 155 S.E.2d 601 (S.C. 1967). For an especially useful discussion of state common law, along with a holding "that a director, who solicits a shareholder to purchase his stock and fails to disclose information not known to the shareholder that bears upon the potential increase in the value of the shares, shall be liable to the shareholder," see Bailey v. Vaughan, 359 S.E.2d 599, 605 (W.Va.1987).

An early line of federal cases arising under Rule 10b–5 applied the special circumstances and, more often, the fiduciary duty rules to face-to-face insider trading transactions. See, e.g., Kohler v. Kohler Co., 319 F.2d 634 (7th Cir.1963); Speed v. Transamerica Corp., 99 F.Supp. 808 (D.Del.1951).

2. See, e.g., Goodman v. Poland, 395 F.Supp. 660, 678–80 (D.Md.1975); Lank v. Steiner, 224 A.2d 242 (Del.1966); Fleetwood Corp. v. Mirich, 404 N.E.2d 38, 46 (Ind.Ct. App.1980); Yerke v. Batman, 376 N.E.2d 1211, 1214 (Ind.Ct.App.1978); Gladstone v. Murray Co., 50 N.E.2d 958 (Mass.1943); cf. Treadway Cos., Inc. v. Care Corp., 638 F.2d 357, 375 (2d Cir.1980) (restating no liability rule as applied by New Jersey state courts, albeit subject to caveat that New Jersey might no longer follow rule).

3. 186 N.E. 659 (Mass.1933).

4. 3A Fletcher Cyc Corp ¶ 1168.1 (Perm. Ed. 1986). But see American Law Institute, Principles of Corporate Governance: Analysis and Recommendations § 5.04 (1992) (opining that a duty to disclose exists in both face-to-face and stock market transactions). Somewhat amusingly, the only state law support offered by the Reporter for the proposition that this duty extends to secondary market transactions is a "but see" cite to *Goodwin*. See id. at 282.

5. In re Cady, Roberts & Co., 40 S.E.C. 907 (1961).

6. See Dirks v. SEC, 463 U.S. 646, 653 (1983).

7. Goodwin v. Agassiz, 186 N.E. 659, 660 (Mass.1933).

All of the cases we have been discussing thus far were brought as direct actions; i.e., cases in which the plaintiff shareholder sued in his own name seeking compensation for the injury done to him by the insider with whom he traded. In derivative litigation, by contrast, the cause of action belongs to the corporation and any recovery typically goes into the corporate treasury rather than directly to the shareholders. One would normally expect the corporation's board or officers to prosecute such suits. Corporate law recognizes, however, that a corporation's managers sometimes may be reluctant to enforce the corporation's rights. This seems especially likely when the prospective defendant is a fellow director or officer. The derivative suit evolved to deal with such situations, providing a procedural device for shareholders to enforce rights belonging to the corporation.

In *Diamond v. Oreamuno*,[8] the leading insider trading derivative case, defendants Oreamuno and Gonzalez were respectively the Chairman of the Board and President of Management Assistance, Inc. ("MAI"). MAI was in the computer leasing business. It sub-contracted maintenance of leased systems to IBM. As a result of an increase in IBM's charges, MAI's earnings fell precipitously. Before these facts were made public, Oreamuno and Gonzalez sold off 56,500 shares of MAI stock at the then-prevailing price of $28 per share. Once the information was made public, MAI's stock price fell to $11 per share. A shareholder sued derivatively, seeking an order that defendants disgorge their allegedly ill-gotten gains to the corporation. The court held that a derivative suit was proper in this context and, moreover, that insider trading by corporate officers and directors violated their fiduciary duties to the corporation.[9]

Diamond has been a law professor favorite ever since it was decided. A plethora of law review articles have been written on it, mostly in a favorable vein. *Diamond* also still shows up in most corporations case books. In the real world, however, *Diamond* has proven quite controver-

---

8. 248 N.E.2d 910 (N.Y.1969).

9. There is a procedural oddity inherent in *Diamond*'s willingness to permit derivative suits against inside traders. As is generally the case in corporate law, New York only allows shareholders to bring a derivative suit if they meet the so-called continuing shareholder test: they held stock at the time the wrong was committed, suit was filed, and judgment reached. See, e.g., Bronzaft v. Caporali, 616 N.Y.S. 2d 863, 865 (N.Y.Sup.Ct.1994) (holding that plaintiffs, who were former shareholders, lacked standing to bring a derivative action after a cash-out merger); Karfunkel v. USLIFE Corp., 455 N.Y.S. 2d 937, 939 (N.Y.Sup.Ct. 1982) (stating "it is settled law that plaintiff must demonstrate that she was a shareholder at the time of the transaction, at the time of trial and at the time of entry of judgment"). In cases like *Diamond*, in which outsiders bought the selling insiders' shares, the purchasers were not shareholders until after the wrong was committed. In the flip category of cases, those in which insiders buy from existing shareholders, the sellers (if they sold all their shares) are no longer shareholders. The effect of the continuing shareholder rule should be obvious: no shareholder in the class most would regard as the inside trader's principal victims can serve as a named plaintiff in a *Diamond*-type suit. Where insiders buy, moreover, the allegedly injured selling shareholders cannot even share in any benefit that might flow from a successful derivative suit.

sial. A number of leading opinions in other jurisdictions have squarely rejected its holdings.[10]

Why has *Diamond* proven so controversial? No one contends that officers or directors never can be held liable for using information learned in their corporate capacities for personal profit. Officers who use information learned on the job to compete with their corporate employer, or to usurp a corporate opportunity, for example, readily can be held liable for doing so. Insider trading differs in an important way from these cases, however. Recall that derivative litigation is intended to redress an injury to the corporate entity. Where employees use inside information to compete with their corporate employer, the injury to the employer is obvious. In *Diamond*, however, the employees did not use their knowledge to compete with the firm, but rather to trade in its securities. The injury, if any, to the corporation is far less obvious in such cases. Unlike most types of tangible property, information can be used by more than one person without necessarily lowering its value. If an officer who has just negotiated a major contract for the corporation thereafter buys some of the firm's stock, for example, it is far from obvious that the officer's trading necessarily reduced the contract's value to the firm.

The *Diamond* court relied on two purportedly analogous precedents to justify allowing a derivative cause of action against inside traders: The Delaware Chancery court's decision in *Brophy v. Cities Service Co.*[11] and the law of agency. On close examination, however, neither provides very much support for *Diamond*.

In *Brophy*, the defendant insider traded on the basis of information about a stock repurchase program the corporation was about to undertake. In a very real sense, the insider was competing with the corporation, which both agency law and corporate law clearly proscribe. While the *Brophy* court did not require a showing of corporate injury, the insider's conduct in fact directly threatened the corporation's interests. If his purchases caused a rise in the stock price, the corporation would be injured by having to pay more for its own purchases. In contrast, the *Diamond* insiders' conduct involved neither competition with the corporation nor a direct threat of harm to it. The information in question related to a historical fact. As such, it simply was not information MAI could use. Indeed, the only imaginable use to which MAI could put this information would be to itself buy or sell its own securities before announcing the decline in earnings. Under the federal securities laws, however, MAI could not lawfully make such trades.

The *Diamond* court made two moves to evade this problem. First, it asserted that proof of injury was not legally necessary, which seems inconsistent with the notion that derivative suits are a vehicle for

10. See, e.g., Freeman v. Decio, 584 F.2d 186 (7th Cir.1978) (Indiana law); Schein v. Chasen, 313 So.2d 739, 746 (Fla. 1975).

11. 70 A.2d 5 (Del.Ch.1949).

redressing injuries done to the corporation. Second, the court inferred that MAI might have suffered some harm as a result of the defendants' conduct, even though the complaint failed to allege any such harm. In particular, the court surmised that the defendants' conduct might have injured MAI's reputation. As we shall see, however, this is not a very likely source of corporate injury. Accordingly, it is quite easy to distinguish *Brophy* from *Diamond*.

Agency law proves an equally problematic justification for the *Diamond* result. According to the Restatement (Second) of Agency, the principal-agent relationship is a fiduciary one with respect to matters within the scope of the agency relationship. More to the point for present purposes, Section 388 of the Agency Restatement imposes a duty on agents to account for profits made in connection with transactions conducted on the principal's behalf. The comments to that section further expand this duty's scope, requiring the agent to account for any profits made by the use of confidential information even if the principal is not harmed by the agent's use of the information. Section 395 provides that an agent may not use for personal gain any information "given him by the principal or acquired by him during the course of or on account of his agency."

One can plausibly argue, however, that the apparent bar on insider trading created by agency law is not as strict as it first appears. The broad prohibition of self dealing in confidential information appears solely in the comments to Sections 388 and 395. In contrast, the black letter text of Section 388 speaks only of profits made "in connection with transactions conducted by [the agent] on behalf of the principal." One must stretch the phrases "in connection with" and "on behalf of" pretty far in order to reach insider trading profits. Similarly, Section 395, which speaks directly to the issue of self dealing in confidential information, only prohibits the use of confidential information for personal gain "in competition with or to the injury of the principal." Arguably, agency law thus requires an injury to the principal before insider trading liability can be imposed.

This argument is supported by *Freeman v. Decio*,[12] the leading case rejecting *Diamond*'s approach. In *Freeman*, the court noted both *Diamond* and the comments to Sections 388 and 395, but nonetheless held that corporate officers and directors could not be held liable for insider trading as a matter of state corporate law without a showing that the corporation was injured by their conduct.[13] *Freeman* conceded that if all confidential information relating to the firm were viewed as a corporate asset, plaintiffs would not need to show an injury to the corporation in order for the insider's trades to constitute a breach of duty. The court said, however, such a view puts the cart before the horse. One should first ask whether there was any potential loss to the corporation before deciding whether or not to treat the information in question as a firm

---

12. 584 F.2d 186 (7th Cir.1978).　　　　**13.** Accord Schein v. Chasen, 313 So.2d 739 (Fla.1975).

asset. The court further concluded that most instances of insider trading did not pose any cognizable risk of injury to the firm. According to the court, any harm caused by insider trading was borne mainly by the investors with whom the insider trades, rather than the firm. Unlike *Brophy*, moreover, there was no competition with the firm or loss of a corporate opportunity, because there was no profitable use to which the corporation could have lawfully put this information.

Which of these cases was correctly decided as a matter of public policy? Unfortunately, we are not yet ready to decide between *Diamond* and *Freeman*. The basic issue that divides them is whether or not all confidential information relating to the firm is treated as a corporate asset. Put another way, did MAI have a protected property right in all such information? Answering that question is a task best deferred until we have examined the arguments in favor of and against regulating insider trading.

§ 11.7 Section 16(b)

In addition to the complicated insider trading rules under § 10(b), Congress has also provided a much simpler prophylactic rule under Securities Exchange Act § 16(b). In brief, § 16(b) holds that any profits an insider earns on purchases and sales that occur within six months of each other must be forfeited to the corporation.[1] As with all prophylactic rules, § 16(b) is both over-and under-inclusive. It captures all sorts of trades unaffected by the use of inside information, while missing many trades flagrantly based on nonpublic information.

§ 11.7

1. Section 16(b) provides:

For the purpose of preventing the unfair use of information which may have been obtained by such beneficial owner, director, or officer by reason of his relationship to the issuer, any profit realized by him from any purchase and sale, or any sale and purchase, of any equity security of such issuer (other than an exempted security) within any period of less than six months, unless such security was acquired in good faith in connection with a debt previously contracted, shall inure to and be recoverable by the issuer, irrespective of any intention on the part of such beneficial owner, director, or officer in entering into such transaction of holding the security purchased or of not repurchasing the security sold for a period exceeding six months. Suit to recover such profit may be instituted at law or in equity in any court of competent jurisdiction by the issuer, or by the owner of any security of the issuer in the name and in behalf of the issuer if the issuer shall fail or refuse to bring such suit within sixty days after request or shall fail diligently to prosecute the same thereafter; but no such suit shall be brought more than two years after the date such profit was realized. This subsection shall not be construed to cover any transaction where such beneficial owner was not such both at the time of the purchase and sale, or the sale and purchase, of the security involved, or any transaction or transactions which the Commission by rules and regulations may exempt as not comprehended within the purpose of this subsection.

See generally Merritt B. Fox, Insider Trading Deterrence Versus Managerial Incentives: A Unified Theory of Section 16(b), 92 Mich. L. Rev. 2088 (1994); Marleen A. O'Connor, Toward a More Efficient Deterrence of Insider Trading: The Repeal of Section 16(b), 58 Fordham L. Rev. 309 (1989); Karl Okamato, Rereading Section 16(b) of the Securities Exchange Act, 27 Ga. L. Rev. 183 (1992); Steve Thel, The Genius of Section 16: Regulating the Management of Publicly Held Companies, 42 Hastings L.J. 391 (1991).

Section 16(a) requires insiders to report monthly any transactions in their company's equity securities. Under § 16(b), any profits earned on purchases and sales within a six month period must be disgorged to the issuer. Shareholders of the issuer may sue insiders derivatively and a shareholder's lawyer can get a contingent fee out of any recovery or settlement.

Unlike Rule 10b–5, § 16(b) applies only to officers, directors, or shareholders who own more than 10% of the company's stock. Determining whether or not one is a shareholder or director is pretty straightforward, of course. In contrast, determining whether or not one is an officer can be pretty tricky. Securities Exchange Act Rule 3b–2 defines an officer as a "president, vice president, secretary, treasury or principal financial officer, comptroller or principal accounting officer, and any person routinely performing corresponding functions. . . ." The latter catch-all phrase is the potential trouble spot. Should the statutory term "officer" be construed narrowly so that objective factors, especially one's title, determine whether or not one was subject to § 16(b)? Or should the term be interpreted more broadly, so as to take into account subjective considerations such as the nature of one's functions and/or whether one's role gave one access to inside information? In a well-known early decision, *Colby v. Klune*,[2] expressed doubt as to whether the SEC had authority to adopt Rule 3b–2. Instead, the court adopted a formulation that looked to subjective considerations, which defined an officer as "a corporate employee performing important executive duties of such character that he would be likely, in discharging those duties, to obtain confidential information that would aid him if he engaged in personal market transactions." The Ninth Circuit later concurred with the view that title alone is not dispositive, but focused on access to information as the relevant consideration: "Liability under § 16(b) is not based simply upon a person's title within his corporation; rather, liability follows from the existence of a relationship with the corporation that makes it more probable than not that the individual has access to inside information."[3] The SEC ultimately intervened by adopting Rule 16a–1(f), under which either one's title or one's function could result in officer status:

> The term "officer" shall mean an issuer's president, principal financial officer, principal accounting officer (or, if there is no such accounting officer, the controller), any vice-president of the issuer in charge of a principal business unit, division or function (such as sales, administration or finance), any other officer who performs a policy-making function, or any other person who performs similar policy-making functions for the issuer. Officers of the issuer's parent(s) or subsidiaries shall be deemed officers of the issuer if they perform such policy-making functions for the issuer. In addition, when the issuer is a limited partnership, officers or employees of the

2.   178 F.2d 872 (2d Cir.1949).

3.   Merrill Lynch, Pierce, Fenner & Smith, Inc. v. Livingston, 566 F.2d 1119 (9th Cir.1978).

general partner(s) who perform policy-making functions for the limited partnership are deemed officers of the limited partnership.

Someone who holds one of the listed titles is likely to be deemed an officer, whether or not he has access to inside information, subject to a "very limited exception applicable only where the title is essentially honorary or ceremonial."[4] (Conversely, the mere fact that one's position is described in, say, the corporate bylaws as that of an officer does not suffice to make one an officer for this purpose.[5]) An executive with policymaking functions that give the executive access to inside information, however, will be deemed an officer even if the executive lacks one of the formal titles usually associated with that position.

Besides the smaller class of prospective defendants, there are several other important limitations on § 16(b)'s scope relative to Rule 10b–5. Section 16(b), for example, also applies only to insider transactions in their own company's stock. There is no tipping liability, no misappropriation liability, and no constructive insider doctrine. Section 16(b) applies only to firms that must register under the Securities Exchange Act. Finally, it applies only to trading in equity securities—such as stocks and convertible debt.

Although there must be both a sale and a purchase within six months of each other in order to trigger § 16(b), it applies whether the sale follows the purchase or vice versa. Accordingly, shares are fungible for § 16(b) purposes. The trader thus need not earn gains from buying and selling specific shares of stock. Instead, if the trader unloads 10 shares of stock and buys back 10 different shares of stock in the same company at a cheaper price, the trader is liable. Some examples will be helpful:

1. Anna is chief financial officer of Acme, Inc. She buys 1,000 Acme shares at $8 on February 1. She sells 1,000 shares at $10 on May 1. Because the sale and purchase took place within six months, § 16(b) is triggered. She has earned a $2 profit per share and therefore must disgorge $2,000 to Acme.

2. Bill is senior vice president of Ajax, Inc. He has owned 10,000 shares for many years. On June 1 he sells 1,000 shares at $10. On September 15 he buys 1,000 shares at $8. He also must disgorge $2,000 to Ajax ($2 per share times 1000 shares).

Courts interpret the statute to maximize the amount the company recovers. Again, an example will be helpful:

3. Carla is president of Acme, Inc. Her transactions were as follows:

   • March 1: bought 100 shares at $10

---

4. National Medical Enterprises, Inc. v. Small, 680 F.2d 83 (9th Cir.1982).

5. Lockheed Aircraft Corp. v. Campbell, 110 F.Supp. 282 (S.D.Cal.1953) (assistant treasurer and assistant secretary not officers for § 16(b) purposes even though their positions were described in the bylaws as those of officers).

- April 1: sold 70 shares at $12
- May 1: bought 50 shares on May 1 at $9
- May 15: sold 25 shares at $13
- December 31: sold 35 shares at $20

The December 31 sale cannot be matched with either the March 1 or May 1 purchase, because they are more than six months apart. The other transactions are all matchable. A court will match them in the way that maximizes Acme's recovery:

- Match the 25 shares sold on May 15 with 25 of the shares bought on May 1, because they have the largest price differential. With a $4 profit per share ($13 minus $9) times 25 shares, Carla owes Acme $100.

- Next match 25 of the shares sold on April 1 with the remaining 25 shares purchased on May 1 for a profit of $75 ($3 per share ($12 minus $9) times 25 shares).

- Now match the remaining 45 shares sold on April 1 with 45 of the shares bought on March 1 for a profit of $90 ($2 per share ($12 minus $10) times 45 shares).

- Carla therefore owes Acme a total of $265.

Form almost always triumphs over substance in § 16(b) cases. There are some exceptions, however, the most notable of which is the unconventional transaction doctrine. The Exchange Act defines "sale" very broadly: it includes every disposition of a security for value. For purposes of § 16(b), however, certain transactions are not deemed sales; namely, so-called unconventional transactions.

The leading case in this area is *Kern County Land Co. v. Occidental Petroleum Corp.*[6] In 1967, Occidental launched a tender offer for 500,000 shares of Kern County Land Co. (Old Kern). The offer later was extended and the number of shares being sought was increased. When the offer closed in June, Occidental owned more than 10% of Old Kern's stock. To avoid being taken over by Occidental, Old Kern negotiated a defensive merger with Tenneco. Under the merger agreement, Old Kern stock would be exchanged for Tenneco stock. In order to avoid becoming a minority shareholder in Tenneco, Occidental sold to a Tenneco subsidiary an option to purchase the Tenneco shares Occidental would acquire in the merger, which could not be exercised until the § 16(b) six month period had elapsed. Tenneco and Old Kern merged during the six month period following Occidental's tender offer. Somewhat later, more than 6 months after the tender offer, Occidental sold Tenneco stock pursuant to the option.

The successor corporation to Old Kern (New Kern) sued under § 16(b). It offered two theories. First, the merger and resulting exchange of Old Kern for Tenneco stock constituted a sale, which had occurred

6.   411 U.S. 582 (1973).

less than six months after the purchase effected by the tender offer. Second, the tender offer constituted a purchase and that the grant of the option (rather than the exercise of the option) constituted a sale. Because the option was granted less than six months after the tender offer, New Kern argued that Occidental was liable for any profit earned on the shares covered by the option. The Supreme Court rejected both of New Kern's arguments, holding that Occidental had no § 16(b) liability. Both the merger and the grant of the option were unconventional transactions and, as such, were not deemed a sale for § 16(b) purposes.

Courts have identified three factors to be considered in deciding whether a transaction is conventional or unconventional: (1) whether the transaction is volitional; (2) whether the transaction is one over which the beneficial owner has any influence; and (3) whether the beneficial owner had access to confidential information about the transaction or the issuer. In the case at bar, Occidental as a hostile bidder had no access to confidential information about Old Kern or Tenneco. In addition, as to the merger, the exchange was involuntary—as the merger had been approved by the other shareholders, Occidental had no option but to exchange its shares.

In closing, a word should be said about the differing treatment of officers and directors on the one hand and shareholders on the other. An officer or director has § 16(b) liability if he is an officer or director at either the time of the purchase or the sale. In contrast, a shareholder has § 16(b) liability only if she owned more than 10 percent of the company's shares both at the time of the purchase and of the sale. In *Reliance Electric Co. v. Emerson Electric Co.*,[7] Emerson bought 13.2 percent of Dodge Manufacturing Co. stock in a hostile tender offer. To avoid being taken over by Emerson, Dodge agreed to merge with Reliance. Emerson gave up the fight and decided to sell its Dodge shares. In an attempt to minimize any potential § 16(b) liability, Emerson first sold Dodge shares representing 3.24 percent of the outstanding common stock. It then sold the remainder, which represented 9.96 percent of the outstanding. When Reliance sued under § 16(b), the Supreme Court held that shareholders are subject to the statute only if they own more than 10 percent of the stock immediately before the sale. Emerson therefore had no liability with respect to its sale of the final 9.96 percent. *Reliance* is a good example of how form prevails over substance in § 16(b)—even though Emerson's two sales were part of a related series of transactions effected pursuant to a single plan, which plausibly could have been deemed a step transaction, the court treated the second sale as having independent legal significance.

Notice that Emerson did not raise, and the Supreme Court thus did not address, the significance of the fact that Emerson had not been a 10 percent shareholder at the time it made its initial tender offer. Instead, that issue came up in *Foremost-McKesson, Inc. v. Provident Securities*

---

7.   404 U.S. 418 (1972).

Co.,[8] in which the Supreme Court held that a purchase by which a shareholder crosses the 10% threshold cannot be matched with subsequent sales for § 16(b) purposes. Again, an example may be helpful:

4. Darla is not an officer or director of Ajax, Inc. At all relevant times, Ajax has 1,000 shares outstanding. Darla's transactions are as follows:

- January 1: buys 50 shares at $10
- February 1: buys 55 shares at $10
- April 1: buys 50 shares at $10.
- May 1: sells 60 shares at $15
- May 2: sells 55 shares at $20

The January 1 purchase cannot be matched with either sale, because on January 1 Darla was not yet a 10 percent shareholder. The February 1 purchase cannot be matched with either sale because it is the transaction by which Darla became a (more than) 10 percent shareholder. Only the April 1 purchase is potentially matchable, because only at the time of that purchase did Darla own more than 10 percent of Ajax's stock. As to the sales, only the May 1 sale can be matched with the April 1 purchase. On May 2, Darla owned less than 10 percent of Ajax's stock. If Darla had been an officer or director on any one of the relevant dates, of course, all of the transactions would have been subject to § 16(b).

§ 11.8 Insider trading policy

The policy case against insider trading traditionally sounded in the language of equity. The SEC, for example, justifies the prohibition as necessary to address "the inherent unfairness" of insider trading.[1] But why is insider trading unfair? In *Texas Gulf Sulphur*, the Second Circuit opined that all investors were entitled to "relatively equal access to material information."[2] But whence comes this entitlement? The difficulty, of course, is that fairness and equality are high-sounding but essentially content-less words. We need some standard of reference by which to measure the fairness or lack thereof of insider trading. This section begins with an examination of the political economy of insider trading—why has the SEC so persistently insisted on an expansive prohibition? It then critically evaluates the various arguments that have been made in favor of and against regulating insider trading. In each case, we will ask two questions: Does the argument make sense? Can it explain the prohibition as it exists?

A. The political economy of insider trading

In evaluating the political economy of insider trading, we rely on a well-established economic model of regulation in which rules are sold by

8. 423 U.S. 232 (1976).

§ 11.8
1. In re Merrill Lynch, 43 S.E.C. 933, 936 (1968).

2. SEC v. Texas Gulf Sulphur Co., 401 F.2d 833, 848 (2d Cir.1968), cert. denied, 394 U.S. 976 (1969).

regulators and bought by the beneficiaries of the regulation.[3] Into that model we can plug slightly different, but wholly compatible, stories about insider trading. One explains why the SEC wanted to sell insider trading regulation,[4] while the other explains to whom it has been sold.[5] By putting these stories together, we obtain a complete answer to the question of why insider trading became a matter of federal concern.

On the supply side, the federal insider trading prohibition may be viewed as the culmination of two distinct trends in the securities laws. First, as do all government agencies, the SEC desired to enlarge its jurisdiction and enhance its prestige. Administrators can maximize their salaries, power, and reputation by maximizing the size of their agency's budget. A vigorous enforcement program directed at a highly visible and unpopular law violation is surely an effective means of attracting political support for larger budgets. Given the substantial media attention directed towards insider trading prosecutions, and the public taste for prohibiting insider trading, it provided a very attractive subject for such a program.

Second, during the prohibition's formative years, there was a major effort to federalize corporation law. In order to maintain its budgetary priority over competing agencies, the SEC wanted to play a major role in federalizing matters previously within the state domain.[6] Insider trading was an ideal target for federalization. Rapid expansion of the federal insider trading prohibition purportedly demonstrated the superiority of federal securities law over state corporate law. Because the states had shown little interest in insider trading for years, federal regulation demonstrated the modernity, flexibility, and innovativeness of the securities laws. The SEC's prominent role in attacking insider trading thus placed it in the vanguard of the movement to federalize corporate law and ensured that the SEC would have a leading role in any system of federal corporations law.

The validity of this hypothesis is suggested by its ability to explain the SEC's devotion of significant enforcement resources to insider trading during the 1980s. During that decade, the SEC embarked upon a

---

3. For a description of this general model, see William A. Landes & Richard A. Posner, The Independent Judiciary in an Interest–Group Perspective, 18 J. L. & Econ. 875 (1975).

4. See generally Michael P. Dooley, Fundamentals of Corporation Law 816–57 (1995).

5. See David D. Haddock and Jonathan R. Macey, Regulation on Demand: A Private Interest Model, with an Application to Insider Trading Regulation, 30 J.L. & Econ. 311 (1987).

6. In the seminal *Cady, Roberts* decision, the Commission acknowledged and embraced the federalization process: "The securities acts may be said to have generated a wholly new and far-reaching body of Federal corporation law." In re Cady, Roberts & Co., 40 S.E.C. 907, 910 (1961). In addition, during the late 1970s the Commission considered imposing a variety of corporate governance rules, which would have essentially superseded state corporation law in many respects. See Stephen M. Bainbridge, The Short Life and Resurrection of SEC Rule 19c–4, 69 Wash. U. L.Q. 565, 603 n.176 (1991).

limited program of deregulating the securities markets. Among other things, the SEC adopted a safe harbor for projections and other soft data, the shelf registration rule, the integrated disclosure system, and expanded the exemptions from registration under the Securities Act. At about the same time, however, the SEC adopted a vigorous enforcement campaign against insider trading. Not only did the number of cases increase substantially, but the SEC adopted a "big bang" approach under which it focused on high visibility cases that would produce substantial publicity.[7] In part this may have been due to an increase in the frequency of insider trading, but the public choice story nicely explains the SEC's interest in insider trading as motivated by a desire to preserve its budget during an era of deregulation and spending restraint.

The public choice story also explains the SEC's continuing attachment to the equal access approach to insider trading. The equal access policy generates an expansive prohibition, which federalizes a broad range of conduct otherwise left to state corporate law, while also warranting a highly active enforcement program. As such, the SEC's use of Rule 14e–3 and the misappropriation theory to evade *Chiarella* and *Dirks* makes perfect sense. By these devices, the SEC restored much of the prohibition's pre-*Chiarella* breadth and thereby ensured that its budget-justifying enforcement program would continue unimpeded.

Turning to the demand side, the insider trading prohibition appears to be supported and driven in large part by market professionals, a cohesive and politically powerful interest group, which the current legal regime effectively insulates from insider trading liability.[8] Only insiders and quasi-insiders such as lawyers and investment bankers have greater access to material nonpublic information than do market professionals. By basing insider trading liability on breach of fiduciary duty, and positing that the requisite fiduciary duty exists with respect to insiders and quasi-insiders but not with respect to market professionals, the prohibition protects the latter's ability to profit from new information about a firm.

When an insider trades on an impersonal secondary market, the insider takes advantage of the fact that the market maker's or specialist's bid-ask prices do not reflect the value of the inside information. Because market makers and specialists cannot distinguish insiders from noninsiders, they cannot protect themselves from being taken advantage of in this way.[9] When trading with insiders, the market maker or

---

7. Stephen M. Bainbridge, Note, A Critique of the Insider Trading Sanctions Act of 1984, 71 Va. L. Rev. 455, 466–67 (1985).

8. See Jonathan R. Macey, Insider Trading: Economics, Politics, And Policy 17–18 (1991). Macey argues that Rule 14e–3, which is so strikingly different than the rest of the federal insider trading prohibition, is designed to protect the interests of target managers, another well-defined and politically powerful interest group. Id. Rule 14e–

3 prohibits the practice of warehousing takeover securities, which hostile bidders otherwise could use to put target company securities into friendly hands before commencing a bid. Id. at 19–20.

9. See William K.S. Wang, Stock Market Insider Trading: Victims, Violators and Remedies—Including an Analogy to Fraud in the Sale of a Used Car with a Generic Defect, 45 Villanova L. Rev. 27, 38–40 (2000).

specialist thus will always be on the wrong side of the transaction. If insider trading is effectively prohibited, however, the market professionals are no longer exposed to this risk.

Professional securities traders likewise profit from the fiduciary-duty based insider trading prohibition. Because professional investors are often active traders, they are highly sensitive to the transaction costs of trading in securities. Prominent among these costs is the specialist's and market-maker's bid-ask spread. If a ban on insider trading lowers the risks faced by specialists and market-makers, some portion of the resulting gains should be passed on to professional traders in the form of narrower bid-ask spreads.

Analysts and professional traders are further benefited by a prohibition on insider trading, because only insiders are likely to have systematic advantages over market professionals in the competition to be the first to act on new information. Market professionals specialize in acquiring and analyzing information. They profit by trading with less well-informed investors or by selling information to them. If insiders can freely trade on nonpublic information, however, some portion of the information's value will be impounded into the price before it is learned by market professionals, which will reduce their returns.

Circumstantial evidence for the demand-side hypothesis is provided by SEC enforcement patterns.[10] In the years immediately prior to *Chiarella*, enforcement proceedings often targeted market professionals. The frequency of insider trading prosecutions rose dramatically after *Chiarella* held insider trading was unlawful only if the trader violated a fiduciary duty owed to the party with whom he trades. Yet, despite that increase in overall enforcement activity, there was a marked decline in the number of cases brought against market professionals.

It is not a very appealing story. Taken together, the demand and supply side stories demonstrate that the insider trading prohibition advances no important federal policy. Instead, the prohibition is driven largely by the venal interests of bureaucrats and the entities they supposedly regulate. The remaining question is whether it is nevertheless possible to identify a public-regarding justification for the federal insider trading prohibition.

B. The case for deregulation

In the policy debate over insider trading, the seminal event was the 1966 publication of Henry Manne's book INSIDER TRADING AND THE STOCK MARKET. It is only a slight exaggeration to suggest that Manne stunned the corporate law world by daring to propose the deregulation of insider trading. The response by most law professors, lawyers, and regulators was immediate and vitriolic rejection.

In one sense, Manne's project failed. Insider trading is still prohibited. Indeed, the sanctions for violating the prohibition have become more

---

10.   See Michael P. Dooley, Fundamentals of Corporation Law 829–34 (1995).

draconian—not less—since Manne's book was first published. In another sense, however, Manne's daring was at least partially vindicated. He changed the terms of the debate. Today, the insider trading debate takes place almost exclusively in the language of economics. Even those who still insist on treating insider trading as an issue of fairness necessarily spend much of their time responding to those who see it in economic terms.

Manne identified two principal ways in which insider trading benefits society and/or the firm in whose stock the insider traded. First, he argued that insider trading causes the market price of the affected security to move toward the price that the security would command if the inside information were publicly available. If so, both society and the firm benefit through increased price accuracy. Second, he posited insider trading as an efficient way of compensating managers for having produced information. If so, the firm benefits directly (and society indirectly) because managers have a greater incentive to produce additional information of value to the firm.

1. *Insider trading and efficient pricing of securities*

Basic economic theory tells us that the value of a share of stock is simply the present discounted value of the stream of dividends that will be paid on the stock in the future. Because the future is uncertain, however, the amount of future dividends, if any, cannot be known. In an efficient capital market, a security's current price thus is simply the consensus guess of investors as to the issuing corporation's future prospects. The "correct" price of a security is that which would be set by the market if all information relating to the security had been publicly disclosed. Because the market cannot value nonpublic information and because corporations (or outsiders) frequently possess material information that has not been made public, however, market prices often deviate from the "correct" price. Indeed, if it were not for this sort of mispricing, insider trading would not be profitable.

No one seriously disputes that both firms and society benefit from accurate pricing of securities. Accurate pricing benefits society by improving the economy's allocation of capital investment and by decreasing the volatility of security prices. This dampening of price fluctuations decreases the likelihood of individual windfall gains and increases the attractiveness of investing in securities for risk-averse investors. The individual corporation also benefits from accurate pricing of its securities through reduced investor uncertainty and improved monitoring of management's effectiveness.

Although U.S. securities laws purportedly encourage accurate pricing by requiring disclosure of corporate information, they do not require the disclosure of all material information. Where disclosure would interfere with legitimate business transactions, disclosure by the corporation is usually not required unless the firm is dealing in its own securities at the time.

When a firm withholds material information, its securities are no longer accurately priced by the market. In *Texas Gulf Sulphur*, when the ore deposit was discovered, TGS common stock sold for approximately eighteen dollars per share. By the time the discovery was disclosed, four months later, the price had risen to over thirty-one dollars per share. One month after disclosure, the stock was selling for approximately fifty-eight dollars per share. The difficulty, of course, is that TGS had gone to considerable expense to identify potential areas for mineral exploration and to conduct the initial search. Suppose TGS was required to disclose the ore strike as soon as the initial assay results came back. What would have happened? Landowners would have demanded a higher price for the mineral rights. Worse yet, competitors could have come into the area and bid against TGS for the mineral rights. In economic terms, these competitors would "free ride" on TGS's efforts. TGS will not earn a profit on the ore deposit until it has extracted enough ore to pay for its exploration costs. Because competitors will not have to incur any of the search costs TGS had incurred to find the ore deposit, they will have a higher profit margin on any ore extracted. In turn, that will allow them to outbid TGS for the mineral rights.[11] A securities law rule requiring immediate disclosure of the ore deposit (or any similar proprietary information) would discourage innovation and discovery by permitting this sort of free riding behavior—rational firms would not try to develop new mines if they knew competitors will be able to free ride on their efforts. In order to encourage innovation, the securities laws therefore generally permit corporations to delay disclosure of this sort of information for some period of time. As we have seen, however, the trade-off mandated by this policy is one of less accurate securities prices.

Manne essentially argued that insider trading is an effective compromise between the need for preserving incentives to produce information and the need for maintaining accurate securities prices. Manne offered the following example of this alleged effect: A firm's stock currently sells at fifty dollars per share. The firm has discovered new information that, if publicly disclosed, would cause the stock to sell at sixty dollars. If insiders trade on this information, the price of the stock will gradually rise toward the correct price. Absent insider trading or leaks, the stock's price will remain at fifty dollars until the information is publicly disclosed and then rapidly rise to the correct price of sixty dollars. Thus, insider trading acts as a replacement for public disclosure of the information, preserving market gains of correct pricing while permitting the corporation to retain the benefits of nondisclosure.[12]

---

11. Suppose TGS spent $2 per acre on exploration costs and is willing to pay $10 per acre to buy the mineral rights from the landowners. TGS must make at least $12 per acre on extracted ore before it makes a profit. Because competitors do not incur any exploration costs, they could pay $11 per acre for the mineral rights and still make a profit.

12. Henry Manne, Insider Trading and the Stock Market 77–91 (1966). On the signaling effect of insider trading, see William J. Carney, Signaling and Causation in Insider Trading, 36 Cath. U. L. Rev. 863 (1987); Dennis S. Corgill, Insider Trading, Price Signals, and Noisy Information, 71 Ind. L.J. 355 (1996); Marcel Kahan, Securi-

Despite the anecdotal support for Manne's position provided by *Texas Gulf Sulphur* and similar cases,[13] empirical evidence on point remains scanty. Early market studies indicated insider trading had an insignificant effect on price in most cases.[14] Subsequent studies suggested the market reacts fairly quickly when insiders buy securities, but the initial price effect is small when insiders sell.[15] These studies are problematic, however, because they relied principally (or solely) on the transactions reports corporate officers, directors, and 10% shareholders are required to file under Section 16(a). Because insiders are unlikely to report transactions that violate Rule 10b–5, and because much illegal insider trading activity is known to involve persons not subject to the § 16(a) reporting requirement, conclusions drawn from such studies may not tell us very much about the price and volume effects of illegal insider trading. Accordingly, it is significant that a more recent and widely-cited study of insider trading cases brought by the SEC during the 1980s found that the defendants' insider trading led to quick price changes.[16] That result supports Manne's empirical claim, subject to the caveat that reliance on data obtained from SEC prosecutions arguably may not be conclusive as to the price effects of undetected insider trading due to selection bias, although the study in question admittedly made strenuous efforts to avoid any such bias.

Does efficient capital markets theory support Manne's hypothesis? Although Manne's assertion that insider trading moves stock prices in the "correct" direction—i.e., the direction the stock price would move if the information were announced—seems intuitively plausible, the anonymity of impersonal market transactions makes it far from obvious that insider trading will have any effect on prices. Accordingly, we need to look more closely at the way in which insider trading might work its magic on stock prices.

If you studied price theory in economics, your initial intuition may be that insider trading affects stock prices by changing the demand for the issuing corporation's stock. Economics tells us that the price of a commodity is set by supply and demand forces. The equilibrium or market clearing price is that at which consumers are willing to buy all of the commodity offered by suppliers. If the supply remains constant, but demand goes up, the equilibrium price rises and vice-versa.

---

ties Laws and the Social Costs of "Inaccurate" Stock Prices, 41 Duke L.J. 977 (1992).

13. Recall that the TGS insiders began active trading in its stock almost immediately after discovery of the ore deposit. During the four months between discovery and disclosure, the price of TGS common stock gradually rose by over twelve dollars. Arguably, this price increase was due to inside trading. In turn, the insiders' profits were the price society paid for obtaining the beneficial effects of enhanced market efficiency.

14. See Roy A. Schotland, Unsafe at Any Price: A Reply to Manne, Insider Trading and the Stock Market, 53 Va. L. Rev. 1425, 1443 (1967) (citing studies).

15. Dan Givoly & Dan Palmon, Insider Trading and the Exploitation of Inside Information: Some Empirical Evidence, 58 J. Bus. 69 (1985).

16. Lisa K. Meulbroek, An Empirical Analysis of Illegal Insider Trading, 47 J. Fin. 1661 (1992).

Suppose an insider buys stock on good news. The supply of stock remains constant (assuming the company is not in the midst of a stock offering or repurchase), but demand has increased, so a higher equilibrium price should result. All of which seems perfectly plausible, but for the inconvenient fact that a given security represents only a particular combination of expected return and systematic risk, for which there is a vast number of substitutes. The correct measure for the supply of securities thus is not simply the total of the firm's outstanding securities, but the vastly larger number of securities with a similar combination of risk and return. Accordingly, the supply/demand effect of a relatively small number of insider trades should not have a significant price effect. Over the portion of the curve observed by individual traders, the demand curve should be flat rather than downward sloping.

Instead, if insider trading is to affect the price of securities, it is through the derivatively informed trading mechanism of market efficiency. Derivatively informed trading affects market prices through a two-step mechanism.[17] First, those individuals possessing material nonpublic information begin trading. Their trading has only a small effect on price. Some uninformed traders become aware of the insider trading through leakage or tipping of information or through observation of insider trades. Other traders gain insight by following the price fluctuations of the securities. Finally, the market reacts to the insiders' trades and gradually moves toward the correct price. The problem is that while derivatively informed trading can affect price, it functions slowly and sporadically. Given the inefficiency of derivatively informed trading, the market efficiency justification for insider trading loses much of its force.

2.   *Insider trading as an efficient compensation scheme*

Manne's other principal argument against the ban on insider trading rested on the claim that allowing insider trading was an effective means of compensating entrepreneurs in large corporations. Manne distinguished corporate entrepreneurs from mere corporate managers. The latter simply operate the firm according to predetermined guidelines. By contrast, an entrepreneur's contribution to the firm consists of producing new valuable information. The entrepreneur's compensation must have a reasonable relation to the value of his contribution to give him incentives to produce more information. Because it is rarely possible to ascertain information's value to the firm in advance, predetermined compensation, such as salary, is inappropriate for entrepreneurs. Instead, claimed Manne, insider trading is an effective way to compensate entrepreneurs for innovations. The increase in the price of the security following public disclosure provides an imperfect but comparatively accurate measure of the value of the innovation to the firm. The entrepreneur can recover the value of his discovery by purchasing the

---

17. See generally Ronald Gilson and Reinier Kraakman, The Mechanisms of   Market Efficiency, 70 Va. L. Rev. 549 (1984).

firm's securities prior to disclosure and selling them after the price rises.[18]

Professors Carlton and Fischel subsequently suggested a further refinement of Manne's compensation argument. They likewise believed *ex ante* contracts fail to appropriately compensate agents for innovations. The firm could renegotiate these contracts *ex post* to reward innovations, but renegotiation is costly and subject to strategic behavior. One of the advantages of insider trading, they argued, is that an agent revises his compensation package without renegotiating his contract. By trading on the new information, the agent self tailors his compensation to account for the information he produces, increasing his incentives to develop valuable innovations.[19]

Manne argued salary and bonuses provide inadequate incentives for entrepreneurial inventiveness because they fail to accurately measure the value to the firm of innovations.[20] Query, however, whether insider trading is any more accurate. Even assuming the change in stock price accurately measures the value of the innovation, the insider's compensation is limited by the number of shares he can purchase. This, in turn, is limited by his wealth. As such, the insider's trading returns are based, not on the value of his contribution, but on his wealth.

Another objection to the compensation argument is the difficulty of restricting trading to those who produced the information. Where information is concerned, production costs normally exceed distribution costs. As such, many firm agents may trade on the information without having contributed to its production.

A related criticism is the difficulty of limiting trading to instances in which the insider actually produced valuable information. In particular, why should insiders be permitted to trade on bad news? Allowing managers to profit from inside trading reduces the penalties associated with a project's failure because trading managers can profit whether the project succeeds or fails. If the project fails, the manager can sell his shares before that information becomes public and thus avoid an other-

---

18. In evaluating compensation-based justifications for deregulating inside trading, it is highly relevant to consider whether the corporation or the manager owns the property right to the information in question. Some of those who favor deregulating insider trading deny that firms have a property interest in information produced by their agents that includes the right to prevent the agent from trading on the basis of that information. In contrast, those who favor regulation contend that when an agent produces information the property right to that information belongs to the firm. As described below, the latter appears to be the better view. The implication of that conclusion for the compensation debate is that agents should not be allowed to set their own compensation by inside trading. Instead, if insider trading is to be used as a form of compensation, it should be so used only with the consent of the firm.

19. Dennis W. Carlton and Daniel R. Fischel, The Regulation of Insider Trading, 35 Stan. L. Rev. 857, 869–72 (1983). But see Saul Levmore, Securities and Secrets: Insider Trading and the Law of Contracts, 68 Va. L. Rev. 117 (1982); Saul Levmore, In Defense of the Regulation of Insider Trading, 11 Harv. J. L. & Pub. Pol. 101 (1988); Robert Thompson, Insider Trading, Investor Harm, and Executive Compensation, 50 Case West. Res. L. Rev. 291 (1999).

20. Henry Manne, Insider Trading and the Stock Market 134–38 (1966).

wise certain loss. The manager can go beyond mere loss avoidance into actual profit-making by short selling the firm's stock.

A final objection to the compensation thesis follows from the contingent nature of insider trading. Because the agent's trading returns cannot be measured in advance, neither can the true cost of his reward. As a result, selection of the most cost-effective compensation package is made more difficult. Moreover, the agent himself may prefer a less uncertain compensation package. If an agent is risk averse, he will prefer the certainty of $100,000 salary to a salary of $50,000 and a ten percent chance of a bonus of $500,000 from insider trading. Thus, the shareholders and the agent would gain by exchanging a guaranteed bonus for the agent's promise not to trade on inside information.

C. The case for regulation

The arguments in favor of regulating insider trading can be separated into one set sounding in economic terms and a second set premised on fairness, equity, and other nonefficiency grounds. The noneconomic arguments break down into two major sets: a claim that regulating insider trading is necessary to protect the mandatory disclosure system and a claim that insider trading is unfair. The economic arguments can be divided as follows: claims that insider trading injures investors; claims that insider trading injures firms; and claims relating to property rights in information.

1. *Mandatory disclosure*

Mandatory disclosure is arguably the central purpose of the federal securities laws. Both the Securities Act and the Exchange Act are based on a policy of mandating disclosure by issuers and others. The Securities Act creates a transactional disclosure regime, which is applicable only when a firm is actually selling securities. In contrast, the 1934 Exchange Act creates a periodic disclosure regime, which requires on-going, regular, disclosures.

As we have seen, neither Act requires a firm to disclose all nonpublic information relating to the firm. Instead, when premature disclosure would harm the firm's interests, the firm is generally free to refrain from disclosing such information. Even proponents of the mandatory disclosure system acknowledge that it is appropriate to strike this balance between investors' need for disclosure and management's need for secrecy.

Some suggest that the federal insider trading prohibition is necessary to the effective working of this mandatory disclosure system. The prohibition supposedly ensures "that confidentiality is not abused and utilized for the personal and secret profit of corporate managers and employees or persons associated with a bidder in a tender offer."[21] Many

21. Roberta S. Karmel, The Relationship Between Mandatory Disclosure and   Prohibitions Against Insider Trading: Why a Property Rights Theory of Insider Infor-

reputable corporate law scholars, of course, doubt whether mandatory disclosure is a sound policy.[22] If the mandatory disclosure system ought to be done away with, this line of argument collapses at the starting gate. For present purposes, however, we will take the mandatory disclosure system as a given and limit our inquiry to whether a prohibition of insider trading is necessary to protect the mandatory disclosure system from abuse.

Insider trading seems likely to adversely affect the mandatory disclosure regime only insofar as it affects managers' incentives to manipulate the timing of disclosure. As the argument goes, managers might delay making federally mandated disclosures in order to give themselves more time in which to trade in company stock before the inside information is announced. As we shall see below, however, it is doubtful whether insider trading results in significant delays in corporate disclosures.

Indeed, insider trading seems more likely to create incentives for insiders to prematurely disclose information than to delay its disclosure. While premature disclosure threatens the firm's interests, that threat has little to do with the mandatory disclosure system. Instead, it is properly treated as a breach of the insider's fiduciary duty.

In any event, concern for ensuring timely disclosure cannot justify a prohibition of the breadth it currently possesses. As we have seen, the prohibition encompasses a host of actors both within and outside the firm. In contrast, only a few actors are likely to have the power to affect the timing of disclosure. A much narrower prohibition thus would suffice if this were the principal rationale for regulating insider trading. Indeed, if this were the main concern, one need not prohibit insider trading at all. Instead, one could strike at the problem much more directly by proscribing failing to disclose material information in the absence of a legitimate corporate reason for doing so.

2. *Fairness*

There seems to be a widely shared view that there is something inherently sleazy about insider trading. Given the draconian penalties associated with insider trading, however, vague and poorly articulated notions of fairness surely provide an insufficient justification for the prohibition. Can we identify a standard of reference by which to demonstrate that insider trading ought to be prohibited on fairness grounds? In short, we cannot.

Fairness can be defined in various ways. Most of these definitions, however, collapse into the various efficiency-based rationales for prohibiting insider trading. We might define fairness as fidelity, for example, by

mation Is Untenable, 59 Brook. L. Rev. 149, 170–71 (1993). See generally James D. Cox, Insider Trading Regulation and the Production of Information: Theory and Evidence, 64 Wash. U. L.Q. 475 (1986).

22. See, e.g., Frank H. Easterbrook & Daniel R. Fischel, The Economic Structure Of Corporate Law 276–314 (1991); Roberta Romano, The Genius Of American Corporate Law 91–96 (1993).

which we mean the notion that agents should not cheat their principal. But this argument only has traction if insider trading is in fact a form of cheating, which in turn depends on how we assign the property right to confidential corporate information. Alternatively, we might define fairness as equality of access to information, as many courts and scholars have done, but this definition must be rejected in light of *Chiarella*'s rejection of the *Texas Gulf Sulphur* equal access standard. Finally, we might define fairness as a prohibition of injuring another. But such a definition justifies an insider trading prohibition only if investors are injured by insider trading, which seems unlikely. Accordingly, fairness concerns need not detain us further; instead, we can turn directly to the economic arguments against insider trading.

3. *Injury to investors*

Insider trading is said to harm investors in two principal ways. Some contend that the investor's trades are made at the "wrong price." A more sophisticated theory posits that the investor is induced to make a bad purchase or sale. Neither argument proves convincing on close examination.

An investor who trades in a security contemporaneously with insiders having access to material nonpublic information likely will allege injury in that he sold at the wrong price; i.e., a price that does not reflect the undisclosed information. If a firm's stock currently sells at $10 per share, but after disclosure of the new information will sell at $15, a shareholder who sells at the current price thus will claim a $5 loss.

The investor's claim, however, is fundamentally flawed. It is purely fortuitous that an insider was on the other side of the transaction. The gain corresponding to the shareholder's loss is reaped not just by inside traders, but by all contemporaneous purchasers whether they had access to the undisclosed information or not.[23]

---

23. To be sure, insider trading results in outside investors as a class reaping a smaller share of the gains from new information. William K. S. Wang, Trading on Material Nonpublic Information on Impersonal Stock Markets: Who Is Harmed, and Who Can Sue Whom Under SEC Rule 10b–5?, 54 S. Cal. L. Rev. 1217, 1234–35 (1981). In Texas Gulf Sulphur Co., for example, the price of TGS's stock rose from about $18 to about $55 during the relevant time period. Assuming all of that gain can be attributed to information about the ore strike, and further assuming that TGS has 1 million shares outstanding, the total gain to be divided was about $37 million. If insiders pocketed $2 million of that gain, there will be $2 million less for outsiders to divide. See William K.S. Wang, Stock Market Insider Trading: Victims, Violators and Remedies—Including an Analogy to Fraud in the Sale of a Used Car with a Generic Defect, 45 Villanova L. Rev. 27, 28–40 (2000) (discussing the "law of conservation of securities"). This is not a strong argument for banning insider trading, however. First, it only asserts that investors as a class are less well-off by virtue of insider trading. It cannot identify any particular investor who suffered losses as a result of the insider trading. Second, if we make the traditional assumption that the relevant supply of a given security is the universe of all securities with similar beta coefficients, any gains siphoned off by insiders with respect to a particular stock are likely to be an immaterial percentage of the gains contemporaneously earned by the class of investors as a whole. (Even in Texas Gulf Sulphur Co., trading by insiders amounted to less than 10% of the trading activity in TGS stock and, of course, a vastly smaller percentage of trading activity in the class of securities with comparable betas.) Finally, although

To be sure, the investor might not have sold if he had had the same information as the insider, but even so the rules governing insider trading are not the source of his problem. On an impersonal trading market, neither party knows the identity of the person with whom he is trading. Thus, the seller has made an independent decision to sell without knowing that the insider is buying; if the insider were not buying, the seller would still sell. It is thus the nondisclosure that causes the harm, rather than the mere fact of trading.[24]

The information asymmetry between insiders and public investors arises out of the mandatory disclosure rules allowing firms to keep some information confidential even if it is material to investor decisionmaking. Unless immediate disclosure of material information is to be required, a step the law has been unwilling to take, there will always be winners and losers in this situation. Irrespective of whether insiders are permitted to inside trade or not, the investor will not have the same access to information as the insider. It makes little sense to claim that the shareholder is injured when his shares are bought by an insider, but not when they are bought by an outsider without access to information. To the extent the selling shareholder is injured, his injury thus is correctly attributed to the rules allowing corporate nondisclosure of material information, not to insider trading.

Arguably, for example, the TGS shareholders who sold from November through April were not made any worse off by the insider trading that occurred during that period. Most, if not all, of these people sold for a series of random reasons unrelated to the trading activities of insiders. The only seller we should worry about is the one that consciously thought, "I'm going to sell because this worthless company never finds any ore." Even if such an investor existed, however, we have no feasible way of identifying him. Ex post, of course, all the sellers will pretend this was why they sold. If we believe Manne's argument that insider trading is an efficient means of transmitting information to the market, moreover, selling TGS shareholders actually were better off by virtue of the insider trading. They sold at a price higher than their shares would have commanded but for the insider trading activity that led to higher prices. In short, insider trading has no "victims." What to do about the "offenders" is a distinct question analytically.

A more sophisticated argument is that the price effects of insider trading induce shareholders to make poorly advised transactions. It is doubtful whether insider trading produces the sort of price effects

---

the law of conservation of securities asserts that some portion of the gains flow to insiders rather than to outside investors, that fact standing alone is legally unremarkable. To justify a ban on insider trading, you need a basis for asserting that it is inappropriate, undesirable, or immoral for those gains to be reaped by insiders. The law of conservation of securities does not, standing alone, provide such a basis.

24. On an impersonal exchange, moreover, the precise identity of the seller is purely fortuitous and it is difficult to argue that the seller who happened to be matched with the insider has been hurt more than any other contemporaneous seller whose sale was not so matched.

necessary to induce shareholders to trade, however. While derivatively informed trading can affect price, it functions slowly and sporadically. Given the inefficiency of derivatively informed trading, price or volume changes resulting from insider trading will only rarely be of sufficient magnitude to induce investors to trade.

Assuming for the sake of argument that insider trading produces noticeable price effects, however, and further assuming that some investors are misled by those effects, the inducement argument is further flawed because many transactions would have taken place regardless of the price changes resulting from insider trading. Investors who would have traded irrespective of the presence of insiders in the market benefit from insider trading because they transacted at a price closer to the correct price; i.e., the price that would prevail if the information were disclosed. In any case, it is hard to tell how the inducement argument plays out when investors are examined as a class. For any given number who decide to sell because of a price rise, for example, another group of investors may decide to defer a planned sale in anticipation of further increases.

An argument closely related to the investor injury issue is the claim that insider trading undermines investor confidence in the securities market. In the absence of a credible investor injury story, it is difficult to see why insider trading should undermine investor confidence in the integrity of the securities markets.

There is no denying that many investors are angered by insider trading. A Business Week poll, for example, found that 52% of respondents wanted insider trading to remain unlawful. In order to determine whether investor anger over insider trading undermines their confidence in the markets, however, one must first identify the source of that anger. A Harris poll found that 55% of the respondents said they would inside trade if given the opportunity. Of those who said they would not trade, 34% said they would not do so only because they would be afraid the tip was incorrect. Only 35% said they would refrain from trading because insider trading is wrong. Here lies one of the paradoxes of insider trading. Most people want insider trading to remain illegal, but most people (apparently including at least some of the former) are willing to participate if given the chance to do so on the basis of accurate information. This paradox is central to evaluating arguments based on confidence in the market. Investors that are willing to inside trade if given the opportunity obviously have no confidence in the integrity of the market in the first instance. Any anger they feel over insider trading therefore has nothing to do with a loss of confidence in the integrity of the market, but instead arises principally from envy of the insider's greater access to information.

The loss of confidence argument is further undercut by the stock market's performance since the insider trading scandals of the mid–1980s. The enormous publicity given those scandals put all investors on notice that insider trading is a common securities violation. At the same time, however, the years since the scandals have been one of the stock market's most robust periods. One can but conclude that insider trading does not seriously threaten the confidence of investors in the securities markets.

In sum, neither investor protection nor maintenance of confidence have much traction as theoretical justifications for any prohibition of insider trading. Nor do they have much explanatory power with respect to the prohibition currently on the books. An investor's rights vary widely depending on the nature of the insider trading transaction; the identity of the trader; and the source of the information. Yet, if the goal is investor protection, why should these considerations be relevant?

Recall, for example, *United States v. Carpenter*:[25] R. Foster Winans wrote the Wall Street Journal's "Heard on the Street" column, a daily report on various stocks that was said to affect the price of the stocks discussed. Journal policy expressly treated the column's contents prior to publication as confidential information belonging to the newspaper. Despite that rule, Winans agreed to provide several co-conspirators with prepublication information as to the timing and contents of future columns. His fellow conspirators then traded in those stocks based on the expected impact of the column on the stocks' prices, sharing the profits. In affirming their convictions, the Second Circuit anticipated *O'Hagan* by holding that Winans's breach of his fiduciary duty to the Wall Street Journal satisfied the standards laid down in *Chiarella* and *Dirks*. From either an investor protection or confidence in the market perspective, however, this outcome seems bizarre at best. For example, any duties Winans owed in this situation ran to an entity that had neither issued the securities in question nor even participated in stock market transactions. What Winans's breach of his duties to the Wall Street Journal had to do with the federal securities laws, if anything, is not self evident.

The incongruity of the misappropriation theory becomes even more apparent when one considers that its logic suggests that the Wall Street Journal could lawfully trade on the same information used by Winans. If we are really concerned with protecting investors and maintaining their confidence in the market's integrity, the inside trader's identity ought to be irrelevant. From the investors' point of view, insider trading is a matter of concern only because they have traded with someone who used their superior access to information to profit at the investor's expense. As such, it would not appear to matter whether it is Winans or the Journal on the opposite side of the transaction. Both have greater access to the relevant information than do investors.

The logic of the misappropriation theory also suggests that Winans would not have been liable if the Wall Street Journal had authorized his trades. In that instance, the Journal would not have been deceived, as

25. United States v. Carpenter, 791   U.S. 19 (1987).
F.2d 1024, 1026–27 (2d Cir.1986), aff'd, 484

O'Hagan requires. Winans' trades would not have constituted an improper conversion of nonpublic information, moreover, so that the essential breach of fiduciary duty would not be present. Again, however, from an investor's perspective, it would not seem to matter whether Winans's trades were authorized or not.

Finally, conduct that should be lawful under the misappropriation theory is clearly proscribed by Rule 14e–3. A takeover bidder may not authorize others to trade on information about a pending tender offer, for example, even though such trading might aid the bidder by putting stock in friendly hands. If the acquisition is to take place by means other than a tender offer, however, neither Rule 14e–3 nor the misappropriation theory should apply. From an investor's perspective, however, the form of the acquisition seems just as irrelevant as the identity of the insider trader.

All of these anomalies, oddities, and incongruities have crept into the federal insider trading prohibition as a direct result of *Chiarella*'s imposition of a fiduciary duty requirement. None of them, however, are easily explicable from either an investor protection or a confidence in the market rationale.

4. Property rights

In short, the federal insider trading prohibition is justifiable solely as a means of protecting property rights in information. There are essentially two ways of creating property rights in information: allow the owner to enter into transactions without disclosing the information or prohibit others from using the information. In effect, the federal insider trading prohibition vests a property right of the latter type in the party to whom the insider trader owes a fiduciary duty to refrain from self dealing in confidential information. To be sure, at first blush, the insider trading prohibition admittedly does not look very much like most property rights. Enforcement of the insider trading prohibition admittedly differs rather dramatically from enforcement of, say, trespassing laws. The existence of property rights in a variety of intangibles, including information, however, is well-established. Trademarks, copyrights, and patents are but a few of the better known examples of this phenomenon. There are striking doctrinal parallels, moreover, between insider trading and these other types of property rights in information. Using another's trade secret, for example, is actionable only if taking the trade secret involved a breach of fiduciary duty, misrepresentation, or theft. This was an apt summary of the law of insider trading after the Supreme Court's decisions in *Chiarella* and *Dirks* (although it is unclear whether liability for theft in the absence of a breach of fiduciary duty survives *O'Hagan*).

In context, moreover, even the insider trading prohibition's enforcement mechanisms are not inconsistent with a property rights analysis. Where public policy argues for giving someone a property right, but the costs of enforcing such a right would be excessive, the state often uses its regulatory powers as a substitute for creating private property rights.

Insider trading poses just such a situation. Private enforcement of the insider trading laws is rare and usually parasitic on public enforcement proceedings. Indeed, the very nature of insider trading arguably makes public regulation essential precisely because private enforcement is almost impossible. The insider trading prohibition's regulatory nature thus need not preclude a property rights-based analysis.

The rationale for prohibiting insider trading is the same as that for prohibiting patent infringement or theft of trade secrets: protecting the economic incentive to produce socially valuable information. As the theory goes, the readily appropriable nature of information makes it difficult for the developer of a new idea to recoup the sunk costs incurred to develop it. If an inventor develops a better mousetrap, for example, he cannot profit on that invention without selling mousetraps and thereby making the new design available to potential competitors. Assuming both the inventor and his competitors incur roughly equivalent marginal costs to produce and market the trap, the competitors will be able to set a market price at which the inventor likely will be unable to earn a return on his sunk costs. *Ex post*, the rational inventor should ignore his sunk costs and go on producing the improved mousetrap. *Ex ante*, however, the inventor will anticipate that he will be unable to generate positive returns on his up-front costs and therefore will be deterred from developing socially valuable information. Accordingly, society provides incentives for inventive activity by using the patent system to give inventors a property right in new ideas. By preventing competitors from appropriating the idea, the patent allows the inventor to charge monopolistic prices for the improved mousetrap, thereby recouping his sunk costs. Trademark, copyright, and trade secret law all are justified on similar grounds.

In many cases, of course, information can be used by more than one person without necessarily lowering its value. If a manager who has just negotiated a major contract for his employer then trades in his employer's stock, for example, there is no reason to believe that the manager's conduct necessarily lowers the value of the contract to the employer. But while insider trading will not always harm the employer, it may do so in some circumstances. This section evaluates several significant potential injuries to the issuer associated with insider trading.

Delay. Insider trading could injure the firm if it creates incentives for managers to delay the transmission of information to superiors. Decisionmaking in any entity requires accurate, timely information. In large, hierarchical organizations, such as publicly traded corporations, information must pass through many levels before reaching senior managers. The more levels, the greater the probability of distortion or delay intrinsic to the system.[26] This inefficiency can be reduced by downward delegation of decisionmaking authority but not eliminated. Even with only minimal delay in the upward transmission of information

---

26. See generally Robert J. Haft, The Effect of Insider Trading Rules on the Internal Efficiency of the Large Corporation, 80 Mich. L. Rev. 1051 (1982).

at every level, where the information must pass through many levels before reaching a decision-maker, the net delay may be substantial.

Managers who discover or obtain information (either beneficial or detrimental to the firm), may delay disclosure of that information to other managers so as to assure themselves sufficient time to trade on the basis of that information before the corporation acts upon it. Even if the period of delay by any one manager is brief, the net delay produced by successive trading managers may be substantial. Unnecessary delay of this sort harms the firm in several ways. The firm must monitor the managers' conduct to ensure timely carrying out of their duties. It becomes more likely that outsiders will become aware of the information through snooping or leaks. Some outsider may even independently discover and utilize the information before the corporation acts upon it.

Although delay is a plausible source of harm to the issuer, its importance is easily exaggerated. The available empirical evidence scarcely rises above the anecdotal level, but does suggest that measurable delay attributable to insider trading is rare.[27] Given the rapidity with which securities transactions can be conducted in modern secondary trading markets, moreover, a manager need at most delay corporate action long enough to place a quick on-line or telephonic order. Delay (either in transmitting information or taking action) also often will be readily detectable by the employer. Finally, and perhaps most importantly, insider trading may create incentives to release information early just as often as it creates incentives to delay transmission and disclosure of information.

Interference with corporate plans. Trading during the planning stage of an acquisition is a classic example of how insider trading might adversely interfere with corporate plans. If managers charged with overseeing an acquisition buy shares in the target, and their trading has a significant upward effect on the price of the target's stock, the takeover will be more expensive. If significant price and volume changes are caused by their trading, that also might tip off others to the secret, interfering with the bidder's plans, as by alerting the target to the need for defensive measures.

The risk of premature disclosure poses an even more serious threat to corporate plans. The issuer often has just as much interest in when information becomes public as it does in whether the information becomes public. Suppose Target, Inc., enters into merger negotiations with a potential acquirer. Target managers who inside trade on the basis of that information will rarely need to delay corporate action in order to effect their purchases. Having made their purchases, however, the managers now have an incentive to cause disclosure of Target's plans as soon as possible. Absent leaks or other forms of derivatively informed trading, the merger will have no price effect until it is disclosed to the market, at

27. Michael P. Dooley, Enforcement of
Insider Trading Restrictions, 66 Va. L. Rev.
1, 34 (1980).

which time there usually is a strong positive effect. Once the information is disclosed, the trading managers will be able to reap substantial profits, but until disclosure takes place, they bear a variety of firm-specific and market risks. The deal, the stock market, or both may collapse at any time. Early disclosure enables the managers to minimize those risks by selling out as soon as the price jumps in response to the announcement.

If disclosure is made too early, a variety of adverse consequences may result. If disclosure triggers competing bids, the initial bidder may withdraw from the bidding or demand protection in the form of costly lock-ups and other exclusivity provisions. Alternatively, if disclosure does not trigger competing bids, the initial bidder may conclude that it overbid and lower its offer accordingly. In addition, early disclosure brings the deal to the attention of regulators and plaintiffs' lawyers earlier than necessary.

An even worse case scenario is suggested by *SEC v. Texas Gulf Sulphur Co.*[28] Recall that insiders who knew of the ore discovery traded over an extended period of time. During that period the corporation was attempting to buy up the mineral rights to the affected land. If the news had leaked prematurely, the issuer at least would have had to pay much higher fees for the mineral rights, and may well have lost some land to competitors. Given the magnitude of the strike, which eventually resulted in a 300–plus percent increase in the firm's market price, the harm that would have resulted from premature disclosure was immense.

Although insider trading probably only rarely causes the firm to lose opportunities, it may create incentives for management to alter firm plans in less drastic ways to increase the likelihood and magnitude of trading profits. For example, trading managers can accelerate receipt of revenue, change depreciation strategy, or alter dividend payments in an attempt to affect share prices and insider returns. Alternatively, the insiders might structure corporate transactions to increase the opportunity for secret-keeping. Both types of decisions may adversely affect the firm and its shareholders. Moreover, this incentive may result in allocative inefficiency by encouraging over-investment in those industries or activities that generate opportunities for insider trading.

Judge Frank Easterbrook has identified a related perverse incentive created by insider trading.[29] Managers may elect to follow policies that increase fluctuations in the price of the firm's stock. They may select riskier projects than the shareholders would prefer, because, if the risks pay off, they can capture a portion of the gains in insider trading and, if the project flops, the shareholders bear the loss. In contrast, Professors Carlton and Fischel assert that Easterbrook overstates the incentive to choose high-risk projects.[30] Because managers must work in teams, the

28. 401 F.2d 833 (2d Cir. 1968), cert. denied, 394 U.S. 976 (1969).

29. Frank H. Easterbrook, Insider Trading, Secret Agents, Evidentiary Privileges, and the Production of Information, 1981 Sup. Ct. Rev. 309, 332.

30. Dennis W. Carlton and Daniel R. Fischel, The Regulation of Insider Trading, 35 Stan. L. Rev. 857, 875–76 (1983). See

ability of one or a few managers to select high-risk projects is severely constrained through monitoring by colleagues. Cooperation by enough managers to pursue such projects to the firm's detriment is unlikely because a lone whistle-blower is likely to gain more by exposing others than he will by colluding with them. Further, Carlton and Fischel argue managers have strong incentives to maximize the value of their services to the firm. Therefore they are unlikely to risk lowering that value for short-term gain by adopting policies detrimental to long-term firm profitability. Finally, Carlton and Fischel alternatively argue that even if insider trading creates incentives for management to choose high-risk projects, these incentives are not necessarily harmful. Such incentives would act as a counterweight to the inherent risk aversion that otherwise encourages managers to select lower risk projects than shareholders would prefer. Allowing insider trading may encourage management to select negative net present value investments, however, not only because shareholders bear the full risk of failure, but also because failure presents management with an opportunity for profit through short-selling. As a result, shareholders might prefer other incentive schemes.

Injury to reputation. It has been said that insider trading by corporate managers may cast a cloud on the corporation's name, injure stockholder relations and undermine public regard for the corporation's securities.[31] Reputational injury of this sort could translate into a direct financial injury, by raising the firm's cost of capital, if investors demand a premium (by paying less) when buying stock in a firm whose managers inside trade. Because shareholder injury is a critical underlying premise of the reputational injury story, however, this argument is a nonstarter. As we have seen, it is very hard to create a plausible shareholder injury story.

Legal liability. Corporations have significant liability exposure when their agents inside trade. First, Section 20(a) of the Securities Exchange Act provides that:

> Every person who, directly or indirectly, controls any person liable under any provision of this chapter or of any rule or regulation thereunder shall also be liable jointly and severally with and to the same extent as such controlled person to any person to whom such controlled person is liable, unless the controlling person acted in good faith and did not directly or indirectly induce the act or acts constituting the violation or cause of action.

Because the corporate employer doubtless controls its employees for this purpose, the corporation faces potential controlling person liability when insiders violate the federal securities laws by, inter alia, insider trading.

generally Lucian Arye Bebchuk and Chaim Fershtman, Insider Trading and the Managerial Choice among Risky Projects, 29 J. Financial & Quantitative Anal. 1 (1994).

31. Compare Diamond v. Oreamuno, 248 N.E.2d 910, 912 (N.Y. 1969) (discussing threat of reputational injury) with Freeman v. Decio, 584 F.2d 186, 194 (7th Cir. 1978) (arguing that injury to reputation is speculative).

The potential for control person liability was expanded following the the 1988 adoption of ITSFEA. The statute created an additional controlling person liability regime specifically applicable to insider trading by controlled persons. Under Securities Exchange Act § 21A(b), the SEC must prove that the controlling person "knew or recklessly disregarded" the fact that one of its employees or other controlled persons was "likely to engage" in illegal insider trading. In addition, the SEC must show that the control person "failed to take appropriate steps" to prevent such trading. If the SEC makes that showing, the control person may be held liable for the greater of $1.1 million or three times the amount of profit gained or loss avoided by the inside trader. See Securities Exchange Act § 21A(a)(3).

Control person liability, of course, arises only where the underlying misconduct is illegal. Legalization of insider trading thus would eliminate this risk of harm. Yet, a securities law-based source of harm would persist even if insider trading were legalized. Evidence of insider transactions is highly relevant to private securities litigation. Conventional wisdom posits that public corporations, especially in technology sectors, have become highly vulnerable to such litigation. At the story usually goes, a technology corporation that fails to meet its quarterly earnings projection will experience a drop in its stock price when that news is announced, and will shortly thereafter be sued for fraud under Rule 10b–5.

In 1995, Congress adopted the Private Securities Litigation Reform Act (PSLRA) to curtail what Congress believed was a widespread problem of merit-less strike suits. Of particular relevance to insider trading compliance programs, one of the PSLRA's provisions established a new (and arguably higher) pleading standard with respect to the scienter element of Rule 10b–5, requiring that a complaint detail facts giving rise to a "strong inference" of scienter.

Post–PSLRA, plaintiffs' securities lawyers have often sought to satisfy the scienter pleading standard by alleging that insiders sold shares in suspicious amounts and/or at suspicious times. Insider sales supposedly provide inferential evidence that senior management knew that earnings forecasts would not be met and sold to avoid the price drop that follows from announcements of lower than expected earnings. According to one report, 57% of "post–PSLRA cases, and 73% of those involving high technology, include allegations of insider sales, whereas only 21% of per–act cases contained such allegations."[32]

* * *

The potential for injury to the issuer perhaps does not provide as compelling a justification for the insider trading prohibition as it does for the patent system. A property right in information should be created

---

32. John L. Latham and Todd R. David, Compliance Programs Curb Risk of Insider Trading, Nat'l L.J., June 28, 1999, at B8.

when necessary to prevent conduct by which someone other than the developer of socially valuable information appropriates its value before the developer can recoup his sunk costs. As we have seen, however, insider trading often has no effect on an idea's value to the corporation and probably never entirely eliminates its value. Legalizing insider trading thus would have a much smaller impact on the corporation's incentive to develop new information than would, say, legalizing patent infringement.

The property rights approach nevertheless has considerable power. Consider the prototypical insider trading transaction, in which an insider trades in his employer's stock on the basis of information learned solely because of his position with the firm. There is no avoiding the necessity of assigning a property interest in the information to either the corporation or the insider. A rule allowing insider trading assigns a property interest to the insider, while a rule prohibiting insider trading assigns it to the corporation.

From the corporation's perspective, we have seen that legalizing insider trading would have a relatively small effect on the firm's incentives to develop new information. In some cases, however, insider trading will harm the corporation's interests and thus adversely affect its incentives in this regard. This argues for assigning the property right to the corporation, rather than the insider.

In any event, whether the corporation is harmed by insider trading is not dispositive. Creation of a property right with respect to a particular asset typically is not dependent upon there being a measurable loss of value resulting from the asset's use by someone else. Indeed, creation of a property right is appropriate even if any loss in value is entirely subjective, both because subjective valuations are difficult to measure for purposes of awarding damages and because the possible loss of subjective values presumably would affect the corporation's incentives to cause its agents to develop new information. As with other property rights, the law therefore should simply assume (although the assumption will sometimes be wrong) that assigning the property right to agent-produced information to the firm maximizes the social incentives for the production of valuable new information.

Because the relative rarity of cases in which harm occurs to the corporation weakens the argument for assigning it the property right, however, the critical issue may be whether one can justify assigning the property right to the insider. On close examination, the argument for assigning the property right to the insider is considerably weaker than the argument for assigning it to the corporation. The only plausible justification for doing so is the argument that legalized insider trading would be an appropriate compensation scheme. In other words, society might allow insiders to inside trade in order to give them greater incentives to develop new information. As we have seen, however, this argument appears to founder because, *inter alia*, insider trading is an inefficient compensation scheme. The economic theory of property rights in information thus cannot justify assigning the property right to insiders rather than to the corporation. Because there is no avoiding the necessity of assigning the property right to the information in question to one of the relevant parties, the argument for assigning it to the corporation therefore should prevail.[33]

The property rights rationale explains many aspects of the (pre-*O'Hagan*) insider trading prohibition far better than do any of the more traditional securities fraud-based justifications.[34] The basic function of a securities fraud regime is to ensure timely disclosure of accurate information to investors. Yet, it seems indisputable that the insider trading prohibition does not lead to increased disclosure. Instead, as we have seen, the disclose or abstain rule typically collapses into a rule of abstention.

Consider also the apparent incongruity that Winans (the defendant in *Carpenter*) could be held liable for trading on information about the Wall Street Journal's "Heard on the Street," but the Journal could have lawfully traded on the same information. This result makes no sense from a traditional securities law perspective. From a property rights perspective, however, the result in *Carpenter* makes perfect sense: because the information belonged to the Journal, it should be free to use the information as it saw fit, while Winans' use of the same information amounted to a theft of property owned by the Journal.

A property rights-based approach also helps make sense of a couple of aspects of *Dirks* that are quite puzzling when approached from a securities fraud-based perspective. One is the Court's solicitude for market professionals. After *Dirks*, market analysts were essentially exempt from insider trading liability with respect to nonpublic information they develop because they usually owe no fiduciary duty to the firms they research. *Dirks* thus essentially assigned the property right to such information to the market analyst rather than to the affected corporation. From a disclosure-oriented perspective, this is puzzling; the analyst and/or his clients will trade on the basis of information other investors lack. From a property perspective, however, the rule is justifiable because it encourages market analysts to expend resources to develop socially valuable information about firms and thereby promote market efficiency.

33. The argument in favor of assigning the property right to the corporation becomes even stronger when we move outside the prototypical situation to cases covered by the misappropriation theory. It is hard to imagine a plausible justification for assigning the property right to those who steal information.

34. To be sure, not all aspects of the federal prohibition can be so explained. For example, because property rights generally include some element of transferability, it may seem curious that federal law, at least in some circumstances, does not allow the owner of nonpublic information to authorize others to use it for their own personal gain. See, e.g., 17 C.F.R. 240.14e–3(d) (a tender offeror may not divulge its takeover plans to anyone likely to trade in target stock). This does not undermine the general validity of the property rights justification. Rather, if protection of property rights is taken as a valid public-regarding policy basis for the prohibition, it gives us a basis for criticizing departures from that norm.

The property rights rationale also supports our view that the fiduciary duty at issue in *Chiarella* and *Dirks* is the duty against self dealing. From a disclosure oriented approach, in which maximizing disclosure is the principal policy goal, reliance on a self dealing duty makes no sense because requiring such a breach limits the class of cases in which disclosure is made. In contrast, from a property rights perspective, an emphasis on self dealing makes perfect sense, because it focuses attention on the basic issue of whether the insider converted information belonging to the corporation.

In *O'Hagan*, the Supreme Court thus could have treated the insider trading prohibition's location in the federal securities laws as a historical accident, which has some continuing justification in the SEC's comparative advantage in detecting and prosecuting insider trading on stock markets. The Court should have then focused on the problem as one of implicating fiduciary duties with respect to property rights in information, rather than one of deceit or manipulation. Unfortunately, the majority chose not to do so.

The majority opinion began promisingly enough with an acknowledgement that confidential information belonging to corporations "qualifies as property."[35] The Court's authorized trading dictum is also consistent with the property rights rationale, while being demonstrably inconsistent with traditional securities law-based policy justifications for the insider trading prohibition. There is a general presumption that property rights ought to be alienable. Accordingly, if we are concerned with protecting the source of the information's property rights, we generally ought to permit the source to authorize others to trade on that information. In contrast, legalizing authorized trading makes little sense if the policy goal is the traditional securities fraud concern of protecting investors and maintaining their confidence in the integrity of the markets. Would an investor who traded with O'Hagan feel any better about doing so if she knew that Dorsey and Whitney had authorized O'Hagan's trades?

Did Justice Ginsburg intend to validate the property rights approach to insider trading? Probably not. The opinion quickly shifted gears towards treating the problem as one sounding in traditional securities fraud: "Deception through nondisclosure is central to the theory of liability for which the Government seeks recognition," and which the majority accepted. Indeed, the incoherence of the majority opinion on policy issues is well-illustrated by its arguable revival of the long-discredited equal access theory of liability. For example, in justifying her claim that the misappropriation theory was consistent with Section 10(b), Justice Ginsburg opined that the theory advances "an animating purpose of the Exchange Act: to insure [sic] honest securities markets and thereby promote investor confidence." She went on to claim that "investors likely would hesitate to venture their capital in a market where trading based on misappropriated nonpublic information is un-

35. U.S. v. O'Hagan, 521 U.S. 642, 654 (1997).

checked by law," because those who trade with misappropriators suffer from an informational disadvantage "that cannot be overcome with research or skill." The parallels to *Texas Gulf Sulphur* are obvious. If we want to protect investors from informational disadvantages that cannot be overcome by research or skill, moreover, the equal access test is far better suited to doing so than the *Chiarella/Dirks* framework.

Yet, predictably, the majority showed no greater fidelity to equality of access to information than it did to protection of property rights. In *O'Hagan*, the majority made clear that disclosure to the source of the information is all that is required under Rule 10b–5. If a misappropriator brazenly discloses his trading plans to the source, and then trades (either with the source's approval or over its objection), Rule 10b–5 is not violated.

This brazen misappropriator dictum is inconsistent with both an investor protection rationale for the prohibition and the property rights justification. As to the former, investors who trade with a brazen misappropriator presumably will not feel any greater confidence in the integrity of the securities market if they later find out that the misappropriator had disclosed his intentions to the source of the information. As to the latter, requiring the prospective misappropriator to disclose his intentions before trading provides only weak protection of the source of the information's property rights therein. To be sure, in cases in which the disclosure obligation is satisfied, the difficult task of detecting improper trading is eliminated. Moreover, as the majority pointed out, the source may have state law claims against the misappropriator. In some jurisdictions, however, it is far from clear whether inside trading by a fiduciary violates state law. Even where state law proscribes such trading, the Supreme Court's approach means that in brazen misappropriator cases we lose the comparative advantage the SEC has in litigating insider trading cases and the benefit of the well-developed and relatively liberal remedy under Rule 10b–5.

In sum, *O'Hagan* fails to cohere as to either policy or doctrine. It forecloses neither the equal access nor the property rights policy rationale for the Rule, while also failing to privilege either rationale. Just as a child might break his toy by attempting to force a square peg into a round hole, the Supreme Court made a farce of insider trading law (and Rule 10b–5 generally) by attempting to force insider trading into securities fraud—a paradigm that does not fit.

D. Scope of the prohibition

In *Diamond v. Oreamuno*,[36] the New York Court of Appeals concluded that a shareholder could properly bring a derivative action against corporate officers who had traded in the corporation's stock. The court explicitly relied on a property rights-based justification for its holding: "The primary concern, in a case such as this, is not to determine

---

36.   248 N.E.2d 910 (N.Y.1969).

whether the corporation has been damaged but to decide, as between the corporation and the defendants, who has a higher claim to the proceeds derived from exploitation of the information." Critics of *Diamond* have frequently pointed out that the corporation could not have used the information at issue in that case for its own profit. The defendants had sold shares on the basis of inside information about a substantial decline in the firm's earnings. Once released, the information caused the corporation's stock price to decline precipitously. The information was thus a historical accounting fact of no value to the corporation. The only possible use to which the corporation could have put this information was by trading in its own stock, which it could not have done without violating the antifraud rules of the federal securities laws.

The *Diamond* case thus rests on an implicit assumption that, as between the firm and its agents, all confidential information about the firm is an asset of the corporation. Critics of *Diamond* contend that this assumption puts the cart before the horse: the proper question is to ask whether the insider's use of the information posed a substantial threat of harm to the corporation. Only if that question is answered in the affirmative should the information be deemed an asset of the corporation.[37]

Proponents of a more expansive prohibition might respond to this argument in two ways. First, they might reiterate that, as between the firm and its agents, there is no basis for assigning the property right to the agent. Second, they might focus on the secondary and tertiary costs of a prohibition that encompassed only information whose use posed a significant threat of harm to the corporation. A regime premised on actual proof of injury to the corporation would be expensive to enforce, would provide little certainty or predictability for those who trade, and might provide agents with perverse incentives.

E. State or federal?

While it seems clear that society needs some regulation of insider trading to protect property rights in corporate information, it is not at all clear that securities fraud is the right vehicle for doing so. Consequently, even among those who agree that insider trading should be regulated on property rights grounds, there is disagreement as to how insider trading should be regulated. Some scholars favor leaving insider trading to state corporate law, just as is done with every other duty of loyalty violation, and, accordingly, divesting the SEC of any regulatory involvement. Others draw a distinction between SEC monitoring of insider trading and a federal prohibition of insider trading. They contend that the SEC should monitor insider trading, but refer detected cases to the affected corporation for private prosecution. A third set favors a federal prohibition enforced by the SEC.

This debate is a wide-ranging one, encompassing questions of economics, politics, and federalism. The analysis here focuses on the ques-

---

37. See, e.g., Freeman v. Decio, 584 F.2d 186, 192–94 (7th Cir.1978).

tion of whether the SEC has a comparative advantage vis-à-vis private actors in enforcing insider trading restrictions. If so, society arguably ought to let the SEC carry the regulatory load.

That the SEC has such a comparative advantage is fairly easy to demonstrate. Virtually all private party insider trading lawsuits are parasitic on SEC enforcement efforts, which is to say that the private party suit was brought only after the SEC's proceeding became publicly known. This condition holds because the police powers available to the SEC, but not to private parties, are essential to detecting insider trading. Informants, computer monitoring of stock transactions, and reporting of unusual activity by self regulatory organizations and/or market professionals are the usual ways in which insider trading cases come to light. As a practical matter, these techniques are available only to public law enforcement agencies. In particular, they are most readily available to the SEC.

Unlike private parties, who cannot compel discovery until a nonfrivolous case has been filed, the SEC can impound trading records and compel testimony simply because its suspicions are aroused. As the agency charged with regulating broker-dealers and self regulatory organizations, the SEC also is uniquely positioned to extract cooperation from securities professionals in conducting investigations. Finally, the SEC is statutorily authorized to pay bounties to informants, which is particularly important in light of the key role informants played in breaking most of the big insider trading cases of the 1980s.

Internationalization of the securities markets is yet another reason for believing the SEC has a comparative advantage in detecting and prosecuting insider trading.[38] Sophisticated insider trading schemes often make use of off-shore entities or even off-shore markets. The difficulties inherent in extraterritorial investigations and litigation, especially in countries with strong bank secrecy laws, probably would preclude private parties from dealing effectively with insider trading involving off-shore activities. In contrast, the SEC has developed memoranda of understanding with a number of key foreign nations, which provide for reciprocal assistance in prosecuting insider trading and other securities law violations. The SEC's ability to investigate international insider trading cases was further enhanced by the 1988 act, which included provisions designed to encourage foreign governments to cooperate with SEC investigations.

---

38. On the relationship between globalization of capital markets and insider trading regulation, see generally Merritt B. Fox, Insider Trading in a Globalizing Market: Who Should Regulate What?, 55 L. & Contemp. Prob. 263–302 (1992); Donald C. Langevoort, Fraud and Insider Trading in American Securities Regulation: Its Scope and Philosophy in a Global Marketplace, 16 Hastings Int'l & Comp. L. Rev. 175 (1993); Steven R. Salbu, Regulation of Insider Trading in a Global Market Place: A Uniform Statutory Approach, 66 Tulane L. Rev. 837 (1992).

Chapter 12

MERGERS AND ACQUISITIONS

Analysis

---

§ 12.1 The urge to merge

The corporation's legal personhood is a fiction, of course, but it is a very useful one. Among the powers thereby granted corporations are the rights to hold, acquire, and dispose of stock of other corporations. As a result, one corporation can acquire control of another through a merger or other acquisition device. To be sure, corporations also can be acquired by natural persons and many other entities, but the vast majority of corporate takeovers are effected by another corporation.

Why would someone want to acquire a corporation? Obviously, there are many potential motivations. Yet, understanding the motivation driving a particular acquisition can help the transaction planner answer two critical questions: (1) What opportunities does the transaction offer by which one or both parties might behave opportunistically? In other words, how might one side try to get more than its "fair" share of the pie? Doing something about strategic behavior is a question as to which we as lawyers have a comparative advantage vis-à-vis other participants in mergers and acquisitions. Our expertise runs towards using laws and contracts to constrain behavior. (Alternatively, we may represent the party that wants to behave strategically, in which case our job is to figure out how to help them get more than their fair share.) (2) How does this transaction create value? This is a pie expansion rather than a pie division question. How can the lawyer expand the pie by adding additional value to the transaction?

A. Do takeovers create wealth?

In evaluating corporate takeovers, one needs to consider the wealth effects of such transactions on three sets of players: (1) target company shareholders; (2) acquiring company shareholders; and (3) society at large, which would include not only net gains to the shareholders of the constituent corporations, but also any externalities imposed on other creditors, employees, communities, and other constituencies. The question here is whether takeovers create new wealth or simply reshuffle existing wealth among the relevant players.[1]

§ 12.1

1. Some commentators contend that the demand curves for stocks slope downwards and may even approximate unitary elasticity (i.e., buying 50% of a company's stock requires a price increase of 50%). See, e.g., Laurie Simon Bagwell, Dutch Auction Re-purchases: An Analysis of Shareholder Heterogeneity, 47 J. Fin. 71 (1992); Andrei Shleifer, Do Demand Curves for Stocks Slope Down?, 41 J. Fin. 579 (1986). If so, little or no new wealth is created by takeovers. Instead, takeover premia are purely an artifact of supply and demand.

1. Target v. acquirer shareholders

Is it possible to have a takeover that increases the wealth of target shareholders, but decreases the wealth of acquiring company shareholders? In brief, sure. An auction of corporate control is the most likely situation in which such an outcome might result. Bidder One makes an offer for Target. Bidder Two then makes a competing, slightly higher bid. Several rounds of competitive bidding follow. In the end, the bidder with the highest reservation price should prevail. Yet, that bidder is the one most likely to overpay. In behavioral economics, this phenomenon is known as the "winner's curse." Suppose Target's stock was trading at $10 before the bidding began. Due to the familiar problems of uncertainty and complexity, nobody knows for sure what Target is really worth. Bidder One's reservation price is $20, Bidder Two's reservation price is $22. All else being equal, Bidder Two should win the auction. Suppose Bidder Two ends up paying its reservation price of $22, but later discovers that Target really was worth no more than $20. Bidder Two has experienced the winner's curse: it won the auction, but lost the war. It overpaid. Target shareholders are better off by $12, but Bidder Two's shareholders are worse off by $2. Net, this is still a value creating acquisition, of course, but that fact may not assuage Bidder Two's shareholders.

The winner's curse does not always occur, even in a multi-bidder auction. The market for corporate control is thin, which reduces the probability that prices will be competed up to the reservation price of the highest-valuing user. Because better information means less risk of error on valuation, moreover, one can reduce the likelihood of bidder overpayment by reducing information asymmetries.[2] Nevertheless, there is evidence the winner's curse operates in the market for corporate control. The successful bidder typically pays a premium of 30–50%, sometimes even higher, over the pre-bid market price of the target's stock.[3] Consequently, target shareholders demonstrably gain substantially—on the

---

2. However, some behavioral economists contend that hubris on the part of acquiring company decisionmakers may cause them to persistently adhere to their chosen reservation price even in the face of objective evidence that they have overvalued the target. See, e.g., Richard Roll, The Hubris Hypothesis of Corporate Takeovers, 59 J. Bus. 197 (1986).

3. Note that this market premium is not inconsistent with the efficient capital markets hypothesis. The pre-bid market price represented the consensus of all market participants as to the present discounted value of the future dividend stream to be generated by the target—in light of all currently available public information. Put another way, the market price represents the market consensus as to the present value of the stream of future cash flows anticipated to be generated by present assets as used in

the company's present business plans. A takeover bid represents new information. It may be information about the stream of future earnings due to changes in business plans or reallocation of assets. In any event, that pre-bid market price will not have impounded the value of that information. To the extent the bidder has private information, moreover, the market will be unable to fully adjust the target's stock price. For contrary arguments, suggesting that mispricing of target securities may explain takeovers, see Reinier Kraakman, Taking Discounts Seriously: The Implications of "Discounted" Share Prices as an Acquisition Motive, 88 Colum. L. Rev. 891 (1988); Lynn A. Stout, Are Takeover Premiums Really Premiums? Market Price, Fair Value, and Corporate Law, 99 Yale L.J. 1235 (1990).

order of hundreds of billions of dollars—from takeovers.[4] In contrast, studies of acquiring company stock performance report results ranging from no statistically significant stock price effect to statistically significant losses.[5] By some estimates, bidders overpay in as many as half of all takeovers.

Even if it is quite common, of course, the winner's curse phenomenon does not preclude a conclusion that takeovers create new wealth. As long as target shareholders gain more than acquiring company shareholders lose, net new value is created. The evidence from the studies cited above suggests that takeovers produce net gains for shareholders.[6]

Should we worry about the distributional consequences of the difference between target and acquiring company shareholders? At first glance, well-diversified investors arguably should be indifferent as to how gains are divided between bidders and targets, because such investors are just as likely to be shareholders of one as the other. Hence, rational investors will prefer rules that maximize the net gain from changes of control. There are two difficulties with this line of reasoning, however. First, the analysis depends on both acquiring and target corporations being publicly held. If bidders are more likely to be privately held than are targets, or vice-versa, rational investors will be concerned with distributional effects. Second, and more important, the evidence recounted above suggests that target shareholders benefit from takeovers but that gains from takeovers are not passed on to acquiring company shareholders. Under such circumstances, rational investors would prefer that gains from takeovers be allocated to targets rather than acquirers. Accordingly, rational investors likely would prefer a rule maximizing the product of the number of takeovers and the average control premium to a rule simply maximizing the number of takeovers.

2. *Investors v. nonshareholder constituencies*

The question remains, whence comes the value created by takeovers? In particular, do takeovers transfer wealth from nonshareholder constituencies of the corporation to target shareholders? If so, takeovers generate negative externalities and the usual sorts of public policy implications follow.

There is a widely shared assumption that takeovers leave nonshareholder constituencies, especially employees, significantly worse off.[7] Ad-

4. See, e.g., Bernard S. Black & Joseph A. Grundfest, Shareholder Gains from Takeovers and Restructurings Between 1981 and 1986, J. Applied Corp. Fin., Spring 1988, at 5; Gregg A. Jarrell et al., The Market for Corporate Control: The Empirical Evidence Since 1980, 2 J. Econ. Persp. 49 (1988); Michael C. Jensen & Richard S. Ruback, The Market for Corporate Control: The Scientific Evidence, 11 J. Fin Econ. 5 (1983).

5. See, e.g., Julian Franks et al., The Postmerger Share–Price Performance of Acquiring Firms, 29 J. Fin. Econ. 81 (1991).

6. After reviewing numerous studies, Professors Gilson and Black conclude "that, on average, corporate acquisitions increase the combined shareholder market value of the acquiring and target companies." Ronald J. Gilson & Bernard S. Black, The Law and Finance of Corporate Acquisitions 309 (2d ed. 1995).

7. See Roberta Romano, The Future of Hostile Takeovers: Legislation and Public

mittedly, a fair bit of anecdotal evidence supports the claim. The AFL–
CIO estimated, for example, that 500,000 jobs were lost as a direct result
of takeover activity between 1983 and 1987 alone.[8] Acquiring companies
also supposedly use funds taken out of the target company's pension
plans to help finance the acquisition.[9] In light of such stories, prominent
management author Peter Drucker spoke for many when he observed
that "employees, from senior middle managers down to the rank and file
in the office or factory floor, are increasingly being demoralized—a
thoughtful union leader of my acquaintance calls it 'traumatized'—by
the fear of a takeover raid."[10]

Corporate takeovers also affect the communities in which the corporation has plants and other facilities. In the wake of Boone Pickens' raid
on Phillips Petroleum, for example, Phillips eliminated 2,700 jobs in its
Bartlesville, Oklahoma headquarters. Because Bartlesville's population
was only 36,000, this downsizing devastated the local community.[11]
Similar tales of woe doubtless could be told of many communities
affected by takeover-related corporate restructurings.

Highly-leveraged takeovers may adversely affect the interests of
bondholders and other corporate creditors. As the theory goes, pre-
takeover creditors assessed the corporation's creditworthiness and set
their loan terms based on the corporation's existing assets and debt-
equity ratios. In a highly-leveraged acquisition, the bidder finances the
acquisition by borrowing against target corporation assets and/or selling
target assets. This significantly lowers the corporation's creditworthiness, yet pre-takeover creditors are not compensated for this loss.
Bondholders are particularly hard hit by this phenomenon. Bond rating
agencies routinely downgrade a corporation's pre-takeover bonds to
reflect the firm's increased riskiness post-takeover, which immediately
reduces those bonds' market value.[12]

A number of commentators have advanced theoretical bases for the
claim that takeovers are detrimental to nonshareholder corporate constituents.[13] As the basic argument goes, many of the contracts making up

Opinion, 57 U. Cin. L. Rev. 457, 490–503
(1988).

8. S. Rep. No. 265, 100th Cong., 1st
Sess. 14 (1987).

9. Leigh B. Trevor, Hostile Takeovers—
The Killing Field of Corporate America, Ad-
dress to the Financial Executives Institute,
Mar. 11, 1986 at 15–16.

10. Peter F. Drucker, Taming the Corporate Takeover, Wall St. J., Oct. 30, 1984,
at 30.

11. S. Rep. No. 265, 100th Cong., 1st
Sess. 77 (1987) (separate views of Senators
Sasser, Sanford, and Chaffee).

12. See Morey W. McDaniel, Bondholders and Stockholders, 13 J. Corp. L. 205
(1988).

13. See, e.g., John C. Coffee, Jr., Share-
holders versus Managers: The Strain in the
Corporate Web, 85 Mich. L. Rev. 1 (1986);
Marleen A. O'Connor, The Human Capital
Era: Reconceptualizing Corporate Law to
Facilitate Labor–Management Cooperation,
78 Cornell L. Rev. 899 (1993); Marleen
O'Connor, Restructuring the Corporation's
Nexus of Contracts: Recognizing a Fiducia-
ry Duty to Protect Displaced Workers, 69
N.C. L. Rev. 1189 (1991); Andrei Shleifer &
Lawrence H. Summers, Breach of Trust in
Hostile Takeovers, in Corporate Takeovers:
Causes and Consequences 33 (Alan J. Auer-
bach ed. 1988). For critiques of such argu-
ments, see William J. Carney, Does Defin-
ing Constituencies Matter?, 59 U. Cin. L.
Rev. 385, 421–22 (1990); Jonathan R. Ma-
cey, Externalities, Firm–Specific Capital In-

the corporation are implicit and therefore judicially unenforceable.[14] Some of these implicit contracts are intended to encourage stakeholders to make firm-specific investments. Consider an employee who invests considerable time and effort in learning how to do his job more effectively. Much of this knowledge will be specific to the firm for which he works. In some cases, this will be because other firms do not do comparable work. In others, it will be because the firm has a unique corporate culture. In either case, the longer he works for the firm, the more difficult it becomes for him to obtain a comparable position with some other firm. An employee will invest in such firm-specific human capital only if rewarded for doing so. An implicit contract thus comes into existence between employees and shareholders. On the one hand, employees promise to become more productive by investing in firm-specific human capital. They bond the performance of that promise by accepting long promotion ladders and compensation schemes that defer much of the return on their investment until the final years of their career. In return, shareholders promise job security.[15] The implicit nature of these contracts, however, leaves stakeholders vulnerable to opportunistic corporate actions.

As the theory goes, this vulnerability comes home to roost in hostile takeovers. In all hostile acquisitions, the shareholders receive a premium for their shares. Where does that premium come from? Recall that the employees' implicit contract involved delaying part of their compensation until the end of their careers. If the bidder fires those workers before the natural end of their careers, replacing them with younger and cheaper workers, or if the bidder obtains wage or other concessions from the existing workers by threatening to displace them or to close the plant, the employees will not receive the full value of the services they provided to the corporation. Accordingly, a substantial part of the takeover premium consists of a wealth transfer from stakeholders to shareholders. Or so the story goes.

There are any number of problems with this thesis, however. For one thing, there is no credible evidence that takeovers transfer wealth from nonshareholder constituencies to shareholders.[16] The theoretical

vestments, and the Legal Treatment of Fundamental Corporate Changes, 1989 Duke L.J. 173.

14. The long-term nature of the relationship between stakeholders and corporations forces the stakeholders to rely on implicit, rather than explicit, contracts. Bargaining is costly, especially where future contingencies are hard to predict. The longer the contractual term, the more costly bargaining becomes. Implicit contracts can be readjusted as needed and thus save all the parties bargaining costs.

15. While the employee-shareholder relationship is the paradigmatic implicit contract, other stakeholders supposedly make similar investments in firms. Communities,

for example, often specialize around a given firm. The community receives a variety of services from the firm, but also provides the firm with a specialized infrastructure, tax breaks, and other benefits.

16. See Ronald J. Gilson & Bernard S. Black, The Law and Finance of Corporate Acquisitions 623–27 (2d ed. 1995) (summarizing evidence); see also Amanda Acquisition Corp. v. Universal Foods Corp., 877 F.2d 496, 500 n. 5 (7th Cir.1989) ("no evidence of which we are aware suggests that bidders confiscate workers' and other participants' investments to any greater degree than do incumbents—who may (and frequently do) close or move plants to follow the prospect of profit").

justification for protecting nonshareholders is equally unpersuasive. Many corporate constituencies do not make firm specific investments in human capital (or otherwise). In contrast, the shareholders' investment in the firm always is a transaction specific asset, because the whole of the investment is both at risk and turned over to someone else's control. Consequently, shareholders are more vulnerable to director misconduct than are most nonshareholder constituencies. Relative to many non-shareholder constituencies, moreover, shareholders are poorly positioned to extract contractual protections. Unlike bondholders or unionized employees, for example, whose term-limited relationship to the firm is subject to extensive negotiations and detailed contracts, shareholders have an indefinite relationship that is rarely the product of detailed negotiations. In general, nonshareholder constituencies that enter voluntary relationships with the corporation thus can protect themselves by adjusting the contract price to account for negative externalities imposed upon them by the firm. Many nonshareholder constituencies have substantial power to protect themselves through the political process. Public choice theory teaches that well-defined interest groups are able to benefit themselves at the expense of larger, loosely defined groups by extracting legal rules from lawmakers that appear to be general welfare laws but in fact redound mainly to the interest group's advantage. Absent a few self-appointed spokesmen, most of whom are either gadflies or promoting some service they sell, shareholders—especially individuals—have no meaningful political voice. In contrast, many nonshareholder constituencies are represented by cohesive, politically powerful interest groups. As a result, the interests of nonshareholder constituencies increasingly are protected by general welfare legislation.

B. Where do takeover gains come from?

Takeovers sometimes create value by allowing the buyer to take advantage of specific legal rules. This is especially true with respect to tax and accounting rules. In the famous business judgment rule decision, *Smith v. Van Gorkom*, for example, the challenged acquisition was motivated by the desire to take advantage of investment tax credits that were about to expire unused.[17] These regulatory sources of value, however, lie outside the scope of this text. Instead, we will focus on two theories of more general application: displacement of inefficient management and strategic acquisitions.

1. *Creating value by displacing inefficient managers*

The agency cost literature describes two basic types of managerial inefficiency. The first is misfeasance: If managers worked harder, were smarter, or were more careful they would earn more money for shareholders. The second is malfeasance: Managers cheat the corporation or lavish perks on themselves. The annals of American business corpora-

17. Smith v. Van Gorkom, 488 A.2d 858, 865 (Del.1985).

tions are replete with examples of both forms of shirking, ranging from congenital unluckiness, to incompetence, to outright theft.

Experience teaches that most successful business people are smart, hard-working, and honest, however. Is it nevertheless possible that smart, hard-working, reasonably honest people might be "inefficient" and therefore in need of replacing? An affirmative answer is suggested by the so-called "free cash flow" theory: Successful managers end up with a lot of cash for which they have no good use. In technical terms, they end up with cash flows greater than the positive net present value investments available to the firm. Disbursing these free cash flows to shareholders in the form of dividends would (a) be costly because of the double taxation on dividends and (b) increase management risks because a smaller asset pool increases the risk of firm failure in the event of financial reverses. Accordingly, even well-meaning managers have an incentive to retain free cash flow by making negative net present value investments. A takeover releases most of those funds, while earning the acquirer a profit from the remainder.[18]

No matter the source or form of director or management shirking, it should be reflected in a declining market price for the stock of the company. Bad management is just another form of information that efficient markets are able to process. When a declining market price signals shirking by directors or management, among those who receive the signal are directors and managers of other firms, who possess the resources to investigate the reason for the potential target's deteriorating performance. Sometimes it will be something that is beyond anybody's ability to control, such as where highly specialized assets are languishing because of a permanent shift in consumer demand. Sometimes, however, it will be due to poor management, which presents real opportunities for gain if the personnel or policies causing the firm to languish can be corrected. A successful takeover gives the acquirer the ability to elect at least a majority of the board of directors and thereby control personnel and policy decisions. The resulting appreciation in value of the acquired shares provides the profit incentive to do so. It is partly for this reason that we refer to the takeover market as "the market for corporate control."[19]

---

18. See generally Michael C. Jensen, The Agency Costs of Free Cash Flow, Corporate Finance, and Takeovers, 76 Am. Econ. Rev. 323 (1986). The free cash flow story seems particularly useful as an explanation for leveraged acquisitions—i.e., those funded by borrowing. A leveraged acquisition results in a one-time disbursement of free cash to the shareholders and, moreover, forces the company to go forward with a highly leveraged capital structure. The additional debt forces the firm's board and management to continuing paying out free cash flows. Dividends are optional and flexible. Debt payments are mandatory and inflexible. You have to make them. Financial flexibility, in the form of free cash flow, large cash balances, and unused borrowing power provides managers with greater discretion over resources that is often not used in shareholders' interests. Debt limits management's discretion in useful ways. In effect, debt becomes a low cost mechanism by which management promises to refrain from spending free cash flows in ways detrimental to shareholder interests.

19. As is so often the case in the law and economics of corporations, the intellectual roots of this theory can be found in one of Henry Manne's articles. See Henry G. Manne, Mergers and the Market for Corpo-

The potential to create value through this market has important transactional and policy implications. The transactional implications should be obvious: nobody likes to be displaced, especially if the explanation for displacing them is their own incompetence or inefficiency. Hence, we can expect incumbent managers to resist takeovers motivated by a desire to displace them. Providing low-cost mechanisms for overcoming management resistance thus is one way in which transactional lawyers can add value to a prospective takeover.[20]

The market for corporate control argument also has important policy implications. Keeping the stock price up is one of the best defenses managers have against being displaced in a takeover. Accordingly, the market for corporate control is an important mechanism for preventing management shirking and thus for minimizing the agency costs associated with conducting business in the corporate form. Indeed, some scholars argue that the market for control is the ultimate monitor that makes the modern business corporation feasible.[21] If true, a variety of policy implications would follow. For example, one might well outlaw any target managerial resistance to takeovers. If there are alternative explanations of how takeovers create value, however, the market for corporate control loses some of its robustness as a policy engine. Put another way, awarding the lion's share of the gains to be had from a change of control to the bidder only makes sense if all gains from takeovers are created by bidders through the elimination of inept or corrupt target managers and none of the gains are attributable to the hard work of efficient target managers.

The empirical evidence suggests that takeovers produce gains for many reasons, of which the agency cost constraining function of the market for corporate control is but one. Studies of target corporation performance, for example, suggest that targets during the 1980s generally were decent economic performers.[22] Second, studies of post-takeover workforce changes find that managers are displaced in less than half of corporate takeovers.[23] Third, as already noted, acquiring company share-

rate Control, 73 J. Pol. Econ. 110 (1965). See also Henry G. Manne, Cash Tender Offers for Shares—A Reply to Chairman Cohen, 1967 Duke L.J. 231. For appreciations of Manne's influence on the subsequent literature, see William J. Carney, The Legacy of "The Market for Corporate Control" and the Origins of the Theory of the Firm , 50 Case W. Res. L. Rev. 215 (1999); Fred S. McChesney, Manne, Mergers, and the Market for Corporate Control, 50 Case W. Res. L. Rev. 245 (1999).

20. Notice the relationship between this issue and the broader question of constraining strategic behavior. Management resistance to takeovers is a form of strategic behavior on their part.

21. See, e.g., Frank H. Easterbrook & Daniel R. Fischel, Auctions and Sunk Costs in Tender Offers, 35 Stan. L. Rev. 1 (1982); Frank H. Easterbrook & Daniel R. Fischel, The Proper Role of a Target's Management in Responding to a Tender Offer, 94 Harv. L. Rev. 1161 (1981); Ronald J. Gilson, The Case Against Shark Repellent Amendments: Structural Limitations on the Enabling Concept, 34 Stan. L. Rev. 775 (1982).

22. See, e.g., Edward S. Herman & Louis Lowenstein, The Efficiency Effects of Hostile Takeovers, in Knights, Raiders & Targets: The Impact of the Hostile Takeover 211 (John C. Coffee, Jr., et al. eds. 1988).

23. See, e.g., David P. Baron, Tender Offers and Management Resistance, 38 J. Fin. 331 (1983); Ralph A. Walkling & Michael S. Long, Agency Theory, Managerial

holders frequently lose money from takeovers. If displacing inefficient managers was the principal motivation for takeovers, acquiring company shareholders should make money from takeovers. Finally, there is little convincing evidence that acquired firms are better managed after the acquisition than they were beforehand. In sum, displacement of inefficient managers is a plausible way in which takeovers create value, but it is hardly the only way—and it may not even be a particularly important way.

2. Strategic acquisitions

One likely candidate as a motivation for many takeovers is the strategic acquisition. The bidder buys a well-managed company because it fits into the bidder's business plan. There are various ways this might happen:

Strategic acquisition for the sake of operating synergy: In a synergistic acquisition, the sum is greater than the whole of the parts. Synergy might be generated if two activities have greater value when conducted within an integrated firm than by separate firms. Suppose a movie studio merged with a magazine publisher, and the combined entity then merged with an internet services provider. The magazines could cover a major movie release, while the ISP provided advertising, ticket sales, and the like. The combined efforts of the various divisions might significantly leverage the value of the movie in a way that a stand-alone studio could not.

Strategic acquisitions to redress potential hold up concerns: A common efficiency-based justification for vertical integration is the elimination of appropriate quasi-rents. Quasi-rents arise where investments in transaction specific assets create a surplus subject to expropriation by the contracting party with control over the assets.[24] A transaction specific asset is one whose value is appreciably lower in any other use than the transaction in question. Once a transaction specific investment has been made, it generates quasi-rents—i.e., returns in excess of that necessary to maintain the asset in its current use.[25] If such quasi-rents are appropriable by the party with control of the transaction specific asset, a hold up problem ensues. Vertical integration brings both parties within a single firm and, accordingly, is a common solution to the hold up problem.

Strategic acquisition for the sake of market power: The bidder might buy one or more of its competitors so as to increase its market share and thus gain a competitive advantage. It is for this reason, of course, that the antitrust laws are concerned with takeovers. A related concept is the acquisition intended to allow entry into related markets with high entry

---

Welfare, and Takeover Bid Resistance, 15 Rand J. Econ. 54 (1984).

24. See Benjamin R. Klein et al., Vertical Integration, Appropriable Rents, and the Competitive Contracting Process, 21 J. L. & Econ. 297, 298 (1978).

25. The asset may also generate true rents—i.e., returns exceeding that necessary to induce the investment in the first place—but the presence or absence of true rents is irrelevant to the opportunism problem.

barriers. An example may be the easiest way to explain this concept: ConAgra is a big agricultural and food products business. It wanted to enter the boxed beef business, which apparently is an industry with very high entry barriers. In other words, it is very difficult to get a new business going in the boxed beef area if one starts from scratch. So ConAgra simply bought an existing boxed beef company.[26]

Strategic acquisition for the sake of diversification: Around the middle of the 20th Century, the idea grew up that good managers could manage anything. This view was operationalized via conglomerate mergers, in which companies intentionally sought to diversify their product lines and business activities horizontally across a wide array of unrelated businesses. The theory was that a cyclical manufacturer could buy a noncyclical business, making the combined company stronger because some division would always be doing well. Diversification necessarily reduces the maximum gains a conglomerate can produce. When one segment is doing well, it is being pulled down by a segment that is doing less well. To be sure, diversification reduced the conglomerate's exposure to unsystematic risk. But so what? Investors can diversify their portfolios more cheaply than can a company, not least because the investor need not pay a control premium. Management of a conglomerate may be better off, because their employer is subject to less risk, but the empirical evidence is compelling that intra-firm diversification reduces shareholder wealth.[27] The self-correcting nature of free markets is demonstrated by what happened next: during the 1980s there was a wave of so-called "bust-up" takeovers in which conglomerates were acquired and broken up into their constituent pieces, which were then sold off. The process resulted in a sort of reverse synergy: the whole was worth less than the sum of its parts.[28]

Strategic acquisition for the sake of empire building: Bigger is typically better from management's perspective. Just like putting oriental rugs down on the floor, bigger organizational charts on the wall are a management perk. If size reduces the chances of firm failure, management even has a financial incentive to pursue such acquisitions. As with acquisitions motivated by a desire for intra-firm diversification, empire building acquisitions doubtless reduce shareholder wealth. Free markets are self-correcting, however. Empirical studies confirm that bidders motivated by considerations other than shareholder wealth maximization themselves tend to become targets.[29]

26. ConAgra Inc. v. Cargill, Inc., 382 N.W.2d 576 (Neb.1986).

27. Yakov Amihud & Baruch Lev, Risk Reduction as a Managerial Motive for Conglomerate Mergers, 12 Bell J. Econ. 605 (1981); R. Hal Mason & Maurice Goudzwaard, Performance of Conglomerate Firms: A Portfolio Approach, 31 J. Fin. 39 (1976).

28. On the conglomerate merger phenomenon and bust-up mergers, see Gerald Davis et al., The Decline and Fall of the Conglomerate Firm in the 1980s: The Deinstitutionalization of an Organizational Form, 59 Am. Soc. Rev. 547 (1994); Andrei Shliefer & Robert W. Vishny, The Takeover Wave of the 1980s, 249 Sci. 745 (1990).

29. Mark L. Mitchell & Kenneth Lehn, Do Bad Bidders Become Good Targets?, 98 J. Pol. Econ. 372 (1990).

3. *Summary*

In sum, we lack a unified field theory of takeovers. We know that target shareholders receive substantial premia in acquisitions—but we do not know why. There is no single compelling explanation of where control premia come from and whether takeovers really create new wealth. Instead, there are probably a host of explanations—ranging from acquiring manager hubris to downward sloping demand curves for stock to capital market inefficiencies to synergies of various forms to constraints on agency costs. The existence of multiple plausible explanations for corporate takeovers has significant policy import. Takeovers present many profound policy choices, which would be far easier to make if we had a robust theory explaining the source of takeover premia. In the absence of such a story, we must frequently settle for second best solutions.

§ 12.2 A typology of acquisition techniques

Corporate acquisitions provide transactional lawyers many opportunities to create value for their clients. One of the most basic is regulatory arbitrage in the choice of acquisition form. If a given substantive deal structure necessarily led to a single legal structure, there would be no issue. But the law provides a number of acquisition forms, providing multiple ways of structuring any given deal. Each form has its own advantages or disadvantages—or, in economic terms, each form has its own transaction cost schedule. The transaction planner's task is to identify, in the context of a particular transaction, the legal form imposing the lowest costs for the deal at hand.

Acquisition techniques can be classified in various ways. One might, for example, distinguish between negotiated and hostile acquisitions. Negotiated acquisitions are those in which the target is willing to be bought—indeed, the target may have initiated the transaction by searching out a buyer. Here the focus is on the mechanics by which the acquisition takes place, the duties of management in selecting and negotiating with a bidder, and the risk that competing bidders will try to buy the target out from under the initial bidder. Hostile acquisitions are those in which the target company's board of directors is unwilling to be acquired. Here the focus will be on how the target can defend itself against the bidder and what the bidder can do to defeat those defenses.

A more useful classification system, however, distinguishes between statutory and nonstatutory acquisition techniques.[1] The former category includes the merger, its variants, and the sale of all or substantially all corporate assets. The latter includes the proxy contest, the tender offer, and stock purchases. The role of the target board of directors is the chief distinction between the two categories. Statutory forms, such as a

---

§ 12.2

1. The statute in question is the corporation code of the relevant state. Although the so-called nonstatutory techniques are largely unregulated by state corporation codes, they are governed by various other statutes, such as the federal securities laws.

merger or asset sale, require approval by the target's board of directors. In contrast, the nonstatutory techniques do not. A proxy contest obviously does not require board approval, although a shareholder vote is still required. A tender offer or stock purchase require neither board approval nor a shareholder vote—if the buyer ends up with a majority of the shares, it will achieve control.

The need for board approval creates insurmountable barriers to use of a statutory form if the bidder is unable to secure board cooperation. The nonstatutory forms eliminate this difficulty by permitting the bidder to bypass the target's board and obtain control directly from the stockholders. But why would a board be unwilling to cooperate? Several reasons suggest themselves: (1) The board may refuse to sell at any price, perhaps out of concern for their positions and perquisites. (2) The board may hold out for a price higher than the bidder is willing to pay. (3) The board may hold out for side-payments.

§ 12.3   Statutory acquisition techniques

A.   The merger

In a merger, two corporations combine to form a single entity. Suppose, for example, Acme Company and Ajax Corporation are about to combine via merger. Their merger is effected by filing the requisite documentation—typically so-called "articles of merger"—with the appropriate state official, not unlike the incorporation process by which the two companies were formed. After the merger, only one of the two companies will survive. But the survivor will have succeeded by operation of law to all of the assets, liabilities, rights, and obligations of the two constituent corporations.[1]

As MBCA § 11.07 more specifically explains, a merger has no fewer than 8 distinct effects on the merging corporations:

- The corporation designated in the merger agreement as the surviving entity continues its existence.

- The separate existence of the corporation or corporations that are merged into the survivor ceases.

- All property owned by, and every contract right possessed by, each constituent corporation is vested in the survivor.

- All liabilities of each constituent corporation are vested in the survivor.

- The surviving corporation's name may be substituted in any pending legal proceeding for the name of any constituent corporation that was a party to the proceeding.

---

§ 12.3

1. As a technical matter, a merger is defined as a combination of two or more corporations in which one of the constituent parties survives. In a consolidation, two or more corporations combine to form a new corporation. Because the articles of consolidation serve as the new entity's articles of incorporation, the distinction is mostly semantic from a corporate law perspective.

- The articles of incorporation and bylaws of the survivor are amended to the extent provided in the merger agreement.

- The articles of incorporation or organizational documents of any entity that is created by the merger become effective.

- The shares of each constituent corporation are converted into whatever consideration was specified in the merger agreement and the former shareholders of the constituent corporations are entitled only to the rights provided them in the merger agreement or by statute.

Under the Model Act, effecting a merger requires four basic steps. First, a plan of merger must be drafted, specifying the deal's terms and conditions.[2] The plan of merger must be approved by the board of directors.[3] The plan then must be approved by the shareholders.[4] Unlike most corporate actions, which only require approval by a majority of those shares present and voting, a merger requires approval by a majority of the outstanding shares.[5] Finally, articles of merger must be filed with the requisite state agency—usually the Secretary of State.

The process is essentially the same in non-Model Act states, with the principal variation being the vote required for the merger to receive shareholder approval. At early common law, a merger required unanimous shareholder approval. The unanimity requirement created the potential for hold up problems, as a dissenting minority could block a transaction in hopes of being assuaged by side-payments. Unanimity gradually gave way to supermajority voting requirements, which in Delaware and Model Act states have further eroded into a mere majority of the outstanding shares. About one-third of the states retain some form of supermajority voting requirement, however, typically two-thirds of the shares entitled to vote.[6]

In most states, a shareholder vote is not required if the transaction qualifies as a so-called short-form merger. The short-form merger statute is a special provision for a merger between a parent corporation and one of its subsidiaries. The statute may be invoked only if the parent corporation owns a high percentage—typically 90%—of the subsidiary's outstanding stock.[7] Early short-form merger statutes typically required

---

2. MBCA § 11.02(c).

3. MBCA § 11.04(a).

4. MBCA § 11.04(b)-(d).

5. MBCA § 11.04(e). The voting requirements become more complex, of course, if group voting is required or if the terms of the deal trigger voting rights for classes of stock that otherwise lack such rights.

6. The most prominent supermajority holdout, New York, amended its statute in 1998 to require approval by a majority of the shares entitled to vote with respect to subsequently formed corporations. N.Y. Bus. Corp. L. § 903. In addition, the New York statute allows pre-existing corporations to opt for a majority vote rule by amending their articles. Id. Given New York's long prominence as a holdout jurisdiction, this action may presage a gradual further erosion of supermajority vote requirements in the remaining holdouts.

7. The statutory elimination of shareholder voting rights makes sense in this context because the outcome of any vote by the subsidiary's shareholders would be a foregone conclusion and because how a parent corporation votes shares of a subsidiary is a business decision for the parent's board rather than the parent's shareholders.

the transaction to be approved by the board of directors of each corporation. Neither corporation's shareholders were allowed to vote. MBCA § 11.05(a) and DGCL § 253(a), however, reflect a modern trend towards even more liberal short-form mergers. Both statutes authorize a short-form merger when the parent owns at least 90% of the subsidiary's stock. If that threshold is met, only the parent corporation's board need approve the merger.[8] Neither the subsidiary's board nor its minority shareholders have any say. The assumption seems to be that both votes would be foregone conclusions.

Under Delaware law, shareholder voting rights also may be eliminated for certain transactions that do not qualify for treatment as short-form mergers if three conditions are met: (1) the agreement of merger does not amend the surviving corporation's articles of incorporation; (2) the outstanding shares of the surviving corporation are unaffected by the transaction;[9] and (3) the transaction does not increase the number of outstanding shares by more than 20%. If all three conditions are satisfied, approval by the surviving corporation's shareholders is not required. Approval by any other constituent corporation's shareholders is still required, however.[10]

B.   The sale of all or substantially all corporate assets

The board of directors has essentially unconstrained authority to sell, lease, mortgage, or otherwise dispose of corporate assets except where the board attempts to dispose of all or substantially all corporate assets. In the latter case, shareholder approval is required.[11] Under DGCL § 271(a), the required vote is a majority of the outstanding voting shares. Under MBCA § 12.02(e), by contrast, the requisite vote is only a majority of those present and voting. In both cases, only the selling corporation's shareholders are entitled to vote.[12]

---

8. If the parent will not survive or the articles of merger will effect a change in the parent's articles of incorporation, however, the parent's shareholders must approve the transaction. DGCL § 253(c); MBCA § 11.05(c).

9. Specifically, DGCL § 251(f) provides that "each share of stock of such constituent corporation outstanding immediately prior to the effective date of the merger is to be an identical outstanding or treasury share of the surviving corporation after the effective date of the merger." This curious language was intended to preclude the use of § 251(f) in so-called reverse triangular mergers. In such a transaction, the target corporation is merged with a subsidiary of the acquiring corporation, with the target surviving. Absent the quoted language, § 251(f) could be invoked to prevent the target corporation's shareholders from voting, provided the other two conditions were satisfied.

10. DGCL § 251(f). Under DGCL § 262, shareholders of the surviving company are denied appraisal rights in such transactions.

11. DGCL § 271. In 1999, the Model Act adopted amendments incorporating a new terminology. Under revised MBCA § 12.02(a), shareholder approval is required if the transaction "would leave the corporation without a significant continuing business activity."

12. Note that we are discussing only dispositions of assets in this section. The decision to purchase assets is vested solely in the board, although shareholder action may be required indirectly by ancillary legal regimes. This is especially likely to be true if the acquiring corporation will issue a substantial amount of stock in connection with the transaction. Under MBCA § 6.21(f)(i)(ii), for example, shareholders must approve an issuance of stock for con-

1.   What does "all or substantially all" mean?

"All or substantially all" is not exactly a bright-line standard. Given the expense and other burdens associated with shareholder approval, and the potentially severe consequences of guessing wrong, determining whether the sale qualifies as "all or substantially all" becomes a critical issue for transaction planners. Two classic Delaware opinions usefully illustrate the problem.

In *Gimbel v. Signal Companies*, the defendant conglomerate had multiple lines of business, including aircraft and aerospace technology, truck manufacturing, and oil.[13] The latter once was Signal's core business, but over time had become something of a side line. The board of directors decided to sell the oil division at a price exceeding $480 million. The plaintiff shareholder challenged the sale on various grounds, including a claim that the transaction constituted a sale of substantially all Signal's assets. The Chancellor used a number of metrics to determine the percentage of assets being sold: revenues, earnings, assets, net worth, return on assets, and return on net worth. In each case, the contribution of the oil business was compared to the other lines of business. The precise percentage attributable to the oil business varied substantially depending on which metric was chosen. For example, the oil business represented 41% of Signal's total net worth, but represented only 26% of total assets, and generated only 15% of revenues and earnings. As a purely quantitative matter, the court therefore held, the sale did not entail a disposition of all or substantially all of Signal's assets. In dicta, however, the court went on to apply a second standard based on qualitative considerations. Signal had become a conglomerate whose main occupation was buying, operating, and selling businesses of various types. Oil may have been where the company started, but it was now just one line of business among many. Selling off the oil subsidiary did not mean that the company was going out of business or even changing the nature of its business. Consequently, the court indicated, the sale did not rise to the level of a sale of all or substantially all Signal's assets.

In *Katz v. Bregman*, the corporation sold off a series of unprofitable divisions.[14] When it proposed to sell one of its principal remaining subsidiaries, however, a shareholder sued claiming the transaction would entail a sale of all or substantially all the remaining assets. Through its various subsidiaries, the company had been in the business of manufacturing steel storage and shipping drums. Using the proceeds of its various sales, the company planned to go into the business of manufacturing plastic shipping and storage drums. In assessing whether share-

siteration other than cash if the shares to be issued "will comprise more than 20 percent of the voting power of the shares of the corporation that were outstanding immediately before the transaction." The major stock exchanges impose similar requirements in their listing standards.

13. Gimbel v. Signal Companies, Inc., 316 A.2d 599 (Del.Ch.1974).

14. Katz v. Bregman, 431 A.2d 1274 (Del.Ch.1981).

holder approval was required, the Chancellor began with quantitative metrics. The subsidiary to be sold represented 51% of the firm's remaining assets, which generated 44.9% of total revenues and 52.4% of pre-tax earnings. Turning to qualitative measures, the court opined that the planned switch from steel to plastic drums would be "a radical departure," by which the corporation would sell off the core part of the business in order to go into an entirely new line of business. Taken together, the nature of the transaction, plus the fairly high percentage of assets being sold, satisfied the "all or substantially all" standard and shareholder approval therefore was required.

The *Katz* opinion seems problematic from a number of perspectives. On the one hand, switching from steel to plastic drums hardly seems like a "radical departure." Imagine a company that for many years profitably manufactured wooden baseball bats. Because almost nobody except professional players uses wooden bats anymore, the business has suffered. The company therefore decides to sell its wood lathes and other manufacturing equipment and to invest the proceeds in equipment for manufacturing aluminum baseball bats. Making this sort of product line decision is a quintessential business judgment for the board of directors. In relying on qualitative considerations, the *Katz* opinion thus improperly inserted shareholders into a decision reserved by statute for the board.[15]

As a transactional planning matter, the absence of a bright-line rule creates unfortunate complications. Consider the plight of a transactional lawyer asked by the seller's board of directors to opine as to the necessity of a shareholder vote. A well-known rule of thumb suggests assuming that a sale of more than 75% of balance sheet assets by market value[16] is a sale of substantially all corporate assets and that a sale of less than 25% is not.[17] Between those yard lines, one must make an educated guess based on qualitative considerations of the sort identified by *Gimbel* and *Katz*. In practice, one throws a few junior associates into the library

---

15. See DGCL § 141(a) ("The business and affairs of every corporation organized under this chapter shall be managed by or under the direction of a board of directors").

16. In general, corporate assets are carried on the books at their historical cost, but current market value obviously is more important and, usually, more accurate. The sale price offers a good proxy for the market value of the assets being sold, of course. As for the value of the assets being retained, one typically obtains an appraisal by an investment banking firm. If litigation results, of course, a battle of expert witnesses as to proper valuation follows. If the assets being sold constitute an identifiable line of business, such as a specific subsidiary or division, some other metrics become available. In these cases, you can often figure out what percentage of your earnings, reve-

nues or sales the assets produce. For example, in *Gimbel*, the firm was selling off its oil subsidiary. So it was fairly easy to compute the percentage of revenues and earnings the subsidiary produced.

17. Leo Herzel et al., Sales and Acquisitions of Divisions, 5 Corp. L. Rev. 3, 25 (1982). The 1999 amendments to the Model Act create a formal safe harbor for transactions below the 25% threshold: "If a corporation retains a business activity that represented at least 25% of total assets at the end of the most recently completed fiscal year, and 25% of either income from continuing operations before taxes or revenues from continuing operations for that fiscal year, in each case of the corporation and its subsidiaries on a consolidated basis, the corporation will conclusively be deemed to have retained a significant continuing business activity." MBCA § 12.02(a).

with instructions to scour the reported decisions looking for cases from the jurisdiction in question—plus all the Delaware cases—that might match up to the facts of the deal at hand. One then writes as narrowly tailored an opinion letter as possible.

2. *Choosing between a merger and an asset sale*

A given transaction often can be accomplished in more than one way. For example, suppose Ajax, Inc., is a unitary corporation with 5 unincorporated divisions: Defense; Consumer Electronics; Computers; Automotive; Trucking. Ajax proposes to sell the Defense division to the Acme Company. Because the divisions are part of a single corporation, it may seem that a sale of assets is the only choice. But the transaction readily could be structured as a merger. The transaction planner will cause Ajax to set up a shell corporation called NewCo. Ajax will then transfer the assets of the Defense division to NewCo in return for NewCo's stock. NewCo and Acme will then merge. Having said that, however, mergers and asset sales do differ in some rather fundamental ways, of which the following seem most significant:

Ease of transferring control: When a merger becomes effective, the separate existence of constituent corporations, except the surviving corporation, comes to an end. As we have seen, a number of key events thereupon take place by operation of law and without the need for further action. In an asset sale, the target company remains in existence with its incumbent directors and shareholders. Virtually nothing happens by operation of law, which significantly raises transaction costs.

Ease of transferring assets: In a merger, title to all property owned by each constituent corporation is automatically vested in the surviving corporation. In an asset sale, documents of transfer must be prepared with respect to each and every asset being sold and those documents must be filed with every applicable agency. For example, a deed of transfer will have to be properly filed with every county in which the target owns real estate.

Ease of passing consideration: In a merger, the consideration passes directly to nondissenting shareholders. In an asset sale, the process of distributing the consideration to the target's shareholders is more complicated. (Assuming this is desired. In some cases, the proceeds will be invested in a new line of business.) Because the selling corporation still exists, one option is to distribute the consideration as a dividend. More often, the target is formally dissolved and liquidated. After creditors have been paid off, any remaining assets (including the consideration paid in the acquisition) are distributed to its shareholders in a final liquidating dividend.

Successor liability: In a merger, the surviving company succeeds to all liabilities of each constituent corporation. In an asset sale, subject to some emerging exceptions in tort law, the purchaser does not take the liabilities of the selling company unless there has been a written assumption of liabilities.

Shareholder voting: Avoiding shareholder voting is the goal of most transaction planners most of the time. In the case of public corporations, the process of obtaining shareholder approval is cumbersome and expensive. Proxies must be solicited, which requires preparation of a proxy statement. Accountants must prepare financial statements and give an accounting opinion. Lawyers must prepare opinion letters on corporate, securities and tax law questions. The lawyers will also draft, or at least review, the proxy statement. The firm typically will hire a proxy solicitation firm to run the shareholder meeting and to solicit proxies. Senior corporate officers must expend time going over documents and gathering materials. And so on. As a result, the cost of the shareholder approval process easily can run well into seven figures. After all of that, moreover, shareholders occasionally do something silly—like not approving the acquisition. In a straight two-party merger, approval by both company's boards and by both company's shareholders is required. In an asset sale, by contrast, the purchasing corporation's shareholders generally are not entitled to vote on the transaction.

Appraisal rights: Appraisal rights give dissenting shareholders the right to demand that the corporation buy their shares at a judicially determined fair market value. The prospect that a significant number of shareholders might force the firm to buy them out for cash can threaten the acquisition, especially if the buyer is strapped for cash. So the transaction planner tries to minimize the availability of appraisal rights. In a straight two-party merger, shareholders of both corporations are eligible for appraisal rights. In most states, shareholders of the selling company are entitled to appraisal rights in a sale of all or substantially all corporate assets, but not the purchasing corporation's shareholders. In Delaware, appraisal is limited solely to mergers. In an asset sale, neither corporation's shareholders are entitled to appraisal.

Summary: On the last three criteria, a sale of all or substantially all corporate assets seems preferable to a merger. An asset sale minimizes successor liability problems and restricts both shareholder voting and appraisal rights relative to a straight two-party merger. Is there a way to get these transaction cost-minimizing advantages of an asset sale, while also getting the advantages of a merger? Indeed, there is a simple solution: the triangular merger.[18]

C. Triangular transactions

In a triangular merger, the acquiring corporation sets up a shell subsidiary. The shell is capitalized with the consideration to be paid to target shareholders in the acquisition—such as cash or securities of the acquiring corporation.[19] The shell is then merged with the target corporation. In a forward triangular merger, the shell is the surviving entity.

---

18. Note that an asset sale also can be structured as a triangular transaction.

19. Formally, the acquiring corporation transfers the consideration to the shell, which in turn issues all of its shares to the parent acquiring company.

In a reverse triangular merger, the target survives. The point is the same in either case. The target company ends up as a wholly owned subsidiary of the acquirer. The former target shareholders either become shareholders of the acquirer or are bought out for cash.

In a triangular merger, nothing changes from the target's perspective. Exactly the same approval process must be followed. From the acquiring corporation's perspective, however, much has changed. Only shareholders of a constituent corporation are entitled to vote or to exercise appraisal rights. In a triangular transaction, the constituent parties are the target and the shell. As a result, the parent acquiring corporation is not a formal party to the transaction, and its shareholders are entitled neither to voting nor appraisal rights.

A triangular merger also addresses the problem of successor liability. After a triangular merger, the target remains in existence as a wholly owned subsidiary of the true acquirer. As such, the target remains solely responsible for its obligations. Unless a plaintiff is able to pierce the corporate veil, and thus reach the parent, the parent acquiring corporation's exposure to successor liability is limited to its investment in the acquired subsidiary.[20]

Again, the take home lesson is that there are many forms a given deal can take. To the extent the law elevates form over substance, as it generally does in this area, the transaction planner has substantial opportunity to engage in regulatory arbitrage. This potentially permits the planner to add substantial value to a transaction. Contrary to conventional wisdom, good lawyering actually can create wealth.

D. Ensuring exclusivity

Announcement of a pending acquisition often leads other bidders to make competing unsolicited offers. Although it is difficult to gauge accurately the likelihood of a competing takeover proposal, conventional takeover wisdom treats competing bids as a serious risk for the initial bidder. The prospective acquirer incurs substantial up-front costs in making the offer, among which are: Search costs entailed in identifying an appropriate target, which can be significant in some circumstances. Once an appropriate target is identified, preparation of the offer typically requires the services of outside legal, accounting, and financial advisers. If all or part of the purchase price is to be paid from sources other than cash reserves, a likely scenario, the bidder incurs commitment and other financing fees. Finally, the bidder may pass up other acquisition opportunities while negotiating with the target. Unfortunately for the bidder, however, the emergence of a competing bid may reduce or eliminate the expected return on its sunk costs. Second bidders prevail in a substantial majority of competitive bidding contests. Even if the initial bidder prevails, the ultimate acquisition price is likely to be substantially higher

20. In addition, leaving the target in place as a separate entity may have other advantages in terms of employee and customer relations.

than the initial bid.[21]

Exclusivity provisions in corporate merger agreements are intended to prevent (or, at least, discourage) competing bids from interfering with the planned transaction. Such provisions may be conveniently divided into two basic categories: performance promises, wherein the target's board agrees to engage (or agrees not to engage) in certain types of conduct prior to the shareholder vote; and cancellation fees, typically a specified amount the target agrees to pay the favored bidder if the transaction does not go forward.

Performance promises can be further broken down into best efforts clauses and the various forms of no shop covenants. A best efforts clause requires both parties to use their "best efforts" to consummate the transaction.[22] It is intended to assure that the target's board of directors will not attempt to back out of the agreement. The best efforts clause also typically imposes corresponding obligations on the favored bidder's board with respect to its shareholders. Even in cases where approval by the bidder's shareholders is not required, such as in a triangular merger, the favored bidder may still agree to use its best efforts to assure that the transaction is consummated.

No shop clauses prohibit the target corporation from soliciting a competing offer from any other prospective bidders, although they allow the target to consider an unsolicited bid and even negotiate with the competing bidder. In contrast, the no negotiation covenant prohibits such negotiations. An intermediary version, the no merger provision, permits the target to negotiate with a prospective competing offeror, but prohibits it from entering into a merger agreement with the competitor until the initial bid has been brought before the shareholders.

Provisions for monetary compensation of the favored bidder in the event the transaction fails to go forward are common in negotiated acquisitions.[23] Cancellation fees, the most widely used member of this category, essentially are liquidated damages payable if the acquirer fails to receive the expected benefits of its agreement. A variation of the

---

21. Richard S. Ruback, Assessing Competition in the Market for Corporate Acquisitions, 11 J. Fin. Econ. 141, 147 (1983) (second bidders prevailed in 75% of the 48 cases examined).

22. In this context, "best efforts" imposes "at a minimum a duty to act in good faith toward the party to whom it owes a 'best efforts' obligation." Jewel Cos., Inc. v. Pay Less Drug Stores Northwest, Inc., 741 F.2d 1555, 1564 n. 11 (9th Cir.1984). But see Great Western Producers Co–op. v. Great Western United Corp., 613 P.2d 873, 878 (Colo.1980) (holding, under Delaware law, that a best efforts clause merely imposed an obligation to "make a reasonable, diligent, and good faith effort"). *Jewel's* interpretation is more consistent with the use

of best efforts terminology in other contexts, where it often is defined to mean "maximizing the contractual benefits of the person to whom the duty is owed, even if the benefits to the one owing the duty have been depleted." See In re Heard, 6 Bankr. 876, 884 (Bankr.W.D.Ky.1980); see generally E. Allan Farnsworth, On Trying to Keep One's Promises: The Duty of Best Efforts in Contract Law, 46 U. Pitt. L. Rev. 1 (1984); Charles J. Goetz & Robert E. Scott, Principles of Relational Contracts, 67 Va. L. Rev. 1089, 1111–26 (1981).

23. See, e.g., Cottle v. Storer Communication, Inc., 849 F.2d 570, 578 (11th Cir. 1988); Beebe v. Pacific Realty Trust, 578 F.Supp. 1128, 1150 n. 7 (D.Or.1984).

cancellation fee arrangement, closely akin to stock lock-ups, involves giving an option to the acquirer pursuant to which the acquirer has the right to purchase a specified number of target shares and also a right to resell those shares to the target at a price higher than the exercise price in the event that an alternative bid is accepted. As such, the target is required to pay some specified dollar amount to the acquirer in the event that the transaction is not consummated, reimbursing the acquirer for out of pocket costs associated with making the offer and perhaps also including an increment reflecting the acquirer's lost time and opportunities.[24] Topping fees are another variation on the basic theme. Instead of specifying the dollar amount to be paid if the merger is not consummated, a topping fee requires that the target pay the defeated offeror a percentage of the victorious bidder's acquisition price.[25] In either case, the fee ordinarily falls in a range of 1 to 5% of the proposed acquisition price.[26] Payment of the fee is commonly triggered by the acquisition of a specified amount of target stock by a third party.[27] Variants include termination of the merger agreement by the target or shareholder rejection of the acquisition proposal.[28]

§ 12.4   The appraisal remedy

Mergers and sales of all or substantially all corporate assets can be likened to a form of private eminent domain. If the transaction is approved by the requisite statutory number of shares, dissenting shareholders have no statutory basis for preventing the merger. Granted, some of the minority shareholders may believe that the merger which is being forced upon them is unfair. They may want to retain their investment in the target or they may believe that the price is unfair. Corporate statutes give hold-out shareholders no remedy where they simply want to keep their target shares—the statutes permit majority shareholders to effect a freezeout merger to eliminate the minority. All the statute gives disgruntled shareholders is a right to complain about the fairness of the price being paid for their shares; namely, the appraisal remedy.

In theory, appraisal rights are quite straightforward. Briefly, they give shareholders who dissent from a merger the right to have the fair

---

24. White knights proposing a leveraged buyout of the target in response to a hostile takeover bid also frequently require an engagement fee, requiring the target to pay a relatively small fee as consideration for the white knight's preparation and submission of its bid. See, e.g., Cottle v. Storer Communication, Inc., 849 F.2d 570, 572 (11th Cir. 1988); Hanson Trust PLC v. ML SCM Acquisition, Inc., 781 F.2d 264, 269 (2d Cir. 1986).

25. See, e.g., In re J.P. Stevens & Co., Inc., 542 A.2d 770, 777 (Del.Ch.1988).

26. See St. Jude Medical, Inc. v. Medtronic, Inc., 536 N.W.2d 24, 27 (Minn.App.

1995) (citing Stephen M. Bainbridge, Exclusive Merger Agreements and Lock–Ups in Negotiated Corporate Acquisitions, 75 Minn. L. Rev. 239, 246 (1990)).

27. See, e.g., Revlon, Inc. v. MacAndrews & Forbes Holdings, Inc., 506 A.2d 173, 178 (Del.1985); Hanson Trust PLC v. ML SCM Acquisition Inc., 781 F.2d 264, 269 (2d Cir.1986).

28. See, e.g., Cottle v. Storer Communication Inc., 849 F.2d 570, 572 (11th Cir. 1988); Beebe v. Pacific Realty Trust, 578 F.Supp. 1128, 1150 (D.Or.1984).

value of their shares determined and paid to them in cash, provided the shareholders comply with the convoluted statutory procedures. Unfortunately, putting this simple theory into practice has proven surprisingly difficult. Indeed, the current status of the appraisal doctrine is best described as "tattered."[1]

A. Mechanics

1. Availability of appraisal

All appraisal statutes authorize appraisal rights in statutory mergers of close corporations. Beyond that, however, it is impossible to generalize. Whether appraisal rights are available for any other type of transaction depends on which state's law governs. In many states, appraisal is available in connection with a wide range of fundamental transactions, including mergers, sales of all or substantially all corporate assets, and even certain amendments to the articles of incorporation. For example, MBCA § 13.02(a)(4) provides appraisal rights in connection with article amendments effecting a reverse stock split.

In contrast, under DGCL § 262, Delaware law provides appraisal rights only in connection with statutory mergers.[2] But not even all mergers are covered. Section 262(b)(1) provides that appraisal rights shall not be available for companies whose stock is listed on a national securities exchange or which has more than 2,000 record shareholders.[3] However, § 262(b)(2) then restores appraisal rights for such firms' shareholders if the consideration paid in the merger is anything other than stock of the surviving corporation, stock of another corporation that is listed on a national securities exchange or held by more than 2,000 record shareholders,[4] and/or cash in lieu of fractional shares.[5]

2. Eligibility for appraisal

In order to be eligible to make use of the appraisal remedy, Delaware § 262(a) requires that a stockholder: (1) hold shares continuously through the effective date of the merger; (2) perfect his appraisal rights by complying with the provisions of Delaware § 262(d) by sending written notice to the corporation, prior to the shareholder vote, that he intends to exercise his appraisal rights (it is not sufficient to merely vote

---

§ 12.4

1. The fiduciary duties of controlling shareholders have laid a significant gloss on the appraisal remedy. The result has been most unfortunate, at least insofar as doctrinal clarity is concerned.

2. Appraisal rights, however, are not available in connection with a short form merger. DGCL § 262.

3. As used here, national securities exchange includes the NASDAQ inter-dealer automated quotation system.

4. This provision would come into play in a triangular merger, in which the surviving corporation ends up as a wholly owned subsidiary of the acquirer. This provision allows the use of acquiring company stock as consideration.

5. The Model Act provides a similar market out, although its version is far more complex by virtue of various exceptions for conflicted interest transactions. MBCA § 13.02(b).

against the merger at the meeting); and (3) neither vote in favor of nor consent in writing to the merger. MBCA § 13.21 is substantially similar.

3. *Exclusivity of appraisal*

A key question is whether appraisal is the exclusive remedy by which a shareholder may challenge a merger. The Delaware supreme court's *Weinberger* decision indicated appraisal would be exclusive except in cases of fraud, misrepresentation, self-dealing, deliberate waste of corporate assets or gross and palpable over-reaching.[6] The subsequent *Rabkin* decision, however, allows plaintiffs to bring a class action for damages whenever the plaintiffs can prove a breach of the duty of fair dealing.[7] Consequently, appraisal is exclusive only in cases in which plaintiff's claims go solely to the adequacy of the price.

B. Valuation in appraisal proceedings

In theory, the value of a share of common stock is the present discounted value of all future dividends to be paid by the corporation.[8] This proposition seems counter-intuitive, because many corporations pay no dividends. As the theory goes, however, in the long run all corporations run out of investment opportunities and begin paying profits out to the shareholders as dividends. It is the expectation of those future dividends that determines the present value of the stock.

The foregoing proposition presents two analytical problems. First, how does one know what dividends are going to be paid in the future? Obviously one cannot project future dividends with certainty and even projecting estimated dividends is a very difficult task to which the full art and science of valuation is devoted. Second, how does one discount the stream of future dividends to present value? This is a far simpler task, involving basic principles arising out of the time value of money.

1. *Valuation basics: The time value of money and discounting to present value*

Even in a world without risk, most people would rather be paid a dollar today than be paid a dollar one year from today. This is why money is said to have a time value: people place a higher value on money to be received today than on money to be received later. The time value of money, along with risk, explains why lenders charge interest and depositors receive interest. Interest on a bank account, just as interest on a loan, is partially compensation for foregoing current consumption.

Suppose Jane deposits one dollar at the First National Bank. The Bank will pay Jane interest to compensate her for giving up the

---

6. Weinberger v. UOP, Inc., 457 A.2d 701 (Del.1983).

7. Rabkin v. Philip A. Hunt Chemical Corp., 498 A.2d 1099 (Del.1985).

8. Accessible introductions to valuation include Jay W. Eisenhofer & John L. Reed,

Valuation Litigation, 22 Del. J. Corp. L. 37 (1997); Samuel C. Thompson, A Lawyer's Guide to Modern Valuation Techniques in Mergers & Acquisitions, 21 J. Corp. L. 459 (1996).

opportunity to spend the dollar today. Assume the Bank pays simple annual interest of 6%. At the end of one year, Jane will receive 6 cents in interest, and the value of her account will grow to $1.06. The formula by which one calculates the future value of a deposit is:

$$FV = A_i(1+\frac{r}{m})^{mn}$$

where FV stands for the value of the deposit at some time in the future; A_i is the amount of the initial deposit; r is the interest rate; m is how many times per year interest compounds; n is the number of years the deposit is left in the account. Suppose Jane deposits $1 today at a bank that pays 6% interest compounding quarterly. At the end of three years the value of Jane's account is $1.20, which is calculated from the foregoing equation as follows:

$$FV = \$1(1+\frac{0.06}{4})^{12} = \$1.$$

The concept of present value, which is critical to corporate valuation, depends on the time value of money. If I promise to pay you $1 in one year, how much is that promise worth to you today? We answer that question by calculating the promise's present value (a.k.a. present discounted value). Instead of asking how much a dollar will be worth in one year, we ask how much one must invest today to receive a dollar in one year. As such, calculating present value simply flips the future value equation around. Put another way, the present value calculation is the inverse of the future value calculation:

$$PV = \frac{A_k}{(1+k)^n}$$

where PV is the present value; A_k is the amount to be received; k is the applicable interest rate, which is now referred to as a discount rate; and n is the number of years before the amount is to be received. Suppose Anita promises to pay Carol $1 in five years. The present value of that promise is 75 cents, which is calculated as follows:

$$PV = \frac{\$1}{(1+0.06)^5} = \frac{\$1}{(1.06)^5} = \frac{\$1}{1.34}$$

The discount rate is simply the opportunity cost of capital, adjusted for risk. This is a very easy concept to articulate, but a very complex one to actually calculate.[9] Opportunity cost is deceptively simple—it is simply

---

9. The CAPM formula is often used to estimate the discount rate. See, e.g., Cede & Co. v. Technicolor, 1990 WL 161084 (Del. Ch.1990); see generally Samuel Thompson,

the rate of return on the next best comparable investment. Unfortunately, it can be very hard to identify the next best comparable investment. Likewise, the question of how much to adjust for risk is a highly subjective question.

2. *Valuation methods based on the present value of future dividends*

As already noted, the theoretical value of a share of stock is the present value of all future dividends. Because the future is uncertain, however, attempting to estimate future dividends obviously is a project fraught with peril. Although a few highly technical and complex valuation methods undertake that project, they are rarely used in legal settings. Instead, far simpler methods are typically used both in planning and litigation. Two such methods use current dividends as a proxy for future dividends. These methods assume that there will be a perpetual dividend stream emanating from the corporation and therefore value the stock using the formula for discounting a perpetuity to present value.

A perpetuity is a stream of income that will be paid perpetually (i.e., indefinitely). The present value of a constant perpetuity is calculated by dividing the value of each installment by the discount rate:

$$PV = \frac{A_i}{k}$$

where PV is the present value of the perpetuity; A_i is the amount of each installment; k is the discount rate. Suppose Ann agrees to pay Barbara $1 per year in perpetuity. Assume the applicable discount rate is 10 percent. The present value of the perpetuity is $1 divided by 0.10, which equals $10.

The zero growth in dividends valuation method assumes that dividends will remain constant in the future. The value of a share of stock is therefore determined by dividing the current per share dividend by an appropriate discount rate:

$$V = \frac{D}{k}$$

where V is the value of the firm; D is the annual dividend; K is the discount rate. Suppose Acme, Inc., pays an annual dividend of one dollar on its common stock. Assuming an 8% discount rate, the value of each share of common stock is $1 divided by 0.08, which equals $12.50.

The preceding method has only limited utility in connection with a rapidly growing company that is retaining all or almost all of its earnings. In such a case, using historical dividend data significantly understates the corporation's value. One solution to that problem is switching the valuation method to the formula used to calculate the present discounted value of a growing perpetuity:

$$V = \frac{D}{k - g}$$

where g is a "growth factor." The most commonly accepted growth factor is return on equity (ROE) times the firm's retention rate. ROE is calculated by dividing earnings by shareholders equity. The retention rate is the percentage of earnings retained by the corporation (i.e., 1 minus the dividend pay out rate). If the dividend and discount rate are held constant, this constant growth formula will produce a higher valuation than the zero growth formula, because the denominator will be smaller. Suppose Acme, Inc., currently pays a $1 dividend per share. Acme's return on equity is 0.05, while its retention rate is 80%. Assuming an 8% discount rate, the value of a share of Acme common stock is $25:

$$V = \frac{\$1}{(0.08 - [0.05 x 0.80])} = \frac{\$1}{0.08 - 0.04} = \frac{\$1}{0.04}$$

3. The Delaware block method

The so-called Delaware block method takes various forms in different states, but generally requires one to take the weighted average of three different valuation measures: net asset value, capitalized earnings, and market value. Net asset value is a variant of the basic book value methodology. Book value is a balance sheet-based valuation method. A corporation's book value is simply its net assets (total assets minus total liabilities). Suppose Acme has total assets of $73,000 and total liabilities of $60,500. Acme's book value is the difference—i.e., $12,500. To determine a per share book value, simply divide the firm's book value by the number of shares of common stock outstanding.

Book value has only one advantage as a valuation methodology, albeit an important one: almost every corporation has a balance sheet no matter how financially unsophisticated the corporation's shareholders may be. Accordingly, the book value of virtually all corporations can be determined quickly and easily. Unfortunately, the valuation obtained by the book value method usually is quite unreliable. Because it is based solely on the balance sheet, book value fails to account for intangible assets that do not appear on the balance sheet, such as goodwill. Book value is also unreliable because assets generally are carried on the balance sheet at their historical cost, which may be wholly unrelated to their current fair market value. Finally, because book value simply involves totaling up assets and liabilities, it fails to account for any synergy resulting from the use of these particular assets by this particular corporation. In other words, book value is based on liquidation value rather than the firm's value as a going concern.[10]

Net asset value tries to correct for these failings. As the Pennsylvania courts have defined the term, for example, it includes "every kind of property and value, whether realty or personalty, tangible or intangible, including good will and the corporation's value as a going concern."[11] Properly understood, net asset valuation thus requires an appraisal of the current fair market value of the corporation's assets on a going concern basis. The Pennsylvania courts nevertheless have cautioned against giving net asset value much weight.[12] In doing so, however, they have confused book value and net asset value. The courts express concern, for example, that net asset value is based on historical cost and excludes going concern values.[13] But net asset value in fact measures both tangible and intangible assets at their current going concern value. The Pennsylvania precedents thus reflect a misunderstanding of their own terminology.

Capitalized earnings are incorporated into all variants of the Delaware block, albeit in subtly different ways. In all its forms, the capitalized earnings valuation method tries to overcome the problems associated with book value by relying on the corporation's income statement rather than on its balance sheet. Value is determined under this method by dividing the corporation's earnings per share by an appropriately chosen capitalization rate.[14] The chief difficulty with this method is determining an appropriate capitalization rate. In theory, the capitalization rate is the reciprocal of the multiplier, which is also known as the price/earnings ratio. The problem, of course, is that one must know the price of the corporation's stock in order to determine the capitalization rate. Yet, this method nevertheless is frequently used to value close corporations, as to which no market price exists. An approximate capitalization rate is chosen by comparing the corporation to similar corporations with known price/earnings ratios.[15]

---

10. Going concern valuation values the company as though it will remain in business after the transaction giving rise to the need for valuation. In other words, the going concern value asks what price the company would command if it were sold as an entity. Liquidation valuation assumes the company will be broken up and all of its assets sold off individually. Generally speaking, going concern values will be higher. If the business is successful, there should be some synergistic effect from the combination of assets, and the whole should be worth more than the sum of the parts. But poor management can accumulate assets that subtract value.

11. In re Watt & Shand, 304 A.2d 694, 698 n. 7 (Pa.1973).

12. See, e.g., In re Watt & Shand, 304 A.2d 694 (Pa.1973); In re Spang Indus., Inc., 535 A.2d 86 (Pa.Super.Ct.1987).

13. In re Watt & Shand, 304 A.2d 694, 700 (Pa.1973).

14. Suppose, for example, that Acme Corporation's earnings last year were $2.10/share. The average price/earnings ratio for comparable corporations is 16. An approximate capitalization rate is estimated by taking the reciprocal of the average price/earnings ratio, which is 0.0625. Acme's earnings per share figure is then divided by the capitalization rate, which equals $33.60/share.

15. See, e.g., Universal City Studios, Inc. v. Francis I. duPont & Co., 334 A.2d 216, 219 (Del.1975) (averaging price-earnings ratios of nine other motion picture companies as of date of merger); Gibbons v. Schenley Indus., Inc., 339 A.2d 460, 471 (Del.Ch.1975) (using price-earnings ratio of the Standard & Poor's Distiller's Index as

The Pennsylvania and Massachusetts precedents illustrate some of the subtle differences in how courts capitalize earnings under the Delaware block method. Massachusetts uses a version known as "earnings value," which is defined as the average corporate earnings for the preceding five years, excluding extraordinary gains and losses.[16] In contrast, Pennsylvania uses a version called "investment value," which requires one to capitalize a representative earnings figure.[17] Investment value thus requires a greater degree of subjective judgment by the appraiser, who must decide what constitutes the requisite representative figure.

Finally, the Delaware Block includes market value. The Delaware block method assumes that no one of the three factors is itself the fair value of the company, but that a weighted average of the three factors is the fair value. Yet, if the company has a market value, how could the fair value and the market value be different? Presumably the answer is either that market value does not reflect a control premium or that the market in which the stock is traded is not efficient. In any event, what does one do if the corporation has no market value, as will be the case for close corporations? Some older Delaware cases suggest that in such cases it may be appropriate to "reconstruct" a market value.[18] The process of doing so is an arcane one, somewhat analogous to determining how many angels can dance on the head of a pin. In practice, it typically involves some variant of either book value or capitalized earnings, thereby giving that element double impact.

None of the three methods is particularly reliable. Net asset value becomes less reliable as it becomes more subjective. To the extent the firm's going concern value diverges from its book value, accordingly, net asset value ought to receive lower weight. Capitalized earnings become less reliable as earnings become more volatile. At one extreme, in a well-established noncyclical firm, earnings should be relatively stable and capitalized earnings should be given a relatively high weight. At the other extreme, in a start-up venture with no earnings history, earnings-based values should get almost no weight. Finally, the weight given market value ought to depend mainly on the thickness of the market for the firm's stock.

In any event, having separately determined the three valuations, one then takes their weighted average. The trial court's assignment of weights to each factor is subject to appellate review under an abuse of discretion standard,[19] which is ironic because the whole process is highly

of date of merger); Felder v. Anderson, Clayton & Co., 159 A.2d 278, 285 (Del.Ch. 1960) (averaging price-earnings ratios of representative stocks over the preceding five-year period).

16. See, e.g., Piemonte v. New Boston Garden Corp., 387 N.E.2d 1145, 1150 (Mass.1979).

17. See, e.g., In re Spang Indus., Inc., 535 A.2d 86, 89–90 (Pa.Super.Ct.1987).

18. Compare In re Delaware Racing Ass'n, 213 A.2d 203, 211–12 (Del.1965) with Universal City Studios, Inc. v. Francis I. duPont & Co., 334 A.2d 216, 222 (Del. 1975).

19. See, e.g., Piemonte v. New Boston Garden Corp., 387 N.E.2d 1145, 1153 (Mass.1979).

arbitrary. In the oft-cited *Spang Industries* decision, for example, the Pennsylvania appeals court opined that net asset value should receive little weight for the reasons discussed above. The court then proceeded to affirm the trial court's assignment of a weight of 80% to net asset value, which in turn the trial court had determined by taking the equally weighted average of three widely divergent expert opinions.[20]

4. Weinberger and its discounted cash flow progeny

The Delaware block method compares apples and oranges. The three factors have very little to do with each other, are based on radically different assumptions and methodologies, and thus can lead to widely divergent results. Courts then blithely proceed to compound the problem by assigning largely arbitrary weights to each factor. The method's sole justification is that the calculations are simple and relevant expert testimony is easy to understand. Accordingly, the block method is easy for nonexpert judges and juries to apply.

As a determiner of value, the Delaware chancery court has significant advantages over courts of other states. As a specialist court, the Delaware chancellors obtain considerable experience with valuation issues. As a court of equity, the expert judge need not fear jury confusion. Accordingly, we might expect that Delaware courts can be more concerned with precision than with ease of calculation.

In *Weinberger*, the Delaware supreme court officially abandoned the block method. (The method's retention of the Delaware name thus is a misnomer.) The court acknowledged that the block method makes little sense from a finance theory perspective. The court therefore set out to up-date Delaware law. Curiously, it did so by throwing open the courthouse door to virtually anything short of the valuation equivalent of junk science: "We believe that a more liberal approach must include proof of value by any techniques or methods which are generally considered acceptable in the financial community and otherwise admissible in court...."[21] Consequently, the court explained, "market value, asset value, dividends, earning prospects, the nature of the enterprise and any other facts which were known or which could be ascertained as of the date of merger and which throw any light on future prospects of the merged corporation are not only pertinent to an inquiry as to the value of the dissenting stockholders' interest, but must be considered...."

In the years following *Weinberger*, the Delaware chancery court has come to rely mainly on the discounted cash flow (DCF) valuation method. DCF has several basic steps:

- Estimate cash flows that the firm will generate over some period of time (the "projection period"). By convention, it is assumed that all cash flows are booked at the end of the fiscal year.

---

20. In re Spang Indus., Inc., 535 A.2d 86, 90–91 (Pa.Super.Ct.1987).

21. Weinberger v. UOP, Inc., 457 A.2d 701, 713 (Del.1983).

- Determine the terminal value (TV), which is the present discounted value, as of the end of the projection period, of the firm's cash flows beyond the projection period. TV can be calculated in one of two ways:
  - Discounting dividends using either the zero growth or constant growth method as appropriate to the company in question.
  - Capitalizing earnings.
- Determine an appropriate discount rate, which is usually set at the firm's estimated cost of capital. The capital asset pricing model (CAPM) is a commonly used means of estimating an appropriate discount rate.
- Discount to present value both the projected cash flows and the TV. This process is represented algebraically as follows:

$$V_f = \left[\sum_0^n \frac{C_n}{(1+k)^n} \right] + \frac{TV}{(1+k)^n}$$

where: V_f is the value of the firm; C_n are the cash flows in each year n; k is the discount rate; n are the years from the present to the end of the projection period; and TV is the terminal value.

An example may be helpful. Assume the appraiser has chosen a four year projection period and has projected cash flows, dividends, and earnings as follows:

Year	Cash Flow	Dividend	Earnings
1	$100	$10	$75
2	$110	$12	$80
3	$125	$12	$85
4	$140	$13	$90

Further assume that the appraiser has used CAPM to estimate a 10% discount rate. A growth rate of 3% has been calculated using the common method of multiplying the return on equity by the retention rate. The appraiser is using a capitalization rate of 15%. Under these assumptions, the DCF value of the firm, using the capitalized earnings method to determine a terminal value, equals $726.52.

$$V = \left[\frac{\$100}{(1+0.10)} \right] + \left[\frac{\$110}{(1+0.10)^2} \right] + \left[\frac{\$125}{(1+0.10)^3} \right] + \left[\frac{\$90 / 0.15}{(1+0.10)^3} \right]$$

The first three sums are the discounted cash flows for each of the first three years in the projection period. The final sum is the terminal value calculated using capitalized earnings. Notice, as is typical, that the terminal value ($450.79) contributed over 60% of the total value of the firm.

The DCF value of the firm, using the constant growth dividend method to calculate the terminal value is the same, except for the final sum. Using the constant growth dividend formula, the terminal value here is calculated by dividing the dividend by the difference of the discount rate and the growth factor:

$$V = \left[\frac{\$100}{(1+0.10)}\right] + \left[\frac{\$110}{(1+0.10)^2}\right] + \left[\frac{\$125}{(1+0.10)^3}\right] + \left[\frac{\$90/0.15}{(1+0.10)^3}\right]$$

The fact that this method resulted in a lower valuation ($415.24) than the capitalized earnings method is purely an artifact of the way the problem is set up.

5. *Elements of value arising from the merger*

DGCL § 262(h) provides that shareholders who succeed in an appraisal proceeding are entitled to the "fair value" of their shares "exclusive of any element of value arising from the accomplishment or expectation of the merger." Query whether that language makes control premia irrelevant? In *Armstrong v. Marathon Oil*, Marathon merged with U.S. Steel on March 11, 1982. U.S. Steel previously had acquired a majority of Marathon's stock in a cash tender offer at $125 per share. In the merger, U.S. Steel paid $100 per share in the form of newly issued U.S. Steel bonds. In a subsequent appraisal proceeding, the Ohio supreme court held that the $125 paid in the cash tender offer was irrelevant to determining the fair value of the shares subject to the appraisal proceeding.[22] Applying the Ohio appraisal statute, which was substantially similar to that of Delaware, the court deemed control premia to be irrelevant to the value of shares by a stockholder who already had control of the company. Instead, the value of plaintiffs' shares was to be determined by their market value on March 10, 1982, which was about $75, adjusted downward to the extent that the market price anticipated the pending merger.

In *Weinberger*, by way of contrast, the Delaware supreme court held that only "speculative elements of value that may arise from the 'accomplishment or expectation' of the merger are excluded" from the determination of fair value under DGCL § 262(h). The word speculative nowhere appears in the statutory text, of course. The court nevertheless went on to describe the disallowance of "speculative elements of value"

22. Armstrong v. Marathon Oil Co., 513 N.E.2d 776 (Ohio 1987).

as "a very narrow exception to the appraisal process, designed to eliminate use of pro forma data and projections of a speculative variety relating to the completion of a merger." The chancery court thus may consider "elements of future value, including the nature of the enterprise, which are known or susceptible of proof as of the date of the merger and not the product of speculation...."[23] As such, evidence of control premia paid in this and comparable acquisitions typically will be relevant.

Despite the Delaware supreme court's departure from the plain language of the statutory text, the court's approach makes substantial policy sense. As we've seen, if the Delaware courts followed the plain language of the statute, they ought to start with the pre-merger market price and adjust it downward to eliminate any appreciation resulting from the merger. One perhaps could justify such a result by the history of the appraisal statute and its supposed purpose of giving dissenting shareholders the same value they would have received had the business remained in existence as a going concern without the merger taking place. Starting with the pre-merger price and working down from there, however, makes little practical sense. Given the universality of control premia, who would invoke the appraisal statute if such a rule were followed? The real issue, moreover, is whether the dissenting shareholders received a fair premium over market. In order to answer that question, one must start with the price paid in the merger and, if appropriate, work up from there.

Suppose there is a significant lapse of time between the initial acquisition and the subsequent freezeout merger, during which the acquirer makes changes in the corporation's business plans that add new value. Suppose plaintiff sought to admit evidence relating to synergistic effects the merger would have, making the combined entity more valuable than the separate companies, such as might be the case if the merger created a vertically integrated company that achieves great economies of scale. What relevance would such information have to valuation in an appraisal proceeding brought in connection with the eventual freezeout merger? In one of its many *Technicolor* decisions, the Delaware supreme court held that in a two-step acquisition value added by the acquiring corporation subsequent to its initial purchase of a controlling block of shares was properly to be considered part of going concern value that dissenting shareholders who sought appraisal were entitled to share. The chancery court had refused to consider such elements of value on grounds that doing so "would be tantamount to awarding [the dissenting shareholder] a proportionate share of a control premium, which the Court of Chancery deemed to be both economically undesirable and contrary" to precedent. The supreme court disagreed, opining that "[t]he underlying assumption in an appraisal valuation is that the dissenting shareholders would [have been] willing to maintain

23. Weinberger v. UOP, Inc., 457 A.2d
701, 713 (Del.1983).

their investment position had the merger not occurred."[24] Note that making such an assumption seemingly leads to the *Marathon* result, as no control premia would have been paid if the merger had not occurred. It seems doubtful, however, that the Delaware supreme court intended that result.

C. Marketability and minority discounts

Minority discounts are at issue when one is valuing the stock of a minority shareholder in a corporation—public or close—that has a controlling shareholder. Minority discounts reduce the appraised value of the minority shareholders' stock to reflect the fact that someone else controls the company. Marketability discounts are at issue when valuing stock that lacks a trading market. Marketability discounts reflect the generally lower value carried by illiquid investments. All else being equal, the lack of a market exit makes such stocks more risky, which causes shareholders to demand a higher return.

Whether one thinks a minority or marketability discount is appropriate in an appraisal proceeding depends in the first instance on what one believes to be the purpose of such a proceeding. In *Cavalier Oil*, the Delaware supreme court stated that appraisal is intended to value the corporate entity, not the shares held by a particular shareholder.[25] If so, this understanding of appraisal's purpose argues against a minority discount, because the question of whether the shares are held by a minority or majority shareholder is irrelevant to the value of the entity as a whole. In contrast, the court's analysis should permit a marketability discount, because the entity as a whole is worth less because the illiquidity of its securities raises its cost of capital and thus reduces its value as a going concern. Curiously, however, the court disallowed both discounts. The opinion treats marketability and minority discounts as though they were one and the same, reflecting a lack of understanding of the conceptual difference between the two types of discounts. In effect, the court mixed apples and oranges.

There is a wide diversity of views on the appropriateness of minority and marketability discounts. In slight contrast to the Delaware view, the American Law Institute Principles of Corporate Governance contend that, in an appraisal proceeding, the corporation's value should be determined "without any discount for minority status or, absent extraor-

---

24. Cede & Co. v. Technicolor, Inc., 684 A.2d 289, 298 (Del.1996).

25. Cavalier Oil Corp. v. Harnett, 564 A.2d 1137, 1144–45 (Del.1989). The court's conclusion seems clearly contrary to the plain text of the statute, which speaks of the fair value of "the shares." Specifically, DGCL § 262(g) requires the court to determine which shareholders are entitled to appraisal. Section 262(g) further provides that the court may order such shareholders to surrender their shares, if held as certifi-

cates, to "the Register in Chancery for notation thereon of the pendency of the appraisal proceedings." DGCL § 262(h) then provides: "After determining the stockholders entitled to an appraisal, the Court shall appraise the shares ... together with a fair rate of interest, if any, to be paid upon the amount determined to be the fair value." The reference to "the shares" clearly refers not to the entity as a whole but rather to the shares held by those stockholders who have perfected their appraisal rights.

dinary circumstances, lack of marketability."[26] The comments to that section define extraordinary circumstances to include "more than the absence of a trading market in the shares; rather, the court should apply this exception only when it finds that the dissenting shareholder has held out in order exploit the transaction giving rise to appraisal so as to divert value to itself that could not be made available proportionately to the other shareholders." The New Jersey supreme court recently adopted the ALI position, holding that extraordinary circumstances could not be found where "the company instigated the restrictions [placed on transfer of the stock] and restructuring; [while] the dissenters merely pursued their lawful options" to, inter alia, institute an appraisal proceeding.[27]

A better approach would focus on case-by-case analysis rather than trying to impose a rule of general applicability. The underlying transaction at issue in *Cavalier Oil*, for example, was a freezeout merger effected by a controlling shareholder who had allegedly usurped a corporate opportunity. The court opined that "to fail to accord to a minority shareholder the full proportionate value of his shares imposes a penalty for lack of control, and unfairly enriches the majority shareholders who may reap a windfall from the appraisal process by cashing out a dissenting shareholder, a clearly undesirable result."[28] In the freezeout merger setting, the desire to prevent the controlling shareholder from reaping a windfall would justify disallowing a minority discount. A marketability discount would be appropriate in such cases, however, because lack of liquidity equally affects the value of both minority and control shares.

Given this analysis, would either a marketability or a minority discount be appropriate in a court-supervised buy back in lieu of dissolution? In this context, a minority shareholder of a close corporation typically invokes the statutory dissolution procedure as a remedy for oppression by the majority shareholders. In many states, the court can allow the majority to buy back the minority's shares in lieu of dissolution. If the court does so, it must appraise the shares to determine their fair value. In such a proceeding, a marketability discount again seems appropriate because illiquidity drives down the value of all shares. In contrast, a minority discount seems even less appropriate in this setting. A minority discount on such facts serves only to reward those whose misconduct gave rise to the finding of oppression in the first place.[29]

§ 12.5 De facto mergers

Transaction planning does not take place in a vacuum, of course. Shareholders denied voting and/or appraisal rights by virtue of the deal's

26. ALI Principles § 7.22 (a).

27. Lawson Mardon Wheaton, Inc. v. Smith, 734 A.2d 738, 749–50 (N.J.1999).

28. Cavalier Oil Corp. v. Harnett, 564 A.2d 1137, 1145 (Del.1989).

29. See, e.g., Brown v. Allied Corrugated Box Co., 154 Cal.Rptr. 170, 176 (Cal.App. 1979).

structure may seek to reclaim those rights by invoking the de facto merger doctrine. This doctrine is based on the principle of equivalence— like things ought to be treated alike. Put another way, the de facto merger doctrine sounds the clarion call of elevating substance over form.

Assume that Buyer Corporation and Target Inc. agree that Buyer will acquire Target via a reverse triangular merger. As a result, Buyer's shareholders will not be entitled to vote on the merger nor will they be eligible for appraisal rights. Disgruntled Buyer shareholders sue, arguing that the reverse triangular merger is a de facto merger. If the court agrees, the court will ignore the form of the transaction, treat the deal as a standard two-party merger, and grant both Buyer and Target share-holders the right to vote and the right to dissent.

In *Hariton v. Arco Electronics*, the Delaware supreme court emphati-cally rejected the de facto merger doctrine.[1] Arco agreed to sell all of its assets to Loral Electronics in return for 283,000 Loral shares. Arco then planned to dissolve, distributing the Loral shares to its shareholders as a final liquidating dividend. An Arco shareholder sued, claiming that the nominal asset sale was, in substance, a merger. The court agreed "that this sale has achieved the same result as a merger," but held that form was to be elevated over substance. The de facto merger doctrine offended the equal dignity of the merger and asset sale provisions of the corpora-tion code. Put another way, the legislature has provided multiple vehi-cles by which to achieve the same substantive outcome. Each statutory acquisition method had "independent legal significance," and the court could not gainsay the legislative decisions to provide different acquisition forms carrying different levels of shareholder protection.

In contrast, the Pennsylvania courts latched onto the doctrine at an early date. Indeed, many of the classic cases are Pennsylvania cases. In 1957, the Pennsylvania legislature amended the state's corporation code with the self-evident intent of eliminating the de facto merger doctrine. Despite clear legislative history indicating such an intent, the Pennsylva-nia supreme court in *Farris v. Glen Alden Corp.* held that the de facto merger doctrine survived the amendment.[2] In 1959, the legislature again amended the statute, this time explicitly entitling the act as "abolishing the doctrine of de facto mergers or consolidation." The Pennsylvania courts subsequently ignored the de facto merger doctrine, leaving it for the Third Circuit sitting in a diversity proceeding to pronounce the doctrine's demise.[3]

Although the de facto merger doctrine apparently is no longer good law in Pennsylvania, the *Glen Alden* decision remains worthy of study. It involved an interestingly structured transaction, which resulted from the planner's imaginative exercise in statutory construction. A company called List owned 38.5% of Glen Alden and wanted to combine the two

§ 12.5

1. Hariton v. Arco Elec., Inc., 188 A.2d 123 (Del.1963).

2. Farris v. Glen Alden Corp., 143 A.2d 25 (Pa.1958).

3. Terry v. Penn Central Corp., 668 F.2d 188, 192 (3d Cir.1981).

companies. In order to do so, List sold its assets to Glen Alden in return for Glen Alden stock. List then liquidated and distributed the Glen Alden stock to its shareholders. Because List was much larger than Glen Alden, the List shareholders wound up owning 76.5% of the Glen Alden stock. The plaintiff, a Glen Alden shareholder, claimed that he was entitled to appraisal rights.

The transaction was structured to fall between the cracks of Delaware and Pennsylvania law. Under Delaware law, shareholders in a merging corporation had appraisal rights, but shareholders in a corporation selling all of its assets did not. Under Pennsylvania law, appraisal rights were available to both constituent parties to a merger, the selling company's shareholders in an asset sale, but not to the purchasing corporation's shareholders in an asset sale. Glen Alden was a Pennsylvania corporation. List was a Delaware corporation. Consequently, if the two companies had merged, both companies' shareholders would get appraisal rights. If Glen Alden sold its assets to List, the Glen Alden shareholders would have appraisal rights under Pennsylvania law. If List sold its assets to Glen Alden, however, neither firm's shareholders would be entitled to appraisal.[4]

In states where the de facto merger doctrine remains good law, courts support the doctrine mainly by platitudes: form should not be elevated over substance, like transactions should be treated alike, and so on. The problem is deciding when two transactions are alike, such that they should be treated alike. The general rule is to ask whether a transaction so fundamentally changes the nature of the business as to cause the shareholder to give up his shares in one company and against his will accept shares in a different enterprise. A relatively standard laundry list of factors to be considered has evolved, including: distribution of consideration to the shareholders; change in board composition; change in shareholder composition; significant changes in share value; and significant changes in the company's lines of business.[5]

Turning to policy concerns, does the de facto merger doctrine make sense? Put another way, why did the Delaware courts and the Pennsylvania legislature reject the de facto merger doctrine? Is it simply that they prefer corporate interests to shareholder interests? No. The statute provides various ways of accomplishing an acquisition. It does so because no one acquisition technique is always appropriate. If we let courts recharacterize the statutory alternatives, we increase uncertainty and we eliminate the wealth-creating advantages of having multiple acquisition formats.

4. Ordinarily, the Glen Alden board alone would have approved the purchase. In this case, however, Glen Alden apparently had insufficient authorized but unissued shares of stock to distribute to List. Accordingly, the shareholders of Glen Alden were allowed to indirectly vote on the transaction, as their approval of an amendment to the articles of incorporation was necessary to authorize more shares.

5. See, e.g., Pratt v. Ballman–Cummings Furniture Co., 495 S.W.2d 509, 511 (Ark. 1973); Good v. Lackawanna Leather Co., 233 A.2d 201, 207–08 (N.J.Ch.1967).

Another useful way of looking at the problem is to compare the de facto merger doctrine to the definition of a sale of substantially all corporate assets. On their face, the two issues seem quite different. In a de facto merger doctrine case, the question is whether the court will recharacterize the transaction. In a sale of substantially all assets case, the transaction remains an asset sale. Note, however, that the remedy is effectively the same. A transaction that was to be effected without shareholder approval now must obtain approval. At a deeper level, there may be a connection between the two problems. Shareholder approval is a way of ensuring accountability. After a successful takeover, the incumbents no longer are subject to either shareholder or market penalties for self-dealing. We might therefore predict that courts will use the de facto merger doctrine in situations where the target is going out of business and management will no longer be subject to the risk of shareholder or market penalties.

§ 12.6 The target board's proper role in statutory acquisitions

The target board of directors' gate-keeping role in statutory acquisitions creates a potential conflict of interest. Because approval by the target's board of directors is a necessary prerequisite to these acquisition methods, the bidder may seek to purchase the board's cooperation by offering directors and/or senior managers side payments, such as an equity stake in the surviving entity, employment or noncompetition contracts, substantial severance payments, continuation of existing fringe benefits or other compensation arrangements.[1] Although it is undoubtedly rare for side payments to be so large as to materially affect the price the bidder would otherwise be able to pay target shareholders, side payments may affect target board decisionmaking by inducing it to agree to an acquisition price lower than that which could be obtained from hard bargaining or open bidding.[2] Even where the board is not consciously seeking side-payments from the bidder, a conflict of interest can still arise: "There may be at work a force more subtle than a desire to maintain a title or office in order to assure continued salary or perquisites. Many people commit a huge portion of their lives to a single large-scale business organization. They derive their identity in part from that organization and feel that they contribute to the identity of the firm. The mission of the firm is not seen by those involved with it as wholly economic, nor the continued existence of its distinctive identity as a matter of indifference."[3] Although such motivations are understanda-

---

§ 12.6

1. E.g., Samjens Partners I v. Burlington Indus., Inc., 663 F.Supp. 614 (S.D.N.Y. 1987) (white knight offered target management equity stake); Singer v. Magnavox Co., 380 A.2d 969 (Del.1977) (target directors offered employment contracts); Gilbert v. El Paso Co., 490 A.2d 1050 (Del.Ch. 1984) (plaintiff alleged tender offeror modified bid to benefit target managers).

2. E.g., Pupecki v. James Madison Corp., 382 N.E.2d 1030 (Mass.1978) (plaintiff claimed that consideration for sale of assets was reduced due to side-payments to controlling shareholder); Barr v. Wackman, 368 N.Y.S.2d 497 (N.Y.1975) (plaintiff claimed target directors agreed to low acquisition price in exchange for employment contracts).

3. Paramount Communications Inc. v. Time Inc., [1989] Fed. Sec. L. Rep. (CCH)

ble, they conflict with the shareholders' economic interests. Corporate acquisitions thus are a classic example of what economists refer to as final period problems. Recall that in repeat transactions the risk of self-dealing by one party is constrained by the threat that the other party will punish the cheating party in future transactions. In a final period transaction, this constraint disappears. Because the final period transaction is the last in the series, the threat of future punishment disappears.

Modern corporation statutes nevertheless give primary responsibility for negotiating a merger agreement to the target's board of directors. The board possesses broad authority to determine whether to merge the firm and to select a merger partner. The initial decision to enter into a negotiated merger transaction is thus reserved to the board's collective business judgment, shareholders having no statutory power to initiate merger negotiations.[4] The board also has sole power to negotiate the terms on which the merger will take place and to arrive at a definitive merger agreement embodying its decisions as to these matters.[5]

To be sure, most mergers require shareholder approval. But we see director primacy at work here, as well. If the target's board rejects the initial bidder, the merger process comes to a halt without shareholder involvement. If the board approves a merger agreement, the shareholders become somewhat more involved, but only slightly. Shareholders have no statutory right to amend or veto specific provisions, their role being limited to approving or disapproving the merger agreement as a whole, with the statute requiring only approval by a majority of the outstanding shares.

Allocating the principal decisionmaking role to the board of directors makes sense. The board knows much more than its shareholders about the company's business goals and opportunities. The board also knows more about the extent to which a proposed merger would promote accomplishment of those goals. The board also is a more manageable body. The familiar array of collective action problems that plague shareholder participation in corporate decisionmaking obviously preclude any meaningful role for shareholders in negotiating a merger agreement. Rational shareholders will expend the effort to make an informed decision only if the expected benefits of doing so outweigh its costs. Because merger proxy statements are especially long and complicated, there are unusually high opportunity costs entailed in attempting to make an informed decision. In contrast, shareholders probably do not expect to discover grounds for opposing the proposed transaction in the proxy statement. Frequently there are none, and even where grounds exist they will often be very difficult to discern from the proxy statement. Accordingly, shareholders can be expected to assign a relatively low value to the expected benefits of careful consideration. As a result, negotiated acquisitions are likely to be approved even where approval is

¶ 94,514, at 93,268–69, 1989 WL 79880 (Del.Ch.1989), aff'd, 571 A.2d 1140 (Del. 1989).

4. Smith v. Van Gorkom, 488 A.2d 858, 873 (Del.1985).

5. DGCL § 251(b).

not the decision an informed shareholder would reach. This is why corporate law gives the board sole power to negotiate mergers. It is also why corporate law requires shareholders to vote on the merger agreement as a whole, rather than allowing them to approve or disapprove specific provisions.

As with any conferral of plenary authority, the board's power to make decisions about negotiated acquisitions gives rise to the potential for abuse. Because mergers must be approved by the target's board of directors before being submitted for shareholder approval, the bidder at the very least may have to compensate the incumbents for the loss of the rents associated with their offices, thereby reducing the amount that can be paid to the target shareholders for the sale of the firm. At the extreme, incumbents may be unwilling to surrender their positions on any terms that are acceptable to the bidder. Despite these concerns, the Delaware cases consistently apply the business judgment rule to board decisions to approve a merger. In the setting at hand, however, the prerequisite of an informed decision takes on particular import. As illustrated by the Delaware supreme court's canonical decision in *Smith v. Van Gorkom*,[6] if the board is grossly negligent in failing to adequately inform itself prior to approving a merger proposal, liability can result. Absent such facts, however, even clear mistakes of judgment thus will not result in liability.

In most cases, the business judgment rule thus ensures that the considerable latitude conferred upon the board by statute may be exercised without significant risk of judicial intervention. Why? In an armslength merger, the board's potential conflict of interest is policed by a variety of nonlegal constraints. Independent directors and shareholders must be persuaded to approve the transaction. The reputational consequences of self-dealing may cause both the directors and managers problems in the internal and external job markets. Ill-advised acquisitions are likely to cause the acquiring firm problems in the capital markets, which may constrain its willingness to divert gains from target shareholders to the target's board and managers. In addition to those monitoring mechanisms, negotiated acquisitions are subject to the constraining influences of the market for corporate control. Where side payments persuade the target's board to accept a low initial offer, a second bidder may—and often does—succeed by offering shareholders a higher-priced alternative. Indeed, to the extent side payments affect the initial bidder's ability to raise its offer in response to a competing bid, the threat of competing bids becomes particularly important. In such cases, the second bidder is almost certain to prevail. True, the competing bidder's transaction can not be structured as a merger or asset sale if it is unable to persuade target management to change sides. But the intervenor has a formidable alternative: the tender offer, which eliminates the need for target board cooperation by permitting the bidder to buy a controlling share block directly from the stockholders.

6. Smith v. Van Gorkom, 488 A.2d 858 (Del.1985).

Do these various monitoring systems perfectly constrain the board's potential conflicted interests? Almost certainly not. Agency cost theory predicts that neither monitoring by the principal nor bonding by the agent can entirely eliminate shirking by the agent. There are always some residual losses. Why does Delaware tolerate such losses in this context by permitting the business judgment rule to shield the board's decisions from judicial review absent clear evidence of self-dealing? In our view, the law governing negotiated acquisitions is a classic example of the Delaware courts' recognition that the perfect must not become the enemy of the good. As always, a balance must be struck between authority and accountability, which necessarily entails less than perfect accountability. So long as nonlegal monitoring mechanisms are judged to provide acceptable levels of accountability, the demands of accountability are met and courts will obey the director primacy model's command to defer to the board's decisions.

§ 12.7   Nonstatutory acquisition techniques

As we have seen, the target corporation's board of directors serves as a gatekeeper in all of the statutory acquisition forms. Target board approval is a condition precedent to putting the transaction to a shareholder vote and, of course, to ultimately closing the transaction to occur. If the board disapproves of a prospective acquisition, an outsider must resort to one of the three nonstatutory acquisitions devices: proxy contests, share purchases, or tender offers.

A.   Share purchases v. tender offers

Absent cumulative voting, ownership of 50.1% of the outstanding voting stock guarantees one the right to elect the entire board of directors. Once the acquirer replaces the incumbent board with new members, the old board's opposition is moot. The acquirer could obtain the necessary shares through purchases on the open market or privately negotiated block transactions. These techniques have significant disadvantages. They are time consuming. The acquisition program eventually must be disclosed, as SEC regulations require disclosure by holders of more than 5% of a company's stock, and may leak even earlier. In either case, news of an acquisition program typically drives up the stock price. Search and other transaction costs may be significant. Privately negotiated block transactions at a premium over market raise fiduciary duty concerns. And so on.

The tender offer was devised as a shortcut to bypass such concerns. A tender offer is a public offer to shareholders of the target corporation in which the prospective acquirer offers to purchase target company shares at a specified price and upon specified terms. The offer is made during a fixed period of time. The offer may be for all or only a portion of a class or classes of securities of the target corporation. Shareholders wishing to accept the offer are said to "tender" their shares to the bidder. Tendered shares are held in escrow until the offer ends. At that time, the bidder may—but need not—"take down" the tendered shares. If the bidder does so, the escrow agent releases the promised consideration to the shareholders. Otherwise, the escrow agent returns the tendered shares to the owners.

B.   Tender offers v. proxy contests

Professor Henry Manne, one of the founders of the law and economics movement, famously described proxy contests as "the most expensive, the most uncertain, and the least used of the various techniques" for acquiring corporate control.[1] Insurgents contemplating a proxy battle face a host of legal and economic disincentives: The incumbents' informational advantages. Long-standing investor perception that proxy insurgents are not serious contenders for control. Classified boards of directors, which mean that even a successful proxy contest can only unseat a minority of the board. Restrictions on reimbursement of the insurgent's expenses, while the incumbent board is allowed essentially unfettered access to the corporate treasury. Rational shareholder apathy.

During the 1960s, the cash tender offer emerged as a potent alternative that suffered from relatively few of these disadvantages. At the time, a principal advantage was the almost total absence of regulation. Since the 1930s, proxy contests have been subject to numerous federal rules imposing substantial disclosure obligations on prospective acquirers. The expensive process of preparing and vetting the requisite disclosure documents directly increases the transaction costs associated with such acquisitions. More subtly, mandatory disclosure rules decrease an insurgent's profit margin by forcing it to reveal the anticipated sources of gain to be had from a change of control. Prior to the 1968 adoption of the Williams Act, in contrast, cash tender offers were essentially unregulated. Accordingly, offers slightly over market could succeed and bidders thus reaped a non-pro rata share of the gains.

After passage of the Williams Act, tender offerors faced disclosure obligations (and thus transaction costs) comparable to those under the proxy rules. Tender offers nevertheless still remained more profitable than proxy contests. Although the Williams Act undoubtedly reduced offerors' profit margins, the tender offeror is still able to reap a non-pro rata share of the gains from a change in control. The changes made by the Williams Act thus reduced, but did not eliminate, the cash tender offer's advantages.

Assume, for example, that the target company has 110 outstanding shares, currently trading at $10 per share, of which the bidder owns ten. The bidder correctly believes that under its management the firm's shares would be worth $20. If the bidder successfully gains control

§ **12.7**

1. Henry G. Manne, Mergers and the Market for Corporate Control, 73 J. Pol.

Econ. 110, 114 (1965).

through a proxy contest, its ten shares will produce a $100 profit when the stock price rises to reflect the company's value under its management. All the other shareholders, however, will also automatically receive a pro rata share of those gains. There is nothing the bidder lawfully can do to capture a non-pro rata share of the gains. As a result, the bidder confers a $1,000 benefit on the other shareholders (many of whom undoubtedly voted for management).

In contrast, if the tender offeror is able to purchase all the outstanding shares it does not already own at a price below $19 per share, its profit will exceed the $100 figure available from a successful proxy contest. To do so, of course, it need not persuade all of the other shareholders to sell. As long as the holders of at least 46 shares are willing to tender at a price below $19 per share, our hypothetical bidder will obtain voting control. It may then freeze out the remaining minority shareholders in a subsequent merger at approximately the same price.

How likely is this scenario? Quite likely. Unlike the proxy contest, the tender offer does not automatically confer a pro rata share of the gains from a change of control on the target's shareholders. Instead, their share of the gains is now determined by the size of the premium paid by the bidder. No rule requires that the premium constitute a pro rata share of the gains. Instead, the premium will be no larger than necessary to obtain a controlling block of target stock. Granted, the disclosures mandated by the Williams Act may enable shareholders to estimate the gains anticipated by the bidder. It is unlikely, however, that shareholders will obtain all of those gains. For one thing, collective action problems preclude the hard bargaining needed to extract a full share of the gains. Absent competing bids or successful management resistance, there is no mechanism for the shareholders to demand a bigger piece of the pie. Rational shareholders thus can be expected to accept a premium reflecting a less than pro rata sharing of the gains, reasoning that some profit is better than none.

In addition to enabling the bidder to obtain a greater share of the gains from a change of control, the tender offer (if followed by a freezeout merger) enables the bidder to eliminate the complications caused by controlling a company with minority shareholders. With minority shareholders remaining in place after a proxy contest, the firm's directors may not benefit the controlling shareholder to the exclusion or at the expense of the minority. With the minority eliminated by a tender offer and freezeout merger, the bidder may do with the target as it will.

In sum, these factors predict that tender offers should succeed far more often than proxy contests. The data confirm this prediction. Proxy contests tend to succeed less than half the time. In contrast, tender offers succeed in the majority of cases. When the tender offer's greater probability of success is coupled with its higher profitability, one would expect bidders to prefer it to proxy contests. Again the data confirm this expectation, both on an absolute scale and when compared to the frequency of tender offers. Although there was an up-tick in proxy contest activity during the 1990s, much of that activity was attributable to the general rise in takeover activity. Indeed, many proxy contests during that period were made in conjunction with tender offers.

§ 12.8 Federal regulation of tender offers

Prior to the 1968 passage of the Williams Act, neither federal securities nor state corporate law regulated tender offers. As already noted, this absence of regulation was one of the intrinsic advantages the tender offer possessed over other acquisition forms and thus led to the enormous growth in the volume of tender offers during the early and middle part of that decade. In 1965, Senator Harrison Williams of New Jersey proposed federal legislation to protect target companies from what he called "industrial sabotage" of hostile corporate raids on "proud old companies."[1] Although the 1965 legislation was not adopted, a second bill was introduced in 1967. The 1967 bill was considerably more balanced and focused primarily on disclosure and antifraud. As Senator Williams and others emphasized, the bill attempted to favor neither the target nor the offeror. As subsequently amended, the Williams Act has four components of principal interest for our purposes:

1. Securities Exchange Act § 13(d) regulates beachhead acquisitions of target stock. (The term beachhead acquisition refers to purchases of an initial block of target stock, either on the open market or privately, before the bidder announces its intent to conduct a tender offer.)

2. Securities Exchange Act § 13(e) regulates self-tender offers by issuers. Among the powers of a corporation is the right to buy its own stock. Stock redemptions and repurchases are subject to the legal capital statute of the state of incorporation. Where effected by means of a tender offer, however, they must also comply with § 13(e).

3. Securities Exchange Act § 14(d) regulates tender offers generally. The statute and the SEC regulations thereunder impose both disclosure and procedural requirements on the offer.

4. Securities Exchange Act § 14(e) prohibits fraud in connection with a tender offer.

There is no doubt that the Williams Act dramatically changed the takeover game. It eliminated such favorite raider tactics as the "Saturday night special"—the surprise offer made over a weekend. It significantly increased the amount of information available to target shareholders, predictably driving up the average control premium paid in

---

§ 12.8

1. Corporate raider is a pejorative dating from the 1960s to describe bidders, especially those who do not actually acquire target companies but rather use the tender offer process to make quick profits through greenmail or by selling blocks of target stocks to other bidders.

takeovers.[2] Finally, it significantly expanded the federal government's role in corporate governance.

A.   Beachhead acquisitions

For the would be acquirer, keeping its interest in the target and takeover plans secret for as long as possible is crucial. As soon as a possible bid is disclosed, the target's stock price jumps. Target management may begin erecting defenses against the bid or seeking alternative transactions. Other potential acquirers may begin looking at the target with the idea of making a competing bid, such that the initial bidder's disclosures may simply serve to identify the target and publicize its vulnerability. In pre-Williams Act days, it was common for a prospective acquirer to quietly buy up substantial amounts of target stock before initiating its public offer. In some cases, bidders managed to acquire de facto control before going public. Today, however, Securities Exchange Act § 13(d) and the SEC rules thereunder form an early warning system effectively mandating early disclosure of impending control contests.

1.   *The obligation to disclose*

Securities Exchange Act § 13(d) requires that any person who acquires beneficial ownership of more than 5% of the outstanding shares of any class of voting equity securities registered under Securities Exchange Act § 12 must file a Schedule 13D disclosure statement within 10 days of such acquisition with the SEC, the issuer, and the exchanges on which the stock is traded.[3] Amendments must be filed within 10 days of any material change in the information in the prior filing. Let's break this requirement down into its component pieces:

Any person: Suppose two corporations or individuals are working together to acquire the target corporation. Each plans to buy just under 5% of the target's stock, thinking that they will thereby get almost 10% without having to file a Schedule 13D disclosure statement. This plan will not work. Section 13(d)(3) provides that when two or more persons act as a group for the purpose of acquiring, holding or disposing of shares of the issuer they will collectively be deemed a "person" under

---

2. A leading empirical study found an average premium of 32.4 percent in successful tender offers made prior to the adoption of the Williams Act, compared to an average premium of 52.8 percent following its adoption. Gregg A. Jarrell & Michael Bradley, The Economic Effects of Federal and State Regulations of Cash Tender Offers, 23 J.L. & Econ. 371 (1980).

3. The § 13(d) reporting requirement also applies to acquisitions of more than 5% of the outstanding shares of any class of voting equity securities of a closed-end investment company registered under the Investment Company Act of 1940 or of an insurance company exempted from registration by Securities Exchange § 12(a)(2)(G).

Certain institutional investors who hold shares with no intent of affecting the control of the issuer may file a short form Schedule 13G, which essentially requires disclosure only of the amount of shares held and the nature of the holder. Rule 13d–1(b). All other 5% holders must file the longer Schedule 13D. Schedule 13D requires substantially greater disclosure (including the purpose of the holding) and must be amended more frequently. (Schedule 13G typically is filed on an annual basis.)

the statute. Accordingly, such a group must file a Schedule 13D report if the members' aggregate holdings exceed the 5% threshold.

Generally speaking, some kind of agreement is necessary before it can be said that a group exists. Not only must there be an agreement, but the agreement must go to certain types of conduct. The relevant statutory provision, Securities Exchange Act § 13(d)(3) identifies "acquiring, holding, or disposing" of stock as the requisite purposes. Shortly after the Williams Act was adopted, the question arose whether two or more persons acting together for the purpose of voting shares, as when they cooperate in conducting a proxy contest, form a group for purposes of this provision. The courts split on that question.[4] The SEC subsequently adopted Rule 13d–5(b)(1), which expanded the statutory list of purposes to include voting. Consequently, a group is formed when two or more shareholders agree to act together for the purposes of voting their shares, even if they do not intend to buy any additional shares. The rule's adoption seems to have resolved the controversy, even if the SEC's authority to effectively amend the statute remains somewhat obscure.

Proving the existence of the requisite agreement is a complex and potentially difficult question of fact. On the one hand, "Section 13(d) allows individuals broad freedom to discuss the possibilities of future agreements without filing under securities laws."[5] On the other hand, an agreement to act in concert need not be formal or written.[6] The existence of such an agreement may be proven by circumstantial evidence.[7] Taken together, these factors create substantial uncertainty for putative group members. Given the minimal penalties for violating § 13(d), one suspects many groups err on the side of not filing.

Who acquires: In cases where a group is at issue, the meaning of the statutory term "acquires" takes on particular import. Suppose the group members' aggregate holdings exceed five percent when they enter into the agreement by which the group is formed for § 13(d) purposes. None of the group members, however, buy any additional shares. Do they have an immediate filing obligation or is their filing obligation only triggered

---

4. Compare GAF Corp. v. Milstein, 453 F.2d 709 (2d Cir.1971) (group exists) with Bath Indus., Inc. v. Blot, 427 F.2d 97 (7th Cir.1970) (no group).

5. Pantry Pride, Inc. v. Rooney, 598 F.Supp. 891, 900 (S.D.N.Y.1984). See also Lane Bryant, Inc. v. Hatleigh Corp., 1980 WL 1412 at *1 (S.D.N.Y.1980) ("Section 13(d) seems carefully drawn to permit parties seeking to acquire large amounts of shares in a public company to obtain information with relative freedom, to discuss preliminarily the possibility of entering into agreements and to operate with relative freedom until they get to the point where they do in fact decide to make arrangements which they must record under the securities laws"). Hence, for example, merely showing the existence of a relationship or the sharing of information or advice between the alleged group members, will not suffice absent some additional evidence that indicates an intention to act in concert. Similarly, investment analysts who follow one another's trades without any agreement so to do, tacit or otherwise, will not be held to be a group. See, e.g., K–N Energy, Inc. v. Gulf Interstate Co., 607 F.Supp. 756 (D.Colo.1983).

6. Morales v. Quintel Entertainment, Inc., 249 F.3d 115, 124 (2d Cir.2001); Wellman v. Dickinson, 682 F.2d 355, 362–63 (2d Cir.1982).

7. Morales v. Quintel Entertainment, Inc., 249 F.3d 115, 124 (2d Cir.2001); SEC v. Savoy Indus., 587 F.2d 1149, 1163 (D.C.Cir.1978).

by further acquisitions of additional shares? The Seventh Circuit early held that the group must acquire additional shares, over and above the shares they own at the time the agreement is made, before the filing obligation is triggered.[8] In contrast, the Second Circuit held that the group acquires stock, and thus triggers the filing obligation, at the moment they enter into an agreement to act in concert, even if the members do not intend to acquire additional shares.[9] In promulgating Rule 13d–5(b), the SEC adopted the Second Circuit position by providing that a group is formed "when two or more persons agree to act together for the purpose of acquiring, holding, voting or disposing of" stock.

Beneficial ownership of more than 5% of any equity security registered under Exchange Act § 12: Rule 13d–3(a) deems a person to be the beneficial owner of stock if he has the power (by contract, understanding, arrangement, relationship or otherwise) to vote or dispose of (or to direct the voting or disposition of) the securities in question. Rule 13d–3(d) further provides that a person shall be deemed the beneficial owner of a security if he has the right to acquire ownership of the security within 60 days (e.g., by exercise of an option, conversion of a convertible security, or revocation or termination of a trust) or acquires such a right (whether or not exercisable within 60 days) with a purpose of affecting control of the issuer. Brokers, pledgees and underwriters are not deemed the beneficial owners of securities when they hold them in the ordinary course of their business. Finally, the SEC long has taken the position that a holding company is the indirect beneficial owner of the securities held by its subsidiaries, so that if the holding company and its subsidiaries hold an aggregate of more than 5% of the outstanding shares of the class in question, they must report. All of the statutory jargon boils down to a very simple point: Beneficial ownership is a broader concept than having title to the securities. Someone can be the beneficial owner of securities even if somebody else actually has title to them. If someone has or shares the power to vote or dispose of the shares, he is their beneficial owner.

Within 10 days after such person crosses the five percent threshold: Under § 13(d), the acquirer has 10 days before it must file a Schedule 13D disclosure statement. The 10 day window begins to run on the day the acquiring person makes an acquisition which puts his holdings over the five percent threshold. Where a group is formed, the 10 day window begins to run on the day they enter into the requisite agreement to act in concert, provided their aggregate holdings exceed 5% on that date.

The statutory framework had a predictable timing effect. A bidder who intends or expects to make a hostile takeover will buy up to 4.9% as quietly as possible. It will not cross the 5% threshold until all its preparations are completed. Once it crosses that threshold, it will begin actively buying stock, attempting to acquire as many shares as possible without alerting the target during the 10 day window. Pre-filing acquisi-

8. Bath Indus., Inc. v. Blot, 427 F.2d 97, 109 (7th Cir.1970).

9. GAF Corp. v. Milstein, 453 F.2d 709, 715 (2d Cir.1971).

tions of 10% of the issuer's stock are common and there are anecdotal accounts of pre-filing acquisitions of as much as 25% or more of the stock.

Amending the disclosure statement: Rule 13d–2(a) requires reporting parties to file an amendment to their Schedule 13D promptly in the event of any material change in the facts set forth in the statement. "Material" is defined to include (but is not limited to) any acquisition or disposition of at least 1% or more of the class of securities in question. "Promptly" is not the most precise term the drafters might have chosen, of course, as it creates a is a question of fact to be determined on a case-by-case basis.[10] As a rule of thumb, most practitioners assume that "promptly" means no more than a couple of days.[11]

2.   *The content of a schedule 13D disclosure statement*

As with other SEC forms, Schedule 13D does not follow the "fill in the box" format familiar from tax returns. Three of the required disclosure items are significant for our purposes: Item 2 on disclosure of identity; Item 4 on disclosure of intent; and Item 6 on disclosure of agreements or understandings.

Item 2—Identity: For individuals, Item 2 disclosure presents no real problem. The individual must disclose such basic items as name, business address, occupation, and whether the individual has ever been found in violation of specified laws. As to the latter point, Item 2 specifically requires disclosure of whether the filer, during the preceding five years, has been convicted in any criminal proceeding, excluding traffic violations or similar misdemeanors. If so, the filer must provide disclosure of the nature and date of the conviction, the name and location of the court, and any penalty imposed. Item 2 also requires disclosure of whether the filer, during the preceding five years, was the subject of a judgment or consent decree enjoining the filer from violating the securities laws in the future or finding a past of such laws.

For corporate parties things get more complicated. In addition to such basic items as identifying the state of incorporation and the like, Instruction C requires Item 2 disclosures with respect to each executive officer and director, and each controlling person. If the controlling person is itself a corporation, Item 2 disclosures are required with respect to each intermediary corporation and each officer and director of the ultimate parent controlling corporation. Surprisingly, it is not clear whether Item 2 disclosures are required with respect to executive officer and director of intermediary corporations.

---

10. Scott v. Multi–Amp Corp., 386 F.Supp. 44, 61 (D.N.J.1974); SEC v. GSC Enterprises, 469 F.Supp. 907, 914 (N.D.Ill. 1979).

11. See, e.g., Kamerman v. Steinberg, 123 F.R.D. 66, 72–73 (S.D.N.Y.1988) (deny-ing motion for summary judgment on ground that a jury reasonably could find that weekend events should have been disclosed at the start of business on the following Monday).

Item 4—Intent: Item 4 is the heart of any Schedule 13D and, along with deciding who is a member of the group, the source of most § 13(d) litigation. The instructions require disclosure of "any plans or proposals which the reporting persons may have which relate to or would result in" any of 9 specified actions or, in a tenth catch-all provision, any "action similar to any of those enumerated above." Among the enumerated actions are: (1) acquisition or disposition of the target's securities; (2) a merger or other extraordinary transaction involving the target or any of its subsidiaries; (3) a sale or transfer of a material amount of the target's assets; (4) changes in the composition of the target's board of directors or management; and so on. In addition to the numerous specifics required by the instructions to Item 4, courts have held that the reporting person must explicitly state whether it intends to seek or is considering seeking control of the issuer.[12]

In practice, Item 4 disclosures tend to be boilerplate and to throw in every possible purpose except the proverbial kitchen sink. The reporting person discloses what options it is considering, but buries its true intent in a lengthy statement of everything it might conceivably do someday. Although courts have occasionally criticized the kitchen sink approach, it remains the safest and most common form of Item 4 disclosure.

Item 6—Contracts and understandings: Item 6 requires disclosure of any contracts, arrangements, understandings, or relationships with respect to the securities of the issuer. At a minimum, Item 6 requires disclosure of the terms of an agreement or understanding among the members of a reporting group. If such an agreement has been reduced to writing, a copy of the agreement must be attached to the disclosure statement as an exhibit pursuant to Item 7.

3.   Section 13(d) litigation

Nobody likes to be fired, so it is hardly surprising that target directors and managers frequently resist unsolicited takeover bids. Among the most common takeover defenses is litigation under § 13(d), typically alleging some form of nondisclosure. Suppose Bidder filed a Schedule 13D disclosure document containing the following Item 4 disclosure: "Bidder has determined to make a large equity investment in Target. From time to time, as market conditions warrant in its view, Bidder may purchase or sell shares of Target's common stock on the open market." Shortly before filing the initial schedule 13D, Bidder entered into a brokerage contract with a well known brokerage firm specializing in takeover stocks. The contract provides: (1) the broker will purchase up to 4.9% of Target's outstanding common stock; (2) Bidder will reimburse the broker for any losses suffered in connection with those acquisitions; and (3) the broker will pay over to Bidder any profits realized in connection with those acquisitions, less its usual brokerage fee plus an additional 5%, including any profits realized by tendering or

---

12. See, e.g., Dan River, Inc. v. Unitex Ltd., 624 F.2d 1216, 1226 n. 9 (4th Cir. 1980); Chromalloy American Corp. v. Sun Chem. Corp., 611 F.2d 240, 247 (8th Cir. 1979); SEC v. Amster & Co., 762 F.Supp. 604, 613–14 (S.D.N.Y.1991).

otherwise selling the shares to Bidder. This so-called "parking" agreement was not disclosed in any of Bidder's filings. The target sues, alleging that Bidder violated § 13(d) by not disclosing the parking arrangement and by not adequately disclosing whether it intended to seek control of Target.

Obviously, the SEC has standing to prosecute violations of the tender offers rules. In a civil proceeding, the SEC may seek a variety of sanctions ranging from disgorgement of profits to corrective disclosures. To be sure, the SEC cannot conduct a criminal prosecution, but the SEC can refer cases to the Justice Department for criminal prosecution, as it frequently did in connection with the insider trading scandals of the 1980s.

Targets of an unsolicited offer frequently inform the SEC of alleged violations and ask that the SEC bring charges against the bidder. This is largely a pro forma act, as the SEC only rarely takes an aggressive posture in prosecuting § 13(d) violations. Instead, most § 13(d) litigation is brought by the target.

Standing presents the initial hurdle for private party litigation under § 13(d). More precisely, there are two distinct issues here, which all too often get bollixed up: (1) Is there an implied private right of action under § 13(d), at all? (2) Assuming that there is an implied private right of action under § 13(d), does this plaintiff have standing to assert that right of action in this case? As to the former question, most courts have found that there is an implied private right of action under § 13(d). As to the latter, we must bifurcate the inquiry. Do shareholders of the target corporation have standing under § 13(d)? Does the target corporation have standing under § 13(d)?

As for shareholder standing, most courts hold that shareholders have standing to seek injunctive but not monetary relief under § 13(d). As a result, shareholders generally cannot receive damages for § 13(d) violations.[13] Shareholders who wish to sue for false or misleading § 13(d) reports thus are relegated to the damage remedies provided by Securities Exchange Act § 18(a) and/or Rule 10b–5. Section 18(a) usually is of limited utility to investors. To recover under Section 18(a), an investor must show actual "eyeball" reliance on the false or misleading report, namely that the investor actually saw the report and relied on it.[14] This requirement has precluded the enforcement of claims under § 18(a) by class action, the only efficient means of litigating such claims. In addition, it can be difficult to show damages under § 18(a), because that section requires the misstatement to have affected the price of the securities (i.e., a causal nexus must be proven between the misrepresen-

---

13. See, e.g., Sanders v. Thrall Car Mfg. Co., 582 F.Supp. 945, 960–61 (S.D.N.Y. 1983), aff'd, 730 F.2d 910 (2d Cir.1984); Rosenbaum v. Klein, 547 F.Supp. 586, 591 (E.D.Pa.1982); Issen v. GSC Enterprises, Inc., 508 F.Supp. 1278, 1295 (N.D.Ill.1981); Myers v. American Leisure Time Enterpris- es, Inc., 402 F.Supp. 213, 214 (S.D.N.Y. 1975), aff'd mem., 538 F.2d 312 (2d Cir. 1976).

14. See, e.g., Gross v. Diversified Mortgage Investors, 438 F.Supp. 190, 195 (S.D.N.Y.1977).

tation and the loss or diminishment of the plaintiff's investment).[15] Rule 10b–5 is also potentially available, but is of limited utility in this context because the investor must prove scienter and must be a purchaser or seller of the security.[16]

As for target corporations, they too lack standing to seek damages for § 13(d) violations. Initially, federal courts almost uniformly granted issuers standing to seek injunctive relief under § 13(d).[17] In the oft-cited *Liberty National* case, however, the standing issue got bollixed up with the issue of allowable remedies. A bit of background on the latter issue is necessary. In *Rondeau v. Mosinee Paper Corp.*, the issuer brought suit for the defendant's failure to file a Schedule 13D. The Seventh Circuit granted an injunction that for a period of 5 years would have prevented the defendant from voting any shares purchased between the date when a Schedule 13D should have been filed and the date on which it was in fact filed. The Supreme Court reversed, on the grounds that the plaintiff had not shown such irreparable harm that a sterilizing injunction was appropriate. The Court suggested that less severe remedies might be available under appropriate fact settings, such as enjoining the defendant from voting, acquiring additional shares or commencing a takeover bid pending compliance.[18] Since *Rondeau*, however, courts finding a § 13(d) violation generally have been quite conservative in fashioning a remedy. Typically, they merely issue an order directing that the violation be cured, either by amending the filing or by filing a Schedule 13D not previously filed. Courts have been unwilling, in the belief that they are unauthorized, to grant more effective relief.[19]

In *Liberty National*, the target corporation sought an aggressive equitable remedy ordering the bidder to divest all of its target stock holdings. In broad language, which lay extensive emphasis on the conflict of interest between target corporation managers and shareholders in the hostile takeover setting, the Eleventh Circuit held that "no cause of action under section 13(d) exists *for the relief Liberty requests*"[20] Notice

---

15. Cramer v. General Telephone & Elec., 443 F.Supp. 516, 525 (E.D.Pa.1977), aff'd, 582 F.2d 259 (3d Cir.1978).

16. See Ernst & Ernst v. Hochfelder, 425 U.S. 185, 193 (1976).

17. See, e.g., Florida Commercial Banks v. Culverhouse, 772 F.2d 1513, 1519 n. 2 (11th Cir.1985) (citing cases in 1st, 2d, 4th, 7th, 8th and 9th Circuits); Portsmouth Square, Inc. v. Shareholders Protective Comm., 770 F.2d 866, 871 n. 8 (9th Cir. 1985); Gearhart Indus., Inc. v. Smith Int'l, Inc., 741 F.2d 707, 714 (5th Cir.1984).

18. Rondeau v. Mosinee Paper Corp., 422 U.S. 49 (1975).

19. See, e.g., Dan River, Inc. v. Icahn, 701 F.2d 278, 287 (4th Cir.1983) (court would not order "sterilization" of shares due to the prior insufficient disclosure); Treadway Companies, Inc. v. Care Corp.,

638 F.2d 357, 380 (2d Cir.1980) (refusing an injunction where defective filing was cured and "shareholders had ample time to digest th[e] information"); Chromalloy American Corp. v. Sun Chemical Corp., 611 F.2d 240, 248–49 (8th Cir.1979) (court would not require "cooling-off" period after submission of corrected Schedule 13D); Energy Ventures, Inc. v. Appalachian Co., 587 F.Supp. 734, 743–44 (D.Del.1984) (interim injunctive relief deemed inappropriate where corrective filing had been made); University Bank & Trust Co. v. Gladstone, 574 F.Supp. 1006, 1010 (D.Mass.1983) (injunction denied where purchaser had made curative disclosure). A rare exception authorized disgorgement in a parking case brought by the SEC. SEC v. First City Fin. Corp., Ltd., 890 F.2d 1215 (D.C.Cir.1989).

20. Liberty Nat'l Ins. Holding Co. v. Charter Co., 734 F.2d 545, 567 (11th Cir. 1984) (emphasis supplied).

how the court blurred three distinct inquiries: the existence of a cause of action, standing of the party at bar; and the remedy being sought. Instructively, a subsequent Eleventh Circuit decision limited *Liberty National* to the relief being sought. Where the target corporation sought only corrective disclosure, the target corporation had standing.[21]

B.   Tender offer disclosure and procedural rules

The Williams Act's announced goal is protection of target shareholders.[22] Disclosure provided the principal vehicle by which this goal was to be achieved; consequently, the Act imposes substantial disclosure requirements on both target management and the bidder.[23] To be sure, the Williams Act also provides a number of procedural protections for shareholders. In general, however, the Act's procedural requirements mainly serve to make the disclosure requirements more effective, as they generally "require or prohibit certain acts so that investors will possess additional time within which to take advantage of the disclosed information."[24]

Accordingly, the bidder must disseminate a Schedule 14D–1 disclosure statement containing, among other things, information relating to the bidder's identity, the source of its funds and any plans to merge with or otherwise make material changes in the target if the bid is successful. If all or part of the tender offer price is to be paid in the form of securities, rather than purely in cash, the bidder likely also will be required to incorporate a Securities Act registration statement in its offering materials and to generally comply with the Securities Act and state blue sky laws on offering securities. Similarly, if the company makes a tender offer for its own shares, it is subject to a series of SEC rules under Exchange Act § 13(e) that basically track the disclosure and procedural rules applicable to third-party tender offers under §§ 14(d) and 14(e).

1. *Definition of tender offer*

Curiously, although the Williams Act establishes an extensive regulatory scheme governing tender offers, the Act never actually defines what constitutes a tender offer subject to the statute and the rules thereunder. The obvious rationale for this failure has been a desire on the part of Congress and the SEC to retain regulatory flexibility to deal

---

21. Florida Commercial Banks v. Culverhouse, 772 F.2d 1513, 1519 (11th Cir. 1985).

22. S. Rep. No. 550, 90th Cong., 1st Sess. 3 (1967); H.R. Rep. No. 1711, 90th Cong., 2d Sess. 3 (1968). See also Rondeau v. Mosinee Paper Corp., 422 U.S. 49, 58 (1975). The extent to which the Williams Act's requirements actually protect target shareholders has been a matter of considerable debate. See, e.g., Daniel R. Fischel, Efficient Capital Market Theory, the Market for Corporate Control, and the Regulation of Cash Tender Offers, 57 Tex. L. Rev. 1 (1978).

23. See Schreiber v. Burlington Northern, Inc., 472 U.S. 1, 8 (1985) ("It is clear that Congress relied primarily on disclosure to implement the purpose of the Williams Act."); see also Piper v. Chris–Craft Indus., 430 U.S. 1, 28 (1977).

24. Schreiber v. Burlington Northern, Inc., 472 U.S. 1, 9 (1985).

with novel transactions that might fall outside the scope of a statutory definition, while still raising the same regulatory concerns as covered transactions. Nobody doubts that the Williams Act applies to "conventional" tender offers, which might be defined as: A public offer to purchase at a specified price and terms during a specified period of time all or part of a class or classes of securities of a publicly held corporation. But what about privately negotiated block purchases or secondary market purchases, as well as other "unconventional" acquisition techniques?

The issue arose during the 1970s and 1980s in connection with two stock purchase techniques: the creeping tender offer and the street sweep. The term "creeping tender offer" is actually a misnomer. The bidder never makes a conventional tender offer. Rather, the bidder directly purchases a sufficient number shares on the open market to give it effective control over the target. Once the bidder has working control over the target, it then effects a merger with the target in order to solidify its control and to eliminate remaining minority shareholders.

In contrast, a street sweep begins with a conventional tender offer that is subsequently withdrawn. The tactic was devised to take advantage of the takeover arbitrageur phenomenon. Arbitrageurs seek profit by buying target company stock on the open market and subsequently tendering the stock to the bidder at the higher tender offer price.[25] Risk averse target shareholders commonly are prompted to sell by the price increase that generally follows announcement of a tender offer. Arbitrageurs, who are willing to take the risk that the deal will not go forward, therefore can acquire substantial blocks of the target's stock. In a street sweep, the nominal bidder withdraws the tender offer and purchases a controlling block of target shares directly from arbitrageurs through open market or privately negotiated transactions. In *Hanson Trust PLC v. SCM Corp.*,[26] for example, Hanson (and affiliated companies) launched a tender offer for all outstanding shares of SCM. After Hanson terminated the tender offer in response to defensive moves by SCM, Hanson made five privately negotiated and one open market purchase from arbitrageurs, totaling 25% of SCM's outstanding common stock.

To determine whether these types of transactions should be deemed tender offers—and thereby subject to § 14(d) and the underlying rules—courts have frequently looked to the eight factors of the so-called *Wellman* test:

> (1) active and widespread solicitation of public shareholders; (2) for a substantial percentage of the issuer's stock; (3) at a premium over the prevailing market price; (4) offer terms fixed, rather than negotiable; (5) offer contingent on the tender of a fixed minimum or limited to a maximum number of shares to be purchased; (6) offer open for only a limited time period; (7) offeree subjected to pressure

---

25. For an overview of takeover arbitrage techniques written by its most infamous practitioner, and insider trading felon, see Ivan Boesky, Merger Mania (1985).

26. Hanson Trust PLC v. SCM Corp., 774 F.2d 47 (2d Cir.1985).

to sell; and (8) public announcement of a purchasing program preceding or accompanying a rapid accumulation of a large amount of the target's securities.[27]

Not all factors need be present for a transaction to be deemed a tender offer. Indeed, one may not even need a majority to be present, as the court emphasized that identifying the determinative factors is to be done on a case-by-case basis. Having said that, however, the factors that usually seem most important are publicity and pressure to sell. These are the factors that make a purchase program most look like a tender offer.

The ambiguity inherent in the *Wellman* test has not precluded its widespread use. Although the SEC has not formally adopted the *Wellman* test, the test was developed by the SEC enforcement staff for use in litigation and the SEC staff has often urged its adoption by the courts on a case-by-case basis.[28] The Ninth Circuit, for example, relied on the *Wellman* test in determining that a creeping tender offer by Carter Hawley Hale was not a tender offer within the meaning of the Act.[29]

In *Hanson Trust*, however, the Second Circuit called the validity of the *Wellman* test into question, arguing that a "mandatory 'litmus test' appears to be both unwise and unnecessary."[30] The issue at bar was whether a street sweep constituted a tender offer subject to the disclosure and procedural mandates of the Williams Act. After Hanson's rapid

27. Wellman v. Dickinson, 475 F.Supp. 783, 823 (S.D.N.Y.1979), aff'd on other grounds, 682 F.2d 355 (2d Cir.1982). Note that Rule 10b–13 prohibits a bidder from making open market or private purchases of target stock during the pendency of a tender offer. Under the rule, a bidder may purchase target stock prior to commencing the tender offer. See, e.g., Heine v. Signal Companies, Inc., [1976–77 Transfer Binder] Fed. Sec. L. Rep. (CCH) ¶ 95,898, 1977 WL 930 (S.D.N.Y.1977) (delaying announcement of a self-tender offer in order to purchase a block of its shares in a privately negotiated transaction did not violate the rule; inter alia, because Signal had obtained a no-action letter from the SEC staff in connection with the proposed series of transactions). Likewise, entering into option agreements to purchase target shares prior to the commencement of a tender offer should not violate the rule, provided the option period does not extend into the tender offer period, since the rule does not prohibit such arrangements until the tender offer period begins to run. Rule 10b–13 obviously will not affect a bidder's ability to conduct a creeping tender offer; it is simply inapplicable to acquisition contests not involving a tender offer. In contrast, the rule will somewhat affect street sweeps: while the initial tender offer is pending, it will prohibit a bidder from entering into ar-

rangements for the private post-offer purchases from arbitrageurs and other shareholders of the target. Its impact on street sweeps, however, is likely to be minimal. In the first instance, it may be difficult to detect and prove the existence of such arrangements. More importantly, bidders and arbitrageurs have demonstrated an ability to come to terms very quickly following the conclusion of a tender offer. For example, in six transactions over a two hour period on the same day that its tender offer was withdrawn Hanson Trust was able to acquire 3.1 million SCM shares (representing approximately 25% of those outstanding). As long as bidders and arbitrageurs are able to move that rapidly, the strictures of Rule 10b–13 will not significantly impede them.

28. David J. Segre, Open–Market and Privately Negotiated Purchase Programs and the Market for Corporate Control, 42 Bus. Law. 715, 727 (1987).

29. The offer in question actually was a defensive stock purchase program effected on the secondary market by the target company for its own stock—a creeping self-tender offer, if you will. SEC v. Carter Hawley Hale Stores, Inc., 760 F.2d 945 (9th Cir.1985).

30. Hanson Trust PLC v. SCM Corp., 774 F.2d 47, 57 (2d Cir.1985).

block purchases following the termination of its tender offer, SCM sought injunctive relief, including enjoining Hanson from acquiring additional shares or voting the shares it held, alleging that Hanson's block purchases were a tender offer in violation of § 14. In lieu of the *Wellman* factors, the Second Circuit invoked the guidelines used to determine whether an offering of securities is eligible for the private placement exemption under Securities Act § 4(1). As such, the main issue is whether the offerees are sophisticated investors who do not need the Williams Act's protections. Applying that standard, the court determined that Hanson Trust's street sweep was neither a new tender offer nor a "de facto" continuation of the withdrawn tender offer. The offerees from whom Hanson Trust bought were all professional investors fully capable of looking out for themselves.

2. *Commencement of a tender offer*

Determining when a tender offer commences is critical for several reasons. For one thing, it tells the bidder when its disclosure obligation triggers. For another, many tender offer rules contain time periods that run from the commencement date. Rule 14d–2 governs the commencement of a tender offer. It identifies two basic events that may constitute the commencement of a tender offer; whichever event takes place first in a particular offer will be the commencement date for that offer. Under Rule 14d–2(a), publishing or transmitting offering materials to the shareholders commences the offer. Under Rule 14a–2(b), subject to a limited exception, any public announcement of takeover plans commences the offer. Hence, if the bidder discloses such information as its identity, the target's identity, the amount of securities it will offer to buy, and the price it is willing to pay—the bidder has just commenced the tender offer. Pre-offer communications are exempted if they (1) do not identify the means by which target shareholders may tender their stock and (2) all written communications are filed with the SEC and issuer.

3. *Content of required disclosure*

On the day the offer commences, the bidder must file a disclosure document on Schedule 14D–1 with the SEC. Most of the information contained in the Schedule 14D–1 also must be disseminated to the target's shareholders, but the Williams Act gives the offeror two options as to how to effect that distribution. The first, and least used option, is so-called long-form publication of the offer in a newspaper. Typically one prepares an advertisement containing all the necessary disclosures and then runs the ad in the Wall Street Journal, New York Times and perhaps one or two other papers of national distribution. This option is unpopular because it is extremely expensive to buy the necessary ad space and, more important, because there is no guarantee that a substantial number of target shareholders will notice the ad or pay much attention to it.

Alternatively, and more commonly, the offeror publishes a summary of the proposal in a newspaper advertisement and then mails a more detailed disclosure statement directly to the shareholders. Although this option is probably at least as expensive as the first, if not more so, there is a fair degree of certainty that all target shareholders will receive notice of the proposal by this means. As with a proxy statement, the issuer must either provide the bidder with a copy of the shareholder list or agree to mail the tender offer materials on behalf of the offeror and at his or her expense.

Most of the disclosures in a tender offer are similar to those required in a Schedule 13D, albeit more detailed, and are fairly mechanical. Counsel just follows the instructions, inserting the usual boilerplate. The most technically difficult issue is the question of soft information disclosure. Consider two companies: Target Corp. and Acquirer Co. Suppose that Target's stock currently is trading at $15 per share. Acquirer does an extensive evaluation of Target. Acquirer prepares business plans for incorporating Target into the existing company, it commissions appraisals of Target's assets, it prepares projections of future income and operating results, and the like. At the end of this process, Acquirer determines on a reservation price of $25 per share. In other words, Acquirer concludes that an acquisition of Target would be profitable at any price up to $25 per share. Clearly, Acquirer is not obliged to disclose its actual reservation price. But what about the appraisals and forecasts from which that price was determined? Must they be disclosed?

Historically, disclosure of soft information was disfavored. In recent years, the SEC has adopted safe harbor rules permitting disclosure of certain soft information, such as appraisals and projections.[31] Because that rule does not mandate disclosure, however, it does not resolve the question at hand. Note that the issue here is different from the run of the mill omissions case under the securities laws, where the initial issue is whether the defendant had a duty to speak. In this context, the bidder has an affirmative obligation to file a Schedule 14D–1 containing significant disclosures. The question here therefore is whether the soft information in question is material, such that it also must be disclosed. Before the Third Circuit's decision in *Flynn v. Bass Brothers*,[32] most courts held that there is no affirmative duty to disclose soft information. In other words, the failure to disclose soft information was not regarded as a material omission. In *Flynn*, however, the Third Circuit held that courts must make a case-by-case determination of whether soft information, such as asset appraisals and projections of future earnings are material. The standard to be applied is whether the benefits to the shareholders will outweigh the harm to the shareholders. The factors the court will consider include: the qualifications of those who prepared the information; the purpose for which it was intended; its relevance to the

---

31. The relevant Securities Exchange Act rule is Rule 3b–6.

32. Flynn v. Bass Bros. Enterprises, Inc., 744 F.2d 978, 988 (3d Cir.1984).

decision; the degree of subjectivity in its preparation; the degree to which the information is unique; and the availability of other more reliable sources of information.

A growing number of courts have followed *Flynn* in holding that soft information must be disclosed in appropriate cases, although some remain skeptical of imposing such a duty.[33] What rule would a diversified investor prefer? Returning to the hypothetical developed above, assume the pre-announcement market price for Target's stock was $15. Assume that Acquirer's appraisal predicts that the deal will be profitable at any price up to $25. The total gain from this transaction is $10 per share: the difference between what the stock is currently trading at and the maximum price Acquirer is willing to pay. Obviously Acquirer doesn't want to pay more than $25 per share. It should be equally obvious that Acquirer would like to pay less than $25 per share. The issue then is how we will divide up the gain from the transaction between the Target shareholders and Acquirer. If Acquirer is forced to disclose the soft information on which its reservation price is premised, several bad things happen: Target shareholders will have a better sense of the company is worth to Acquirer and therefore will demand a higher price. Target might itself adopt any value-enhancing ideas disclosed by Acquirer or use the disclosures as a means of persuading competing bidders to enter the picture.

Disclosure thus forces the bidder to share information its worked to acquire, resulting in a transfer of wealth from the first bidder to target shareholders and/or subsequent bidders. This wealth transfer discourages prospective bidders from investing in takeover activity, reducing the overall number of takeovers. Put another way, the lower the bidder's return, the lower the level of investment. Mandatory disclosure thus results in fewer deals but higher prices in those that take place.[34] Once

33. For a useful head count and discussion of the competing standards, see Walker v. Action Indus., Inc., 802 F.2d 703, 708–09 (4th Cir.1986).

34. This argument was put forward quite early by Professor Daniel Fischel, who argued that the cash tender offer is "the most effective means now available for wresting control from a resisting management." Daniel R. Fischel, Efficient Capital Market Theory, the Market for Corporate Control, and the Regulation of Cash Tender Offers, 57 Tex. L. Rev. 1, 2 (1978). Fischel contended that the tender offer premium usually results from the offeror's "belief that it can manage the target company more efficiently than present managers." Id. Hence, he asserted, "the firm and society in general ... benefit from a transfer of control to more capable management." Id. To explain Fischel's analysis with a mathematical hypothetical, assume that under current management, the target's shares are priced at $100 per share and that under

the offeror's management, they would trade at $200 per share. Thus, if the offer is successful there is a net increase in social welfare of $100 per share. Fischel argues that the disclosure requirements of the Williams Act force the offeror to "alert the [target] shareholder that his shares will be worth more under new management." Id. at 25. This increases the cost of the tender offer by increasing the premium the offeror must pay, thereby "greatly reduc[ing] the incentive to undertake a takeover attempt." Id. at 14. It is this disincentive that produces regulatory inefficiency. Expanding the hypothetical, further assume that there are 100 companies that are potential targets, each with 100 shares, and that each would be subject to a successful offer in the absence of regulation. Thus, when all offers are completed, there will be a net social gain of one million dollars. Now assume that regulation of tender offers will deter 10% of all offers, because of the increased costs of completing the offer. Thus, there

again, we are required to determine whether diversified investors are better off with a rule that maximizes the control premium in a given case or a rule that maximizes the number of takeovers. As before, some scholars argue that, because a diversified investor is as likely to be a shareholder of Acquirer as of Target, such an investor should be indifferent to how takeover gains are distributed. Instead, such an investor should prefer a rule maximizing the number of deals, which in this context is a rule permitting acquirers to withhold soft information.

This analysis depends in the first instance on an assumption that the rules of the takeover game ought to be drafted without regard for their effect on nondiversified investors. This assumption is admittedly controversial,[35] but seems a logical extension of portfolio theory. The risk of being on the "wrong" side of a takeover is akin to the risk of owning stock in a company whose sole line of business is outlawed. In other words, it is an unsystematic risk, which the investor could eliminate through diversification. Accordingly, portfolio theory posits, investors need not—and should not—be compensated for voluntarily assuming nondiversified unsystematic risk. Because mutual funds and similar investments offer readily available opportunities for diversification at low cost, the law should not create special protections for investors who refuse to protect themselves by diversifying. Put another way, just as the tort law doctrine of assumption of risk bars recovery, the law should treat nondiversified investors as having "assumed the risk." Where a rule would benefit nondiversified investors at the expense of those who have diversified, the case for protecting the former seems particularly weak.

Conceding that we ought to privilege diversification, however, does not resolve the debate. As before, the analysis may change if certain conditions are not satisfied. If acquirers are systematically more likely to be privately held than are targets, for example, rational diversified investors could prefer a rule maximizing premiums. More important, if rational diversified investors believe that acquirer company boards and managers will fritter away the gains of takeovers in ways that do not benefit their shareholders, such investors may prefer to maximize cash in hand. Recall the evidence that acquiring company shareholders on average do not gain from takeovers, which suggests that such frittering occurs. If so, rational investors will prefer a rule that maximizes the product of the number of deals and the average premium over rules that

would be a $100,000 reduction in net social welfare. It is this reduction to which Fischel objects. "By increasing the cost of making a tender offer and by reducing the exchange value of privately produced information, the Williams Act limits the effectiveness of cash tender offers and thereby undermines a check against entrenched inefficient management to the detriment of current shareholders." Id. at 26, 45.

35. See, e.g., Victor Brudney, Equal Treatment of Shareholders in Corporate Distributions and Reorganizations, 71 Cal. L. Rev. 1072, 1100 n.85 (1983) ("The morality of a proposal which requires investors to diversify in order to protect themselves against the appropriative behavior of controllers, but which does not seek to prevent the appropriative behavior itself, is not self-evident."); Morey W. McDaniel, Bondholders and Stockholders, 13 J. Corp. L. 205, 243 (1988) ("investors should not be penalized because they are not diversified or because they are not diversified enough").

maximize one at the expense of the other. This analysis suggests a slightly different balancing test than the one adopted in *Flynn*. The appropriate balancing test weighs the "potential aid such information will give a shareholder" against the extent of the acquirer's proprietary interest in the information.

4. Procedural rules

In addition to the basic disclosure provisions, the Williams Act provides a number of procedural protections for target shareholders. For example, shareholders are permitted to withdraw shares tendered to the bidder at any time prior to the closing of the offer. In Section 14(d)(5), the statute actually provides that tendered shares may only be withdrawn during the 7 days after the offer commences and at any time 60 days after commencement of the bid (assuming that the offer has not been closed and the shares taken up during that 60 day period). SEC Rule 14d–7, however, permits withdrawal for up to 15 days after commencement of the offer. The rule triggers withdrawal rights if a competing bid is made during the tender offer period. Shareholders thus have substantial opportunity to change their minds, especially if a better offer comes along.

Rule 14e–1 obligates the bidder to keep the tender offer open for at least 20 business days. In addition, the bidder must further extend the tender offer period by at least 10 business days after material changes in the offer's terms. In particular, the bidder must extend the offer by 10 days if it raises the offering price.

In partial tender offers, if more than the specified number of shares are tendered Rule 14d–8 requires the offeror to take up the tendered shares on a pro rata basis. This ensures that all shareholders who tender get a chance to receive a premium for at least part of their shares. The rule eliminates a favorite pre-Williams Act tactic, in which bidders made a partial offer on a first come-first served basis. This tactic pressures shareholders to tender, so as to avoid being left as minority shareholders in a company under new control. To eliminate a similar tactic, Rule 14d–10 provides that if the bidder, during the pendency of the offer, increases the consideration to be paid, shareholders who have already tendered their shares are entitled to receive that additional consideration.

5. Target obligations

As long as they are acting in good faith, the target's directors have no legal duty to negotiate with a prospective acquirer. The target's board likewise has no duty to make a detailed response to hypothetical questions or hypothetical offers. Once a firm, bona fide offer is on the table, however, the target's board has a state corporate law-based fiduciary obligation to consider carefully the proposed acquisition.[36] To be sure,

---

36. See, e.g., Norlin Corp. v. Rooney, Pace Inc., 744 F.2d 255, 267 (2d Cir.1984) ("we have required corporate managers to examine carefully the merits of a proposed change in control ... [and] have also urged consultation with investment specialists in

the "business judgment" rule "leaves relatively wide discretion in management to act in what it considers to be the best interests of the corporation."[37] Recall, however, that an informed decision is an essential prerequisite for the rule's application.[38]

In evaluating a bona fide proposal, the following factors are legitimate and relevant considerations:

1. The adequacy of the offering price in terms of variables such as (i) current and past market prices of the target's stock,[39] (ii) book value and replacement cost of assets, (iii) earnings projections, (iv) "hidden" or off balance sheet assets, (v) future prospects for improvements in earnings or market value, (vi) market conditions, (vii) liquidation value of assets, (viii) if all shares are sought, the potential sales price of the business (a full financial picture of the target should be prepared), (ix) recent sales prices of other similarly situated companies, (x) premiums over book value paid in recent "friendly" acquisitions and hostile takeovers of other similar companies, and (xi) the probability that a higher price could be obtained from another offeror.

2. The nature of the consideration offered, e.g., cash or securities (and, if securities, the prospects of the company to which they relate).

3. Whether the acquirer is seeking all or a portion of the target stock; if a partial offer, the effect upon remaining shareholders, i.e., what generally would be the prospects for the minority in

undertaking such analysis.... [t]he purpose of this exercise ... is to insure a reasoned examination of the situation before action is taken, not afterwards"); Smith v. Van Gorkom, 488 A.2d 858, 872 (Del.1985) ("Representation of the financial interests of others imposes on a director an affirmative duty to protect those interests and to proceed with a critical eye in assessing information of the type and under the circumstances present....").

37. Berman v. Gerber Products Co., 454 F.Supp. 1310, 1319 (W.D.Mich.1978).

38. Smith v. Van Gorkom, 488 A.2d 858, 872 (Del.1985) (directors must inform themselves of "all material information reasonably available to them"). Depending on the circumstances, the views of non-management directors with regard to any proposal may be given particular weight. See Panter v. Marshall Field & Co., 646 F.2d 271, 294 (7th Cir.1981) ("The presumption of good faith the business judgment rule affords is heightened when the majority of the board consists of independent outside directors.").

39. In evaluating the adequacy of an offer, the mere fact that a target's shares may trade below the offer price does not mean that the price was sufficient, since the ordinary trading market does not reflect the target's value in an acquisition. The proper comparison is not between the price of the stock in the market and the offer price, but rather between the offer price and the price which could otherwise be obtained upon a sale of the entire company. As the Delaware supreme court has noted, "[a] substantial premium may provide one reason to recommend a merger, but in the absence of other sound valuation information, the fact of a premium alone does not provide an adequate basis upon which to assess the fairness of an offering price.... [Because] the Board had made no evaluation of the Company designed to value the entire enterprise, nor had the Board ever previously considered selling the Company or consenting to a buy-out merger ... the adequacy of a premium is indeterminate unless it is assessed in terms of other competent and sound valuation information that reflects the value of the particular business." Smith v. Van Gorkom, 488 A.2d 858, 875–76 (Del.1985).

the case of a successful partial offer, and in particular, whether there would be a subsequent merger and if so, on what terms.[40]

4. If applicable, the regulatory implications of the offer and the likelihood that the suitor could obtain regulatory approvals.

5. The offeror's background, business practices and intention towards the company.

The latter two considerations are especially pertinent with respect to the target board's potential duty to affirmatively oppose an offer. Where the directors know or have reason to know that a potential acquirer would loot or mismanage the target company, for example, they have a duty to oppose the offer.[41] Likewise, where the target's directors believe that an offer is illegal for regulatory reasons, they also have a duty to oppose it.[42]

Where the initial offer by the suitor includes an invitation to negotiate, the directors of the target may enter into negotiations if they so choose, of course. Negotiation may disclose useful information, as well as providing the target company more time to evaluate and respond to the situation. The target company may condition its willingness to enter into negotiations on the suitor's agreement not to make an unfriendly offer. On the other hand, there are several potential disadvantages to entering into negotiations with an unwanted suitor. Negotiating could also give the suitor the impression that an offer might be accepted if the terms were different. This could encourage the suitor to disbelieve management objections and to pursue its proposal persistently when it might otherwise withdraw. Any counter-offer made by the target could undermine subsequent arguments to shareholders attacking the suitor. If discussions included a consideration of management's or the directors' future with the target company, claims could be raised that management or directors received improper benefits.

Once the target board has carefully considered the offer, and the offer has commenced, the Williams Act mandates a target board disclosure statement on Schedule 14D–9.[43] Before filing the Schedule 14D–9, the target may only send communications to its shareholders if those communications are limited to three matters: (i) identifying the offeror; (ii) stating that the target is studying the tender offer and will, before a specified date, advise as to its position; and (iii) requesting shareholders to defer making a determination on whether to accept or reject the

---

40. For example, the directors should consider the likely market liquidity of the shares held by the remaining shareholders, and whether this is the first step in a "freezeout" of the minority in light of Weinberger v. UOP, Inc., 457 A.2d 701 (Del.1983).

41. Harman v. Willbern, 374 F.Supp. 1149, 1158–59 (D.Kan.1974), aff'd, 520 F.2d 1333 (10th Cir.1975).

42. Panter v. Marshall Field & Co., 646 F.2d 271, 297 (7th Cir.1981); Berman v. Gerber Products Co., 454 F.Supp. 1310, 1323 (W.D.Mich.1978).

43. Before the offer has actually commenced, the issue is whether a proposal is material information the target is required to disclose. In general, no announcement need be made of invitations to negotiate or of casual inquiries. Panter v. Marshall Field & Co., 646 F.2d 271, 296 (7th Cir.1981) ("Directors are under no duty to reveal every approach made by a would-be acquiror or merger partner.").

tender offer until they have been advised of the target's position. Under SEC Rule 14e–2, the target must disclose to shareholders within 10 business days of the commencement of a tender offer whether the target's board: (i) recommends acceptance or rejection of the tender offer; (ii) expresses no opinion and is remaining neutral with respect to the tender offer; or (iii) is unable to take a position with respect to the tender offer. The statement also must include the board's reason or reasons for its position. Pursuant to Rule 14d–9(f), this communication is deemed to be a recommendation or solicitation and therefore requires the filing of Schedule 14D–9 with the SEC. The Schedule 14D–9 must disclose: (i) the reasons supporting the board's recommendations, (ii) any arrangements or understandings between members of management or the board and the offeror, (iii) the identity and employment capacity of the persons making the recommendations, and (iv) information as to all transactions by officers or directors effected during the 60 days prior to the filing of the Schedule 14D–9 in the securities that are the subject of the offer.

C. Tender offer litigation

Tender offers generate a lot of litigation: the target sues the bidder; the bidder sues the target; target shareholders sue both the target board and the bidder; the SEC sues the target and/or the bidder. It is a litigator's dream and a transactional lawyer's nightmare. None of the relevant statutes explicitly grant a cause of action to private parties. As with § 13(d) litigation, the questions therefore are (1) whether an implied private right of action exists and (2) if so, does the party in question have standing?

In its infinite wisdom, the United States Supreme Court has seen fit over time to offer up at least four distinct approaches to creating implied private rights of action:

1. The old *Borak* rule, under which the court creates an implied right of action whenever private enforcement of the statute is necessary to supplement SEC efforts.[44] Although *Borak* has not been expressly overruled, it has been effectively limited to the proxy setting.[45]

2. A four factor standard announced in *Cort*,[46] which asks: "First, is the plaintiff one of the class for whose especial benefit the statute was enacted …? Second, is there any indication of legislative intent, explicit or implicit, either to create such a remedy or to deny one? … Third, is it consistent with the underlying purposes of the legislative scheme to imply such a

---

44. J.I. Case Co. v. Borak, 377 U.S. 426 (1964).

45. See, e.g., Reschini v. First Fed. Sav. & Loan Ass'n of Ind., 46 F.3d 246, 255 (3d Cir.1995) (holding that *Borak* "is still good law as a construction of the 1934 Act and Rule 14a–9," but noting that "it is not clear that *Borak*, if it arose for the first time today, would be decided the same way").

46. Cort v. Ash, 422 U.S. 66 (1975).

remedy for the plaintiff? ... And finally, is the cause of action one traditionally relegated to state law, in an area basically the concern of the States, so that it would be inappropriate to infer a cause of action based solely on federal law?"[47]

3. The strict constructionist approach announced in *Touche Ross*, which mandates a very narrow focus on legislative intent.[48]

4. The legal context approach of *Curran*, also known as the re-enactment approach, which asks whether Congress has amended the statute in question without overruling judicial decisions creating an implied right of action under a federal statute.[49] If so, it will be assumed that Congress expressly intended to preserve the implied remedy.

Unfortunately, the only Supreme Court guidance on implied private rights of action under the Williams Act pre-dates the latter two approaches. In *Piper v. Chris–Craft*, the Court addressed the standing of a defeated tender offeror to sue a successful competing bidder and the target for damages under § 14(e)'s antifraud provision. In late 1968, Chris–Craft mounted a takeover bid for Piper. The Piper board of directors enlisted Bangor–Punta as a white knight—a competing bidder more acceptable to the target's incumbent directors and managers. By the time Bangor–Punta's competing offer commenced, Chris–Craft had already acquired about 13% of Piper's outstanding shares. Bangor–Punta ultimately prevailed, acquiring just over 50% of the stock. Chris–Craft was left owning just over 40% of the shares. Chris–Craft sued Piper, its underwriter, and Bangor–Punta. Chris–Craft's main allegation was that Bangor–Punta listed a railroad as a subsidiary in a filing sent to Piper's shareholders in connection with the exchange offer. Chris–Craft alleged that Bangor–Punta failed to disclose that the railroad was about to be sold at a loss, which allegedly violated § 14(e)'s prohibition of fraud in connection with a tender offer. This nondisclosure allegedly caused Piper's shareholders to accept Bangor–Punta's offer in reliance on misleading disclosures relating to Bangor–Punta's fixed assets.

It is important to understand the nature of the alleged injury at issue in this case. Bear in mind that Chris–Craft ended up as the minority shareholder of Piper, with Bangor–Punta as the controlling shareholder. Chris–Craft, of course, had paid a substantial premium over market in buying its Piper shares. But once the Bangor–Punta offer succeeded, the value of Chris–Craft's Piper holdings fell sharply. As we know, the value of any share of stock reflects the market's consensus as to the present value of the bundle of rights conferred by stockownership. Among the relevant valuation factors are: the value of the stream of future dividends, voting rights, and the probability of future takeover attempts at a premium. The decline in value of Chris–Craft's holdings

---

47. California v. Sierra Club, 451 U.S. 287, 293 (1981).

48. Touche Ross & Co. v. Redington, 442 U.S. 560 (1979).

49. Merrill Lynch, Pierce, Fenner & Smith, Inc. v. Curran, 456 U.S. 353 (1982).

reflected two basic facts of takeover life: First, Bangor–Punta now had a controlling stock position, such that the voting rights of the minority shareholders were now essentially worthless. Second, since Bangor–Punta had a controlling stock position, nobody could obtain control by buying the rest of Piper's outstanding stock. Thus, the possibility of future takeover premiums was also lost.

The lower court held that Chris–Craft had a cause of action for damages against Bangor–Punta and Piper under § 14(e). The court measured the amount of Chris–Craft's damages by the difference between what Chris–Craft paid to buy its block and the much lower price Chris–Craft could have obtained by selling that block in a public offering immediately after Bangor–Punta obtained control, which worked out to about $37 per share. The Supreme Court reversed on standing grounds—defeated tender offerors lack standing to sue for damages arising out of a violation of § 14(e).

Two years before *Piper*, the Supreme Court had decided *Cort v. Ash*, in which it created a four factor test to be used by courts in creating new implied private rights of action. Post-*Piper* cases have purported to overrule *Cort*. As Justice Scalia has explained, the Court "effectively overruled the *Cort v. Ash* analysis in *Touche Ross* ... and *Transamerica* ... converting one of [*Cort*'s] four factors (congressional intent) into the *determinative factor*."[50] Having said that, however, the other three *Cort* factors remain relevant insofar as they assist in determining congressional intent.[51] Consequently, it is still useful to analyze *Piper* by working through the original four factor test.

The first *Cort* factor asks whether plaintiff was part of the class for whose especial benefit the statute was enacted. Chris–Craft was a Piper shareholder—it started out owning about 13% and ended up owning over 40% of Piper's stock. Chris–Craft, however, was not the kind of shareholder which Congress wanted to protect. Congress was worried about public shareholders caught between the offeror and management. Congress was trying to regulate offerors for the benefit of independent shareholders. Chris–Craft was thus part of the regulated class, not the benefited class, and, as such, was not part of the especial class.

The second *Cort* factor, now deemed determinative, is whether there is any indication of a legislative intent, explicit or implicit, either to create or deny a remedy. The strongest argument for Chris–Craft's position is based on the claim that the Williams Act was intended to be neutral as between bidders and target management. In order to preserve a level playing field between the contending parties, a frequently used analogy, Congress must have wanted the courts to let managers and bidders sue each other for violations of the statute so as to ensure that the competition is fair. The Court acknowledged that Congress adopted a policy of neutrality as between bidders and target management, but said

50. Thompson v. Thompson, 484 U.S. 174, 189 (1988) (Scalia, J., concurring) (emphasis in original).

51. Touche Ross & Co. v. Redington, 442 U.S. 560, 575–76 (1979).

the neutrality policy has nothing to do with the protection of tender offerors or their standing to sue for violations of the statute. Rather, the neutrality policy was designed to help achieve the principal purpose of the Williams Act; namely, the protection of independent shareholders through a regime of full and fair disclosure by offerors. It also was intended to rebut criticisms that the legislation favored target management. Because Congress' intent was to regulate the previously unregulated conduct of bidders, it is hard to see why Congress would have wanted to give bidders an additional weapon. The whole point was to protect shareholders from offerors—not to enhance the rights of offerors.

The third *Cort* factor is whether it is consistent with the underlying purposes of the legislative scheme to imply such a remedy for the plaintiff. Chris–Craft lost on this point too. The court emphasized that it was difficult to accept the contention Chris–Craft's recovery would benefit the other Piper shareholders. Although a recovery would benefit the old Piper shareholders who are now shareholders of Chris–Craft, it would harm the larger group of old Piper shareholders who are now shareholders of Bangor–Punta and who would therefore bear the burden of the damages payment. The Supreme Court's argument made sense in this case, because the Bangor–Punta tender offer was an exchange offer in which the consideration was paid in the form of Bangor–Punta shares. Would the court's argument still make sense if Bangor–Punta had paid cash, such that the old Piper shareholders would not now be Bangor–Punta stockholders? Yes, although you lose the make-weight argument that a recovery would harm the majority of old Piper shareholders. The point is that a recovery by Chris–Craft would benefit Chris–Craft and Chris–Craft alone—this was not a class action brought to champion the rights of all Piper shareholders.[52] This was a lawsuit arising out of the fact that Chris–Craft was stuck with a minority position and had lost the difference between the price it paid for Piper stock and the present value of Piper shares. Thus, even if Bangor–Punta's offer had been for cash, a Chris–Craft recovery would not have benefited the old Piper shareholders.

The fourth *Cort* factor is whether the cause of action is one traditionally relegated to state law. The Supreme Court held that granting Chris–Craft a cause of action on these facts would be tantamount to creation of a federal cause of action for tortious interference with a prospective commercial advantage. This cause of action has traditionally been a matter of state tort law. Hence, so offerors should be relegated to their state law remedies, if any, until Congress acts.

---

52. Chris-Craft could not have brought its suit as a class action on behalf of all Piper shareholders, because nobody but Chris–Craft was injured. The shareholders who sold to Chris–Craft got a premium from Chris–Craft, and in any event obviously didn't rely on the alleged misstatements. The shareholders who sold to Piper also weren't injured—selling the railroad at a loss caused the value of their new Bangor–Punta shares to rise, not fall. The shareholders who didn't sell to either side also weren't injured, as there is nothing to suggest that the misstatement caused them to hold on to their shares.

So on all the relevant factors, Chris–Craft lost. Hence, no standing for tender offerors for damages. As one might expect, lower courts have extended *Piper* to preclude standing by target companies to bring an implied private right of action for damages under all of the applicable statutes. In doing so, they have relied mainly on *Piper*'s emphasis on the notion that target managers and bidders were part of the regulated class, not the special class benefited by the statute. As for shareholders, the majority rule denies damages standing to target shareholders under virtually all provisions except § 14(e). As with § 13(d) litigation, all three relevant players—bidders, targets, and target shareholders—generally have been given standing to bring an implied private right of action for equitable relief under all of the Williams Act's various provisions.

The distinction between equitable and damage remedies makes sense. Since *Borak*, the basic justification for implied private rights of action has been the concept of private attorneys general. As Chris–Craft argued, defeated bidders have a special interest in uncovering violations. Consequently, granting Chris–Craft standing to bring a cause of action will benefit shareholders by furthering enforcement of the federal securities laws. Yet, while deterrence is desirable, it ought to be achieved in an efficient manner. Deterrence is a function of the nominal sanction imposed and the probability of detection and conviction. When detection is costly or difficult and hence unlikely, the nominal sanction must increase to compensate and effect deterrence. In the case of Williams Act violations, the probability of detection is relatively high. The offeror must file with the SEC and both target and bidder have plenty of incentive to look for illegal conduct. Consequently, the nominal sanction does not need to be very large in order for there to be adequate levels of deterrence. Indeed, if the sanction is large in these cases you may have over-deterrence—you may deter beneficial conduct that falls close to the line between legal and illegal actions. If we think takeovers, especially takeovers in which there is competitive bidding, are a good thing, we don't want too much deterrence. This principle explains why damage relief is uniformly denied—the courts, following the Supreme Court's lead in *Piper*, must believe that damage penalties would create too high a level of deterrence. Conversely, if one side is free to lie and cheat, subject only to the risk of SEC enforcement, the level playing field may tip in that party's favor. Injunctive relief—especially when limited to corrective disclosure—seems like a fairly nonintrusive means of helping to maintain the level playing field envisioned by the Act. The party with the most incentive to seek legal relief will be given an opportunity to prevent misstatements and other violations, while not creating excessive levels of deterrence.

In any event, having identified who has standing to seek what remedies for violations of the tender offer statutes, the obvious next task is identifying the elements of the cause of action. The elements of the injunctive action are essentially the same as those for injunctive relief under the proxy rules—assuming you can show the traditional grounds for equitable relief, all you have to show is that the defendant failed to file a required document or that the defendant's filing contains a material misstatement or omission.

§ 12.9 Takeover defenses: The arsenal

As we have seen, the target's board of directors functions as a sort of gatekeeper in statutory acquisitions. A key feature of the nonstatutory acquisition forms, from the acquirer's perspective, thus is the ability to bypass the target board and make an offer directly to the target's shareholders. When the hostile tender offer emerged in the 1970s as an important acquirer tool, lawyers and investment bankers working for target boards began to develop defensive tactics designed to impede such offers. Takeover defenses reasserted the board's primacy, by extending their gatekeeping function to the nonstatutory acquisition setting. The takeover arms race remains unrelenting. As fast as new acquisition techniques are developed, new defenses spring up.

A. Shark repellents

A shark repellent is an amendment to the firm's articles of incorporation designed to persuade potential bidders to look elsewhere. Broadly speaking, shark repellents fall into two principal categories: provisions relating to the board of directors and supermajority voting requirements for certain transactions.

1. Classified boards

Classified board provisions, which are also known as staggered boards, divide the board of directors into three classes of which only one is elected annually. The offeror thus must go through two annual meeting cycles before it has elected a majority of the board. This defense will be most effective as to an acquirer who needs quick access to target assets to pay off acquisition debt. If the acquirer can wait out the current board, the provisions will be of little benefit. Many factors will tend to lead the current board to play along with a successful acquirer—even if the board has the right to hold-out. Why should any director, except maybe an insider, risk being sued by the acquirer every time they do something he or she opposes?[1]

The classification scheme must be protected from the possibility that the acquirer will (1) remove the directors without cause or (2) pack the board with his or her own appointments. This can be done by reserving to the board the sole right to determine the number of directors and the sole right to fill any vacancies. If permitted by state law, also limit or abolish the right of shareholders to call a special shareholders meeting or

---

§ 12.9

1. Ronald J. Gilson, The Case Against Shark Repellent Amendments: Structural Limitations on the Enabling Concept, 34 Stan. L. Rev. 775, 793 (1982). Although the classified board seemingly has limited utility standing alone, we shall see below that it can become a very effective device when coupled with a poison pill. See generally John C. Coates IV, Takeover Defenses in the Shadow of the Pill: A Critique of the Scientific Evidence, 79 Tex. L. Rev. 271, 325–28 (2000).

to remove directors without cause (defining cause as narrowly as possible).

2. *Supermajority vote requirements*

Supermajority provisions focus on preventing back-end freezeout mergers. It is rare for even a highly successful hostile tender offeror to purchase 100% of the shares. The bidder therefore will usually follow a successful offer with a freezeout merger to eliminate any remaining minority shareholders.

In some cases, a bidder may intentionally use a back-end merger to ensure success. In a so-called "two-tier offer," the bidder makes a partial tender offer and simultaneously announces its intention to subsequently acquire the remaining shares of the company in a subsequent merger. Often, the price paid in the second step merger will be lower than the tender offer price and/or be paid in a less desirable form of consideration. Such offers are said to be structurally coercive.[2] Such an offer works because collective action problems preclude shareholders from communicating with each other and from credibly binding themselves to reject offers not in their collective best interests. Suppose the bidder makes a tender offer for 51% of the target's stock at $50 per share in cash, while announcing an intent to follow up a successful offer with a freezeout merger at $40 per share to be paid in the form of subordinated debt securities. An individual shareholder might believe that the offer is unacceptable, but worry that a majority of the other stockholders will accept the offer. A shareholder who does not tender thus risks having all of his shares acquired in the less desirable back-end transaction, which creates an incentive to tender into the front-end transaction. If the shareholder tenders, however, some pro rata portion of his shares will be taken up in the higher paying front-end.

A freezeout merger generally only requires approval by a majority of the outstanding shares. As a result, the outcome of the shareholder vote often will be a foregone conclusion in light of the acquirer's holdings. Supermajority voting shark repellents erect barriers to second-step transactions by imposing a supermajority voting requirement for mergers, asset sales, and like transactions. A typical formulation requires that any merger be approved by 80% of all outstanding shares and a majority of the outstanding shares not owned by the bidder. Such provisions are authorized by DGCL § 102(b)(4), which authorizes the articles of incorporation to include: "Provisions requiring for any corporate action, the vote of a larger portion of the stock or of any class or series thereof...."[3]

---

2. See, e.g., Chesapeake Corp. v. Shore, 771 A.2d 293, 331 (Del.Ch.2000); City Capital Assoc. Ltd. Partnership v. Interco Inc., 551 A.2d 787, 797 (Del.Ch.1988).

3. See Seibert v. Milton Bradley Co., 405 N.E.2d 131 (Mass.1980) (upholding by-law requiring 75% approval of a merger unless the merger was approved by a two-thirds vote of the board of directors); Seibert v. Gulton Indus., Inc., 1979 WL 2710 (Del.Ch.1979) (upholding a supermajority vote shark repellent requiring an 80% vote to approve mergers with another person or entity owning 5% or more of the outstanding stock).

Supermajority vote shark repellents usually provide that the supermajority provision can be deleted or amended only by a vote equal to the supermajority vote. Hence, for example, amending an 80% vote requirement would have to be approved by 80% of all outstanding shares. This requirement is obviously intended to prevent the offeror from avoiding the supermajority vote by the simple expedient of amending the charter. In order to permit friendly transactions, most of these provisions provide that transactions approved by a majority or supermajority of the continuing directors—those in office when the raider first acquired a substantial interest in the target (say 10%)—shall not be subject to the supermajority shareholder vote requirement.

3.   The fair price variant

Fair price shark repellents are a variant on the supermajority vote provision. This version exempts transactions from the supermajority vote where the price to be paid exceeds a specified amount. The specified "fair price" usually is not less than the price paid in the first-step transaction. In addition, fair price provisions also typically require that the second-step payment be made in the same form of consideration. Hence, they prevent the offeror from paying cash in the first-step and junk bonds in the second. A related alternative is a compulsory redemption provision that allows minority shareholders to demand to be bought out at a price at least equal to the price paid in the first-step transaction.

4.   Supermajority and fair price provisions in action

The supermajority vote and fair price variants of shark repellents will be most effective when the aggregate holdings of insiders and persons with demonstrated loyalty to present management are sufficient to block the second-step transaction. If the necessary vote is 80% of the outstanding shares, for example, and insiders own more than 20%, it will be difficult for an acquirer to obtain the necessary approval. Supermajority vote shark repellents, however, are effective only against bidders who want to acquire 100% ownership. If the acquirer is willing to live with a frozen-in minority, the second-step barrier is essentially meaningless. Note that compulsory redemption provisions may deter even that class of raiders, because they require the bidder to buy out the minority at a fair price.

The effectiveness of these provisions largely depends on the minority having not only the power, but also the will, to exercise their rights. Exercising one's rights under these charter provisions often results in current managers being frozen into a substantially less liquid minority investment. In many cases, management may not want to be caught in that position. As with staggered board provisions, they may prefer to waive their rights and get out from under a determined bidder, albeit at a price.

B. Poison pills

Poison pills take a wide variety of forms, but today most are based on the class of security known as a right. Hence, the pill's official name, the "shareholder rights plan." A traditional right, such as a warrant, grants the holder the option to purchase new shares of stock of the issuing corporation. The modern poison pill adds three additional elements not found in traditional rights: a "flip-in" element; a "flip-over" element; and a redemption provision.[4]

1. *First generation pills*

The first poison pill was adopted in 1983 by Lenox. Like most of the first generation pills, the Lenox plan was based on so-called blank check preferred stock. Many corporate charters authorize a class of preferred stock whose rights are not detailed in the articles. Instead, the preferred stock's rights are defined by the board of directors at the time the stock is issued. Typically, these provisions do not require any shareholder action—hence, the name "blank check." The Lenox pill was issued as a special dividend consisting of nonvoting convertible preferred stock, the dividend issuing at the ratio of one preferred share for every forty shares of common stock.

The anti-takeover effect of the preferred stock lay in the conversion rights conferred on its holders. If Lenox was merged into another corporation, the preferred stock became convertible into common stock of the acquiring corporation at a price well below market. Any such conversion would result in undesirable balance sheet effects for the bidder and dilute the holdings of pre-existing bidder shareholders, which would make an acquisition of Lenox less attractive.

The Lenox plan was an early variant of what are now known as flip-over plans. Modern flip-over plans start not with preferred stock as did the Lenox pill, but with the issuance of rights as a pro rata dividend on the common stock to the shareholders of the target corporation. Rights are corporate securities that give the holder of the right the option of purchasing shares. Because issuance of rights does not require shareholder approval, a rights-based pill may be adopted by the board of directors without any shareholder action.[5] When adopted, the rights initially attach to the corporation's outstanding common stock, cannot be traded separately from the common stock, and are priced so that exercise of the option would be economically irrational. The rights become exercisable, and separate from the common stock, upon a so-called distribution event, which is typically defined as the acquisition of,

---

4. Warrants are traded as separate securities, having value because they typically confer on the holder the right to buy issuer common stock at a discount from the prevailing market price. In contrast, the poison pill right usually is "stapled" to the common stock and does not trade separately until some triggering event occurs.

5. See Account v. Hilton Hotels Corp., 780 A.2d 245 (Del.2001) (noting the power of "directors of a Delaware corporation" to "adopt a rights plan unilaterally").

or announcement of an intent to acquire, some specified percentage of the issuer's stock by a prospective acquirer. (Twenty percent is a commonly used trigger level.) Although the rights are now exercisable, and will remain so for the remainder of their specified life (typically ten years), they remain out of the money.

The pill's flip-over feature typically is triggered if, following the acquisition of a specified percentage of the target's common stock, the target is subsequently merged into the acquirer or one of its affiliates. In such an event, the holder of each right becomes entitled to purchase common stock of the acquiring company, typically at half-price, thereby impairing the acquirer's capital structure and drastically diluting the interest of the acquirer's other stockholders. In other words, once triggered, the flip-over pill gives target shareholders the option to purchase acquiring company shares at a steep discount to market. As with the older style preferred stock pills, this causes dilution for the bidder's pre-existing shareholders and may have undesirable balance sheet effects.

The first generation flip-over pills were largely ineffective in deterring takeovers. Bidders continually found flaws in the plans. The classic example of a bidder turning such a pill to its own advantage was Sir James Goldsmith's takeover of Crown Zellerbach. Like most first generation pills, the Crown Zellerbach pill only kicked in if the bidder sought to effect a freezeout merger. Goldsmith acquired a controlling interest in Crown Zellerbach, but decided not to squeeze out the remaining Crown Zellerbach shareholders. This had a rather nifty effect. Since Goldsmith wasn't going to do a merger, he didn't suffer any poisonous effects. On the other hand, since the rights were now exercisable in the event of a merger, what had happened? The pill had become a double-edged sword, which Goldsmith had redirected at the target's throat. By triggering the pill, Goldsmith precluded anyone from merging with Crown Zellerbach— any merger partner would suffer the poisonous effects. As a result, he had effectively precluded the board from attracting a white knight.

There were other ways around the first generation plans. For example, the Goldsmith strategy only worked because the Zellerbach pill was not redeemable. Suppose the target included a redemption provision, which would allow the board to repurchase the preferred shares at a nominal cost. That would defeat the Goldsmith strategy, but created its own set of problems. The bidder could simply condition its tender offer on the redemption of the plan by the target's board of directors. If the board refused to redeem the pill in the face of a fair any and all cash offer, the board took a substantial risk with its constituency.[6]

In *Moran v. Household International*, the Delaware supreme court upheld a flip-over pill against challenges based on both the board's

---

6. One could also get around a flip-over pill by placing anti-dilution provisions into the bidder's corporate charter. This would involve the issuance of shares to preexisting acquirer shareholders in proportion to the shares issued to target shareholders exercising their flip-over rights. Another possible defense to the flip-over pill involved the acquirer's giving itself a call on any shares issued in a merger at below-market prices.

authority and the board's fiduciary duties.[7] Household's poison pill was a flip-over pill, albeit with a few bells and whistles. There were two triggering events: (1) the making of a tender offer for 30 percent or more of Household's shares; and (2) the acquisition of 20% or more of Household's outstanding shares by any person or group. If issued, the rights were immediately exercisable and would entitle the holders to purchase 1/100th of a share of Household preferred stock at a price of $100. Because that price was way out of the money, there was no expectation that the rights would be exercised.

Why were the underlying rights initially stapled to the common stock? This common provision is intended to ensure that the rights trade with the common. If the rights traded separately, the potential target corporation would have to issue a separate security. More important, if the rights did not trade with the common, holders might sell common without selling the rights—or vice-versa if a separate secondary trading market developed for the rights.

Why are the rights detached from the rights in a way that initially makes them unattractive to exercise? By detaching the rights once a bidder is on the scene, the target ensures that the bidder has to buy up the rights separately. Some stockholders will tender their common or sell their common shares on the market, but retain the rights. Consequently, the bidder has to deal with two distinct groups. As for the provision under which the rights are initially convertible into preferred (out of the money) and only convertible into common (in the money) in the event of a second-step transaction, it is intended to preclude an argument that the right was a sham security. DGCL § 157 allows the corporation to issue rights, but does not facially authorize the issuance of rights for takeover defenses purposes. Presumably, the transaction planner who devised the pill intended that this provision would make it appear as though the rights had economic value.

Note that the Household pill, if triggered by the making of a tender offer for 30% or more of the stock, was redeemable. The board could redeem the rights at a price of 50 cents per right at any time prior to their being exercised. If the pill was triggered by the acquisition of 20% or more of the stock, however, the rights were not redeemable. The transaction planner presumably intended this distinction to deter hostile beachhead acquisitions exceeding 20% of the shares, while still allowing a friendly deal to be accomplished by means of a tender offer.

In *Moran*, plaintiff argued that the board lacked authority to adopt a poison pill. Plaintiff contended, for example, that Delaware law, if it

---

7. Moran v. Household Int'l, Inc., 500 A.2d 1346 (Del.1985). The Delaware supreme court recently invoked the principle of stare decisis to reject a post-*Moran* challenge to poison pills: "It is indisputable that *Moran* established a board's authority to adopt a rights plan." Account v. Hilton Hotels Corp., 780 A.2d 245 (Del.2001). "To recognize viability of the [plaintiff's] claim would emasculate the basic holding of *Moran*, both as to this case and *in futuro*, that directors of a Delaware corporation may adopt a rights plan unilaterally. The Chancellor determined that the doctrine of *stare decisis* precluded that result and we agree." Id.

allowed poison pills, would be preempted by the Williams Act. The Delaware court brushed this argument off by positing that there was no state action where private parties act pursuant to a state statute authorizing their conduct.

Plaintiff also contended that DGCL § 157 did not authorize the issuance of the rights. As we've already seen, Household's poison pill was structured so as to avoid the anticipated § 157–based claim that the rights were a sham security. A second issue, however, was presented by § 157's authorization of rights "entitling the holders thereof to purchase from the corporation any shares of *its* capital stock."[8] How could Household issue rights that purport to give its shareholders the right to buy shares of another corporation? In *Moran*, the court analogized the Household pill to the anti-destruction provisions commonly found in convertible securities. Anti-destruction clauses are a common feature of convertible securities. They give holders of target company convertible securities the right to convert their securities into whatever securities the acquiring company is offering in exchange for target company common stock. Because anti-destruction provisions are valid, and the right was not a sham security, the court upheld the pill.

Plaintiffs' final broad category of authority arguments asserted that the board has no power to block shareholders from receiving tender offers. Although the *Moran* decision recognized that the board can erect defenses that deter certain types of bids, it implied that the board must leave some mechanism by which the bidder can present an offer to the shareholders. The court thus upheld the Household pill because there were several methods by which one could structure the offer so as to avoid the pill's poisonous effects, including conditioning the offer on redemption of the pill by board, soliciting written consents to remove board at same time that the offer is made, and conducting a proxy contest to oust the incumbent board.[9]

2. *Second generation pills*

As the defects in the first generation of pills became increasingly obvious, takeover lawyers developed new features to close the various loopholes that had been identified. Among the most important of these was the so-called flip-in element, which prevents a bidder from implementing the Goldsmith strategy. In a flip-in plan, rights again are issued

---

8. DGCL § 157 (emphasis supplied).

9. Plaintiff argued that Household's pill precluded shareholders from exercising their right to conduct a proxy contest. Delaware law provides that a board may not erect takeover defenses that disenfranchise its shareholders without a "compelling justification." See, e.g., Unitrin, Inc. v. American Gen. Corp., 651 A.2d 1361, 1379 (Del. 1995); Stroud v. Grace, 606 A.2d 75, 92 n. 3 (Del.1992); Blasius Indus., Inc. v. Atlas Corp., 564 A.2d 651 (Del.Ch.1988). While the board thus cannot preclude proxy contests, the *Moran* court concluded that Household's pill did not do so. Soliciting proxies did not trigger the pill, even if the challenger held proxies for more than 20% of the shares. Moreover, the court concluded that even though the pill would effectively prohibit one from buying more than 20% of the shares before conducting a proxy contest that restriction was unlikely to have a significant impact on the success rate of such contests. Moran v. Household Int'l, Inc., 500 A.2d 1346, 1355 (Del.1985).

and become exercisable upon the same sort of triggering events. The difference between the two plans is that the flip-in plan enables shareholders of the target to purchase target stock at a discount. Today, they are usually adopted in tandem with flip-over plans.

The second generation pill's flip-in element is typically triggered by the actual acquisition of some specified percentage of the issuer's common stock. (Again, 20 percent is a commonly used trigger.) If triggered, the flip-in pill entitles the holder of each right—except, and this is key, the acquirer and its affiliates or associates—to buy shares of the target issuer's common stock or other securities at half price. In other words, the value of the stock received when the right is exercised is equal to two times the exercise price of the right. The flip-in plan's deterrent effect thus comes from the dilution caused in the target shares held by the acquirer. For example, in Grand Metropolitan's bid for Pillsbury, Pillsbury's flip-in plan would have reduced Grand Met's interest in Pillsbury from 85% to 56 percent. The value of Grand Met's holdings would have declined by more than $700 million dollars.

3. *Redemption provisions*

Proponents of poison pills argue that such plans give the target bargaining leverage that it can use to extract a higher price in return for redeeming the pill. Because the rights trade separately from the issuer's common stock, an acquirer remains subject to the pill's poisonous effects even if an overwhelming majority of the target's shareholders accept the bidder's tender offer. In the face of a pill, a prospective acquirer thus has a strong incentive to negotiate with the target's board.

Flexible redemption provisions are imperative for this purpose; the transaction planner must give the board the option of redeeming the rights at a nominal cost in order to allow desirable acquisitions to go forward. Typical redemption provisions include: the window redemption provision, in which the board retains the ability to redeem the rights for a specified time period following the issuance of the rights, and the white knight redemption provision, in which the target may redeem the rights in connection with a transaction approved by a majority of the continuing directors.

Note that combining a poison pill with a classified board shark repellent gives the board an especially powerful negotiating device. The pill will deter the bidder from buying a control block of stock prior to the pill being redeemed. Instead, in the face of board resistance, the acquirer must go through two successive proxy contests in order to obtain a majority of the board. Prevailing in two such successive contests, without owning a controlling block of stock, would be a significant obstacle.

4. *Variants on the second generation pill*

Back-end plans involve issuing rights to the shareholders upon some triggering event—normally the acquisition of a specified percentage of the target's shares. The target's shareholders may then exchange their rights for a package of target company securities valued at the present minimum fair value of the target. The back-end plan thus establishes a minimum takeover price for the target, since such pills typically are redeemable if the bidder's offer meets or exceeds the price set by the board.

Back-end plans are designed to deter partial tender offers, structurally coercive two-tier tender offers, and open-market purchases by establishing a minimum fair price at which the holders of the rights may be cashed out. Moreover, the debt securities to be issued under the plan typically include provisions precluding the bidder from selling target assets or taking on additional debt. This prevents the bidder from using the target's own resources as collateral for financing the acquisition.

Poison debt relies solely on debt securities. The target issues bonds or notes whose terms are designed to deter a hostile takeover. The indentures for such debt forbid the acquirer from burdening the target with further debt. They also usually forbid the bidder from selling target assets. Poison debt also usually makes a change of control an event of default. As a result, the bondholders may accelerate the loan and force the bidder to immediately redeem the bonds, which has a significant adverse effect on the company's cash flow.

Poison debt is an effective defense against leveraged takeovers. In a leveraged acquisition, the bidder borrows funds to finance the acquisition. These loans are typically given with the assumption that the bidder will be able to sell off target assets and make use of the target's cash flow in order to repay the debt. The theory is that the bidder will not be able to get financing if lenders know about the restrictive provisions of the poison debt.

Voting plans were briefly in vogue during the late 1980s. In some respects, they were a return to the first generation pills. Most voting plans go back to the idea of using preferred stock. One version gives the preferred shares the right to vote, but denies that right to bidders who acquire more than a specified percentage of the common or preferred stock. An alternative version permits the preferred shareholders, other than the bidder, to vote as a separate class in electing directors and gives them the right to elect a specified number of directors to represent their interests.

5.   *The third generation: Dead hand and no hand pills*

In *Carmody v. Toll Brothers*, the Delaware chancery court (per Vice Chancellor Jack Jacobs) cast considerable doubt on the validity of so-called dead hand poison pills.[10] In addition to fairly standard flip-in and

---

10. Carmody v. Toll Bros., Inc., 723 A.2d 1180 (Del.Ch.1998). Cases from other jurisdictions are divided on the validity of such pills. Compare Bank of N.Y. Co., Inc. v. Irving Bank Corp., 139 Misc.2d 665, 528 N.Y.S.2d 482 (N.Y.Sup.Ct.1988) (dead hand pill violated New York law), with Invacare Corp. v. Healthdyne Technologies. Inc., 968 F.Supp. 1578 (N.D.Ga.1997) (applying Georgia law; dead hand pill permissible). See generally Peter V. Letsou, Are Dead

flip-over features, the Toll Brothers pill provided that it could be redeemed only by those directors who had been in office when the shareholder rights constituting the pill had become exercisable (or their approved successors). This provision was intended to foreclose a loophole in standard poison pills. Most pills are subject to redemption at nominal cost by the target's board of directors. Such redemption provisions purportedly allow the target's board to use the pill as a negotiating device: The poison pill makes an acquisition of the target prohibitively expensive. If the prospective acquirer makes a sufficiently attractive offer, however, the board may redeem the pill and allow the offer to go forward unimpaired by the pill's dilutive effects. Although such redemption provisions gave the target's board considerable negotiating leverage, and were one of the justifications used to defend the whole idea of the poison pill, they also made the target vulnerable to a combined tender offer and proxy contest. The prospective acquirer could trigger the pill, conduct a proxy contest to elect a new board, which, if elected, would then redeem the pill to permit the tender offer to go forward. The dead hand pill was intended to close this loophole by depriving any such newly elected directors from redeeming the pill. A shareholder sued, alleging both lack of authority and breach of fiduciary duty claims.

In denying Toll Brothers' motion to dismiss, Vice Chancellor Jacobs indicated that dead hand pills likely ran afoul of several aspects of Delaware law. First, such pills implicated the Delaware statutes governing the powers of directors: "Absent express language in the charter, nothing in Delaware law suggests that some directors of a public corporation may be created less equal than other directors, and certainly not by unilateral board action." Second, by deterring proxy contests by prospective acquirers, the dead hand pill effectively disenfranchised shareholders who wished to elect a board committed to redeeming the pill. Accordingly, the shareholder stated a claim under *Stroud v. Grace*, in which the Delaware supreme court held that defensive measures that disenfranchise shareholders are strongly suspect and cannot be sustained absent a compelling justification.[11] Finally, Vice Chancellor Jacobs concluded that the plaintiff-shareholder had stated a "far from conclusory" breach of fiduciary duty claim. Although standard pills had been upheld against such claims, the dead hand pill was both preclusive and coercive. It was coercive because the pill effectively forced shareholders to re-elect the incumbent directors if they wished to be represented by a board entitled to exercise its full statutory powers. The pill was preclusive because the added deterrent effect of the dead hand provision made a takeover prohibitively expensive and effectively impossible.

In *Mentor Graphics v. Quickturn Design Systems*, Vice Chancellor Jacobs likewise invalidated a so-called no hand pill.[12] Unlike Toll Brother's pill, Quickturn's pill contained no provision for redemption by

Hand (and No Hand) Poison Pills Really Dead?, 68 U. Cin. L. Rev. 1101 (2000).

11. Stroud v. Grace, 606 A.2d 75, 92 n. 3 (Del.1992).

12. Mentor Graphics Corp. v. Quickturn Design Sys., Inc., 728 A.2d 25 (Del.Ch. 1998).

continuing directors. Instead, it made the pill nonredeemable for six months after a change in control of the board. Vice Chancellor Jacobs concluded that the no hand pill violated the target board's fiduciary duties and, accordingly, declined to address plaintiff's authority-based claims.

The Delaware supreme court affirmed, but on different grounds.[13] The supreme court's opinion focused on the board's authority. According to the court's opinion, Delaware law "requires that any limitation on the board's authority be set out in the" articles of incorporation. The no hand pill limited a newly elected board's authority by precluding redemption of the pill—and thereby precluding an acquisition of the corporation—for six months. Consequently, the no hand pill tended "to limit in a substantial way the freedom of [newly elected] directors' decisions on matters of management policy." Accordingly, it violated "the duty of each [newly elected] director to exercise his own best judgment on matters coming before the board." Absent express authorization of such a limitation in the articles, the no hand pill was invalid as beyond the board's authority.

Dead hand and no hand pills unquestionably raise very serious issues of target director fiduciary duty. But the Delaware supreme court's emphasis on the board's authority is highly problematic. Dead hand and no hand pills are a type of precommitment strategy. In *The Odyssey*, Homer tells a classic story of using a precommitment strategy to achieve a desired goal. Circe warned Odysseus that his course would lead him past the Sirens, whose song famously enchanted all who passed near them. Once trapped, the passerby would be warbled to death by the sweetness of their song. Following Crice's advice, Odysseus adopted a plan by which he would be able to hear the Sirens' song but still escape their trap. Odysseus charged his men to lash him to the mast of their boat and not to release him until they were far beyond the Sirens. Odysseus then stopped up his sailor's ears with beeswax, so they could hear nothing. As his ship passed the Sirens, their song overwhelmed Odysseus' will power and he tried desperately to get his men to approach the Sirens. Unable to hear the song, and thus being free of its enchantment, however, his men merely tied him even more tightly to the mast and sailed on. Only once they were safely past the Sirens did they release Odysseus.

Homer's tale illustrates the use of a precommitment strategy to solve the problems known to behavioral economists as time inconsistent discount rates and multiple selves.[14] The discount rate an individual applies when making net present value calculations often declines as the date of the reward recedes. Professors Korobkin and Ulen offer the following example: "Suppose that an individual is to choose between

---

13. Quickturn Design Sys., Inc. v. Shapiro, 721 A.2d 1281 (Del.1998).

14. See generally Russell B. Korobkin and Thomas S. Ulen, Law and Behavioral Science: Removing the Rationality Assumption from Law and Economics, 88 Cal. L. Rev. 1051, 1119–24 (2000).

Project A, which will mature in nine years, and Project B, which will mature in ten years. Suppose, further, that an individual who compares the two projects across all their different dimensions prefers Project B to A. Now suppose that we bring the dates of maturity of the two projects forward while maintaining the one-year difference in their maturity dates. Because discount rates increase as maturity dates get closer, it is possible that the individual's preference will switch from Project B to Project A as the dates of maturity decline (but preserving the one-year difference)." One effect of time inconsistent discount rates is that people "always consume more in the present than called for by their previous plans."[15]

The somewhat related multiple selves phenomenon posits that individuals do not have a single utility function, but rather multiple competing utility functions. Because each "self" orders preferences differently, there is an ever-present risk that the self predominating at a given moment may make decisions not in the complete individual's best interest. Again, Korobkin and Ulen explain: "A stiff tax on cigarettes, to take an obvious example, can be viewed as aiding the future-oriented self in its battle with a more present-oriented self that values immediate gratification over long-term health. . . . Today's self can attempt to make commitments that either will completely bind tomorrow's self or, at least, raise the cost of taking action that today's self wishes to avoid." In Homer's tale, Odysseus had himself lashed to the mast precisely so that his present-oriented self could not satisfy its desire to prolong exposure to the Sirens' song. Being lashed to the mast was a precommitment strategy by which he avoided making an unwise decision in the future. Hence, Odysseus privileged the desires of his farsighted "planner" self, who was concerned with lifetime utility, over those of his myopic and selfish "doer" self. Bank Christmas Clubs are predicated on the same idea. By prohibiting the withdrawal of funds until late November, Christmas Clubs prevent people from acting on hyperbolic discounting proclivities, and assure the future availability of funds to pay for Christmas presents. In general, precommitment strategies are desirable because they disempower the myopic "doer" self. As such, "people rationally chose to impose constraints on their own behavior."[16]

Accordingly, there are many situations in which both individuals and organizations make enforceable precommitments.[17] Such precommitments are beneficial because they protect ourselves against passion and time inconsistency. In using contractual devices to make a precommitment, the incumbent board likewise binds itself—and future boards—to a particular strategy. In striking down the dead hand and no hand poison pills on authority grounds, the Delaware courts seemingly have

15. Richard H. Thaler, The Winner's Curse 98 (1992).

16. See generally Richard H. Thaler & H.M. Shefrin, An Economic Theory of Self–Control, 89 J. Pol. Econ. 392 (1981).

17. A political constitution can be considered a special species of precommitment that protects the body politic "against its own predictable tendency to make unwise decisions." Jon Elster, Ulysses Unbound: Studies in Rationality, Precommitment, and Constraints 88 (2000).

limited the use of such precommitment strategies by adopting a broad principle that boards have an ongoing duty to constantly re-evaluate their decisions.

Boards commonly enter into contracts limiting their future authority to varying degrees. Bond indentures commit the board to long-term obligations that will continue to bind future boards for many years. To be sure, the constraint on the authority of future boards is relatively modest, as such boards could always choose to breach the contractual obligations imposed by the indenture, but it nevertheless remains the case that their authority has been constrained.

Merger agreements likewise commonly contain provisions by which the board of directors binds itself to particular courses of conduct. A best efforts clause, for example, obliges the target's board to use its "best efforts" to consummate the transaction. No shop clauses prohibit the target corporation from soliciting a competing offer from any other prospective bidders. The no negotiation covenant, a variant on the no shop theme, goes further to prohibits negotiations with unsolicited bidders.

As we saw in the preceding section, fair price shark repellents commonly include continuing director provisions. Like the dead hand pill, the continuing director provision of a fair price shark repellent allows a bid to go forward only if approved by those members of the board of directors who were on the board when the acquirer first triggered the defensive provision. If the fair price shark repellent was included in the articles of incorporation, rather than the bylaws, it might satisfy the supreme court's view that "any limitation on the board's authority be set out in the" articles of incorporation.[18] Query, however, whether a typical fair price provision would contain language explicitly authorizing a limitation of the board's authority and whether the Delaware courts would require an explicit statement to that effect.

All such corporate actions would be vulnerable to an authority-based challenge if the supreme court's reference to "*any* limitation on the board's authority" is to be taken literally. Yet, if the word "any" is not to be taken literally, where is the firebreak between permissible and impermissible limitations? A better solution to the problem would begin with the sweeping grant of authority made by DGCL § 141(a): "The business and affairs of every corporation organized under this chapter shall be managed by or under the direction of a board of directors...." To be sure, DGCL § 141(a) authorizes such exceptions to the board's authority as may set forth in the statute or the corporation's articles of incorporation. But why read that authorization as a negative prohibition of self-imposed limitations?

In fact, the most plausible reading of DGCL § 141(a) is that the statute simply does not address the problem at hand. In pertinent part, the statute provides: "If any such provision is made in the certificate of

---

18. Quickturn Design Sys., Inc. v. Shapiro, 721 A.2d 1281, 1291 (Del.1998).

incorporation, the powers and duties conferred or imposed upon the board of directors by this chapter shall be exercised or performed to such extent and by such person or persons as shall be provided in the certificate of incorporation." This language clearly reflects a concern with the special problems of close corporations, whose articles often include provisions allowing the corporation's shareholders to run the firm as though it were a partnership. Taken as a whole, DGCL § 141(a)'s language regarding exceptions to the board's authority is concerned with ensuring the validity of such close corporation governance provisions. On its face, nothing in the statute compels a conclusion that the board cannot create self-imposed limitations on its authority.

C. Other defenses

The most common response to a hostile takeover bid is litigation, usually raising some violation or another of the tender offer rules we studied earlier. In this section, we consider some other commonly used defenses.

1. Pre-offer planning

In olden days, say circa 1980, corporations would develop so-called "black books" that provided a pre-determined set of responses to unsolicited offers. Today, however, most takeover lawyers recommend against pre-planned defensive packages. In reviewing target board actions, courts have emphasized the board's duty to evaluate a particular offer.[19] Canned responses will fail the "smell test" many courts seem to use when reviewing the consistency of a defense with the fiduciary duties of management.[20]

2. Early warning systems

In order to successfully resist an unsolicited takeover, the target must know at the earliest possible moment that a bid is being planned. Waiting for a Schedule 13D to be filed could mean the difference between a successful defense and a successful takeover. Counsel commonly advise potential targets to conduct daily reviews of trading in the company's stock to detect unusual price or volume movements. Regular contact with the firm's market maker or floor specialists was encouraged so as to alert the target of any large block transactions. The target was advised to regularly review the stockholder lists, looking for concentrated accumulations under individual or nominee names.

---

19. See, e.g., Moran v. Household Int'l, Inc., 500 A.2d 1346, 1354 (Del.1985) ("When the Household Board of Directors is faced with a tender offer and a request to redeem the Rights, they will not be able to arbitrarily reject the offer.").

20. See E. Norman Veasey, The New Incarnation of the Business Judgment Rule in Takeover Defenses, 11 Del. J. Corp. L. 503, 512 (1986) (noting that a defense may fail the "smell test" if "it looks like an effort to entrench the incumbents and ... there is a reasonable likelihood that stockholders are not getting the best price obtainable").

Today, most takeover lawyers recommend against pre-planned defensive packages. In reviewing target board actions, courts have emphasized the board's duty to evaluate a particular offer. Canned responses will fail the "smell test" many courts seem to use when reviewing the consistency of a defense with the fiduciary duties of management. On the other hand, the early warning system is still strongly encouraged.

3. *Defensive acquisitions*

In the old days, a potential target would try to create barriers for potential purchasers by acquiring companies that cause antitrust problems for the most likely bidders. In the 1970s, for example, the Marshall Field & Co. department store chain acquired numerous other retail chains for the purpose of creating such antitrust barriers. Although the acquisitions were uniformly unprofitable, the acquired chains operated in the same geographic areas as the most probable potential bidders for Marshall Field.[21] An obvious problem with this tactic is that unprofitable defensive acquisitions will cause the target's stock price to fall, which may make the target more vulnerable to potential buyers who will not face antitrust concerns.[22]

4. *Dual class stock plans*

In the early decades of the last century, the capital structure of many corporations included multiple classes of common stock having disparate voting rights. Classes of nonvoting common were especially common. Such dual class stock capital structures fell into disfavor around the time of the Great Depression but returned to prominence in the 1980s due to their considerable potential as an anti-takeover device. An incumbent who cannot be outvoted, after all, cannot be ousted. In the early 1980s, a growing number of companies therefore adopted dual class capital structures to concentrate voting control in management's hands. This effect is most easily demonstrated by considering the simplest type of disparate voting rights plan—a charter amendment creating two classes of common stock. The Class A shares are simply the preexisting common stock, having one vote per share. The newly created Class B shares, distributed to the shareholders as a stock dividend, have most of the attributes of regular common stock, but possess an abnormally large number of votes (usually 10) per share. Class B shares typically are not transferable, but may be converted into Class A shares for sale. Normal shareholder turnover thus concentrates the superior voting shares in the hands of long-term investors, especially incumbent managers, giving them voting control without the investment of any additional funds.

As a result of regulatory developments in the late 1980s, dual class stock has lost much of its utility as a takeover defense. Under current stock exchange listing standards, dual class stock plans generally must

---

21. Panter v. Marshall Field & Co., 646 F.2d 271 (7th Cir.1981) (holding that the defensive acquisition strategy did not violate the target board's fiduciary duties).

22. See Mark L. Mitchell & Kenneth Lehn, Do Bad Bidders Become Good Targets?, 98 J. Pol. Econ. 372 (1990).

be implemented before the corporation goes public. Post–IPO charter amendments effecting a disparate voting rights plan thus are precluded. The difficulty of marketing dual class stock in an IPO has largely limited this technique to companies whose existing dual class structures was grandfathered by the stock exchanges.

5. Stock repurchases

Stock repurchase programs involve setting up a regular program to buy target shares on the open market from time to time. Such programs should have the desirable effect of supporting the company's stock price by (1) lessening the number of outstanding shares and (2) acting as a signal that management is supportive of shareholder interests. As a high stock price is an excellent takeover defenses, such repurchase programs have become a common feature of corporate governance.

As a takeover defense, stock repurchases will be most effective when the corporation has a large amount of free cash (cash for which there are no positive NPV transactions), but no substantial free cash flows. If the corporation has on-going free cash flows, a one-time stock repurchase is unlikely to have a permanent stock price effect. In order to make such a target a less attractive takeover candidate, an on-going program of regular stock repurchases will be necessary.

There are some potential problems associated with stock repurchase programs. Securities fraud liability is a major risk. Issuers can be held liable for securities fraud under Rule 10b–5 when they purchase shares while in possession of material nonpublic information, just as officers and directors can be held liable for inside trading. In any repurchase plan, the corporation therefore must be careful to analyze whether there would be any basis for an insider trading claim. In large companies with diverse information flows, this can obviously be very difficult. The best times to engage in repurchases are therefore immediately after annual and quarterly disclosure reports are filed with the SEC, as there is somewhat less likelihood of undisclosed material information at those times.

A stock repurchase plan reduces the number of shares the bidder has to buy in order to achieve control. If the price effect of the repurchase plan is not substantial, the plan may backfire. This risk can be alleviated by having a friendly or controlled entity purchase the stock. Some firms therefore effect repurchases through a pension plan or employee stock ownership plan. In that way, the shares remain outstanding, with full voting rights, instead of becoming nonvoting treasury shares.

6. Lock-ups

Both negotiated acquisitions and unsolicited tender offers may trigger competitive bidding for control of the target. Like exclusivity provisions in a merger agreement, the lock-up developed as a response to these risks. A lock-up is any arrangement or transaction by which the target corporation gives the favored bidder a competitive advantage over other bidders.[23] So defined the term includes such tactics as an unusually large cancellation fee or an agreement by the target to use takeover defenses to protect the favored bid from competition. Lock-up options refer more narrowly to agreements (usually separate from the merger agreement) granting the acquirer an option to buy shares or assets of the target. The option commonly becomes exercisable upon the acquisition by some third party of a specified percentage of the target's outstanding shares.[24]

Stock lock-up options give the favored bidder an option to purchase treasury or authorized but unissued target shares. If the option is exercised prior to the shareholder vote on the merger agreement, the favored bidder can vote the additional shares in favor of the merger, helping to assure that the requisite approval will be obtained. If a competing bidder prevails, the favored bidder can exercise the option and sell the additional shares on the open market or tender them to the successful bidder, thereby recouping some or all of its sunk costs. Finally, the risk that the option will be exercised, thereby driving up the number of shares that must be acquired in order to obtain control and thus increasing the overall acquisition cost, may deter competing bids in the first instance.

Asset lock-up options grant the favored bidder an option to purchase a significant target asset. While asset lock-ups often are used to entice a prospective bidder, they are principally intended to end or prevent competitive bidding for the target. Accordingly, the subject of the option is usually either the assets most desired by a competing bidder or those essential to the target's operations.[25] Asset lock-ups are sometimes referred to as "crown jewel options," the name coming from the notion that the asset subject to the option is the target's crown jewel, i.e., its most valuable or desirable asset.

§ 12.10 The propriety of target board resistance to unsolicited offers

At the heart of the academic debate over corporate takeovers lies the basic question of corporate governance: who decides? The shareholders or, as with all other important policy questions, is it initially a decision for the board? Virtually all academic commentators insist on the former answer, while the Delaware courts persistently adhere to the latter. Our analysis of target board resistance to unsolicited takeover bids proceeds from the same basic premise that has pervasively informed our analysis

---

23. See generally Stephen M. Bainbridge, Exclusive Merger Agreements and Lock–Ups in Negotiated Corporate Acquisitions, 75 Minn. L. Rev. 239 (1990).

24. E.g., Hanson Trust PLC v. ML SCM Acquisition Inc., 781 F.2d 264, 267 (2d Cir. 1986); Mobil Corp. v. Marathon Oil Co., 669 F.2d 366 (6th Cir.1981), cert. denied, 455 U.S. 982 (1982); DMG, Inc. v. Aegis Corp., 1984 WL 8228 (1984).

25. See, e.g., Hanson Trust PLC v. ML SCM Acquisition Inc., 781 F.2d 264, 267 (2d Cir.1986); Mobil Corp. v. Marathon Oil Co., 669 F.2d 366 (6th Cir.1981), cert. denied, 455 U.S. 982 (1982).

of corporate law; namely, the constant tension between authority and accountability. Seeking to hold directors accountable for their decisions necessarily reduces the efficiency of corporate decisionmaking. Conversely, deference to the board's authority necessarily entails a risk of opportunism and even plain carelessness.

Strongly influenced by the agency cost branch of New Institutional Economics, academic commentary on takeover defenses is concerned almost solely with the need to deter and remedy misconduct by the firm's decisionmakers and agents. But while the separation of ownership and control in modern public corporations indisputably implicates important accountability concerns, accountability standing alone is an inadequate normative account of corporate law. A fully specified account of corporate law must incorporate the value of authority—i.e., the need to develop a set of rules and procedures that provides the most efficient decisionmaking system. In turn, corporate decisionmaking efficiency can be ensured only by preserving the board's decisionmaking authority from being trumped by courts under the guise of judicial review.

Achieving an appropriate mix between these competing models of corporate governance is a daunting—but necessary—task. Ultimately, authority and accountability cannot be reconciled. At some point, greater accountability necessarily makes the decisionmaking process less efficient, while highly efficient decisionmaking structures necessarily involve reduced levels of accountability. Making corporate law thus requires a careful balancing of these competing values. Nowhere has this proven more challenging than with respect to corporate takeover defenses.

Although the partition admittedly is somewhat artificial, it is useful to begin with the distinction between judicial review of operational issues, such as whether to install lighting in a baseball park, and structural choices, especially those creating a final period situation, such as takeovers.[1] The former typically (and appropriately) receive much less probing review than do the latter. This result is tolerable because most operational decisions do not pose much of a conflict between the interests of directors and shareholders. Operational decisions are a species of repeat transactions. Where parties expect to have repeated transactions, the risk of self-dealing by one party is constrained by the threat that the other party will punish the cheating party in future transactions. To be sure, shareholder discipline is not a very important check on directorial self-dealing. Yet, shareholder voting is just one of an array of extrajudicial constraints that, in totality, give directors to exercise reasonable care in decisionmaking. True, these constraining forces do not eliminate the possibility of director error. The directors will still err from time to time. That is precisely the sort of error, however, that the courts traditionally—and appropriately—eschew reviewing.

§ 12.10

1. See E. Norman Veasey, The Defining Tension in Corporate Governance in Amer-
ica, 52 Bus. Law. 393, 394 (1997) (drawing a similar distinction between "enterprise" and "ownership" decisions).

In contrast, structural decisions—such as corporate takeovers—present a final period problem entailing an especially severe conflict of interest. Successful bids undoubtedly produce positive abnormal returns for target shareholders. In contrast, in today's hostile takeover environment, target directors and officers know that a successful bidder is likely to fire many of them. Any defensive actions by the incumbent board and management are thus tainted by the specter of self-interest. As Judge Richard Posner explains:

> When managers are busy erecting obstacles to the taking over of the corporation by an investor who is likely to fire them if the takeover attempt succeeds, they have a clear conflict of interest, and it is not cured by vesting the power of decision in a board of directors in which insiders are a minority.... No one likes to be fired, whether he is just a director or also an officer. The so-called outsiders moreover are often friends of the insiders. And since they spend only part of their time on the affairs of the corporation, their knowledge of those affairs is much less than that of the insiders, to whom they are likely therefore to defer.[2]

Because corporate takeovers are a species of final period transactions, the various constraints imposed on target directors management in the operational context break down. Target boards and management are no longer subject to shareholder discipline because the target's shareholders will be bought out by the acquirer. Target directors and managers are no longer subject to market discipline because the target by definition will no longer operate in the market as an independent agency. Accordingly, in the structural context there is good reason to be skeptical of incumbents' claims to be acting in the shareholders' best interests.

A.   *Cheff v. Mathes*: **Delaware's first try**

Holland Furnace marketed its products using a set of remarkably fraudulent tactics. Holland salesmen went door to door posing as government or utility inspectors. Once they had received access to the homeowner's furnace, the salesmen would dismantle the furnace and refuse to reassemble it. The salesmen would inform the homeowner that the furnace was unsafe and that parts necessary to make it safe were unavailable. The homeowner would then be sold a replacement Holland furnace.[3] Because of government investigations into these unsavory practices, the firm was under-performing.

Arnold Maremont proposed a merger between Holland and Maremont's Motor Products Corporation. Holland's president, one Cheff, rejected Maremont's overtures. Maremont then began buying Holland stock. When he announced his purchase publicly and demanded a place on the board, Cheff again refused. Holland claimed Maremont often

---

2.   Dynamics Corp. of Am. v. CTS Corp., 794 F.2d 250, 256 (7th Cir.1986), rev'd on other grounds, 481 U.S. 69 (1987).

3.   Holland Furnace Co. v. FTC, 295 F.2d 302 (1961).

bought corporations to liquidate them for a profit. Because of this reputation, Cheff claimed, Holland employees who were aware of Maremont's interest were beginning to show signs of discontent.

Having met resistance, Maremont offered to sell his stock to the firm at a premium over his purchase price and over the current market price.[4] Holland's board agreed, causing the corporation to repurchase Maremont's shares using corporate funds. Other shareholders then challenged that repurchase transaction in a derivative suit.

In *Cheff v. Mathes*, the Delaware supreme court announced the so-called "primary purpose test" for review of takeover defenses. Under that standard, the court did not give the directors the immediate benefit of the business judgment rule's presumption of good faith. Rather, the directors had the initial burden of showing that they had reasonable grounds to believe that a danger to corporate policy and effectiveness existed and did not act for the primary purpose of preserving their own incumbency. Only if the board could make such a showing would they be entitled to the business judgement rule's protection. However, the directors merely had to show good faith and reasonable investigation; they could not be held liable for an honest mistake of judgment.[5]

The *Cheff* court was well aware of the conflict of interest inherent in target resistance to unsolicited bids. Hence, its imposition of the primary purpose test. To be sure, the Court downplayed the conflict slightly by comparing the conflict posed by takeovers to that "present, for example, when a director sells property to the corporation." As we shall see below, however, this comparison is a perfectly plausible one, although it also is one that has essentially escaped most academic commentators.

---

4. During the 1980's, the purchase by a corporation of a potential acquirer's stock, at a premium over the market price, came to be called "greenmail." Buying off one person, however, provides no protection against later pursuers, except possibly to the extent that the premium paid to the first pursuer depletes the corporate resources and makes it a less attractive target. Such reduction in corporate resources could, of course, be achieved by managers simply by paying a dividend to all shareholders or by buying the corporation's shares from all shareholders wanting to sell. Section 5881 of the Internal Revenue Code, enacted in 1987, imposes a penalty tax of 50 percent on the gain from greenmail, which is defined as gain from the sale of stock that was held for less than two years and sold to the corporation pursuant to an offer that "was not made on the same terms to all shareholders." Despite its many critics, greenmail actually may be beneficial in that it may allow the board to seek higher bids or to enhance value (above the greenmail bidder's price) by making changes in management or strategy. The question whether greenmail deserves its

bad reputation therefore is essentially an empirical one. The evidence supports the proposition that greenmail actually benefits nonparticipating shareholders overall, and does not appear to be a device for entrenching incumbent management. Consequently, a greenmailer may be a catalyst for change from within or for a bidding war and may therefore deserve to make a profit. Jonathan R. Macey & Fred S. McChesney, A Theoretical Analysis of Corporate Greenmail, 95 Yale L.J. 13 (1985); Fred S. McChesney, Transaction Costs and Corporate Greenmail: Theory, Empirics, and a Mickey Mouse Case Study, 14 Managerial & Decision Econ. 131 (1993).

5. See Cheff v. Mathes, 199 A.2d 548 (Del.1964); see also Royal Indus., Inc. v. Monogram Indus., Inc., [1976–1977 Transfer Binder] Fed. Sec. L. Rep. (CCH) ¶ 95,-863 at 91,136–38, 1976 WL 860 (C.D.Cal. 1976) (applying Delaware law); Bennett v. Propp, 187 A.2d 405, 408 (Del.1962); Kors v. Carey, 158 A.2d 136, 140–42 (Del.Ch. 1960).

In practice, however, the burden placed on target directors by the primary purpose test proved illusory. Liability could be imposed only if entrenching the incumbent officers and directors in office was the primary motive for the defensive actions.[6] Management therefore simply directed its counsel to carefully scrutinize the bidder's tender offer documents to find some issue of policy as to which they differed. And, of course, it was always possible to find some policy disagreement between incumbent management and the outside bidder. Why else would the bidder be trying to oust the incumbents? Once found, such a policy difference was all that was necessary to justify the use of defensive tactics, because the board could not be held liable for its actions, even if hindsight showed them to be unwise, so long as they were motivated by a sincere belief that they were necessary to maintain proper business policy and practices.[7] The primary purpose analysis thus added little to the highly deferential treatment of board decisions mandated by the traditional business judgment rule and therefore proved an ineffective response to the conflict of interest present when target boards and management respond to a takeover bid.

B. The academic critique of *Cheff*

In the early 1980s, a veritable flood of academic writing began on target board resistance to unsolicited takeover bids. Despite the voluminous debate, however, a relatively narrow set of policy proposals emerged. Professor Ronald Gilson was the early spokesman for what might be termed the auction model.[8] After arguing that *Cheff* failed to adequately constrain management's conflict of interest in takeover contests, Gilson proposed a substantially more limited role for takeover defenses than the Delaware courts had contemplated. Under Gilson's proposal, the incumbent board would be allowed to use only those tactics intended to secure a better offer for the shareholders, such as releasing information relevant to the offer's adequacy or delaying an offer while an alternative bidder is sought. While Gilson's concern for management's conflict of interest is apparent, his approach did not effectively

---

6. Royal Industries, Inc. v. Monogram Industries, Inc., [1976–1977 Transfer Binder] Fed. Sec. L. Rep. (CCH) ¶ 95,863 at 91,136–38, 1976 WL 860 (C.D.Cal.1976) (applying Delaware law); Condec Corp. v. Lunkenheimer Co., 230 A.2d 769 (Del.Ch. 1967).

7. See Ronald J. Gilson, A Structural Approach to Corporations: The Case Against Defensive Tactics in Tender Offers, 33 Stan. L. Rev. 819, 829 (1981).

8. See, e.g., Ronald J. Gilson, Seeking Competitive Bids Versus Pure Passivity in Tender Offer Defense, 35 Stan. L. Rev. 51 (1982); Ronald J. Gilson, The Case Against Shark Repellent Amendments: Structural Limitations on the Enabling Concept, 34

Stan. L. Rev. 775 (1982). Professor Lucian Bebchuk was another early spokesman for a variant of the auction model. Unlike Gilson, however, Bebchuk was so concerned with the target incumbent's conflict of interest that he rejected allowing the incumbents to use defenses to promote an auction. Instead, he proposed statutory rules intended to allow an auction to develop on its own. See, e.g., Lucian A. Bebchuk, The Case for Facilitating Competing Tender Offers: A Reply and Extension, 35 Stan. L. Rev. 23 (1982); Lucian A. Bebchuk, The Case for Facilitating Competing Tender Offers, 95 Harv. L. Rev. 1028 (1982); see generally Michael P. Dooley, Fundamentals of Corporation Law 549–55 (1995).

resolve that problem. It is very difficult to distinguish ex ante between defensive tactics that will promote a corporate auction and those that will preserve target board independence. In addition, because Gilson's proposal only addressed incumbent tactics undertaken after an unsolicited offer is expected, it did nothing to prevent incumbent directors and managers from erecting defenses long before any offer is on the horizon.

Professors Frank Easterbrook and Daniel Fischel were the leading early spokesmen for what might be termed the passivity or no resistance rule. Easterbrook and Fischel would allow incumbent directors and managers of a target company no role in unsolicited offers: they argued for complete passivity on the part of target incumbents in the face of a hostile tender offer.[9] In their view, the tender offer is the critical constraint on unfaithful or inefficient corporate managers. Their no resistance rule was thus designed to render management's conflict of interest irrelevant. Having no legitimate decisionmaking role, management is powerless to affect the bid's outcome.

Easterbrook and Fischel argued that takeovers generate social welfare from both ex ante and ex post perspectives. First, the mere threat of corporate takeovers acts as an important check on agency costs that overcomes the collective action problems that plague shareholder oversight. The company is most vulnerable to hostile bids when its stock price is low due to management incompetence and there is room for improving the company's value by displacing the incumbent management team. Put another way, a company will only appear attractive, and therefore will only be acquired, if the stock is undervalued compared to its potential. Knowing this, corporate managers will pursue superior performance and high stock prices to preserve their own jobs. Hence, "investors benefit even if their corporation never becomes the subject of a tender offer." Second, Easterbrook and Fischel argue that successful takeovers benefit all parties ex post. The target's shareholders are better off, as they receive a premium over the market price. The bidder gains the difference between price paid for the target's shares and the value of the firm once its performance improves. Finally, any nontendering shareholders participate in the appreciation of the price of shares.

Given this analysis, Easterbrook and Fischel's hostility to management resistance to takeovers is hardly surprising. They argue that defensive tactics make "monitoring by outsiders less profitable and thus also less common." Put another way, takeover defenses attenuate outsiders' incentives to play a monitoring role by eroding the expected return on identifying suitable takeover targets. Instead of being able to capture the returns of their monitoring activities, bidders are forced to share their gains with shareholders of the target company and with other bidders.

9. See, e.g., Frank H. Easterbrook & Daniel R. Fischel, Auctions and Sunk Costs in Tender Offers, 35 Stan. L. Rev. 1 (1982); Frank H. Easterbrook & Daniel R. Fischel, The Proper Role of a Target's Management in Responding to a Tender Offer, 94 Harv. L. Rev. 1161 (1981).

In contrast to Gilson's preference for auctions, Easterbrook and Fischel contend that defensive tactics that induce auctions are especially problematic. The first bidder expends time and effort monitoring potential targets. Second bidders essentially free ride on the first bidder's efforts. If the first bidder is unable to earn an adequate return on its efforts, however, the incentive to bid is reduced. In response, Lucian Bebchuk and Ronald Gilson argued that first bidders' costs are not that large and are easily offset by the tendering their shares to a successful bidder. They also argued that an auction leads to greater productivity improvements, because auctions direct assets to the highest valuing user, who may not be the first bidder.

The Delaware supreme court has explicitly rejected Easterbrook and Fischel's passivity approach.[10] Before considering the merits of Easterbrook and Fischel's approach in detail, accordingly, it will be instructive to first explore the current state of Delaware law. At this point, however, it is worth noting an apparent disconnect between their analysis of takeovers and their analysis of corporate law generally. Over the years, Easterbrook and Fischel have been among the most outspoken proponents of the nexus of contracts model. Yet, they depart from the contractarian fold when it comes to takeover resistance.

As a general matter, Easterbrook and Fischel contend that "anything goes—that managers should be allowed to exploit any available devices ... while being bound to respect any contractual limits on their powers. Courts' only role would be to enforce the contracts."[11] Hence, why should the incumbent management team be barred from adopting contractual terms that allow resistance to unsolicited takeover bids? Easterbrook and Fischel justify their localized apostasy by explaining that "the contractual model draws much of its power because managers and entrepreneurs must 'pay' for any inefficient terms by accepting lower prices for the securities they sell." In the context of takeover defenses, however, "[c]ontractual arguments become especially difficult [as] many of the provisions in question are latecomer terms not 'priced' when adopted." As these terms often are adopted after securities have been sold, they escape the "market test" that validates conditions in place when a firm first issues securities.

In the first instance, their defense of the passivity position only justifies a prohibition of latecomer terms. If firms go public with takeover defenses in place, as many do, the market will price those defenses. In the second, they are wrong in asserting that the market does not price latecomer terms. Rational prospective buyers of a firm's securities will determine the price they are willing to pay based not only on the takeover defenses that a firm has already implemented, but also on those

---

10. Unocal Corp. v. Mesa Petroleum Co., 493 A.2d 946, 955 n. 10 (Del.1985) (noting academic suggestions that "a board's response to a takeover threat should be a passive one," the court opined that "that clearly is not the law of Delaware")

11. Frank H. Easterbrook & Daniel R. Fischel, The Economic Structure of Corporate Law 166 (1991).

that a firm may implement in the future.[12] The underlying principle—that economic actors base their decisions on rational expectations of other actors' future behavior—is a staple of Easterbrook and Fischel's scholarship elsewhere but curiously disappears in this context.

C. *Unocal* and *Revlon*: Delaware tries again

The Delaware supreme court never adopted either the auction or the passivity model.[13] At the same time, however, the court early recognized that the traditional doctrinal options were inadequate to the task at hand. Characterizing the action of a corporation's board of directors as a question of care or of loyalty has vital—indeed, potentially outcome determinative—consequences.[14] If the court treated takeover defenses as a loyalty question, with its accompanying intrinsic fairness standard, takeover defenses would rarely pass muster. The defendant directors would be required, subject to close and exacting judicial scrutiny, to establish that the transaction was objectively fair to the corporation.[15] Because this burden is an exceedingly difficult one to bear, and thus would likely result in routine judicial invalidation of takeover defenses, a duty of loyalty analysis makes sense only if we think all takeovers are socially desirable and that all takeover defenses are therefore bad social policy.

On the other hand, if the court treated takeover defenses as a care question, virtually all takeover defenses would survive judicial review. Before the target's directors could be called to account for their actions, plaintiff would have to rebut the business judgment rule's presumptions by showing that the decision was tainted by fraud, illegality, self-dealing, or some other exception to the rule. Absent the proverbial smoking gun, plaintiff is unlikely to prevail under this standard. A duty of care

12. In game theory terms, pricing of securities can be expected to coordinate on a Nash equilibrium—i.e., a set of strategies in which each player's strategy is set to be optimal to other players' strategies. Suppose investors recognize that adoption of takeover defenses is privately optimal for management and that shareholders cannot effectively restrain management from adopting such defenses. In this event, even if takeover defenses harm shareholder value, investors will pay the same price for the shares of a firm with takeover defenses and those of a second firm that is otherwise identical but has not yet implemented defenses. Investors will assume that rationally self-interested incumbents will adopt takeover defenses when the firm is threatened. There is no reason, therefore, to pay a significant premium for his company's shares over those of a company that has already adopted such defenses. Only if a firm could credibly commit to a policy of never adopting takeover defenses would investors be willing to pay a premium for the firm's shares. Yet, there is no mechanism by which a firm can make such a commitment.

13. Unocal Corp. v. Mesa Petroleum Co., 493 A.2d 946, 955 n. 10 (Del.1985).

14. Both the Delaware supreme and chancery courts have recognized that choice of standard can be outcome determinative in this context. Mills Acquisition Co. v. Macmillan, Inc., 559 A.2d 1261, 1279 (Del. 1989); AC Acquisitions Corp. v. Anderson, Clayton & Co., 519 A.2d 103, 111 (Del.Ch. 1986).

15. See Robert M. Bass Group, Inc. v. Evans, 552 A.2d 1227, 1239 (Del.Ch.1988); cf. Sinclair Oil Corp. v. Levien, 280 A.2d 717 (Del.1971) (application of intrinsic fairness standard to fiduciary duties of majority shareholders).

analysis thus makes sense only if we think management resistance to takeovers is always appropriate.

1. Unocal

In *Unocal v. Mesa Petroleum*,[16] the Delaware supreme court attempted to steer a middle course by promulgating what has been called an "intermediate" or "enhanced business judgment" standard of judicial review, but is perhaps best described as a "conditional business judgment rule."[17] Famed corporate raider T. Boone Pickens, whom the court referred to as having "a national reputation as a 'greenmailer,'" owned via his main corporate vehicle, Mesa Petroleum, 13% of Unocal's voting stock. Mesa launched a hostile two-tiered tender offer, pursuant to which it offered to buy slightly over 37% of the remaining shares for $54 per share. It would then eliminate the remaining shares by means of a freezeout merger, in which the consideration would be junk bonds ostensibly worth $54 per Unocal share.

Two-tier offers like Mesa's are structurally coercive. Suppose Target's pre-bid stock price was $50. Bidder 1 makes a two-tier offer with differing prices: $80 cash in the first step tender offer and $60 cash in the second step freezeout merger. Assuming the first step tender offer seeks 50% of the shares plus one, the blended offer price is $70 with a blended premium of $20 per share (calculated by taking the weighted average of the two steps). Bidder 2 offers $75 in cash for any and all shares tendered, a premium of $25 per share. As a group shareholders are better off with Bidder 2. Yet, Bidder 1's offer creates a prisoners' dilemma. Those shareholders who "cheat," by taking Bidder 1's front end offer, end up with $80 rather than $75. With a large noncohesive group in which defectors bear no cost—such as shame or reprisals— rational investors should defect. Because everyone's individual incentive is to defect, the shareholders end up with the offer that is worst for the group. Mesa's offer differed from this example by offering the same price in both steps, but the far less attractive form of consideration to be paid in the second step would have similarly coercive effects.

To stop the Mesa takeover, Unocal made a self-tender offer for its own stock. Under Unocal's counter offer, if Mesa's front end tender offer succeeded in giving Mesa a majority of Unocal's stock, Unocal would repurchase the remaining minority shares with debt securities worth $72. This self-tender offer was discriminatory because Pickens could not tender into it. It would leave the company drained of significant assets and burdened by substantial debt. Even more cleverly, however, Unocal might never need actually complete the self-tender offer. Its offer only

---

16. Unocal Corp. v. Mesa Petroleum Co., 493 A.2d 946 (Del.1985).

17. Michael P. Dooley, Fundamentals of Corporation Law 547 (1995). Like the traditional business judgment rule, the conditional *Unocal* rule can be applied only to actions that are within the power or au-

thority of the board. As a preliminary inquiry one thus must ask whether the board had the authority under the governing statutes and the corporation's organic documents to take this specific action. Moran v. Household Int'l, Inc., 500 A.2d 1346, 1350 (Del.1985).

applied if Mesa acquired more than 50% of Unocal's voting stock. Because Unocal offered a higher price than did Mesa, however, Unocal's shareholders were likely to tender to it rather than to Mesa. If no shareholders tendered to Mesa, Mesa would not acquire 50%, and Unocal would be able close its offer without taking down any of the tendered shares. When Unocal's shareholders complained about this aspect of the defense, Unocal agreed to buy 50 million of the shares tendered to it the stock tendered to it even if Mesa did not acquire 50%.

Mesa sued, arguing that Unocal's board owed Mesa the same fiduciary duties they owed all other shareholders. If they arranged for Unocal to repurchase the other shareholders' stock at advantageous prices, they owed Mesa same treatment. The Delaware supreme court rejected that argument.[18] Given the coercive nature of Mesa's bid, the bid's probable price inadequacy, and Pickens' reputation as a greenmailer, Unocal was entitled to take strong measures to defeat the Mesa offer. Because excluding Mesa from the self-tender offer was essential to making the defense work, the directors could discriminate against Mesa without violating their fiduciary duties.[19]

In *Unocal*, the Delaware supreme court reaffirmed the target's board general decisionmaking primacy, which includes an obligation to determine whether the offer is in the best interests of the shareholders. In light of the board's potential conflict of interest vis-à-vis the shareholders, however, judicial review was to be somewhat more intrusive than under the traditional business judgment rule: "Because of the omnipresent specter that a board may be acting primarily in its own interests, rather than those of the corporation and its shareholders, there is an enhanced duty which calls for judicial examination at the threshold before the protections of the business judgment rule may be conferred."

The initial burden of proof is on the directors, who must first show that they had reasonable grounds for believing that a danger to corporate policy or effectiveness existed. The directors satisfy this burden by showing good faith and reasonable investigation. The good faith element requires a showing that the directors acted in response to a perceived threat to the corporation and not for the purpose of entrenching themselves in office. The reasonable investigation element requires a demonstration that the board was adequately informed, with the relevant

---

18. After the *Unocal* decision, the SEC demonstrated its disapproval of discriminatory tender offers by amending its Williams Act rules to prohibit tender offers other than those made to all shareholders. See Exchange Act Rule 13e–4(f)(8) (issuer self-tender offers); Exchange Act Rule 14d–10(a)(1) (third party offers).

19. Unocal and Mesa eventually negotiated an agreement that allowed Mesa to participate in Unocal's self-tender. A Unocal shareholder then sued Mesa under the short swing profit provisions of Securities Exchange Act § 16(b). Mesa argued that the self-tender qualified as an unorthodox transaction exempt from § 16(b). In Colan v. Mesa Petroleum Co., 951 F.2d 1512 (9th Cir.1991), however, the court rejected that argument, holding that the so-called *Kern County* exception applies solely to involuntary transactions. Mesa's decision to tender to Unocal was voluntary and, therefore, subject to § 16(b) liability.

standard being one of gross negligence. Assuming the directors carry their initial burden, they next must prove that the defense was reasonable in relationship to the threat posed by the hostile bid. Note that both the decision to adopt and any subsequent decision to implement a set of takeover defenses are subject to challenge and judicial review.[20]

Not surprisingly, the board's "initial" burden of proof quickly became the whole ball game. If the directors carried their two-step burden, the business judgment rule applied, but if the directors failed to carry their initial burden, the duty of loyalty's intrinsic fairness test applied.[21] It is for this reason that the *Unocal* test is more properly seen as a conditional version of the business judgment rule, rather than an intermediate standard. The *Unocal* rule solved the problem of outcome determination not so much by creating a different standard of review, as by creating a mechanism for determining on an individual basis which of the traditional doctrinal standards was appropriate for the particular case at bar.

2. Revlon

In *Revlon v. MacAndrews & Forbes Holdings*, the Delaware supreme court developed a modified version of the *Unocal* to deal with a particular problem; namely, the use of takeover defenses to ensure that a white knight would prevail in a control auction with the hostile bidder.[22] In response to an unsolicited tender offer by Pantry Pride, Revlon's board undertook a variety of defensive measures, culminating in the board's authorization of negotiations with other prospective bidders. Thereafter the board entered into a merger agreement with a white knight, which included a lock-up arrangement, as well as other measures designed to prevent Pantry Pride's bid from prevailing. Revlon's initial defensive tactics were reviewed (and upheld) under standard *Unocal* analysis. In turning to the lock-up arrangement, however, the Court struck out in a new direction:

> The Revlon board's authorization permitting management to negotiate a merger or buyout with a third party was a recognition that the company was for sale. The duty of the board had thus changed from the preservation of Revlon as a corporate entity to the maximization of the company's value at a sale for the stockholders' benefit. This significantly altered the board's responsibilities under the *Unocal* standards. It no longer faced threats to corporate policy and effectiveness, or to the stockholders' interests, from a grossly inadequate bid. The whole question of defensive measures became moot. The directors' role changed from defenders of the corporate bastion to auctioneers charged with getting the best price for the stockholders at a sale of the company.

20. Moran v. Household Int'l, Inc., 500 A.2d 1346 (Del.1985).

21. Shamrock Holdings, Inc. v. Polaroid Corp., 559 A.2d 257, 271 (Del.Ch.1989).

22. Revlon, Inc. v. MacAndrews & Forbes Holdings, Inc., 506 A.2d 173 (Del. 1985).

Because the lock-up ended the auction in return for minimal improvement in the final offer, it was invalidated.

Revlon proved surprisingly troublesome. For example, did it establish special duties to govern control auctions or are the so-called "*Revlon* duties" really just the general *Unocal* rules applied to a special fact situation? The courts have waffled on this issue, although the latter interpretation seems to have ultimately prevailed. In 1987, for example, the Delaware supreme court drew a rather sharp distinction between the *Unocal* standard and what it then called "the *Revlon* obligation to conduct a sale of the corporation."[23] Two years later, however, the court indicated that *Revlon* is "merely one of an unbroken line of cases that seek to prevent the conflicts of interest that arise in the field of mergers and acquisitions by demanding that directors act with scrupulous concern for fairness to shareholders."[24] The doctrinal differences between *Unocal* and *Revlon* still loom quite large at times or, at least, in some eyes.

Whether the *Revlon* duties were distinct or just a sub-set of *Unocal*, what exactly were directors supposed to do once their role changes from "defenders of the corporate bastion to auctioneers"? Prior to the pivotal *Paramount* decisions discussed below, we thought a few things could be said with confidence. We knew, for example, that target directors need not be passive observers of market competition.[25] The board's objective, however, "must remain the enhancement of the bidding process for the benefit of the stockholders."[26] Favored treatment of one bidder at any stage of the process was therefore subjected to close scrutiny. Ultimately, the board's basic task was to get the best possible deal, which usually but not always meant the best possible price, for their shareholders. Directors did not need to blindly focus on price to the exclusion of other relevant factors. The board could evaluate offers on such grounds as the proposed form of consideration, tax consequences, firmness of financing, antitrust or other regulatory obstacles, and timing.[27] Easy standards to state perhaps, but often quite difficult ones to apply.

Finally, and even more fundamentally, when did directors stop being "defenders of the corporate bastion" and become "auctioneers"? Again, prior to the *Paramount* decisions, it seemed well-settled that the auctioneering duty is triggered when (but apparently only when) a proposed transaction would result in a change of control of the target corporation. For example, if a defensive recapitalization, which most of these cases involved, transferred effective voting control to target management, or some other identifiable control block, the courts treated the transaction as a "change in control" of the corporation requiring adherence to

23. Ivanhoe Partners v. Newmont Mining Corp., 535 A.2d 1334, 1338 (Del.1987).

24. Barkan v. Amsted Indus., Inc., 567 A.2d 1279, 1286 (Del.1989).

25. CRTF Corp. v. Federated Dep't Stores, Inc., 683 F.Supp. 422, 441 (S.D.N.Y. 1988) (applying Delaware law).

26. Mills Acquisition Co. v. Macmillan, Inc., 559 A.2d 1261, 1287 (Del.1989).

27. Cottle v. Storer Communication, Inc., 849 F.2d 570, 577 (11th Cir.1988).

Revlon's auction rule.[28] If no identifiable control block formed (or changed hands), however, defensive measures were subject solely to standard *Unocal* review.[29]

D. Striking a balance between authority and accountability

Given the Delaware courts' normal sensitivity to conflicts of interests, the clear evidence that management resistance to unsolicited tender offers is at best a risky proposition for shareholders and at worst economically disastrous, and the undeniable fact that the no resistance rule does a more thorough job of removing management's conflicted interests from the tender offer process than does *Unocal*, is it not surprising that Delaware courts adopted a standard that permits target resistance? The Delaware courts' consistent rejection of the no resistance rule suggests that the courts have perceived some dimension to the puzzle that has escaped the attention of academics.

Analysis should begin with the proposition that all doctrinal responses to corporate conflict of interest transactions have two features in common. First, so long as the board of directors is disinterested and independent, it retains full decisionmaking authority with respect to the transaction.[30] Second, the board's independence and decisionmaking process is subject to judicial scrutiny. Here, as ever, we see the competing influences of authority and accountability.

In a sense, Delaware's takeover cases do no more than to simply bring this traditional corporate governance system to bear on target resistance to tender offers.[31] Admittedly, the form of review is unique, but so too is the context. Just as has been the case with all other corporate conflicts of interest, Delaware decisions in the unsolicited tender offer context strive to find an appropriate balance between authority and accountability. We see the courts' concern for accountability in, for example, *Unocal*'s explicit recognition of the conflict of interest

---

28. Mills Acquisition Co. v. Macmillan, Inc., 559 A.2d 1261, 1285 (Del.1989) (holding that the requisite "sale" could take "the form of an active auction, a management buyout or a 'restructuring' "); see also Robert M. Bass Group, Inc. v. Evans, 552 A.2d 1227, 1243 (Del.Ch.1988); cf. Ivanhoe Partners v. Newmont Mining Corp., 535 A.2d 1334, 1345 (Del.1987) (*Revlon* not triggered where management ally had less than 50% voting control after defensive recapitalization); accord Black & Decker Corp. v. American Standard, Inc., 682 F.Supp. 772, 781 (D.Del.1988) (reading Delaware law to require directors of a company to maximize the amount received by shareholders once it is clear to them that the "corporation is to be subject to a change of control").

29. Paramount Communications, Inc. v. Time Inc., [1989 Transfer Binder] Fed. Sec. L. Rep. (CCH) ¶ 94,514 at 93,279–80, 1989 WL 79880 (Del. Ch.), aff'd on other grounds, 571 A.2d 1140 (Del.1989).

30. See Michael P. Dooley, Two Models of Corporate Governance, 47 Bus. Law. 461, 490 (1992).

31. The point is made obvious by the Delaware supreme court's decision in Williams v. Geier, 671 A.2d 1368 (Del.1996), in which an anti-takeover dual class stock plan received approval by the disinterested shareholders. In light of the shareholder action, the court held that the *Unocal* standard was "inapplicable here because there was no unilateral board action." Id. at 1377. In other words, as with all other conflicted interest transactions, shareholder approval provides substantial protection from judicial review for the board's decision.

that target directors and officers face in an unsolicited takeover bid. Of course, it is one thing to recognize this conflict of interest and quite another to do something about it. As a doctrinal matter, the Delaware supreme court concretely demonstrated its sensitivity to management's conflicted interests by placing the preliminary burden of proof on the board. This action demonstrated considerable judicial sensitivity to the board's conflicted interests, because outside of areas traditionally covered by the duty of loyalty, putting the initial burden of proof on the board of directors is a very unusual—indeed, essentially unprecedented—step.

At the same time, however, we see the value of authority reflected in, for example, *Unocal*'s express rejection of the passivity model. Even plainer evidence of the Delaware courts' concern for authority came when Chancellor Allen wrote that unless *Unocal* was carefully applied "courts—in exercising some element of substantive judgment—will too readily seek to assert the primacy of their own view on a question upon which reasonable, completely disinterested minds might differ."[32] Is it not striking how precisely Allen echoes our argument that one cannot make an actor more accountable without simultaneously transferring some aliquot of his decisionmaking authority to the entity empowered to hold him to account?

In contrast, virtually all of the policy prescriptions to emerge from the academic accounts of the tender offer's corporate governance role would create an entirely corporate governance system, in which the board is stripped of some or all of its normal decisionmaking authority. Recast in our terminology, the academic proposals reflect an overriding concern with accountability. There is no room in the academic account for the value of authority. Indeed, the academic proposals reject the very notion that authority has any legitimate role to play in developing takeover doctrine. Deciding whether the judiciary or the ivory tower has the better argument is the task to which the remainder of this section is devoted.

We approach the problem by asking whether the unsolicited tender offer differs in kind, not just degree, from any other conflicted interest transaction. If so, perhaps a special governance scheme applicable only to unsolicited tender offers can be justified. If not, however, we would expect the law to treat unsolicited tender offers just as it treats other conflicted interest transactions. In other words, the law can be expected to develop mechanisms for policing incumbent conflict of interests, but cannot be expected to deny incumbents a role in the process.

1. The question of comparative advantage

According to most critics of Delaware's takeover jurisprudence, corporate law gives the board decisionmaking authority because in most

---

32. City Capital Assoc. Ltd. Partnership v. Interco Inc., 551 A.2d 787, 796 (Del.Ch. 1988).

situations the directors have a competitive advantage vis-a-vis the shareholders in choosing between competing alternatives. They then argue that directors have no such competitive advantage when it comes to making tender offer decisions and, accordingly, reject granting the board decisionmaking authority in the tender offer context. Certainly it is true that even the most apathetic investor is presumably capable of choosing between an all-cash bid at $74 per share and an all-cash bid at $76. This analysis, however, obscures two important rationales for granting the board decisionmaking authority in the tender offer context.

At the outset, it is important to recognize that unsolicited tender offers and negotiated acquisitions have a good deal in common. From a practical perspective, it is often increasingly difficult to tell the two apart. In today's market place most takeovers follow a fairly convoluted path. They start out quasi-hostile, but end up as quasi-friendly, or vice-versa. They start out as a merger proposal, which is restructured as a tender offer for tax or other business reasons, or vice-versa. The problem is usefully illustrated by Chancellor Allen's opinion in *TW Services v. SWT Acquisition*.[33] SWT's unsolicited partial tender offer for TW Services was subject to a number of conditions, including a requirement that the transaction be approved by TW Services' board of directors. The TW Services' board saw the tender offer as a ruse designed to extort greenmail or to put the company into play. Accordingly, the board declined to redeem the company's outstanding poison pill. SWT filed a lawsuit seeking invalidation of the pill. Because SWT conditioned its offer on the TW Service board's support, the case presented a problem of characterization that the legal literature largely ignores. If the transaction is characterized as a merger, then most commentators would permit the board an active decisionmaking role. Conversely, if the transaction is characterized as a tender offer, they would preclude the board from exercising decisionmaking authority. Categorizing this transaction, however, is a non-trivial task.[34] Attempting to define the scope of the board's authority by the nature of the transaction at hand thus quickly proves an unsatisfactory resolution.

Even if one were wholly confident of one's ability to appropriately characterize transactions, however, the comparative advantage argument still would not justify precluding the board from exercising decisionmaking authority in tender offers. Consider transactions like the defensive restructuring at issue in *City Capital Associates v. Interco*. In the face of an all-cash hostile bid at $74 per share, Interco's board of directors proposed to sell certain assets and to borrow a substantial amount of money. The joint proceeds of those transactions would then be paid out to Interco's shareholders as dividends. The dividends would be paid in three forms: cash, bonds, and preferred stock. The dividends' total value

33. TW Servs., Inc. v. SWT Acquisition Corp., 1989 WL 20290 (Del.Ch.1989).

34. Chancellor Allen treated the transaction as a merger proposal. This result makes sense. After all, the bidder controls the conditions to which the tender offer is subject. If SWT had wished to trigger *Unocal*-based review, for example, it could have done so by merely waiving the requirement for board approval.

was said to be $66 per share. Interco's investment banker opined that, after this series of transactions, Interco's stock would trade at no less than $10 per share. The proposed defensive measures thus purportedly would give Interco's shareholders a total value of $76—$2 more than the hostile bid. In rebuttal, the bidder's investment bankers valued the defensive plan at $68–$70 per share.[35] It is precisely because passive, widely dispersed shareholders have neither the inclination nor the information necessary to decide between these sort of alternatives that the corporate law in other contexts allocates the decision to the board.[36] Only compelling accountability concerns can justify treating tender offers differently. The comparative advantage argument thus collapses into a variant of the agency cost arguments discussed below.

2. *The bypass argument*

An alternative justification for treating the tender offer differently than negotiated acquisitions rests on the former's elimination of the need for target management's cooperation. As we saw above, the target board's gatekeeper role in negotiated acquisitions creates a conflict of interest, which is constrained principally by the ability the tender offer gives a bidder to bypass the target's board by purchasing a controlling share block directly from the stockholders. According to some academics, authority values thus are only appropriate in the negotiated acquisition context if the board is denied the ability to resist tender offers.[37]

This argument looks good on paper, but ultimately is unpersuasive. In the first place, it too ignores the problem of characterization alluded

---

35. City Capital Assoc. Ltd. Partnership v. Interco, Inc., 551 A.2d 787 (Del.Ch.1988). If the reader is not fully persuaded by the Interco example, consider that of the well-known Time–Paramount contest. Time received an initial bid from Paramount of $175, later raised to $200. Time's board was advised by its investment bankers, however, that if the company were to be sold it would likely command in excess of $250 per share. Time's shares had traded in a range of 103 5/8 to 113 3/4 in February and rose to 105–122 5/8 in March and April, after the announcement of the Warner merger. The investment bankers further advised that the shares of the combined Time–Warner could be expected to trade initially around $150 and, based on projected cash flows, would steadily increase over the next three years until trading in the range of $208–402 per share in 1993. As Chancellor Allen dryly observed, the latter was a "range that Texas might feel at home on." Paramount Communications, Inc. v. Time Inc., [1989 Transfer Binder] Fed. Sec. L. Rep. (CCH) ¶ 94,514 at 93,273, 1989 WL 79880 (Del. Ch.), aff'd, 571 A.2d 1140 (Del.1989).

36. Cf. Dynamics Corp. of Am. v. CTS Corp., 794 F.2d 250, 254 (7th Cir.1986) (shareholders "know little about the compa-

nies in which they invest or about the market for corporate control"), rev'd on other grounds, 481 U.S. 69 (1987). In addition, management often has information about the firm's value that is difficult to communicate effectively to shareholders in the middle of a takeover fight. E.g., Shamrock Holdings, Inc. v. Polaroid Corp., 559 A.2d 278, 289–90 (Del.Ch.1989) (target company had large, but unliquidated, asset in the form of a damage claim for patent infringement). In such cases, management does have a competitive advantage vis-a-vis the shareholders in making tender offer decisions.

37. See, e.g., Ronald J. Gilson, A Structural Approach to Corporations: The Case Against Defensive Tactics in Tender Offers, 33 Stan. L. Rev. 819, 850 (1981) ("Restricting management's role in a tender offer does not deny the value of management's expertise in evaluating and negotiating complex corporate transactions, but rather validates the unfettered discretion given management with respect to mergers and sales of assets.").

to in the preceding section. In addition, tender offers are not the only vehicle by which outsiders can appeal directly to the shareholders. Proxy contests similarly permit a would-be acquirer to end-run management. How a shareholder votes in director elections seems just as an individual decision as that of whether to tender to a hostile bidder. Yet, nobody expects a board to be passive in the face of a proxy contest. To the contrary, the incumbent board's role is very active indeed. Why? Because the incumbent board members remain in office and therefore also continue to be legally responsible for the conduct of the business until they are displaced. Complete passivity in the face of a proxy contest thus would be inconsistent with the directors' obligation to determine and advance the best interests of the corporation and its shareholders.[38]

The same is true of a tender offer. While the analogy between tender offers and proxy contests is unconvincing for most purposes, the courts may have correctly sensed a fit at this most basic level. The directors will remain in office unless the offer succeeds and they thereafter resign or are removed by the new owner. As a doctrinal matter, the board of directors has a "fundamental duty" to protect shareholders from harm, which can include an unsolicited tender offer that the directors truly believe is not in the shareholders' best interests. As *Unocal* recognized, complete passivity in the face of such an offer would be inconsistent with their fiduciary duties.[39] To the contrary, their on-going fiduciary duty obliges them to seek out alternatives. At the bare minimum, it thus would be appropriate for the board to use takeover defenses to delay an inadequate bid from going forward while the board seeks out an alternative higher-valued offer, because until the board has time to arrange a more attractive alternative there is a risk that the shareholders will "choose an inadequate tender offer only because the superior offer has not yet been presented."[40]

3. *The structural argument (a.k.a. shareholder choice)*

A more substantial argument against authority values in the unsolicited tender offer context contrasts the board's considerable control in negotiated acquisitions with the board's lack of control over secondary market transactions in the firm's shares. Corporate law generally provides for free alienability of shares on the secondary trading markets. Mergers and related transfers of control, however, are treated quite differently. As we saw above, corporate law gives considerable responsibility and latitude to target directors in negotiating a merger agreement. The question then is whether unsolicited tender offers are more like secondary market trading or mergers.

The so-called structural argument—also known as the shareholder choice argument—asserts that the tender offer is much more closely

---

38. See Michael P. Dooley, Two Models of Corporate Governance, 47 Bus. Law. 461, 516 (1992).

39. See Unocal Corp. v. Mesa Petroleum Co., 493 A.2d 946, 954 (Del.1985).

40. Shamrock Holdings, Inc. v. Polaroid Corp., 559 A.2d 278, 289 (Del.Ch.1989).

analogous to the former. According to its proponents, an individual shareholder's decision to tender his shares to the bidder no more concerns the institutional responsibilities or prerogatives of the board than does the shareholder's decision to sell his shares on the open market or, for that matter, to sell his house.[41] Both stock and a home are treated as species of private property that are freely alienable by their owners.

The trouble is that none of the normative bases for the structural argument prove persuasive. That shareholders have the right to make the final decision about an unsolicited tender offer does not necessarily follow, for example, from the mere fact that shareholder have voting rights. While notions of shareholder democracy permit powerful rhetoric, corporations are not New England town meetings. Put another way, we need not value corporate democracy simply because we value political democracy.[42]

Indeed, we need not value shareholder democracy very much at all. In its purest form, our authority-based model of corporate decisionmaking calls for all decisions to be made by a single, central decisionmaking body—i.e., the board of directors. If authority were corporate law's sole value, shareholders thus would have no voice in corporate decisionmaking. Shareholder voting rights thus are properly seen not as part of the firm's decisionmaking system, but as simply one of many accountability tools—and not a very important one at that.

Nor is shareholder choice a necessary corollary of the shareholders' ownership of the corporation. The most widely accepted theory of the corporation, the nexus of contracts model, visualizes the firm not as an entity but as a legal fiction representing a complex set of contractual relationships. Because shareholders are simply one of the inputs bound together by this web of voluntary agreements, ownership is not a meaningful concept under this model. Each input is owned by someone, but no one input owns the totality. A shareholder's ability to dispose of

---

41. E.g., Dynamics Corp. of America v. CTS Corp., 794 F.2d 250, 254 (7th Cir. 1986), rev'd on other grounds, 481 U.S. 69 (1987); Hanson Trust PLC v. ML SCM Acquisition Inc., 781 F.2d 264, 282 (2d Cir. 1986); Norlin Corp. v. Rooney, Pace Inc., 744 F.2d 255, 258 (2d Cir.1984). In addition to the normative arguments we discuss in the text, Professor Bebchuk advances two other justifications for shareholder choice: moving corporate assets to their highest valued user and encouraging optimal levels of investment in target companies. See Lucian A. Bebchuk, Toward Undistorted Choice and Equal Treatment in Corporate Takeovers, 98 Harv. L. Rev. 1693, 1765–66 (1985). Neither of these legitimate goals, however, requires shareholder choice. Rather, they require only a competitive process that produces the highest-valued bid; in

other words, they require only fair competition for control.

42. The analogy between political and corporate voting rights is especially inapt in light of the significant differences between the two arenas. First, voting rights are much less significant in the corporate than in the political context. Second, unlike citizens, shareholders can readily exit the firm when dissatisfied. Third, the purposes of representative governments and corporations are so radically different that there is no reason to think the same rules should apply to both. For example, if the analogy to political voting rights was apt, it would seem that the many corporate constituents affected by board decisions would be allowed to vote. Yet only shareholders may vote. Bondholders, employees and the like normally have no electoral voice.

his stock thus is not defined by notions of private property, but rather by the terms of the corporate contract, which in turn are provided by the firm's organic documents and the state of incorporation's corporate statute and common law. The notion of shareholder ownership is thus irrelevant to the scope of the board's authority. As Vice Chancellor Walsh observed, "shareholders do not possess a contractual right to receive takeover bids. The shareholders' ability to gain premiums through takeover activity is subject to the good faith business judgment of the board of directors in structuring defensive tactics."[43]

Finally, and most importantly, the structural argument also ignores the risk that restricting the board's authority in the tender offer context will undermine the board's authority in other contexts. Even the most casual examination of corporate legal rules will find plenty of evidence that courts value preservation of the board's decisionmaking authority. The structural argument, however, ignores the authority values reflected in these rules. To the contrary, if accepted, the structural argument would necessarily undermine the board's unquestioned authority in a variety of areas. Consider, for example, the board's authority to negotiate mergers. If the bidder can easily by-pass the board by making a tender offer, hard bargaining by the target board becomes counterproductive. It will simply lead to the bidder making a low-ball tender offer to the shareholders, which will probably be accepted due to the collective action problems that preclude meaningful shareholder resistance. Restricting the board's authority to resist tender offers thus indirectly restricts its authority with respect to negotiated acquisitions.[44]

Indeed, taken to its logical extreme, the structural argument requires direct restrictions on management's authority in the negotiated acquisition context. Suppose management believes that its company is a logical target for a hostile takeover bid. One way to make itself less attractive is by expending resources in acquiring other companies. Alter-

---

43. Moran v. Household Int'l, Inc., 490 A.2d 1059, 1070 (Del.Ch.), aff'd, 500 A.2d 1346 (Del.1985) (affirmed post-*Unocal*). Accord Shamrock Holdings, Inc. v. Polaroid Corp., 559 A.2d 257, 272 (Del.Ch.1989).

44. Many acquisitions are initiated by target managers seeking out potential acquirers. A no resistance rule would discourage these takeovers, thus harming shareholders. No sensible seller would seek out potential buyers unless it is able to resist low-ball offers. Note that there is a subtle difference between our position and what might be called the "management as negotiator" model of takeover jurisprudence. Under this model, management can resist a tender offer in order to extract a better offer from the bidder. While this model can be found in some of the Delaware cases, it poses some difficulties. Just how target directors are supposed to use takeover defenses as a negotiating tool, for example, never

has been made entirely clear. Unless the directors can plausibly threaten to preclude the bid from going forward, their defensive tactics have no teeth and thus provide no leverage. Yet, in light of management's conflict of interest, a board refusal to drop its defenses is necessarily suspect. Judicial review of such a refusal, moreover, would require courts to pursue some very thorny lines of inquiry: Is target management correct in believing that they are better managers than the bidder. Or would the company, in fact, be better off with the bidder at the helm? Neither is the sort of question courts are comfortable asking about business decisions, even decisions involving self-dealing. As described below, our approach therefore centers not on how the board used takeover defenses, but rather on whether the board's decisions were tainted by conflicted interests.

natively, the board could effect a preemptive strike by agreeing to be acquired by a friendly bidder. In order to assure that such acquisitions will not deter unsolicited tender offers, the structural argument would require searching judicial review of the board's motives in any negotiated acquisition.

To take but one more example, it is quite clear that managers can make themselves less vulnerable to takeover by eliminating marginal operations or increasing the dividend paid to shareholders and thus enhancing the value of the outstanding shares. A corporate restructuring thus can be seen as a preemptive response to the threat of takeovers. It is hard to imagine valid objections to incumbents securing their position through transactions that benefit shareholders.[45] Why then should it matter if the restructuring occurs after a specific takeover proposal materializes? The structural argument not only says that it does matter, but taken to its logical extreme would require close judicial scrutiny of all corporate restructurings.

4. The conflicted interest argument

The final and perhaps most important argument for treating negotiated and hostile acquisitions differently with respect to the scope of the target board's authority comes down to the conflicted interests inherent in corporate takeovers. Put in our terminology, the argument is that accountability concerns are so severe in this context that they must trump authority values. Unsolicited tender offers implicate accountability concerns in at least two ways, which might be referred to respectively as transactional and systemic. The former relates to the effect of a hostile takeover on the target in question, while the latter relates to the effect resistance to hostile takeovers can have on public corporations as a whole. Neither justifies wholly barring authority values from playing a part in developing the governing legal rules.

Transactional accountability. As with business judgment rule scholarship generally, a failing of the academic literature on takeovers is the almost universal tendency to conflate the roles of corporate officers and directors. The legal literature speaks of "management resistance" and "management defensive tactics," rarely recognizing any separate institutional role for the board. Most commentators simply assume that even independent directors are in thrall to senior managers and will ignore shareholder interests if necessary to preserve their patrons' jobs.[46]

---

45. Cf. Shamrock Holdings, Inc. v. Polaroid Corp., 559 A.2d 257, 276 (Del.Ch. 1989) (upholding an employee stock ownership plan despite its anti-takeover effects, because the plan was "likely to add value to the company and all its stockholders").

46. E.g., Dynamics Corp. of Am. v. CTS Corp., 794 F.2d 250, 256 (7th Cir.1986), rev'd on other grounds, 481 U.S. 69 (1987); Norlin Corp. v. Rooney Pace, Inc., 744 F.2d 255, 266 n. 12 (2d Cir.1984); Panter v.

Marshall Field & Co., 646 F.2d 271, 300 (7th Cir.) (Cudahy, J., dissenting), cert. denied, 454 U.S. 1092 (1981). Professor Michael Dooley notes that management resistance to unsolicited tender offers may not deserve the opprobrium to which it is usually subjected. Dooley acknowledges that it seems inappropriate even to raise this question, because it suggests tolerance for a clear managerial conflict of interest. As suggested by our discussion of the motives

In contrast, the Delaware courts take the board's distinct role quite seriously, especially with respect to its independent members. As a doctrinal matter, the board's burden of proof is more easily carried if the key decisions are made by independent directors.[47] As a practical matter, the court's assessment of the outside directors' role often is outcome-determinative.[48]

driving corporate acquisitions, however, it would be naive to assume that takeovers displace only "bad" or "inefficient" managers. While blamelessness does not eliminate the managers' conflict of interest, it does suggest that resistance may not deserve the opprobrium usually attached to self-dealing transactions. Indeed, Dooley observes, it may often be shareholders rather than managers who act opportunistically in the takeover context. Much of the knowledge a manager needs to do his job effectively is specific to the firm for which he works. As he invests more in firm-specific knowledge, his performance improves, but it also becomes harder for him to go elsewhere. An implicit contract thus comes into existence between managers and shareholders. On the one hand, managers promise to become more productive by investing in firm-specific human capital. They bond the performance of that promise by accepting long promotion ladders and compensation schemes that defer much of the return on their investment until the final years of their career. In return, shareholders promise job security. See Stephen M. Bainbridge, Interpreting Nonshareholder Constituency Statutes, 19 Pepperdine L. Rev. 971, 1004–08 (1992). Viewed in this light, the shareholders' decision to terminate the managers' employment by tendering to a hostile bidder seems opportunistic and a breach of implicit understandings between the shareholders and their managers. Shareholders can protect themselves from opportunistic managerial behavior by holding a fully diversified portfolio. By definition, a manager's investment in firm-specific human capital is not diversifiable. Shareholders' ready ability to exit the firm by selling their stock also protects them. In contrast, the manager's investment in firm-specific human capital also makes it more difficult for him to exit the firm in response to opportunistic shareholder behavior. See John C. Coffee, Jr., Shareholders versus Managers: The Strain in the Corporate Web, 85 Mich. L. Rev. 1, 73–81 (1986). Dooley concedes that this analysis certainly helps explain the courts' greater tolerance of conflicted interests in this context than in, say, garden variety interested director transactions. But he also argues that the possibility that the shareholders' gains come at the expense of

the managers does not justify permitting management to block unsolicited tender offers. Rather, he argues, the managers' loss of implicit compensation appears to be a particularly dramatic form of transaction costs, which could be reduced by alternative explicit compensation arrangements, such as payments from shareholders to managers who lose their jobs following a takeover. It thus may be that courts tolerate management involvement in the takeover process not because they perceive management as having a right for management to defend its own tenure, but rather a right to compete with rival managerial teams for control of the corporation. By allowing management to compete with the hostile bidder for control, the courts provide an opportunity for management to protect its sunk cost in firm-specific human capital without adversely affecting shareholder interests. Indeed, allowing them to compete for control will often be in the shareholders' best interests. There is strong empirical evidence that management-sponsored alternatives can produce substantial shareholder gains. See Michael C. Jensen, Agency Costs of Free Cashflow, Corporate Finance, and Takeovers, 76 Am. Econ. Rev. 323, 324–26 (1986) (summarizing studies of shareholder gains from management-sponsored restructurings and buyouts). A firm's managers obviously have significant informational advantages over the firm's directors, shareholders, or outside bidders, which gives them a competitive advantage in putting together the highest-valued alternative. Management may also be able to pay a higher price than would an outside bidder, because to a firm's managers' the company's value includes not only its assets but also their sunk costs in firm-specific human capital. Shareholders thus have good reason to want management to play a role in corporate takeovers, so long as that role is limited to providing a value-maximizing alternative. See Michael P. Dooley, Fundamentals of Corporation Law 561–63 (1995).

47. Moran v. Household Int'l, Inc., 500 A.2d 1346, 1356 (Del.1985); Unocal Corp. v. Mesa Petroleum Co., 493 A.2d 946, 955 (Del.1985).

48. See Michael P. Dooley, Two Models of Corporate Governance, 47 Bus. Law. 461,

Why have the Delaware courts insisted on drawing such sharp distinctions between the board's role and that of management? Because while the conflict of interest unsolicited tender offers pose for the target company's managers is inescapable, the independent director's conflict of interest is merely a potential problem. For the independent directors, the conflicts posed by unsolicited tender offers are no different than those posed by freezeout mergers, management buyouts, interested director transactions, or a host of similar situations. Corporate law neither prohibits these transactions, nor requires complete board passivity in connection with them, simply because they potentially involve conflicts of interest. Instead, it regulates them in ways designed to constrain self-interested behavior. Unless one makes a living on the buy-side of corporate takeovers, it is not clear why hostile takeovers should be treated differently.

Consider, for example, the somewhat analogous case of management-sponsored leveraged buyouts. Like unsolicited tender offers, these transactions inherently involve a strong risk of management self-dealing. While management is acting as the sellers' agents and, in that capacity, is obliged to get the best price it can for the shareholders, it is also acting as a purchaser and, in that capacity, has a strong self-interest to pay the lowest possible price. Like unsolicited tender offers, management buyouts also create conflicts of interest for the independent directors. Just as an independent director may resist an unsolicited tender offer to avoid being fired by the hostile bidder, he may go along with a management buyout in order to avoid being fired by the incumbent managers. Alternatively, if an independent director is inclined to resist a hostile takeover because of his friendship with the insiders, why should he not go along with a management-sponsored buyout for the same reason? Strikingly, however, the empirical evidence indicates that shareholder premiums are essentially identical in management-sponsored leveraged buyouts and arms-length leveraged buyouts.[49] This evidence suggests that the potentially conflicted interests of independent directors are not affecting their ability to successfully constrain management misconduct. Accordingly, while judicial review of management buyouts tends to be rather intensive, courts have not prohibited such transactions, but have addressed the problem of conflicted interests by encouraging an active role for the firm's independent directors in approving a management buyout proposal.[50] Why should the same not be true of the board's response to unsolicited tender offers?

In sum, the conflict of interest present when the board responds to an unsolicited tender offers thus differs only in degree, not kind, from

---

518–19 (1992); see also William T. Allen, Independent Directors in MBO Transactions: Are They Fact or Fantasy?, 45 Bus. Law. 2055, 2060 (1990).

49. Jeffrey Davis & Kenneth Lehn, Information Asymmetries, Rule 13e–3, and Premiums in Going–Private Transactions, 70 Wash. U.L.Q. 587, 595–96 (1992).

50. See, e.g., In re RJR Nabisco, Inc. Shareholders Litigation, [1988–89 Transfer Binder] Fed. Sec. L. Rep. (CCH) ¶ 94,194, 1989 WL 7036 (Del.Ch.1989); Freedman v. Restaurant Assoc. Indus., Inc., [1987–88 Transfer Binder] Fed. Sec. L. Rep. (CCH) ¶ 93,502, 1987 WL 14323 (Del.Ch.1987).

any other corporate conflict. Although skepticism about their motives is thus appropriate, their conflict of interest does not necessarily equate to blameworthiness. Rather, it is simply a state of affairs inherently created by the necessity of conferring authority in the board of directors to act on behalf of the shareholders. To be sure, proponents of the no resistance rule will respond that such a state of affairs could be avoided by declining to confer such authority on the board in this context. Yet, if the legal system deprives the board of authority here, it will be hard-pressed to decline to do so with respect to other conflict transactions. As has been the case with other situations of potential conflict, we therefore would expect the courts to develop standards of review for takeover defenses that are designed to detect, punish, and deter self-interested behavior. Because the risk may be greater in this context, stricter than normal policing mechanisms may be required, but this does not mean that we must set aside authority values by divesting the board of decisionmaking authority.

Systemic accountability. Because the incumbent directors and management's transactional conflict of interest is neither so severe nor unusual as to justify a wholly new governance system for tender offers, opponents of target resistance to tender offers must find some other basis for depriving the board of its normal decisionmaking authority. For most critics of takeover defenses, such a basis is to be found in the systemic agency cost effects of management resistance.

In agency cost theory, disciplinary actions against employees and mid-level managers are expected to take the form of dismissals, demotions, or salary adjustments imposed by senior management. Where it is senior management that requires discipline, however, alternative mechanisms become necessary. According to the standard academic account, hostile takeover bidders provide just such a mechanism. Making the standard efficient capital market assumption that poor corporate performance will be reflected in the corporation's stock price, opponents of target resistance claim that a declining market price sends a signal to prospective bidders that there are gains to be had by acquiring the corporation and displacing the incumbent directors and managers. Of course, the signal will not always be correct. Sometimes the firm's market price may be declining despite the best efforts of competent management, as where some exogenous shock—such as technological change or new government regulation—has permanently altered the corporation's fundamentals. If close examination by a prospective bidder reveals that the declining market price is in fact attributable to shirking by senior management, however, a disciplinary takeover could produce real gains for division between the target's shareholders and the successful acquirer. This prospect creates positive incentives for potential bidders to investigate when the market signals a firm is in distress. Conversely, because keeping the stock price up is the best defense managers have against being displaced by an outside searcher, the market for corporate control—more specifically, the unsolicited tender offer—is an important mechanism for preventing management slacking.

Indeed, some would argue, the market for control is the ultimate monitor that makes the modern business corporation feasible.

By making possible target resistance to unsolicited takeover bids, so the theory goes, takeover defenses thus undermine the very foundations of corporate governance. The first prospective bidder to identify a prospective target incurs significant search costs, which become part of the bidder's overall profit calculation. By announcing its offer, however, the first bidder identifies the prospective target to all other potential bidders. Subsequent bidders thus need not incur the high search costs carried by the first bidder, perhaps allowing them to pay a higher price than is possible for the first bidder. If target resistance delays closing of the offer, subsequent bidders have a greater opportunity to enter the fray. At the very least, target resistance may force the initial bidder to raise its offer, reducing the gains to search. Target resistance therefore reduces bidders' incentives to search out takeover targets. Reductions in bidders' search incentives results in fewer opportunities for shareholders to profit from takeover premia. More important, a reduction in search incentives also reduces the effectiveness of interfirm monitoring by outsiders. In turn, that reduces the market for corporate control's disciplinary effect. A rule prohibiting target resistance is therefore likely to decrease agency costs, and increase stock prices, benefiting shareholders of all firms, even those whose companies are never targeted for a takeover bid.[51]

All well and good, but who died and left the unsolicited tender offer in charge? A no resistance rule in effect creates a kind of private eminent domain: bidders can effectively "condemn" target shares by offering even a slight premium over the current market price.[52] Awarding the lion's share of the gains to be had from a change of control to the bidder, however, only makes sense if all gains from takeovers are created by bidders through the elimination of inept or corrupt target managers and none are attributable to the hard work of efficient target managers.

---

51. Frank H. Easterbrook & Daniel R. Fischel, The Proper Role of a Target's Management in Responding to a Tender Offer, 94 Harv. L. Rev. 1161 (1981). Some commentators who generally accept the this account nonetheless have rejected the no resistance rule. These critics concede that the rule maximizes search incentives, but question the amount of search activity that is socially desirable. In particular, they assert, the benefits of increased search must be compared with the costs imposed on target companies if shareholders are coerced into selling at a price that they do not perceive to be higher than the value of the target to them. See, e.g., Lucian A. Bebchuk, The Case for Facilitating Competing Tender Offers: A Reply and Extension, 35 Stan. L. Rev. 23, 33–38 (1982). Alternatively, they posit that the benefits of permitting corporate control auctions can out-

weigh the costs of doing so. E.g., Jonathan R. Macey, Auction Theory, MBOs and Property Rights in Corporate Assets, 25 Wake Forest L. Rev. 85 (1990). We need not resolve this dispute within the ranks, because we believe that both sides have missed the central point by focusing solely on accountability concerns and ignoring the equally important role of authority values.

52. Lucian Arye Bebchuk, The Sole Owner Standard for Takeover Policy, 17 J. Leg. Stud. 197, 200 (1988). As Bebchuk notes, the taking implications of the no resistance rule are inconsistent with the passivity model's chief proponents' strong preference in other contexts for property rights and freedom of contract. Id. at 200–03. See generally Michael P. Dooley, Fundamentals of Corporation Law 552 (1995) (discussing Bebchuk's analysis).

Unfortunately for proponents of the no resistance rule, the evidence is that takeovers produce gains for a variety of reasons that are likely to differ from case to case.[53]

In order for a no resistance rule to make sense, the unsolicited tender offer also must be the critical mechanism by which incumbents are disciplined. In fact, however, unsolicited tender offers are so rare and sporadic that a director or manager who shirks his responsibilities by playing golf when he should be working is undoubtedly more likely to be struck by lightening while on the course than to be fired after a hostile takeover. As a result, the disciplinary effect of takeovers has been grossly overstated by proponents of the no resistance rule. Instead, as our analysis of Delaware's takeover jurisprudence will suggest, the critical disciplinary mechanism is the board of directors, especially the independent directors. In turn, the tenure and reputation of outside board members are determined by the performance of the inside managers, which gives independent directors incentives to be vigilant in overseeing management's conduct.

If independent directors were the sole bulwark against managerial shirking, concerns about structural and actual bias might be troubling, but they do not stand alone. Important accountability mechanisms are supplied by the product market in which the firm operates and the internal and external job markets for the firm's managers.[54] Corporate directors and managers do not get ahead by being associated with sub-par performance in the product markets. Indeed, as between shareholders and managers, it is the latter who have the greatest incentives to ensure the firm's success. Shareholders can and should hold diversified portfolios, so that the failure of an individual firm will not greatly decrease their total wealth, while managers cannot diversify their firm-specific human capital (or their general human capital, for that matter). If the firm fails on their watch, it is the incumbent directors and managers who suffer the principal losses.

It is for this reason that the capital markets also have a disciplinary function. Incompetent or even unlucky management eventually shows up in the firm's performance. These signs are identified by potential debt or equity investors, who (if they are willing to invest at all) will demand a higher rate of return to compensate them for the risks of continued

---

53. Useful summaries of the empirical literature include Bernard S. Black, Bidder Overpayment in Takeovers, 41 Stan. L. Rev. 597 (1989); Roberta Romano, A Guide to Takeovers: Theory, Evidence, and Regulation, 9 Yale J. Reg. 119 (1992). Among the more intriguing, albeit controversial, aspects of the empirical puzzle are the findings of industrial organization economists that takeovers and mergers generally do not result in increased revenues, market share, profitability, or cost efficiency on the target's part. See, e.g., David J. Ravenscraft & F.M. Scherer, Mergers and Managerial Performance, in Knights, Raiders, and Targets: The Impact of the Hostile Takeover (John C. Coffee et al. eds., 1988). But see Paul M. Healy et al., Does Corporate Performance Improve after Mergers?, 31 J. Fin. Econ. 135 (1992) (answering their titular question affirmatively and criticizing Ravenscraft and Scherer's work).

54. See Barry D. Baysinger & Henry N. Butler, Antitakeover Amendments, Managerial Entrenchment, and the Contractual Theory of the Corporation, 71 Va. L. Rev. 1257, 1272 (1985).

suboptimal performance. In turn, this makes the firm more likely to flounder—taking the incumbent managers down with it.

Our point is not that the tender offer has no disciplinary effect, but merely that the tender offer is only one of many mechanisms by which management's behavior is constrained. Once we view corporate governance as a system in which many forces constrain management behavior, the theory of the second best becomes relevant. In a complex, interdependent system, it holds that inefficiencies in one part of the system should be tolerated if "fixing" them would create even greater inefficiencies elsewhere in the system as a whole.[55] Even if we concede the claim that a no resistance rule would reduce agency costs, such a rule would still be inappropriate if it imposes costs in other parts of the corporate governance system. By restricting the board's authority with respect to tender offers, the various academic proposals impose just such costs by also restricting the board's authority with respect to the everyday decisions upon which shareholder wealth principally depends. Accordingly, it is not surprising that Delaware has rejected the academic approach to the unsolicited tender offer. This half of Delaware's takeover jurisprudence, like that regulating negotiated acquisitions, is best explained as implicitly concluding that the benefits of preserving authority outweighs the costs of doing so.

E. Evaluating Delaware's balance

In its takeover jurisprudence, Delaware has balanced the competing claims of authority and accountability by varying the standard of review according to the likelihood that the actions of the board or managers will be tainted by conflicted interests in a particular transactional setting and the likelihood that nonlegal forces can effectively constrain those conflicted interests in that setting. In other words, the Delaware cases suggest that motive is the key issue. As former Delaware Chancellor Allen explained in the closely related context of management buyout transactions: "The court's own implicit evaluation of the integrity of the . . . process marks that process as deserving respect or condemns it to be ignored." Assuming that a special committee of independent directors would be appointed to consider the proposed transaction, Allen went on to explain: "When a special committee's process is perceived as reflecting a good faith, informed attempt to approximate aggressive, arms-length bargaining, it will be accorded substantial importance by the court. When, on the other hand, it appears as artifice, ruse or charade, or when the board unduly limits the committee or when the committee fails to correctly perceive its mission—then one can expect that its decision will be accorded no respect."[56] Our claim is the same is true with respect to

---

55. See Michael P. Dooley, Two Models of Corporate Governance, 47 Bus. Law. 461, 525 (1992).

56. William T. Allen, Independent Directors in MBO Transactions: Are They

Fact or Fantasy?, 45 Bus. Law. 2055, 2060 (1990); see generally Michael P. Dooley, Two Models of Corporate Governance, 47 Bus. Law. 461, 517–24 (1992) (discussing board resistance to unsolicited tender offers. If the conflict of interest inherent in such resistance has matured into actual self-dealing, the court will invalidate the defensive tactics. If the board acted from proper motives, even if mistakenly, however, the court will leave the defenses in place.

Former Delaware supreme court Justice Moore argued, for example, that his court's "decisions represent a case-by-case analysis of some difficult and compelling problems."[57] He later elaborated:

> We did not approach [takeover] cases with the question of whether to allow the corporation to continue in its present form or to permit someone else to acquire the company.... [T]he question before the Court was whether the directors acted properly in accepting or rejecting the competing offers.... As long as the directors adhered to their fiduciary duties, it would have been most inappropriate for any court to intrude upon a board's business decision. No court has a role in disciplining directors for the proper exercise of business judgment, even if it turns out to be wrong.[58]

Former Delaware Chancellor Allen made much the same point in *RJR Nabisco*, where he indicated that the basic question is whether the board acted with due care and in good faith:

> Surely the board may not use its power to exercise judgment in [an auction of control] as a sham or pretext to prefer one bidder for inappropriate reasons.... But the board of directors continues, in the auction setting as in others, to bear the burden imposed and exercise the power conferred by Section 141(a). Assuming it does exercise a business judgment, in good faith and advisedly, concerning the management of the auction process, it has, in my opinion, satisfied its duty.[59]

A federal court similarly described the *Unocal* standard as asking "whether a fully informed, wholly disinterested, reasonably courageous director would dissent from the board's act in any material part."[60] Motive is the consistent theme throughout these summations of Delaware law.

1. The evolution towards a motive-based inquiry

As the *Unocal* rules evolved, two recurring questions arose. First, what threats to the corporation and its shareholders were legally cogni-

---

the significance of board motives in Delaware's takeover jurisprudence).

57. Andrew G.T. Moore, II, State Competition: Panel Response, 8 Cardozo L. Rev. 779, 782 (1987).

58. Andrew G.T. Moore, II, The 1980s— Did We Save the Stockholders While the Corporation Burned?, 70 Wash. U.L.Q. 277, 287–89 (1992).

59. In re RJR Nabisco, Inc. Shareholders Litigation, [1988–89 Transfer Binder] Fed. Sec. L. Rep. (CCH) ¶ 94,194 at 91,715, 1989 WL 7036 (Del.Ch.1989).

60. Southdown, Inc. v. Moore McCormack Resources, Inc., 686 F.Supp. 595, 602 (S.D.Tex.1988).

zable under the first prong? Second, what defenses were proportional to a given threat?

At least for a time, the Delaware chancery court defined the category of cognizable threats quite narrowly. Only threats to shareholder interests had any real analytical significance. Nor were all threats to shareholder interests cognizable. Rather, at least in the context of an offer for all of the target's outstanding shares, the trend was towards limiting cognizable threats to inadequate value and structural coercion.[61] Inadequate value refers, obviously enough, to a claim that the price offered by the bidder is too low. Structural coercion refers to bidder tactics creating a "risk that disparate treatment of non-tendering shareholders might distort shareholders' tender decisions."[62]

The Delaware courts gave target directors a more-or-less free hand to deal with structurally coercive bidder tactics. Defenses designed to preclude such offers, to minimize their coercive effect, or to provide a more viable alternative to the shareholders all were deemed proportional. Indeed, when structural coercion was the identified threat, proportionality review usually was perfunctory at best.[63]

When inadequate value was the sole threat, however, proportionality review became more exacting. As most observers interpreted the so-called poison pill cases,[64] *Unocal* permitted target management to use takeover defenses as negotiating leverage to obtain a better deal for the shareholders or, more realistically, to delay the hostile offer while an

---

61. See, e.g., City Capital Assoc. Ltd. Partnership v. Interco Inc., 551 A.2d 787, 797 (Del.Ch.1988).

62. Ronald J. Gilson & Reinier Kraakman, Delaware's Intermediate Standard for Defensive Tactics: Is there Substance to Proportionality Review, 44 Bus. Law. 247, 267 (1989). Two-tier tender offers are perhaps the most commonly recognized form of structural coercion. If shareholders believe that the offeror is likely to obtain a controlling interest in the front-end transaction, they face the risk that they will be squeezed out in the back-end for less desirable consideration. Thus they are coerced into tendering into the front-end to avoid that risk, even if they believe the front-end transaction itself is undesirable.

63. In *Unocal*, for example, the court's proportionality analysis can be described most charitably as concise. See Unocal Corp. v. Mesa Petroleum Co., 493 A.2d 946, 956 (Del.1985). Note that Delaware law on coercive bidder tactics is easily squared with our authority-accountability framework. On the one hand, corporate law grants sweeping powers to the board in part so that the board can protect shareholder financial interests. If a coercive bid threatens those interests, authority values thus justify board resistance. On the other hand,

giving the board power to resist coercive offers does not implicate significant accountability concerns. To be sure, the board's decision to resist a structurally coercive bid may be motivated by personal considerations unrelated to shareholder welfare. But so what? In the first place, the category of structurally coercive tactics is a well-defined one, making it possible to objectively determine whether the board was responding to a true threat to shareholder interests. In the second, why should it matter that incumbents get some protection if resistance also protects shareholder interests? The bidder, after all, controls its own fate in this regard. If the bidder drops the structurally coercive aspects of its offer, this justification for defensive tactics is no longer availing.

64. The name refers to a group of cases in which targets used poison pills to protect a restructuring plan from interference by a hostile bidder. See, e.g., Grand Metropolitan PLC v. Pillsbury Co., 558 A.2d 1049 (Del.Ch.1988); City Capital Assoc. Ltd. Partnership v. Interco Inc., 551 A.2d 787 (Del.Ch.1988); see also BNS Inc. v. Koppers Co., Inc., 683 F.Supp. 458 (D.Del.1988) (applying Delaware law); CRTF Corp. v. Federated Dep't Stores, Inc., 683 F.Supp. 422 (S.D.N.Y.1988) (same).

alternative transaction was arranged. In either case, however, target management supposedly had to let the shareholders make the ultimate decision.[65] According to the conventional wisdom, once it became clear the best possible alternatives were on the table, the board was required to redeem the pill and permit the shareholders to choose between the available alternatives. The target board could neither "just say no," nor could it structure the transaction in such a way as to force shareholders to accept a management-sponsored alternative.

A superficial reading of these cases might lead one to conclude that the Delaware courts have embraced the structural argument described above. Proponents of the structural argument would insist that the critical doctrinal factor is whether shareholders were allowed to make the ultimate decision between the course of action proposed by management and that opposed by management. On close examination, however, this reading misses a subtle, but important nuance.

In *Interco*, the leading poison pill case, the target's board of directors refused to redeem its poison pill. By doing so, the board prevented a hostile bid from going forward until a management-sponsored restructuring could be completed, which would make Interco an unattractive takeover target. Chancellor Allen enjoined the board's obstructive tactics, using dicta that broadly endorsed the shareholder choice position.[66] Tellingly, however, he concluded "that reasonable minds not affected by an inherent, entrenched interest in the matter, could not reasonably differ with respect to the conclusion that the [bidder's] $74 cash offer did not represent a threat to shareholder interests sufficient in the circumstances to justify, in effect, foreclosing shareholders from electing to accept that offer." If the right to decide belongs to the shareholders, however, what relevance does the board's motives have? A motive analysis is only necessary—or appropriate, for that matter—if the board in fact has decisive authority in takeover battles.[67]

The emphasis on motive is further confirmed by a case outside the line of poison pill decisions: the Delaware supreme court's *Macmillan* decision.[68] In May 1987, Macmillan's senior management recognized that

---

65. Cases purporting to stand for the proposition that the board must ultimately permit the shareholders to choose include: Shamrock Holdings, Inc. v. Polaroid Corp., 559 A.2d 257 (Del.Ch.1989); Grand Metropolitan PLC v. Pillsbury Co., 558 A.2d 1049, 1058 (Del.Ch.1988); City Capital Assoc. Ltd. Partnership v. Interco Inc., 551 A.2d 787, 799–800 (Del.Ch.1988); AC Acquisitions Corp. v. Anderson, Clayton & Co., 519 A.2d 103, 113–14 (Del.Ch.1986). But see Moran v. Household Int'l, Inc., 490 A.2d 1059, 1070 (Del.Ch.), aff'd, 500 A.2d 1346 (Del. 1985).

66. City Capital Assoc. Ltd. Partnership v. Interco, Inc., 551 A.2d 787 (Del.Ch.1988). See generally Michael P. Dooley, Two Mod-

els of Corporate Governance, 47 Bus. Law. 461, 519–21 (1992).

67. This reading of Allen's *Interco* opinion is supported by his subsequent *TW Services* decision, in which he distinguished *Interco* and the other poison pill cases from the case at bar on the ground that the former did not "involve circumstances in which a board had in good faith (which appears to exist here) elected to continue managing the enterprise in a long term mode and not to actively consider an extraordinary transaction of any type." TW Servs. v. SWT Acquisition Corp., 1989 WL 20290 (1989).

68. Mills Acquisition Co. v. Macmillan, Inc., 559 A.2d 1261, 1265 (Del.1989).

it was a likely takeover target. Management therefore began studying a restructuring plan that would effectively transfer voting control to senior managers. Before the restructuring could be completed, the Robert M. Bass Group emerged as a potential bidder. The board then lowered the threshold at which its poison pill would become operative and took various other defensive steps designed to stave off the Bass Group until the restructuring could be completed. Unfortunately for Macmillan's management, Vice Chancellor Jacobs found that the restructuring was not only economically inferior to the Bass Group bid, but also was designed to preclude the shareholders from accepting that bid.[69] Concluding that *Unocal* obliged Macmillan's directors to give their shareholders "a choice," the Vice Chancellor enjoined the restructuring. So far all is perfectly consistent with the conventional wisdom.

Undaunted by their initial failure, the Macmillan board immediately began exploring a management-sponsored leveraged buyout. Shortly thereafter, a company controlled by Robert Maxwell entered the fray. Early negotiations with Maxwell were largely conducted by Macmillan's incumbent CEO. Maxwell was misled, while information about his bid was tipped to management's leveraged buyout partner. Nor did the Macmillan board of directors act to restrain management; instead, the board essentially abdicated its oversight function, allowing management to skew the auction process in favor of their partner. Finally, the board granted a lock-up option to management's partner, effectively precluding Maxwell from presenting a competing tender offer to the target's shareholders. The ultimate decision thus was made not by the disinterested board members or the shareholders, but by the same managers who were trying to buy the company.

Now we reach the point at which the conventional wisdom begins to unravel. In the course of invalidating the lock-up, the supreme court distinguished between lock-ups that draw an otherwise unwilling bidder into the contest and those that end an active auction by effectively foreclosing further bidding. While neither type is per se unlawful, the latter is subject to exacting judicial scrutiny. Where the target obtains only a minimal increase in the final bid in return for an auction-ending lock-up, the agreement is unlikely to pass muster. On the other hand, where the favored bidder offers a significant price increase in return for an end to competitive bidding, judicial review will be more favorable.

If this distinction is to be taken seriously, *Macmillan* effectively permits the board to foreclose shareholder choice.[70] Lock-ups can pose a severe threat both to free shareholder choice and to continued competitive bidding. While *Macmillan* holds bid-preclusive lock-ups to a high standard, it also leaves open the possibility that the board can justify

---

69. Robert M. Bass Group, Inc. v. Evans, 552 A.2d 1227, 1241–44 (Del.Ch.1988).

70. In theory, of course, shareholders retain some degree of choice even in this context. They can reject the favored bidder's proposal, by voting down a merger agreement or refusing to sell into a tender offer, in the hopes that competing bids will then be made. In practice, however, the factors outlined in the text often render even this vestige of shareholder choice illusory.

their use in appropriate cases. What then happened to the principle of free shareholder choice? The answer is that *Macmillan* rested not on shareholder choice but on motive. *Macmillan* implies that the board retains full decisionmaking authority—including the authority to foreclose shareholder choice—unless it acted from improper motives.

This interpretation of *Macmillan* is forcefully confirmed by the contrast between that decision and Chancellor Allen's opinion in the RJR Nabisco takeover fight. Drawn with a broad brush, these cases appear to be quite similar. In both, the sequence of events opened with a proposal to give incumbent management control of the company. In both, a competing bid then emerged. In both, an auction of corporate control developed. In both, the board ultimately had to select between two bids that were quite close in price. Yet the results were quite different. In *Macmillan*, the board selected the nominally higher bid, but was found guilty of breaching its fiduciary duties. In *RJR Nabisco*, the board rejected the nominally higher bid, but its decision was protected by the business judgment rule. Why this disparity of result? As always, the answer is in the details.

In *RJR Nabisco*, a special committee of outside directors was formed as soon as the board was told that a group led by Russ Johnson, the President and Chief Executive Officer, wanted to take the company private in a management-sponsored leveraged buyout.[71] The board carefully did not permit Johnson to have any role in the selection of the special committee; nor did the committee permit Johnson any role in selecting its financial or legal advisers. No member of the special committee had any direct or indirect financial interest in the transaction. The committee's independence paid off handsomely in its insistence on fair competition. The management group's role in the auction was limited to that of a bidder, with no special advantages. Indeed, plaintiffs asserted that the committee and the board were biased against management, a claim Chancellor Allen found "baseless." As a result, there was no basis for believing that the board's decisions were motivated by self-interest.

In *Macmillan*, by contrast, there was a lengthy delay before a special board committee was formed. The special committee was "hand picked" by the incumbent chief executive officer, who along with Macmillan's other senior managers was to receive up to a 20 percent equity stake in the firm if their leveraged buyout proposal succeeded. The supposedly independent committee, moreover, included a former college classmate of the CEO's father. The committee's financial and legal advisers were selected by the CEO. Not surprisingly, the committee failed to adequately oversee the competitive process, allowing management to skew the process in its favor.

71. RJR Nabisco, [1988–89 Transfer   91,703.
Binder] Fed. Sec. L. Rep. (CCH) ¶ 94,194 at

Circumstantial evidence of the board's motives thus proved critical to the outcomes of both cases. In *RJR Nabisco*, for example, Chancellor Allen ultimately treated plaintiff's complaint as "an attack upon a decision made by an apparently disinterested board in the exercise of its statutory power to manage the business and affairs of the corporation." Finding no evidence that undermined the appearance of disinterest, Chancellor Allen upheld the RJR Nabisco board's conduct even though the two bids were substantially equivalent. He did so even though the nominally higher bid was rejected. He did so even though the board expressly refused to reopen the bidding. This last is particularly striking. The stated reason for the board's refusal to reopen the bidding, despite the closeness of the two bids, was a concern that the non-management bidder would drop out if the auction was extended. Although Allen believed that was unlikely, in light of the absence of any evidence that the board had acted from conflicted interests he deferred to the board's decision to endorse one of the bids, just as our analysis suggests he should have done. In contrast, the strong evidence of self-interested behavior by Macmillan's officers and directors rendered the board's decisions unworthy of deference.[72] Shareholder choice thus is not important in its own right, but rather has significance only because attempts to foreclose it may suggest that the board of directors' inherent conflict of interest has shifted from being a potential problem to an actual one.

2. *The merits of a motive-based inquiry*

Our evaluation of the balance thus struck by the Delaware courts between authority and accountability depends on the merits of the motive-based analysis they have adopted. Some observers will concede that target managers and directors do not always pursue their own self-interest, but argue that the difficulty of distinguishing between proper and improper motives is so great in this context that courts should simply eschew a motive-based analysis. Granted, motive analysis is always difficult, but in every other conflicted interest context the board's authority to act depends upon the validity of the directors' motives.[73] Unless we are to accept the passivity model and strip the board of

---

72. Other examples of the outcome-determinative nature of motive include Gilbert v. El Paso Co., 575 A.2d 1131, 1146 (Del.1990) (upholding settlement of a hostile takeover contest because "there is not a scintilla of evidence to intimate that this arrangement was the result of improper motives" on the board's part); Ivanhoe Partners v. Newmont Mining Corp., 535 A.2d 1334, 1344 (Del.1987) (upholding defensive tactics because the "board acted to maintain the company's independence and not merely to preserve its own control"); Henley Group, Inc. v. Santa Fe Southern Pacific Corp., 13 Del J. Corp. L. 1152, 1178 (Del.Ch.1988) (upholding corporate restructuring where the board's "diligent efforts" to sell the company before embarking on the restructuring "deprive[d] the plaintiffs' argument—that the defendants were motivated to entrench themselves—of its force."); Freedman v. Restaurant Assoc. Indus., [1987–1988 Transfer Binder] Fed. Sec. L. Rep. (CCH) ¶ 93,502, 1987 WL 14323 (Del.Ch.1987) (board committee's handling of management-led leveraged buyout proposal to be reviewed under the business judgment rule because plaintiffs had "failed utterly to offer any legal justification for the court's second-guessing of the special committee.").

73. Michael P. Dooley, Two Models of Corporate Governance, 47 Bus. Law. 461, 518 (1992).

decisionmaking authority in the takeover context, a motive-based inquiry is inescapable.

In multiple bidder settings, moreover, the board's conduct in overseeing the competition between the management-sponsored alternative and the hostile bid provides more-or-less objective insights into the board's motives. Suppose for example that the Macmillan board had conducted a fair auction, in which neither side had any special advantages. At the end of this process, one of the competing bidders offered a substantial increase in price in return for a lock-up option. On these facts, it seems unlikely that a board decision to grant the option is tainted by improper motives. As the Eleventh Circuit has noted:

> All auctions must end sometime, and lock-ups by definition must discourage other bidders. The question therefore is not whether the asset lock-up granted to [the favored bidder] effectively ended the bidding process. The question is whether [the target] conducted a fair auction, and whether [the favored bidder] made the best offer.[74]

If those questions can be answered in the affirmative, we have more or less objective evidence that the board acted from proper motives even though their actions effectively precluded anyone other than the favored bidder from acquiring the company. The use of a lock-up or other defensive tactics to foreclose shareholder choice in such situations thus no longer raises a presumption of self-interest. The superiority of the prevailing proposal will have been demonstrated by the competitive process.[75]

3. *The pivotal Paramount cases*

The ability of Delaware's takeover doctrine to address cases in which improper motives tainted the board's decisionmaking process was at first undermined but ultimately restored in a pair of well-known cases involving Paramount Communications. In the first of these cases, *Paramount Communications v. Time Inc.*,[76] the Delaware courts addressed a takeover struggle between Time, Warner Communications, and Paramount. After first developing a long-term strategic plan and searching for acquisitions that would advance that plan, Time's board of directors agreed to a merger with Warner Communications in which former

---

74. Cottle v. Storer Communication, Inc., 849 F.2d 570, 576 (11th Cir.1988) (citations omitted).

75. That this principle can be generalized to a wide range of takeover actions is illustrated by Henley Group, Inc. v. Santa Fe Southern Pacific Corp., 1988 WL 23945 (1988). The defendant corporation adopted a poison debt plan pursuant to which pay-in-kind debentures were distributed to the company's shareholders as part of a restructuring. A variety of anti-takeover provisions were built into the debentures, making the company a much less attractive takeover candidate. Id. at 1174–75. Vice Chancellor Jacobs, however, deemed the debentures to be valid under *Unocal*. The Vice Chancellor's conclusion was driven in large part by the board of directors' "diligent efforts" to sell the company prior to embarking upon the restructuring. Id. at 1178. Those efforts "deprive[d] the plaintiffs' argument—that the defendants were motivated to entrench themselves—of its force." Id.

76. Paramount Communications, Inc. v. Time Inc., [1989 Transfer Binder] Fed. Sec. L. Rep. (CCH) ¶ 94,514, 1989 WL 79880 (Del.Ch.), aff'd, 571 A.2d 1140 (Del.1989).

Warner shareholders would receive newly issued Time shares representing approximately 62 percent of the shares of the combined entity. As is typical in negotiated acquisitions, the parties also sought "to discourage any effort to upset the transaction" by agreeing to a lock-up option giving each party the option to trigger an exchange of shares. In addition, the merger agreement included a no shop clause in the merger agreement, which they supplemented by obtaining commitments from various banks that they would not finance a takeover bid for Time.

Shortly before Time' shareholders were to vote on the merger agreement,[77] Paramount made a cash tender offer for Time. Time's board rejected the offer as inadequate, without entering into negotiations with Paramount. To forestall Paramount, the Time and Warner boards then agreed to a new structure for the transaction, under which Time would make a cash tender offer for a majority block of Warner shares to be followed by a merger in which remaining Warner shares would be acquired, thus obviating the need for shareholder approval. The new plan required Time to incur between 7 and 10 billion dollars in additional debt. Finally, and perhaps most damningly from the perspective of a Time shareholder, it foreclosed the possibility of a sale to Paramount. If the new plan succeeded, Time's shareholders therefore would end up as minority shareholders in a company saddled with substantial debt and whose stock price almost certainly would be lower in the short run than the Paramount offer.

The substantial differences in shareholder wealth likely to result from a decision to merge with Warner rather than to sell to Paramount forcefully presented the question of who should make that decision. As Chancellor Allen put it, the "overarching question is where legally (an easy question) and equitably (more subtle problem) the locus of decision-making power does or should reside in circumstances of this kind." Paramount naturally insisted that Time's board had an obligation to give the "shareholders the power and opportunity to decide whether the company should now be sold." Chancellor Allen, however, squarely rejected that proposition. Allen acknowledged that reasonable people could believe that the Paramount offer was the better deal for the shareholders, that many of Time's shareholders undoubtedly so believed, and that the Time directors' preference for the Warner deal might turn out to be a terrible mistake. Having said all that, however, the board nonetheless had the authority to go forward with the Warner acquisition:

> [T]he financial vitality of the corporation and the value of the company's shares is in the hands of the directors and management of the firm. The corporation law does not operate on the theory that directors, in exercising their powers to manage the firm, are obligat-

77. The plan of merger called for Warner to be merged into a Time subsidiary in exchange for Time common stock. Although Time was not formally a party to the merger and approval by its shareholders therefore was not required under Delaware law, New York Stock Exchange rules required a vote of Time shareholders because of the number of shares to be issued.

ed to follow the wishes of a majority of shares. In fact, directors, not shareholders, are charged with the duty to manage the firm.[78]

So much for the structural argument. By now it should not be surprising that we, unlike proponents of the structural argument, are not troubled by *Time*'s emphasis on board prerogative at the expense of shareholder choice. Because we regard shareholder choice as having little, if any, independent normative significance, the question for us is whether the Time board's foreclosing of shareholder choice was based on proper or improper motives. In other words, did the board exercise its prerogative in ways suggesting that the transaction was driven by management self-interest?

Granted, Time's decisions were made by a board comprised principally of outsiders with no readily apparent conflicts of interest. Once the Paramount bid emerged, however, the directors undertook a drastic course of action whose sole purpose was preventing their shareholders from accepting Paramount's offer. As in *Macmillan* and *Interco*, the attempt to foreclose shareholder choice without first conducting a fair competition for control implicates accountability concerns because it provides circumstantial evidence from which one might reasonably infer the presence of self-interested decisionmaking.

Both decisions in *Time* responded at least implicitly to this concern. Both courts concluded that the Time board's initial decision to merge with Warner was protected by the business judgment rule. Both courts also concluded that the lock-up, the decision to recast the transaction as a tender offer for Warner, and the various other measures undertaken to stave off Paramount's competing bid involved a conflict of interest sufficiently severe to require application of a more exacting standard of review. The preliminary question then was whether the *Unocal* or *Revlon* standard governed.

For somewhat different reasons both Chancellor Allen and the supreme court concluded that *Revlon* had not triggered. Chancellor Allen followed the poison pill cases by holding that *Revlon* applies to any transaction constituting a change in control, but he determined that the merger agreement would not result in a transfer of control because

---

78. Paramount Communications, Inc. v. Time Inc., [1989 Transfer Binder] Fed. Sec. L. Rep. (CCH) ¶ 94,514 at 93,284, 1989 WL 79880 (Del.Ch.1989). The Supreme Court agreed: "Delaware law confers the management of the corporate enterprise to the stockholders' duly elected board representatives.... That duty may not be delegated to the stockholders." Paramount Communications, Inc. v. Time Inc., 571 A.2d 1140, 1154 (Del.1989). The Supreme Court further observed, however, that courts should not substitute their "judgment as to what is a 'better' deal for that of a corporation's board of directors." Id. at 1153. Unfortunately, the Delaware supreme court there-upon accused the Chancery Court of having done so in *Interco* and its progeny, id., which is neither fair nor accurate. While Chancellor Allen observed in *Interco* that the actual value of the restructuring was "highly debatable," he did not attempt to resolve the valuation dispute. City Capital Assoc. Ltd. Partnership v. Interco Inc., 551 A.2d 787, 799 (Del.Ch.1988). Instead, Chancellor Allen determined (as we read his opinion) that the board of directors was disabled from acting because of their demonstrated conflict of interest. *Interco* thus is not inconsistent with the authority values *Time* reflects, but rather brought into play accountability concerns *Time* downplayed.

control of the combined entity remained "in a large, fluid, changeable and changing market."

Although the Delaware supreme court indicated Allen's analysis was correct "as a matter of law," it rejected plaintiff's *Revlon* claims on "different grounds":

> Under Delaware law there are, generally speaking and without excluding other possibilities, two circumstances which may implicate *Revlon* duties. The first, and clearer one, is when a corporation initiates an active bidding process seeking to sell itself or to effect a business reorganization involving a clear break-up of the company. However, *Revlon* duties may also be triggered where, in response to a bidder's offer, a target abandons its long-term strategy and seeks an alternative transaction also involving the breakup of the company.[79]

This passage is not exactly crystal clear. What are the other possibilities the court did not exclude? What is the difference between the first and second identified possibilities? If they were deciding the case on broader grounds than Allen, can change of control transactions not involving a break-up of the company still trigger *Revlon*?[80] In particular, does *Revlon* apply when the target "initiates an active auction process seeking to sell itself," but the auction participants do not contemplate breaking-up the company?[81] What does the Court mean by a break-up of the company?[82] One could spin out such questions indefinitely, but the key point remains that the Court appears to have used *Time* as a vehicle for sharply limiting *Revlon*'s scope, albeit in an unusually murky manner.

---

79. Paramount Communications, Inc. v. Time Inc., 571 A.2d 1140, 1150 (Del.1989).

80. Suppose the target company, which is following some long-term business strategy, receives a hostile takeover bid. In response, the target's board decides to effect a recapitalization, which will transfer control to an identifiable control block comprised of target management and its allies, but will not require the sale of any target assets. Does *Revlon* apply? Arguably not. Even if this is a business reorganization, it does not involve a break-up of the company, so neither the first nor the second prong appear to be triggered.

81. Suppose that a target company sought out a white knight bid. Assume the white knight intends to keep the target intact and to continue the target's long-term strategy. Does *Revlon* apply? The second prong of the court's test is inapplicable, because there has been no abandonment of the strategy and there is to be no break up of the company. The answer therefore depends on how you read the first prong. The target has "initiate[d] an active bidding process seeking to sell itself." But query

whether this prong triggers Revlon in the absence of an intention to break up the company. Does the language "involving a clear break-up of the company" in that sentence modify both clauses or only the latter? In this regard, note that the Court premised its rejection of plaintiff's Revlon argument on "the absence of any substantial evidence to conclude that Time's board, in negotiating with Warner, made the dissolution or breakup of the corporate entity inevitable, as was the case in Revlon." Paramount Communications, Inc. v. Time Inc., 571 A.2d 1140, 1150 (Del.1989).

82. Presumably they have in mind the species of transactions commonly referred to as "bust-up" takeovers, in which a bidder finances the transaction through highly leveraged debt securities and then sells substantial portions of the target's assets in order to help finance the acquisition. If so, however, it also remains unclear what percentage of the firm must be sold off in order for the transaction to be regarded as a break-up. See Marc I. Steinberg, Nightmare on Main Street: The Paramount Picture Horror Show, 16 Del. J. Corp. L. 1, 16–17 (1991).

The court's rejection of *Revlon* is curious because *Revlon*, as it had been interpreted before *Time,* seemed well-designed to address the problem at hand. There was a growing recognition that the *Revlon* "duties" were in fact simply the general *Unocal* rules applied to a special fact situation. Consistent with our analysis of *Unocal* and its progeny, there also was growing recognition that *Revlon* is principally concerned with capturing cases of conflicted interests.[83] Hence, *Revlon* did not create a special duty of the board, and corresponding right of the shareholders, to maximize the short-term value of the target company's shares through a control auction.[84] *Revlon* thus provided a useful vehicle by which the court might have determined whether the board had acted from improper motives. But the *Time* court not only ignored this option, its limitation of *Revlon*'s doctrinal scope restricted the ability of Delaware courts to do so in future cases. This weakening of *Revlon* thus threatened to permit cases in which the board acted from improper motives to escape judicial review.

To be sure, the *Time* courts did not leave the lock-up and other bid-preclusive measures immune from challenge. Instead, both courts concluded that the lock-up and Time's subsequent recasting of the acquisition as a tender offer were defensive measures to be analyzed under *Unocal.* Relying on *Interco* and its progeny, Paramount argued that bid-preclusive defensive tactics were excessive in light of the minimal threat of inadequate value posed by a non-coercive tender offer at a substantial premium. Chancellor Allen distinguished those cases on the grounds that the original decision to merge with Warner was motivated by Time's long-term business plan. Unlike the poison pill cases, in which the management-sponsored transaction was principally intended to defeat an unsolicited tender offer, Chancellor Allen saw the revised structure of the Time–Warner transaction as being principally intended to facilitate accomplishment of the board's long-term strategy. Given that the tender offer thus arose out of preexisting legitimate, non-defensive business considerations, Time had a "legally cognizable interest" in going forward with the acquisition of Warner, which satisfied the first prong of *Unocal.*

Allen believed the second prong of the *Unocal* analysis required him to evaluate, among other things, the importance of the corporate policy at stake and the impact of the board's actions. With respect to the first point, Chancellor Allen reiterated his view that pursuing the board's long-term strategy was a legitimate and important corporate goal. As to

---

83. See, e.g., Barkan v. Amsted Indus., Inc., 567 A.2d 1279, 1286 (Del.1989); In re J.P. Stevens & Co., Inc. Shareholders Litig., 542 A.2d 770, 778 (Del.Ch.1988).

84. From this perspective, *Revlon* itself can be seen as a case in which the board's actions strongly suggest self-interest. Why else would an honest auctioneer approve a transaction other than the highest bid if not for improper motives, at least assuming the competing proposals are identical in all respects other than price? While the court did not find that the board acted out of self-interest, the inherently conflicted position of a target board coupled with the suggestive conduct of the board at hand sufficed to taint their course of action. In fact, it appears that Revlon's directors were mainly concerned with protecting themselves from litigation by the company's debtholders. See Revlon, Inc. v. MacAndrews & Forbes Holdings, Inc., 506 A.2d 173 (Del.1985).

the latter, he observed that the offer for Warner "was effective, but not overly broad." Time's board thus "did only what was necessary to carry forward a preexisting transaction in an altered form."

As with Allen's *Revlon* analysis, the supreme court affirmed his *Unocal* analysis, but once again did so with important differences. The supreme court expressly rejected Paramount's argument that structural coercion and inadequate value were the only threats cognizable under *Unocal*. Instead, *Unocal* was to be applied on a case-by-case basis and in a flexible, open-ended manner. Among the flexible, open-ended threats the court identified in this case were the possibility that shareholders might incorrectly value the benefits of sticking with management's long-term business plan, the difficulty of comparing Paramount's bid to the benefits of the Warner acquisition, and the possibility that Paramount's bid might "upset, if not confuse," the shareholder vote. Applying the second, proportionality prong of the *Unocal* analysis, the court found that Time's recasting of the transaction was a reasonable response to the identified threats.

Just as had been the case with its analysis of *Revlon*, the supreme court's approach marked a major turning point in the evolution of *Unocal*. It expanded the list of cognizable threats and arguably weakened the proportionality standard. In doing so, it appeared to undermine the ability of the *Unocal* framework to capture cases in which conflicted interests drove the board's decisionmaking process.

Consider, for example, that many commentators concluded that *Time* validated the so-called "just say no" defense, pursuant to which the target's board simply refuses to allow the firm to be acquired, backing up that refusal by a poison pill or other takeover defenses.[85] We find this reading unpersuasive. At the Chancery Court level, Allen's analysis hinged on his observation that Time's acquisition of Warner did not legally preclude "the successful prosecution of a hostile tender offer" for the resulting entity. More important, he also indicated that defensive tactics used against a hostile offer by Paramount or some other bidder for the combined entity after Time's acquisition of Warner would present a different issue.

The supreme court's opinion is similarly limited. While it is true that the court rejected any inference that directors are obliged to abandon a pre-existing business plan in order to permit short-term shareholder gains, Time's plan was deemed reasonable and proportionate to the Paramount threat precisely because it was "not aimed at 'cramming down' on its shareholders a management-sponsored alternative," but was only intended to carry forward "a preexisting transaction in an altered form." The supreme court also expressly affirmed Chancel-

---

85. See Wall St. J., Feb. 28, 1990, at A3. Prior cases had at least implicitly rejected the just say no defense. In *Interco*, for example, Chancellor Allen indicated that "in most instances" the use of takeover defenses was only legitimate in connection with attempts by the board to negotiate with the unsolicited bidder or to assemble an alternative transaction. City Capital Assoc. Ltd. Partnership v. Interco Inc., 551 A.2d 787, 798 (Del.Ch.1988). In other words, the board can not simply just say no.

lor Allen's finding that Time's actions "did not preclude Paramount from making an offer for the combined Time–Warner company."

These limitations on the court's holding are important, because they eliminate the just say no defense, as well as some of the other more apocalyptic interpretations of *Time*. The just say no defense does cram down a particular result—independence—on the shareholders, and also attempts to preclude anyone from making an offer for the combined company, both of which the court said management could not do. *Time* thus does not necessarily compel one to conclude that the just say no defense will be deemed to be proportional to an adequate, non-coercive offer.

The trouble is that this limitation on *Time*'s scope is not sufficient, because it in fact creates it own problems. The courts' concern with the legal effect of Time's actions appeared to signal a retreat from the use of *Unocal* to constrain target defensive measures. Consider, for example, the poison pill cases. Suppose management responds to an unsolicited tender offer by proposing a restructuring that effectively transfers voting control to the incumbent management team. The target's board endorses this proposal and, to insure its success, refuses to redeem the target's outstanding poison pill. Because of the substantial financial injury a pill would work on the bidding company and its shareholders, a bidder rarely seeks to complete its tender offer while an effective pill remains in place. Unless there has been a fair competition between the competing proposals, this course of conduct necessarily permits an inference of management self-interest. Yet, just as Time's actions did not legally preclude Paramount from pursuing a bid for the combined Time–Warner entity, a poison pill does not legally preclude a bidder from going forward. Accordingly, one could have plausibly argued that it was proper under *Time*'s interpretation of *Unocal*.

Although *Time*'s doctrinal implications are troubling, the actual result in that case is far less troubling. In most of the poison pill cases, for example, the pill was deployed in order to delay a hostile bid while the target undertook a defensive restructuring intended to give management effective voting control or to otherwise make the target unpalatable to potential bidders.[86] Such a restructuring's deterrent effect is not

---

86. In a typical defensive restructuring, the target company pays a dividend consisting of cash (often borrowed) and debt securities, reducing the post-dividend value of the target's stock to the extent of the distribution. While the process is usually rather complex, target managers and/or the target's employee stock ownership plan effectively receive the dividend in the form of stock, rather than cash or debt, at an exchange rate based on the stock's post-dividend value. E.g., Black & Decker Corp. v. American Standard, Inc., 682 F.Supp. 772 (D.Del.1988); Ivanhoe Partners v. Newmont Mining Corp., 535 A.2d 1334, 1345 (Del.

1987); Robert M. Bass Group, Inc. v. Evans, 552 A.2d 1227, 1243 (Del.Ch.1988). Alternatively, the target may conduct a tender offer in which public shareholders exchange their stock for cash and debt. E.g., AC Acquisitions Corp. v. Anderson, Clayton & Co., 519 A.2d 103 (Del.Ch.1986). In either case, management's equity interest increases substantially vis-a-vis public shareholders. In *AC Acquisitions*, for example, the restructuring would have transferred 25% of the firm's voting stock to a newly formed employee stock ownership plan. Coupled with management's stock holdings, this

dependent upon the target's size; it works even for very small companies. In contrast, the success of Time's defensive actions depended almost wholly on the combined entity's great size. While the extent of the combined entity perhaps made it unlikely that a subsequent buyer would emerge to unwind the transaction, the possibility existed. The market for corporate control thus could exert some constraining influence on Time's board, which reduced the likelihood that the board was acting for improper motives, especially in comparison to the defensive restructurings just described.

A variety of other factors could be cited to distinguish *Time* from *Macmillan*, *Interco*, and their ilk. Time's business strategy was motivated by a desire to advance legitimate corporate interests; in particular, it had not been cobbled together simply to justify takeover defenses. As a result, Paramount was essentially asking the court to enjoin Time's board from continuing to operate the corporation's business and affairs during the pendency of the takeover bid. The Delaware courts were properly reluctant to do so, as a hostile bidder has no right to expect the incumbent board of directors to stop an ongoing business strategy in mid-stream.[87]

In sum, *Time* presented a highly unusual set of facts, which rebutted the inference that the board acted from improper motives and rendered the result—if not the reasoning—in that particular case relatively unobjectionable. Many fruitful avenues for limiting *Time*'s reasoning thus presented themselves. The question was whether the Delaware supreme court would avail themselves of those options or would continue down the road of retreat *Time*'s reasoning appeared to mark out.

Ironically, the vehicle by which the Delaware supreme court revisited its *Time* decision was provided by Paramount, which now found itself playing Time's role and advocating the very same arguments that had been its downfall in the prior case.[88] Paramount, run by Martin Davis, entered into merger negotiations with Viacom, run and largely owned by Sumner Redstone. The parties sought to preclude competing bids with an array of defensive measures, including: (1) A no shop clause in their merger agreement, pursuant to which Paramount's board could not discuss any business combination with a third party unless (i) the third party could show that its proposal was not subject to financial contingencies, and (ii) the Paramount board decided that its fiduciary duties

---

would have created a formidable barrier for any post-transaction bidder.

87. *Time* also was distinguishable from negotiated acquisitions in which the target board used a lock-up to preclude competing bids. Time was the putative acquirer in what was really a merger of equals, unlike the typical fact pattern, in which the competing bid is directed to the shareholders of the merger target. As such, there is a lower than normal risk that the merger was motivated by side payments to Time's managers. Moreover, Time's board could have structured the Warner acquisition as a tender offer from the outset, borrowing several billion dollars in the junk bond market to pay cash for Warner's shares, and thereby complete the acquisition without ever having to getting shareholder approval. Had they done so, Paramount would have been powerless to prevent the acquisition except by getting control of Time's board before the Warner acquisition could be completed.

88. Paramount Communications Inc. v. QVC Network Inc., 637 A.2d 34 (Del.1994).

required it to talk to the third party. (2) A termination fee, under which Paramount was obliged to pay Viacom $100 million if the Paramount–Viacom deal fell through. The termination fee was payable regardless of whether the deal cratered because Paramount terminated the Viacom deal to accept a competing offer or the Paramount stockholders voted down the Viacom deal. (3) A stock lock-up option, under which, if the Viacom deal fell through for any reason that triggered the termination fee, Viacom would have the option of buying 24 million shares of outstanding Paramount stock at $69 per share (roughly 20% of the outstanding shares). Viacom could buy these shares with a senior subordinated note or could demand instead that Paramount pay it the difference between $69 and the market price of the stock for 24 million shares.

Despite this seemingly formidable array of defenses, QVC made a competing offer. Hollywood egos seem to have played some role, as QVC's CEO and major shareholder, Barry Diller, had once been fired by Davis and the two apparently hated each other. Following several rounds of bidding, Paramount's board announced that it would recommend acceptance of the Viacom proposal and would continue to resist QVC's offer.

In the inevitable litigation, Paramount relied on *Time* to argue that the *Revlon* duties had not triggered. Given *Time*'s description of the requisite triggering events, this was not an implausible argument. Paramount had neither initiated an active bidding process nor approved a breakup of the company.

QVC thus sharply illustrated the potential mischief done by *Time*. Assuming that *Revlon* had not triggered, the issue would be whether Paramount's defensive actions could be sustained under a *Unocal*-style analysis, which would have raised the distinction between legally and factually precluding competing bids. A successful Paramount–Viacom merger would not have legally precluded QVC from attempting to purchase the combined Viacom–Paramount entity. Accordingly, there was a strong argument that Paramount's actions should pass muster under *Time*'s reading of *Unocal*.

Even assuming QVC could have financed a bid for the combined entity, however, its efforts to acquire Paramount would have faced an insurmountable practical barrier; namely, the presence of Sumner Redstone. As controlling shareholder of Viacom, Redstone would have controlled the combined Paramount–Viacom entity. The presence of a controlling shareholder substantially changes the conflict of interest mix.

In theory, so long as acquisitions of publicly held corporations are conducted by other publicly held corporations, diversified shareholders will be indifferent as to the allocations of gains between the parties. Assume that the typical acquisition generates gains equal to 50 percent of the target's pre-mid market price. A fully diversified investor is just as likely to own acquiring company shares as target shares. Indeed, he may own both. Allocation of the available gain between targets and acquirers is thus irrelevant to the diversified shareholder. Increasing the target's share of the gains by increasing the premium the acquirer pays to obtain control necessarily reduces the acquirer's share, which from the shareholder's perspective is simply robbing Peter to pay Paul. Worse yet, to the extent that gain allocation rules increase transaction costs, they leave a fully diversified shareholder worse off. In practice, of course, this argument is undermined by the implicit assumption that gains to the acquirer flow through to its shareholders.

Whatever one makes of the theory, however, situations like *QVC* unquestionably raise serious gain allocation concerns for target shareholders. If the acquiring entity is privately held, even a fully diversified shareholder by definition cannot be on both sides of the transaction. If the acquiring entity is publicly held, but is controlled by a single very large shareholder, a fully diversified shareholder may not be able to fully share in the gains to be reaped by the acquiring company because the large shareholder's control enables it to reap a non-pro rata share of any such gains. In the *QVC* situation, shareholders therefore would not be indifferent to gain allocation. Instead, they would prefer to see gains allocated to the target.

For this reason, *QVC* raised accountability concerns in a way that *Time* simply did not. There is special reason to fear that the controlling shareholder's positional and informational advantages will affect the allocation of gains. In particular, the controlling shareholder's ability to reap a disproportionate share of post-transaction gains gives it an unusually high incentive to cause the acquiring entity to offer side-payments to target directors in order to obtain their cooperation. In turn, the controlling shareholder's ability to reject acquisition proposals insulates the combined entity from the constraining influence of the market for corporate control.[89] As a result, the normal conflict of interest to be found in any acquisition is substantially magnified in the *QVC* situation.

In *QVC*, the Delaware supreme court demonstrated its sensitivity to this concern. Consider the otherwise rather obscure way in which the court described the nature of the shareholder interest that was imperiled by the Paramount board's conduct. As Professor Michael Dooley has observed, the court several times "noted that voting control is generally achieved only at the price of paying a 'premium' to the minority shareholders for the loss of their voting influence (fluid and dispersed though it is), and that public shareholders lose the expectation of receiving any such premium once control has been transferred to and consolidated in a majority shareholder."[90] In addition, the court offered an equally curious explanation of why board action in a sale of control

---

89. While a controlling shareholder owes fiduciary duties to the minority, it would not be obliged to sell its shares to another bidder. Indeed, the Delaware supreme court has held that *Revlon* duties do not apply when a controlling shareholder effects a cash-out merger with the subsidiary target corporation. Bershad v. Curtiss–Wright Corp., 535 A.2d 840, 844–45 (Del. 1987).

90. Michael P. Dooley, Fundamentals of Corporation Law 577 (1995).

context is subject to enhanced judicial scrutiny: "Such scrutiny is mandated by: (a) the threatened diminution of the current stockholders' voting power; (b) the fact that an *asset belonging to public shareholders (a control premium)* is being sold and may never be available again; and (c) the traditional concern of Delaware courts for actions which impair or impede stockholder voting rights."[91] If generalized to all takeovers, these references are rather puzzling. As Dooley observes, they have little to do with the conflicted-interest focus of *Unocal* and *Revlon* and, in fact, might presage some new analytic mode in which the principal emphasis will be on protecting shareholder property rights in control premia. As applied to the specific facts of *QVC*, however, references to the shareholders' interest in the control premium make perfect sense. They reflect the possibility that conflicted interests on the part of Paramount's directors would lead them to take actions that transferred gains from their shareholders to Viacom and Redstone.

Of course, it is not enough to recognize a conflict of interest, one must go on to do something about it. The *QVC* court not only recognized the enhanced conflict of interest present in this situation, but also seemingly recognized the doctrinal limitations *Time* imposed on efforts to deal with this conflict. Granted, the court did not overrule *Time*, but it did limit *Time* to its unique facts. It did so by rejecting Paramount's reading of *Time*. Recall the relevant passage from *Time*: "Under Delaware law there are, generally speaking and *without excluding other possibilities*, two circumstances which may implicate *Revlon* duties," which are initiation of an active bidding process and approval of a break-up of the company.[92] In *QVC*, the court emphasized the phrase "without excluding other possibilities." In this case, the court opined, one of the other possibilities was present; namely, a change of control. Accordingly, *Revlon* was triggered.[93]

The court's analysis of *Time*, of course, was disingenuous at best. In *Time*, the court had passed over the change of control test in favor of the break-up and self-initiated auction triggers. The "other possibilities" language was little more than judicial boilerplate. Yet, from a precedential perspective, that boilerplate became the mechanism by which the court was able to avoid the need to overrule its own *Time* decision while still repairing the damage that decision had done to *Unocal* and *Revlon*.

The end, however, perhaps justifies the means. By rehabilitating Chancellor Allen's *Time* opinion, which the *QVC* court went out of its way to describe as "well-reasoned," and by resurrecting the change of control test, *QVC* specifically addressed the potential for conflicted interests on the part of directors in transactions like the one at hand. Indeed, the court laid great stress on the fact that a transaction in which

---

91. Paramount Communications Inc. v. QVC Network Inc., 637 A.2d 34, 45 (Del. 1994) (emphasis supplied).

92. Paramount Communications, Inc. v. Time Inc., 571 A.2d 1140, 1150 (Del.1989) (emphasis supplied).

93. Paramount Communications Inc. v. QVC Network Inc., 637 A.2d 34, 46–48 (Del. 1994).

control changes hands to an identifiable owner leaves the target's shareholders vulnerable to both ex ante and ex post misconduct by the incumbent directors and the new owner.

In addition to consigning *Time*'s interpretation of *Revlon* to the dust bin of history, the court made a subtle but very important doctrinal shift. Where *Time* had treated *Unocal* and *Revlon* as involving separate modes of inquiry directed at distinct issues, *QVC* restored the pre-*Time* view that they are part of a single line of cases in which the significant conflict of interest found in certain control transactions justified enhanced judicial scrutiny. The court, for example, opined that "the general principles announced in *Revlon*, in *Unocal v. Mesa Petroleum Co.*, and in *Moran v. Household International, Inc.* govern this and every case in which a fundamental change of corporate control occurs or is contemplated."

Likewise, while *Time* had emphasized the formal tests announced in *Unocal* and *Revlon*, the *QVC* court struck out in a less rigid direction. As described by *QVC*, the enhanced scrutiny test is basically a reasonableness inquiry to be applied on a case-by-case basis: "The key features of an enhanced scrutiny test are: (a) a judicial determination regarding the adequacy of the decisionmaking process employed by the directors, including the information on which the directors based their decision; and (b) a judicial examination of the reasonableness of the directors' action in light of the circumstances then existing." The burden of proof is on the directors with respect to both issues. They need not prove that they made the right decision, but merely that their decision fell within the range of reasonableness.

The new reasonableness standard is a logical culmination of our argument that motive is what counts. While a cynic might argue that it is merely a way of justifying a particular result, the reasonableness test in fact is well-calibrated to preventing improper motives from skewing the competition for control. Notice that the reasonableness test parallels the definition of fairness used in the former Revised Model Business Corporation Act provisions governing interested director transactions, namely, whether the transaction in question falls "within the range that might have been entered into at arms-length by disinterested persons."[94] Both standards seem designed to ferret out board actions motivated by conflicted interests by contrasting the decision at hand to some objective standard. The implicit assumption is that a reasonable decision is unlikely to be motivated by conflicted interest or, at least, that improper motives are irrelevant so long as the resulting decision falls within a range of reasonable outcomes. The operating norm seems to be "no harm, no foul," which seems sensible enough.

QVC, moreover, strongly indicated that a court should not second-guess a board decision that falls within the range of reasonableness, "even though it might have decided otherwise or subsequent events may have cast doubt on the board's determination." In *Interco*, Chancellor

94. Rev. Model Bus. Corp. Act § 8.31
cmt. 4 (1984).

Allen had warned that "Delaware courts have employed the Unocal precedent cautiously.... The danger that it poses is, of course, that courts—in exercising some element of substantive judgment—will too readily seek to assert the primacy of their own view on a question upon which reasonable, completely disinterested minds might differ."[95] *QVC* made clear that, so long as the board's conduct falls within the bounds of reasonableness, Delaware courts will not second-guess the board's decisions.

4. *Unitrin*

If that point was insufficiently clear after *QVC*, it was driven home in unmistakable terms by the Delaware supreme court's subsequent decision in *Unitrin v. American General Corp.*, in which the court approved an everything but the kitchen sink array of defensive tactics.[96] Unitrin's board adopted a poison pill, amended the bylaws to add some shark repellent features, and initiated a defensive stock repurchase. The chancery court found the latter "unnecessary" in light of the poison pill. The supreme court reversed. The court deemed "draconian" defenses— those which are "coercive or preclusive"—to be invalid. (Note the parallel to our discussion of the post-*Time* status of the just say no defense.) Defenses that are not preclusive or coercive are to be reviewed under *QVC*'s "range of reasonableness" standard. On the facts before it, the court concluded that the shareholders were not foreclosed from receiving a control premium in the future and that a change of control was still possible. Accordingly, the defensive tactics were neither coercive nor preclusive. More important, the supreme court held that the chancery court had "erred by substituting its judgment" for that of the board. The court explained:

> The *ratio decidendi* for the "range of reasonableness" standard is a need of the board of directors for latitude in discharging its fiduciary duties to the corporation and its shareholders when defending against perceived threats. The concomitant requirement is for judicial restraint. Consequently, if the board of directors' defensive response is not draconian (preclusive or coercive) and is within a "range of reasonableness," a court must not substitute its judgment for the board's.

Note, once again, how the balance tips towards authority values even in a context charged with conflicts of interest. Given the significant conflicts of interest posed by takeovers, courts recognize the need for some review. But the Delaware courts also seemingly recognize that their power of review easily could become the power to decide. To avoid that unhappy result, they are exercising appropriate caution in applying the *Unocal* standard.

---

95. City Capital Assoc. Ltd. Partnership v. Interco, Inc., 551 A.2d 787, 796 (Del.Ch. 1988).

96. Unitrin, Inc. v. American General Corp., 651 A.2d 1361 (Del.1995).

5. *Summation*

In sum, the search for conflicted interests reflects the Delaware courts' solution to the irreconcilable tension between authority and accountability. Concern for accountability drives the courts' expectation that the board will function as a separate institution independent from and superior to the firm's managers. The court will inquire closely into the role actually played by the board, especially the outside directors, the extent to which they were supplied with all relevant information and independent advisors, and the extent to which they were insulated from management influence. Only if the directors had the ultimate decision-making authority, rather than incumbent management, will the board's conduct pass muster. But if it does, respect for authority values will require the court to defer to the board's substantive decisions. The board has legitimate authority in the takeover context, just as it has in proxy contests and a host of other decisions that nominally appear to belong to the shareholders. Nor can the board's authority be restricted in this context without impinging on the board's authority elsewhere. Authority thus cannot be avoided anymore than can accountability; the task is to come up with a reasonable balance. Properly interpreted, that is precisely what the Delaware cases have done.

§ 12.11 Consideration of nonshareholder constituency interests

The takeover wars of the 1980s produced a host of target corporation defensive tactics. Early on, so-called nonmonetary factor provisions were a fairly common variant on the shark repellent theme. They permit, and in some cases require, directors to consider a variety of nonprice factors in evaluating a proposed acquisition. In particular, most allow directors to consider "the social, legal and economic effects of an offer upon employees, suppliers, customers and others having similar relationships with the corporation, and the communities in which the corporation conducts its business."[1]

From management's perspective, nonmonetary factor provisions have two principal drawbacks. First, except in the case of a newly incorporated firm, they must be adopted as amendments to the corporation's charter, which requires shareholder approval. Shareholder resistance to shark repellents steadily grew throughout the 1980s, especially among institutional investors. By 1989, for example, over half of the institutional investors responding to an industry survey reported that they had opposed some nonmonetary factors provisions, while another one-quarter reported that they did so routinely.[2] This growing opposition

---

§ 12.11

1. Proxy Statement and Text of Amendment for Nortek, Inc. (May 26, 1982), reprinted in Robert L. Winter et al., 1 Shark Repellents and Golden Parachutes: A Handbook for the Practitioner 197 (1983 and supp.) The full laundry list also usually included the legality of the offer, the bidder's financial condition, prospects, and reputation, the offer's structure, and the bidder's intentions for the target. See id. at 194.

2. Lauren Krasnow, Voting by Institutional Investors on Corporate Governance Issues in the 1989 Proxy Season 37 (1989).

made nonmonetary factors provisions far less attractive and helped contribute to their apparent decline in popularity.

Second, and more seriously, state law arguably does not permit corporate organic documents to redefine the directors' fiduciary duties. In general, a charter amendment may not derogate from common law rules if doing so conflicts with some settled public policy.[3] In light of the well-settled shareholder wealth maximization policy, nonmonetary factors charter amendments therefore appeared vulnerable. As the 1980s wound down, this problem seemed especially significant for Delaware firms, as Delaware law became increasingly hostile to directorial consideration of nonshareholder interests in the takeover decisionmaking process.

A.   Delaware case law

The business judgment rule typically precludes courts from reviewing board of director decisions that take into account the interests of nonshareholder constituencies. Once Delaware adopted *Unocal's* conditional business judgment rule as the standard of review for management resistance to takeovers, however, such decisions were no longer automatically protected. To be sure, under its first prong, *Unocal* apparently allowed directors to consider interests other than short-term shareholder wealth maximization. Under *Unocal*, target directors may balance the takeover premium a bidder offers shareholders against the bid's potential effects on the corporate entity. Among other factors, the board was explicitly permitted to consider "the impact of the bid on 'constituencies' other than shareholders (i.e., creditors, customers, employees, and perhaps even the community)."[4]

Unfortunately, *Unocal* was not entirely clear as to what the language just quoted meant. Unocal's board was faced with a structurally coercive bid by "a corporate raider with a national reputation as a 'greenmailer.' "[5] Accordingly, the directors reasonably believed that the bid was not in the best interests of any corporate constituency and, on the facts before the court, there arguably was no conflict between shareholder and stakeholder interests. Other situations are less clear-cut. Suppose, for example, the bidder makes a fairly priced, noncoercive

---

3. Sterling v. Mayflower Hotel Corp., 93 A.2d 107, 118 (Del.1952); Ernest L. Folk, III, The Delaware General Corporation Law: A Commentary and Analysis 10 (1972).

4. Unocal Corp. v. Mesa Petroleum Co., 493 A.2d 946, 955 (Del.1985). Several judicial opinions outside Delaware suggest that nonshareholder interests may be considered in making structural decisions. See, e.g., Norlin Corp. v. Rooney, Pace, Inc., 744 F.2d 255 (2d Cir.1984); Herald Co. v. Seawell, 472 F.2d 1081 (10th Cir.1972); GAF Corp. v. Union Carbide Corp., 624 F.Supp. 1016 (S.D.N.Y.1985); Enterra Corp. v. SGS As-

soc., 600 F.Supp. 678 (E.D.Pa.1985); Abramson v. Nytronics, Inc., 312 F.Supp. 519 (S.D.N.Y.1970). It is difficult to form a coherent picture from these cases, as most courts outside of Delaware face corporate law issues on a sporadic basis, which precludes sustained doctrinal development. Cf. Treadway Cos., Inc. v. Care Corp., 638 F.2d 357, 382 (2d Cir.1980) (stating that "[t]he law in this area is something less than a seamless web").

5. Unocal Corp. v. Mesa Petroleum Co., 493 A.2d 946, 956 (Del.1985).

offer, but also announces plans to close plants and lay off numerous workers. The target's board of directors reasonably concludes that the negative impact on its employees exceeds the gains shareholders will garner. Did *Unocal* permit the board to turn down such an offer?

In *Revlon, Inc. v. MacAndrews and Forbes Holdings, Inc.*, the Delaware supreme court concluded that *Unocal* did not.[6] *Revlon* added two crucial provisos to *Unocal*'s treatment of nonshareholder constituencies. The first is of general applicability, dealing with all structural decisions except those in which the so-called *Revlon* duties have triggered. If *Unocal* arguably allowed target boards to trade off a decrease in shareholder wealth for an increase in stakeholder wealth, *Revlon* forecloses that interpretation. *Revlon* expressly forbids management from protecting stakeholder interests at the expense of shareholder interests. Rather, any management action benefiting stakeholders must produce ancillary shareholder benefits.[7] In other words, directors may only consider stakeholder interests if doing so would benefit shareholders.[8]

Second, where the *Revlon* duties have triggered, stakeholders become entirely irrelevant. Once a *Revlon* auction begins, it no longer matters whether benefiting nonshareholder interests may also benefit shareholders. Instead, shareholder wealth maximization is the board's only appropriate concern.[9] Indeed, in *Revlon* land,[10] considering any factors other than shareholder wealth violates the board's fiduciary duties.[11]

In sum, *Revlon* sharply limits directors' ability to consider nonshareholder interests in structural decisions.[12] Moreover, by withholding the

---

6. Revlon, Inc. v. MacAndrews & Forbes Holdings, Inc., 506 A.2d 173 (Del.1985). In Newell Co. v. Vermont American Corp., 725 F.Supp. 351 (N.D.Ill.1989), the court, applying the *Unocal* test, determined that the offer would maximize short-term shareholder profits, but nevertheless upheld the target's defensive measures. Although the principal threat appeared to be to nonshareholder interests, the court avoided the question posed in the text by finding that long-term shareholder interests were threatened. See id. at 372–76.

7. "A board may have regard for various constituencies in discharging its responsibilities, provided there are rationally related benefits accruing to the stockholders." Revlon, Inc. v. MacAndrews & Forbes Holdings, Inc., 506 A.2d 173, 182 (Del.1985). A somewhat weaker formulation was used in Mills Acquisition Co. v. Macmillan, Inc., 559 A.2d 1261 (Del.1989), which allows consideration of nonshareholder interests provided they bear "some reasonable relationship to general shareholder interests." Id. at 1282 n. 29.

8. Compare Buckhorn, Inc. v. Ropak Corp., 656 F.Supp. 209, 231–32 (S.D.Ohio),

aff'd, 815 F.2d 76 (6th Cir.1987) (employee stock ownership plan invalidated because there was "no evidence in the record as to how the ESOP would benefit the stockholders nor as to how Ropak's tender offer posed a threat to Buckhorn's employees") with Shamrock Holdings, Inc. v. Polaroid Corp., 559 A.2d 257, 276 (Del.Ch.1989) (employee stock ownership plan upheld because it was "likely to add value to the company and all of its stockholders").

9. Revlon, Inc. v. MacAndrews & Forbes Holdings, Inc., 506 A.2d 173, 182 (Del. 1985).

10. "*Revlon* land" is the emerging term of art for corporate control contests in which the so-called *Revlon* duties have triggered.

11. Black & Decker Corp. v. American Standard, Inc., 682 F.Supp. 772, 786–87 (D.Del.1988); C–T of Virginia, Inc. v. Barrett, 124 Bankr. 689 (W.D.Va.1990); Revlon, Inc. v. MacAndrews & Forbes Holdings, Inc., 506 A.2d 173, 185 (Del.1985).

12. To be sure, some commentators contend that *Time* implicitly allows target managers greater freedom to consider non-

business judgment rule's protections from directors, *Revlon* puts considerable teeth into the shareholder wealth maximization norm. Unlike the operational context, directors who make structural decisions based on stakeholder interests rather than shareholder interests face the very real threat of personal liability.

B.   A note on the ALI Principles' approach

The ALI Principles adopted a rule bearing substantial similarity to *Unocal* minus the *Revlon* limitations thereon. Section 6.02 provides that the board, when making takeover decisions, may "have regard for interests or groups (other than shareholders) with respect to which the corporation has a legitimate concern if to do so would not significantly disfavor the long-term interests of shareholders."[13] Unlike *Unocal*, the burden is on plaintiff to prove that the defendant directors acted unreasonably. This rule applies to all takeover situations, including those in which a *Revlon*-like control auction has begun.

Section 6.02 is a very odd formulation; indeed, even the ALI's reporter seems puzzled by it. For one thing, the shareholders have long-term interests in the takeover context only if the target remains independent. The standard thus seems to put the cart before the horse. Additionally, how much injury to the shareholders can the target board work before the shareholders are "significantly disfavor[ed]"? The ALI failed to coherently answer that question. The unsatisfactory treatment of this issue by the ALI becomes more explicable when one realizes that Section 6.02 was one of the most hotly debated sections of the entire project. The final version is a compromise that seems to have satisfied no one.[14]

C.   Nonshareholder constituency statutes

Thirty-one states have adopted nonshareholder constituency statutes that authorize directors to consider nonshareholder interests when making corporate decisions, typically by amending the existing statutory statement of the director's duty of due care. These statutes provide that, in discharging their duty of care, directors may consider the effects of a decision on not only shareholders, but also on a laundry list of other constituency groups, commonly including employees, suppliers, customers, creditors, and the local communities in which the firm does business. In the operational setting, these statutes rarely will change the

shareholder interests. See, e.g., Alan E. Garfield, *Paramount*: The Mixed Merits of Mush, 17 Del. J. Corp. L. 33, 57–58 (1992); Lyman Johnson & David Millon, The Case Beyond *Time*, 45 Bus. Law. 2105 (1990); David Millon, Redefining Corporate Law, 24 Ind. L. Rev. 223, 237–38 (1991). But see Jeffrey N. Gordon, Corporations, Markets, and Courts, 91 Colum. L. Rev. 1931, 1951–71 (1991).

13.   ALI Principles § 6.02(b)(2).

14.   See Steven M. H. Wallman, Section 6.02: Is ALI Provision on Director Duties Consistent with Evolution in Thinking about Takeovers?, Corp. Couns. Wkly. (BNA) at 8 (Aug. 7, 1991).

outcome of shareholder litigation. Because the business judgment precludes courts from deciding whether directors violated their duty of care, the court will not even reach the statutory issue in most cases.

In the structural setting, however, the statutes could have outcome determinative effects. Despite some judicial holdings to the contrary,[15] it seems clear that nonshareholder constituency statutes were intended to reject *Revlon*'s constraints on director decisionmaking. Like most state takeover laws, nonshareholder constituency statutes are typically adopted at the request of target corporation management actively engaged in resisting a hostile takeover bid. Unquestionably, the legislative intent was to make takeovers harder.[16] What better way do so than by tempering the shareholder wealth norm exemplified by *Revlon*? This interpretation is especially apt for those statutes that expressly permit directors to consider the corporation's long-term interests even in takeover contests. These statutes can only be read as implicitly rejecting *Revlon*'s command that short-term shareholder wealth maximization be the director's sole concern once a corporate control auction begins.

The rejection of *Revlon* implicit in most statutes was made explicit by Indiana's nonshareholder constituency statute. The legislation was obviously drafted in response to a pair of Seventh Circuit decisions striking down a series of poison pills adopted by a target corporation.[17] Because Indiana had no applicable precedents, the Seventh Circuit looked to *Unocal* and *Revlon* for guidance. The Indiana nonshareholder

---

15. See, e.g., Hilton Hotels Corp. v. ITT Corp., 978 F.Supp. 1342 (D.Nev.1997); Amanda Acquisition Corp. v. Universal Foods Corp., 708 F.Supp. 984, 1009 (E.D.Wis.), aff'd on other grounds, 877 F.2d 496 (7th Cir.1989).

16. In a legislative debate on Pennsylvania's package of takeover laws, which included a new nonshareholder constituency statute, one of the bill's sponsors observed, "To Sam Belzberg, to Carl Icahn, to Boone Pickens, to the Bass Brothers, to Don Trump and all you other corporate raiders, you do not have a friend in Pennsylvania." Pa.Legis.J., Sen., Dec. 13, 1989, at 1539 (Sen. Armstrong). See also id. at 1507 ("legislation in defense from corporate raiders is no vice") (Sen. Williams); Pa.Legis.J.House, Apr. 24, 1990, at 778 ("By passing this antitakeover measure, we will send a loud and clear message to those who would make our Pennsylvania corporations simple, quick-profit chop shops, and that is, Pennsylvania is no longer your playground."). Professors Johnson and Millon have argued that state takeover laws are generally intended "to protect nonshareholders from the disruptive impact of ... hostile takeovers." Lyman Johnson & David Millon, Missing the Point About State Takeover Statutes, 87 Mich. L. Rev. 846, 848 (1989).

Whether or not this claim is true of state takeover laws generally, it is difficult to reject as to nonshareholder constituency statutes. See Robert D. Rosenbaum & L. Stevenson Parker, The Pennsylvania Takeover Act of 1990: Summary and Analysis 28–30 (1990) ("The basic argument made in support of the new [Pennsylvania] stakeholder provision was that public corporations are and should be more than vehicles to generate maximum profits—particularly in the short term—for shareholders.").

17. Dynamics Corp. of Am. v. CTS Corp., 805 F.2d 705 (7th Cir.1986), prior op., 794 F.2d 250 (7th Cir.1986), rev'd on other grounds, 481 U.S. 69 (1987). This takeover battle went on to fame as CTS Corp. v. Dynamics Corp. of Am., 481 U.S. 69 (1987), in which the Supreme Court upheld the constitutionality of a different Indiana takeover statute. No decision to date has squarely addressed the constitutionality of nonshareholder constituency statutes. In the course of upholding a different type of state takeover statute, however, Judge Easterbrook offered the following noteworthy dictum: "States could choose to protect 'constituencies' other than stockholders." Amanda Acquisition Corp. v. Universal Foods Corp., 877 F.2d 496, 500 n. 5 (7th Cir.), cert. denied, 493 U.S. 955 (1989).

constituency statute was specifically intended to reverse that approach, giving courts astonishingly blunt guidance:

> Certain judicial decisions in Delaware and other jurisdictions, which might otherwise be looked to for guidance in interpreting Indiana corporate law, including decisions relating to potential change of control transactions that impose a different or higher degree of scrutiny on actions taken by directors in response to a proposed acquisition of control of the corporation, are inconsistent with the proper application of the business judgment rule under this article.[18]

Revlon is the statute's clear target, for the statute goes on to expressly reject the primacy of shareholder interests: "directors are not required to consider the effects of a proposed corporate action on any particular corporate constituent group or interest as a dominant or controlling factor." Moreover, the board's determinations in this respect are conclusive unless a challenger proves that the board did not act "in good faith after reasonable investigation."

So interpreted, these statutes are very unsound as a matter of public policy. To be sure, there is a lot of anecdotal evidence suggesting that corporate takeovers generate negative externalities with respect to nonshareholder constituencies. Yet, there is little systematic evidence that takeover bidders do any more damage to the interests of such constituencies than do entrenched "incumbents—who may (and frequently do) close or move plants to follow the prospect of profit."[19]

By contrast, there is a well-documented managerial conflict of interest in the takeover setting. There is a very real possibility that unscrupulous directors will use nonshareholder interests to cloak their own self-interested behavior. Selfish decisions easily could be justified by an appropriate paper trail of tears over the employees' fate. This then is the real vice of nonshareholder constituency statutes. While they allow honest directors to act in the best interests of all the corporation's constituents, they also may protect dishonest directors who are acting solely in their own interest. All of this tends to suggest that legislatures ought to think twice about adopting nonshareholder constituency statutes without first addressing management's conflict of interest.

What then should we do about the statutes that are on the books? Whatever the theoretical merits of a rule requiring management passivi-

---

18. Ind. Code Ann. § 23–1–35–1(f) (West 1990). Pennsylvania's nonshareholder constituency statute largely tracks the Indiana statute. Like Indiana, Pennsylvania makes the board's determinations conclusive unless a challenger proves that the board did not act "in good faith after reasonable investigation." 15 Pa. Cons. Stat. § 1721 (Supp.1991). Similarly, Pennsylvania also precludes courts from imposing any burden greater than the business judgment rule on directors seeking to justify takeover defenses. Id. Finally, the Pennsylvania stat-ute does not require directors to treat any corporate constituency interest as having paramount importance. See id. Although Pennsylvania omitted any direct reference to Delaware law, the prohibition on imposition of a higher standard of review is clearly intended to follow Indiana in precluding courts from adopting *Unocal* or *Revlon*.

19. Amanda Acquisition Corp. v. Universal Foods Corp., 877 F.2d 496, 500 n. 5 (7th Cir.), cert. denied, 493 U.S. 955 (1989).

ty in the face of a hostile takeover bid, the nonshareholder constituency statutes plainly reject any such requirement. Rather, their very premise is that shareholder and stakeholder interests conflict in corporate takeovers and that the target's directors are in the best position to reconcile those competing interests.

While the nonshareholder constituency statutes clarify that it is appropriate for directors to consider the interests of those constituencies in making structural decisions, corporate law need not ignore the very real risk that the directors' proffered justification is a ruse. Enabling directors to transfer part of the pie from shareholders to stakeholders is the stated purpose of nonshareholder constituency statutes. Courts must be true to that purpose, but they need not interpret nonshareholder constituency statutes as allowing directors and managers to reallocate a bigger piece of the pie to themselves. In structural decisions, corporate law therefore should separate instances of honest director concern for nonshareholder interests from selfish director concern for their own positions. Happily, a mechanism for doing so is close at hand: *Unocal*'s shifting burdens of proof will do quite nicely by analogy.

To be sure, nonshareholder constituency statutes reject the *Revlon* gloss on *Unocal*. Absent the unique provisions found in the Indiana and Pennsylvania statutes, however, the nonshareholder constituency statutes need not be interpreted as barring a *Unocal*-type test. An apt precedent for this thesis is provided by the prevailing judicial interpretation of interested director transaction statutes. Not every interested director transaction involves self dealing, but the high probability of misconduct in this context led courts to permit review even of transactions that are properly ratified and to impose a very exacting standard on transactions that are not ratified. The significant risk of self-interested director behavior in corporate acquisitions similarly justifies exacting judicial scrutiny of claims that the directors were acting to protect nonshareholder interests. Accordingly, unless the legislature has clearly prohibited courts from imposing a heightened standard of review, courts should read a *Unocal*-type standard into the nonshareholder constituency statutes.

By analogy to the first *Unocal* prong, a court should first require the directors to show that the takeover bid poses a threat to one of the enumerated nonshareholder interests. Presumably, the requisite threats could take a variety of forms: lay-offs, plant closings, downgrading of bonds, and the like. A court should also require directors to show that they acted in good faith and after a reasonable investigation. The good faith element requires a showing that the directors acted in response to a perceived threat to the corporation and not for the purpose of entrenching themselves in office. As such, this element necessarily involves a subjective inquiry into the directors' motives. Absent the proverbial smoking gun it may be difficult to distinguish cases involving self-interested director behavior from cases involving legitimate director concern for stakeholders. Nonetheless, retaining a subjective component to the analysis can be justified on several grounds. First, judicial review is better than no review. Many takeover decisions are subject to review by the market. For example, when a board agrees to merge with one of several potential bidders, motive analysis is unnecessary. As long as the board fairly conducted an auction amongst the competing bidders, the market will have demonstrated the merger's fairness. However, when a board rejects a hostile takeover bid on nonmonetary grounds, by definition a market test is unavailable. In effect, the directors are asking to be exempted from a market test because of the takeover's alleged impact on nonshareholder constituents. As such, a motive based inquiry becomes more justifiable. At the very least, it captures gross cases in which there is good evidence—either direct or circumstantial—that the board acted for its own interest. Second, the test proposed here is not limited to a subjective motive analysis. Instead, the good faith element is primarily intended to force the directors to articulate a nonself-interested rationale for their action. The directors' stated rationale can then be tested against the model's objective standards, which have the primary responsibility for capturing cases of director misconduct. Finally, as further described below, the obligation to construct a disinterested rationale for the decision may deter many boards from self-interested behavior in the first place.

The second *Unocal* prong is the critical one if self-interested management behavior is to be controlled. Unless the requirement of proportionality between threat and response has real teeth, management can still use a threat to nonshareholder interests as a cloak for protecting their own jobs. Absent an effective proportionality standard, any threat to nonshareholder interests, no matter how mild or insignificant, would give management a free hand to develop takeover defenses to kill the hostile takeover bid. Because one cannot reasonably interpret the nonshareholder constituency statutes as codifying *Revlon*, the statute must be interpreted as allowing directors to make trade-offs between shareholder and stakeholder interests. At the same time, however, an effective proportionality standard requires that directors minimize the effect of their decision on shareholders. In other words, their decision must impose no greater burden on the shareholders than necessary to protect the nonshareholder constituencies. If measures less harmful to the shareholders' interest would have adequately protected the nonshareholder interests at stake, the target's chosen defensive measures should be invalidated.

Similar tests are used in other corporate conflict of interest transactions. Under Massachusetts law, for example, when a minority close corporation shareholder alleges a breach of fiduciary duty by the firm's controlling shareholder, the controlling shareholder must first demonstrate a legitimate business purpose for its actions. If the controlling shareholder does so, the minority shareholder can still prevail by showing that the same objective could have been accomplished through an alternative course less harmful to the minority's interest.[20]

The precise application of this standard will obviously vary from case to case. In general, however, judicial review should focus on questions of process. In making proportionality assessments, the court should thus scrutinize closely management's arguments and require a convincing demonstration that no less restrictive defense is available. In doing so, the court should look to such evidence as the specificity of management's plans, the record of the board's deliberations, and expert testimony from both sides. A showing that the directors were aware of and considered the threat to nonshareholder interests at the time they decided to resist the takeover bid is particularly important, because it lowers the likelihood that the threat is an ex post facto justification for selfish behavior.

Courts also should examine closely the negotiations, if any, between the bidder and target management. If there is any evidence that target management would set aside its concern for stakeholders in exchange for a higher acquisition price or side payments for itself, management's purported fears for nonshareholder interests should be seen as mere pretence.

The most important evidence probably will be the history of the firm's treatment of nonshareholder constituencies. A long history of board concern for the firm's workers tells a more plausible story than a sudden interest in their welfare. This is particularly relevant for firms that have previously used threats to nonshareholder constituencies to justify takeover defenses. Not infrequently, an unsuccessful hostile bid will be followed months or years later by another hostile bid from a new bidder. If management has largely ignored stakeholder concerns in the interim, it will be hard for them to use those concerns to justify resisting the new bid.

By carrying its burden of proof under both prongs of this test, the board of directors demonstrates that it is not disabled by a conflict of interest. Absent a disabling conflict, courts generally defer to board decisions. Accordingly, if the board carries its burden, the court should not inquire into the reasonableness of the board's decision unless the plaintiff is otherwise able to rebut the business judgment rule's presumptions. But if the board fails to carry its burden, the court should enjoin the proposed corporate action and/or grant other appropriate relief.

An effective proportionality requirement may reduce management's ex ante incentives to cheat. Dishonest management may find it difficult to construct a plausible story of nonshareholder injury. Dishonest management may not be able to locate experts who can or will support credibly a false nonshareholder injury story; indeed, stakeholders themselves may decline to support dishonest management's story. Independent directors may be unwilling to risk the reputational injury of

---

20. Wilkes v. Springside Nursing Home, Inc., 353 N.E.2d 657 (Mass.1976).

supporting a false story. Finally, the hostile bidder will be actively seeking to rebut management's story and, perhaps, will be recruiting stakeholder support. All of these factors should deter management misconduct and, moreover, give management incentives to evaluate fairly whether shareholder and stakeholder interests in fact diverge.

§ 12.12   State anti-takeover legislation

Although its intensity has varied from year to year, the takeover arms race remains unrelenting. As fast as new acquisition techniques are developed, new defenses spring up. In the quest for more effective defenses, legislative avenues were by no means ignored. Although Congress remains on the sidelines, the states are active players. The states normally can be found on management's end of the playing field; state takeover laws are almost uniformly anti-takeover laws. Although the state law front has been relatively quiet since the mid–1990s, the old statutes remain on the books. Under current law, moreover, there are few obstacles to renewed state activism.

A.   The first generation and *MITE*

Simultaneously with Congress' adoption of the Williams Act, the states began adopting what are now known as first generation state takeover laws.[1] Like the Williams Act, the first generation state laws were mainly disclosure statutes. Unlike the Williams Act, the first generation statutes also imposed certain procedural and substantive requirements creating substantial obstacles for takeover bidders.

The Illinois Business Takeover Act (IBTA), which the Supreme Court invalidated in *Edgar v. MITE Corp.*,[2] was typical of the first generation statutes. It differed from the Williams Act in three critical ways. First, the IBTA required bidders to notify the target and the Illinois Secretary of State twenty days before the offer's effective date. Second, the IBTA permitted the Secretary of State to delay a tender offer by holding a hearing on the offer's fairness. Moreover, the Secretary was required to hold such a hearing if one was requested by shareholders owning ten percent of the class of securities subject to the offer. Finally, the Secretary of State could enjoin a tender offer on a variety of bases, including substantive unfairness.

1.   *Preemption standards*

Three basic preemption tests are currently in use. First, the federal regulatory scheme may so thoroughly pervade the field as to suggest Congress left no room for concurrent state regulation.[3] Nobody seriously

---

§ 12.12

1. Indeed, Virginia's first generation statute was adopted several months prior to the William Act's passage. Stephen M. Bainbridge, State Takeover and Tender Offer Regulations Post–MITE: The Maryland, Ohio and Pennsylvania Attempts, 90 Dickinson L. Rev. 731, 736 (1986).

2. Edgar v. MITE Corp., 457 U.S. 624 (1982).

3. Rice v. Santa Fe Elevator Corp., 331 U.S. 218, 230 (1947) (whether federal regu-

contends that state takeover regulation is preempted by the Williams Act under this standard. Congress has never attempted broadly to supplant state regulation of corporate governance.[4] A cursory comparison of the federal tender offer rules and any state's corporation code demonstrates that the former occupies only a relatively small portion of the field. Among the many issues left to state law are the fiduciary duties of managers, the validity of post-offer freezeout mergers, and so on. Federal regulation is thus by no means sufficiently pervasive as to justify preemption under this prong.

Second, where it is physically impossible for an actor to comply with both federal and state regulations, the supremacy of federal law requires that the actor comply with the federal rule.[5] This is a fairly constrained standard, however. The question here is not whether the state statute deters rational actors from going forward. Rather, the question is whether an actor could comply with both the federal and state laws if it chose to make the attempt.

Finally, state statutes are preempted by federal law if they are inconsistent with the purposes of the relevant federal law. Here the relevant standard is whether the state law "stands as an obstacle to the accomplishment and execution of the full purposes and objectives of Congress."[6] This preemption standard requires a court to resolve two questions: (1) What are the intended Congressional purposes of federal tender offer regulation? (2) Does the state statute under review interfere with the accomplishment of those purposes?

2. Did the Williams Act preempt the IBTA?

Lower courts were divided on the constitutionality of state takeover legislation pre-*MITE*, but the trend was decidedly hostile towards state regulation.[7] Courts found such statutes problematic under both the physical incompatibility and frustration of Congressional intent standards. The potential for delay inherent in the advance filing and the administrative review requirements of many state statutes were found to excessively tilt the balance sought by the Williams Act to the side of target management.[8] The administrative review process, which could

---

lation is "so pervasive as to make reasonable the inference that Congress left no room for the States to supplement" federal law).

4. CTS Corp. v. Dynamics Corp. of Am., 481 U.S. 69, 85–86 (1987); Business Roundtable v. SEC, 905 F.2d 406, 411–13 (D.C.Cir.1990).

5. Florida Lime & Avocado Growers, Inc. v. Paul, 373 U.S. 132, 142–43 (1963).

6. Hines v. Davidowitz, 312 U.S. 52, 67 (1941).

7. Pre-*MITE* decisions invalidating state takeover statutes included: Kennecott Corp. v. Smith, 637 F.2d 181 (3d Cir.1980);

Natomas Co. v. Bryan, 512 F.Supp. 191 (D.Nev.1981); Canadian Pac. Enter. (U.S.) Inc. v. Krouse, 506 F.Supp. 1192 (S.D.Ohio 1981); Kelly v. Beta–X Corp., 302 N.W.2d 596 (Mich.Ct.App.1981). But see AMCA Int'l Corp. v. Krouse, 482 F.Supp. 929 (S.D.Ohio 1979); City Investing Co. v. Simcox, 476 F.Supp. 112 (S.D.Ind.1979), aff'd, 633 F.2d 56 (7th Cir.1980).

8. In 1979, the SEC had promulgated Rule 14d–2(b), which requires that a bidder meet the SEC's dissemination and Schedule 14D–1 disclosure requirements within five days of the announcement of the offer. The rule created a direct conflict between the federal tender offer rules and the first gen-

result in the state barring the tender offer on "fairness" or other grounds, was also found to conflict with a purported Congressional intent that shareholders make the decision as to whether to tender or not.

On January 19, 1979, MITE Corporation filed a Schedule 14D–1 with the SEC, indicating its intent to make a $28 per share cash tender offer for Chicago Rivet & Machine Company. On February 1, 1980, Illinois officials notified MITE that the proposed offer violated the IBTA and issued a cease and desist order and a notice of an administrative hearing. Chicago Rivet then notified MITE that it would file suit under the IBTA to restrain the tender offer. MITE thereupon sued in federal court, seeking to have the IBTA declared unconstitutional on both preemption and commerce clause grounds. The district court struck down the statute on both grounds and the Seventh Circuit affirmed.

Although the circuit court recognized that the federal scheme of regulating tender offers is not so pervasive that an implicit congressional intent to preempt parallel state legislation could be inferred from the Williams Act, it found that the IBTA empowered the Illinois Secretary of State to pass upon the substantive fairness of a tender offer and to prohibit it from going forward, if the Secretary judged the offer inequitable. Thus, the circuit court stated, "Illinois' substitution of the judgment of its Secretary of State for an investor's own assessment of the equitability of a tender offer is patently inconsistent with the Williams Act, . . . which contemplates unfettered choice by well-informed investors." Consequently, the IBTA was preempted by the Williams Act. The circuit court also found that the IBTA unconstitutionally burdened interstate commerce. The circuit court relied on the balancing standard set forth by the Supreme Court in *Pike v. Bruce Church*: "Where the statute regulates evenhandedly to effectuate a legitimate local public interest, and its effects on interstate commerce are only incidental, it will be upheld unless the burden imposed on such commerce is clearly excessive in relation to the putative local benefits."[9] Illinois asserted two interests: protection of resident shareholders and regulation of the internal affairs of Illinois corporations. The circuit court rejected both arguments. It found that the IBTA provided shareholders "marginal" benefits and that Illinois' "tenuous interest" was counterbalanced by the statute's "global impact" and its "significant potential to cause commercial disruption"

---

eration of state takeover laws. Because most first generation statutes required a substantial delay between the announcement and dissemination of the offer, it was no longer possible to time an offer to comply with both federal and state law. After Rule 14d–2(b) was promulgated, the clear trend was towards finding state takeover statutes unconstitutional. See Mark A. Sargent, On the Validity of State Takeover Regulation: State Responses to *MITE* and *Kidwell*, 42 Ohio St. L.J. 689, 696–97 (1981).

9. Pike v. Bruce Church, Inc., 397 U.S. 137, 142 (1970) (citation omitted). The commerce clause of the U.S. constitution is both a grant of power to Congress and a limitation on state power. Under the supremacy clause a valid congressional exercise of the commerce power will preempt conflicting state regulation. However, even in the absence of congressional legislation, the "dormant" commerce clause bars direct state regulation of commerce. Edgar v. MITE Corp., 457 U.S. 624, 640 (1982) (White, J.).

by blocking an offer "even if it received the enthusiastic endorsement of all other States." Consequently, because the IBTA substantially obstructed interstate commerce, without significant countervailing local benefits, it violated the dormant commerce clause.

The Supreme Court affirmed in a badly divided opinion.[10] Rejecting an argument that the preliminary injunction rendered the case moot, the plurality reached the constitutional issues. Among the substantive portions of Justice White's opinion, only the *Pike* commerce clause analysis commanded a majority. On that issue, the Court found that Illinois had "no legitimate interest in protecting non-resident shareholders," and offered only "speculative" protection for resident shareholders. The Court agreed with the circuit court "that the possible benefits of the potential delays as required by the Act may be outweighed by the increased risk that the tender offer will fail due to defensive tactics employed by incumbent management." The Court also rejected Illinois' "internal affairs" argument, noting that: "[t]ender offers contemplate transfers of stock by stockholders to a third party and do not themselves implicate the internal affairs of the target company. Furthermore, . . . Illinois has no interest in regulating the internal affairs of foreign corporations." The Court therefore concluded that the IBTA was unconstitutional under the dormant commerce clause because it imposed a substantial burden on interstate commerce that outweighed the putative local benefits.

Writing for a plurality of the court, Justice White also argued that the Williams Act preempted IBTA. According to White, the Williams Act adopted a policy of neutrality as between bidders and targets. In an oft-used metaphor, Congress supposedly intended to create a level playing field for takeover contests. The IBTA's prenotification and hearing requirements imposed significant delays before a bid could commence, during which management could erect defenses and take other measures designed to prevent the offer from going forward, and thus frustrated Congressional purpose by tipping the playing field in target management's favor. Drawing on the Williams Act's legislative history, White noted that Congress had rejected an advance filing requirement precisely because "Congress itself 'recognized that delay can seriously impede a tender offer' and sought to avoid it." In addition, White concluded that the administrative veto granted the Secretary of State conflicted with a Congressional intent that shareholders be allowed make the final decision as to whether to accept a tender offer.

The *MITE* decision's immediate impact was unclear. Only those statutes with similarly "global" ability to block tender offers were directly rendered unconstitutional by the opinion of the Court. Because

---

10. Edgar v. MITE Corp., 457 U.S. 624 (1982). In his lead opinion, Justice White determined that the IBTA was preempted by the Williams Act and also invalid under the commerce clause because (1) the IBTA directly regulated interstate commerce and (2) the IBTA's legitimate local benefits did not outweigh its indirect burden on interstate commerce. Only the latter holding, however, commanded a majority of the Court.

Justice White's preemption analysis commanded the votes of only two other Justices, it seemed possible that state statutes with a more narrow jurisdictional basis but still having a pro-target bias could pass constitutional muster. Indeed, in refusing to join the preemption analysis, Justice Stevens expressly stated that he was "not persuaded ... that Congress' decision to follow a policy of neutrality in its own legislation is tantamount to a federal prohibition against state legislation designed to provide special protection for incumbent management." Similarly, Justice Powell declined to join the preemption analysis, observing that the Court's "Commerce Clause reasoning leaves some room for state regulation" and that "the Williams Act's neutrality policy does not necessarily imply a congressional intent to prohibit state legislation [protecting] interests that include but are often broader than those of incumbent management." Surprisingly, however, subsequent lower court decisions almost uniformly adopted the plurality's preemption analysis.

B. The second generation and *CTS*

Justice White's *MITE* opinion left open a narrow window of opportunity for states to regulate takeovers: the internal affairs doctrine, pursuant to which the state of incorporation's law governs questions of corporate governance. The second generation of state takeover statutes was carefully crafted to fit within that loophole.

1. *The second generation statutes*

The so-called "second generation" statutes were, for the most part, cautiously tailored to avoid direct regulation of tender offers. Instead, they addressed issues purporting to fall within the sphere of corporate governance concerns traditionally subject to state law. In the years between 1983 and 1987, many of these statutes were challenged and almost uniformly were struck down by the lower courts as unconstitutional. That trend was reversed following the Supreme Court's decision in *CTS Corp. v. Dynamics Corp.*,[11] however.

There are four principal variants of "second generation" statutes: Control share acquisition statutes rely on the states' traditional power to define corporate voting rights as a justification for regulating the bidder's right to vote shares acquired in a control transaction. A "control share acquisition" is typically defined as the acquisition of a sufficient number of target company shares to give the acquirer control over more than a specified percentage of the voting power of the target. The triggering level of share ownership is usually defined as an acquisition which would bring the bidder within one of three ranges of voting power: 20 to 33 1/3%, 33 1/3 to 50% and more than 50%. Most control share acquisition laws provide that shares acquired in a control share acquisition shall not have voting rights unless the shareholders approve a resolution granting voting rights to the acquirer's shares.[12] The shares

11. CTS Corp. v. Dynamics Corp. of Am., 481 U.S. 69 (1987).

12. E.g., Ind. Code Ann. § 23–1–42. A few states took a slightly different ap-

owned by the acquirer, officers of the target and directors who are also employees of the target may not be counted in the vote on the resolution.

The stated purpose of control share statutes is providing shareholders with an opportunity to vote on a proposed acquisition of large share blocks which may result in or lead to a change in control of the target. These statutes are premised on the assumption that individual shareholders are often at a disadvantage when faced with a proposed change in control. If the target's shareholders believe that a successful tender offer will be followed by a purchase by the offeror of non-tendered shares at a price lower than that offered in the initial bid, for example, individual shareholders may tender their shares to protect themselves from such an eventuality, even if they do not believe the offer to be in their best interests.

By requiring certain disclosures from the prospective purchaser and by allowing the target's shareholders to vote on the acquisition as a group, control share acquisition statutes supposedly provide the shareholders a collective opportunity to reject an inadequate or otherwise undesirable offer. For example, since control share acquisition statutes generally require the offeror to disclose plans for transactions involving the target that would be initiated after the control shares are acquired, shareholders presumably would be unlikely to approve a creeping tender offer or street sweep which would be followed by a squeezeout back-end merger at a price less than or in a consideration different than that paid by the acquirer in purchasing the initial share block.

Fair price statutes are modeled on the approach taken in company charters that include fair price provisions. These statutes provide that certain specified transactions, sometimes called "Business Combinations," involving an "interested shareholder" must be approved by a specified supermajority shareholder vote unless certain minimum price and other conditions are met. The term "interested shareholder" is typically defined by statute as a shareholder owning more than some specified percentage, often 10%, of the outstanding shares of the target.

Business combination statutes are an extension of the fair price statute concept, providing substantially greater teeth. The typical statute prohibits a target from engaging in any business combination with an interested shareholder of the target corporation for a set period of time, often five years, following the date on which the interested shareholder achieved such status. Following the initial freeze period, a business combination with an interested shareholder is still prohibited unless the business combination is approved by a specified vote of the outstanding shares not beneficially owned by the interested shareholder or the business combination meets specified fair price and other criteria.[13] The

proach, under which the shareholders determine whether or not the proposed acquisition may be made. E.g., Ohio Rev. Code Ann. § 1701.831. This is a slightly more aggressive position than the more usual ap-

proach, which simply requires shareholder approval for voting rights to be accorded to the acquirer's shares.

13. See, e.g., N.Y. Bus. Corp. Law § 912(c). Delaware § 203 is similar to the

definition of interested shareholder typically is comparable to that used in fair price statutes. As with fair price statutes, the term "business combination" typically is defined to include a broader variety of transactions than just a statutory merger.

Cash-out statutes require an acquirer of more than a threshold percentage of a target's stock to offer to purchase the remaining shares of all of the other shareholders at a price which reflects the highest premium paid by the acquirer in accumulating target stock. Cash-out statutes typically apply to so-called "control transactions," which are defined as acquisitions by a person or group who, after the acquisition, will have the status of a "controlling person or group." A "controlling person or group" is a person who has, or a group of persons acting in concert that has, voting power over voting shares that would entitle the holders thereof to cast at least a specified percentage of votes that all shareholders would be entitled to cast in the election of directors.

2. *Powell's CTS opinion*

In *CTS Corp. v. Dynamics Corp.*,[14] the Supreme Court upheld an Indiana control share acquisition statute. Justice Powell's majority opinion began by noting that the *MITE* plurality's preemption analysis was not binding on the Court, but he declined to explicitly overrule it. Instead, Powell claimed that the Indiana Act passed muster even under White's interpretation of the Williams Act's purposes. It is perhaps instructive, however, that Justice White was the lone dissenter from Powell's preemption holding.

In fact, *CTS'* preemption analysis differed from *MITE*'s in at least two key respects. Where Justice White emphasized Congress' neutrality policy, Justice Powell emphasized Congress' desire to protect shareholders.[15] Where Justice White would preempt any state statute favoring management, Justice Powell upheld the Indiana Act even though he recognized that it would deter some takeover bids. Justice Powell did so because he believed that, despite the Indiana statute's deterrent effect,[16]

---

original business combination statutes in a number of respects, but there is no requirement of shareholder approval after the freeze period expires. Shareholder voting may still occur, however, because the freeze period will be waived if at any time during it a proposed transaction is approved by the board of directors and by the two-thirds of the outstanding shares not owned by the bidder. DGCL § 203.

14. CTS Corp. v. Dynamics Corp. of Am., 481 U.S. 69 (1987).

15. In dissent, Justice White argued that the Williams Act was primarily intended to protect individual investors. CTS Corp. v. Dynamics Corp. of Am., 481 U.S. 69, 98–99 (1987) (White, J., dissenting). In contrast, Justice Powell believed that the Williams Act was intended to protect share-

holders. Id. at 82. The difference between investors and shareholders is more than just semantic. Under Justice White's view, a statute will be preempted if it interferes with an individual investor's ability to freely make his own decision. In contrast, Justice Powell would uphold state takeover statutes that make shareholders as a group better off, even if the wishes of some individual investors are thereby frustrated.

16. Arguably, the control shareholder acquisition statutes are an ineffective takeover deterrent. The bidder's ability to request a special shareholder meeting to consider its proposed acquisition provides corporate raiders with an opportunity to cheaply advertise a target's takeover vulnerability. Likewise, a bidder can reduce the impact of a control share acquisition

Justice Powell believed that it protected shareholders by permitting them collectively to evaluate an offer's fairness. He laid particular emphasis on a bidder's ability to coerce shareholders into tendering, such as by making a two-tier tender offer. By allowing shareholders collectively to reject such offers, the Indiana statute defuses their coercive effect. That the statute also deters takeovers and thereby protects incumbent managers is merely incidental to its primary function of protecting shareholders. The Indiana act therefore did not conflict with the Williams Act; to the contrary, Justice Powell concluded that it furthered Congress' goal of protecting shareholders.

Although Justice Powell acknowledged the Indiana act imposed a substantial delay on bidders, he reinterpreted *MITE* to only bar states from injecting unreasonable delay into the tender offer process. He then concluded that a potential 50 day waiting period was not unreasonable. Justice Powell noted that a variety of state corporate laws, such as classified board and cumulative voting statutes, limit or delay the transfer of control following a successful tender offer: "[T]he Williams Act would pre-empt a variety of state corporate laws of hitherto unquestioned validity if it were construed to pre-empt any state statute that may limit or delay the free exercise of power after a successful tender offer.... The longstanding prevalence of state regulation in this area suggests that, if Congress had intended to pre-empt all state laws that delay the acquisition of voting control following a tender offer, it would have said so explicitly."

Justice White's analysis implied that the Williams Act's neutrality policy meant that any state laws which derogated from the level playing field established by the Williams Act were to be preempted. However, there was another, perhaps equally plausible, interpretation of the Act; namely, that Congress wanted to assure that the Act itself not affect the balance of power between bidders and targets but did not intend to prohibit all state laws that affected that balance. Powell's opinion implicitly embraced the latter view.

Turning to the commerce clause issues, Powell held that the Indiana statute also passed muster under the dormant commerce clause. The statute did not discriminate against out of state entities. It did not bar tender offers, leaving a meaningful opportunity for the offeror to succeed. Because the statute was limited to Indiana corporations, the statute did not have significant extraterritorial effects. As to the local benefits aspect of the balancing test, Justice Powell held that the state had a legitimate interest in defining the attributes of its corporations and protecting shareholders of its corporations. He opined, for example,

---

statute by simply delaying consummation of a purchase until a shareholder vote has been held and requiring a favorable vote as a condition to its tender offer. Most control share statutes prohibit both bidders and target insiders from voting on the resolution, but do not impose any minimum holding period on the "disinterested" shareholders in order for them to be eligible to vote. As a result, the outcome of the vote likely will depend in large part on the views of takeover arbitragers and other speculators who can be expected to favor the bidder over target management.

that "[n]o principle of corporation law and practice is more firmly established than a State's authority to regulate domestic corporations, including the authority to define the voting rights of shareholders."[17] Accordingly, it "is an accepted part of the business landscape in this country for States to create corporations, to prescribe their powers, and to define the rights that are acquired by purchasing their shares."[18]

C. Interpreting *CTS*

Clearly *CTS* contemplated a greater degree of state regulation than did *MITE*, but how much greater remained uncertain. Because Justice Powell so narrowly focused on the specific provisions of the Indiana Act, he failed to provide a generally applicable analysis. Indeed, both proponents and opponents of state takeover legislation can mine *CTS* for support for their arguments. Faced with this uncertainty, two distinct lower court readings of *CTS*'s preemption analysis developed.

1. *A meaningful opportunity for success*

The more restrictive interpretation of *CTS* requires states to preserve a meaningful opportunity for successful hostile bids. This standard is most fully developed in a trilogy of cases involving the Delaware takeover statute's constitutionality.[19] DGCL § 203 is a variant on the older business combination statutes. Section 203 prohibits a Delaware corporation from entering into a business combination for a period of three years after an offeror becomes an interested stockholder. Business combination is defined to include freezeout mergers and other common post-acquisition transactions.[20] Interested shareholder is defined, subject to various exceptions, as the owner of 15% or more of the target's outstanding shares.

Unlike the older business combination statutes, the Delaware statute does not impose either a supermajority approval or a fair price requirement in connection with business combinations after the freeze

---

17. CTS Corp. v. Dynamics Corp. of Am., 481 U.S. 69, 89 (1987).

18. Some ten years after the Supreme Court's decision, CTS Corporation (the target) agreed to acquire Dynamics Corporation of America (the bidder) for $210 million in cash and stock. Dynamics still owned a 44 percent stake in CTS, which dated back to the contested control share acquisition. Ironically, the CTS acquisition was intended to thwart WHX Corporation's hostile takeover bid for Dynamics. CTS' chairman described the acquisition as a major benefit to "our shareholders." He also observed that the two companies' product families were complementary. The deal was structured as a cash tender for part of the Dynamics shares, to be followed by a stock swap for the rest of the shares, which gave Dynamics shareholders an opportunity to reject the cash end and take CTS shares, thereby avoiding tax on unrealized gain. Wall St. J., May 12, 1997, at B9.

19. City Capital Assoc. Ltd. v. Interco, Inc., 696 F.Supp. 1551 (D.Del.1988), aff'd on other grounds, 860 F.2d 60 (3d Cir. 1988); RP Acquisition Corp. v. Staley Cont'l, Inc., 686 F.Supp. 476 (D.Del.1988); BNS Inc. v. Koppers Co., Inc., 683 F.Supp. 458 (D.Del.1988).

20. Section 203 puts fewer restrictions on the raider's use of target assets to finance an acquisition than do the older business combination statutes. For example, it permits the raider to sell off target assets to third parties (subject to the usual fiduciary duty and voting rules).

period expires. Thus, once the three-year period expires, the interested stockholder may complete a second-step business combination on whatever terms and conditions would be lawful under applicable corporate and securities law provisions. In addition, the three-year freeze period is waived if any of four conditions are satisfied: (1) prior to the date on which the bidder crosses the 15% threshold, the business combination or the triggering acquisition is approved by the target's board of directors; (2) the bidder, in a single transaction, goes from a stock ownership level of less than 15% to more than 85% of the target's voting stock (not counting shares owned by inside directors or by employee stock plans in which the employees do not have the right to determine confidentially whether shares held by the plan will be tendered); (3) during the three year freeze period, the transaction is approved by the board of directors and by two-thirds of the outstanding shares not owned by the bidder; or (4) the target's board of directors approves a white knight transaction. Section 203(b) also sets forth various other conditions under which the statute will not apply, most prominently an opt-out provision pursuant to which a corporation may exempt itself from the statute through appropriate charter or bylaw provisions.

In the leading case of the trilogy, *BNS Inc. v. Koppers Co.*,[21] Chief District Judge Schwartz began by interpreting *CTS* as meaning that neutrality between bidders and targets was no longer regarded as a purpose of the Williams Act in itself, but rather merely as a means towards the true congressional end of shareholder protection. State statutes having a substantial deterrent effect are now permissible, as are statutes favoring management, so long as these effects are merely incidental to protecting shareholders.[22] This proviso, however, is critical. As Chief Judge Schwartz saw it, *CTS* does not permit states to eliminate hostile takeovers. Rather, states must preserve a "meaningful opportunity" for hostile offers that are beneficial to target shareholders to succeed. Chief Judge Schwartz offered a four part test to decide whether a state law did so: (1) does the state law protect independent shareholders from coercion; (2) does it give either side an advantage in consummating or defeating an offer; (3) does it impose an unreasonable delay; and (4) does it permit a state official to substitute his views for those of the shareholders. Concluding that Section 203 probably satisfied these standards, Chief Judge Schwartz declined to enjoin its enforcement.

2. *Amanda Acquisition*

The 1980s takeover wars took many a surprising turn. Perhaps none was more surprising, however, than Judge Frank Easterbrook's decision in *Amanda Acquisition Corp. v. Universal Foods Corp.*[23] Judge Easter-

---

21. BNS Inc. v. Koppers Co., Inc., 683 F.Supp. 458 (D.Del.1988).

22. Accord Hyde Park Partners, L.P. v. Connolly, 839 F.2d 837, 850 (1st Cir.1988) ("protection of management that is incidental to protection of investors does not per se

conflict with the purpose or purposes of the Williams Act.").

23. Amanda Acquisition Corp. v. Universal Foods Corp., 877 F.2d 496 (7th Cir. 1989).

brook is an unabashed proponent of hostile takeovers, of course. Indeed, *Amanda Acquisition* itself sings their praises. Yet in upholding the Wisconsin business combination statute, Judge Easterbrook authored the most permissive preemption analysis of state takeover legislation to date.[24]

Like most post-*MITE* state takeover statutes, the Wisconsin law deters tender offers by regulating freezeout mergers and other post-acquisition transactions. Like most business combination statutes, it imposes a statutory freeze period, here three years, following the acquisition during which business combinations are prohibited. The sole viable exception to the freeze period is prior approval by the incumbent directors: "In Wisconsin it is management's approval in advance, or wait three years."

Judge Easterbrook began with the Williams Act's neutrality policy. Congress unquestionably expected the federal tender offers rules to be neutral as between bidders and targets. In *MITE*, Justice White read that expectation as forbidding state statutes from tipping the balance between them. Both Justices Powell and Stevens rejected that reading in their concurrences. And, of course, *CTS* implicitly backpedals from the spirit of Justice White's analysis. Judge Easterbrook recognized that all of this might open the door for nonneutral state laws, but he claimed to "stop short of th[at] precipice." At a minimum, however, *Amanda Acquisition* implicitly treats neutrality as a means rather than an end in itself. Easterbrook's decision to uphold the Wisconsin statute in the face of its admitted deterrent effects only makes sense if he has rejected Justice White's analysis in *MITE* of the neutrality policy's preemptive power.

In any case, Judge Easterbrook thereafter essentially ignored the Williams Act's neutrality policy. Instead, he asserted that Congress intended the Williams Act to regulate the process by which tender offers take place and the disclosures to which shareholders are entitled. He then used this reading of congressional purpose to distinguish *MITE* from *CTS*. The IBTA threatened to preclude a bidder from purchasing target shares even if the bidder complied with federal law. In contrast, the Indiana control share acquisition statute did not interfere with the federally mandated tender offer process; indeed, it did not even come into play until that process was completed and the shares acquired.

---

24. Some observers posit that Judge Easterbrook did not mean what he said, but said it only to goad the Supreme Court or Congress into preempting state takeover legislation. Perhaps so, but then why did he not simply say so, instead of creating an elaborate justification for state takeover regulations? It is not uncommon for lower court judges to follow Supreme Court precedents they disagree with, while expressly urging the Supreme Court to reconsider its prior holdings. No one doubts the appropriateness of such behavior. At the very least, however, there would be something unseemly about a judge deliberately misrepresenting his position in an attempt to force the Supreme Court to reverse him. Accordingly, it seems better to take Judge Easterbrook at his word, as several subsequent cases have done. E.g., Hoylake Investments Ltd. v. Washburn, 723 F.Supp. 42, 48 (N.D.Ill.1989); Glass, Molders, Pottery, Plastics and Allied Workers Int'l Union v. Wickes Co., Inc., 578 A.2d 402, 406 (N.J.Super.1990).

The Wisconsin business combination statute, like the Indiana Act, left the tender offer process alone. According to Judge Easterbrook, the Wisconsin statute therefore could be preempted only if the Williams Act gives investors a federal right to receive tender offers. He determined, however, that no such federal right exists: "Investors have no right to receive tender offers. More to the point—since Amanda sues as bidder rather than as investor seeking to sell—the Williams Act does not create a right to profit from the business of making tender offers. It is not attractive to put bids on the table for Wisconsin corporations, but because Wisconsin leaves the process alone once a bidder appears, its law may coexist with the Williams Act." The state statute need not even leave the bidder an opportunity—meaningful or otherwise—for success. Accordingly, the issue is not whether the statute deters tender offers. The issue is whether the state law directly interferes with an undeterred bidder's ability to go forward on schedule and in compliance with federal law.

3. *Choosing a standard*

Selection of the standard of review is often determinative. Plausible arguments can be made for both the meaningful opportunity for success standard and *Amanda Acquisition*. On balance, however, *Amanda Acquisition* seems preferable. The meaningful opportunity for success standard inherently poses difficult interpretative problems for legislators attempting to remain within constitutional bounds and for judges reviewing new statutes. More important, *Amanda Acquisition* is a logical extension of the Supreme Court's recent trend in drawing the dividing line between state corporate law and federal securities law.

As for ease of application. what does "meaningful opportunity for success" mean? Against what potential injuries may the state guard shareholders? Which proxy contests are "beneficial to shareholders"? How much deterrence is too much? How open must the window of opportunity be to be meaningful? Admittedly, stringing together rhetorical questions is not the most powerful of argumentative devices, but each of these is critical to application of the standard. Yet, each also has no readily apparent answer.[25] *Amanda Acquisition* thus offers courts a standard posing much simpler questions.

---

25. Recall that Chief Judge Schwartz offered a four part test in *BNS* to supplement the meaningful opportunity for success standard. BNS Inc. v. Koppers Co., Inc., 683 F.Supp. 458, 469 (D.Del.1988). Unfortunately, there are several problems with that attempted clarification. First, several of the prongs are as unclear or as uncertain as the basic standard; so too is the question of how many prongs must be satisfied. Second, neither *BNS* nor its progeny solely operated within this framework. Finally, the second prong—whether the law gives one side an advantage—may be incon-sistent with *CTS*. Justice Powell had asked whether the Indiana Act gave either side an advantage in communicating with shareholders; Chief Judge Schwartz recast that question to essentially ask whether the statute helped either side prevail. *BNS* thus "restated the question much more broadly and gave greater weight to the neutrality principle than the Court in *CTS* may have intended." Evelyn Sroufe & Catherine Gelband, Business Combination Statutes: A "Meaningful Opportunity" for Success?, 45 Bus. Law. 891, 917 n.119 (1990).

As for consistency with *CTS*, there are perhaps as many theories about what the Supreme Court did in *CTS*, why it did it, and whether it should have done it as there are corporate law professors. While disputes as to the latter two questions were unavoidable in light of the hot debate over corporate takeovers, disagreement as to the former was avoidable. The disparate readings offered by *BNS* and *Amanda Acquisition* were only possible because Justice Powell failed to face and resolve the tensions inherent in his analysis.

On the one hand, recall that Justice Powell argued that the Indiana statute actually furthered the Williams Act's purpose. While the *MITE* plurality had emphasized Congress' neutrality policy, Justice Powell emphasized Congress' desire to protect shareholders. Because he believed that the Indiana act protected shareholders by giving them a collective opportunity to pass on a tender offer, he concluded that the state statute was consistent with congressional intent. Chief Judge Schwartz used this aspect of *CTS* as the intellectual underpinnings of the meaningful opportunity for success standard.

On the other hand, however, there is Justice Powell's broad language about the traditional primacy of state regulatory authority in the corporate governance field. Recall that Justice Powell limited his preemption analysis by noting the "long-standing prevalence of state regulation."[26] Accordingly, absent express congressional direction, he declined to interpret the Williams Act in a manner that might permit it to preempt any state law that interfered with tender offers. Justice Powell's commerce clause analysis even more strongly endorsed the primacy of the states in corporate governance regulation. Proponents of state takeover regulation seize on that language to argue for a broad reading of *CTS*. Correspondingly, opponents of an active state role feared that subsequent decisions might make this aspect of *CTS* the basis for preemption analysis in this area. In *Amanda Acquisition*, that chicken came home to roost.

The case for *Amanda Acquisition* begins with the burden of proof in preemption litigation. When a state takeover law is challenged, the challenger bears the burden of proof. This is not an easy burden to carry. The Supreme Court is generally reluctant to infer preemption.[27] This is especially true in areas traditionally regulated by the states.[28] That corporate law is such an area goes a long way towards explaining *CTS*.

States have been in the business of regulating corporate governance since before the United States was founded. Throughout that same time span, many have argued for federalizing corporate law. Yet, the federal government did not enter the picture until the New Deal securities legislation of the 1930s and 1940s. Moreover, when Congress finally did get involved, it did so in a fairly limited way. Congress was mainly

---

26. CTS Corp. v. Dynamics Corp. of Am., 481 U.S. 69, 86 (1987).

27. Exxon Corp. v. Governor of Md., 437 U.S. 117, 132 (1978).

28. California v. ARC America Corp., 490 U.S. 93 (1989).

concerned with disclosure and with providing procedural safeguards to make the disclosure requirements more effective.

In a long line of cases, the Supreme Court has respected the balance created by Congress by holding that the federal securities laws merely place a limited gloss on state corporate law.[29] Unless federal law expressly governs some corporate law question, the court will treat state law as controlling.[30] The corporation thus is recognized as a creature of the state, "whose very existence and attributes are a product of state law."[31] The court therefore acknowledges that states have legitimate interests in overseeing the firms they create and in protecting the shareholders of their corporations. Finally, the *CTS* court further accepted a state's "interest in promoting stable relationships among parties involved in the corporations it charters, as well as in ensuring that investors in such corporations have an effective voice in corporate affairs." If so, state regulation not only protects shareholders, but also protects investor and entrepreneurial confidence in the fairness and effectiveness of the state corporation law.[32]

The country as a whole benefits from state regulation in this area, as well. The markets that facilitate national and international participation in ownership of corporations are essential for providing capital not only for new enterprises but also for established companies that need to expand their businesses. This beneficial free market system depends at its core upon the fact that corporations generally are organized under, and governed by, the law of the state of their incorporation.[33]

This is so in large part because ousting the states from their traditional role as the primary regulators of corporate governance would eliminate a valuable opportunity for experimentation with alternative solutions to the many difficult regulatory problems that arise in corpo-

---

29. E.g., Kamen v. Kemper Fin. Servs. Inc., 502 U.S. 974 (1991); Burks v. Lasker, 441 U.S. 471 (1979); Santa Fe Indus., Inc. v. Green, 430 U.S. 462 (1977); Piper v. Chris–Craft Indus., Inc., 430 U.S. 1 (1977); Cort v. Ash, 422 U.S. 66 (1975).

30. Cort v. Ash, 422 U.S. 66, 84 (1975).

31. CTS Corp. v. Dynamics Corp. of Am., 481 U.S. 69, 89 (1987). There is an ongoing debate within academia as to "whether the modern corporation is essentially a matter of public or private concern." Lawrence E. Mitchell, Private Law, Public Interest?: The ALI Principles of Corporate Governance, 61 Geo. Wash. L. Rev. 871, 876 (1993). For those who come down on the public side of the debate, the *CTS* arguments about the states' interests in regulating the corporation should be conclusive. For them the corporation, and thus corporate law, is a matter of public concern that the state has a strong interest in regulating. For those on the private law side of the

debate, however, the *CTS* arguments also should prove persuasive. They acknowledge that the state has an interest in ensuring that the gains of private transacting are maximized and further acknowledge that state regulation is more likely to maximize those gains than is national regulation.

32. Some argue that the state also has an interest in corporations that make a substantial contribution to the state. Corporations provide employment, a crucial tax base, sell and purchase goods and services, and supply support for community activities. This interest in any corporation will vary from case to case, but it is a real interest, deriving from the corporation's existence as a tangible economic entity created by state law. See Mark A. Sargent, Do the Second Generation State Takeover Statutes Violate the Commerce Clause?, 8 Corp. L. Rev. 3, 23 (1985).

33. CTS Corp. v. Dynamics Corp. of Am., 481 U.S. 69, 90 (1987).

rate law. As Justice Brandeis pointed out many years ago, "It is one of the happy incidents of the federal system that a single courageous State may, if its citizens choose, serve as a laboratory; and try novel social and economic experiments without risk to the rest of country."[34] So long as state legislation is limited to regulation of firms incorporated within the state, as it generally is, there is no risk of conflicting rules applying to the same corporation. Experimentation thus does not result in confusion. In contrast, a uniform federal standard would preclude experimentation with differing modes of regulation.

In this light, *MITE* can be seen as an aberration that *CTS* corrected. If read broadly, *MITE* threatened to preempt any state corporate law that affected control contests. As Justice Powell recognized, much of state corporate law was potentially vulnerable to challenges based on such a reading of *MITE*. By limiting the Williams Act's preemptive force, Justice Powell prevented this scenario. The tensions and contradictions in Justice Powell's preemption arguments resulted from his failure to face the full implications of his own analysis. In contrast, Judge Easterbrook saw and accepted those implications. Judge Easterbrook was unable to find a firebreak between preemption of the Wisconsin business combination statute and preemption of the host of state corporate laws that affect tender offers. If the Williams Act preempted the Wisconsin statute, there was no principled basis upon which to preserve classified boards, cumulative voting, supermajority voting requirements, dual class voting rights, and takeover defenses. While *BNS* essentially ignores this risk, *Amanda Acquisition* drew the logical conclusion from Justice Powell's refusal to preempt that body of state law.

4.   Commerce clause issues

As illustrated by both *CTS* and *MITE*, challenges to state takeover laws typically entail not only preemption but also dormant commerce clause claims. Recall that there are three core commerce clause questions: (1) does the state statute discriminate against interstate commerce; (2) does the state statute subject interstate commerce to inconsistent regulation; and (3) do the local benefits of the statute outweigh the burdens it places on interstate commerce (the legitimacy of this third test is a matter of considerable debate among constitutional scholars, but let's leave it in their capable hands).[35] Post-*CTS*, commerce clause challenges have not had much traction. As long as the state statute treats in-state bidders and out-of-state bidders the same, the statute will pass muster under the first test. Provided the state law applies only to firms incorporated within the regulating state, there is no possibility of inconsistent regulation and it will pass muster under the second test. Some state takeover law decisions have declined to apply the third test, concluding that even statutes whose costs exceed their benefits are

---

34. New State Ice Co. v. Liebmann, 285 U.S. 262, 311 (1932) (Brandeis, J., dissenting).

35. See CTS Corp. v. Dynamics Corp. of Am., 481 U.S. 69, 87–93 (1987).

constitutional.[36] Even those that retain the third test, however, generally uphold state takeover laws in light of the substantial state interest in regulating corporate governance.[37]

D. The third generation

Following *CTS*, many states began adopting increasingly draconian takeover statutes. Perhaps none was more blatantly anti-takeover, however, that the statute adopted by Pennsylvania in 1990.[38] The statute contained no fewer than five distinct anti-takeover provisions. First, pursuant to a fairly standard nonshareholder constituency statute, directors are allowed to take account of the interests not only of shareholders but also of "employees, suppliers, customers and creditors of the corporation, and ... communities in which offices or other establishments of the corporation are located." Perhaps even more significantly, however, target company directors are expressly relieved of any obligation to treat the interests of shareholders as "dominant or controlling." These rules expressly apply to takeover defenses, such as a board refusal to redeem a poison pill. To be sure, the statute requires that directors act in "good faith," but their lack of good faith must be proved by "clear and convincing evidence."

Second, Pennsylvania adopted a control share acquisition statute largely modeled on the Indiana statute upheld in *CTS*. A control share acquisition must be approved by a majority of the "disinterested" shares and a majority of all shares (other than those of the bidder). If approval is not forthcoming, the bidder's shares are stripped of their voting rights. Disinterested shares are defined by statute as those that have been held by their owner for (i) twelve months before the record date for voting or (ii) five days prior to the first disclosure of the takeover bid. This provision apparently is intended to address a perceived loophole in second generation control share acquisition statutes; namely, the fact that takeover speculators often buy up large blocks of stock after a bid is announced.

Third, the statute contains a so-called "tin parachute" provision, under which an employee who is fired after a takeover is entitled to a week's pay for each year of prior employment to a maximum of 26

36. E.g., Amanda Acquisition Corp. v. Universal Foods Corp., 877 F.2d 496, 505–09 (7th Cir.1989).

37. See, e.g., City Capital Assoc. L.P. v. Interco, Inc., 696 F.Supp. 1551, 1555 (D.Del.1988), aff'd on other grounds, 860 F.2d 60 (3d Cir.1988); RP Acquisition Corp. v. Staley Cont'l, Inc., 686 F.Supp. 476, 487–88 (D.Del.1988).

38. On Pennsylvania's various takeover statutes, see Stephen M. Bainbridge, Redirecting State Takeover Laws at Proxy Con-

tests, 1992 Wis. L. Rev. 1071 (discussing 1990 legislation, especially with respect to its effect on proxy contests); Stephen M. Bainbridge, State Takeover and Tender Offer Regulations Post-*MITE*: The Maryland, Ohio and Pennsylvania Attempts, 90 Dickinson L. Rev. 731 (1986) (discussing earlier cash out statute); John Pound, On the Motives for Choosing a Corporate Governance Structure: A Study of Corporate Reaction to the Pennsylvania Takeover Law, 8 J. L. Econ. & Org. 656 (1992).

weeks' pay. In a related provisions, the statute provides that after a takeover all labor contracts are to remain in force.

Finally, and perhaps most innovatively, a target corporation (or one of its shareholders suing derivatively) may sue a controlling person or group for disgorgement of any profits realized upon disposition of the latter's shares in the target if the disposition occurs within 18 months after the person or group achieved control status. The shares also must have been acquired by the controlling person or group within 24 months before or 18 months after they acquired control status. A person or group achieves control status by disclosing an intent to seek control of the firm or by acquiring, offering to acquire or disclosing an intent to acquire "voting power over voting shares of a registered corporation that would entitle the holder thereof to cast at least 20% of the votes that all shareholders would be entitled to cast in an election of directors of the corporation." A registered corporation is one registered with the SEC under the Securities Exchange Act of 1934. Control is defined as the "power, whether or not exercised, to direct or cause the direction of the management and policies of a person, whether through the ownership of voting shares, by contract or otherwise."

Note that the statutory definition of control status picks up not only successful bidders but also the holder of proxies representing more than 20 percent of the outstanding shares. It does so because such a proxy holder has the power to cast "at least twenty per cent of the votes that all shareholders would be entitled to cast in the election of directors of the corporation."[39] As originally introduced, the statute thus imposed the disgorgement penalty not only on tender offerors, but also on anyone soliciting proxies for any purpose from more than 20 percent of the target's shareholders. As adopted, however, the statute expressly exempted all management proxy solicitations. It also provided a safe harbor for insurgent solicitations satisfying two conditions: (1) the solicitation is made in accordance with applicable federal proxy rules; and (2) the proxies given do not empower the holder to vote the covered shares on any matter except those described in the proxy statement and in accordance with the instructions of the giver of the proxy. The first condition is problematic because it opens the door for application of the disgorgement remedy not only to fraudulent proxy solicitations, but also to those that fail to comply with some technical aspect of the federal proxy rules. The second is equally problematic. Proxies normally grant the holder discretionary authority to vote on procedural and other unanticipated matters that arise during a shareholders' meeting. The second condition precludes insurgents (but not management) from seeking that normal discretionary authority.[40]

39. "Voting power" is not a defined term in the disgorgement statute. Pennsylvania's older cash-out statute defines it as the power to direct the voting of the shares "through any option, contract, arrangement, understanding, conversion or relationship." One or more of these should cover the proxy relationship, which is usually regarded as being a sub-species of agency relationships. Parshalle v. Roy, 567 A.2d 19, 27 (Del.Ch.1989).

40. Although Pennsylvania's cash-out statute provides no comparable safe harbor for proxy solicitations, it does exempt per-

Some insurgents no doubt can live with these conditions. Perhaps anticipating just such insurgents, the safe harbor was carefully crafted to exclude insurgents waging a proxy contest for control of the target. Recall that there are two ways one becomes a controlling person: (1) by acquiring voting power over 20% or more of the stock and (2) by announcing an intent to seek control. The safe harbor is only applicable to persons achieving control status by virtue of the first method. As such, the disgorgement remedy still applies to any insurgent that announces an intent to seek control of the company.[41]

Would the Pennsylvania statute pass constitutional muster? Several of the provisions clearly would do so on an individual basis. Because it was closely patterned after the Indiana statute, the control share acquisition provision's constitutionality should follow as a matter of course from *CTS*. Likewise, nobody seriously doubts the constitutionality of nonshareholder constituency statutes. In contrast, the tin parachute

---

sons who hold shares as an agent or nominee of a beneficial owner. The holder of a revocable proxy thus should fall within the literal definition of a controlling person, but be exempted by the exception for agents. In fact, it makes little sense to extend the cash-out statute to proxy contests. A proxy solicited under the Exchange Act is only a temporary transfer of voting power and an easily revocable one at that. Moreover, subject to the limited exception for discretionary voting authority, an Exchange Act proxy only authorizes the holder to vote the shares as directed by their beneficial owner. Control of the company will not change hands unless the insurgent succeeds and, even then, voting power returns to the shares' beneficial owner after the shareholder meeting. In a remarkably opaque opinion, however, U.S. District Court Judge Gawthorp apparently interpreted the statute as being triggered by a proxy solicitation. Centaur Partners wanted to call a special shareholders meeting to remove Pennwalt Corporation's incumbent directors and replace them with Centaur nominees. In order to demand a special meeting, it needed consents from 20 percent of the outstanding shares. Apparently Centaur did not own sufficient shares to demand a meeting by itself, as it solicited consents from other Pennwalt shareholders. The solicitation provided that the consents would be nullified if a court determined that execution of the consent made the shareholder a member of a controlling group for purposes of the cash-out statute. Pennwalt, of course, contended that Centaur and the signing shareholders were acting in concert and therefore constituted a control group. Judge Gawthorp agreed. In so doing, he implied that the statute applies to proxy contests. He also appeared to hold

that the agency exception did not apply to Centaur. Pennwalt Corp. v. Centaur Partners, 710 F.Supp. 111, 115 (E.D.Pa.1989). If *Pennwalt* stands for the proposition that the cash-out statute applies to proxy solicitations, an almost insurmountable deterrent to proxy contests arises. Because the statute is triggered by voting power over 20 percent of the shares, an insurgent could lose the proxy contest and still be obliged to offer to buyout all the remaining shareholders. In effect, the statute gives the other shareholders a put, which rational shareholders will exercise if the statutorily defined fair price exceeds the current market price. Presumably no rational insurgent would conduct a proxy contest under those circumstances.

41. A bidder who seeks to evade the disgorgement remedy by failing to disclose a control intent likely will run afoul of the federal securities laws. Any person who acquires more than 5% of a class of a corporation's equity securities must file a Schedule 13D with the SEC within 10 days after crossing the 5% threshold. Item 4 of Schedule 13D effectively requires the filer to state whether it intends to seek control. Even if the filer does not intend to seek control at the time the statement is first filed, a change in that intent would require filing of an amendment to the schedule to disclose the new intent. As Schedule 13Ds are publicly available documents, disclosure of a control intent therein will trigger this method of acquiring control status. So too would disclosure of an intent to seek control pursuant to Pennsylvania's control share acquisition statute, which requires such disclosures by persons seeking to acquire 20 percent or more of the firm's voting shares.

provision seems particularly vulnerable. A similar provision in Massachusetts law was held preempted by the federal Employee Retirement Income Security Act (ERISA), which explicitly preempts "any and all State laws" that "relate to any employee benefit plan."[42]

The disgorgement provision presents the most serious constitutional questions. Under *Amanda Acquisition*, of course, the provision doubtless passes muster. Provided a state statute does not interfere with the tender offer process (or, by way of analogy, the proxy solicitation process) if a bid appears, the statute's effectiveness in deterring bidders is irrelevant. As the Pennsylvania statute affects neither the federal tender offer nor the proxy solicitation process, a court following *Amanda Acquisition* must uphold it.

The meaningful opportunity for success standard poses significantly greater problems for the disgorgement provision. Applying *BNS'* four-pronged test, note that the provision does not delay a tender offer (or proxy contest) nor provides any role for state officials. The third and fourth *BNS* prongs are thus not applicable to this provision. Under the first prong, the question is whether the Pennsylvania statute's primary effect is to protect shareholders. Yet the word shareholder does not even appear in the act's statement of purpose. According to that statement, the statute protects the corporation and its constituents—which presumably includes, but is not limited to shareholders—from greenmail and the hazards of having the company put in play. Those hazards supposedly include instability and loss of confidence, the risk that speculators will appropriate corporate values at the expense of the corporation and its constituents, and reaping short term profits. Because this statement of purpose emphasizes potential harms to nonshareholder interests, it may prove problematic under the meaningful opportunity for success standard.

Under the second *BNS* prong, the question is whether the statute gives either side an advantage. The question here is whether the disgorgement provision provides sufficient loopholes that an "appreciable number" of bidders will be able to proceed.[43] It seems unlikely. Other than some minor exceptions unlikely to be of significant utility to bidders, there are four principal exemptions. First, the safe harbor for proxy contests not involving control. By definition, this loophole is useless to bidders seeking control. Second, disgorgement is waived if the bidder's acquisition of shares receives prior approval of both the board of directors and the shareholders owning a majority of the outstanding shares. It is difficult to imagine the board of directors that would agree ex ante to exempt acquisitions by a potential bidder, so this exemption's utility is also minimal. Third, disgorgement is waived if the bidder's disposition of shares receives prior approval by both the board of directors and shareholders owning a majority of the outstanding shares, provided that the bidder controlled the corporation at the time the

42. Simas v. Quaker Fabric Corp. of Fall River, 6 F.3d 849 (1st Cir.1993).

43. BNS, Inc. v. Koppers Co., Inc., 683 F.Supp. 458, 470 (D.Del.1988).

disposition was approved. This exemption is potentially useful to hostile bidders, but in order to make use of it they must prevail. Moreover, because they must be able to prove they controlled the corporation at the time they sought to dispose of their shares, successful bidders who own less than 50 percent of the outstanding shares prior to the disposition face some uncertainty when the question of whether they have control is inevitably litigated. Finally, a corporation may opt out of the statute by adopting an appropriate charter provision in its original articles of incorporation. A bidder could therefore urge that the firm be reincorporated, so as to exempt any subsequent dispositions of shares.[44] Because reincorporation requires board of director approval, the bidder effectively must prevail in order to have a meaningful opportunity to exercise this loophole. Because reincorporation also requires shareholder approval, however, the loophole's availability is not guaranteed even if the bidder prevails. In sum, all of the meaningful exemptions are available only to bidders insurgents who prevail—the class least likely to trigger the statute by disposing of their shares.[45] In contrast, all management proxy solicitations are specifically exempted from the disgorgement penalty. Even before considering the other statutory obstacles Pennsylvania has erected, the disgorgement statute thus may fail the *BNS* test.

The Delaware trilogy holds out one ray of hope for proponents of the Pennsylvania statute. Since *CTS*, courts faced with state takeover statutes have been disinclined "to second-guess the empirical judgments of lawmakers concerning the utility of [takeover] legislation."[46] In *BNS*, for example, Chief Judge Schwartz opined that the Delaware statute's plausible exemptions are stacked in the target's favor.[47] After reviewing the conflicting evidence on a bidder's prospects under the statute, however, Chief Judge Schwartz concluded that he could not conclusively predict whether a meaningful opportunity for success remained. He therefore deferred to the state legislature's implicit judgment that the statute's benefits outweighed its costs. Schwartz left open an opportunity for reconsideration of the statute's constitutionality if conclusive evidence subsequently developed. In each of the next two installments of the trilogy, hostile bidders offered substantial new evidence on the exemptions' pro-management effects. In each, the court again rejected the bidder's preemption arguments.[48] The disgorgement statute's exemp-

---

44. Alan R. Palmiter, The *CTS* Gambit: Stanching the Federalization of Corporate Law, 69 Wash. U.L.Q. 445, 541 (1991).

45. A nonprevailing insurgent that made a sufficient nuisance of itself might be able to obtain the incumbent board's cooperation by agreeing to go away in return. Such agreements, would have to be disclosed, however, lowering the likelihood of shareholder approval where that is necessary and opening the insurgent to the legal consequences of greenmail.

46. CTS Corp. v. Dynamics Corp. of Am., 481 U.S. 69, 92 (1987). Although this

quotation is taken from the commerce clause portion of the majority opinion, other takeover cases have applied it to the preemption analysis as well. E.g., Amanda Acquisition Corp. v. Universal Foods Corp., 708 F.Supp. 984, 1000 (E.D.Wis.), aff'd, 877 F.2d 496 (7th Cir.1989), cert. denied, 493 U.S. 955 (1989).

47. BNS, Inc. v. Koppers Co., Inc., 683 F.Supp. 458, 470 (D.Del.1988).

48. City Capital Assoc. Ltd. v. Interco, Inc., 696 F.Supp. 1551, 1554–55 (D.Del. 1988), aff'd on other grounds, 860 F.2d 60 (3d Cir.1988); RP Acquisition Corp. v. Sta-

tions raise a similar empirical issue: will bidders prevail frequently enough to say they have a viable opportunity to make use of these exemptions.

When the Pennsylvania statute is taken as a whole, moreover, its viability under the meaningful opportunity for success standard becomes even more problematic. Consider a bidder who owns less than 20 percent of the target's shares prior to initiating a contest for control. Such a bidder faces both the disgorgement and the cash-out statutes. A bidder who purchases more than twenty percent of the target's shares before beginning a control contest faces the disgorgement statute, the cash-out statute, and the control share acquisition statute. Then too, the nonshareholder constituency statute will help validate target defensive tactics. The proverbial kitchen sink necessarily comes to mind.

As one might expect, the share prices of Pennsylvania corporations subject to the 1990 statute declined dramatically.[49] In a rare example of investor muscle flexing, a number of financial institutions announced that they would not invest in Pennsylvania corporations that did not opt out of the law. Under pressure from such investors, several large Pennsylvania corporations, including Westinghouse Electric Corp. and H.J. Heinz Co., in fact opted out.[50] An unpublished study of 96 Pennsylvania corporations found that 27 opted out of all of the statute's provisions, while only 17 opted out of none. The most common decision, selected by 45% of the firms, was to opt out of the control share acquisition and disgorgement provisions, but retain coverage under the nonshareholder constituency statute.

ley Cont'l, Inc., 686 F.Supp. 476, 482–86 (D.Del.1988). See also West Point–Pepperell, Inc. v. Farley Inc., 711 F.Supp. 1096, 1100–06 (N.D.Ga.1989) (in light of inconclusive evidence as to bidder's chances for success, presumption of constitutional validity used to uphold Georgia takeover statute).

49. See Samuel H. Szewczyk & George P. Tsetsekos, State Intervention in the Market for Corporate Control, 31 J. Fin. Econ. 3 (1992) (estimating an aggregate loss to shareholders of $4 billion).

50. Many Companies in Pennsylvania Reject State's Takeover Protection, N.Y. Times, July 20, 1990, at 1.

Chapter 13

DIVIDENDS AND OTHER LEGAL
CAPITAL ARCANA

Analysis

---

§ 13.1 Introduction

State legal capital rules remain an important component of the regulatory regime governing the issuance of equity securities, albeit an outdated (and even annoying) one.[1] Those same rules also govern the disbursement of corporate profits and assets to shareholders. The good news is that many states have followed the MBCA's lead and have substantially modernized their legal capital rules. The bad news is that many states, most notably Delaware, have not. Numerous traps for the unwary thus continue to lurk within the arcana of legal capital.

Recall that a corporation's balance sheet "balances" when assets (the left side) equal the sum of liabilities and shareholder equity (the

§ 13.1

1. See Chapter 3.

right side). Shareholder equity thus consists of the corporation's net assets—the (hopefully positive) difference between assets and liabilities. Consequently, we speak of an "equity cushion." Because creditors have a prior claim on the corporation's assets, a fall in the value of those assets comes out of shareholder equity before it impairs the corporation's ability to repay its liabilities.

At common law, the corporation's shareholder equity thus was viewed as a "trust fund" held by the corporation for the benefit of its creditors. This doctrine received its classic expression in the early 19th century decision of *Wood v. Dummer*.[2] The Hallowell and Augusta Bank paid out the bulk of its assets in dividends to its shareholders. As a result, when the Bank later became insolvent, insufficient assets remained to pay its creditors. Trying the case in his capacity as a circuit judge, U.S. Supreme Court Justice Story held that "the capital stock of banks is to be deemed a pledge or trust fund for the payment of the debts contracted by the bank."[3] Suppose, for example, that the Bank issued 2,000 shares of common stock having a par value of $100. On those facts, its capital equaled $200,000. Accordingly, the Bank was obliged to maintain net assets of at least $200,000.

The trust fund concept made some sense. Corporate insolvencies obviously entail high transaction costs, but they also generate considerable externalities. An insolvency not only affects creditors and shareholders, but also employees who lose their jobs, communities that lose an employer and part of their tax base, customers and suppliers who lose a business partner, and so on. If we could come up with a regulatory regime that ensured solvency, as by requiring firms to maintain a certain equity cushion, these costs would be averted.

The trust fund doctrine also could be justified as a means of deterring opportunistic conduct by shareholders vis-à-vis creditors. The corporation's decisionmaking and financial apparatus is controlled by the board of directors, elected by and responsible to the shareholders. In close corporations, the problem is especially pronounced because the shareholders and the board members likely will be one and the same. One obvious risk is that shareholders will divert cash flows to their own pockets in the form of salaries, bonuses, dividends, and the like. A more subtle problem is that limited liability creates incentives for shareholders to cause the company to invest in higher risk projects than the firm's creditors would like. As the firm's residual claimants, shareholders will not be paid until all creditor claims are satisfied. Shareholders thus will prefer that the corporation select high risk projects that promise high returns. Because limited liability means that shareholders only put at risk what funds they have invested in the firm, moreover, they are able to effectively externalize some of the risk associated with such projects to

---

2. 30 F.Cas. 435 (C.C.D.Me.1824).

3. Id. at 436. By capital stock Justice Story likely meant what we today call "stat-ed capital," i.e., the aggregate par value of the shares.

creditors. If the high risk project fails, the creditors may not be paid, but cannot collect any unpaid debt from the shareholders.

In the nineteenth century, many states gave teeth to the trust fund doctrine through minimum capital requirements. Over time, however, it became obvious that one size does not fit all and minimum capital requirements have faded from view. Few states have them today and those that do set the minimum at nominal amounts.

Instead, legal capital rules tried to implement the trust fund concept by deterring shareholders from impairing the corporation's equity cushion. One prong of this approach regulated the flow of money into the corporation, while the other regulated the flow of money out. Requiring that stock be fully paid and nonassessable was an effort to ensure that the assets of which the corporation's shareholder equity purportedly consisted actually existed and, in fact, had been paid in. Restricting the payment of dividends was an effort to ensure that the corporation maintained some equity cushion.[4] Neither effort turned out very well, however, and today the once proud trust fund doctrine is but a tattered shadow of its former self. Instead, modern creditors must rely on self-help. They protect themselves through private contracting (such as negative pledge covenants in bond indentures or loan agreements), credit investigations, and charging higher interest rates.

§ 13.2 Money in: Herein of watered stock

If the corporation wishes to raise capital by selling equity securities, it is the board of directors that makes that determination and also decides the amount and form of consideration to be received in exchange for the shares to be issued.[1] Accordingly, so long as the charter authorizes the class of shares in question and there are sufficient authorized but unissued shares, the board is free to sell shares for any lawful purpose, provided that the corporation receives adequate consideration for the shares. That latter proviso leads us to the questions of par value and watered stock.

At one time, all stock had a "par value," stated in the articles of incorporation, which was the price at which the corporation initially sold shares to the public. A firm could not sell shares for less than par value and, at least in its initial offering, usually did not sell shares for more than par value. A vast and arcane body of law grew up to implement these so-called legal capital requirements. Today, however, most of that law has fallen into decrepitude. Virtually all states allow one to sell stock with low or even no par value. The MBCA has gone even further and simply abolished the entire concept of par value. Yet, because it is difficult to understand today's legal capital regime without understanding that regime's historical antecedents, we begin with a brief lesson on the history of par value and "watered stock."

---

4. A dividend is a distribution of firm assets to shareholders, usually in the form of cash, although sometimes in property.

§ 13.2

1. DGCL § 153(a).

Recall that the corporation's capital—i.e., the aggregate par value of its outstanding stock—was viewed as a trust fund for the protection of creditors. If a corporation claimed that it had sold 2,000 shares of stock with a par value of $100 per share, for a total capital of $200,000, the trust fund concept necessitated some mechanism for ensuring that the full value of the purported capital in fact had been paid into the corporation. Suppose Shareholder bought 100 shares of the corporation's stock. Shareholder should have paid at least $10,000 for her shares. If Shareholder paid less than that amount, her stock was said to be "watered." If Shareholder actually paid only $4,000, for example, she could be held liable to the firm's creditors for the $6,000 "water."[2]

Failure to pay in full for shares probably was rare. Because corporation statutes allowed corporations to issue stock in return for noncash forms of consideration, such as property or services rendered, however, disputes over the valuation of such consideration were not uncommon.[3] Suppose the board accepted an offer from a prospective shareholder to exchange an acre of land for 500 shares of stock having a par value of $100 per share. The corporation later became insolvent and creditors claimed that the acre of land in question was really worth only $20,000. If true, the shareholder's stock was watered to the tune of $30,000.

Several factors combined to effectively eliminate the watered stock problem. One was the decline of par value as a meaningful concept. Par value always was an arbitrary figure. With the development of secondary trading markets for corporate stock, the market price (and thus the value) of outstanding corporate stock rarely coincided with its par value. As a result, par value simply had no relation whatsoever to the price shares would command on a secondary trading market or the price at which shares subsequently might be issued by the corporation. States began to permit corporations to issue low par value stock (such as shares with par value of a penny) and most states eventually permitted corporations to issue shares having no par value whatsoever. Consequently, today, watered stock is largely a dead issue. Corporations issue no par or low par stock and sell it at the highest price the shares will bring in the primary market. As long as the investor pays something for his shares, the par value requirement will be satisfied.

A. Watered stock in Delaware law today

All statutes permit the corporation to issue shares in return for not only cash, but also property and past uncompensated services. Traditional legal capital statutes prohibit a corporation, however, from accepting certain forms of consideration for shares. Delaware's statute is typical of this group: only cash, services rendered, and personal or real property

---

2. They still arise today. See, e.g., Hanewald v. Bryan's Inc., 429 N.W.2d 414 (N.D. 1988).

3. Valuation disputes were (and are) especially likely when a promoter receives stock from the corporation in return for noncash consideration. These situations are governed by the fiduciary duties of promoters. See Chapter 2.

constitute lawful consideration for stock.[4] Other forms of consideration are not permitted. In particular, Delaware does not permit its corporations to issue stock in return for a promise of future services, which can have significant planning consequences.[5]

When a corporation issues shares for unlawful or inadequate consideration, the other shareholders are injured because the value of their stock is diluted. This is of particular concern when shares are issued for noncash consideration, because of the potential for valuation disputes. Traditional legal capital statutes require the board of directors to place a value on noncash consideration. In the absence of actual fraud, however, the value set by the board is conclusive on all parties—the corporation, its shareholders and its creditors.[6] Obviously, water cannot exist if the board has conclusively determined that the price paid equals the price required. Allegations that the board acted improperly in assigning a value to the consideration are therefore relegated to tort fraud rules and corporate fiduciary duties.

B. Watered stock under the MBCA today

The trend away from par value was taken to its logical conclusion in the MBCA, under which par value has no legal significance. The MBCA, moreover, goes even further than Delaware law towards eliminating concerns about the propriety and adequacy of consideration for shares. Section 6.21(b) allows the corporation to accept just about any form of consideration: tangible or intangible property, cash, promissory notes, services performed, contracts for future services or other securities of the corporation. Section 6.21(c) then provides that the board must determine whether the consideration is adequate. If the board so determines, their conclusion is conclusive. Once the corporation receives the agreed consideration, the shares are regarded as fully paid and nonassessable.

§ 13.3 Money out: Dividend statutes

From the trust fund perspective, it is not enough to ensure that the corporation's allegedly paid-in capital actually exists, one must also

---

4. DGCL § 152.

5. See, e.g., Maclary v. Pleasant Hills, Inc., 109 A.2d 830 (Del.Ch.1954).

6. DGCL § 152. In most states, constructive fraud can be found where the board grossly overvalued the property. See, e.g., McManus v. American Exp. Tax and Business Services, Inc., 67 F.Supp.2d 1083, 1089 (D.Ariz.1999) (holding that to establish constructive fraud the plaintiff needs to show a fiduciary relationship and all elements of fraud except for intent); Daibo v. Kirsch, 720 A.2d 994, 998 (N.J.Super.Ct.App.Div.1998) (stating that a finding of equitable fraud does not require knowledge of the falsity of the misrepresentation and intent to obtain an advantage from the misrepresentation); In re Tri–Star Pictures, Inc., Litigation, 634 A.2d 319 (Del.1993) (holding a cause of action existed when the plaintiff, a minority shareholder, suffered harm from voting power dilution when the defendant issued too many shares in exchange for overvalued property); cf. Haft v. Dart Group Corp., 841 F.Supp. 549 (D.Del. 1993) (stating that gross overvaluation establishes constructive fraud but that this is not enough to indicate actual fraud without other factors); Efron v. Kalmanovitz, 38 Cal.Rptr. 148 (Cal.Ct.App.1964) (holding that constructive fraud can be found when the overvaluation constitutes conduct that is not fraudulent but a breach of fiduciary duty).

prevent the shareholders from draining assets out of the corporation. Preventing shareholders from doing so in the form of dividends is the function of the second set of legal capital rules—the dividend statutes.

A. Modern dividend statutes

Our analysis focuses on two representative examples of modern dividend statutes—the MBCA and Delaware. In working through the statutes, we will concentrate on two issues: (1) when may the corporation properly pay dividends; and (2) who can be held liable if dividends are paid improperly.

The following sample problem will facilitate our discussion of the statutes: Assume Acme Corporation issued 1,000 shares of stock (par value $1.00). Five years later the balance sheet reads as follows:

Assets		*Liabilities and Shareholder Equity*	
Cash	$2,000	Current liabilities	$2,000
Accounts receivable	$2,000	Long-term liabilities	$13,000
Inventory	$6,000	Total liabilities	$15,000
Total current assets	$10,000	Capital	$1,000
		Surplus	$4,000
Building	$10,000	Total shareholder equity	$5,000
Total fixed assets	$10,000		
Total assets	$20,000		

Can Acme pay a dividend under these circumstances? If Acme pays an illegal dividend, who can be held liable by whom?

1. Delaware

DGCL § 170(a)(1) provides, in pertinent part:

> The directors of every corporation, subject to any restrictions contained in its certificate of incorporation, may declare and pay dividends upon the shares of its capital stock ... either (1) out of its surplus ... or (2) in case there shall be no such surplus, out of its net profits for the fiscal year in which the dividend is declared and/or the preceding fiscal year.

Some of the statutory terminology should be familiar from our treatment of corporate finance, but understanding how the statute works requires us to use the more precise definitions set out in DGCL § 154. *Capital*: the amount allocated to the capital account depends on whether the stock has a par value. In the case of par value shares, the minimum amount of capital is determined by multiplying the number of shares issued by their par value. In addition, the board may (but need not) designate an additional portion of the consideration received by the corporation when shares are issued as capital. In the case of no-par shares, capital is simply that part of the consideration received designated by the board as capital. If the board fails to designate part of the consideration as capital, than capital is determined by the amount of the consideration received. Notice the potential trap for the unwary. It is important for the board to always designate some portion of the consideration as capital or all of the consideration goes into capital. *Net assets*: the difference between total assets and total liabilities. *Surplus*: The difference between the corporation's net assets at any time and the amount of capital. The following examples may shed some light on how these statutes work in practice:

1.　At t=0, ABC Corporation has no assets, no liabilities, and no shareholder equity. At t=1, ABC sells 1,000 shares of common stock at the stock's par value of $1 per share. After giving effect to this transaction, ABC's balance sheet will read as follows:

Assets	*Liabilities + Shareholder Equity*
Cash $1,000	Liabilities 0 Capital $1,000

Legal capital statutes, such as Delaware's, divide shareholder equity into two basic categories: capital and surplus. Per DGCL § 154, capital, in the case of par value shares, is the aggregate par value of the outstanding shares. Accordingly, ABC has capital of $1,000 (1000 shares issued x $1 per share par value).

2.　At t=0, XYZ Corporation has no assets, no liabilities, and no shareholder equity. At t=1, XYZ sells 1,000 shares of common stock. Each share of stock has a par value of $1. XYZ is able to sell the stock for more than par value: $10 per share. (No law says a corporation cannot sell stock for more than its par value.) After giving effect to that transaction, XYZ's balance sheet will read as follows:

Assets	*Liabilities + Shareholder Equity*
Cash $10,000	Liabilities 0 Capital $1,000 Surplus $9,000

Again, because we are dealing with par value shares, capital is the aggregate par value of the outstanding shares, which here is $1,000 (1000 shares issued x $1 per share par value). In addition, because XYZ sold the shares for more than their par value, the board had the option to designate as capital an additional portion of the consideration received. Assume XYZ's board did not do so. Accordingly, the remainder of the consideration XYZ received for its shares ($9,000) will be allocated to the surplus account.

3. At t=0, 123 Corporation has no assets, no liabilities, and no shareholder equity. At t=1, 123 sells 1,000 shares of "no par" common stock. 123 is able to sell the stock at $10 per share. In the case of no-par shares, capital is simply that portion of the consideration received designated by the board as capital. The board could put as little as $1 into the capital account. If the board fails to designate part of the consideration as capital, however, the entire consideration received is deemed to be capital.

Pursuant to DGCL § 170, the board of directors may cause the corporation to pay a dividend out of the corporation's surplus up to the full amount of any such surplus. If the corporation has no surplus, or has negative surplus, the board can cause the corporation to pay a so-called nimble dividend out of its net profits for the fiscal year in which the dividend is paid or for the preceding fiscal year.[1]

In our principal example, Acme has net assets of $5,000. How did we determine that amount? The accounting distinction between current and fixed assets has no legal significance under Delaware law, so we have total assets of $20,000. Likewise, the accounting distinction between current and long-term liabilities has no legal significance, so we have total liabilities of $15,000. Subtracting total liabilities from total assets gives us net assets of $5,000. Subtracting the $1,000 capital (1,000 shares times a par value of $1 per share) from our net assets of $5,000, leaves us with a total of $4,000 in surplus. Hence, Acme can pay a dividend of up to $4,000 out of surplus.

DGCL § 174 provides that if there is a willful or negligent illegal dividend payment the directors under whose administration the payment occurs are jointly and severally liable to the corporation or directly to its creditors in the event of dissolution or insolvency. A director can avoid liability by timely causing his dissent to be noted on the corporation's books. Section 172 also protects a director who in good faith relies on reports of corporate officers, legal counsel or accountants. The amount for which directors can be held liable is the amount of the dividend that was improperly paid plus prejudgment interest. There is no express provision for holding liable those shareholders who receive the improper dividend, although directors are entitled to contribution from sharehold-

---

§ 13.3

1. Note the nimble dividend provision raises the prospect of double-dipping for dividends. Assume the corporation has both surplus and net profits in the current fiscal year. A fair reading of DGCL suggests that such a corporation could maximize its dividend by breaking the dividend declaration process into two stages. The corporation's board of directors would first declare a divi- dend under DGCL § 170(a)(1) equal to the full amount of the corporation's surplus. At that point, the corporation no longer has any surplus. Accordingly, DGCL § 170(a)(2) permits the corporation to pay a nimble dividend out of its profits for the current fiscal year. Nothing on the face of Section 170(a) prohibits such a tactic, although there are no reported decisions on point.

ers who knowingly received the illegal dividend. Worse yet, from the creditor's perspective, standing under § 174 is limited to the corporation (and, presumably, shareholders suing derivatively). Creditors are given standing only where the corporation is insolvent. In effect, creditors are limited to their fraudulent conveyance remedies.

2. *MBCA: Old and new*

The 1969 version of the MBCA was a legal capital statute, not unlike (but somewhat more complicated than) the Delaware statute. The MBCA (1969), like Delaware, used surplus as the basic test for the legality of dividends. The MBCA (1969), however, recognized two distinct types of surplus: earned surplus and capital surplus. The definition of capital surplus was straightforward: it was any surplus that was not earned surplus. Earned surplus was a somewhat complex concept, but basically one added up all of the corporation's profits and other gains (if any) from the date of incorporation. One then subtracted from that figure any losses from the date of incorporation. Finally, one further deducted any distributions to shareholders or amounts transferred to stated capital or capital surplus. What was left was earned surplus.

Under the MBCA (1969), there were two distinct tests for the legality of dividends. First, an equity insolvency test that prohibited the corporation from paying dividends if the firm was insolvent or if the payment would render the corporation insolvent. Second, a balance sheet test that allowed dividends to be paid only out of surplus. Earned surplus could be freely used for dividends, up to the full amount thereof. In contrast, MBCA (1969) § 46 permitted a "distribution" to be paid out of capital surplus only if a number of conditions were satisfied, most importantly: (1) no dividend could be paid if the corporation was insolvent or the payment would render the corporation insolvent; (2) the articles of incorporation authorized the board to pay dividends out of capital surplus or, in the alternative, the shareholders approved such payment by a majority of the outstanding shares; and (3) the rights of preferred shareholders were protected.

All such complications went out the window with the 1984 promulgation of the MBCA's current version. Indeed, MBCA § 6.40 is the simplest of all the modern statutory limitations on the payment of dividends. Section 6.40 governs a class of transactions referred to as "distributions," a term defined in § 1.40(6) to include not only the traditional cash dividend but also any direct or indirect transfer of money or other property (except the firm's own shares) or incurrence of debt to or on behalf of shareholders. The term thus includes cash dividends, distribution of noncash assets, repurchase or redemption of shares, and distribution of debt securities.

Like the MBCA (1969), the current version imposes a two-part test to determine the legality of a distribution. First, an equity insolvency test under which the corporation, after giving effect to the distribution,[2]

---

2. Under MBCA § 6.40(e)(3), when the effect of a cash dividend is measured depends on the time span between the date the distribution is authorized and the date

must be able to pay its debts as they become due in the usual course of business.[3] Second, a balance sheet test under which, after giving effect to the distribution, the corporation's total assets must exceed the sum of total liabilities plus the amount required to satisfy any liquidation preference of preferred stock.[4] Both tests must be satisfied, as MBCA § 6.40(c) is phrased in the disjunctive, or the distribution may not be made. In our principal example, assuming Acme can satisfy the equity insolvency test and has no preferred stock to worry about, Acme could make a distribution of up to $5,000, which is the amount by which total assets exceed total liabilities.

MBCA § 8.33(a) provides that a director who votes for, or assents to, an improper distribution is personally liable to the corporation for the amount of the distribution that exceeds that which could have properly been paid out. Plaintiff must also show that the director did not comply with the standards of conduct set forth in § 8.30. In turn, MBCA § 8.30(a) requires that the director act in good faith, with the care that an ordinarily prudent person in a like position would exercise under similar circumstances and in a manner he reasonably believes to be in the best interests of the corporation. MBCA § 8.30(b) further provides that a director is entitled to rely on reports from corporate officers, legal counsel and accountants. A director who relies in good faith on an accounting opinion stating that neither of the § 6.40(b) tests are met and a legal opinion that the dividend is proper therefore may not be held liable.

As an example, assume that prior to making a distribution, Acme Corporation had total assets of $10,000 and total liabilities of $8,000. Assume that payment of the distribution will not prevent the corporation from paying its debts as they come due. If the corporation makes a $4,000 distribution, the directors' potential § 8.33(a) liability is $2,000. The MBCA's liability provision thus takes into account that some portion of the distribution may have been proper. The corporation could properly make a $2,000 distribution, because that is the amount by which total assets exceeded total liabilities, and only the excess over that amount is the extent of the liability.

MBCA § 8.33(b) provides that a director who is held liable for an unlawful distribution is entitled to contribution from (1) any other director who voted for or assented to the distribution and also failed to live up to the standards of section 8.30, and (2) from each shareholder who accepted the distribution knowing that it was improper. Although the MBCA imposes a contribution obligation on shareholders who knowingly receive an improper distribution, it does not otherwise impose any liability on shareholders. If a creditor wishes to recover the amount of the unlawful distribution from the shareholders, its remedy lies in the

---

it is actually paid. If that time span is less than 120 days, the effect is measured as of the date of authorization; if the span is more than 120 days, however, the effect is measured on the date of payment.

3. MBCA § 6.40(c)(1).

4. MBCA § 6.40(c)(2).

fraudulent conveyance laws, not the MBCA. This is a significant change from the common law rule that all shareholders had corporate law liability for improper distribution.

It is noteworthy that under MBCA § 8.33, the cause of action for an unlawful distribution belongs to the corporation. A shareholder therefore could bring a derivative action against the responsible directors. Because creditors generally have no standing to sue derivatively, however, only rarely will they be able to bring suit under MBCA § 8.33. The MBCA's distribution rules thus provide creditors with few protections.

B. Dividends and asset revaluation

A sad truth is that 90 percent of what we do as corporate lawyers is not very creative. Indeed, creativity is affirmatively discouraged. If you doubt that claim, wait until the first time you have to prepare an SEC filing, do a 50 state blue sky memorandum, or blackline a document. Figuring out ways for a company to pay a dividend despite the literal terms of the statute and the present state of the firm's balance sheet, however, is one item that falls within the 10 percent or so where creativity is desirable. And lawyers have gotten quite good at what accountants would see as juggling the books.

Consider a relatively simple balance sheet:

Assets			*Liabilities and Shareholder equity*	
Land		$ 9,000	Total liabilities:	$38,000
Other		$24,000	Capital:	$15,000
	Total	$33,000	Surplus	($20,000)
			Total shareholder equity	($ 5,000)

This corporation could not pay a dividend under either the MBCA or Delaware approach. Under the MBCA, total liabilities already exceed total assets, so a distribution could not be made. Under Delaware law, the corporation has no surplus and, assuming it could not pay a nimble dividend, thus could not pay a dividend.

Notice, however, that the corporation owns real property being carried on the balance sheet at $9,000. Because assets generally are carried on the books at their historical cost, and land tends to appreciate in value, it is a fair supposition that the land may be worth much more than $9,000. Suppose the fair market value of the land in fact is $30,000. If we "write up" the value of the land to $30,000, the corporation will have total assets of $54,000, and now may pay a dividend. Under the MBCA, total assets exceed total liabilities by $16,000, which is available for distribution. Under Delaware law, net assets are now $16,000, which results in a surplus of $1,000, which is available for payment of a dividend.

Generally accepted accounting principles (GAAP) require that most assets be carried on the books at historical cost less depreciation.

Accordingly, you may not write up assets to reflect an increase in their fair market value, but must write them down to reflect depreciation. In contrast, state corporate law generally does not require adherence to GAAP in determining whether a dividend lawfully may be paid. Indeed, MBCA § 6.40(d) expressly authorizes a corporation to use "a fair valuation or other method that is reasonable under the circumstances" in determining the amount of total assets and total liabilities. Accordingly, while the corporation may rely on financial statements prepared in accordance with GAAP, there is no requirement that it do so. The drafters' comments on § 6.40, moreover, go on to state that the statute authorizes departures from historical cost accounting in determining the funds available for distribution. The comments further indicate that a corporation generally may not selectively revalue assets, however. If it is going to revalue some assets, all must be reappraised and adjusted to their fair market value. Delaware and New York reach the same result through case law.[5]

C. A critique of modern dividend statutes

Our analysis of the various dividend rules began with the assumption that they are a response to the shareholders' incentive to drain funds out of the firm to the detriment of creditors. The final question we therefore need to ask is how effective the statutes are in protecting creditors. The answer is, not very. There are a variety of reasons for this failure, of which the following are just a few:

Limited scope: Although creditors are likely to be concerned about the risk that excessive dividends may be paid, they are likely to be at least as concerned about the possibility that the corporation will incur additional debt. Creditors will be especially concerned about the creation of new secured debt, which will have a prior claim on corporate assets. Dividend statutes do nothing to address these concerns.

Control is vested in the shareholders or their representatives: Control over the dividend machinery is vested in the hands of directors who are elected by, and therefore may be inclined to favor the interests of the shareholders, rather than creditors. In close corporations, where the controlling shareholders typically are also board members, the unity of ownership and control ensures that creditor interests are at risk.

Meaningless concepts: Capital, which is the linchpin of traditional statutes, is a wholly arbitrary number. If you were considering lending money to General Motors, you would not care what the par value of a share of GM stock was back when the stock was issued 50 years ago. In

---

5. See, e.g., Morris v. Standard Gas & Electric, 63 A.2d 577, 582 (Del.Ch.1949) (the board of directors has a "duty to evaluate the assets on the basis of acceptable data and by standards which they are entitled to believe reasonably reflect present values"); Randall v. Bailey, 23 N.Y.S.2d 173, 183 (N.Y.Sup.1940) (rejecting contention that "cost and not value must be used in determining whether or not there exists a surplus out of which dividends can be paid"); see also Klang v. Smith's Food & Drug Centers, Inc., 702 A.2d 150 (Del.1997) (authorizing revaluation of assets for purposes of determining whether a repurchase of shares complied with DGCL § 160).

any case, the availability of low par or no par stock means that only a minimal amount need be treated as capital. The requirement that stock be fully paid and nonassessable has thus lost all substantive content.

Lack of a time dimension: Dividend statutes wholly lack any time dimension—ancient, present, and future economic events are scrambled together without regard for their current economic significance. In computing the availability of "surplus," for example, there is no difference between a debt due next week and one due 20 years from now; but to a lender there may be a great deal of difference.

Lack of attention to liquidity: Dividend statutes treat all assets the same, irrespective of their relative liquidity. Creditors, however, view different types of assets differently.

Ease of evasion: With competent legal counsel, the board of directors often can readily evade dividend restrictions. The nimble dividend rule in Delaware lets a heavily indebted firm pay dividends, for example, as long as it has one year of profitability.[6] The concept of revaluation surplus as a source of dividends expressly allows the corporation to juggle the books in determining whether a dividend is legally payable. Thus, any semi-competent lawyer can usually arrange things so that the firm can pay dividends, as long as the firm is not actually insolvent.

Given the relative ineffectualness of dividend statutes in protecting creditor interests, self-help has become the rule of the day. A creditor makes loans based on its own assessment of the corporation's ability to repay. If the creditor is worried that the directors will drain funds from the corporation by paying large dividends, the creditor protects itself by charging a higher interest rate or by conditioning its extension of credit on a contractual prohibition on payment of dividends.

At worst, the dividend statutes are a historical anachronism. At best, they promote a psychological inhibition against indiscriminate distribution of assets to shareholders. The bottom line, however, is that the statutes are still on the books and corporate lawyers still need to know about them if their clients are going to stay out of trouble. While creative lawyering can usually end run all dividend problems except true insolvency, the statutes are a trap for the unwary.

§ 13.4 Redemptions and repurchases

Redemptions and repurchases by a corporation of its own stock are an alternative way of getting funds out of the corporation and into the

---

6. Although the introduction of nimble dividends substantially eroded the common law notion that a corporation's capital represented a trust fund for creditors, the Delaware legislature presumably believed that allowing nimble dividends would produce offsetting benefits. As a practical matter, a corporation that has accumulated large deficits and has a heavy burden of unpaid debt has little prospect of obtaining further credit unless new equity can be attracted to the enterprise. In turn, there is little hope of attracting new equity investments unless there is some prospect that dividends will be paid. The Delaware legislature seemingly concluded that old deficits must not be allowed to block future dividends, as long as the corporation was not insolvent. Thus, it allowed a currently profitable firm to pay dividends, even though the old deficits had not been eliminated.

hands of shareholders. Again, we will focus on the Delaware and MBCA statutes as examples.

A. Delaware law

DGCL § 160 provides that a corporation may repurchase its own stock, provided that it may not do so if its capital is impaired or if the redemption would cause its capital to be impaired.[1] This means, in effect, that repurchases are made out of surplus rather than capital. Note that there is no equivalent of the nimble dividend concept, so a corporation with no surplus may not repurchase shares. Presumably this requirement reflects some residual notion of capital as a trust fund for the benefit of creditors.

Suppose the corporation has 4,000 shares of stock outstanding, each share of stock having a par value of $5. Prior to the repurchase the corporation's balance sheet read as follows:

Assets	*Liabilities/Shareholder Equity*
Cash $100,000	Liabilities $50,000
	Capital $20,000
	Surplus $30,000

The corporation then redeems 1,000 shares, paying $10 per share.[2] After giving effect to that transaction, the balance sheet will read as follows:

Assets	*Liabilities/Shareholder Equity*
Cash $90,000	Liabilities $50,000
	Capital $20,000
	Surplus $20,000

Unless the firm reduces its capital pursuant to DGCL §§ 243 and 244, the stated capital for the repurchased shares thus remains on the books.

Suppose the corporation in our example subsequently wanted to issue the repurchased shares for less than par value and/or for an

---

§ 13.4

1. Section 160 does permit the corporation to repurchase its own stock out of capital provided the corporation reduces its capital pursuant to DGCL §§ 243 and 244.

2. Note that there is no legal obstacle to paying more than par value in a repurchase transaction. Par value solely relates to the price that the corporation must receive when it sells shares.

impermissible form of consideration (such as a promise of future services). Ordinarily such a sale would present watered stock problems, but the use of repurchased shares can obviate those concerns. Recall that authorized but unissued shares are shares authorized by the charter that have not been sold by the firm. Suppose the charter authorizes the firm to issue up to 20,000 common shares. The firm sells 4,000 shares to investors. At that point it has 4,000 outstanding shares and 16,000 authorized but unissued shares. Treasury shares are shares which were once issued and outstanding, but have been repurchased by the corporation. If, in the preceding example, the corporation bought back 1,000 of its outstanding shares, it would now have 3,000 outstanding shares, 16,000 authorized but unissued shares, and 1,000 treasury shares. Treasury shares may not be voted, do not count towards a quorum, and do not receive dividends.[3] The stated capital for those shares is still on the books, however, so treasury shares are still deemed fully paid and nonassessable even after they are repurchased. Accordingly, "[t]reasury shares may be disposed of by the corporation for such consideration as may be determined from time to time by the board of directors...."[4] The statute thus allows the board to issue treasury shares for less than their par value and/or in return for forms of consideration not lawful with respect to newly-issued shares.

B. MBCA

MBCA § 1.40(6) defines the term distribution to include a redemption of shares. Consequently, redemptions are subject to the same statute—§ 6.40—as dividends. Returning to the example used in the preceding section, the firm could lawfully repurchase the shares in question. After giving effect to the transaction, which you will recall requires payment of $10,000 to the shareholders, total assets would still exceed total liabilities. Consistent with its abolition of the par value concept, the MBCA has also eliminated the concept of treasury shares. Reacquired shares under the RMBCA are simply classified as authorized but unissued shares.

C. Note on related legal issues

Courts sometimes order an involuntary redemption of stock as a remedy in close corporation cases. Redemption is commonly ordered as an alternative to dissolution of the corporation in cases in which a minority shareholder has been oppressed by the majority.[5] Redemption is also sometimes used as a remedy for breach of the fiduciary duties owed by controlling shareholders.

Where the corporation voluntarily goes into the market to repurchase stock a couple of issues may arise. One is the validity of selective

---

3. DGCL § 160(c).

4. DGCL § 153(c).

5. See, e.g., Alaska Plastics, Inc. v. Coppock, 621 P.2d 270 (Alaska 1980); see also MBCA § 14.34 (authorizing such a remedy).

repurchases from specific shareholders, which is mostly a problem in close corporations. In *Donahue v. Rodd Electrotype*,[6] for example, Electrotype's controlling shareholder, Harry Rodd, wished to retire from the business. Harry gave some his stock to his sons and daughter. One of his sons, Charles Rodd, was then elected president of the corporation. Harry and Charles (the latter acting on behalf of the firm) reached an agreement whereby the corporation purchased the remainder of Harry's stock. Donahue, a minority shareholder, asked that his shares be redeemed by the corporation on the same terms as those given Harry, but was refused. Donahue claimed this selective repurchase violated the fiduciary duties owed by the controlling shareholders of a closely held corporation to the minority shareholders thereof. The Massachusetts court agreed, holding that shareholders of a close corporation must deal with one another with "utmost good faith and loyalty."[7] The purchase of Harry's shares, coupled with the refusal to buy Donahue's shares, constituted a breach of this duty because it gave Harry (but only Harry) a market for his shares and also constituted a diversion of corporate assets to the personal use of a controlling shareholder. While *Donahue* thus suggests that majority shareholders cannot use their control of the firm to, in effect, create a market for their shares without extending the same opportunity to the minority,[8] one should not treat *Donahue* as precluding selective repurchases. *Donahue* arose in the close corporation context and the court's decision is expressly limited to that context. Subsequent Massachusetts decisions, moreover, have backed away from the strong fiduciary duty announced in *Donahue*.[9]

Selective repurchases by a public corporation are generally insulated from judicial review by the business judgment rule. Challenges to such repurchases, moreover, bump up against the various obstacles to derivative litigation. Where selective repurchases are used as a takeover defense, however, either by repurchasing shares from the would-be takeover raider (so-called "greenmail") or as part of a recapitalization designed to impede a takeover bid, the heightened judicial scrutiny applicable to such cases poses more serious problems for the board.[10] In *Strassburger v. Earley*,[11] for example, Vice Chancellor Jacobs thus held that a corporation generally may repurchase shares of particular stockholders selectively, without being required to offer to repurchase the shares of all stockholders generally. Where the repurchase was effected for the "primary purpose" of entrenching the incumbent board or managers in control of the corporation, however, the transaction is unlawful even if the price paid was fair.

---

6.   328 N.E.2d 505 (Mass.1975).

7.   Id. at 593 (quoting Cardullo v. Landau, 105 N.E.2d 843, 845 (Mass.1952)).

8.   A proposition also supported by Jones v. H.F. Ahmanson & Co., 460 P.2d 464 (Cal.1969).

9.   See, e.g., Wilkes v. Springside Nursing Home, Inc., 353 N.E.2d 657 (Mass. 1976).

10.   See, e.g., Unocal Corp. v. Mesa Petroleum Co., 493 A.2d 946 (Del.1985) (discriminatory self-tender offer); Cheff v. Mathes, 199 A.2d 548 (Del.1964) (greenmail).

11.   752 A.2d 557 (Del.Ch.2000).

The other major legal hurdle to redemptions, even as to a repurchase program open to all shareholders, is the risk of insider trading liability on the issuer's part for illegally trading in its own stock.[12] In any repurchase plan, counsel therefore must be careful to ensure that the issuer does not possess any material nonpublic information that could give rise to an insider trading claim. In large companies with diverse information flows, this can obviously be very difficult. Under basic principles of agency law, information known even to a single officer can be attributed to the corporation.[13] The safest times to engage in repurchases therefore are immediately after annual and quarterly disclosure reports are filed with the SEC, as there is less likelihood of undisclosed material information at those times.

§ 13.5   Stock splits and dividends

A stock dividend is not really a dividend at all. Instead, a stock dividend is the issuance of additional shares of the corporation to its shareholders at no charge to the shareholders.[1] Assume, for example, that ABC Corp sells 2,000 shares of $5 par value stock at a price of $10 per share. Its balance sheet reads as follows:

Assets	*Liabilities/Shareholder Equity*
Cash $20,000	Liabilities 0
	Capital $10,000
	Surplus $10,000

A.   Stock dividends

If ABC now declares a share dividend of 200 shares, what effect will that transaction on the corporation's balance sheet? DGCL § 173 pro-

---

12. If the issuer repurchase program is deemed to be a self-tender offer, the issuer will also have to comply with the disclosure and procedural requirements of Securities Exchange Act Section 13(e) and the SEC rules thereunder.

13. See, e.g., Magnum Foods, Inc. v. Continental Cas. Co., 36 F.3d 1491, 1501 (10th Cir.1994) (stating that information gained by supervisory employees, including officers and directors, can be imputed to the corporate employer); Hercules Carriers, Inc. v. Claimant State of Fla., Dept. of Transp., 768 F.2d 1558, 1574 (11th Cir.1985) (holding that with regard to corporations, knowledge of managers and officers are attributable to the corporation); Continental Oil Co. v. Bonanza Corp., 706 F.2d 1365, 1377 (5th Cir.1983) (holding that when an employee is granted managerial power, the employee's knowledge and privity may be attrib-

uted to the corporation); Pheasant Ridge Associates Ltd. Partnership v. Town of Burlington, 506 N.E.2d 1152 (Mass.1987) (stating that the actions, words, and knowledge of employees acting within the scope of their employment can be attributed to the corporation).

§ 13.5

1. Note, however, that a distribution of stock of another company would be treated as a distribution of property subject to the dividend statute. Suppose Acme Corporation owned 100,000 shares (representing 51 percent of the equity) of Ajax corporation. If Acme distributed the Ajax shares it owned to its shareholders, a so-called "spin-off transaction," that distribution would be a dividend subject to the dividend statute of Acme's state of incorporation.

vides that: "If the dividend is to be paid in shares of the corporation's theretofore unissued capital stock the board of directors shall, by resolution, direct that there be designated as capital in respect of such shares an amount which is not less than the aggregate par value of par value shares being declared as a dividend and, in the case of shares without par value being declared as a dividend, such amount as shall be determined by the board of directors." Accordingly, in ABC's case, the effect of the stock dividend is to transfer $1,000 (200 shares times $5 par value per share) from surplus to capital. It has no other effect on the balance sheet. Because a stock dividend has no significant balance sheet effects, in most states they are not subject to the statutory restrictions on dividends.[2]

B. Stock splits

In colloquial speech, the term "stock split" is often used to describe a stock dividend in which the number of shares issued equals or exceeds the number of shares outstanding. In legal capital terms, however, this is a misuse of terminology. A stock dividend is an issuance of authorized but unissued stock to the shareholders and may be effected by the board of directors acting alone. A stock split, in contrast, is effected by amending the articles of incorporation to reduce the par value. Suppose ABC's board wanted to effect a 2:1 split, in which each shareholder will end up owning 2 "new" shares post-split for every one pre-split share. ABC's board would recommend that the shareholders approve an amendment to the articles of incorporation reducing the par value from $5 to $2.50 per share. Each shareholder will then receive two "new" shares of common stock for each "old" share they previously owned. Because a stock split is effected via a reduction in the par value, it has no impact on the corporation's balance sheet. Accordingly, the board need not redesignate surplus "as capital . . . if shares are being distributed by a corporation pursuant to a split-up or division of its stock rather than as payment of a dividend declared payable in stock of the corporation."[3] This is so because the capital is the aggregate par value of all outstanding shares. Here the number of outstanding shares went up by 2 but the par value is ½ its former value, so capital is unchanged.

Given that stock splits have no meaningful balance sheet or income statement effects, why do companies make use of them? Studies of the stock market price effect of splits show that they have limited informational content. While a stock split is usually interpreted as a signal that management expects continued strong earnings performance, event studies confirm that announcement of a split has almost no impact on

---

2. Which is not to say that the board may issue stock dividends will-nilly. In Reiss v. Superior Indus., Inc., 466 So.2d 542 (La.Ct.App.1985), for example, a close corporation issued a share dividend to two living shareholders but not to heirs of a deceased shareholder. The court invalidated the dividend on grounds that it constituted a breach of fiduciary duty.

3. DGCL § 173.

returns.[4] The market seemingly has already detected the good earnings news and the split, at most, confirms the market's expectation.

A more plausible explanation for splits therefore focuses on their liquidity effect. Stock generally trades in "round lots" of 100 shares. As a company's stock price rises, small investors thus get squeezed out of the market for the firm's stock. At a market price of $100 per share, after all, buying a round lot would cost $10,000. Setting aside any signaling effect it might have, a 2:1 split should cut the stock price in half. There has been no change in the corporation's fundamentals, but now the pie is being divided into twice as many pieces. A split thus enhances the stock's liquidity by making it possible for small investors to trade in the stock and thereby increasing the pool of potential investors.[5]

C.   Reverse stock splits and freeze-outs

An interesting wrinkle on this class of transactions is provided by the so-called "reverse stock split." Consider *Leader v. Hycor, Inc.*,[6] for example, in which the corporation's shareholders approved an amendment to the articles of incorporation changing the par value from one cent to $40 per share. As with a regular stock split, the transaction had no impact on Hycor's balance sheet. Hycor shareholders, however, received one new post-split share for every 4,000 "old" shares they owned pre-split. What happened, you may ask, to shareholders who owned less than 4,000 shares? If you owned 1,000 shares, would you have received a quarter share? Like most states, Massachusetts allows but does not require a corporation to issue fractional shares. Where a corporate transaction would leave some shareholders with fractional shares, the corporation may cash out the holders of such shares by paying them the fair value of their fraction of a share. The effect (and presumably the intent) of Hycor's reverse stock split thus was to squeeze-out the firm's minority shareholders, all of whom owned less than 4,000 shares. Such transactions are thus subject to review under the fiduciary duty standards applicable to freeze-out mergers or close corporation squeeze-outs.[7]

---

4.   Michael P. Dooley, Fundamentals of Corporation Law 476–77 (1995) (summarizing studies).

5.   See Christopher G. Lamoureux and Percy Poon, The Market Reaction to Stock Splits, 42 J. Fin. 1347 (1987) (finding that the number of shareholders increases following a split, which tends to confirm the liquidity explanation); see also Josef Lakonishok and Baruch Lev, Stock Splits and Stock Dividends: Why, Who, and When, 42 J. Fin. 913 (1987) (supporting liquidity explanation for splits).

6.   479 N.E.2d 173 (Mass.1985).

7.   *Hycor* involved a going private transaction by a Massachusetts corporation. Without deciding whether Hycor should be treated as a close corporation and thus be subjected to the exacting fiduciary duties applied by Massachusetts to such firms, the court concluded that Hycor had met that standard. Eliminating the costs associated with being a public corporation was a legitimate business purpose and that the objecting minority could show no less harmful alternative. Id. at 177–78. See also Goldman v. Union Bank and Trust, 765 P.2d 638 (Colo.Ct.App.1988) (courts reviewing freeze-outs effected by a reverse stock split usually require defendants to show a legitimate business purpose for the transaction); Teschner v. Chicago Title & Trust Co., 322 N.E.2d 54 (Ill.1974) (plaintiff not entitled to relief in connection with a freeze-out effected by reverse stock split where plaintiff failed to show that the transaction was fraudulent, unfair, or had an improper pur-

The use of reverse stock splits to squeeze-out minority shareholders is also mitigated somewhat by the fact that such transactions require an amendment to the articles of incorporation. Indeed, under the MBCA a reverse stock split triggers both group voting and appraisal rights.[8]

§ 13.6 Dividends on preferred stock

Preferred stock with a dividend preference is entitled to receive its specified dividend before any dividends are paid on the common stock. The dividend preference stated in the articles of incorporation, of course, does not trump the statutory limitations on payment of dividends. Just as with dividends on the common, dividends on the preferred must pass muster under the relevant statute.

Recall that dividends differ significantly from interest payable on a bond. Payment of interest on debt obligations is not discretionary— failure to pay interest when due is a default. Payment of dividends, in contrast, is discretionary. In order to make preferred stock more attractive to investors, however, issuers generally assume contractual obligations that give the preferred shareholders some assurance that they will in fact receive the stated dividend.

A. Cumulative dividends

A very common dividend protection is the so-called cumulative dividend. Assume that the issuer's articles of incorporation provide that the preferred stock is entitled to a dividend of $1 in each calendar quarter. If the corporation fails to pay a dividend for a given quarter, the missed dividend "accumulates." This is true even if the corporation could not lawfully pay a dividend for the given quarter. Although the corporation may accumulate missed dividends for an indefinite period, all accumulated dividends on the preferred must be paid before any dividend is paid to the common.

Suppose the issuer has failed to pay any dividends for four quarters. In such a situation, the corporation would have to pay the missed dividends ($4) before it can pay any dividends to the common. Indeed, if the dividend for the current quarter is already due, it will have to pay that dividend, as well, for a total of $5 per share, before paying anything to the common.

Outside venture capital transactions, noncumulative preferred stock is rare. If the articles specify that the dividend is noncumulative, however, a couple of interesting questions arise. First, suppose the issuer had sufficient funds to pay the noncumulative dividend to the preferred but decided not to do so. Instead, the board opted to retain those funds for internal purposes. Do the preferred stockholders have a cause of action against the board? Second, suppose the issuer had sufficient funds

pose); Lerner v. Lerner, 511 A.2d 501 (Md. 1986) (freeze-out by reverse stock split enjoined on fiduciary duty grounds).

8. See MBCA § 10.04(a)(4) (group voting); MBCA § 13.02(a)(4) (appraisal rights).

to pay a dividend on the noncumulative preferred but lacked funds to pay a dividend on the common. If the board paid a dividend on the former but not the latter, do the common shareholders have a cause of action against the board? The latter question is easy. The business judgment rule would preclude bringing such a claim.

As to the former question, the majority rule is that payment of noncumulative dividends is within the board's discretion. Liability arises only if the board abused its discretion in declining to pay such dividends.[1] If no dividend is declared on noncumulative dividends for a given fiscal year, "the claim for that year is gone and cannot be asserted at a later date."[2] Indeed, while payment of a noncumulative dividend for a given fiscal year is discretionary, once that fiscal year has ended, the directors are "left with no discretion ever to pay any such dividend."[3] Or, as Berle put it, the "popular interpretation" is that "dividends on noncumulative preferred stock, once passed or omitted, are 'dead'; can never be made up."[4]

Suppose, for example, that the articles of incorporation provide for an annual noncumulative dividend of $8 per share of preferred. The issuer's board failed to declare dividends in Years 1 and 2. In Year 3, the board wishes to declare a dividend on both the common and the preferred. A holder of the noncumulative preferred asserts, however, that the issuer owes the preferred $24: $8 for each of Years 1 to 3. The issuer's board replies that it need only pay the $8 dividend for Year 3. Under the majority rule, the board will prevail.

The principal exception to the foregoing is the so-called dividend credit rule followed by New Jersey.[5] This approach interprets a noncu-

§ 13.6

1. Guttmann v. Illinois Central Railroad Co., 189 F.2d 927, 928 (2d Cir.1951). It is curious that *Guttmann* invoked an abuse of discretion standard rather than the business judgment rule. Yet, it seems that abuse of discretion is the usual standard in this area. See, e.g., Smith v. Southern Foundry Co., 179 S.W. 205, 207 (Ky.1915) (holding that even though plaintiff was a preferred stockholder, declaration of a dividend rested in the discretion of the board unless the board is guilty of bad faith or a willful abuse of discretion); Crocker v. Waltham Watch Co., 53 N.E.2d 230, 233 (Mass. 1944) (stating that, absent a contractual provision, the general rule, which applies to both preferred and common stock, is that the declaration of a dividend is within the discretion of the board and that courts will not interfere absent a showing of an abuse of discretion); Morse v. Boston & Maine R.R., 160 N.E. 894, 896 (Mass.1928) (holding that the declaration of dividends on noncumulative preferred stock is within the discretion of the board of directors and that plaintiff had not demonstrated that the di-

rectors had abused their discretion); Agnew v. American Ice Co., 66 A.2d 330, 334 (N.J. 1949) (holding noncumulative preferred shareholders do not have an absolute rights to dividends and that absent an abuse of discretion, failure to pay a dividend is within the discretion of the board). In at least some of these cases, however, the courts seem to be using the term "abuse of discretion" to describe the proof necessary to overcome the presumption against review of the business judgment rule. Given that the purpose of the business judgment rule is to preclude judicial review of the merits of the directors' decision and that an abuse of discretion standard appears to go to the merits, however, the standard remains problematic.

2. Wabash Railway Co. v. Barclay, 280 U.S. 197, 203 (1930).

3. *Guttmann*, 189 F.2d at 929.

4. Adolf Berle, noncumulative Preferred Stock, 23 Colum. L. Rev. 358, 364–65 (1923).

5. See, e.g., Sanders v. Cuba Railroad Co., 120 A.2d 849 (N.J.1956).

mulative dividend provision as precluding accumulation of dividends only in years in which the corporation had insufficient earnings to pay the specified dividend. In the preceding example, if the corporation had sufficient earnings in Years 1 and 2 to pay a noncumulative dividend, but chose to retain those earnings for reinvestment, the preferred would get a credit for the unpaid dividends and the board would indeed have to declare a $24 dividend on the preferred before paying anything to the common.

It is possible to achieve the New Jersey result by contract using a so-called cumulative to the extent earned dividend preference.[6] Where the articles of incorporation do not so provide, however, the New Jersey rule is absurd. The preferred shareholders bought stock that said "noncumulative." The price they were willing to pay for such stock presumably was discounted to reflect the lack of protection resulting from the absence of a cumulative preference. They made their bed, so they should lie in it. As Judge Frank famously put it, "the preferred stockholders are not—like sailors or idiots or infants—wards of the judiciary. As courts on occasions have quoted or paraphrased ancient poets, it may not be inappropriate to paraphrase a modern poet, and to say that 'a contract is a contract is a contract'."[7]

B. Contingent voting rights

Contingent voting rights are the other common protection given preferred stock's dividend preference. In other words, so long as dividends specified by the articles are paid, the preferred will have no voting rights. If a specified number of dividends are missed, however, the preferred is given the right to elect some or all of the members of the board of directors. Four to six missed quarterly dividends seems to be typical. The precise voting rights given the preferred will be specified in the articles of incorporation. Commonly used options include giving the preferred shareholders the right to elect a specified number of directors, giving convertible preferred shares the right to vote on a fully-diluted basis—i.e., casting the number of votes they would have been entitled to cast if they converted into common, and allowing the preferred to vote as a separate class.

§ 13.7 Does dividend policy affect firm value?

Conventional wisdom long claimed that changes in dividend policy could affect firm value, which implied that boards of directors could identify some optimal dividend policy. In a justly famous article, Nobel economics prize laureates Miller and Modigliani contended that dividend

---

6. In Kern v. Chicago & Eastern Illinois Railroad Co., 285 N.E.2d 501 (Ill.App.1972), the court considered the meaning of a provision under which the preferred stock's dividends were "cumulative but only to the extent that there are 'net earnings available for dividends.'" Id. at 502. The court reject-ed plaintiff's claim that undistributed earnings of a wholly owned subsidiary should have been considered in determining whether the parent had net earnings for a given year. Id. at 504.

7. *Guttmann*, 189 F.2d at 930.

policy is irrelevant to firm value, albeit assuming away taxes, transaction costs, and other market imperfections.[1] At the core of their model is the plausible assumption that the firm wishes to maintain a constant level of investment. Assume the firm has annual earnings of $1,000, which are retained for capital investment. If the firm begins a $100 annual dividend, its retained earnings will fall to $900. In order to maintain the prior level of capital investment, $1,000, the firm will have to borrow or sell new equity to replace the amount paid out as a dividend.

Put another way, Miller and Modigliani observed that firms can either finance their operations through retained earnings or through a combination of paying dividends and raising additional capital. Further, they offered a mathematical proof of the proposition that the choice between those options has no affect on the firm's value. For our purposes, however, that proof is less important than the assumptions that underlie it. They assume (sometimes explicitly and sometimes implicitly): (1) zero transaction costs and no taxes; (2) rational shareholder behavior; (3) perfect certainty; (4) homogenous expectations, which means that all investors have the same beliefs concerning future investments, profits and dividends; (5) management faithfulness to shareholder interests; (6) no changes in firm investment policy; (7) firms and shareholders can generate the same rate of investment; and (8) the firm has no intrinsic value, but rather the firm is worth only what somebody is willing to pay for its shares.

Let's start to relax the assumptions a little bit. Assume a firm is trying to choose between two dividend policies: (1) a high dividend policy in which most earnings are paid out; and (2) a low dividend policy in which most earnings are retained. When we relax Miller and Modigliani's assumptions, does one policy lead to a higher firm value than the other? Let's first take away the assumption of no taxes. Obviously, there are taxes in the real world, but which policy—low or high dividends—makes sense in a world with both corporate and personal taxes? The intuitive answer may be that low dividends make sense because dividend payments are subject to double taxation—they are taxed at the corporate level as profits and as ordinary income to the shareholders. Actually, however, the effect of taxes on dividend policy is more subtle. It depends on the relative levels of personal and corporate tax rates. Generally speaking, high dividend strategies maximize shareholder wealth when personal tax rates are lower than corporate tax rates; while low dividend strategies maximize shareholder wealth when personal tax rates are significantly higher than corporate tax rates.

This holds true, however, only if capital gains and ordinary income are taxed at the same rate. If capital gains are taxed at a lower rate than ordinary income, which is generally the case, retention is favored be-

§ 13.7   Valuation of Shares, 34 J. Bus. 411 (1961).
   1.   Merton H. Miller and Franco Modigliani, Dividend Policy, Growth and the

cause dividends are taxed as ordinary income, while proceeds from sales of stock are taxed as capital gains. Firms could maximize shareholder wealth by retaining earnings and then either having the shareholder sell the stock or having the firm redeem the stock. In addition, capital gains are not taxed until they are realized when the asset is sold, while dividends are taxed upon receipt. Capital gains taxes may also be avoided through careful estate planning, because persons who inherit capital assets get a stepped-up basis in the asset equal to the fair market value at the time of the testator's death.

Our discussion of the tax implications of dividend policy reflected another key assumption; namely, that the firm is able to invest retained earnings at the same pre-tax rate as shareholders. Setting aside tax questions for the moment, if the firm is able to generate higher rates of return than the shareholders are able to generate, the firm should retain earnings. One can readily imagine such cases: as where the firm can use the retained earnings to buy a new asset, which will have a synergistic effect when tied to the firm's existing assets. Conversely, if shareholders are able to generate a higher rate of return than the firm is, the firm should pay out dividends. If a mature business in a mature industry reinvests retained earnings in its own industry, those investments are likely to produce a sub-market rate of return. If that business makes investments outside its industry, transaction costs may result in the firm's rate of return being lower than that which could be generated by shareholders. Because of higher transaction costs and the need to pay a premium for control, it is cheaper (on a per share basis) to buy one share of stock than to buy the whole company.

This point segues nicely into a discussion of the assumption that transactions costs are zero. Paying out dividends entails transmission, mailing, and other costs. Shareholders who are going to reinvest dividends they receive also incur transaction costs in making the new investment (e.g., brokerage commissions). For a mature business, however, the transaction costs of reinvesting within the firm may be higher than the transaction costs associated with paying a dividend that is reinvested by the shareholders.

The assumption that the firm's investment policy is stable is critical to the irrelevance hypothesis. As we have seen, if the firm pays out dividends, it will have to raise new capital to maintain the same level of investment. Yet, this assumption often may not hold. A mature business in a mature industry, for example, may not need to maintain the same level of investment. Instead, it may be reducing new investments and paying out cash flow as dividends.

One can also readily imagine situations in which the firm could sensibly increase the dividend at the same time that it is increasing its level of investment, without borrowing or selling new equity. If the firm's managers expect earnings to rise, it will have sufficient funds to pay the higher dividend and maintain (or even increase) reinvestment. This observation suggests that dividends can act as a signaling device, alerting investors that management believes the firm's future is promising. Such a signal will increase the stock price and, hence, the value of the firm. But why is increasing the dividend a necessary signal? Why not just announce that management expects the future to be rosy and announce the basis for management's expectations? In many cases, management may not be able to announce the information in question for legal or business reasons. Even if management could release the information, however, the market may not regard management's claims as credible. An increased dividend acts as a bond, showing that management's expectations are credible.

The latter point segues into the assumption of management faithfulness, which our knowledge of agency cost economics suggests is flawed. Managers may prefer to retain earnings, because their compensation is often linked to firm size and to stock price, both of which go up with retained earnings. This has become an increasingly plausible scenario in recent years, given the rising importance of stock options as form of management compensation. Indeed, in recent years there has been a trend away from high dividend payout policies even among the very largest firms.[2]

Finally we come to the assumption of rational behavior and homogeneous expectations. Taken together, these assumptions suggest investors will not prefer stocks paying high dividends over stocks paying low dividends (or vice-versa). In the real world, however, might investors in fact have preferences? Sure. Retired investors may want current income over capital appreciation. (Which brings to mind a joke that has become a staple of elderly comedians: "At my age, I don't even buy green bananas.") On the other hand, such investors could, at relatively low cost, sell their shares and thus manufacture tax-advantaged home made dividends.

Young investors may prefer low dividend stocks, because they avoid the transaction costs associated with reinvesting dividends. On the other hand, they may prefer current income if they expect tax rates to rise in the future.

If we relax the rational behavior and homogeneous expectation assumptions, some investors will have different preferences about dividend policy than other investors. If so, might a firm add value by changing its dividend policy to appeal to a new clientele of shareholders? No. This strategy will only work if there is an unsatisfied clientele, but the law of supply and demand predicts that there should be no such unsatisfied clientele. Suppose the firm perceives a change in investor preference towards high dividends—in effect, a rightward shift in the demand curve for high dividend stocks. If so, the price of high dividend firms should rise relative to those of low dividend firms. Once equilibrium is restored, however, which should happen quickly absent some

---

2. Kathy Jones & James Ramage, Remember Dividends?, 53 Kiplinger's Personal Finance (1999) (stating that "dividend yields have shrunk to the point of invisibility" and that they are "at a near-record low").

market failure, no unsatisfied clientele will remain and no firm will be able to increase stock prices by changing its dividend policy.

Let's pull it all together. Once we relax the assumptions underlying the irrelevance hypothesis, what can we say about dividend policy? It may be relevant to firm value, but it is awfully hard to predict with confidence how a change in dividend policy will cut in any given setting. What is the legal implication of that conclusion? Mainly that courts should not second-guess director decisions about dividend payout policy, because courts are no more likely to get it "right" than is the board.

§ 13.8 Suits to compel declaration of a dividend

Stockholders have no right to dividends. The decision of whether, when, and how much of a dividend should be paid is reserved to the discretion of the board.[1] Despite this clear and well-accepted principle, one occasionally sees suits brought by shareholders to compel the board to declare a dividend. Such suits rarely succeed, however, because the decision to declare a dividend (or not to do so) is protected by the business judgment rule.[2]

§ 13.8

1. See, e.g., Liebman v. Auto Strop Co., 150 N.E. 505, 506 (N.Y.1926) ("It is a fundamental rule relating to the management of corporations that it is within the discretion of the directors to determine when and to what extent a dividend shall be made, subject of course to the qualification that the same shall not encroach on the capital.... It is for the directors to say, acting in good faith of course, when and to what extent dividends shall be declared."); see also Kamin v. American Express Co., 387 N.Y.S.2d 993 (App.Div.1976). The situation is rather different once the board has declared a dividend. If the board declares a dividend, but fails to pay it, the court will treat the shareholder as having a contractual right to receive the dividend and order the corporation to pay it. See, e.g., Bulger Block Coal Co. v. U.S., 48 F.2d 675, 680 (Ct.Cl.1931) (holding that once a dividend has been declared, it becomes an indebtedness to the stockholders); Wheeler v. Northwestern Sleigh Co., 39 F. 347, 348 (C.C.Wis. 1889) (holding that once a certain dividend has been declared, shareholders become creditors of the corporation for that amount); Lockhart Iron & Steel Co. v. O'Toole, 22 F.Supp. 919, 920 (D.C.Pa.1938) (stating that a declaration of a dividend creates a debtor-creditor relationship between the corporation and the shareholder); McLaren v. Crescent Planing Mill Co., 93 S.W. 819 (Mo.Ct.App.1906) (holding that once a dividend is declared it becomes a debt of the corporation to the shareholders and, accordingly, may not be revoked by the board); State by Parsons v. Standard Oil

Co., 74 A.2d 565, 575 (N.J.1950) (stating that declaring a dividend gives rise to a debt in favor of stockholders and that once money has been set aside for the payment of dividends, it is held in trust and can not be reached by other creditors).

2. See, e.g., In re Tube Methods, Inc., 73 Bankr. 974 (Bankr.E.D.Pa.1987) (holding that, under Pennsylvania law, the decision to declare a dividend is vested in the discretion of the board and that judicial review of board decisions is subject to the business judgment rule); Barnes v. State Farm Mut. Auto. Ins. Co., 16 Cal.App.4th 365, 378 (Cal.Ct.App.1993) (stating that the declaration of dividends falls under the business judgment rule and courts will not interfere with the board's discretion absent a showing of an abuse of discretion); New England Trust Co. v. Penobscot Chemical Fibre Co., 50 A.2d 188, 190 (Me.1946) (stating that absent fraud, bad faith, or abuse of discretion, the judgment of the board to not pay dividends is conclusive unless the discretion is limited by charter, bylaw, or statute); Dodge v. Ford Motor Co., 170 N.W. 668 (Mich.1919) (applying business judgment rule to board dividend decisions); Hassett v. S.F. Iszard Co., 61 N.Y.S.2d 451, 455 (N.Y.Sup.Ct.1945) (holding, after an examination of the corporation's financial condition, that absent a showing of bad faith or an abuse of discretion, failure to pay a dividend is within the discretion of the board); cf. Hirsch v. Cahn Elec. Co., 694 So.2d 636, 643 (La.Ct.App.1997) (holding that courts may order the corporation to

As between shareholders and directors, the allocation of decision-making authority to the board makes sense. The decision whether to declare a dividend differs but little from any other board decision. Absent facts indicating that the decision was tainted by a conflict of interest, the principle of respecting the board's decisionmaking authority predominates over accountability concerns and the board's decision appropriately is insulated from review by shareholders and courts. With respect to suits to compel declaration of a dividend, moreover, the usual justifications for judicial abstention are buttressed by our lack of confidence in our ability to predict the effect a change in dividend policy will have on firm value. Courts are no more likely to get dividend policy right than are directors.

Cases involving self-dealing thus seem the most likely scenario in which a suit to compel a dividend will succeed. The Delaware Supreme Court, for example, has noted that structuring a dividend so that it is paid only to a controlling shareholder could involve self-dealing sufficient to set aside the business judgment rule:

> For example, suppose a parent dominates a subsidiary and its board of directors. The subsidiary has outstanding two classes of stock, X and Y. Class X is owned by the parent and Class Y is owned by minority stockholders of the subsidiary. If the subsidiary, at the direction of the parent, declares a dividend on its Class X stock only, this might well be self-dealing by the parent. It would be receiving something from the subsidiary to the exclusion of and detrimental to its minority stockholders. This self-dealing, coupled with the parent's fiduciary duty, would make intrinsic fairness the proper standard by which to evaluate the dividend payments.[3]

Where the minority shareholders get their pro rata share of any dividends, however, there is no self-dealing and the business judgment rule applies.

Self-dealing might also be found where the board suspended regular payment of a dividend for the benefit of a controlling shareholder. In

declare a dividend if it seems "there is capricious, arbitrary, or discriminating management"); Giannotti v. Hamway, 387 S.E.2d 725, 735 (Va.1990) (stating that generally the declaration of dividends is under the discretion of the board unless the refusal to declare a dividend is "so arbitrary" or "so unreasonable"). If brought, a suit to compel declaration of a dividend typically is regarded as direct rather than derivative. Sobel v. Whittier Corp., 95 F.Supp. 643, 645 (D.Mich.1951); Gordon v. Elliman, 119 N.E.2d 331, 334 (N.Y.1954) (stating that since "a corporation has no right to compel itself to pay a dividend, the stockholders' right cannot possibly 'derive' from it"); cf. Stevens v. United States Steel Corp., 59 A. 905, 906 (N.J.Ch.1905) (stating that a dividend, as a debt owed by the corporation, is owed to stockholders severally as individuals).

Note that in close corporations courts may order payment of a dividend as a remedy for oppression of minority shareholders by the majority. See, e.g., Miller v. Magline, Inc., 256 N.W.2d 761 (Mich.App.1977); Patton v. Nicholas, 279 S.W.2d 848 (Tex.1955); see also Gottfried v. Gottfried, 73 N.Y.S.2d 692 (N.Y.Sup.Ct.1947) (recognizing remedy but declining to grant it on facts); Zidell v. Zidell, 560 P.2d 1086 (Or.1977) (same).

3. Sinclair Oil Corp. v. Levien, 280 A.2d 717, 722 (Del.1971). See also Reiss v. Superior Indus., Inc., 466 So.2d 542 (La.App. 1985) (selective distribution of stock to some but not all close corporation shareholders was breach of fiduciary duty).

Gabelli & Co. v. Liggett Group, Inc.,[4] for example, Liggett was the subject of a takeover bid by Grand Metropolitan Ltd. ("Grand Met"). Grand Met first acquired roughly 85 percent of Liggett's outstanding stock through a tender offer. Grand Met planned to eliminate the remaining minority shareholders through a reverse triangular merger— Ligget would merge with GM Sub, a wholly-owned subsidiary of Grand Met, with Liggett as the surviving corporation. While the merger was pending, Liggett's board suspended payment of its regular quarterly dividend (62.5 cents per share). The Chancery Court held that the decision to suspend a regularly paid dividend is protected by the business judgment rule. Consequently, "it is settled law in Delaware that the Court of Chancery will not compel payment of a dividend unless the corporation is in the proper business and financial posture to do so, and if the failure to declare the dividend is the result of an 'oppressive or fraudulent abuse of discretion.' " The case at bar, however, involved a freeze-out merger by a controlling shareholder and therefore implicated that shareholder's fiduciary duties. Accordingly, the question was whether the merger price was fair. In other words, did the merger price reflect and include the value of the foregone dividend? If so, no harm—no foul.

An interesting twist on the problem was presented by *Baron v. Allied Artists Pictures Corp.*[5] Allied's articles of incorporation provided that if six or more quarterly dividends were missed the preferred shareholders, voting as a class, would have the right to elect a majority of the board of directors. Allied missed the requisite number of preferred dividends, triggering the preferred shares' contingent voting rights. The idea behind contingent voting rights, of course, is that the preferred shareholders' board representatives will change corporate policy so that the firm can begin paying dividends on the preferred. Once the missed dividends are caught up, the preferred shareholders' representatives step down and control returns to the common. (Classically minded readers will note the parallel to the story of Cincinnatus, the Roman general who left his farm to defeat the Aequi and Volscians and, after victory, went back to his farm.) In Allied's case, however, the board failed to begin paying dividends on the preferred stock. As a result, the preferred retained their right to elect a majority of the board—for a period of ten years.

Plaintiff was a common shareholder who sued, in effect, to compel the board to declare such dividends as would be necessary to return control to directors elected by the common. The Chancery Court rejected plaintiff's claim, holding that the directors have discretion to declare dividends or to refrain from doing so. The exercise of that discretion is not unbounded, of course. A board elected by the preferred "does have a fiduciary duty to see that the preferred dividends are brought up to date

4. 444 A.2d 261 (Del.Ch.1982), aff'd, 479 A.2d 276 (Del.1984). Cf. Dodge v. Ford Motor Co., 170 N.W. 668 (Mich.1919) (ordering reinstatement of routinely paid "special dividends" suspended by controlling shareholder who thought minority shareholders "should be content to take what he chooses to give them").

5. 337 A.2d 653 (Del.Ch.1975), appeal dismissed, 365 A.2d 136 (Del.1976).

as soon as possible in keeping with prudent business management."[6] Note, however, that the latter qualification substantially eviscerates the scope of the stated duty. The board need not begin paying dividends on the preferred the moment sufficient funds have become available, so long as there is a good business reason for retaining earnings. Worse yet, the business judgment rule precludes the court from second-guessing the board's decision absent "fraud or gross abuse of discretion."[7] In light of the volatile nature of the motion picture business and the resulting need to retain sufficient reserves against major losses, the court refused to grant relief.

Two conceptions of the business judgment rule compete in the cases—some view it as a rule of abstention, while others treat it as a substantive standard of review? As their invocation of an "abuse of discretion" standard suggests, both *Gabelli* and *Allied Artists* lean towards the view that the business judgment rule is a substantive standard of review, albeit a quite deferential one. That impression perhaps is confirmed by the relatively extensive analysis in both decisions of the respective firms' ability to pay a dividend in the circumstances. In *Gabelli*, such an intrusive review perhaps was justified in light of the conflict of interest created by Grand Met's status as a controlling shareholder. As the court phrased the problem in *Allied Artists*, however, there was no conflict of interest. Hence, instead of reviewing the merits of Allied's dividend policy, the court could have (and should have) simply abstained.

Ironically, however, everyone seems to have ignored the fact that over half of Allied's preferred stock was owned by a single shareholder—Kalvex, Inc.—who owned almost none of Allied's common stock. Because the preferred voted as a class without benefit of cumulative voting, Kalvex controlled the outcome of board elections, despite owning only 7 percent of Allied's total equity. As a result, there was a substantial interlock between the two companies' boards and management. Allied's president, for example, was also the president of Kalvex. Although Kalvex was mainly a preferred shareholder, it could have (and should have) been treated as Allied's controlling shareholder subject to the attendant fiduciary duties. Under the duty of loyalty applicable to controlling shareholders, the question would be whether Kalvex received a benefit at the expense of and to the exclusion of the other shareholders. If so, Kalvex would have to justify that benefit under the intrinsic fairness standard. Plaintiff would have argued that control of the corporation is itself a benefit, which the preferred shareholders seized to the exclusion of the common, and also pointed to the highly remunerative compensation Kalvex's officers received by virtue of their positions at Allied. Would plaintiff have won? Maybe not, but certainly plaintiff's chances would have been far greater than under the theory actually used.

6. Id. at 660.   **7.** Id. at 659.

Chapter 14

CLOSE CORPORATIONS

Analysis

---

§ 14.1   Exit versus voice

A "close corporation is one in which the stock is held in a few hands, or in a few families, and wherein it is not at all, or only rarely, dealt in by buying or selling."[1] The firm's size thus is not determinative, al-

§ 14.1

1.   Galler v. Galler, 203 N.E.2d 577, 583 (Ill.1964). See also G & N Aircraft, Inc. v. Boehm, 743 N.E.2d 227, 236 n. 2 (Ind.2001) ("A minimum requirement is a lack of a public market for the shares, and most would require a small number of shareholders as well."). A number of states have adopted special statutes for close corporations, commonly modeled on the ABA's Model Close Corporation Supplement. Promoters of a close corporation may opt into coverage by such statutes through an express designation of such status in the arti-

though most close corporations tend to be small, local businesses. Instead, the hallmarks of the closely held corporation are the small number of shareholders and, most important, the absence of a secondary market in which its stock is traded.

This definition emphasizes a critical difference between the public and close corporation; namely, the absence of a market out. If shareholders of a public corporation are unhappy with the firm's management, they can easily exit via the stock market. Consequently, they can simply sell out and put the unhappy experience behind them. Shareholders of a close corporation, in contrast, have no access to a secondary trading market for their shares and, as a result, may find it very difficult to locate a buyer for their shares. Where exit is precluded, dissatisfied constituencies of an organization must resort to voice; that is, because they cannot escape from the unsatisfactory situation, they must seek to change it through internal governance mechanisms.[2]

Unlike a large public corporation, where collective action problems preclude shareholders from bargaining with one another, the small group of investors in a close corporation permits them to bargain at comparatively law cost. Investors would be foolish to agree to invest in the business, but leave planning the details about the firm until the future. Instead, they should settle the critical questions in advance— before they've invested money in the business.

The small number of shareholders typical of close corporations also vitiates the efficiency rationale for separating ownership and control. To the contrary, shareholders of close corporations are far less likely to be passive investors than is the case with respect to public corporations. (These are exceptions, of course, as many close corporations have "silent partners.") A desire for active involvement follows directly from the lack of a market out. If the shareholders cannot protect themselves by selling out, they are wise to want an effective voice in how the firm is operated.

Earning a return on one's investment provides yet another reason for shareholders to be actively involved in running the close corporation. Most close corporations do not pay significant dividends. Instead, for tax reasons, the shareholders' principal return on their investment comes in the form of salary and bonuses. Dividends are not deductible by the firm, so they are subject to double taxation, once at the firm level and again

---

cles of incorporation. The regulatory regime for statutory close corporations is substantially more liberal in a variety of ways than is mainstream corporate law. Yet, courts frequently grant comparable benefits to nonstatutory close corporations. In Ramos v. Estrada, 10 Cal.Rptr.2d 833 (Cal.App. 1992), defendants noted that California's close corporation statute authorizes vote pooling agreements but the general corporation statute was silent. Defendants inferred that vote pooling agreements were invalid in close corporations that had not opted into the special statute. The court rejected that argument, upholding vote pooling agreements as valid even in nonstatutory close corporations. See also Zion v. Kurtz, 428 N.Y.S.2d 199 (1980) (similar holding under Delaware law). In addition, very few corporations have opted into the special close corporation statutes. Accordingly, separate treatment of those statutes is omitted in this text.

2. See generally Albert O. Hirschman, Exit, Voice, and Loyalty (1970).

when received by the shareholder. In contrast, reasonable salary and bonuses are deductible by the firm, so they are taxed only once (at the shareholder/employee level). Because of these tax consequences and the resulting practice of not paying dividends, a denial of employment to a minority shareholder may deny that shareholder a fair return on his investment.

Finally, unlike the public corporation context, it is often practical for the shareholders to be actively involved in running the store. In many closely held corporations, all shareholders are employees and/or directors of the firm, which means that they are in a much better position to monitor the firm's performance and the performance of other firm employees than their public corporation counterparts.

The difficulty, of course, is that the corporation statutes fail to take this into account. Recall that shareholders have no meaningful management rights. Instead, once they have elected the directors, the firm is run by the board of directors. As we have just seen, however, this approach makes very little sense in the context of a small firm where the managers, directors, and shareholders are likely to be one and the same.

There are a wide variety of techniques by which close corporation shareholders can be given effective control over firm management. Most entail some degree of private ordering. Will courts enforce private contracts that derogate from the statutory allocation of powers and rights? If private ordering fails, what ex post extra-contractual rights do allegedly injured shareholders possess?

§ 14.2   Private ordering in close corporations

A.   Private ordering of voting rights

Whether a corporation is public or close, the most important thing shareholders do as shareholders is the election of directors. Shareholder voting on such matters as dissolution, mergers, and the like runs a reasonably close second. In the close corporation, with its limited number of shareholders, voting can prove problematic in a variety of ways. If shareholders are evenly divided on some issue, deadlock may ensue.[1] More likely, a majority faction may use its voting power to oppress the minority. The majority might, for example, decline to elect minority representatives to the board of directors. The law provides two contractual solutions to this problem: the voting trust and the vote pooling agreement.

---

§ 14.2

1. A creative solution to the deadlock problem was validated in Lehrman v. Cohen, 222 A.2d 800 (Del.1966). The Lehrman and Cohen families were equal partners in a grocery store corporation. The corporation had three classes of stock. One class was owned solely by the Lehrman family and gave them the right to elect two directors. A second class was owned solely by the Cohen family and gave them the right to elect two directors. A third class with very limited economic rights but also the right to elect one director was issued to the corporation's legal counsel, who thus functioned as a tie-breaker between the two families. The Delaware supreme court held that the third class was a valid class of stock and that the agreement did not constitute an illegal voting trust.

1. Voting trusts

A voting trust is an agreement among shareholders under which all of the shares owned by the parties are transferred to a trustee, who becomes the nominal, record owner of the shares. The trustee votes the shares in accordance with the provisions of the trust agreement, if any, and is responsible for distributing any dividends to the beneficial owners of the shares.

At common law, voting trusts originally were suspect. Early courts believed that the power to vote stock was an essential incident of owning shares and that separating voting rights from ownership therefore violated public policy.[2] This oddly formalistic approach ran counter to the basic corporate law principle allowing separation of ownership and control. Because it impeded private ordering, the policy also was inconsistent with basic principles of freedom of contract. Legislatures uniformly have overruled the common law, adopting statutes authorizing voting trusts.[3] Lingering judicial hostility to voting trusts can be seen in cases invalidating voting trusts for relatively trivial failures to comply with statutory requirements.[4] In recent years, however, courts have been more tolerant of minor deviations from the statute. In *Goldblum v. Boyd*,[5] for example, a shareholder sought to invalidate a voting trust for failure to comply with a statutory requirement that voting trusts be filed with the corporation's office. Because the parties had kept a photocopy of the trust agreement in the office, the court deemed them to have substantially complied with the statutory requirement and upheld the trust. In *Oceanic Exploration Co. v. Grynberg*,[6] the Delaware chancery court invalidated a voting trust for failure to comply with several statutory requirements. The Delaware supreme court reversed, excusing noncompliance with those requirements by recharacterizing the instrument as a vote pooling agreement.

The chief advantage of a voting trust is that it eliminates the possibility of shareholder deadlock, because all shareholders put their shares in the trust and only the trustee votes. The disadvantages are more numerous. Shareholders experience a significant loss of control. Most states limit the duration of a voting trust to ten years, after which time it must be renegotiated.[7] Finally, the voting trust does not fully prevent oppression of the minority. A majority coalition of directors still could use its powers on the board to oppress the minority.

---

2. See, e.g., Luthy v. Ream, 110 N.E. 373, 375 (Ill.1915); Warren v. Pim, 59 A. 773, 789 (N.J.1904).

3. Only Massachusetts has not done so. See MBCA § 7.30 cmt. On the other hand, Massachusetts courts have long recognized the validity of voting trusts even without statutory authorization. See, e.g., Colbert v. Hennessey, 217 N.E.2d 914, 920 (Mass. 1966).

4. See, e.g., Christopher v. Richardson, 147 A.2d 375, 376 (Pa.1959) (invalidating a voting trust whose term exceeded the statutory ten year limit).

5. 341 So.2d 436 (La.App.1976).

6. 428 A.2d 1 (Del.1981).

7. See, e.g., MBCA § 7.30.

2. *Vote pooling agreements*

Suppose four friends—Alpha, Beta, Charlie, and Delta—form a corporation in which each owns 25% of the voting common shares. They sign a contract pursuant to which each agrees to vote for the others when electing the board of directors, thereby ensuring that all will be elected. Would such an agreement be enforceable? In brief, yes. Given that a single majority shareholder validly could decide in advance whom to elect, the courts allow several shareholders to decide together in advance whom to elect.[8]

Such a vote pooling agreement differs from a voting trust in that there is no transfer of legal title to the stock in question. As such, the historic prejudice against voting trusts generally was not extended to vote pooling agreements.[9] A notable exception to this general rule was the Delaware supreme court's decision in *Abercrombie v. Davies*,[10] in which the court recharacterized a vote pooling agreement as a voting trust and held it invalid for failure to comply with the voting trust statute. Consequently, where the substantive effect and purpose of the agreement is "sufficiently close to the substance and purpose of [the voting trust statute] to warrant its being subjected to the restrictions and conditions imposed by that Statute," the court will recharacterize the agreement.[11] In contrast, however, the Delaware supreme court's subsequent decision in *Oceanic Exploration Co. v. Grynberg*[12] recognized the ongoing liberalization of judicial attitudes towards voting trusts and pooling agreements. In that case, the court recharacterized a voting trust as a vote pooling agreement. To be sure, *Oceanic Exploration* did not overrule *Abercrombie*. In *Oceanic Exploration*, however, the court acknowledged that judicial hostility towards private ordering was unsound, which signaled a move towards freedom of contract.

Today, a vote pooling agreement is most likely to be recharacterized as a voting trust where some provision separates the right to vote the shares from the other incidents of stock ownership. Suppose two shareholders holding an equal number of shares enter into a vote pooling agreement. Recognizing the risk of deadlock, they agree to submit any disagreements as to how the shares should be voted to a third-party arbitrator. They further grant the arbitrator an irrevocable proxy to vote the shares, so as to provide a mechanism for enforcing the arbitrator's decisions. Such an agreement resembles the definition of a voting trust implied by DGCL § 218, which applies to written agreements by which the shareholders "transfer capital stock to any person" and vest that person with the right to vote that stock. As with a voting trust, they

8. See, e.g., McQuade v. Stoneham, 189 N.E. 234, 236 (N.Y.1934) (noting the "well settled" rule that shareholders may "combine to elect directors").

9. See, e.g., Luthy v. Ream, 110 N.E. 373, 376 (Ill.1915) ("the pooling of stock for the purpose of electing directors and officers and controlling the management and business of the corporation is not necessarily illegal").

10. 130 A.2d 338 (Del.1957).

11. Lehrman v. Cohen, 222 A.2d 800, 806 (Del.1966).

12. 428 A.2d 1 (Del.1981).

have divorced the right to vote their shares from the other incidents of stockownership and vested that right in some third party. Such an agreement thus is a likely candidate for recharacterization as a voting trust, at least under the illiberal rules laid out in cases like *Abercrombie*.[13] In light of the hyper-technical approach many courts take to voting trusts, under which minor deviations from the statutory provisions are sufficient grounds for invalidating the trust, a recharacterized agreement is very vulnerable. It would be surprising if the drafter of a vote pooling contrast will have bothered to comply with every statutory requirement for a voting trust.

Vote pooling agreements present a number of significant planning and drafting considerations. Should the agreement attempt to specify how the parties will vote their shares (for example, by stating that Alpha agrees to vote for Beta, Charlie, and Delta as directors)? If the agreement does not specify how the shares should be voted, what mechanisms might be adopted to facilitate achieving consensus on that issue? How can one prevent defection by shareholders party to the agreement? Should courts use specific performance to enforce such agreements?

The classic voting pooling decision remains the Delaware supreme court's opinion in *Ringling Bros.-Barnum & Bailey Combined Shows v. Ringling*.[14] When our story began, the circus was owned by descendants of the eponymous Ringling Brothers. The family had split into three factions. Edith Ringling and Aubrey Ringling Haley each owned 315 of the 1000 outstanding shares. The remaining 370 shares were owned by John Ringling North. In 1941, Edith and Aubrey entered into a vote pooling agreement, apparently codifying an earlier agreement dating from 1934, pursuant to which they sought "to act jointly in all matters relating to their stock ownership." More specifically, the agreement required them to "consult and confer" before voting. If they were unable to agree as to how their shares should be voted, the issues was to be referred to a designated arbitrator, one Karl D. Loos, who was also their lawyer.[15] Loos' decision was "binding" on the ladies.

The corporation used cumulative voting in the election of directors. If each shareholder voted separately, Aubrey and Edith could each elect two directors, while John could elect three. If properly cumulated, however, Edith's and Aubrey's shares empowered them to elect five of the seven directors.[16] In 1946, however, Aubrey and Edith had a falling

---

13. Cf. Galler v. Galler, 203 N.E.2d 577, 586 (Ill.1964) (refusing to recharacterize a vote pooling agreement as a voting trust on grounds that it was "a straight contractual voting control agreement which does not divorce voting rights from stock ownership").

14. 53 A.2d 441 (Del.1947).

15. Although Loos did not violate any ethical standards by serving as both the parties' lawyer and their arbitrator, such a dual role is imprudent. Loos was the lawyer for both parties, but this agreement inevitably put him in the middle of an increasingly embittered personal conflict—an outcome any sensible lawyer would try to avoid.

16. Edith and Aubrey were each entitled to 2205 votes (multiply their 315 shares by the seven vacancies to determine the number of votes). Acting together, they could therefore cast 4410 votes, which could be divided so as to allow 882 votes for each of 5 candidates. (Note that at least one of the five would have to receive votes from

out and were unable to agree on the identity of the fifth director to be elected by their block.[17] Edith demanded arbitration by Loos, who directed that Edith should vote her shares as follows: 882 votes for Edith herself, 882 for her son Robert, and 441 for a Mr. Dunn. At the meeting, Edith did so. Loos also directed that Aubrey vote her shares as follows: 882 for Aubrey, 882 for her husband James, and 441 for Dunn. At the meeting, Aubrey was represented by her husband James, who refused to comply with Loos' direction. Instead, James cast 1103 votes for Aubrey and 1102 for himself. John divided his votes across three candidates, casting 864 votes for a Mr. Wood, 863 for a Mr. Griffin, and 863 for himself.

If the votes had been cast as directed by Loos, the now defunct Edith–Aubrey coalition would have elected its usual five directors: Edith, Robert, Aubrey, James, and Dunn. If the votes stood as cast, however, Dunn would not be elected. Instead, John would elect all three of his candidates. Edith sought judicial review of the election under what is now DGCL § 225, which authorizes the chancery court to determine the validity of a director election. The vice chancellor upheld the agreement, finding that where one party refused to comply with the arbitrator's judgment the agreement gave the willing party an irrevocable proxy to vote the recalcitrant party's shares as directed by the arbitrator.[18] The vice chancellor proposed to enforce this decree by ordering a new

both Edith and Aubrey.) John, by virtue of his 370 shares, was entitled to cast 2590 votes, a total that could not be divided so as to give to more than two candidates as many as 882 votes each.

17. The falling out apparently grew out of intra-family disputes triggered by the aftermath of a disastrous fire in the circus big top. Henry Ringling North & Alden Hatch, The Circus Kings: Our Ringling Family Story (1960).

18. Why didn't the parties avoid the problem by giving Loos an irrevocable proxy? Several answers suggest themselves. First, they may not have wished to give up that much control. Second, they may have been concerned that including an irrevocable proxy might make it more likely that the agreement would be recharacterized as a voting trust on grounds that such a proxy would separate the right to vote their shares from the other incidents of stock ownership that they retained. Third, the common law strongly disfavors irrevocable proxies. To be deemed irrevocable, a proxy must state that it is irrevocable and be coupled with an interest. See, e.g., Calumet Indus. v. MacClure, 464 F.Supp. 19, 26 (N.D.Ill.1978); Abercrombie v. Davies, 123 A.2d 893, 906 (1956), rev'd on other grounds, 130 A.2d 338 (Del.1957). "The 'interest' necessary in order to support irrevocability may be, for example, security for a

loan, title to the stock itself, or, in more recent cases, an employee's interest in the corporation." *Calumet Indus.*, 464 F.Supp. at 26. Common law courts divided as to whether the requisite interest must be one in the shares or merely in the corporation. Compare In re Chilson, 168 A. 82, 86 (Del. Ch.1933) (requiring "some recognizable property or financial interest in the stock in respect of which the voting power is to be exercised") with Deibler v. Chas. H. Elliott Co., 81 A.2d 557, 561 (Pa.1951) (asserting the "rule in general" to be "that the interest which will support an irrevocable proxy need not be in the stock itself"). Under *Chilson*, which was still good law in Delaware when *Ringling* was decided, any proxy given Loos likely would be deemed revocable. In Haft v. Haft, 671 A.2d 413, 420 (Del.Ch.1995), however, the Delaware chancery court recognized that *Chilson* had been overruled by statute. Today, for example, MBCA § 7.22(d)(5) expressly recognizes that the requisite interest arises in connection with the appointment of a party in connection with a vote pooling agreement. The Delaware code contains no such express provision, but one suspects that Delaware courts would enforce an irrevocable proxy created in connection with such an agreement.

election to be held before a special master who would give effect to the agreement. The newly-formed Aubrey–John coalition appealed.[19]

On appeal, the Aubrey–John coalition argued that vote pooling agreements were illegal. The only way for shareholders to precommit to a particular voting scheme, they contended, was through a voting trust that fully complied with the various statutory requirements. The Delaware supreme court squarely rejected that argument, distinguishing voting trusts from vote pooling agreements and upholding the validity of the latter.[20] Although the opinion contains sweeping language with respect to the validity of vote pooling agreements, the court's enthusiasm for contractual enforcement mechanisms was more restrained. "*Reasonable* provisions for cases of failure" to agree "seem unobjectionable," the supreme court opined, which invited other courts to invalidate unreasonable anti-defection provisions. If so, however, courts have declined to accept that invitation.[21]

Curiously, the court failed to grapple with the most significant objection to the agreement's validity. One of the supposed evils of voting trusts is the potential for "secret, uncontrolled combinations of stockholders" to collectively "acquire control of the corporation to the possible detriment of non-participating shareholders."[22] Hence, presumably, such statutory requirements as the obligation to file the trust agreement with the corporation's principal office.[23] If this concern has merit, is not a vote pooling agreement equally problematic? Creating a "combination" to acquire greater control of the corporation was the very purpose of the Edith–Aubrey agreement. To be sure, in this instance, the agreement was open and notorious. But public notoriety is not demanded by

---

19. Why did John care? After all, assuming the Haleys were now firmly on his side, he would control the board by a 4–3 margin. The new coalition apparently intended to install John as President. If the board was elected as specified by Loos, the coalition would have had only 4 votes to Edith Ringling's 3 (assuming Dunn would side with Edith). The vote would be 4–3 for John as President, but only by counting John's own vote. Suppose Edith challenged the election on conflict of interest grounds. Assuming John's position as President carried with it a salary or other benefits, his election to that position would implicate the interested director transaction provisions of what is now DGCL § 144. Although § 144(a) allows the board to approve conflicted interest transactions, John's vote could not count for that purpose. Consequently, the vote would split 3–3. To be sure, his appointment likely would have passed muster under § 144(a)(3) on grounds that it was fair to the corporation at the time it was approved, but that approach invited further litigation. Obtaining a fifth vote would avoid that problem, by allowing the board to approve the transaction 4–2 (with John abstaining). (Note that this analysis assumes the current state of the law on director voting and conflicts of interest.)

20. Ringling Bros.-Barnum & Bailey Combined Shows v. Ringling, 53 A.2d 441, 447 (Del.1947). See also Nixon v. Blackwell, 626 A.2d 1366, 1380 (Del.1993) (positing the validity of "definitive stockholder agreements, and such agreements may provide for elaborate earnings tests, buy-out provisions, voting trusts, or other voting agreements").

21. In Ramos v. Estrada, 10 Cal.Rptr.2d 833 (Cal.App.1992), for example, the contract provided for a mandatory buyout of the defecting shareholders' stock at the disadvantageous price of cost plus 8 percent annual interest. Despite that rather onerous anti-defection provision, the court exhibited no qualms about upholding the agreement.

22. Oceanic Exploration Co. v. Grynberg, 428 A.2d 1, 7 (Del.1981),

23. DGCL § 218(a).

Ringling or its progeny. The answer presumably is that the supposed concern lacks merit. After all, if directors favored by a particular group of shareholders keep getting elected at the annual stockholders' meeting, even the densest of investors will eventually figure out that a "combination" has acquired control of the corporation. If we are going to let an individual majority shareholder to control the corporation, as we do, there seems no reason that a group of shareholders should not be allowed to the same through collective action without regard to whether they put their fellow shareholders on notice. If the excluded shareholders feel aggrieved, let them induce one or more of the contracting shareholders to defect or, in appropriate cases, pursue claims for breach of fiduciary duty or dissolution.

Equally curiously, having upheld the agreement, the *Ringling* court failed to provide the obvious remedy. Edith and Aubrey surely intended that, in the event of disagreement, Loos' decision would be binding and the shares voted as he directed. The easiest way for a court to effect that intent would be to order specific performance of the agreement. Many courts have granted specific performance of vote pooling agreements and the MBCA provision validating such agreements expressly authorizes specific performance.[24] In *Ringling*, however, the court apparently felt constrained by the nature of the proceeding. In a review of an election, the court opined, the chancellor may reject votes cast in violation of a vote pooling agreement. As a result, the Haley votes should be rejected and not counted. The effect was that six people were elected—John's three nominees, the two Ringlings, and Dunn. The result seems objectionable on several grounds: It disenfranchised the Haleys. It is almost surely not the outcome the parties intended. It elevates a formalistic concern with the nature of the proceeding over the basic principle of freedom of contract. Specific performance seems clearly preferable.

To be sure, specific performance is a relatively rare remedy in contract law. Yet, investments in close corporations are unique. There is no readily available substitute for the investment, which is typical of contracts for which specific performance is awarded (the classic example being real estate contracts). In addition, damages for breach of a shareholder agreement often would be speculative. How can we monetize the injury Edith suffered from the Haleys' defection?

Before finally endorsing specific performance, however, a word or two needs be said about the relationship of that doctrine to the concept of efficient breach.[25] In some cases, it will be more efficient for a party to

---

24. MBCA § 7.31. For decisions granting specific performance of a vote pooling agreement, see, e.g., Ramos v. Estrada, 10 Cal.Rptr.2d 833 (Cal.App.1992); Weil v. Beresth, 220 A.2d 456 (Conn.1966); Galler v. Galler, 203 N.E.2d 577 (Ill.1964).

25. On the economic analysis of specific performance generally, see Thomas S. Ulen, The Efficiency of Specific Performance: To-

ward a Unified Theory of Contract Remedies, 83 Mich. L. Rev. 341 (1984). For an argument that courts should not grant relief requiring "parties to go on doing business together on terms that are unacceptable to one or more of them," with specific application to vote pooling agreements, see Abram Chayes, Comment, Madame Wagner

breach than to perform—i.e., where the costs of performing exceed the benefits to all parties. Specific performance may seem inconsistent with the principle of efficient breach, because it gives the promisee a right to the promised performance without regard to cost-benefit analysis. Assuming transaction costs are low, however, the Coase theorem predicts that private ordering will result in efficient renegotiation of the contractual obligation. In this sense, specific performance merely has distributional consequences in favor of the party who does not defect. Accordingly, given the equities and the high cost of calculating monetary damages in this setting, the specific performance remedy remains attractive. To be sure, Edith and Aubrey arguably found themselves in a bilateral monopoly, which implies high transaction costs. On the other hand, it is precisely the nature of the bilateral monopoly in question that excludes good market substitutes for the promised performance and thus occasions the need for specific performance rather than money damages or other forms of relief.

B. Private ordering re decisionmaking authority

A vote pooling agreement—even if it ensures that all shareholders are elected to the board—cannot fully protect minority shareholders from oppression by the majority. A majority of the directors has the power to take such actions as ceasing the payment of dividends, refusing to elect minority shareholders as corporate officers,[26] or terminating a minority shareholder's employment with the corporation. Consequently, shareholders frequently adopt agreements restricting director discretion. Such agreements typically provide that all shareholders shall be appointed as officers. They also commonly set out specific requirements as to salary, dividends, pensions, tenure in office, and the like.

Private ordering affecting the directors' powers runs afoul of the foundational principle that the corporation is "managed by or under the direction of a board of directors."[27] This principle is so strongly ensconced in corporate law that courts originally were quite hostile to shareholder agreements purporting to limit the board's powers.

The classic expression of such hostility is the New York Court of Appeals' decision in *McQuade v. Stoneham*.[28] Charles Stoneham was the majority shareholder of the corporation that owned the New York Giants baseball team. He entered into a shareholders agreement with John McGraw, the team's manager, and Francis McQuade, a New York City magistrate. Under the contract, the three agreed to use their best efforts to elect each other directors and appoint each other as officers at specified salaries. McQuade later fell out of favor with Stoneham, who thereupon engineered McQuade's ouster as officer and director.

---

and the Close Corporation, 73 Harv. L. Rev. 1532, 1536 (1960).

26. In a number of states, the articles of incorporation or the bylaws may authorize election of officers by shareholders. A vote pooling agreement with respect to such election should be valid.

27. DGCL § 141(a).

28. 189 N.E. 234 (N.Y.1934).

McQuade sued, seeking specific performance of the agreement. The court agreed with Stoneham that the contract was invalid. Directors must exercise their independent business judgment on behalf of all shareholders. If directors agree in advance to limit that judgment, shareholders do not receive the benefit of their independence, and the agreement is therefore void as against public policy.[29]

McQuade's analysis doubtless seems formalistic, but it finds some support in two basic precepts of corporation law and economics. First, under the nexus of contracts model, shareholders own the residual claim on the corporation but not the corporation itself. If so, by what right do shareholders exercise the ownership-like right of restricting the board's discretion? Second, as we have seen repeatedly, there is a powerful economic rationale for separating ownership of the residual claim from control of the corporation. The separation of ownership and control and the consequent principle of director primacy thus emerge as essential attributes of the corporation, which perhaps should be immune from private ordering by the residual claimants. DGCL § 141(a) arguably embraces such an understanding of the respective shareholder and director roles by providing for director primacy except as "otherwise provided in [the code] or [the corporation's] certificate of incorporation."

On the other hand, the close corporation is closer to being an "incorporated partnership" in substance, if not in form, than a true corporation.[30] As in a partnership, "the investment interests are interwoven with continuous, often daily, interaction among the principals."[31] Put another way, ownership of the residual claim and management are united. To be sure, such union exists de jure in the partnership and only de facto in the close corporation. Moreover, in many settings, it is important to draw clear distinctions between partnerships and close corporations. Yet, some regard for the practicalities of the organizational form seems warranted.[32]

---

29. The court carefully distinguished the agreement before it from vote pooling agreements. "Stockholders may, of course, combine to elect directors. . . . The power to unite is, however, limited to the election of directors and is not extended to contracts whereby limitations are placed on the power of directors to manage the business of the corporation by the selection of agents at defined salaries." Id. at 236.

30. Cf. Meiselman v. Meiselman, 307 S.E.2d 551, 557 (N.C.1983) (observing that "the commentators all appear to agree that '[c]lose corporations are often little more than incorporated partnerships'"); see also Helms v. Duckworth, 249 F.2d 482, 486 n. 6 (D.C.Cir.1957); Donahue v. Rodd Electrotype Co. of New England, Inc., 328 N.E.2d 505, 512 (Mass.1975); Ripin v. Atlantic Mercantile, 98 N.E. 855, 856 (N.Y.1912).

31. Comment, Deadlock and Dissolution in the Close Corporation: Has the Sacred Cow Been Butchered?, 58 Neb. L. Rev. 791, 795 (1979). Or, as the Illinois supreme court opined, the shareholder of a close corporation "often has a large total of his entire capital invested in the business and has no ready market for his shares should he desire to sell. He feels, understandably, that he is more than a mere investor and that his voice should be heard concerning all corporate activity." Galler v. Galler, 203 N.E.2d 577, 584 (Ill.1964).

32. The task thus is to distinguish settings in which shareholders should be allowed to act as owners of the entity from those in which they should be treated as merely owners of the residual claim. The Model Act's drafters struck a sensible enough balance by validating shareholder agreements only with respect to corporations whose shares are not listed from trading on a stock exchange or regularly traded over-the-counter in a market maintained by

Once we decide to treat close corporations as though they were incorporated partnerships, at least for this purpose, the case for freedom of contract becomes quite compelling. Welfare economics contends that market failure is a necessary (but not sufficient) justification for government regulation of private ordering. In turn, welfare economics classically recognizes four basic sources of market failures: producer monopoly; externalities; the good to be produced is a public good; and informational asymmetry between producer and consumer. In this setting, only external effects on third parties loom large as a source of concern. Unlike vote pooling agreements, shareholder agreements restricting the powers of the board work material changes in the organic fiber of the corporation. Hence, only where the agreement adversely affects the interests of shareholders not party thereto, should a court decline to enforce it.[33]

In *Clark v. Dodge*,[34] the New York Court of Appeals revisited this issue, striking a new balance between freedom of contract and constraining externalities. Clark and Dodge jointly owned two drug companies, with Clark owning 25% of the stock and Dodge owning the remaining 75%. Pursuant to a shareholders agreement, they jointly decided whom to elect as directors and officers of the firms. After a falling out, Dodge used his voting control to oust Clark. When Clark sued, Dodge cited *McQuade* for the proposition that the agreement was void. The court rejected Dodge's argument, holding that *McQuade* was intended to protect minority shareholders not party to the agreement. Where the corporation has no minority shareholders, as was the case here, the prohibition is unnecessary. Absent potential harm "to bona fide purchasers of stock or to creditors or to stockholding minorities," i.e. externalities, there was no justification for invalidating the contract even though it "impinges slightly" on the principle of director primacy.[35]

---

a national securities exchange. Whether a corporation's shares are publicly traded seems a reasonable proxy for the extent to which management and ownership are united or separated. MBCA § 7.32(d). Note that, in practice, most corporations will be unable to avail themselves of § 7.32 long before they get big enough to be publicly traded. Under § 7.32(b)(1), such an agreement must be unanimously adopted. Once the number of investors gets into triple (or maybe even double) figures, the unanimity requirement likely will become problematic. In any case, courts have tended to be less precise. In *Galler*, for example, the Illinois supreme court validated shareholder agreements within close corporations, which it defined as firms "in which the stock is held in a few hands or in a few families." Galler v. Galler, 203 N.E.2d 577, 583 (Ill.1964).

33. On the other hand, a vote pooling agreement that gives control of the board to one faction may lead to the same sort of adverse consequences for the minority. Does it matter all that much whether the directors' conduct is limited by a contract or by de facto control?

34. 199 N.E. 641 (N.Y.1936).

35. Id. at 642. See also Adler v. Svingos, 436 N.Y.S.2d 719 (App.Div.1981) (upholding a shareholder agreement effectively giving each shareholder a veto over board decisions); Zion v. Kurtz, 428 N.Y.S.2d 199 (1980) (reaching same result under Delaware law). Agreements that impinge more significantly on the board of directors' powers, however, may still be vulnerable under New York law. See, e.g., Long Park v. Trenton–New Brunswick Theatres Co., 77 N.E.2d 633 (N.Y.1948), in which the court of appeals invalidated a shareholders' agreement purporting to delegate "full authority and power to supervise and direct the operation and management" of the business to one of the shareholders. Distinguishing Clark v. Dodge, 199 N.E. 641 (N.Y. 1936), as involving only "a slight impingement" on the board's powers, the *Long Park* court invalidated the agreement on

Is unanimity required? Conversely, does unanimity suffice? In *Galler v. Galler*,[36] the Illinois supreme court answered both questions in the negative. Benjamin and Isadore Galler ran a wholesale drug company. Benjamin and his wife Emma owned 47.5% of the shares; Isadore and his wife Rose owned 47.5%. An employee named Rosenberg owned the remaining 5 percent. Benjamin and Isadore entered into a shareholders agreement, to which Rosenberg was not a party, pursuant to which: (i) the two families would each have two seats on a four-person board of directors, even if one of the brothers died; (ii) the firm would pay specified dividends, subject to minimum-earned-surplus limitations; and (iii) the firm would pay a specified death benefit to the widow of either brother. After Benjamin died, Emma tried to enforce the agreement. When Isadore and his son Aaron refused to comply, Emma sued. (In July 1961, before the case was tried, Isadore and Rose bought Rosenberg's shares.)

The *Galler* court held that a nonunanimous shareholders agreement could be (specifically) enforced where: (1) the corporation is closely held, (2) the minority shareholder does not object, and (3) the terms are reasonable.[37] On the facts before it, the court deemed the agreement's terms to be reasonable. The duration of the agreement was limited (to the lifetimes of the parties). The company had no obligation to pay dividends if it lacked sufficient earned surplus. Providing a death benefit for surviving spouses of key employees was a legitimate corporate expenditure and the amount payable under the contract was reasonable in amount. Indeed, the stipend for his widow doubtless constituted an important part of Benjamin's compensation. Such a death benefit (called a salary continuation agreement for tax reasons) is akin to so-called "key

---

grounds that it violated the statutory assignment of managerial authority to the board.

36. 203 N.E.2d 577 (Ill.1964).

37. Illinois law now provides two statutory solutions to the *Galler* problem. Section 7.70 of the Illinois Business Corporation Act of 1983, applicable to all corporations except statutory close corporations, generally authorizes voting agreements among shareholders, without any of the limitations inherent in *Galler*. Section 7.71 even more specifically authorizes unanimous shareholder agreements as to matters concerning the management of the corporation, so long as there is no fraud or apparent injury to the public or to creditors. Some claim that Section 7.71 was a legislative compromise intended to codify *Galler*. See Donald R. Tracy & Stephen A. Tsoris, Illinois Close Corporation Law: To Elect or Not to Elect, 80 Ill. B.J. 552 (1992). By negative implication, however, § 7.71(b) goes beyond *Galler* to provide that a shareholder agreement is effective as against a shareholder who is not a party to the contract so long as the shareholder had actual knowledge of the agreement at the time he became a shareholder or the agreement is conspicuously noticed on the certificate of incorporation. The principal limitation on shareholder agreements now contemplated by Illinois law is that only statutory close corporations may properly replace the board of directors with direct shareholder governance (see Illinois Business Corporation Act (§ 8.05(a)), although § 7.71(c) provides that an agreement which improperly attempts to do so shall not be grounds for piercing the corporate veil. There do not appear to be any Illinois decisions attempting to reconcile these statutory provisions with *Galler*. For statutory close corporations (which are reportedly quite rare in Illinois), Illinois Business Corporation Act §§ 2A.40 and 2A.45 also broadly authorize unanimous shareholder agreements relating to the management of the corporation, specifically including both agreements that limit director discretion and ones that provide for direct shareholder management.

man" life insurance. So long as the firm benefits from the executive's services and death benefits help secure those services most cheaply, it is hard to see why such an agreement should not be enforced.

Galler rests explicitly on a conception of the close corporation as a sui generis entity having more in common with a partnership than a public corporation: "the shareholders of a close corporation are often also the directors and officers thereof. With substantial shareholding interests abiding in each member of the board of directors, it is often quite impossible to secure, as in the large public-issue corporation, independent board judgment free from personal motivations concerning corporate policy."[38] In embracing freedom of contract within such firms, *Galler* is consistent with the trend in the law governing unincorporated business organizations. Section 103 of the UPA (1997), for example, provides that the partnership agreement trumps contrary provisions of the partnership statute, subject to certain enumerated exceptions relating mainly to fiduciary duties and rights of third parties. Section 1101(b) of Delaware's Limited Liability Company Act goes even further, expressly adopting freedom of contract as the core policy of the act.

In contrast, the Model Act's provisions on shareholder agreements are significantly less liberal. Under MBCA § 7.32(b), shareholder agreements must be unanimous and (like voting trusts) are limited to 10 years duration. The agreement's existence must be conspicuously noted on the stock certificates, per § 7.32(c), and any purchaser who takes without notice of the agreement is entitled to rescission. Section 7.32(a) enumerates seven specific provisions an agreement may properly include, including restrictions on the discretionary powers of directors, before concluding with a broad catchall for agreements governing "the exercise of the corporate powers or the management of the business affairs of the corporation or the relationship among the shareholders, the directors and the corporation, or among any of them, and is not contrary to public policy." The drafters acknowledge that this creates uncertainty as to the permissible scope of shareholders agreements, but suggest that "in defining the outer limits, courts should consider whether the variation from the Model Act under consideration is similar to the variations permitted by the first seven subsections."[39] As an example of an agreement falling outside § 7.32(a)'s limits, the drafters cite a contract purporting to eliminate the duty of care and/or loyalty.

C. Private ordering re exit rights

The absence of a market out for close corporation shareholders presents a number of difficult business planning issues: Should the shareholders be free to sell to an outsider without the consent of their fellow shareholders? If so, should the other shareholders get a right of first refusal? Under what circumstances and upon what terms or conditions should shareholders be able to liquidate their investment?

---

38. Galler v. Galler, 203 N.E.2d 577, 584 (Ill.1964).

39. MBCA § 7.32 cmt. 1.

1. *Restrictions on transferability*

In general, one of the great advantages of the corporate form is that shares of stock are freely transferable. Any such transfer has no effect or impact on the corporation, except that there is now a new voter of the transferred shares. In contrast, partnership law is far more restrictive. Absent agreement to the contrary, no one can become a partner without the unanimous consent of all other partners.[40] A partner may assign his interest to another party, but the assignee does not become a partner of the firm and has no rights vis-à-vis the firm other than the right to receive whatever income the assignor partner would have been entitled to.[41] For a typical partnership, these rules make sense because the identity of one's fellow partners often matters a great deal. The success or failure of a small business depends largely on the ability of its owners to cooperate.

The role of trust between the parties is an especially important consideration justifying partnership law's restrictions on transferability. Contracts are a useful, but ultimately imperfect, device for minimizing transaction costs. Because of the now familiar triad of uncertainty, complexity, and opportunism, contracts are necessarily incomplete. Because ex ante contracting therefore is an imperfect solution, parties frequently rely on trust as a lubricant to reduce social friction. If I trust you to refrain from opportunistic behavior, I will not invest as many resources in ex ante contracting. If you prove trustworthy, I will not need to incur ex post enforcement costs. Because trust is developed over time through experience, the identity of one's partners matters a lot. Partners likely would not want the composition of the partnership subject to willy-nilly changes. Instead, they will want some control over the make-up of the partnership, which the default rules provide.

Because the close corporation resembles an "incorporated partnership," it seems safe to assume that trust and, accordingly, the identity of one's fellow shareholders likewise matters in that setting.[42] Again, private ordering comes to the rescue. Close corporation shareholders often include restrictions on share transferability in the articles of incorporation or in a shareholder agreement. These restrictions commonly take the form of either a right of first refusal or, more aggressively, an outright prohibition of transfer without the consent of the other shareholders. A right of first refusal is triggered when a shareholder receives an offer from an outsider. The right gives either the corporation and/or the other shareholders an option to purchase the shares on the same terms and conditions offered by the outsider.[43] For example, if Purchaser

---

40. UPA (1914) § 18(g); UPA (1997) § 401(i).

41. UPA (1914) § 25–27; UPA (1997) §§ 502–04.

42. Cf. Donahue v. Rodd Electrotype Co. of New England, Inc., 328 N.E.2d 505, 512 (Mass.1975) ("Just as in a partnership, the relationship among the stockholders must be one of trust, confidence and absolute loyalty if the enterprise is to succeed.").

43. An alternative, sometimes referred to as the right of first option, gives the corporation and/or other shareholders the right to purchase the would be seller's stock on terms and conditions specified in the governing documents.

offers Shareholder $120,000 for the latter's stock, the right of first refusal gives the corporation and/or other shareholders an option to buy the stock for $120,000.

At common law, some courts viewed such restrictions as a restraint on alienation—indeed, some still do so. In *Ogden v. Culpepper*,[44] for example, a Louisiana court opined: "Restrictions on the transfer of corporate stock are to be strictly construed as they unduly restrict the free flow of commerce." In general, however, most courts uphold transferability restrictions so long as they are "reasonable" and the complaining shareholder took the stock with notice of the restriction.[45] Applying this standard, rights of first refusal have been routinely upheld.[46] In contrast, outright prohibitions of transfer absent consent often have been struck down as unreasonable.[47] MBCA § 6.27 authorizes both types of restrictions, with respect to persons on notice of thereof, so long as they are adopted for a reasonable purpose and, with respect to consent requirements, their terms are not manifestly unreasonable.

2. Buyout agreements

The well-drafted shareholders agreement always contains some sort of buyout provision. Such provisions can provide a contractual exit for close corporation shareholders, giving them liquidity, while also ensuring that the remaining shareholders have some control over who owns stock in the corporation. The critical "deal points" are three-fold: What events trigger a buyout? Does the buyout create a put (giving the shareholder the right to force a sale), a call (giving the corporation the right to mandate a sale), or both? How are the shares to be valued?

A right of first refusal is a commonly used solution to these problems. Typically, the would-be seller is obliged notify the corporation and/or his fellow shareholders of the terms of the proposed sale. Some rights of first refusal allow the corporation and/or its shareholders to purchase the would-be seller's stock at book value.[48] Book value is likely

44. 474 So.2d 1346, 1350 (La.App.1985).

45. See, e.g., Allen v. Biltmore Tissue Corp., 161 N.Y.S.2d 418, 422 (1957).

46. See, e.g., Groves v. Prickett, 420 F.2d 1119 (9th Cir.1970); Allen v. Biltmore Tissue Corp., 161 N.Y.S.2d 418, 422 (1957); In re Estate of Spaziani, 480 N.Y.S.2d 854 (N.Y.Surrogate Ct.1984); In re Mather's Estate, 189 A.2d 586 (Pa.1963); Bruns v. Rennebohm Drug Stores, Inc., 442 N.W.2d 591 (Wis.App.1989). On the other hand, some courts still hold that rights of first refusal are to be strictly construed. See, e.g., Frandsen v. Jensen–Sundquist Agency, Inc., 802 F.2d 941, 946 (7th Cir.1986). In Winter v. Skoglund, 404 N.W.2d 786 (Minn.1987), for example, the court invalidated a right of first refusal on grounds that it had not been signed by all shareholders.

47. Compare Hill v. Warner, Berman & Spitz, P.A., 484 A.2d 344, 351 (N.J.App.Div. 1984) (invalid); Rafe v. Hindin, 288 N.Y.S.2d 662, 665 (App.Div.1968) (same) with Colbert v. Hennessey, 217 N.E.2d 914, 920 (Mass.1966) (valid).

48. Note that a repurchase of shares by the corporation will be subject to the relevant legal capital statute of the state of incorporation. The well-drafted buyout agreement therefore typically allows the nonselling shareholders to buy the stock in question, in case the corporation lacks sufficient surplus to effect the purchase. See Van Kampen v. Detroit Bank & Trust Co., 199 N.W.2d 470 (Mich.App.1972) (holding that the board of directors acted properly in refusing to buyback shares when the corporation's capital was impaired, even though doing so violated shareholder buyout agreement).

to be far less than fair market value, of course, given its focus on historical cost and disregard of going concern values. Because book value thus is almost certain to be much lower than the price an otherwise willing buyer likely would pay, such a provision deters outsiders from bidding. Why should an outsider invest time and effort in making a deal when the other shareholders can almost certainly under-bid the outsider's offer? As a result, such provisions substantially limit shareholder liquidity.[49] (Of course, as we saw in the preceding section, restrictions on liquidity are often desirable in small businesses where the identity of one's co-venturers is important.)

A seemingly more transfer-friendly pricing provision requires the corporation and/or other shareholders to purchase the would-be seller's stock at the same price offered by the prospective purchaser. One key advantage of such a provision is that it, in effect, creates a market price for the shares, which allows one to avoid messy valuation questions. The price an outsider is willing to pay, however, likely will reflect both a marketability and minority discount. In addition, the outsider still must invest time and resources in deciding what to pay. This is a sunk cost. The right of first refusal means that the outsider likely won't get the shares, however, so the outsider will be unwilling to invest significant sunk costs in accurately pricing the shares. In turn, this means that the outsider will further discount the price for uncertainty. Accordingly, relying on a right of first refusal to create a "market" price is likely to result in a value much lower than the shares' fair value. Finally, such a provision does not fully resolve the liquidity problem, as a shareholder can only get out by finding a willing buyer.

Identifying the transactions that trigger the right of first refusal is a critical drafting issue. Judge Richard Posner's decision in *Frandsen v. Jensen–Sundquist Agency, Inc.*[50] nicely illustrates the key issues. The Jensen family owned 52 percent of the Jensen–Sundquist Agency, Inc. (JSA), which in turn owned a majority of the shares of the First Bank of Grantsburg (FBG). Dennis Frandsen owned 8 percent of JSA. The parties' shareholders agreement contained a right of first refusal pursuant to which the Jensen family was obliged to offer their shares to Frandsen before selling to an outsider. If Frandsen exercised the right of first refusal, he was obliged to pay the same price as that offered by the prospective purchaser. If Frandsen did not exercise his right of first refusal, however, the Jensen family was obliged to offer to buy Frandsen's stock at that price. This is a so-called "take-me-along" or "equal sharing" provision.

First Wisconsin Corp. wanted to buy FBG. If First Wisconsin had directly bought the FBG shares from JSA, no problems would have

49. Note that there is no legally "correct" pricing term. Setting the buyout price is a matter of business discretion for the client. See Nichols Construction Corp. v. St. Clair, 708 F.Supp. 768, 771 (M.D.La.1989), aff'd mem., 898 F.2d 150 (5th Cir.1990) (holding that "the mere failure to pay 'fair value' for stock under a stock redemption agreement" does not amount "to fraud or breach of fiduciary duty"); see also Palmer v. Chamberlin, 191 F.2d 532 (5th Cir.1951).

50. 802 F.2d 941 (7th Cir.1986).

arisen. The right of first refusal only applied to a sale of the Jensen's family's JSA stock, not to a sale of FBG stock by JSA. For reasons that remain unclear, however, the parties initially structured as a merger in which all of the JSA shareholders would be bought out for cash. Frandsen objected, claiming the merger triggered the right of first refusal and that he was therefore entitled to purchase the Jensen family's JSA shares. The Jensen family and First Wisconsin thereupon restructured the deal so that First Wisconsin would buy the FBG stock directly from JSA. The issue presented was whether the court should construe the right of first refusal clause as being triggered by a merger in which all shareholders would participate. (Although the merger would give Frandsen cash for his shares, he apparently preferred owning FGB to being cashed out.) Judge Posner held that the right of first refusal was not triggered. The clause stated that if the Jensen family "at any time [should] offer to sell their stock" in JSA, they had to give Frandsen a right of first refusal. Because a merger has different legal implications than a sale of stock, and because an experienced businessman like Frandsen should have recognized that distinction and protected himself, the court declined to give the term "offer to sell" an expansive construction encompassing a merger. (Note the similarity to de facto merger doctrine, in that the court is elevating form over substance.[51]) Other courts have likewise tended to give rights of first refusal fairly narrow constructions,[52] thereby putting a premium on careful ex ante negotiation and drafting.

An alternative to the right of first refusal as a solution to the problem of setting the price at which the buyout is to occur is illustrated by the agreement at issue in *Helms v. Duckworth*.[53] The agreement included a buyout provision applicable when one of the two shareholders died. The buyout clause provided: "The price which the surviving

---

51. In Seven Springs Farm, Inc. v. Croker, 748 A.2d 740 (Pa.Super.2000), for example, the Pennsylvania court held that a buyout provision in a shareholders agreement did not apply to a cash-out merger. The court found that the merger was structured so as to avoid triggering a right of first refusal contained in the buyout agreement, but the court thought that fact irrelevant to the task of interpreting the contract. The court interpreted the agreement as being limited to acts of a shareholder, such as a sale of stock to a third party, while a merger was deemed a corporate act. In thus elevating form over substance, the court opined: "formalities are crucial in corporate law.... It has been said of corporate law that it is not so much what is done, but how it is done." Id. at 749. See also Frandsen v. Jensen–Sundquist Agency, Inc., 802 F.2d 941 (7th Cir.1986), in which Posner explained that corporate law "is an area of law where formalities are important, as they are the method by which sophisticated businessmen make their contractual rights definite and limit the authority of the courts to redo their deal." Id. at 947.

52. See, e.g., Engel v. Teleprompter Corp., 703 F.2d 127 (5th Cir.1983) (under Texas law the merger of subject corporation's wholly owned subsidiary with corporate majority shareholder was not a sale, transfer, assignment, or other disposition of stock of subject corporation within meaning of the right of first refusal); Louisiana Weekly Pub. Co., Inc. v. First Nat'l Bank of Commerce, 483 So.2d 929 (La.1986) (right of first refusal restricting sales of stock not triggered by a gift of stock); Helfand v. Cohen, 487 N.Y.S.2d 836 (App.Div.1985) (right of first refusal limiting sales of stock was not triggered by sale of corporation's sole asset); In re Estate of Spaziani, 480 N.Y.S.2d 854 (Surr.1984) (right of first refusal limiting sales of stock was not triggered by bequest of shares).

53. 249 F.2d 482 (D.C.Cir.1957).

stockholder shall pay for the stock of the deceased stockholder shall be at the rate of $10.00 per share; provided, however, that such sale and purchase price may, from time to time, be re-determined and changed in the following manner: During the month of January in any year while this agreement remains in force, the parties of the first and second part shall have the right to increase or decrease the sale and purchase price by an instrument in writing. . . ." What happens if one of the parties refuses to bargain in good faith, as in fact did happen in *Helms v. Duckworth*? Defendant Duckworth's lawyer made a serious tactical error in allowing Duckworth to sign an affidavit stating that the price had never been renegotiated and, worse yet, that Duckworth never intended to allow a change in the initial price. In light of that testimony, the court declined to enforce the buyout agreement. The court held that Duckworth had a fiduciary duty to bargain in good faith. Duckworth's secret intent not to bargain violated that duty.

It is unclear what a duty to bargain in good faith means in this context. Did Duckworth have a duty to raise the issue, even if the other shareholder did not? A better basis for the result thus is the court's alternative holding that Duckworth had a duty at the time the contract was signed to disclose his intention to refuse to allow an increase in the buyout price. His failure to disclose that intention constituted fraud, which created an independent and sufficient basis for holding the contract unenforceable.

A third approach simply establishes a valuation formula in the buyout agreement. The agreement might provide, for example, that the corporation should be valued at some contractually specified multiple of earnings. Buyout agreements taking this tack tend to use relatively unsophisticated valuation techniques. One rarely sees close corporation buyout agreements using discounted cash flow valuation, for example. In part, this may be attributable to a lack of sophistication on the part of the drafting attorney. Even if the lawyer understands valuation, the clients may not have the financial sophistication necessary to understand the document or to later apply it. Even relatively simple valuation formulas, such as capitalized earnings, moreover, can require forecasts of uncertain future events and lots of subjective judgments. (What multiple shall we select? Will that multiple still be relevant 20 years from now? How do we measure earnings? etc.) One either gets very high ex ante bargaining costs or lots of ex post disputes or both. As in most drafting matters, the lawyer must strike a balance between accuracy and certainty, which arguably ought to tip in favor of certainty.

The need for certainty and predictability may also explain why one rarely sees valuation provisions that require hiring an appraiser. The value appraisers or arbitrators put on the company will depend in large part on the methodology used by the appraiser, which means the drafter either needs to select an appraiser in advance or face grave uncertainty.

A final issue with respect to buyout agreements is the extent to which courts will apply them in settings not contemplated by the agreement. In *In re Pace Photographers, Ltd.*,[54] for example, the parties' shareholder agreement contained a right of first refusal under which sales of stock made during the first five years would be priced at a steep discount to fair value. Three years into the deal one shareholder had a falling out with his fellows and brought an action for involuntary dissolution. Invoking a New York statute under which the corporation could elect to buyout the complaining shareholder's stock in lieu of dissolution, the other shareholders contended that the valuation set by the shareholder agreement should control. Acknowledging that shareholders in theory could contractually set a price to be applied in an involuntary dissolution proceeding, the court held that such an agreement needed to do so explicitly. A valuation provision applicable on its face solely to voluntary sales thus did not control judicial valuation in a dissolution proceeding.

§ 14.3 Fiduciary duties in close corporations

At early common law, shareholders as such owed no fiduciary duties to the corporation or to other shareholders. Consequently, when acting in their capacity as shareholders, the shareholders were free to vote or otherwise to act in their own self interest. We have already observed some erosion of this doctrine in the context of a majority shareholder of a public corporation. *Sinclair Oil*, for example, prohibits controlling shareholders from benefiting themselves at the expense of the minority in connection with ordinary business decisions.[1]

A similar erosion of the common law rule has occurred in the close corporation context. Indeed, the concept of shareholder fiduciary duties is most highly developed in closely held corporations. This is not surprising when one considers the superficial similarities between the close corporation and partnership forms of organization. Recall Judge Cardozo's opinion in *Meinhard*,[2] which exemplifies the strong fiduciary duty concepts courts have created in the partnership setting.

A. The (in)famous Massachusetts line of cases

1. *The fiduciary duties of majority shareholders*

Massachusetts has been by far the leader in imposing partnership type fiduciary duties on close corporation shareholders, so our discussion will initially focus on a series of cases decided by its courts. The series began with *Donahue v. Rodd Electrotype*.[3] Harry Rodd, the controlling shareholder of the eponymous Rodd Electrotype corporation, wished to retire. Harry gave some his stock to his sons and daughter. One of his sons, Charles Rodd, was then elected as president of the corporation.

---

54. 530 N.Y.S.2d 67 (1988).

§ 14.3

1. Sinclair Oil Corp. v. Levien, 280 A.2d 717 (Del.1971).

2. Meinhard v. Salmon, 164 N.E. 545 (N.Y.1928).

3. Donahue v. Rodd Electrotype Co. of New England, Inc., 328 N.E.2d 505 (Mass. 1975).

Harry then negotiated with Charles, who acted on behalf of the firm, an agreement whereby the corporation would purchase the remainder of Harry's stock. Donahue, a minority shareholder, objected. Donahue requested that the corporation redeem his shares on the same terms as those given Harry, a request the firm refused. Donahue sued, claiming the firm's refusal to accord him an equal right to sell his shares constituted a breach of the controlling group's fiduciary duties (the group now being composed mainly of Harry's children).

In *Donahue*, the Massachusetts supreme judicial court began by describing the close corporation as an incorporated partnership. In the court's view, the shareholders adopted the corporate form to obtain, among other advantages, tax benefits and limited liability. But while its form may be corporate, in substance the firm remains a partnership. Accordingly, the court opined that shareholders of a close corporation owe one another the same fiduciary duties as partners owe to one another. More specifically, the court adopted Judge Cardozo's *Meinhard* formulation, holding that shareholders of a close corporation must deal with one another with the "utmost good faith and loyalty." On the facts before it, the court concluded that the purchase of Harry's shares, coupled with the refusal to buy Donahue's shares, constituted a breach of this duty because it gave Harry—but only Harry—a market for his shares. The court thus held that the majority could not use its control of the firm to, in effect, create a market for their shares, without extending the same opportunity to the minority.[4]

---

4. In Jones v. H.F. Ahmanson & Co., 460 P.2d 464 (Cal.1969), the California supreme court, per Chief Justice Traynor, likewise limited the ability of controlling shareholders to create a market for their shares without providing comparable liquidity for the minority. The United Savings and Loan Association of California was a closely held financial institution. The defendants owned about 85 percent of United's shares. Defendants wished to create a public market for their shares, a task that could have been accomplished using any of several methods, most of which would have created a market for all shareholders' stock. Instead of adopting any of those options, however, the defendants set up a holding company, to which they transferred their shares. The holding company then conducted a public offering of its stock, which created a secondary trading market for that stock. The 15 percent of United's stock that was not owned by the holding company was thus left without a viable secondary market. The California supreme court held that when no active trading market for the corporation's shares exists, the controlling shareholders may not use their power over the corporation to promote a marketing scheme that benefits themselves alone to the exclusion and detriment of the minori-

ty. It once seemed likely that *Ahmanson* would become an important precedent, perhaps precluding a wide range of transactions including sales of control blocks at a premium. At least outside California, that has not happened. See Nixon v. Blackwell, 626 A.2d 1366 (Del.1993); Toner v. Baltimore Envelope Co., 498 A.2d 642 (Md. 1985); Delahoussaye v. Newhard, 785 S.W.2d 609 (Mo.App.1990). Even in California, there seems to be something of a trend towards limiting *Ahmanson* to its unique facts and procedural posture. See, e.g., Miles, Inc. v. Scripps Clinic and Research Foundation, 810 F.Supp. 1091 (S.D.Cal. 1993) ("The *Jones* case did give the narrow circumstance in which a fiduciary duty may be imposed: when a majority shareholder usurps a corporate opportunity from or otherwise harms the minority shareholder."); Kirschner Bros. Oil, Inc. v. Natomas Co., 229 Cal.Rptr. 899 (Cal.App.1986) (noting that *Ahmanson*'s sweeping dicta must be "carefully related" to the facts before a violation can be found; hence, plaintiffs must explain with "specificity what they . . . might have been entitled to that they did not receive"). If *Ahmanson* is to remain on the books, a debatable proposition, it should be so limited. The case was decided

In reaching that result, *Donahue* used language so broad as to imply that the majority must always subordinate their interests to those of the minority. Arguably, a relatively strong set of fiduciary duties is justified in the close corporation setting, because of the risk that the majority shareholder will use its control to oppress the minority shareholder. Even so, it is far from clear that one should go as far as the court did in *Donahue*. In *Wilkes v. Springside Nursing Home*,[5] the Massachusetts supreme judicial court in fact reconsidered and retrenched. Plaintiff Wilkes, one of four shareholders in a close corporation, had been a director and salaried officer of the corporation. Relations between Wilkes and the other shareholders deteriorated to the point that Wilkes gave notice of intent to sell his shares. Wilkes was then stripped of his salary and offices.

The Massachusetts supreme judicial court held that the denial of employment constituted a freezing out of the minority shareholder. Indeed, Wilkes lost both the return on his labor and on his investment in the nursing home. The former he could recoup by finding another job, but the latter he would lose entirely unless the firm repurchased his stock or began paying dividends.

Under *Donahue*, this is an easy case. If the majority must always subordinate its interests to those of the minority, the actions of the majority shareholders in *Wilkes* clearly breached that duty. But while the court did not disavow *Donahue*, it did tweak—and limit—the rule substantially. According to *Wilkes,* there must be a balance between the fiduciary duty of the majority and its right to selfish ownership, which gives the controlling group "some room to maneuver" in setting policy. In most cases, the majority will have made a larger investment, by which it effectively purchased the right to control. Hence, the majority should have a greater voice in setting corporate policy.[6] In addition, the minority shareholders presumably knew a controlling block existed when they bought into the firm. The minority shareholders therefore assumed the risk that some decisions would be adverse to their interests.

Wilkes held that the controlling group must first demonstrate some legitimate business purpose for its action. If such a showing is made, the

---

on appeal from the trial court's grant of a motion to dismiss. Interpreting the facts most favorably for the plaintiffs, the defendants went out of their way to deprive the minority shareholders of a market for their shares, reduced the dividend in order to deprive the minority shareholders of any economic return, at least in the short run, and displayed their true objective by offering a low price for the minority shares. In short, this is just a run of the mill squeeze-out case. Unfortunately, there is much broader dicta in the opinion—and it is that dicta for which the case is frequently cited.

5. Wilkes v. Springside Nursing Home, Inc., 353 N.E.2d 657 (Mass.1976).

6. *Wilkes* does not offer controlling shareholders of close corporations anywhere near the level of protection the business judgment rule gives to directors and controlling shareholders of public corporations, however. The initial burden of proof is on the controlling shareholders and, even if they meet that burden, the court will go on to compare their action against alternatives they might have selected. On the other hand, the *Wilkes* formulation does not give minority shareholders as much protection as partners receive under cases like *Meinhard*.

burden then shifts to the minority shareholder to show that the legitimate purpose could have been achieved through an alternative less harmful to the minority's interest. The court must then attempt to balance the legitimate business purpose against the practicability of the proposed less harmful alternative.[7]

A legitimate business purpose could have been shown on the facts of this case if Wilkes had been negligent in failing to perform his duties or in failing to perform them with due care. Wilkes, however, had been competent and remained willing to perform his tasks. Instead, the shareholders for personal reasons had forced Wilkes out by denying him any return on his investment and then offering to buy his shares at a price they admitted they would not accept.[8]

7. See also Zimmerman v. Bogoff, 524 N.E.2d 849, 853 (Mass.1988) (noting that "the *Donahue* remedy is not intended to place a strait jacket on legitimate corporate activity"). A number of other jurisdictions have adopted *Wilkes*, with varying degrees of fidelity. See, e.g., Hollis v. Hill, 232 F.3d 460 (5th Cir.2000) (interpreting Nevada law); W & W Equip. Co. v. Mink, 568 N.E.2d 564, 570 (Ind.App.1991); Daniels v. Thomas, Dean & Hoskins, Inc., 804 P.2d 359, 366 (Mont.1990); Crosby v. Beam, 548 N.E.2d 217, 220 (Ohio 1989); Duncan v. Lichtenberger, 671 S.W.2d 948 (Tex.App. 1984); Masinter v. WEBCO Co., 262 S.E.2d 433 (W.Va.1980); see also Long v. Atlantic PBS, Inc., 681 A.2d 249, 256 n. 8 (R.I.1996) (dicta). In Nelson v. Martin, 958 S.W.2d 643 (Tenn.1997), the Tennessee supreme court approvingly cited *Wilkes* but then substantially abrogated the force of that doctrine by further holding that if the defendants "were protecting the interests of the corporation, the presence of spite or ill will would not render them or the corporation liable." Id. at 650. "The burden was on [plaintiff] Nelson to produce evidence that they were not acting in good faith in furtherance of the corporation's best interest." Id.

8. The existence of a low-ball buyout offer did not assume any particular significance in *Wilkes*. To the contrary, the court expressly referred not only to conduct by which the majority freezes out the minority, but also more generally to conduct by which the majority oppresses or otherwise disadvantages the minority. Wilkes v. Springside Nursing Home, Inc., 353 N.E.2d 657, 662 (Mass.1976). In contrast, a subsequent federal decision applying Massachusetts law in a diversity case, Sugarman v. Sugarman, 797 F.2d 3 (1st Cir.1986), raised the existence of such a low-ball offer to an essential element of the claim. Three Sugarman brothers, Joseph, Samuel, and Myer formed the Statler Corp. By the time of the dispute at bar, Leonard Sugarman, son of Myer,

owned 61 percent of the shares. Samuel's shares had passed to his three grandchildren, Jon, James, and Marjorie Sugarman, who together owned another 21.8 percent. Marjorie wanted to work for the firm but Leonard would not hire her; Jon once worked for the firm but Leonard fired him. The company did not pay dividends. Leonard offered to buy Jon's and Marjorie's stock at a "grossly inadequate" price. Jon, James, and Marjorie sued, raising various claims, of which the most pertinent for our purposes is their allegation that Leonard had attempted a freeze-out in violation of *Wilkes*. The court agreed. Yet, it is difficult to figure out what Leonard did wrong. Absent some shareholder or employment agreement, a minority shareholder has no right to a job with the firm. Likewise, a minority shareholder has no legal entitlement to dividends, which are vested in the discretion of the board. Instead, "the minority shareholder must first establish that the majority shareholder employed various devices to ensure that the minority shareholder is frozen out of any financial benefits from the corporation through such means as the receipt of dividends or employment, and that the offer to buy stock at a low price is the 'capstone of the majority plan' to freeze-out the minority." Id. at 8 (quoting Donahue v. Rodd Electrotype Co. of New England, Inc., 328 N.E.2d 505 (Mass. 1975)). Accordingly, the key fact seems to be the attempt to buy out the minority at a low price, which implies Leonard would have escaped liability if he had refrained from making an offer to buy their shares. This result, of course, is nonsensical. If the majority makes a below-market offer, it at least offers the plaintiff something. A controlling shareholder more ruthless (or more cunning) than Leonard could instead have forced the minority shareholders to hang on to shares that have become close to worthless. It is hard to see why a plaintiff should

Wilkes is subject to criticism from a variety of perspectives. On the facts at bar, the parties had an agreement—or, at least, an oral understanding—pursuant to which all were to be directors and salaried officers. Accordingly, this case could have been decided as a simple breach of contract.[9] It is not at all clear why fiduciary duty concepts even come into the picture.

Assuming the relevance of fiduciary obligation, should partnership-like fiduciary duties be imposed in the close corporation setting? On the one hand, the court rightly notes that close corporations operate much like partnerships, and face the same practical constraints. If so, why is there any difference in the duties? Neither partners nor shareholders in closely held corporations have a ready market for their investments.[10] If partners need stringent legal protection, so too do shareholders; if shareholders need managerial flexibility, so too do partners.

On the other hand, while the partnership analogy is a useful one, we should not overstate it. Investors are heterogeneous and the best approach may be to offer them standard form contracts—off the rack rules—that provide significant choice.[11] Corporate and partnership law differs in many respects. Courts will maximize investor welfare by letting investors choose the form best suited to their business. If investor choice is a virtue, in other words, Massachusetts' decision to harmonize close corporation and partnership law was wrongheaded. A better ap-

---

have a better claim when the defendant makes a low-ball offer than when the defendant makes no offer at all.

9. Likewise, in A.W. Chesterton Co., Inc. v. Chesterton, 951 F.Supp. 291 (D.Mass.), aff'd, 128 F.3d 1 (1st Cir.1997), the court enjoined a transfer of shares of a closely held corporation where the transfer would have terminated a subchapter S tax election. The defendant, whose proposed transfer was at issue, had played a key role in the adoption of the election and was well aware of the adverse tax effects of termination. The court stated that when the shareholders approved the S election (unanimously, as required by subchapter S), they "demonstrated a general agreement they would do nothing that would adversely affect the Company's S status." There was no express agreement to that effect, however, and the Articles did grant the shareholders the right to transfer their shares, subject to a right of first refusal for any sale outside the Chesterton family. Probably the key fact in the case was that the defendant proposed to transfer his shares to his wholly owned, newly formed shell corporations and had no good reason for doing this. So it was clear that his proposed transfer was a straw man transaction intended to force the company to buy him out. But the company lacked the cash to do this. In finding for the company, the court relied on *Donahue*,

Wilkes, and *Atlantic Properties*: "By unanimously electing S status, the shareholders agreed that they would not act in any way that would cause the Company to lose the considerable benefits of S status. This agreement was memorialized by the signed consent forms executed by each shareholder, as well as the subsequent yearly tax returns." On appeal Chesterton argued that the district court had "resurrected a contract claim that the plaintiffs voluntarily dismissed." The appellate court rejected this argument, stating that in context the statements of the district court relate to "the expectations and understanding of the shareholders [which are] relevant to a breach of fiduciary duty determination." So the courts once again turned a weak contract claim into a breach of fiduciary obligation claim and bailed out investors who were the victims of bad lawyering (in this case the failure to back up the S election with an adequate restriction on transfer of shares).

10. Note that the power of partners to dissolve at will partnerships gives them somewhat greater de jure liquidity than is possessed by shareholders of a close corporation.

11. See Frank H. Easterbrook and Daniel R. Fischel, Close Corporations and Agency Costs, 38 Stan. L. Rev. 271 (1986).

proach would be to retain a real choice by not imposing higher fiduciary duties on close corporation shareholders. To be sure, in the past, some investors probably preferred partnership rules but felt it necessary to incorporate so as to get the benefit of limited liability. These days, such investors can form a limited liability company, which combines a more-or-less partnership-like governance structure with limited liability.[12] Accordingly, the case for maintaining a clear distinction between partnership and corporate law has become even stronger.

2.   *The fiduciary duties of minority shareholders*

Ownership of voting stock is not the only basis on which control may rest. In the close corporation, a shareholder agreement may give minority shareholders considerable power. A Massachusetts appellate court evaluated the implications of *Donahue* and *Wilkes* for such a situation in *Smith v. Atlantic Properties*.[13] Four shareholders bought equal amounts of stock in a real estate venture. A supermajority provision was included in both the articles of incorporation and bylaws, under which no corporate action could be taken without the approval of 80% of the outstanding shares. As such, each shareholder could effectively veto any proposed corporate action. Shareholder Wolfson used his veto power to prevent the corporation from paying dividends. Wolfson claimed he wanted to spend the firm's earnings on maintaining and improving the firm's property, but the other shareholders were unwilling to do so. In fact, Wolfson's reluctance to permit dividends most likely arose out of tax considerations. In the years at issue, the maximum marginal individual tax rate was 90 percent (1954–1963) or 70 percent (after 1963) but the maximum capital gain rate was 25 percent. Wolfson apparently was a high bracket taxpayer, so that payment of dividends would leave him little after taxes. If Atlantic Properties retained its profits, increasing the value of the shares, however, the increased value could be realized by selling the shares and the resulting gain would be taxed at the much lower capital gains rate.

Because the firm was unable to pay dividends over Wolfson's veto, however, another tax issue arose. The accumulated earnings tax penalizes corporations that accumulate excess earnings that are neither paid out to shareholders nor otherwise spent. Due to the deadlock between Wolfson and the other shareholders, the firm was unable either to spend its earnings on improvements or to pay them out as dividends. As a result, the firm eventually incurred the accumulated earnings tax penalty. The other shareholders sued, alleging that Wolfson's use of his veto power constituted a breach of fiduciary duty. The Massachusetts court agreed, holding that minority shareholders, at least where they have a veto power over corporate action, are subject to the same fiduciary duties as those imposed by *Donahue* and *Wilkes*. On the facts before it, the court held that Wolfson's use of his veto power violated those duties

12.   See § 14.5.

13.   Smith v. Atlantic Properties, Inc., 422 N.E.2d 798 (Mass.App.1981).

because it subjected the corporation to an unnecessary assessment of penalty taxes.

The basic proposition—that a veto power vested in the majority shareholders should be subject to fiduciary analysis—seems unobjectionable.[14] On the facts, however, it is inapt. Wolfson no more caused the firm to incur the accumulated earnings tax than did the other three shareholders. To be sure, Atlantic could have avoided the tax by paying dividends, but it could just as well have avoided that tax by reinvesting the money in the firm's real estate. The court implied that Wolfson opposed the dividends because he was in a higher tax bracket than the others. But so what? It was just as selfish for the others to vote for dividends because they were in a lower bracket. In this instance, each of the four shareholders rationally voted his individual self-interest. It was because each side refused to compromise that the firm was liable for the tax penalty. The *Wilkes* line of cases simply has no application where the issue is deadlock, which was the case here.

B. Delaware law

In *Nixon v. Blackwell*,[15] the Delaware supreme court faced a very common close corporation problem. The founder of a closely held business died, leaving behind a messy estate. Control of the corporation passed to a group of loyal employees, who received all of the voting stock. The founder's family received nonvoting stock, which left them with a significant equity stake in the business but without any control rights. The employee block tried to buyout the family block, which rejected the offer as too low. The corporation paid modest dividends, leaving the minority with virtually no economic return on their shares. Meanwhile, the controlling group of employees adopted an ESOP and took out so-called key man life insurance policies on themselves. Under such policies, in the event one of the shareholders dies, the proceeds go to the corporation, which then uses the proceeds to buy the shares from the dead employee's estate.

The minority sued, alleging a breach of the controlling group's fiduciary duties. The Delaware supreme court used this opportunity to expressly reject any special fiduciary duties applicable only to close corporations. The decision does not leave the minority shareholders without a remedy, however. The court noted that standard corporate law fiduciary duty principles constrain the conduct of both directors and controlling shareholders. Because the ESOP and key man life insurance

---

14. Some cases suggest that minority control through a veto provision may not be necessary to impose fiduciary obligations on the minority. See, e.g., A.W. Chesterton Company, Inc. v. Chesterton, 951 F.Supp. 291 (D.Mass.), aff'd, 128 F.3d 1 (1st Cir. 1997) (holding that a minority shareholder's proposed sale of his shares to other corporations, which would terminate the corporation's favorable tax status as subchapter S corporation, would constitute a breach of fiduciary duty); see also Zimmerman v. Bogoff, 524 N.E.2d 849 (Mass.1988) (holding that "fiduciary obligations may arise regardless of percentage of share ownership").

15. 626 A.2d 1366 (Del.1993).

policies entailed conflicted interest transactions, they were to be reviewed under the entire fairness standard applicable to duty of loyalty claims. On the facts before it, the court deemed that test to be satisfied. ESOPs and key man insurance policies are a normal corporate benefit, but in this case they also were a reasonable way of pursuing the founder's intent that the business continue as an employee-controlled corporation.

The court made something of a production out of its rejection of special fiduciary duties for close corporations. But does it matter? Under *Wilkes*, the majority could have shown a legitimate business purpose for what it did. ESOPs and key man insurance policies provide important benefits to the corporation. How could the minority have shown a less restrictive way of accomplishing these purposes? Unless we read *Wilkes* to say that the minority has a right to liquidity, plaintiffs probably would have lost even under *Wilkes*.

As a practical matter, it thus is not clear that the Delaware and Massachusetts approaches are all that dissimilar. These cases typically involve situations in which the majority has benefited itself at the minority's expense. In almost all such cases, the majority shareholders are also directors or control the directors. Given the absence of a disinterested decisionmaker and the presence of the majority on both sides of the transaction, Delaware courts would apply the entire fairness standard to most of the cases litigated under the Massachusetts standard. Accordingly, while the doctrine differs, the results may not.

C. Private ordering of fiduciary obligation

Partnership and corporate law each provide standard form contracts, whose terms differ in many significant ways. One can debate the extent to which the close corporation is a hybrid of the two and, if so, the extent to which such corporations should be subject to default terms closer to those of partnership law than to corporate law. What is not debatable is that one size does not fit all. Rules that work well for some investors will prove a straightjacket for others. The contractarian model contends, of course, that corporate law should consist mostly of defaults that the parties are free to modify as they see fit. Modern partnership law explicitly embraces this freedom of contract approach. UPA (1997) § 103(b)(3), for example, provides that a partnership agreement may not eliminate the duty of loyalty, but may "identify specific types or categories of activities that do not violate the duty of loyalty, if not manifestly unreasonable," or specify a mechanism for approving or ratifying transactions that "otherwise would violate the duty of loyalty." Do we stretch the partnership analogy too far when we urge that corporate law do likewise?

Suppose a businessman hired a key employee and, as part of the employment bargain, caused the corporation to issue stock to that newly hired employee. At the time of hiring, they also enter into a shareholder agreement under which if the employee should "cease to be an employee of the Corporation for any reason," the controlling shareholder has the right to buy the new employee's shares at a specified price. After several years, the controlling shareholder brings his two sons into the business and fires the employee. The businessman then claims his firing of the employee triggered the buyout provision of the shareholder agreement. The employee asserts that, as a shareholder, he has a "fiduciary-rooted protection against being fired." Does the contract trump the fiduciary duties of a controlling shareholder?

On these precise facts, the New York court of appeals, in *Ingle v. Glamore Motor Sales,* expressly rejected the Massachusetts approach: "No duty of loyalty and good faith akin to that between partners, precluding termination except for cause, arises among those operating a business in the corporate form who 'have only the rights, duties and obligations of stockholders' and not those of partners."[16] Despite his shareholder status, Ingle was still an employee-at-will with no contractual guarantee of continued employment. When he was fired, he ceased to be an employee, and the divestiture of his shares followed as a logical matter by virtue of the shareholders agreement.

Because the court enforced the buyout provision, *Ingle* arguably stands for the proposition that you can contract around fiduciary duties.[17] Admittedly, *Ingle*'s facts differ from those of *Wilkes* in several respects. In *Wilkes* all the shareholders started out together and formed a new business, while in *Ingle* Glamore was the original owner who brought in Ingle as an employee. Put another way, employment followed from stockownership in *Wilkes*, while stockownership followed from employment in *Ingle*. The partnership analogy thus works a lot better for *Wilkes* than it does for *Ingle*. Yet, courts have not tried to make this sort of fine distinction. Distinguishing close from public corporations can be tricky enough, without adding further refinements to the mix.

Private ordering has also been validated in Massachusetts, albeit less emphatically. On the one hand, *Donahue* itself suggested that fiduciary obligation would not stand in the way of an otherwise valid shareholder agreement providing for, inter alia, a stock repurchase plan.[18] In *Blank v. Chelmsford Ob/Gyn*, the court interpreted this aspect of *Donahue* as standing for the proposition that "questions of good faith and loyalty with respect to rights on termination or stock purchase do not arise when all the stockholders in advance enter into agreements concerning termination of employment and for the purchase of stock of a withdrawing or deceased stockholder."[19] Accordingly, the plaintiff, a

16. Ingle v. Glamore Motor Sales, Inc., 535 N.E.2d 1311 (N.Y.1989).

17. In Gallagher v. Lambert, 549 N.Y.S.2d 945 (1989), the New York court of appeals even more explicitly embraced that proposition. Observing that shareholder "agreements define the scope of the relevant fiduciary duty and supply certainty of

obligation to each side," the court further opined that such agreements "should not be undone simply upon an allegation of unfairness." Id. at 947.

18. Donahue v. Rodd Electrotype Co., 328 N.E.2d 505, 518 n. 24 (Mass.1975).

19. Blank v. Chelmsford Ob/Gyn, P.C., 649 N.E.2d 1102, 1105 (Mass.1995). Simi-

minority shareholder of an incorporated medical practice, who was terminated in accordance with the terms of an employment agreement and whose shares were redeemed under the terms of a stock repurchase agreement, had no remedy. On the other hand, the Massachusetts courts also have held that the existence of an employment agreement or otherwise valid shareholder agreement does not divest shareholders of the *Donahue*-based fiduciary duty they owe to one another.[20] The precise degree to which parties have freedom of contract in Massachusetts thus remains somewhat uncertain. Both clarity and efficiency would be promoted if Massachusetts courts clearly held that contract trumps fiduciary obligation.

§ 14.4   Dissolution

As we have seen, close corporations entail significant agency costs, especially the risk of oppression of minority interests by majority shareholders. One way in which corporate law has sought to limit agency costs in this context is through imposition of fiduciary duties going well beyond those imposed in the public corporation context. This method, however, is far from satisfactory as a general solution to the problem. In the first instance, fiduciary duty cases necessarily involve relatively high costs of judicial enforcement. More importantly, it often may be very difficult to construct a remedy for breach of fiduciary duty. To what compensation is someone entitled when they are squeezed out of employment with the close corporation?

As an alternative to suit for breach of fiduciary duty, the disgruntled minority shareholder may seek judicial dissolution of the corporation.[1]

larly, in Merola v. Exergen Corp., 668 N.E.2d 351 (Mass.1996), the court denied a remedy to a 4.1 percent shareholder who allegedly had been terminated because of a personal conflict with the majority shareholder rather than for any legitimate corporate purpose. The court explained: "Not every discharge of an at-will employee of a close corporation who happens to own stock in the corporation gives rise to a successful breach of fiduciary duty claim. The plaintiff was terminated in accordance with his employment contract and fairly compensated for his stock." Id. at 355. See also Vakil v. Anesthesiology Assoc., Inc., 744 N.E.2d 651, 655 (Mass.App.2001) (holding that "[w]here there was no evidence that the plaintiff's compensation or employment was conditioned on his ownership of stock in the corporation or that the majority stockholders acted out of a desire to increase their financial gain in the corporation, the majority stockholders' termination of the plaintiff's employment and repurchase of his stock in accordance with the agreements into which the plaintiff had freely entered did not constitute a breach of fiduciary duty"); Evangelista v. Holland, 537 N.E.2d

589 (Mass.App.1989) (enforcing buyout provision of shareholder agreement even though the actual value of the stock was far higher than the price set in the agreement); Olsen v. Seifert, 1998 WL 1181710 at *5 n. 5 (Mass.Super.1998) ("The Delaware court's concern that duties owed to shareholders or to shareholder employees should not be implied so as to override express contractual provisions has a corollary in a *Donahue/Wilkes* analysis under Massachusetts law."); cf. In re Wet–Jet Int'l, Inc., 235 Bankr. 142, 149–50 (Bankr.D.Mass. 1999) (contending that Massachusetts courts draw a distinction "between disputes arising from actions relating to the subject matter of a shareholder agreement, and those stemming from shareholder dealings in matters outside of the agreement").

20. See, e.g., King v. Driscoll, 638 N.E.2d 488 (Mass.1994).

§ 14.4

1. Various other grounds for dissolution are created by statute. A corporation that has not issued shares or commenced business may be dissolved by the incorporators

All states have provisions under which a shareholder may seek an involuntary dissolution of the corporation.[2] If granted, dissolution leads to a winding up and liquidation of the firm, followed by a distribution of the firm's remaining assets to creditors and then to shareholders.

MBCA § 14.40 is typical of these statutes. It provides four grounds upon which a court may dissolve the corporation at a shareholder's request: (1) Deadlock among the directors. The directors must be evenly divided and therefore unable to make corporate decisions. The shareholders must be unable to resolve the deadlock. The deadlock must threaten irreparable injury to the corporation or prevent the business of the corporation from being conducted to the advantage of the shareholders. Director deadlock seemingly will not justify a dissolution where the firm is still making a profit—it goes to situations in which the deadlock is preventing the firm from functioning at all. (2) Waste of corporate assets. (3) Deadlock among the shareholders. The shareholders must be evenly divided and, because of their division, unable to elect a board of directors for a period covering at least two annual meeting dates. (4) Dissolution is authorized where the directors or controlling shareholders have acted in a manner that is illegal, oppressive or fraudulent. The fourth basis has provided the most fertile ground for creative lawyering.

Interpreting the comparable New York statute, the New York Court of Appeals defined oppression as conduct that substantially defeats a minority shareholder's reasonable expectations.[3] Reasonable expectations, in turn, are those that objectively viewed were reasonable under the circumstances, known (or should have been known) to the majority, and were central to the petitioner's decision to join the venture. Oppression thus is something more than mere disappointment, it must mean that the very reasons for participating have been defeated.

or initial board of directors by filing articles of dissolution with the secretary of state. MBCA § 14.01. The board and shareholders may approve a voluntary dissolution. MBCA § 14.02. The secretary of state may commence an involuntary dissolution proceeding if the corporation, for example, fails to pay its franchise taxes. MBCA § 14.20. In this section, we focus solely on judicial proceedings for involuntary dissolution initiated by a shareholder.

2. In most states dissolution is a matter of statute—there is no common law cause of action for dissolution of the firm. A few states, like New York, preserve a dissolution remedy available in equity. According to In re Kemp & Beatley, Inc., 473 N.E.2d 1173 (N.Y.1984), an equitable decree of dissolution is still available in New York when the directors have committed a palpable breach of the fiduciary duty for which there is no adequate remedy in law, such as a shareholder derivative suit for damages.

3. In re Kemp & Beatley, Inc., 473 N.E.2d 1173 (N.Y.1984). Similarly, in interpreting a North Carolina statute authorizing dissolution where it is "reasonably necessary" for the protection of the "rights or interests" of the complaining shareholder, the North Carolina supreme court held that those rights and interests include the "reasonable expectations" the complaining shareholder has in the corporation. "Only expectations embodied in understandings, express or implied, among the participants should be recognized by the court." Meiselman v. Meiselman, 307 S.E.2d 551, 563 (N.C.1983). But see Kiriakides v. Atlas Food Sys. & Serv., Inc., 541 S.E.2d 257, 264–66 (S.C.2001) (rejecting *Meiselman's* reasonable expectation approach in favor of an "elastic" and "fact-specific" approach to defining oppression). For a critique of the reasonable expectations approach on grounds that it is "based on false premises, invites fraud, and is an unnecessary invasion of the rights of the majority," see J.C. Bruno, "Reasonable Expectations"—A Primer on an Oppressive Standard, 71 Mich. B.J. 434 (1992).

On the facts before it in *Kemp*, the court concluded that the minority had in fact been oppressed. The firm had a long-standing policy of awarding de facto dividends in the form of bonuses based on stock ownership. This practice was a known incident of stock ownership. If you owned stock, you participated in firm management and were paid salary and profits in the form of bonuses. This policy was changed after the minority shareholders left the firm, so that bonuses were dependent on services rendered to the corporation. This change in policy was deemed an attempt to exclude the minority shareholders from gaining any return on their investment. Note the parallel to the fiduciary duty analysis in cases like *Wilkes v. Springside Nursing Home*.[4] Although *Wilkes* and *Kemp* involved different remedies, they shared an analytical assumption that shareholders of a close corporation can reasonably expect to receive a return on their investment in the form of salary, bonuses, and retirement benefits. By denying these benefits, the majority defeated those reasonable expectations and opened itself to suit.

Dissolution is an extreme remedy. Many firms will be worth more as going concerns than if they were split up and sold off in pieces. This fact counsels against granting dissolution, which would lower the value of the firm to everyone—both the complaining shareholder and the defendants. In recognition of that fact, MBCA § 14.34 grants the noncomplaining shareholders the right to buyout the complaining shareholders in lieu of dissolution. If the parties are unable to agree on a price, the court will determine the fair value of the shares.[5] The share repurchase option effectively creates a market out for the complaining shareholders by coercing the majority into buying the minority's shares, while also preserving the going concern value of the firm.

In *Alaska Plastics v. Coppock*, the Alaska supreme court concluded that judges have equitable discretion to order a stock buyback in lieu of dissolution even in the absence of express statutory authorization.[6] Three investors originally owned Alaska Plastics, but one transferred half of his shares (or a 1/6 interest in the firm) to his ex-wife (Muir) in a divorce settlement. The three original owners paid themselves directors' fees, but paid no dividends. Muir eventually sued, alleging various causes of action. The lower court ordered Alaska Plastics to buy Muir's shares at their fair value.

The supreme court reversed and remanded. Alaska corporate law permits shareholders to sue for dissolution and, if a plaintiff meets the requirements for dissolution, Alaska courts have equitable power to order such a buyback in lieu of dissolution. To obtain a decree of

4. 353 N.E.2d 657 (Mass.1976).

5. See, e.g., Brown v. Allied Corrugated Box Co., 154 Cal.Rptr. 170 (Cal.App.1979); In re Gift Pax, Inc., 475 N.Y.S.2d 324 (Sup. Ct.1984), aff'd, 486 N.Y.S.2d 272 (App.Div. 1985); Charland v. Country View Golf Club, Inc., 588 A.2d 609 (R.I.1991).

6. Alaska Plastics, Inc. v. Coppock, 621 P.2d 270 (Alaska 1980). Other courts have concluded that they have equitable power to order an even broader range of alternative remedies, such as compelling the board to declare dividends. See, e.g., In re Kemp & Beatley, Inc., 473 N.E.2d 1173 (N.Y.1984); Baker v. Commercial Body Builders, Inc., 507 P.2d 387 (Or.1973).

dissolution in the first place, however, the plaintiff-shareholder must show oppression or fraud. Because the lower court made no finding of oppression, the supreme court sent the case back for further proceedings.

On remand, Muir prevailed, which seems surprising. To be sure, the directors arguably breached their fiduciary duties to Muir by paying themselves fees, while denying any return to Muir.[7] Her ex-husband, Crowe, moreover, only owned one-sixth of the shares, but received the same "dividend" as the other majority shareholders, who each owned one-third. The majority, moreover, offered her an unacceptable price for her shares. The majority also failed to notify Muir of shareholder meetings. But does all that amount to oppression? What reasonable expectations of Muir, known to and accepted by the majority, had been substantially frustrated? Muir could have sued derivatively to recover the fees improperly paid the majority. Alternatively, she could have sued directly for her share of the de facto dividends. She could have sued her divorce lawyer for getting her into this mess in the first place. It is hard to see how she was oppressed, however, at least under the reasonable expectations standard.

The best way to solve a freeze-out is to avoid it from the start, by negotiating a buyout agreement with the majority shareholders or the corporation. Not all shareholders are so farsighted, however, and when shareholders have negotiated no such agreement, freeze-outs become even less tractable than usual. In such cases, the parties may use corporate dissolution statutes as low-budget alternatives to the buyout agreements they should have negotiated but did not. All of which leads to the interesting question of whether it was appropriate for the Alaska supreme court to create a buyback remedy when the statute didn't provide one?

Serious questions of institutional competence are raised when court engage in interstitial lawmaking of the sort exemplified by Alaska Plastics, but those issues lie far outside our field of inquiry. Instead, our attention must turn to more pragmatic matters. One could argue, for example, that a buyout order is unnecessary given the practical effect of a decree of dissolution. Where dissolution would destroy the firm's going-concern value, the majority likely will prefer to prevent dissolution. The dissolution remedy thus has the virtue of forcing the majority to bargain with the frozen-in minority. Indeed, one would expect the majority to offer to buy the minority's stock—and, according to the leading empirical study, that is exactly what happens.[8]

---

7. Embracing the Massachusetts approach as set out in Donahue v. Rodd Electrotype Co., 328 N.E.2d 505 (Mass.1975), the Alaska supreme court indicated that the payment of directors fees and other benefits to the shareholders other than Muir violated her right to "equal treatment." If the other shareholders received disguised dividends (e.g., directors' fees), Muir should receive them as well. Because the other shareholders did not have the right to sell their stock to the firm, however, equal treatment does not require the firm to buy Muir's stock. Alaska Plastics, Inc. v. Coppock, 621 P.2d 270, 276–77 (Alaska 1980).

8. J.A.C. Hetherington & Michael P. Dooley, Illiquidity and Exploitation: A Proposed Statutory Solution to the Remaining

One might also object to *Alaska Plastics* on the ground that ordering a buyout in lieu of dissolution really is no less drastic than dissolution. The virtue of such an order is that it settles the dispute quickly and forever. Yet, it also has draconian result. By virtue of arguably minor transgressions, the majority was forced to buy out Muir.

A third objection is that liberal dissolution rights allow minority shareholders to hold up the firm or the other shareholders. Because few firms ordinarily hold large amounts of liquid assets, the threat of filing a dissolution proceeding is often powerful. In effect, liberal dissolution coupled with a buyout order in lieu of dissolution gives a powerful gun for minority shareholders to hold to the head of the majority. There is some substantial risk that the minority will use that power to extract a nonpro rata share of corporate benefits.

The latter objection to *Alaska Plastics* leads to the broader question of whether courts and legislatures should create an even more liberal dissolution regime than currently exists, thereby allowing minority shareholders even greater freedom to dissolve the firm over the majority's opposition.[9] A recurrent theme of this text is that firms are essentially contractual in nature. A key insight flowing from our contractarian approach, which we have seen on many occasions, is that the corporation statutes are analogous to off the rack rules or, put another way, standard form contracts that the parties are largely free to adopt or modify as they see fit. As with any standard form contract, corporate statutes thus serve to reduce bargaining costs.

A key corollary of contractarian theory is that courts should avoid interpreting the corporation statute in ways that make it more closely resemble the partnership statute and vice-versa. Preserving clear-cut choices between the various standard form contracts by preserving sharply delineated differences between their rules usually should lower bargaining costs. Partnership law provides very liberal dissolution rights.[10] A liberal approach to dissolution is appropriate for the typical partnership—a small firm in which all of the owners have roughly equal economic stakes and are actively involved in firm management on a more or less equal basis. Personal conflict will be highly disruptive to such a firm. At the very least, such conflict adversely affects decision-making by interfering with the consensus-building process. At worst, it can have devastating economic consequences, as when the conflict becomes public and drives away customers (as happens all too frequently, especially in service businesses). Consequently, rational partners will prefer liquidity to stability. In hypothetical bargain terminology, liberal

---

Close Corporation Problem, 63 Va. L. Rev. 1 (1977).

9. See, e.g., Meiselman v. Meiselman, 307 S.E.2d 551, 560 (N.C.1983) (noting a "trend toward enactment of more liberal grounds under which dissolution will be granted to a complaining shareholder").

10. Indeed, unless the parties have expressly or implicitly agreed on a definite term for the enterprise, partnerships exist "at will" and may be dissolved without cause at any time. See, e.g., Page v. Page, 359 P.2d 41 (Cal.1961).

dissolution rules will emerge as the majoritarian default because they create de facto liquidity.

In contrast, corporation law is designed for large firms with many owners. Corporation law rests on an assumption that ownership is separated from control and, moreover, that ownership will be essentially passive. Interpersonal relations between the firm's owners are thus irrelevant to the economic viability of the firm, which is a key factor distinguishing the corporation from the partnership, and a strong argument against allowing shareholders to force a dissolution of the corporation. We therefore expect that corporation law would make dissolution considerably more difficult than does partnership law. Consistent with that prediction, MBCA § 14.30 leaves shareholders of a public corporation essentially powerless to dissolve it.

The standard form contracts thus seem well-designed for the firms for which they were designed. But what about the hybrid close corporation? Is this an instance in which we ought to treat the close corporation as an "incorporated partnership" and therefore provide liberal partnership-like dissolution rights? Like partners, investors in close corporations may prefer liquidity to stability, but the standard form contract gives them stability rather than liquidity.

There are at least three reasons to reject the argument for liberal dissolution rights, two of which have already been noted. First, liberal dissolution rights allow the minority to hold up the majority and, as such, may frustrate the majority's reasonable expectations. Second, parties who want liberal dissolution rights may bargain for them by insisting on an appropriate buyout agreement before investing. As to close corporations, the default rules of corporate law operate as a penalty default encouraging parties to bargain, while preserving the desirable distinction between partnership and corporation law.

The remaining reason for denying liberal partnership-like dissolution rights in the close corporation context is that such rights will create a significant negative externality. An important function of organization law is to provide affirmative asset partitioning, which refers to the principle that creditors of the firm have prior access to firm assets vis-à-vis both the firm's equity investors and the personal creditors of such investors.[11] Affirmative asset partitioning thus allows the firm to create a pool of assets that serves as a bond for all the firm's contracts. Protecting the firm's going concern value is another significant benefit of affirmative asset partitioning. Creditors of a corporation (close or public) make lending decisions mainly on financial factors such as net assets and cash flows. By virtue of affirmative asset partitioning, creditors of a corporation need not be concerned with such other considerations as the interpersonal relations among equity investors.[12] Under a regime of

---

11. Henry Hansmann & Reinier Kraakman, The Essential Role of Organization Law, 110 Yale L.J. 387 (2000).

12. Without this protection, the creditors of a bankrupt minority shareholder could force the inefficient liquidation of a firm in order recoup the value of the minor-

liberal dissolution rights, however, creditors of the corporation may find the corporation dissolving unexpectedly due to a relatively trivial falling out among the equity investors. Liberal dissolution rights thus undercut the benefits of affirmative asset partitioning, disadvantaging creditors of the corporation, requiring them to monitor factors as to which they lack a comparative advantage, increasing creditor costs, and thus raising the cost of capital.

§ 14.5   The limited liability company alternative

One of the most important ways in which transactional lawyers can create value for their clients is by helping them choose appropriate organizational structures for their businesses. In considering the problems that arise in this area, the nexus of contracts model again proves most useful. Recall that we can think of the statutes governing different types of business organizations as standard form contracts. When two or more persons enter into a business relationship, they are undertaking an inherently contractual act. They must specify a host of rules to govern their relationship: what are their respective rights and duties, powers and obligations. If the parties choose to structure their relationship as a particular type of business organization, much of this work will already have been accomplished. The statute provides a sort of standardized contract, which lowers bargaining and other transaction costs by providing a set of default rules the parties can adopt off-the-rack. At the same time, because most statutory rules in this area are merely default rules, it is possible to modify the standard form contract when and as necessary to more closely tailor the firm to the clients' needs.

Until recently, the only important standard form contracts provided by most states were the corporation and the general partnership. During the 1990s, however, most states have added a third standard form contract to this short list of options: the limited liability company (LLC).[1] To be sure, LLCs have been around for a couple of decades. Prior to 1988, however, only a few states had adopted LLC statutes and very few had been formed. In that year, the situation changed dramatically because the Internal Revenue Service concluded that LLCs could be classified as a partnership for federal tax purposes.[2] With that development, the concept took off. LLCs provide a standard form contract that incorporates many of the most attractive features of partnerships and

ity shareholder's ownership in the firm. With the protection provided by affirmative asset partitioning, however, creditors are only able to claim the same rights as the minority shareholder held pre-bankruptcy.

§ 14.5

1. See generally William J. Carney, Limited Liability Companies: Origins and Antecedents, 66 U. Colo. L. Rev. 855 (1995); Wayne M. Gazur, The Limited Liability Company Experiment: Unlimited Flexibility, Uncertain Role, 58 Law and Contemp. Probs. 135 (1995); Robert R. Keatinge et al., The Limited Liability Company: A Study of the Emerging Entity, 47 Bus. Law. 375 (1992); Larry E. Ribstein, The New Choice of Entity for Entrepreneurs, 26 Cap. U. L. Rev. 325 (1997); Larry E. Ribstein, The Emergence of the Limited Liability Company, 51 Bus. Law. 1 (1995).

2. Rev. Rul. 88–76, 1988–2 Cum. Bull. 360. See generally William A. Klein & Eric Zolt, Business Form, Limited Liability, and Tax Regimes: Lurching Toward a Coherent Outcome?, 66 U. Colo. L. Rev. 1001 (1995).

corporations. In particular, they combine the latter's limited liability with the former's pass through tax treatment.

A. What is a LLC?

The LLC is an unincorporated business organization that can provide its members with pass through tax treatment, limited liability, and the ability to actively participate in firm management.[3] Because it is thus a unique entity, differing in important ways from other types of business organizations, it is important to avoid thinking of the LLC as, for example, a partnership with limited liability.[4] Doing so is likely to lead to analytical errors. The LLC is sui generis and should be treated as such.

B. Choice of form

In choosing an appropriate business structure for one's clients, there are four factors traditionally considered: taxation; transferability of ownership interests; flexibility of organizational structure; and liability.[5]

1. Taxation

Structuring a business relationship as a corporation potentially opens the owners to the risk of double taxation. If a corporation is profitable, and the owners wish to pay a dividend, taxes will be paid both

---

3. Some early LLC statutes required that, like a general partnership, a LLC had to have two or more members. More recent statutes, however, permit single member LLCs. See, e.g., ULLCA § 202(a).

4. Despite the many similarities between LLCs and general partnerships, it is not quite accurate to think of LLCs as general partnerships with limited liability tacked on. Such things do exist elsewhere, however. A growing number of states have now adopted a Limited Liability Partnership (LLP) statute. Unlike the traditional limited partnership, a LLP is a true general partnership in all respects, except that the partners can obtain the benefit of limited liability by filing a certificate of organization with the state. Most LLP statutes provide limited liability only for partnership debts arising from negligence and similar misconduct (other than misconduct for which the partner is directly responsible), not for contractual obligations, although a few provide protection for both contract and tort liabilities. The principal impetus for the enactment of the first LLP legislation, in Texas in 1991, was the concern of lawyers for malpractice liability, following the collapse of the savings and loan industry and the potentially devastating effect of the collapse of one such institution on a

leading Dallas law firm. See Robert W. Hamilton, Registered Limited Liability Partnerships: Present at the Birth (Nearly), 66 U. Colo. L. Rev. 1065, 1069 (1995). Hamilton observes that "more than 1,200 law firms, including virtually all of the state's largest firms, elected to become LLPs within one year after ... enactment" of the Texas LLP statute. Id. at 1065. In other states having a LLP statute and professional rules that allow attorneys and accountants to organize in limited liability firms, the LLP likewise appears to becoming the preferred organizational structure for professional firms.

5. Other factors worthy of consideration, but omitted here are the flexibility of capital structure, duration, and the consequences of dissolution of the business. Finally, one should also be aware of the still unresolved issue of whether LLC membership interests are securities for purposes of state and/or federal law. For an overview of the relevant issues, see Mark A. Sargent, Are Limited Liability Company Interests Securities?, 19 Pepperdine L. Rev. 1069 (1992). See also Great Lakes Chem. Corp. v. Monsanto Co., 96 F.Supp.2d 376 (D.Del. 2000) (detailed treatment concluding that LLC interests in case at bar were not securities).

by the corporation and the shareholders. From the corporation's perspective, the dividends are not deductible because they are regarded as being paid from after-tax profits. From the shareholder's perspective, the dividends are regarded as ordinary income and are taxed as such.

In contrast, partnerships and LLCs usually are not treated as taxable entities. Initially, the IRS determined the tax status of LLCs under the so-called Kintner regulations, which specified six factors in determining whether an unincorporated association should be taxed as though it were a corporation: (1) associates; (2) a business purpose; (3) continuity of life; (4) centralization of management; (5) limited liability; and (6) free transferability of ownership. Because all partnerships and most LLCs (excepting only single owner firms) meet the first two requirements, they could be disregarded.[6] If the entity in question met more than two of the remaining criteria, it would be treated as a corporation for tax purposes.[7] So-called "bullet proof" LLC statutes contained mandatory rules designed to ensure that the LLC would meet the Kitner regulations.

In 1996, the IRS adopted so-called "check the box" regulations that allow the LLC's members to elect between corporate and partnership tax treatment. Because the check the box regulations allow greater organizational flexibility, recent LLC statutes have tended towards default rules that the parties are free to modify as they see fit.

Assuming the LLC's members elect to be taxed as though they were a partnership, the LLC merely files an informational return, reporting any gain or loss. If the firm is profitable, its gains are "passed through" to the owners as ordinary income. At first blush, these pass through entities appear to be attractive choices because they allow one to eliminate the double taxation of corporate profits. At least insofar as income tax is concerned,[8] however, it is easy to overstate the importance of tax treatment in choosing a business structure. Many small businesses can readily qualify for treatment as a S corporation, which is taxed on a pass through basis. To be sure, S corporation status carries with it various restrictions that may make it inappropriate in some cases. If the corporation could not meet those restrictions and thus could not qualify as a S corporation, however, there are a variety of well-established methods by

---

6. Under the Kintner regulations, it was important that the transaction planner structure the entity so as to avoid at least two of the other three characteristics that distinguish partnerships from corporations for tax purposes; namely, free transferability of ownership, continuity of life, and centralized management. In general, it was fairly easy to impose necessary restrictions on transferability of ownership in the LLC context. If continuity of life was desired, one therefore had to provide sufficiently decentralized management to ensure that the entity will qualify for pass through tax treatment. Usually it was fairly easy to

minimize the impact of the continuity of life factor, however, thereby allowing for centralization of management. Under the check the box regulations, these concerns are no longer salient.

7. See generally Treas. Reg. § 301–7701–2.

8. Income tax is not the only relevant issue. One should also consider filing fees and franchise taxes, to which even S corporations are subject. In many cases, however, these will be de minimis.

which closely held corporations can reduce the impact of double taxation to a de minimis level, such as paying substantial salary and bonuses.

2. *Transferability of ownership interests*

One of the great advantages of the public corporation as an investment vehicle is the free transferability of shares. In contrast, an ownership interest in a partnership is essentially nontransferable. In this respect, the LLC more closely resembles the partnership. Admission of a new member requires unanimous consent, unless the operating agreement provides to the contrary. The assignee of an ownership interest receives only an entitlement to the assignor's share of profits.

The degree to which ownership interests are freely transferable, however, rarely will be dispositive of the choice of form issue. Although shares of stock in a closely held corporation are freely transferable in theory, the lack of a readily available secondary trading market for such shares means that in practice they are seldom easily transferable. Moreover, investors in a closely held corporation will often prefer to restrict transferability. Like any other personal relationship, the success or failure of a small business often depends upon maintaining a rather delicate balance between the owners. Free transferability of ownership interests can threaten that balance. In closely held corporations, accordingly, the standard form contract is often modified in ways that make it closely resemble partnerships or LLCs.

Conversely, the partnership and LLC rules are merely default rules. In both cases, the rules restricting transferability are subject to any contrary agreement the founders wish to make. If your clients want free transferability, you can thus provide it within the partnership or LLC context, subject of course to tax considerations and the practical limitations imposed by the absence of a secondary trading market.[9]

3. *Flexibility of organizational structure*

As we have repeatedly observed, the decisionmaking processes of business enterprises fall on a spectrum between two poles that might be labeled consensus and authority. In small business firms, those who own the firm usually also are the firm's decisionmakers. Their decisionmaking processes tend to be based on consensus, lacking formality or hierarchy. This is possible because there is a limited number of owner-managers who share the same basic goal and have more or less the same level of information about the firm. Equality of information ensures that each partner can correctly determine the course of action that best advances his interests; commonality of interest ensures that the partners usually will agree on the course of action to be pursued.

---

9. In setting up a partnership or closely held corporation, the transaction planner should normally ask the client to consider an appropriate buyout agreement. Unlike its corporate and partnership counterparts, the LLC statute includes a default buyout provision pursuant to which a member who resigns is entitled to the fair value of his interest in the firm. See, e.g., ULLCA §§ 701–02.

As firms become larger, however, consensus becomes increasingly impractical. By the time we reach the public corporation, it becomes essentially impossible. At the most basic level, the sheer mechanics of achieving consensus amongst thousands of decisionmakers preclude an active role for shareholders. Yet, even if those mechanical obstacles could be overcome, active shareholder participation in corporate decisionmaking would still be precluded by the shareholders' widely divergent interests and distinctly different levels of information. The decisionmaking processes of large corporation are thus based on authority models. Formality and hierarchy are the orders of the day.

This economic reality is reflected in the default rules provided by the various statutes. State law allows one to choose between off-the-rack governance systems ranging from an almost purely consensus-based model to an almost purely authority-based model. At one extreme, the default decisionmaking structure provided by partnership law is a consensus model. Partners have equal rights to participate in management of the firm on a one-vote per partner basis. This rule makes sense for most small businesses because all partners are also entitled to share equally in profits and losses, giving them essentially identical interests (namely higher profits), and are entitled to equal access to information, giving them essentially identical levels of information.

At the other extreme, a publicly held corporation's decisionmaking structure is principally an authority-based one. As a practical matter, most public corporations are marked by a separation of ownership and control. Shareholders, who are said to "own" the firm, have virtually no power to control either its day-to-day operation or its long-term policies. Instead, as we saw in Chapter 5, the statutory model contemplates that the vast majority of corporate decisions shall be made by the board of directors (or their subordinates) acting alone. The default corporate decisionmaking model thus is one in which the board acts and shareholders, at most, react. This statutory framework is given teeth by the rules governing corporate limited liability. Under state corporate law, failure to comply with corporate formalities of this sort is one of the factors to be considered when a creditor seeks to pierce the corporate veil.

Both the corporation and partnership statutes provide substantial flexibility to vary from the default rules provided by statute. Under partnership law, the statutory one-partner/one-vote model is subject to "*any*" contrary agreement amongst the partners.[10] A general partnership thus can have any decisionmaking structure upon which its members are able to reach agreement. This flexibility is particularly valuable for mid-sized firms, in which formal corporate-like decisionmaking remains inappropriate but some degree of centralized decisionmaking is nevertheless desirable. Similarly, under many corporation statutes, a shareholder agreement may treat the corporation as though it were a partnership for this purpose.

---

10. UPA § 18 (1914) (emphasis supplied).

The LLC statute provides similar flexibility. The default rule is comparable to the general partnership form, vesting management in the LLC's members, except that the number of votes cast by each member is determined by his proportional share in the book value of the membership interests.[11] In general, both of these rules are subject to any contrary provisions of the articles of organization and operating agreement. The LLC thus provides substantial flexibility in structuring the firm's decisionmaking processes. If desired, for example, one could establish a virtual dictatorship. If the articles of organization so provide, the members may elect a manager who shall have such authority and responsibility as the members may delegate in the operating agreement or articles of organization.[12] Unless specifically retained by them therein, the members thereby lose control over areas delegated to the manager. Alternatively, because one can have multiple managers, it is be possible to operate by committee or even to set up a corporate-like board of managers. Unfortunately, however, the flexibility provided by the LLC statute is achieved at the cost of specificity. If the LLC's decisionmaking structure is to vary from the standard form contract, detailed contractual provisions are thus essential if later disputes are to be avoided.

4. *Limited liability*

In a general partnership, the partners are personally liable to creditors of the firm in the event that the firm's assets are insufficient to satisfy the creditor's claim. In contrast, shareholders of a corporation are not personally liable to the firm's creditors. A shareholder of a corporation thus puts at risk only the funds invested in purchasing shares, while a partner puts at risk his entire estate. Seemingly, this makes the corporation a far more attractive choice than the partnership. On closer examination, however, the differences are more apparent than real. On the one hand, corporate limited liability often will be unavailing. Many contract creditors, for example, will insist that shareholders of a closely held corporation guarantee the firm's loans and other obligations. In addition, the common law doctrine of veil piercing enables courts to impose personal liability on shareholders in appropriate cases. On the other hand, adequate levels of insurance can provide partners with substantial protection despite their nominally unlimited liability.

The adoption of the LLC does not disturb this equation. Under the LLC statute, members of a LLC—like shareholders of a corporation—are not personally liable for the firm's obligations.[13] Some LLC statutes, however, invite courts to extend the corporate veil piercing rules to the LLC context. Similarly, contract creditors frequently insist on personal guarantees from LLC members.

5. *Summary*

One of the great advantages of thinking of business firms in a contractual sense is that one quickly realizes that the standard form

---

11. ULLCA § 404.

12. ULLCA § 404.

13. ULLCA § 303.

contracts provided by statute almost always can be manipulated into a result that meets the client's needs. From this perspective, the LLC offers little that was not already achievable under the existing corporation and partnership statutes. To be sure, the LLC combines pass-through taxation with limited liability, thereby achieving two of the transaction planner's key goals, but such a structure could be created under the prior statutes.

Having said that, the LLC statute nevertheless can play a useful role in transaction planning. While we could provide clients with pass through taxation, relatively informal decisionmaking, restricted membership, and limited liability, we could do so only by substantially modifying the default rules governing corporate operation. From the client's perspective, extensive modifications of the default statutory rules are always problematic. Acceptable modifications must be bargained out, which is costly and may result in disagreements that prevent the relationship from ever getting off the ground. Agreed-upon modifications must be spelled out in detail to reduce the risk of future disagreements and, even if this is done, disputes over the parties' intent may nevertheless arise. By providing a set of default rules meeting these four criteria, the LLC statutes allow many small business relationships to adopt the statutory rules "off-the-rack."

C. Veil piercing in the LLC context

Recall that corporate law insulates shareholders from personal liability. Under the doctrine of limited liability, shareholders of a corporation generally are not liable for debts incurred or torts committed by the firm. Shareholder losses when the firm faces financial difficulties are limited to the amount the shareholder has invested in the firm—the amount initially paid by the shareholder to purchase his stock.

As we have seen, LLCs similarly provide limited liability for their members. ULLCA § 303 provides, for example, that "the debts, obligations, and liabilities of a limited liability company, whether arising in contract, tort, or otherwise, are solely the debts, obligations, and liabilities of the company. A member or manager is not personally liable for a debt, obligation, or liability of the company solely by reason of being or acting as a member or manager."

Query whether corporate law's veil piercing rules also carry over to the LLC context? In some cases, that question is resolved (affirmatively) by statute. Minnesota's LLC statute provides, for example, that "case law that states the conditions and circumstances under which the corporate veil of a corporation may be pierced under Minnesota law also applies to limited liability companies."[14] Absent such a statute mandating the use of corporate veil piercing precedents in determining the personal liability of members of a LLC, however, should a court import the corporate law doctrine into the LLC arena? Given the availability of

---

14. Minn. Stat. § 322B.303(2) (1996).

corporate law doctrines as a ready-made body of law close at hand, doing so has proven an irresistible impulse for some courts.[15]

As a normative matter, however, courts ought to refrain from extending the veil piercing doctrine to the LLC context. In the first instance, it depends on what one thinks the legislature intended. If one defines the null hypothesis to be incorporation of corporate law doctrine into LLC and LLP law, one can point out that there is no legislative evidence to the contrary. Suppose, however, we define the null hypothesis to be that the legislatures intended for LLC and LLP law to be distinct and independent from corporate law. If that is the null hypothesis, the burden is on those who favor incorporating the corporate veil piercing doctrine to find evidence that the legislature intended to do so. One could make a good argument for the latter, in which case courts should not look to the corporate law model. If the legislature intended to incorporate the corporate law doctrines, they easily could have done so explicitly—as Minnesota did. Indeed, given the availability of such models, one could argue that subsequently adopted statutes were not intended to incorporate corporate law rules in the absence of explicit Minnesota-like language.

An additional reason for treating LLCs differently than corporations is suggested by the nexus of contracts theory of the firm. Recall that the contractarian model views statutes governing business organizations as a set of off the rack default rules. One advantage to having multiple forms of business organizations is that parties can select the set of rules that most closely tracks their needs and, accordingly, reduces their bargaining costs. Put another way, because investors are heterogeneous the best approach may be to offer them a significant choice. Courts may maximize investor welfare by letting investors choose the form best suited to their business, and different legal rules for LLCs and corporations would do just that.

Finally, the LLC context gives us an opportunity to break away from the pre-occupation with side issues like compliance with corporate formalities that has bedeviled veil piercing in the corporate context. Recall from Chapter 4 that limited liability is a social concern mainly because it permits equity investors to externalize risk. If so, what on earth does failure to observe organizational formalities have to do with anything? Setting aside the rare cases in which failure to observe organizational formalities misleads a creditor into believing it is dealing with an individual rather than a corporation, there simply is no causal link between the creditor's injury and the shareholder's (or member's) mis-

---

15. See, e.g., Hamilton v. AAI Ventures, L.L.C., 768 So.2d 298 (La.App.2000). Indeed, some courts have done even stranger things when it comes to veil piercing in the LLC context. In New Horizons Supply Cooperative v. Haack, 590 N.W.2d 282 (Wis. App.1999), the trial court decided to treat the LLC as though it were a partnership, and imposed personal liability on the members, mainly because the LLC was treated as a partnership for tax purposes! The appeals court reversed that holding, but imposed personal liability on the alternative grounds that the member did not follow proper procedures for dissolution and did not prove that the amounts distributed to her on dissolution were less than the amount of the debt to New Horizons. Id.

conduct. Perhaps courts believe a failure to observe the requisite organizational formalities inferentially indicates a potential disregard for creditors' interests—if you play fast and lose with formalities, maybe courts suspect that you are likely to play fast and loose with your bills, as well. But even that explanation seems tenuous, at best.

The ULLCA's drafters seemingly recognized the desirability of getting away from an emphasis on compliance with formalities. ULLCA Act § 303(b) provides, in fact, that: "The failure of a limited liability company to observe the usual company formalities or requirements relating to the exercise of its company powers or management of its business is not a ground for imposing personal liability on the members or managers for liabilities of the company." Unfortunately, in the absence of such statutory guidance, some courts are importing corporate law's insistence on compliance with such formalities into the LLC context.[16]

D. Freedom of contract

Many LLC statutes stand as exemplars of the contractarian principle that organizational law ought to consist mostly of default rules that the parties are free to vary or even derogate. The ULLCA, for example, allows variations on and departures from the statute in all but a handful of areas.[17] The Delaware statute goes even further, expressly providing that: "It is the policy of this chapter to give the maximum effect to the principle of freedom of contract and to the enforceability of limited liability company agreements."[18]

In *Elf Atochem North America v. Jaffari*,[19] Elf and Jaffari formed a joint venture formally structured as a Delaware LLC. The operating agreement contained an arbitration clause requiring that any arbitration (and/or any judicial proceeding to enforce an arbitral award) take place in California. Elf claimed that Jaffari had breached his fiduciary obligations and filed a derivative suit against Jaffari in Delaware. Citing the Delaware statutory provision on freedom of contract, and the social policies favoring arbitration as a mode of dispute resolution, the court held that the operating agreement was binding on both the LLC and its several members. "The basic approach of the Delaware Act is to provide members with broad discretion in drafting the Agreement and to furnish default provisions when the members' agreement is silent." Analogizing LLCs to limited partnerships for this purpose, and noting the policy of freedom of contract recognized by Delaware limited partnership law, the court further noted that "[o]nce partners exercise their contractual

16. See, e.g., Hollowell v. Orleans Regional Hosp., 1998 WL 283298 (E.D.La. 1998), aff'd, 217 F.3d 379 (5th Cir.2000); Hamilton v. AAI Ventures, L.L.C., 768 So.2d 298 (La.App.2000).

17. ULLCA § 103(b).

18. Del. Code Ann., tit. 6, § 18–1101(b). In general, however, the Delaware LLC code is a bare bones statute, which puts a high premium on preformation planning and creates a strong incentive for the use of detailed operating agreements. In contrast, the ULLCA lends itself to "off-the-rack" use by virtue of its numerous and highly detailed default rules.

19. Elf Atochem North America, Inc. v. Jaffari, 727 A.2d 286 (Del.1999).

freedom in their partnership agreement, the partners have a great deal of certainty that their partnership agreement will be enforced in accordance with its terms."

The *Jaffari* result is consistent not only with the statutory policy of freedom of contract, but also with the nexus of contracts theory of the firm. Default statutory rules provide cost savings comparable to those provided by standard form contracts, because both can be accepted without the need for costly negotiation. At the same time, however, because the default rule can be modified by contrary agreement, idiosyncratic parties wishing a different rule can be accommodated. Given these advantages, a fairly compelling case ought to be required before we impose a mandatory rule. In my view, mandatory rules are justifiable only if a default rule would demonstrably create significant negative externalities or, perhaps, if one of the contracting parties is demonstrably unable to protect itself through bargaining.

An interesting question is whether the fiduciary duties of LLC members should be subject to contractual variation and/or derogation.[20] The ULLCA permits variation, but not derogation of the duty of loyalty. The operating agreement thus may not "eliminate the duty of loyalty" but may "identify specific types or categories of activities that do not violate the duty of loyalty, if not manifestly unreasonable. . . ."[21] In addition, the operating agreement may "specify the number or percentage of members or disinterested managers that may authorize or ratify, after full disclosure of all material facts, a specific act or transaction that otherwise would violate the duty of loyalty."[22] The agreement may modify, but not "unreasonably reduce the duty of care. . . ."[23] In contrast, the Delaware LLC statute far more permissively provides that fiduciary "duties and liabilities may be expanded or restricted by provisions in a limited liability company agreement."[24]

Although it is still early days, courts appear to be giving full effect to the principal of freedom of contract even in this controversial area. A widely-cited Ohio decision, *McConnell v. Hunt Sports Enterprises*,[25] for example, involved the formation of a LLC to buy a NHL hockey expansion franchise to be located in Columbus, Ohio. After the LLC's members failed to obtain public financing of a hockey arena, Nationwide Insurance offered to build an arena that would be leased to the LLC. LLC member Lamar Hunt, purporting to act on the LLC's behalf but without authority to do so, rejected the offer. In a series of meetings over the next several weeks, Hunt and his cronies persisted in rejecting that offer, while LLC member John McConnell and his supporters wanted to accept it. McConnell and his supporters thereupon formed a separate team ownership group that accepted Nationwide's offer and, moreover, was

20. See generally Larry E. Ribstein, Fiduciary Duty Contracts In Unincorporated Firms, 54 Washington & Lee L. Rev. 537 (1997).

21. ULLCA § 103(b)(2).

22. ULLCA § 103(b)(2)(ii).

23. ULLCA § 103(b)(3).

24. Del. Code Ann., tit. 6, § 18–1101(c)(2).

25. 725 N.E.2d 1193 (Ohio App.1999).

awarded the franchise. Hunt sued, alleging breach of fiduciary duty and contract claims.

The court noted that the LLC operating agreement expressly allowed members to compete with the LLC. Focusing on the plain language of the relevant provision, which authorized LLC members to engage in "any other business venture of any nature," the court held that McConnell's group was free to pursue their own bid for the NHL franchise despite being members of a LLC that had been formed for that same purpose. Unfortunately, in going on to discuss Hunt's contract-based claims, the court muddied the waters somewhat by implying that the result might have been different if Hunt had not rejected the Nationwide proposal. The opinion is nevertheless significant for its strong "affirmative" answer to "the question [of whether] an operating agreement of a limited liability company may, in essence, limit or define the scope of the fiduciary duties imposed upon its members."

As with *Jaffari*, this result is consistent not only with the statute but also with contractarian theory. The phenomena of bounded rationality, complexity, and uncertainty coalesce to ensure that the set of contracts making up the firm are necessarily incomplete. Hence, fiduciary duties are properly viewed as gap-fillers that substitute for the missing terms. Using the hypothetical bargain methodology, the court should determine the rule to which most parties would have agreed to govern such disputes. Alternatively, the court can make use of the flexibility inherent in the ambiguous language of fiduciary obligation to tailor a default rule for the specific parties at bar. In either case, the chosen default defines the scope of fiduciary obligation in the situation at hand. As with all default rules, the use of fiduciary obligation as a gap-filler reduces transactions costs by, inter alia, reducing the amount of bargaining necessary to form a business organization. In this specific context, moreover, well-chosen defaults should have the added benefit of deterring opportunism by punishing specific examples of strategic behavior and, as a result, should also reduce transaction costs by constraining agency costs.

Where the parties have gone to the effort of bargaining over specific matters, however, there is no gap to be filled. Instead, absent negative externalities or other forms of market failure, the basic principle of freedom of contract mandates that courts respect the bargain struck by the parties.[26] Consequently, to invoke fiduciary obligation to trump actual contracts sets the process on its head. Worse yet, doing so often results in an unjustified windfall. When the parties entered into their bargain, the price paid by each member for a LLC interest (or what have you) reflected their estimate of the trade-offs inherent in that investment, including the protections (or lack thereof) provided by the op-

---

26. Compare Frank H. Easterbrook & Daniel R. Fischel, The Corporate Contract, 89 Colum. L. Rev. 1416 (1989) (making a strong case for freedom of contract even as applied to fiduciary duties) with Jeffrey N. Gordon, The Mandatory Structure of Corporate Law, 89 Colum. L. Rev. 1549 (1989) (contending that fiduciary duty rules should be mandatory in nature).

erating agreement.[27] Allowing parties to subsequently invoke fiduciary obligation to escape a bargain that turned out badly gives them an undeserved second bite at the apple. Put another way, the parties made their bed and courts ought to let them—indeed, make them—lie in it.

---

27. This analysis assumes transaction costs are low, so that the parties can meaningfully price contract terms and bargain over them. In ex ante face-to-face bargaining, that condition probably holds. Once the parties enter into an agreement, however, transaction costs may rise if, inter alia, they form a bilateral monopoly. Consequently, ex post changes in the contract may deserve closer judicial scrutiny than ex ante terms.

TABLE OF CASES

References are to Pages.

INDEX

References are to pages.

†